Nineteenth-Century Literature Criticism

Topics Volume

Guide to Gale Literary Criticism Series

For criticism on	Consult these Gale series
Authors now living or who died after December 31, 1959	*CONTEMPORARY LITERARY CRITICISM (CLC)*
Authors who died between 1900 and 1959	*TWENTIETH-CENTURY LITERARY CRITICISM (TCLC)*
Authors who died between 1800 and 1899	*NINETEENTH-CENTURY LITERATURE CRITICISM (NCLC)*
Authors who died between 1400 and 1799	*LITERATURE CRITICISM FROM 1400 TO 1800 (LC)* *SHAKESPEAREAN CRITICISM (SC)*
Authors who died before 1400	*CLASSICAL AND MEDIEVAL LITERATURE CRITICISM (CMLC)*
Black writers of the past two hundred years	*BLACK LITERATURE CRITICISM (BLC)*
Authors of books for children and young adults	*CHILDREN'S LITERATURE REVIEW (CLR)*
Dramatists	*DRAMA CRITICISM (DC)*
Hispanic writers of the late nineteenth and twentieth centuries	*HISPANIC LITERATURE CRITICISM (HLC)*
Poets	*POETRY CRITICISM (PC)*
Short story writers	*SHORT STORY CRITICISM (SSC)*
Major authors from the Renaissance to the present	*WORLD LITERATURE CRITICISM, 1500 TO THE PRESENT (WLC)*

ISSN 0732-1864

Volume 44

Nineteenth-Century Literature Criticism

Topics Volume

Excerpts from Criticism of Various
Topics in Nineteenth-Century Literature,
including Literary and Critical Movements,
Prominent Themes and Genres, Anniversary
Celebrations, and Surveys of National Literatures

Joann Cerrito
Editor

James Andrew Edwards
Judith Galens
Alan Hedblad
Michael W. Jones
Jelena O. Krstović
Brian St. Germain
Lawrence J. Trudeau
Associate Editors

 **Gale Research Inc.** • DETROIT • WASHINGTON, D.C. • LONDON

STAFF

Joann Cerrito, *Editor*

James Edwards, Judith Galens, Alan Hedblad, Jelena O. Krstović, Marie Lazzari, Brian St. Germain, Lawrence J. Trudeau, *Associate Editors*

Deron Albright, Thomas Carson, Catherine C. DiMercurio, Kathryn Horste, Daniel Marowski, Sean McCready, Paul Sassalos, Debra A. Wells, *Assistant Editors*

Jeanne A. Gough, *Permissions & Production Manager*
Linda M. Pugliese, *Production Supervisor*
Donna Craft, Paul Lewon, Maureen A. Puhl, Camille P. Robinson, Sheila Walencewicz, *Editorial Associates*

Sandra C. Davis, *Permissions Supervisor (Text)*
Maria L. Franklin, Josephine M. Keene, Michele Lonoconus, Shalice Shah, Kimberly F. Smilay, *Permissions Associates*
Jennifer A. Arnold, Brandy C. Merritt, *Permissions Assistants*

Margaret A. Chamberlain, *Permissions Supervisor (Pictures)*
Pamela A. Hayes, Keith Reed, *Permissions Associates*
Susan Brohman, Arlene Johnson, Barbara A. Wallace, *Permissions Assistants*

Victoria B. Cariappa, *Research Manager*
Maureen Richards, *Research Supervisor*
Kelly Hill, Mary Beth McElmeel, Donna Melnychenko, Tamara C. Nott, Jaema Paradowski, *Editorial Associates*
Julie A. Kriebel, Stefanie Scarlett, *Editorial Assistants*

Mary Beth Trimper, *Production Director*
Catherine Kemp, *Production Assistant*

Cynthia Baldwin, *Art Director*
Barbara J. Yarrow, *Graphic Services Supervisor*
Sherrell Hobbs, *Macintosh Artist*
Willie F. Mathis, *Camera Operator*

Library of Congress Catalog Card Number 84-643008
ISBN 0-8103-8477-9
ISSN 0732-1864

Printed in the United States of America
Published simultaneously in the United Kingdom
by Gale Research International Limited
(An affiliated company of Gale Research Inc.)
10 9 8 7 6 5 4 3 2 1

The trademark **ITP** is used under license.

Contents

Preface   vii

Acknowledgments   xi

Irish Nationalism and Literature

Travel Writing in the Nineteenth Century

Preface

Since its inception in 1981, *Nineteenth-Century Literature Criticism* has been a valuable resource for students and librarians seeking critical commentary on writers of this transitional period in world history. Designated an "Outstanding Reference Source" by the American Library Association with the publication of its first volume, *NCLC* has since been purchased by over 6,000 school, public, and university libraries. The series has covered more than 300 authors representing 26 nationalities and over 15,000 titles. No other reference source has surveyed the critical reaction to nineteenth-century authors and literature as thoroughly as *NCLC*.

Scope of the Series

NCLC is designed to introduce students and advanced readers to the authors of the nineteenth century, and to the most significant interpretations of these authors' works. The great poets, novelists, short story writers, playwrights, and philosophers of this period are frequently studied in high school and college literature courses. By organizing and reprinting commentary written on these authors, *NCLC* helps students develop valuable insight into literary history, promotes a better understanding of the texts, and sparks ideas for papers and assignments. Each entry in *NCLC* presents a comprehensive survey of an author's career or an individual work of literature and provides the user with a multiplicity of interpretations and assessments. Such variety allows students to pursue their own interests; furthermore, it fosters an awareness that literature is dynamic and responsive to many different opinions.

Every fourth volume of *NCLC* is devoted to literary topics that cannot be covered under the author approach used in the rest of the series. Such topics include literary movements, prominent themes in nineteenth-century literature, literary reaction to political and historical events, significant eras in literary history, prominent literary anniversaries, and the literatures of cultures that are often overlooked by English-speaking readers.

NCLC continues the survey of criticism of world literature begun by Gale's *Contemporary Literary Criticism (CLC)* and *Twentieth-Century Literary Criticism (TCLC)*, both of which excerpt and reprint commentary on authors of the twentieth century. For additional information about *TCLC*, *CLC*, and Gale's other criticism series, users should consult the Guide to Gale Literary Criticism Series preceding the title page in this volume.

Coverage

Each volume of *NCLC* is carefully compiled to present:

- criticism of authors, or literary topics, representing a variety of genres and nationalities
- both major and lesser-known writers and literary works of the period
- 7-10 authors or 4-6 topics per volume
- individual entries that survey critical response to an author's work or a topic in literary history, including early criticism to reflect initial reactions, later criticism to represent any rise or decline in reputation, and current retrospective analyses.

Organization

An author entry consists of the following elements: author heading, biographical and critical introduction, list of principal works, excerpts of criticism (each preceded by an annotation and followed by a bibliographic citation), and a bibliography of further reading.

- The **Author Heading** consists of the name under which the author most commonly wrote, followed by birth and death dates. If an author wrote consistently under a pseudonym, the pseudonym will be listed in the author heading and the real name given in parentheses on the first line of the biographical and critical introduction. Also located at the beginning of the introduction to the author entry are any name variations under which an author wrote, including transliterated forms for an author whose language uses a nonroman alphabet.

- The **Biographical and Critical Introduction** outlines the author's life and career, as well as the critical issues surrounding his or her work. References are provided to past volumes of *NCLC* in which further information about the author may be found.

- Most *NCLC* entries include a **Portrait** of the author. Many entries also contain reproductions of materials pertinent to an author's career, including manuscript pages, title pages, dust jackets, letters, and drawings, as well as photographs of important people, places, and events in an author's life.

- The list of **Principal Works** is chronological by date of first publication and identifies the genre of each work. In the case of foreign authors with both foreign-language publications and English translations, the English-language version is given in brackets. Unless otherwise indicated, dramas are dated by first performance, not first publication.

- **Criticism** in each author entry is arranged chronologically to provide a perspective on changes in critical evaluation over the years. All titles of works by the author featured in the entry are printed in boldface type to enable the user to easily locate discussion of particular works. Also for purposes of easier identification, the critic's name and the publication date of the essay are given at the beginning of each piece of criticism. Unsigned criticism is preceded by the title of the journal in which it appeared. Publication information (such as publisher names and book prices) and parenthetical numerical references (such as footnotes or page and line references to specific editions of works) have been deleted at the editors' discretion to provide smoother reading of the text.

- Critical excerpts are prefaced by **Annotations** providing the reader with information about both the critic and the criticism that follows. Included are the critic's reputation, individual approach to literary criticism, and particular expertise in an author's works. Also noted are the relative importance of a work of criticism, the scope of the excerpt, and the growth of critical controversy or changes in critical trends regarding an author. In some cases, these annotations cross-reference excerpts by critics who discuss each other's commentary.

- A complete **Bibliographic Citation** designed to facilitate location of the original essay or book follows each piece of criticism.

- An annotated list of **Further Reading** appearing at the end of each entry suggests secondary sources on the author. In some cases it includes essays for which the editors could not obtain reprint rights.

Cumulative Indexes

■ Each volume of *NCLC* contains a cumulative **Author Index** listing all authors who have appeared in Gale's Literary Criticism Series, along with cross-references to such biographical series as *Contemporary Authors* and *Dictionary of Literary Biography*. Useful for locating authors within the various series, this index is particularly valuable for those authors who are identified with a certain period but who, because of their death dates, are placed in another, or for those authors whose careers span two periods. For example, Fyodor Dostoevsky is found in *NCLC*, yet Leo Tolstoy, another major nineteenth-century Russian novelist, is found in *TCLC* because he died after 1899.

■ Each *NCLC* volume includes a cumulative **Nationality Index** which lists all authors who have appeared in *NCLC*, arranged alphabetically under their respective nationalities, as well as Topics volume entries devoted to particular national literatures.

■ Each new volume in Gale's Literary Criticism Series includes a cumulative **Topic Index**, which lists all literary topics treated in *NCLC, TCLC, LC 1400-1800*, and the *CLC* Yearbook.

■ Each new volume of *NCLC*, with the exception of the Topics volumes, contains a **Title Index** listing the titles of all literary works discussed in the volume. In response to numerous suggestions from librarians, Gale has also produced a **Special Paperbound Edition** of the *NCLC* title index. This annual cumulation lists all titles discussed in the series since its inception and is issued with the first volume of *NCLC* published each year. Additional copies of the index are available on request. Librarians and patrons have welcomed this separate index: it saves shelf space, is easy to use, and is recyclable upon receipt of the following year's cumulation. Titles discussed in the Topics volume entries are not included in the *NCLC* cumulative index.

Citing *Nineteenth-Century Literature Criticism*

When writing papers, students who quote directly from any volume in Gale's Literary Criticism Series may use the following general forms to footnote reprinted criticism. The first example pertains to material drawn from periodicals, the second to material reprinted from books:

[1]T.S. Eliot, "John Donne," *The Nation and Athenaeum*, 33 (9 June 1923), 321-32; excerpted and reprinted in *Literature Criticism from 1400-1800*, Vol. 10, ed. James E. Person, Jr. (Detroit: Gale Research, 1989), pp. 28-9.

[2]Clara G. Stillman, *Samuel Butler: A Mid-Victorian Modern* (Viking Press, 1932); excerpted and reprinted in *Twentieth-Century Literary Criticism*, Vol. 33, ed. Paula Kepos (Detroit: Gale Research, 1989), pp. 43-5.

Suggestions Are Welcome

In response to suggestions, several features have been added to *NCLC* since the series began, including annotations to excerpted criticism, a cumulative index to authors in all Gale literary criticism series, entries devoted to criticism on a single work by a major author, more illustrations, and a title index listing all literary works discussed in the series.

Readers who wish to suggest authors or topics to appear in future volumes, or who have other suggestions, are cordially invited to write the editors.

Acknowledgments

The editors wish to thank the copyright holders of the excerpted criticism included in this volume, the permissions managers of many book and magazine publishing companies for assisting us in securing reprint rights, and Anthony Bogucki for assistance with copyright research. We are also grateful to the staffs of the Detroit Public Library, the Library of Congress, the University of Detroit Mercy Library, Wayne State University Purdy/Kresge Library Complex, and the University of Michigan Libraries for making their resources available to us. Following is a list of the copyright holders who have granted us permission to reprint material in this volume of *NCLC*. Every effort has been made to trace copyright, but if omissions have been made, please let us know.

COPYRIGHTED EXCERPTS IN *NCLC*, VOLUME 44, WERE REPRINTED FROM THE FOLLOWING PERIODICALS:

American Literature, v. 23, January, 1952. Copyright 1952, renewed 1980 Duke University Press, Durham, NC. Reprinted by permission of the publisher.—*American Studies,* v. XXIV, Fall, 1983 for "Romantic Travelers in the Adirondack Wilderness" by Philip G. Terrie; v. 32, Spring, 1991 for "Eighteenth-Century Aesthetic Theory and the Nineteenth-Century Traveler in Trans-Allegheny America: F. Trollope, Dickens, Irving and Parkman" by Kris Lackey. Copyright © Mid-America American Studies Association, 1983, 1991. Both reprinted by permission of the publisher and the respective authors.—*Ariel: A Review of International English Literature,* v. 17, April, 1986 for "Lucie Duff Gordon's 'Letters from Egypt' " by Charisse Gendron; v. 21, October, 1990 for "First Impressions: Rhetorical Strategies in Travel Writing by Victorian Women" by Eva-Marie Kröller. Copyright © 1986, 1990 The Board of Governors, The University of Calgary. Both reprinted by permission of the publisher and the respective authors.—*The Emerson Society Quarterly,* n. 35, II Quarterly, 1964 for "Uncharted Interiors: The American Romantics Revisited" by James E. Miller, Jr. Copyright © 1964, renewed 1992, Kenneth Walter Cameron. Reprinted by permission of the publisher and the author.—*Essays in Arts and Sciences,* v. XIV, May, 1985. Copyright © 1985 by the University of New Haven. Reprinted by permission of the publisher.—*Essays in Criticism,* v. XLI, April 2, 1991 for "Death on the Nile: Fantasy and the Literature of Tourism 1840-1860" by John Barrell. Reprinted by permission of the Editors of *Essays in Criticism* and the author.—*German-Canadian Yearbook,* v. VII, 1983. Reprinted by permission of the publisher.—*Modern Drama,* v. 9, September, 1966; v. XXI, June, 1978. Copyright 1966, 1978 *Modern Drama,* University of Toronto. Both reprinted by permission of the publisher.—*Mosaic: A Journal for the Interdisciplinary Study of Literature,* v. XIV, Spring, 1981. © Mosaic 1981. Acknowledgment of previous publication is herewith made.—*New Literary History,* v. VIII, Winter, 1977. Copyright © 1977 by *New Literary History.* Reprinted by permission of the publisher.—*The Personalist,* v. XLVI, January, 1965. Reprinted by permission of the publisher.—*SHAW,* v. 11, 1991. Copyright © 1991 The Pennsylvania State University. All rights reserved. Reproduced by permission of The Pennsylvania State University Press.—*Studies in Romanticism,* v. 15, Fall, 1976. Copyright 1976 by the Trustees of Boston University. Reprinted by permission of the publisher.—*The Victorian Newsletter,* n. 79, Spring, 1991 for "Image of Middle-Eastern Women in Victorian Travel Books" by Charisse Gendron. Reprinted by permission of *The Victorian Newsletter* and the author.—*The Yale Review,* v. 76, September, 1987 for "Two Vulgar Geniuses: Augustin Daly and David Belasco" by Stanley Kauffmann. Copyright 1987, by Yale University. Reprinted by permission of the editors and Brandt & Brandt Literary Agents, Inc.

COPYRIGHTED EXCERPTS IN *NCLC*, VOLUME 44, WERE REPRINTED FROM THE FOLLOWING BOOKS:

Andrews, William, L. From "The Representation of Slavery and the Rise of Afro-American Literary Realism, 1865-1920," in *Slavery and the Literary Imagination.* Edited by Deborah E. McDowell and Arnold Rampersad. Johns Hopkins University Press, 1989. © 1989 The Johns Hopkins University Press. All rights reserved. Reprinted by

American Abolitionism

INTRODUCTION

A political and moral crusade to defeat what contemporaries called the "peculiar institution" of American slavery, abolitionism exerted a significant impact on nineteenth-century literature. Comprising novels, poetry, sermons, essays, and political orations, as well as such African-American genres as spirituals, slave narratives, and folk tales, abolitionist literature abounded after 1831, when the South intensified its system of slave control in response to a bloody insurrection led by slave leader and religious fanatic Nat Turner.

Although some early antislavery leaders had advocated an unhurried end to slavery and supported the return of African-Americans to their native homeland, both proposals were generally met with public indifference. Realizing the failure of gradualism and repatriation efforts, many formerly ambivalent social reformers now wholeheartedly embraced the abolitionist cause and called for slavery's immediate extinction. To that end, one of the most strident proponents of the cause, William Lloyd Garrison, founded the abolitionist journal *The Liberator* in 1831 and the American Anti-Slavery Society two years later. Some leaders, including William Ellery Channing, Theodore D. Weld, and Theodore Parker, were drawn from the ranks of the clergy. Distinguished literary figures such as James Russell Lowell, Lydia Maria Child, and Ralph Waldo Emerson also made important contributions to the antislavery crusade, underscoring in their writings and lectures the evils of slavery and pointing to the unconstitutional persecution of abolitionist leaders. One of the most prominent among these authors was John Greenleaf Whittier, whose antislavery poetry and tracts are considered among the most significant works of the period. Many fugitive slaves also devoted their rhetorical and literary skills to the abolitionist movement, recounting their servitude in song, verse, and autobiographical narratives. Among these latter works, Frederick Douglass's *Narrative of the Life of Frederick Douglass, an American Slave, Written by Himself* (1845) is regarded as one of the era's most compelling antislavery documents and is valued as an eloquent argument for human rights. As such, it has transcended its immediate historical milieu and is now considered a landmark in American autobiography.

The abolitionist movement gained momentum in 1850 with the passage of the Fugitive Slave Act, which required runaway slaves to be returned to their owners. Repulsed by this law and the ruthless tactics of slavehunters, Harriet Beecher Stowe published *Uncle Tom's Cabin; or, Life among the Lowly* (1852), its strong humanitarian tone and antislavery theme making it one of the most popular and influential works of the nineteenth century. Tensions were further heightened in 1859 when John Brown, an abolitionist with extreme views, was executed for inciting a slave revolt at Harpers Ferry, Virginia. Like many other authors, Transcendentalist writer Henry David Thoreau, stirred by the bloody raid on Brown's men and the harshness of Brown's sentence, composed three essays decrying the "peculiar institution" and the legal prosecution of abolitionists. In 1860, shortly after the election of antislavery advocate Abraham Lincoln to the presidency, the Civil War commenced, eventually resulting in the liberation of four million slaves. Lincoln's *Proclamation of Emancipation by the President of the United States, January 1st, 1863,* as well as his other speeches and writings on the slavery issue, are also counted among the key works of abolitionist literature.

REPRESENTATIVE WORKS

Channing, William Ellery
  Slavery 1835
Child, Lydia Maria
  An Appeal in Favor of That Class of Americans Called Africans 1833
Douglass, Frederick
  Narrative of the Life of Frederick Douglass, an American Slave, Written by Himself 1845
Garrison, William Lloyd
  "Words of Encouragement to the Oppressed" 1833
Jacobs, Harriet A.
  Incidents in the Life of a Slave Girl 1861
Lincoln, Abraham
  "Gettysburg Address" 1863
  Proclamation of Emancipation by the President of the United States, January 1st, 1863 1863
Lowell, James Russell
  "The Present Crisis" 1844
Parker, Theodore
  "The Present Aspect of Slavery in America and the Immediate Duty of the North" 1858
  The Rights of Man in America [first publication] 1911
Stowe, Harriet Beecher
  Uncle Tom's Cabin; or, Life among the Lowly 1852
Thoreau, Henry David
  "The Last Days of John Brown" 1860
Weld, Theodore D.
  American Slavery as It Is: Testimony of a Thousand Witnesses 1839
Whittier, John Greenleaf
  "Justice and Expediency" 1833
  "To William Lloyd Garrison" 1833

OVERVIEWS

Louis Ruchames

[In the following essay, Ruchames offers an overview of the antislavery movement, focusing on its leading political and literary figures.]

"The character of a city is determined by the character of the men it crowns," once remarked Wendell Phillips, quoting the Greek orator Aeschines. Applying the lesson to modern times, there are few periods in American history that offer as remarkable an opportunity for the molding of American character to the highest standards of humanity as that in which the men and women known as Abolitionists lived and wrought. Devoted to the ideals of brotherhood and equality of opportunity for all men, their consciences seared by the heartlessness of slavery in the South and racial prejudice in the North, they consecrated their lives to the eradication of both evils. Encompassed by both indifference and hostility, subjected to social ostracism, economic sanctions and physical violence for daring to condemn institutions and customs which were regarded as vital to the welfare of American society and therefore sacrosanct, they stubbornly and heroically continued their efforts until victory in the war against slavery was achieved.

The nature of the revolution wrought by the Abolitionists may best be assessed by placing ourselves in the year 1829, immediately before the rise of the modern Abolitionist movement. In December of that year, the American Convention for Promoting the Abolition of Slavery and Improving the Condition of the African Race held its twenty-first biennial convention at Washington, D. C., with delegates present from New York, Pennsylvania, Maryland, Washington, D. C., and Alexandria, Virginia. Formed thirty-five years earlier in an attempt to unite the efforts of existing state and local anti-slavery groups, the organization's successes and failures during the intervening years were highlighted in three notable reports to the convention.

In the first, Benjamin Lundy, one of the great anti-slavery pioneers, enumerated its successes. These were an increase in the number of anti-slavery advocates from very few to thousands, some of them "among the most influential characters in the nation"; the complete abolition of slavery in certain states, particularly Rhode Island, Connecticut, New York, New Jersey, Pennsylvania, Ohio, Indiana and Illinois; and the passage of the Missouri Compromise in 1820 which had prohibited the extension of slavery north of 36° 30'.

The failures were detailed in two other reports which noted no visible improvement in the treatment of the slave since 1790, the year of the first census, but rather an alarming increase in the number of slaves from 694,280 to about 2,000,000 and a tripling in the area devoted to slavery from an original 212,000 to nearly 600,000 square miles. Most disturbing, however, one report noted, was

the public apathy toward all efforts to help the slave, which "are viewed in the light of encroachment on the established order of society, for so deeply has the system of slavery become rooted in the soil, that even those who are not directly interested in its continuance, are not disposed to aid by their countenance, or afford us assistance in pecuniary manner—and thus our usefulness is checked, and our endeavors to lay before the public the train of evils attendant on a state of slavery are retarded. . . . "

That the anti-slavery movement, in the light of its own statements in 1829, had marched into a cul-de-sac which required heroic efforts on its part to extricate itself, seems evident today. The greatest need was a re-examination of its basic strategy which had been based upon "moderation" and "temperance" in describing the nature of slavery and the responsibility of the slaveholder; the espousal of "gradualism" and colonization of former slaves to areas outside the United States as the most feasible methods of hastening the end of slavery; and an emphasis upon convincing the slaveholder that it was to his economic interest to liberate the slave and utilize free labor instead.

The results of this strategy were the very opposite of what its proponents had intended. The recourse to a very cautious "moderation" in language, and the avoidance of any language likely to antagonize the slaveowner, simply minimized the inherent evils of the institution and the responsibility of the slaveowner for the suffering of the slave and made it more difficult to awaken the public conscience to a recognition of the evil; the appeal to self-interest foundered upon the reality of slavery as a source of wealth to the master and his family; the policy of gradual emancipation provided an excuse for doing nothing immediately and salved the consciences of those who were indisposed to take vigorous action; while colonization, recommended by the American Colonization Society since 1816—and by many who were sincerely interested in helping the slave—actually hindered emancipation and the struggle for equal rights for the Negro. For colonization assumed the inferiority of the Negro and regarded his presence in this country as a danger to white American society and thus reinforced the very arguments which were being used to keep him in slavery and to deprive him, when free, of the rights of a white man.

The resulting situation has been perceptively summarized by Albert Bushnell Hart [in his *Slavery and Abolition, 1831-1841,* 1906].

> When Jackson became president, in 1829, anti-slavery seemed, after fifty years of effort, to have spent its force. The voice of the churches was no longer heard in protest; the abolitionist societies were dying out; there was hardly an abolitionist militant in the field; the Colonization Society absorbed most of the public interest in the subject, and it was doing nothing to help either the free Negro or the slave; in Congress there was only one anti-slavery man, and his efforts were without avail. It was a gloomy time for the little band of people who believed that slavery was poisonous to the south, hurtful to the north, and dangerous to the Union.

It was at this point that William Lloyd Garrison appeared

with a revolutionary philosophy that challenged every basic assumption of the existing anti-slavery societies, and building upon new foundations, created a movement which ultimately brought about the destruction of slavery. Harriet Martineau, the English author, in her little volume entitled *The Martyr Age of the United States* [1839], has called Garrison "the mastermind of the great revolution." He was indeed that and more. Born in 1805 to a mother who was a pious Baptist and a father who deserted his family when the boy was three years old, Garrison early sought to prepare himself for the profession of writing. A newspaper apprentice at thirteen, he later edited newspapers in Newburyport, Boston and Bennington. In 1827, in Boston, he met Benjamin Lundy, a New Jersey Quaker who had been carrying on a one-man crusade against slavery for more than fifteen years. Lundy had formed anti-slavery societies throughout the country, had promoted schemes for Negro colonization in Mexico and Haiti, and had been editing the *Genius of Universal Emancipation* since 1821. Lundy persuaded Garrison to move to Baltimore in the fall of 1829 and join him in editing his newspaper, which then became a weekly. Several months later the partnership was interrupted when Garrison, convicted of libel by a Baltimore jury for excoriating a Massachusetts shipowner who had been transporting slaves for the South, was jailed upon failure to pay the fine of $50 and costs. Upon his release—the fine having been paid by Arthur Tappan, a New York merchant and anti-slavery philanthropist—he made plans to issue his own newspaper, which he realized with the appearance of the *Liberator* in Boston on January 1, 1831. Starting without capital and aided by Isaac Knapp, a printer, Garrison relied for financial support primarily upon Negro contributions and subscriptions, supplemented by those of a few white sympathizers.

The revolutionary nature of Garrison's thought, made manifest in the first pages of the *Liberator,* was summarized years later by Wendell Phillips in his comment that Garrison "undertook to look at the slave question as the Negro looked at it." Identifying himself completely with the slave, Garrison saw and felt slavery in all its terror and misery, refused to accept as valid any excuse for its continuance, and demanded its immediate and total abolition. Identifying himself, too, with the free Negro, he affirmed the latter's right to complete equality of opportunity and condemned the American Colonization Society for viewing the Negro as a danger to American society, to be freed from slavery only if he left the country. Indeed, within a few years after he had begun to expose the pernicious nature of this philosophy, an anti-slavery man who defended the American Colonization Society became a rarity. One aspect of Garrison's philosophy was his refusal to bate one jot or tittle from the deserved condemnation of either slavery or the slaveholder. Viewing slavery as a crime against millions of human beings which contravened the established moral and religious principles of decent humanity, to Garrison the slaveholder was a criminal whose piety as a Christian and respectability as citizen, husband and father, did not palliate in the slightest the horror of his action toward the slave. So accustomed was American society of that day—including many who were honestly anti-slavery—to speak in soft tones of slavery and the slave-

holder, that Garrison's language seemed outlandish and violent. Yet what he wrote was never coarse or vulgar, and to the fair-minded observer today, remembering the villainy that had to be described and the indifference to be overcome, it appears appropriate and necessary.

Through the cogency of his arguments and the sincerity and vitality of his writings and speeches, Garrison soon attracted to himself a varied group of friends and associates.

Harriet Martineau once wrote:

> There is a remarkable set of people now living and vigorously acting in the world, with a consonance of will and understanding which has perhaps never been witnessed among so large a number of individuals of such diversified powers, habits, opinions, tastes and circumstances. The body comprehends men and women of every shade of color, of every degree of education, of every variety of religious opinion, of every gradation of rank, bound together by no vow, no pledge, no stipulation but of each preserving his individual liberty; and yet they act as if they were of one heart and of one soul. Such union could be secured by no principle of worldly interest; nor, for a term of years, by the most stringent fanaticism. A well-grounded faith, directed towards a noble object, is the only principle which can account for such a spectacle as the world is now waking up to contemplate in the abolitionists of the United States. [*The Martyr Age of the United States,* 1839]

Among the first to be deeply influenced were Samuel J. May, of Brooklyn, Connecticut, the only Unitarian minister then in the state; May's brother-in-law Bronson Alcott; and Samuel E. Sewall, May's cousin, a young Boston lawyer who was a descendant of Judge Samuel Sewall of Colonial fame and a member of one of the most prominent families of the Commonwealth. The three had attended a lecture by Garrison in Boston in October 1830 at which Garrison had argued the doctrine of immediate emancipation. They had been deeply impressed, had offered Garrison their cooperation, and had invited him to Bronson Alcott's home where they spent several hours. So great was the impact of that meeting that almost forty years later May still retained much of his original fervor when he wrote [in his *Some Recollections of our Antislavery Conflict,* 1869]: "That night my soul was baptized in his spirit, and ever since I have been a disciple and fellow-laborer of William Lloyd Garrison." May helped in the formation of the American Anti-Slavery Society, served as general agent and secretary of the Massachusetts Anti-Slavery Society, and in the midst of a busy ministerial career devoted to many causes, achieved a notable reputation as a reformer and friend of the slave. Others who joined Garrison's standard were John Greenleaf Whittier, whose poems Garrison was the first to publish in the Newburyport *Herald,* and who became an early and devoted friend, though the two later differed on the question of political action; Ellis Gray Loring, a rising young Boston lawyer of a socially prominent family, who took his place as a leader in the Massachusetts Anti-Slavery Society; Oliver Johnson, born and raised in Vermont, who was first influenced by Garrison's *Journal of the Times,* and who later, in 1831, as editor of the *Christian Soldier*—with an office in the building in which the *Liberator* was published—became his devoted friend, collaborator and the author of his first full-length biography; Arnold Buffum, a Quaker hat manufacturer who became the first president of the New England Anti-Slavery Society, although he later left the Garrison camp for political action with the Liberty Party; and David and Lydia Maria Child, husband and wife, the former a journalist, teacher, lawyer and for a short period a member of the Massachusetts legislature, the latter a popular novelist and publicist whose *An Appeal in Favor of that Class of Americans Called Africans,* published in July 1833, gained many new converts for the anti-slavery movement.

The first organizational result of Garrison's teaching was the formation, after several meetings, of the New England Anti-Slavery Society on January 6, 1832. Its constitution, adopted on that day, was the first to avow the principle of immediate emancipation. Among the twelve who signed it were Garrison, Johnson, Buffum, Knapp and Joshua Coffin. Although David Child, Sewall and Loring at first objected to the inclusion of the immediate emancipation clause on grounds of expediency and refused to sign, they did so soon after and assumed leading posts in the organization.

Of great significance to the cause was the publication in 1832 of a pamphlet by Garrison entitled "Thoughts on African Colonization," which exposed the pretensions of the American Colonization Society and condemned it out of the writings and speeches of its leaders as an anti-Negro, pro-slavery organization. The pamphlet had a wide impact, influencing such men as Elizur Wright, Jr. and Beriah Green, two professors at Western Reserve College who were later to play a prominent part in the anti-slavery movement, as well as Lewis and Arthur Tappan, the influential businessmen-philanthropists of New York.

Anti-slavery sentiment now increased in different parts of the country and voices were raised in favor of forming a national anti-slavery organization upon the principles of immediate, unconditional emancipation. The publication in 1833 of Whittier's pamphlet, "Justice and Expediency" and of Lydia Maria Child's *Appeal,* further stirred public opinion and gained new converts. So did the persecution of Prudence Crandall by leading public officials of the State of Connecticut for seeking to educate Negro girls in her school in Canterbury, Connecticut. At this time, too, there emerged in New York City a group of anti-slavery men of ability and vision who began to agitate for the formation of anti-slavery societies in New York City and nationally. These included, along with the Tappans, William Goodell, an editor of the *Genius of Temperance* and later of the *Emancipator,* established in 1833; Isaac T. Hopper, a radical Quaker of Philadelphia who had moved to New York, and who had been helping escaped slaves and free Negroes for many years; Joshua Leavitt, editor of the *Evangelist* and subsequently of the *Emancipator;* and William Jay, author and reformer, the son of Chief Justice John Jay. These took the lead in forming a New York anti-slavery society in October 1833.

On October 29, 1833, a month after Garrison's return from England, where he had spent several months securing the support of English Abolitionists for the American anti-slavery movement and their condemnation of the American Colonization Society, a call for a national convention was issued. According to varying estimates, between 50 and 60 delegates, among whom were several Negroes, met in Philadelphia on three days in early December. Beriah Green, then president of Oneida Institute, acted as president, with Lewis Tappan and Whittier as secretaries. Garrison, May and Whittier were chosen to draw up a declaration of principles. Asked by the other two to write a draft, Garrison wrote through the night at the home of his host, Frederick A. Hinton—a Negro Abolitionist of Philadelphia and a delegate to the convention—and completed it by morning. Samuel J. May had this to say about the impact of the declaration upon the delegates: "Never in my life have I seen a deeper impression made by words than was made by that admirable document upon all who were there present . . . We felt that the word had just been uttered which would be mighty, through God, to the pulling down of the strongholds of slavery."

The formation of the national society gave an additional fillip to growing anti-slavery sentiment. From New England to the Mississippi River, anti-slavery organizations mushroomed into being. In 1835, Garrison referred to "our 4 or 500 societies." During that year alone, 328 new societies were formed, 254 of which boasted 27,182 members. By 1838, there were 1,350 societies in the national organization, with a membership of about 250,000. In Massachusetts, in 1837, there were 145 local societies, in New York 274 societies, and in Ohio, the most ardent anti-slavery state in the West, 213.

In 1834, a *cause célèbre* occurred near Cincinnati that proved of immense significance to the anti-slavery movement, especially in the West. The locale was Lane Seminary, which had been founded to prepare young men for the ministry and whose president was the eminent Boston minister, Lyman Beecher. In 1834, as a result of the publication of Garrison's *Thoughts on African Colonization* and the founding of the American Anti-Slavery Society, discussions arose among the students concerning the aims and methods of the anti-slavery enterprise. It was decided to debate two questions: the validity of immediate, unconditional emancipation and the worthwhileness of the American Colonization Society. The upshot was a debate extending over eighteen evenings; the result, the passage of resolutions approving immediate emancipation and condemning the American Colonization Society. Reports of the proceedings were published throughout the country, with ensuing public pressure which impelled the faculty and board of overseers to ban the newly formed student anti-slavery society as well as a previously approved colonization society. Most of the students resigned in protest, and many—including several Southerners—became active Abolitionists and leaders in the American Anti-Slavery Society. Among these were Amos Dresser, who received twenty lashes on his back when found with anti-slavery literature in Tennessee; James A. Thome, son of a Kentucky slaveholder; Henry B. Stanton, who was appointed agent and lecturer for the American Anti-Slavery

Society; and most prominent of all, Theodore D. Weld, regarded by the trustees as instigator of the entire episode, of whom Samuel J. May has written that "no one except Garrison and Phillips had done more for the abolition of American slavery." It was partly as a result of the Lane episode, as well as the impact of the formation of the American Anti-Slavery Society, that James G. Birney of Kentucky was led to abandon the American Colonization Society and to participate actively in the anti-slavery movement.

As the Abolitionist movement grew, so did the fears of the friends of slavery and their hatred of the Abolitionists. The outcome included frequent mob riots, beatings and even killings. On October 21, 1835, a Boston mob consisting mostly of "gentlemen of property and influence" broke up a meeting of the Boston Female Anti-Slavery Society, which was to be addressed by George F. Thompson, a well-known English Abolitionist. In the course of the riot, Garrison was almost hanged and was finally saved by being lodged in jail. On the same day, in Utica, a meeting of 600 delegates assembled to form a New York State anti-slavery society was broken up by rioters. It was as a result of this riot that Gerrit Smith, a prominent reformer and philanthropist, joined the American Anti-Slavery Society. Henry B. Stanton is supposed to have been mobbed at least two hundred times, Theodore Weld's speeches were frequently disrupted, and in 1837 Owen Lovejoy, the anti-slavery editor, was slain at Alton, Illinois, while trying to prevent the destruction of his fourth newspaper press. It was at a meeting in Boston, called to memorialize Lovejoy's death, that Wendell Phillips, then twenty-six years old, made an impromptu address and began a career which in anti-slavery importance was second perhaps only to Garrison's.

Until 1837, the history of the anti-slavery movement was one of a continuously growing and united movement despite religious, political and social differences among its members. In that year, however, the first of a number of schisms, which ultimately were to lead to a divided movement, appeared. In Massachusetts, an "Appeal of Clerical Abolitionists on Anti-Slavery Measures," which criticized some of Garrison's tactics, was followed by another statement by the Abolitionists of Andover Theological Seminary which objected to Garrison's language, his attacks upon church ministers who refused to cooperate with the Abolitionists, and his espousal of public lectures by women.

These attacks soon involved several of the New York anti-slavery leaders and others of the national organization who refused to come to Garrison's defense and were therefore, in Garrison's opinion, giving tacit approval to his critics. These included the Tappans, Birney, Elizur Wright, Leavitt and others who did not share Garrison's views on the place of women in the anti-slavery movement, who thought his attacks on the churches ill-considered, his language abusive and his negative attitude toward certain kinds of political action a deterrent to the further development of the anti-slavery movement. The conflict came to a head at the annual convention of the national organization in 1840, when Garrison and his follow-

ers elected Abby Kelley to the society's business committee. Thereupon, Lewis Tappan, who had been the society's president, led his followers from the convention and formed the American and Foreign Anti-Slavery Society. The *Emancipator,* the official newspaper of the original organization, had been transferred earlier to the New York Anti-Slavery Society, which was controlled by anti-Garrison forces. In its place, Garrison and his group established the *National Anti-Slavery Standard* under the aegis of the American Anti-Slavery Society. Lydia M. Child soon assumed the duties of editor, was followed by her husband David Lee Child and then by Sydney Gay, who edited the paper with the help of Edmund Quincy and James Russell Lowell.

It may be noted that while the American Anti-Slavery Society carried on with undiminished vigor until after the Civil War, the American and Foreign Anti-Slavery Society, though it held annual meetings and issued some effective pamphlets, gradually dwindled in strength and passed out of existence in the 1850's, while the *Emancipator* stopped publication even earlier. Years later, Lewis Tappan, in the biography of his brother Arthur, implied that, judged by its results, the secession was not as well-advised as it seemed to be at the time. For though the secessionists adopted "such language and such measures as Christians could not reasonably object to, those who had been loudest in their opposition and most offended with what they termed the unchristian spirit of the Abolitionists, kept aloof as well from the American and Foreign Anti-Slavery Society . . ." It seems reasonable to conclude that it was not Garrison's language or his espousal of the rights of women or his attacks upon the churches for their indifference to slavery which brought down upon the Abolitionists the wrath of so many of America's political, economic and religious leaders, but the doctrine of immediate and unconditional emancipation, which was indeed a revolutionary doctrine for its time and represented a threat to what many believed to be the foundation of the existing social and economic order.

The year 1840 marks a watershed in the history of the anti-slavery movement. Besides witnessing the division already mentioned, it also saw the formation of the Liberty Party, with the selection of Birney and Thomas Earle, a Philadelphia Quaker, as the party's candidates for President and Vice-President. The party had been formed by such anti-slavery stalwarts as Myron Holley, who had had a distinguished carreer in public affairs, Joshua Leavitt, Elizur Wright, Henry B. Stanton and Alvan Stewart, a leader in the New York State Anti-Slavery Society. In time it was absorbed by the Free-Soil Party, which in turn gave way to the Republican Party.

A decisive event in Abolitionist history was Garrison's decision, in 1843, that slavery could not be eliminated as long as the North remained in the Government of the United States and thereby cooperated with the South, under the Constitution, in the maintenance of slavery. The Constitution, Garrison came to believe, assumed the existence of slavery, gave the institution its sanction, and could not be changed without the consent of a considerable portion of the slave states themselves, which therefore made the abolition of slavery by constitutional means impossible. The Constitution, he concluded, was—in the words of the prophet Isaiah whom he quoted—"a covenant with death and an agreement with hell." Indeed "the free states," by upholding the Constitution, "are guardians and essential supports of slavery. We are the jailers and constables of the institution." The only moral and just course for the North was disunion or secession, which would ultimately result in the fall of slavery.

Garrison first began to broach this point of view in the *Liberator* in 1842. In the spring of 1843, the Massachusetts Anti-Slavery Society affirmed that "the compact . . . between North and South . . . should be immediately annulled." When the issue was raised in 1844 before the national organization, a long and heated discussion ensued which culminated in a vote of 59 to 21 in favor of disunion. Soon thereafter the entire Garrisonian movement gave its approval to the slogan of "No union with slaveholders" and remained committed to it until the Civil War.

The late 1840's and 50's saw no important changes in antislavery theory or practice. The Abolitionists continued their work of arousing public opinion to the increasing advances of slavery, and played a prominent part in the many crises which shook the country to its foundations—the war with Mexico, the Fugitive Slave Law, the Kansas-Nebraska Act and the conflict over control of Kansas, the Dred Scott decision and John Brown's raid on Harpers Ferry. On all of these issues, the Abolitionists acted vigorously to awaken the anti-slavery conscience of America and to convince the North of the imperative necessity of abolishing slavery if the rights of all Americans were to be maintained. They thus helped to mold that public opinion which ultimately resulted in the abolition of slavery in the United States.

On April 6, 1865, in Petersburg, Virginia, Abraham Lincoln spoke with Daniel H. Chamberlain, ex-Governor of North Carolina. In the course of the conversation, Lincoln summed up what he and the entire country owed to Garrison and the anti-slavery movement: "I have been only an instrument," he said. "The logic and moral power of Garrison, and the anti-slavery people of the country and the Army, have done all."

> *Louis Ruchames, in an introduction to his* The Abolitionists: A Collection of Their Writings, *G. P. Putnam's Sons, 1963, pp. 13-24.*

Melvin Dixon

[*An American educator, translator, and author, Dixon was well regarded for his works on African and African-American literature. In the following essay, he examines slave narratives and Negro spirituals as descriptive social history and as an innate revolt against the "peculiar institution."*]

The fabric of tradition in Afro-American literature is woven from slave narratives and Negro spirituals, the earliest and most significant forms of oral and written literature created by blacks during slavery. Not only did the spirituals identify the slave's peculiar syncretistic religion,

sharing features of Protestant Christianity and traditional African religions, but they became an almost secretive code for the slave's critique of the plantation system and for his search for freedom in *this* world. Similarly, the narratives identified the slave's autobiographical and communal history as well as his active campaign against the "peculiar institution." Both forms of cultural expression from the slave community create a vision of history, an assessment of the human condition, and a heroic fugitive character unlike any other in American literature.

Critical studies of this material as literature or history have been slow to appreciate its distinctive cultural voice. Marion Starling has argued [in his "The Slave Narrative: Its Place in American Literary History," 1946] that slave narratives are of "sub-literary quality" and that their chief importance lies "in their genetic relationship to the popular slave novels of the 1850s," most notably Harriet Beecher Stowe's *Uncle Tom's Cabin.* And historians, until recently, have ignored them as genuine documents because of their subjectivity and possible "inauthenticity."

Further scholarship, such as Charles Nichols' *Many Thousand Gone,* has produced important reconsiderations of the slave community and of the relations between masters and slaves by using slave literature as a primary source. Through the study of black and white autobiographies, folklore, music, religion and art by such historians as John Blassingame, Eugene Genovese, and Lawrence Levine, the black past is now recognized as an active, vital, creative element in American history and literature. Furthermore, we are finding that "slavery was never so complete a system of psychic assault that it prevented slaves from carving out independent cultural forms" that preserve some degree of personal autonomy and a range of positive self-concepts [see Levine in his "Slave Songs and Slave Consciousness", in *American Negro Slavery,* 2nd ed., edited by Allen Weinstein and Frank Otto Gatell, 1973].

Through American slave culture we uncover the roots of the many recurring images and metaphors used to describe the black experience on both a group and individual level. The spirituals and the narratives constitute a literature in that they are deliberate creations of the slaves themselves to express their moral and intellectual universe. These forms of communication, what W.E.B. Du Bois called "the sorrow songs," what Benjamin Mays [in his *The Negro's God as Reflected in His Literature,* 1968] referred to as "mass" literature, and what Saunders Redding [in his *To Make a Poet Black,* 1968] has identified as a "literature of necessity," remind us that they were created out of the practical need to adjust to the American environment with a burning passion to be free.

Slave narratives were published from 1703 until the first forty years of the twentieth century, when former slaves, interviewed in the Federal Writers' Project, furnished volumes of historical testimony and when men such as Booker T. Washington and George Washington Carver published autobiographies drawn from their childhood experiences during slavery. Published in single volumes both in England and the United States and reaching a height of popularity and commercial success after 1840 when antislavery sentiment was strongest, narratives and autobiographical sketches of slaves appeared in abolitionist newspapers such as Garrison's *Liberator, The National Anti-Slavery Standard, The Quarterly Anti-Slavery Magazine* in New York, *The National Enquirer* in Philadelphia, and *The Observer* in St. Louis. Narratives also appeared in judicial records, broadsides, and church records. Slave songs were less widely popularized, and no major effort to collect them was made until after the Civil War when William Francis Allen and Lucy McKim Garrison published *Slave Songs of the United States* in 1867.

Both narratives and songs are seminal to the development of Afro-American autobiography, fiction, and poetry. By infusing the dynamic vestiges of an oral tradition and culture into a more formal written literary mode, they create an important slave literature in the United States.

This literature has been called native, naïve and childlike by critics who wish to limit the songs and narratives to one dimensional meaning. Granted the "native imagery and emphasis in the spirituals are selected elements that helped the slave adjust to his particular world" [G. R. Wilson, *Journal of Negro History* VII (January, 1923)], but it is precisely in the slave's pattern of acculturation that the student of black history and culture finds specific ideologies for survival. That Christianity is easily recognizable in the language of the songs and narratives has led many critics to emphasize the spiritual docility and other-worldliness of slave thought. However, a deeper study of the dual aspects of culture contact and acculturation between European and African belief structures reveals that slaves needed a language and a flexible vocabulary more for communication than for belief. Thus it is more realistic to examine how Christianity was "the nearest available, least suspect, and most stimulative system for expressing their concepts of freedom, justice, right and aspiration." In the literature, that Christian imagery becomes "an arsenal of pointed darts, a storehouse of images, a means of making shrewd observations" [John Lovell, Jr., "The Social Implications of the Negro Spiritual," in *The Social Implications of Early Negro Music in the United States,* edited by Bernard Katz, 1969].

Revolutionary sentiments, plans for escape, and insurrection were often couched in the religious imagery which was the slave community's weapon against despair and moral degradation. This literature contained ideas that reached the masses of slaves primarily through the "church" within the slave community and the men and women preached, testified, and told God all their troubles.

Using the Bible as a storehouse of myth and history that could be appropriated for religious syncretism and a practical philosophy based on historical immediacy, the slave community identified with the children of Israel; but they did not stop there. Slaves knew that deliverance would come, as proven by their African assurance of intimacy and immortality with the Supreme Being, and by the wider implications of the biblical past. Both systems of belief helped the slave know that he could actively participate in deliverance and judgment by joining God's army, singing with a sword in his hand, or walking in Jerusalem just like John. The slave was sure he was experiencing all of history: the past, present and future. Moses very often

came to slaves in the person of Harriet Tubman and other ex-slaves who went back into Egypt, heard the children "yowlin'," and led them to the promised land in the North. Historical immediacy created and sustained through the oral tradition that healing moment of deliverance and salvation:

> O Mary don' you weep don' you moan
> Pharaoh's army got drownded.

Upon the rock that was traditional African religion as well as American Christianity, the slave community built a church. Out of religious syncretism and an oral literature they established an active contemporary apocalypse in the realm of their own daily experiences. The historical moment for the slave was never abstract, but imminent. The time for deliverance and witness was now. The complexity of the religious experience, as well as the complexity of the day-to-day social experience in the slave quarters, centered in a conversion-like initiation, became further testing grounds for individual and corporate faith in the possibility of freedom. And as the slave lived, he would reckon with time, community, and his own life journey. He sang:

> God dat lived in Moses' time
> Is jus' de same today.

Slavery had brought black men and women face to face with the extreme fact of their wretchedness as individuals. Conversion to an inner cult, an in-group morality, provided the very real awareness that individual loneliness and despair could be resolved in group solidarity. The conversion experience emphasized a person's recognition of his own need for deliverance from sin and bondage into a holy alliance with God as the avenging deity:

> My God He is a Man—a Man of War,
> An' de Lawd God is His name.

> I'm a soljuh in the Army of thuh Lawd,
>   I'm a soljuh in this Army.

> Hold out yo' light you heav'n boun' soldier
>   Let yo' light shine around the world.

> We are the people of God.

Conversion also provided for socio-religious mobility and status within the slave community. Conversion also confirmed an African orientation of personal duty on both a ritualistic and humanistic level. Ritual, duty, and creative expression all served as outlets for individual expression without disturbing communal solidarity. Song and personal testimony, as forms of an oral literature, allowed for individual interpretation while they "continually drew [the slave] back into the communal presence and permitted him the comfort of basking in the warmth of the shared assumptions of those around him" [Levine]. Conversion to these shared assumptions provided a basis for self-esteem, new values, and an important defense against degradation. Slaves were initiated through the spiritual potency of personal testimony. They prepared themselves to fight for freedom by becoming morally free of an intrusive and debilitating white out-group and by becoming more responsible to the inner slave community.

Slaves demanded of each other explicit principles of character and right living: for the "soul" to be a "witness for my Lord." This was no mystical yearning, but a real test of character and conviction. As realists, slaves demanded that they be struck dead to sin in order to live again in freedom. In order for this transformation to be real enough to connect with the vital image of deliverance, "conversion had to be in the nature of a stroke of lightning which would enter at the top of their head and emerge from their toes." Slaves, as Paul Radin continues [in his "Status, Phantasy, and the Christian Dogma"], "had to meet God, be baptized by him in the river of Jordan, personally, and become identified with him."

The status slaves gained as a result was both inward and outward, sometimes manifesting itself in change of behavior from mild submission to active resistance. Here it is necessary to distinguish an important feature of the slave's conversion. Knowing the deep need for community and the deprived sense of belonging for slaves isolated in bondage, and knowing the utter contempt with which whites regarded black spiritual welfare (despite a very false "Christian" religious education), it is obvious that through the religious organization in the slave quarters, the slaves were not converting themselves to God, but *were converting themselves to each other.* As a result, slaves converted God to their new identity and community in the New World and made God active in their struggle for freedom. This syncretic African-Christian God became "a fixed point within and without [the slave] and all that God commanded was unqualified faith and throwing away of doubt," which was what slaves demanded of each other. Both God and man experienced conversion. Together they struggled for self-expression and the fulfillment of human destiny. "The sins would take care of themselves," Radin has argued, but more importantly a socio-religious mobility has been set in motion, unifying the community. Frederick Douglass himself confirmed, "we were generally a unit, and moved together."

Conversion as rebirth or transformation was a central event in the slave's recorded life. In this way it gave individuals an outline of personal history and made them aware of their part in the larger history of the racial group. In fact, by achieving a personal witness (a personal historical sense or vision in which man is the essential binder of time and space), individual men and women could participate in the larger history and further regenerate themselves by attaining freedom and salvation. Testimonies in the narratives speak directly to this transformation and regeneration [Fisk University, *God Struck Me Dead,* 1945]:

> I was born a slave and lived through some very hard times. If it had not been for *my God,* I don't know what I would have done. Through his mercy I was lifted up. My soul began singing and I was told that I was one of the elected children and that I would live as long as God lives. . . . A building is waiting for me way back in eternal glory and I have no need to fear. He stood me on my feet and told me that I was a sojourner in a weary land. I came from heaven and I am now returning.

And he sang:

> I'm er rollin', I'm er rollin'
> Through an unfriendly world.

When slaves came to write their formal autobiographies they emphasized a conversion-like model of personal experience and testimony to construct their own "witness" to the horrors of slavery and the regenerative joy of freedom. The conversion experience helped to organize the individual life and unite it with time and the eternal presence of God. As one slave testified to this historical pattern:

> The soul that trusts in God need never stumble nor fall, because God being all wise and seeing and knowing all things, having looked down through time before time, foresaw every creeping thing and poured out His spirit on the earth. The earth brought forth her fruits in due season. In the very beginning every race and every creature was in the mind of God and we are here, not ahead of time, not behind time, but just on time. It was time that brought us here and time will carry us away.

The use of historical and religious language and symbol is seen most clearly in the escape episode in slave narratives. The nearby woods or the wilderness into which the fugitive escapes becomes the testing ground of his faith in God and in himself:

> If you want to find Jesus, go in de wilderness
> Go in de wilderness, go in de wilderness
> Mournin' brudder, go in de wilderness
> To wait upon de Lord.

The scenes of self-revelation and the experience of grace and a final rebirth become as characteristic to the narratives as they are to the songs. What is developed from this imagery, shared between oral and written modes, is a literature of struggle and fulfillment. The thematic transformation in the text parallels the transformation in its creators. The change is from chattel status, unholiness, and damnation in the hell which was slavery to the integrity of being a man and a saved child of God now walking the paved streets of a heavenly city, the promised North. The slave has been delivered. Conversion was the correlative for a subjective synthesis of history; earning freedom through escape (or insurrection) was heroic action.

That religion and freedom went hand in hand is evidenced by the entire experience of the fugitive slave. Often poorly equipped for long journeys and with few geographic aids, he was alone with only God to help him endure the wilderness. Often leaders of fugitive parties were ministers themselves. One preacher, a Methodist, tried to persuade John Thompson to join his band of runaways. Thompson was unwilling to escape with them, and only several months later did he attempt his escape alone, once he was assured of God's presence. Thompson [in his *The Life of John Thompson,* 1856] described the occasion and method of that first fugitive group and his own skepticism:

> The Methodist preacher . . . urged me very strongly to accompany them, saying that he had full confidence in the surety of the promises of God . . . he believed he was able to carry him safely to the land of freedom, and accordingly he was determined to go. Still I was afraid to risk

myself on such uncertain promises; I dared not trust an unseen God.

On the night on which they intended to start . . . they knelt in prayer to the great God of Heaven and Earth, invoking Him to guard them . . . and go with them to their journey's end.

Most often the slave's idea of freedom was a consequence of his recognition of his slave status. He needed little outside influence to convince him of the advantages of freedom. Even as far south as Louisiana and in as isolated a region as Bayou Boeuf to which Solomon Northup was kidnapped, the idea of freedom was a regular topic among the slaves, as Northup writes [in his "Twelve Years as a Slave," in *Puttin' on Ole Massa,* edited by Gilbert Osofsky, 1969]:

They understand the privileges and exemptions that belong to it—that it would bestow upon them the fruits of their own labor, and that it would secure to them the enjoyment of domestic happiness. They do not fail to observe the difference between their own condition and the meanest white man's and to realize the injustice of the laws.

Thus, freedom, an essential aspect of human development, was a value within the slave community which also outlined a socio-religious mobility for its attainment. The mobility established in the slave's conversion experience became the philosophical model for further initiation into free status and identity.

The first step in this mobility on the personal level involved a recognition of one's wretchedness as a slave, a realization that one is different and deprived. "I was born a slave," wrote Harriet Jacobs [in *Black Men in Chains,* edited by Charles Nichols, 1972], "but I never knew it till six years of happy childhood had passed away . . . When I was six years old, my mother died; and then, for the first time, I learned by the talk around me, that I was a slave."

Henry Bibb of Kentucky had a similar rude awakening; "I knew nothing of my condition as a slave. I was living with Mr. White, whose wife had died and left him a widower with one little girl, who was said to be the legitimate owner of my mother and all her children. This girl was also my playmate when we were children." When he was eight or ten years old Bibb discovered that his wages were being spent for the education of his playmate. It was then that he realized his slave labor was profitless for himself. "It was then I first commenced seeing and feeling that I was a wretched slave" [in *Puttin' on Ole Massa*].

Former slave Thomas Jones [in his *The Experience of Thomas H. Jones,* 1862] began his narrative with the following recognition: "I was born a slave. My recollections of early life are associated with poverty, suffering and shame. I was made to feel in my boyhood's first experience that I was inferior and degraded and that I must pass through life in a dependent and suffering condition."

The Negro spirituals speak to the same sense of wretchedness in slavery as the singers sought deliverance:

Oh, wretched man that I am;

Oh, wretched man that I am;
Oh, wretched man that I am,
Who will deliver poor me?

I am bowed down with a burden of woe;
I am bowed down with a burden of woe;
I am bowed down with a burden of woe;
Who will deliver poor me?

My heart's filled with sadness and pain;
My heart's filled with sadness and pain;
My heart's filled with sadness and pain;
Who will deliver poor me?

The moment of self-discovery has been one of the more dramatic turning points in the personal history of every black American. The moment called for new tactics or behavior that would help the individual come to grips with his feelings of difference and alienation from the society at large. William Du Bois [in his *The Souls of Black Folk,* 1903] once wrote of his own experience that:

Then it dawned upon me with a certain suddenness that I was different from the others; or like, mayhap in heart and life and longing, but shut out from their world by a vast veil. I had therefore no desire to tear down that veil, to creep through; I held all beyond it in common contempt, and lived above it in a region of blue sky and great wandering shadows.

That crucial self-discovery, which can happen suddenly and by accident, is nonetheless the beginning of a collective consciousness and group identity. As poet Margaret Walker once wrote in her more contemporary account [*For My People,* 1947], it was a bitter hour "when we discovered we / were black and poor and small and different and / nobody cared and nobody / wondered and nobody understood."

By the force of this personal alienation the individual began to see himself as a member of an oppressed group. Within the group experience, perhaps because of it, the individual resolved to remedy the situation for himself and the others who were joined to him by the extreme pressures of racial oppression. The slave could openly rebel or secretly escape. He could also accommodate himself to the subservient role slavery defined for him, as no doubt some slaves did. Whatever action the slave finally took was considered not the end of experience, but the beginning of a long confrontation from which he hoped to wrench his freedom.

Black religion told the slave where to seek liberation: "Jesus call you, go in the wilderness." There a man will be tested, tried and "be baptized." Religion agitated the slave's search. Preachers like Nat Turner and Denmark Vesey conspired to gain it. Other leaders urged slaves to run away. Turner himself often secreted himself in the woods where he communed with the Spirit and returned with the fresh assurance that his struggle had divine sanction [*The Confessions of Nat Turner,* in *Nat Turner's Slave Rebellion,* edited by Herbert Aptheker, 1968]:

. . . I saw white spirits and black spirits engaged in battle, and the sun was darkened—the thunder rolled in the heaven, and blood flowed in streams—and I heard a voice saying, "Such is your luck, such you are called to see, and let it come rough or smooth, you must surely have it." I now withdrew myself as much as my situation would permit, from the intercourse of my fellow servants, for the avowed purpose of serving the Spirit more fully—and it appeared to me and reminded me of the things it had already shown me, and that it would then reveal to me the knowledge of the elements. After this revelation in the year of 1825 . . . I sought more than ever to obtain true holiness before the great day of judgement should appear, and then I began to receive the true knowledge of faith.

On the night of his rebellion, Turner met again in the woods with his co-conspirators, where they shared cider and roasted pork as sacraments to their mission.

Other slaves often secreted themselves in the woods, even if only to meditate on their condition. In the wilderness of nature, freedom was revealed as a man's right in the natural harmony of God's created world. Henry Bibb meditated in the woods and wrote: "I thought of the fishes of the water, the fowls of the air, the wild beasts of the forest, all appeared to be free to go where they pleased, and I was an unhappy slave." Nature furnished the slave with examples of freedom and the harmony of all life with God just as his African religious tradition continued to inform him. In the new American environment, the harmony of the natural world was easily given religious significance. Natural imagery was analogous to freedom and revealed a point of contact between man and God. The slave resolved to seek that contact and unity in the wilderness. Frederick Douglass [in his *Life and Times of Frederick Douglass,* 1881] once described this communion: "I was in the wood, buried in its somber gloom and hushed in its solemn silence, hidden from all human eyes, shut in with nature and with nature's God, and absent from all human contrivances. Here was a good place to pray, to pray for help, for deliverance.

From the slave's point of view, the life pilgrimage of man was possible only through a renewed contract with nature, and by so doing he could effect a new covenant with God. This qualification of the life experience is evident in the ordinary day-to-day struggle of the slave in the hot fields and dramatized vividly in the plight of the fugitive. In nature the slave found a guide for the fulfillment of his identity; once he saw himself as a wretched slave, then too, even as he saw himself as a child of God, for the power of God as reflected in the world around him was strong enough to deliver him from slavery. This was one basic element of the slave's belief pattern, and he responded accordingly when Jesus called him into the woods. Thus the slave felt himself converted to the community of believers and to the mission of freedom. In this same wilderness, Henry Bibb stood on the bluff of the Ohio River, perhaps knowing then that in African beliefs, water, as well as the wilderness, was a place of divine power: wells, springs, rivers and streams. There he meditated and formed his resolution to seek freedom. He wrote:

> Sometimes standing on the Ohio River bluff, looking over on a free State, and as far north as my eyes could see, I have eagerly gazed upon the

blue sky of the free North, which at times constrained me to cry out from the depths of my soul, Oh Canada, sweet land of rest—Oh! that I had the wings of a dove, that I might soar away to where there is no slavery; no clanking of chains, no captives, no lacerating of backs, no parting of husbands and wives; and where man ceases to be the property of his fellow man.

In a similar way Douglass resolved to seek freedom. He cried: "O God save me! God deliver me! Let me be free. . . . Only think of it: one hundred miles north, and I am free. . . . It cannot be that I shall live and die a slave. I will take to the water. This very bay shall yet bear me into freedom." For Josiah Henson, freedom in the North was heaven. He resolved: "Once to get away with my wife and children, to some spot where I could feel that they were indeed *Mine*—where no grasping master could stand between me and them, as arbiter of their destiny—was a heaven yearned after with insatiable longing" [*Father Henson's Story of His Own Life,* 1858]. Henry "Box" Brown felt called to escape with the same fervor that he felt called upon to serve God. The revelation also told him how he could escape successfully:

> One day, while I was at work and my thoughts were eagerly feasting upon the idea of freedom, I felt my soul called out to Heaven to breathe a prayer to Almighty God. I prayed fervently that he who seeth in secret and knew the inmost desires of my heart would lend me his aid in bursting my fetters asunder and in restoring me to possession of those rights of which men had robbed me; when suddenly, the idea flashed across my mind of shutting myself *up in a box,* and getting myself conveyed as dry goods to a free state.

The impulse for freedom was very often the beginning of a change in the slave's character. He began to strengthen himself for the difficulties which he would have to endure. Gustavas Vassa, one of the earliest narrators who vividly remembered his African heritage, wrote [in his *The Interesting Narrative of Olaudah Equiano, or Gustavas Vassa, the African. Written by Himself,* 1791] that in the midst of his thoughts on slavery and freedom his immediate impulse was to look "up with prayers anxiously to God for my liberty; and at the same time [use] every honest means and [do] all that was possible on my part to obtain it."

James W.C. Pennington, the fugitive "blacksmith," had a clear idea of what lay beyond his resolution to free. He knew that the time had come for him to act:

> . . . and then when I considered the difficulties of the way—the reward that would be offered— the human bloodhounds that would be set upon my track—the weariness—the hunger—the gloomy thought of not only losing all one's friends in one day, but of having to seek and make new friends in a strange world. . . . But, as I have said, the hour was come, and the man must act or forever be a slave.

The moment of decision and action was sometimes taken in flight from cruel treatment. William Parker once fought his master when the master tried to whip him: "I let go of my hold—bade him goodbye, and ran for the woods. As I went by the field, I beckoned to my brother, who left work and joined me at rapid pace." Parker's escape brought him to the verge of a new era in his life, one that would sustain him over many years because of the very impulse of freedom:

> I was now at the beginning of a new and important era in my life. Although upon the threshold of manhood, I had, until the relation with my master was sundered, only dim perceptions of the responsibilities of a more independent position. I longed to cast off the chains of servitude because they chafed my free spirit, and because I had a notion that my position was founded in injustice . . . The impulse of freedom lends wings to the feet, buoys up the spirit within, and the fugitive catches glorious glimpses of light through rifts and seams in the accumulated ignorance of his years of oppression. How briskly we traveled on that eventful night and the next day.

The same impulse for freedom was so strong in Henry Bibb that he "learned the art of running away to perfection." He continues: "I made a regular business of it and never gave it up until I had broken the bonds of slavery and landed myself in Canada where I was regarded as a man and not as a thing."

Often the fugitives' only companion was God, and they believed that it was He alone who could deliver man from the death and hell experience of slavery and escape. One recalls John Thompson's reluctance to escape with the Methodist preacher because he doubted an unseen God. But because membership in the community of believers, in God's army, required an unconditional faith in God's power and willingness to deliver his children, Thompson had to be converted. He had to hear God's voice and believe. When saved from a dangerous situation, Thompson began to believe in God's presence and then, started his life pilgrimage toward the salvation and freedom slaves felt was theirs to achieve. Thompson's personal witness united him to his community and to the cause of freedom that he now has the strength and guidance to seek alone:

> I knew it was the hand of God, working in my behalf; it was his voice warning me to escape from the danger towards which I was hastening. Who would not praise such a God? Great is the Lord, and greatly to be praised.

> I felt renewed confidence and faith, for I believed that God was in my favor, and now was the time to test the matter . . . I fell upon my knees, and with hands uplifted to high heaven, related all the late circumstances to the Great King, saying that the whole world was against me without a cause, besought his protection, and solemnly promised to serve him all the days of my life. I received a spiritual answer of approval; a voice like thunder seeming to enter my soul, saying, I am your God and am with you; though the world be against you, I am more than the world; though wicked men hunt you, trust in me, for I am the Rock of your Defense.

> Had my pursuers then been near, they must have heard me, for I praised God at the top of my voice. I was determined to take him at his word, and risk the consequences.

> I retired to my hiding place in the woods.

Once united with God, man shared in a specific moral code that sanctioned his escape and other tactics to insure success. The ethos of the fugitive was as practical as it was unique. In describing the tactics of Harriet Tubman, Sarah Bradford recognized this aspect of the fugitives' experience as perhaps a consequence of fear during their dangerous plight. "They had a creed of their own," Bradford writes [in her *Harriet—The Moses of Her People,* 1886], "and a code of morals which we dare not criticize till we find our own lives and those of our dear ones similarly imperiled." It was this moral code that helped the fugitive identify people along the escape route who could be trusted to help.

William Wells Brown once indicated his indictment of all people as victims of slavery and found most of them unworthy of his trust:

> I had long since made up my mind that I would not trust myself in the hands of any man, white or colored. The slave is brought up to look upon every white man as an enemy to him and his race; and twenty-one years in slavery had taught me that there were traitors, even among colored people.

The slave on the run was constantly on his guard. John Thompson used his unique "Christian" experience as a criterion for seeking help from others. He was referred to people of *true* Christian character, meaning those who would aid a fugitive. Of one man who offered his aid, Thompson writes: "I knew this man was a Christian, and therefore that it was safe to trust him, which is not true of all, since there are many treacherous colored, as white men." In another instance Thompson inquired, "I asked what I should do; to which he replied he could not tell, but pointing to a house nearby, said 'There lives Mrs. R., a free woman, and one of *God's true children,* who has travelled there many times and can direct you. You can depend upon what she tells you' " (emphasis mine). When suddenly accosted by a party of potentially dangerous white men, Thompson passed among them unharmed and calm. He attributed this to God's grace:

> . . . they did not molest us, although they followed us with their eyes, as far as they could see us. This was another Ebeneezer for us to raise, in token of God's deliverance, we knelt and offered up our thanksgiving to God for this great salvation.

Slaves believed that God moved through nature to help the fugitive. Moreover, through nature, God made his presence known by presenting obstacles and avenues for deliverance during the fugitive's journey. Most often the same natural force, such as a wide river, was both obstacle *and* aid. The dual quality of nature in the slave's thought makes it more crucial for man to take an active part in seeking deliverance, for he must be capable of identifying the voice as he did through his conversion experience and those good people who share in God's word: the children of God, the *true* believers. These barriers become an important test of man's faith in the power of God to make possible the freedom and salvation the slave seeks. Again, man must earn his freedom.

When Henry Bibb attempted escape alone, nature was his guide: "I walked with bold courage, trusting in the arm of Omnipotence; guided by the unchangeable North Star by night, and inspired by an elevated thought that I was fleeing from a land of slavery and oppression, bidding farewell to handcuffs, whips, thumbscrews and chains." Once having gained freedom for himself, he returned to rescue his wife and child. Caught again in slave territory, he felt he had to renew his covenant with God; he "passed the night in prayer to our Heavenly Father, asking that He would open to me even the smallest chance for escape."

In the woods following their escape, Bibb and his wife and child encounter nature at its harshest level:

> So we started off with our child that night, and made our way down to Red River swamps among the buzzing insects and wild beasts of the forest. We wandered about in the wilderness for eight or ten days. . . . Our food was parched corn . . . most of the time we were lost. We wanted to cross the Red River but could find no conveyance to cross it. I recollect one day of finding a crooked tree which bent over the river. . . . When we crossed over on the tree . . . we found that we were on an island surrounded by water on either side. We made our bed that night in a pile of dry leaves. . . . We were much rest-broken, wearied from hunger and travelling through briers, swamps and cane breaks. . . .

Then Bibb encountered the wolves who lived there and who came howling out of the night close to them:

> The wolves kept howling. . . . I thought that the hour of death for us was at hand . . . for there was no way for our escape. My little family were looking up to me for protection, but I could afford them none. . . . *I was offering up my prayers to that God who never forsakes those in the hour of danger who trust in him.* . . . I was surrounded by those wolves. But it seemed to be the will of a merciful providence that our lives should not be destroyed by them. I rushed forth with my bowie knife in hand. . . . I made one desperate charge at them . . . making a loud yell at the top of my voice that caused them to retreat and scatter which was equivalent to a victory on our part. *Our prayers were answered,* and our lives were spared through the night. (Emphasis mine.)

Through prayer Bibb was able to unite himself to the greater force of God and thus renew his own life force. However, his escape with his family had further complications and eventually they were recaptured. Once again Bibb escaped alone and began a new life in free territory without them. This last escape found Bibb secreted aboard a ship which conveyed him out of the waters of slavery and trial and into the promised North:

> When the boat struck the mouth of the river

Ohio, and I had once more the pleasure of looking on that lovely stream, my heart leaped up for joy at the glorious prospect that I should again be free. Every revolution of the mighty steam-engine seemed to bring me nearer and nearer the "promised land."

Henry Bibb's narrative is characteristic of the many slave autobiographies in which the protagonist confronts and is confronted by the challenge of survival and deliverance from the wilderness. Man, here, endures the test of the wilds in order to reap his reward of freedom, which is a direct result of his alliance with God. In the end he will be delivered on foot or aboard a particular conveyance which will provide a secret cover for his rebirth.

The escape episode in nature or secreted aboard a ship is an experience of the womb, the woods, or a dark cover that will give birth to a new man. Escape, then, is the central transforming episode in the death-rebirth cycle of life as viewed by the slave. By dint of his escape and his hiding, man becomes enlightened about his condition and reborn through his confrontation fighting his own fear, the wolves, the deep water of Jordan or the slave "patrollers."

The Reverend Thomas Jones recorded in his narrative that he hid aboard a ship until the time was right, until nature intervened by making the tide flow in his favor, and he gained his free identity:

> Here [in the hold of the ship] I was discovered by the Captain. He charged me with being a runaway slave, and said he should send me back by the first opportunity that offered. That day a severe storm came on and for several days we were driven by the gale. I turned to and cooked for the crew. The storm was followed by a calm of several days; and then the wind sprung up again and the Captain made for port at once. . . . While the Captain was in the city . . . I made a raft of loose board as I could get and hastily bound them together, and committing myself to God, I launched forth upon the waves. The shore was about a mile distant; I had the tide in my favor.

In the *Life and Adventure of Robert* [1829] the narrator hid in a "cave surrounded by a thick hedge of wild briars and hemlock" in Fox Point, Providence, Rhode Island, when his life in free territory was further complicated by slave catchers. Robert was a slave in Princeton, New Jersey, and engineered his escape by secreting himself aboard a sloop bound for Philadelphia. When his family was threatened and then separated by slave catchers, Robert made a final retreat into the wilderness. He returned to the womb of nature, his cave; as he told his amanuensis, "I felt but little desire to live, as there was nothing then to attach me to this world—and it was at that moment that I formed the determination to retire from it—to become a recluse, and mingle thereafter as little as possible with human society."

Henry "Box" Brown made more poignant use of the death-rebirth theme. He nailed himself up in a box and shipped himself to free territory as cargo. During the long journey he experienced the physical effects of dying: "I felt a cold sweat coming over me which seemed to be a warning that death was about to terminate my earthly miseries; but as I feared even that less than slavery, I resolved to submit to the will of God, and, under the influence of that impression, I lifted up my soul in prayer to God, who alone was able to deliver me. My cry was soon heard." When the box arrived at its destination a friend knocked to see if Brown was still alive inside. Brown's rebirth began: "The joy of the friends was very great. When they heard that I was alive they soon managed to break open the box, and then came my resurrection from the grave of slavery. I rose a free man; but I was too weak, by reason of long confinement in that box, to be able to stand, so I immediately swooned away."

By all accounts the God of the fugitive is a God who offers immediate freedom and deliverance to his chosen people. But this deliverance is on the condition of man's trial— man's willingness to be struck dead and achieve enlightenment through his despair, fear and solitude. Man with God conquers Egypt and death so that a freeman can be born.

In their long search for freedom, as in their religion and literature, slaves defined life as a pilgrimage. Just as life for the African was a continual practice of maintaining harmony and force within the ontological hierarchy established between man, the ancestors, and natural phenomena, so too was life for the Afro-American a pilgrimage toward renewed contact with God. The slave narrators preserve the dualism between the African and the Christian components in black religious syncretism, and we find through their emphasis on the escape experience that the narrators and bards gave the wilderness confrontation a central place in recounting the progress of their lives. For the narrators, this crucial moment of escape is also symbolic of the fusion of the two divergent cultural modes: the African and the American. Out of this cultural confrontation and, in some cases, moral entanglement the slave is converted and reconverted to himself, his community, his God. By engaging the wilderness the slave, as fugitive, renews his primal covenant with God through nature and becomes a freeman. From this primary connection with spiritual and natural forces, man derives his creativity, his freedom, and his spiritual redemption. His self and soul are strengthened.

In song and narrative, through the unifying image and actual experience of deliverance and survival—a life-affirming ideology—the slaves themselves have defined heroic value as an essential aspect of human character. The journey of the fugitive is but a microcosm of the entire life experience of men in search of freedom, which is also salvation. Samuel Ringgold Ward, himself a fugitive when just a child, has written [in his *Autobiography of a Fugitive Negro*, 1865] that men entrusted with such a mission grow with it heroically, and thus the fugitive becomes an exemplar of individual and group ideals:

> The fugitive exercises patience, fortitude, and perseverance, connected with and fed by an ardent and unrestrained and resistless love of liberty, such as cause men to be admired everywhere . . . the lonely toiling journey; the endurance of the excitement from constant danger; the hearing the yell and howl of the blood-

hound, the knowledge of close hot pursuit. . . . All these furnaces of trial as they are, purify and ennoble the man who has to pass through them. . . . All these are inseparable from the ordinary incidents in the northward passage of the fugitive; and when he reaches us, he is, first, what the raw material of nature was; and secondly, what the improving process of flight has made him.

Thus, the life of man that the spirituals and the narratives create for us is one which is grounded in concrete action and one which follows the highest moral persuasions. Man, as conceived within the slave's mythos and ethos, progresses toward spiritual regeneration. Through the test and trial of his faith he has fixed time and space in his quest; he has conquered the future by realizing it now; he has gained free territory by stepping forth from bondage; he has conquered life as a slave by being struck dead. Rebirth and immortality are his rewards. What gave the slave the surety of his life convictions and what made real the possibility of regeneration in this life and a positive, functional immortality in the next, was religion. The slave's religion, indeed his corporate faith that joined one to the other by the example of trial and the witness of death, was a joy and a healing fortune. And the slave has become free by first singing with a sword in his hand.

> *Melvin Dixon, "Singing Swords: The Literary Legacy of Slavery," in The* Slave's Narrative, *edited by Charles T. Davis and Henry Louis Gates, Jr., Oxford University Press, 1985, pp. 298-317.*

Marion Wilson Starling

[*In the following essay, Starling presents an overview of the various kinds of slave narratives that were popular in the nineteenth century, contending that although they have little artistic merit, they were nevertheless effective weapons in the abolitionist crusade.*]

The slave narratives, on the whole, are admittedly low in artistic value. Their primary significance, their picture of the institution of slavery as seen through the eyes of the bondsman himself, concerns the social historian. Some of the narratives achieve a degree of literary distinction in some passages, and the narratives of Equiano and Douglass are readily acceptable as literary achievements. But the untutored condition of the slave authors and the rush market for their stories as abolitionist propaganda militated against the development of literary excellence in the slave narratives. Social history apart, therefore, the significance of the narratives rests largely upon their germinating influence on American letters in the 1850s and 1860s and upon their revelation of the mind of the American Negro author as a slave.

Popular interest in the life of the Negro slave extends further back than the history of the narrative by a slave or an ex-slave. It seems to have begun in the latter part of the seventeenth century with the publication in 1688 of Mrs. Behn's *Oroonoko*, the story of an idealized African slave martyr, recently described [by George B. Woods, Homer A. Watt, and George B. Anderson, in their *The Literature of England,* Vol. 1, 1966] as notable "for its early statement of a theme that was to become the darling of the revolutionary novelists during the romantic movement—the theme of the noble savage and of the tyranny that afflicted him." The interest waned during the first half of the eighteenth century, when urbanization became a chief concern, but it waxed strong again in England toward the end of the century. The slave poetry of Cowper and Blake and the narratives of Gronniosaw and Equiano brought the slave into the picture of the common man then occupying the central position. With the rise of periodical literature in America as well as in England during the first quarter of the nineteenth century, the slave's story reached the journals.

Two types of slave narrative appeared side by side in the periodicals until 1852. The formula that Mrs. Behn had launched nearly a century and a half before was the basis for an idealized portrait of a cultured and sensitive slave bearing wrongs from his oppressor with remarkably Anglo-Saxon philosophizing. At the same time, there appeared the realistic portrait of the ambitious but frustrated slave finding his way out of slavery into freedom. Fusion of the two types appeared but rarely before the 1850s. The idealized narrative generally went its highly polished way with much style and little substance, and the "natural" narrative blundered along with inept expressions.

Idealized slave narrative sketches formed an important part of the contents of the antislavery periodicals, from the opening pages of Elihu Embree's *The Emancipator* in April of 1820 to the closing pages of Garrison's *The Liberator* in December of 1865. Often highly sentimental in tone, the sketches were written by leading abolitionist writers of the day: Mrs. Child, Edmund Quincy, Harriet Martineau, Maria Weston Chapman, Isaac Hopper, Julia Griffiths, William Adam, and others. Even more highly sentimentalized poems in the style of Cowper appeared beside the narratives, contributed to the periodicals by William Cullen Bryant, Whittier, Elizabeth Barrett Browning, Longfellow, and numerous poetasters. Created by authors almost totally ignorant of the actual slave scene, these slave narrative sketches and poems lacked life, though as literary exercises they were sometimes admirable.

Collection of these "parlor" pieces on the life of the slave were reprinted in permanent book form as early as 1826, when Abigail Field Mott published the first of five series of *Biographical Sketches and Interesting Anecdotes of Persons of Color.* This was followed by Harriet Martineau's sketches of slaves of Columbia, South Carolina, reprinted in her two-volume account of *Society in America,* published in London in 1932. Adopting the format of the elegant "gift books" in vogue in the 1830s, Mrs. Child brought together a group of the sketches and poems, published as *The Oasis,* in 1834. Her lead was followed by Mrs. Chapman, who, with the aid of a talented editorial board united under the name "Friends of Freedom," prepared handsome volumes of the antislavery "gift book" annual, *The Liberty Bell,* for sale in connection with the annual Massachusetts Anti-Slavery Fair. *The Liberty Bell* appeared annually from 1839 to 1858, except for the years

1840, 1850, 1854, 1855, and 1857. Other antislavery "gift books" made sporadic appearances, including the volumes entitled *Freedom's Gift* (1840), *North Star* (1840), *Star of Emancipation* (1841), *Liberty Chimes* (1845), and *Autographs for Freedom* (1853 and 1854). A collection of slave narrative sketches designed for children was gathered from the pages of *The Slave's Friend* and other periodicals and printed as *The Anti-Slavery Alphabet* for sale at the antislavery fair at Philadelphia in 1847. From first to last, these treatments of the noble savage theme attest to the efforts of authors of the day to interpret the plight of the slave in the only way they could, by imaginatively identifying themselves with persons they had never really known and the like of whose besetting problems they had never even seen. What these authors lacked in verity they endeavored to make up for with fine writing. The paper upon which their pieces were printed was also very fine, and the bindings and other subsidiary attractions were generally elegant.

Contrasting sharply with these pieces were the undressed narratives of the slave by the slave, after the school of Arthur and Venture Smith, William Grimes, and Richard Allen. Nearly three hundred slave stories of this type appear in the pages of *The Liberator.* Other antislavery periodicals contain an additional hundred. Theodore Weld gathered approximately a hundred more to include among his "thousand witnesses" of *Slavery as It Is.* This accounts in large measure for the amazing popularity of that "antislavery handbook" from the time of its publication in 1839. The printer J. W. Barber contributed thirty-six real-life sketches of slaves direct from Africa to the growing store of slave testimonials in his publication of the result of his personal interviews (with the aid of an African who understood a number of native dialects and spoke English) with the insurgents on the *Amistad* slave ship. These appeared together with phrenological studies of the captives in New Haven in 1840, under the title, *The History of the Amistad Captives.* By the 1840s, therefore, readers of the various antislavery publications were being copiously supplied with the raw materials of the slave's story, direct from his lips to the reporter's page.

The authors of the idealized slave sketches were the quickest of all the friends of the fugitives to appreciate the superior strength of the real slave story in comparison with the imagined one. Some of them at once became scribes and editors for the slaves' narrations. Whittier recorded the ill-starred story of James Williams. Joseph Lovejoy acted as scribe for the Clarke brothers. Wendell Phillips consulted with Douglass over his manuscript. Edmund Quincy helped William Wells Brown with his. The obviously tampered state of Zamba's narrative is the work of its many different editors, whose liberties with Zamba's text were taken as an excuse by the last editor, Peter Neilson, for additional changes of his own. Samuel Eliot prepared Josiah Henson's story; Olive Gilbert wrote Sojourner Truth's; Chamerovzow wrote John Brown's. Mrs. Child edited Harriet Jacobs's. Although it is plain that the hand of the scribe was sometimes taking down dictation from his own brain, especially in introductory and transitional passages, even cursory comparison of the content material of the abolitionist author's signed slave story with the slave story he edited will discourage belief that he was the creator of the latter. A recent student of the slave narratives, who is by no means inclined towards allowing the slave author undue credit, presents his decision as to the genesis of those writings [John Herbert Nelson, in his *The Negro in American Fiction*]:

> Curiously enough, of the many slave autobiographies, or biographies—for they were often "edited" by friends of the slave—all but three or four seem to be forgotten. For this neglect students of literature are easily excusable, because the narratives are seldom works of art; not so the historians, however, whose need is always for just such illuminating documents. Although filled with the most vociferous propaganda, in parts embittered and untrue, even the worst of them record as nothing else does the workaday life of the ante-bellum South. A reader soon learns to distinguish, in the large, the true portions from the falsified, and having done so, he finds himself confronted with pictures of slavery as it was; he discovers how both slaves and masters of the old South actually talked, dressed, carried on their occupations, amused themselves—in short, what their social background was, the world in which they moved.

Dearth of attention to the slave narratives as literature was not a characteristic of contemporary chronicles, however. The tenor of the frequent reviews and criticisms in current periodicals of all types ranged from highest praise to dire disgust. One of the most sustained of the contemporary studies was an article by a Reverend Ephraim Peabody, entitled "Narratives of Fugitive Slaves," which appeared in the *Christian Examiner* in July, 1849. The article was published shortly after publication of the narrative of Josiah Henson, which had produced a profound effect upon the writer because it had seemed to him to contain all of the points of strength of the slave narratives previously published but was free from their chief defect, a one-sided picture of the slaveholder.

Describing the recent vogue of narratives by slaves, Peabody placed their volumes "without hesitation among the most remarkable productions of the age—remarkable as being pictures of slavery by the slave, remarkable as disclosing under a new light the mixed elements of American civilization, and not less remarkable as a vivid exhibition of the force and working of the native love of freedom in the individual mind." Ordinary romances were tame, he thought, by the side of the incredible adventures of the fugitive slaves. Dwelling further upon the nature of the slave experience, Peabody writes:

> [The fugitive slaves] encounter a whole Iliad of woes, not in plundering and enslaving others, but in recovering for themselves those rights of which they have been deprived from birth. Or if the Iliad should be thought not to present a parallel case, we know not where one who wished to write a modern Odyssey could find a better subject than in the adventures of a fugitive slave. What a combination of qualities and deeds and sufferings most fitted to attract human sympathy in each particular case!

Five slave narratives are included in Peabody's specific discussion of the "very wide influence on public opinion" exerted by the slave narratives "scattered over the whole of the North," compared with which, he believed, "all theoretical arguments for or against slavery" were "feeble." The narratives were the autobiographies of Douglass (1845 version), Lewis and Milton Clarke (1846), William Wells Brown (1847), James W. C. Pennington (1849), and Josiah Henson (1849). Concerning Douglass and Henson, both of whom he declared he had known personally. Peabody says, "Apart from the internal evidence of truth which their stories afford, we have every reason to put confidence in them as men of veracity." Most of the thirty-pages of this article are devoted to analysis of their books.

Douglass's narrative was somewhat of a disappointment to Peabody, who was sorry to find in the "life of a superior man" like Douglass a "severity of judgment and a one-sidedness of view." Peabody believed that a person with Douglass's ability to "make all he says effective, through candor and a just appreciation of the difficulties that beset the subject of emancipation" should be careful not to diminish his power as an advocate of the antislavery cause by alienating antislavery sympathizers in the South. He inserted a personal message to Douglass in his article, directing his attention to the discussion that followed of the two kinds of slaveholders. Without minimizing the perpetual danger to the slave inherent in the system under which he existed, even under the best of slave environments, Peabody pleaded earnestly for a more understanding attitude toward the Southerners who recognized slavery as "a per-

Frederick Douglass.

nicious institution, injurious to the higher interests of all who are affected by it." Though fewer in number than those who cared only for "the advantages which they imagine may accrue to themselves personally from the present state of things," such slaveholders did exist, he pointed out, and it was vitally important to early solution of the problem of emancipation that pivotal figures like Douglass learn to regard "the friends of freedom at the South with the profoundest interest and sympathy." In fact, Peabody concluded in this connection that such Southerners composed "the only class of antislavery men whose existence is absolutely vital and essential to freedom—freedom can dispense with the efforts of others, but not with theirs."

Peabody objected to the narratives of the Clarkes, Brown, Pennington, and Douglass because of the impression they give that "the Slave States constitute one vast prison-house, of which all the whites without exceptions are the mere keepers, with no interest in the slaves further than they can be made subservient to the pleasure or profit of their owners." But the objection did not extend to the narrative of Josiah Henson. Declaring that he considered that narrative "to be the best picture of the evils incident to slave life on the plantations which can be found," Peabody devoted the entire second half of his essay to analysis of that individual, for whom he recommended the title of "Moses of the regenerated Africans in Canada." It might be interesting to the reader to compare Peabody's conception of Henson with the reader's own impressions from the narrative. To be sure, Peabody had the added advantage of personal acquaintance with the man, which we may keep in mind as we read his summary of Henson's treatment of slavery as a system:

> Those who know Henson will not doubt his statement of facts; and there is a freedom of [sic] exaggeration, a tolerance of judgment, and an absence of personal bitterness which give additional weight to his testimony. He does not represent all the whites in the Slave States as demons; but they appear in his narrative such as they are in reality,—human beings with the average virtues and vices of mankind, but their characters modified by the institutions under which they live. Among the whites he had kind friends—he knew those who were opposed to slavery; even those among his several masters who, in particular cases, treated him the worst, he looks upon with kindness. He sees that the masters, in their worst vices, are hardly less the victims of this disastrous institution than are the slaves in their degradation. There is no disposition to nurse his indignation against the wrongs he has received, or to bring them forward as a complete picture of slavery.

The "peculiar air of trustworthiness to what he says" had the effect of making more emphatic the evils inherent in the slave system, particularly that chief fear of the slave even on happy plantations—the fear of being sold away from his loved ones. Concerning this evil, so clearly depicted in Henson's story, Peabody writes:

> If we leave out of view the physical horrors of the Middle Passage, we believe that this internal

slave trade is a system more accursed, more deserving of execration, the cause of more suffering, than the direct trade from Africa. It is a horrible phantom, making miserable the whole slave population of the South. They who are never made the victims of this traffic, who live and die on the same plantation, know that, at any moment,—sometimes from the selfishness of avaricious masters, sometimes from the misfortunes or death of the kind-hearted,—they are liable to be sold to the slave-dealer who will bid highest, and sent to some other region. . . . When added to all other deprivations and sufferings, this horrible fear, weighing incessantly on the thoughts of millions of men and women, is in itself an evil of terrible magnitude.

Considered as an ideational unit, Peabody's analysis of the narratives of fugitive slaves pulses with suggestions for a subject-hunting fiction writer in that crucially important year of the slavery question, 1849 to 1850. Therefore, since Mrs. Harriet Beecher Stowe did come forth before the public in 1857 with the dramatic declaration that Josiah Henson was the prototype for her immortal Uncle Tom, and since for various reasons it is inconceivable that her interpretation of that character would have accidentally conformed to the fifteen-page interpretation of the Reverend Mr. Peabody rather than to a somewhat less myopic view of the contents of Henson's narrative, we believe that Mrs. Stowe found the ideational groundwork for her masterpiece in Peabody's study.

Mrs. Stowe's career as a fiction writer had been launched in the middle 1840s in the pages of *Godey's Lady's Book*. The editor of that "monthly annual" was the enterprising Mrs. Sarah Josepha Hale, author of the first slave novel written in America, *Northwood; or, Life North and South* (1827), the success of which had brought prominence to the little woman who was also owner and editor of the first "female" monthly magazine in the country, published in Boston. Louis Godey had bought out her magazine and transported Mrs. Hale to Philadelphia to become the editor of his new magazine for the rapidly expanding public of women readers. By 1850, Mrs. Hale had built up the subscription list to the fashionable *Godey's Lady's Book* to a monthly circulation of 150,000 copies and had presented to the public, through its pages, such outstanding literary "finds" as the Carey sisters, the Warner sisters, and Margaret Fuller. It is to be imagined that Mrs. Stowe, with her inherited "Beecher" ambition and eye for opportunities, was on the lookout for the formula underlying the sensational successes of some of her associates on Mrs. Hale's staff. Nor would it take long to ascertain the ingredients of the Susan Warner success motif: the domestic scene, sentiment "Dickenized into sentimentality," predominating femininity, and "always the humanitarian motif," as [Fred Pattee, in his *First Century of American Literature*, 1935] has analyzed the best-seller of the day.

For the indispensable humanitarian theme, nothing could have suggested itself to a subject-hunting novelist as more likely to attract the masses than the slave story, given the inflamed state of popular opinion in the North in the days surrounding the passage of the drastic Fugitive Slave Law of 1850. As to precedents in use of the theme in fiction, there was Mrs. Hale's own first novel, which had gone through four editions in a few years, and there was Richard Hildreth's slave novel, *Memoirs of Archy Moore,* which had enjoyed even wider success. The autobiographies of popular fugitive slave lecturers had been occupying the limelight in the 1840s, but their public was largely limited to the antislavery world. Borrowing their materials, rich in the ingredients of "sentiment-jerkers," as Peabody had so clearly pointed out, it would be possible to graft the slave's theme upon the *Wide, Wide World* formula and, instead of thousands of readers, capture tens of thousands! Thus do we imagine the course of Mrs. Stowe's musing in her quest for a theme rivaling that of her co-workers in appeal. At about that time she must surely have come upon Peabody's article in a magazine that few people besides preachers like her husband read.

This is not the place to trace exhaustively the apparently seminal relationship between Peabody's "Narratives of Fugitive Slaves" and *Uncle Tom's Cabin.* In the *Key to Uncle Tom's Cabin* which Mrs. Stowe prepared for the publishers directly after the appearance of her novel in order to satisfy the avalanche of requests from the reading world that she present the "original facts and documents upon which the story is founded, together with corroborative statements verifying the truth of the work," there is no mention of the Reverend Ephraim Peabody. On the other hand, the narrative of Josiah Henson, which in 1857 she cited as the chief original source for her book in her glowing introduction to the special "Harriet Beecher Stowe Edition" dedicated to her and republished in that year, receives less space in the *Key, etc.,* than do any of the other four slave narratives which Mrs. Stowe acknowledged as the source of her main materials. These same five narratives were the ones that Peabody had presented from among a number of popular narratives by fugitives. . . . In so hectic a period as the 1850s, when escaping slaves were shooting up one street and slave hunters down another, when the emissaries of the law were ordered to be extra vigilant lest any but the latter be served, a matter like the genesis of Mrs. Stowe's great idea seemed trifling. Nearly a hundred years later, however, in the course of tracing ideational growth from 1830 to the 1860's, it becomes important to examine the notion that Mrs. Stowe simply "thought up" her novel, after the day's dishes were done and the children tucked safely in bed, that she drew it from the depths of her great compassion for the slaves she often saw and helped on their hurried passage northward through Cincinnati.

First described by Mrs. Stowe [in *The Liberator* (17 September 1852)] as "simply a *tale,* a story, the scenes of which lie among a race hitherto ignored by the associations of polite and refined society," *Uncle Tom's Cabin* brought about a fusion of the two types of slave story: the raw material of the slave's account and the sentimental material of the imagined account. As Peabody had observed, the lives of the struggling slaves made the ordinary characters of romance seem dull and tame. He did not know "where one who wished to write a modern Odyssey could find a better . . . combination of qualities and deeds and sufferings . . . fitted to attract human sympathy." We have been on the Shelby plantation before—at the Lloyd

plantation in Douglass's narrative, at the Campbell plantation in the Clarke brothers' story, and at the Tilghman plantation in Pennington's narrative. George Harris is a composite picture of Douglass and William Wells Brown; Legree combines Messrs. Gore and Covey; Mr. St. Clair looks like Mr. Freeland; and we met Haley and Marks and Tom Loker when we went down to New Orleans with Henson. Clarke's sister Delia looks out from Cassy's eyes; Eliza is Henson's Charlotte; Little Evas run through dozens of slave testimonials telling of the loyalty and affection of the children of the Big House, who would openly defy the scorn of older members of their family to go dress the wounds of a favorite slave beaten dreadfully for some trifle or other and run the risk of punishment themselves for slipping off to teach slave children the rudiments of learning denied them. Mrs. Stowe's New England need not be looked to as the only possible source for Ophelia and St. Clair's Yankee brother; New Englanders appear on a number of the plantations, in the narratives of the slaves. The scenes on the cotton field, in front of the cabins, on the auction block, and beside the whipping post are made up of authentic details repeatedly corroborated in the mass slave records. The distress of the separated members of the loving slave family, the outrageous nature of punishments administered because of the slave's refusal to bend as low as the master's command, the hairbreadth escapes and breathtaking adventures of the spirited young slave, the transcendent power of religious faith over the degradation of the slave experience—from a mass of real happenings teeming with sensation the inspired author created unity by means of the idealized figure of Uncle Tom.

Uncle Tom was Peabody's conception of Josiah Henson, not Henson's. Mrs. Stowe must have realized this after she met the interesting "ambassador for the fugitives" in England in the course of her triumphal tour. Wishing to find a slave sufficiently philosophical in his thinking to look at the slave scene steadily and see it in terms of a whole, Peabody found passages enough in Henson's narrative to satisfy him. He completely missed this man's irony, it would seem, as well as the picture of a slaveholder given by Douglass in Mr. Freeland, which is superior to Henson's Master Amos or any of the others. Henson's remarkable description of his conversion deeply affected Peabody and inspired a moving interpretation of the very able and by no means self-effacing plantation overseer.

The idealized Henson becomes Mrs. Stowe's Uncle Tom. His ending cannot be the same. George Harris escapes to a colony in Liberia (in deference, perhaps, to the cherished antislavery plan of Mr. Birney, who was the first buyer of Mrs. Stowe's story), but Uncle Tom must die a victim of the system that he understood too profoundly to pack his children in a duffel bag and flee to the north, like the real Josiah Henson! In his concern that the slave narrative serve the antislavery cause effectively, stirring all hearts by the compelling power of true revelations of evils but at the same time avoiding "censorious, loose, and violent treatment" of the slaveholders as a class, the Reverend Mr. Peabody unwittingly joined hands with those who wrote of the "noble savage" with more style than substance. The one step remaining to be taken to weld fact and fancy into the novel of novels is the step taken by Mrs. Stowe.

Thus, to the student of the slave narrative, the novel that, according to Lincoln, started the Civil War is an intriguing composite of two literary streams: the sentimentally imagined slave story and the real slave autobiography. None of the events in the whole eventful story is without its parallel in the slave records. But whereas the slave author, in the full flush of his release from the dreadful reality of slavery, felt its wrongs too deeply for tears, the sentimental writer required equal portions of fact and tears to fulfill the stock formula. How well Mrs. Stowe succeeded in meeting the requirements we can deduce from the chiding of her master in the field of the sentimental novel, Charles Dickens. Asked by Mrs. Stowe for an opinion of *Uncle Tom's Cabin,* he is said to have written:

> You go too far and seek to prove too much. The wrongs and atrocities of slavery are, God knows! case enough. I doubt if there be any warrant for making out the African race to be a great race, or for supposing the future destinies of the world to lie in that direction [Pattee].

It was to an antislavery paper, we will do well to remember, not to *Godey's Lady's Book,* that Mrs. Stowe sold the serial rights to her slave novel. The conservative abolitionists, Mr. and Mrs. James G. Birney, bought her story for the journal they had founded in 1846, *The National Era,* a paper forever to be distinguished among antislavery publications as the medium through which the reading world first obtained Whittier's *Leaves from Margaret Smith's Journal in the Province of Massachusetts Bay, 1678-1679* (1849) and Hawthorne's *The Scarlet Letter* (1850), as well as *Uncle Tom's Cabin,* which was the serial feature from June 5, 1851, until April 1, 1852. Just before the appearance of the last installment as a serial, on March 12, 1852, the novel was published reluctantly in book form by the firm of John P. Jewett and Company of Boston.

The history of the popular reception of this book almost exceeds belief. Early newspaper reports credited its "immense circulation" to the "extraordinary exertion of the abolitionists" who, according to one paper, were everywhere "exulting in the sale of this pernicious work," and, according to another, were rejoicing over the cause "this admirable work" was serving—the downfall of slavery. By the first of May, the publishers canceled all other printing orders, busying themselves for the next eleven months with turning out nothing but copies of the novel they were loathe to publish in the first place for fear that they would lose money on the venture. Ten thousand copies per week were printed, fifty thousand having already been sold by the first of May. Extant copies of issues from the John P. Jewett press with the 1852 imprint give the information "10th thousand," "30th thousand," "40th thousand," "70th thousand," "85th thousand," "100th thousand," "120th thousand," "183rd thousand," and "285th thousand"! Reporting the sale of the novel in England, an authority states that between April and December, 1852, eighteen different publishing houses had reprinted and sold one-and-a-half million copies of *Uncle Tom's Cabin.* One publisher sending out to his agents as many as 10,000 copies per day. In conclusion, [Clarence Gohdes, in his *American Literature in Nineteenth Century England,* 1944] says:

> Of all the American works reprinted in Great Britain during the century, by all odds *Uncle Tom's Cabin* had the largest immediate or relatively immediate sale. Indeed, this work supplied the English booktrade with its first example of "best sellerism" in the modern sense, far surpassing anything by Scott or Dickens in its initial success.

In 1853, the book was being issued in translations to German, French, Flemish, Dutch, Italian, Spanish, Portuguese, Greek, and Celtic, in editions ranging in price from thirty-seven-and-a-half cents to five dollars. A letter sent to Garrison from Constantinople, in midsummer of 1853, reported that *Uncle Tom's Cabin,* which was being published in that city by a Greek newspaper as a weekly serial, was "taking the literary world by storm" and that "Shelby, St. Clair, 'Uncle Tom.' Casey, and Legree [had become] household words." In May of 1853, Mrs. Stowe's *Key to Uncle Tom's Cabin* was ready for distribution. Jewett and Company announced that 59,300 copies of the initial edition of 80,000 copies had been ordered in advance of publication. The book was soon issued in bindings conforming to the various bindings for the novel as a companion-piece, in editions ranging from the twenty-five cent copy "for the million," to the five-dollar, turkey-red octavo for the luxury-minded. Translations of the *Key, etc.* were published in German, French, and Celtic.

Miniature "Uncle Tom flags" were being circulated as choice souvenirs at church fairs, and the praises of "the story of the age" were being sung either *ex tempore* or in the words of Whittier's poem "Little Eva, Uncle Tom's Guardian," as set to music by Manuel Emilio in July of 1852. Meanwhile, a grumbling undercurrent in opposition to the novel was striving to make itself felt. One newspaper correspondent denounced the book as a "mischievous, dangerous work, got up on purpose for evil," and considered Eve's sinful sharing of the apple the only adequate parallel to the harm done. The students of the University of Virginia, learning that Mrs. Stowe was visiting in the neighborhood, got up a great mock serenade and burnt her in effigy. A black man in Dorchester County, Maryland, received a sentence of ten years in the State Penitentiary for having "incendiary publications"—that is, a copy of *Uncle Tom's Cabin*—in his house, though it was not proved that he had read it to any other black people in the neighborhood or even that he knew how to read it himself. A curious group of opposers to the novel consisted of radical abolitionists of the type that had fought Douglass's ransoming of himself. They were greatly disturbed by Mrs. Stowe's "gentle" handling of the slaveholder. One irate correspondent, after having declared himself "an abolitionist heart and soul," wound up a heated letter with the following splutter [*The Liberator* (22 October 1852)]:

> I fear the book will raise jeers and jests. . . . If this book be really a faithful record of what slavery is in America, and of what slaves are, let slavery remain and work out its own cure. No missionaries will ever make the converts which

the "niggers" will of their masters, if they are like Uncle Tom, and no laborers in our European countries lead half such happy lives as the majority of "niggers" do in the slave States, according to this novel.

The reaction of readers in New Orleans, as avowed in a letter from a resident of that city to the editor of the *New York Independent,* shows a viewpoint among Southerners that Peabody had discussed. Writing from New Orleans, August 18, 1852, the resident says:

> When *Uncle Tom's Cabin* was first issued, it was predicted in your paper that it would be read in New Orleans; and it has indeed found its way here, and numbers of our citizens have, as with avidity they persued its deeply interesting narratives, been alternately moved to tears, or convulsed with laughter. I sent to New York for the book, and when I carried it home and laid it upon the table, it was taken up and read by a young Southern friend then present, who has trafficked in slaves; and he soon remarked, 'This description is true to the life; the writer must have had some personal experience of slavery!' He asked and obtained the first loan of the book. Since then, it has been going the rounds, and before one is through, it is engaged by another.
>
> Our papers occasionally copy notices of the work, such as the extent of the sales, the profits of the author, etc.,—but I have seen only one notice upon the merits of the book, and that was in the *Bulletin,* whose editor pronounced it "a pack of lies." But I will venture the assertion, that he never read the book, and probably never saw it. My own view is, that Mrs. Stowe has presented the institution of slavery in too favorable a light. As to the truthfulness of the barbarities she describes, abundant confirmation may be had by any one who will take the trouble to collect the facts. This very day, a Southern lady, a slaveholder, detailed to me scenes of cruelty she had witnessed, equaling in atrocity the worst representation in *Uncle Tom's Cabin.*

The whole front page of *The Liberator* for the issue of March 4, 1853, was devoted to reprintings of reviews of *Uncle Tom's Cabin* from newspapers throughout the world in honor of the phenomenal first-year record of that best-selling novel. At the same time that Garrison was glorying in the book's power, George R. Graham, owner, publisher and editor of *Graham's Magazine,* was sending slips to the nineteen hundred editors with whom he exchanged," in order to "make clear the principles" of his periodical in connection with the current "incursion of the blacks" into the pressroom. Among other things, Graham tells the editors:

> Mrs. Stowe's *Uncle Tom's Cabin* is a *bad book.* It is badly constructed, badly timed, and made up for a bad purpose. The work has been successful pecuniarily—but there is such a thing as blood money, speedily gained by nefarious doings. . . . Uncle Tom has served its purpose—it has made excitement and money—but we must be excused from falling down and worshiping so false and mean a thing. . . . Our female agitators have abandoned Bloomers in despair, and

are just now bestride a new hobby—an intense love of black folks, in fashionable novels. A plague of all black faces!

Two months earlier, after a long stampede on *Uncle Tom's Cabin* in particular and the interest of the public in "black letters" in general, including interest in the "literary nigritudes" and "tadpoles of the press" in the form of the slave autobiographies, the sad-hearted author posed a worried query in an unsigned article appearing in *Graham's Magazine* for January of 1853, entitled "Black Letters; or, Uncle Tom-foolery in Literature":

> The population of reader has gone a woolgathering. . . . Seriously speaking—our writers who would take the public ear, would turn to something worthier than these Negro subjects. Where is the great need of going to the black section of the population in quest of themes, while the broader and richer domains of the better races lie before them?

Despite such pleas to the writers of the day, however, the "great need" of taking advantage of Mrs. Stowe's popular invention of the stickily sentimental novel based on the actual and grotesque facts of the slave system struck antislavery agitators, proslavery agitators, and writers in search of good potboilers. Because it was a formula that almost any writer of the day might imitate to some sort of advantage, a flurry of imitations of *Uncle Tom's Cabin* rose like dust particles, many of them settling again almost as quickly. In superficial design, these "poor relations of Uncle Tom," as one recent critic has named the slave novels deluging the market in the 1850s, resembled each other. The front matter of the volumes usually announced the author's purpose of portraying "slavery in the cabins and the mansions of the South as it really is" or something very similar. And in their final effect, probably, the import of the novels by antislavery or proslavery thinkers was probably very similar: the focusing of the world's attention on the lives of four million human beings who, whether oppressed by direst sufferings or pampered with luxury, were one and all denied the freedom of movement of other human beings. In their advertised purpose, however, the basic unity of the slave story was divided into two treatments: books denying or books affirming cruelty to the slave by the slave system.

Literary and social historians of the 1850s have adopted the rather obvious statement that "at least fourteen proslavery novels" followed close upon publication of *Uncle Tom's Cabin.* At least fourteen have *survived.* Judging from contemporary notices, the actual number that appeared must have been wearying. The best, like Mrs. Eastman's *Aunt Phillis' Cabin* (1852), J. Thornton Randolph's *The Cabin and the Parlor* (1852), Mrs. Emily Pearson's *Cousin Frank's Household* (1852), J. P. Kennedy's 1852 revision of *Swallow Barn* (originally published in 1832), and J. H. Ingraham's *The Sunny South* (1860), received wide recognition for their "corrections" of Mrs. Stowe's pictures of the South's "patriarchal institution." The worst, like W.L.G. Smith's *Uncle Tom's Cabin as It Is* (1852) and Wilson's *Our Nig* (1853), provoked the ridicule of the press for conspicuous wasting of fine paper and good ink in printing them. On the whole, however, the many "answers to *Uncle Tom's Cabin*" that appeared, particularly in 1852 and from 1859 to 1860, in the wake of the John Brown tragedy, were of run-of-the-mill quality, no better and no worse than the second- and third-rate fiction of any literary period. As social documents revealing the mental atmosphere of the decade, they are of value today, for they show the unthinking sentimentality with which millions of Americans glossed over the evils of slavery rather than be faced with the troublesome task of changing the status quo. From a historical point of view, one of the most enlightening of the proslavery publications was the republishing in 1857 of *Northwood; or, Life North and South,* which had appeared in 1827 as the first slave novel. Originally written in the hope of improving the understanding of the difference between social conditions north and south of the Mason-Dixon line, Mrs. Hale's novel was antislavery in tone but stressed preservation of the Union through appreciation of sectional problems. In 1857, in her introduction to the revised edition, which enjoyed great financial success because of the important position of its author and the nature of its publication history, Mrs. Hale expressed regret that the humanitarian question at the basis of the vogue for novels on slavery was being confused with political issues. Forced to take a stand, therefore, either for or against "the South," she was now launching her previously antislavery book on the side of the proslavery sympathizers.

Meanwhile, the abolitionists were also "answering" *Uncle Tom's Cabin* with fewer volumes, distinctly belligerent in tone. Mrs. Stowe's treatment of certain aspects of slavery had troubled many in the antislavery ranks, and there was sharp purpose behind the didactic "fiction" that resulted. Richard Hildreth's *Memoirs of Archy Moore,* which had never really left the book stands from the time of its appearance in 1836, came forth in 1852 in a new version, buttressed with a "key" to its sources in the newly added appendix and variously titled *The White Slave: or, Memoirs of a Fugitive; The Slave: or, Memoirs of Archy Moore;* and, *The White Slave: or, Negro Life in the Slave States of America.* William Wells Brown, from his exiled position in England as a fugitive from slavery, adopted the slave novel form for his own picture of the life of the mulatto slave in *Clotel: or, The President's Daughter,* a very popular addition to antislavery publications in England in 1853. Mrs. Stowe's *Dred,* which appeared in 1856 and sold 165,000 copies within the course of three months, no longer "straddled the fence" after the manner of Peabody's wishes (and with the certain result of catapulting her masterpiece into fame and fortune). Based on the *Confessions of Nat Turner* and attentive to the complaints of abolitionists concerning the "milk of human kindness" that they felt unnecessary and even harmful to antislavery literature, *Dred* was a much stronger novel than *Uncle Tom's Cabin* and makes for better reading today. But the change in the formula from her initial combination of ingredients left only the facts and kept *Dred* from becoming popular outside of abolitionist groups, except on the basis of "another novel by the author of *Uncle Tom's Cabin.*"

The slave narratives were closely imitated by the abolitionist authors of slave novels after 1852, and it was frequently impossible to tell one from the other when the author was not publicly known. The anonymous *Autobiography of a Female Slave* (1856) was probably the most successfully disguised of the slave novels. Its author, Mattie Griffiths Browne, was a young white woman, a former slaveholder in Kentucky, who had enlisted wholeheartedly in the abolitionist cause and had emancipated all of her slaves, even though she was thus confronted with the prospect of poverty and the derision of the only society she had ever known. Befriended in Boston by Mrs. Child, the young woman wrote short sketches and antislavery poems for the journal Mrs. Child was editing, *The National Anti-Slavery Standard,* before preparing one of the most powerfully authentic of the slave novels. Sentiment-ridden and intolerant of slavery, the book still possesses strength as a work of fiction, and its details, which Mrs. Browne declared were true in every respect, are authenticated in the mass testimony of the slave records. It was long believed to be an actual autobiography. During the late 1850s and early 1860s, few readers stopped to investigate or to care. The annals of the lowly slave were eagerly sought and were so strange even in mild histories that whether a work was factual or fictional or a combination ceased to concern the popular mind. In an atmosphere saturated with slave stories, fact and fancy came together to form one thing: books on slavery.

Commingling of the materials continued throughout the nineteenth century in post-Civil War stories of the slave. With the disappearance from sight and memory of the harassed, hunted fugitive, popular conception in the North of the Negro as a "brother but in chains" faded, and a stereotyping along the line of the "Topsy" motif began to take place. In the South, the wreck of the entire social fabric and the poverty everywhere precluded interest in the ubiquitous black man as a man. Social research in the present day, however, is leading to analyses that separate fact and fancy in the social history of the slave. In the field of his literary history, equal advances can be made.

This pioneer study of the slave narratives must be considered as merely "getting our guns into position" for projecting the mind of the slave into the records of American literary history. The narratives before 1836 and after 1865 reveal the same person that we find in the autobiographies winnowed from the stacks of slave literature of the 1830s to the 1860s: the American Negro, without benefit of society.

He is a very thoughtful individual, this American Negro slave. Saffin's Adam, Gronniosaw, Equiano, Venture Smith, Robert Voorhis, Solomon Bayley, Richard Allen, William Grimes, Lunceford Lane, Henry Bibbs, Austin Steward, John Thompson—the mere names call forth their sensitive reflections on the nature of the environment in which fate had placed them, on plans for effecting an improvement in their lot, on analysis of their fellow man. The absence of humor in their narratives does not mean an absolute absence of that essential quality in their lives. In the process of focusing their attention upon the underlying pattern of their experiences as slaves, in meeting the demands of the autobiography as a literary form, humor would assume a very negative position. Unconsciously, however, the slave narrator sometimes reveals the very soul of humor, even in the midst of harrowing experiences: Solomon Bayley's overhearing of the slavehunters coming back from their search for him, or the little dog that worried Pennington as he lay afraid even to tremble on the bed of cornshucks that crackled like pistols when he but breathed, or Lunceford Lane's indecision in choosing to work all night to earn money to buy himself or to sleep all night so that he would not get beaten for not working fast enough during the day.

The ambition of the slave of the narratives and his struggle against dreadful odds to achieve learning, decent standards of living, security, and freedom make the slave narratives an impressive record of human behavior. Undoubtedly, the record concerns superior slaves in the main, especially in the book-length narratives. It is probable that only superior slaves were able to inspire enough interest in themselves to bring the story of their lives to permanent records. Nonetheless, the narrators Venture Smith and Tom Jones, James Curry and Moses Grandy, Henry Watson and Henry Box Brown were not telling of themselves alone. With very few exceptions, the narratives tell of the ambitions of other slaves on the plantation, of cooperation between slaves within a plantation and between plantations. The mysterious "grapevine" that carried slave messages so bafflingly in all parts of the slave area was a monument to the slaves' interest and desire to help others acquire the opportunity to escape from slavery if humanly possible. There are numerous accounts of the ways in which house slaves steared the projects of escaping slaves, welcoming their opportunity to keep informed at the Big House of happenings of importance to the slaves in general. They ran the risk of being whipped to death for learning to read, in order that they might convey to the other slaves information from the newspapers and other printed matter. Thousands of slaves who attempted flight were caught, beaten, "demoted" to harder work, sold to the deep South. Only a relative few, an estimated sixty thousand, managed to reach free soil.

The slave authors were a select group of that number of successful fugitives. It is possible that they were not fewer proportionally, however, than the percentile relationship between authors and readers in the free world of their time. Ideationally, the slave narrator and the slave seem to be one.

Present-day reviewers are complaining, with increasing frequency, of the "bitterness" and "emotion" expressed in the writings of Richard Wright, Chester Himes, W.E.B. DuBois, Langston Hughes, J. Saunders Redding, and most of the rest of the growing circle of popular Negro authors. Their market, today, reminds us of the market of the fugitive slave one hundred years ago. A crusade is again in process, this time for the purpose of emancipating humankind from the neurosis of racial prejudice. A Mrs. Stowe is again needed to fuse the Negro's story and the imaginings of wishful thinkers.

Marion Wilson Starling, "The Literary Significance of the Slave Narratives," in her The Slave Narrative: Its Place in American History, *G. K. Hall and Co., 1981, pp. 294-310.*

William L. Andrews

[In the following essay, Andrews examines how the themes of slavery and freedom were treated differently in African-American literature before and after the Civil War and emancipation.]

The most famous metaphor of slavery in the history of Afro-American literature appears in the climax of the *Narrative of the Life of Frederick Douglass, an American Slave,* in which Douglass reconstructs the significance of his struggle with the slave-breaker, Edward Covey, on a hot August morning in 1834. Triumph over Covey, known as "the snake" among his slaves, became Douglass's "glorious resurrection, from the tomb of slavery, to the heaven of freedom." A little more than a half century after Douglass's *Narrative* was published, the most infamous metaphor of slavery in the history of black American literature appeared in the first chapter of Booker T. Washington's *Up from Slavery.* When we "look facts in the face," Washington states, "we must acknowledge that, notwithstanding the cruelty and moral wrong of slavery, the ten million Negroes inhabiting this country, who themselves or whose ancestors went through the school of American slavery, are in a stronger and more hopeful condition, materially, intellectually, morally, and religiously, than is true of an equal number of black people in any other portion of the globe." The disparities between these two metaphors are striking. The antebellum writer says slavery was like a tomb, in which he languished in what Orlando Patterson [in his *Slavery and Social Death,* 1982] would call "social death" and from which he was resurrected only by rebellious effort. The postbellum writer, on the other hand, compares slavery to a school, in which he and his fellows received, rather than lost, social purpose and from which they graduated not by violence but by sanctioned behavior like industry and dutifulness. I do not call attention to this difference between Douglass and Washington in order to question the reliability of one or the other as historian of slavery. The metaphorical shift between the two most influential slave narratives in American literature urges a more important inquiry, I believe, into the dynamics of Afro-American literary, rather than sociopolitical, history.

Throughout the nineteenth century and well into the twentieth, autobiographies of former slaves dominated the Afro-American narrative tradition. Approximately sixty-five American slave narratives were published in book or pamphlet form before 1865. Between the Civil War and the onset of the depression, at least fifty more ex-slaves saw their autobiographies in print, to a large extent eclipsing in their own time the influence, if not the memory, of their antebellum predecessors. Yet with the exception of criticism on *Up from Slavery,* there has been little investigation into what I shall call the postbellum slave narrative, nor has there been any serious study of the large number of black autobiographies in the late nineteenth and early twentieth centuries that were written in the shadow of the postbellum slave narrative, especially Washington's. It is imperative to read the slave narrative tradition wholly, however, if we wish to reckon with the significance of the crucial shift in the metaphor of slavery that highlights the Douglass and Washington texts. If we read the Afro-

American autobiographical tradition from 1765 to 1920 in toto, we can see that major parameters of this tradition—such as the representation of slavery—underwent revision, not only according to the differing perspectives of individual writers but also in relation to the changing social and political priorities of successive generations of freedmen and freedwomen.

The slave narrative took on its classic form and tone between 1840 and 1860, when the romantic movement in American literature was in its most influential phase. Transcendentalists like Theodore Parker welcomed antebellum slave narratives (and Douglass's in particular) into the highest echelon of American literature, insisting that "all the original romance of Americans is in them, not in the white man's novel" [in his "The American Scholar," in *The American Scholar*, edited by George Willis Cooke, vol. 8 of *Centenary Edition of Theodore Parker's Writings*, 1907]. Douglass's celebration of selfhood in his 1845 *Narrative* might easily be read as a black contribution to the literature of romantic individualism and anti-institutionalism. Ten years later Douglass's second autobiography, *My Bondage and My Freedom*, deconstructs his 1845 self-portrait with typical romantic irony. The idea of heroic slaves like Douglass resurrecting themselves from graves of the spirit by forceful resistance to authority undoubtedly appealed to an era fascinated by the romantic agon, the life-and-death contest of the spirit of revision against all that represses it. But after the Civil War, few ex-slave autobiographers recounted their lives in the manner of Douglass. The stunningly different treatments of bondage and selfhood in *Up from Slavery* [1901], for instance, signal a new wave of revisionism in postbellum Afro-American literature, instanced in the reaction of later slave autobiographers to what they perceived as romanticized interpretations of the pre-emancipation past, whether by black or white writers. By the turn of the century, slave narrators viewed slavery and its significance to the advancement of black people in an increasingly pragmatic perspective, delineated most effectively in *Up from Slavery*. This immensely influential slave narrative articulates a quasi-literary realism whose rhetoric, conventions, and cultural import need to be examined if we are to reckon adequately with the effort on the part of turn-of-the-century black novelists to make fiction address matters of fact.

The antebellum slave narrative was the product of fugitive bondmen who rejected the authority of their masters and their socialization as slaves and broke away, often violently, from slavery. Since the slave's right to rebel was a hotly debated issue in the 1840s and 1850s, the classic antebellum slave narrative highlights the brutalizing horrors of slavery in order to justify forcible resistance and escape as the only way a black could preserve his or her humanity. Through an emphasis on slavery as deprivation—buttressed by extensive evidence of a lack of adequate food, clothing, and shelter; the denial of basic familial rights; the enforced ignorance of most religious or moral precepts; and so on—the antebellum narrative pictures the South's "peculiar institution" as a wholesale assault on everything precious to humankind. Under slavery, civilization reverts to a Hobbesian state of nature; if left to its own

devices slavery will pervert master and mistress into monsters of cupidity and power-madness and reduce their servant to a nearly helpless object of exploitation and cruelty. Ultimately this objectifying power of slavery is what the antebellum slave narrative protests against most eloquently by demonstrating the evolution of a liberating subjectivity in the slave's life, up to and including the act of writing autobiography itself.

Antebellum slave narrators like Douglass and Henry Bibb trace their salvation back to an intuition of individual uniqueness and a sense of special destiny which they claim has inspired them since their early youth. "The fire of liberty," Bibb states [in his *Narrative of the Life and Adventures of Henry Bibb*, 1849], "seemed to be a part of my nature; it was first revealed to me by the inevitable laws of nature's God." The slave's outward struggle for physical freedom emanates from an inner conflict played out in the arena of his consciousness, where the fire of his Promethean self contends with the "mental and spiritual darkness" (in James Pennington's typical image [in his *The Fugitive Blacksmith*, in *Great Slave Narratives*, edited by Arna Bontemps, 1968]) of slavery. Ironically, however, the enlightenment provided by the Promethean fire within only reveals the tremendous gulf between the slave's subjective view of himself as a unique essence and slavery's objectified view of him as a thing. As a result of such revelations, the slave's world takes on an absolute, binary character. The only way he can assert his existence as a subject is by rebelling against the system that renders him an object. In the act of rebellion, the slave realizes himself, gives order to the chaos of his condition, and claims what we might call an existential authenticity and freedom while still in bondage.

What the slave rebel seeks in his flight to the North, however, is much more than an existential alternative to the non-being of slavery. The quest is for an ideal of freedom, a condition in which one may liberate the essential self within through expressive action and the power of the word. Few fugitive slaves say that their goal, when they fled the South, was to make a name for themselves as speakers and / or writers in the North. Still, the most memorable antebellum slave narrators treat their arrival on the abolitionist lecture platform or their acceptance of the antislavery pen as the fulfillment of their destiny. Literacy is considered the ultimate form of power in the antebellum slave narrative, for at least two reasons. First, language is assumed to signify the subject and hence to ratify the slave narrator's humanity as well as his authority. Second, white bigotry and fear presumably cannot withstand the onslaught of the truth feelingly represented in the simple personal history of a former slave. This romantic trust in the power of language did not go unchallenged in the antebellum black autobiography, as I have argued in my book *To Tell a Free Story* [1986]. Still, given the paucity of alternative weapons for blacks in the antislavery struggle, the idea that the word could make them free remained an article of faith in Afro-American literature of the antebellum era.

The abolition of involuntary servitude in 1865 forced the slave narrator in the postwar era to reevaluate the purpose of his or her prospective literary enterprise. Since ex-slaves no longer needed to denounce slavery to white America, the story of their past no longer carried the same social or moral import. Upon the demise of Reconstruction, however, and the rise of reactionary racism in the New South, many ex-slaves felt a renewed sense of purpose as first-hand commentators on the South before and after the war. The author of the new slave narrative, however, was no longer the rebel-fugitive whose ascent to freedom in the North had been celebrated in romantic fashion in the antebellum era. The large majority of postbellum ex-slave autobiographers—three out of every four, to be more exact—take pride in having endured slavery without having lost their sense of worth or purpose and without having given in to the despair that the antebellum narrator pictures as the lot of so many who languished in slavery. Acknowledging that rare "moral courage" was required to engineer a successful escape from slavery, the typical postbellum narrator insists that slaves who never took such a step could still claim a dignity and heroism of their own. "There were thousands of hightoned and high-spirited slaves," Henry Clay Bruce recalls in his 1895 narrative [*The New Man: Twenty–Nine Years a Slave, Twenty–Nine Years a Free Man*], "who had as much self-respect as their masters, and who were industrious, reliable and truthful. . . . These slaves knew their own helpless condition" and understood that "they had no rights under the laws of the land." Yet "they did not give up in abject servility, but held up their heads and proceeded to do the next best thing under the circumstances, which was, to so live and act as to win the confidence of their masters, which could only be done by faithful service and an upright life." When these "reliables," as Bruce terms them, were "freed by the war, the traits which they had exhibited for generations to such good effect, were brought into greater activity, and have been largely instrumental in making the record of which we feel so proud to-day."

These remarks from Bruce's autobiography . . . exemplify the pragmatism of the postbellum slave narrative in several respects. Bruce implicitly rejects the existential thesis of the antebellum narrative, namely, that because slavery was inimical to a slave's intellectual, moral, and spiritual development, rebellion was necessary to the slave's assertion and preservation of selfhood. Bruce argues that slaves could and did achieve "self-respect" without rebelling or running away to the North. Instead of the "either-or" conditions of the antebellum narrator—either self-affirming rebellion or self-abnegating acceptance of chattelism—Bruce, like most postbellum narrators, stresses that slaves could and did choose "the next best thing" according to relative, rather than absolute, standards of value. There is ample evidence of forcible, as well as passive, resistance to mean-spirited masters in slave narratives like Bruce's, a testimony to the fact that slaves in the postbellum narrative treasure their dignity as much as their counterparts in the antebellum narrative. But in the postbellum narrative, the measure of a slave's dignity is much more pragmatic than existential, more public than private, and more tangible and considerably less ideal than it is in the most famous antebellum narratives. Thus, while Douglass's fight with Covey epitomizes the antebellum ideal of "manhood," a typical postbellum slave narrator like George

Henry [in his *The Life of George Henry,* 1894] sets out to prove "that though black I was a man in every sense of the word" by recalling his superlative achievements as a hostler, a ship's captain, even as overseer, in slavery. In the postbellum narrative, a slave does not have to fight back to claim a free man's sense of empowering honor; diligence in his duties and pride in a task well done say as much or more about a black man's respectability as running away, especially if that black man is also a family man. Ultimately, men like Bruce and Henry appeal to the pragmatic test of history to vindicate their sense of honor. The success stories that these "new men" chronicle in their post-emancipation years are designed to demonstrate that the course they followed as slaves prepared them well to seize opportunity in freedom and turn it to honorable account, both socially and economically.

The pragmatism of the postbellum slave narrator stems primarily from his willingness to interpret and evaluate slavery according to its practical consequences in the real world of human action. While the antebellum narrative did not ignore the practical effects of slavery on blacks and whites in the South, it rested its antislavery case on religious and ethical absolutes like Bibb's "inevitable laws of Nature's God," or what William Craft called [in his *Running a Thousand Miles for Freedom*, in *Great Slave Narratives*, edited by Arna Bontemps, 1968] "the sacred rights of the weak." The postbellum narrator rarely appeals to such ideals or to the righteous indignation that let his antebellum predecessor condemn slavery so categorically. Instead he asks his reader to judge slavery simply and dispassionately on the basis of what Booker T. Washington liked to call "facts," by which the Tuskegean meant something other than empirical data. In *Up from Slavery,* as in many other postbellum slave narratives, a factual evaluation of slavery exploits what William James [in his "What Pragmatism Means," in *American Thought: Civil War to World War I,* edited by Perry Miller, 1954] would later call the "practical cash-value" of the word, its significance in the present day. What slavery was in the past is not so important as what slavery means, or (more importantly) can be construed to mean, in the present. A factual view of slavery, for Washington, is concerned less with a static concept of historical truth, frozen in the past, than with the need for rhetorical power in the ever-evolving present. To the postbellum slave narrator, particularly Washington, slavery needed to be reviewed and reempowered as a concept capable of effecting change, of making a difference ultimately in what white people thought of black people as freedmen, not slaves. The facts of slavery in the postbellum narrative, therefore, are not so much what happened *then*—bad though it was—as what *makes* things, good things, happen now.

Looking the facts of the present (more than the past) in the face, Washington could justifiably call slavery a school in which black Americans had learned much about the necessity of hard work, perseverance, and self-help as survival skills in their difficult passage in the antebellum South. The fact of turn-of-the-century American "scientific" racism, which stereotyped "the Negro" as degraded, ignorant, incompetent, and servile, demanded that slavery be re-presented anew, not as a condition of deprivation and degradation, but as a period of training and testing, from which the slave graduated with high honors and even higher ambitions. Given the changed sociopolitical circumstances, it is not surprising to find the postbellum slave narrator treating slavery more as an economic proving ground than an existential battleground for southern black people. The slave past, if effectively represented, could provide the freedman and freedwoman with credentials that the new industrial-capitalist order might respect. By the turn of the century, blacks were realizing their need for a usable American past on which they could build. They could also see that southern whites needed to be reminded of who had built the Old South and who could help to build a New South as well. The agenda of the postbellum slave narrative thus emphasizes unabashedly the tangible contribution that blacks made to the South, in and after slavery, in order to rehabilitate the image of the freedman, not the idea of slavery, in the eyes of business America.

Although in some ways a typical postbellum slave narrative, *Up from Slavery* stands out today, as always, because of its articulation of an accommodationist strategy that, though by no means original, Washington managed to identify as his own. What we would call accommodationism, however, is what the Tuskegean would have termed realism. What are the sources of real power in the real world? asks the writer of *Up from Slavery*. In the antebellum slave narrative, as I have already noted, the answer is almost unanimous. Knowledge is power, and the fundamental source of knowledge is literacy, the ability to open one's mind to the words of others and to liberate other minds with a text of one's own. As an ex-slave and an educator, Washington pays lip service to the importance of reading in his own life and in the training of his people. But in his preferred persona as pragmatic student of power, he demotes men of the word and elevates men of action to the putative leadership of his people. The irony of the preeminent black speaker and writer of his day identifying himself as a man of real acts, not mere words, should not prevent us from recognizing the literary significance of Washington's antiliterary thesis. *Up from Slavery* is, in its own quiet and indirect—should I say sly?—way, a manifesto of a quasi-literary realism that attempts to restrict the traditional sovereignty of the black wordsmith by chaining the signifier to a preexistent signified and thus making the word merely reflective, rather than constitutive, of reality.

Washington's realism entails a radical distinction between deeds and words. "The actual sight of a first-class house that a Negro has built is ten times more potent than pages of discussion about a house that he ought to build, or perhaps could build." Action, Washington insists, produces things; discussion, by contrast, produces only more discussion. "Instead of studying books so constantly, how I wish that our schools and colleges might learn to study men and things!." The men Washington studies are, of course, white men of action and substance, like Andrew Carnegie, Collis P. Huntington, and William McKinley. In stark contrast with them are black men of words—in particular, southern politicians, preachers, and educators. These men, Washington argues, have too often made

speaking and writing a refuge from doing, from working productively for the good of the race. As he surveys the recent history of his people, he finds that politicians stirred up in the people only an "artificial" desire to hold public office; preachers inspired in literate black men only a self-serving "call to preach"; teachers merely pandered to "the craze for Greek and Latin learning" among pathetically ignorant blacks. Instead of doing tangible good, all this preaching and teaching and speechmaking created in the minds of rural southern blacks a pernicious notion, namely, that an alternative resource of power existed to what Washington called the "real, solid foundation" of black advancement, the agrarian life. Even Washington had to acknowledge that the black community had traditionally revered the man of the word as "a very superior human being, something bordering almost on the supernatural" in the case of those who understood the mystery of foreign languages. Such men seemed not to require "the sold and never deceptive foundation of Mother Nature", that is, a grounding in the life of "the soil," to exercise power and excite envy among southern blacks. Washington's fear was that the example of Afro-American men of the word would encourage young blacks to believe that the route to black power was not hand-to-mouth, from act to word, but rather just the reverse, from performing word to reforming act. Washington pays inadvertent tribute to these black masters of the speech-act by noting that they "live by their wits" instead of by their hands and that the white South regards them with a perplexed and uneasy suspicion.

Few can read *Up from Slavery* today without recognizing that Washington also lived by his wits and in a consummate manner. A former political stump speaker and student of the ministry, Washington clearly understood the power of the word in the mouth of an artful and ambitious black man. "I never planned to give any large part of my life to speaking in public," he blandly remarks, adding, "I have always had more of an ambition to *do* things than merely to talk *about* doing them". Yet no black man could have built Tuskegee Institute without knowing that action proceeds from speech and that speech is itself a most potent form of action. Washington acknowledges that he authorized the erection of Porter Hall, the first building on the Tuskegee campus, before he had the money to pay for it. He relied on his charm and good name in the community to secure loans to complete the edifice. He had no capital at all when he conceived of putting up a second building, but, as he offhandedly comments, "We decided to give the needed building a name" anyway. Naming the building Alabama Hall proved, of course, a shrewd political maneuver that helped to ensure the continuation of the state funding on which Washington depended so much in the early years. This speech-act alone, so reminiscent of the talismanic power of naming in the slave narrative tradition, belies Washington's insistence that words merely publicize deeds. Thus, even though he claims that he always "had a desire to do something to make the world better, and *then* be able to speak to the world about that thing," Washington had the wit to see that speaking makes doing possible and that reality is contingent on language, not the other way around.

Nevertheless, in an effort to subvert the "almost supernatural" status of the man of words in the black community, the author of *Up from Slavery* presents himself as a naturalist, arguing that only from a rootedness in "nature" does he derive the "strength for the many duties and hard places that await me" in the real world. Washington is not talking about communing with Nature in some romantic fashion. His need is more immediate and tangible: "I like, as often as possible, to touch nature, not something that is artificial or an imitation, but the real thing." Hence it is no surprise to find Washington depreciating belles-lettres and enthusing over newspapers as "a constant source of delight and recreation." Obviously, fiction, poetry, and drama are artificial and merely imitative of "the real thing." Only one kind of storytelling can satisfy Washington's appetite for realism, namely, "biography," for which he claims "the greatest fondness." Why he should prefer biography to all other kinds of reading is plain enough: "I like to be sure that I am reading about a real man or a real thing." But the way Washington prefaces his predictable desire for the "real thing"—"I like to be *sure*"—suggests that he knows that readers of biography do not always get what they expect or want, nor does biography always assure its readers of their ability to distinguish between the real and the artificial. Maybe this is one reason why Washington is at such pains in writing his own biography to portray himself as a plain and simple man of facts, "the real thing" among autobiographers, a man who represents himself as no more than what he is. Washington *knows* the prejudice in his white audience against black men of words as truth-tellers; this is a major reason why he claims he is a man of acts and facts. By repeatedly declaring his "great faith in the power and influence of facts" and his conviction that one can touch the real thing in biography, Washington acts to shore up the foundation of *Up from Slavery,* which we can see is not so much grounded in real things as in linguistic demonstrations of realism.

Capitalizing on the postbellum slave narrator's pragmatic revision of the facts of slavery, *Up from Slavery* promulgates a concept of realism which challenges the traditional status of the sign in the Afro-American narrative tradition. By claiming a radical distinction between action and speech and by disclaiming language as anything more than a referential medium, Washington denies the performative dimension of representation. The consummate rhetorician, he tries to pass for a realist, we might say, since this lets him keep his agenda masked behind a semblance of nonrhetorical *vraisemblance.* If Washington could define the terms by which realism would be judged in Afro-American writing, then he could consign literary representation to a *reactive* status in Afro-American culture, thereby robbing it of the expressive power that the word had held in the black community since the antebellum era. The rise of Tuskegee realism then, foregrounded by the postbellum slave narrative and reinforced by numerous autobiographies of Washington's protégés, imitators, and admirers, discounts the hard-won victory of antebellum narratives like *My Bondage and My Freedom* and *Incidents in the Life of a Slave Girl,* texts that liberated black narrative from an alienating and objectifying focus on the sign as a referent to an object—slavery—rather than a sub-

ject—the questing consciousness of the former slave. Tuskegee realism, ever respectful of Washington's much-heralded "gospel of the toothbrush," sanitizes the mouth of the speaking subject until it attains that acme of "unselfishness" which is, in Washington's eyes, the hallmark of every successful man of action.

Neither the rise of pragmatism in the slave narrative nor the articulation of Tuskegee realism in *Up from Slavery* exerted a profound impact on the idealism of the protest fiction that dominated much late nineteenth- and early twentieth-century black belletristic prose in America. Protest romances from Frances Ellen Watkins Harper's *Iola Leroy* (1892) to Du Bois's *The Quest of the Silver Fleece* (1911) answer the call that Pauline Hopkins delivered in the preface to her novel *Contending Forces* (1900): "We must ourselves develop the men and women who will faithfully portray the inmost thoughts and feelings of the Negro with all the fire and romance which lie dormant in our history." The problem with devoting the novel to romances of racial uplift, however, was that this could easily play into the hands of Tuskegee realism. Washington would have been happy to see the novel in its place, as a defensive, (merely) inspirational reaction to unjust realities. The way to combat Tuskegee realism was not to justify romance, however well intentioned. Black wordsmiths needed to decertify—literally, to make *un*certain—the "real, solid foundation" on which Tuskegee realism claimed its hegemony. This is what happens in two prominent fictive texts of this period, Charles W. Chesnutt's *The Conjure Woman* (1899) and James Weldon Johnson's *The Autobiography of an Ex-Coloured Man* (1912).

As fictive autobiographies, both of these books exploit the anxiety that Washington expressed about biography as a representation of "a real man or a real thing." *The Conjure Woman* purports to be a collection of dictated slave narratives transcribed by a white entrepreneur from Ohio. However, by mediating his intention through Uncle Julius McAdoo's narratives and the conflicting interpretations of them offered by the Ohioan and his wife, Chesnutt made it hard for many readers to tell what the man behind all these masks really meant. Reviewers who did not know that Chestnutt was an Afro-American (neither Chesnutt nor his publishers mentioned this fact when *The Conjure Woman* came out) extrapolated from the text an implied author who, though a Northerner, had thoroughly immersed himself in the local color of the South and had written to entertain his white readership with the quaint customs and folklore of the southern Negro. Comparatively few reviewers perceived a "dark side" and tragic note in Chesnutt's representation of the slavery past. The disparity between the two implied authors attributed to *The Conjure Woman* demonstrated that the real is not a constant but a function of words like "Negro" and "white" which are themselves but traces of racial *différance* in the cultural text of the racist American reading community.

Even more destabilizing of black biographical reality is Johnson's *Autobiography of an Ex-Coloured Man.* Published anonymously, the novel was designed by its author to be taken as a real, not a fictive, work. Most reviewers, as well as a large part of the black reading community, were taken in by the *vraisemblance* of the novel, which, if one were to analyze it in detail, reads almost like a catalog of the stock in trade of nineteenth-century realism. What distinguishes the ex-colored man as a persona is not his storytelling but his leisurely digressions from the facts of his life into the realm of social and cultural commentary. His breadth of experience, his criticism of whites and blacks alike, and his almost Olympian detachment from racial loyalties give him an objectivity toward the whole race question that sounds almost Tuskegean. Moreover, Washington would surely have concurred with the ex-colored man's regretful judgment of his having passed for white as a selfish and socially unproductive act. An even more obvious invocation of the Tuskegee line comes at the end of the novel, when Washington himself makes a cameo appearance representing all the "earnestness and faith" of a progressive race, as contrasted with the self-protective cynicism of the ex-colored man.

What do these apparent endorsements of Tuskegee realism mean, however, if the narrator who makes them is not a "real man"? Does the fictiveness of the narrator invalidate the authority of what he says? Does fictive language have less—or perhaps more—performative potential than natural language? Did Johnson invent a fictive character like the ex-colored man out of a belief that such a vehicle could actually represent certain facts more fully and freely than an actual man? If so, is this a testimonial to the strength of the Afro-American novel or the weakness of Afro-American autobiography? However we answer these questions posed by the problematic "author-function" of *The Autobiography of an Ex-Coloured Man,* we can see clearly enough that the novel does not leave unscathed many of the assumptions about realism—how to recognize it, how to read it—that Washington held dear. If Johnson wrote the ex-colored man's story with no other purpose than to unveil the cultural conventions that predisposed his readership to believe an "autobiography" by a doubly phony white man over a novel authored by a real black man, namely, Johnson himself, his effort must be considered a signal success in the history of Afro-American autobiography, as well as fiction.

The pragmatic reassessment of slavery and the rise of Afro-American realism illustrate a process of revisionism at work in black narrative of the late nineteenth century that exempted virtually nothing in the past from being remade anew. Whatever black reality *was* historically, whatever one generation of black narrators said it was, their successors refused to be bound by it. First pragmatic slave narrators, then the Tuskegee realists, and then novelists like Chesnutt and Johnson insisted on their right to reappropriate the signifying potential of black reality and, through what we might call deconstructive acts, prepare the discursive ground once again for a new assay of the basis on which a usable truth could be constructed. From the perspective of the New Negroes of the Harlem Renaissance, Johnson had only begun to probe the deeper resources of subjective consciousness in *The Autobiography of an Ex-Coloured Man;* Chesnutt had only glimpsed the import of black folk culture in the magical realism of *The Conjure Woman.* Nevertheless, in their revisionistic atti-

tude toward prevailing notions of the real, and in their emphasis on reality as a function of consciousness mediated through language, these were enabling texts. They not only pointed new directions for the Harlem Renaissance; they bore witness to the postbellum slave narrators' determination to keep the past alive and meaningful to the present. In short, the work of Chesnutt and Johnson helped preserve Afro-American realism as a literary tradition, a bridge between the antebellum and modern eras, that makes Tuskegee available for the Invisible Man to reinvent and enables the transposing of the "apparently incoherent" slave songs of Douglass's *Narrative* into the *Song of Solomon.*

> *William L. Andrews, "The Representation of Slavery and the Rise of Afro-American Literary Realism, 1865-1920," in* Slavery and the Literary Imagination, *edited by Deborah E. McDowell and Arnold Rampersad, The Johns Hopkins University Press, 1989, pp. 62-80.*

ABOLITIONIST IDEALS

William E. Channing

[*Heralded as the "apostle of Unitarianism," Channing was a distinguished American clergyman who spoke and wrote extensively on the social and philanthropic issues of his day. In the following essay from his acclaimed work* Slavery (1835), *he lauds the abolitionists' philosophical and political purposes, decrying their persecution as immoral and unconstitutional.*]

The word ABOLITIONIST in its true meaning comprehends every man who feels himself bound to exert his influence for removing slavery. It is a name of honorable import, and was worn, not long ago, by such men as Franklin and Jay. Events, however, continually modify terms; and, of late, the word ABOLITIONIST has been narrowed from its original import, and restricted to the members of associations formed among us to promote Immediate Emancipation. It is not without reluctance that I give up to a small body a name which every good man ought to bear. But to make myself intelligible and to avoid circumlocution, I shall use the word in what is now its common acceptation.

I approach this subject unwillingly, because it will be my duty to censure those whom at this moment I would on no account hold up to public displeasure. The persecutions, which the abolitionists have suffered and still suffer, awaken only my grief and indignation, and incline me to defend them to the full extent which truth and justice will admit. To the persecuted of whatever name my sympathies are pledged, and especially to those who are persecuted in a cause substantially good. I would not for worlds utter a word to justify the violence recently offered to a party, composed very much of men blameless in life, and holding the doctrine of nonresistance to injuries; and of women, exemplary in their various relations, and acting, however mistakenly, from benevolent and pious impulses.

Of the abolitionists I know very few; but I am bound to say of these, that I honor them for their strength of principle, their sympathy with their fellow-creatures, and their active goodness. As a party, they are singularly free from political and religious sectarianism, and have been distinguished by the absence of management, calculation, and worldly wisdom. That they have ever proposed or desired insurrection or violence among the slaves there is no reason to believe. All their principles repel the supposition. It is a remarkable fact, that, though the South and the North have been leagued to crush them, though they have been watched by a million of eyes, and though prejudice has been prepared to detect the slightest sign of corrupt communication with the slave, yet this crime has not been fastened on a single member of this body. A few individuals at the South have, indeed, been tortured or murdered by enraged multitudes, on the charge of stirring up revolt; but their guilt and their connexion with the abolitionists were not, and from the circumstances and the nature of the case could not be, established by those deliberate and regular modes of investigation, which are necessary to an impartial judgment. Crimes, detected and hastily punished by the multitude in a moment of feverish suspicion and wild alarm, are generally creatures of fear and passion. The act which caused the present explosion of popular feeling was the sending of pamphlets by the Abolitionists into the slave-holding States. In so doing, they acted weakly and without decorum; but they must have been insane, had they intended to stir up a servile war; for the pamphlets were sent, not by stealth, but by the public mail; and not to the slaves, but to the masters; to men in public life, to men of the greatest influence and distinction. Strange incendiaries these! They flourished their firebrands about at noon-day; and, still more, put them into the hands of the very men whom it is said they wished to destroy. They are accused, indeed, of having sent some of the pamphlets to the free colored people, and if so, they acted with great and culpable rashness. But the publicity of the whole transaction absolves them of corrupt design.

The charge of corrupt design, so vehemently brought against the abolitionists, is groundless. The charge of fanaticism I have no desire to repel. But in the present age it will not do to deal harshly with the characters of fanatics. They form the mass of the people. Religion and Politics, Philanthropy and Temperance, Nullification and Antimasonry, the Levelling Spirit of the working man, and the Speculating Spirit of the man of business, all run into fanaticism. This is the type of all our epidemics. A sober man who can find? The abolitionists have but caught the fever of the day. That they should have escaped it would have been a moral miracle. I offer these remarks simply from a sense of justice. Had not a persecution, without parallel in our country, broken forth against this society, I should not have spoken a word in their defence. But whilst I have power I owe it to the Persecuted. If they have laid themselves open to the laws, let them suffer. For all their errors and sins let the tribunal of public opinion inflict the full measure of rebuke which they deserve. I ask no favor for them. But they shall not be stripped of the

rights of man, of rights guarantied by the laws and Constitution, without one voice, at least, being raised in their defence.

The abolitionists have done wrong, I believe; nor is their wrong to be winked at, because done fanatically or with good intention; for how much mischief may be wrought with good design! They have fallen into the common error of enthusiasts, that of exaggerating their object, of feeling as if no evil existed but that which they opposed, and as if no guilt could be compared with that of countenancing or upholding it. The tone of their newspapers, as far as I have seen them, has often been fierce, bitter, and abusive. Their imaginations have fed on pictures of the cruelty to which the slave is exposed, till they have seemed to think that his abode was perpetually resounding with the lash, and ringing with shrieks of agony; and accordingly, the slaveholder has been held up to execration, as a monster of cruelty. I know that many of their publications have been calm, well considered, and abounding in strong reasoning. But those, which have been most widely scattered and are most adapted to act on the common mind, have had a tone unfriendly both to manners and to the spirit of our religion. I doubt not that the majority of the abolitionists condemn the coarseness and violence of which I complain. But in this, as in most associations, the many are represented and controlled by the few, and are made to sanction and become responsible for what they disapprove.

One of their errors has been the adoption of "Immediate Emancipation" as their motto. To this they owe not a little of their unpopularity. This phrase has contributed much to spread far and wide the belief, that they wished immediately to free the slave from all his restraints. They made explanations; but thousands heard the motto who never saw the explanation; and it is certainly unwise for a party to choose a watchword, which can be rescued from misapprehension only by labored explication. It may also be doubted whether they ever removed the objection which their language so universally raised, whether they have not always recommended a precipitate action, inconsistent with the well-being of the slave and the order of the state.

Another objection to their movements is, that they have sought to accomplish their objects by a system of Agitation; that is, by a system of affiliated societies, gathered, and held together, and extended, by passionate eloquence. This, in truth, is the common mode by which all projects are now accomplished. The age of individual action is gone. Truth cannot be heard unless shouted by a crowd. The weightiest argument for a doctrine is the number which adopts it. Accordingly, to gather and organize multitudes is the first care of him who would remove an abuse or spread a reform. That the expedient is in some cases useful is not denied. But generally it is a showy, noisy mode of action, appealing to the passions, and driving men into exaggeration; and there are special reasons why such a mode should not be employed in regard to slavery; for slavery is so to be opposed as not to exasperate the slave, or endanger the community in which he lives. The abolitionists might have formed an association; but it should have been an elective one. Men of strong principles, judiciousness, sobriety, should have been carefully sought as members. Much good might have been accomplished by the coöperation of such philanthropists. Instead of this, the abolitionists sent forth their orators, some of them transported with fiery zeal, to sound the alarm against slavery through the land, to gather together young and old, pupils from schools, females hardly arrived at years of discretion, the ignorant, the excitable, the impetuous, and to organize these into associations for the battle against oppression. Very unhappily they preached their doctrine to the colored people, and collected these into their societies. To this mixed and excitable multitude, minute, heartrending descriptions of slavery were given in the piercing tones of passion; and slaveholders were held up as monsters of cruelty and crime. Now to this procedure I must object as unwise, as unfriendly to the spirit of Christianity, and as increasing, in a degree, the perils of the slaveholding States. Among the unenlightened, whom they so powerfully addressed, was there not reason to fear that some might feel themselves called to subvert this system of wrong, by whatever means? From the free colored people this danger was particularly to be apprehended. It is easy for us to place ourselves in their situation. Suppose that millions of white men were enslaved, robbed of all their rights, in a neighbouring country, and enslaved by a black race, who had torn their ancestors from the shores on which our fathers had lived. How deeply should we feel their wrongs! And would it be wonderful, if, in a moment of passionate excitement, some enthusiast should think it his duty to use his communication with his injured brethren for stirring them up to revolt?

Such is the danger from abolitionism to the slaveholding States. I know no other. It is but justice to add, that the principle of nonresistance, which the abolitionists have connected with their passionate appeals, seems to have counteracted the peril. I know not a case in which a member of an anti-slavery society has been proved by legal investigation to have tampered with the slaves; and after the strongly pronounced and unanimous opinion of the free States on the subject, this danger may be considered as having passed away. Still a mode of action, requiring these checks, is open to strong objections, and ought to be abandoned. Happy will it be, if the disapprobation of friends, as well as of foes, should give to abolitionists a caution and moderation, which would secure the acquiescence of the judicious, and the sympathies of the friends of mankind! Let not a good cause find its chief obstruction in its defenders. Let the truth, and the whole truth, be spoken without paltering or fear; but so spoken as to convince, not inflame, as to give no alarm to the wise, and no needless exasperation to the selfish and passionate.

I know it is said, that nothing can be done but by excitement and vehemence; that the zeal which dares every thing is the only power to oppose to long rooted abuses. But it is not true that God has committed the great work of reforming the world to passion. Love is a minister of good only when it gives energy to the intellect, and allies itself with wisdom. The abolitionists often speak of Luther's vehemence as a model to future reformers. But who, that has read history, does not know that Luther's reformation was accompanied by tremendous miseries and

crimes, and that its progress was soon arrested? and is there not reason to fear, that the fierce, bitter, persecuting spirit, which he breathed into the work, not only tarnished its glory, but limited its power? One great principle, which we should lay down as immovably true, is, that if a good work cannot be carried on by the calm, self-controlled, benevolent spirit of Christianity, then the time for doing it has not come. God asks not the aid of our vices. He can overrule them for good, but they are not the chosen instruments of human happiness.

We, indeed, need zeal, fervent zeal, such as will fear no man's power, and shrink before no man's frown, such as will sacrifice life to truth and freedom. But this energy of will ought to be joined with deliberate wisdom and universal charity. It ought to regard the whole, in its strenuous efforts for a part. Above all, it ought to ask first, not what means are most effectual, but what means are sanctioned by the Moral Law and by Christian Love. We ought to think much more of walking in the right path than of reaching our end. We should desire virtue more than success. If by one wrong deed we could accomplish the liberation of millions, and in no other way, we ought to feel that this good, for which, perhaps, we had prayed with an agony of desire, was denied us by God, was reserved for other times and other hands. The first object of a true zeal is, not that we may prosper, but that we may do right, that we may keep ourselves unspotted from every evil thought, word, and deed. Under the inspiration of such a zeal, we shall not find in the greatness of an enterprise an apology for intrigue or for violence. We shall not need immediate success to spur us to exertion. We shall not distrust God, because he does not yield to the cry of human impatience. We shall not forsake a good work, because it does not advance with a rapid step. Faith in truth, virtue, and Almighty Goodness, will save us alike from rashness and despair.

In lamenting the adoption by the abolitionists of the system of agitation or extensive excitement, I do not mean to condemn this mode of action as only evil. There are cases to which it is adapted; and, in general, the impulse which it gives is better than the selfish, sluggish indifference to good objects, into which the multitude so generally fall. But it must not supersede or be compared with Individual action. The enthusiasm of the Individual in a good cause is a mighty power. The forced, artificially excited enthusiasm of a multitude, kept together by an organization which makes them the instruments of a few leading minds, works superficially, and often injuriously. I fear that the native, noble-minded enthusiast often loses that single-heartedness which is his greatest power, when once he strives to avail himself of the machinery of associations. The true power of a Reformer lies in speaking truth purely from his own soul, without changing one tone for the purpose of managing or enlarging a party. Truth, to be powerful, must speak in her own words, and in no other's, must come forth with the authority and spontaneous energy of inspiration from the depths of the soul. It is the voice of the Individual giving utterance to the irrepressible conviction of his own thoroughly moved spirit, and not the shout of a crowd, which carries truth far into other souls, and insures it a stable empire on earth. For want of this, most which is now done is done superficially. The progress of society depends chiefly on the honest inquiry of the Individual into the particular work ordained him by God, and on his simplicity in following out his convictions. This moral independence is mightier, as well as holier, than the practice of getting warm in crowds, and of waiting for an impulse from multitudes. The moment a man parts with moral independence; the moment he judges of duty, not from the inward voice, but from the interests and will of a party; the moment he commits himself to a leader or a body, and winks at evil, because division would hurt the cause; the moment he shakes off his particular responsibility, because he is but one of a thousand or million by whom the evil is done; that moment he parts with his moral power. He is shorn of the energy of singlehearted faith in the Right and the True. He hopes from man's policy what nothing but loyalty to God can accomplish. He substitutes coarse weapons forged by man's wisdom for celestial power.

The adoption of the common system of agitation by the abolitionists has proved signally unsuccessful. From the beginning it created alarm in the considerate, and strengthened the sympathies of the free States with the slaveholder. It made converts of a few individuals, but alienated multitudes. Its influence at the South has been evil without mixture. It has stirred up bitter passions and a fierce fanaticism, which have shut every ear and every heart against its arguments and persuasions. These effects are the more to be deplored, because the hope of freedom to the slave lies chiefly in the dispositions of his master. The abolitionist proposed, indeed, to convert the slaveholders; and for this end he approached them with vituperation, and exhausted on them the vocabulary of abuse! And he has reaped as he sowed. His vehement pleadings for the slaves have been answered by wilder ones from the slaveholder; and, what is worse, deliberate defences of slavery have been sent forth, in the spirit of the dark ages, and in defiance of the moral convictions and feelings of the Christian and civilized world. Thus, with good purposes, nothing seems to have been gained. Perhaps (though I am anxious to repel the thought) something has been lost to the cause of freedom and humanity.

I earnestly desire that abolitionism may lay aside the form of public agitation, and seek its end by wiser and milder means. I desire as earnestly, and more earnestly, that it may not be put down by lawless force. There is a worse evil than abolitionism, and that is the suppression of it by lawless force. No evil greater than this can exist in the State, and this is never needed. Be it granted, that it is the design, or direct, palpable, tendency, of abolitionism, to stir up insurrection at the South, and that no existing laws can meet the exigency. It is the solemn duty of the Chief Magistrate of the State to assemble immediately the legislative bodies, and their duty immediately to apply the remedy of Law. Let every friend of freedom, let every good man lift up his voice against mobs. Through these lies our road to tyranny. It is these which have spread the opinion, so common at the South, that the free States cannot long sustain republican institutions. No man seems awake to their inconsistency with liberty. Our whole phraseology is in fault. Mobs call themselves, and are called, the People,

when in truth they assail immediately the sovereignty of the People, involve the guilt of usurpation and rebellion against the People. It is the fundamental principle of our institutions, that the People is Sovereign. But by the People we mean not an individual here and there, not a knot of twenty or a hundred or a thousand individuals in this or that spot, but the Community formed into a body politic, and expressing and executing its will through regularly appointed organs. There is but one expression of the will or Sovereignty of the People, and this is Law. Law is the voice, the living act of the People. It has no other. When an individual suspends the operation of Law, resists its established ministers, and forcibly substitutes for it his own will, he is a usurper and rebel. The same guilt attaches to a combination of individuals. These, whether many or few, in forcibly superseding public law and establishing their own, rise up against the People, as truly as a single usurper. The People should assert its insulted majesty, its menaced sovereignty, in one case as decidedly as in the other. The difference between the mob and the individual is, that the usurpation of the latter has a permanence not easily given to the tumultuary movements of the former. The distinction is a weighty one. Little importance is due to sudden bursts of the populace, because they so soon pass away. But when mobs are organized, as in the French Revolution, or when they are deliberately resolved on and systematically resorted to, as the means of putting down an odious party, they lose this apology. A conspiracy exists against the Sovereignty of the People, and ought to be suppressed, as among the chief evils of the state.

In this part of the country our abhorrence of mobs is lessened by the fact, that they were thought to do good service in the beginning of the Revolution. They probably were useful then; and why? The work of that day was Revolution. To subvert a government was the fearful task to which our fathers thought themselves summoned. Their duty they believed was Insurrection. In such a work mobs had their place. The government of the State was in the hands of its foes. The People could not use the regular organs of administration, for these were held and employed by the power which they wished to crush. Violent, irregular efforts belonged to that day of convulsion. To resist and subvert institutions is the very work of mobs; and when these institutions are popular, when their sole end is to express and execute the will of the People, then mobs are rebellion against the People, and as such should be understood and suppressed. A people is never more insulted than when a mob takes its name. Abolition must not be put down by lawless force. The attempt so to destroy it ought to fail. Such attempts place abolitionism on a new ground. They make it, not the cause of a few enthusiasts, but the cause of freedom. They identify it with all our rights and popular institutions. If the Constitution and the laws cannot put it down, it must stand; and he who attempts its overthrow by lawless force is a rebel and usurper. The Supremacy of Law and the Sovereignty of the People are one and indivisible. To touch the one is to violate the other. This should be laid down as a first principle, an axiom, a fundamental article of faith which it must be heresy to question. A newspaper, which openly or by innuendo excites a mob, should be regarded as sounding the tocsin of insurrection. On this subject the public mind slumbers, and needs to be awakened, lest it sleep the sleep of death.

How obvious is it, that pretexts for mobs will never be wanting, if this disorganizing mode of redressing evils be in any case allowed! We all recollect, that when a recent attempt was made on the life of the President of the United States, the cry broke forth from his friends, "that the assassin was instigated by the continual abuse poured forth on this distinguished man, and especially by the violent speeches uttered daily in the Senate of the United States." Suppose, now, that his adherents, to save the Chief Magistrate from murder, and to guard his constitutional advisers, had formed themselves into mobs, to scatter the meetings of his opponents. And suppose that they had resolved to put to silence the legislators, who, it was said, had abused their freedom of speech to blacken the character and put in peril the life of the Chief Magistrate. Would they not have had a better pretext than mobs against abolition? Was not assassination attempted? Had not the President received letters threatening his life unless he would change his measures? Can a year or a month pass, which will not afford equally grave reasons for insurrections of the populace? A system of mobs and a free government cannot stand together. The men who incite the former, and especially those who organize them, are among the worst enemies of the state. Of their motives I do not speak. They may think themselves doing service to their country, for there is no limit to the delusions of the times. I speak only of the nature and tendency of their actions. They should be suppressed at once by law, and by the moral sentiment of an insulted people.

In addition to all other reasons, the honor of our nation, and the cause of free institutions should plead with us to defend the laws from insult, and social order from subversion. The moral influence and reputation of our country are fast declining abroad. A letter, recently received from one of the most distinguished men of the continent of Europe, expresses the universal feeling on the other side of the ocean. After speaking of the late encroachments on liberty in France, he says, "On your side of the Atlantic, you contribute, also, to put in peril the cause of liberty. We did take pleasure in thinking that there was at least in the New World a country, where liberty was well understood, where all rights were guarantied, where the people was proving itself wise and virtuous. For some time past, the news we receive from America is discouraging. In all your large cities we see mobs after mobs, and all directed to an odious purpose. When we speak of liberty, its enemies reply to us by *pointing to America.*" The persecuted abolitionists have the sympathies of the civilized world. The country which persecutes them is covering itself with disgrace, and filling the hearts of the friends of freedom with fear and gloom. Already despotism is beginning to rejoice in the fulfilment of its prophecies, in our prostrated laws and dying liberties. Liberty is, indeed, threatened with death in a country, where any class of men are stripped with impunity of their constitutional rights. All rights feel the blow. A community, giving up any of its citizens to oppression and violence, invites the chains which it suffers others to wear.

William E. Channing, "Abolitionism," in his Slavery, *James Munroe and Company, 1835, pp. 130-48.*

Len Gougeon

[*Gougeon was an American educator, author, and a founding member of the Ralph Waldo Emerson Society. In the following essay from his study* Virtue's Hero: Emerson, Antislavery, and Reform, *(1990), he evaluates Emerson's dedication to the antislavery campaign.*]

Ralph Waldo Emerson was a committed social reformer all of his life. He was deeply concerned with and involved in the major social reform movement of his time, antislavery. Throughout his lifetime Emerson never wavered in his commitment to clearly defined principles of human liberty, equality, and equal rights. The only serious doubts he ever felt in the matter concerned how *he* might best make his contribution to the cause. He did not wish to waste his energies in unproductive enterprises for which he was not fit. Also, he was always convinced, radical that he was, that American society could only be reformed by striking at the *roots* of social evil rather than simply pruning an occasional branch. For Emerson, the major cause of America's moral malaise was its gross materialism—the general tendency to place the value of things above people—and slavery was the epitome of this corrupt philosophy. Against this formidable brick-and-stone opponent Emerson fired the artillery of sympathy, emotion, and idealism, in the hope of precipitating a cultural revolution that would have the effect of elevating the civilization of America to a higher moral plane. He was quintessentially American in his reform efforts. Like the Founding Fathers whom he admired and the Declaration of Independence, which he once described as the "greatest achievement of American literature," he recognized that ideas can be powerful in shaping the course of things. He always believed, as he told the graduates of Harvard in 1837, that "this time, like all times, is a very good one, if we but know what to do with it." And, for the most part, Emerson usually did.

It was as a scholar, an American scholar, that Emerson believed his best contribution could be made in the effort to reform and redeem American society. But he also recognized that while a scholar can enlighten the minds and move the hearts of others, a more specific instrumentality would be necessary to effect specific changes—to make the law of the heart the law of the land also. For Emerson, this instrumentality was the political process. While often critical of politicians for their numerous failures, especially the tendency to compromise principles in the name of expediency, Emerson never eschewed the political process itself. Whatever its shortcomings, the system established by the Founding Fathers had contributed enormously to the evolution of American greatness, and would continue to do so if leaders could be made to lead properly. Government, he felt, had the capacity to relieve social ills. As he noted in 1844, "Government exists to defend the weak and the poor and the injured party." However, he also realized that an effort was often required to compel the government to use its power wisely. He was well aware, as he pointed out in 1854, of the "worthlessness of good tools to bad workmen." He believed that citizens must imbue themselves with the best spirit of American democracy, must thereby become "citadels and warriors . . . declarations of Independence, the charter, the battle and the victory," and must demand that elected representatives follow this example themselves. Emerson always recognized that in America, "what great masses of men wish done, will be done" if the people themselves insist upon it. Change, and for Emerson, evolutionary progress, was always possible in America because "a Congress is a standing insurrection," and no matter how firmly entrenched a given political position, party, or policy is, it can be uprooted, overthrown, and abolished. As a means toward this end Emerson generally favored the ballot box. He always voted and always encouraged others to do so. An enlightened mind and sensitive heart could do much to improve society by the casting of a conscientious vote. Also, he was not above participating directly in a political campaign when it seemed appropriate for him to do so.

Emerson recognized that the casting of votes was not always in itself enough. At times, opposition to the social and moral reform of America appeared in a more violent guise than that of political party. Sometimes, as in Boston in 1835 and 1860, and Alton, Illinois, in 1837, the face of opposition appeared as a violent mob. Opposition to this form of evil often required a violence of its own, at times accompanied by self-sacrifice and even the sacrifice of others. Emerson applauded the heroic action of Elijah Lovejoy, as other abolitionists did, and Lovejoy would be but the first of many heroes who, for Emerson, "put their creed into their deed" and were willing to make the ultimate sacrifice for the moral values they held dear. There would be others, including the Free Soil farmers of Kansas, for whom Emerson would provide Sharpe's rifles; the noble Charles Sumner, struck down on the floor of the Senate; John Brown, executed in 1859; President Lincoln, the victim of an assassin's bullet; and finally, the entire generation of brave young men who willingly gave their lives in the Civil War. To Emerson, all of these were ultimately transcendental heroes, individuals who were prepared to sacrifice all in the name of principle.

Emerson also recognized in the 1850s that government itself may not at all times be susceptible to change through traditional political means. With the shocking passage of the Fugitive Slave Law in 1850 he realized that it would be necessary to step outside the bounds of constitutional law in order to oppose that immoral measure. A "higher law" than the Constitution must prevail in such cases, and he willingly and openly urged a defiant civil disobedience and practiced it himself. For him, the sacredness of individual moral conscience would always be infinitely more important than any institution, including the government of the United States. Even at this time, however, he would have preferred that the system correct itself, using the means available to it. He was bitterly disappointed when Massachusetts Chief Justice Lemuel Shaw refused to challenge the federal statute in the several opportunities provided to him. He consistently maintained that both legal tradition and human nature dictate that "you cannot

enact a false thing to be true and a wrong thing to be right."

Emerson lived to see what he considered to be the "second American Revolution" correct the one glaring deficiency of the first, the catastrophic compromise with slavery. The Civil War represented the triumph of principle in a society that had become mired in a corrupt materialistic skepticism. He was optimistic that the war had redeemed America from the sinful corruption of the institution of slavery, and he looked forward to a glorious flowering of the American ideal in the post-Civil War period. In one of his last speeches, "Fortune of the Republic" (1878), he described the triumph of the liberal spirit in America in the following terms: "The genius of the country has marked out our true policy,—opportunity. Opportunity of civil rights, of education, of personal power, and not less of wealth; doors wide open. If I could have it,—free trade with all the world without toll or custom-houses, invitation as we now make every nation, to every race and skin, white men, red men, yellow men, black men; hospitality of fair field and equal laws to all."

In the light of this, it is profoundly ironic that the image of Emerson that would emerge in the closing decades of the nineteenth century would be quite the opposite of the liberal, activist reformer and moralist that he truly was . . . [The] Holmes biography in 1884 was undoubtedly influential in creating a very conservative view of Emerson, but the times themselves reinforced this inclination. In the waning years of the nineteenth century the concept of rugged individualism, reinforced by Darwinian science and Herbert Spencer's social philosophy, came increasingly to dominate American consciousness. By this time Emerson's reputation as a great American thinker was firmly established, and many individuals looked to Emersonian philosophy for an understanding of, and justification for, what seemed to be inevitable developments in American society. Unfortunately, to many, Emerson's early essays like "Self-Reliance," and later ones like "Power" and "Wealth," from *Conduct of Life* (1860), as well as longer works like *Representative Men* (1850), seemed to endorse the deeds of self-made entrepreneurs like Andrew Carnegie, John D. Rockefeller, J. P. Morgan, and others. As a result, Emerson's words were often invoked to justify what Emerson himself would have considered blatant corruptions of the American spirit.

A typical example of this tendency appears in the pronouncements and preachings of the Right Reverend William Lawrence, Methodist bishop of Massachusetts. In his 1901 essay "The Relation of Wealth to Morals" Bishop Lawrence makes the following statement: " 'Man,' says Emerson, 'is born to be rich. He is thoroughly related, and is tempted out by his appetites and fancies to the conquest of this and that piece of Nature, until he finds his well-being in the use of the planet, and of more planets than his own.' " To this the bishop adds his own observation that "man draws to himself material wealth as surely, as naturally, and as necessarily as the oak draws the elements into itself from the earth," and therefore, "in the long run, it is only to the man of morality that wealth comes." Reinforced by his invocation of Emersonian philosophy, the

Reverend Lawrence concludes with the assertion that "Godliness is in league with riches."

Because of perversions such as this, as the historian Daniel Aaron points out [in his *Men of Good Hope,* 1951], in some quarters Emerson came to occupy the role of "seer of laissez-faire capitalism and the rampant individual." Aaron also notes that even though "Emerson . . . never intended his exhortations to justify the practices of the 'Robber Barons,' " his political philosophy seemed to do just that. "Strongly individualistic, it also spoke for equality of opportunity in economic and political affairs, and it lent support to the belief in laissez-faire and the necessity of the minimized state." Other scholars have also drawn attention to this development and have noted, for example, that "Emerson's essay 'Self-Reliance' . . . provided another ideal justification for what the strong man was going to do anyhow, willy-nilly. And the gentle Emerson, who had grandly declared, 'Let man stand erect, go forth and possess the universe,' lived on into the time when Diamond Jim Brady and Jim Fisk took his advice quite literally and exhibited the success of his doctrine to a pitch appallingly beyond his wildest dreams" [see "The New Consciousness: 1861-1914," in *American Literature: The Makers and the Making,* 2 vols., edited by Cleanth Brooks, R. W.B. Lewis, and Robert Penn Warren, 1973].

Perry Miller also points out [in *The Responsibility of a Mind in a Civilization of Machines,* edited by John Crowell and Stanford J. Searl, Jr., 1979] that despite Emerson's early reputation as a revolutionary, "in the course of time, his preaching of individualism, especially 'self-reliance,' came to seem not at all dangerous, but rather the proper code for a young businessman with get-up and go." Miller adds that Emerson's "essay 'Napoleon' in *Representative Men, . . .* is in substance his love letter to the entrepreneurs, to the practical men who brushed aside the 'old legislation' and were building railroads." One of the most prominent spokespersons for this view of Emerson at the turn of the century was Charles W. Eliot, president of Harvard University. President Eliot's commentary on Emerson, celebrating the centenary of his birth, was by far the most widely publicized of the time. It was delivered as part of the Emerson Centennial exercises in Boston, sponsored by the American Unitarian Association, on 24 May 1903. The address was delivered at Symphony Hall and was reported and substantially reproduced in many places, including virtually all of the major newspapers in New York and Boston. In his presentation President Eliot presents an image of Emerson that might be described as a cross between a conservative Boston Brahmin and a captain of industry.

Among other things, Eliot suggests that contemporary American efforts to colonize Cuba and the Philippines would be applauded by Emerson because he believed in education as "the only sure means of permanent and progressive reform," and since "the Cubans are to be raised in the scale of civilization and public happiness," and "the Filipinos, too, are to be developed after the American fashion; . . . we send them 1,000 teachers of English."

Regarding rampant racism in the South, Eliot suggests that through education "the Southern States can be res-

cued from the persistent poison of slavery . . . after forty years of failure with political methods." The particular type of education that Eliot has in mind, however, focuses on "manual training schools" and, he says, the education of men by manual labor "was a favorite doctrine with Emerson," and Emerson "saw clearly that manual labor might be made to develop not only good mental qualities but good moral qualities."

President Eliot also addressed the question of the distribution of wealth within American society. At a time when American labor, responding to decades of exploitation by the captains of industry, was demanding a minimum wage and improved working conditions, President Eliot indicates that Emerson's position on such questions was clear. "It is interesting, at the state of industrial warfare which the world has now reached, to observe how Emerson, sixty years ago, discerned clearly the absurdity of paying all sorts of services at one rate, now a favorite notion with some labor unions." According to Eliot, such misinformed egalitarianism would not be appreciated by the great bard, and he notes that Emerson himself had observed that "even when all labor is temporarily paid at one rate, differences in possessions will instantly arise: 'In one hand the dime became an eagle as it fell, and in another hand a copper cent. For the whole value of the dime is in knowing what to do with it.' " Eliot concludes his point with a statement that clearly underscores his own conservative attitude toward the major social problems of the time. He asserts flatly and firmly that "Emerson was never deceived by a specious philanthropy or by claims of equality which find no support in the nature of things" [Charles W. Eliot: *The Man and His Beliefs,* 2 vols., edited by William Allan Nielson, 1926].

One might add as a footnote that nowhere in his lengthy memorial address does President Eliot allude to Emerson's extensive efforts as a social reformer or his active participation in the abolition movement. In fact, Eliot states bluntly that "although a prophet and inspirer of reform, Emerson was not a reformer. He was but a halting supporter of the reforms of his day; and the eager experimenters and combatants in actual reforms found him a disappointing sort of sympathizer. . . . When it came to action . . . he was surprisingly conservative." He also notes that Emerson "was intimate with many of the leading abolitionists; but no one has described more vividly their grave intellectual and social defects." For Eliot, Emerson was clearly only a theoretical reformer who "laid down principles which, when applied, would inevitably lead to progress and reform; but he took little part in the imperfect step-by-step process of actual reforming." Finally, he suggests that Emerson "probably would have been an ineffective worker in any field of reform." To reinforce this conservative image of his subject Eliot adds the totally erroneous statement that, despite his well-known religious radicalism, Emerson "attended church on Sundays all his life with uncommon regularity." Not surprisingly, at the conclusion of his memorial address Eliot notes that in his youth he was not fond of Emerson's thinking because it seemed too idealistic. But in his later years he has come to discover a "practical" element in

Emerson that places the bard in a new and, apparently, more satisfactory light.

The image of Emerson as an idealist and active social reformer was not entirely lost, however. The Emerson Memorial School, which was held simultaneously in Concord and Boston 13-31 July 1903, was probably the most ambitious effort to set the record straight regarding Emerson's sentiments and activities as a social reformer and abolitionist. The memorial was sponsored by the Free Religious Association of America, of which Emerson was a co-founder and longtime vice president. It consisted of some thirty lectures spread over the two weeks of the gathering. The committee that organized the series included such well-known social activists as Franklin Sanborn and Moorfield Storey. Not surprisingly, many of the talks centered on Emerson's reform activities, and included Julia Ward Howe's "A Century from the Birth of Emerson"; Franklin B. Sanborn's "Emerson and the Concord School of Philosophy"; Francis E. Abbot's "Emerson the Anti-imperialist or Prophet of the Natural Rights of Man"; William M. Salter's "Emerson's Aim and Method in Social Reform"; William Lloyd Garrison II's "Emerson and the Anti-slavery Movement"; and Moorfield Storey's "Emerson and the Civil War." The presentations most significant in projecting an image of Emerson as a reformer and abolitionist were those of Abbot, Garrison, and Storey.

Dr. Francis E. Abbot, who was one of the founders, with Emerson, of the Free Religious Association and a former editor of the *Index,* spoke directly of Emerson's career as an agitator. His concern, as one newspaper put it [*Boston Evening Transcript* (22 July 1903)], was to rebut "certain criticisms recently made upon Emerson as having taught a different sort of equality than appears in the Declaration of Independence." Dr. Abbot spoke at some length about Emerson's service in the antislavery cause, stressing that "his [Emerson's] conception of Americanism was entirely in accord with the teachings of Jefferson and Lincoln, in urging at all times an equal freedom under law for all," and that this was a significant contrast to "the Jefferson Davis concept of a purely white man's rule." Additionally, in an obvious reference to commentaries such as Eliot's regarding the relationship of Emersonian philosophy to the social problems of the present age, he adds emphatically, "Nowhere does he [Emerson] do aught but condemn the modern concept of moral law that grows indignant at restrictions on the game of exploiting other men."

The presentation of William Lloyd Garrison II offered, in the words of one newspaper account [*Springfield Republican* (30 July 1903)], "a remarkable consideration of the way in which a scholar and a man of letters so notably gentle and retiring as Emerson should nevertheless be inseparably linked in history with the aggressive opponents of American slavery." Garrison's lecture provides some interesting insights into the relationships among noted abolitionists, based upon his personal experience in his father's household, and suggests that a lack of personal intimacy did not mean a lack of involvement with the cause, as some critics had maintained was the case with Emerson. The newspaper account indicates that "Mr. Garrison

noted the interesting fact that several of the prominent men associated with closely in history for their connection with the anti-slavery movement seldom met: Phillips, Garrison, and Parker held neighborhood and household intimacy; Edmund Quincy was familiar; but Whittier, Mr. Garrison remembers at his father's house only once." The reporter then quotes Garrison. "Lowell [a most active Boston abolitionist] I never saw at an anti-slavery meeting or in [an] anti-slavery household, I never knew him in companionship with my father." Of Emerson, Garrison says, "I think my father spent but a single night under his roof." While useful for personal reminiscences, Garrison's presentation is less than complete in indicating the length and depth of Emerson's abolition service. Undoubtedly this was due to the fact that his specific knowledge of such activities on Emerson's part was largely limited to the biographical resources available at the time, which were . . . less than all-encompassing in this regard.

The presentation of Moorfield Storey, on the other hand, is much more effective in dealing with the specifics of Emerson's thought on the questions of slavery, abolition, and human rights. One major reason for this is that Storey had the advantage of quoting directly from Emerson's famous "lost journal," *WO Liberty,* which he had borrowed for this purpose from the Emerson family, and which would remain thereafter unaccounted for among his papers until 1966.

Moorfield Storey was a longtime friend of the Emerson family. He had been a classmate of Edward Waldo Emerson at Harvard and later collaborated with him on a biography of the venerable Ebenezer Rockwood Hoar of Concord. Storey came to know Ralph Waldo Emerson as a result of this association, and at this time, the early 1860s, Emerson was deeply involved in the abolition movement and its aftermath. Storey's own abolitionist heritage was significant. As one biographer points out [William B. Hixson, Jr., *Moorfield Storey and the Abolitionist Tradition,* 1972], his mother was "an outright abolitionist," and the two acquaintances of his father whom Storey claimed most influenced him, after Emerson, were James Russell Lowell, who once served on the *National Anti-slavery Standard* and in other abolitionist capacities, and Charles Sumner, senator from Massachusetts and one of the Senate's most outspoken opponents of slavery. Storey served as Sumner's personal secretary from 1867 to 1869.

After rising to prominence as a successful Boston attorney and eventually becoming president of the American Bar Association in 1896, Storey began to turn his attention to America's pressing social problems. In 1898 he became president of the Massachusetts Reform Club, in 1905 vice president of the National Civil Service Reform Association, and, also in 1905, president of the Anti-imperialist League. Storey's longtime battle for the rights of the Negro, which he considered to be the legacy of the abolitionists he admired, culminated with his election in 1910 as the first president of the National Association for the Advancement of Colored People.

Given his interests in social reform, his friendship with the Emerson family, and his respect for the abolitionist tradition, it is not surprising that Storey should be most interested in maintaining the image of Emerson as an active social reformer with a strong interest in human rights. Storey's address describes Emerson as a poet-reformer. In this capacity "it was possible for him [Emerson] to make his position absolutely clear, to stand ready as a citizen to bear his testimony against slavery whenever occasion demanded, but not to abandon the other work of his life for the purpose of leading the anti-slavery crusade." Storey recognized that much had been made of Emerson's lack of personal sympathy with some individual abolitionists and that this criticism had been extrapolated by some commentators to include the cause itself. In response to this, after taking note of representative comments by Emerson in this regard, Storey states, "But great injustice would be done to Emerson if it were supposed that such words as these expressed his real attitude towards the opponents of slavery." While Emerson could "appreciate their weaknesses" and could "point out their faults," he respected the abolitionists' efforts and their cause, and he once referred to them as individuals "who see the faults and stains of our social order, and who pray and strive incessantly to right the wrong." At another point he quotes from "The Young American" (1844) Emerson's dictum that we must not "throw stumbling blocks in the way of the abolitionist [and] the philanthropist as the organs of influence and opinion are swift to do." He concludes this aspect of his presentation with the assertion that while Emerson at times adopted an "attitude of semi-humorous criticism" toward them, he felt a "real respect towards the anti-slavery leaders."

At other points in his talk Storey alludes to Emerson's earliest associations with the abolition movement in the 1830s and his later alliance and friendship with Charles Sumner. Sumner was most zealous in the cause of freedom and "impatient of apathy or indifference" in the matter, and "in Emerson he found a thoroughly congenial soul; . . . the absolute sympathy that existed between them is proof that Sumner recognized in Emerson as intense a love of freedom as his own."

Storey's lengthy address notes several other aspects of Emerson's thinking on the need to abolish slavery and assert human rights, and the methodology to be employed in reaching these goals, drawing freely from Emerson's journal to support his points. As might be expected, Storey's account of Emerson's commitment to the basic integrity of all individuals and his consequent vigorous opposition to all efforts to enslave and exploit others was directly related to his own concern with contemporary social problems in America, especially racism. Thus at one point Storey notes Emerson's hopeful belief that the very qualities of benevolence, docility, and industriousness that led to the exploitation of the Negro race in the nineteenth century, "in a more moral age will not only defend their independence but will give them a rank among nations." Recognizing the sad truth that twentieth-century America was manifestly *not* moving toward the fulfillment of this dream, Storey is led to exclaim: "How full of inspiration are these words to every lover of freedom and justice! How ineffably sad it is to read them now and to reflect as we listen to the cries of the mob at Wilmington and Evansville and read of the horrors committed in Luzon that ours is

a less moral age, and that punishment waits upon our sins as it did of our fathers."

Overall, Storey's address was quite successful in identifying Emerson's strong commitment to the abolition cause and his equally strong belief in the sacredness of the individual and the natural rights, such as freedom and self-determination, that accrue from this belief. Indeed, in this respect the entire Memorial School series was similarly successful. In a commentary in the *Springfield Republican* in July, Franklin Sanborn noted that Storey's presentation contributed significantly to the public's understanding of Emerson because the speaker "had the advantage of access to the private journals of Emerson, and quoted freely therefrom," and hence "was able to do more than rehearse well known opinions." Clearly, Emerson's ideas were "much in advance of those which the educated men of the country in general held at that time." Without referring directly to the proper Boston Brahmins, Sanborn notes that while "the scholarly class in America have usually followed the multitude and not led them, the exceptions [are] Emerson, Parker, Thoreau, Wendell Phillips and Lowell."

Unfortunately, despite such efforts to preserve the legacy of Emerson's campaign for social justice, the works and writings of men like Higginson, Sanborn, and Storey for the most part died with them, their words entombed in the dusty volumes of nineteenth-century newspapers and long-forgotten periodicals. The result is that the image of the serenely disengaged Emerson remains very much with us today. Nevertheless, there are undoubtedly those who, having been stimulated and excited by Emerson as undergraduates, still read the "American Scholar" and the 1844 "Emancipation in the British West Indies" address as moving statements of a pure American idealism. It was this idealism, stimulated by a genuine love for mankind and commitment to human virtue, that fueled Emerson's long and inevitable campaign against slavery, and remains alive and well in his words today.

> Len Gougeon, in a conclusion to his Virtue's Hero: Emerson, Antislavery, and Reform, *The University of Georgia Press, 1990, pp. 337-48.*

Theodore Parker

[*Parker was a prominent Unitarian clergyman who became widely known in the United States during the 1840s and 1850s for his espousal of Transcendentalism and for his outspoken opposition to slavery. In the following speech, originally delivered before the New England Anti-Slavery Convention in 1848, he outlines the abolitionists' political and moral objectives.*]

The design of the abolitionists is this,—to remove and destroy the institution of slavery. To accomplish this well, two things are needed, ideas and actions. Of the ideas first, and then a word of the actions.

What is the idea of the abolitionists? Only this, That all men are created free, endowed with unalienable rights; and in respect of those rights, that all men are equal. This is the idea of Christianity, of human nature. Of course, then, no man has a right to take away another's rights; of course, no man may use me for his good, and not my own good also; of course, there can be no ownership of man by man; of course, no slavery in any form. Such is the idea, and some of the most obvious doctrines that follow from it.

Now, the abolitionists aim to put this idea into the minds of the people, knowing that if it be there, actions will follow fast enough.

It seems a very easy matter to get it there. The idea is nothing new; all the world knows it. Talk with men, Democrats and Whigs, they will say they like freedom in the abstract, they hate slavery in the abstract. But you find that somehow they like slavery in the concrete, and dislike abolitionism when it tries to set free the slave. Slavery is the affair of the whole people; not Congress, but the nation, made slavery; made it national, constitutional. Not Congress, but the voters, must unmake slavery; make it unconstitutional, un-national. They say Congress cannot do it. Well, perhaps it is so; but they that make can break. If the people made slavery, they can unmake it.

You talk with the people; the idea of freedom is there. They tell you they believe the Declaration of Independence—that all men are created equal. But somehow they contrive to believe that negroes now in bondage are an exception to the rule, and so they tell us that slavery must not be meddled with, that we must respect the compromises of the Constitution. So we see that respect for the Constitution overrides respect for the inalienable rights of three millions of negro men.

Now, to move men, it is necessary to know two things—first, What they think, and next, Why they think it. Let us look a little at both.

In New England, men over twenty-one years old may be divided into two classes. First, the men that vote, and secondly, the men that choose the Governor. The voters in Massachusetts are some hundred and twenty thousand; the men that choose the Governor, who tell the people how to vote, whom to vote for, what laws to make, what to forbid, what policy to pursue—they are not very numerous. You may take one hundred men out of Boston, and fifty men from the other large towns in the State—and if you could get them to be silent till next December, and give no counsel on political affairs, the people would not know what to do. The Democrats would not know what to do, nor the Whigs. We are a very democratic people, and suffrage is almost universal; but it is a very few men who tell us how to vote, who make all the most important laws. Do I err in estimating the number at one hundred and fifty? I do not like to exaggerate—suppose there are six hundred men, three hundred in each party; that six hundred manage the political action of the State, in ordinary times.

I need not stop to ask what the rest of the people think about freedom and slavery. What do the men who control our politics think thereof? I answer, They are not opposed to slavery; to the slavery of three millions of men. They may not like slavery in the abstract, or they may like it,

I do not pretend to judge; but slavery in the concrete, at the South, they do like; opposition to that slavery, in the mildest form, or the sternest, they do hate.

That is a serious charge to bring against the prominent rulers of the State. Let me call your attention to a few facts which prove it. Look at the men we send to Congress. There are thirty-one New England men in Congress. By the most liberal construction you can only make out five anti-slavery men in the whole number. Who ever heard of an anti-slavery Governor of Massachusetts in this century? Men know what they are about when they select candidates for election. Do the voters always know what they are about when they choose them?

Then these men always are in favour of a pro-slavery President. The President must be a slave-holder. There have been fifteen presidential elections. Men from the free States have filled the chair twelve years, or three terms; men from the slave States forty-four years, or eleven terms. During one term, the chair was filled by an amphibious presidency, by General Harrison, who was nothing but a concrete availability, and John Tyler, who was—John Tyler. They called him an accident; but there are no accidents in politics. A slave-holder presides over the United States forty-eight years out of sixty! Do those men who control the politics of New England not like it? It is no such thing. They love to have it so. We have just seen the Democratic party, or their leaders, nominate General Cass for their candidate—and General Cass is a Northern man; but on that account is he any the less a pro-slavery man? He did oppose the South once, but it was in pressing a war with England. Everybody knows General Cass, and I need say no more about him. But the Northern Whigs have their leaders—are they anti-slavery men? Not a whit more. Next week you will see them nominate, not the great Eastern Whig, though he is no opponent of slavery, only an expounder and defender of the Constitution; not the great Western Whig, the compromiser, though steeped to the lips in slavery; no, they will nominate General Taylor, a man who lives a little further South, and is at this moment dyed a little more scarlet with the sin of slavery.

But go a step further as to the proof. Those men who control the politics of Massachusetts, or New England, or the whole North, they have never opposed the aggressive movements of the slave power. The annexation of Texas, did they oppose that? No, they were glad of it. True, some earnest men came up here in Faneuil Hall, and passed resolutions, which did no good whatever, because it was well known that the real controllers of our politics thought the other way. Then followed the Mexican war. It was a war for slavery, and they knew it; they like it now—that is, if a man's likings can be found out by his doings, not his occasional and exceptional deeds, but his regular and constant actions. They knew that there would be a war against the currency, a war against the tariff, or a war against Mexico. They chose the latter. They knew what they were about.

The same thing is shown by the character of the press. No "respectable" paper is opposed to slavery; no Whig paper, no Democratic paper. You would as soon expect a Catholic newspaper to oppose the Pope and his church, for the slave power is the pope of America, though not exactly a pious pope. The churches show the same thing; they also are in the main pro-slavery, at least not anti-slavery. There are some forty denominations or sects in New England. Mr President, is one of these anti-slavery? Not one! The land is full of ministers, respectable men, educated men— are they opposed to slavery? I do not know a single man, eminent in any sect, who is also eminent in his opposition to slavery. There was one such man, Dr Channing; but just as he became eminent in the cause of freedom, he lost power in his own church, lost caste in his own little sect; and though men are now glad to make sectarian capital out of his reputation after he is dead, when he lived, they cursed him by their gods! Then, too, all the most prominent men of New England fraternize with slavery. Massachusetts received such an insult from South Carolina as no State ever before received from another State in this Union; an affront which no nation would dare offer another, without grinding its sword first. And what does Massachusetts do? She does—nothing. But her foremost man goes off there, "The schoolmaster that gives no lessons," to accept the hospitality of the South, to take the chivalry of South Carolina by the hand; the Defender of the Constitution fraternizes with the State which violates the Constitution, and imprisons his own constituents on account of the colour of their skin.

Put all these things together, and they show that the men who control the politics of Massachusetts, of all New England, do not oppose or dislike slavery.

So much for what they think; and now for the why they think so.

First, there is the general indifference to what is absolutely right. Men think little of it. The Anglo-Saxon race, on both sides of the water, have always felt the instinct of freedom, and often contended stoutly enough for their own rights. But they never cared much for the rights of other men. The slaves are at a distance from us, and so the wrong of this institution is not brought home to men's feelings as if it were our own wrong.

Then the pecuniary interests of the North are supposed to be connected with slavery, so that the North would lose dollars if the South lost slaves. No doubt this is a mistake; still, it is an opinion currently held. The North wants a market for its fabrics, freight for its ships. The South affords it; and, as men think, better than if she had manufactures and ships of her own, both of which she could have, were there no slaves. All this seems to be a mistake. Freedom, I think, can be shown to be the interest of both North and South.

Yet another reason is found in devotion to the interests of a party. Tell a Whig he could make Whig capital out of anti-slavery, he would turn abolitionist in a moment, if he believed you. Tell a Democrat that he can make capital out of abolition, and he also will come over to your side. But the fact is, each party knows it would gain nothing for its political purposes by standing out for the rights of man. The time will come, and sooner too than some men think, when it will be for the interest of a party to favour abolition, but that time is not yet. It does seem strange, that

while you can find men who will practise a good deal of self-denial for their sect or their party, lending, and hoping nothing in return, you so rarely find a man who will compromise even his popularity for the sake of mankind.

Then, again, there is the fear of change. Men who control our politics seem to have little confidence in man, little in truth, little in justice, and the eternal right. Therefore, while it is never out of season to do something for the tariff, for the moneyed interests of men, they think it is never in time to do much for the great work of elevating mankind itself. They have no confidence in the people, and take little pains to make the people worthy of confidence. So any change which gives a more liberal government to a people, which gives freedom to the slave, they look on with distrust, if not alarm. In 1830, when the French expelled the despotic king who encumbered their throne, what said Massachusetts, what said New England, in honour of the deed? Nothing. Your old men? Nothing. Your young men? Not a word. What did they care for the freedom of thirty millions of men? They were looking at their imports and exports. In 1838, when England set free eight hundred thousand men in a day, what did Massachusetts say about that? What had New England to say? Not a word in its favour from these political leaders of the land. Nay, they thought the experiment was dangerous, and ever since that it is with great reluctance you can get them to confess that the scheme works well. In 1848, when France again expels her king, and all the royalty in the kingdom is carted off in a one horse cab—when the broadest principles of human government are laid down, and a great nation sets about the difficult task of moving out of her old political house, and into a new one, without tearing down the old, without butchering men in the process of removal,—why, what has Boston to say to that? What have the political leaders of Massachusetts, of New England, to say? They have nothing to say for liberty; they are sorry the experiment was made; they are afraid the French will not want so much cotton; they have no confidence in man, and fear every change.

Such are their opinions, to judge by what they do; such the reasons thereof, judging by what they say.

But how can we change this, and get the idea of freedom into men's minds? Something can be done by the gradual elevation of men, by schools and churches, by the press. The churches and colleges of New England have not directly aided us in the work of abolishing slavery. No doubt by their direct action they have retarded that work, and that a good deal. But indirectly they have done much to hasten the work. They have helped educate men; helped make men moral, in a general way; and now this moral power can be turned to this special business, though the churches say, "No, you shall not." I see before me a good and an earnest man [Rev. Cyrus Pierce], who, not opening his mouth in public against slavery, has yet done a great service in this way: he has educated the teachers of the Commonwealth, has taught them to love freedom, to love justice, to love man and God. That is what I call sowing the seeds of anti-slavery. The honoured and excellent Secretary of Education [Horace Mann], who has just gone to stand in the place of a famous man, and I hope to fill it nobly, has done much in this way. I wish in his reports on education he had exposed the wrong which is done here in Boston, by putting all the coloured children in one school, by shutting them out of the Latin school and the English high school. I wish he had done that duty, which plainly belongs to him to do. But without touching that, he has yet done, indirectly, a great work towards the abolition of slavery. He has sown the seeds of education wide spread over the State. One day these seeds will come up; come up men, men that will both vote and choose the Governor; men that will love right and justice; will see the iniquity of American slavery, and sweep it off the continent, cost what it may cost, spite of all compromises of the Constitution, and all compromisers. I look on that as certain. But that is slow work, this waiting for a general morality to do a special act. It is going without dinner till the wheat is grown for your bread.

So we want direct and immediate action upon the people themselves. The idea must be set directly before them, with all its sanctions displayed, and its obligations made known. This can be done in part by the pulpit. Dr Channing shows how much one man can do, standing on that eminence. You all know how much he did do. I am sorry that he came so late, sorry that he did not do more, but thankful for what he did do. However, you cannot rely on the pulpit to do much. The pulpit represents the average goodness and piety; not eminent goodness and piety. It is unfair to call ordinary men to do extraordinary works. I do not concur in all the hard things that are said about the clergy, perhaps it is because I am one of them; but I do not expect a great deal from them. It is hard to call a class of men all at once to rise above all other classes of men, and teach a degree of virtue which they do not understand. But you may call them to be true to their own consciences.

So the pulpit is not to be relied on for much aid. If all the ministers of New England were abolitionists, with the same zeal that they are Protestants, universalists, Methodists, Calvinists, or Unitarians, no doubt the whole State would soon be an anti-slavery State, and the day of emancipation would be wonderfully hastened. But that we are not to look for.

Much can be done by lecturers, who shall go to the people and address them, not as Whigs or Democrats, not as sectarians, but as men, and in the name of man and God present the actual condition of the slaves, and show the duty of the North and South, of the nation, in regard to this matter. For this business, we want money and men, the two sinews of war; money to pay the men, men to earn the money. They must appeal to the people in their primary capacity, simply as men.

Much also may be done by the press. How much may be done by these two means, and that in a few years, these men [Garrison, Phillips, and Quincy] can tell; all the North and South can tell. Men of the most diverse modes of thought can work together in this cause. Here on my right is Mr Phillips, an old-fashioned Calvinist, who believes all the five points of Calvinism. I am rather a new-fashioned Unitarian, and believe only one of the five points, the one Mr Phillips has proved—the perseverance

of the saints; but we get along without any quarrel by the way.

Some men will try political action. The action of the people, of the nation, must be political action. It may be constitutional, it may be unconstitutional. I see not why men need quarrel about that. Let not him that voteth condemn him that voteth not, nor let not him that voteth not condemn him that voteth, but let every man be faithful to his own convictions.

It is said, the abolitionists waste time and wind in denunciation. It is partly true. I make no doubt it inspires the slave-holder's heart to see division amongst his foes. I ought to say his friends, for such we are. He thinks the day of justice is deferred, while the ministers thereof contend. I do not believe a revolution is to be baptized with rose-water. I do not believe a great work is to be done without great passions. It is not to be supposed that the Leviathan of American slavery will allow himself to be drawn out of the mire in which he has made his nest, and grown fat and strong, without some violence and floundering. When we have caught him fairly, he will put his feet into the mud to hold on by; he will reach out and catch hold of everything that will hold him. He has caught hold of Mr Clay and Mr Webster. He will catch hold of General Cass and General Taylor. He will die, though slowly, and die hard. Still it is a pity that men who essay to pull him out, should waste their strength in bickerings with one another, or in needless denunciation of the leviathan's friends. Call slave-holding, slave-holding; let us tell all the evils which arise from it, if we can find language terrible enough; let us show up the duplicity of the nation, the folly of our wise men, the littleness of our great men, the baseness of our honourable men, if need be; but all that with no unkind feelings toward any one. Virtue never appears so lovely as when, destroying sin, she loves the sinner, and seeks to save him. Absence of love is absence of the strongest power. See how much Mr Adams lost of his influence, how much he wasted of his strength, by the violence with which he pursued persons. I am glad to acknowledge the great services he performed. He wished to have every man stand on the right side of the anti-slavery line; but I believe there were some men whom he would like to have put there with a pitchfork. On the other hand, Dr Channing never lost a moment by attacking a personal foe; and see what he gained by it! However, I must say this, that no great revolution of opinion and practice was ever brought about before with so little violence, waste of force, and denunciation. Consider the greatness of the work; it is to restore three millions to liberty; a work, in comparison with which the American Revolution was a little thing. Yet consider the violence, the denunciation, the persecution, and the long years of war, which that Revolution cost. I do not wonder that abolitionists are sometimes violent; I only deplore it. Remembering the provocation, I wonder they are not more so and more often. The prize is to be run for, "not without dust and heat."

Working in this way, we are sure to succeed. The idea is an eternal truth. It will find its way into the public mind, for there is that sympathy between man and the truth, that he cannot live without it and be blessed. What allies we have on our side! True, the cupidity, the tyranny, the fear, and the atheism of the land are against us. But all the nobleness, all the honour, all the morality, all the religion, are on our side. I was sorry to hear it said, that the religion of the land opposed us. It is not true. Religion never opposed any good work. I know what my friend meant, and I wish he had said it, calling things by their right names. It is the irreligion of the land that favours slavery; it is the idolatry of gold; it is our atheism. Of speculative atheism there is not much; you see how much of the practical!

We are certain of success; the spirit of the age is on our side. See how the old nations shake their tyrants out of the land. See how every steamer brings us good tidings of good things; and do you believe America can keep her slaves? It is idle to think so. So all we want is time. On our side are truth, justice, and the eternal right. Yes, on our side is religion, the religion of Christ; on our side are the hopes of mankind, and the great power of God.

> *Theodore Parker, "Speech at Faneuil Hall before the New England Anti-slavery Convention, May 31, 1848," in* The Collected Works of Theodore Parker, *edited by Frances Power Cobbe, Trübner & Co., 1863, pp. 93-102.*

Harriet Beecher Stowe

[*Stowe was an important nineteenth-century abolitionist and writer. Her famous novel* Uncle Tom's Cabin; or, Life among the Lowly *(1852), which is noted for its humanitarian tone and antislavery message, became one of the most popular and profoundly influential novels of the period. In the following 1851 letter to African-American abolitionist Frederick Douglass, she requests information on slave life for her impending work and defends the church's role in the antislavery crusade.*]

Frederick Douglass, Esq.:

Sir,—You may perhaps have noticed in your editorial readings a series of articles that I am furnishing for the *Era* under the title of *Uncle Tom's Cabin, or Life among the Lowly.*

In the course of my story the scene will fall upon a cotton plantation. I am very desirous, therefore, to gain information from one who has been an actual laborer on one, and it occurred to me that in the circle of your acquaintance there might be one who would be able to communicate to me some such information as I desire. I have before me an able paper written by a Southern planter, in which the details and *modus operandi* are given from his point of sight. I am anxious to have something more from another standpoint. I wish to be able to make a picture that shall be graphic and true to nature in its details. Such a person as Henry Bibb, if in the country, might give me just the kind of information I desire. You may possibly know of some other person. I will subjoin to this letter a list of questions, which in that case you will do me a favor by inclosing to the individual, with the request that he will at earliest convenience answer them.

For some few weeks past I have received your paper through the mail, and have read it with great interest, and desire to return my acknowledgments for it. It will be a pleasure to me at some time when less occupied to contribute something to its columns. I have noticed with regret your sentiments on two subjects,—the church and African colonization, . . . with the more regret because I think you have a considerable share of reason for your feelings on both these subjects; but I would willingly, if I could, modify your views on both points.

In the first place you say the church is "proslavery." There is a sense in which this may be true. The American church of all denominations, taken as a body, comprises the best and most conscientious people in the country. I do

---

> **William Lloyd Garrison on his rhetorical style (1831):**
>
> I am aware, that many object to the severity of my language; but is there not cause for severity? I will be as harsh as truth, and as uncompromising as justice. On this subject, I do not wish to think, or speak, or write, with moderation. No! no! Tell a man, whose house is on fire, to give a moderate alarm; tell him to moderately rescue his wife from the hands of the ravisher; tell the mother to gradually extricate her babe from the fire into which it has fallen; but urge me not to use moderation in a cause like the present! I am in earnest. I will not equivocate—I will not excuse—I will not retreat a single inch—AND I WILL BE HEARD. The apathy of the people is enough to make every statue leap from its pedestal, and to hasten the resurrection of the dead.
>
> It is pretended, that I am retarding the cause of emancipation by the coarseness of my invective, and the precipitancy of my measures. The charge is not true. On this question, my influence, humble as it is, is felt at this moment to a considerable extent, and shall be felt in coming years—not perniciously, but beneficially—not as a curse, but as a blessing; and POSTERITY WILL BEAR TESTIMONY THAT I WAS RIGHT. I desire to thank God, that he enables me to disregard "the fear of man which bringeth a snare" and to speak his truth in its simplicity and power.
>
> > "Oppression!" I have seen thee, face to face,
> > And met thy cruel eye and cloudy brow;
> > But thy soul-withering glance I fear not now—
> > For dread to prouder feelings doth give place,
> > Of deep abhorrence! Scorning the disgrace
> > Of slavish knees that at thy footstool bow,
> > I also kneel—but with far other vow
> > Do hail thee and thy herd of hirelings base:
> > I swear, while life-blood warms my throbbing
> >   veins,
> > Still to oppose and thwart, with heart and hand,
> > Thy brutalizing sway—till Afric's chains
> > Are burst, and Freedom rules the rescued land,
> > Trampling Oppression and his iron rod:
> > Such is the vow I take—so help me God!
>
> *William Lloyd Garrison, in his "Commencement of the 'Liberator'," in* The Abolitionists: A Collection of Their Writings, *edited by Louis Ruchames, G. P. Putnam's Sons, 1963.*

not say it comprises none but these, or that none such are found out of it, but only if a census were taken of the purest and most high-principled men and women of the country, the majority of them would be found to be professors of religion in some of the various Christian denominations. This fact has given to the church great weight in this country,—the general and predominant spirit of intelligence and probity and piety of its majority has given it that degree of weight that it has the power to decide the great moral questions of the day. Whatever it unitedly and decidedly sets itself against as moral evil it can put down. In this sense the church is responsible for the sin of slavery. Dr. Barnes has beautifully and briefly expressed this on the last page of his work on slavery, when he says: "Not all the force out of the church could sustain slavery an hour if it were not sustained in it." It then appears that the church has the power to put an end to this evil and does not do it. In this sense she may be said to be pro-slavery. But the church has the same power over intemperance, and Sabbath-breaking, and sin of all kinds. There is not a doubt that if the moral power of the church were brought up to the New Testament standpoint it is sufficient to put an end to all these as well as to slavery. But I would ask you, Would you consider it a fair representation of the Christian church in this country to say that it is pro-intemperance, pro-Sabbath-breaking, and pro everything that it might put down if it were in a higher state of moral feeling? If you should make a list of all the abolitionists of the country, I think that you would find a majority of them in the church,—certainly some of the most influential and efficient ones are ministers.

I am a minister's daughter, and a minister's wife, and I have had six brothers in the ministry (one is in heaven); I certainly ought to know something of the feelings of ministers on this subject. I was a child in 1820 when the Missouri question was agitated, and one of the strongest and deepest impressions on my mind was that made by my father's sermons and prayers, and the anguish of his soul for the poor slave at that time. I remember his preaching drawing tears down the hardest faces of the old farmers in his congregation.

I well remember his prayers morning and evening in the family for "poor, oppressed, bleeding Africa," that the time of her deliverance might come; prayers offered with strong crying and tears, and which indelibly impressed my heart and made me what I am from my very soul, the enemy of all slavery. Every brother I have has been in his sphere a leading anti-slavery man. One of them was to the last the bosom friend and counselor of Lovejoy. As for myself and husband, we have for the last seventeen years lived on the border of a slave State, and we have never shrunk from the fugitives, and we have helped them with all we had to give. I have received the children of liberated slaves into a family school, and taught them with my own children, and it has been the influence that we found in the church and by the altar that has made us do all

this. Gather up all the sermons that have been published on this offensive and unchristian Fugitive Slave Law, and you will find that those against it are numerically more than those in its favor, and yet some of the strongest opponents have not published their sermons. Out of thirteen ministers who meet with my husband weekly for discussion of moral subjects, only three are found who will acknowledge or obey this law in any shape.

After all, my brother, the strength and hope of your oppressed race does lie in the church,—in hearts united to Him of whom it is said, "He shall spare the souls of the needy, and precious shall their blood be in his sight." Everything is against you, but Jesus Christ is for you, and He has not forgotten his church, misguided and erring though it be. I have looked all the field over with despairing eyes; I see no hope but in Him. This movement must and will become a purely religious one. The light will spread in churches, the tone of feeling will rise, Christians North and South will give up all connection with, and take up their testimony against, slavery, and thus the work will be done.

Harriet Beecher Stowe, "Brunswick," in Life and Letters of Harriet Beecher Stowe, *edited by Annie Fields, Houghton, Mifflin and Company, 1897, pp. 122-61.*

Henry D. Thoreau

[*Regarded as one of the key figures of the American Transcendentalist movement, Thoreau is best known for his* Walden, or Life in the Woods *(1854), as well as for his numerous poems and essays, especially "Civil Disobedience" (1849). In the following essay, originally composed in 1860, he offers some retrospective reflections on John Brown, an American abolitionist who was condemned to death in 1857 for inciting a slave insurrection at Harpers Ferry, Virginia.*]

John Brown's career for the last six weeks of his life was meteor-like, flashing through the darkness in which we live. I know of nothing so miraculous in our history.

If any person, in a lecture or conversation at that time, cited any ancient example of heroism, such as Cato or Tell or Winkelried, passing over the recent deeds and words of Brown, it was felt by any intelligent audience of Northern men to be tame and inexcusably far-fetched.

For my own part, I commonly attend more to nature than to man, but any affecting human event may blind our eyes to natural objects. I was so absorbed in him as to be surprised whenever I detected the routine of the natural world surviving still, or met persons going about their affairs indifferent. It appeared strange to me that the 'little dipper' should be still diving quietly in the river, as of yore; and it suggested that this bird might continue to dive here when Concord should be no more.

I felt that he, a prisoner in the midst of his enemies, and under sentence of death, if consulted as to his next step or resource, could answer more wisely than all his countrymen beside. He best understood his position; he contemplated it most calmly. Comparatively, all other men, North and South, were beside themselves. Our thoughts could not revert to any greater or wiser or better man with whom to contrast him, for he, then and there, was above them all. The man this country was about to hang appeared the greatest and best in it.

Years were not required for a revolution of public opinion; days, nay, hours, produced marked changes in this case. Fifty who were ready to say on going into our meeting in honor of him in Concord, that he ought to be hung, would not say it when they came out. They heard his words read, they saw the earnest faces of the congregation; and perhaps they joined at last in singing the hymn in his praise.

The order of instructors was reversed. I heard that one preacher, who at first was shocked and stood aloof, felt obliged at last, after he was hung, to make him the subject of a sermon, in which, to some extent, he eulogized the man, but said that his act was a failure. An influential class-teacher thought it necessary, after the services, to tell his grown-up pupils, that at first he thought as the preacher did then, but now he thought that John Brown was right. But it was understood that his pupils were as much ahead of the teacher, as he was ahead of the priest; and I know for a certainty, that very little boys at home had already asked their parents, in a tone of surprise, why God did not interfere to save him. In each case, the constituted teachers were only half conscious that they were not *leading,* but being *dragged,* with some loss of time and power.

The more conscientious preachers, the Bible men, they who talk about principle, and doing to others as you would that they should do unto you,—how could they fail to recognize him, by far the greatest preacher of them all, with the Bible in his life and in his acts, the embodiment of principle, who actually carried out the golden rule? All whose moral sense had been aroused, who had a calling from on high to preach, sided with him. What confessions he extracted from the cold and conservative! It is remarkable, but on the whole it is well, that it did not prove the occasion for a new sect of *Brownites* being formed in our midst.

They, whether within the Church or out of it, who adhere to the spirit and let go the letter, and are accordingly called infidel, were as usual foremost to recognize him. Men have been hung in the South before for attempting to rescue slaves, and the North was not much stirred by it. Whence, then, this wonderful difference? We were not so sure of *their* devotion to principle. We made a subtle distinction, forgot human laws, and did homage to an idea. The North, I mean the *living* North, was suddenly all transcendental. It went behind the human law, it went behind the apparent failure, and recognized eternal justice and glory. Commonly, men live according to a formula, and are satisfied if the order of law is observed, but in this instance they, to some extent, returned to original perceptions, and there was a slight revival of old religion. They saw that what was called order was confusion, what was called justice, injustice, and that the best was deemed the worst. This attitude suggested a more intelligent and generous spirit than that which actuated our forefathers, and

the possibility, in the course of ages, of a revolution in behalf of another and an oppressed people.

Most Northern men, and a few Southern ones, were wonderfully stirred by Brown's behavior and words. They saw and felt that they were heroic and noble, and that there had been nothing quite equal to them in their kind in this country, or in the recent history of the world. But the minority were unmoved by them. They were only surprised and provoked by the attitude of their neighbors. They saw that Brown was brave, and that he believed that he had done right, but they did not detect any further peculiarity in him. Not being accustomed to make fine distinctions, or to appreciate magnanimity, they read his letters and speeches as if they read them not. They were not aware when they approached a heroic statement—they did not know when they *burned.* They did not feel that he spoke with authority, and hence they only remembered that the *law* must be executed. They remembered the old formula, but did not hear the new revelation. The man who does not recognize in Brown's words a wisdom and nobleness, and therefore an authority, superior to our laws, is a modern Democrat. This is the test by which to discover him. He is not wilfully but constitutionally blind on this side, and he is consistent with himself. Such has been his past life; no doubt of it. In like manner he has read history and his Bible, and he accepts, or seems to accept, the last only as an established formula, and not because he has been convicted by it. You will not find kindred sentiments in his common-place book, if he has one.

When a noble deed is done, who is likely to appreciate it? They who are noble themselves. I was not surprised that certain of my neighbors spoke of John Brown as an ordinary felon, for who are they? They have either much flesh, or much office, or much coarseness of some kind. They are not etherial natures in any sense. The dark qualities predominate in them. Several of them are decidedly pachydermatous. I say it in sorrow, not in anger. How can a man behold the light, who has no answering inward light? They are true to their *right,* but when they look this way they *see* nothing, they are blind. For the children of the light to contend with them is as if there should be a contest between eagles and owls. Show me a man who feels bitterly toward John Brown, and let me hear what noble verse he can repeat. He'll be as dumb as if his lips were stone.

It is not every man who can be a Christian, even in a very moderate sense, whatever education you give him. It is a matter of constitution and temperament, after all. He may have to be born again many times. I have known many a man who pretended to be a Christian, in whom it was ridiculous, for he had no genius for it. It is not every man who can be a freeman, even.

Editors persevered for a good while in saying that Brown was crazy: but at last they said only that it was 'a crazy scheme,' and the only evidence brought to prove it was that it cost him his life. I have no doubt that if he had gone with five thousand men, liberated a thousand slaves, killed a hundred or two slaveholders, and had as many more killed on his own side, but not lost his own life, these same editors would have called it by a more respectable name. Yet he has been far more successful than that. He has lib-

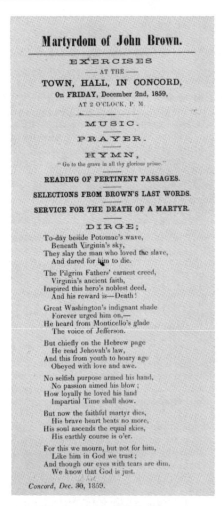

John Brown broadside by Thoreau.

brated his martyrdom, so called, by an annual service. What a satire on the Church is that!

Look not to legislatures and churches for your guidance, nor to any soulless, *incorporated* bodies, but to *inspirited* or inspired ones.

What avail all your scholarly accomplishments and learning, compared with wisdom and manhood? To omit his other behavior, see what a work this comparatively unread and unlettered man wrote within six weeks. Where is our professor of *belles lettres* or of logic and rhetoric, who can write so well? He wrote in prison, not a history of the world, like Raleigh, but an American book which I think will live longer than that. I do not know of such words, uttered under such circumstances, and so copiously withal, in Roman or English or any history. What a variety of themes he touched on in that short space! There are words in that letter to his wife, respecting the education of his daughters, which deserve to be framed and hung over every mantlepiece in the land. Compare this earnest wisdom with that of Poor Richard.

The death of Irving, which at any other time would have attracted universal attention, having occurred while these things were transpiring, went almost unobserved. I shall have to read of it in the biography of authors.

Literary gentlemen, editors and critics, think that they know how to write, because they have studied grammar and rhetoric; but they are egregiously mistaken. The *art* of composition is as simple as the discharge of a bullet from a rifle, and its master-pieces imply an infinitely greater force behind them. This unlettered man's speaking and writing are standard English. Some words and phrases deemed vulgarisms and Americanisms before, he has made standard American; such as '*It will pay.*' It suggests that the one great rule of composition—and if I were a professor of rhetoric, I should insist on this—is to *speak the truth.* This first, this second, this third; pebbles in your mouth or not. This demands earnestness and manhood chiefly.

We seem to have forgotten that the expression, a *liberal* education, originally meant among the Romans one worthy of *free* men; while the learning of trades and professions by which to get your livelihood merely, was considered worthy of *slaves* only. But taking a hint from the word, I would go a step further and say, that it is not the man of wealth and leisure simply, though devoted to art, or science, or literature, who, in a true sense, is *liberally* educated, but only the earnest and *free* man. In a slaveholding country like this, there can be no such thing as a *liberal* education tolerated by the State; and those scholars of Austria and France who, however learned they may be, are contented under their tyrannies, have received only a *servile* education.

Nothing could his enemies do, but it redounded to his infinite advantage—that is, to the advantage of his cause. They did not hang him at once, but reserved him to preach to them. And then there was another great blunder. They did not hang his four followers with him; that scene was still postponed; and so his victory was prolonged and completed. No theatrical manager could have arranged things

erated many thousands of slaves, both North and South. They seem to have known nothing about living or dying for a principle. They all called him crazy then; who calls him crazy now?

All through the excitement occasioned by his remarkable attempt and subsequent behavior, the Massachusetts Legislature, not taking any steps for the defence of her citizens· who were likely to be carried to Virginia as witnesses and exposed to the violence of a slaveholding mob, was wholly absorbed in a liquor-agency question, and indulging in poor jokes on the word 'extension.' Bad spirits occupied their thoughts. I am sure that no statesman up to the occasion could have attended to that question at all at that time,—a very vulgar question to attend to at any time.

When I looked into a liturgy of the Church of England, printed near the end of the last century, in order to find a service applicable to the case of Brown, I found that the only martyr recognized and provided for by it was King Charles the First, an eminent scamp. Of all the inhabitants of England and of the world, he was the only one according to this authority, whom that church had made a martyr and saint of; and for more than a century it had celeso wisely to give effect to his behavior and words. And who, think you, *was* the manager? Who placed the slave woman and her child, whom he stooped to kiss for a symbol, between his prison and the gallows?

We soon saw, as he saw, that he was not to be pardoned or rescued by men. That would have been to disarm him, to restore to him a material weapon, a Sharps' rifle, when he had taken up the sword of the spirit—the sword with which he has really won his greatest and most memorable victories. Now he has not laid aside the sword of the spirit, for he is pure spirit himself, and his sword is pure spirit also.

> 'He nothing common did or mean
> Upon that memorable scene,
> Nor called the gods with vulgar spite,
> To vindicate his helpless right;
> But bowed his comely head
> Down as upon a bed.'

What a transit was that of his horizontal body alone, but just cut down from the gallows-tree! We read, that at such a time it passed through Philadelphia, and by Saturday night had reached New York. Thus, like a meteor it shot through the Union from the southern regions toward the north! No such freight had the cars borne since they carried him southward alive.

On the day of his translation, I heard, to be sure, that he was *hung,* but I did not know what that meant; I felt no sorrow on that account; but not for a day or two did I even *hear* that he was *dead,* and not after any number of days shall I believe it. Of all the men who were said to be my contemporaries, it seemed to me that John Brown was the only one who *had not died.* I never hear of a man named Brown now,—and I hear of them pretty often,—I never hear of any particularly brave and earnest man, but my first thought is of John Brown, and what relation he may be to him. I meet him at every turn. He is more alive than ever he was. He has earned immortality. He is not confined to North Elba nor to Kansas. He is no longer working in secret. He works in public, and in the clearest light that shines on this land.

> *Henry D. Thoreau, "The Last Days of John Brown," in* Henry D. Thoreau: Reform Papers, *edited by Wendell Glick, Princeton University Press, 1973, pp. 145-53.*

Wendell Phillips

[*An American reformer, Phillips was a prominent abolitionist and president of the American Anti-Slavery Society from 1865 to 1870. In the following remarks made at the funeral of William Lloyd Garrison in 1879, Phillips acknowledges Garrison's dedication to the abolitionist movement, lauding him as the "noblest of Christian men."*]

It has been well said that we are not here to weep, and neither are we here to praise. No life closes without sadness. Death, after all, no matter what hope or what memories surround it, is terrible and a mystery. We never part hands that have been clasped life-long in loving tenderness but

---

Lydia Maria Child's preface to the 1836 edition of An Appeal in Favor of That Class of Americans Called Africans:

Reader, I beseech you not to throw down this volume as soon as you have glanced at the title. Read it, if your prejudices will allow, for the very truth's sake:—If I have the most trifling claims upon your good will, for an hour's amusement to yourself, or benefit to your children, read it for *my* sake:—Read it, if it be merely to find fresh occasion to sneer at the vulgarity of the cause:—Read it, from sheer curiosity to see what a woman (who had much better attend to her household concerns) will say upon such a subject:—Read it, on any terms, and my purpose will be gained.

The subject I have chosen admits of no encomiums on my country; but as I generally make it an object to supply what is most needed, this circumstance is unimportant; the market is so glutted with flattery, that a little truth may be acceptable, were it only for its rarity.

I am fully aware of the unpopularity of the task I have undertaken; but though I *expect* ridicule and censure, it is not in my nature to *fear* them.

A few years hence, the opinion of the world will be a matter in which I have not even the most transient interest; but this book will be abroad on its mission of humanity, long after the hand that wrote it is mingling with the dust.

Should it be the means of advancing, even one single hour, the inevitable progress of truth and justice, I would not exchange the consciousness for all Rothschild's wealth, or Sir Walter's fame.

> *L. Maria Child, in her Preface to* An Appeal in Favor of That Class of Americans Called Africans, *1836. Reprint. Arno Press and The New York Times, 1968.*

---

the hour is sad; still, we do not come here to weep. In other moments, elsewhere, we can offer tender and loving sympathy to those whose roof-tree is so sadly bereaved. But in the spirit of the great life which we commemorate, this hour is for the utterance of a lesson; this hour is given to contemplate a grand example, a rich inheritance, a noble life worthily ended. You come together, not to pay tribute, even loving tribute, to the friend you have lost, whose features you will miss from daily life, but to remember the grand lesson of that career; to speak to each other, and to emphasize what that life teaches,—especially in the hearing of these young listeners, who did not see that marvellous career; in their hearing to construe the meaning of the great name which is borne world-wide, and tell them why on both sides the ocean, the news of his death is a matter of interest to every lover of his race. . . . [We] have no right to be silent. Those of us who stood near him, who witnessed the secret springs of his action, the consistent inward and outward life, have no right to be silent. The largest contribution that will ever be made by any single man's life to the knowledge of the working of our institutions will be the picture of his career. He sounded the depths of the weakness, he proved the ultimate strength, of republican institutions; he gave us to know the perils that confront us; he taught us to rally the strength that lies hid.

To my mind there are three remarkable elements in his career. One is rare even among great men. It was his own moral nature, unaided, uninfluenced from outside, that consecrated him to a great idea. Other men ripen gradually. The youngest of the great American names that will be compared with his was between thirty and forty when his first anti-slavery word was uttered. Luther was thirty-four years old when an infamous enterprise woke him to indignation, and it then took two years more to reveal to him the mission God designed for him. This man was in jail for his opinions when he was just twenty-four. He had confronted a nation in the very bloom of his youth. It could be said of him more than of any other American in our day, and more than of any great leader that I chance now to remember in any epoch, that he did not need circumstances, outside influence, some great pregnant event to press him into service, to provoke him to thought, to kindle him into enthusiasm. His moral nature was as marvellous as was the intellect of Pascal. It seemed to be born fully equipped, "finely touched." Think of the mere dates; think that at some twenty-four years old, while Christianity and statesmanship, the experience, the genius of the land, were wandering in the desert, aghast, amazed, and confounded over a frightful evil, a great sin, this boy sounded, found, invented the talisman, "Immediate, unconditional emancipation on the soil." You may say he borrowed it—true enough—from the lips of a woman on the other side of the Atlantic; but he was the only American whose moral nature seemed, just on the edge of life, so perfectly open to duty and truth that it answered to the far-off bugle-note, and proclaimed it instantly as a complete solution of the problem.

Young men, you have no conception of the miracle of that insight; for it is not given to you to remember with any vividness the blackness of the darkness of ignorance and indifference which then brooded over what was called the moral and religious element of the American people. When I think of him, as Melancthon said of Luther, "day by day grows the wonder fresh" at the ripeness of the moral and intellectual life that God gave him at the very opening.

You hear that boy's lips announcing the statesmanlike solution which startled politicians and angered church and people. A year afterwards, with equally single-hearted devotion, in words that have been so often quoted, with those dungeon doors behind him, he enters on his career. In January, 1831, then twenty-five years old, he starts the publication of *The Liberator,* advocating the immediate abolition of slavery; and, with the sublime pledge, "I will be as harsh as truth and as uncompromising as justice. On this subject I do not wish to speak or write with moderation. I will not equivocate—I will not excuse—I will not retreat a single inch—AND I WILL BE HEARD."

Then began an agitation which for the marvel of its origin, the majesty of its purpose, the earnestness, unselfishness and ability of its appeals, the vigor of its assault, the deep national convulsion it caused, the vast and beneficent changes it wrought, and its wide-spread, indirect influence

on all kindred moral questions, is without a parallel in history since Luther. This boy created and marshalled it. His converts held it up and carried it on. Before this, all through the preceding century, there had been among us scattered and single abolitionists, earnest and able men; sometimes, like Wythe of Virginia, in high places. The Quakers and Covenanters had never intermitted their testimony against slavery. But Garrison was the first man to begin a *movement* designed to annihilate slavery. He announced the principle, arranged the method, gathered the forces, enkindled the zeal, started the argument, and finally marshalled the nation for and against the system in a conflict that came near rending the Union.

I marvel again at the instinctive sagacity which discerned the hidden forces fit for such a movement, called them forth, and wielded them to such prompt results. Archimedes said, "Give me a spot and I will move the world." O'Connell leaned back on three millions of Irishmen, all on fire with sympathy. Cobden's hands were held up by the whole manufacturing interest of Great Britain; his treasury was the wealth of the middle classes of the country, and behind him also, in fair proportion, stood the religious convictions of England. Marvellous was their agitation; as you gaze upon it in its successive stages and analyze it, you are astonished at what they invented for tools. But this boy stood alone; utterly alone, at first. There was no sympathy anywhere; his hands were empty; one single penniless comrade was his only helper. Starving on bread and water, he could command the use of types, that was all. Trade endeavored to crush him; the intellectual life of America disowned him.

My friend Weld has said the church was a thick bank of black cloud looming over him. Yes. But no sooner did the church discern the impetuous boy's purpose than out of that dead, sluggish cloud thundered and lightened a malignity which could not find words to express its hate. The very pulpit where I stand saw this apostle of liberty and justice sore beset, always in great need, and often in deadly peril; yet it never gave him one word of approval or sympathy. During all his weary struggle, Mr. Garrison felt its weight in the scale against him. In those years it led the sect which arrogates to itself the name of Liberal. If this was the bearing of so-called Liberals, what bitterness of opposition, judge ye, did not the others show? A mere boy confronts church, commerce, and college; a boy with neither training nor experience! Almost at once the assault tells; the whole country is hotly interested. What created such life under those ribs of death? Whence came that instinctive knowledge? Where did he get that sound common-sense? Whence did he summon that almost unerring sagacity which, starting agitation on an untried field, never committed an error, provoking year by year additional enthusiasm; gathering, as he advanced, helper after helper to his side! I marvel at the miraculous boy. He had no means. Where he got, whence he summoned, how he created, the elements which changed 1830 into 1835— 1830 apathy, indifference, ignorance, icebergs, into 1835, every man intelligently hating him, and mobs assaulting him in every city—is a marvel which none but older men than I can adequately analyze and explain. He said to a friend who remonstrated with him on the heat and severity of his language, "Brother, I have need to be all on fire, for I have mountains of ice about me to melt." Well, that dungeon of 1830, that universal apathy, that deadness of soul, that contempt of what called itself intellect, in ten years he changed into the whole country aflame. He made every single home, press, pulpit, and senate-chamber a debating society, with *his* right and wrong for the subject. And as was said of Luther, "God honored him by making all the worst men his enemies."

Fastened on that daily life was a malignant attention and criticism such as no American has ever endured. I will not call it a criticism of hate; that word is not strong enough. Malignity searched him with candles from the moment he uttered that God-given solution of the problem to the moment when he took the hand of the nation and wrote out the statute which made it law. Malignity searched those forty years with candles, and yet even malignity has never lisped a suspicion, much less a charge—never lisped a suspicion of anything mean, dishonorable, dishonest. No man, however mad with hate, however fierce in assault, ever dared to hint that there was anything low in motive, false in assertion, selfish in purpose, dishonest in method—never a stain on the thought, the word, or the deed.

Now contemplate this boy entering such an arena, confronting a nation and all its forces, utterly poor, with no sympathy from any quarter, conducting an angry, widespread, and profound agitation for ten, twenty, forty years, amid the hate of everything strong in American life, and the contempt of everything influential, and no stain, not the slightest shadow of one, rests on his escutcheon! Summon me the public men, the men who have put their hands to the helm of the vessel of state since 1789, of whom that can be said, although love and admiration, which almost culminated in worship, attended the steps of some of them.

Then look at the work he did. My friends have spoken of his influence. What American ever held his hand so long and so powerfully on the helm of social, intellectual, and moral America? There have been giants in our day. Great men God has granted in widely different spheres; earnest men, men whom public admiration lifted early into power. I shall venture to name some of them. Perhaps you will say it is not usual on an occasion like this, but long-waiting truth needs to be uttered in an hour when this great example is still absolutely indispensable to inspire the effort, to guide the steps, to cheer the hope, of the nation not yet arrived in the promised land. I want to show you the vast breadth and depth that this man's name signifies. We have had Webster in the Senate; we have had Lyman Beecher in the pulpit; we have had Calhoun at the head of a section; we have had a philosopher at Concord with his inspiration penetrating the young mind of the Northern States. They are the four men that history, perhaps, will mention somewhere near the great force whose closing in this scene we commemorate to-day. Remember now not merely the inadequate means at this man's control, not simply the bitter hate that he confronted, not the vast work that he must be allowed to have done,—surely vast, when measured by the opposition he encountered and the strength he held in his hands,—but dismissing all those considerations, mea-

suring nothing but the breadth and depth of his hold, his grasp on American character, social change, and general progress, what man's signet has been set so deep, planted so forever on the thoughts of his epoch? Trace home intelligently, trace home to their sources, the changes social, political, intellectual and religious, that have come over us during the last fifty years,—the volcanic convulsions, the stormy waves which have tossed and rocked our generation,—and you will find close at the sources of the Mississippi this boy with his proclamation!

The great party that put on record the statute of freedom was made up of men whose conscience he quickened and whose intellect he inspired, and they long stood the tools of a public opinion that he created. The grandest name beside his in the America of our times is that of John Brown. Brown stood on the platform that Garrison built; and Mrs. Stowe herself charmed an audience that he gathered for her, with words which he inspired, from a heart that he kindled. Sitting at his feet were leaders born of *The Liberator,* the guides of public sentiment. I know whereof I affirm. It was often a pleasant boast of Charles Sumner that he read *The Liberator* two years before I did, and among the great men who followed his lead and held up his hands in Massachusetts, where is the intellect, where is the heart that does not trace to this printer-boy the first pulse that bade him serve the slave? For myself, no words can adequately tell the measureless debt I owe him, the moral and intellectual life he opened to me. I feel like the old Greek, who, taught himself by Socrates, called his own scholars "the disciples of Socrates."

This is only another instance added to the roll of the Washingtons and the Hampdens, whose root is not ability, but *character;* that influence which, like the great Master's of Judea (humanly speaking), spreading through the centuries, testifies that the world suffers its grandest changes not by genius, but by the more potent control of *character.* His was an earnestness that would take no denial, that consumed opposition in the intensity of its convictions, that knew nothing but right. As friend after friend gathered slowly, one by one, to his side, in that very meeting of a dozen heroic men, to form the New England Anti-Slavery Society, it was his compelling hand, his resolute unwillingness to temper or qualify the utterance, that finally dedicated that first organized movement to the doctrine of immediate emancipation. He seems to have understood—this boy without experience—he seems to have understood by instinct that righteousness is the only thing which will finally compel submission; that one, with God, is always a majority. He seems to have known it at the very outset, taught of God, the herald and champion, God-endowed and God-sent to arouse a nation, that only by the most absolute assertion of the uttermost truth, without qualification or compromise, can a nation be waked to conscience or strengthened for duty. No man ever understood so thoroughly—not O'Connell, nor Cobden—the nature and needs of that *agitation* which alone, in our day, reforms states. In the darkest hour he never doubted the omnipotence of conscience and the moral sentiment.

And then look at the unquailing courage with which he faced the successive obstacles that confronted him! Modest, believing at the outset that America could not be as corrupt as she seemed, he waits at the door of the churches, importunes leading clergymen, begs for a voice from the sanctuary, a consecrated protest from the pulpit. To his utter amazement, he learns, by thus probing it, that the church will give him no help, but, on the contrary, surges into the movement in opposition. Serene, though astounded by the unexpected revelation, he simply turns his footsteps, and announces that "a Christianity which keeps peace with the oppressor is no Christianity," and goes on his way to supplant the religious element which the church had allied with sin by a deeper religious faith. Yes, he sets himself to work, this stripling with his sling confronting the angry giant in complete steel, this solitary evangelist, to make Christians of twenty millions of people! I am not exaggerating. You know, older men, who can go back to that period; I know that when one, kindred to a voice that you have heard to-day, whose pathway Garrison's bloody feet had made easier for the treading, when he uttered in a pulpit in Boston only a few strong words, injected in the course of a sermon, his venerable father, between seventy and eighty years, was met the next morning and his hand shaken by a much moved friend. "Colonel, you have my sympathy. I cannot tell you how much I pity you." "What," said the brusque old man, "what is your pity?" "Well, I hear your son went crazy at 'Church Green' yesterday." Such was the utter indifference. At that time, bloody feet had smoothed the pathway for other men to tread. Still, then and for years afterwards, insanity was the only kind-hearted excuse that partial friends could find for sympathy with such a madman!

If anything strikes one more prominently than another in this career—to your astonishment, young men, you may say—it is the plain, sober common-sense, the robust English element which underlay Cromwell, which explains Hampden, which gives the color that distinguishes 1640 in England from 1790 in France. Plain, robust, well-balanced common-sense. Nothing erratic; no enthusiasm which had lost its hold on firm earth; no mistake of method; no unmeasured confidence; no miscalculation of the enemy's strength. Whoever mistook, Garrison seldom mistook. Fewer mistakes in that long agitation of fifty years can be charged to his account than to any other American. Erratic as men supposed him, intemperate in utterance, mad in judgment, an enthusiast gone crazy, the moment you sat down at his side, patient in explanation, clear in statement, sound in judgment, studying carefully every step, calculating every assault, measuring the force to meet it, never in haste, always patient, waiting until the time ripened,—fit for a great leader. Cull, if you please, from the statesmen who obeyed him, whom he either whipped into submission or summoned into existence, cull from among them the man whose career, fairly examined, exhibits fewer miscalculations and fewer mistakes than this career which is just ended.

I know what I claim. As Mr. Weld has said, I am speaking to-day to men who judge by their ears, by rumors; who see, not with their eyes, but with their prejudices. History, fifty years hence, dispelling your prejudices, will do justice to the grand sweep of the orbit which, as my friend said, to-day we are hardly in a position, or mood, to measure.

As Coleridge avers, "The truth-haters of to-morrow will give the right name to the truth-haters of to-day, for even such men the stream of time bears onward." I do not fear that if my words are remembered by the next generation they will be thought unsupported or extravagant, When history seeks the sources of New England character, when men begin to open up and examine the hidden springs and note the convulsions and the throes of American life within the last half century, they will remember Parker, that Jupiter of the pulpit; they will remember the long unheeded but measureless influence that came to us from the seclusion of Concord; they will do justice to the masterly statesmanship which guided, during a part of his life, the efforts of Webster, but they will recognize that there was only one man north of Mason and Dixon's line who met squarely, with an absolute logic, the else impregnable position of John C. Calhoun; only one brave, far-sighted, keen, logical intellect, which discerned that there were only two moral points in the universe, *right* and *wrong;* that when one was asserted, subterfuge and evasion would be sure to end in defeat.

Here lies the brain and the heart; here lies the statesman-like intellect, logical as Jonathan Edwards, brave as Luther, which confronted the logic of South Carolina with an assertion direct and broad enough to make an issue and necessitate a conflict of two civilizations. Calhoun said, Slavery is *right.* Webster and Clay shrunk from him and evaded his assertion. Garrison, alone at that time, met him face to face, proclaiming slavery a sin and daring all the inferences. It is true, as New Orleans complains to-day in her journals, that this man brought upon America everything they call the disaster of the last twenty years; and it is equally true that if you seek through the hidden causes and unheeded events for the hand that wrote "emancipation" on the statute-book and on the flag, it lies still there to-day.

I have no time to number the many kindred reforms to which he lent as profound an earnestness and almost as large aid.

I hardly dare enter that home. There is one other marked, and, as it seems to me, unprecedented, element in this career. His was the happiest life I ever saw. No need for pity. Let no tear fall over his life. No man gathered into his bosom a fuller sheaf of blessing, delight, and joy. In his seventy years, there were not arrows enough in the whole quiver of the church or state to wound him. As Guizot once said from the tribune, "Gentlemen, you cannot get high enough to reach the level of my contempt." So Garrison, from the serene level of his daily life, from the faith that never faltered, was able to say to American hate, "You cannot reach up to the level of my home mood, my daily existence." I have seen him intimately for thirty years, while raining on his head was the hate of the community, when by every possible form of expression malignity let him know that it wished him all sorts of harm. I never saw him unhappy; I never saw the moment that serene, abounding faith in the rectitude of his motive, the soundness of his method, and the certainty of his success did not lift him above all possibility of being reached by any clamor about him. Every one of his near friends will agree with me that this was the happiest life God has granted in our day to any American standing in the foremost rank of influence and effort.

Adjourned from the stormiest meeting, where hot debate had roused all his powers as near to anger as his nature ever let him come, the music of a dozen voices—even of those who had just opposed him—or a piano, if the house held one, changed his mood in an instant, and made the hour laugh with more than content; unless indeed, a baby and playing with it proved metal even more attractive.

To champion wearisome causes, bear with disordered intellects, to shelter the wrecks of intemperance and fugitives whose pulse trembled at every touch on the door-latch—this was his home; keenly alive to human suffering, ever prompt to help relieve it, pouring out his means for that more lavishly than he ought—all this was no burden, never clouded or depressed the inextinguishable buoyancy and gladness of his nature. God ever held over him unclouded the sunlight of his countenance.

And he never grew old. The tabernacle of flesh grew feebler and the step was less elastic. But the ability to work, the serene faith and unflagging hope suffered no change. To the day of his death he was as ready as in his boyhood to confront and defy a mad majority. The keen insight and clear judgment never failed him. His tenacity of purpose never weakened. He showed nothing either of the intellectual sluggishness or the timidity of age. The bugle-call which, last year, woke the nation to its peril and duty on the Southern question, showed all the old fitness to lead and mould a people's course. Younger men might be confused or dazed by plausible pretensions, and half the North was befooled; but the old pioneer detected the false ring as quickly as in his youth. The words his dying hand traced, welcoming the Southern exodus and foretelling its result, had all the defiant courage and prophetic solemnity of his youngest and boldest days.

Serene, fearless, marvellous man! Mortal, with so few shortcomings!

Farewell, for a very little while, noblest of Christian men! Leader, brave, tireless, unselfish! When the ear heard thee, then it blessed thee; the eye that saw thee gave witness to thee. More truly than it could ever heretofore be said since the great patriarch wrote it, "the blessing of him that was ready to perish" was thine eternal great reward.

Though the clouds rest for a moment to-day on the great work that you set your heart to accomplish, you knew, God in his love let you see, that your work was done; that one thing, by his blessing on your efforts, is fixed beyond the possibility of change. While that ear could listen, God gave what He has so rarely given to man, the plaudits and prayers of four millions of victims, thanking you for emancipation, and through the clouds of to-day your heart, as it ceased to beat, felt certain, *certain,* that whether one flag or two shall rule this continent in time to come, one thing is settled—it never henceforth can be trodden by a slave!

> *Wendell Phillips, "Appendix," in* W. L. Garrison and His Times, *by Oliver Johnson, Mnemosyne Publishing Co., 1969, pp. 455-68.*

THE LITERATURE OF ABOLITIONISM

American Anti-Slavery Society

[*In the following declaration adopted at the formation of the American Anti-Slavery Society in 1833, the members condemn slavery on biblical and legal grounds and call for its immediate abolition.*]

The Convention, assembled in the city of Philadelphia, to organize a National Anti-Slavery Society, promptly seize the opportunity to promulgate the following *Declaration of Sentiments,* as cherished by them, in relation to the enslavement of one-sixth portion of the American people.

More than fifty-seven years have elapsed since a band of patriots convened in this place to devise measures for the deliverance of this country from a foreign yoke. The cornerstone upon which they founded the Temple of Freedom was broadly this—"that all men are created equal; that they are endowed by their Creator with certain inalienable rights; that among these are life, *Liberty,* and the pursuit of happiness." At the sound of their trumpet-call, three millions of people rose up as from the sleep of death, and rushed to the strife of blood; deeming it more glorious to die instantly as freemen, than desirable to live one hour as slaves. They were few in number—poor in resources; but the honest conviction that *Truth, Justice,* and *Right* were on their side, made them invincible.

We have met together for the achievement of an enterprise without which that of our fathers is incomplete, and which, for its magnitude, solemnity, and probable results upon the destiny of the world, as far transcends theirs as moral truth does physical force.

In purity of motive, in earnestness of zeal, in decision of purpose, in intrepidity of action, in steadfastness of faith, in sincerity of spirit, we would not be inferior to them.

Their principles led them to wage war against their oppressors, and to spill human blood like water, in order to be free. *Ours* forbid the doing of evil that good may come, and lead us to reject, and to entreat the oppressed to reject, the use of all carnal weapons for deliverance from bondage; relying solely upon those which are spiritual and mighty through God to the pulling down of strongholds.

Their measures were physical resistance—the marshalling in arms—the hostile array—the mortal encounter. *Ours* shall be such only as the opposition of moral purity to moral corruption—the destruction of error by the potency of truth—the overthrow of prejudice by the power of love—and the abolition of slavery by the spirit of repentance.

Their grievances, great as they were, were trifling in comparison with the wrongs and sufferings of those for whom we plead. Our fathers were never slaves—never bought and sold like cattle—never shut out from the light of knowledge and religion—never subjected to the lash of brutal taskmasters.

But those for whose emancipation we are striving—constituting, at the present time, at least one-sixth part of our countrymen—are recognized by the law, and treated by their fellow-beings, as marketable commodities, as goods and chattels, as brute beasts; are plundered daily of the fruits of their toil, without redress—really enjoying no constitutional nor legal protection from licentious and murderous outrages upon their persons; are ruthlessly torn asunder—the tender babe from the arms of its frantic mother—the heart-broken wife from her weeping husband—at the caprice or pleasure of irresponsible tyrants. For the crime of having a dark complexion, they suffer the pangs of hunger, the infliction of stripes, and the ignominy of brutal servitude. They are kept in heathenish darkness by laws expressly enacted to make their instruction a criminal offence.

These are the prominent circumstances in the condition of more than two millions of our people, the proof of which may be found in thousands of indisputable facts, and in the laws of the slaveholding States.

Hence we maintain, that in view of the civil and religious privileges of this nation, the guilt of its oppression is unequalled by any other on the face of the earth; and therefore,

That it is bound to repent instantly, to undo the heavy burdens, to break every yoke, and to let the oppressed go free.

We further maintain, that no man has a right to enslave or imbrute his brother—to hold or acknowledge him, for one moment, as a piece of merchandise—to keep back his hire by fraud—or to brutalize his mind by denying him the means of intellectual, social, and moral improvement.

The right to enjoy liberty is inalienable. To invade it is to usurp the prerogative of Jehovah. Every man has a right to his own body—to the products of his own labor—to the protection of law, and to the common advantages of society. It is piracy to buy or steal a native African, and subject him to servitude. Surely the sin is as great to enslave an *American* as an *African.*

Therefore, we believe and affirm, That there is no difference, *in principle,* between the African slave-trade and American slavery.

That every American citizen who retains a human being in involuntary bondage as his property, is, according to Scripture (Ex. xxi. 16), a *man-stealer.*

That the slaves ought instantly to be set free, and brought under the protection of the law.

That if they lived from the time of Pharaoh down to the present period, and had been entailed through successive generations, their right to be free could never have been alienated, but their claims would have constantly risen in solemnity.

That all those laws which are now in force admitting the right of slavery, are therefore before God utterly null and void; being an audacious usurpation of the Divine prerogative, a daring infringement on the law of nature, a base overthrow of the very foundations of the social compact, a complete extinction of all the relations, endearments,

and obligations of mankind, and a presumptuous transgression of all the holy commandments; and that, therefore, they ought instantly to be abrogated.

We further believe and affirm, That all persons of color who possess the qualifications which are demanded of others, ought to be admitted forthwith to the enjoyment of the same privileges, and the exercise of the same prerogatives, as others; and that the paths of preferment, of wealth, and of intelligence, should be opened as widely to them as to persons of a white complexion.

We maintain that no compensation should be given to the planters emancipating the slaves—

Because it would be a surrender of the great fundamental principle that man cannot hold property in man;

Because *slavery is a crime, and therefore is not an article to be sold;*

Because the holders of slaves are not the just proprietors of what they claim; freeing the slaves is not depriving them of property, but restoring it to its rightful owners; it is not wronging the master, but righting the slave—restoring him to himself;

Because immediate and general emancipation would only destroy nominal, not real property; it would not amputate a limb or break a bone of the slaves; but, by infusing motives into their breasts, would make them doubly valuable to the masters as free laborers; and

Because, if compensation is to be given at all, it should be given to the outraged and guiltless slaves, and not to those who have plundered and abused them.

We regard as delusive, cruel, and dangerous, any scheme of expatriation which pretends to aid, either directly or indirectly, in the emancipation of the slaves, or to be a substitute for the immediate and total abolition of slavery.

We fully and unanimously recognize the sovereignty of each State to legislate exclusively on the subject of the slavery which is tolerated within its limits; we concede that Congress, *under the present national compact,* has no right to interfere with any of the Slave States in relation to this momentous subject.

But we maintain that Congress has a right, and is solemnly bound, to suppress the domestic slave-trade between the several States, and to abolish slavery in those portions of our territory which the Constitution has placed under its exclusive jurisdiction.

We also maintain that there are, at the present time, the highest obligations resting upon the people of the free States to remove slavery by moral and political action, as prescribed in the Constitution of the United States. They are now living under a pledge of their tremendous physical force, to fasten the galling fetters of tyranny upon the limbs of millions in the Southern States; they are liable to be called at any moment to suppress a general insurrection of the slaves; they authorize the slave-owner to vote on three-fifths of his slaves as property, and thus enable him to perpetuate his oppression; they support a standing army at the South for its protection; and they seize the slave who has escaped into their territories, and send him back to be tortured by an enraged master or a brutal driver. This relation to slavery is criminal and full of danger: *it must be broken up.*

These are our views and principles—these our designs and measures. With entire confidence in the overruling justice of God, we plant ourselves upon the Declaration of our Independence and the truths of Divine Revelation, as upon the Everlasting Rock.

We shall organize Anti-Slavery Societies, if possible, in every city, town, and village in our land.

We shall send forth agents to lift up the voice of remonstrance, of warning, of entreaty, and rebuke.

We shall circulate, unsparingly and extensively, antislavery tracts and periodicals.

We shall enlist the pulpit and the press in the cause of the suffering and the dumb.

We shall aim at a purification of the churches from all participation in the guilt of slavery.

We shall encourage the labor of free men rather than that of slaves, by giving a preference to their productions; and

We shall spare no exertions nor means to bring the whole nation to speedy repentance.

Our trust for victory is solely in God. *We* may be personally defeated, but our principles, never. *Truth, justice, reason, humanity,* must and will gloriously triumph. Already a host is coming up to the help of the Lord against the mighty, and the prospect before us is full of encouragement.

Submitting this *Declaration* to the candid examination of the people of this country, and of the friends of liberty throughout the world, we hereby affix our signatures to it; pledging ourselves that, under the guidance and by the help of Almighty God, we will do all that in us lies, consistently with this Declaration of our principles, to overthrow the most execrable system of slavery that has ever been witnessed upon earth—to deliver our land from its deadliest curse—to wipe out the foulest stain which rests upon our national escutcheon—and to secure to the colored population of the United States all the rights and privileges which belong to them as men and as Americans—come what may to our persons, our interests, or our reputation—whether we live to witness the triumph of *liberty, justice,* and *humanity,* or perish untimely as martyrs in this great, benevolent, and holy cause.

> *"Appendix," in* W. L. Garrison and His Times, *by Oliver Johnson, Mnemosyne Publishing Co., 1969, pp. 473-79.*

John Greenleaf Whittier

[*A distinguished American abolitionist, poet, journalist, and critic, Whittier is considered one of the most influential figures of the nineteenth century. His works, informed by his Quaker faith, are noted for their humanitarianism, moral tone, and simple expression of senti-*

ment. *The following poem, "To William Lloyd Garrison," was read at the convention which formed the American Anti-Slavery Society in Philadelphia, in December, 1833.*]

Champion of those who groan beneath
  Oppression's iron hand:
In view of penury, hate, and death,
  I see thee fearless stand.
Still bearing up thy lofty brow,
  In the steadfast strength of truth,
In manhood sealing well the vow
  And promise of thy youth.

Go on, for thou hast chosen well;
  On in the strength of God!
Long as one human heart shall swell
  Beneath the tyrant's rod.
Speak in a slumbering nation's ear,
  As thou hast ever spoken,
Until the dead in sin shall hear,
  The fetter's link be broken!

I love thee with a brother's love,
  I feel my pulses thrill,
To mark thy spirit soar above
  The cloud of human ill.
My heart hath leaped to answer thine,
  And echo back thy words,
As leaps the warrior's at the shine
  And flash of kindred swords!

They tell me thou art rash and vain,
  A searcher after fame;
That thou art striving but to gain
  A long-enduring name;
That thou hast nerved the Afric's hand
  And steeled the Afric's heart,
To shake aloft his vengeful brand,
  And rend his chain apart.

Have I not known thee well, and read
  Thy mighty purpose long?
And watched the trials which have made
  Thy human spirit strong?
And shall the slanderer's demon breath
  Avail with one like me,
To dim the sunshine of my faith
  And earnest trust in thee?

Go on, the dagger's point may glare
  Amid thy pathway's gloom;
The fate which sternly threatens there
  Is glorious martyrdom!
Then onward with a martyr's zeal;
  And wait thy sure reward
When man to man no more shall kneel,
  And God alone be Lord!

> *John Greenleaf Whittier, "Anti-Slavery Poems," in his* The Complete Poetical Works of Whittier, *Houghton Mifflin Company, 1894, pp. 262-63.*

Samuel J. May

[*A Unitarian clergyman, May became a confirmed abolitionist after meeting William Lloyd Garrison in 1830. His* Recollections of Our Antislavery Conflict *(1869) has been praised as a clear and insightful response to the moral issues of slavery. In the following excerpt from that work, May acknowledges the literary community's*

Frederick Douglass clarifies the meaning of African-American independence (1848):

In the Northern states, we are not slaves to individuals, not personal slaves, yet in many respects we are the slaves of the community. We are, however, far enough removed from the actual condition of the slave to make us largely responsible for their continued enslavement, or their speedy deliverance from chains. For in the proportion which we shall rise in the scale of human improvement, in that proportion do we augment the probabilities of a speedy emancipation of our enslaved fellow-countrymen. It is more than a mere figure of speech to say, that we are as a people, chained together. We are one people—one in general complexion, one in a common degradation, one in popular estimation. As one rises, all must rise, and as one falls all must fall. Having now, our feet on the rock of freedom, we must drag our brethren from the slimy depths of slavery, ignorance, and ruin. Every one of us should be ashamed to consider himself free, while his brother is a slave. The wrongs of our brethren, should be our constant theme. There should be no time too precious, no calling too holy, no place too sacred, to make room for this cause. We should not only feel it to be the cause of humanity, but the cause of christianity, and fit work for men and angels. We ask you to devote yourselves to this cause, as one of the first, and most successful means of self improvement. In the careful study of it, you will learn your own rights, and comprehend your own responsibilities, and, scan through the vista of coming time, your high, and God-appointed destiny. Many of the brightest and best of our number, have become such by their devotion to this cause, and the society of white abolitionists. The latter have been willing to make themselves of no reputation for our sake, and in return, let us show ourselves worthy of their zeal and devotion. Attend Anti-slavery meetings, show that you are interested in the subject, that you hate slavery, and love those who are laboring for its overthrow. Act with white Abolition societies where-ever you can, and where you cannot, get up societies among yourselves, but without exclusiveness. It will be a long time before we gain all our rights; and although it may seem to conflict with our views of human brotherhood, we shall undoubtedly for many years be compelled to have institutions of a complexional character, in order to attain this very idea of human brotherhood. We would, however, advise our brethren to occupy memberships and stations among white persons, and in white institutions, just so fast as our rights are secured to us.

Never refuse to act with a white society or institution because it is white, or a black one, because it is black; but act with all men without distinction of color. By so acting, we shall find many opportunities for removing prejudices and establishing the rights of all men. We say, avail yourselves of *white* institutions, not because they are white, but because they afford a more convenient means of improvement.

Frederick Douglass, in "An Address to the Colored People of the United States," in Witness for Freedom, *edited by C. Peter Ripley, The University of North Carolina Press, 1993.*

contribution to the abolitionist crusade and singles out American poet John Greenleaf Whittier as the "laureate" of the antislavery movement.]

All great reformations have had their bards. The Hebrew prophets were poets. They clothed their terrible denunciations of national iniquities and their confident predictions of the ultimate triumph of truth and righteousness in imagery so vivid that it will never fade. Mr. Garrison was bathed in their spirit when a child by his pious mother. He is a poet and an ardent lover of poetry. The columns of *The Liberator,* from the beginning, were every week enriched by gems in verse, not unfrequently the product of his own rapt soul. No sentiment inspires men to such exalted strains as the love of liberty. Many of the early Abolitionists uttered themselves in fervid lines of poetry,—Mrs. M. W. Chapman, Mrs. E. L. Follen, Miss E. M. Chandler, Miss A. G. Chapman, Misses C. and A. E. Weston, Mrs. L. M. Child, Mrs. Maria Lowell, Miss Mary Ann Collier, and others, male and female. In 1836—the time that tried men's souls—Mrs. Chapman gathered into a volume the effusions of the above-named, together with those of kindred spirits in other lands and other times. The volume was entitled, *Songs of the Free and Hymns of Christian Freedom.* Many of these songs and hymns will live so long as oppression of every kind is abhorred, and men aspire after true liberty. This book was a powerful weapon in our moral welfare. My memory glows with the recollections of the fervor, and often obvious effect, with which we used to sing in true accord the 13th hymn, by Miss E. M. Chandler:

> Think of our country's glory
>   All dimmed with Afric's tears!
> Her broad flag stained and gory
>   With the hoarded guilt of years!

Or the 15th, by Mr. Garrison:

> The hour of freedom! come it must.
>   O, hasten it in mercy, Heaven!
> When all who grovel in the dust
>   Shall stand erect, their fetters riven.

Or the 7th, by Mrs. Follen:

> 'What mean ye, that ye bruise and bind
>   My people,' saith the Lord;
> 'And starve your craving brother's mind,
>   That asks to hear my word?'

Or the 102d, by Mrs. Chapman:

> Hark! hark! to the trumpet call,
>   'Arise in the name of God most high!'
> On ready hearts the deep notes fall,
>   And firm and full is the strong reply:
> 'The hour is at hand to do and dare!
>   Bound with the bondmen now are we!
> We may not utter the patriot's prayer,
>   Or bend in the house of God the knee!'

Or that stirring song, by Mr. Garrison:

> I am an Abolitionist;
>   I glory in the name.

The singing of such hymns and songs as these was like the bugle's blast to an army ready for battle. No one seemed unmoved. If there were any faint hearts amongst us, they were hidden by the flush of excitement and sympathy.

In 1838 or 1839 Mrs. Chapman, assisted by her sisters, the Misses Weston, and Mrs. Child, commenced the publication of *The Liberty Bell.* A volume with this title was issued annually by them for ten or twelve years, especially for sale at the yearly antislavery fair. These volumes were full of poetry in prose and verse. The editors levied contributions upon the true-hearted of other countries besides our own, and enriched their pages with articles from the pens of all the above-named, and from Whittier, Pierpont, Lowell, Longfellow, Phillips, Quincy, Clarke, Sewall, Adams, Channing, Bradburn, Pillsbury, Rogers, Wright, Parker, Stowe, Emerson, Furness, Higginson, Sargent, Jackson, Stone, Whipple, our own countrymen and women; and Bowring, Martineau, Thompson, Browning, Combe, Sturge, Webb, Lady Byron, and others, of England; and Arago, Michelet, Monod, Beaumont, Souvestre, Paschoud, and others, of France. It would not be easy to find elsewhere so full a treasury of mental and moral jewels.

The names of most of our illustrious American poets appear in *The Liberty Bell* more or less frequently. To all of them we were and are much indebted. James Russell Lowell was never, I believe, a member of the Antislavery Society. He was seldom seen at our meetings. But his muse rendered us essential services. His poems—"The Present Crisis," "On the Capture of Fugitive Slaves near Washington," "On the Death of Charles T. Torrey," "To John G. Palfrey," and especially his "Lines to William L. Garrison," and his "Stanzas sung at the Antislavery Picnic in Dedham, August 1, 1843"—committed him fully to the cause of freedom,—the cause of our enslaved countrymen.

Rev. John Pierpont gave us his hand at an earlier day. He took upon himself "our reproach" in 1836, when we most needed help. I have already made grateful mention of his "Word from a Petitioner," sent to me by the hand of the heroic Francis Jackson in the midst of the convention of the constituents of Hon. J. Q. Adams, called at Quincy to assure their brave, invincible representative of their deep, admiring sense of obligation to him for his persistent and almost single-handed defence of the sacred right of petition on the floor of Congress.

Mr. Pierpont's next was a *tocsin* in deed as well as in name. He was impelled to strike his lyre by the alarm he justly felt at the tidings from Alton of the destruction of Mr. Lovejoy's anti-slavery printing-office, and the murder of the devoted proprietor. His indignation was roused yet more by the burning of "Pennsylvania Hall" in Philadelphia, and the shameful fact that at the same time, 1838, no church or decent hall could be obtained in Boston for "love or money," in which to hold an anti-slavery meeting; but we were compelled to resort to an inconvenient and insufficient room over the stable of Marlborough Hotel.

His next powerful effusion was *The Gag,* a caustic and scathing satire upon the Hon. C. G. Atherton, of New Hampshire, for his base attempt in the House of Representatives at Washington to put an entire stop to any discussion of the subject of slavery.

His next piece was *The Chain,* a most touching comparison of the wrongs and sufferings of the slaves with other evils that injured men have been made to endure.

Then followed *The Fugitive Slave's Apostrophe to the North Star,* which showed how deeply he sympathized with the many hundreds of our countrymen who, to escape from slavery, had toiled through dismal swamps, thickset canebrakes, deep rivers, tangled forests, alone, by night, hungry, almost naked and penniless, guided only by the steady light of the polar star, which some kind friend had taught them to distinguish, and had assured them would be an unerring leader to a land of liberty. They who have heard the narratives of such as have so escaped need not be told that Mr. Pierpont must have had the tale poured through his ear into his generous heart.

But of all our American poets, John G. Whittier has from first to last done most for the abolition of slavery. All my antislavery brethren, I doubt not, will unite with me to crown him our laureate. From 1832 to the close of our dreadful war in 1865 his harp of liberty was never hung up. Not an important occasion escaped him. Every significant incident drew from his heart some pertinent and often very impressive or rousing verses. His name appears in the first volume of *The Liberator,* with high commendations of his poetry and his character. As early as 1831 he was attracted to Mr. Garrison by sympathy with his avowed purpose to abolish slavery. Their acquaintance soon ripened into a heartfelt friendship, as he declared in the following lines, written in 1833:

> Champion of those who groan beneath
>   Oppression's iron hand:
> In view of penury, hate, and death,
>   I see thee fearless stand.
> Still bearing up thy lofty brow,
>   In the steadfast strength of truth,
> In manhood sealing well the vow
>   And promise of thy youth. . . .
>
> I love thee with a brother's love;
>   I feel my pulses thrill,
> To mark thy spirit soar above
>   The cloud of human ill.
> My heart hath leaped to answer thine,
>   And echo back thy words,
> As leaps the warrior's at the shine
>   And flash of kindred swords! . . .
>
> Go on—the dagger's point may glare
>   Amid thy pathway's gloom,—
> The fate which sternly threatens there
>   Is glorious martyrdom!
> Then onward with a martyr's zeal;
>   And wait thy sure reward,
> When man to man no more shall kneel,
>   And God alone be Lord!

Mr. Whittier proved the sincerity of these professions. He joined the first antislavery society and became an active official. Notwithstanding his dislike of public speaking, he sometimes lectured at that early day, when so few were found willing to avow and advocate the right of the enslaved to immediate liberation from bondage without the condition of removal to Liberia. Mr. Whittier attended the convention at Philadelphia in December, 1833, that formed the American Antislavery Society. He was one of the secretaries of that body, and a member, with Mr. Garrison, of the committee appointed to prepare the "Declaration of our Sentiments and Purposes." Although, as I have elsewhere stated, Mr. Garrison wrote almost every sentence of that admirable document just as it now stands, yet I well remember the intense interest with which Mr. Whittier scrutinized it, and how heartily he indorsed it.

In 1834, by his invitation I visited Haverhill, where he then resided. I was his guest, and lectured under his auspices in explanation and defence of our abolition doctrines and plans. Again the next year, after the mob spirit had broken out, I went to Haverhill by his invitation, and he shared with me in the perils which I have described on a former page.

In January, 1836, Mr. Whittier attended the annual meeting of the Massachusetts Antislavery Society, and boarded the while in the house where I was living. He heard Dr. Follen's great speech on that occasion, and came home so much affected by it that, either that night or the next morning, he wrote those "Stanzas for the Times," which are among the best of his productions:

> Is this the land our fathers loved,
>   The freedom which they toiled to win?
> Is this the soil whereon they moved?
>   Are these the graves they slumber in?
> Are *we* the sons by whom are borne
> The mantles which the dead have worn?
>
> And shall we crouch above these graves
>   With craven soul and fettered lip?
> Yoke in with marked and branded slaves,
>   And tremble at the driver's whip?
> Bend to the earth our pliant knees,
> And speak but as our masters please? . . .
>
> Shall tongues be mute when deeds are wrought
>   Which well might shame extremest hell?
> Shall freemen lock the indignant thought?
>   Shall Pity's bosom cease to swell?
> Shall Honor bleed? Shall Truth succumb?
> Shall pen and press and soul be dumb?
>
> No;—by each spot of haunted ground,
>   Where Freedom weeps her children's fall,—
> By Plymouth's rock and Bunker's mound,—
>   By Griswold's stained and shattered wall,—
> By Warren's ghost,—by Langdon's shade,—
> By all the memories of our dead! . . .
>
> By all above, around, below,
> Be our indignant answer,—NO!

I can hardly refrain from giving my readers the whole of these stanzas. But I hope they all are, or will at once make themselves, familiar with them. As I read them now, they revive in my bosom not the memory only, but the glow they kindled there when I first pored over them. Then his lines entitled "Massachusetts to Virginia," and those he wrote on the adoption of Pinckney's Resolution, and the passage of Calhoun's Bill, excluding antislavery newspapers and pamphlets and letters from the United States

Mail,—indeed, all his antislavery poetry helped mightily to keep us alive to our high duties, and fired us with holy resolution. Let our laureate's verses still be said and sung throughout the land, for if the portents of the day be true, our conflict with the enemies of liberty, the oppressors of humanity, is not yet ended.

> *Samuel J. May, "John G. Whittier and the Antislavery Poets," in his* Some Recollections of Our Antislavery Conflict, *1869. Reprint by Arno Press, 1968, pp. 259-66.*

William Lloyd Garrison

[An American journalist and reformer, Garrison was the first publisher of the abolitionist journal The Liberator *(1831), as well as the founder of the American Anti-Slavery Society (1833). In the following introduction to Frederick Douglass's autobiography,* Narrative of the Life of Frederick Douglass, an American Slave *(1845), Garrison relates his first encounter with Douglass as a fugitive slave and sums up his value to the abolitionist enterprise.]*

In the month of August, 1841, I attended an anti-slavery convention in Nantucket, at which it was my happiness to become acquainted with Frederick Douglass, the writer of the [*Narrative of the Life of Frederick Douglass, An American Slave*]. He was a stranger to nearly every member of that body; but, having recently made his escape from the southern prison-house of bondage, and feeling his curiosity excited to ascertain the principles and measures of the abolitionists,—of whom he had heard a somewhat vague description while he was a slave,—he was induced to give his attendance, on the occasion alluded to, though at that time a resident in New Bedford.

Fortunate, most fortunate occurrence!—fortunate for the millions of his manacled brethren, yet panting for deliverance from their awful thraldom!—fortunate for the cause of negro emancipation, and of universal liberty!—fortunate for the land of his birth, which he has already done so much to save and bless!—fortunate for a large circle of friends and acquaintances, whose sympathy and affection he has strongly secured by the many sufferings he has endured, by his virtuous traits of character, by his ever-abiding remembrance of those who are in bonds, as being bound with them!—fortunate for the multitudes, in various parts of our republic, whose minds he has enlightened on the subject of slavery, and who have been melted to tears by his pathos, or roused to virtuous indignation by his stirring eloquence against the enslavers of men!—fortunate for himself, as it at once brought him into the field of public usefulness, "gave the world assurance of a MAN," quickened the slumbering energies of his soul, and consecrated him to the great work of breaking the rod of the oppressor, and letting the oppressed go free!

I shall never forget his first speech at the convention—the extraordinary emotion it excited in my own mind—the powerful impression it created upon a crowded auditory, completely taken by surprise—the applause which followed from the beginning to the end of his felicitous remarks. I think I never hated slavery so intensely as at that moment; certainly, my perception of the enormous outrage which is inflicted by it, on the godlike nature of its victims, was rendered far more clear than ever. There stood one, in physical proportion and stature commanding and exact—in intellect richly endowed—in natural eloquence a prodigy—in soul manifestly "created but a little lower than the angels"—yet a slave, ay, a fugitive slave,—trembling for his safety, hardly daring to believe that on the American soil, a single white person could be found who would befriend him at all hazards, for the love of God and humanity! Capable of high attainments as an intellectual and moral being—needing nothing but a comparatively small amount of cultivation to make him an ornament to society and a blessing to his race—by the law of the land, by the voice of the people, by the terms of the slave code, he was only a piece of property, a beast of burden, a chattel personal, nevertheless!

A beloved friend from New Bedford prevailed on Mr. Douglass to address the convention. He came forward to the platform with a hesitancy and embarrassment, necessarily the attendants of a sensitive mind in such a novel position. After apologizing for his ignorance, and reminding the audience that slavery was a poor school for the human intellect and heart, he proceeded to narrate some of the facts in his own history as a slave, and in the course of his speech gave utterance to many noble thoughts and thrilling reflections. As soon as he had taken his seat, filled with hope and admiration, I rose, and declared that Patrick Henry, of revolutionary fame, never made a speech more eloquent in the cause of liberty, than the one we had just listened to from the lips of that hunted fugitive. So I believed at that time—such is my belief now. I reminded the audience of the peril which surrounded this self-emancipated young man at the North,—even in Massachusetts, on the soil of the Pilgrim Fathers, among the descendants of revolutionary sires; and I appealed to them, whether they would ever allow him to be carried back into slavery,—law or no law, constitution or no constitution. The response was unanimous and in thunder-tones—"NO!"

"Will you succor and protect him as a brother-man—a resident of the old Bay State?" "YES!" shouted the whole mass, with an energy so startling, that the ruthless tyrants south of Mason and Dixon's line might almost have heard the mighty burst of feeling, and recognized it as the pledge of an invincible determination, on the part of those who gave it, never to betray him that wanders, but to hide the outcast, and firmly to abide the consequences.

It was at once deeply impressed upon my mind, that, if Mr. Douglass could be persuaded to consecrate his time and talents to the promotion of the anti-slavery enterprise, a powerful impetus would be given to it, and a stunning blow at the same time inflicted on northern prejudice against a colored complexion. I therefore endeavored to instil hope and courage into his mind, in order that he might dare to engage in a vocation so anomalous and responsible for a person in his situation; and I was seconded in this effort by warm-hearted friends, especially by the late General Agent of the Massachusetts Anti-Slavery Society, Mr. John A. Collins, whose judgment in this instance entirely coincided with my own. At first, he could give no encouragement; with unfeigned diffidence, he expressed his conviction that he was not adequate to the performance of so great a task; the path marked out was wholly an untrodden one; he was sincerely apprehensive that he should do more harm than good. After much deliberation, however, he consented to make a trial; and ever since that period, he has acted as a lecturing agent, under the auspices either of the American or the Massachusetts Anti-Slavery Society. In labors he has been most abundant; and his success in combating prejudice, in gaining proselytes, in agitating the public mind, has far surpassed the most sanguine expectations that were raised at the commencement of his brilliant career. He has borne himself with gentleness and meekness, yet with true manliness of character. As a public speaker, he excels in pathos, wit, comparison, imitation, strength of reasoning, and fluency of language. There is in him that union of head and heart, which is indispensable to an enlightenment of the heads and a winning of the hearts of others. May his strength continue to be equal to his day! May he continue to "grow in grace, and in the knowledge of God," that he may be increasingly serviceable in the cause of bleeding humanity, whether at home or abroad!

It is certainly a very remarkable fact, that one of the most efficient advocates of the slave population, now before the public, is a fugitive slave, in the person of Frederick Douglass; and that the free colored population of the United States are as ably represented by one of their own number, in the person of Charles Lenox Remond, whose eloquent appeals have extorted the highest applause of multitudes on both sides of the Atlantic. Let the calumniators of the colored race despise themselves for their baseness and illiberality of spirit, and henceforth cease to talk of the natural inferiority of those who require nothing but time and opportunity to attain to the highest point of human excellence.

It may, perhaps, be fairly questioned, whether any other portion of the population of the earth could have endured the privations, sufferings and horrors of slavery, without having become more degraded in the scale of humanity than the slaves of African descent. Nothing has been left undone to cripple their intellects, darken their minds, debase their moral nature, obliterate all traces of their relationship to mankind; and yet how wonderfully they have sustained the mighty load of a most frightful bondage, under which they have been groaning for centuries! To illustrate the effect of slavery on the white man,—to show that he has no powers of endurance, in such a condition, superior to those of his black brothers,—Daniel O'Connell, the distinguished advocate of universal emancipation, and the mightiest champion of prostrate but not conquered Ireland, relates the following anecdote in a speech delivered by him in the Conciliation Hall, Dublin, before the Loyal National Repeal Association, March 31, 1845. "No matter," said Mr. O'Connell, "under what specious term it may disguise itself, slavery is still hideous. *It has a natural, an inevitable tendency to brutalize every noble faculty of man.* An American sailor, who was cast away on the shore of Africa, where he was kept in slavery for three years, was, at the expiration of that period, found to be imbruted and stultified—he had lost all reasoning power; and having forgotten his native language, could only utter some savage gibberish between Arabic and English, which nobody could understand, and which even he himself found difficulty in pronouncing. So much for the humanizing influence of THE DOMESTIC INSTITUTION!" Admitting this to have been an extraordinary case of mental deterioration, it proves at least that the white slave can sink as low in the scale of humanity as the black one.

Mr. Douglass has very properly chosen to write his own Narrative, in his own style, and according to the best of his ability, rather than to employ some one else. It is, therefore, entirely his own production; and, considering how long and dark was the career he had to run as a slave,—how few have been his opportunities to improve his mind since he broke his iron fetters,—it is, in my judgment, highly creditable to his head and heart. He who can peruse it without a tearful eye, a heaving breast, an afflicted spirit,—without being filled with an unutterable abhorrence of slavery and all its abettors, and animated with a determination to seek the immediate overthrow of that execrable system,—without trembling for the fate of this country in the hands of a righteous God, who is ever on the side of the oppressed, and whose arm is not shortened that it cannot save,—must have a flinty heart, and be qualified to act the part of a trafficker "in slaves and the souls of men." I am confident that it is essentially true in all its statements; that nothing has been set down in malice, nothing exaggerated, nothing drawn from the imagination; that it comes short of the reality, rather than overstates a single fact in regard to SLAVERY AS IT IS. The experience of Frederick Douglass, as a slave, was not a peculiar one; his lot was not especially a hard one; his case may be regarded as a very fair specimen of the treatment of slaves in Maryland, in which State it is conceded that they are better fed and less cruelly treated than in Georgia, Alabama, or Louisiana. Many have suffered incomparably more, while very few on the plantations have suffered less, than himself. Yet how deplorable was his situation! what terrible chastisements were inflicted upon his person! what still more shocking outrages were perpetrated upon his mind! with all his noble powers and sublime aspirations, how like a brute was he treated, even by those professing to have the same mind in them that was in Christ Jesus! to what dreadful liabilities was he continually subjected! how destitute of friendly counsel and aid, even in his greatest extremities! how heavy was the midnight of woe which shrouded in blackness the last ray of hope, and filled the future with terror and gloom! what longings after freedom took possession of his breast, and how his misery augmented, in proportion as he grew reflective and intelligent,—thus demonstrating that a happy slave is an extinct man! how he thought, reasoned, felt, under the lash of the driver, with the chains upon his limbs! what perils he encountered in his endeavors to escape from his horrible doom! and how signal have been his deliverance and preservation in the midst of a nation of pitiless enemies!

This Narrative contains many affecting incidents, many passages of great eloquence and power; but I think the most thrilling one of them all is the description Douglass gives of his feelings, as he stood soliloquizing respecting his fate, and the chances of his one day being a freeman, on the banks of the Chesapeake Bay—viewing the receding vessels as they flew with their white wings before the breeze, and apostrophizing them as animated by the living spirit of freedom. Who can read that passage, and be insensible to its pathos and sublimity? Compressed into it is a whole Alexandrian library of thought, feeling, and sentiment—all that can, all that need be urged, in the form of expostulation, entreaty, rebuke, against that crime of crimes,—making man the property of his fellow-man! O, how accursed is that system, which entombs the godlike mind of man, defaces the divine image, reduces those who by creation were crowned with glory and honor to a level with four-footed beasts, and exalts the dealer in human flesh above all that is called God! Why should its existence be prolonged one hour? Is it not evil, only evil, and that continually? What does its presence imply but the absence of all fear of God, all regard for man, on the part of the people of the United States? Heaven speed its eternal overthrow!

So profoundly ignorant of the nature of slavery are many persons, that they are stubbornly incredulous whenever they read or listen to any recital of the cruelties which are daily inflicted on its victims. They do not deny that the slaves are held as property; but that terrible fact seems to convey to their minds no idea of injustice, exposure to outrage, or savage barbarity. Tell them of cruel scourgings, of mutilations and brandings, of scenes of pollution and blood, of the banishment of all light and knowledge, and they affect to be greatly indignant at such enormous exaggerations, such wholesale misstatements, such abominable libels on the character of the southern planters! As if all these direful outrages were not the natural results of slavery! As if it were less cruel to reduce a human being to the condition of a thing, than to give him a severe flagellation, or to deprive him of necessary food and clothing! As if whips, chains, thumb-screws, paddles, bloodhounds, overseers, drivers, patrols, were not all indispensable to keep the slaves down, and to give protection to their ruthless oppressors! As if, when the marriage institution is abolished, concubinage, adultery, and incest, must not necessarily abound; when all the rights of humanity are annihilated, any barrier remains to protect the victim from the fury of the spoiler; when absolute power is assumed over life and liberty, it will not be wielded with destructive sway! Skeptics of this character abound in society. In some few instances, their incredulity arises from a want of reflection; but, generally, it indicates a hatred of the light, a desire to shield slavery from the assaults of its foes, a contempt of the colored race, whether bond or free. Such will try to discredit the shocking tales of slaveholding cruelty which are recorded in this truthful Narrative; but they will labor in vain. Mr. Douglass has frankly disclosed the place of his birth, the names of those who claimed ownership in his body and soul, and the names also of those who committed the crimes which he has alleged against them. His statements, therefore, may easily be disproved, if they are untrue.

In the course of his Narrative, he relates two instances of murderous cruelty,—in one of which a planter deliberately shot a slave belonging to a neighboring plantation, who had unintentionally gotten within his lordly domain in quest of fish; and in the other, an overseer blew out the brains of a slave who had fled to a stream of water to escape a bloody scourging. Mr. Douglass states that in neither of these instances was any thing done by way of legal arrest or judicial investigation. The *Baltimore American,* of March 17, 1845, relates a similar case of atrocity, perpetrated with similar impunity—as follows:—"*Shooting a Slave.*—We learn, upon the authority of a letter from Charles county, Maryland, received by a gentleman of this city, that a young man named Matthews, a nephew of General Matthews, and whose father, it is believed, holds an office at Washington, killed one of the slaves upon his father's farm by shooting him. The letter states that young Matthews had been left in charge of the farm; that he gave an order to the servant, which was disobeyed, when he proceeded to the house, *obtained a gun, and, returning, shot the servant.* He immediately, the letter continues, fled to his father's residence, where he still remains unmolested."—Let it never be forgotten, that no slaveholder or overseer can be convicted of any outrage perpetrated on the person of a slave, however diabolical it may be, on the testimony of colored witnesses, whether bond or free. By the slave code, they are adjudged to be as incompetent to testify against a white man, as though they were indeed a part of the brute creation. Hence, there is no legal protection in fact, whatever there may be in form, for the slave population; and any amount of cruelty may be inflicted on them with impunity. Is it possible for the human mind to conceive of a more horrible state of society?

The effect of a religious profession on the conduct of southern masters is vividly described in the following Narrative, and shown to be any thing but salutary. In the nature of the case, it must be in the highest degree pernicious. The testimony of Mr. Douglass, on this point, is sustained by a cloud of witnesses, whose veracity is unimpeachable. "A slaveholder's profession of Christianity is a palpable imposture. He is a felon of the highest grade. He is a man-stealer. It is of no importance what you put in the other scale."

Reader! are you with the man-stealers in sympathy and purpose, or on the side of their down-trodden victims? If with the former, then are you the foe of God and man. If with the latter, what are you prepared to do and dare in their behalf? Be faithful, be vigilant, be untiring in your efforts to break every yoke, and let the oppressed go free. Come what may—cost what it may—inscribe on the banner which you unfurl to the breeze, as your religious and political motto—"NO COMPROMISE WITH SLAVERY! NO UNION WITH SLAVEHOLDERS!"

William Lloyd Garrison, in a preface to Narrative of the Life of Frederick Douglass, an American Slave, *edited by Benjamin Quarles, Cambridge, Mass.: The Belknap Press of Harvard University Press, 1960, pp. 3-15.*

Benjamin Quarles

[*An American scholar and educator, Quarles is considered a major contributor to the recording of the African-American experience, having written several pioneering studies on the abolitionist movement and on major anti-slavery figures. In the following essay, he discusses the impact of Frederick Douglass's lectures and autobiography on the abolitionist cause.*]

The time and place—August 11, 1852, at the Masonic Hall in Pittsburgh. The occasion—the national convention of the Free Soil party, a political group that four years previously had been formed to combat the extension of slavery into the territories. The afternoon meeting had been in progress for more than an hour when a Negro, wearing a white linen coat and dark blue trousers, entered the hall. Before he could find a seat someone shouted his name, and others spontaneously took up the cry. The presiding officer, his voice drowned out, resorted to sign language to welcome the visitor and invite him to speak. Amid cheers, the newcomer proceeded down the aisle.

Facing the audience, he showed no sign of nervousness— he had a talent for talking fluently. For the space of a few moments, however, he said nothing, as if to satisfy those among the two thousand spectators who might wish to size him up as a physical specimen. Broad-shouldered, six feet tall and in the prime of manhood, he could bear scrutiny. His skin was bronze-colored and his mass of black hair was neatly parted on the left. His eyes were deep-set and steady. But at the moment they were less expressive than his well-formed nose that now, as he prepared to say his first words, inhaled deeply, almost critically, as though the air might offer to nonwhites an inferior oxygen, if vigilance were relaxed.

"Gentlemen, I take it that you are in earnest, and therefore I will address you," he began in low but carrying tones that searched the recesses of the auditorium, hinting of a readiness to defy faulty acoustics. But there was no answering challenge to this voice that had tested itself in damp groves, in tents and on ship decks. "I have come here, not so much of a free soiler as others have come," he continued. "I am, of course, for circumscribing and damaging slavery in every way I can. But my motto is extermination—not only in New Mexico, but in New Orleans, not only in California but in South Carolina." The theme was a familiar one with the speaker, but he saw no need of talking about new wrongs as long as the old ones still existed.

He proceeded to criticize the Fugitive Slave Law. Because an alleged runaway might be carried away without trial by jury, "the colored man's rights are less than those of a jackass," since the latter could not be seized and taken away without submitting the matter to twelve men. He had a solution, said the speaker: "The only way to make the Fugitive Slave Law a dead letter is to make half a dozen or more dead kidnappers. The man who takes the office of a bloodhound ought to be treated as a bloodhound." The crowd applauded, many of them knowing that the speaker's strong language resulted in part from his twenty-year experience as a slave.

When the noise died down, the speaker continued along a different line—denunciation was but one of his weapons. The Constitution, he contended, was against slavery inasmuch as "human government is for the protection of rights and not for the destruction of rights." But even if the Founding Fathers had expressly said that one man had the right to possess another man, such a stipulation would lack the binding quality of rationality: "Suppose you and I made a deed to give away two or three acres of blue sky; would the sky fall, and would anybody be able to plough it?" The speaker's sentences had now gained momentum. Those who were listening to him for the first time became aware of a voice that employed every degree of light and shade, a rich baritone giving emotional vitality to every word.

He resumed in a conversational manner—he had all the gifts requisite to an orator—"You are about to have a party, but I want to be independent and not hurried to and fro into the ranks of Whigs and Democrats." Possibly some in the audience may have reflected that it was this desire for independence that had led him to break with his slave past and to strike out on his own.

Now that he was at the point of bringing his remarks to a close, he had a parting bit of advice. "It has been said that we ought to take the position of the greatest number of voters. That is wrong. Numbers should not be looked to so much as right. The man who is right is a majority. If he does not represent what we are, he represents what we ought to be."

The crowd cheered again and again as the speaker concluded in this high strain. He had difficulty making his way down the aisle, past those who wished to shake his hand. The clapping and shouting, however, were not primarily an approval of what the speaker had said. Rather they were a personal tribute to a man who had devoted his talents to the building of a better America.

For to Frederick Douglass this address differed from his others only in externals. All his public appearances grew out of a career that had sought the storms in a period that was itself shaped by stress and passion. By the time he delivered this impromptu speech his career had been inexorably charted, Douglass having become a reformer of the first water.

Douglass acquired prominence in his day because of his qualities of mind and spirit and the fact that he was a Negro. These two outstanding causative factors may be examined in turn.

Douglass had become a professional reformer by having come to the attention in August 1841 of the Massachusetts school of abolitionists, headed by William Lloyd Garrison and Wendell Phillips. Persuaded to join the cause as a paid lecturer, Douglass cut loose from his odd-jobs work in New Bedford to become a careerist in reform. To say that Douglass became an abolitionist solely as an alternative to sawing wood, sweeping chimneys, and blowing bellows is to venture beyond the record. Outward circumstance may have been reinforced by inner calling. But whatever the motivation, Douglass had no difficulty in internalizing his role, becoming a typical reformer in outlook and style.

As one who was single-mindedly bent on wiping out institutions he regarded as outworn, Douglass viewed things with an almost theological purity. He was given to abso-

lutes of feeling, making him tend to overstate his case. To him the slave system was "a grand aggregation of human horrors." For the master class he had no charity: "Every slaveholder is the legalized keeper of a house of ill-fame, no matter how high he may stand in Church or State. He may be a Bishop Meade or a Henry Clay—a reputed saint or an open sinner—he is still the legalized head of a den of infamy" [Philip S. Foner, in his *The Life and Writings of Frederick Douglass,* 4 vols., 1950-55].

But if Douglass tended to overreact, it was due to the failure of the great majority to react at all. Charged with irritating the American people, Douglass [in a speech before the American Anti-Slavery Society (11 May 1847)] replied that this was what they deserved: "The conscience of the American public needs this irritation. And I would blister it all over, from center to circumference, until it gives signs of a purer and better life than it is now manifesting to the world."

Douglass was not a gradualist, prepared to await for abuses to be corrected "in the fulness of time." At one of the reformist gatherings Henry Ward Beecher stated that rather than see slavery abolished as a result of mercenary motives, he would prefer to wait seventy-five years to have the evil struck down by the power of Christian faith. Douglass, who followed Beecher on the program, immediately replied that "if the reverend gentleman had worked on plantations where I have been, he would have met overseers who would have whipped him in five minutes out of his willingness to wait for liberty" [*Annual Report of the American Anti-Slavery Society for 1853*].

Douglass' whole philosophy of reform was one of no quarter. He had little patience with well-intentioned men like the influential Unitarian pastor, William Ellery Channing, who deplored harsh language, seeking instead to win over the slaveholder by a policy of sweet reasonableness. Douglass, in a West India Emancipation celebration speech in August 1857, pointed out that "those who profess to favor freedom and yet deprecate agitation are men who want rain without thunder and lightning. Power concedes nothing without a demand. It never did and it never will."

Douglass brought more to the reform movement than a "hard line" against the opposition. He had the gift of words. His sentences, although sonorous as befit the style of his day, arrested the attention. One example may suffice. Speaking in Rochester in 1852 on "The Meaning of July Fourth to the Negro," he posed a long rhetorical question concerning the "equal manhood of the Negro race":

> Is it not astonishing that, while we are ploughing, planting, and reaping, using all kinds of mechanical tools, erecting houses, constructing bridges, building ships, working in metals of brass, iron, copper, silver and gold; that, while we are reading, writing and ciphering, acting as clerks, merchants and secretaries, having among us lawyers, doctors, ministers, poets, authors, editors, orators and teachers; that, while we are engaged in all manner of enterprises common to other men, digging gold in California, capturing the whale in the Pacific, feeding sheep and cattle on the hill-side, living, moving, acting, thinking,

planning, living in families as husbands, wives and children, and, above all, confessing and worshipping the Christian's God, and looking hopefully for life and immortality beyond the grave, we are called upon to prove that we are men!

Douglass tinged his eloquence with humor. When Stephen A. Douglas was debating with Abraham Lincoln in 1858, Douglass had this to say of the Illinois Senator: "Once I thought he was about to make the name respectable, but now I despair of him, and must do the best I can for it myself." In mockery Douglass was devastating, as evidenced in an address at Faneuil Hall on a June day in 1849: "I want to say a word about the Colonization Society of which Henry Clay is President. He is President of nothing else." Cheers and applause greeted this quip at Clay's long-held White House ambitions. A clever mimic, Douglass was often called upon to deliver his "slaveholder's sermon"—a white clergyman's address to the bondmen.

A typical example of Douglass' raillery was his account of the plight of Bishop James O. Andrew, whose family holdings in slaves precipitated the shattering sectional split in Methodism at the General Conference in New York in 1844:

> A slaveholding bishop, Bishop Andrew of South Carolina, married a slaveholding wife and became the possessor of fifteen slaves. At this time the Methodist Church in the North was of the opinion that bishops should not hold slaves. They remonstrated with the Conference to induce Bishop Andrew to emancipate his slaves. The Conference did it in this way. A resolution was brought in, when the Bishop was present, to the following effect: "Whereas Bishop Andrew has connected himself with slavery, and has thereby injured his itinerancy as a bishop . . ." It was not, "Whereas Bishop Andrew has connected himself with slavery, and has thereby become guilty, or has done a great wrong," but "has thereby injured his itinerancy as a bishop, we therefore resolve that Bishop Andrew be, and he hereby is,"—what?—"requested to suspend his labors as a bishop until he can get rid of "—what?—slavery?—"his impediment." (Laughter.) This was the name given to slavery. One might have inferred from the preamble that it was to get rid of his wife. (Laughter and loud cheers.)

Douglass' considerable abilities as an abolitionist lecturer were heightened by the fact that he was a Negro. Here was no stammering fugitive from the South; here was no shiftless former slave unable to cope with the responsibilities of freedom. Here was a different breed of Negro, a different brand of abolitionist—a symbolic figure in race relations and in reform.

Douglass' accomplishments were trumpeted by abolitionists as an example of Negro improvability. As no other colored man or woman, Douglass was a challenge to the widespread belief that the Negro was innately inferior in character, intelligence, and ability. To those who held that the rightness or wrongness of slavery pivoted on the ca-

pacity of the colored man, Douglass was a figure who could not be overlooked.

This image of Douglass as an able Negro had owed much to the publication of his autobiography, *Narrative of the Life of Frederick Douglass,* in 1845. Slave narratives were effective weapons in the abolitionist crusade. "It is often said that the evils of slavery are exaggerated. This is said by the masters," wrote Theodore Parker in 1847, after reading a number of slave narratives. Douglass' book was by far the most effective of the lot, in part because he had written every line. If its prose was simple and unadorned, the Douglass autobiography was forceful and vivid, a tribute to a man who less than seven years previously had been a slave calker in a Baltimore shipyard. Aside from what it said in the text, the *Narrative* spoke volumes for the capacity of the Negro. Indeed, Douglass always recognized that whatever he said or wrote had a meaning beyond the letter. When he launched his own weekly in Rochester in 1848, he appended his initials to his editorials in order to demonstrate that a former slave could write good English.

If others saw him as a Negro before all else, the maturing Douglass never sought to escape such an identification. If some Negroes affected a studied indifference to race problems, he did not. He had no trace of the self-hate that leaves its mark on many members of an oppressed minority. "Whatever character or capacity you ascribe to us, I am not ashamed to be numbered with this race," he said in an address to the American and Foreign Anti-Slavery Society in May 1853. "I shall bring the Negro with me," he once wrote in response to an invitation to lecture. " 'I am black, but comely,' is as true now as it was in the days of Solomon," he wrote in April 1849 in reviewing Wilson Armistead's lengthy book, *A Tribute for the Negro.*

Douglass' sense of identification with his Negro fellows expressed itself in his concern over their plight. In the August 10, 1849 issue of his newspaper, *The North Star,* he proposed that an organization be formed exclusively of Negroes, for the purpose of opposing slavery and improving their own condition. The society would bear the title "The National League," with the motto "The union of the oppressed for the sake of freedom." After more than two months the suggestion had met with almost no response in Negro circles, much to the mortification of its sponsor. "We have among us our little Popes and Bishops," Douglass wrote in an acid editorial on October 26, 1849.

Although Douglass had proposed an all-colored improvement society, he never thought of the Negro as apart from the mainstream of American life. As he put it, it was better to be a part of the whole than the whole of a part. "We are Americans, and as Americans we would speak to Americans," ran a sentence in a statement which the Colored Convention of 1853, meeting in Rochester, addressed to "the People of the United States." This lengthy address, composed in the main by Douglass, was entitled, "The Claims of Our Common Cause," and its insistent theme was the Americanism of the Negro.

To Douglass one of the best ways that the Negro could exercise his full rights as an American citizen was to make contacts across the color line. Setting an example himself, he made it a point to defy Jim Crow practices in restaurants and on common carriers. To be "roughed up" for seeking service in places open to the public was no novelty to Douglass. Prominent Negroes who accepted segregation drew his fire. He wrote a bitter editorial chastising Elizabeth Taylor Greenfield (the "Black Swan") for giving a concert at Metropolitan Hall in New York in April 1853, to which whites only were admitted.

Douglass was a protagonist for "integrated" schools. When his nine-year-old daughter was put in a room and taught separately at Seward Seminary in Rochester, his protest could be heard throughout the city. But his indignation did not spring solely from the protective sympathies of a parent. "If this were a private affair, only affecting myself and family, I should possibly allow it to pass without attracting public attention to it; but such is not the case," he wrote to the editor of the *Rochester Courier* on March 30, 1849. "It is a deliberate attempt to downgrade and injure a large class of persons, whose rights and feelings have been the common sport . . . for ages."

Because he mixed with whites as a matter of principle, the Douglass of the abolitionist crusade felt no uneasiness in their presence. Within a few years after his flight from his master, his slavery-days dislike of whites had evaporated. His close association with them as fellow reformers left him permanently shorn of racist thinking. He viewed whites individually, not lumping them together.

By the time he had reached his prime as a man and as a reformer, Douglass had placed himself "upon grounds vastly higher and broader than any founded upon race or color," to use his own language. His own freedom from preconceptions enabled him to view things in the round. To him the abolitionist crusade had become less a separate movement than a national impulse; to him the struggle of the Negro was more of a human struggle than one of race. Paradoxically, it would seem, his belonging to a despised group had given him a deeper, more inclusive sense of human brotherhood. This broad concern led him to take an active role in reforms that were not Negro-centered, among them the woman's rights movement.

In the closing years of the abolitionist crusade, Douglass was one of its chief ornaments. He carried himself with the assurance of one who had risen above obscure birth, color prejudice and all the Pandora's box of human besettings. Of the many assessments made of him by contemporaries, the words of Albion W. Tourgée [in his *A Memorial of Frederick Douglas from the City of Boston*, 1896] would not seem wide of the mark: "Three classes of the American people are under special obligations to him: the colored bondman whom he helped to free from the chains which he himself had worn; the free persons of color whom he had helped make citizens; the white people of the United States whom he sought to free from the bondage of caste and relieve from the odium of slavery."

Douglass' chief claim to enduring recollection has been voiced by a present-day poet, Robert E. Hayden, akin to Douglass by color if not by century. When freedom, writes Hayden, is finally won:

this man, this Douglass, this former slave,
        this Negro
beaten to his knees, exiled, visioning a world
where none is lonely, none hunted, alien,
this man, superb in love and logic, this man
shall be remembered . . .

> *Benjamin Quarles, "Abolition's Different Drummer: Frederick Douglass," in* The Antislavery Vanguard: New Essays on the Abolitionists, *edited by Martin Duberman, Princeton University Press, 1965, pp. 123-34.*

Moira Davison Reynolds

[*In the following essay, Reynolds elucidates the background of Harriet Beecher Stowe's antislavery novel* Uncle Tom's Cabin *(1852) and relates the work's initial reception.*]

In the Hall of Fame for Great Americans, along with the busts of Thomas Paine, Abraham Lincoln, George Washington Carver, and others who have influenced the course of this nation, stands the bust of Harriet Beecher Stowe. Cited as the author of the antislavery novel *Uncle Tom's Cabin,* written before the Civil War, Mrs. Stowe exemplified the power of the pen in reaching the conscience of the North. . . .

A northeaster was lashing the town of Brunswick, Maine, when Harriet arrived there on May 22, 1850. She was 39 and expecting her seventh child in about six weeks. Her husband, the Reverend Calvin Stowe, was finishing the school year at Lane Theological Institute in Cincinnati and would arrive later. His new position would be Collings Professor of Natural and Revealed Religion at Bowdoin College in Brunswick.

Harriet's 18 years in Cincinnati were not uneventful. Like her brothers and sisters, she had gone there because her famous father, Dr. Lyman Beecher, had dreamed of creating a New England-type of seminary in what was then considered the West. In Cincinnati she had taught school and had had her first literary successes; it was there she married, bore six children and buried one. In Cincinnati she had come face-to-face with slavery; she had become aware of fugitives fleeing from slave states to the free soil of Ohio. In Cincinnati she had witnessed the birth of a special type of abolitionism. She had also seen in that northern city violent and shocking acts committed against those who dared to speak against slavery.

The journey east from Ohio had been an adventure for the children with her—to Pittsburgh by river steamboat and then by canalboat, and finally by train to Philadelphia. They visited their Uncle Henry Ward Beecher in Brooklyn, New York, and spent a week in Hartford, Connecticut. In Boston they paid a visit to another uncle, the Reverend Edward Beecher. Edward was an abolitionist; in fact, he had belonged to an antislavery association as early as 1825. His wife Isabella shared his views, and their home was a gathering place for people with similar sentiments. Harriet perceived their consternation at proposed legislation about fugitive slaves. This legislation did pass Congress and was the trigger that induced Harriet to write

A portrait of Harriet Beecher Stowe.

Uncle Tom's Cabin. We shall digress here in order to gain more familiarity with the historic background.

When Alabama entered the Union in 1819, it preserved the balance between free and slave-holding states. (There were eleven of each.) With this balance, slavery would gain no increased support in the Senate, where each state had equal representation. The North, with its greater population, had more members in the House of Representatives; but bills had to pass both houses. There was much dissention over Missouri, which had petitioned to come in as a slave state. Before the matter was settled, Maine applied to enter as a free state. So a compromise was agreed upon, allowing Missouri in as a slave state, Maine as free, and stipulating that in the future slavery could not exist in all other parts of the Louisiana Purchase north of the line 36° 30'. (This meant that slavery could be extended only into what is now Arkansas and Oklahoma. The original territory obtained from France extended from the Mississippi River to the Rocky Mountains and from the Gulf of Mexico to British North America. Louisiana and Mississippi had already been admitted as slave states.)

For 30 years this "Missouri Compromise" was in effect, but the Mexican War Treaty brought fresh problems. The United States gained the territories of New Mexico, California, and Utah. Anti-slavery forces were determined to curb the spread of slavery into the newly acquired land, but the war had been supported by those who wished to see it extended. The independent republic of Texas had been admitted as a slave state in 1845. California came in as free in 1850 and would remain so, but California's application for admission in 1849 had caused a grave crisis.

Henry Clay, now old and ailing, was serving as a senator from Kentucky. Determined to preserve the Union, he was instrumental in shaping another compromise whereby the status of the New Mexico and Utah territories would be worked out when application for statehood was submitted. In addition, the slave trade in the District of Columbia would be abolished, and the fugitive slave laws of 1793 enforced throughout the nation.

A federal act of 1793 provided for the return of escaped slaves. In the free states this was largely disregarded, and by the middle of the nineteenth century, aid to fugitive slaves had become a commitment of the abolitionist movement. To appease the South, the new compromise provided for strict enforcement: "all good citizens" were to assist federal marshals and their deputies in returning fugitives to their owners. There would be no trial for an apprehended black—the word of a master claiming ownership would be final. In the case of free blacks, tragic mistakes might be made, with these legally emancipated Negroes being arrested as runaways and having no redress. Most Northerners tended to agree with the 1816 pronouncement of George Bourne, a Presbyterian minister who did not countenance slavery: "No human law must be obeyed when it contravenes the divine command."

In the biography of his mother, Charles Stowe wrote: "her soul was all on fire with indignation at this new indignity and wrong about to be inflicted by the slave-power on the innocent and helpless." But apparently Harriet listened well and said little on the subject.

The house the Stowes had arranged to rent was more than 40 years old and seems to have been in need of repairs. Henry Wadsworth Longfellow had lived there as a sophomore at Bowdoin College, but Harriet was probably less interested in its history than in getting it ready for occupancy for her family before the baby arrived. (In 1963, Stowe House was designated a Registered National Landmark.) The storm lasted for several days and delayed the arrival of the family's household effects. A friendly professor and his wife opened their home to the Stowes until the sailing ship with their goods arrived from Boston. Somehow Harriet got everything settled before the birth on July 8 of Charles Edward, who was her last child, and who, incidentally, would write her approved biography. Calvin had arrived only a few days before the birth.

According to *Crusader in Crinoline,* Harriet's biography by Forrest Wilson, Lane had not found a replacement for Calvin, and he had promised to teach there during the coming winter session. Bowdoin graciously granted him a three-month leave of absence for this; but now Andover Theological Seminary in Massachusetts offered him an attractive position as Professor of Sacred Literature. For years Calvin had failed to earn the salary he knew he was worth, and he was determined to have the Andover professorship regardless of any obligations to Lane or Bowdoin. After much discussion, Bowdoin again released him for a period to be spent at Andover during the winter of 1852. It was agreed that in the following summer he could begin full-time work at the Massachusetts institution. But meanwhile, the Stowes' financial position was as precarious as ever, and in the fall of 1850 Harriet was running a school of sorts in her home. She was also writing regularly for the *National Era,* an anti-slavery publication in Washington, D.C. Edited by the well-known abolitionist Gamaliel Bailey, the *Era*'s aim was "to mingle literature with politics." Indeed, Harriet was in good company—Whittier was an associate editor, while contributors included Hawthorne, Melville, and Lowell.

Brunswick is on the Androscoggin River, very close to the coast. Its prosperity was in part based on shipbuilding. Iron and later steel would replace wooden ships, but the sailing ships made of timber from the woods that surrounded the town were still being produced in the mid-1800s. In fact, the Stowes sometimes watched launchings. Harriet was happy to be back in her native New England. She soon became familiar with the bays, coves, and islands near Brunswick, and in time they and the Maine people would be portrayed in her writings.

Congress passed the Fugitive Slave Act in the fall of 1850. Massachusetts's Daniel Webster had backed Clay's compromise with his last eloquent oration, which began, "I speak today for the preservation of the Union. Hear me for my cause." Because this stand permitted the spread of slavery, Webster was reviled by the anti-slavery forces. Although the enactment was expected, the abolitionists were outraged. Isabella Beecher wrote to her literary sister-in-law: "Hattie, if I could use a pen as you can, I would write something that will make this whole nation feel what an accursed thing slavery is."

Harriet's reply was: "As long as the baby sleeps with me nights I can't do much at any thing—but I shall do it at last. I shall write that thing if I live . . . "

Calvin left in December for Cincinnati. Early in January, 1851, Henry Ward visited Harriet, arriving by train during a wild blizzard. The handsome brother whom she loved so dearly was becoming famous. Three years before, he had accepted a call to Plymouth Church in Brooklyn. His preaching had tremendous appeal (it has been described as spellbinding), his articles were well received by a substantial Congregational publication named the *Independent,* and he was giving lectures such as the one he had just delivered in Boston's Tremont Temple. Even the finances of his church were in good shape; so he felt himself in a position to make positive contributions to the antislavery cause. In 1848 he had held a slave "auction"—the practice of selling a slave for liberty. He would continue this at Plymouth Church, collecting the money at Sunday service, with the subject present. He knew very well that such an emotional and dramatic act would publicize the evil of slavery, besides, of course, making a free Negro of a slave. Beecher had already welcomed the able abolitionist orator, Wendell Phillips, to his pulpit, a pulpit to which the eyes of the nation were beginning to turn.

Harriet mentioned Isabella's letter and told him that she too intended to fight slavery—and by writing something. Henry encouraged her, but he was an egotist, absorbed in his own affairs, and it is likely that he regarded his sister's intention as inconsequential.

According to members of the Stowe family, some weeks later at church Harriet had a vision. She saw a Negro being flogged viciously at the order of his master. As the man died, he prayed that those who had wronged him would be forgiven. Harriet participated in the communion service in a mechanical, distracted manner, and afterwards walked home. Later that day she wrote out her vision, using names. The saint-like man was Uncle Tom, the owner was Simon Legree, and his henchmen were Sambo and Quimbo. Then she added something: the Christ-like action of Uncle Tom made converts of Sambo and Quimbo. (Today Pew 23 of Brunswick's First Parish Church, where Harriet sat, is marked with a bronze plaque.)

Stowe family biographers contend that when Calvin returned from Ohio, he found the manuscript. It moved him to tears, and he urged his wife to use her vision as the climax to her "thing" that would condemn slavery.

On March 9 Harriet wrote to the editor of the *National Era:*

> Mr. Bailey, Dear Sir:
>
> I am at present occupied upon a story which will be much longer than any I have ever written, embracing a series of sketches which give the lights and shadows of the "patriarchal institution," written either from observation, incidents which have occurred in the sphere of my personal knowledge, or in the knowledge of my friends. I shall show the *best side* of the thing, and something *faintly approaching the worst.*
>
> Up to this year I have always felt that I had no particular call to meddle with the subject, and I dreaded to expose even my own mind to the full force of its existing power. But I feel now that the time is come when even a woman or a child who can speak for freedom and humanity is bound to speak. The Carthagenian women in the last peril of their state cut off their hair for bow-strings to give the defenders of their country; and such peril and shame as now hangs over this country is worse than Roman slavery, and I hope every woman who can write will not be silent . . .
>
> My vocation is simply that of a *painter,* and my object will be to hold up in the most lifelike and graphic manner possible Slavery, its reverses, changes, and the negro character, which I have had ample opportunities for studying. There is no arguing with *pictures,* and everyone is impressed by them, whether they mean to be or not.
>
> I wrote beforehand, because I know that you have much matter to arrange, and I thought it might not be amiss to give you a hint. The thing may extend through three or four numbers. It will be ready in two or three weeks. . . .

For the projected three-or-four-part serial, Dr. Bailey was willing to pay $300, a generous sum for that day. But the work became about ten times the length anticipated, and Bailey appears to have stuck to his original price.

The *National Era* was a magazine (really more like a weekly newspaper) that came out every Thursday. On May 8 it announced a new story by Mrs.

H. B. Stowe—*Uncle Tom's Cabin* or *The Man That Was a Thing,* to be published at a later date. (A serialized story or novel was not unusual; indeed, it was common for Dickens to publish in this manner.) When the first part finally appeared in the issue of June 5, the subtitle had been changed to *Life Among the Lowly.*

An unsigned letter to the editor in the July 1 issue gave hint of what was to come:

> Sir: *Uncle Tom's Cabin* increases in interest and pathos with each successive number. None of thy various contributions, rich and varied as they have been, have so deeply interested thy female readers of this vicinity as this story of Mrs. Stowe has so far done and promises to do.

Soon *Uncle Tom*'s author was having difficulty producing the required weekly installments. In addition to all the usual demands imposed upon her by a large and active family, there was another obstacle. Her father, the distinguished Lyman Beecher, now 75, was visiting. His chief interest just then was to prepare his views on theology for publication, and to help him, he had on hand one of the stepdaughters by his third marriage. (The current Mrs. Beecher was also a visitor.) There is small likelihood that he had any idea that his daughter's publication would far outshine his, and he cannot be blamed for not realizing what would happen. Apparently Harriet wrote whenever and wherever she could, refusing to be deterred by trivial events. She often used the kitchen table as her desk. And aside from the considerable stress of having to produce, Harriet found that summer in Maine very pleasant. But there were undercurrents that she could not escape; for instance, one of the Bowdoin professors maintained that blood would be shed before the slavery problem was solved.

The installment (really a chapter) for July 24 arrived late. Most of the other material for the issue was already set up, leaving insufficient space for the complete installment. So the editor was forced to divide it, much to the author's chagrin. On August 21 a notice advised that " 'Uncle Tom's Cabin' reached us at too late an hour for insertion this week. Mrs. Stowe having requested that it should not be divided, our readers may look for the entire chapter in the next *Era*."

In the issue of September 4, Dr. Bailey noted that, in answer to inquiries, *Uncle Tom* would appear in book form; that Mrs. Stowe had taken out a copyright, but the publication date and cost were not yet made public.

Harriet's oldest sister Catherine was another visitor to Brunswick that summer. She read Harriet's work as far as it was written and was impressed. Phillips, Samson and Company of Boston had recently published her own *True Remedy of the Wrongs of Women,* and she thought they might be interested in *Uncle Tom.* So, with Harriet's permission, she approached them. However, the house had a large southern following and turned down the suggestion.

Another Boston publisher was more courageous. He was John P. Jewett, definitely antislavery and friendly with Gamaliel Bailey. In Jewett's own words, "my attention

was called to this story [*Uncle Tom*] by my noble and gifted wife, to whom the entire credit is due for its publication in book form. . . . " But this takes us ahead of the story.

Harriet's literary project was demanding more and more of her time and energy. The narrative grew and grew, with the author unwilling or unable to control it. She had little time for revision. Later she admitted that she "no more thought of style or literary excellence than the mother who rushes into the street and cries for help to save her children from a burning house thinks of the teachings of the rhetorician or the elocutionist." Catherine, if no one else, realized her sister's predicament. She agreed to spend a year in the Stowe household in order to help Harriet. Here is a portion of a letter written to her by her sister, Mary Perkins, in September, 1851: "At eight o'clock we are through with breakfast and prayers and then we send off Mr. Stowe and Harriet both to his room in the college. There is no other way to keep her out of family cares and quietly at work, and since this plan is adopted, she goes ahead finely." Calvin's "room" was in Appleton Hall. Women rarely frequented campus buildings, but now one did. Later, when Calvin went to Andover, she had the office to herself.

Sometimes Harriet shared her chapters with some of their faculty friends. Her own family was, of course, a captive audience to whom she could read each installment as she composed it. But the Stowes needed no encouragement to listen—they, like the *Era*'s readers, were impatient to know what was going to happen.

There were irate protests to the *Era* when the October 30 issue failed to carry a chapter of *Uncle Tom.* (Bear in mind that readers of that day had no television to occupy their leisure hours.) There were also protests when the magazine published the suggestion that Mrs. Stowe's long story could be finished quickly with a brief summary. Apparently the readership not only wanted to know what happened, but also wanted to be informed in the style to which they had become accustomed. Here is a letter from one *Era* subscriber:

> Please signify to Mrs. Stowe that it will be quite agreeable to the wishes of the many readers of the *Era* for her *not to hurry through* "Uncle Tom". We don't get sleepy reading it. Having resided many years among slaves and being familiar with their habits, thoughts, feelings, and language, I have not been able to detect a single mistake in her story in any of these respects—'tis perfect in its way—will do great good.

The issue of December 18 carried this announcement:

> We regret, as much as any of our readers can regret, that Mrs. Stowe had no chapter in this week's *Era*. It is not our fault, for up to this hour we have nothing from her. As she is generally so punctual, we fear that sickness may have prevented. We feel constrained to make this apology, so profound is the interest taken in her story by nearly all our readers.

After that, the author managed not only to keep up but to have a few installments ready in advance of the deadline. It was at the end of the fortieth "number" (the book has 44 chapters) that she wrote *finis* to the story line. With regard to length, the finished work was, of course, a far cry from what Harriet had originally proposed to Dr. Bailey.

There is considerable doubt about the exact date of the signing of the book contract. John Jewett offered 50 percent of the profits if the Stowes could pay 50 percent of the publication cost. Calvin had no money, so settled for a ten percent royalty on all sales. (As to the *Uncle Tom* plays, the first law to grant dramatic rights so as to secure a percentage on all presentations of dramatizations did not pass until 1856. Likewise, the foreign copyright act was not in effect until about 40 years later.)

The publication day was March 20, 1852. (Curiously, the last installment in the *Era* appeared on April 1.) The book consisted of two volumes with a woodcut of a cabin as the frontispiece. There were three styles of bindings: paper cover, selling at $1; cloth at $1.50; and cloth full-gilt at $2. Calvin returned to Brunswick with a supply of early copies, including some cloth full-gilt, the cloth being lavender. The original run produced 5,000 copies. Three thousand sold on the first day, and it became clear that filling orders would be a problem. Jewett got out more printings, and in three weeks 20,000 copies had sold. The *Boston Traveller* noted "three power presses running twenty-four hours a day (except Sundays), one hundred bookbinders at work, three mills running to supply the paper." By January, 1853, 200,000 copies had sold in this country, and this was only the beginning.

Harriet did not own a silk dress and had high hopes that the royalties would make it possible for her to buy a black one; she was not disappointed. She received $10,300 as her copyright premium on three months' sales of *Uncle Tom,* believed at the time to be the largest sum ever received by an American or European author from the sale of a single work in so short a period of time. The book was enormously popular in England; the *London Times* of September 3, 1852, noted that "*Uncle Tom's Cabin* is at every railway book-stall in England, and in every third traveller's hand. The book is a decided hit." (Eventually *Uncle Tom* was translated into many foreign languages.)

By April, 1852, laudatory responses were pouring in. The reviewer of the influential *Independent* wrote: "This book is full of the intensest Truth . . . Let ALL MEN read it!" Kudos arrived from Longfellow and Whittier. Senator Charles Sumner of Massachusetts wrote his praises, while Senator William Seward of New York claimed *Uncle Tom* as "the greatest book of all times." And so it went.

Later the people of the South woke up. The comment of the *Southern Literary Messenger* was a forerunner of the mounting conflict:

> Let it be bourne in mind that this slanderous work has found its way to every section of our country, and has crossed the water to Great Britain, filling the minds of all who know nothing of slavery with hatred for that institution and those who uphold it. Justice to ourselves would seem to demand that it should not be suffered to circulate longer without the brand of falsehood upon it. . . . [Mrs. Stowe deserves criticism] as

the mouthpiece of a large and dangerous faction which if we do not put down with the pen, we may be compelled one day (God grant that day may never come!) to repel with the bayonet.

(October, 1852)

Moira Davison Reynolds, "Written in the Book of Fate," in her "Uncle Tom's Cabin" and Mid-Nineteenth Century United States: Pen and Conscience, McFarland & Company, Inc., 1985, pp. 1-12.

John L. Thomas on Garrison's success and failure:

The American abolitionists constituted a religion, and Garrison the leader of a schismatic sect within that religion. He took the formula for salvation of the religious revivalists of his day and applied it directly to slavery. "Immediate emancipation" as he taught it was not a program but an attitude, an urgent warning that shut out thoughts of expediency or compromise. Applied to politics, it fostered an apocalyptic view of the world and released in him hidden desires for perfection. Christian perfection, in turn, offered the comforting ideal of the perfect society, harmonious, self-regulating, free from the demonic aspects of power. Garrison's experiment in practical piety carried him out of the anti-slavery camp, beyond the Jacksonian compass to the very borders of Christian anarchy. It took secession and the coming of a war he had predicted to recall him to the realities of institutionalized slavery and the task of abolishing it. For the failure of his generation to achieve the racial democracy which the Civil War made possible he must be held accountable. He made the moral indictment of slavery which precipitated the war, but he lacked the understanding and sustaining vision to lead his countrymen toward the kind of democratic society in which he believed. Both in his great achievement and in his tragic failure he spoke for his age.

John L. Thomas, in his The Liberator: William Lloyd Garrison, A Biography, *Little, Brown, and Company, 1963.*

Karen Sánchez-Eppler

[*In the following essay, Sánchez-Eppler analyzes Harriet Jacobs's* Incidents in the Life of a Slave Girl *(1861), noting that Jacobs's description of slavery primarily in terms of sexual experience was a way of capturing her readers' attention and thereby furthering her abolitionist goals.*]

In her letters, Harriet Jacobs repeatedly voices the wish that her story conform better to prevailing feminine mores. The task of writing *Incidents in the Life of a Slave Girl* [1861], Jacobs explains to the abolitionist Amy Post, would be less daunting "dear Amy if it was the life of a Heroine with no degradation associated with it," but it is not, and she finds it difficult to depict the degradations that a heroine would have no occasion to speak: "There are somethings I might have made plainer I know— Woman can whisper—her cruel wrongs into the ear of a very dear friend—much easier than she can record them for the world to read." As she describes her reluctance to write about her life, and particularly as her stress on deg-radations and cruel wrongs suggests, to write about her sexual experiences, Jacobs substitutes the general figures of "Woman" and "Heroine" for her individual "I." The moment when she alludes to incidents so private that they ought to be whispered in the intimacy of friendship, rather than recorded for a reading world, is the moment when the intimate confessions of her letters give way to a gener-alized claim about feminine discourse.

Jacobs's book is not an intimate utterance but a highly public document; she explicitly enlists her words in anti-slavery reform. In particular, the sexual experiences on which her narrative centers fulfill an abolitionist agenda of displaying the horror and corruption of slavery. Thus, as all her readers have noted, the story Jacobs has to tell may well be unique among slave narratives in that it de-scribes slavery primarily in terms of sexual experience. The pseudonymous Linda Brent, harassed by the sexual attentions of her master, Dr. Flint, evades his designs by becoming the concubine of a neighboring white gentleman to whom she bears two children. After hiding for seven years in her grandmother's attic, and after Mr. Sands—her white lover—buys their children from a deceived and enraged Dr. Flint, Linda escapes to the North, where she can again see her children but cannot provide them with a home. As such a plot summary makes clear, sexual ha-rassment, sexual intercourse, and childbirth are not tan-gential to a narrative of enslavement, escape, and emanci-pation; they are that narrative.

In Jacobs's *Incidents in the Life of a Slave Girl* the insights into the corporeality of identity that feminist-abolitionists discovered in describing the physical otherness of the slave come to occupy the more threatening space of the writer's own body. The merger of the personal and the political, the writer and the social world . . . are literally enacted by Jacobs's narrative, as her personal and bodily experi-ences stand as evidence of the oppressions of slavery. Thus the ways in which the body of the slave grounds antebel-lum discourses of identity has another, and more ominous, meaning for the slave author. In Jacobs's narrative the constraints of her body and the constraints of her writing replicate each other. The loss entailed in producing a slave narrative derives from the idea, as Henry Louis Gates puts it [in his Introduction to *Figures in Black: Words, Signs, and the "Racial" Self,* 1987], "that any human being would be demanded to write him or herself into the human community," and beyond this, from the recogni-tion that such an act of self-writing assumes the same pos-sessive and negating attitudes toward the body and bodily experience as slavery itself. As Jacobs's distress at record-ing her personal experience in a public and political docu-ment demonstrates, many of the characteristics of slavery (degradation, exposure, exploitation) are implicated in the act of writing down those experiences. For Jacobs the act of writing is affiliated alternately with both self-mastery and enslavement.

Jacobs had not originally intended to tell her story herself. She had hoped that Harriet Beecher Stowe would write it for her. Indeed she offered Stowe not only her own history as a possible subject for the novelist's pen, but also the ser-vices of her daughter Louisa during Stowe's intended voy-age to England. As Jacobs explained to Amy Post, "I thought Louisa would be a very good representative of a Southern Slave. She has improved much in her studies and I think she has energy enough to do something for the cause." Stowe rejected both offers: she desired only to in-clude Jacobs's story among the substantiating anecdotes compiled in her *Key to Uncle Tom's Cabin,* and "she was afraid," Jacobs wrote, angrily summarizing Stowe's objec-tions, that such a journey "would subject [Louisa] to much petting and patronizing which would be more pleas-ing to a young Girl than useful and the English very apt to do it and [Mrs. Stowe] was very much opposed to it with this class of people." Ironically, in treating both her life and her daughter as "representative" of Southern slav-ery, Jacobs anticipates the terms of Stowe's insult. In using this vocabulary, Jacobs reveals her desire to change how slavery is represented and the slave understood. Jacobs sees her own and Louisa's intelligence and energy as suit-ing them for the role of representative: she recognizes her-self and her daughter as articulate, individualized advo-cates for the slave, rather than simply as sample slaves. To be representative, as Jacobs understood it, meant being presentable.

In seeing the mother as an apt illustration for her *Key* and the daughter as a member of a preconceived "class," Stowe reads this representativeness differently. It is be-cause she claims the role of representative slave that Ja-cobs's experiences can be alienated from her person and recast into the exemplary facts of Stowe's *Key.* Racist as-sumptions about the representative character of the slave permit Stowe confidently to predict Louisa's foibles. Moreover, the symmetry of Stowe's response to the double offer of daughter and tale reveals the symmetrical situa-tions of servitude and narrative. In Stowe's response both the representative slave girl and the representation of a slave girl are denied the integrity of individuation.

Only after Stowe had refused to write Jacobs's story as "a history of my life entirely by itself " did Jacobs begin her work on *Incidents.* It could be argued that she set about recounting her life as an antidote to Stowe's denigrating response. In writing the story herself, however, Jacobs cannot completely avoid the problems posed by her claim to presentable representativeness. Although Jacobs's "conversation and manners inspire . . . confidence," al-though she "has so deported herself as to be highly es-teemed," although, in short, she was an eminently present-able black woman, the sexual story she wished to tell ren-dered her not presentable at all.

Analogies between representation and slavery, the story and the slave woman, pervade Jacobs's writings, so it is hardly surprising that the tactics by which she ultimately escaped from slavery come to inform her treatment of her new narrative confines. "I had no motive for secrecy on my own account," Jacobs insists in her "Preface" as she defends the fact that she has "concealed the names of places, and given persons fictitious names." Lydia Maria Child, who edited and introduced the anonymous *Inci-dents,* advised such concealments "out of delicacy to Mrs. Willis," Jacobs's employer and the woman who had procured her freedom. That Jacobs's identity had to be occluded to protect the name of a mistress, however generous and beloved, illustrates the easy expendability of black identities. Yet clearly Jacobs's use of the pseudonym "Linda Brent," which provides a mechanism of escape highly valued by any fugitive, is not without advantages. She had, after all, admitted to finding the secrecy of whispers easier than public utterance. Jacobs signed the name "Linda" to an antislavery letter she wrote to the *Liberator;* one she sent to the *New York Tribune* is simply signed "a fugitive," and her own strategy for escaping from slavery bears a marked similarity to her mode of pseudonymous authorship. Jacobs hid for seven years in the attic of her grandmother's house, watching the master from whom she fled through a hole bored in the wall of her hiding place. Like her grandmother's attic, the figure of Linda Brent places Jacobs in close proximity to those who are seeking her and yet leaves her carefully concealed. And like this attic—"a very small garret . . . only nine feet long and seven feet wide. The highest part was three feet high, and sloped down abruptly to the loose board floor"—the refuge Jacobs finds in *Incidents* proves a confining one.

The analogy between how Jacobs manages to escape from slavery and how she comes to represent it emphasizes not only the equation for the slave author of the position of the slave and that of the literary subject, but also the literary ramifications of such an equation. Jacobs's narrative provides a particularly appropriate site for my inquiry both because her attention to the sexual aspects of slavery necessarily insists on its bodily implications and because this sexual concern has resulted in a certain generic instability. The anomalous product of a slave woman, Jacobs's text juxtaposes the traditionally male adventures of the slave narrative with the white middle-class femininity of the domestic novel. As Jacobs writes her story, Linda Brent acts out the problems inherent in this hybridization of slave and domestic narrative forms.

Unlike the heroes of slave narratives, Linda escapes not by fighting or running but by burrowing into domestic spaces. Besides the "loophole of retreat," as Jacobs calls the secret garret, Linda hides beneath the kitchen floorboards and atop the spare featherbeds in the home of a sympathetic, but slave-owning, white woman. She locates freedom in feminized spaces; but while she haunts these houses, she cannot occupy them. She never comes to inhabit the domestic; rather, as a slave and particularly as a female slave she *is* the domestic. In her effort to escape, her body literally lines the floors and ceilings of houses, just as in servitude her body and its labor sustains the Southern home. Significantly, the peephole she bores in the wall of her grandmother's attic does not provide her with a view of the house's interior. She cannot watch her grandmother care for her children; instead she watches the street where, powerless to intervene, she sees her son attacked by a dog or threatened by her master.

The domestic scene she cannot see from her attic remains just as elusive in the freedom of her final page:

> Reader, my story ends with freedom; not in the usual way, with marriage. I and my children are now free! We are as free from the power of slaveholders as are the white people of the north; and though that, according to my ideas, is not saying a great deal, it is a vast improvement in *my* condition. The dream of my life is not yet realized. I do not sit with my children in a home of my own. I still long for a hearthstone of my own, however humble. I wish it for my children's sake far more than for my own.

Fairy tales traditionally grant three wishes, and Jacobs repeats hers three times, but ultimately "children," "home," and the thrice reiterated "my own" prove a single, continuously denied dream. As Jacobs sees it, only in claiming possession, only by inhabiting rather than making the domestic, can she assure that she and her children are not property. Apologizing for the inadequacies of her style, Jacobs explains in her preface that she was "compelled . . . to write these pages at irregular intervals, whenever I could snatch an hour from household duties." Although the domestic constitutes the conditions under which she writes, the feminine travails that order her plot, and the locus and the goal of the story she tells, Jacobs's narrative is nevertheless a document of exclusion from the domestic. Melding the slave narrative and the domestic novel, Jacobs reveals the social and political paradox behind her problem of genre: slavery can create the private, domestic realm precisely because the slave has no privacy and no claim on domestic space or domestic utterance. Might Jacobs conceive of feminine discourse as whispers because she cannot properly occupy domestic space or speak out loud there? In the harsh confines of her grandmother's attic Linda felt "a very painful sensation of coldness in my head; even my face and tongue stiffened, and I lost the power of speech."

Desiring a home for her "children's sake far more than for [her] own," and concluding her narrative with the solace that "all the gloomy recollections" of slavery required by the task of writing are accompanied by "tender memories of my good old grandmother," Jacobs postulates maternity as a rejoinder to slavery. Maternity is, of course, an alternative means of locating the domestic: children replace houses as signs of a title to domesticity and an ability to engage in feminine discourse or to claim the status of a virtuous and valuable woman. In Jacobs's book, however, motherhood, like home, provides only the most paradoxical of refuges. Describing her own childhood, Jacobs explains:

> When I was six years old, my mother died; and then, for the first time, I learned, by the talk around me, that I was a slave. My mother's mistress was the daughter of my grandmother's mistress. She was the foster sister of my mother; they were both nourished at my grandmother's breast. In fact, my mother had been weaned at three months old, that the babe of the mistress might obtain sufficient food. They played together as children; and, when they became women, my mother was a most faithful servant to her whiter foster sister. On her death-bed her mistress promised that her children should never suffer for any thing; and during her lifetime she kept her word. They all spoke kindly of my dead mother, who had been a slave merely in name,

but in nature was noble and womanly. I grieved
for her, and my young mind was troubled with
the thought who would now take care of me and
my little brother. I was told that my home was
now to be with her mistress; and I found it a
happy one. . . .

When I was nearly twelve years old, my kind
mistress sickened and died. As I saw the cheek
grow paler, and the eye more glassy, how earnestly I prayed in my heart that she might live!
I loved her; for she had been almost like a mother to me.

The roles of mother, sister, slave, and mistress tangle in
this report. The assumption that infants who suckle at the
same breast become sisters, or that the woman who
"take[s] care of me" and provides "my home" is "almost"
a mother, derives from a familial conception of social relations, a desired fusion of slavery and maternal domesticity. But if the young Linda suggests the naivete of one just
learning her social place, the irony of her confusion is,
nevertheless, perfectly clear. In her will the mistress who
is "almost like a mother" bequeaths Linda to her five-
year-old niece. Her mistress had taught her the scriptural
precept to "love thy neighbor as thyself," but, Jacobs concludes, "I was her slave, and I suppose she did not recognize me as her neighbor." The asymmetry of social place
that allows the mistress to appear almost as a mother
while the slave is not recognizable as a neighbor instantly
disentangles familial and plantation relations, revealing
the difference and distance hidden in the word "almost."
In fact it is with the death of this mistress, rather than that
of her mother, that Linda can be said to learn that she is
a slave; and it is with the death of this mistress that the
first chapter, "Childhood," ends.

This rupture of the felt similitude between mother and
mistress reiterates a division already discernible in their
suckling. To call mother and mistress "foster-sisters" is to
suggest that a certain parity and relatedness adhere to
sharing the same breast. But the story Jacobs tells reveals
that rather than produce social equality, sharing the same
breast becomes itself a means of imposing the hierarchies
of slavery. Weaning the slave in order to provide more
milk for the mistress denies both sisterhood and the presumed primacy of familial or maternal ties; it subjugates
the claims of biological and emotional relations to the economic relations of the plantation.

In Jacobs's narrative the act of breast-feeding proves emblematic of plantation society, demonstrating how slavery
denies the possibility of separating the personal from the
political, since the body itself, and all that makes and
maintains it, remains constantly liable to commodification. The slave nurse is not simply a completely corporeal
person; she is, beyond that, comestible, literally consumed
by her owners and their offspring. The ability to nurse, like
the ability to bear children and to provide sexual gratification, manifests the particular utility of the female slave, a
utility resulting not simply from the labor performed by
her body but rather from her body itself. That this grandmother, whose body nourished the bodies of both of
Linda's mistresses, also provided "for all [Linda's] comforts, spiritual or temporal," reveals, however, that the

commodification of her capacity for generation and nurturance does not destroy its potential for empowerment. The
meals and clothes the grandmother makes for Linda, coming as they do despite plantation prohibitions, grant Linda
a source of sustenance external to the domestic economy
of the plantation. Although obviously tenuous and limited, these acts of nurturance nevertheless provide a degree
of autonomy sufficient to affirm for Linda that her body
and her identity are not completely subsumed into her position as slave. In revealing the maternal to be simultaneously a means of subverting the plantation economy and
a commodity within that economy, Jacobs discovers the
limits of her own proposal for a domestic liberty.

The connections Jacobs draws between public records and
intimate whispers, liberty and domesticity, derive from
the dual nature of her narrative task: to depict the inter-
section of slavery and sexual exploitation. Jacobs's conflation of the two creates an explicitly textual dilemma, one
that functions both thematically and structurally. The
narration of this "life of a slave girl," and particularly of
the events that comprise Linda's harassment by Dr. Flint
and resultant sexual relation with Mr. Sands, is interspersed with incidents and even whole chapters at best pe-
ripheral to Linda's personal story. For example, within a
single chapter, the story of Linda's first sexual confrontation with Dr. Flint intertwines with the stories of her uncle
Benjamin's much thwarted but ultimately successful escape to the North and of her brother William's resistance
to the taunts and cuffings instigated by his young master.
On a larger scale, between a chapter devoted to Dr. Flint's
angry refusal to allow Linda to wed a free-born black man
and the chapter in which, in an effort to protect herself
from and to spite Dr. Flint, she decides to become Mr.
Sands's lover, Jacobs places a chapter entitled "What
Slaves Are Taught to Think of the North" and another
called "Sketches of Neighboring Slaveholders." Similarly,
between the two chapters which recount the births of
Linda's two children, fathered by Mr. Sands, Jacobs in-
serts a chapter-length discussion of Southern responses to
Nat Turner's rebellion (an addition that Child had suggested might be of interest to a Northern audience), and
a chapter on "The Church and Slavery." The content of
these digressive chapters largely conforms to the descriptions of slavery regularly published in abolitionist pamphlets.

Like the strategy of displacement employed in her letter
to Post, Jacobs's narrative digressions disperse and so conceal issues of sexuality within the more general political
context of slavery. But, considering that accounts of all
the lies, violence, surveillance, and religious justification
that buttress the institution of slavery constitute the essential and ubiquitous abolitionist narrative, it is equally valid
to read the story of Linda's sexual experiences as a series
of digressions within this more general abolitionist text. In
juxtaposing these generic exposés of the horrors of slavery
with the individual and more personal account of Linda's
sexual experiences, Jacobs's text raises questions about the
adequacy of abolitionist reportage. Yet, as Houston Baker
points out [in his *Blues, Ideology, and Afro-American Literature,* 1984], by calling her narrative the life of *a* slave
girl she generalizes her personal experience, implying that

such sexual exploitation may define slavery for any, or even all, slave girls. Jacobs's narrative strategies evince a desire to have it both ways, to hide her story, and hence her sexual vulnerability, within the general rubric of slavery's atrocities, and to rupture the normative abolitionist accounts of cruel masters and suffering slaves by interposing within it the private discourse of female sexuality.

Jacobs's two-part title, *Incidents in the Life of a Slave Girl, Written By Herself,* reveals more than convention, since the book is as much about the act of writing these incidents of sexual exploitation as it is about the incidents themselves. Jacobs's anxiety over literacy strikingly differentiates her text from the majority of slave narratives, in which command over letters frequently serves as a tool and symbol of liberation. Only rarely does Jacobs celebrate the cunning and skill that permitted Frederick Douglass to write his own pass or reveal the educational bravado with which William Wells Brown tricked white schoolchildren into teaching him letters by showing off the nonsense "writing" he had scratched with a stick into the dirt road. Hiding in her grandmother's attic, Linda does send Dr. Flint taunting letters with misleading Northern postmarks. But in general the trickery and authority of literacy do not remain in her control, for at the very moments that she gains literacy she finds these new skills turned against her. Linda is taught to read and spell by the almost motherly mistress whose written will bequeaths her to the Flints, and when Dr. Flint discovers her teaching herself to write he twists this accomplishment to serve his own plans and begins to slip her threatening and lascivious notes. Thus Jacobs's abolitionist text must also be seen as a site of bondage and sexual degradation. Just as Linda's liaison with Mr. Sands succeeds in challenging the authority of her master at the cost of "womanly virtue," telling her sexual story both emancipates and exploits. The strained relations between the public record of slavery and the intimate whispers of sexuality are reenacted in the scene of writing.

In her introduction to this slave narrative, Lydia Maria Child states that the sexual dimensions of slavery have "generally been kept veiled" but that she, in her role as editor, "willingly take[s] the responsibility of presenting them with the veil withdrawn." In heralding the narrative as a form of undressing, a discursive striptease, Child also records the resistance that awaits the sexual exposure of reading and writing. She explains that her "sisters in bondage . . . are suffering wrongs so foul that our ears are too delicate to listen to them." At work here is not only the solipsism that replaces the suffering of the slave woman with the suffering of her auditor, but also a recognition, even in critique, that the act of narration is itself a sexual act—that though, as Child asserts, Jacobs's experiences may be called "delicate subjects," issues of delicacy are also entailed in their transmission. Urging female readers to the exertion of "moral influence" and exhorting male readers to actively "prevent" the implementation of the fugitive slave laws, Child concludes with a distinctly conservative vision of the gendering of abolitionist response. Out of keeping with her usual feminist posture, Child's insistence that the reading of this slave narrative will work to produce traditional gender norms testifies to

her sense of the story's threatening indelicacy—its siege on sexual order and conventional morality.

Anxieties over the obstacles to transmission posed by the delicate ears of a Northern audience are directly thematized within Jacobs's text as she repeatedly restages the scene of telling: the abusive erotics of narration become the subject of her narration. The first of these restagings is initiated by the jealous interrogations of Linda's mistress, Mrs. Flint. In one of his many schemes of harassment, Dr. Flint decides to take his young daughter to sleep in his room as a pretext for requiring Linda's presence there throughout the night. The doctor's room and the mistress's room, the would-be scene of harassment and the scene of narration, vie with each other as the locus of Jacobs's text.

> After a while my mistress sent for me to come to her room. Her first question was, "Did you know you were to sleep in the doctor's room?"
>
> "Yes, ma'am."
>
> "Who told you?"
>
> "My master."
>
> "Will you answer truly all the questions I ask?"
>
> "Yes, ma'am."
>
> "Tell me, then, as you hope to be forgiven, are you innocent of what I have accused you?"
>
> "I am." . . .
>
> "If you have deceived me, beware! Now take this stool, sit down, look me directly in the face, and tell me all that has passed between your master and you."
>
> I did as she ordered. As I went on with my account her color changed frequently, she wept, and sometimes groaned. She spoke in tones so sad, that I was touched by her grief. The tears came to my eyes; but I was soon convinced that her emotions arose from anger and wounded pride. She felt that her marriage vows were desecrated, her dignity insulted; but she had no compassion for the poor victim of her husband's perfidy. She pitied herself as a martyr; but she was incapable of feeling for the condition of shame and misery in which her unfortunate, helpless slave was placed.

The scene has virtually no content: the accusation and the account given are not voiced within Jacobs's text. Instead of describing the events told, Jacobs represents the form of their telling, the dynamics of the discourse of female sexual experience. What Mrs. Flint requires from Linda is finally not a protestation of Linda's sexual innocence, but the titillation of being told all. Yet despite her request, Mrs. Flint refuses to listen to Linda's account; she replaces what Linda would say with her own groans, so that she becomes the martyred subject of the only story she is willing to hear. As in Child's introduction, the experience of the auditor all too easily supplants the sufferings of the slave.

For Linda, moreover, this enforced act of recounting her

sexual victimization repeats the scene of sexual abuse. The descriptions of Dr. Flint's efforts to harass Linda provided within *Incidents* focus primarily on his corrupting words: "My master, whose restless, craving vicious nature roved about day and night, seeking whom to devour, had just left me, with stinging, scorching words; words that scathed ear and brain like fire;" "My master began to whisper foul words in my ear. . . . He peopled my young mind with unclean images, such as only a vile monster could think of;" "When I succeeded in avoiding opportunities for him to talk to me at home, I was ordered to come to his office, to do some errand. When there, I was obliged to stand and listen to such language as he saw fit to address to me." Linda observes that Mrs. Flint's tears and groans derive from her own sense of martyrdom and not from sympathy with the position of her slave. Nevertheless, as this scene is portrayed, Mrs. Flint's position becomes that of the slave woman listening to Dr. Flint's "foul words." "Her color," Jacobs notes, "changed frequently." But though Linda's narration may thus seem to function as a medium of revenge, a way of wounding her cruel auditor, this inversion does not serve to empower Linda, to grant her the authority or dominance of the master. In speaking Dr. Flint's words, Linda both obeys the orders of her mistress, complying with Mrs. Flint's solipsistic and voyeuristic needs, and reveals the extent to which her master's words have indeed scathed her ear and brain. Linda, who met Dr. Flint's speeches with her own words of resistance, conforms to his language, yielding as it were to the dynamics of the sexual scene, only when she recreates it for Mrs. Flint. Rather than redress her sufferings, the act of voicing her sexual experiences enforces and realizes the abuses of which she speaks.

Finally it is Mrs. Flint and not her husband who takes Linda to sleep "in a room adjoining her own."

> There I was an object of her especial care, though not of her especial comfort, for she spent many a sleepless night to watch over me. Sometimes I woke up, and found her bending over me. At other times she whispered in my ear, as though it was her husband who was speaking to me, and listened to hear what I would answer. If she startled me, on such occasions, she would glide stealthily away; and the next morning she would tell me I had been talking in my sleep, and ask who I was talking to. At last I began to be fearful for my life.

As she bends over her sleeping slave, her mouth at Linda's ear, Mrs. Flint occupies precisely the position of erotic dominance repeatedly denied the doctor. This is the most explicitly and graphically sexual representation in the entire narrative; while Jacobs depicts Mrs. Flint in the dark, bending over Linda's supine body, she does not present either the doctor or the more sexually successful Mr. Sands in any similarly intimate posture. Since this scene, despite all of its overtly erotic content, purports to represent jealousy rather than lust, it falls safely within the bounds of acceptable feminine discourse. Modestly "veiled" by jealousy the scene offers no affront to "delicacy."

Such an explanation for the displacement of the role of rapist from husband to wife does not, however, fully account for Jacobs's description of these nocturnal encounters. In casting this scene of sexual domination between slave and mistress, rather than, as her plot would indicate, between slave and master, Jacobs collapses female sexual experience into the problems associated with feminine discourse and the telling of that experience. Mrs. Flint's midnight whisperings imitate both Dr. Flint's harassments and Linda's account of those harassments. The story Linda must tell and the act of telling it combine in this life-threatening figure. "Woman can whisper—her cruel wrongs into the ear of a very dear friend," Jacobs had written to Amy Post. Yet it is in this very image of an intimately whispering woman that Jacobs comes closest to depicting the scene of rape. In short, she identifies sexual oppression less with any physical act than with the representation of that act.

The rapes of narration and reenactment that Jacobs shows to be inherent in the discourse of sexuality occupy the place of the unspeakable event of male sexual violence and its institutionalization in the plantation economy, where illicit offspring become property. This does not mean, of course, that the compulsions of slavery and the threat of male violence have disappeared. After all, this nightmare scene explicitly reenacts Dr. Flint's efforts to harass Linda. He is never really absent from these apparently female interactions: in Linda's responses to the command that she tell all, and in Mrs. Flint's nocturnal visits, the doctor's lewd speech threatens, and indeed usurps, the identities of both women. As Mrs. Flint whispers "as though it were her husband who was speaking," the discourse of female sexuality or female power finds itself hopelessly mired in the master's words.

Explicitly written for a Northern, white, female readership, *Incidents* bears a strained and strange relation to feminine domestic norms. The narrator frequently turns to address her readers, calling attention to her abolitionist purpose and to the fact that this textual account, like the scenes of narration presented within it, relies upon the responsive presence of an audience. This general tendency to address the reader becomes, however, unusually pronounced when Linda explains her attachment to Mr. Sands and her "plunge into the abyss" of sexual activity. While such passages of direct address usually function as a relatively detached form of commentary on the events described—a plea for action or an attack on Northern complicity not directly related to the incidents at hand—in the pages that discuss Linda's decision to become Mr. Sands's lover the reader's role seems less that of an audience than that of an essential actor in the scene. The plot of Linda's explanations to her judgmental readers largely overwhelms the plot of Mr. Sands's eloquence and Linda's gullible calculations. The presumed rejections and resistances of her readers quite literally replace the story of her sexual choices: "I will not try to screen myself behind the plea of compulsion from a master," she writes, "for it was not so,"

> Neither can I plead ignorance or thoughtlessness. . . . I knew what I did and I did it with deliberate calculation.
>
> But, O, ye happy women, whose purity has been

sheltered from childhood, who have been free to choose the objects of your affection, whose homes are protected by law, do not judge the poor desolate slave girl too severely!

If Jacobs's narrative puts the white woman's expectations in the place of her own sexuality, she nevertheless insists that such displacements are finally untenable. After describing Mr. Sands's flattering attentions, and asserting the "something akin to freedom" in taking as a lover a man who is not her master, Linda concludes "there may be sophistry in all this; but the condition of a slave confuses all principles of morality, and, in fact, renders the practice of them impossible."

> Pity me, and pardon me, O virtuous reader! You never knew what it is to be a slave; to be entirely unprotected by law or custom; to have the laws reduce you to the condition of a chattel, entirely subject to the will of another. . . . I know I did wrong. No one can feel it more sensibly than I do. The painful and humiliating memory will haunt me to my dying day. Still, in looking back, calmly, on the events of my life, I feel that the slave woman ought not to be judged by the same standard as others.

Linda's stress on the wrongful humiliation of her past actions conforms to the moral code of her happy and virtuous readers. Yet though she asks for their pity and their pardons, she also repeatedly and explicitly disqualifies them and their code of sexual morality for the task of judgment. It is not the protected reader, but only the slave woman, writing from the calm vantage of her experiences, who can articulate an appropriate standard. The sexual experience she decries and would repress provides the only available ground of judgment and therefore the only means of validation and liberation. If Linda's sexual relations with Mr. Sands tend to dissolve in this chapter into the narrative act of explaining and justifying those relations, the explanations offered invariably point back to the realm of experience. Asking for her readers' pity and yet denying their ability to comprehend her choices, Jacobs suggests that the experiences of slavery remain precisely what cannot be explained. Transgressing social norms, slavery threatens to foreclose communication. Just as Jacobs hopes that her narrative will redefine slavery, and perhaps even help to abolish it, slavery challenges the bounds of feminine discourse and the grounds of feminine judgment and hence redefines Jacobs's relation to her sexuality, her text, and the white women whose decorum would censor them both.

Within the text, Linda's attempts to tell this portion of her sexual history demonstrate the cultural pervasiveness of such censorship among black listeners as well as white. Newly arrived in Philadelphia, she is taken into the home of "a respectable-looking colored man," the Rev. Jeremiah Durham, where his questions reveal some of the limits of her Northern freedom.

> Mr. Durham observed that I had spoken to him of a daughter I expected to meet; that he was surprised, for I looked so young he had taken me for a single woman. He was approaching a subject on which I was extremely sensitive. He

would ask about my husband next, I thought, and if I answered him truly, what would he think of me? He asked some further questions, and I frankly told him some of the most important events of my life. It was painful for me to do it; but I would not deceive him. If he was desirous of being my friend, I thought he ought to know how far I was worthy of it. "Excuse me, if I have tried your feelings," said he. "I did not question you from idle curiosity. I wanted to understand your situation, in order to know whether I could be of any service to you, or your little girl. Your straight-forward answers do you credit; but don't answer every body so openly. It might give some heartless people a pretext for treating you with contempt."

Linda's sensitivity on this subject, her concern with what her auditor will think, her insistence that such narrations are painful to her, and her allusion to a scale of worthiness in which the illegitimacy of her children functions as a demerit all indicate her wish to comply with nineteenth-century standards of chastity. Yet despite these symptoms of internal censorship, Linda bristles at Rev. Durham's suggestion that she suppress the sexual aspects of her history:

> That word *contempt* burned me like coals of fire. I replied, "God alone knows how I have suffered; and He, I trust, will forgive me. If I am permitted to have my children, I intend to be a good mother, and to live in such a manner that people cannot treat me with contempt."

The words that had burned her under slavery were the "scorching words" of Dr. Flint. The language of sexual harassment and the language of sexual suppression impose comparable scars. Even before this quite sympathetic audience, Linda finds that the act of telling her sexual story subtly reenacts that story.

Linda's response proposes the role of the "good mother" as a substitute for chastity. Such a redefinition of sexual morality casts the children whose illegitimate birth attest to her sexual activity as the signs and sources of her moral virtue. Abolitionist writings consistently offer the light-skinned child of the slave woman as proof of the miscegenating economy of slavery, so that the child stands as evidence of the gap between plantation life and the ideology of the sacrosanct bourgeois family. Inverting this system of bodily signs, Jacobs presents the slave-child, even the interracial slave-child, as a potential means of access to a virtuous, respectable domesticity. Rather than signifying her difference from the middle-class white woman, Linda recognizes her children as signs of her sameness, and as barriers against the contempt that comes with differentiation. This reinterpretation depends upon viewing the child not as a product of sexual activity, but as an object of maternal nature. Jacobs has used this defense before under antithetical circumstances. Threatened by the completion of the cabin where Dr. Flint proposes to keep her as his concubine, Linda asserts, "I will never go there. In a few months I shall be a mother." Motherhood replaces sexuality.

Significantly, this maternal elision of sexuality characterizes Linda's attempt to tell her sexual history to her daughter Ellen. Her final restaging of the scene of sexual narration appears in a very brief chapter entitled "The Confession," only two chapters away from the end of the volume. But even here, with the book nearly completed, and with her daughter's loving acceptance of Linda's choices "making," as Hazel Carby argues [in her *Reconstructing Womanhood,* 1987], "external validation unnecessary and unwarranted," the act of telling her sexual story remains ambivalent. In fact Linda hardly manages to tell her story at all:

> I recounted my early sufferings in slavery, and told her how nearly they had crushed me. I began to tell her how they had driven me into a great sin, when she clasped me in her arms, and exclaimed, "O, don't, mother! Please don't tell me any more."
>
> I said, "But my child, I want you to know about your father."
>
> "I know all about it, mother," she replied.

As Ellen goes on to deny the claims of her father and affirm her love for her mother, the story of her parental allegiances silences the story of her mother's sexual experience. The ploy of denying parental sexuality emancipates through repression, granting respectability to the freed woman by forgetting the sexual vulnerability of the slave. Linda is empowered in this chapter not by her confession, as the title implies, but rather by the child's will to absolve by denial.

Jacobs hopes that the feminine discourse of domesticity and motherhood might serve to rectify the sexual story that is "the life of a slave girl." Her narrative, however, ultimately fails to displace the sexual experiences it describes. Instead it repeats them, as the act of telling this story results in rape, shame, contempt, and denial—results, that is, in the painful attributes of slavery's degrading sexuality. But if Jacobs's narration takes on the suffering and vulnerability of sexuality, it also commands a measure of its pleasures and its power. Before Child's introduction to *Incidents,* with its anxious but enticing promise of a story that would "unveil" the experiences of a slave girl, Jacobs places two epigraphs and a preface that locate the threat of sexual objectification differently.

The two epigraphs that introduce Jacobs's book discretely suggest that the reader shares in this story's sexual risk. "Northerners know nothing at all about Slavery," she quotes from a woman of North Carolina, "they have no conception of the depth of *degradation* involved in that word, SLAVERY." The epigraph promises a lesson in reading, in the belief that the comprehension of a word would produce abolitionist action. Yet, as her emphasis insists, all that would replace the "nothing" of ignorance and apathy must be recognized as *degradation.* Once fully read the word SLAVERY threatens to rape the "too delicate" ears of Jacobs's Northern audience. Indeed, the second epigraph to *Incidents* links the possibility of white women's political "rise" to Jacobs's ability to gain access to this eroticized narrative orifice: "Rise up, ye women that are at ease! Hear my voice, ye careless daughters! Give ear unto

my speech" (Isaiah 32:9). P. Gabrielle Foreman [in her "Manuscript in *Signs*"] calls attention to the subsequent lines of Isaiah pointedly not printed on Jacobs's page: "Tremble, you women who are at ease, Shudder you complacent ones. Strip and make yourself bare, and gird sackcloth upon your loins" (Isaiah 32:11). If Jacobs forbears from stripping her auditors, this suppressed threat nevertheless marks the potential reversibility of the circuits of narrative eroticism, destabilizing, as Foreman argues, "the very category of racially determined sexual objectification."

Such reversals do not attempt to deny or evade the patterns of dominance and submission inherent in the erotics of narration, but they do imagine a form of telling that rather than merely unveil the slave girl who is its subject would also work to reveal its Northern audience. "I have not written my experiences in order to attract attention to myself," Jacobs states in her preface,

> on the contrary, it would have been more pleasant to me to have been silent about my own history. Neither do I care to excite sympathy for my own sufferings. But I do earnestly desire to arouse the women of the North to a realizing sense of the condition of two millions of women at the South, still in bondage, suffering what I suffered, and most of them far worse.

In presenting herself to a Northern female readership as the representative of two million slave women, Jacobs makes her private history into a public and emblematically political document, but beyond this she defines the political purposes and forum for which she writes as female. The forbidden politics and the forbidden sexuality are conflated: throughout this statement her political goals assert an erotic urgency. Reiterating Isaiah's injunction to "rise up," Jacobs forfeits a "pleasant" silence, and demurs "to excite sympathy" because of her "desire to arouse the women of the North." The arousal entailed in reading this "Life of a Slave Girl," the sexual charge of abolitionist politics, eroticizes Jacobs's Northern audience by equating their reading with the perverse interrogations of a Mrs. Flint. In constructing an equation between her jealous mistress, her Northern audience and, by extension, that suspect figure, the white critic, myself, Jacobs presents the sexual dynamics of narration with the "veil withdrawn." As she "desires" the arousal of her readers, she makes use of the erotic power of narration instead of being employed by it. Thus in telling the story of her own sexual exploitation Jacobs enlists both the sexual responses of her readers and the threat of their similar sexual vulnerability for her own abolitionist purposes. The act of narration may be a striptease, and so, like Linda's sexual relations with Mr. Sands, it may appear a source of shame. But such degradations may, nevertheless, prove tactical. Jacobs's conflation of sex and writing establishes both her sexual story and her telling of it as acts of defiance, as a means of resisting—however inadequately—the oppressions, even the sexual oppressions, of slavery.

Karen Sánchez-Eppler, "Righting Slavery and Writing Sex: The Erotics of Narration in Harriet Jacobs's 'Incidents',' in her Touching Liberty: Abolition, Feminism, and the Politics of the Body, *University of California Press, 1993, pp. 83-104.*

John Hope Franklin

[*A modern historian, Franklin is the author of numerous studies of American history, including* From Slavery to Freedom: A History of American Negroes *(1947),* The Militant South: 1800-1861 *(1956),* Reconstruction: After the Civil War *(1961), and* The Emancipation Proclamation *(1963). In the following excerpt from the last-named work, Franklin portrays Lincoln's edict as a powerful document that far surpassed its immediate purpose as a war measure and ultimately served to validate and extend the principles of democracy and equality expressed in the Declaration of Independence.*]

The character of the Civil War could not possibly have been the same after the President issued the *Emancipation Proclamation* as it had been before January 1, 1863. During the first twenty months of the war, no one had been more careful than Lincoln himself to define the war merely as one to save the Union. He did this not only because such a definition greatly simplified the struggle and kept the border states fairly loyal, but also because he deeply felt that this was the only legitimate basis for prosecuting the war. When, therefore, he told Horace Greeley that if he could save the Union without freeing a single slave he made the clearest possible statement of his fundamental position. And he was holding to this position despite the fact that he had written the first draft of the *Emancipation Proclamation* at least six weeks before he wrote his reply to Greeley's famous "Prayer of Twenty Millions."

Lincoln saw no contradiction between the contents of his reply to Greeley and the contents of the *Emancipation Proclamation.* For he had come to the conclusion that in order to save the Union he must emancipate *some* of the slaves. His critics were correct in suggesting that the Proclamation was a rather frantic measure, an act of last resort. By Lincoln's own admission it was, indeed, a desperate act; for the prospects of Union success were not bright. He grabbed at the straw of a questionable victory at Antietam as the occasion for issuing the *Preliminary Proclamation.* If anything convinced him in late December that he should go through with issuing the final Proclamation, it was the ignominious defeat of the Union forces at Fredericksburg. *Something* needed to be done. Perhaps the *Emancipation Proclamation* would turn the trick!

The language of the Proclamation revealed no significant modification of the aims of the war. Nothing was clearer than the fact that Lincoln was taking the action under his authority "as Commander-in-Chief of the Army and Navy." The situation that caused him to take the action was that there was an "actual armed rebellion against the authority and government of the United States." He regarded the *Emancipation Proclamation,* therefore, as "a fit and necessary war measure for suppressing said rebellion." In another place in the Proclamation he called on the military and naval authorities to recognize and maintain the freedom of the slaves. Finally the President declared, in the final paragraph of the Proclamation, that the measure was "warranted by the Constitution upon military necessity." This was, indeed, a war measure, conceived and promulgated to put down the rebellion and save the Union.

Nevertheless, both by what it said and what it did not say, the Proclamation greatly contributed to the significant

President Abraham Lincoln gives the first reading of the Preliminary Emancipation Proclamation to his cabinet on 22 July 1862.

shift in 1863 in the way the war was regarded. It recognized the right of emancipated slaves to defend their freedom. The precise language was that they should "abstain from all violence, unless in necessary self-defence." It also provided that former slaves could now be received into the armed services. While it was clear that they were to fight to save the Union, the fact remained that since their own fate was tied to that of the Union, they would also be fighting for their own freedom. The Negro who, in December 1862, could salute his own colonel instead of blacking the boots of a Confederate colonel, as he had been doing a year earlier, had a stake in the war that was not difficult to define. However loyal to the Union the Negro troops were— and they numbered some 190,000 by April 1865—one is inclined to believe that they were fighting primarily for freedom for themselves and their brothers in the months that followed the issuance of the *Emancipation Proclamation*.

Despite the fact that the President laid great stress on the issuance of the Proclamation as a military necessity, he did not entirely overlook the moral and humanitarian significance of the measure. And even in the document itself he gave some indication of his appreciation of this particular dimension that was, in time, to eclipse many other considerations. He said that the emancipation of the slaves was "sincerely believed to be an act of justice." This conception of emancipation could hardly be confined to the slaves in states or parts of states that were in rebellion against the United States on January 1, 1863. It must be recalled, moreover, that in the same sentence that he referred to emancipation as an "act of justice" he invoked "the considerate judgment of mankind and the gracious favor of Almighty God." This raised the Proclamation above the level of just another measure for the effective prosecution of the war. And, in turn, the war became more than a war to save the integrity and independence of the Union. It became also a war to promote the freedom of mankind.

Throughout the previous year the President had held to the view that Negroes should be colonized in some other part of the world. And he advanced this view with great vigor wherever and whenever possible. He pressed the Cabinet and Congress to accept and implement his colonization views, and he urged Negroes to realize that it was best for all concerned that they should leave the United States. It is not without significance that Lincoln omitted from the *Emancipation Proclamation* any reference to colonization. It seems clear that the President had abandoned hope of gaining support for his scheme or of persuading Negroes to leave the only home they knew. Surely, moreover, it would have been a most incongruous policy as well as an ungracious act to have asked Negroes to perform one of the highest acts of citizenship—fighting for their country—and then invite them to leave. Thus, by inviting Negroes into the armed services and omitting all mention of colonization, the President indicated in the Proclamation that Negroes would enjoy a status that went beyond mere freedom. They were to be free persons, fighting for their *own* country, a country in which they were to be permitted to remain.

The impact of the Proclamation on slavery and Negroes

was profound. Negroes looked upon it as a document of freedom, and they made no clear distinction between the areas affected by the Proclamation and those not affected by it. . . . The celebration of the issuance of the Proclamation by thousands of Negroes in Norfolk illustrates the pervasive influence of the document. President Lincoln had said that Norfolk slaves were not emancipated by his Proclamation. Norfolk Negroes, however, ignored the exception and welcomed the Proclamation as the instrument of their own deliverance.

Slavery, in or out of the Confederacy, could not possibly have survived the *Emancipation Proclamation.* Slaves themselves, already restive under their yoke and walking off the plantation in many places, were greatly encouraged upon learning that Lincoln wanted them to be free. They proceeded to oblige him. There followed what one authority has called a general strike and another has described as widespread slave disloyalty throughout the Confederacy. Lincoln understood the full implications of the Proclamation. That is one of the reasons why he delayed issuing it as long as he did. Once the power of the government was enlisted on the side of freedom in one place, it could not successfully be restrained from supporting freedom in some other place. It was too fine a distinction to make. Not even the slaveholders in the excepted areas could make it. They knew, therefore, that the *Emancipation Proclamation* was the beginning of the end of slavery for them. . . .

The critics of the Lincoln Administration stepped up their attack after January 1, 1863, because they fully appreciated the fact that the Proclamation changed the character of the war. Orestes A. Brownson, Clement L. Vallandigham, William C. Fowler, Samuel S. Cox, and others insisted that the Proclamation represented a new policy that made impossible any hasty conclusion of the struggle based on a compromise. The President had become the captive of the abolitionists who had persuaded him to change the war aims from preservation of the Union to abolition of slavery. . . .

In the light of the demands they had been making, the language of the *Emancipation Proclamation* could hardly have been the source of unrestrained joy on the part of the abolitionists. The Proclamation did not represent the spirit of "no compromise" that had characterized their stand for a generation. There was no emancipation in the border states, with which the abolitionists had so little patience. Parts of states that were under Union control were excepted, much to the dismay of the abolitionists, whose view was ably set forth by Chase. Obviously, the President was not completely under their sway, despite the claims of numerous critics of the Administration. For the most part, the Proclamation represented Lincoln's views. It was in no sense the result of abolitionist dictation.

And yet, when the Proclamation finally came, the abolitionists displayed a remarkable capacity for accommodating themselves to what was, from their point of view, an obvious compromise. . . .

For thirty years William Lloyd Garrison had never been known to make concessions as far as slavery was concerned. Yet, he declared the *Emancipation Proclamation* to be a measure that should take its place along with the Declaration of Independence as one of the nation's truly important historic documents. Frederick Douglass, the leading Negro abolitionist, said that the Proclamation changed everything. "It gave a new direction to the councils of the Cabinet, and to the conduct of the national arms." Douglass realized that the Proclamation did not extend liberty throughout the land, as the abolitionists hoped, but he took it "for a little more than it purported, and saw in its spirit a life and power far beyond its letter. Its meaning to me was the entire abolition of slavery," he concluded, "and I saw that its moral power would extend much further." . . .

The enthusiasm of the abolitionists was greater than that of a group that had reached the conclusion that half a loaf was better than none. Their initial reaction of dissatisfaction with the [*Preliminary Emancipation Proclamation*] had been transformed into considerable pleasure over the edict of January 1. Most of them seemed to agree with Douglass that the Proclamation had, indeed, changed everything. Even if the Proclamation did not free a single slave, as Henry Ward Beecher admitted, it gave liberty a moral recognition. It was a good beginning, the most significant step that had been taken in a generation of crusading. . . .

[Britons] made known their enthusiastic support of the Lincoln policy in a dozen different ways. As Henry Adams, writing from London, put it, the Proclamation was creating "an almost convulsive reaction in our favor all over this country." He chided the London *Times* for behaving like a "drunken drab," but he was certain that its hostility represented no substantial segment of the middle and lower classes. "Public opinion is deeply stirred here and finds expression in meetings, addresses to President Lincoln, deputations to us, standing committees to agitate the subject and to affect opinion, and all the other symptoms of a great popular movement peculiarly unpleasant to the upper classes here because it rests on the spontaneous action of the laboring classes and has a pestilous squint at sympathy with republicanism."

Within a few weeks after the issuance of the Proclamation, some important public figures in Britain began to speak out in public—at first timidly, then more boldly—in support of the Northern policy. In late March, the Prime Minister, speaking in Edinburgh on the Civil War, expressed a feeling of horror of any war that brought in its wake so much suffering and bloodshed. This was the Palmerston style, to which the people had become accustomed. But this time there was a reply. On the following evening the Duke of Argyll said that when civil wars involved a high moral purpose, he for one was not ashamed of the ancient combination of the Bible and the sword. . . . Soon the British government became more respectful of what Argyll had called the combination of the Bible and the sword.

The broadening of the Union's war aims to include a crusade against slavery coincided with another important development. Serious grain shortages at home were forcing the British to look elsewhere for foodstuffs. . . . [The]

British had come to rely heavily on Northern wheat. Indeed, many thought it was indispensable. Perhaps, under the circumstances, the British government should not risk a rupture with the North, some leaders began to reason. As Her Majesty's Government began to look seriously at this problem, it also began to take cognizance of the pressures of the rank and file of the British people and the pressures of the Washington government. Hope for recognition of the Confederacy by Britain and the Continental powers faded away. The *Emancipation Proclamation* had played an important role in achieving this signal diplomatic victory. . . .

The President hoped that the Proclamation would be the instrument for the further prosecution of the war and the emancipation of slaves in states and parts of states excepted by the Proclamation. He followed with great interest the recruitment and activity of Negro troops that followed in the wake of emancipation. He noticed that the Confederates attacked Negro troops fiercely, and that was to be expected. "It is important to the enemy that such a force shall *not* take shape, and grow, and thrive, in the South; and in precisely the same proportion, it is important to us that it shall." In May the President said he would gladly receive "ten times ten thousand" colored troops and would protect all who enlisted. . . .

[Lincoln] praised the conduct of Negroes under fire and said that some of the generals who had been most successful in the field "believe the emancipation policy, and the use of colored troops, constitute the heaviest blow yet dealt to the rebellion; and that, at least one of those important successes, could not have been achieved when it was, but for the aid of black soldiers." The President had no doubt of the loyalty of Negroes to the Union, but he felt that their interest in their own freedom was an additional motive. This grew out of the government's emancipation policy, the wisdom of which Lincoln was even more certain before the end of the year.

Although the Proclamation did not apply to the border slave states—Missouri, Kentucky, Maryland, and Delaware—Lincoln hoped that it would be a stimulus for the development of emancipation policies in those areas. He was pleased to learn in the spring of 1863 that the state of Missouri was considering a plan for gradual emancipation. . . .

Despite the fact that the immediate results of the *Emancipation Proclamation* were not always measurable, Lincoln was pleased with what he had done. Over and over again he expressed the view that he had done the right thing. It had not had an adverse effect on the course of the war. The war, he told a correspondent in the summer of 1863, had "certainly progressed as favorably for us, since the issue of the proclamation as before." The Proclamation was valid, and he would never retract it. Moreover, it reflected his own repugnance to slavery. As an antislavery man, he wrote Major General Nathaniel P. Banks, he had a motive for issuing the Proclamation that went beyond military considerations. At last he had been able to strike the blow for freedom that he had long wanted to do.

Finally, Lincoln hoped that the Proclamation would provide the basis for a new attitude and policy for Negroes. That all slaves would soon be free was a reality that all white men should face. "Those who shall have tasted actual freedom I believe can never be slaves, or quasi slaves again." He hoped, therefore, that the several states would adopt some practical system "by which the two races could gradually live themselves out of their old relation to each other, and both come out better prepared for the new." He hoped that states would provide for the education of Negroes, and he went so far as to suggest to Governor Michael Hahn of Louisiana that his state might consider extending the franchise to free Negroes of education and property.

Thus, in many ways the Proclamation affected the course of the war as well as Lincoln's way of thinking about the problem of Negroes in the United States. Abroad, it rallied large numbers of people to the North's side and became a valuable instrument of American foreign policy. At home it sharpened the issues of the war and provided a moral and humanitarian ingredient that had been lacking. It fired the leaders with a new purpose and gave to the President a new weapon. Small wonder that he no longer promoted the idea of colonization. Small wonder that he began to advocate education and the franchise for Negroes. They were a new source of strength that deserved to be treated as the loyal citizens that they were.

For the last hundred years the *Emancipation Proclamation* has maintained its place as one of America's truly important documents. Even when the principles it espoused were not universally endorsed and even when its beneficiaries were the special target of mistreatment of one kind or another, the Proclamation somehow retained its hold on the very people who saw its promises unfulfilled. It did not do this because of the perfection of the goal to which it aspired. At best it sought to save the Union by freeing *some* of the slaves. Nor did it do it by the sublimity of its language. It had neither the felicity of the Declaration of Independence nor the simple grandeur of the "Gettysburg Address." But in a very real sense it was another step toward the extension of the ideal of equality about which Jefferson had written.

Lincoln wrote the *Emancipation Proclamation* amid severe psychological and legal handicaps. Unlike Jefferson, whose Declaration of Independence was a clean break with a legal and constitutional system that had hitherto restricted thought and action, Lincoln was compelled to forge a document of freedom for the slaves within the existing constitutional system and in a manner that would give even greater support to that constitutional system. This required not only courage and daring but considerable ingenuity as well. As in so many of Lincoln's acts the total significance and validity of the measure were not immediately apparent, even among those who were sympathetic with its aims. Gradually, the greatness of the document dawned upon the nation and the world. Gradually, it took its place with the great documents of human freedom.

When English America was settled in the seventeenth century it soon became the haven for people who were religiously and socially discontent, economically disadvan-

taged, and politically disoriented. It was not until they broke away from the mother country that they began effectively to realize the existence of which they had dreamed. The break was so complete and the ideology of the break so far-reaching that the only valid base on which to build the New World republic was one characterized by democracy and equality. The tragedy of this republic was that as long as human slavery existed its base had a fallacy that made it both incongruous and specious. The great value of the *Emancipation Proclamation* was that in its first century it provided the base with a reinforcement that made it at long last valid and worthy. Perhaps in its second century it would give real meaning and purpose to the Declaration of Independence. . . .

> *John Hope Franklin, "Victory More Certain," in his* The Emancipation Proclamation, *Doubleday & Company, Inc., 1963, pp. 136-54.*

FURTHER READING

Bontemps, Arna. "The Slave Narrative: An American Genre." In *Great Slave Narratives,* edited by Arna Bontemps, pp. vii-xix. Boston: Beacon Press, 1969.
> Contends that although the slave narrative is a forgotten nineteenth-century literary genre, it had tremendous impact on subsequent American writing and should be valued as an important part of the nation's cultural history.

Davis, Charles T. "The Slave Narrative: First Major Art Form in an Emerging Black Tradition." In his *Black Is the Color of the Cosmos: Essays on Afro-American Literature and Culture, 1942-1981,* edited by Henry Louis Gates, Jr., pp. 83-119. New York: Garland Publishing, 1982.
> Analyzes the relationship between the slave narrative and the abolitionist movement, contending that the genre has had "an enduring effect upon the shape of the tradition of black expression in America."

Dillon, Merton L. *The Abolitionists: The Growth of a Dissenting Minority.* DeKalb: Northern Illinois University Press, 298 p.
> Examines the historical literature devoted to the antislavery movement, from the Enlightenment-inspired abolitionism of the Revolutionary period to the religiously-motivated antislavery ethos of the pre-Civil War era.

Fellman, Michael. "Theodore Parker and the Abolitionist Role in the 1850s." *The Journal of American History* LXI, No. 3 (December 1974): 666-84.
> Maintains that although religious leaders like Theodore Parker were instrumental in the abolitionist crusade, they were motivated by their theological—rather than humanitarian—interest in the slavery issue.

Filler, Louis, ed. *The Crusade against Slavery, 1830-1860.* New York: Harper & Brothers, 1960, 318 p.
> Investigates the case against slavery as depicted in the writings of seminal antislavery figures William Lloyd

Garrison, Theodore D. Weld, Joshua R. Giddings, and others.

Friedman, Lawrence J. *Gregarious Saints: Self and Community in American Abolitionism, 1830-1870.* Cambridge: Cambridge University Press, 1982, 344 p.

Scrutinizes the piety and social psychology of the first generation of immediatist abolitionists—those who took up the cause in the 1830s.

Hart, Albert Bushnell. *Slavery and Abolition, 1831-1841.* New York: Harper & Brothers, 1906, 306 p.

Highly regarded early-twentieth-century study that describes "the conditions of slavery and the state of mind of those interested for it or against it, and at the same time of recording the events which mark the antislavery agitation."

Hawkins, Hugh, ed. *The Abolitionists: Immediatism and the Question of Means.* Lexington, Mass.: D. C. Heath and Co., 1964, 103 p.

Includes contemporary historical interpretations of the abolitionists as well as several nineteenth-century essays on the antislavery movement's philosophy.

Kraditor, Aileen S. *Means and Ends in American Abolitionism: Garrison and His Critics on Strategy and Tactics, 1834-1850.* 1967. Reprint. New York: Pantheon Books, 1969, 296 p.

Discusses differences that arose within the antislavery establishment and public reception of the crusade, observing that the abolitionists were "people intensely earnest in their struggle against slavery but also capable of poking fun at their own seriousness and laughing at their own vagaries."

Loggins, Vernon. *The Negro Author: His Development in America to 1900.* 1931. Reprint. Port Washington, N.Y.: Kennikat Press, 1964, 480 p.

Explains the African-American contribution to nineteenth-century literature, citing the artistic merits of the slave narrative, spiritual, and folk tale.

Nye, Russel B. *William Lloyd Garrison and the Humanitarian Reformers.* Boston: Little, Brown and Co., 1955, 215 p.

Surveys the reformer's life and career, noting his involvement in such humanitarian and philanthropic issues of his day as abolition, temperance, and universal education.

Olney, James. " 'I Was Born' ": Slave Narratives, Their Status as Autobiography and as Literature." In *The Slave's Narrative,* edited by Charles T. Davis and Henry Louis Gates, Jr., pp. 148-75. Oxford: Oxford University Press, 1985.

Assesses the slave narrative's status in the history of American literature and, particularly, in the African-American literary tradition.

————. "The Founding Fathers—Frederick Douglass and Booker T. Washington." In *Slavery and the Literary Imagi-*

nation, edited by Deborah E. McDowell and Arnold Rampersad, pp. 1-24. Baltimore, Md.: The John Hopkins University Press, 1989.

Examines the relationship between leading African-American autobiographers Douglass and Washington, noting their works' artistic, historical, and cultural value.

Stewart, James Brewer. *Holy Warriors: The Abolitionists and American Slavery.* New York: Hill and Wang, 1976, 226 p.

General overview of the antislavery campaign with attention to its salient political, religious, and literary figures.

Sundquist, Eric J. "Slavery, Revolution, and the American Renaissance." In *The American Renaissance Reconsidered,* edited by Walter Benn Michaels and Donald E. Pease, pp. 1-33. Baltimore, Md.: The John Hopkins University Press, 1985.

Analyzes the antislavery orations of Abraham Lincoln and Daniel Webster, traces the events and ideas that led to slavery, and examines the significant literature that the crisis produced.

————, ed. *Frederick Douglass: New Literary and Historical Essays.* Cambridge: Cambridge University Press, 1990, 295 p.

Collection of essays by several leading scholars—Eric J. Sundquist, Henry Louis Gates, Jr., Wilson J. Moses, among others—dealing with a variety of issues surrounding African-American abolitionist, lecturer, and author Douglass.

Thomas, John L., ed. *Slavery Attacked: The Abolitionist Crusade.* Englewood Cliffs, N.J.: Prentice-Hall, 1965.

Contains numerous antislavery polemics by the movement's outstanding figures and includes an introductory essay outlining the campaign's political and moral objectives.

Wilson, Henry. *History of the Rise and Fall of the Slave Power in America.* 3 vols. Boston: James R. Osgood and Co., 1872.

Comprehensive nineteenth-century study of the origin and growth of American slavery and the abolitionist response.

Winks, Robin W. "The Making of a Fugitive Slave Narrative: Josiah Henson and Uncle Tom—A Case Study." In *The Slave's Narrative,* edited by Charles T. Davis and Henry Louis Gates, Jr., pp. 112-46. Oxford: Oxford University Press, 1985.

Probes the influence of fugitive slave Henson's autobiography, *The Life of Josiah Henson, formerly a Slave, Now an Inhabitant of Canada* (1849), on Harriet Beecher Stowe's antislavery novel, *Uncle Tom's Cabin* (1852).

American Romanticism

INTRODUCTION

Literary Romanticism flourished in America during the period between the War of 1812 and the Civil War. Encompassing a broad range of subjects and styles, Romanticism is a category that defies concise definition; it is possible, however, to identify in American Romanticism certain recurring themes, many of which were derived from the writings of the European Romantics. Prominent among these themes are the value of the individual and the rejection of restrictions on individual freedom, whether from societal institutions or traditional literary conventions; an emphasis on the expression of emotion and the de-emphasis of reason as a means of apprehending the world; and recognition of the need for a personal relationship with God and with nature.

The movement in America was, however, more than an imitative response to the works of the European Romantics; American Romanticism was shaped by social forces unique to the New World. American democracy offered the prospect of an egalitarian society in which the citizenry would possess political power and be freed from the rule of King and nobility. The frontier, with its seemingly unlimited room for settlers, offered the means for an individual to establish a simple homestead away from the restrictions of civilization. In addition, the absence of an established national literary tradition resulted in a greater willingness to experiment with literary forms and styles. Thus, the social, political, and cultural climate in America was one in which the Romantic imagination could thrive. As the nation grew in scope, population, and economic power, patriotic pride resulted in a perceived need for a national literature to rival that of England and to complement the nation's other achievements. As a result, American authors sought to utilize American settings and themes, and Romanticism provided a means for these authors to respond to the political ideals and natural beauty of their developing nation.

OVERVIEWS

Paul Kaufman

[*Kaufman was an American educator and critic. In the following essay, he surveys the history and characteristics of the Romantic movement in America.*]

A generation ago, in the last decade of the nineteenth century, the laconic announcement of the passing of the fron-

tier inspired an interpretation of American civilization almost as novel and sweeping as the pioneer movement itself. Today we accept the facts which this interpretation has illumined and arranged in panoramic perspective; we recognize the unique shaping influence of the frontier, in its various aspects and meaning, upon our national outlook and upon our literature.

In the same decade American scholarship produced the first volumes recognizing and describing in English literature a movement which was then beginning to be termed romantic. And since that time the designation has persisted, however controversially, as the counter of criticism and literary history. Yet only within a year or two has any one definitely proposed that in American letters also could be discovered a "romantic" period. Hitherto we have called our literature between the Revolutionary and the Civil Wars by the noncommittal chronological name Early National, or we have made geographical divisions and naturally spoken of the New England school or the New York group; and if we have hazarded a descriptive epithet at all we have spoken of our "classic period." Inner coherence, prevailing tendencies we have not discovered or at least been willing to conceive in terms universally applied to contemporary European literature in the earlier part of the nineteenth century.

That our prose fiction and drama during this period was romantic is well recognized. That the most conspicuous single concerted movement, Transcendentalism, was romantic in a different sense, that it represents the most complete counterpart of various European romanticisms, is equally clear. That the personalities of the time which appear now as the most important, Emerson, Thoreau, Hawthorne, Poe, Melville, Whitman, likewise embodied in their several fashions new movements which we label romantic cannot be questioned. Still we have hesitated to apply the inclusive designation, partly perhaps because our literature has seemed at once so diverse and so largely imitative, formal, reticent. At all events we have not seen an underlying unity which would warrant the single descriptive term applied to European literatures.

Not even although America has traditionally incarnated the romantic in almost every sense. Not even although we still speak with reason of the American adventure, the great democratic experiment, both of which are the essence of romanticism. But is it not strange that the migratory impulse which sprang from revolt against the disintegrating authorities and institutions of Europe and which found unique opportunity for unlimited expression should not have been called romantic? For American civilization detaching itself from the old world and developing new forms of social life has been essentially a quest, the most recent racial struggle for individual freedom. Its distinctive type is represented by the pioneer with boundless opportunity stretching out before him in every direction and ever-expanding frontiers luring him on. What could be more romantic? Nothing, assuredly, at least to men of the old world from the moment when the marvels of the tropical wilderness first broke upon their view; and still at the present time, when we are reproached for our vulgarity and greed, we are to them as romantic in the Volstead Act and in our reckless waste as once we were in our scenery and our capture of a continent.

But perhaps we may urge that the spirit of freedom and experiment has so thoroughly pervaded American civilization that no single period can properly be termed romantic. This is only partially true. Since the war between the states we have become an increasingly bourgeois industrial empire immersed in the business of getting on. Prior to the war of independence the settlers along the seaboard were still transplanted Europeans looking backward rather than forward and not inspired with visions of great adventure or with passion for experiment. Can we then find in the intervening early national epoch a prevailing spirit which distinguishes it from the other two? Recent historical criticism has formulated just such a distinction and two volumes bear witness in their titles to belief in the new historical orientation: one boldly proclaims its belief in "the romantic revolution" [Vernon Louis Parrington's *The Romantic Revolution in America, 1800-1860,* 1927] and the other announces that "the golden day" dawned, flourished, and waned [Louis Mumford's *The Golden Day,* 1926]. It was, says Mr. Mumford,

> the period of an Elizabethan daring on the sea, of a well-balanced adjustment of farm and factory in the East, of a thriving regional culture . . . an age in which the American mind had flourished and had begun to find itself. . . . The Civil War cut a white gash through the history of the country. . . . When the curtain rose on the post-bellum scene this old America was for all practical purposes demolished.

So, too, most recent historians have found unity in an age of diverse and tumultuous expansion. The Jacksonian consummation of the ideal of complete political equality arrived significantly in the very middle of the period, and the last barriers of aristocratic control in both traditional and newer senses were swept away. This all-important revolution, combined with sudden floods of immigration, the spread of industrialism, and the westward migrations, produced

> vigorous mass movements marked by lectures, public schools, circuses, museums, penny newspapers, varied propaganda, political caucuses, woman suffrage conventions, temperance reform, labor organization, Mormonism, Millerism, mesmerism—the martial notes of the agitator mingled with the vibrant tones of the moralist, preacher, and educator—pioneers in opinion marching forward, sometimes inspired, often ignorant and usually crotchety, to the conquest of the future in America. [Charles and Mary Beard, *The Rise of American Civilization,* 1927].

As Professor Parrington has written:

> It needs no uncommon eyes, surely, to discover

in the swift changes that came to America in the wake of the second English war, the seed-bed of those ebullient romanticisms which in politics and economics, in theology and literature, turned away so contemptuously from the homespun past. . . . The ideal of a static society having been put away, progress was assumed to be the first law of nature, and innovation was accepted as the sign and seal of progress. It was our first great period of exploitation, and from it emerged . . . the spirit of romance, gross and tawdry in vulgar minds, dainty and refined in the more cultivated. . . . But always romance.

Granted, then, that this period manifests a persistent impulse of enthusiastic expansion in every field of American activity, do we find a corresponding expression of coherent character in literature? An answer in the affirmative depends upon the recognition of the fact that American romanticism is both imitative and independent, exhibiting all degrees between extremes—to take major personalities, between Longfellow and Whitman in poetry or between Irving and Emerson in prose. The differences between these two in both instances are comprehensive: in content, in form, and in temper. But the mere mention of these names raises the fundamental question of defining the limits of romanticism. Rather obviously, an initial confusion has arisen from the elementary ambiguity of the adjective which must refer both to romance and romanticism. By the first we mean either the temper or the expression in literature of some form of idealization, of departure from the commonplace and portrayal of the exceptional, the marvelous, the mysterious; of life conceived in high colors and in more striking aspects. This we mean when we characterize the American drama and prose fiction during the period in question as romantic. But the romantic movement in Europe expresses far more than this quality; and no simple formula will comprehend its varied impulses. Let us say that it includes a recovery of the past as an effort to broaden emotional and imaginative outlooks; the revolt against tradition and authority in whatever area of human concern; humanitarian sympathy including new interests in humble life and assertion of individual rights; a fresh perception of nature; the renascence of wonder; and in general an ascendancy of feeling and imagination. And all these we may properly apply in testing American literature. To these we may add what we may call a patriotic romanticism, expressing itself in declarations of literary independence, which began during the Revolution, and also deliberately expressing American scenes and themes, in which latter respect it bears striking parallel to the first stages of German romanticism.

To analyze these aspects in both major and minor writers, to essay and synthesize, pointing out their absence or prevalence together with indications of originality, is to write the history of the romantic movement of America; and this long-delayed undertaking urgently invites the best efforts of present-day students. Within the present limits I can only outline the approach here suggested and describe the main results. Fortunately the facts are so well recognized that most critical assertions need no demonstration, and hence my assignment is to show the facts in a new setting.

To attempt discovery of the beginnings of American romanticism is even more futile than the same endeavor in English literature. Yet as definite new tendencies appear in England during the third quarter of the eighteenth century, so similar expressions with definite applications to the American scene emerge at the same time. Crèvecœur represents a significant realization of radical differences between the civilizations of the Old and the New World. In his very question, What is an American? appears new consciousness of the separation which dates from 1620; and his answer that the American is a "new man who acts upon new principles" shows distinctly formulated belief. Crèvecœur is a pioneer in his vision of a material and cultural civilization, rich in promise for all. It is this promise which, with varied emphasis, during the Revolutionary period and the years following, is insistently voiced. In the decorous neoclassical style of Trumbull, Dwight, and Barlow is celebrated the glowing prospect of future glory. In many a Revolutionary song and ballad is more positively proclaimed revolt against tyranny and a new liberty hailed with vigorous enthusiasm. Tom Paine may be claimed for American literature as powerful spokesman of the "common sense" yet none the less novel contention for human rights. And indeed the Declaration of Independence belongs to the same movement.

Among these must be ranked high in importance Philip Freneau, who is the most versatile and pronounced exponent of dawning nationalism, as well as a pioneer in poetic appreciation of the sea, of native Indian civilization, and of natural scenes on the new continent. Beginning as he did in his commencement poem at Princeton on "The Rising Glory of America" before the Revolution and living on to 1832, he represents the most complete embodiment of this period of nationalistic romanticism. In literary importance he is the greatest forerunner of that vigorous independence which is given a universal philosophic sanction by Emerson's "American Scholar" and which culminates in the rhapsodies of Whitman.

The second stage is more distinctly literary and traditional. After the Revolution the three founders of American prose fiction turned to romance in the older sense. Charles Brockden Brown found his models in the Gothic tale which was enjoying wide popularity in Europe and produced American versions designed to inspire entertaining terror. In much more original fashion Cooper was moved to surpass the English stories of stirring adventure, first naturalizing the sea in American prose and then portraying indigenous types of Indian and scout in the light of virile yet romantic idealization. Often vividly faithful in representing details of action and natural environment, he may be most fairly estimated by recalling that to the European readers of his time he seemed to reflect the distinctive romantic elements of the new world scene. Of quite different temperament was Irving who found himself much more at home socially and intellectually in the old world. Deriving his literary nourishment from the urbanity of an Addison, lacking strong convictions, and possessing notably charm of style, he was hardly a romanticist, rather a genial romancer. Yet he does belong to literary romance in his discovery of the old world picturesqueness, notably of course in Spain; and he inaugurated the American tra-

dition of recovering both the European and the American past and presenting them as more or less colorful and glamorous.

Out of these beginnings were developed various types of prose romance which have flourished luxuriantly to the present time. To the early popularity of such fiction significant testimony was recorded by Royall Tyler in his preface to *The Algerine Captive* in 1797 when he observed that after an absence of seven years he was impressed with "the extreme avidity with which books of mere amusement were purchased and perused by all ranks of his countrymen." When he left New England, "books of biography, travels, novels and modern romance were confined to our seaports." But on his return he found "the whole land" filled "with modern travels and novels almost as incredible." In the last decade of the eighteenth century apparently the young nation had discovered romance, which was inevitably imported wholesale from Europe. Tyler deplored the fact that "they are not of our own manufacture," and as if to remove the reproach and meet a new demand, the important writers of the first three decades of the nineteenth century provided the various types of romantic narrative, both imitative and original.

Within two more decades two greater personalities made permanent contributions not only to American but to world literature. Both Hawthorne and Melville were romancers par excellence, both voyaging into strange seas of thought alone, the one exploring intensively the inner realms of the soul, the other ranging extensively over the earth and in his most important work finding a certain cosmic meaning in man's deeds of daring adventure. Hawthorne explicitly termed several of his narratives romance, but into traditional form he infused profound brooding and achieved the new distinction of making romance profoundly subjective. Hitherto this genre both in prose and verse had been, in the psychological phrase of our day, of extrovert nature. He created an original introvert form true to his own character, thus introducing the recent romantic preoccupation with individual feeling and imagination into the traditional type.

Sharing the same aloofness from the American environment and the same passionate artistic impulses, Poe also, with obvious differences, inaugurated his own adaptations of romantic tale, working in his own original technique to produce a *frisson* of the imagination and the feelings both in prose and verse. In his poetry Poe transcends the spirit of older romance as he catches the new English accent of mystery, vague longing for some shadowy ideal of beauty, and the haunting sense of frustration, found in Coleridge, Shelley, or Keats. Although some of his lyric work is timeless and cannot happily be confined within a formula, his distinctive and perhaps best self is Israfel.

> If I could dwell
> Where Israfel
>   Hath dwelt, and he where I,
> He might not sing so wildly well
>   A mortal melody,
> While a bolder note than this might swell
>   From my lyre within the sky.

In complete contrast stands Longfellow, our most wide-ranging purveyor of European song and story. From Portugal, Spain, and Italy, Germany, Belgium, and France, from Lapland and Scandinavia, he brought rich store and naturalized it all by the hospitable hearth of the New England Wayside Inn. Between him and Poe the difference may be most simply dramatized in the contrast between the two poems of quest and of aspiration, "Eldorado" and "Excelsior": the one earnestly moral, with obvious human theme moving with some metrical ineptitude and commonplace rime to a definite conventional ending in a Christian setting; the other quite unmoral, seeking subtle emotional effects by sheer rhythm and melody, the vague quest unfinished somewhere in a land of supernatural fantasy. Nor would I discredit Longfellow. His services to American poetry are undeniably impressive, and he did far more than translate European literature. Gracefully and entertainingly he rendered the Indian into romance. He domesticated in mildly and harmlessly sentimental forms scenes of early colonial days. But except for the handful of poems on slavery he reveals almost as little interest in the turbulent expanding civilization about him as did Poe himself. Although he could appreciate the poetry of the new European romanticism, he appears to have felt none of the new powerful impulses which inspired its spokesmen. He was too much absorbed in the past, both of Europe and of America. Even nature moved him little. He understood Dante better.

Longfellow represents in graciously academic tone the milder romance themes which dominate our literature throughout the whole period. In much cruder fashion our prose fiction and drama produced a vigorous rank growth which partially replaced the stream of imported novels recorded by Royall Tyler. In the preface to *The Yemassee* (1835) William Gilmore Simms notes that "modern Romance is the substitute which the people of the present day offer for the ancient epic," but as Mr. Carl Van Doren has suggested [in the *Cambridge History of American Literature*], Simms meant by epic not Homer but Froissart. "The sudden onslaught—the retreat as sudden—the midnight tramp—the moonlight bivouack—the swift surprise—and, amid the fierce and bitter warfare, always, like a sweet star shining above the gloom, the faithful love, the constant prayer, the devoted homage and fond allegiance of the maiden heart"—such was Simms' own cherished formula, which he repeatedly applied to his Revolutionary romances. So, increasingly amid the westward march, romance sprang up in the footsteps of the pioneer. Over the mountains not of the moon but of the Alleghanies lay Eldorados called Kentucky, Ohio, and Wisconsin; and the gallant knights who rode forth were named Daniel Boone and David Crockett. While Hawthorne brooded over the secret ways of the heart in Salem and while Melville roved the South Seas or sought Moby Dick, an increasing number of forgotten chroniclers were discovering new romance in the rude democracy pushing its way toward the Pacific. They were not Dumas or Scotts, but they bore testimony to America's own original romantic movement, which continues in various frontiers to this day.

So too in the drama the tradition of romance, particularly in tragedy, was maintained. During the first quarter of the nineteenth century many European themes, ancient and modern, were presented in native versions, but more and more American playwrights turned to the scenes of their own history, producing nearly two hundred plays on American subjects before 1860. "As was natural," observes Professor Quinn [in the *Cambridge History of American Literature*], "the Revolution was the most appealing theme. Practically every great event from the Boston Tea Party to the Battle of Yorktown was dramatized." That the stage vogues corresponded to the trend of the prose fiction may be demonstrated by the constant dramatization of the current novels, notably those of Cooper. However conventional and imitative was our theater, American playwrights achieved all that could be expected in presenting native subjects. What concerns us here is the comparatively slight proportion of realistic comedy. The drama was prevailingly romantic.

Amid all this American adaptation of romance in the older meaning, our literature betrays little consciousness of the new powerful forces in Europe until the fourth decade of the century. But when in 1836 the little volume entitled simply *Nature* appeared, we can now see that a certain individualistic impulse of Puritanism, developing for two centuries on American soil and at last expanded by new English and German outlooks, suddenly issued its own original manifesto: "Why should not we also enjoy an original relation to the universe? . . . There are new lands, new men, new thoughts. Let us demand our own works and laws and worship." This earliest version of Emerson in which his whole future writing is implicit is at once social, individual, national. In the familiar, more explicitly national note of the following year, he declared, "Our long apprenticeship to the learning of other lands draws to a close. The millions that around us are rushing into life cannot always be fed on the sere remains of foreign harvests." Likewise, in the same address he exalted "everything which tends to insulate the individual . . . so that each man shall feel the world as his, and man shall treat with man as a sovereign state with a sovereign state." Each man, he declared, finds the world of truth in "his own bosom alone." These words, ringing with new authority, proclaimed that a new romanticism had arrived in America.

To prove this were unnecessary here, Emerson focuses in himself most of the important elements of English romanticism: revolt against tradition and authority and the assertion of individual rights, the fresh perception of nature, the renascence of wonder, and the reliance upon feeling and imagination. Philosophically of course he assimilated the German doctrine that the world is intuitively created by the individual self, which, together with the belief that the Over-Soul dwells in every man, constitutes the core of Transcendentalism. The only elements in the English romanticism lacking in Emerson were positive humanitarian sympathy and concern with humble life. Otherwise it is hardly too much to say that in the range of his writing both in prose and verse he is a whole romantic movement in himself! He combined both the varied aspects of the English and German movements in an original synthesis which is both a culmination and, in America, at least, a new inspiration of various movements.

Were it not for this overshadowing importance of Emerson, half a dozen or more of his contemporary Transcendentalists would doubtless loom up in more impressive proportions today. As is well known, several of them manifested eccentricities characteristic of the more extreme European romanticists. One went insane, one followed certain German romanticists into the Roman church, and the leading woman of the group married an Italian count! To stray further from New England norms, intellectual, religious, social, were impossible. Only in their rectitude and moral idealism could they be called "correct." They were certainly original and not conventional. And if they left little enduring literature, some of the more ardent among them dared to attempt the realization of the Coleridgean dream of an earthly Utopia. Perhaps this transitory experiment at Brook Farm is more significant than we think. May it not symbolize the whole democratic experiment in social idealism, romantic in the deepest sense, fulfilling the dream of many centuries?

Just as insurgent as the Transcendentalists but facing everyday actualities with far more vigor and courage, Thoreau takes his place beside Emerson as a prophet of individualism. But his distinction consists in his total lack of mistiness and sentimentalism. As no other American, perhaps no man recorded in history, he committed himself to the belief that "the most live is the wildest"—not in mere craving for adventure, not misled by any primitivistic fallacy or lured by the luxury of vague revery, but because he believed that "man is a part and parcel of Nature rather than a member of society." In the pungent expression of his convictions and experiences he "nailed worlds to their primitive senses" and "transplanted" them to his page with the earth which he loved so intensely adhering to their roots. Extreme certainly in his disdain for society, in his devotion to nature, and in his eccentric aloofness, Thoreau differs from most romanticists in his calm stability. He was not given to "causes" of any kind. There is so much of the realist, the universal and timeless in him that one hesitates to label him at all except as "bachelor of nature."

Between Longfellow and the Transcendental group Whittier occupies a middle ground. In his Quaker dependence upon the "inner light" he belongs obviously to the latter, while as a genial balladist of New England life and of older times he rivals the Cambridge poet. Yet deriving his first creative inspiration from Burns, who taught him to see

> through all familiar things
> The romance underlying,

he was by the circumstances of his life able to celebrate more intimately and completely than a college professor the scenes of humble life. Far more intensely than the Transcendentalists, on the other hand, he flamed in noble ire against the evil of slavery. In his own words, he was

> a dreamer born,
> Who with a mission to fulfil,
> Had left the Muses' haunts to turn
> The crank of an opinion-mill.

Out of the opinion-mill, however, came much of the expression of his intense faith in equality and in the dignity

of labor. In his simplicity and childlike convictions Whittier was a great social romanticist.

The poetic energy not only of Whittier but of other Northern writers was evoked by the growing menace of slavery. In fact the strange anomaly of negro bondage in the first democratic state became the motive force of a humanitarian protest which may be called the second wave of the romantic movement in the social realm, and which gathered intensity second only to the original agitation for human rights in the eighteenth century. Abolition and the frontier perhaps constitute America's most distinctive contribution to the progress of romanticism. Yet apart from the slavery issue the chief American writers before the Civil War were astonishingly oblivious to the turbulent and bewildering expansion of the nation on all frontiers, geographical, political, industrial. Emerson and Thoreau did catch the thrill of this new civilization suddenly spreading over the whole continent, and they reflected their vision in occasional memorable passages. But their feeling of kinship with the masses who were creating this crude, eagerly acquisitive society was limited to the small farmers about Concord. They could not become intoxicated merely by crossing Brooklyn ferry, "one of that centripetal and centrifugal gang." They could only point the way to one "turbulent, fleshly, sensual, eating, drinking, and breeding," and when he arrived, exclaim, "Unto us a man is born!"

> I am of old and young, of the foolish as much
>   as the wise, . . . a child as well as a man,
> Stuff'd with the stuff that is coarse and stuff'd
>   with the stuff that is fine, . . .
> A Southerner soon as a Northerner, . . .
> A Kentuckian walking the vale of the Elkhorn
>   in my deerskin leggings, a Louisianian or
>   Georgian,
> A boatman over lakes or bays or along coasts,
>   a Hoosier, Badger, Buckeye; . . .
> Comrade of Californians, comrade of free
>   North-Westerners, (loving   their   big
>   proportions) . . .
> Of every hue and caste am I, of every rank and
>   religion,
> A farmer, mechanic, artist, gentleman, sailor,
>   quaker,
> Prisoner, fancy-man, rowdy, lawyer, physician,
>   priest.

This is the meaning of Walt Whitman. No one ever reached out and embraced the whole, good and bad, coarse and fine, with such universal enthusiasm. In him culminated more completely than in any other American all the elements of romanticism. But he transcends previous expression of these elements with prodigal originality. Equality took on new and startling literalness in his mind; democracy became mystic and even cosmic in its significance; the academic doctrine of brotherhood proclaimed in rhapsodic accent as incarnate in the very tides of American life. So entirely committed was he to the independent destiny of his country that he dared to repudiate even Shakespeare as narrowly aristocratic and carried out to extreme (we can hardly say logical) conclusion Emerson's plea for a new American literature in his contention for novel literary forms. His own innovations in unrimed, endlessly enumerative style undeniably expressive of the teeming life of the nation (we need not explain) not only inaugurated a new movement in poetry but emphasized the realistic and naturalistic tendencies developing out of certain aspects of romanticism.

So much of a comprehensive sketch has been useful, I hope, in assembling the facts, which are familiar enough, but which hitherto have not been isolated and rearranged in the present pattern. Thus presented in brief survey, one or more elements of romanticism stand out pervasively in the work of each of the principal writers. Colonial romanticism begins in the perception of vision of "a new man who acts upon new principles," possible only amid the unique opportunities of the New World. During the Revolution and in the earliest years of the nation these new principles become more definitely and independently formulated as the confession of faith of a new society. Only in a general sense were they derived from the Old World. It was America which showed the way not only in applying but in shaping visions of political and social individualism.

In the first stages, then, American romanticism was as independent as English, French, or German. During the following decades our literature naturally absorbed ideas, impulses, forms, from current English writing. But some it simulated and reproduced in both derivative and original fashion; others it rejected. Romance in the older sense it fed upon with eagerness, reproducing romance themes in fiction and drama, but also reflecting distinctively American scenes in romantic manner. Of the new romanticism the various elements reappear sometimes in derivative, often in more original forms modified by the American environment. Revolt against tradition and authority takes the form of asserting national independence in social and political, but not in literary or esthetic ideals. Until the present generation our literature shows extraordinarily little experiment in forms. Among other elements enumerated, the fresh perception of nature is pervasive, although often failing of memorable expression; the sense of wonder is rather surprisingly absent, seldom rising to the level of ecstasy; and in general our literature does not attain intensity in expression of the emotions and of imagination. The recovery of a more remote past as stimulus to emotional and imaginative outlooks is moreover comparatively unimportant. Far more characteristic is the reflection of humanitarian sympathies and the assertion of individual rights, though these are often implicit rather than explicit.

If the evidence appears somewhat negative, it is important to realize that our literature, although less romantic in degree, is prevailingly romantic in character. The romantic movement in America was wide in range and rich in achievement. But this general assertion and more specific critical contentions here made must be carefully tested. We need much detailed investigation of each aspect of romanticism and detailed final appraisals of the relative prevalence or absence of these aspects in each writer. We need also close comparisons between European and American romanticism. Only when such investigations are made can we formulate an intelligent critical estimate of American literary achievement during its most productive period.

Paul Kaufman, "The Romantic Movement," in The Reinterpretation of American Literature: Some Contributions Toward the Understanding of Its Historical Development, *edited by Norman Foerster, Harcourt Brace Jovanovich, 1928, pp. 114-38.*

Robert E. Spiller

[*Spiller, an American educator and critic, is the author of numerous studies of American literature and the co-editor of the* Literary History of the United States *(1946). He has devoted his career to the exploration of the relationship between literary and cultural history. In the following essay, he contends that American Romanticism was comprised of two separate trends: one imitative of European Romanticism and the other a uniquely American reaction against such imitation.*]

I

The search for the critical standards which guided the romantic movement in the United States is an even more difficult task than a similar search for the contemporaneous standards in European literatures. Not only must one take into account the criteria of romanticism throughout the Western world, but one must also recognize the differences between Europe and America.

In its broader historical terms, the romantic movement in western European literatures may be regarded as the literary expression of the revolutionary political, social, religious, and other ideas which attempted to overthrow traditional patterns of society and thought during the latter part of the eighteenth and the early part of the nineteenth centuries. In this sense, the very existence of the United States as a nation was a product of romanticism. In its specifically literary sense, the movement was a revolution against neoclassical standards and forms of expression and became itself a more or less stable body of ideas and attitudes which spread from literature to literature.

The distinguishing features of the movement in America are not, however, at first apparent. Regarded as a body of developing ideas in a historical period, with specific reference to literature, romanticism in America seems at casual glance to parallel closely the movement in European literatures. When I first wrote this paper, more than two years ago, I showed it to a friend, who pointed out that, in his opinion, there was in America a first phase of pseudoclassicism; then an intermediate stage of pouring new ideas into old molds; and then, around 1840, the full blossoming of the truly romantic movement. He further pointed out that in both Europe and America there was a close relationship between the political and the aesthetic problems and that in America as in Europe political liberalism was parallel to aesthetic liberalism.

This line of reasoning is historically sound as far as it goes and may even be documented by the evidence which I shall here present in an attempt to shift the focus of the problem and to gain a slightly different perspective. Romanticism was a movement which followed a fairly consistent pattern of development throughout occidental literatures and in which America, as an offshoot of western Europe, participated fully. A stimulating paper could be written on this parallelism. Historical sequences would be subordinated to organic forces, and it would be discovered that the same factors were operative in all cases.

But it is precisely because such correlations are so easy to establish that this argument blocks a full understanding of American romanticism as an indigenous movement. In this paper, therefore, I shall concern myself mainly with those factors which distinguish American romanticism from its European analogues and perhaps overstate my case in order to make my point more clear. We can assume the parallels; let us see whether there are differences. I shall attempt to show that there was no regular progress in America from an indigenous pseudo-classicism to a mature and native romanticism and that the correlation of political and aesthetic factors in Europe and America is therefore imperfect and misleading.

II

Our starting point is a recognition of one fundamental difference between Europe and America. Europe in the eighteenth century was an old and familiar land with rooted traditions and cultures; America was a new land without indigenous traditions and cultures other than those of the Indians, which were at first totally rejected and have only recently been faintly recognized and absorbed into our cultural stream. For the European immigrant in early America, even to the third or fourth generation of settlers, the cultures of Europe were still the dominant and shaping inheritance. The life that he knew and the land that he wished to describe and interpret were alien to the modes of thought and the forms of writing to which he was habituated. In no country of Europe was the gulf between the materials to be expressed and the available forms of expression so vast. To be sure, shifting populations and the creation of new nations gave rise to somewhat parallel circumstances in European literary history between 1760 and 1860, but for the most part they were incidental and sporadic. In America, the discrepancy between material and form is the central and overwhelmingly significant factor at this stage of our literary history.

There did not occur, therefore, in America a first phase of pseudo-classicism in the sense in which one occurred in Europe. During the seventeenth and eighteenth centuries, when pseudo-classicism reigned, the colonies of the eastern seaboard were still more or less distinct entities, each with closer cultural ties to the country of its origin than to any other colony in this hemisphere. Neoclassicism appeared sporadically in American literature toward the end of the eighteenth century, but it never took hold and never became a part of our indigenous literary history. The whole concept of romanticism as a revolt against neoclassicism is invalid for our literature because we had no common literary criteria, no schools, and no traditions of our own at the time when the revolt was taking place in Europe. There was no neoclassical movement as such in American literature because there were virtually no literary traditions.

Similarly, our romantic movement in its earlier phases was either completely lacking in literary self-consciousness or was overwhelmingly imitative. There was no unified romantic movement because there was no indigenous neoclassicism for it to revolt against. Prior to the occurrence of the movement, there was an English, a French, a German, and Italian, a Spanish, a Russian literature, whether the peoples concerned had achieved political autonomy or not. Each of these consisted of a tradition of expression coming from a people who spoke more or less a common language, had lived for some generations in a single locale, had suffered the same political and religious vicissitudes, and had a common sense of cultural heritage. The romantic movement in Europe was therefore an alteration—in some cases a reversal—of existing cultural patterns.

In America there was no such common cultural heritage except as it was imported. Political independence from England established the need rather than the actuality of cultural unity. Without the background of a rooted cultural tradition, a literary movement of any kind, in the usual sense in which historians use the term, was impossible. The significant dichotomy in American literary history is therefore that between imitative romanticism (including an addendum of imitative pseudo-classicism) and an organic and emotional romanticism of slow but indigenous growth and closely related to the American adventure. This dichotomy can be followed through the nineteenth century and down even to our own day. It established the conservative and the liberal traditions in our literary history.

It is somewhat misleading, therefore, to proceed by the customary methods in our examination of the evidences of romanticism in American literature in the century from 1760 to 1860. Because American literature was, during that period, undergoing a basically formative process, the generally accepted symptoms of romanticism might be found, but they would not have the same meaning that they had in the established literatures of older countries. The problem of tracing the indigenous romantic movement in American literature cannot be divorced from the problem of describing the beginnings of our national literature. These two problems are not identical, but they are closely interrelated.

The errors a historian might be subjected to were he to ignore this fact are easily illustrated. Take, for example, three generally accepted identification tags of romanticism at this period: medievalism, awareness of primitive nature, and experimentation in form. In European literatures, medievalism represented the desire for escape from the stereotyped uses of classical material to the material of a Christian and as yet unexploited culture. The new anthropomorphic view of nature was in part a reaction against the artificial code of nature-appreciation which had become stereotyped on neoclassical models in the seventeenth and eighteenth centuries. Experimentation in form was an effort to discover new ways of saying old things.

All three of these trends are found in American literature of the period, but the motivation behind each of them is different from that behind European authors, sometimes,

Ralph Waldo Emerson.

indeed, quite the reverse. Classicism and medievalism were equally meaningless against an American background; neither had any roots in this hemisphere. The shift from the use of one of these traditional cultures to that of the other was merely the change from the imitation of one kind of material to that of another, both imported. In both cases, the compelling motivation was imitation rather than increased freedom, and the resultant American writing in the medieval mode should not be called romanticism in an organic sense of the word. Medievalism in Freneau or Brown has not the same significance as has medievalism in Keats or Scott.

Similarly, motives for the expression of the grand and rugged in nature were different, though the results were similar. Europeans were reacting against conventions, whereas Americans were striving to make articulate their feelings about the untamed world at their doorstep. And, while in Europe experimentation in form was an effort to discover new ways of saying old things, in America it was more often an effort to make the *old ways* say new things.

The usual orientation for the discussion of such movements as neoclassicism and romanticism cannot therefore be applied without a great deal of limitation and modification when the scene is moved across the Atlantic. A new orientation must be found by an examination of the whole process of building a new literature rather than of that of reforming an old one. New terms must be discovered and new charts drawn.

A suggestion for this new orientation has already been noted in the urge to create and the urge to imitate. By its very nature, an emergent literature should be romantic because the opening of a new continent is a great adventure. The demand for a new national literature distinct from those of the old world is in itself a romantic motivation. On the other hand, the earliest writings of conscious art in a new civilization are likely to be imitative and deferential. The poles of reference for the romantic movement in America are therefore *imitation* and *nationalism,* existing contemporaneously rather than in sequence. The desire to create literature distinct from European importations, and better than any of them, was its primary incentive; the inevitable servility to European forms and modes, whether neoclassical or romantic, even to European materials and ideas, was its chief obstacle.

Even a casual reading of the periodicals between 1790 and 1830 will demonstrate that this view of the movement is historically accurate. One finds practically no articles dealing with problems of pure literary criticism before Bryant and Poe began to write in the thirties. The controversy between neoclassicism and romanticism, which was shaping the literatures of Europe, found no echo in our press. Our writers seem scarcely to have been aware of it, and they formed no schools in these terms. The radical Barlow and the conservative Dwight were literary bedfellows, and Cooper fought Scott's feudalism without being aware of his own debt to the romantic theory of the "Great Unknown."

On the other hand, it is quite easy to distinguish schools of critical thought in terms of imitation and nationalism. In the period between 1812 and 1825, American periodicals were crowded with articles proclaiming and demanding a "national literature." G. H. Orians has assembled an impressive list of such articles by Neal, Paulding, Ingersoll, Everett, Cooper, Bryant, Longfellow, Flint, Channing, and a host of others. The rallying cry of early romanticism in this country is summed up by Walsh in 1827: "There is no objective more worthy the exercise of the highest attributes of the mind, than that of administering to the just pride of national character, inspiring a feeling for the national glory and inculcating a love of our country." And Emerson's *American Scholar,* ten years later, was a mature philosophical statement of the same defensive national pride.

III

In this new orientation of the romantic movement, the tendency toward imitation of European forms and modes takes the place, in America, of neoclassicism as the reactionary factor against which the movement developed. The model for imitation may be either romantic or neoclassic; the act of imitation puts the imitator into the class of reactionaries rather than into that of experimenters.

Any careful study of literary trends in the early days of American independence should start with an analysis of book importations and popular reading. This could be done by an examination of the catalogues of the early libraries and of booksellers, of excerpts from and notices in periodicals and newspapers, and of contemporary letters and journals. No such systematic study is available, but one can form general impressions from the evidence provided by such books as Mott's history of magazines, Raddin's study of Caritat's library, such biographies as Ellis' *Dennie,* Leary's *Freneau,* Cowie's *Trumbull,* and Adkins' *Halleck,* and from the published memoirs, letter collections, and journals of such men as Goodrich or Putnam. The impression which the reader of such sources will inevitably get is that few original books were published in this country, that periodicals and publishers followed the current English listings and republished popular work quickly, that the classics of English literature were still read but that books of only secondary literary interest were even more general, and that taste was largely dictated from London.

The eclectic character of American reprinting and reading during this period has frequently been noted. Importation and imitation alike reflected the judgment of the English upper middle class, and the popularity of a given author or work in the mother country or in France or Germany seems to have been the only and sufficient reason for introducing him or it to American readers by reprint or imitation.

The result was an undue degree of reverence for Dryden, Pope, Addison, and those other neoclassical authors who had become established as dictators of taste by a previous generation abroad. The American method of learning to write was still that proposed by Franklin in his youthful imitation of Addison: "By comparing my work afterwards with the original, I discovered many faults and amended them." Even Americans like Barlow and Hopkinson, who had radical things to say, felt that these things could not be made into literature unless they were coerced into the conventional forms of the epic, the satire, and the periodical essay.

Where departure was made from these fixed standards, it tended backward to the Elizabethans, now of established respectability, as in Godfrey's love lyrics, or into the late eighteenth century or contemporary English romantics who were approved by bourgeois taste abroad. Such English nature poets as Cowper and Goldsmith enjoyed wide American popularity, and Dwight's *Greenfield Hill* is a good example of the direct imitation of this school. The more sentimental of the *fin de siècle* poets were likewise read and imitated: Burns, Campbell, the then popular James Montgomery, Samuel Rogers, and Tom Moore; as was the graveyard school: Blair, Young, and Gray. And, in the newer generation of English romantics, Byron, Hunt, and Wordsworth passed the dual test of popularity and propriety; whereas little attention was paid to Keats, Shelley, and even Coleridge, who was soon to be discovered by the Transcendentalists as a philosophical rather than as a literary influence. Freneau's "Beauties of Vera Cruz" and "The House of Night," Halleck's "Alnwick Castle," even Bryant's "Thanatopsis," can hardly lay claim to being fresh products of American soil.

Although there was comparatively little imitation of the familiar essay of Lamb and Hazlitt, the American periodical essay was as numerous as a family of guinea pigs and as strict in following the inheritance of dominant charac-

teristics. Like its English parent, it was concerned with morals and manners, taste and character. Even the boisterous "Salmagundi" group could not break entirely with the precedents established by "Timothy Timbertoes," the "Visitant," and Brockden Brown's "Rhapsodist."

In fiction, Cooper's gesture of defiance in throwing aside an English novel, probably *Persuasion,* with the remark, "I could write a better book myself," is symptomatic of the formative period from 1790 to 1830. The result was little more than a transposition of the letters in the title to form *Precaution* and a similar but more clumsy treatment of English country life, which he had drawn from this and other reading and of which he knew nothing. Brown calls himself "a story telling moralist" and boasts that he employs "the European models merely for the improvement of his taste," but his novels, original and dynamic as they are in comparison with those of his contemporaries, are Godwinian and Gothic to an incongruous degree. Even the nationalistic Breckenridge wrote in 1795 from Pittsburgh, "Nature intended me for a writer, and it has always been my ambition. How often have I sighed for the garrets of London; where I have read histories, manners, and anecdotes of Otway, Dryden, and others, who have lived in the upper stories of buildings, writing paragraphs, or essays in prose and verse."

And the influence of Hallam's so-called "American Company" during the days of our youth guided our native drama into the molds of the popular English social comedy of Sheridan and Goldsmith and the sentimental melodrama of more antique ancestry.

In all such embryonic attempts to form a national literature prior to 1820, there was an almost complete absence of developed literary criteria. A largely indiscriminate copying of models, accidentally selected, cannot be said to provide a set of critical standards, whether of classicism or of romanticism, however much a given work may seem to belong to one school or the other. Imitation, as such, is a reactionary rather than a revolutionary force in literary history and, as such, the seeming romantic elements which we have reviewed can be relegated to the class of spurious or at best secondary romanticism if they can be placed in that category at all.

IV

It was against this background, however, that the genuine American romantic movement came into being. In most of the writers mentioned above, as in their fellows whom we have not discussed, there is an element of impatience with their own imitation, on two counts: first, they had difficulty in adapting native American material to their models; and, second, the social, political, and religious ideas expressed in these models seemed narrow and reactionary. Against the trend of imitation can be set, even in our earliest literature, the romantic motivation of nationalism, which demanded the use of American materials and the expression of American ideas. The result was, in some cases, a strange and incongruous mixture, but the desire for novelty and freedom, which is characteristic of any romantic movement, is here apparent, even though in an elementary form.

The earlier writers were naïve in their belief that the task of adapting new materials to old forms was simple. Brown turned from "puerile superstition and exploded manners, Gothic castles and chimeras" to "the incidents of Indian hostility, and the perils of the wilderness" as more suitable means "of calling forth the passions and engaging the sympathy of the reader" in his stories of romantic terror. Barlow clothed his Adam in the costume of Columbus and gave him an Archangel Hesperus to take him to a height and point out to him the future glories of America. Tyler put the blunt Bob Acres into Yankee homespun and called him Jonathan. The banks of the Schuylkill and the Hudson were lined with sylvan bowers and peopled with imps and kelpies, while Drake, as late as 1835, cried out for "a seat on Appalachia's brow" (or one on the Palisades' lofty brow would do as well) so that he might "scan the glorious prospect round" and "sing the beauteous scenes of nature's loveliest land."

This desire to use familiar materials is a common characteristic of the romantic movement. Crabbe wrote of the village, Wordsworth of the country folk and the beauties of the Lakes. But it has an added significance in America as a basic and easily appreciated aspect of a growing national consciousness. Obvious as it is, it furnishes us with the first and most elementary factor in our own romantic movement.

There is but a short step from this demand for an objective treatment of the American landscape and the American people to an effort to explore and define the principles underlying an American national being. Without the traditions of race and habit, the only grounds our early writers could discover for national autonomy of mind and spirit lay in what they soon came to call "American principles." One should not merely accept these principles in theory; they must be in the very bone. "Her poets and artists," wrote Simms, "to feel her wants, her hopes, her triumphs, must be born of the soil and ardently devoted to its claims." Jonathan must not only wear homespun; he must speak to his servant as to an equal.

Yet the exact definition of these principles was vague. They constituted a common feeling rather than an agreement on a system of thought. Whether of political, economic, or religious implications, they invariably conveyed the concepts of novelty and freedom. Crèvecoeur wrote, back in 1782: "The American is a new man, who acts upon new principles. . . . . From involuntary idleness, servile dependence, penury, and useless labour, he has passed to toils of a very different nature, rewarded by ample subsistence." "The leading distinctive principle of this country," added Cooper in 1838, "is connected with the fact that all political power is strictly a trust, granted by the constituent to the representative." And Channing gave the same concepts a moral and religious setting:

> The great distinction of our country is, that we enjoy some peculiar advantages for understanding our own nature. . . . . Man is not hidden from us by so many disguises as in the old world. The essential quality of all human beings, founded on the possession of a spiritual, progressive, immortal nature, is, we hope, better understood.

Liberty, equality, fraternity—the trio of Revolution—formed the tripod of democracy and erected a new man upon it. Whatever his race, creed, or color, he became an American as soon as he had absorbed the principles of democracy into his blood stream.

Four principal qualities made up this American democratic man. First, and most important, he was an intense individualist with a belief in his rights, his opportunities, his powers, and his destiny. Second, he had an almost equally intense social conscience, not in the modern sense of granting a common destiny to society as a state at a sacrifice of individualism, but in the sense that by developing his individualism he could help others do the same and lead society toward a perfection of the whole through a perfection of each of the parts. Third, he had a sound practical sense, born of his pioneering, which made him hospitable to "common-sense" philosophies from utilitarianism to pragmatism. And, finally, he offset this common sense by an idealism which shaped his religion and his ethics, his politic and his personal relationships, without ever becoming a systematic philosophy. The contradictions in these traits did not worry him because of his underlying certainty of inexhaustible spiritual and material resources. Rather the four added up to a buoyant nationalism which identified the destiny of the individual with that of the group, promised a vital present and a glowing future, and provided the instrument of common sense to make their attainment possible.

In Europe, these principles had been the stuff of revolution, the battle cry of the underprivileged. In America, they formed the established code of the ruling and the professional classes, whether of Federalist or Republican caste, Calvinist or Transcendentalist belief. For this reason, as Charvat has pointed out, the privileged classes, mainly men of legal or religious training, gave them a judicial and moral tone and brought literature close to the world of affairs on the one hand and to that of traditional religion on the other. The revolutionary code, stemming as it did from European disorder, had become the mark of respectability, the unique gift which America felt it her mission to contribute to the world currents of civilization.

The word "nationalism," when applied to this movement, has a meaning very different from that which it carries today. Recent events have given it the connotation of self-seeking, destructive imperialism. In the United States of 1840, its meaning was the contrary. Pride in the nation was pride in the democratic ideal, the property of the free man everywhere but native to America only, because there circumstances had provided the free environment necessary to its growth. The new American culture was to be different from any the world had ever known because it was founded on the political principle of the sovereignty of the people, the religious principle of liberty of conscience, and the economic principle of free use of apparently inexhaustible natural resources. In this ideal, America found the mainspring of its own romantic movement. The American man, once recognized and defined, must find his own means and his own forms of expression. That was the task which the authors of the period following the War of Independence set themselves.

V

By 1840, therefore, the romantic movement was fairly launched in America and was ready to provide the young nation with a literature of its own. The next two decades produced, for the first time on this side of the Atlantic, a half dozen or more writers worthy of a place in world literature. Obviously, tradition and originality have become reconciled.

The two trends which we have been following are still apparent in this mature literature. Each had deepened and become richer, more sure of itself, as the American democratic man gained confidence in himself. No longer was imitation a mere copying of models; no longer was nationalism a childish faith in the new nation. The one had become the tradition of conservatism, a deep awareness of the continuation of the culture of western Europe, and even of Asia, in this hemisphere; the other a bold and confident grappling with life's major problems in terms of the American experience.

Thus, in the perspective of a century, such writers as Longfellow and Lowell, who seemed in their own day to represent the culmination of the struggle toward a national literature in the romantic mode, appear to us in their truer colors as spokesmen for the culture of Europe transplanted to these shores. And such writers as Emerson, Thoreau, Melville, and Whitman, who seemed to their contemporaries to be eccentrics in many respects, protesting against currents of the times, reveal to us today the deeper forces of a romanticism at once indigenous and universal.

Enough has been said, I hope, to indicate that the search for the critical standards of romanticism in the United States as a historical movement must be undertaken with reference to the basic and self-conscious difference between that literature and those of Europe. A great deal of false speculation has resulted from the assumption on the part of historians that American literature, in the century between 1760 and 1860, was merely one more strand of European literature. Against the American background the movement developed a pattern of growth which should be and can be clearly distinguished from its European analogues.

Robert E. Spiller, "Critical Standards in the American Romantic Movement," in College English, *Vol. 8, No. 7, April, 1947, pp. 344-52.*

SOCIOPOLITICAL INFLUENCES

Walter Fuller Taylor

[Taylor was an American educator and critic. In the following excerpt, he discusses the social forces that made American Romanticism differ from the European movement.]

ROMANTICISM AS A PERMANENT LITERARY QUALITY. Romanticism may refer to a quality which is present to some degree in all human thought of all ages, or it may refer more narrowly to a historical movement of the late eighteenth and early nineteenth centuries. In the former sense, romanticism means simply creating a vision or interpretation of life as we should like to have it, could our human wishes be fulfilled. In these our visions, life is sometimes made more exciting than it actually is, sometimes more beautiful, sometimes a thing simply of greater depth or dignity. Romanticism thus represents our human vision of what life might be, ideally, not our sober sense of what the actualities of life really are. Such romance is created by a process of imaginative idealizing. That is, those phases of life which we dislike, or to which we are indifferent, are minimized, while those which we enjoy are selected and recombined by the imagination in novel and pleasing forms. Romantic writing is, then, a literature of wish fulfillment, through which we enjoy in imagination a life of adventure, of loveliness, or of achievement, to which men rarely attain in reality.

ROMANTICISM AS A HISTORICAL MOVEMENT: INDIVIDUALISM. Historically, the romantic period was one in which men's interest in the ideal exceeded their interest in the actual; in which literature ministered to their need for vision rather than their need for fact. Of all the romantic visions of the age, the most profound and far-reaching was the vision of a broader freedom—of a larger scope for growth—for the individual human being. Unlike the theologian Calvin, the typical romanticist regarded human nature as fundamentally good, and therefore worthy of all possible opportunity for individual growth. This attitude toward human nature had been of slow development, and its causes were both numerous and obscure. Economically, romantic individualism grew out of the steadily increasing wealth and power of the middle classes, who now found it possible to loosen or shake off the control of king and noble. In a second line of descent, romantic individualism came from the Renaissance, with its assumption of the excellence of man's life in this world, as opposed to the world to come. In a third, it came from the Lutheran Reformation, which had emphasized the dignity of the individual soul in its immediate relationship with God. In a fourth, it grew naturally from the enlightenment—in part from that scientific deism which assumed that man shared in the benevolence of his Creator; and in part from the associational psychology of Locke and Hartley and Helvétius, which, by maintaining that the mind is formed wholly by environment, made it appear that all men were created equal, and that a wise education, by controlling men's environment, could indefinitely improve the race. In a fifth, it proceeded from the personality and eloquence of Rousseau, who, without exhaustively reasoning the matter, simply *felt,* with all the ardor of his passionate nature, that man was good, that his natural goodness should not be imprisoned within arbitrary conventions, and that the evils of society came from institutions rather than from human nature itself. Finally, it represented simply a reaction against the rationalism and formality which, in the neoclassic age, had laid rigid restrictions on the individual's inner life. From these and possibly other causes, the romanticist came to desire above all else the free exercise of his individual powers, whether of thought, or action, or imagination. Whatever oppressed them, he frowned upon; whatever gave them full expression, he approved. Trust in the human spirit, and freedom for that spirit to develop and exercise itself—this was his profoundest and most far-reaching dream.

In society in general, the leaven of individualism worked as powerfully as it did in the narrower field of literature. Political economy, for instance, saw the destruction of mercantilist restrictions on commerce and the substitution in their place of the individualistic doctrine of *laissez faire.* Metaphysics, meanwhile, was witnessing the overthrow of eighteenth-century rationalism by the forces set in motion by Immanuel Kant's *Critique of Pure Reason* (1781). In regard to government, the romanticists had no little trouble in deciding whether the largest individual freedom was to be obtained under a benevolent despotism, a constitutional oligarchy like that of England, or a democracy like that of Jeffersonian America. Such was the incompetence of European rulers, however, and so strong the trust in the individual citizen, that the tide finally set in overwhelmingly toward democracy. By the close of the nineteenth century, suffrage in England had become substantially democratic, France had succeeded in erecting a stable republic, and the constitution of every important European state had been to some degree liberalized.

In religion, the romanticism of England and America made two alliances. Its emotional fervor and its reaction from reason toward faith allied it with the pietistic-evangelical sects like the Methodists. Its emphasis on human excellence allied it, on the contrary, with the Unitarians, who were abandoning the evangelical doctrines of the depravity of man and the consequent necessity of a divine Saviour. In morals, too, the romantic spirit operated in paradoxically different directions. On the one hand, the assertion of individualism led to an attack on all those moral conventions and institutions which, like marriage, tended to restrain men's desires. Authors like Mary Wollstonecraft, Godwin, and Shelley preached and practiced a type of free love; Friedrich Schlegel, in his *Lucinde,* issued an impassioned apology for the senses. On the other hand, romanticism was directed toward social ends in the great humanitarian movements of the age. If the individual man is naturally excellent, he is excellent even in the degradation of the prison or slave ship, and he is worthy of all practical efforts to improve his condition. Hence the romantic period is rich in philanthropic efforts to relieve the sufferings of the submerged classes. Howard, in his efforts to lessen the inhumanities of English prisons; Wilberforce, in his struggles on behalf of the slaves in the English colonies; Whittier, in his antislavery propaganda in America—all these and other humanitarian reformers assumed the romantic doctrine of the worth and excellence of the individual man.

THE ENLARGEMENT OF THE BOUNDS OF EXPERIENCE: (I) THE EMOTIONS. In the presence of a movement of thought so pervasive, literature not only responded to the time spirit, but in its turn stimulated and helped create it. The art of writing, no less than the business of government, felt the impulse toward the liberation and enlarge-

ment of the individual being. And in that enlargement, authors naturally sought for experiences that lay outside of the comparatively narrow bounds of the older neoclassic literature. With some exceptions, neoclassic writing had been limited to observations of contemporary life and manners, to satire, and to rather obvious reflections; and in all these it was inclined to exalt reason at the expense of emotion. Gradually, however, the emotions were discovered anew as a profound source of literary power; alongside the eighteenth-century ideal of the man of good sense arose the ideal of the "Man of Feeling."

The germs of "sensibility"—for this was the eighteenth-century name for emotional indulgence—may certainly be traced as far back in English literature as the bourgeois drama of George Lillo, a contemporary of Pope. The genuine rediscovery of the heart, however, was made by Samuel Richardson, the founder of the English novel, in such works as *Pamela* (1740) and *Clarissa Harlowe* (1748). Not long afterward, Rousseau, with his wonderfully eloquent descriptions of romantic love and suffering, awakened the *blasé* society of France to the great, primitive emotions. And Burns, with his command of tenderness, pathos, and broad, homely mirth, recovered channels of feeling that had been lost to English literature for over a century.

Among numerous results of the growth of sentimentalism, one was the development of a new type of heroine and hero, distinguished chiefly by susceptibility to feeling. The ancient epic and medieval romance had portrayed characters who appealed by virtue of their courage, their prowess, their piety, or their chivalry; it remained for romanticism to develop a character whose appeal was based on his sensibility. And how extremely sentimental some of these characters are! There is Mrs. Radcliffe's Emily, who habitually blushes and faints, and plays the lute in a lonely Gothic tower; or Goethe's Werther, who shoots himself because of a conflict of love and friendship; or Mackenzie's man of feeling, Harley, who dies from the press of his emotions upon learning that he is beloved of a fair Scotch maiden. There is, above all, the proud, egotistical hero of Byron or Chateaubriand, nursing in solitude, or amid some savage tribe, his grievance against civilization and his despairing faithfulness to some fatal love. But the romantic indulgence in feeling did not always assume these extreme forms. Virtuosos in sentiment, the romanticists were capable, like skillful musicians, of sounding the whole range of emotions, the mild as well as the strong. Now they offer a stirring ballad of heroic adventure, now a wild Gothic tale of mystery and terror, now a chivalric story of romantic love, now a hymn of passionate defiance of tyranny, and now a familiar essay in which pathos and whimsical humor are delicately mingled. The romanticists became, in short, explorers of the inner life, discovering new worlds of mystery, of wonder, of suffering, and of aspiration; and often they succeeded in transmuting emotion into forms of enduring beauty.

(2) REMOTE TIMES AND PLACES. Nor was the romantic search for novel experiences confined to the empire of emotion. The romanticists did not always look inward. They looked outward also, seeking the exotic charm of remote times and places. Interest in the Middle Ages, for in-

stance, had not been important or extensive during the neoclassic age. But from the mid-eighteenth century on, interest in the picturesque past, the past of medieval chivalry and of Gothic architecture, continually increased. Because of its very remoteness from the present, the past was more easily subjected to romantic idealization; so that the Middle Ages, which were in many respects barbarous enough, rose before the romantic imagination as an era of chivalric idealism, of strange yet beautiful superstitions, of a Catholic faith that touched deep chords of wonder and of awe.

The antiquarian revival—for so the movement is called—was the source of several divergent streams of literature and art. One was the revival of a taste for Gothic instead of classical architecture. Another was the revival of the popular ballad, with its compound of naïveté, adventure, and superstition. A third was the development of the Gothic novel of Horace Walpole and Mrs. Radcliffe—"Gothic" because the setting is so often a ruinous Gothic castle with mysterious passages, trap doors, and subterranean vaults. A fourth was the growth of the historical novel of love and adventure, which was first extensively popularized by Walter Scott, and which, in the hands of Scott, Cooper, Victor Hugo, and others, was established as a permanent literary form. Numerous miscellaneous works of thought and art, also, were produced under the inspiration of the medieval spirit. The strange opulent beauty of Keats's "The Eve of St. Agnes," the moralized romance of Tennyson's "Morte d'Arthur," and the reversion to Catholicism known as the Oxford movement, all owe much to that same return to the past which had produced the romantic ballad, Gothic fiction, and the historical novel.

The romantic interest in the past, it should be understood, was not often scientific or scholarly. The romanticists went to the past not for facts but for ideally picturesque forms of beauty or adventure. And, if they found it attractive to invest remote times with picturesque glamour, they found it easy to invest remote places with a similar charm. Hence they turned to Oriental civilizations as a richly colored background for romantic tales, and produced works like Byron's *The Bride of Abydos.* Or they turned to the remote Occident, to the great rivers and solitary forests of interior America, for the majestic setting of tales like the *Atala* of Chateaubriand. Or, with Herman Melville, they went even farther to the demiparadise of the South Sea Islands. The motive which led the romantic imagination into such remote quarters of the globe was precisely that which had led it to the past—the thirst for enlargement of experience, for the thrill of novelty, for the enjoyment of exotic forms of beauty. The romanticists desired less to know than to live, and to live intensely.

(3) NATURE. But it was not always necessary, in the conquest of new materials for experience, to go so far afield. Within reach of everyone, even the most urban Londoner, lay a broad and fascinating and almost undiscovered country, the outdoors. The neoclassic treatment of nature, like that of the past, had not been extensive. When the neoclassicist referred to "unerring Nature," he was speaking in the eighteenth-century manner of the orderly uni-

verse as a whole, operating under natural laws with admirable mechanical precision; and his interest in the outdoors seldom led him outside of his carefully cultivated English garden. But beginning as far back as the early eighteenth century, and stimulated doubtless by the deistic conception of nature as the handiwork of God, an interest in the outdoors began to reappear in English literature. The world of woodland and meadow, of river and sea and mountain, of cloud and sunshine and rain, was gradually rediscovered as a fruitful source of beauty. The realization grew that some of the deepest human satisfactions were to be had from the sights and sounds and odors of the open fields or forests, where man had lived from immemorial antiquity; and that there was something in man which responded to the homely beauty of a wild flower, no less than to the rich adornments of a Gothic cathedral.

Nor was this all. It was assumed, in a manner that the romanticists probably found less vague than we, that nature is a moral teacher. The romanticists were, of course, unacquainted with the biological revelation of "natural" morality as a ruthless struggle for survival. Instead, they interpreted nature against the background of Rousseau's eloquent celebration of the simple life. If, as Rousseau felt, the source of evil really lay in corrupt institutions rather than in human character, then it followed that the human virtues flourished best in the solitudes, away from the swarming centers of society. To return to nature was to return to whatever was most instinctive and spontaneous (and therefore to what was best) in humanity. Communion with nature tended to develop fundamental virtues such as religious reverence, courage, self-reliance, and integrity. Consequently, the Indians, and other people who lived simply and intimately with nature, were likely to produce splendid examples of manhood—the "Noble Red Men" of fiction and poetry. This primitivist conception of nature as a moral teacher colors deeply the frontier romances of Cooper and the nature essays of Thoreau.

(4) THE COMMON MAN. Quite as close as nature to the romanticist's door, lay another undiscovered country, the life of the common man. The conscious literary employment of the common man may be said to have begun with Thomson, to have given rise to literature of high excellence with Burns, and to have become a sort of literary creed with Wordsworth. With less subtlety, and with fewer possible situations than could be had among the nobility, the life of the common man was thought to be richer in plain humanity, unrepressed by the artificial restraints of cultivated society. Wordsworth, in his heavy but solidly reasoned explanation of his *Lyrical Ballads,* states the case:

> Humble and rustic life was generally chosen, because in that condition the essential passions of the heart find a better soil in which they can attain their maturity, are less under restraint, and speak a plainer and more emphatic language . . . and . . . because in that condition the passions of men are incorporated with the beautiful and permanent forms of nature.

The study of the common man was thus to be, no less than that of nature or the storied past, a romantic exploration. Richer ores of human experience, less diluted by artificial customs, were to be found in the cottage than in the court. After all, was not a deep interest in the common man an integral part of the romantic pattern of ideas? Romanticism approved the simple life, demanded respect for the individual human soul, trusted common human nature, and looked on man with humanitarian sympathy. Romanticism demanded, moreover, intensity of feeling, and where was this better to be found than among simple folk who responded uncritically but powerfully to the great human emotions of love, hatred, jealousy, and superstitious fear? Hence it was that the same enlargement of spirit which revived an interest in nature and the past, included within its pale the poignant sufferings and joys of the common man. Thus, as the nineteenth century wore on, the treatment of common everyday life in literature became as familiar as it had once been novel.

AMERICAN INFLUENCES AND THE ROMANTIC MOVEMENT. To anyone familiar with American writings of the later eighteenth century, it is plain that the romantic movement was definitely maturing in the United States before 1800. Jefferson, Paine, Barlow, Freneau, and Brown in their political liberalism; Freneau in his love of the remote and exotic; Freneau and Brown in their fondness for mystery and terror, all bear the imprint of romanticism. But American romanticism was not, even then, duplicating European, nor was it destined to do so between 1820 and 1870, when grown to its full stature. For romanticism in America was molded by social forces that had come to vary widely from those of Europe; and romantic writings took on, consequently, forms that were equally distinct. So widely, indeed, does American romanticism vary from European, that only within the last decade have scholars come to lay stress on the existence of an American romantic period at all.

(1) AN ACHIEVED DEMOCRACY. Among many social forces that influenced American romanticism, several contributed to restrain the belligerent radicalism and the moral anarchy with which the movement was accompanied in Europe. In Europe, literary romanticism came to flower before political, so that the celebration of freedom characteristic of poets like Byron assumed a violently defiant tone. In America, on the other hand, both independence and substantial democracy were achieved before the height of the romantic movement in literature was reached. Among American romantic poets only Freneau resembles, in his aggressive support of liberty, such English radicals as Hunt and Byron and Shelley. Later American poets, from Bryant through Whitman, turned to the milder task of glorifying the national past or of developing a set of social and literary ideals suitable to a democratic people.

(2) THE FRONTIER. Another restraining force, which lessened the economic incentive to political radicalism, was the existence of enormous tracts of public land along the frontier. Throughout the early nineteenth century the frontier acted as a kind of safety valve for economic discontent. So rapid was the westward trend of population, and so enormous the drain of labor from the eastern centers, that the supply of labor was kept low and wages correspondingly high. Hence the evils of capitalistic

Nathaniel Hawthorne.

industrialism—unemployment, starvation wages, and the herding of working people in unspeakable slums—developed more slowly in America than in England. Not until after the Civil War were these problems a matter of deep or widespread concern. Prior to 1860, America was still the land of opportunity; the welfare of the industrious citizen was assured; and the temper of the American people was accordingly buoyant and hopeful. In the midst of this environment, American romanticism could hardly fail to be more optimistic than European, more self-satisfied, less radical and challenging. The fierce social invective of Carlyle's *Past and Present* is unimaginable in youthful America.

(3) EVANGELICAL RELIGION. Just as political radicalism was made somewhat pointless by the achievement of democracy and a moderate prosperity, so moral radicalism was restrained by other forces. Public opinion in America, far more than in Europe, was under the control of aggressively Protestant religious sects. Among these were the Congregationalists, the direct descendants of the Puritans; and, more widely dispersed, the evangelical denominations—Presbyterian, Methodist, and Baptist—whose power had been founded during the eighteenth century by the use of the Edwardean revival system. American moral ideals were, therefore, largely Puritan; for the Evangelicals, though by no means in agreement on theo-

logical matters, insisted as stoutly as the Puritans upon a rigorous personal morality. Together with the Congregationalists, they frowned on any amusement that smacked of carnal indulgence, and they dealt resounding blows at the sins of the flesh. Sexual laxity they especially abhorred. They upheld the sanctity of marriage and the permanent solidarity of the home. And they were remarkably successful in forming the moral opinions of the nation. The force of those opinions, and the control they exercised over American literature, may be judged from the relative importance of the theme of illicit love in European and American romanticism. The lawless passion which was hymned by Bürger and Byron, and which became a veritable staple of French romance, left no more than the faintest echo in American literature before 1870. If treated at all, it was handled, as in Cooper and Hawthorne, with such delicacy as to avoid giving offense to the most fastidious churchgoer. And woe to the unfortunately frank author who, like Melville or Whitman, violated this convention of reserve.

In positive ways, too, as well as in merely negative, American romanticism adapted itself to American moralism. Polite literature had long been under suspicion from the devout, as being frivolous if not pernicious. When Reverend Timothy Dwight protested against the light reading which young people were prone to, he only gave voice to this widespread suspicion of pure literature: "When the utmost labor of boys is bounded by history, biography, and the pamphlets of the day: girls sink down to songs, novels, and plays." In view of this feeling, those who were interested both in piety and in "songs, novels, and plays" were moved to reconcile their two interests by making literature serve as a moral teacher. Whittier, for example, desired to purvey both beauty and goodness; he wished his readers to be both amused and improved. Now the use of literature as a vehicle for moral teaching is not exclusively romantic, or exclusively American; the moralistic tendency is present to some extent in the literature of all ages and places. Nevertheless, nineteenth-century literature in America does carry an unusually heavy load of didacticism. Poe and Irving might protest against the "heresy of the didactic," but Cooper, Bryant, Emerson, Thoreau, Longfellow, Lowell, Holmes, Mrs. Stowe, Whittier, and others were all moved to elevate their readers, as well as to entertain them.

Because of its social environment, then, American romanticism was destined to more decorum and less exuberance than European—a statement especially true of the mild romancing of Irving and Longfellow, and in a measure true even of the more daringly original Emerson and Thoreau. But the American environment did more with romanticism than curb it; that environment also provided romantic literature with a distinctly American content.

(4) THE AMERICAN OUTDOORS. To illustrate:—our conscious literary interest in nature was derived chiefly from the English nature poets; but no sooner were American authors awakened to the beauties of nature than fiction and poetry became full of distinctly American scenes. To foreign readers of Cooper, not the least charm of his fiction lay in his majestic descriptions of America's limitless

forests and broad blue inland lakes. Thoreau and Emerson and Hawthorne filled their pages with native pictures— woodlands and meadows about Concord, the Concord river at flood, and the rugged seacoasts near Salem. Irving drew scenes from the Hudson valley, Bryant from the still unpeopled Western prairie, and Lanier from the subtropical luxuriance of the Georgia marshes. Not a few Old World favorites of poetry, like the skylark and the nightingale, had to be given up, but their places were soon filled with the thrush and mockingbird.

(5) THE AMERICAN PAST. Moreover, interest in the picturesque past, though derived from European romanticism, was often directed toward native materials. Two hundred years, though not so long as Europe's storied ages, constitute no mean antiquity. The American people came into the nineteenth century really richer in traditions than many an older nation. They had faced difficulties and conquered them together, driving the Indians westward, stubbornly subduing the wilderness, contesting the possession of the new continent with the French, and finally wresting themselves free from the English soldiery. Bloody and brutally realistic as these struggles had been, they contained in the rough the jewel of romantic adventure. No medieval knight had been more valorous than many a rude pioneer in buckskin; no castled crag on the Rhine had seen more heroic defense than many a frontier blockhouse; nothing among the Scottish highlands promised more of mystery than a solitary bridle path among Indian-haunted forests. Stories of the Revolution, the Settlement, and the Frontier came therefore to form a large part of American fiction. And even the quieter scenes of Dutch or Puritan colonial life could be invested, as Irving and Hawthorne found, with their own peculiar charm.

(6) DISTINCT NATIONAL IDEALS. Out of the American past had also come a distinct set of national ideals. Until far into the nineteenth century, America was the only important nation with an achieved and stable democracy. The romantic ideal of civic freedom—at least in its democratic expression—could long be regarded as our peculiar charge. It became the task of our romantic poets to define our national ideals, to exalt them, and to broaden their application from political to general social fields. To what extent are our national ideals compatible with slavery? With the imitation of feudal manners? With the growing divergence of the rich and the poor? Considerations of this sort echo through our literature, reaching their peak of influence in the grandiose visions and searching criticisms of Walt Whitman.

(7) AN AGRARIAN SOCIETY. The young republic, it should be further observed, remained predominantly rural. The great majority of its people lived on farms or in small villages. As late as 1860, only one sixth of the population lived in towns of eight thousand inhabitants or more. The influence of agrarianism, while less tangibly evident in American literature than in American politics, is still discernible. In not a few instances, American authors applied the romantic tendency toward idealization to the materials of rural life. Fenimore Cooper, idealizing the country gentry of New York, stoutly fought their battles against the rising commercial classes. Whittier drew idyl-

lic pictures of the homely New England farms. Southern authors wrote panegyrics to the plantation system. Moreover, farm life could be treated humorously, as in the *Biglow Papers* of Lowell, or with a bluff unsophisticated realism, as in the *Georgia Scenes* of A. B. Longstreet. More philosophically considered, the Jeffersonian ideal of a society of independent farmers fitted in well with other traits of American romanticism—democracy, personal freedom, and the return to nature.

(8) AN IMMATURE CULTURE—THE "COLONIAL COMPLEX." More evidently than by agrarianism, American writings were influenced by our cultural immaturity as a nation. Ours was a vigorous, fast-growing, adolescent civilization, with a full measure of that adolescent self-consciousness which V. F. Calverton has called the Colonial Complex. In every state, it is true, a remnant of patricians preserved the well-bred, cosmopolitan spirit of the eighteenth-century gentleman. But the great mass of well-to-do citizens, while eager to possess themselves of the supposed refinements of an advanced civilization, were by no means sure of the route that led to culture. As was natural, they came to attach an undue importance to "elegant accomplishments" and the possession of artistic bric-a-brac. In literature, they preferred a stilted, formal, and somewhat florid style, the style of Brockden Brown's *Wieland*. They reveled in eighteenth-century "sensibility"; to the cultured young female, tender emotions were as essential as good manners. When John Howard Payne was compelled to admit to Mary Shelley that American manners were often crude, he was constrained to add, as a sufficient defense, "We have refined feelings." In assuming that American sensibility was accompanied by "refinement," Payne was right. Anything that savored of coarseness was studiously avoided by the culturally aspiring. Illicit sex, drunkenness, and profanity alike came under the ban. When Mrs. Stowe described a profane slave trader, she contrived to avoid soiling her pages with a single oath:—"His conversation was garnished at intervals with sundry profane expressions, which not even the desire to be graphic shall induce us to transcribe for our readers." In fine, the literature of American romanticism was produced in a social atmosphere of somewhat specious elegance, sentimentalism, and prudery—the atmosphere of an aspiring, but immature and highly self-conscious, society.

Our national self-consciousness was not lessened by the attitude of European critics. If America found sympathetic interpreters in De Tocqueville and Von Raumer, American people were perhaps more conscious of the sneers of English observers like Mrs. Trollope. The witty Sydney Smith, in spite of his sympathy with American political institutions, probably succeeded better than anyone else in ruffling the American temper. "In the four quarters of the globe," he wrote in 1820, "who reads an American book? Or goes to an American play? Or looks at an American picture or statue? What does the world yet owe to American physicians or surgeons? What new substances have their chemists discovered? Or what old ones have they analyzed? What new constellations have been discovered by the telescopes of Americans? What have they done in mathematics? . . . " Furious at this indictment, the American press kept returning for decades to the task of defending American culture against Smith's aspersions. The result of such criticisms and recriminations was to accentuate, in American letters, an aggressively national spirit. Cultural independence, no less than political, must be won. America must have a literature commensurate with her material greatness. American themes and scenes must be exploited, an American literature created for patriotic ends. Cooper's amusingly inverted comparison, "A fairer morning never dawned upon the Alleghenies than that which illumined the Alps," illustrates perfectly the national self-consciousness of the twenties and early thirties. But as the century advanced, and Americans were yearly creating indisputable proof that their democracy could bear cultural fruitage, the adolescent self-consciousness of earlier years was largely outgrown.

(9) SECTIONAL DIFFERENCES. In so large a country, sectional influences were almost as deeply felt as national. Writers of the Middle States—Poe especially—worked in closest touch with the commercialized, professionalized literature of the time, and by consequence, in closest touch with the tastes of the popular reader. Writers of New England, though they too addressed the popular reader, responded also to the more philosophic influences of the New England renaissance. Southern literature, on the other hand, was conditioned by the agrarian, semifeudal society of the planters, or by the rough democracy of the back country. In studying the literature of romanticism, then, we shall find our way most clearly by a sectional division, considering first the literature of the Middle States, then of New England, and finally of the South.

(10) AMERICAN CONDITIONS OF PUBLICATION. No influence, sectional or national, lay closer to American literature than the conditions of publication under which American authors worked. Increasing wealth and increasingly widespread popular education furnished a steadily enlarging reading public. Publication became a large commercial venture, a development which increased the rewards of authorship, but which tended at the same time to enslave the professional author to contemporary standards of taste. The possession of the language of English literature both helped and hindered American writers. On the one hand, they had the privilege of addressing an English, as well as American, audience. On the other, they were faced at home with an involuntary competition from English authors, whose works, in the absence of an international copyright law, were pirated by unscrupulous publishers. American writers, however, more than held their own. In 1820, in the estimate of Charles and Mary Beard, "not quite one-third of the publications issued in the United States came from American writers; before the middle period had reached its close more than four-fifths were of domestic origin. Thus the profession of letters was put on a firm economic basis. . . . "

Financial support for the profession of letters came perhaps more from periodicals than from separately published books. Newspapers were numerous and widely read, and though often up to the ears in political controversies, they found space for an occasional poem. Magazines were especially numerous between the Revolution and the War of 1812; but they were widely scattered and financially uncertain. After 1812, magazines which wielded more influence and showed more stamina began to appear. The *North American Review,* founded at Boston in 1815 under the editorship of William Tudor, served as a dignified medium for conservative New England opinion. Near the opposite pole in interests was the entertaining *Godey's Lady's Book,* which divided its space among light refined fiction, sentimental poems, fashions, and articles on household management suited to polite circles. Midway between these two stood the more miscellaneous *Knickerbocker Magazine,* and *Graham's,* which announced itself on its title page as a "Monthly Magazine of Literature and Art, Embellished with Mezzotint and Steel Engravings, Music, etc." Not long before the Civil War, two longer-lived magazines of general literature were established: *Harper's Magazine* (New York, 1850), and the *Atlantic Monthly* (Boston, 1857).

Authors received substantial returns not only from the better-established magazines, but from a kind of periodical now almost extinct—the annual. Originating in Germany, the publication of annual miscellanies of literature had spread to England and thence to America. In the United States, annuals became so popular that more than sixty a year were produced between 1846 and 1852. The annuals, one suspects, were more often designed to be given away than to be read. The costlier were bound in leather, were hand-tooled, and were inlaid with mother-of-pearl; the cheaper were inexpensive enough to be given away wholesale as presents to Sunday school classes. Adjuncts to a polite and formal society, they fed the contemporary taste for sentimental refinement, as is shown by such titles as *Keepsake, Souvenir, Token, Gem, Friendship's Garland,* and *Rose of Sharon.* Nevertheless, they afforded publication to many an American classic from Poe, Longfellow, and Hawthorne.

A CONCLUDING SUMMARY. The foregoing description of the romantic impulse, and of the American environment which modified it, has anticipated developments in American literature ranging through half a century. Romanticism in general, it has appeared, consists simply in the portrayal of life as men would like to have it, instead of as it is. The romantic movement, considered historically, was an enlargement or expansion of the individual human spirit, in revolt against whatever might cramp its free expression. The movement wrought profound changes in politics, economics, philosophy, religion, and morals; and it made possible a more adequate treatment of the emotions, remote times and places, nature, and the common man. In America, the romantic movement was both held in check and outfitted with new materials by a number of distinctly American factors:

(1) The prior achievement of democracy.
(2) The frontier.
(3) Evangelical religion.
(4) American, rather than European, nature.
(5) The American, rather than the European, past.
(6) The national ideals.
(7) An agrarian economic structure.

(8) An immature, oversentimental, and self-conscious society.
(9) Certain sectional divergencies.
(10) Certain conditions of publication.

This consideration of the romantic impulse and the American environment can . . . serve as a ground plan for the whole story of American literature to 1870. For the history of pre-Civil War literature is largely the history of these romantic impulses, and these native influences, as they were colored by the personalities of American authors and transmuted into art.

> *Walter Fuller Taylor, "The Romantic Impulse and the American Environment," in his* A History of American Letters, *American Book Company, 1936, pp. 75-92.*

R.A. Yoder

[In the following essay, Yoder discusses the political concerns that he contends are embodied in the fictional and historiographic writings of the American Romantics.]

It is impossible today, as it must have been one hundred and fifty years ago, to think of the American Revolution without thinking of the Adams legacy. Historians have revived the Whig interpretation of the Revolution, and they like to quote John Adams, who said it was a change "in the minds and hearts of the people" that occurred well before the war for independence began. Writing retrospectively, during the last decade of his long life, Adams passed over the spirit of '76 and the heroism of his contemporaries; instead he praised the achievement of national unity (with his famous metaphor of thirteen clocks striking together) and warned that revolutions should never be undertaken rashly. Indeed, old Adams saw the character of the American people and their politics already in decline, and a dangerous tendency toward "disaggregation" setting in. Hope for America lay in the spirit of Union, he thought, and in the checks and balances of the Constitution, which in his later life Adams interpreted socially, in a British and Romantic sense, as an idea embodying the historical cohesiveness of the nation, rather than as a prescription for government.

In this respect the elder Adams was a precursor of American Romanticism; his son, as statesman and man of letters, was one of its spokesmen. In 1811 John Quincy Adams wrote to his father from St. Petersburg: "*Union* is to me what the *balance* is to you, and as without this there can be no good government among mankind in any state, so without that there can be no good government among the people of North America." What served as an axiom of politics for the Adamses was also to become an axiom of Romantic art in America.

When he spoke of the Revolution, on July 4, 1821, John Quincy Adams attributed its success to the feelings of the American people and to the natural laws of association on which written compacts like the Declaration of Independence must be founded. Developing his father's viewpoint, he interpreted the achievements of the revolutionary period with the fully Romantic sensibility of a Wordsworth or Burke:

It is a common government that constitutes our *country*. But in THAT association, all the sympathies of domestic life and kindred blood, all the moral ligatures of friendship and of neighbourhood, are combined with that instinctive and mysterious connexion between man and physical nature, which binds the first perceptions of childhood in a chain of sympathy with the last gasps of expiring age, to the spot of our nativity, and the natural objects by which it is surrounded.

Because Americans in 1775 were already a country in this sense, they were able to act in concert to secure their independence. When they were left without an effective government in the critical period after 1782, the people acted again, "with guarded and cautious deliberation," "without tumult" and "without violence," to establish the Constitution and guarantee an enduring union. In the midst of the Nullification controversy Adams again spoke at an Independence Day celebration in Quincy, July 4, 1831. He interpreted the Declaration of Independence as affirming the long standing union of the colonies as a "whole people," and insisted that "to this compact, union was as vital as freedom or independence." John Adams had toasted "INDEPENDENCE FOREVER" on the day of his death; John Quincy Adams, at the close of his oration, offered "INDEPENDENCE AND UNION FOREVER."

Both Adamses built their careers as Unionists opposed to parties, factions, and sections. As a matter of principle, then, Quincy Adams viewed the Constitution as the fulfillment of the Revolution, a greater achievement than the Declaration of Independence or victory in the war. The circumstances of his life reinforced this kind of judgment. A beleaguered president in 1826, he seems to have had little taste for the festivities marking the jubilee of American independence. Later he learned of the death of his father and Thomas Jefferson on that very day, July 4, 1826, and while this coincidence was generally regarded as providential, the younger Adams in his bereavement read into it an elegy for his own career and hopes for the nation. Thirteen years later, remarkably reinvigorated in the House of Representatives, Adams delivered the oration for the Jubilee of the Constitution in New York City. Alluding grandly to Hebrew and classical works, he portrayed the Constitution as the perfect completion of independence, and at dinner following the ceremonies he complimented the art of Trumbull (who was present) but complained that "the heroic age of our revolutionary history has not yet been celebrated in poetry with a dignity suitable to the grandeur of the subject."

This remark was appropriate, perhaps even prophetic in 1839, just before the flowering of New England literature, for despite the many works that touch on the times of struggle for American independence no suitable literary monument to the Revolution, in poetry or prose, emerged from the Romantic era. Adams might have known why, for if he truly admired Trumbull's battle-pieces in the Capitol rotunda, he also knew that the foremost Romantic artist of that day had serious misgivings about the subject and rejected a similar commission. Romantic writers and Romantic painters were uncomfortable with revolutionary themes. Like the Adamses they were preoccupied with the idea of "constitution"—that is, the organic relation of parts as a whole, and of past and present—and with the idea of "union," generalized and lifted above a narrowly political context. The real literary monuments of American Romanticism are dedicated to "the perfect whole" [Emerson, "Each and All"], the "transcendental Union" [Whitman, "Thou Mother With Thy Equal Brood"], or "the mysterious federation" [Melville, *Mardi*] that is a replica of organic nature. They justified the American Revolution, then, by showing that it was no revolution at all but a natural growth, and they used symbols of natural wholeness almost as charms against the dissolution Americans always feared. In 1850 a thorough crack in the Union seemed inevitable and irreparable, but not new; the threat of "Disunion" had been constant, almost since the day independence had been declared, and its implications were perennially discussed, especially in the period between the election of Jefferson and the War of 1812 and then again when the controversy over slavery assumed its inexorable course after 1820. These are the formative years of the Romantic movement in America, and although it was common then to refer to the war for independence as "almost bloodless," the first Romantics did not have to be reminded that their Revolution, however unique, had the essential aspects of a civil war. In addition, they grew up in the shadow of the French Revolution, which was elaborated for them with all the elements of Gothic terror, and so they looked on the dissolution of political and legal order as nearly the worst of all possible social ills. They worried about the consequences of the liberty and equality which, they believed, Americans had imported from France, and they were not altogether sanguine about a future of popular democratic politics.

In short, Romantics wanted to feel certain that the first American Revolution was also the last, and therefore they had rather mixed feelings about celebrating it with dignity and grandeur. This reluctance was apparent from the start, for the first Romantics were all intellectual sons of Adams, and their concern for the integrity of the United States overshadowed themes of liberty and independence when they wrote about the birth of the nation.

I

In looking back at the Revolution, Romantics were guided by the Adamses and the earliest American historians who set forth what has become known as the "Federalist-Whig" interpretation. Briefly, it blames the British crown and ministry for subverting liberal practices, long established in England as well as in the colonies and legitimized by the Whigs in the Glorious Revolution of 1688, and thereby leaving the Americans with no choice but to rebel. Federalists like John Adams, a little chary of Whig liberties after 1790, nevertheless agreed that the reluctant colonists were driven to rebellion in 1775 and that they were justified by principles and practices dating from the earliest settlements in the new world. Federalists tended to shift the emphasis—slightly but significantly—from the fact that *libertarian* principles had been established to the fact that principles of government were *established* independently in the colonies, and whatever those principles were they could not be suddenly uprooted. The argument thus became nationalist or cultural rather than democratic.

The Whig interpretation allowed Federalists to admire their own heritage of English law and custom while insisting that the tyrannies of George III and his ministers could never occur again—their own achievement repaired, even perfected, the British Constitution. The first American Romantics—Cooper and Irving in New York, Bryant, the elder Dana, the Channings, and Allston in Massachusetts—were all of Federalist families, often with fathers who had been Revolutionary activists and members of the first congresses. After the first decade of the nineteenth century, however, the Federalist party and its dynasties had disintegrated, certainly in terms of national politics. Federalism survived not as a political force but in social and literary circles as a way of life dedicated to preserving national unity and personal integrity at a time when American politics was first gaining a reputation for unsavoriness. If not wholly corrupt, politics was certainly confusing to a man of principle during the period of ideological patchwork between 1810 and 1828 when some Federalists were pleading states' rights and castigating the dynasty of Virginia, while Jeffersonians embraced the Bank and schemes of national improvement. Irving's Geoffrey Crayon speaks for the old Federalist mind when he confesses, "The more I have considered the study of politics, the more I have found it full of perplexity" [*Bracebridge Hall,* 1822]. So the sons of Federalists, having no reasonable expectation of office, spurned office entirely, and even refused literary posts or commissions that might have compromised their integrity. Edward Everett could write to an English friend in 1828 that office was everything, there was nothing else to aspire to in America; but Everett had missed the point of the Romantics, who aspired to be acknowledged legislators of the world as poets and men of letters. William Ellery Channing [in his essay "Remarks on National Literature" (1830)] reaffirmed their conviction: "Political life is less and less regarded as the only or chief sphere for superior minds . . . influence and honor are more and more accumulated in the hands of literary and thinking men." Politics, being outward and transitory, reflected only superficially what the nation was; Romantics hoped to reform politics through a literature that conveyed the inner spirit of America. No wonder, then, that like John Adams, they saw the American Revolution established in the minds of the people long before the external event took place, or that they admired the Constitution as the embodiment of the mysterious unity that "constituted" the nation.

The first Romantics had to interpret the Revolution as an act of continuity because what they did inherit from their fathers was the Federalist fear of revolution or civil disturbance in general, of democracy and despotism, all identified in the immediate, livid example of Napoleonic France. To the small group of Harvard undergraduates who met to read Southey and the English Gothic writers in 1807, France became the sort of monstrosity they encountered in fiction. Washington Allston imagined France as the invader of Eden returned:

> Then from his throne stepped forth
> The King of Hell, and stood upon the Earth:
> But not, as once, upon the Earth to crawl.
> A Nation's congregated form he took,
> Till drunk with sin and blood, Earth to her centre shook.
>
> [*Lectures on Art, and Poems,* 1850]

Perhaps they had been startled by Burke into a heightened sense of what was suddenly lost and what was utterly changed as a result of the French Revolution, for they exaggerated both the dangers of innovation and the desirability of the *status quo,* and they made the strongest possible distinction between the deliberate, conservative action of America and the madness in France.

Americans in 1776 were not fighting "in the expectation that the whole order of society were to be changed," but "to secure rights which were as old as society itself." So said Edward Tyrell Channing [in his *Oration Delivered July 4, 1817*], to whom the French Revolution showed precisely the mischief of excessive freedom and irresponsible reasoning. Channing in 1817 could look back on two decades during which New England Federalists opposed France as a matter of principle. In 1812 many of them had wondered if taking arms against an "intestine foe" wasn't preferable to another fight with England. The Federalist party was already doomed by then, but its back was surely broken in this crisis, when loyalty to the Union it had created seemed at odds with the principles of social order and personal integrity it held dear. Just after war had been declared, William Ellery Channing preached against hostilities in which neither justice nor expediency was on the American side. England was provocative and England was corrupt, he admitted, but the institutions that America had inherited from England were the best that men had yet devised and constituted a natural bond between the two countries. The Whig interpretation implied that American independence from England was accidental, but the independence of traditional liberties she shared with England was essential. Thus, Channing argued, Americans could not justly side with despotic France to destroy libertarian England.

> To see [the war] in its true character, we must consider *against what nation it is waged, and with what nation it is connecting us.* We have selected for our enemy the nation from which we sprang, and which has long afforded and still offers us a friendly and profitable intercourse—a nation, which has been, for ages, the stronghold of Protestant Christianity—which every where exhibits temples of religion, institutions of benevolence, nurseries of science, the aids and means of human improvement—a nation, which, with all the corruptions of her government, still enjoys many of the best blessings of civil liberty, and which is now contending for her own independence, and for the independence of other nations, against the oppressor of mankind.
>
> [*Sermon Preached in Boston July 23, 1812*]

Channing upheld the principles of Federalism against the current national government, but he was unwilling to countenance resistance or the secessionist movement in

New England. He reminded his listeners that civil commotion was the worst evil to befall the country (except slavery). And he warned them that though we had "passed through one civil war without experiencing the calamitous consequences of which I have spoken," that was because the government we rebelled against was not in our midst, and because in 1776 "our manners and habits tended to give a considerateness and a stability to the publick mind, which can hardly be expected in a future struggle." In addition, "we were favoured by heaven with a leader of incorruptible integrity." To the Federalist mind deference and integrity had already passed from public life by 1812; Channing was satisfied that no true Federalist would foment an insurrection with analogies from the last revolution.

The progress of the war drained some of New England's sympathy for Great Britain, but not among those who were to become the first literary Romantics. Richard Henry Dana on the 4th of July, 1814, produced the most somber reflections on the American Revolution:

> The day which we have met to celebrate, we once vainly imagined, was to work an universal change in the condition and character of man; that it was to spread its light over the nations which we supposed were sitting in the gloom of slavery, ignorance and crime; and that they were to come forth the renovated beings of freedom, wisdom and virtue. In vision, the very face of nature was changing; every weak thing was waxing strong, and every dry thing green. The world, with its swamps and deserts, was shooting forth in all the beauty and freshness of Eden; and man walking in the midst, sinless and free as Adam. But alas! all that our fevered imaginations pictured out was but a dream. The physical and moral world have undergone no change—notwithstanding the American Revolution, Arabia still has its deserts, and mankind their sins.
>
> [*An Oration,* 1814]

It was not that Dana scorned the dream of paradise regained; indeed he longed for an older way of life rooted in the natural world and child-like in its simplicity, as his Romantic criticism shows. But he identified the imagery of Eden with "visionary schemes" that he profoundly distrusted, since they aimed to dissolve long established ways of government and substitute a system based on the assumption that society is "one indiscriminate mass." Dana believed that any society had to take account of the differences between men in order to remain virtuous. Too much of the spirit of 1776 denied this, he thought, and so he did not spare from his description of the American Revolution the terror and violence that orators usually reserved for the French. He gave credit to Washington for withstanding revolutionary radicalism and for later preventing the people from doing violence to the Constitution, but since the death of Washington the French influence had crept over the land again. Dana could only hope that with the overthrow of Napoleon "old fashioned principles" would return.

If Dana meant to imply that the Federalists would be returned to power, he was of course disappointed. Monroe was elected in 1816, and the following summer he made a grand conciliatory tour of New England. In Boston he shook hands with many of the Old Federalists and visited their homes; but he did not appoint them to office. Edward Tyrell Channing, who gave his 4th of July oration in Monroe's presence, happily noted "the stillness of the world, and the spirit of conciliation, that prevails in our own country"; it lent quiet dignity to the occasion usually marked by exuberance and a declamatory spirit. Channing preferred to speak in a more deliberative style which he ascribed to the Revolutionary leaders. He reminded the assembly that, though our country represented politically "a new order of things," our forefathers had kept their old feelings and character, an essentially English character:

> We need not speak of our ancestors as Englishmen, if we are not yet old enough in our sovereignty to talk safely and proudly of English freedom and virtue: only let us feel the early character of our own countrymen. Though our nation be young, and its establishments recent, though it be unfurnished with the decayed grandeur or lumber of antiquity—we have still an old and honoured character to study and be proud of; we are connected with the oldest supporters of enlightened freedom in Europe, and are accomplishing here their great work of raising the nature and condition of man.

For Dana and Channing English freedom was not democratic or libertarian but rather the traditional idea of an equitable and enduring balance between the different orders of society, knitting men together in a varied unity, not separating them as monotonously identical units. They had listened to the Fathers of 1787 who voiced "prophetic fears" for the Union, and like John Adams, they admired the "Stupendous fabric" of the English Constitution written into the history of the nation. Their charge against democracy was the same one they levelled at the poetry of Pope and neoclassical poetics in general—too monotonous and mechanical, hence never touching the heart but attaching to the trivial, external concerns of life. France was again the culprit, since it was the luxurious refinement of French society that had corrupted both politics and poetry in eighteenth-century England. As editors of the *North American Review* Dana and Channing idealized the simple, parochial life of Elizabethan England and rejected the kind of Augustan Age their predecessors in the *Monthly Anthology* had predicted for America. They gladly blamed the Augustan spirit, manifested in an imperious, self-indulgent British court, for driving the American colonies to rebellion; thus they could praise the "true" spirit of England in its poetic age, for which they retained a natural filial affection.

This regard sometimes carried the early Romantics a step further to the idea of reconciliation with England, especially after the War of 1812 had ended. They did not propose political reunion, but emphasized the fact of cultural interdependence: political separation, even the recent war could not undo the deeper, older union of a people in manners, language, affection, and blood. American artists whose careers had flourished in England were the most outspoken. In 1817, the year that Channing spoke of conciliation in Boston, Coleridge included in his *Sybilline Leaves* a poem titled "America to Great Britain," written by his friend Allston seven years earlier when relations between the two countries were at the worst:

> Though ages long have past
>   Since our Fathers left their home,
> Their pilot in the blast,
>   O'er untravelled seas to roam,
> Yet lives the blood of England in our veins!
>
>   . . . . .
>
> While the manners, while the arts,
>   That mould a nation's soul,
> Still cling around our hearts,—
>   Between let Ocean roll,
> Our joint communication breaking with the Sun:
> Yet still from either beach
> The voice of blood shall reach,
> More audible than speech,
>   "We are One."

In claiming that the ties of spirit are stronger than external barriers, Allston in effect denied one of the common apologies for the Revolution, America's natural or geographic distance from England. Later he added in a note that his closing line alluded only to "moral union," not political reunion. Clearly, though, it is the same union that Burke had appealed to under the Empire and the British Constitution—America's interest in England "is in the close affection which grows from common names, from kindred blood, from similar privileges, and equal protection. These are ties which, though light as air, are as strong as links of iron."

Allston's promotion of cultural alliance was for the most part private and theoretical; through him the main principles of Coleridgean criticism filtered back to his friends and family in Boston. Irving, who collaborated with Allston while they were both living in London, made the most influential and popular appeal for transatlantic cultural union in *The Sketch Book* and *Bracebridge Hall*. At a time when Americans bitterly resented the contemptuous treatment their writings received in Britain, Irving took a neutral ground between the two sides, opposed to British asperity and to American retaliation in kind. He assured the English of a more than favorable predisposition toward them on the part of Americans, urging them not to destroy "the ancient tie of blood" or the "natural alliance of affection" between the two countries. Americans looked to England

> with a hallowed feeling of tenderness and veneration, as the land of our forefathers—the august repository of the monuments and antiquities of our race—the birthplace and mausoleum of the sages and heroes of our paternal history. After our own country, there was none in whose glory we more delighted—none whose good opinion we were more anxious to possess—none toward which our hearts yearned with such throbbings of warm consanguinity. Even during the late war, whenever there was the least opportunity for kind feelings to spring forth, it was the delight of the generous spirits of our country to show that, in the midst of hostilities, they still kept alive the sparks of future friendship.
>
> Is all this to be at an end? Is this golden band of kindred sympathies, so rare between nations, to be broken forever? Perhaps it is for the best; it may dispel an illusion which might have kept us in mental vassalage, which might have interfered occasionally with our true interests, and prevented the growth of proper national pride. But it is hard to give up the kindred tie. And there are feelings dearer than interest—closer to the heart than pride—that will still make us cast back a look of regret, as we wander farther and farther from the paternal roof and lament the waywardness of the parent that would repel the affections of the child.
>
>   [*The Sketch Book*]

The rhetoric and cadences of Burke are unmistakably present in this passage, and the encomiums of Geoffrey Crayon on the old rural life, the ancient houses, and the social orders of England suggest that Irving sincerely admired the British Constitution as Burke construed it.

The themes of union and reconciliation, and the reluctance to admit any break with the past in the American Revolution are undoubtedly legacies from the Federalists of the 1790's. For the first American Romantics the myth of the American Adamses was far more comforting and pertinent than the old story of Adam. Looking at their country with an imaginative eye, they did not see the First Man alone in his garden; instead they saw the myriad children of Adam and marvelled at the "mystery of unity" implied and so they believed the Adamses who placed the Union above all other values. Social order was more important than individual liberty, and revolution was the most dangerous calamity men faced because it so easily destroyed what was so difficult to build. They praised the Constitution, not the Revolution. A constitution, like a great cathedral, was an extraordinary work of art and nature, a symbol of true unity. William Ellery Channing [in "The Duty of the Free States" (1842)] summarized these feelings about the origins of the nation when he wrote: "The federal Constitution was a higher achievement than the assertion of our independence in the field of battle. If we can point to any portion of our history as indicating a special Divine Providence, it was the consent of so many communities to a frame of government combining such provisions for human rights and happiness as we now enjoy."

II

Hoping to dissuade John Quincy Adams from going back into the arena of politics in 1831, his family asked if he could not stick to literature, for "the nation wants a national literature." Literature may not yet have been a viable alternative career, but Ellery Channing argued that it was a means to national culture, and it promised to be at least as effective as the government under Adams had been. Surely Federalists had learned the value of detachment from the political process whose centrifugal tendencies disturbed the Adamses, and early Romantic writers like Irving and Dana were not simply masking but pointing to their true perspective when they analyzed society under the *persona* of Geoffrey Crayon or the "Idle Man." They wanted to speak as the natural aristocrats the country desperately needed but had proscribed from office, and it seemed fitting that a speaker off-stage or a traveller abroad or a hero surviving as an anachronism in the present day should tell how much the times and ways of the United States were out of joint. Thus sketch and legend combined to produce Rip Van Winkle and Old Esther Dudley, both symbolic mediators between the past and present and between opposing political factions. The War of Independence passes them by, they are wholly unaware of any change, and when they refuse to break with the past their discomfiture reflects the failings of post-Revolutionary society—contrary to progressive history, perhaps, but not out of keeping with the idea that the Revolution brought no essential change in American practices. In these mild critiques of Jeffersonian democracy Irving and Hawthorne reiterate the Adams theme: the nation existed before the Revolution, and as an integral culture it must be wider than any single ideological or legal strand that could be isolated after 1776.

Cooper, too, has been placed in the Adams line, because he insisted that the Revolution was founded in the colonies' long experience as an independent culture, and because he hoped to find a creative balance between the antagonistic forces in America, which he and Adams defined most simply as the forces of democracy and aristocracy. His fiction swung to both sides, toward democracy in the European novels of the 1830's, and toward aristocracy in the later Littlepage trilogy; but the hero his imagination sought is in the Leatherstocking tales. Natty Bumppo is the *"beau ideal"* who transcends the dichotomies of American experience, teaching true civility to both civilization and the wilderness. Cooper's early Revolutionary novels should be read as sketches preparatory to this por-

trait of an ideal American. The war and the historical issues involved in it are really incidental, and the narratives that superficially support the American cause always discover unresolved ambiguities at a deeper level. The primary thematic issue is how to sustain personal virtue, on which society is founded, through a time when society is torn apart and men readily degenerate. Cooper was especially conscious of the Revolution as a civil war, perhaps because marriage connected him with the loyalist De Lanceys, perhaps also because the specter of disunion was rising over America in the 1820's. The war, then, is a moral testing ground, where neither side is absolutely right or wrong, and where the hero cannot be a conventional conqueror but rather a man able to sort out the moral dilemmas inherent in divided loyalty and to preserve a common good that division might otherwise have cost. He must act essentially in a private capacity, behind the central historical or political scenery, and, like the symbolic figures of Irving and Hawthorne who pass unconsciously through the Revolution, he must transcend the immediate conflict and stand for the necessary continuity of values that makes a culture whole. Of the Revolutionary heroes Cooper delineated by 1825, Lionel Lincoln clearly fails to transcend the conflict he internalizes, and John Paul Jones in *The Pilot* reveals precisely the moral dangers of the central historical stage. Only Harvey Birch approaches the ideal that Cooper would later embody in Leatherstocking, and *The Spy* was and remains the most successful of his Revolutionary tales.

This success, however, is at the expense of Revolutionary history, and the only one of the novels that brings the patriots' cause into the foreground is *Lionel Lincoln,* which Cooper admitted (and nearly everyone else has agreed) to be a literary failure. When he later wrote [in *Notions of the Americans*] that "all the attempts to blend history with romance in America have been comparative failures," primarily because the subjects were too familiar to be treated with the freedom that imagination requires, he was probably thinking of *Lionel Lincoln,* where the strain between the actual and the imaginary is extreme. One of the early chapters is devoted to the two histories—one private and imaginary, the other public and actual—that the novel intertwines: first, the genealogy of the Lincoln family, and then a summary of the relations between America and Great Britain until April 1775, the time when Lionel arrives in Boston. This summary expounds the Whig view, as Cooper does in *Notions of the Americans,* suggesting that natural or geographic reasons made separation inevitable but laying the blame primarily on the "machinations," "intrigues," and "unconstitutional attempts" of the British ministry to oppress the colonists. Americans are portrayed as reluctant to fight, even more so to rebel and secede, since, as Cooper believed, they were loyal subjects to George III even while they resisted Parliamentary acts. Cooper's hero admires the deliberateness of the Sons of Liberty, who are described as respectful in their remonstrances and bold in their assertions of constitutional principle, and as a major in the British army Lionel has to praise the ability and bravery of Americans on the battlefield even while he must oppose them. Cooper's authorial comment on Bunker Hill ascends nearly to the level of commemorative oratory:

James Fenimore Cooper.

This firmness, however, was not like the proud front which high training can impart to the most common mind: for, ignorant of the glare of military show; in the simple and rude vestments of their call; armed with such weapons as they had seized from the hooks above their own mantels; and without even a banner to wave its cheering folds above their heads, they stood, sustained only by the righteousness of their cause, and those deep moral principles which they had received from their fathers, and which they intended this day should show were to be transmitted untarnished to their children.

Contrasted with this is the behavior of the British soldiery, shocking to the two central characters of the book who are technically American-born Tories. Barely disembarked in Boston, Lionel confronts troops of his own regiment flogging Job Pray (the idiot "boy" who is actually Lionel's older half-brother), and just after her marriage to Lionel, Cecil Dynevor defends Job from the cruelty of the Irish grenadiers. The rioting and abuse by common soldiers is matched by intemperance and tactlessness on the part of the British officers. Lionel is shocked when the British "fire at unoffending men" on Lexington Green, and appalled by the senseless insult of using Old South Meeting House for indoor cavalry exercises. Against the sordidness of life in Dock Square during the siege, Cooper sets the ostentatious civilities of the Province House; against the petty rivalries of the proud British generals, the service of Putnam or Washington under great hardship and with little promise of reward other than securing the principles for which they fought.

Objectively, then—that is, measured by inserted historical accounts, authorial commentary, and the responses of sympathetic characters—*Lionel Lincoln* is a strong justification of the American Revolution. It is the private story of Lionel and his family that casts doubt on Revolutionary principles and ultimately wrecks the novel for most readers who feel that its only structurally coherent conclusion would be Lionel's conversion to the American cause. The "heir-loom" of the Lincolns is a morbid sensibility that seems to have worked against the establishment of this ancient and wealthy family. Lionel's great-grandfather, a younger son, became by virtue of a gloomy mind and a widower's grief "an ascetic puritan and an obstinate predestinarian." He left England for America in "revolt at the impure practices of the court of Charles" after 1660. This pattern is repeated two generations later with the landing of a ship in Boston Harbor at the beginning of the novel: Ralph—in reality Lionel's father, born in the colonies but called to England as the family heir—has returned to America as a matter of principle to be part of the Revolution.

In *Lionel Lincoln* Ralph takes on the role that Harvey Birch and John Paul Jones have already played in Cooper's fiction. He is a mysterious, nearly supernatural manipulator, working behind the scenes with Gothic machinery to advance the Revolutionary cause. In his aged appearance (he is actually under fifty) and prophetic tirades against the confines of civilization, he also anticipates Natty Bumppo as the trapper in *The Prairie,* but there is a significant difference in their responses: Ralph's

is to invade history, Natty's is to evade and go beyond it. Early in the novel Ralph tells Lionel that he really belongs to another world, tarrying here only "because there is a great work to be done, which cannot be performed without me." He envisions this work as a "mighty convulsion" that will shake Europe and regenerate the American continent. Ralph would be, like Birch and Jones, a pilot, and when no longer active enough to be a pilot, a beacon serving the Revolutionary cause. He is a fanatic on the subject of freedom, and far more zealous than the Sons of Liberty as they are presented by Cooper. For, as Cooper and his contemporaries maintained, the colonists acted out of principle, not against actual or unbearable oppressions; that Ralph has been oppressed in a most literal sense is implied by his responses to Lionel's inquiry:

> "Have you ever known slavery, in your travels, more closely than in what you deem the violation of principle?"
>
> "Have I not?" said the stranger, smiling bitterly. "I have known it as man should never know it—in act and will. I have lived days, months, and even years, to hear others coldly declare my wants; to see others dole out their meager pittances to my necessities, and to hear others assume the right to express the sufferings and to control the enjoyments of sensibilities that God has given to me only! . . . infidels, that denied the precepts of our blessed Redeemer; and barbarians, that treated one having a soul, and possessing reason like themselves, as a beast of the field."

Lionel's father, we learn at the end of the novel, had been preyed upon by his wicked aunt Mrs. Lechmere to the point where his inherited morbidity gave way to madness and he was confined to an asylum in England. Whether he was or still is a madman (authorially Cooper implies that he is), he is certainly confused in relating the principle of liberty in America to the fact of his confinement in England. His appeal for Lionel to join the side of the colonies is allegedly based on ties of blood and country, but in the end he asks Lionel to swear "eternal hatred to that country and those laws by which an innocent and unoffending man can be levelled with the beasts of the field." Cooper was not as friendly to England as some of the New England Federalists were, but he shared their respect for the British Constitution, as well as their misgivings about revolutionary excesses. Ralph's feelings are the result, not of calm deliberation, but of his peculiar temperament and personal experience. Thus, though his prophecies and actions serve a cause that is justified by history, his Revolutionary role is suspect: he is like Jones in *The Pilot,* who preached an excessive doctrine of liberty and whose "devotion to America proceeded from desire of distinction, his ruling passion, and perhaps a little also from resentment at some injustice which he claimed to have suffered from his countrymen." Ralph's ruling passion is different, but he too is a revolutionary out of a sense of private injustice, not for public reasons.

Hence Ralph, though he is Lionel's father, cannot properly be the mainspring of Lionel's conversion to the American cause, and the novel never reaches its anticipated consummation. In the denouement Lionel does swear that he "will league with this rebellion," but this is in the midst of a "tempest of passions" when he has nearly given way to the morbid tendency of the Lincolns. To do so would be to destroy his own character which has been from early youth a fortification against an aspect of his mind that is "a little romantic, if not diseased":

> He was certainly not entirely free from a touch of that melancholy and morbid humor which has been mentioned as the characteristic of his race, nor did he always feel the less happy because he was a little miserable. However, either by his activity of intellect or that excellent training in life he had undergone, by being required to act early for himself, he had so far succeeded in quelling the evil spirit within him, as to render its influence quite imperceptible to others, and nearly so to himself.

Lionel has lived an internal strife, with reason and will engaged against the mists and shadows of irrationality that represent the constitutional weakness of his family. When he reaches the breaking point and the Revolution calls from the side of irrationality, Lionel momentarily falters, but with the help of Cecil he quickly regains his self-possession. Objectively the Revolution is justified, but subjectively it is dangerous to the stability of the hero; in this sense, Lionel's return to England is a logical (though unprepared and mismanaged) conclusion to the novel. Training and usage have kept him from the protestant, revolutionary ways of his great-grandfather and father, and the outward manifestation of his defenses against internal disorder has been an unwavering allegiance to what he has called the "blessed Constitution of England," particularly to its sovereign and its law. Lionel could not league with Ralph because Ralph has denied what the Whig apology for the Revolution always maintained, the fundamental justice and liberty of the English system.

In another passage of historical commentary Cooper alludes to this common ground shared by both sides in the civil war: "So long as none but men who had been educated in those acknowledged principles of justice and law, known to both people, where admitted to the contest, there were visible points, common to each, which might render the struggle less fierce, and in time lead to a permanent reconciliation." Americans were long accustomed to English law, and they remained loyal to the Crown until the introduction of foreign mercenaries into "a quarrel purely domestic" so embittered them that they looked on the King as no different from Parliament or his ministers: ". . . as the minds of men began to loosen from their ancient attachments and prejudices, they confounded, by a very natural feeling, the head with the members. . . . Allegiance to the prince was the last and only tie to be severed; for the colonies already governed themselves in all matters, whether of internal or foreign policy, as effectually as any people could, whose right to do so was not generally acknowledged." The implication is that, apart from the question of sovereignty, all ties between America and England, including the *"principles of justice and law known to both people"* (emphasis added), remained in effect. Thus Cooper indirectly affirms that the Revolution

preserved the very traditions that Ralph's animus would have destroyed.

The idea of a shared tradition is actually stronger in Cooper's two earlier novels about the Revolution, but there it is also more remote from the issues that separated the colonies and England. Much more emphatically than Allston, Cooper would have opposed any idea of political reunion. Yet in *The Pilot* he pointed to the kind of reconciliation that he thought was possible. Reconciliation does not suit the main actors in that novel—the desperately egoistical Jones, the equally desperate and treacherous Kit Dillon, or the somewhat wooden American officers Griffith and Barnstable. But it does penetrate a subordinate narrative, in which the humors of typed characters displace the political and psychological conflicts of the main plot. A camaraderie of spirits (madeira from Colonel Howard's cellars at St. Ruth's Abbey) joins the English captain Borroughcliffe and the American marine Manual. They drink together and fight each other in a succession of Falstaffian escapades that have less to do with the war than with their private notions of honor, and finally they pledge to meet again as friends after the hostilities have ended. It is within the customary license of recapitulatory epilogues, we must suppose, that they do in fact meet years later as the respective commanders of British and American fortresses on either side of the Canadian border. A river marks that border, and on one of its islands Borroughcliffe and Manual build a cabin "as a sort of neutral territory" where the concerns of the spirit may be pursued in relative freedom from the claims of national service. The fruit of their renewed intercourse is a "most perfect harmony . . . between the two posts, notwithstanding the angry passions that disturbed their respective countries."

Borroughcliffe and Manual are absurdly comic figures, but Cooper carefully adds touches to show them both to be sensitive and decent men. Borroughcliffe is genuinely moved by Manual's sorrow for his subordinates killed in the battle, and Burroughcliffe also commiserates with Tom Coffin, the coxswain who becomes a prisoner when Dillon violates his pledge to be exchanged. The desire for advancement that leads Borroughcliffe to elaborate freely on the glory of his military successes is an excusable foible beside the cruel ambition of Dillon or the more mysterious passion of Jones for "the path of glory." Borroughcliffe and Manual are honorable, if lesser, men, and the narrative that leads to reconciliation in a neutral territory gives needed reinforcement to the moral theme that just barely emerges from the main plot: honor, decency, fidelity to one's word must come before national or political loyalty; when he learns that lesson in what amounts to a death-bed conversion, Colonel Howard willingly leaves his niece and ward under charge of the two rebel officers, and the adventure story is neatly resolved. The marriage of Celia Howard to Griffith stands for the larger union of the United States, and their fortune is secured by the restoration of the Howard estates in America and by the establishment of the confederate government. These happy gentry trust to the wisdom of Washington, whose devotion to his country was selfless; the motives of the Pilot, Griffith explains to Celia, were not so pure, and though "he was greatly instrumental in procuring our sudden union," he is left nameless and in the last sentence of the book is dismissed from their joint consciousness.

The themes of conciliation and union, for which there is really no adequate vehicle in *The Pilot,* had already been given a suitable hero and appropriate symbols in Cooper's very first Revolutionary novel. In *The Spy* Cooper addressed and, within limited aesthetic terms, resolved what were really contemporary national problems of 1820. He treated the war most explicitly as a civil war by focusing on a divided family and disputed land, and by making the main action the rescue of a British officer by an American spy, thus taking all the edge out of the American-British conflict. The dangers of any kind of civil disruption are heightened by the activities of the Skinners, the irregular Americans whose savagery and avarice tarnish the cause they ostensibly serve. So the "Neutral Ground" is, as Donald Ringe has described it [in his *James Fenimore Cooper* (1962)], a place of moral confusion where appearances and reality are not readily distinguished. Cooper's first description of the Westchester valley in *The Spy* shows how this setting is like the frontier in *The Prairie* and later Leatherstocking novels; it ends with this summary: "In short, the law was momentarily extinct in that particular district, and justice was administered subject to the bias of personal interests, and the passions of the strongest." The Neutral Ground is to become a synecdoche for all of America; it is, in a larger sense than the veteran Colonel Singleton intends, "an appellation that originates with the condition of the country."

There is one passage—dialogue, not commentary—that elaborates on the issues of the Revolution in *The Spy,* and even that bears out Cooper's concern for a primary social compact. Dr. Sitgreaves engages the British Colonel Wellmere on the causes of discontent:

> "We deem it a liberty to have the deciding voice in the councils by which we are governed. We think it a hardship to be ruled by the king of a people who live at a distance of three thousand miles, and who cannot, and who do not, feel a single political interest in common with ourselves. I say nothing of oppression; the child was of age, and was entitled to the privileges of majority. In such cases, there is but one tribunal to which to appeal for a nation's rights—it is power, and we now make that appeal."

> "Such doctrines may suit your present purposes," said Wellmere, with a sneer; "but I apprehend it is opposed to all the opinions and practices of civilised nations."

Scoundrel that he is, Wellmere has a point; for even though Sitgreaves is awarded victory by the author, he has certainly gone beyond respectable Whig grounds. And the effect of this colloquy is not so much to justify the Revolution as to open up Cooper's reiterated theme that the Neutral Ground is like a state of nature or lawless wilderness where power does indeed appear to be the sole tribunal. That is underlined in the succeeding chapter when the Skinners loot the Birch cottage after the death of Harvey's father. To Katy Haynes's indignant cry for law, their leader answers, "The law of the neutral ground is the law of the strongest." The same lesson is plain to Mr. Wharton,

who has determined to maintain a strict neutrality in the contest over which his children are taking opposite sides. An essentially decent but not very strong character, Mr. Wharton knows that, whoever wins, the most probable consequence of the insurrection for himself will be the loss of property and wealth. His predicament is symbolized early in the novel by his ineffectual attempts to repair broken china.

In portraying the lawlessness of the Neutral Ground and an understandable moral confusion as the result of the Revolutionary War, Cooper follows in a general way the warning of Gentz about the evils of insurrection in a mixed form of government, and of course this warning would apply to any latter disruption under the American republic. Thus *The Spy* admonishes, but it also celebrates contemporary America. As his gloss in *The Pilot* suggests, Cooper already conceived of the neutral territory as a landscape of opportunity and a place where the ground of agreement between two opposing parties might be reaffirmed. In *The Spy* that ground is the same as in the main narrative of *The Pilot*—the principles of integrity and honor that Henry Wharton shares with his southern kinsman Peyton Dunwoodie, though they now serve under opposing flags. All through the novel personal virtue cuts across the lines of opposition in the war, so that the true opposition between virtue and vice can be discerned by any close observer: Harper, who is Washington in disguise, promises not to betray young Wharton; Captain Lawton of the Virginia dragoons flogs the Skinners; Dunwoodie inters Wharton, acting according to a code they both respect, and the American spy rescues both Tory Whartons, Sarah from the clutches of the bigamist Wellmere and Henry from the Americans whose duty is to execute him. Honor and decency transcend political loyalties; the Whartons and Dunwoodies, divided over the war, nevertheless share this older and deeper allegiance. Through the confusion of mists and masks in *The Spy* virtue is finally sustained: Henry Wharton, obviously innocent of spying, is saved, and the divided family is symbolically reunited in the epilogue. Cooper's point is that the Neutral Ground also holds the promise of America; the message for the 1820s is that the divisions of the nation can be healed and its destiny is with the union.

Ultimately, then, the law that rules the Neutral Ground is not strength but virtue. Virtue rules, in part, because it is established in the minds of the people—not just the well-to-do Whartons, but "low" characters like the servant Caesar or Betty Flanagan recognize principles that are independent of the war; as Betty moralizes, " 'a tief 's a tief, any way; whether he steals for King George or for Congress.' " But virtue unaided is sorely tried by the circumstances of the war, and in fact it could not be sustained simply by the ordinary recognition and observances of society. The trial of Henry Wharton, for example, is conducted by decent men and according to "principles which long usage had established" (the same ones that hanged Andre), so that the very forms of justice constrain men to impose an injustice they do not desire. Even Washington, the historical hero, cannot directly intervene because to do so publicly in his office of commander-in-chief would dangerously undermine American discipline and morale.

Therefore the survival of virtue depends upon the intervention of a unique agent, a private hero who combines virtue with power. (In the other Revolutionary novels, Jones has power without virtue, Lionel Lincoln virtue without power.) Harvey Birch is, in Cooper's repeated epithet, a "mysterious being" who defies calculation—an itinerant peddler and man of the people, yet an aristocrat of talent in the hills and valleys of Westchester. Like the Neutral Ground itself, which becomes a proper noun in the course of the book, Harvey grows into the role of an archetypal American hero, the tamer of the wilderness. To Birch the strange, ambiguous landscape is not a threat but a refuge; as he explains to Wharton, who is terrified by the sight of the gallows, " . . . Captain Wharton, you see it where the setting sun shines full upon you; the air you breathe is clear and fresh from the hills before you. Every step that you take leaves that hated gallows behind; and every dark hollow, and every shapeless rock in the mountains, offers you a hiding place from the vengeance of your enemies." Necessity has made Harvey a close observer, a consummate actor, and "a dexterous pilot among these hills." And though we are told of his invaluable service to his country as a double agent, in the novel his work is to repair the incivilities and injustice the Revolution has provoked.

Harvey's work succeeds, finally, because it is providential. In the last part of *The Spy* Cooper appeals beyond history, beyond popular tradition and heroic exploits, to the Christian identification of divine goodness in an ordinary man. At this stage of the action Washington is (as he might well have seemed to Cooper's Federalist contemporaries) a *deus absconditus,* a god withdrawn from the world that suffers in the absence of his spirit. It is Birch who descends into the Neutral Ground, serves it not in uniform or office but privately, behind the scenes, and is hunted like a sacrificial beast by the world he struggles to redeem. This Christological gloss is reinforced by Cooper's introduction of sublime machinery connecting the Neutral Ground to the higher, unimpeachable territory of the divine. The design that saves Wharton originates in a "mysterious residence" on a mountaintop that overlooks "the imperfect culture of the neutral ground." From this hut, which contains a wardrobe of disguises and a Bible, Washington and Harvey Birch operate their cosmic masquerade. By not allowing Washington to intervene, Cooper keeps him as a hero of character, which Romantics distinguished from a hero of action like Napoleon. Ellery Channing, for example, wrote [in "Remarks on Napoleon" (1828)] that the American Revolution was successful because it was diffused among the whole people and needed no political savior. Washington in *The Spy* is a sublime, hence remote moral example; Birch is a savior, but private rather than political, and as a Revolutionary he is one of the anonymous heroes who demonstrate, for writers like Channing, the greatness of a whole people. His humility, his refusal of a fortune, and his willingness to suffer a fate of infamy or at best oblivion distinguish Harvey Birch from patriots of a Napoleonic mold like Ralph or the Pilot. For Americans of the Federalist mind in 1821 he was the incarnation of all that they wished to recover from the Revolutionary past.

Harvey is the first of many American heroes to light out for the frontier, which is his symbolic home, but in the epilogue of *The Spy* he returns to American history, an anachronism in 1814 and looking more like Natty Bumppo than ever. Cooper apparently wanted to leave no doubt about the meaning of Harvey's Revolutionary work: Harvey finds the fruit of his Westchester labors in the golden youth Wharton Dunwoodie, who must stand for the reunion of a divided people and for the continuing promise of America. The Neutral Ground is still imperfect, but it is "improving with time," and in the passing of Birch's secret to young Dunwoodie there is hope of personal virtue transcending the political infirmities of the age. Cooper's best contribution to Revolutionary literature circumvented the event, immortalizing instead the perilous experiment of union and what an Adams could never have been, a hero who brings us together.

III

Both Cooper and the earliest Romantics in New England struggled to cast the very act of fracturing a culture as a holistic event. What happened to the nation between 1830 and 1850 seems only to have strengthened this tendency of Romantic writers to echo the Adams cry of "Union forever." Poe's Roderick Usher or even *Moby-Dick* read as political allegory testifies to the demonic terror that images of a house divided held for the American Romantic imagination. Certainly, until there was no longer any use in denying it, threatening disunion chilled any real literary enthusiasm for the Revolution. Emerson and later Whitman remarked upon the lack of "interpenetration" in America, whose separate parts were not yet fused and knitted into a single web. Both of them preached the Adams legacy, that the nation would be connected by a system of internal improvements wrought by scientific technology; but both also worried that the spiritual union might lag behind its physical counterpart. When an older Cooper returned to the Revolutionary theme in 1842, he told quite bluntly the dark truth of the borders or neutral ground where the most just cause in the world has "its evil aspects." In *Wyandotte* the Hutted Knoll is a frontier-paradise, with Captain Willoughby as decent and right-minded an owner as any of Irving's lords of the manor, until the Revolution substitutes "discontent for subordination in the settlement," and both Willoughby and his order are destroyed through the treachery of the demagogue Joel Strides. These are the "unpleasant" and "pernicious" effects of the Revolution that Hawthorne in his fiction preferred to ignore, except in the ambiguous tale "My Kinsman, Major Molineux." Hawthorne understood that a revolution was always a civil war, and when America faced its second, he appealed to the spirit of union and the Constitution, defending Webster on the Compromise and his college classmate Franklin Pierce as one who "dared to love that great and sacred reality—his whole, united native country—better than the mistiness of a philanthropic theory." Hawthorne thought that by apprehending the principle unity in history and thus joining the present to the past, Pierce made "history as a living tutor." [*Life of Franklin Pierce*]. This was just what young Americans (like his own Robin Molineux) needed, and Hawthorne provided them with *Grandfather's Chair,* a child's history of America written in 1840. Its significance lies less in the narrative than in the attempt to comprehend the whole of American history and to offer a general principle that gives it coherence. The chair, which has stood through many vicissitudes of government, is a symbol of historical continuity; in his preface Hawthorne explains the mechanism of that continuity. The American past is seen as a dialectical process, an epoch of stern asceticism followed by an antithetical epoch of worldliness and military adventure. The epoch of the Revolution itself, Hawthorne suggests, is a period of synthesis and integration, in which opposite energies are fused in an ascendant nation: "Perhaps, in a third Epoch, we shall find in individuals, and the people at large, a combination of ideal principle and adventurous action. . . ." In the narrative, then, Hawthorne stresses the way men differing widely in character or class were brought together in the Revolution, and how the people, who acted first as a mob, grew calm and orderly under the influence of wise leaders. Quite in character with his creator, Grandfather skimps the details of the war after the British have evacuated Boston. But one important fact is underlined. When one of the children asks who governed Massachusetts until its constitution was settled upon in 1780, Grandfather replies that the Legislature ruled and "the people paid obedience of their own accord": "It is one of the most remarkable circumstances in our history, that, when the charter government was overthrown by the war, no anarchy nor the slightest confusion ensued. This was a great honor to the people." This wonderful, apparently spontaneous deference, which gave society unity and order instead of anarchy and confusion, was for Hawthorne the finest achievement of the Revolutionary epoch.

Fear of social disorder and faith in the orderliness of nature left later American Romantics really no choice but to follow their predecessors and diffuse the Revolution into its own past. Hurtling toward the abyss of 1861, they clutched the Adams talisman—their independence was the corollary of their union, established well before 1776 and guaranteed by the Revolutionary epoch ending in the Constitution—and long afterwards they clung to the myth of a conservative, dialectically conciliatory democracy. The man who insured the efficacy of this myth, and who may have provided the broad outlines of Hawthorne's American history, was both a first and a last Romantic. Born in 1800 and in the midst of his *Wanderjahre* when Romantic ideas were taking hold in New England, George Bancroft was a thoroughgoing democrat for nearly all of his long life; but like Hawthorne and other literary men who had intermittently served Jacksonian interests, he was not bound to Jackson's brand of populism, and, most important, he never threw off the aesthetic perspective of his literary youth. Thinking himself a failure as a poet, he nevertheless aspired to be a poetic and Emersonian scholar, to be among the "great high-priests of nature who unfold truths of universal importance, discover powers which give man mastery over his destiny." This early Romanticism tempered his politics and eventually directed his comprehensive approach to American history.

Bancroft's 4th of July oration at Northampton in 1826 is often taken as his first enunciation of *vox populi, vox dei,*

the spirit that oversees his *History of the United States.* While that is probably true, it is important to note the terms in which Bancroft describes the voice of the people, for they are crucial and remained consistent throughout his work:

> The popular voice is all powerful with us; this is our oracle; this, we acknowledge, is the voice of God. Invention is solitary; but who shall judge of its results? Inquiry may pursue truth apart; but who shall decide, if truth is overtaken? There is no safe criterion of opinion but the careful exercise of the public judgment; and in the science of government as elsewhere, the deliberate convictions of mankind, reasoning on the cause of their own happiness, their own wants and interests, are the surest revelations of political truth.

"Careful" and "deliberate" are Bancroft's favorite adjectives in this context, and already they imply that the people must be conceived temporally rather than formally or numerically, and that their judgment is a gradual, winnowing process, not a poll or tally on any one occasion. At Williamstown in 1835 Bancroft was even more explicit in praising the people for the "natural dialectics" that made them act with moderation and resist innovation or frequent change.

> True political science does indeed venerate the masses. It maintains, not as has been perversely asserted, that "the people can make right," but that the people can DISCERN right. Individuals are but shadows, too often engrossed by the pursuits of shadows; the race is immortal: individuals are of limited sagacity; the common mind is infinite in its experience: individuals are languid and blind; the many are ever wakeful: individuals are corrupt; the race has been redeemed. . . . Truth is not to be ascertained by the impulses of an individual; it emerges from the contradictions of personal opinions; it raises itself in majestic serenity above the strifes of parties and the conflict of sects; it acknowledges neither the solitary mind, nor the separate faction as its oracle; but owns as its only faithful interpreter the dictates of pure reason itself, proclaimed by the general voice of mankind.

Unity and continuity, then, are requisites to a people's perception of truth. Here Bancroft approaches Burke's own definition of a nation as "an idea of continuity, which extends in time as well as in numbers and space." Both Burke and Bancroft distinguish between the individual and the species in almost identical language; the difference is that Bancroft, like John Adams, was able to conceive of the process as more rational and universal than Burke would ever admit.

Yet Bancroft's idea of reason was tinged by post-Kantian German idealism and what Burke called the "method of nature." In his *History* there are many instances of the people's firm and tranquil movement, but none so remarkable as the one that Hawthorne also had singled out, the way Massachusetts created her own government at the time of the Revolution. In 1774 Massachusetts, desiring to "guard against anarchy," had instituted a government of its own, and again in 1775, after the war had begun, the

Herman Melville.

people elected a representative government "according to their usage and their charter." Completing the last volumes of the *History* after the Civil War, Bancroft focused on the way the Massachusetts constitutional convention acted to preserve all former laws and still reject the institution of slavery:

> The history of the world contains no record of a people which in the institution of its government moved with the caution which now marked the proceedings of Massachusetts. . . . So calm and effortless was the act by which slavery fell away from Massachusetts. Its people wrought with the power of nature, which never toils, never employs violence in arms, but achieves its will through the might of overruling law. There is in the world a force tending to improvement, and making itself felt in us and around us, with which we can work, but which it is above our ability to call into being or to destroy.

Bancroft's rhetoric rides on universals and an unflagging optimism, but beneath that is his essential agreement with Burke and the English tradition of common law, that decreed laws simply cannot violate natural law: in Bancroft's words, slavery was doomed by history, even though few in 1776 recognized "that an ordinance of man can never override natural law, and that in the high court of Eternal

Providence justice forges her weapons long before she strikes."

For all his insistence that liberty was the transcendent, vital principle of world history since the Reformation, Bancroft was also able to imagine the American past as a conflict of forces, neither of which is good or bad, working toward a conciliatory harmony rather than the triumph of a single principle. This more relativist view derives from Bancroft's idea, expressed in "The Office of the People," that truth emerges from the contradictions of opinion. In his 1854 address to the New York Historical Society he elaborated from this idea an historical dialectic consonant with the aesthetic theories of the American Romantics and in particular with Hawthorne's figure of a neutral territory where the actual and the ideal meet. "The course of human destiny is ever a rope of three strands," Bancroft's figure began;

> Without all three, the fates could not spin their thread. As the motions of the solar world require the centripetal force, which, by itself alone, would consolidate all things in one massive confusion; the centrifugal force, which, if uncontrolled, would hurl the planets on a tangent into infinite space; and lastly, that reconciling adjustment, which preserves the two powers in harmony; so society always has within itself the elements of conservatism, of absolute right, and of reform.

And in a passage that sounds as much like Emerson's "Fate" as Bancroft's earlier evocation of the scholar-poet resembled young Emerson's American Scholar, Bancroft once again assured his audience of ultimate harmony in the movement of the spheres, though individual mortals might not hear it:

> The system of the universe is as a celestial poem, whose beauty is from all eternity, and must not be marred by human interpolations. Things proceed as they were ordered, in their nice, and well-adjusted, and perfect harmony; so that as the hand of the skilful artist gathers music from the harp-strings, history calls it forth from the well-tuned chords of time. Not that this harmony can be heard during the tumult of action. Philosophy comes after events, and gives the reason of them, and describes the nature of their results. The great mind of collective man may, one day, so improve in self-consciousness as to interpret the present and foretell the future; but as yet, the end of what is now happening, though we ourselves partake in it, seems to fall out by chance. All is nevertheless one whole; individuals, families, peoples, the race, march in accord with the Divine will; and when any part of the destiny of humanity is fulfilled, we see the ways of Providence vindicated. The antagonisms of imperfect matter and the perfect idea, of liberty and necessary law, become reconciled. What seemed irrational confusion, appears as the web woven by light, liberty and love. But this is not perceived till a great act in the drama of life is finished.

The office of the historian, then, is to put the finishing, artistic touch to the drama of life by showing that freedom and necessity are reconciled in this beneficent web.

Two years before this speech Bancroft had published the first volumes of his *History* that treat the era of the Revolution. He conceived it in the broadest context as representing the progress of universal reason, not just because it secured the principle of government by ever-renewed consent of the people but also because it demonstrated the inevitable and increasing "connection" of cultures throughout the world. In his 1836 4th of July oration at Springfield Bancroft had amended the Adams cry to "union and progress," and in 1852 that rule took on even larger proportions: "for the world of mankind does not exist in fragments, nor can a country have an insulated existence. . . . The very idea of the progress of an individual people, in its relation to universal history springs from the acknowledged unity of the race." American progress, moreover, was never radically disjunctive: "Its political edifice rose in lovely proportions, as if to the melodies of the lyre," because it built upon the past and not upon theory alone. Quoting Pascal on the union of all human generations in "one identical man," Bancroft acknowledged that there can be no progress without continuity.

> It is this idea of continuity which gives vitality to history. No period of time has a separate being; no public opinion can escape the influence of previous intelligence. We are cheered by rays from former centuries, and live in the sunny reflection of all their light. . . . We are the children and the heirs of the past, with which, as with the future, we are indissolubly linked together; and he that truly has sympathy with every thing belonging to man, will, with his toils for posterity, blend affection for the times that are gone by, and seek to live in the vast life of the ages. It is by thankfully recognising those ages as a part of the great existence in which we share, that history wins power to move the soul.

Romantic poets like Dana or Bryant could not quarrel with this passage. The fact is that Bancroft's progressivism was organic and conciliatory, and though he chastised Burke for clinging to old and really transient theories, he too sanctified the past because permanent truths are there beside transient ones, and can be observed gaining wider recognition and embodiment in the historical process.

By 1860 the dialectic Bancroft expounded in 1854 was clearly guiding his *History of the United States*. Equating the development of political institutions with that of natural phenomena, Bancroft analyzed the social organism into its "three strands": "Law which restrains all, and freedom which adheres to each individual, and the mediation which adjusts and connects these two conflicting powers." In its most general structure, government is composed of opposite tendencies, "attraction" opposed to "repulsion," or "central power" opposed to "individuality," and without an established balance between the two, civil order would disintegrate. Applying this theory to the issue between Britain and America, Bancroft gave the classic Whig exposition: George III (whom Bancroft called "the author of American independence") and his ministers chose to enforce an extreme despotism rather than to reform, according to long established principles of representation, government in the colonies and at home; thus civil order was inevitably dissolved, and the Ameri-

cans went reluctantly to war in order to repair the balance of the constitution they had long shared with the English people. The Declaration of Independence, wrote Bancroft, promulgates universal and eternal rights, but at the same time "avoiding specious and vague generalities, grounds itself with anxious care upon the past, and reconciles right and fact." The reconciliation is crucial to Bancroft's vision of order in history.

As Romantic historian, his theory matured and he reached the climax of his one great work just as the United States came to the edge of civil war. It is therefore not surprising that Bancroft, like Hawthorne, reconstructed the Revolutionary period as primarily a time of synthesis and "connection." The strands of American destiny, as Bancroft presents them, do not readily fit the labels "conservatism" and "absolute right" that he used in the 1854 speech on the progress of mankind, but there are clearly "centrifugal" and "centripetal" tendencies, toward absolute individual liberty on the one hand and toward national consolidation on the other.

Bancroft defined the two major phases of American history—from the discovery to 1688, and from 1688 to 1776—according to these tendencies. The second volume closed with this explicit distinction: "The period through which we have passed shows why we are a free people; the coming period will show why we are a unified people." He also recognized a natural antagonism between them. Men, especially uneducated men in a hardly settled land, are quick to defend their independence but "less capable of union and perseverance." Part of the precedent for American liberty was the reluctance of its colonies to join together; of Franklin's plan for union in 1754, Bancroft wrote, "The fervid attachment of each colony to its own individual liberties repelled the overruling influence of a central power. Yet central authority was necessary to the preservation of liberty, even when it impinged on some individual liberties. Thus Bancroft explained the early religious intolerance of the Puritan theocracy, a "system inflexibly established and regarded as the only adequate guarantee of the rising liberties of Massachusetts"—Massachusetts, an organism convalescing, not yet in full health, could not tolerate the risk of greater freedom or new infections of English oppression. Until the era of the Revolution the idea of a union and consolidation of authority remained an effective but not wholly desirable remedy against aggression by the Indians and French and by the British themselves.

The Revolutionary War, however, made confederation an obvious necessity, the more obvious to Bancroft who looked back on it from the perspective of the Civil War. He turned again to the language that had excused the Puritan theocracy. Traditions of local liberty and the spirit of separatism—especially "a dread of interference with the peculiar institutions of each colony—darkened the prospect "of that energetic authority which is the first guaranty of liberty." Although he alluded to the differences between North and South, Bancroft acknowledged the historical resistance in all of the colonies to "an overruling central force," which the people believed was inherently hostile to "their vital principle of self-direction." The people could not see how authority guaranteed liberty, and in the first efforts to form a constitution they jealously withheld the power of taxation from the confederated government. To deny authority to fairly elected representatives as if they were no different from an hereditary king or corrupt parliament was, in Bancroft's view, to sink "back into bondage to the past." Clearly the vital principle of individuality needed to be tempered by the development of unified or centralized organization that perpetuates life in the whole.

But the giant, generative process that Bancroft made of history was not yet ready to be delivered of such a union. The birth of a nation in 1776 was in this sense premature, because the nation was little more than a "chaotic mass" in which only the "rudiments of a spinal cord" could be discerned. "The child that was then born was cradled between opposing powers of evil"—so Bancroft raised his narrative to mythic level—"if it will live, its infant strength must strangle the twin serpents of separatism and central despotism." Bancroft's serpents are centrifugal and centripetal forces in their extreme, unmodified forms. In 1776 the people, on whom History had long relied, distrusted Congress, and Bancroft was persuaded that Congress merited distrust; neither could be father to this young country, which needed a national regulating principle to modify and balance the extremes within it. Precisely that became Washington's office, according to every Romantic summary of his career: Bancroft concurred in the judgment of literary men that Washington was above all a hero of character, whose providential role had been to unite the colonies by "combining the centripetal and the centrifugal forces in their utmost strength and in perfect relations."

It can hardly be said that Bancroft avoided details of the Revolutionary War as Hawthorne did, or that he ever sidetracked the ideological oppositions as Cooper had in his novels. But, to use his own expression, the vital force seems to be lost in his long chronicle of battles, probably because Bancroft believed that liberty was inevitable in America, that it was rooted so deep that even British victory could not eradicate it, and because the historian of inevitability must always be ahead of himself, sowing seeds of a future epoch while those already planted are yielding fruit. Thus in the war narrative Bancroft's underlying, dynamic principle is no longer liberty but Washington's crusade for union. Washington was far ahead of the people or Congress in his conception of national unity, and the most significant interruptions and authorial comments in the War volumes deal with Washington's unflagging defense of union against the entrenched principle of local sovereignty or against the self-interest of factions and the cabal. Washington once compared the emerging union to the mechanism of one great clock, only lacking a mainspring; for Bancroft Washington was that mainspring or regulating principle because he saw what Bancroft saw in the history of politics, namely, the interdependency of opposites like liberty and authority.

By the time Bancroft came to write about the end of the war he knew that the history of the American Revolution could not end there. The last sentences of his tenth volume, published in 1874, point to the fulfillment of his dialectical process. The Revolution would be completed only when the "organization" of the United States caught up with its "vital force," when individual liberty was tempered by the authority of the whole; this was the "reconciling adjustment" that, according to Bancroft's theory of 1854, would preserve opposing forces in harmony and make possible an enduring union. The Constitution was a great compromise between stability and progress, between freedom and authority, and although the subject of its formation is inherently less dramatic than the Revolutionary War, Bancroft orchestrated it with his grand theme of the connection and ultimate identity of all men. At the culmination of his work he stood beside Emerson and Whitman as a poetic high-priest, unfolding the lesson of transcendent union, and eliciting truth from the critical period of the new nation that his own age of crisis badly needed to hear. In his extraordinary summary Bancroft imagined the Constitution as a fully developed spinal cord or central nervous system regulating a whole organism, and again as an instrument of musical harmony:

> The states and the United States are members of one great whole; and the one is as needful as the other. The powers of government are not divided between them; they are distributed; so that there need be no collision in their exercise. The union without self-existent states is a harp without strings; the states without union are as chords that are unstrung. . . . In short, the constitution knows nothing of United States alone, or states alone; it adjusts the parts harmoniously in an organized unity. Impair the relations or the vigor of any part, and disease enters into the veins of the whole. That there may be life in the whole, there must be healthy life in every part. The United States are the states in union; these are so inwrought into the constitution that the one cannot perish without the other.

Bancroft's dialectic of opposing forces that must be modified to work as a bipolar unity takes its final form in the constitutional relationship between the states and the federal government. The whole is a self-regulating system able to adapt itself to changes but always according to the tranquil, circumspect pace of the people.

> To perfect the system and forever prevent revolution, power is reserved to the people by amendments of their constitution to remove every imperfection which time may lay bare, and adapt it to unforeseen contingencies. But no change can be hastily made. . . . America, being charged with the preservation of liberty, has the most conservative polity in the world, both in its government and in its people. . . .

> For Europe, there remained the sad necessity of revolution. For America the gates of revolution are shut and barred and bolted down, never again to be thrown open.

With this conclusion to the work of an entire lifetime, George Bancroft gave to the American Revolution the dignity and grandeur that the Adamses and their contemporaries thought fitting. Both John Adams and Quincy Adams wanted to be Orpheus or Amphion to their country, but they could not be legislators and poets, too. Bancroft understood the vocation of the artist in America as the first Romantics had conceived it. Adapting the role of scholar to the higher calling of the Orphic Poet, he plied the lyre of Union and would have tamed every faction with his litany of conservative, historical democracy. The fulfillment of the Revolution was to "forever prevent revolution." Grass had grown over the graves of Revolutionaries and Romantics alike by 1885, when the old historian finally assured that their rest would be undisturbed.

R. A. Yoder, "The First Romantics and the Last Revolution," in Studies in Romanticism, *Vol. 15, No. 4, Fall, 1976, pp. 493-529.*

Russel Blaine Nye on Romanticism and nationalism in America:

Romanticism and nationalism in American literature . . . developed together—unlike Europe, where England, France, Germany, and Spain already possessed strongly identifiable national characteristics before Romanticism came. In the United States, which had no native literary tradition, the Romantic movement supplied both means and vehicle for creating one. True, American Romanticism drew its central ideas from British and European sources—from Wordsworth, Coleridge, and Carlyle in England; from Herder, Schelling, and the Schlegels in Germany; from Taine and others in France. Traces of nearly every major Romantic critic or philosopher could be found in the essays and reviews published in American periodicals after 1820. But American critics and authors put these ideas to their own uses. The American variety of Romanticism was not simply a mélange of British and European principles and practices transported across the Atlantic, for though Americans may have imported them, they utilized them within an American environment, and within the context of a different past.

Russel Blaine Nye, in his Society and Culture in America: 1830-1860, *Harper & Row, 1974.*

ROMANTICISM AND THE AMERICAN FRONTIER

Bernard Rosenthal

[*In the following excerpt, Rosenthal contends that American Romantic authors used the conquest of the American wilderness as a metaphor for a personal quest for spiritual regeneration.*]

The common denominator of American Romanticism, probably of all Romanticism, may be found in the attempt to create a private world free from the constraints of time and history. Romantic writers want to reject predestina-

tion, mechanism, or any theory of history that denies individual preeminence in the shaping of events. Accordingly, in articulating a theory of history, Emerson found an understandable appeal in a rhetorical question Napoleon asked: "What is history . . . but a fable agreed upon?" In the same essay, "History" (1841), Emerson further concludes that "All history becomes subjective; in other words there is properly no history, only biography." If history as an absolute process could be turned to private biography, malleable in the mind of the poet, the individual would be free to enter a world of infinite possibility—the location of Romanticism.

But the Romantic writer is also compelled to acknowledge the constraints imposed by linear history, as Emerson indeed does in "History":

> But along with the civil and metaphysical history of man, another history goes daily forward—that of the external world—in which he is not less strictly implicated. He is the compend of time; he is also the correlative of nature. His power consists in the multitude of his affinities, in the fact that his life is intertwined with the whole chain of organic and inorganic being.

Out of the vast quantity of critical study on American Romanticism, agreement has emerged on at least one point: American Romantics experienced a conflict between themselves and the culture within which they lived, between the myth they sought to create and the historical world in which they were "implicated." Whether, as A N Kaul [in his *American Vision,* 1963] argues, they sought to resolve this through creating an ideal of community, or whether, as Richard Poirier [in his *A World Elsewhere,* 1966] affirms, they looked for "a world elsewhere," modern scholarship has correctly acknowledged the fundamental tension between the Romantics and their "external world." But the relationship between the two has been only partially understood, since comprehensive attempts at examining such American concepts as "nature," the "garden," or the "city" have generally presupposed that these terms had meanings common to the Romantics and to the other people who inhabited the country in which they shaped their art. If such a supposition is false, then the definitions need to be clarified, and the premises underlying the "tension" between the artist and society require reexamination.

American Romantics, being "implicated" in linear history, took their language, their metaphors, their tropes, from the "external world." Primarily, they shaped into private meanings American categories of thought centering on images of nature. Stated another way, Americans of the day generally held a set of myths about nature, and from these public myths the Romantics reconstructed a vocabulary to express radically different private myths. Regardless of how odd their definitions of nature may appear upon close examination, the people who inhabited Emerson's "external world" had reasonably common understandings of nature's meanings. These understandings differed profoundly from romantic perceptions of nature, even though romantic writers appropriated national images of nature to their own ends.

The Americans of Emerson's "external world" perceived nature primarily as participating in a teleological process shaped in part by man and culminating in civilization. Nature in its most important and pervasive metaphorical use connoted the values of civilization and often implied civilization itself. In its purest form, nature took the shape of urban America, and the journey to nature became the journey to the city. In a world that held to this sensibility, Emerson and his contemporaries came of age. Because of their implication in an "external world," the American Romantics defined their interior journeys in a language that also brought them from nature to the city. If Leo Marx [in his *The Machine in the Garden,* 1964] has drawn different conclusions from observing this pattern of their journeys, he has nevertheless accurately noted that "our American fables" lead heroes through "a raw wilderness . . . back toward the city."

But toward what city, and through what nature do our fables lead us? The answer to this depends on whether the journey occurs in historic America or in private myth, a distinction Thoreau suggests in his essay "Walking":

> I walk out into *a* [my italics] nature such as the old prophets and poets, Menu, Moses, Homer, Chaucer walked in. You may name it America, but it is not America; neither Americus Vespucius, nor Columbus, nor the rest were the discoverers of it. There is a truer account of it in mythology than in any history of America, so called, that I have seen.

The truest history of nature, Thoreau tells us, cannot be found in any history of America. Nor is nature one phenomenon, as his indefinite article indicates. Thoreau walks to "a" nature, discovered earlier by poets, explorers of man's interior world. In the region of romantic myth, Thoreau can walk the same ground they did. But it is a different ground from that upon which the people of his day walk. Put another way, Thoreau has not simply posed history against myth; he has confronted his myth with his culture's myth. Americans had constructed a story about nature, which Thoreau rejected, though he would use the frame of that story in describing his own interior journey. This story of nature in early nineteenth-century America, whether told in novels, travel narratives, or political orations, recounted the transformation of nature into its purest form, civilization. It was not the only story of the time, but it was the most pervasive, and it found its greatest teller in James Fenimore Cooper, to whom I shall return at length.

The counterpart to the myth Cooper essentially endorsed exists in the myth of nature as spiritual place, the region comparable to where Thoreau walks in the paths of Menu, Moses, Homer, and Chaucer. One does not need trees or lakes here, although one may certainly use them, as one uses whales. Similarly, one may use America, as Whitman does in "Passage to India," as he passes through America's historical triumph over the West to embark on a "Passage to more than India," to a mythic sphere that leaves the linear history of America behind. It is an interior journey to a private place, one that ultimately takes the poet as far from an American location as Thoreau takes the reader in "Walking," where he finds the "truer account"

of "nature" in "mythology" rather than in America. All our classic writers of the Romantic period, except for Cooper, explored mythic regions analogous to those found by Whitman and Thoreau.

Although the journey motif has a history older than America, writers understandably fashioned their literary enterprises after the models of their day. Consequently, while our classic writers differed radically in their intentions from their compatriots in the "external world" of America, they found their metaphors in the ordinary myths of society. When juxtaposed, private myth against national myth, interior myth against exterior myth, the language of each illuminates the other. Concepts of nature and the city emerge from seemingly indiscriminate language and form definable patterns of thought that would defy coherent analysis without the recovery of lost definitions. The reacquisition of these meanings, bearing crucially on America's exterior political journey and the interior literary ones, requires an examination of forgotten fiction, travel narratives, newspapers, and magazines, as well as belles-lettres. As in the present, popular images are discovered, by definition, quantitatively rather than qualitatively. For common attitudes of the nineteenth century, we look to Timothy Flint before examining Thoreau. But we can understand neither without studying both.

All writers, of course, do not fit neatly into one category or the other, nor is the canon of any given author ever wholly devoted to a single view. Yet, broadly speaking, a distinction may be made between those primarily concerned with the "external world" and those who sought to find a different order of understanding in a new religious myth generally called Romanticism.

It is no understatement to say that Romanticism has many connotations, but without entering into the debate Arthur O. Lovejoy [in *PMLA* 39 (June 1924)] precipitated by his moderate insistence that the term requires definition, I want to cite Northrop Frye's *A Study of English Romanticism* to establish my own use of the term. According to Professor Frye, the

> Middle Ages itself, like all ages, had its own antimimetic tendencies, which it expressed in such forms as the romance, where the knight turns away from society and rides off into a forest or other "threshold symbol" of a dream world. In Romanticism this romance form revives, so significantly as to give its name to the whole movement, but in Romanticism the poet himself is the hero of the quest, and his turning away from society is to be connected with . . . the demoting of the conception of man as primarily a social being living in cities. He turns away to seek a nature who reveals herself only to the individual.

Additionally, "the great Romantic theme is the attaining of an apocalyptic vision by a fallen but potentially regenerate mind."

Literary historians reasonably enough associate this regeneration with an "Adamic myth," but there must be no misunderstanding about the state of Adam in this myth as it took shape in America. Adam was fallen and not innocent. The successful romantic quests, such as those found in *Nature, Walden,* or "Song of Myself," all posit the fallen figure seeking to *restore* a diminished or lost spirituality. Conversely, the quests of Melville, Hawthorne, and Poe generally reveal probings at regeneration accompanied by a failure to achieve it, at least if one reads these writers as governed by Melville's "blackness." But whether finding success or failure in the quest for regeneration, all of them—Emerson, Thoreau, Whitman, Melville, Hawthorne, Poe—explore "the great Romantic theme."

Cooper, however, does not, although he misleads the reader who has not taken into account typologies of nature basic to Cooper and his contemporaries. Cooper writes primarily in Emerson's "external world." His heroes and heroines, Natty Bumppo included, perceive nature as existing in America rather than in mythology, to use Thoreau's dichotomy.

The "mythology" in which Thoreau found his true account of nature may certainly have been a timeless one, as he suggests, but it was probably most accessible to him and other Romantics as part of what Northrop Frye calls "an encyclopedic myth."

> In Western Europe [this] myth, derived mainly from the Bible, dominated both the literary and the philosophical tradition for centuries. I see Romanticism as the beginning of the first major change in this pattern of mythology, and as fully comprehensible only when seen as such.

This new mythology does not reject the past. On the contrary, it seeks to recapture something that has slipped away. While romantic concepts of *apocalypse, fall,* and *regeneration* lost much of their traditional meaning as speculations about them moved from historical Christianity, the continuing vitality of the ideas, particularly those of *fall* and *regeneration,* strongly indicate an adherence to Christian categories if not to Christian history. As M. H. Abrams [in his *Natural Supernaturalism,* 1971] cogently observes, the basic thrust of Romanticism is conservative: "Despite their displacement from a supernatural to a natural frame of reference, . . . the ancient problems, terminology, and ways of thinking about human nature and history survived. . . . " The observation is as appropriate to American Romantics as to English ones.

This "displacement" had little to do with Cooper or with most of the people living in the geographical location of America because for them the concepts of *fall* and *regeneration* required no radical redefinitions. While many Americans had modified the theological rigor of their forebears, they basically held to the old beliefs. Emerson's myth of man as a ruined divinity, his Adamic myth, carried a theology antithetical to the beliefs of most Americans, including James Fenimore Cooper, the great articulator of a secular American myth of nature. Cooper tells adventure stories, and sometimes very good ones. He comments extensively on the society in which he lives. He is attracted to the magic of the wilderness, and if this is Romanticism then Cooper is a Romantic. But by no stretch of the imagination does Cooper or his most venturesome soul, Natty, seek to reconstruct Christian categories into a new theological myth. None of his "good" people are ruined divinities, and his "bad" people are simply ruined.

Cooper, alone, among the major American writers of his day, created relatively innocent individuals in the wilderness, a tangible region comprehensible in terms of America's idea of nature as process tending toward civilization and incorporating its values. The obligation of individualists inhabiting Cooper's nature is to disappear. Which Natty does. He lives in linear history, lives out its joys and sadnesses, and then moves on before an advancing civilization. The inhabitants of Cooper's world do not whittle sticks, as Thoreau's artist of Kouroo does, while eons pass. Unlike Emerson, Cooper does not seek to build a new world. God had built him a fine one already. He would justify it in his writings.

Although America was obviously not of one mind in the early nineteenth century, readers charmed by the novelty and freshness of Cooper's writings generally shared the underlying premises of his Leatherstocking stories. Written as historical fiction—for the events Cooper chronicles had long since passed—the Leatherstocking stories combine two visions of America, both very familiar to his audience. One treats the West and nature as a region that inevitably must and should be transformed into civilization. The other constructs the fantasy wilderness of noble savages, a location imaged first in Europe. But American readers knew which was fantasy and which was not, and Americans in general, Romantics included, had few illusions about geographical America as an Edenic region. Although various Europeans fixed their view on the Edenic mirage they had long seen in the American wilderness, few Americans succumbed to images of primitive utopianism. Many, however, did see in America the old European image of endless possibility for new beginnings. Seen this way, America was a vast region into which one could journey either to escape the past or to create a new future, or both. The geographical space offered room for establishing or reestablishing social, economic, political, or religious order suitable to individual desire. But central to this image, no matter how ecstatic, was the idea of America as a geographic place, the outcome of history's most recent revelation.

The Romantics found such a view of the new world constrained and insufficient. For them, the newness was spiritual rather than geographical, apart from America rather than of it. In Melville's words, "You must have plenty of sea-room to tell the Truth in; especially when it *seems* [my italics] to have an aspect of newness, as America did in 1492, though it was then just as old, and perhaps older than Asia, only those sagacious philosophers, the common sailors, had never seen it before, swearing it was all water and moonshine there." Only in the context of this perception can we comprehend his often-quoted statement that the "world is as young today as when it was created; and this Vermont morning dew is as wet to my feet as Eden's dew to Adam's." *His* Vermont belongs to Thoreau's "mythology." The "Idea of Man," as Roy Harvey Pearce calls it in his *Continuity of American Poetry,* takes precedence over the idea of America, even in the basic Adamic formulation. Readers having noted England's Adamic motif, if only in Mary Shelley's *Frankenstein,* understand how remote from nationality and America's newness the myth of "Adam's" regenerative quest was in the nineteenth century. The great "experience" of American Romantics was private rather than national; it was visited upon individuals caught in that moment of history when, even prior to Nietzsche's crystallization of the idea, the possibility of God's death haunted the poetic imagaination. In response, a new religious pattern began to emerge, even among writers like Longfellow and Whittier, who waivered between newer and older myths, just as the major Romantics did.

At some point in the nineteenth century, and historians may debate exactly when, the American journey into nature ended. The political frontiers had been conquered, and Western man, as Whitman affirms in "Passage to India," had circumnavigated the globe. If the American West was not a totally idyllic place, it nevertheless essentially redeemed the pledge of material prosperity nature had held. Political and economic problems remained, but the American journey to nature had been relatively successful. The romantic journey was also largely over in the sense that new methods of literary exploration engaged the attention of leading writers such as Adams, Crane, James, and Twain, although inquiries into the meaning of being remained fundamental to their writing. What had generally changed was the pattern of metaphor. Whether coincidental or not, the *romantic* trope of a journey to nature in search of salvation ended at about the time that America fully possessed the promised land.

Except for Melville's *Clarel* and *Billy Budd,* the last richly poetic nineteenth-century exploration of what had already become an old dream appeared in Whitman's "Passage to India." The poem, dated 1871, explores again the romantic myth that by then bordered on nostalgia. Since Melville's later writings offer only bleak possibilities, "Passage to India" remains as the final great nineteenth-century example of the romantic dream that in the "Passage to more than India," as Whitman phrased it in his poem, a truly new metaphysical and redemptive frontier could emerge. Melville, as early as 1849, had insisted in *Mardi* that such quests led to places other than those Whitman imagined in his poem. Yet both writers probed the "mythology" of Thoreau's "Walking." In the polarities of human possibility outside of geographical America, one thrusting toward hope and the other toward a hopeless endurance, "Passage to India" and *Mardi* exemplify the similar meanings to be found in so many journeys to nature taken by romantic writers.

Both narratives recognize that, in Whitman's words, "the shores of America," or of this world, are too confining, that "this separate Nature," as Whitman calls the tangible world, is "so unnatural." One must shed the temporal, as the poet does in seizing command of his soul and launching "out on trackless seas" in search of "unknown shores." Whitman is "bound where mariner has not yet dared to go," and is ready to "risk the ship, ourselves and all." Whitman's "trackless seas" may be equated with Melville's "endless sea" and "chartless' voyage across "untracked" waters. Whitman, who will "steer for the deep waters only," is like Melville's hero Taji, who grasps possession of his own soul, seizes the helm of his ship with "eternity . . . in his eye," and daringly plunges forth. Before the final moment of these two journeys, where the he-

roes leave all temporal things behind and move toward the mystical "unknown shores," each author has first taken the reader through a linear history. Both writers have invoked Europe and America; each has found them "so unnatural"; each has sought to redefine the self in a region beyond the world of physical things, regardless of different expectations. In "Passage to India" an old Walt Whitman still follows the promise that

> Nature and Man shall be disjoin'd and diffused
>   no more,
> The true Son of God [the poet] shall absolutely
>   fuse them.

We recognize in the vision its kinship to Emerson's prophecy of 1836 [in his essay *Nature*] that the "problem of restoring to the world original and eternal beauty is solved by the redemption of the soul." This world defined by Emerson as one that "lacks unity, and lies broken and in heaps" will be put together again. Melville, in sending his hero across the "endless sea," makes no such promise. But the quests are similar in their intentions, and they have little to do with Cooper's American journeys.

In 1855 when Whitman announced himself to the world in *Leaves of Grass* he did so with the implicit promise that the words of Emerson would be validated. In "Passage to India" he was still uttering the promise, as if by a kind of Shelleyan incantation he could make it happen. Emerson was saying little at this time about putting the world back together again. By 1871, for a generation of writers, the restless, longing dream that art might in some way make coherent the incoherent world was for the most part over.

Their dream had generally implied that if science rendered chaotic the old divine order, perhaps the world might yet be held together by something called *nature.* Not the nature that Whitman thought of as "unnatural," but something else: the peculiar amalgam of all tangible things seen through the religious eye that transformed them into an idea whereby nature would transcend its physical qualities. To this region of nature beyond India, heroes of a literary era embarked on their inner journeys to Walden, or to Ishmael's sea, or to the "place" in *Nature* where Emerson's "poet" found a way of knowing that would transform old beliefs into a new myth. Such explorations are neither peculiar to America nor to the nineteenth century. But the American writers who created such journeys drew heavily from an image fundamental to those living in their "external world." The discovery of nature became the discovery of civilization, or the self, as the Romantics modified the pattern.

The American journey was successful; it was a rewarding passage whereby a nation transformed the wilderness into something approximating the urban dream it held for nature. The romantic journey had a different outcome. Cast often in the lyric language of success, as in *Walden, Nature,* or "Passage to India," the inner quest for what these works of art prophesied was generally unfulfilled, and nature rarely kept the promise it had seemed to make. Indeed, nature often evoked a threatening myth, often suggested that all the seas might not be those of God. On the other side of Walden Pond one might find "A Winter Walk," where Thoreau thinly covers with snow the death and decay he implicitly defines as something other than nature:

> The wonderful purity of nature at this season is a most pleasing fact. Every decayed stump and moss-grown stone and rail, and the dead leaves of autumn, are concealed by a clean napkin of snow.

This world of death and decay lurked just underneath the "clean napkin" of nature. When the "napkin" was probed, however, when the world was explored, it often appeared in its ambiguity of whiteness. "Think what a mean and wretched place this world is," writes the creator of *Walden* in another book [*A Week on the Concord and Merrimack Rivers*],

> that half the time we have to light a lamp that we may see to live in it. This is half our life. Who would undertake the enterprise if it were all? And, pray, what more has day to offer? A lamp that burns more clear, a purer oil, say winter-strained, that so we may pursue our idleness with less obstruction. Bribed with a little sunlight and a few prismatic tints, we bless our Maker, and stave off his wrath with hymns.

"Who would undertake the enterprise if it were all?" That was the crucial question, and the Romantics hoped that it would not be "all." Somewhere there might be something else; not in the realm of America's nature, but in the private vision of the questing individual. This is by no means to say that all the Romantics spent their entire lives monomaniacally searching for God or some equivalent. Obviously, they found other satisfactions. But when nature served as the metaphor for the regenerative quest, when artists sought their location in the universe, the passage took them to a region away from geographical America, away from any geographical place, to a mythic nature where they could escape from an "unnatural" plight. And they dared the search, even though the "seas of God" proclaimed by Whitman in 1871 had too often proved to be, in Melville's words, the "realm of shades" [*Mardi*]. They searched in the region of Thoreau's "mythology" rather than in the America from which they took much of the imagery that described their separate journey.

> *Bernard Rosenthal, "Introduction: Journeys to Nature," in his* City of Nature: Journeys to Nature in the Age of American Romanticism, *University of Delaware Press, 1980, pp. 15-27.*

Lewis Mumford

[*Mumford was an American sociologist, historian, philosopher, and critic whose primary interest was the relationship between the modern individual and his or her environment. In the following excerpt, he contrasts the American pioneering spirit with the idyllic "back to nature" theme of the European Romantics.*]

I

The pioneer has usually been looked upon as a typical product of the American environment; but the truth is that he existed in the European mind before he made his appearance here. Pioneering may in part be described as the Romantic movement in action. If one wishes to fathom the pioneer's peculiar behavior, one must not merely study his relations with the Indians, with the trading companies, and with the government's land policies: one must also understand the main currents of European thought in the Eighteenth Century. In the episode of pioneering, a new system of ideas wedded itself to a new set of experiences: the experiences were American, but the ideas themselves had been nurtured in Savoy, in the English lake country, and on the Scots moors. Passing into action, these ideas became queerly transmogrified, so that it now takes more than a little digging to see the relation between Chateaubriand and Mark Twain, or Rousseau and William James. The pioneer arose out of an external opportunity, an unopened continent, and out of an inward necessity. It is the inward necessity that most of our commentators upon him have neglected.

In the Eighteenth Century, Europe became at last conscious of the fact that the living sources of its older culture had dried up; and it made its first attempt to find a basis for a new culture. Many of its old institutions were already hollow and rotten. The guilds had become nests of obsolete privileges, which stood doggedly in the way of any technical improvement. The church, in England and in France, had become an institution for providing support to the higher ranks of the clergy, who believed only in the mundane qualities of bread and wine. In fact, all the remains of medieval Europe were in a state of pitiable decay; they were like venerable apple-trees, burgeoned with suckers and incapable of bearing fruit. A mere wind would have been enough to send the old structure toppling; instead of it, a veritable tempest arose, and by the time Voltaire had finished with the Church, Montesquieu and Rousseau with the State, Turgot and Adam Smith with the old corporations, there was scarcely anything left that an intelligent man of the Eighteenth Century would have cared to carry away. Once the old shelters and landmarks were gone, where could people turn? The classic past had already been tried, and had been found—dull. Medievalism was not yet quite dead enough to be revived; *chinoiseries* were merely amusing. There remained one great and permanent source of culture, and with a hundred different gestures the Eighteenth Century acclaimed it—Nature.

The return to Nature occurred at the very climax of an arranged and artificial existence: trees had been clipped, hedges had been deformed, architecture had become as cold and finicking as a pastrycook's icing, the very hair of the human head had been exchanged for the white wig of senility. Precisely at this moment, when a purely urbane convention seemed established forever, a grand retreat began. In the Middle Ages such a retreat would have led to the monastery: it now pushed back to the country, by valiant mountain paths, like Rousseau's, or by mincing little country lanes, like that which led Marie Antoinette to build an English village in Versailles, and play at being a milkmaid. Nature was the fashion: "every one did it." If one had resources, one laid out a landscape park, wild like the fells of Yorkshire, picturesque like the hills of Cumberland, the whole atmosphere heightened by an artificial ruin, to show dramatically the dominance of Nature over man's puny handiwork. If one were middle class, one built a villa, called Idle Hour, or The Hermitage; at the very least, one took country walks, or dreamed of a superb adventurous manhood in America.

In the mind of the great leader of this movement, Jean-Jacques Rousseau, Nature was not a fresh element in the tissue of European culture: it was a complete substitute for the existing institutions, conventions, habits, and histories. Rousseau began his career with an essay on the question whether the restoration of the arts and sciences had the effect of purifying or corrupting public morals: he won the prize offered by the academy at Dijon by affirming their tendency to corrupt; and from that time onward (1750) he continued to write, with better sense but with hardly any decrease in his turbulent conviction, upon the worthlessness of contemporary civilization in Europe. His prescription was simple: return to Nature: shun society: enjoy solitude. Rousseau's Nature was not Newton's Nature—a system of matter and motion, ordered by Providence, and established in the human mind by nice mathematical calculations. By Nature Rousseau meant the mountains, like those which shoulder across the background of his birthplace; he meant the mantle of vegetation, where one might botanize, and see "eternity in a grain of sand, and heaven in a wild flower;" he meant the fields, like those of Savoy, where a simple peasantry practiced the elementary routine of living.

The return to Nature, in Rousseau's sense, was not a new injunction; nor was it an unsound one. As an aid to recovery in physical illness and neurosis, its value was recognized at least as early as Hippocrates, and as a general social formula it has played a part in the life and literature of every finished civilization. The Georgics, the Bucolics, and the idylls of classic culture belong to its sophisticated moments: after the formalities of the Confucian period Lao-tse's philosophy developed a similar creed and persuaded its individualistic adherents to renounce the sterile practices of the court and the bureaucracy and bury themselves in the Bamboo Grove. Nature almost inevitably becomes dominant in the mind when the powers of man himself to mold his fortunes and make over his institutions seem feeble—when, in order to exist at all, it is necessary to accept the wilderness of Nature and human passion as "given," without trying to subdue its disorder.

What made the authority of Rousseau's doctrine so immense, what made it play such a presiding part in European life, echoing through the minds of Goethe, Herder, Kant, Wordsworth, and even, quite innocently, Blake, was the fact that there awaited the European in America a Nature that was primitive and undefiled. In the purely mythical continent that uprose in the European mind, the landscape was untainted by human blood and tears, and the Red Indian, like Atala, led a life of physical dignity and spiritual austerity: the great Sachem was an aborigine with the stoic virtues of a Marcus Aurelius. Rousseau's glorification of peasant life was after all subject to scrutiny, and by the time the French Revolution came, the peasant had a word or two to say about it himself; but the true child of Nature in the New World, uncorrupted by the superstitions of the Church, could be idealized to the heart's content: his customs could be attributed to the unhindered

spontaneity of human nature, his painfully acquired and transmitted knowledge might be laid to instinctive processes; in short, he became a pure ideal. Even William Blake could dream of liberty on the banks of the Ohio, if not on the banks of the Thames.

In America, if society was futile, one had only to walk half a day to escape it; in Europe, if one walked half a day one would be in the midst of another society. In Europe one had to *plan* a retreat: in America one simply encountered it. If Nature was, as Wordsworth said, a world of ready wealth, blessing our minds and hearts with wisdom and health and cheerfulness, what place could be richer than America? Once Romanticism turned its eyes across the ocean, it became a movement indeed. It abandoned culture to return to Nature; it left a skeleton of the past for an embryo of the future; it renounced its hoarded capital and began to live on its current income; it forfeited the old and the tried for the new and the experimental. This transformation was, as Nietzsche said, an immense physiological process, and its result was "the slow emergence of an essentially super-national and nomadic species of man, who possesses, physiologically speaking, a maximum of the art and power of adaptation as his typical distinction."

The Romantic Movement was thus the great formative influence which produced not merely the myth of pioneering, but the pioneer. But it was not the sole influence upon the scene. Human society was divided in the Eighteenth Century between those who thought it perfectible, and those who thought that the existing institutions were all essentially rotten: the Benthams and the Turgots were on one side, the Rousseaus and Blakes on the other, and the great mass of people mixed these two incompatible doctrines in varying proportions. The perfectionists believed in progress, science, laws, education, and comfort; progress was the mode and comfort the end of every civil arrangement. The followers of Rousseau believed in none of these things. Instead of sense, they wanted sensibility; instead of education, spontaneity; instead of smokeless chimneys and glass windows and powerlooms, a clear sky and an open field.

If the pioneer was the lawfully begotten child of the Romantic Movement, he belonged to the other school by adoption. He wanted Nature; and he wanted comfort no less. He sought to escape the conventions of society; yet his notion of a free government was one that devoted itself to a perpetual process of legislation, and he made no bones about appealing to the Central Government when he wanted inland waterways and roads and help in exterminating the Indian. Society was effete: its machinery could be perfected—the pioneer accepted both these notions. He believed with Rousseau that "man is good naturally, and that by institutions only is he made bad." And if the Yankees who first settled in Illinois were looked upon as full of "notions" because they were wont to take thought for the morrow and to multiply mechanical devices, these habits, too, were quickly absorbed. As Nature grew empty, progress took its place in the mind of the pioneer. Each of these ideas turned him from the past, and enabled him to speculate, in both the commercial and philosophic senses of the word, on the future.

II

In America the return to Nature set in before there was any physical necessity for filling up the raw lands of the West. The movement across the Alleghanies began long before the East was fully occupied: it surged up in the third quarter of the Eighteenth Century, after the preliminary scouting and road-building by the Ohio Company, and by the time the Nineteenth Century was under way, the conquest of the Continent had become the obsession of every progressive American community.

This westward expansion of the pioneer was, without doubt, furthered by immediate causes, such as the migration of disbanded soldiers after the Revolution, endowed with land-warrants; but from the beginning, the movement was compulsive and almost neurotic; and as early as 1837 Peck's New Guide to the West recorded that "migration has become almost a habit." External matters of fact would perhaps account for the New England migration to Ohio: they cease to be relevant, however, when they are called upon to explain the succession of jumps which caused so many settlers to pull up stakes and move into Illinois—and then into Missouri—and so beyond, until finally the Pacific Coast brought the movement temporarily to an end. This restless search was something more than a prospecting of resources; it was an experimental investigation of Nature, Solitude, The Primitive Life; and at no stage of the journey, however much the story may be obscured by land-booms and Indian massacres and gold rushes, did these things drop out of the pioneer's mind. Charles Fenno Hoffmann, in *A Winter in the West* (1835), was only echoing the unconscious justification of the pioneer when he exclaimed: "What is the echo of roofs that a few centuries since rung with barbaric revels, or of aisles that pealed the anthems of painted pomp, to the silence which has reigned in these dim groves since the first fiat of Creation was spoken?"

Mark the difference between this movement and that which first planted the colonists of Massachusetts or Pennsylvania in the New World. In the first period of the seaboard settlement, America was a place where the European could remain more nearly his proper self, and keep up the religious practices which were threatened by economic innovations and political infringements in Europe. The Puritans, the Moravians, the Dunkers, the Quakers, the Catholics, sought America as a refuge in which they could preserve in greater security what they dearly valued in Europe. But with the drift to the West, America became, on the contrary, a place where the European could be swiftly transformed into something different: where the civil man could become a hardy savage, where the social man could become an "individual," where the settled man could become a nomad, and the family man could forget his old connections. With pioneering, America ceased to be an outpost of Europe. The Western communities relapsed into an earlier and more primitive type of occupation; they reverted to the crude practices of the hunter, the woodman, and the miner. Given the occasion and the environment, these were necessary occupations; the point to be noted, however, is that, uninfluenced by peasant habits or the ideas of an old culture, the work of the miner, wood-

man, and hunter led to unmitigated destruction and pillage. What happened was just the reverse of the old barbarian invasions, which turned the Goths and the Vandals into Romans. The movement into backwoods America turned the European into a barbarian.

The grisly process of this settlement was described by Crèvecœur and Cooper long before Professor Turner summed them up in his classic treatise on the passing of the frontier. "In all societies," says Crèvecœur,

> there are off-casts; this impure part serves as our precursors or pioneers. . . . By living in or near the woods, their actions are regulated by the neighborhood. The deer often come to eat their grain, the wolves to destroy their sheep, the bears to kill their hogs, the foxes to catch their poultry. The surrounding hostility immediately puts the gun into their hands; they watch these animals; they kill some; and thus, by defending their property, they soon become professed hunters; this is the progress; once hunters, farewell to the plow. The chase renders them ferocious, gloomy, unsociable; a hunter wants no neighbors, he rather hates them because he dreads competition.

Equipped with his ax and his rifle, the two principal weapons of the pioneer, he carried on his warfare against Nature, cutting down the forest and slaughtering its living

Henry Wadsworth Longfellow.

creatures. Instead of seeking Nature in a wise passiveness, as Wordsworth urged, he raped his new mistress in a blind fury of obstreperous passion. No one who has read *The Pioneers* can forget Cooper's account of the sickening massacre of wild pigeons, carried on long after the need for food had been satisfied. In these practices, the ordinary farmer and tradesman of the old country went back to a phase of European experience which had lingered on chiefly in the archaic hunts of a predatory aristocracy; and in the absence of any restraints or diversions, these primitive practices sank more deeply into the grain.

The apology for this behavior was based upon the noblest grounds; one can scarcely pick up a contemporary description of the pioneering period without finding a flowery account of the new life, put in contrast to wretched, despotic, foolishly beautiful Europe; and this animus was echoed even in the comments that Hawthorne and Emerson, to say nothing of such a real pioneer as Mark Twain, made upon the institutions of the Old World. Let me put the contemporary apology and criticism side by side. The first is from a pamphlet by George Lunt called *Three Eras of New England* (1857):

> Whenever this is the state of man the impertinent fictions and sophisms of life die out. The borrowings and lendings of the human creature fall away from him under the rigid discipline of primeval necessities, as the encrusting dirt, which bedimmed the diamond, is removed by the hard process which reveals and confirms its inestimable price. The voice of the mountain winds would mock at the most indispensable and best recognized trappings of polished society as they rent them away and fastened them fluttering in the crevices of a cliff, or bore them onwards to the unknown wilderness, and would hail its very discomforts with the shout and laughter of derision. . . . So far, therefore, as our familiar and inherent characteristics, which form the foundation of our nature, and make us good and make us great, are liable to become diluted or perverted by the sophistications of social being, they may require an actual refreshment and renewal, under the severe and inevitable trials of colonial existence. . . . This, then, is the absolute law of all legitimate migration, that it leaves behind it the weaknesses, the concretions and superfluities of artificial life, and founds its new existence upon an appeal to the primordial elements of natural society.

Against this apology for the deprivations of the pioneer life, let me set the comment of a young English settler named Fordham, who had come face to face with the untrammeled Children of Nature; this passage occurs on the page after that in which he records the amiable slaughter of six Indians, men and women, on English Prairie, in the spring of 1817:

> Instead of being more virtuous, as he is less refined, I am inclined to think that man's virtues are like the fruits of the earth, only excellent when subjected to culture. The force of the simile you will never feel, until you ride in these woods over wild strawberries, which dye your horses' fetlocks like blood, yet are insipid in

flavour; till you have seen wagon-loads of grapes, choked by the brambles and the poisonous vine; till you find peaches, tasteless as a turnip, and roses throwing their leaves of every shade upon the wind, with scarcely a scent upon them. 'Tis the hand of man that makes the wilderness shine.

The hand of man was of course busy, and here and there, particularly in Ohio, Kentucky and Tennessee, villages and cities grew up which carried on, for a generation or so in the Nineteenth Century, the tradition that the seaboard knew in an earlier day; but like a river that, rushing onwards, deposits its heaviest burdens first, the best people and the soundest traditions tended to be deposited in the tracts that adjoined the original colonies, and as the stream moved further west, the traditions of a civil life disappeared, and the proportion of scalawags, cut-throats, bruisers, bullies, and gamblers tended to increase, and the wilderness got the upper hand. There are plenty of exceptions to this generalization, it goes without saying; but Texas and Nevada were the poles towards which pioneer effort tended to run. The original process has been obscured in many places by a second and third wave of agriculturists: but it is not hard to get below the surface and see what the original reality was.

III

The shock of the pioneer's experience left its mark in one or two gestures of anticipation, and in an aftermath of regretful reminiscence. The post-Civil War writers who deal with *Roughing It, A Son of the Middle Border,* or *A Hoosier Schoolmaster,* to mention only a few examples, had already abandoned the scene of the pioneer's efforts and had returned to the East: they made copy of their early life, but, though they might be inclined to sigh after it, because it was associated with their youth, they had only a sentimental notion of continuing it. For them, the pioneering experience could be recapitulated in a night around a camp-fire or a visit to the Wild West Show, which the astute Barnum had introduced to the denizens of New York in a day when the West was still in fact wild. A genuine culture and a relevant way of life do not lose their significance so easily; and the thin-skinnedness of the pioneer in the face of criticism, and the eagerness of the post-pioneer generation—*The Inheritors* of Susan Glaspell's play—to identify themselves with the culture of the past, shows, I think, that at bottom the pioneer realized that his efforts had gone awry.

One is faced by the paradox that the formative elements in the pioneer's career expressed themselves in literature almost at the very outset of the movement, in the works of men who were in fact almost as aloof from the realities of the western exodus as Chateaubriand himself; and although the pioneer types and the pioneer adventures have been repeated in literature of the rubber-stamp pattern from Gustave Aimard to Zane Grey, what was valid and what was peculiar in the pioneer regime was embodied, once for all, by James Fenimore Cooper. These new contacts, these new scenes, these adventures, served to create just three genuine folk-heroes. In these heroes, the habits of the pioneer were raised to the plane of a pattern.

Cooper's Leatherstocking was the new *NaturMensch,* established on a platform of simple human dignity. He was versed in the art of the woods, with the training of the aborigine himself; he shared the reticence and shyness that the Amerind perhaps showed in the company of strangers; and above the tender heart he exhibited mutely in *The Deerslayer,* he disclosed a leathery imperturbability. His eye was unerring; and it was only in instinct that Chingachgook, the Indian, sometimes surpassed this great hunter and warrior. Leatherstocking's bullet, which drives the bullet that has already hit the bull's eye still deeper into the target is, of course, no ordinary bullet: it shared the inevitable enlargement of the hero's powers. Not every pioneer, needless to say, was a Natty Bumpo; but the shy, reserved, taciturn, dryly humorous hunter was the sort of being the pioneer tended, under the first stress of his new association, to become. Cooper himself painted other pioneer types, the sullen squatter, Ishmael, the fur trader, the frontier soldier, the woodman, the bee-hunter; but the fact that he had already outlined the character of Leatherstocking in the equally shrewd and reserved Spy of the Neutral Ground, Harvey Birch, showed, I believe, that this figure had become a property of his unconscious.

First a hunter, then a scout, then a trapper, Leatherstocking encompassed the chief pioneering experiences; it required a generation or two before the trader became the boomtown manufacturer, and the manufacturer the realtor and financier, dealing only with the tokens of industry. Like the first pioneers, Leatherstocking fled before the smoke of the settler's domestic fire, as before the prairie fire itself. With all the shoddiness of Cooper's imaginative constructions, he was plainly seized by a great character: his novels live solely through their central conception of Leatherstocking. The hard man, a Sir Giles Overreach, or the cunning man, Ulysses, had been portrayed before in literature; but the hardness and craft of Leatherstocking brought forth a new quality, which came directly from the woods and the prairies. When the pioneer called his first political hero Old Hickory he poetically expressed this new truth of character: barbarians or outlaws they might be, these pioneers, but their heroes grew straight. This straightness is the great quality one feels in Lincoln. It was as if, after centuries of clipping and pruning, we had at last allowed a tree to grow to its full height, shaped only by snow, rain, sun, wind, frost. A too timid and complacent culture may sacrifice the inner strength to an agreeable conformity to a common mold, a little undersized. These Old Hickories, on the other hand, grew a little scraggly and awkward; but in their reach, one would catch, occasionally, a hint of the innate possibilities of the species.

In the course of the Nineteenth Century, Leatherstocking was joined by an even more authentic folk hero, Paul Bunyan, whose gigantic shape, partly perhaps derived from Gargantua through his French-Canadian forebears, took form over the fire in the logger's shack. Paul Bunyan, properly enough, was an axman; and, as if to complete the symbolism and identify himself more completely with the prime activities of the new American type, he was also a great inventor. He figures on a continental scale. All his prowess and strength is based upon the notion that a thing becomes a hundred times as important if it is a hundred times as big. The habit of counting and "calculating" and "figuring" and "reckoning" and "guessing"—the habit, that is, of exchanging quality for number—is expressed in nearly all of Bunyan's exploits. In a day when no one dared point to the string of shacks that formed the frontier town as a proof of the qualitative beauties and delights of a pioneer community, the popular imagination took refuge in a statistical criterion of value: they counted heads: they counted money: they counted miles: they counted anything that lent itself to large figures.

This habit grew to such an extent that people began to appreciate its comic quality; in the Bunyan tales it is a device of humor as well as of heroic exaggeration. For many years, as the legend was quietly growing and expanding, Paul Bunyan lurked under the surface of our life: we lived by his light, even if we were ignorant of his legend. He, too, like Leatherstocking, was aloof from women; and this fact is not without significance; for with the woman the rough bachelor life must come to an end, and though the pioneer might carry his family with him, bedstead, baby, and all, they were sooner or later bound to domesticate him, and make him settle down. Woman was the chief enemy of the pioneer: she courageously rose to the burdens of the new life, and demanded her place side by side in the legislature: but in the end she had her revenge, in temperance clubs, in anti-vice societies, or in the general tarnation tidiness of Tom Sawyer's aunt. When Whitman sang of the Perfect Comrade, he did not at first think of woman: so far from indicating a special sexual anomaly in Whitman, it is rather a tribute to his imaginative identification with the collective experience of his generation.

At the same time, another folk-hero arose in literature, at first sight an incomprehensible one. He was neither heroic, nor, on the surface, a pioneer; and the story that brought him forth was a rather commonplace fantasy of an earlier day. Yet the history of Rip Van Winkle shows that he has had a deep hold on the American mind: Irving's tale itself remains a popular legend, and the play that was written about him as early as the eighteen-thirties was remodeled by succeeding generations of American actors, until given its classic form by Joseph Jefferson. How did this happen? The reason, I think, was that Rip's adventures and disappointments stood for that of the typical American of the pioneer period. Inept at consecutive work, harried by his wife, and disgusted with human society, he retires to the hills with his dog and his gun. He drinks heavily, falls asleep, and becomes enchanted. At the end of twenty years he awakes to find himself in a different society. The old landmarks have gone; the old faces have disappeared; all the outward aspects of life have changed. At the bottom, however, Rip himself has not changed; for he has been drunk and lost in a dream, and for all that the calendar and the clock records, he remains, mentally, a boy.

There was the fate of a whole generation: indeed, is it not still the fate of perhaps the great majority of Americans, lost in their dreams of a great fortune in real-estate, rubber, or oil? In our heroic moments, we may think of ourselves as Leatherstockings, or two-fisted fellows like Paul Bunyan; but in the bottom of our hearts, we are disconsolate Rips. In this process of uneasy transition, in the endless experimentalism and externality of the American scheme, the American came to feel that something was wrong. He saw no way of rectifying the fact itself; the necessity to be "up and moving" seemed written in the skies. In his disappointment and frustration, he became maudlin. It is no accident that our most sentimental popular songs all date back to the earlier half of the Nineteenth Century. At the moment when the eagle screamed loudest, when the words Manifest Destiny were put into circulation, when Colonel Diver, the fire-eater, Jefferson Brick, the editor of the Rowdy Journal, and Scadder, the real-estate gambler, were joining voices in a Hallelujah of triumph,—it was then that the tear of regret and the melancholy clutch of the Adam's apple made their way into the ballad.

The great song of the mid-century was "Don't you remember Sweet Alice, Ben Bolt?" but the truth is that Alice was merely a name to start the tears rolling. It was not over the fate of Alice that the manly heart grieved: what hurt was the fact that in the short space of twenty years, the mill-wheel had fallen to pieces, the rafters had tumbled in, the cabin had gone to ruin, the tree had been felled, and "where once the lord of the forest waved" were grass and golden grain. In short, ruin and change lay in the wake of the pioneer, as he went westering. "There is change in the things I loved, Ben Bolt, they have changed from the old to the new," and somehow this progressive generation had an uneasy suspicion that they were not changing altogether for the better. What a conflict was in the pioneer's bosom! He pulls up stakes, to the tune of Home Sweet Home. He sells his parcel of real estate to the next gambler who will hold it, still sighing "there is no place like home." He guts out the forest: "Woodman, spare that tree, touch not a single bough, in youth it sheltered me, and I'll protect it now." And in the struggle of scalping one of the Red Varmints he is driving to the Land of the Sunset the Song of Hiawatha slips from his hip-pocket.

Does this seem to exaggerate the conflict? Be assured that it was there. The Mark Twains, Bret Hartes, and Artemus Wards would not have found the old solidities of Europe so ingratiating, taught as they were to despise Europe's cities and institutions as the relics of a miserable and feudal past, if the life they had known had not too often starved their essential humanity.

IV

With the experience of the Great War behind us, we can now understand a little better the psychal state of our various American communities, whilst they were immersed in their besetting "war against Nature." A war automatically either draws people into the service, or, if they resist, unfits them for carrying on their civil duties in a wholehearted manner. In the pioneer's war against Nature, every member of the community was bound to take part, or be branded as a dilettante, a skulker, a deserter. The phrases that were used in justification of pioneering during the Nineteenth Century were not those which set the Romantic Movement in action in the Eighteenth: these newcomers sought to "conquer a wilderness," "subdue Nature," "take possession of the continent." "To act that each to-morrow finds us *farther* than to-day," was the very

breath of the new pioneer mores: the Psalm of Life was the sum of the pioneer's life.

The throb and urge of this grand march across the continent communicated itself to those who remained in the East. The non-combatants in Boston, Philadelphia, and New York were as uneasy and hesitating in their activities as a conscript who expects at any moment to be called to the colors. Some of them, like C. F. Adams, were only too happy when the Civil War turned the call of the pioneer into a command; others, like George Perkins Marsh, confessed that "in our place and day the scholar hath no vocation," and made plain with what reluctance they turned their backs upon science and the humane arts to struggle in the world of business; others, like William Cullen Bryant, threw a handful of Nature poems into the scales, to weigh over against a life of zealous energy in newspaperdom. In these, and many other equally irritating biographies, one finds that the myth of the Pioneer Conquest had taken possession of even the finer and more sensitive minds: they accepted the uglinesses and brutalities of pioneering, even as many of our contemporaries accepted the bestialities of war, and instead of recognizing no other necessity than their best desires, they throttled their desires and bowed to an imaginary necessity. In the end, the pioneer was as far from Rousseau and Wordsworth as the inventor of poison gas was from the troubadour who sang the Song of Roland.

The effect of the pioneer habits upon our culture has become a commonplace of literary criticism during the last half-generation; the weakness of this criticism has been the failure to grasp the difference in origin between the puritan, the pioneer, and the inventor-business man. The Puritan did indeed pave the way for the extroverts that came after him; but what he really sought was an inner grace. The pioneer debased all the old values of a settled culture, and made the path of a dehumanized industrialism in America as smooth as a concrete road; but it was only in the habits he had developed, so to say, on the road, that he turned aside from the proper goal of the Romantic Movement, which was to find a basis for a fresh effort in culture, and gave himself over to the inventor-businessman's search for power. All three, Puritan, pioneer, and businessman came to exist through the breakdown of Europe's earlier, integrated culture; but, given the wide elbow room of America, each type tended to develop to its extreme, only to emerge in succeeding generations into the composite character of that fictitious person, the Average American.

In the end, the pioneer was as far from Rousseau and Wordsworth as the inventor of poison gas was from the troubadour who sang the Song of Roland.

—Lewis Mumford

In order to appreciate the distance between the America of the Eighteenth Century, which was still attached umbilically to the older Europe, and the America of the pioneer, tinctured by the puritan and the industrialist, one might perhaps compare two representative men, Thomas Jefferson and Mark Twain. When Mark Twain went to Europe during the *Gilded Age,* he was really an innocent abroad: his experience in *Roughing It* had not fitted him for any sort of seasoned contact with climates, councils, governments. When Jefferson went to Paris from the backwoods of Virginia, a hundred years earlier, he was a cultivated man, walking among his peers: he criticized English architecture, not as Mark Twain might have done, because it was effete and feudal, but because it was even more barbarous than that of the American provinces. To Mark Twain, as to most of his contemporaries, industry appeared in the light of what sporting people call a good thing; when, after sinking a small fortune in a new typesetting machine, he approached his friend H. H. Rogers with another invention, the chief attraction he emphasized was its potential monopoly. Jefferson's concern with the practical arts, on the other hand, was personal and esthetic: he was an active farmer, with a carefully kept nursery book, and he brought back to America prints and measurements of public buildings, which served him in the design of his own.

The death of Jefferson, the scholar, the artist, the statesman, and agriculturist—one of the last true figures of the Renaissance—was symbolic; for it came in 1826, just at the moment when the great westward expansion began. In two men of the following generation, S. F. B. Morse and Edgar Allan Poe, we find the new pioneer mores working towards their two legitimate goals. Morse defended his preoccupation with criticism, instead of painting, in words that might have been framed as an illustration of the mood I have been trying to describe. "If I am to be the Pioneer, and am fitted for it, why should I not glory as much in felling trees and clearing away rubbish as in showing the decorations suited to a more advanced state of culture?" As for Poe, the Walpole of a belated Gothic revival, he recorded in literature the displacement and dissociation that was taking place in the community's life.

With no conscious connection with the life about him, Poe became nevertheless the literary equivalent of the industrialist and the pioneer. I have no desire to speak lightly of Poe's capacities as a critic of literature, which were high, nor of his skill in the formal exercises of literary composition. Poe was the first artist consciously to give the short-story a succinct and final form; and as an esthetic experimentalist his own arrangements in prose prepared the way, among other things, for Baudelaire's prose poems. Yet Poe's meticulous and rationalistic mind fitted his environment and mirrored its inner characteristics far more readily than a superficial look at it would lead one to believe. In him, the springs of human desire had not so much frozen up as turned to metal: his world was, in one of his favorite words, plutonian, like that of Watt and Fulton and Gradgrind: the tears that he dropped were steel beads, and his mind worked like a mechanical hopper, even when there were no appropriate materials to throw into it. It happened to be a very good mind; and when it had some-

thing valuable to work upon, as in literary criticism, the results were often excellent. Left to himself, however, he either spent his energies on small ingenuities like ciphers and "scientific" puzzles, or he created a synthetic world, half-pasteboard and half-perfume, whose thinness as an imaginative reality was equaled only by its apparent dissociation from the actualities that surrounded him. The criticism of Poe's fantasies is not that they were "unreal": Shakespeare's are equally so: the criticism is that they have their sources in a starved and limited humanity, the same starved and limited humanity in which Gradgrind devoted himself to "hard facts," and the frontier fighter to cold steel. Terror and cruelty dominated Poe's mind; and terror and cruelty leave a scar on almost every tale and anecdote about pioneer life.

The emotional equivalence of Poe's fiction and the pioneer's fact was perhaps a matter of chance; I will not strain my point by trying to make out a case for anything else. That the equivalence is not a meretricious presumption on my part, is attested, I think, by the fact that it was corroborated a generation later in the anecdotes of Mark Twain and the short stories of Ambrose Bierce. No sensitive mind can undergo warfare or pioneering, with all the raw savagery of human nature developed to the full, without undergoing a shock. The massacres, the banditries, even the coarse practical jokes, all left their detestable impressions. There is a mock-sinister side to the Romantic Movement in European literature in the horror stories of Walpole and Mrs. Radcliffe; but these stories are mere pap for infants alongside those Mark Twain was able to recount in almost every chapter of *Roughing It* and *Life on the Mississippi.*

Poe, perhaps, had never heard one of these stories; but the dehumanized world he created gave a place for terrors, cruelties, and murders which expressed, in a sublimated and eminently readable form, the sadisms and masochisms of the pioneer's life. Man is, after all, a domestic animal; and though he may return to unbroken nature as a relief from all the sobrieties of existence, he can reside for long in the wilderness only by losing some of the essential qualities of the cultivated human species. Poe had lost these qualities, neurotically, without even seeing the wilderness. Cooper's generation had dreamed of Leatherstocking; in realization, the dream had become the nightmare world of Poe. There is scarcely a page of reliable testimony about pioneer life which does not hint at this nightmare. The testimony is all the more salient when one finds Mark Twain reciting his horrors in a vein of pure innocence, without a word of criticism, and then, by a psychic transfer, becoming ferociously indignant over the same things when he finds them in his imaginary Court of King Arthur.

V

The vast gap between the hope of the Romantic Movement and the reality of the pioneer period is one of the most sardonic jests of history. On one side, the bucolic innocence of the Eighteenth Century, its belief in a fresh start, and its attempt to achieve a new culture. And over against it, the epic march of the covered wagon, leaving behind it deserted villages, bleak cities, depleted soils, and the sick and exhausted souls that engraved their epitaphs in Mr. Masters' *Spoon River Anthology*. Against the genuine heroism and derring-do that accompanied this movement, and against the real gains that it achieved here and there in the spread of social well-being, must be set off the crudities of the pioneer's sexual life, his bestial swilling and drinking and bullying, and his barbarities in dealing with the original inhabitants—"a fierce dull biped standing in our way." The gun and the ax and the pick, alas! had taught their lessons only too well; and the more social and coöperative groups, like the Mormons, were attacked violently, but always under the cover of high moral indignation, by belligerent worthies whose morals would have given a bad odor to a hangman's picnic.

The truth is that the life of the pioneer was bare and insufficient: he did not really face Nature, he merely evaded society. Divorced from its social context, his experience became meaningless. That is why, perhaps, he kept on changing his occupation and his habitat, for as long as he could keep on moving he could forget that, in his own phrase, he was not "getting anywhere." He had no end of experiences: he could shoot, build, plant, chop, saw, dicker: he was Ulysses, Nimrod, Noah, and Cain all bundled into one man. But there was, all too literally, no end to these activities—that is, no opportunity to refine them, to separate the ore from the slag, to live them over again in the mind. In short, the pioneer experience did not produce a rounded pioneer culture; and if the new settler began as an unconscious follower of Rousseau, he was only too ready, after the first flush of effort, to barter all his glorious heritage for gas light and paved streets and starched collars and skyscrapers and the other insignia of a truly high and progressive civilization. The return to Nature led, ironically, to a denatured environment, and when, after the long journey was over, the pioneer became conscious once more of the social obligation, these interests manifested themselves in covert pathological ways, like campaigns to prohibit the cigarette or to prescribe the length of sheets for hotel beds, or to promote institutions of compulsory good fellowship. So much for an experience that failed either to absorb an old culture or create a new one!

Lewis Mumford, "The Romanticism of the Pioneer," in his The Golden Day: A Study in American Experience and Culture, *Boni & Liveright Publishers, 1926, pp. 47-84.*

THEMATIC CONCERNS

Robert N. Hertz

[*In the following essay, Hertz examines the themes of individualism and democracy in the works of the American Romantics.*]

The period of American Romanticism, which may be said to extend beyond the first half of the nineteenth century, has close affiliations with the corresponding, if slightly earlier movement in Europe. We associate with both movements a renewed concern for idealism and individualism; we find fresh emphasis on the dignity of each man and his possibility for self realization, creative expression, and rewarding intuitive knowledge of life. In general, however, we characterize the Romantics of the United States as men of affirmation, optimism, and healthy vision of the certain glory which lies a little beyond. By implication, the English Romantics are brilliant but effete aristocrats rather than men of the People or great souls of quiet meditation and discovery. Hawthorne and Melville are presented as the "other side" of the affirmative American picture: the side which temporarily faces the wall.

It is a familiar and partly accurate critical generalization that even the nineteenth century pessimists of the still New World affirmed in their varying degrees of disillusionment the possibility of "self-realization." Certainly Hawthorne is not a writer of Despair. Man's blemishes of sin and evil can be beauty spots if he will not attempt to remove them or cover them with a patch; and if happiness hardly seems a reality, at least unhappiness is not inevitable for everyone. Hepsibah [in *The House of the Seven Gables*] would certainly find fulfillment if she had her life to live over; that she has only one sad life is "compensated" for by the fact that Phoebe and Holgrave have the fresh blood of a young America to build houses with nice gardens instead of with superfluous gables.

The question once again arises, however, of just how healthy is the affirmative impulse. Were Americans once more seeking fulfillment where it was least likely to be found? What did it mean to be an "individual" saying Yes to democracy and envisioning the realization of the ideal, the American dream of equality, of perfectability, or of something?

Perhaps we begin to offer a possible answer to these questions if we repeat with different illustrations the fact that American writers, rebels, and thinkers were futilely advocating the pursuit of simply a metaphysical concept of The Dream—the "little beyond"—rather than presenting for contemplation and action a real goal based on the observed facts of experience. Abstract conceptions of Destiny, Brotherhood, Individualism, Affirmation, and Democracy seem to have been expressed without consideration of the impulses which give rise to such ideals, or of their meaning in a social context. Manifest Destiny where? Brotherhood of whom? Which individuals? Affirmation of what? Although we respond with pleasure and sympathy to our Romantics partially because they do not feel the need to answer very precisely these questions, we must nonetheless acknowledge that our nineteenth century writers often seem to emerge as eccentric and unconscious self-deceivers, moving toward a goal of fulfillment that ends in the same terrible isolation with which it began.

Such a judgment may achieve the clarity it needs if we attempt to discover at least one specific difference between the English Romantics and our own writers in the period of American Romanticism. Perhaps most evident is a significant difference in emphasis between English obsession with the unavoidable disparity between the Real and the Ideal, and American assurance that such disparity marks only a temporary and bridgeable gap. We note that Shelley, for example, has no real desire to become the skylark whose exquisite song he admires. In "To a Skylark" Shelley is not affirming possibilities. He is melancholy about the regrettable hiatus between human aspiration and attainment, and his poem of the unseen bird makes possible one kind of pleasure or fulfillment in the face of life's very real unfulfillment. Some of the more personal poetry of Wordsworth, Coleridge, and Byron is also in part a lament for some acknowledged loss of unattainment. Our own Romantics—Emerson and Thoreau, for instance—tend to affirm an attainable perfection by conceiving of the Idea as Thing, while the English produce lovely music over the lugubrious verity that the best things in life will never be.

Our comparison is at best imperfect; *The Prelude* and *Walden,* let us say, would probably defy easy juxtaposition even by Mr. Spiller. Still, suppose we presume to risk one merely suggestive observation: Wordsworth's ponderous iambics on "the growth of a poet's mind" seem substantially more terrestrial than Henry David's careful prose account of his life in the woods. This is neither to imply that Wordsworth's head is ever very far beneath the cloudy miasma of metaphysical confusion, nor to disparage the "symbolic" import of Thoreau's masterpiece. In fact, critics are usually quite swift to proclaim that Thoreau had not the slightest intention of contributing to the world's knowledge of flora and fauna. Rather, Thoreau apparently hoped that the relentlessly minute description of his private universe would provide a fitting context for his assaults on Conventional Man: beneath the "mud and slush of opinion," if we can uncover it, is a fundamental "reality." Beneath "poetry and philosophy" and most other human artifice and institutions is the hard rock bottom of that which is Real. The paradox, of course, is that *Walden* itself is "poetry and philosophy" and that Thoreau's "reality" is defined, or conceived, in terms of a reader's response to the author's unique combinations of language and perceptions, his response to word allegories. "Making the earth say beans instead of grass": this, said Thoreau, was his daily work. *Walden* must also have once been Thoreau's daily work: a work of imagination, mind, and idea no less than *The Prelude* is such a work. The difference is that Thoreau's prose poem is a self-contained, abstract, aesthetic monument to the ideal of human aspiration and individual possibility. Wordsworth's verse is a narrative of real life experience, of the specific aspirations of a single human being—not merely of the notion of possibilities.

As for "Romantic" writers of fiction, Edgar Allan Poe and Emily Bronte should provide an interesting contrast between American and English "Gothic." Although Mr. Parrington has disposed of Poe's literary production as the "atrabilious wretchedness of a dipsomaniac," the more sophisticated critical line is that Poe's metaphysical "quest for experience" encompasses a vision of the ideal, a penetration of the reality of death (not to mention the illusion of reality), and even a serious consideration of freedom and fate. W. H. Auden, for instance, writes of "the relation of will to environment" in *The Narrative of A. Gordon Pym.* In a far more extensive commentary than that of Mr. Auden, Edward Davidson describes *Pym* as an "elaborate

symbolic allegory" of the "sinkage of reality into the terror of . . . dream" and death; a "rotting corpse" in disguise helps save the lives of "two men against thousands. . . ." Mr. Davidson does not call *A. Gordon Pym* the *Moby Dick* of the southland, though he reminds us suggestively of "the blinding white" toward which Poe's characters sail "without any willing of their own." Of these characters, the two central ones, Pym himself and his friend Peters, are "typical, headstrong, and heedless American go-getters." Where they go, of course, is to a chimerical polar strand inhabited by natives whom Swift might have used in *Gulliver's Travels.* And what the American go-getters find there is a hostile, nearly fatal welcome. Pym alone escaped to tell us.

The "metaphysic of death" in *Wuthering Heights,* on the other hand, is given in terms of love. Miss Bronte seems to say that we can understand something of the meaning of death—of the unknown reality—when love in its most passionate intensity becomes a kind of madness in which eternity is not inconceivable: it is continuous with the present. Since love for another human being is usually a part of the felt experience of life, we are able to accept the metaphysic of death as "somehow" a concomitant or aspect of living. The madness that Poe describes, however, seems removed from experience. Pym's incarceration in the ship's hold, his journey to an arctic wonderland, Miss Usher's exhumation, and the pit beneath the pendulum—these hardly represent the intelligent grappling with felt experience so much as they suggest the distorted representation of imagined abnormalities. Poe called *A. Gordon Pym* a "silly book." A number of "literary psychologists," however, would sooner call it sick.

Whether or not the psychologists have for us any insights from their "discipline," we are not likely to say we know "somehow" the experience of death as Pym makes numerous, prolonged dives into the flooded hold. Most readers will probably be interested, and only mildly, in finding out if he comes up again with something to eat or drink. On the other hand, when Heathcliff lies prostrate on Catherine's grave we are prepared to accept the emotional validity and "full" knowledge of death as it is experienced by one who is alive.

This is more than saying simply that Poe is a lesser craftsman than Miss Bronte. It is to suggest that, if we accept Poe as an important and representative American writer, we must recognize the literal absurdity of most of his fiction. Mr. Davidson's alternative to reading *Pym* as a "silly" adventure story, as we have discovered, is to read it as elaborate symbolic allegory. Such an alternative in itself is not quite satisfactory, however, because allegories are normally little tales without a country. Thus, Mr. Davidson—somewhat incongruously, inaccurately, and unnecessarily—outfits the ship "Jane Guy" with typical, heedless, headstrong American go-getters. The paradox of Poe is that most of his fiction is too grotesque and inconsistent to be allegorical, too "allegorical" to be American, and to haphazardly bizarre to be remarkable as "art" of even a minor order. Whatever makes Edgar Allan Poe so inordinately interesting to so many readers, he has little to do with either the American dream or a southern night-

Edgar Allan Poe.

mare. In fact, his detachment from actual human experience is almost complete.

But he will be read, quoth the critic, Evermore.

Emerson, Thoreau, Whitman, Hawthorne, and Melville are certainly much more "American," much more "universal" than is Poe. The first three of these names, of course, are associated particularly with such favorably toned concepts as individualism, democracy, vision, and the like. Such associations may reveal, though, that we tend to laud or emulate our Romantic writers too quickly as shaping spirits of purpose and profundity concerning the New World—as men whose writings are interpreted to be indigenously and fundamentally "American doctrine." Perhaps, after all, their America was as often Nowhere as it was Here. If they wished to show the way to fulfillment for all men, we must acknowledge that they were prone unwittingly to show the way to that fulfillment where it was least likely to be found, except maybe to a few.

In this respect, suppose we begin by noting several gnawing paradoxes which Emerson presents. A teacher who wishes to help his students penetrate the writings of Emerson is obliged to preface his reading assignments with a reminder that Emerson's prose, after all, is impenetrable—in the usual expository sense. The students, then, must have some knowledge of the subtle metaphysical distinction between the "Me" and the "Not Me," a distinction

that helps to make philosophically plausible, if not precisely meaningful, apparently incongruous or bizarre statements. ("We think of nature as an appendix to the soul.") Although Emerson is personally sensitive to actual life experience and even to the unalterability of the universal course of things, his affirmation of the "private infinitude" of each man is a response in terms of "idea" to the "things" of our world. In his essay "Experience," for example, Emerson catalogues such mundane human "obstacles" as illusion, temperament, mood fluxes, and skepticism; each of these is known by every reader in its personally felt manifestation. The world of such obstacles, however, is not the world "I *think,*" Emerson concludes. "Why not realize your world?" Our world, both private and shared, is one of unpredictable tribulations and limitations; the essay "Fate" tells us so. But the same essay urges us, finally, to "build altars to the Beautiful Necessity." We are left with the cryptic poetry of the metaphysician, whose words themselves are allegories of the "Divine Unity" of things.

The poetry is beautiful, it is true. Many readers are surely moved by Emerson's affirmation of limitless human "possibility." They are moved even if that possibility should mean only an individual's capacity for feeling, and attempting to communicate (or create) in language, a reality—an idea of faith—which transcends experience without ignoring it. But can we reconcile Emerson the poet of "inifinitude" and Emerson the pamphleteer of practicality? Unfortunately, one has learned to feel guilty if he fails to read Emerson's essays without wrenching his psyche into the proper *metaphysical* position in order to get the message as a perfectly *applicable* guide to life. Can a poem both mean and be?

Having arrived at this juncture between the physical and the metaphysical, so to speak, let us explore the implications of Emerson's concepts of "Love" and "Thinking." Love is clearly not a major concern of Emerson's prose. Yet his journals frequently refer to the sense of possible fulfillment attainable in the communication based upon friendship. He occasionally describes people whom he has briefly met, talked to, even walked with in long forest strolls. Regretting the transitory and imperfect pleasure of these contacts, Emerson has written in a kind of lamentation, "But how insular and pathetically solitary are all the people we know." The presumable inference is that men ought not to be islands divided from themselves, for solitude is not the same as loneliness. Still we must see that Emerson's view of life contradicts this implication. For he treats love, or friendship, more as a concept than as an actual fact to be reckoned with. That is, human alliances are imperfect because the only genuine alleviation of loneliness occurs in that solitude which promotes the apprehension of spiritual truth. If we share with all men the Divine essence which is heavenly as well as mundane, anything so earthly as a single human bond is imperfect precisely as it is only a symbolic representation of perfect "wholeness." Such wholeness, or unity, is an unrealizeable idea of the mind. It is an irony and no small wonder that the metaphysician should feel the loneliness of incommunication in a world in which every man is an island, even if inhabiting the same spiritual sea.

It has already been suggested that the "egalitarianism" of Original Sin provided for a minority of the "elect" who were implicitly "better" than the rest of society because Divine Grace had destined them for the fulfillment of an eternal reward. Emerson's "better" class of thinking men, especially as they reflect the philosophy of Transcendentalism, is a secular counterpart of that distinctive minority. The fulfillment that the "scholar" experiences is one in which he is able to conceive that God is in him, that in some intuitively affirmable sense he *is* God. Just as the Deists removed God from paradise and placed Him in the world's garden and man's Reason, Emerson has put Him into men's souls—into man's very Being. And just as Jonathan Edwards advocated complete submission to the God above, Emerson advocates total submission to the God within. And Emerson's God seems almost unqualifiedly to be Self. The passive egoism of the Deists is now the aggressive "self-reliance" of American scholars.

Scholars and students of Emerson, of course, are the first to point out that Emerson's "scholar" is not the pale bibliophile or harmless academic drudge which the term usually connotes. We are told, moreover, that "The American Scholar" is a classic statement of America's revolutionary and quite "shocking" intellectual purposes. Instead of bookworms transcribing stale ideas from yellowed library books, our scholars would be "Men Thinking." Besides reading and studying, the "new" intellectual would cultivate his creative impulses, learn to labor with his hands, and strive for a philosophic mind: one which sees Truth beyond sham and pretension.

Emerson's famous address to a group of Harvard initiates into Phi Beta Kappa is indeed a kind of triumphantly original statement of American intellectual policy. It is a policy, however, which is presented mainly in the imagery and allegorical language of disengagement from actuality. The scholar, Emerson writes, "is to find consolation in exercizing the highest functions of human nature. . . . He is the world's eye . . . the world's heart." The scholar's task is "observation," "patience," entrance into the "Divine flux" of things. One is reminded of Matthew Arnold's series of apparently synonymous ambiguities in *Culture and Anarchy:* "culture"; "sweetness and light"; "reason and the will of God"; and "our own best self." The difference between Emerson and Arnold, however, is that Arnold was quite unequivocally turning to the actions and ideas of the past while Emerson was vaguely announcing an unformulated future.

As a message of "liberation" and private infinitude, "The American Scholar" is probably unexcelled in our national writing. But liberation and private infinitude, however majestic is the idealism they project, express nothing of the actual character of America herself; nor do they provide the scholar with very much more than a kind of "religious" incantation of "possibility." Some will say that liberty and possibility are truly the components of the American dream. We can only agree a little musingly and wonder if the land between freedom and possibility is not a Dreamland indeed. A land, as Keats might say, of sleep and poetry.

Whitman's affirmation is often more exquisite than Emerson's because Whitman's intensity is movingly translated into the lyricism and expansiveness of inspired verse. Yet the democratic idealism, individualism, and optimism he expounds as the bard of the American dream seem to begin and end in loneliness and ineffectuality. As an inspiration toward a way of life which can lead to increased humanity and progress toward an ideal, Whitman's poetry is, paradoxically, futile. Suppose we acknowledge, for instance, that the Romantic "Myself " is an expansive symbol of all mankind, and that Whitman's impulse to assume such a universally inclusive identity were allegedly ones of love and humanity. To participate emotionally in the universal "I," however, may only be an effective way for us to ignore the troublesome personal identity that places us in the actual body of men. Even as the Deists find God everywhere precisely because He is nowhere, the reader of Whitman becomes all men only as he avoids being anyone in particular. It appears unflatteringly probable that when we "celebrate" ourselves along with Whitman, we are probably celebrating our own fantasy or ideal which would render us part of the minority of the Elect. "Democratic Vistas," after all, is a plea for a few bards to sing of the dream of America rather than a call for brawn to till and excavate our good earth. It is not the individual butcher or prostitute, after all, who is beautiful or divine. We love the "idea" of them. We love to hear the words that help us think of America as more than a dream.

Similar points have already been made about Thoreau; that his celebration of the gift of life marks a retreat from most of the "things" of experience to their ideal or symbolic properties. Thus, the individualism and affirmation of his philosophy have far less to do with American life and the American dream than they do with the urgency which draws one toward the ideal by emerging *from* the province of the Imperfect rather than by working *through* it: an emergence into the symbol of language, often very beautiful language.

Thoreau's visit to Walden Pond—like Pym's voyage to the Arctic, and Emerson's spiritual space flight, and Whitman's passage to India, and Ahab's white whaling—is essentially imaginary. That is, we can apprehend these places and events only by not actually being there, even dramatically; we conceive the *idea* of them. And ideas, after all, occupy the realm of intelligence, whether American or Greek or Japanese. I think we delude ourselves and promote a kind of unconscious hypocrisy to praise these writers as purveyors of a purely American blueprint for the future, as builders and nourishers of those virtues of individualism, democracy, and affirmation we associate with the greatness of America. They were Americans even as Plato was a Greek. Yet we are quite content to talk of Platonism and rarely of Greek Platonism, while the "American Transcendentalists" are lumped in with the Federalists and Republicans and Confederates and Jacksonian agrarians, as if they were congressional lobbyists.

If our literature of the past hundred years has been one of disillusionment and futility and escape from the actual facts of experience on our continent, perhaps it is merely a more overt manifestation of a desperate quest for that creative and intellectual aristocracy, the impulse toward which we still overlook in our evaluation of American letters. There is not a great difference between Walt Whitman and Norman Mailer. Whether one sings of oneself or "advertises," the struggle is purportedly for individual freedom and creative self-expression, the struggle for a few born equal to die supreme. The point, however, is not that the American artist is unfree, as his passion for Possibility perhaps indicates: he is *too* free. And his search has always been for the confinement of a place in which to belong—in the recognized aristocracy of talent, among the scholars and bards whose frontier is verbal. How interesting it is that the American artist presents himself as one of the elect, the chosen, the inheritor of truth and guide to salvation through the things, or better yet, through the symbols, of the spirit. At the same time his writing, openly or in disguise, is a cry of anguish that the philistine materialists do not accord him that recognition which is presumably bestowed by the very nature of his "calling," whether or not the call of his voice is heeded. If Mr. Mailer has made advertising copy out of Whitman's song, may we not suggest that the pavement on Kerouac's road marks the major difference from the path of Roger Williams, in spite of the fact that the Howlers do not end up in Rhode Island?

And Holden Caulfield is surely not the last of our Antinomians.

> Robert N. Hertz, "English and American Romanticism," in The Personalist, *Vol. XLVI, No. 1, January, 1965, pp. 81-92.*

R. P. Adams

[*In the following essay, Adams contends that the works of the American Romantics are informed by their perception of the universe as an organic, dynamic whole.*]

Morse Peckham, in a recent paper [in *PMLA* LXVI, March 1951], proposes a definition of romanticism which I believe may prove highly useful, not only in the study of nineteenth-century English literature, to which he chiefly applies it, but perhaps even more in the investigation of literary history in the United States. It is my present intention to test this proposition by applying Peckham's theory to some works of the period (1850-1855) which F. O. Matthiessen has called the "American Renaissance."

I

Peckham deals in his article only with the historical meaning of romanticism, not with its general meaning, and he concentrates mainly though not exclusively on its meaning for the study of literature. A definition of romanticism covering this ground should, he says, do two things: first, help us to classify works historically as romantic or other, and second, help us to understand and properly appreciate those classified as romantic. After the usual clearing of the ground, he introduces a theoretical definition which, I agree with him in believing, will do these things—not absolutely, to be sure, but well enough to make the concept extremely valuable for criticism and, especially, for historical research. I wish first to recapitulate, very briefly in my

own words, the main points of the definition and then to show how I think it may be applied to the works of a few outstanding American writers of the mid-nineteenth century.

Historically, Peckham says, romanticism consists in the shift which Arthur O. Lovejoy describes in the last three chapters of *The Great Chain of Being*, a shift away from thinking of the universe as a static mechanism, like a clock, to thinking of it as a dynamic organism, like a growing tree. This shift took place in a few minds at about the end of the eighteenth century, and its implications have been developing in various fields of art, thought, and action ever since. For those who make the shift, the values of static mechanism—reason, order, permanence, and the like—are replaced by their counterparts in an organic universe—instinct or intuition, freedom, and change. Romantic thought is relativistic and pluralistic; it rejects absolute values, formal classifications, and exclusive judgments; it welcomes novelty, originality, and variety. It is less interested in distinctions than in relationships, particularly in the organic relationship which it posits between man and nature, or the universe, and (less often) between the individual and society. The great chain of being is replaced by an indefinitely extended and complicated live network of connecting filaments, as in the vascular system of a plant or in a mass of animal nerve tissue, by which every phenomenon is tied by countless direct and indirect contacts to every other. When a new fact appears, it is not just another link in the chain or cog in the machine; it is an evidence of organic growth and development, and its emergence changes every previously existing aspect of the universe. A new characteristic is evidence of a totally new and different world.

Therefore a romantic artist will strive, not to imitate an ideal perfection of form which has always existed, but to originate a form which has never existed before and which will uniquely express what he alone feels and knows. To do so, he will rely more on imagination than on logic, more on symbols than on signs or allegories, more on unconscious than on conscious powers. He will believe that he is creating a genuinely new thing and thereby changing and renewing the whole of his organic universe. His attitude, given the premise, is perfectly reasonable. One of Peckham's most useful contributions, I think, is that he goes farther than anyone else I know to demonstrate that the romantic artist occupies, philosophically, a very respectable position.

It seems to me obvious that such a change or shift in thinking took place in America between, say, Edwards and Emerson, or Franklin and Whitman, much as it did in England between Pope and Wordsworth. The conservative effort of Edwards to revive Puritanism by reconciling Calvin's theology with Newton's physics and Locke's psychology in a single, permanent metaphysical system is about as characteristic as anything could be of static mechanistic thinking, notwithstanding that it is rather strongly colored by Edwards's emotional and sometimes mystical attitude toward God. Franklin, whose deistic beliefs preclude anthropomorphism, is even more easily identified as a static mechanist. His youthful (and, of course, almost entirely derivative) thinking about the freedom of the will brings him to the conclusion [in his *Dissertation on Liberty and Necessity, Pleasure and Pain*] that "As Man is a Part of this great Machine, the Universe, his regular Acting is requisite to the regular moving of the whole." Otherwise, he says, it would be "as if an ingenious Artificer, having fram'd a curious Machine or Clock, and put its many intricate Wheels and Powers in such a Dependance on one another, that the whole might move in the most exact Order and Regularity, had nevertheless plac'd in it several other Wheels endu'd with an independent *Self-Motion,* but ignorant of the general Interest of the Clock. . . . " The position was a little too rational, perhaps, even for Franklin; certainly most of his contemporaries preferred not to expose the antihuman implications of mechanism quite so nakedly. But those implications could not ultimately be either concealed or accepted. Sooner or later static mechanism had to be abandoned.

In America it was abandoned later and by fewer people, probably, than in England or Germany. The organicism which had begun to replace it abroad was not effectively adopted here until the 1830's, when the short stories of Hawthorne began to appear and Emerson (possibly the first American to go abroad in search of new rather than old ideas) visited Europe and met Landor, Coleridge, Carlyle, and Wordsworth. His publication of Carlyle's *Sartor Resartus* and his own *Nature* at Boston in 1836 makes that year as good a date as any for the beginning of the romantic movement in the United States. In my opinion, however, the greatest works of early American romanticism are not those of Emerson and Hawthorne or of the 1830's, but Melville's *Moby-Dick* (1851), Thoreau's *Walden* (1854), and Whitman's "Song of Myself" (1855). It is to these works that I wish to apply Peckham's theory.

II

Peckham demonstrates very satisfactorily, it seems to me, that *The Ancient Mariner, The Prelude,* and *Sartor Resartus* are all "about spiritual death and rebirth, or secular conversion." That is, they render in various ways the experience that some people have of abandoning one kind of belief in the universe, passing through a period of doubt, despair, and spiritual wandering, and arriving at another kind of belief. Specifically, these works record the breakdown of static mechanism, the search for a new metaphysic to replace it, and the adoption of more or less dynamic interpretations of organicism. I believe that *Moby-Dick, Walden,* and "Song of Myself" are also about the same experience, and that they make use of the same devices of structure and imagery to communicate their meaning.

In *Moby-Dick,* as in *The Ancient Mariner,* the chief metaphor of death and rebirth is the ocean voyage, which Ishmael says "is my substitute for pistol and ball." On this voyage Ishmael becomes involved, inadvertently, in Ahab's mad pursuit of the white whale, a symbol of life like the albatross in Coleridge's poem. And, just as the Mariner's crossbow is a mechanical instrument, Ahab is described several times in mechanistic language. Once Ishmael hears him "lowly humming to himself, producing a sound so strangely muffled and inarticulate that it seemed the mechanical humming of the wheels of his vitality in

him." Speaking of his dominance over the crew, Ahab says, "I thought to find one stubborn, at the least; but my one cogged circle fits into all their various wheels, and they revolve." Ahab's ideal man, to be made by a blacksmith Prometheus, is "fifty feet high in his socks; then, chest modelled after the Thames Tunnel; then, legs with roots to 'em, to stay in one place; then, arms three feet through the wrist; no heart at all, brass forehead, and about a quarter of an acre of fine brains. . . . " What all this means is that Ahab, with his ivory leg and his harpoon baptized with fire in the name of the devil, is in part literally and in the whole figuratively a mechanical man, at deadly enmity with life.

Ishmael, for a time, is carried away by Ahab's intensity and gives himself up with the rest of the crew to revenge and madness. But he has known better things, notably in his relations with the tolerant and tolerable savage Queequeg, and he alone in the world of the ship is able to break away from Ahab's influence. He does so one night when, on duty as helmsman, gazing at the red light of the tryworks, he sees "the rushing Pequod, freighted with savages, and laden with fire, and burning a corpse, and plunging into that blackness of darkness," as "the material counterpart of her monomaniac commander's soul." Lapsing into a hypnotic trance, he loses sight of the compass. "Nothing seemed before me but a jet gloom, now and then made ghastly by flashes of redness. Uppermost was the impression, that whatever swift, rushing thing I stood on was not so much bound to any haven ahead as rushing from all havens astern. A stark, bewildered feeling, as of death, came over me." He finds that he has turned round facing the stern of the ship. Unconsciously he has dissociated himself from its impious quest and its captain's destructive madness. When the ship is stove and sunk by the hunted whale, Ishmael, clinging to the lifebuoy made of Queequeg's coffin, is saved while the rest perish. Out of death he is reborn.

There are many subtle and complicated reasons for this rebirth, which can perhaps be most nearly, though inadequately, expressed by reference to the subtle and complicated attitude that Ishmael develops toward life and toward the white whale as a symbol of life. Without ever denying for a moment that the whale is full of power, malice, and evil, Ishmael realizes, as Ahab does not, that it is also full of goodness, beneficence, and beauty. On his first view of Moby-Dick he says that:

> A gentle joyousness—a mighty mildness of repose in swiftness, invested the gliding whale. Not the white bull Jupiter swimming away with ravished Europa clinging to his graceful horns . . . not that great majesty Supreme! did surpass the glorified White Whale as he so divinely swam. . . . for an instant his whole marbleized body formed a high arch, like Virginia's Natural Bridge, and warningly waving his bannered flukes in the air, the grand god revealed himself, sounded, and went out of sight. Hoveringly halting, and dipping on the wing, the white seafowls longingly lingered over the agitated pool that he left.

A few minutes later the whale, swiftly rising again, crushes Ahab's boat in its jaws.

The unresolved complexity of Ishmael's attitude here is consistent with his views on other matters. He paradoxically exalts the nobility of "the kingly commons" of Nantucket's ocean empire. He respects both the beauty and the fierce, tigerish power of the sea, but he is not afraid to dive "among the unspeakable foundations, ribs, and very pelvis of the world" to discuss its monsters, its sharks, whales, giant squids and krakens, finding in it a "visible image of that deep, blue, bottomless soul, pervading mankind and nature; and every strange, half-seen, gliding, beautiful thing that eludes him; every dimly-discovered, uprising fin of some undiscernible form, seems . . . the embodiment of those elusive thoughts that only people the soul by continually flitting through it." Above all, he understands that man's life is an unending movement of change, with nothing fixed or safe, no haven on a lee shore. He sees even, as very few people have the courage to conceive, that "there is no steady unretracing progress in this life; we do not advance through fixed gradations, and at the last one pause:—through infancy's unconscious spell, boyhood's thoughtless faith, adolescence' doubt (the common doom), then scepticism, then disbelief, resting at last in manhood's pondering repose of If. But once gone through, we trace the round again; and are infants, boys, and men, and Ifs eternally." Because he knows life thus in all its complexity of organic, incessantly changing relatedness and because he accepts it and loves it in its evil and terrible as well as in its good and joyful aspects, and also because he sees and loves the nobility mingled with the savagery of a Queequeg, the weakness of a Starbuck, the thoughtlessness of a Stubb or a Flask, or even the crazed evil of an Ahab, he is worthy of his own life and of being reborn, as he is, from the deadly encountering shock of the most irreconcilable opposites.

In *Walden,* as in *Moby-Dick,* the pattern of symbolic death and rebirth is used to express a revolt against static mechanism in favor of dynamic organicism. Thoreau begins by saying, in effect, that most men, involved in the mechanical activities of commerce, do not live. They are "so occupied with the factitious cares and superfluously coarse labors of life that its finer fruits cannot be plucked by them." A laboring man "has no time to be anything but a machine," and "men have become the tools of their tools." To this mechanistic image of man as he is Thoreau opposes an organic image of man as he might be and as the romantic believes he should be. "The soil, it appears, is suited to the seed, for it has sent its radicle downward, and it may now send its shoot upward also with confidence. Why has man rooted himself thus firmly in the earth, but that he may rise in the same proportion into the heavens above?" Man, having died, should be reborn.

The purpose of Thoreau's experiment at Walden is accordingly to discover whether, once a man "has obtained those things which are necessary to life, there is another alternative than to obtain the superfluities; and that is, to adventure on life now, his vacation from humbler toil having commenced." Believing that "the cost of a thing is the amount of what I will call life which is required to be ex-

changed for it, immediately or in the long run," he plans to reduce his material wants, trade as little time as possible for mere subsistence, and devote the rest to the organic process of life itself.

The basic structure of the book may be most clearly understood in the fact that Thoreau, "for convenience," condenses his two years' experience at Walden into one, and describes it beginning with summer and proceeding through fall and winter to spring. The turning seasons thus define a process of symbolic death and rebirth which, for Thoreau as for other romantics, represents the character of personal development. In the summer chapters, which take up most of the room in the book, he discusses chiefly the relationships between man and nature and between the individual and society, alternating between the two themes in "Reading" and "Sounds," "Solitude" and "Visitors," "The Bean-Field" and "The Village," "The Ponds" and "Baker Farm," and "Higher Laws" and "Brute Neighbors." In the fall chapter, "House-Warming," he reluctantly goes indoors, to something like hibernation. In the three winter chapters he discusses "Former Inhabitants; and Winter Visitors," "Winter Animals," and "The Pond in Winter." He is most interested in this section in history and metaphysics, and in harmonies of relationship which he infers from the regularity of the pond in this comparatively static season and from the fact that ice from it is to be shipped as far away as India.

His climax is the chapter on "Spring," a paean of rebirth in which he carries the organic metaphor to its ultimate conclusion. Seeing how the clay on the bank of a railroad cut flows under the rays of the spring sun he announces roundly that "there is nothing inorganic. . . . The earth is not a mere fragment of dead history, stratum upon stratum like the leaves of a book, to be studied by geologists and antiquaries chiefly, but living poetry like the leaves of a tree, which precede flowers and fruit,—not a fossil earth, but a living earth; compared with whose great central life all animal and vegetable life is merely parasitic." He is impressed particularly by the grass, which he says "flames up on the hillsides like a spring fire . . . not yellow but green is the color of its flame;—the symbol of perpetual youth," and it assures him of his own rebirth after death. "So our human life but dies down to its root, and still puts forth its green blade to eternity." As for the pond, he simply remarks, "Walden was dead and is alive again."

Life, as Thoreau understands it, is not only organic but very explicitly dynamic as well. That is why he says that "in any weather, at any hour of the day or night, I have been anxious to improve the nick of time, and notch it on my stick too; to stand on the meeting of two eternities, the past and future, which is precisely the present moment; to toe that line." His business, he explains, is "to anticipate, not the sunrise and the dawn merely, but, if possible, Nature herself! How many mornings, summer and winter, before yet any neighbor was stirring about his business, have I been about mine!" Morning is Thoreau's most frequent symbol for the moving present moment, which continually supersedes tradition and the past. The most important thing is always life in the present; "alert and healthy natures remember that the sun rose clear. It is never too late to give up our prejudices. No way of thinking or doing, however ancient, can be trusted without proof." And Thoreau also very well understands that this dynamic aspect of life implies diversity; change leads naturally to variety; the new thing is a different thing. Therefore he cautions his reader that "I would not have any one adopt *my* mode of living on any account; for, beside that before he has fairly learned it I may have found out another for myself, I desire that there may be as many different persons in the world as possible; but I would have each one be very careful to find out and pursue *his own* way, and not his father's or his mother's or his neighbor's instead."

It should hardly be necessary to point out how closely, in the terms of Peckham's theory of romanticism, *Walden* is related to Carlyle's *Sartor Resartus* in theme, structure, and imagery. And, for once, it is probably safe to suppose that the relationship is largely a result of direct influence, for it was at Walden that Thoreau wrote his very perceptive and enthusiastic essay on "Thomas Carlyle and His Works." In that essay Thoreau says that Carlyle's "earlier essays reached us at a time when Coleridge's were the only recent words which had made any notable impression so far . . . and he has no doubt afforded reasonable encouragement and sympathy to many an independent but solitary thinker." One of those who benefited most from this transatlantic tutelage was surely Thoreau himself.

He was never merely a follower, however, and he seems to have gone considerably farther than Carlyle in his belief that each individual life is a process of continual change, continual growth, continual rebirth. Every morning, he says, is an occasion for complete renewal "to a higher life than we fell asleep from. . . . That man who does not believe that each day contains an earlier, more sacred, and auroral hour than he has yet profaned, has despaired of life, and is pursuing a descending and darkening way." And morning need not be confined to an hour only. "To him whose elastic and vigorous thought keeps pace with the sun, the day is a perpetual morning. . . . Morning is when I am awake and there is a dawn in me." And he adds, "To be awake is to be alive." He is not content, after his experimental rebirth at Walden, to rest on that achievement. "I left the woods," he explains, "for as good a reason as I went there. Perhaps it seemed to me that I had several more lives to live, and could not spare any more time for that one." He left for the same reason he went, that is, to seek rebirth in a new phase of life, growth, and development. Like Melville, he tells us that life does not advance in a single straight line but through a series of mornings, or springs, each novel, unpredictable, and intensely interesting.

Whitman's use of symbolic death and rebirth as a structural pattern in "Song of Myself" is less obvious than either Melville's or Thoreau's in the works we have examined, but it is none the less effective. Like Thoreau he finds a prime symbol of regeneration in the grass, which he guesses is "the flag of my disposition, out of hopeful green stuff woven," or "itself a child. . . . the produced babe of the vegetation," or "the beautiful uncut hair of graves," growing from the bodies of the dead, "from under the faint red roofs of mouths," and he exclaims, "O I perceive after

all so many uttering tongues" which "do not come from the roofs of mouths for nothing." Death has no terrors for Whitman because he believes that it is a phase of a cycle, that it always leads to rebirth and more life. "The smallest sprout shows there is really no death," he says. "All goes onward and outward. . . . and nothing collapses, / And to die is different from what any one supposed, and luckier." Throughout the poem grass is consistently presented as an organic metaphor of rebirth, of communication after death, and of immortality in that communication. Whitman makes his meaning clearest when he says near the end, "I bequeath myself to the dirt to grow from the grass I love, / If you want me again look for me under your bootsoles." What this tells us, plainly and emphatically, is that Whitman himself is reborn in his poetry, which is for that reason called *Leaves of Grass* and which we may quite soberly say has kept him in a very real sense alive to our thought and imagination.

Whitman, like Thoreau and Melville, prepares for this rebirth in communication by saying early in the poem that he will withdraw from "houses and rooms" (though he does not reject them) and "go to the bank by the wood and become undisguised and naked," seeking, like the others, to establish his relationship with nature before attempting a return to society through the medium of his work. He finds this relationship to be organic, and he is confident, sometimes serenely, more often enthusiastically, that it includes all things, himself, the world, God, and other people, "that the spirit of God is the eldest brother of my own, / And that all the men ever born are also my brothers. . . . and the women my sisters and lovers, / And that a kelson of the creation is love. . . ." The universe, to Whitman as to other romantics, is alive, and he is passionately in love with it, longing to embrace the "barebosomed night," the "voluptuous coolbreathed earth," the "Capricious and dainty sea." Being alive, it is naturally dynamic; it grows and changes. Whitman describes its evolution in sexual terms, the changing present being characterized for him, as it hardly is for Thoreau, by "the procreant urge of the world." But he is no more interested than Thoreau in "the beginning or the end," concentrating instead on a dialectic process of change which is the very essence of dynamic organicism. "Out of the dimness opposite equals advance. . . . Always substance and increase, / Always a knit of identity. . . . always distinction. . . . always a breed of life."

Whitman's emphasis on the "distinction" is to many people his most outstanding characteristic; so much so that the structural organization of his poems, especially "Song of Myself," has not been sufficiently noticed. He is of course a fascinated diversitarian, reveling through endless catalogues in the greatest possible variety of relationships and activities, entering at great length, by sympathy and by empathy, into the lives and feelings of people in all places and occupations. "I resist anything," he confesses, "better than my own diversity," and he is resolved that every aspect of it shall be represented. He is the poet of evil as well as of good, and a vehicle for "Voices of sexes and lusts. . . . voices veiled, and I remove the veil, / Voices indecent by me clarified and transfigured." Out of this vast variety, and specifically out of the dialectic of good and evil, also comes developing life. "The pleasures of heaven are with me, and the pains of hell are with me, / The first I graft and increase upon myself. . . . the latter I translate into a new tongue." Though he is less easy to analyze or to quote than Thoreau or Melville, partly because of this almost explosive diversitarianism, Whitman is if anything an even more consistent and radical positive romanticist. His determined insistence on variety as well as on change and his lavish use of organic imagery make him an almost perfect exemplar of Peckham's definition.

III

That definition, however, is not complete, as Peckham says, without the concept of negative romanticism, which is needed as much in the study of American as of English literature. Positive romanticism will not account for Poe any better than it will for Byron, many of whose attitudes Poe shared and continued, and transmitted to the French romantics who took him for their prophet. And I think it is important that such writers as Byron, Poe, and Baudelaire be firmly placed in the romantic movement, and that the character of their romanticism be clearly understood. Peckham defines negative romanticism as the attitude of those who have rejected the old static mechanistic world order but who have not, for whatever reasons, arrived at a satisfactorily dynamic and organic metaphysic to replace it. They are often haunted by feelings of guilt, alienation, and fear, none of which appear to have any adequate cause, until we realize that negative romanticists inhabit a universe without purpose or meaning. They have, therefore, no sufficient sense of place or direction, or feeling of relationship to their environment. Their world is a place of confusion, of uncertainty, and very often, quite understandably, of terror. Most recent critics and historians of literature have found them easiest to understand as weaklings, sick men, and neurotics, which many of them certainly were. But their position is none the less valid or interesting for that, and their work, I suspect, is negative and often morbid as much for philosophic as for psychiatric reasons. I find it very hard to believe that neuroticism equals genius, as one extreme kind of psychological interpretation tends to imply, or that a man's work may be good because he is ill.

The negative characteristics of Poe's work are obvious enough in his preoccupation with themes of crime, terror, incest, burial alive, and forbidden knowledge, and in his strong affinity to the Gothic tradition and the Byronic pose. At the same time he is obviously romantic in his appreciation and use of Keats and Coleridge, in his partial subscription to an organic theory of form in literature, and most of all in his practical use of symbolism to express ideas and feelings of which he is largely unconscious and apparently very much afraid. It might be said most simply, perhaps, that his indirect and, as it were, inadvertent self-expression through symbolism constitutes him a romantic and that his fear of self-expression, his insistence on the purely conscious and intentional character of his work, his refusal in "The Philosophy of Composition" to examine the sources of his inspiration, and his very superficial notion of originality show that his romanticism is negative. The fundamental contradiction may be seen in

much of his critical writing, as when he remarks in "Marginalia" that:

> To see distinctly the machinery—the wheels and pinions—of any work of Art is, unquestionably, of itself, a pleasure, but one which we are able to enjoy only just in proportion as we do *not* enjoy the legitimate effect designed by the artist:—and, in fact, it too often happens that to reflect analytically upon Art, is to reflect after the fashion of the mirrors in the temple of Smyrna, which represent the fairest images as deformed.

The difficulty seems to be partly that Poe is thinking of a work of art as an organism and trying to analyze it into "wheels and pinions" as if it were a machine. The deformation results not so much from the fact of analysis as from the fact that the analysis is made in the wrong terms. It might indeed be better not to analyze at all, but it would be better still to analyze correctly, that is organically. The same kind of inconsistency may be found in *Eureka,* where Poe concludes that "all is Life—Life—Life within Life," but where life is described in completely static terms. Poe's "living" universe proceeds from a normal and right state of unity through an abnormal and wrong phase of diversity to its original unity again, the whole process being an absolutely orderly and logical result of a single act of will on the part of God. Poe is pathetically certain that in this formulation he has discovered the ultimate truth, which can never be altered, "since," as he remarks in passing, "Truth and Immutability are one." And so, in Poe's metaphysic, are life and death.

IV

In this country, as in Europe, the ideas of positive romanticism have been cogently developed by only a very few people. The great majority of Americans have remained static mechanists or, at the most, negative romanticists, and they have generally succeeded in making life uncomfortable for those who, in the interests of organicism, dynamism, and diversitarianism, have refused to conform to majority mores and opinions. The struggle has been aggravated here by the relatively long persistence of Puritan and Fundamentalist theology, by the overwhelming predominance of middle-class commercial interests, and more recently by the tremendous growth of technological skill and industrial power. Static mechanism has never been more apparently successful than in the United States over the past century and a half, or enjoyed greater prestige except, perhaps, among the dialectical materialists of the Soviet Union. Therefore, probably, its defects have never been more clearly apparent than to those few Americans who have been courageously independent enough to examine it critically in the light of romantic ideas.

This very limited and superficial examination of the American Renaissance with reference to Peckham's theory indicates two rather important conclusions, both of which are in some quarters considered unorthodox. The first is that the independent, self-sustaining American literature which arose during the middle years of the nineteenth century was not so much the result of American writers' rejection of European models and devotion to native themes as it was of their somewhat belated rejection of static mechanism and adoption of dynamic organicism, in which they were greatly aided and encouraged by the example of such Europeans as Goethe, Wordsworth, Coleridge, and Carlyle. The second is that, partly because they had the firm foundation of European romanticism to build on and partly, perhaps, because they were so clearly and completely in opposition to the predominant forces in their own society, these Americans carried the romantic revolution farther and developed its implications more consistently than the writers of any other national literature in their own time or, I am inclined to think, since then.

R. P. Adams, "Romanticism and the American Renaissance," in American Literature, Vol. 23, No. 4, January, 1952, pp. 419-32.

Richard Moody on characteristics of American Romanticism:

The clearest and most colorful traits of the romanticist are his loving and longing looks into the past and into the future, his delight in rosy recollections and fervid hopes, his easy and fanciful dreams of distant place and distant clime, and his preoccupation with the curious, the strange, and the mysterious. His revolutionary spirit prefers to act on faith, to trust the inner experiences of life, to follow the sentimental longings of his heart. He distrusts the strictures and painful rigidities of reasoned behavior. Inherited laws and customs, rules of conduct for life and art, and the barriers which would bind, encompass, and confine him to an earthbound and prosaic existence fall before his insurgent protests. But vigorous as his insurgent rebellions may and do become, he remains a common man, tenderhearted and sentimental in his expansive love for his fellows and in his unshakable belief in a glorious future. When his dreams demand expression in painting, in literature, or in the theatre, he revolts against any calculated classical forms and delights in seemingly indissoluble mixtures, in the blends of contraries, in the irregularities of nature. He relies on each work to achieve its own form from its inherent association of ideas and the pervading atmosphere it creates, not from any traditional concepts. His art must be new, fresh, and persistently retentive of the illusion of the "first time."

Richard Moody, in his America Takes the Stage: Romanticism in American Drama and Theatre, 1750-1900, Indiana University Press, 1955.

Tony Tanner

[*Tanner is an English educator and critic. In the following essay, he explores ways in which the American and European Romantics differed in their attitudes toward nature, society, and the past.*]

I

Animals have often provided Romantic writers with important images. Blake's tiger and Melville's whale are both used to focus on the awesome and ambiguous energies at the heart of creation. Insects, too, have often been invoked

for the purposes of emulation or identification. Wordsworth gathers visual pleasures 'like a bee among the flowers'; Emerson admires the 'Humble-Bee' in his 'sunny solitudes':

Sailor of the atmosphere;
Swimmer through the waves of air;
Voyager of light and noon;

Emily Dickinson cries 'Oh, for a bee's experience / Of clovers and of noon'; Rilke writes 'We are the bees of the Invisible. Nous butinons éperdument le miel du Visible pour l'accumuler dans la grande ruche d'or de l'invisible.' It is an attractive and understandable image for any Romantic writer who seeks to assimilate the pollen of perception in order to transmute it into the honey of his art. But more unusual perhaps is the attraction which the spider has held for American writers from Jonathan Edwards to Robert Lowell. Thus Edwards starts one of his earliest pieces of writing, 'Of Insects': 'Of all Insects no one is more wonderfull than the Spider especially with Respect to their sagacity and admirable way of working.' Edwards was particularly struck to see spiders apparently 'swimming in the air' (like Emerson's bee), and he describes how he watched and experimented to see how they managed to sustain themselves in space. The secret, the marvel, was the way they 'put out a web at their tails' which was so light that the wind took it, and held up the spider at the same time; then

If the further End Of it happens to catch by a tree or anything, why there's a web for him to Go over upon and the Spider immediately perceives it and feels when it touches, much after the same manner as the soul in the brain immediately Perceives when any of those little nervous strings that Proceed from it are in the Least Jarrd by External things.

Pausing to notice how the Puritan imagination effortlessly makes the external fact emblematic of an inner process, I want to juxtapose Whitman's poem on 'A Noiseless Patient Spider' where the spider's emblematic significance is fully developed:

A Noiseless patient spider,
I mark'd where on a little promontory it stood isolated,
Mark'd how to explore the vacant vast surrounding,
It launched forth filament, filament, filament, out of itself,
Ever unreeling them, ever tirelessly speeding them.

And you O my soul where you stand,
Surrounded, detached, in measureless oceans of space,
Ceaselessly musing, venturing, throwing, seeking the spheres to connect them,
Till the bridge you will need be form'd, till the ductile anchor hold,
Till the gossamer thread you fling catch somewhere, O my soul.

We could scarcely hope to find a better image of the American Romantic writer, which is almost to say the American writer, than this. Isolated and secreting filament, filament, filament (think of Whitman's constantly renewed stream of notations and enumerations) to explore, to relate to, and to fill 'the vacant vast surrounding'. America is the 'measureless oceans of space'; the web is the private creation of the writer, constructed with a view of attaching himself somehow to reality, a world of his own making in which he can live on his own terms, assimilating and transforming what the outside world brings his way. Emily Dickinson, too, obviously saw something of her own poetic activity in the movements of the spider, as in the famous poem which starts:

> A spider sewed at night
> Without a light
> Upon an arc of white.

And in other poems, for example, 'The spider . . . —dancing softly to Himself / His Coil of Pearl— unwinds.' She elsewhere calls the spider an artist of 'surpassing merit' whose tapestries, wrought in an hour, are 'Continents of Light'; but also very ephemeral. 'He plies from Nought to Nought / In insubstantial Trade.' A not dissimilar image occurs to Henry Adams in the crucial chapter in his *Education* on 'A Dynamic Theory of History':

> For convenience as an image, the theory may liken man to a spider in its web, watching for chance prey. Forces of nature dance like flies before the new, and the spider pounces on them when it can . . . The spider-mind acquires a faculty of the memory, and, with it, a singular skill of analysis and synthesis, taking apart and putting together in different relations the meshes of its trap.

And in a comparably important statement in Henry James's essay 'The Art of Fiction' the work of the spider receives perhaps its finest transformation:

> Experience is never limited, and it is never complete; it is an immense sensibility, a kind of huge spider-web of the finest silken threads suspended in the chamber of consciousness, and catching every air-borne particle in its tissue. It is the very atmosphere of the mind; and when the mind is imaginative . . . it takes to itself the faintest hints of life, it converts the very pulses of the air into revelations.

The emblem has become a metaphor; the web has been internalized and experience has become the atmosphere of the mind.

Now it is a truism that one of the recurrent features of Romantic art is the elevation of inner activity over external reality. Hegel's is only the most sweeping of many such generalizations, when he says in the Introduction to the *Philosophy of Art*:

> In brief, the essence of Romantic art lies in the artistic object's being free, concrete, and the spiritual idea in its very essence—all this revealed to the inner rather than to the outer eye . . . This inner world is the content of Romantic art; Romantic art must seek its embodiment in precisely such an inner life or some re-

flection of it. Thus the inner life shall triumph over the outer world . . .

But since for Hegel Romantic art included nearly everything since Classical art, this panoramic view of the internalization or subjectivization of reality (examined brilliantly and at length by Erich Heller in *The Artist's Journey into the Interior*) will not help us very much in an attempt to suggest some of the differences between American and European Romanticism. This analogy between the American writer and the spider may at least provide a specific point of departure.

II

One of the formative experiences of all those early American writers was of a sense of space, of vast unpeopled solitudes such as no European Romantic could have imagined. As the hero of Chateaubriand's *René* says to his American auditors: 'Europeans constantly in a turmoil are forced to build their own solitudes.' The reverse was true for the American Romantic. Solitude was all but imposed on him. Nothing seemed easier for him than to take a few steps to find himself confronting and caught up in those measureless oceans of space where Whitman found his soul both surrounded and detached. This gravitation towards empty space is a constant in American literature, even if it appears only in glimpses, as for instance when the narrator of *The Sacred Fount* turns away from the crowded house of Newmarch and staring up at the sky finds the night air 'a sudden corrective to the grossness of our lustres and the thickness of our medium'; or when the narrator of *The Last Tycoon* says 'It's startling to you

Walt Whitman.

sometimes—just air, unobstructed, uncomplicated air.' Charles Olson is justified in starting his book on Melville (*Call me Ishmael*) with the emphatic announcement: 'I take SPACE to be the central fact to man born in America, from Folsom cave to now. I spell it large because it comes large here. Large, and without mercy.' But like those spiders who came under Jonathan Edwards's formidable scrutiny, the American artist, once he found himself at sea in space, had to do something to maintain himself, and one instinctive response was to expand into the surrounding space. William Cullen Bryant writes of 'The Prairies': 'I behold them from the first, / And my heart swells, while the dilated sight / Takes in the encircling vastness'; Whitman claims 'I chant the chant of dilation'; Emerson records how 'the heart refuses to be imprisoned; in its first and narrowest pulses it already tends outward with a vast force and to immense and innumerable expansions . . . there is no outside, no inclosing wall, no circumference to us'. Emerson's eye, and his mind after it, was continually drawn to the remotest horizons; the only true encirclement to a man obsessed with circles was earth's vanishing point, the very perimeter of the visible world where sight lost itself in space. When he writes about 'The Poet' and his attraction to narcotics of all kinds Emerson says: 'These are auxiliaries to the centrifugal tendency of a man, to his passage out into free space, and they help him to escape the custody of that body in which he is pent up, and of that jail-yard of individual relations in which he is enclosed.' Near the end of *Walden* Thoreau has some marvellous lines about the 'ethereal flight' of a hawk which sported alone 'in the fields of air'. 'It appeared to have no companion in the universe . . . and to need none but the morning and the ether with which it played.' Thoreau ends the book, appropriately enough, with the parable of the bug which hatches out in an old table and breaks free into 'beautiful and winged life', and Whitman at the end of *Song of Myself* literally feels himself diffused back into the elements: 'I depart as air . . .' In these three seminal American Romantics we find a similar 'centrifugal tendency'; a dilation of self, which can become an abandoning of self, into the surrounding vastness. But of course if this were all we would have had no record of the movement since words are not carefully strung together by a man in the process of being metamorphosed into the circumambient air, as Emerson seems to recognize in a letter to Samuel Gray Ward: 'Can you not save me, dip me into ice water, find me some girding belt, that I glide not away into a stream or a gas, and decease in infinite diffusion?' Like those spiders swimming in the air, the American writer throws out filament, filament, filament, and weaves a web to sustain himself in the vastness. Paradoxically these webs are often notable for being composed of many very concrete particulars and empirically perceived facts (thus Thoreau is also one of the earthiest of writers); it is as though these solid details offered some anchoring attachment. When Frost described a poem as a stay against confusion, he might have more accurately phrased it, for the American writer, as a stay against diffusion.

The web is the writer's style; the concrete details are the nourishing particles which the web ensnares and transforms. And what extraordinary webs the American Romantics (and indeed post-Romantics) have spun: Emerson's essays for instance, which often seem to tremble and blur with the very vertigo they were written to counteract, or *Walden* and *Moby-Dick* which, although they seem to repeat stock Romantic themes—the return to nature, the voyage—are of a stylistic idiosyncrasy which can scarcely be paralleled in European writing. And much of that style is not being used to explore self or environment so much as to fill in the spaces between self and environment. Again, *Song of Myself* might at first glance appear to have much in common with *The Prelude,* and the phrase 'egotistical sublime' which Keats applied to Wordsworth could certainly be extended to Whitman. And yet the sense of harmonious reciprocities between mind and landscape, that 'intimate communion' which, says Wordsworth, 'our hearts / Maintain with the minuter properties / Of objects which already are belov'd', is absent from Whitman's more desperate and sometimes hysterical ecstasies. 'My voice goes after what my eyes cannot reach, / With the twirl of my tongue I encompass worlds and volumes of worlds.' This verbal and visual pursuit of objects and worlds to fill up his void is somewhat different from the serene stealth with which, for Wordsworth, 'the visible scene / Would enter unawares into his mind / With all its solemn imagery'.

Among American Romantics there is an unusual stress on a visual relationship with nature. 'I am becoming a transparent eyeball; I am nothing; I see all'—Emerson's famous formulation is relevant for much subsequent American writing. Thoreau, whose other senses were active enough, puts the emphasis on sight: 'We are as much as we see.' Whitman asks himself 'What do you see Walt Whitman?' in 'Salut au Monde' and answers literally and copiously, using the phrase 'I see' eighty-three times. Obviously new habits of attention, recovered visual intimacies with nature, were crucial for European Romantics as well (and Ruskin was to make of sight an instrument arguably more sensitive than anything to be found in American writing). But more often than in America, the English Romantic's response was also auditory. Keats listening darkling to his nightingale is only one of the many English Romantic poets whose ears were highly receptive to any vibrations or music that reached them. 'With what strange utterance did the loud dry wind / Blow through my ears', 'I heard among the solitary hills / . . . sounds / of undistinguishable motion', 'Then sometime, in that silence, while he hung / Listening, a gentle shock of mild surprise / Has carried far into the heart the voice / Of mountain torrents'—these examples from Wordsworth of the voice and utterances of landscape may be readily multiplied, perhaps the most famous being 'The Solitary Reaper', where the sound of the woman's song provides lasting nourishment for the poet:

> The music in my heart I bore,
> Long after it was heard no more.

The American Romantics do not give the impression of valuing auditory responses in quite this way. More to the point, for the English Romantics a purely visual relationship to the outside world betokened a state of deprivation, a loss of intimacy, a failure of poetic vision. Coleridge's 'Dejection: an Ode' hinges on this severance between self and surrounding things: 'I see them all so excellently fair,

/ I see, not feel, how beautiful they are!' And Shelley's 'Stanzas Written in Dejection', by lamenting the absence of some other 'heart' to 'share in my emotion' as he looks at the scene in front of him, is also asserting the insufficiency of mere sight. A purely or predominantly visual relationship with nature in fact can indicate a state of alienation or detachment from it. An auditory response suggests that the sounds of the environment mean something to the hearer, something within becomes alert to something without which seems to speak a comprehensible language. This suggests at least the possibility of communication, of significant relationship, perhaps even of a kind of dialogue. To be linked to a thing only by sight is at the same time to be severed from it, if only because the act of purely visual appropriation implies a definite space between the eye and the object. And American writers have been predominantly watchers. Thoreau, supposedly so immersed in his environment, can still use this strange image: 'I enter some glade in the woods . . . and it is as if I had come to an open window. I see out and around myself.' Having left man-made dwellings behind him, he reintroduces part of their architecture to describe his feelings. To be in the midst of nature and yet to see it as through an open window is surely in some way also to feel cut off from it. Emerson often refers to the world as 'spectacle' and is extremely sensitive to all shades of visual experience, as when he says it is enough to take a coach ride to have the surrounding world 'wholly detached from all relation to the observer'. He said of the soul: 'It is a watcher more than a doer, and it is a doer, only that it may the better watch.' This in turn anticipates James, whose central figures are all great watchers, thereby excluded from participation in the world they survey—like James himself, leaning intently out of one of the many windows in his house of fiction. Again, in Hemingway's characters their visual alertness and acuity is in part a symptom of their alienation.

Those American writers we associate with the New England Renaissance (and many subsequently) most typically felt themselves to be swimming in space; not, certainly, tied fast into any society, nor really attached very firmly to the vast natural environment. In many ways this state was cherished and preferred; to sport in fields of air could be the ultimate ecstasy. On the other hand there was the danger of, as it were, vanishing or diffusing altogether. The emergent strategy, variously developed by different writers, was to spin out a web which could hold them in place, which would occupy the space around them, and from which they could look out into the world. But even when they scrutinized their environment with extreme care, and took over many of its details to weave into their webs of art, they were seldom in any genuine communion with nature. European Romantics, on the other hand, do seem to have enjoyed moments of reciprocal relationship with nature and could speak truly of what they 'half perceive and half create'. With Wordsworth they could consider 'man and nature as essentially adapted to each other'. In discovering nature they were at the same time discovering themselves; in internalizing what was around them they were at the same time externalizing what was within, as Coleridge often described. 'The forms / Of Nature have a passion in themselves / That intermingles with

those works of man / To which she summons him.' That is Wordsworth, and it is just that sort of fruitful *intermingling* of Nature's and Man's creative potencies that is absent from American Romantic writing, which tends, rather, to testify that Nature holds off from man's approaches. Nature is indeed seen, seen with intense clarity through the intervening air, but it leaves precisely that intervening space to be filled by the writer's own filament. That marriage between subject and object, mind and nature, which is an abiding Romantic dream, is seldom consummated in the work of the American Romantics. When Emerson speaks of 'the cool disengaged air of natural objects' he is pointing to a perceptual experience which makes for important differences in American Romanticism.

Of course it would be an unacceptable simplification of Emerson's strangely fluid writing to fix on any one of his descriptions of nature as his definitive attitude. But in his first famous essay on 'Nature' we find a conception of nature markedly different from any to be found in any comparable European documents. Above all it is the fluidity, the insubstantiality, the transparency of nature which is stressed. Emerson may sound like Wordsworth when he talks of 'that wonderful congruity which subsists between man and the world'—so much was a stock Romantic piety, or hope. But what a strange congruity Emerson's is. To the poet, he says, 'the refractory world is ductile and flexible'. When a poetic mind contemplates nature, matter is 'dissolved by a thought'. The Transcendentalist, says Emerson (and Transcendentalism was pertinently described as 'that outbreak of Romanticism on Puritan ground' by James Elliot Cabot [Quoted by Henry James in his essay 'Emerson']) has only to ask certain questions 'to find his solid universe growing dim and impalpable'. The 'poet turns the world to glass'; when he looks at nature he sees 'the flowing or the Metamorphosis'. 'The Universe is fluid and volatile': 'this surface on which we now stand is not fixed, but sliding'. If there is any 'fixture or stability' in all this sliding, dissolving, melting world, it is 'in the soul'. 'We are not built like a ship to be tossed, but like a house to stand', says Emerson. Since his Nature is distinctly watery, and the 'ethereal tides' seem at times almost to inundate him as he opens himself to them, we may wonder what will be the origin of this stable house of self which can stand firm in the flowing flux of Existence.

Although Emerson is sometimes very specific about individual facts and perceptions, the nature he refers to has no autonomy and very little local identity. It is a mental fabrication. We look in vain for the specificity of all those place-names which are so common in European Romanticism, whether it is Tintern Abbey or Mont Blanc or 'Lines Composed while Climbing the Left Ascent of Brockley Coome, Somersetshire, May 1795' (Coleridge). Emerson says that America's 'ample geography. dazzles the imagination' and a dazzled imagination may respond in unusual ways. His own response, more often than not, is to treat nature as a flimsy, flowing tissue of appearances. He is concerned either to see through it, or withdraw from it. It is indeed a source of emblems, but he tends only to assert this emblematical quality. Perhaps the difference between an emblem and a metaphor is that an emblem is a sign existing at a definite remove from what it signifies and composed of different material; while a metaphor merges the sign and the thing signified. For Emerson Nature was more a matter of emblems than metaphors; it provided no final resting place, no home, for the mind. Here, perhaps, we can detect vestiges of the old Puritan suspicion of matter as fallen, flawed, and misleading—despite Emerson's programmatic optimism about the essential benevolence of all creation. However it is, Emerson's Nature lacks the substantiality, the local external reality, to be found in many European Romantic writers. In Emerson Nature may be a symbol for the mind, or a manifestation of the invisible Over-Soul. What it tends not to be is its own solid self. Children, said Emerson, 'believe in the external world'. When we grow older we realize that it 'appears only'. Perhaps Emerson found no more dramatic phrase for his concept of Nature than when he suggested it might be 'the apocalypse of the mind'.

What Emerson has done is to interpose his version of a ductile, transparent, fluid, apparitional nature between himself and the hard, opaque, refractory (and dazzling) otherness of the real American landscape. This way he makes Nature amenable to himself and his purposes. It is notable how often he talks of playing with Nature as if it were a collection of baubles and toys. The genius, he writes in his journal, 'can upheave and balance and toss every object in Nature for his metaphor'; we must be like Shakespeare, he says, who 'tosses the creation like a bauble from hand to hand'. Anything less tossable from hand to hand, less bauble-like, than the American landscape in the mid-nineteenth century would be hard to think of. But Emerson is swimming in air; and this Nature, this flowing stream of soft transparent playthings, is the web he has created to keep himself afloat. By contrast Wordsworth's or Keats's poetic Nature is, if not the apocalypse of reality, at least its consecration. More recent American writers have not found themselves in exactly the same vast otherness as the mid-nineteenth-century writers. If anything they have to deal with a congestion which would squash them rather than an emptiness which might swallow them, though of course there is a kind of crowdedness which feels like a vacancy. But when Wallace Stevens says that 'resistance to the pressure of ominous and destructive circumstance consists of its conversion, so far as possible, into a different, an explicable, an amenable circumstance', he seems to be placing the emphasis in a way which is typical of the American Romantic attitude, which has so often 'converted' the given environment into something amenable, not necessarily benevolent if we think of Poe, Hawthorne, Melville, but amenable—ductile to the weavings of their art.

III

Emerson tells his American poet-figure 'Thou shalt leave the world', adding: 'the impressions of the actual world shall fall like summer rain, copious, but not troublesome to thy invulnerable essence'. Reality becomes something like a light shower, easily disregarded. In its place, as he says at the end of 'Nature', 'Every spirit builds itself a house'. This is the house (or the web) which we have already seen the American artist constructing for his own stability, sustenance and unhindered development. 'Build

therefore your own world', Emerson goes on to admonish his readers in a phrase which has given Richard Poirier a starting-point for his exciting book *A World Elsewhere.* Poirier's more fully developed ideas, as in such a passage as the following, corroborate my suggestion that the creation of a verbal web, safe for habitation and the expansion of consciousness, is a major characteristic of American Romanticism:

> The books which in my view constitute a distinctive American tradition within English literature are early, very often clumsy examples of a modernist impulse in fiction: they resist within their pages the forces of environment that otherwise dominate the world. Their styles have an eccentricity of defiance, even if the defiance shows sometimes as carelessness. Cooper, Emerson, Thoreau, Melville, Hawthorne, Mark Twain, James—they both resemble and serve their heroes by trying to create an environment of 'freedom', though as writers their efforts must be wholly in language. American books are often written as if historical forces cannot possibly provide such environment, as if history can give no life to 'freedom', and as if only language can create the liberated place.

Elaborating on the Emersonian image of the house, Poirier comments: '*Walden* is only one of the examples of something like an obsession in American literature with plans and efforts to build houses, to appropriate space to one's desires'; he mentions the houses in Cooper, Mark Twain, *The House of the Seven Gables,* Fawns in *The Golden Bowl,* Sutpen's Hundred, Silas Lapham's house, Gatsby's estate, even Herzog's country house, and of course the work of crucial architects like Frank Lloyd Wright, and he adds 'the building of a house is an extension and an expansion of the self, an act by which the self possesses environment otherwise dominated by nature'. It is certainly a way of interposing your world between yourself and the given world and obviously of particular importance in America where the unparalleled freedom, and need, to erect habitations of one's own design has produced unique architectural and literary structures alike. Poirier could have developed his point further. When Emily Dickinson says 'I dwell in Possibility—a Fairer House than Prose' we can see that it is also the house of her own style. Similarly all those extremely ornate and cunningly decorated, coloured, and upholstered interiors in Poe's stories (which Baudelaire commented on enthusiastically), are surely images of his own pure art style which he so defiantly opposed to the unpoetical barrenness of contemporary America. (One might note in passing Edith Wharton's enthusiastic writing on house decoration which preceded her fictional works.) The opening stanza of Wallace Stevens's 'Architecture' (in *Opus Posthumous*) admirably evokes this whole attitude:

> What manner of building shall we build?
> Let us design a chastel de chasteté.
> De pensée . . .
> Never cease to deploy the structure.
> Keep the laborers shouldering plinths.
> Pass the whole of life hearing the clink of the
> Chisels of the stone-cutters cutting the stones.

Let us build a castle of thought (just as James speaks of 'a palace of thought'); what is more, let us build it of any materials we please, arranged in any fashion that pleases us. The suggestion is that for these and comparable writers, art is a continuous building of a private edifice; and the process of building—of playing with the available materials, as Emerson's poet plays with the baubles of nature, as Stevens plays with rare exotic things and words (like 'chastel')—is perhaps more important than the product. Build therefore your own world, or weave your own web—here is a key cry of the American writer, particularly those writers we designate as being in one way or another Romantic. The same sort of idea is of course also to be found in Europe, in Coleridge's 'stately pleasure-dome' and Tennyson's 'Palace of Art', for instance. But these are different sorts of building, built for a different purpose (to explore the world of the creative unconscious among other things), and in both cases the edifices represent dreams from which there has to be a waking.

A good visual example of this sort of private 'architecture' in American art is provided by an amazing picture by Erastus Field called 'Historical Monument of the American Republic'. It shows the most extraordinary mélange of heterogeneous architectural styles of building from various cultures and various ages, all connected up at the top by tenuous little bridges—filaments, really, of the painter's fantasy. The result is that although the various specific contents of the work are public and historical, the over-all effect is private and fanciful. Field is building his own world and its relation to the actual world is more apparent than real. Among poets, Stevens can be such an architect. Pound and Eliot likewise use fragments of the world's past and disparate cultures to build their own private worlds. This sort of relatively unfettered eclecticism when dealing with the past is peculiarly American and an utterly different thing from the European writer's sense of the past. If anything it negates the historical sense—Pound plays with the cultures of the past, tossing pieces from hand to hand, just as Emerson played with images of Nature. The results and new juxtapositions can be brilliant, breathtakingly original, and very un-European. As in Field's painting, images of the real past are dislodged and reassembled at the whim of the poet as he spins out his web. And there is another aspect to this almost forceful gathering together of human culture into one web through the sheer effort of style. Faulkner often repeats a sentiment that 'I'm trying to say it all in one sentence, between one Cap and one period . . . I don't know how to do it. All I know is to keep on trying in a new way.' This ambition to 'put all mankind's history in one sentence' partly explains some of the Gargantuan qualities to be found in many American writers—for example, an unprecedented omnivorousness which affects syntax as well as length. Wallace Stevens reveals his own tendency towards this when he writes in a letter, 'for me the important thing is to realize poetry . . . it is simply the desire to contain the world wholly within one's own perception of it'. This pre-empting of the world and history, this making it over on your own terms, is necessarily a condition of much art anywhere. But nowhere do you find this will to reconstitute and contain the world and the past in the web of an individual style more strong than in certain American writers.

A final point about this private house of the American Romantic, again from Emerson: 'It is awful to look into the mind of man and see how free we are . . . Outside, among your fellows, among strangers, you must preserve appearances, a hundred things you cannot do; but inside, the terrible freedom.' The notion that the house which the spirit builds for itself may become a place of terror is deftly conceded by Emily Dickinson with her trenchant economy:

> One need not be a chamber to be haunted,
> One need not be a house;
> The brain has corridors surpassing
> Material place.

Robert Frost's 'Bereft' suggests similar terrors, when the wind turns threatening and the leaves hiss at him:

> Something sinister in the tone,
> Told me my secret must be known:
> Word I was in the house alone
> Somehow must have gotten abroad,
> Word I was in my life alone,
> Word I had no one left but God.

The horrors which take place in Poe's secluded rooms also emphasize how often the American writer is to be found sitting alone in the house which his soul has made for him and which is so often and so singularly haunted.

Alone in his house or sporting in fields of air alone, the American writer seems to have taken his cue from Emerson's axiom, 'Alone is heaven.' The word, and the aspiration, recur constantly, and it is most apt that the first sentence of Emerson's first major essay should define the conditions for the procurement of solitude: 'To go into solitude, a man needs to retire as much from his chamber as from society.' As Emily Dickinson puts it, 'the soul selects her own society / Then shuts the door.' No single sentence differentiates Emerson more clearly from a writer like Wordsworth than this (it follows after Emerson has been discussing the grandeur of nature): 'Yet this may show us what discord is between man and nature, for you cannot freely admire a noble landscape if laborers are digging in the field hard by. The poet finds something ridiculous in his delight until he is out of the sight of men.' But Wordsworth does not. For Wordsworth to encounter the shepherd, the leech-gatherer, the reaper, or anyone else living in intimacy with nature, could be the occasion of an epiphany, a visionary gleam. Emerson reveals a more Oriental streak in the American response to landscape when he emphasizes the discrepancy between tiny man and the vast dissolving grandeur of nature. Indeed, he would even banish those tiny figures which Oriental painters include to remind one of that discrepancy. For Emerson the ideal landscape was the unpeopled landscape. Thoreau does meet people in the woods, yet his instinct is for solitude. 'It would be sweet to deal with men more, I imagine, but where dwell they? Not in the fields which I traverse.' Whitman seems to reach out to embrace the whole continent; his imagination is crowded with electric, tactile contacts. Yet it seems to be more a dream of contact; for the most part he is 'out of the game', 'apart from the pulling and hauling', looking, peering, beholding, watching—one of those great lonely voyeurs who recur in American literature. At the end of the poem it is his evasive solitariness which we feel as he promises to 'stop somewhere waiting for you' and then vanishes without even waiting to close off his poem with a full stop. Carlyle's warning to Emerson could be extended to cover other American writers: 'We find you a Speaker indeed, but as it were a Soliloquizer on the eternal mountain-tops only, in vast solitudes where men and their affairs all lie hushed in a very dim remoteness. . . .' By contrast, 'The Prelude' starts and ends with an address to 'my Friend' (Coleridge, of course).

All Romantics are supposed to be soliloquizers, enraptured by their own potency, yet a good deal of European, certainly of English, Romantic poetry is addressed to friends, or presupposes or involves them. These Romantics cherished company, even if it had to be very select, just as they seem more interested in women than were their American counterparts. And the implications of this go beyond the relatively trivial question of whether the European Romantic had more friends than the American. It involves a difference in their relative conceptions of their own role in relation to their societies. 'The poet', says Wordsworth, 'binds together by passion and knowledge the vast empire of human society'; poets, says Shelley, 'are the unacknowledged legislators of the world', Wordsworth's poet is a 'man speaking to men'; by contrast the American Romantic seems more to be a man speaking to himself. William Cullen Bryant stands in the American woods and dreams of a future civilization: [I] 'think I hear / The sound of that advancing multitude / Which soon shall fill these deserts'; but his poem ends, 'A fresher wind sweeps by, and breaks my dream, / And I am in the wilderness alone.' The European Romantic did not have to dream of crowds and societies and civilizations, they were everywhere he turned; and despite the fixed image of the European Romantics as escapists, most of them were very politically minded and concerned with the development of society. Ever since Rousseau had shown that society was an arbitrary, man-made structure, the idea had been gaining ground that man could reshape society according to the demands and dictates of his imagination. Mental structures might precede and ordain political structures. The French Revolution demonstrated both the will and the ability of men to actively reshape their society. In a rich and authoritative article on 'English Romanticism: The Spirit of the Age', M. H. Abrams demonstrates conclusively that for the English Romantics the French Revolution was the single most formative experience of their lives. The great outburst of social or anti-social energy provoked and encouraged a similar release of personal creative energy. Millennial hopes and apocalyptic expectations ran high. The advent of the New Jerusalem or Paradise on Earth was prophesied. English Romantics argued from the French Revolution to the Book of Revelation, and prophesied liberating changes in the 'vast empire of human society'. The poet's role was to offer the shaping vision, to produce imaginative constructs which would provide models for social constructs. Acknowledged or not, they felt themselves to be, or potentially to be, the legislators of the world. Most European Romantics were implicitly if not explicitly revolutionary; as Hazlitt shrewdly commented on the Lake School, 'regular metre was abolished with regular government'. Of course, disillusion with the French Revolution set in, and it is precisely a part

of Professor Abrams's story to show how the English Romantics experienced a loss of hope, gave up their expectations of a specific historical revolution in the near future, and concentrated on what Abrams calls 'the apocalypse of imagination'. I quote one of his conclusions, concerning this shift of emphasis. 'The hope has been shifted from the history of mankind to the mind of a single individual, from militant external action to an imaginative act; and the marriage between the Lamb and the New Jerusalem has been converted into a marriage between subject and object, mind and nature, which creates a new world out of the old world of sense.'

In America, the writing of the Transcendentalists, and all those we may wish to consider as Romantics, did not have this revolutionary social dimension. It was not rooted in the energizing conviction that the poet's imaginative visions, in one way or another, could vitally influence and enhance the conditions of life of their fellow men. Whitman certainly talks of the great 'en-masse' and has dreams of a harmonious collectivity, yet even here the strongest emphasis is on 'the centripetal isolation of a human being in himself'. Between that centrifugal tendency into space I mentioned earlier, and this centripetal isolation of the human being in himself, the American artist spins his self-sustaining web, with society usually excluded, ignored, or unenvisaged. Appropriately enough the most famous use of the image of the spider's web in nineteenth-century English literature is in George Eliot's *Middlemarch,* where she uses it to illustrate the complex and ramifying interrelatedness of all human relationships, that 'stealthy convergence of human lots'. What in English literature has here provided an image of our unavoidable involvement in the lives of other people, in American literature has typically been the image for the patterns and strategies with which the American artist both fills and preserves his radical solitude. The contrast has at least some parabolic aptness.

IV

While dealing with attitudes towards society and civilization, another point is worth making, which is put clearly in the poem written by Bryant for the painter Thomas Cole as the latter was about to leave for Europe. First Bryant reminds Cole of the wonderful wild and savage landscapes which he has painted (and which indeed he loved), then he warns him of what he will see in Europe:

> Fair scenes shall greet thee where thou goest—
>   fair,
> But different—everywhere the trace of men,
> Paths, homes, graves, ruins, from the lowest glen
> To where life shrinks from the fierce Alpine
>   air—
> Gaze on them, till the tears shall dim thy sight
> But keep that earlier, wilder image bright.

In Europe, 'everywhere the trace of men': in America, 'that wilder image'. Bryant himself is clearly appreciative of both, but he more particularly wants to retain 'that wilder image' which the as-yet uncivilized landscape of America can provide. The wildness of this landscape was felt to have values and provide spiritual nourishment not available in Europe. 'We need the tonic of wildness', says

Thoreau, while Cole, in his 'Essay on American Scenery' (1835), insists that 'the wilderness is YET a fitting place to speak of God'. Against those who prefer Europe, Cole argues that 'the most impressive characteristic of American scenery is its wildness', while in 'civilized Europe the primitive features of scenery have long since been destroyed or modified'. He instances some of the splendid wildness of America, for example Niagara: 'in gazing on it we feel as though a great void had been filled in our mind—our conceptions expand—we become a part of what we behold'. (It is amusing to recall that when Chateaubriand first saw Niagara he was so overwhelmed that he wanted to throw himself in, and indeed did nearly fall over the edge—a pregnant Romantic anecdote. And it was in the wild American woods, Chateaubriand says, a new, an 'unknown muse appeared to me'. Such wildness, he felt, would provoke a new poetry.) At the same time anyone writing in America then was aware that the rapid 'improvements of cultivation' were inevitably replacing 'the sublimity of the wilderness'. Here was a difficulty. The American wilderness was a source of visionary exaltation. Unlike Europe, the land was not scarred and stained by the intolerable crimes of history: 'You see no ruined tower to tell of outrage—no gorgeous temple to speak of ostentation.' But if American landscape was not suffused with a sense of the past it was full of what Cole calls 'associations . . . of the present and future'. 'And in looking over the yet uncultivated scene, the mind's eye shall see far into futurity. Where the wolf roams, the plough shall glisten; on the gray crag shall rise temple and tower. . . .' There is a problem for the American Romantic. Blessedly, there are no man-made towers marring the American landscape; but happily there will soon be towers springing up. The wonder and richness of America is its wildness, but wonderfully, the wildness will soon be put to the plough. As soon as Cole has outlined his optimistic vision of a civilized society living in a domesticated landscape, he goes on 'yet I cannot but express my sorrow that the beauties of such landscapes are quickly passing away—the ravages of the axe are daily increasing—the most noble scenes are made desolate and often times with a wantonness and barbarism scarcely credible in a civilized nation'. Where the European Romantic, used to the 'traces of men', might look forward to an imagined millennium for human society, the American was very aware of increasing depredations of the precious wildness. He might cling to images of idealized pastoral domesticity, or indulge in pieties about manifest destiny or the melting-pot, but his strategy on the whole was to seek out that solitude, those unpeopled landscapes, prescribed by Emerson—in reality, or in art. That is why while European Romanticism characteristically looks to the past and to the future, American Romanticism seeks to move out of time altogether, out of time and into some sort of space. For time means history, and history means 'traces of men' and society, and society means not only the loss of 'that wilder image' but also the spaces it provided and the limitless freedom to sport in air.

'The great discovery of the eighteenth century is the phenomenon of memory,' says Georges Poulet, and certainly the attempt to renew contact with one's individual past and the past of society is a decisive factor in the literature of Europe we call Romantic. Chateaubriand's René, who laid down so many of the behaviour patterns for subsequent Romantic poets and heroes, is exemplary in this. Accounting for his melancholy in the depths of the American woods, René recalls his European past. In one early phrase he anticipates many subsequent works: 'Memories of these childhood adventures still fill my soul with delight.' Another key word is introduced when he describes how the sound of bells in his native land awakens the happiest associations in later life. 'All is contained in these delicious reveries into which we are plunged by the sound of our native bells.' Revery, first eulogized by Rousseau, is a word which appears very frequently in European nineteenth-century literature, and René's sentiment is echoed by Wordsworth and Proust to mention only the most obvious. To cope with his misery—caused by that favourite Romantic frustration, hopeless incestuous love—René has recourse to the Romantic antidote of travel. 'I went and sat among the ruins of Rome and Greece: countries of strong and productive memory.' In particular he favours moon-lit meditations: 'Often, by the rays of this star which nourishes our reveries, I thought I saw the Spirit of Memory seated in deep thought by my side.' I need hardly point out what a wealth of Romantic iconography is here assembled. And when René cries out, 'Is it my fault, if I find limits everywhere, if what is finite has no value for me?', and 'I lacked something that could fill the emptiness of my existence', he articulates archetypal Romantic feelings. Having left Europe after the death of his sister and come to the depths of the American woods, he does not find anything to fill that emptiness and indeed he is said to die shortly after completing his tale, his recollection. A recollection, not quite in tranquillity, but one which suggests that what meaning and content there was to his life is all in the past. There is nothing emptier than the present. René also affords us an excellent picture of a typical European Romantic as he sits at the edge of the sea when his sister has immolated herself in a convent after confessing her illicit love. René is awaiting his ship, knowing that his life henceforward will always be incomplete, unfilled. As he describes the contrast between the convent behind him and the ocean in front, we can see him hanging between two worlds. On the one side there is the place, the symbol, of infinity, calm, refuge, timeless knowledge, and unfaltering motionless light; on the other, the unceasing tides of Time, the place of storm, of shipwreck, of uncertain navigation, and moving beacon lights which shift and sway with the swell of the sea. And in between, drawn to both, full inhabitant of neither, is the unappeasable, the European, René.

René, it is true, does not find something to fill his inner emptiness in past, present, or future. He perhaps qualifies as one of those who, as Georges Poulet puts it, in an effort to create their identities out of the past and present or future time, risk a 'double tearing of the self' by finally feeling themselves cut off from both. But if nearly all Romantics have felt what Poulet calls 'the infinite deficiency of the present moment', some of them have indeed managed to reconstitute a more lasting self out of remembrance. For memory proved to be one of the major defences against the disintegration of the self and its endless diffusion into innumerable unrelated moments. As Poulet puts it, 'all at once the mind is able to feel an entire past reborn within itself. This past, together with the whole train of its emotions, surges up in the moment and endows it with a life that is not momentary.' Instead of being a mere creature of intermittent and discrete sensations, the writer, through this remembering, recapturing, re-experiencing of the past, discovers the miracle of his own duration. It would be out of place and unnecessary to embark on any sketch of the role of memory in European Romanticism; but this deliberate cultivation of an awareness and a sense both of society's historical past and the past of the individual provided the European Romantic with one of his main themes and activities. Let Wordsworth suffice as an obvious example:

> But a sense
> Of what had been here done, and suffer'd here
> Through ages, and was doing, suffering, still
> Weigh'd with me, could support the test of
> thought,
> Was like the enduring majesty and power
> Of independent nature; and not seldom
> Even individual remembrances,
> By working on the Shapes before my eyes,
> Became like vital functions of the soul;
> *(Prelude,* VIII, *781-9)*

and again:

> There are in our existence spots of time,
> Which with distinct pre-eminence retain
> A vivifying Virtue, whence . . .
> our minds
> Are nourished and invisibly repair'd . . .
> *(Prelude,* XI, *258-65)*

In the rediscovery of the Middle Ages in German Romanticism, or in the Hellenism of poets like Shelley and Byron, European Romanticism was as retrospective as it was revolutionary.

A few quotations from Emerson will suggest how radically different was the American Romantic's attitude towards memory and the past. 'But why should you keep your head over your shoulder? Why drag about this corpse of your memory . . .?'; 'In nature every moment is new; the past is swallowed and forgotten; the coming only is sacred'; 'how easily we might walk onward into the opening landscape . . . until by degrees the recollection of home was crowded out of the mind, all memory obliterated by the tyranny of the present, and we are led in triumph by nature'. Emerson described himself as 'an endless seeker with no Past at my back', and in his funeral address on Thoreau he said of him, 'he lived for the day, not cumbered and mortified by his memory'. This antipathy to memory, the resolute rejection of the past, is of course connected to America's national growth. For the past was Europe, that old world whose influence America had to escape if it was to discover itself. It is part of the American genius not to be dominated and held back by the inertia of the past, to feel that the future is still full of infinite possibilities, that, as Stevens put it, 'the vegetation still abounds with forms'—new forms, not copies of the old forms of the past. However, this denial of memory seems to rob most American writers of any experience of duration. Henry Miller is only an extreme form of the many

Henry David Thoreau.

American writers, Romantic and otherwise, who seem to experience life as an unrelated series of spasmodic 'nows'. 'There is nothing else than now', says the Hemingway hero to himself. The past can certainly be every kind of burden, a real load of nightmare and repression. But to lack any sense of the past can be impoverishing, and to live in a pure present can have its terrors. Certainly it must lead to a much less stable sense of self. As I suggested earlier, the tendency of certain American writers to dilate into the space around them, even to dissolve into their environment, is related to this flight from the past which is a flight out of time.' 'WHAT SCARED YOU ALL INTO TIME?, . . . COME OUT OF TIME AND INTO SPACE. FOREVER. THERE IS NO THING TO FEAR. THERE IS NO THING IN SPACE.' William Burroughs's message to Allen Ginsberg effectively sums up a position held intermittently by American writers over the last hundred years. Of course if the American artist did manage to vanish out of time and into space he would not write anything. First, because, as Burroughs points out, there is no thing in space and you cannot have art without things any more than you can have consciousness without things. Secondly, because it is doubtful whether the pure present, a series of spatial moments utterly cut off from the past, can mean anything at all. Needless to say, Emerson, Whitman, and Thoreau did not vanish in this way, and even Burroughs is still writing. But Emerson and Whitman, for example, get very repetitive; indeed at times it seems as if Emerson's prose loses inner direction, as if the words at least had got out of time and into space where they are sporting in air. And the American novelist had to turn to the past before he could find any subjects productive of drama and significance. Hawthorne sitting in the customs house sifting through those old papers is the precise image of the American artist looking for some sort of American past which will provide the dynamic for his art. Mark Twain and Melville both looked back for the material of their greatest works, while James's fiction begins and ends with the introduction of an American sense of the present into European territories drenched with the past. Today, young American poets like Ed Dorn are trying to isolate and imaginatively use the figure of the Indian and his culture—the true historic past of America.

For good or bad the American Romantic writers do not have that sense of the past which was so important for their European counterparts. Of course, they faced a landscape devoid of 'traces of men': clean, 'dazzling', but humanly speaking empty—potentially alien in a way that the European landscape, so saturated with history, legend, myth, could never be. This perhaps partially explains why the European writer can seem to be more genuinely intimate with his landscape than the American with his, why it offers him so much in the way of suggestions, associations, and consolations, while the American landscape, 'that wilder image', tends to hold off from its watcher as pure obdurate fact. Of course there is a whole tradition of sublime writing celebrating nature in American Romantic poetry. Josephine Miles has described it in her excellent *Eras and Modes in English Poetry* (London, 1977), but she also, most interestingly, notes that the whole vocabulary of subtle 'psychological discriminations' which was developed by the English Romantics was not adopted or developed in America. This corresponds to my sense that the American Romantic feels nature to be something so vast as to be almost beyond him; he does not feel that sort of psychological intimacy with his environment, that sense of reciprocities between man and man, man and nature, which marks much European Romantic writing. For Emerson, despite his celebratory euphoria, the actual surrounding world could often seem 'an Iceland of negations' from which he would habitually escape into his visions of 'infinitude'. Similarly, Wallace Stevens uses the image of a barren wintry landscape to describe his sense of a world which has not been supplemented and illuminated by some imaginary construct invented by the poet himself. The world unmediated or unmodified by Imagination is perhaps a cold and empty place for most Romantics. But whereas the European seems to draw help from history, legend, memory, from friends (and lovers), from visions of future societies, from the landscape itself, as he strives to fill that emptiness, the American Romantic seems to be thrown back much more on his own resources, the devices and designs of his own style. To consider American Romantic literature from Emerson to Wallace Stevens in this light is to realize anew how very remarkable and inventive those resources are.

That recurrent image of the spider, drawing the filament

out of himself alone, weaving his private web, provides an illuminating analogy for the situation, and secretion, of the American writer. His delight (or is it sometimes his desperation?) is to put together his own unique verbal structure; and in this activity, the ingredients which go into the making of each piece of filament are perhaps less important than the fact of the web itself which sustains the writer in the real and imagined spaces of America. The visions of the European Romantic interpenetrated on all sides with their natural and human surroundings. It is just this feeling of *interpenetration* that seems to me to be missing in the work of the American Romantic. If we seek him out we are most likely to find him as Emily Dickinson found her spider—dancing softly to himself, unwinding his coil of Pearl. The wonder is what 'continents of light' he thus manages to summon into being.

> *Tony Tanner, "Notes for a Comparison between American and European Romanticism," in his* Scenes of Nature, Signs of Men, *Cambridge University Press, 1987. Reprint by Cambridge University Press, 1988, pp. 25-45.*

James E. Miller, Jr.

[Miller is an American educator and critic. In the following essay, he discusses works of the American Romantics as explorations of the "enigmatic, symbolic landscape" of the unconscious.]

As any graduate student knows, American literature is schizophrenic. It is held paralyzed between hope and despair, between the affirmative and negative, between illusion and fact, between optimism and pessimism, between the ideal and the real. The split is down the middle and the major writers may be divided: Emerson, Thoreau, and Whitman on the one side; Poe, Hawthorne, and Melville on the other. The origins of a divided taproot have been traced back incredible distances, but in America itself there are, for the sons of light, eighteenth-century rationalism, deism, and Quakerism, and for the sons of darkness, seventeenth-century puritanism and Calvinism. Our own twentieth century has looked back on this split personality in American literature, and has declared the chasm unbridgeable. Indeed if we would be frank, we should acknowledge that the twentieth century has most frequently found its own dark features best reflected in Hawthorne and Melville, and even in Poe when he sounds most like Kafka. And the contemporary critic of Emerson and Whitman has found himself apologizing for the smiling countenance of his subject, and the commentator on Thoreau has had to stress that the woodsdweller is not a hermit permanently committed to his pond-side solitude.

In short, modern criticism, whatever its protestations, has judged the American Romantics not on their art but their attitudes. The bad guys are those who embraced life with a gusto, vigour, and virility that jar the anxiety-ridden modern sensibility; the good guys are those who held life at a distance because of its horror, hostility, and evil—the twentieth century's view of its own predicament. No one writer can be cited as the cause of the shift in critical view, but one can be named as pivotal: T. S. Eliot. After "Tradition and the Individual Talent" (1920), few critics seemed able to take seriously Emerson's call for the American to establish his own original relation with the universe. After *The Waste Land* (1922), few poets seemed able to listen seriously to the barbaric yawp of Whitman. And it is, surely, no accident that it was precisely at this period that American criticism discovered it had been overlooking perhaps its greatest writer, Herman Melville.

Whatever the causes—and they surely run deep in political, social, philosophical, and religious undercurrents—the fact remains, there was a massive shift in American critical outlook between the 1850's and the 1920's. The benign optimism of one prince of American letters, Ralph Waldo Emerson, was transmogrified into the scowling gloom of his successor to the crown, T. S. Eliot. And even now, after our precarious entry into the second half of the tentative twentieth century, we have not escaped the shadow of that long scowl. We accept as our own, too often without question, judgments that hardened into dogma almost a half-century ago. We have been timid in questioning the established gospel; we have been afraid to see the world anew with our own eyes.

It is time that we re-examined the schizoid character of American literature and set about discovering those elements that would make it an integrated personality. But at the outset of such a search, we should agree that writers of genius—and this category would include Emerson, Thoreau, Whitman, Poe, Hawthorne, and Melville—are distinguished by their uniqueness, by their separateness from all that has come before or after. To make categorical and inflexible groupings is false; to make rigid alignments and alliances is phony. If we explore relationships of these American Romantics, we are not seeking a single pool from which they all sipped, but a subterranean torrent that quenched their varied thirsts.

What I propose is not a conclusion but a beginning, not a discovery but an exploration. As a context for a new perspective, a number of quotations from twentieth century psychology may best be introduced forthwith.

> I cannot but think that the most important step forward that has occurred in psychology since I have been a student of that science is the discovery, first made in 1886, that, in certain subjects at least, there is not only the consciousness of the ordinary field, with its usual centre and margin, but an addition thereto in the shape of a set of memories, thoughts, and feelings which are extra-marginal and outside of the primary consciousness altogether, but yet must be classed as conscious facts of some sort, able to reveal their presence by unmistakable signs . . . generalizing this phenomenon, Mr. Myers has given the name of *automatism,* sensory or motor, emotional or intellectual, to this whole sphere of effects, due to 'up-rushes' into the ordinary consciousness of energies originating in the subliminal parts of the mind (William James, *The Varieties of Religious Experience*).

> A more or less superficial layer of the unconscious is undoubtedly personal. I call it the *personal unconscious.* But this personal uncon-

scious rests upon a deeper layer, which does not derive from personal experience and is not a personal acquisition but is unborn. This deeper layer I call the *collective unconscious.* I have chosen the term 'collective' because this part of the unconscious is not individual but universal; in contrast to the personal psyche, it has contents and modes of behavior that are more or less the same everywhere and in all individuals. It is, in other words, identical in all men and thus constitutes a common psychic substrate of a suprapersonal nature which is present in every one of us (C. G. Jung, *The Basic Writings*).

> Heaven, hell, the mythological age, Olympus and all the other habitations of the gods, are interpreted by psychoanalysis as symbols of the unconscious. The key to the modern systems of psychological interpretation therefore is: the metaphysical realm—the unconscious. Correspondingly, the key to open the door the other way is the same equation in reverse: the unconscious—the metaphysical realm. 'For,' as Jesus states it, 'behold, the kingdom of God is within you' (Joseph Campbell, *The Hero with a Thousand Faces*).

Additional quotations could be cited, especially from Sigmund Freud or D. H. Lawrence, but these few should serve our purposes. The hypothesis I wish to offer, with no hope of testing it in this short space, derives from the kind of thinking, with its strong psychoanalytic drift, embodied in the foregoing quotations. In brief it runs as follows: the meeting ground of Emerson, Thoreau, and Whitman is in their transcendental mysticism—spirit; while the meeting ground of Poe, Hawthorne, and Melville is in their psychological drama—mind; when the one group leaps high enough in the spirit, and the other delves deep enough in the mind, they find themselves on the same enigmatic, symbolic landscape. Whether exploring the hills of heaven or the pits of hell, the landscape lies within. In short, what all these American Romantics knew and explored together was what the modern psychologists think they have newly discovered—the unconscious. The vocabulary has shifted, but the fundamental visions remain.

Emerson's thought has so long been considered derivative, connecting as it does with Plato, with Oriental philosophy, with Kant, with Carlyle, that attention has been deflected from its possible relationship with modern psychological thought. Quotation after quotation might be culled from his essays to show a kind of prophecy of contemporary concepts of the conscious and the unconscious.

> But when, following the invisible steps of thought, we come to inquire, Whence is matter? and Whereto? many truths arise to us out of the recesses of consciousness. . . . As a plant upon the earth, so a man rests upon the bosom of God; he is nourished by unfailing fountains, and draws at his need inexhaustible power (*Nature*).

> What is the aboriginal Self, on which a universal reliance may be grounded? . . . The inquiry leads us to that source, at once the essence of genius, of virtue, and of life, which we call Spontaneity or Instinct. We denote this primary wis-

dom as Intuition, whilst all later teachings are tuitions. In that deep force, the last fact behind which analysis cannot go, all things find their common origin ("Self-Reliance").

On my saying, 'What have I to do with the sacredness of traditions, if I live wholly from within?' my friend suggested,—'But these impulses may be from below, not from above.' I replied, 'They do not seem to me to be such; but if I am the Devil's child, I will live then from the Devil.' No law can be sacred to me but that of my nature. Good and bad are but names very readily transferable to that or this; the only right is what is after my constitution; the only wrong what is against it ("Self-Reliance").

Translated into the modern psychological idiom, this conversation might be conceived as resting on the distinction between Freud's personal unconscious, with all its suppressed sexual emotion, and Jung's collective unconscious, with its universal racial memory.

It is possible, even, to see Emerson's terms of soul and oversoul verging on transfiguration into modern psychology's conscious and unconscious, or the personal as differentiated from the collective unconscious.

The philosophy of six thousand years has not searched the chambers and magazines of the soul. In its experiments there has always remained, in the last analysis, a residuum it could not resolve. Man is a stream whose source is hidden. . . . When I watch that flowing river, which, out of regions I see not, pours for a season its streams into me, I see that I am a pensioner; not a cause but a surprised spectator of this ethereal water; that I desire and look up and put myself in the attitude of reception, but from some alien energy the visions come. . . . We live in succession, in division, in parts, in particles. Meantime within man is the soul of the whole; the wise silence; the universal beauty, to which every part and particle is equally related; the eternal ONE ("The Over-Soul").

Like Emerson, Thoreau discovered the deepest mysteries of life not without but within, and within those very "chambers and magazines" of the soul which have always baffled philosophy.

I found myself, and still find, an instinct toward a higher, or, as it is named, spiritual life, as do most men, and another toward a primitive rank and savage one, and I reverence them both. . . . We are conscious of an animal in us, which awakens in proportion as our higher nature slumbers. It is reptile and sensual, and perhaps cannot be wholly expelled; like the worms which, even in life and health, occupy our bodies. Possibly we may withdraw from it, but never change its nature. I fear that it may enjoy a certain health of its own; that we may be well, yet not pure (*Walden*).

Freud would have no difficulty here in identifying his id, ego, and superego, and Jung would have no trouble in identifying, in the following quotation, his collective unconscious:

Time is but the stream I go a-fishing in. I drink at it; but while I drink I see the sandy bottom and detect how shallow it is. Its thin current slides away, but eternity remains. I would drink deeper; fish in the sky, whose bottom is pebbly with stars (*Walden*).

As transcendentalism moved closer to the twentieth century and found its finest poetic expression in Walt Whitman, it seemed to become more self-consciously psychological. Whitman himself was a believer in the psychology of his day, phrenology, and prided himself on his own poetically favorable chart of bumps. It is of considerable significance that Whitman saw the attributes of the poet in psychological terms (the words have special phrenological meanings):

Extreme caution or prudence, the soundest organic health, large hope and comparison and fondness for women and children, large alimentiveness and destructiveness and causality, with a perfect sense of the oneness of nature and the propriety of the same spirit applied to human affairs . . . these are called up of the float of the brain of the world to be parts of the greatest poet from his birth out of his mother's womb and from her birth out of her mother's (1855 Preface).

"The float of the brain of the world" needs only the slightest modification to become Jung's collective unconscious, with all its racial residue of myths and archetypes. In the opening section of "Song of Myself," the poet says:

Creeds and schools in abeyance,
Retiring back a while sufficed at what they are,
    but never forgotten,
I harbor for good or bad, I permit to speak at
    every hazard,
Nature without check with original energy.

In Jungian terms, the poet seems to be voiding his mind in preparation for the invading floods from the unconscious. And later on, fragmentary visions seem to surge to surface and flash out in momentary brilliance:

Urge and urge and urge,
Always the procreant urge of the world.

Out of the dimness opposite equals advance, always substance and increase, always sex,
Always a knit of identity, always distinction, always a breed of life.

The very substance of the imagery in such passages as this suggests a strong affinity with modern psychological thought. Although the vision is sexual, it appears to drive deeper than the personal, to that line where levels of the unconscious mingle, where sex itself begins to generate myth.

In many ways the entire work of Poe can be seen as a probing of the dark "chambers and magazines" of the soul or mind. As a foundation stone of his work stands that curious prose-poem, *Eureka,* with its strange mixture of science, philosophy, religion, and psychology. Observe: "We walk about, amid the destinies of our world-existence, encompassed by dim but ever present *Memories* of a Destiny more vast—very distant in the bygone time, and infinitely awful." Here the Jungian racial memory lurks in embryo. And more:

> . . . that nothing is, or can be, superior to any one soul; that each soul is, in part, its own God—its own Creator;—in a word, that God—the material *and* spiritual God—*now* exists solely in the diffused Matter and Spirit of the Universe; and that the regathering of this diffused Matter and Spirit will be but the re-constitution of the *purely Spiritual* and Individual God.

The whole tendency of such a passage is to throw the individual back into himself—the soul is "its own Creator"—in the search for the profundities of being. All of Poe's imaginative writing represents in some sense an exploration of hidden labyrinths of the interior; hence his recurring use of the dream as dramatic structure. In "Dream-Land":

> By a route obscure and lonely,
> Haunted by ill angels only,
>   Where an Eidolon, named NIGHT,
>   On a black throne reigns upright,
>   I have reached these lands but newly
>   From an ultimate dim Thule—
> From a wild weird clime that lieth, sublime,
>   Out of SPACE—out of TIME.

The poem is filled with a bizarre symbolism—vales, caves, mountains toppling, seas surging, lakes outspread—that begins to make sense only in terms of psychoanalytic interpretation. And that King of the black throne, "who hath forbid / The uplifting of the fring'd lid," is surely related, however distantly, to the psychologist's Censor. As has been frequently noted, the house in Poe often becomes the controlling symbol of a work, and is nearly always equated with the mind. Jung himself could not have discovered a better metaphor for his meanings than the school house in "William Wilson":

> But the house!—how quaint an old building was this!—to me how veritably a palace of enchantment! There was really no end to its windings—to its incomprehensible subdivisions. It was difficult, at any given time, to say with certainty upon which of its two stories one happened to be. From each room to every other there were sure to be found three or four steps either in ascent or descent. Then the lateral branches were innumerable—inconceivable—and so returning in upon themselves, that our most exact ideas in regard to the whole mansion were not very far different from those with which we pondered upon infinity. During the five years of my residence here, I was never able to ascertain with precision, in what remote locality lay the little sleeping apartment assigned to myself and some eighteen or twenty other scholars.

Like Poe's stories, Hawthorne's tales often are basically psychological structures with objects, places, or characters functioning symbolically, leading the reader not outward into the world of reality but inward into the mazes of the mind. A typical Hawthorne protagonist may be delineated as suffering from a paralysis of the imagination as he fixes his gaze in horror on the personal unconscious, filled as it is with all of the individual's suppressed and un-

speakable desires. Unable either to extricate himself from his gaze or to penetrate to the profounder levels of the unconscious, he becomes sick in his obsession with his own and mankind's evil. In "Egotism; or, The Bosom Serpent," Roderick Elliston is such a protagonist who broadcasts to the community that he is being gnawed by a snake in his breast:

> The symptoms caused them endless perplexity. They knew not whether ill health were robbing his spirits of elasticity, or whether a canker of the mind was gradually eating, as such cankers do, from his moral system into the physical frame, which is but the shadow of the former. . . . Some thought that their once brilliant friend was in an incipient stage of insanity.

In "The Birthmark," the mad scientist, Aylmer, obsessed like Roderick with the world's imperfection, kills his wife in his attempt to remove the disfiguration from her face:

> Yet, had Aylmer reached a profounder wisdom, he need not thus have flung away the happiness which would have woven his mortal life of the self-same texture with the celestial. The momentary circumstance was too strong for him; he failed to look beyond the shadowy scope of time, and, living once for all in eternity, to find the perfect future in the present.

In Jungian terms, Hawthorne's obsessed heroes have found imprisonment and not freedom in the labyrinths of the unconscious. Theirs is a shallow penetration into the hidden recesses of the mind.

Like Whitman, Melville strikes us as closer to the modern psychological point of view than his predecessors, Poe and Hawthorne. Indeed, in that astonishing chapter called "Dreams" in the middle of *Mardi*, Melville seems to be penetrating and exploring the depths of the unconscious much as Whitman does in his poem, "The Sleepers." Melville:

> Dreams! dreams! golden dreams: endless, and golden, as the flowery prairies . . . my dreams herd like buffaloes, browsing on to the horizon, and browsing on round the world; and among them, I dash with my lance, to spear one, ere they all flee.

And Whitman:

> I wander all night in my vision,
> Stepping with light feet, swiftly and noiselessly
>   stepping and stopping,
> Bending with open eyes over the shut eyes of
>   sleepers. . . .

Both writers seem to be released from the bonds of earth and time. Melville: " . . .with all the past and present pouring in me, I roll down my billow from afar." Whitman: "I descend my western course, my sinews are flaccid, / Perfume and youth course through me and I am their wake."

In *Mardi*, too, Babbalanja seems consciously to tap the resources of wisdom which lie in the collective unconscious as he attunes himself to his mysterious interior "devil," Azzageddi. In his seizures by Azzageddi, Babbalanja always speaks with a more cryptic, profounder insight than he knows. Of all Melville's novels, however, *Pierre* seems most directly to anticipate modern psychology's theories of the unconscious. Its *Ambiguities* (the subtitle) are all of the mind, and in following the "endless, winding way,— the flowing river in the cave of man," Melville discovered complexities of motivation in the depths of the mind that Freud and Jung could have cited as the basis for their theories. But Melville's understanding of the depths of the psyche can best be suggested by a neglected passage from that novel of novels, *Moby Dick,* a passage with an intricate series of metaphors and symbols well worth close study:

> This is much; yet Ahab's larger, darker, deeper part remains unhinted. But vain to popularize profundities, and all truth is profound. Winding far down from within the very heart of this spiked Hotel de Cluny where we here stand— however grand and wonderful, now quit it;— and take your way, ye nobler, sadder souls, to those vast Roman halls of Thermes; where far beneath the fantastic towers of man's upper earth, his root of grandeur, his whole awful essence sits in bearded state; an antique buried beneath antiquities, and throned on torsoes! So with a broken throne, the great gods mock that captive king; so like a Caryatid, he patient sits, upholding on his frozen brow the piled entablatures of ages. Wind ye down there, ye prouder, sadder souls! question that proud, sad king! A family likeness! aye, he did beget ye, ye young exiled royalties; and from your grim sire only will the old State-secret come.

The structure symbolism is reminiscent of Poe's houses of the mind, but Melville seems to conceive the structure of the psyche in more grandiose and awesome terms. And as we wind our way into the depths, we cannot help but feel that we are approaching, however obliquely and obscurely, the deepest and most ancient sources of being, out of space, out of time—a landscape that is all mankind's ("a family likeness") as much as Ahab's.

It is, of course, one thing to discover in the American Romantics some prophetic suggestions of modern psychological concepts; it is another to find patterns in these suggestions that might prove significant and illuminating in approaching individual works. It is, then, appropriate to sketch a tentative pattern here, offered more as hypothesis than as an inflexible formula. One characteristic of the monomyth (according to Joseph Campbell in *The Hero with a Thousand Faces*) is withdrawal and the journey, for which the self's retreat into and exploration of the unconscious is the paradigm. Departure and travel seem to constitute a major recurring metaphor in the work of all six of the American writers we have examined. In Emerson, the metaphor is not overt so much as everywhere implied, as in such sentences as: "Books are for the scholar's idle times. When he can read God directly, the hour is too precious to be wasted in other men's transcripts of their readings" ("The American Scholar"). Emerson's call to communion with the "aboriginal self," in "Self-Reliance," is clearly the call to a spiritual exploration. Thoreau's trip to Walden pond, however short the distance, may yet

prove the longest in America; and in his chapter on "Solitude" he asked: "Why should I feel lonely? is not our planet in the Milky Way?" Whitman said, in "Song of Myself": "I tramp a perpetual journey, (come listen all!) / My signs are a rain-proof coat, good shoes, and a staff cut from the woods." Poe's narrators in "The Fall of the House of Usher" and "Ulalume" tell us in their opening sentences that they are journeying over strange landscapes; and Arthur Gordon Pym voyages forth in exploration of places never before seen by man. Hawthorne's "Young Goodman Brown" and Robin (in "My Kinsman, Major Molineaux") withdraw from home and venture forth on journeys that subtly merge nightmare and reality. And Melville's Ishmael, with the "damp, drizzly November" in his soul, accounts it "high time to get to sea" as soon as he can.

Clearly all of these journeys are in some sense symbolic journeys, and represent to some degree a descent into the depths of the "aboriginal Self." The discoveries are diverse, but are they as antithetical as we have always assumed? The psyche in its labyrinthine maze contains many truths; to emerge with one is not to deny others. Thoreau as he sets off for Walden has much in common with Ishmael as he sets off on the *Pequod*. As Thoreau goes about making the familiar exotic, and Melville the exotic familiar, we begin to detect a subterranean identity in the substance of their explorations. Similarly, the dream-worlds explored by Whitman in "The Sleepers" and by Hawthorne in "Young Goodman Brown" have much in common, however different the ultimate effects on the mature poet and the young man. Emerson's prose poem *Nature* shares much in the contours of its landscape with Poe's prose poem, *Eureka*. Isolated sentences, flashing forth from the deepest intuition, might well win the signature of both.

To suggest connections is not to deny differences. Genius by definition is unique. But it is true that scholarly ways of thinking may drift into rigidity, and what was originally brilliance of insight may in the repetition become exhausted cliché. The differences among these six American Romantics are clear, detectable, permanent. We would not want it otherwise. But as readers in depth, we might well want to ponder some compelling likenesses as we journey with them through uncharted interiors and view the remarkable continents they have discovered.

> *James E. Miller, Jr., "Uncharted Interiors: The American Romantics Revisited," in* The Emerson Society Quarterly, *No. 35, II Quarter, 1964, pp. 34-9.*

FURTHER READING

Barbour, James, and Quirk, Thomas, eds. *Romanticism: Critical Essays in American Literature.* New York: Garland Publishing, 1986, 344 p.

    Anthology of critical essays on six works of American

Romanticism: Ralph Waldo Emerson's *Essays,* Henry David Thoreau's *Walden,* Edgar Allan Poe's *Short Stories,* Nathaniel Hawthorne's *The Scarlet Letter,* Herman Melville's *Moby-Dick,* and Walt Whitman's *Leaves of Grass.*

Bickman, Martin. *The Unsounded Centre: Jungian Studies in American Romanticism.* Chapel Hill: The University of North Carolina Press, 1980, 182 p.

Psychoanalytic discussion of selected works of American Romantic writers.

Boas, George, ed. *Romanticism in America.* New York: Russell & Russell, 1961, 202 p.

Collection of essays discussing the influence of Romanticism on American arts and culture.

Brantley, Richard E. *Coordinates of Anglo-American Romanticism: Wesley, Edwards, Carlyle, and Emerson.* Gainesville: University of Florida Press, 1993, 207 p.

Explores links between four American and English philosophical writers in the era of Romanticism.

Chai, Leon. *The Romantic Foundations of the American Renaissance.* Ithaca, N.Y.: Cornell University Press, 1987, 438 p.

Traces the use of various "governing concepts" of European Romanticism by American Romantic writers.

Foster, Edward Halsey. *The Civilized Wilderness: Backgrounds to American Romantic Literature, 1817-1860.* New York: The Free Press, 1975, 220 p.

Focuses on the relationship between wilderness and civilization in the works of the American Romantics.

Hoffman, Michael J. *The Subversive Vision: American Romanticism in Literature.* Port Washington, N.Y.: Kennikat Press, 1972, 160 p.

Proposes a theory of Romanticism that encompasses both the European and American movements, suggesting a "continuity in consciousness on both sides of the Atlantic."

Lieber, Todd M. *Endless Experiments: Essays on the Heroic Experience in American Romanticism.* Columbus: Ohio State University Press, 1973, 277 p.

Contends that the Romantic hero is motivated by a need to reconcile the dualisms of "mind and object, spirit and matter, human and absolute, man and God."

Matthiessen, F.O. *American Renaissance: Art and Expression in the Age of Emerson and Whitman.* London: Oxford University Press, 1941, 678 p.

Influential study of the major figures in the American Romantic period.

Miller, Perry. *Nature's Nation.* Cambridge, Mass.: Belknap Press of Harvard University Press, 1967, 298 p.

Collection of Miller's essays tracing the development of American culture. Includes essays on Emerson, Thoreau, and Melville, and on the Romantic concept of nature.

Morse, David. *American Romanticism.* 2 vols. Hampshire, England: Macmillan, 1987.

Discusses the major American Romantic writers. Morse contends that "of all societies, the United States is the one that has been most deeply marked by the impact of Romanticism."

Parrington, Vernon Louis. *Main Currents in American Thought. Volume Two: 1800-1860, The Romantic Revolution in America.* New York: Harcourt Brace Jovanovich, 1927, 486 p.

Examines the intellectual background of American Romanticism.

Spiller, Robert E., et al., eds. *Literary History of the United States.* Fourth edition, revised. New York: Macmillan Publishing, 1974, 1556 p.

Includes chapters on the major figures of the American Romantic period.

Strout, Cushing, ed. *Intellectual History in America: Contemporary Essays on Puritanism, the Enlightenment, and Romanticism, Vol. I.* New York: Harper & Row, 1968, 258 p.

Anthology includes John L. Thomas's "Reform in the Romantic Era" and other essays dealing with Romantic authors and themes.

Yoder, R.A. "The Equilibrist Perspective: Toward a Theory of American Romanticism." *Studies in Romanticism* 12, No. 4 (Fall 1973): 705-40.

Characterizes the American Romantics as "Equilibrists"—passive figures who seek balance with nature rather than control over it.

Dramatic Realism

INTRODUCTION

Realism was an artistic and literary movement that reacted against the conventions of neoclassicism and romanticism and attempted to create a style that better reflected the facts of human existence. Influenced by the rise of modern science, realist writers sought to examine society and human behavior objectively and to delineate exactly what they discovered. Realism first had a great impact on novel writing and only later spread to drama, where, championed by such notable figures as Anton Chekhov, Henrik Ibsen, and August Strindberg, it revolutionized the construction of plays as well as acting and staging.

Written in a style that attempts to imitate the form and tone of everyday speech, realist works for the theater are generally prose rather than verse dramas, and they dispense with what their authors perceived to be artificial stage conventions such as soliloquies and asides. Their plots do not always follow the ancient unities, which require that the entire action of the play occurs in one place over the course of one day; indeed, they need not possess any rigidly formal structure at all. Intended to provide a closely observed slice of life, realist dramas eschew traditional denouements, particularly happy endings. Their authors considered them more than simple entertainment; often pessimistic in outlook, these plays were meant to leave the audience with an uncomfortable feeling that would stimulate them to social action.

The realist emphasis on the presentation of precise details also affected the production of the plays. The environment, regarded as an important determinant of characters' behavior or as a force with which they came into conflict, was carefully and minutely represented. The fantastic painted canvases of earlier eras, forming backgrounds for actors who stood well to the front of the stage, gave way to the box set surrounding the players. These three-walled "rooms" were filled with real furniture to create a natural setting. The proscenium arch formed the invisible "fourth wall" through which the audience viewed the scene. At times furniture was lined against this "wall" to enhance the illusion of real life under observation. Sound effects, too, like the hoof beats of approaching horses, were used, as well as other devices, like the scent of fresh cherries that wafted over the audience during a 1926 performance of Chekhov's *The Cherry Orchard* at the Moscow Art Theater.

The realist movement also had a great impact on acting styles and methods. Much as in life, characters' thoughts and interior lives were projected not by great speeches, but by subtleties in their behavior and conversation, facial expressions and gestures, voice inflections and evocative uses of silence. Sustaining the illusion of real-life space created by the box set, the actors ignored the audience and spoke directly to each other in a conversational tone.

Despite the wide diffusion of realist drama throughout Europe and America, by the end of the nineteenth century there emerged a significant reaction against it. Some critics maintained that realist techniques do not reflect life but only the authors' own philosophies, which tend to be materialistic and deterministic. William Butler Yeats, for example, asserted that realist dramas ignore the spiritual dimension of life, and he deplored their failure to present an ennobling ideal. In spite of such criticisms, however, realism has proven to be more than just a nineteenth-century trend, as the work of successful twentieth-century realist playwrights from Arthur Miller to Harold Pinter demonstrates. It has fundamentally affected the way in which drama is conceived.

REPRESENTATIVE WORKS

Becque, Henri
  Les corbeaux 1882
  [*The Vultures,* 1913]
Belasco, David
  The Girl of the Golden West 1905
Chekhov, Anton
  Chayka 1896
  [*The Sea Gull,* 1912]
  Djadja Vanya 1897
  [*Uncle Vanya,* 1912]
  Tri sestry 1901
  [*The Three Sisters,* 1941]
  Visnoyovy sad 1904
  [*The Cherry Orchard,* 1908]
Hauptmann, Gerhart
  Die Weber 1892
  [*The Weavers,* 1899]
Ibsen, Henrik
  Et dukkehjem 1879
  [*A Doll's House,* 1882]
  Gengangere 1881
  [*Ghosts,* 1890]
  Vilanden 1884
  [*The Wild Duck,* 1890]
  Hedda Gabler 1890
  [*Hedda Gabler,* 1891]
Jones, Henry Arthur
  Michael and His Lost Angel 1896
Pinero, Arthur Wing
  The Profligate 1889

The Second Mrs. Tanqueray 1893
The Notorious Mrs. Ebbsmith 1895
The Benefit of the Doubt 1895
Trelawny of the "Wells" 1898
Mid-Channel 1909
Strindberg, August
  Fadren 1887
    [*The Father,* 1907]
  Kamraterna 1888
    [*Comrades,* 1919]
  Fordingsägare 1888
    [*Creditors,* 1910]
  Fröken Julie 1888
    [*Miss Julie,* 1913]
  Till Damascus 1898
    [*To Damascus,* 1933-35]
Tolstoy, Leo
  Vlast tmy 1886
    [*The Power of Darkness,* 1888]
Zola, Émile
  Thérèse Raquin 1873
    [*Thérèse Raquin,* 1891]

OVERVIEWS

Robert D. Boyer

[*In the excerpt below, Boyer provides an introductory
survey of realist drama, identifying a number of social
and cultural influences on its growth and development.*]

In 1748, the French encyclopedist Denis Diderot argued
that "the perfection of a spectacle consists in the imitation
of an action so exact that the spectator, deceived without
interruption, imagines himself present at the action itself."
Curiously, the eighteenth-century stagecraft with which
Diderot was familiar, replete with artifice and spectacular
fakery on all levels, exhibited this ideal of imitation so
minimally that Diderot's vision can only be seen as a remarkable prophecy of a profound and lasting movement,
but one that would not be felt in European theatres for another hundred years.

The history of theatre in Europe may be depicted as a broken series of overlapping, often disorderly, experiments
seeking a completely appropriate and fully satisfying rhetoric of imitation by which the entire length and breadth
of man's experience—or that portion of it deemed "suitable" by the authorities—can be interpreted by actors for
an audience. Each generation has explored anew the potentialities of imitation—inventing, refining, and discard-
ing innumerable rules, formulas, conventions, and other
artifices. When the concerted efforts of theatre artists produced a recognizably consistent mode of dramaturgy and
stagecraft, lasting at least a few generations, subsequent
theatre historians have pronounced its special collection
of techniques and principles "a style."

In the middle of the nineteenth century, a few daring playwrights, concerned with the banality that had overwhelmed the popular stages of Europe, began to develop
a new style, almost unnoticed. Influenced by the unusual
honesty of the prose writers of France and Russia, they
began to discern the artistic merit of imitating life, on
stage, with greater exactitude, allowing the daily experience of man, in all of its detail, to be the compelling example. The goal of these authors was to reproduce life—that
is, to imitate action flawlessly—without the artifices and
fakery and without the philosophic and moral prejudices
typical of romantic writing. Russian playwrights led their
European contemporaries toward this ideal of uncon-
trived dramaturgy, because, as John Gassner has written
[in his *Treasury of the Theatre,* Volume 1, 1959], the Rus-
sians "thought not of theatrical effect but of life first." The
style of dramatic writing that they developed came to be
known as Realism, and it would shortly engender an offshoot called Naturalism.

DEFINITION OF TERMS

Both the term "Realism" and the term "Naturalism" had
been part of philosophic jargon for some years when they
were introduced into the vocabulary of the drama. Their
usage in dramatic criticism, however, is little illuminated
by their established philosophic usage. Dramatic Realism
is most simply defined as the set of artistic strategies designed to achieve verisimilitude on stage, to create the appearance of the life that is, with no discernible artifice, no
self-justifying poesy, no pretty illusions, and most importantly, no lies. The subject matter is hard material fact (as
opposed to the soft, dreamy illusion of Romanticism),
which is crafted into a unique form, carefully disguised.
William Gerhardie, in his seminal work on Chekhov
[*Anton Chekhov: A Critical Study,* 1923], expressed this
objective, with special insight, as

> extracting from life . . . its characteristic
> features—for life outside the form of art is like
> the sea, blurred, formless and with no design—
> and the replacing of them in a design calculated
> to represent, within art's focus, life that is like
> the sea, blurred, formless and with no design.

Naturalism is an extreme form of Realism in which observation and reproduction of detail often become ends in
themselves, and for which the subject matter chosen is
typically the seamier side of the human condition. All
form or design is denied and traditional ideas of art are
held to be inimical to the desired end; thus, art approaches
science, and the drama becomes documentary—little
more than extremely accurate reportage. Emile Zola, announcing the introduction of Naturalism in his Preface to
Therese Raquin (1873), made clear that the model was to
be life itself, "an immense field where each may study and
create as he likes," not corrupted by the artist's imagination, selection or arrangement:

> I am for no school, because I am for human
> truth, which excludes all sects and all sys-
> tems. . . . The word *art* displeases me; it con-
> tains the idea of . . . necessary arrangement and
> absolute ideal. To make art, is that not outside
> of man and of nature?

The impulse, however, is the same for both Realism and Naturalism—Gerhardie neatly described it as the desire "to resurrect the complete illusion of real life, using the things characteristic of real life." The results are clearly comparable, although the techniques vary by degree and occasionally by philosophic justification. Thus, for the sake of convenience, I shall use the term "Realism" as inclusive of Naturalism in the remainder of this essay.

THE REVOLT AGAINST MELODRAMA

To understand the emergence of the realistic urge in the theatre, one must investigate the condition of dramatic art at the time Realism first appeared and attempt to comprehend the prevailing taste of the mid-nineteenth-century audience. Realism was a radical response, an undisguised reaction, to Romanticism in the popular theatre—which meant, for the most part, melodrama. Likewise, it was a rebuke to the value system that lay behind the literary impulse on which that popular genre was based, an impulse described by Hippolyte Taine (writing of English literature specifically) as, "always moral, never psychological, bent on exactly measuring the degree of human honesty, ignorant of the mechanisms of our sentiments and faculties."

Melodrama depicted the irrational, dreamy side of life, and postulated a world of absolute values, governed by a just and omnipotent God, who regularly intervened in the affairs of men. Man himself was seen as a perfectable being, a child of God, especially created by divine plan, and thereby endowed with inherent dignity. The universe was perceived as an innately good and congenial environment for the stalwart and God-fearing. The good man might suffer temporarily, but he would ultimately see justice done, for virtue must inevitably triumph if Nature's God loves virtue; moreover, evil doers would be punished in proportion to their misdeeds.

Since the appeal of melodrama was primarily to the impoverished and downtrodden, particularly to the urban proletariat, the plays provided escapist theatre, turning the playhouse into a never-never land where the reality of vermin-ridden and cheerless slums could be repressed for a few hours of moral uplift, haloed by the almost constant music from which the genre takes its name. Faraway settings, narratives from history, and exotic characters helped the spectator to forget his life in the fetid streets and sweatshops of Paris or Petersburg, London or Glasgow. The theatre provided a lively emotional experience—a "culinary experience," to use Brecht's phrase. The spectator could check his intelligence, along with his coat, at the playhouse door. He would be asked to feel, not to think, to forget, not to confront the realities of nineteenth-century urban existence. The overwhelming evidence that most playwrights were no longer attempting to touch the contemporary condition of man, but were supplying a mindless, amnesic experience in the theatre, struck the early Realists as an abdication of a central commitment of the drama: to present the truth of human experience on the stage. Emile Zola, in the preface to *Therese Raquin,* certainly with more hope than objective evidence, declared that the "despicable melodrama," along with historical drama, was dead in the hearts of the general public.

If Realism grew out of an immediate need to provide an alternative to the primary dramatic style of the popular theatre, its philosophical roots and intellectual impetus came not so much from theatrical tradition as from social conditions and intellectual currents being profoundly felt throughout Europe. No earlier style of dramaturgy can be demonstrated more strongly to be a product of the *Zeitgeist* ("the spirit of the times") in which it flourished as can Realism. From the beginning, its writers and sympathetic critics turned to intellectual ideals, not theatrical effect, as justification for their cause. Although aimed at remedying maladies of the popular, commercial theatre, Realism managed, paradoxically, to cultivate a relatively small *coterie* audience: the literati, plus the sophisticated upper-middle class—an audience, in temperament and education, not unlike the playwrights and critics themselves.

The intellectual currents that intermingled in nineteenth-century Europe, and that gave nerve and justification to the new drama, cannot be discretely segmented, but we can isolate the most important and relate these influences directly to dramatic practice.

INFLUENCE: NEW THEOLOGICAL IDEAS

Across the Continent, new theological ideas were being debated and embraced by serious scholar and dilettante alike. Søren Kieregaard and Friedrich Nietzsche laid the foundations for modern existentialism. Their emphasis on individual responsibility, their rejection of systematic philosophy, and their refusal to accept the comforting illusions of institutional Christianity—different as their ultimate conclusions were—challenged the world of theology. By daring to question the traditionally accepted "meaning of existence," Nietzsche, Kierkegaard, and their comrades opened the door to greater freedom of decision, but, often, to a greater sense of personal alienation. Atheism found a new, broader audience and a new name: free-thinking. For many serious men and women, like Ibsen's Mrs. Alving, the existence of a benevolent and interventionist God was no longer necessary as a basic axiom of universal truth. Whatever became of the Everlasting Arms? Karl Marx, likewise, argued that religions were merely socially expedient ideologies used by the economic establishment to pacify the working class, which had no hope of social progress or justice in this life, with dreams of rest and happiness in the afterlife. Flaubert, in his short story "A Simple Heart," told of an old woman who believed her stuffed parrot to be the Holy Ghost; were man's religious myths really the product of his own deranged imagination? In the latter part of the century, there was serious debate over the place of Christianity in the modern scientific world. Charles Péguy, a socialist and a Christian mystic, summed up one reasoned position in his novel *Clio* (1910):

> What we wish to say . . . is that the modern world has renounced the system altogether, as well as the mystique. . . . [From now on] there is another world, a modern world, and this modern world is not simply an evil Christian world, a world of bad Christianity . . . but an un-Christian world, absolutely de-Christianized, literally, totally un-Christian. That is what must be said, what must be believed. That is what must be seen. If it were only the old story . . .

that sin had once again intruded, that would be nothing. We have become used to that; the world is used to that . . . one more bad Christian century like many others. If people knew history as well as I know it, they would know that it has always been thus, that all of those centuries, those twenty centuries, have always been centuries of miserable Christianity.

What is interesting, what is new, is that there is no longer any Christianity at all. That expresses not only the extent but the type and nature of the disaster.

We have seen instituted before our eyes a world both viable and entirely un-Christian. It is necessary to admit that; those who deny it are wretched.

Péguy, the editor of the prestigious *Cahiers de la Quinzaine,* France's leading journal of literature and ideas, thus gave voice to the religious malaise that had gripped Europe for half a century.

In the serious theatre, this spiritual doubt and religious degeneration were in great part responsible for the repudiation of melodrama, which had postulated its world view on traditional religious foundations and comforts. The realistic writers typically pictured a world without God and without the consoling illusions of religion, often a world of accident and chaos. The portraits they produced of the clergy (like Hauptmann's Pastor Kittelhaus and Ibsen's Pastor Manders) were uncomplimentary, depicting guileful or insipid men dispensing false comforts. Moral judgments, the stock-in-trade of conservative religion, were no longer supplied by playwrights—heroes and villains no longer had to be clearly labeled. What meaning have Vice and Virtue in a godless chaos? Naturalism, especially, carried the pessimistic inference of an indifferent universe, uncaring and uncongenial, operating on the impersonal laws of cause and effect, not by benign intention.

INFLUENCE: THE SCIENTIFIC OUTLOOK

The scientific method, glorified in the late nineteenth century as the salvation of man, implied that truth was a product of experiment and not of revelation. Careful observation and reportage led to empirical truth, and empirical truth could, it was believed, answer all the needs of mankind. Ernest Renan wrote in 1849 [in his *L'Avenir de la Science*] that "science alone could ameliorate the unhappy state of man." The chemist Berthelot asserted that "science possesses a moral force capable of aiding society to attain, with but a brief delay, the blessed age of equality and fraternity," and the physicist Laplace conceived of a Being who would know the position and momentum of every particle of the universe, together with the laws governing such particles. The scientific ideal of observation and reportage was assimilated by the realistic playwrights, as was the optimism over the possibilities for improving the human condition. On this theme, Zola wrote, "the experimental and scientific spirit of the century will enter the domain of the drama, and in it lies its only salvation" [cited in H. Barrett Clark's *European Theories of the Drama,* 1918], and several years later, he added,

We have come to an age of method, of experi-

mental science. We have, above all, the need for precise analysis. We should show little appreciation of the freedom won if we wished to wrap ourselves in a new tradition. The terrain is free; we can return to man and to nature. [*Oeuvres Completes,* Vol. 11, 1968]

The powerful influence of scientific method and discovery on the realistic drama makes it necessary to emphasize the overwhelming spirit of optimism that surrounded scientific activity in this period—particularly since, in the twentieth century, reasonable men have developed serious reservations as to the "moral force" of science and its potential for salvation. Three major writers, credited with popularizing the scientific outlook by writing eloquently of its future horizons, remind us of the excitement and hope. David Masson, in his *Recent British Philosophy* (1869), wrote,

There has been . . . in consequence of the revelations of science . . . some most notable enlargements of our views of physical nature and of history—enlargements even to the breaking down of what had been a wall in the minds of most and the substitution on that side of a sheer vista of open space.

Masson went on to specify some of the problems that lay ahead; they included the battle between empiricism and transcendentalism and the question of the place of man in the natural scheme. Ernest Renan in *L'Avenir de la Science* ("The Future of Science," 1849), intoned,

The true world which science reveals to us is much superior to the fantastic world created by the imagination. . . . Let us say without fear that if the marvels of fiction seemed up to now necessary for poetry, the marvels of nature, when laid bare in all of their splendor, will constitute a poetry a thousand times more sublime, a poetry which will be reality itself, which will be, simultaneously, science and philosophy.

Thirty years later, Emil du Bois-Reymond would match Renan's enthusiasm, in *Natural Science and the History of Culture* (1878), as he concluded that,

scarcely anything in the heights or depths remains a mystery. . . . Only in scientific research and power over nature is there no stagnation: knowledge grows steadily, the creative strength develops unceasingly. Here, alone, each generation stands on the shoulders of the preceding one.

Is it any wonder that the realistic playwrights, determined as they were to improve the condition of human life, would attempt to join a movement of such vigor, confidence, and hope?

INFLUENCE: ADVANCES IN PSYCHOLOGY

European dramaturgy, grounded as it was in traditional Judeo-Christian morality, historically envisioned character motivation in terms of choice, the conscious decision to do good or evil. Man, possessed of a conscience and "free will," could freely pursue options of behavior, and thus was responsible for his actions and their results. Discoveries in the emerging science of psychology brought into question this easy assumption about the underlying sources of behavior, and, in so doing, required a reassessment of the ideas of sin and guilt. Messmer, Freud, Charcot, Janet, and other pioneer psychologists began to investigate the realm of the subconscious, a vague and almost unfathomable world, revealed to be the well-spring of human action. Joseph Breuer, an associate of Freud, in the period 1880-82, stumbled upon the method of approaching mental disturbance by unearthing a blurred memory, often under hypnosis, and having the patient "talk it out," a technique now attributed in popular belief to Freud alone. Breuer's process, much refined and debated, became fashionable psychoanalysis by the end of the century. Psychologists spoke of human behavior—particularly aberrant, antisocial, "unnatural" behavior—in terms of subconscious drives, not conscious choices; the action itself became less important than the motives, conscious and unconscious, that engendered it.

The cardboard, one-dimensional characters of melodrama, and the patent naivete of traditional dramatic motivation, began to look pathetically frail and dishonest to the early realistic playwrights in light of contemporary psychology. Fully dimensioned characters, developed with a recognition of current psychological understandings, became a requirement of the new dramaturgy early on. If a man's actions were truly the product of deep, unconscious, and only vaguely understandable causation, could sin have meaning any longer? Or punishment? Poetic justice—the principle that virtue must triumph, that good must be rewarded and evil punished in perfect proportion—lost its appeal to writers, not only because the principle was incompatible with the new concepts of psychological motivation, but because it quite simply was incompatible with the day-to-day experience of real life. Because psychologists faced, with honesty, the seamier side of human behavior, the distasteful and the abhorrent, playwrights found themselves challenged to portray similar behavior, to force their audiences to confront the unpleasant and ugly in human experience.

As with the depiction of behavior, all themes and subject matter, no matter how lurid or objectionable, were justified. Sexuality, a subject considered so intrinsically private at the time that "decent people" dared not even whisper about it if they valued their reputations, was made stageworthy. Even a partial list of the subjects investigated in the domestic dramas of Ibsen, "the best-hated writer of the nineteenth century," is revealing: the innocence of women, hereditary syphilis, political corruption, euthanasia, incest, suicide, religious hypocrisy. Life, these writers asserted, should be portrayed as it is lived, and to the Naturalist, particularly, the stage should provide an objective *tranche da vie* ("slice of life"), without glossing over the distasteful.

Predictably, the Romanticists, the Sentimentalists, and the Moral Guardians bruited their displeasure, accusing the Realists of gratuitously revealing festering sores to public view. Ibsen responded that he descended into the sewers not to bathe, but to cleanse them. And Chekhov, answering a correspondent's charge that he concentrated on the filth of life at the expense of the "pearls," wrote,

Indeed, to think that literature bears the responsibility of digging up the "pearl" from the muck heap would amount to rejecting literature itself. Literature is called artistic because it depicts life as it actually is. . . . Surely a man of letters is not a confectioner, nor a dealer in cosmetics. . . . He is compelled to struggle with his fastidiousness and soil his imagination with the dirt of life . . . [to] realize that dung heaps play a very respectable role in the landscape and that evil passions are as inherent in life as good ones [cited in Ernest J. Simmons's *Chekhov: A Biography,* 1962].

Psychology had taught the theatre not only crucial lessons in characterization, but also the artist's responsibility to refuse his audience the Romantic comfort of faraway places and times, in favor of the here and now.

INFLUENCE: NEW THEORIES IN ANTHROPOLOGY

The publication of Charles Darwin's *The Origin of Species,* in which natural selection was credited with the evolution of the lower animals, initiated a wider investigation of the generative past of all animate nature. Darwin's revolutionary study of 1859 was followed by Thomas Huxley's *Man's Place in Nature* (1863) and Darwin's *The Descent of Man* (1871), in which man was firmly placed in the evolutionary process. According to traditional Judeo-Christian teaching, based on the early chapters of Genesis, God had created man as a separate species in His own image. This myth had evolved into a fundamental doctrine of Christianity, Special Creation, which endowed man with dignity and his earthly presence with divine authority. In the popular imagination, the importance of evolutionary theory was that it gave all mankind a simian ancestor. Not Old Adam, but a monkey! Where, it was asked, was man's dignity, if his progenitor was an ape? The dramaturgic result of evolutionary theory (coupled with new understandings in genetics) was the portrayal of man without inherent dignity. Authentic heroes and heroines, a staple feature of melodrama and the popular historical drama, virtually disappear. How could a human being, the product of immutable genetic codes, intrinsically selfish, lacking free will, and surviving by animal instincts, possibly be heroic?

Darwin had also emphasized the adaptation to environment and the survival of the fittest. Realistic, and especially, naturalistic playwrights depicted men attempting to cope with depraved environments and frequently failing. Set designers relished the opportunity to reproduce detailed squalor on stage, whether it was the stinking beef carcasses in the setting for Antoine's production of *The Butcher* in 1888 or the closely observed flophouse conditions that constituted the *mise-en-scène* for the Moscow Art Theatre's original production of Gorky's *The Lower Depths* in 1902. Stock settings, pulled from storage, the weary contrivances of hack scene painters, would no longer do. A character both created, and was created by, his surroundings, "the landscape of his soul." Following social and literary theory, espoused by Taine and Stendhal, among earlier critics, the Naturalists believed that man was inseparable from his environment—indeed, from his "national characteristics" as well. A man's "exterior life," his milieu, leaves imprints on his character, just as surely as a man has an impact on his surroundings.

INFLUENCE: SOCIAL AND POLITICAL FACTORS

The nineteenth century witnessed unparalleled civil disorder and social upheaval. The traditional forms of civil governance, and the economic system that had dominated Europe since the decline of feudalism, were challenged in print by imaginative and influential political theorists and in the streets by charismatic, often violent, revolutionaries. The surviving monarchies, facing the twilight of their epoch, teetered uneasily between ancient arrogance and painful compromise. In England, the Chartist movement, seeking rights for the working class, slowly gained significant victories. The incubating socialist movement met its first rigorous test of strength in the Paris uprising of 1848, an insurrection of workers under Alexandre Herzen. This bloody revolt, brutally put down by the military, pitted the bourgeois French legislature against the fearsome reality of proletarian demands. In the same year, similar uprisings hit other capitals of Europe, as though by contagion.

Moreover, Karl Marx published *The Communist Manifesto* in London in that troubled year, and later *A Contribution to the Critique of Political Economy* (1859), and, with Friedrich Engels, issued *Capital* (1867), the three primers of classic Marxist theory. Marx wrote ominously, "a spector is haunting Europe; it is the spector of Communism." The short-lived revolutionary and egalitarian government of France, established in 1871 and known as the Paris Commune, gave additional evidence of proletarian muscle and potential popular support. Marx outlined the basic lessons of the Commune in an address to the General Council of the First International, later published as *The Civil War in France.* In this speech, he portrayed the "struggle of the producing against the appropriating class," and championed "the economic emancipation of labor." The spreading claims of communism and socialism, coupled with the sordid realities of the industrial revolution, hardened class barriers throughout Europe, and hastened a breakdown in society, in part by denying ancient privilege. Dialectical materialism, the basic Marxist system of reasoning, denied permanence and a priori values, and thus was incompatible with the philosophy that sustained melodrama.

In the Realistic theatre, the results of this social unrest and political debate were numerous. Chekhov wrote, "Everything in this world is relative and approximate." Writers like Gerhart Hauptmann, in *The Weavers,* and Maxim Gorky, in *The Lower Depths,* experimented with the "mass hero"; a number of suffering, alienated workers provide the focus of interest, rather than a single character. The breakdown of class barriers was mirrored seriously in Strindberg's *Miss Julie* and humorously in Bernard Shaw's *Pygmalion,* among other works. Ibsen investigated the corruption of capitalist enterprise in *The Wild Duck* and *An Enemy of the People,* and joined other playwrights with similar concerns in portraying the chaos of a fragmented citizenry.

Social concerns, the center of liberal (or, as it was often called in the period, Progressive) thinking, found their greatest theatrical expression in the development of the social problem play (*pièce à thèse*)—that is, a work that takes as its theme a specific blight on society, such as prostitution, infidelity, alcoholism, or unwed motherhood, and dramatically demonstrates its causes and effects, and suggests solutions. De Toqueville generalized in 1840 [in his *Democracy in America,* Volume 1], "no portion of literature is connected closer or with more numerous ties with the present state of society than the drama," and the writers of social problem plays in the ensuing century would more than justify this claim. These playwrights sought immediate redress for grievous social ills. The intensity of their desire for direct action on the part of the audience is clearly demonstrated by Eugène Brieux's *Damaged Goods,* a dramatic treatise on venereal disease. Before the curtain goes up, the stage manager appears and cautions the audience,

> Ladies and Gentlemen, I beg to inform you, on behalf of the author and the management, that the object of the play is a study of the disease of syphillis and its bearing on marriage.

The play portrays the ravages of "loves mischances" in the life of a young French woman. At the final curtain, the doctor, who has served as a *raisonneur* (or spokesman for the author), addresses M. Loches, a member of the Chamber of Deputies:

> This poor girl is typical. The whole problem is summed up in her: she is at once the product and the cause. We set the ball rolling, and others keep it up and it runs back to bruise our own shins. . . . But if you give a thought or two to what you have just seen when you are sitting in the Chamber, we shall not have wasted our time.

In Bernard Shaw's commentary on his *Widowers' Houses* (1892), an attack on slums and absentee landlords, he boldly informed the reader that the play "deals with a burning social question and is deliberately intended to induce people to vote on the Progressive side in the next City Council election in London."

CONCLUSION

The emergence of realistic dramaturgy in the playhouses of Europe was, demonstrably, a product of the complex mingling of the nontheatrical influences described above. However, much established theatre practice, originally unrelated to realistic production, must also be credited with numerous contributions. The serious domestic drama of T. W. Robertson in England, and the *pièce bien fait* ("the well-made play") in France, the rising popularity of the convincing "box set," the concern for authenticity in the setting and costuming of historical drama, even the technology developed to achieve realistic special effects in melodrama, were appropriated by the new movement. Among other influences, which had nonrealistic origins, were the adaptation of electric lighting for stage use, the construction of more intimate theatres with diminished forestages, the emergence of the director as a unique artist, and the conscious efforts by prominent actor-managers to gain a new respectability for the theatre. The list is seemingly endless, and I have been able, in a paper of intentional brevity, hardly to touch the multifarious ways in which the theories and influences that engendered Realism were translated into stage practice; nor could I treat the important power that Realism exerted in the theatre and cinema of the twentieth century.

> Robert D. Boyer, *"The Emergence of Realism in the European Theatre," in his* Realism in European Theatre Drama, 1870-1920: A Bibliography, *Greenwood Press, 1979, pp. xv-xxv.*

Martin Esslin

[*Esslin, a prominent and sometimes controversial critic of contemporary theater, is perhaps best known for coining the term "theatre of the absurd." His* Theatre of the Absurd *(1961) is a major study of the avant-garde drama of the 1950s and early 1960s, including the works of Samuel Beckett, Eugene Ionesco, and Jean Genet. In this essay, Esslin analyzes realism and the revolutionary impact it had upon the theater.*]

Nothing tastes staler than the revolutions of the day before yesterday; the bitter flavor of great expectations disappointed clings to them; they make us feel superior for having seen through their ridiculous pretensions and sorry for our fathers and grandfathers for having been taken in by them. That naturalism in the novel and in the theatre still leaves such an aftertaste on our palates is, in a way, a tribute to the intensity of emotion it aroused in its day and the length of time during which it acquired and held a dominant position. After all, it was in the 1870s that Zola shocked the world with his new concept of naturalism; Ibsen's *Ghosts* was first published in 1881; Strindberg's *Father* in 1887, his *Miss Julie* in 1888; Hauptmann's *Vor Sonnenaufgang* had its first performance in 1889; Chekhov's *Seagull* in 1896. Yet the expressionism of the 1920s, Brecht's epic theatre of the thirties and forties, the Theatre of the Absurd of the fifties and sixties were still, essentially, reactions *against* naturalism, or at least against its latter-day exponents who still dominated—almost to this day—the more conservative sector of our theatre: Broadway, the London West End, and the Paris boulevard, not to speak of Moscow. What started out as a furious attack on the conventions of what was then regarded as the well-made play, as an iconoclastic, revolutionary onslaught against the establishment, has now turned into the embodiment of "squareness," conservatism, and the contemporary concept of the well-made play. In the West End of London early Shaw and Ibsen have become safe after-dinner entertainment for the suburban business community, the equivalents of Scribe, Sardou, and Dumas fils in their own day—the very authors whom they wanted to replace because they were safe and establishment-minded.

Such, however, is the dialectical law of historical development: each hour has its own necessity, its own imperative; and what is essential is precisely the insight and the courage needed to obey it. Once the hour is passed, the new molds have been created, lesser spirits will inevitably continue to use them; and that is how the revolutionary contents and forms of yesteryear turn into the safe, conservative clichés of today.

What matters, therefore, for any objective assessment of a movement like naturalism is to see it in its historical context; to understand the moral and artistic impulse behind it; and to pursue its manifestations into our own time. We shall then find that the impulse behind the naturalist movement is still very much alive, very relevant for our own time, and well worth our study and understanding.

The mid-nineteenth century was one of dismal stagnation in the European theatre; the achievements of the classical and romantic movement in Germany, of the romantic revolution in France had frozen into an empty routine; the theatre was discredited as a serious art form. Looking back on those days, Strindberg reported that

> . . . if one wanted to submit a play to the Royal Dramatic Theatre in the sixties and seventies the following conditions had to be met to get it performed: the play had to have five acts, each act had to run to about six sheets of writing paper, thus the whole play to 5 times 24 = 120 foolscap pages. Changes of scene within the acts were not liked and were considered a weakness. Each act had to have a beginning, a middle, and an end. The curtain lines had to give rise to applause through oratorical figures; if the play was in unrhymed verse, the last two lines had to rhyme. In the play there had to be "turns" for the actors which were called "scenes"; the monologue was permissible and often constituted a highlight; a longish emotional outburst or invective, a revelation, were almost compulsory; there also had to be narrative passages—a dream, an anecdote, an event. . . . This dramaturgy had a certain justification and even a certain beauty; it stemmed in the last resort from Victor Hugo and had been a reaction against the obsolete abstractions of Racine and Corneille in the thirties. But this art form degenerated like all others when it had had its day, and the five-act form was used for all kinds of subjects, even for insignificant minor history or anecdote. . . .

Strindberg here confirms the diagnosis Zola made in his preface to *Thérèse Raquin* (dated July 25, 1873):

> Drama is dying of its extravagances, its lies, and its platitudes. If comedy still keeps on its feet in the collapse of our stage, that is because it contains more of real life, because it is often true. I defy the last of the romantics to put onto the stage a heroic drama; the old iron of the Middle Ages, the secret doors, the poisoned wines and all the rest would only make one shrug one's shoulders. Melodrama, the bourgeois offspring of romantic drama, is even more dead in the affection of the people; its false sentiment, its complications of stolen children and recovered documents, its impudent grandiloquence have brought it, at long last, into such disrepute that one holds one's ribs at any attempt to resuscitate it. The great works of the 1830s will remain as milestones of a struggle, as literary red-letter days, as superb efforts that brought down the classical trappings. But now that all this is overturned, the cloaks and the daggers have become unnecessary. The time has come to create works of truth. To replace the classical tradition by a romantic tradition would amount to a failure to

make use of the freedom which our elders won for us. There must be no more schools, no more formula, no more literary panjandrums of any kind. There is just life itself, an immense field where everybody can explore and create to his heart's content.

No more schools, no more formula, no more literary panjandrums of any kind! Here lies the impetus behind the naturalist movement which is still alive, still active, still immensely relevant today. No wonder that Zola's impassioned manifesto reads so well, that it seems fresh and topical to us, almost a hundred years after it was written. The romantic movement had overthrown the dominance of the rigid formula of French classical drama; but it had imposed its own narrow conception of subject matter, technique, and objective on all serious drama. Comedy, stemming from Molière and his realism of observation and language, had remained much freer from the blight of the schoolmen. Now the naturalists called for a fresh start in *complete* freedom; art, like philosophy, was making the transition from a *closed* to a totally *open* system. The naturalists were the first to formulate such a new, open view of aesthetics.

It had taken half a century for Auguste Comte's positivist philosophy to be taken up by the creative artists—Comte's *Système de philosophie positive* had appeared in 1824. It reached Zola via the works of a physiologist, Claude Bernard, notably his *Introduction à l'étude de la médecine expérimentale* (1865), and a literary and social historian, Hippolyte Taine, whose epoch-making *Histoire de la littérature anglaise* had appeared in 1864. What Zola took from Claude Bernard is no more and no less than the basic concept of the *scientific method* of painstaking inquiry through observation, hypothesis, and the testing of hypotheses through experiment. Zola's essay *Le Roman expérimental,* the basic formulation of the naturalists' creed, is little more than an anthology of quotations from Claude Bernard's book on experimental medicine. "All experimental reasoning must be founded on doubt, for the experimenter must have no preconceived ideas when confronting nature; he must always preserve his freedom of mind."

Bernard had stressed that the scientific, experimental method implied a *determinist* view of nature; experimentation uncovers the chain of cause and effect behind seemingly arbitrary phenomena. But it was from Taine that Zola took his own specific determinism. In his history of English literature Taine sought to explain each writer through three main factors that determined his nature and his style: *race, milieu, moment*—race, environment, and the particular historical circumstances of his time. This concept allowed the naturalists to reintroduce the classical source of tragedy, preordained, inescapable *fate,* into the drama in a new and highly respectable "scientific" guise. Men were predetermined, their individual fate was preordained through a combination of heredity, environment, and history. (Taine's ideas of race and heredity came to hideous fruition in Hitler's racialism and the extermination camps of the Second World War.) It was this idea of heredity that stalked through Ibsen's *Ghosts* and Gerhart Hauptmann's *Vor Sonnenaufgang* or Strindberg's *Miss Julie.*

Taine's determinism was an oversimplification and in itself scientifically untenable. (Modern genetics soon showed that the real workings of heredity were far more complex than Taine, or even Darwin, had imagined, that neither Oswald's syphilis nor the alcoholism Hauptmann's Helene in *Vor Sonnenuntergang* seemed destined to inherit would in fact have been transmitted from father to son, from father to daughter.) But—and this must be stressed again and again in the face of a present-day tendency to scoff at the naturalists precisely for being scientifically out of date—these mistakes of scientific detail are not of the essence of their attitude. Their fundamental and essential belief has not become obsolete:

> Naturalism, in literature . . . is the return to nature and to man, direct observation, correct anatomy, the acceptance and the depiction of that which *is*. The task is the same for the scientist as for the writer. Both have to abandon abstractions for realities, ready-made formulas for rigorous analysis. Hence no more abstract characters in our works, no more mendacious inventions, no more absolutes, but real people, the true history of everyone, the web and woof of daily life. It was a matter of a totally new start, of getting to know man from the very wellsprings of his being, before reaching conclusions in the manner of the idealists who invent their types. Writers from now on are constrained to build from the foundation upward, by bringing us the largest possible number of human documents, presented in their logical order . . . (Zola, *Le Naturalisme au théâtre*).

This spirit of free inquiry, totally unprejudiced, unburned by preconceived ideas, liberated immense energies. That it consciously aimed beyond the immediate techniques and subject matters of the moment is clearly shown by, for example, the manifesto with which Otto Brahm, the great critic and director of German naturalist drama, opened the Berlin *Freie Bühne* (Free Stage) on January 29, 1890:

> Once upon a time there was an art which avoided the present and sought poetry only in the darkness of the past, striving in a bashful flight from reality to reach ideal distant shores where in eternal youth there blooms what has never happened anywhere. The art of our time embraces with its clasping organs everything that lives, nature and society; that is why the closest and subtlest relations bind modern art and modern life together; and anyone who wants to grasp modern art must endeavor to penetrate modern life as well in its thousand merging contours, in its intertwined and antagonistic instincts. The motto of this new art, written down in golden characters by our leading spirits, is one word: truth; and truth, truth on every path of life, is what we are striving for. Not the objective truth, which escapes the struggling individual, but individual truth, freely arrived at from the deepest convictions, freely uttered: the truth of the independent spirit who has nothing to explain away or hide; and who therefore knows only one adversary, his archenemy and mortal foe: the lie in all its forms.

No other program is to be recorded in these

pages. We swear by no formula and would not dare to chain into the rigid compulsion of rules that which is in eternal flux—life and art. Our striving is for that which is in the act of becoming and our eyes are directed far more attentively onto the things which are about to arise than onto those elements of an eternal yesterday which have the presumption to tie down in conventions and rules once and for all time mankind's infinite potential. We bow in reverence before all the greatness that past epochs have preserved for us, but it is not from them that we draw the lodestone and the norms of life; for it is not he who ties himself to the views of a dead world, but only he who freely feels the demand of the present hour, who will penetrate the spiritual powers activating our age as a truly modern man. . . . No barrier of theory, no sanctified model of the past must inhibit the infinity of development, which constitutes the essence of our species. . . . Friends of naturalism, we want to stride along with it for a fair stretch of the way, but we shall not be astonished if in the course of this journey, at a point we cannot as yet foresee, the road might suddenly turn, opening up surprising new vistas in art or life. For the infinite development of human culture is bound to no formula, not even the newest; and in this confidence, in this faith in infinite potentiality, we have erected a free stage for modern life.

These are noble words; they show the genuine freedom of the spirit, transcending all the narrow dogmatism of literary movements or coteries, that inspired the best minds among the champions of naturalism. Seldom in the history of literature has the call for *absolute truth* been voiced with such uncompromising conviction, such absolute courage.

> Artistic literature is called so [wrote Chekhov in 1887] because it depicts life as it really is. Its aim is truth—unconditional and honest. . . . I agree with you that the "cream" is a fine thing, but a littérateur is not a confectioner, not a dealer in cosmetics, not an entertainer; he is a man bound, under compulsion, by the realization of his duty, and by his conscience; having put his hand to the plow, he must not plead weakness; and no matter how painful it is to him, he is constrained to overcome his aversion and soil his imagination with the sordidness of life. He is just like an ordinary reporter. What would you say if a newspaper reporter, because of his fastidiousness or from a wish to give pleasure to his readers, were to describe only honest mayors, high-minded ladies, and virtuous railroad contractors? To a chemist nothing on earth is unclean. A writer must be as objective as a chemist; he must abandon the subjective line; he must know that dung heaps play a very respectable part in a landscape and that evil passions are as inherent in life as good ones . . . (letter to M. V. Kiselev, January 14, 1887).

The decisive and truly revolutionary element in this attitude—this I believe must be stressed above all—was its passionate proclamation of the *primacy of content over form*, the conviction that any subject matter could be treated, and that each subject matter would call for the form most adequate and suitable to express it. Artistic form thus came to be seen as the *organic expression* of its content.

> We are through with intrigue, with artificial plot, through with the play as a kind of chess game; the ability to perceive and to express, which is the secret of each true artist, is his natural style, his inner form, his inner turn of phrase. In these the great rhythm and the great dynamism of life are reduced to an individual rhythm, an individual dynamism. There may be a tradition in this, but it has become flesh and blood, a tradition that, like those of eating and drinking, is carried by ever new hunger and thirst. Traditional, external dogmas cannot have a bearing on this process. Such useless and pointless external dogmas are: the dogma of plot, the dogma of the unities of space and time, the dogma of exposition in twenty to thirty lines at the opening of the first act, and others (Gerhart Hauptmann, c. 1910).

Yet in their demand for truth, for the primacy of subject matter over form, the naturalists were never—as is nowadays often thoughtlessly assumed—naïve enough to believe in the possibility of a truly objective representation of nature. In the above quotation Hauptmann insists on the artist's individual ability to perceive and to express as the starting point. And Zola himself coined the famous slogan: "*Il est certain qu'un oeuvre ne sera jamais qu'un coin de la nature vu à travers un tempérament*" ["A work of art cannot but be a corner of nature seen through a temperament"]. This recognition of the subjective nature of all perception marks the really decisive breach with any theory of art that believed in the possibility of embodying absolutes, eternal verities, in great enduring works. As such the naturalists were the first conscious existentialists in the realm of aesthetics. (The link from Kierkegaard to his fellow Scandinavian Ibsen is only too clear, although Ibsen was at pains to stress that he had "read little and understood less" of Kierkegaard. Mere awareness of the debate around Kierkegaard must have been enough to acquaint him with the essence of his ideas. While denying that Kierkegaard had been the model for Brand, Ibsen added: "But, of course, the depiction of a man whose sole aim in life is to realize his ideals will always bear a certain resemblance to Kierkegaard's life.")

There is no contradiction between the ruthless pursuit of truth, observed, scientifically tested, experimental truth on the one hand, and the continual awareness of a subjective point of view on the part of the observer. Indeed, the notion that the observer's subjectivity will always have to be reckoned with is the hallmark of a truly scientific attitude. Zola used the term *document humain* to show that any truthful description of human experience, however subjective, also has an objective value as a contribution to man's knowledge of himself. Hence Strindberg's violent denunciation of the tyranny of women over men could be seen as equally valid as Ibsen's and Shaw's passionate advocacy of the rights of women. Each one of these dramatists was ruthlessly truthful, precisely *because* he gave the fullest possible expression to nature seen through *his* temperament.

From this acceptance of the individual's point of view there also follow the rejection of any ethical absolutes, the denial of the previously held notion that it was art's purpose to propagate the accepted moral code. "The idealists," says Zola, "pretend that it is necessary to lie in order to be moral, the naturalists assert that one cannot be moral outside the truth. . . ." Truthfulness, accuracy of observation, and the courage to confront the results of this observation thus become the only moral absolutes of the artist. And this is the impulse that inspires the literature of today—as indeed it does all the other arts.

Once one realizes that the view of naturalism as a mere attempt to create photographic reproductions of external reality is a very superficial one; that, indeed, the essence of the naturalists' endeavor was an existential, value-free, scientific, and experimental exploration of reality in its widest possible sense (including the subjective reality of the artist's temperament through which he perceives external reality), and that this approach logically led to the rejection of all ready-made formal conventions and implied the acceptance of organic form dictated by the nature of the subject matter—all else follows.

The earliest naturalists did not, to be sure, all have the ability or the desire to follow the theoretical implications of their views to their logical consequence. Zola's own *Thérèse Raquin* had more in common with a well-made play à la Dumas fils than with later naturalist drama (while its basic highly effective melodramatic image, the paralyzed observer unable to communicate his knowledge of a crime to his visitors, comes directly from that archromantic novel by Dumas père, *The Count of Monte Cristo*). Ibsen's great social dramas used the stage technique of Sardou, while Shaw openly proclaimed his determination to use the convention of popular drama to put over modern ideas in a play like *You Never Can Tell.* But who, on the other hand, would doubt that Ibsen's later symbolic myths were the direct and logical development of his determination to explore his inner as well as his external reality; that Strindberg's dream plays did not continue the impulse behind his naturalistic explorations?

As early as 1887 Georg Brandes pointed out that Zola constantly invested the nature he was describing and exploring with symbolical, mythical significance; that in fact his naturalism took far more from Zola's own poetic temperament, his way of looking at the world, than from the mere transcription of external phenomena. Art, unlike experimental science, deals with a reality that includes the *emotional* reaction of the observer; even the most prosaic object, seen in a human context, becomes a symbol: Hedda Gabler's pistols, Solness' church tower, Hedwig Ekdahl's wild duck transform themselves into images of inner, psychological realities, become the embodiments of dreams and dark desires.

It is often said that naturalism soon lost its impact because its main practitioners turned to symbolism and neo-romanticism. This is true only in so far as the dramatists concerned—Ibsen, Strindberg, Hauptmann—followed

their initial impulse to its logical conclusion. In Hauptmann's *Hannele* the sick child's dream vision leads us straight from the ultra-naturalist environment of a workhouse into the poetic world of neo-romantic visions of the Savior surrounded by angels. Likewise Strindberg in plays like *Ghost Sonata* or *To Damascus* merely translated the psychological situation of the chief character of a play like *The Father* into a direct concrete image of his nightmares and obsessions. Oscar Wilde's *Salomé* (1892) and Hugo von Hofmannsthal's *Elektra* (1903) are both clearly derived from naturalism in their ruthless determination to delve into the depths of human nature, yet at the same time they also bear the mark of aestheticism and neoromanticism. Max Reinhardt, the greatest of the neoromantic directors, took over from Otto Brahm, the founder of the *Freie Bühne,* and also excelled as the interpreter of the naturalists. He can, indeed, be regarded as the founder of the truly naturalist style of acting by his creation of the *Kammerspiele,* a chamber theatre specially designed for intimate dialogue and subtle psychological effects (1907). Quite analogously, Stanislavsky, the other great originator of naturalistic acting and production, developed his style toward neo-romanticism and invited Gordon Craig to direct a highly stylized neo-romantic *Hamlet* (1912). "The theory of environment ends where the subconscious starts," Stanislavsky declared—in other words, the naturalism of external reality merges into the dreamlike reality of man's inner life.

This, of course, is not to say that symbolism, neoromanticism, and expressionism are *identical* with naturalism in its accepted sense, but merely to draw attention to the fact that once the basic position of the naturalists had been reached a *new phase* of art history had begun, a phase in which the same basic impulse carried all before it so that—as indeed Otto Braham had predicted—new vistas quite naturally opened up at bends in the road and the wayfarers traveling on it naturally entered a succession of new landscapes: Ibsen, who had consciously chosen the path of realism with *Pillars of Society* ("I believe I may say with certainty that we shall both be satisfied with this play of mine. It is modern in all respects and completely in tune with the times . . ." Letter to F. Hegel, July 29, 1877—six years after Zola's *Thérèse Raquin*), almost imperceptibly turned into a symbolist; Hauptmann into a neo-romantic; while Strindberg gradually evolved from a ruthless naturalist (*Miss Julie* was subtitled "A Naturalistic Tragedy") into the first expressionist; and at the end of *The Cherry Orchard* even Chekhov, the most rigorous naturalist, could not resist introducing that famous, mysterious symbolic sound, like the breaking of a string.

This line of evolution was dictated not only by the logic behind the basic philosophical concept that had inspired the naturalist movement but also by the parallel logic of the development of the *organic form* which, of necessity, had to follow the subject matter. Zola, Becque, Ibsen followed the formal pattern of the well-made social melodrama of the Parisian boulevard. Yet with the gradual implementation of the underlying theory with its rejection of intrigue and artificial shape, dramatists tried to implement Jean Jullien's slogan that drama should become a *tranche de vie*—a slice of life.

It was Hauptmann who perfected this new technique in plays like *Die Weber* (*The Weavers*) or *Florian Geyer.* Each act of these massive dramas became a series of loosely connected snapshots, with characters emerging from the crowd and then sinking back into it, half-finished episodes out of which the total picture gradually coalesced, like a mosaic, which is composed of thousands of tiny colored stones. These plays could dispense with the old division of the cast into heroes and supporting actors. *The Weavers* has no hero; its principal character is the mass of the Silesian weavers, just as the subject of the play is not the fate of one man but that of a whole social class. This is the multifocal technique of playwriting that was used with such immense effect by Gorky in *The Lower Depths* (triumphantly produced by both Stanislavsky and Reinhardt) and by Chekhov. (Elmer Rice's *Street Scene,* Saroyan's *The Time of Your Life* and O'Neill's *The Iceman Cometh* belong in the same category. O'Neill is, of course, also a notable example of the closeness of the naturalistic and the expressionist impulse; his development closely parallels Strindberg's.)

The multifocal snapshot technique makes the playwright concentrate on a single, static segment of *time.* Hauptmann tended to build his plays in this style from a sequence of such static pictures. But he was at the same time aware that there might be subjects requiring a completely different approach. In a note dated August 9, 1912, he remarked: "The modern dramatist, being a biologist, may sometimes strive for a drama which like a house, a work of architecture, stands still in one spot without moving from its position. Or he may have cause to comprehend life in a horizontal direction, having already grasped it in the vertical. He might prefer the *epic flow* of life to its *dramatic stasis.* The true biologist will not want to do without either of these two possibilities of form. . . ." Here Hauptmann clearly anticipates Brecht's idea of an epic theatre in which the loving depiction of multifarious minute detail gives way to the swift flow of action in a horizontal direction through time. That Brecht's concept of the theatre as a sociological laboratory also stems from the original impulse of the naturalist's experimental concept hardly needs to be stressed. His demand for a theatre that would be able to deal with reality in an age of science very closely resembles Zola's original manifesto. Equally his view that drama should be used to stimulate thinking in the audience has much in common with Hauptmann's view—which he expressed in 1912—that "drama as literature is not so much the ready-made result of thought as the *thinking process* itself. It is the living presentation of the socially manifested content of consciousness. From this it follows that none of the truths it presents can lay claim to final, absolute, self-contained validity. Each is valid only in so far as it is conditioned by the inner drama," i.e., the particular conception of a particular poet's consciousness of a particular event.

Hauptmann saw the dramatist as a biologist, Zola took his basic concepts from the physiologist Claude Bernard. It is surely no coincidence that Georg Büchner (1813-37), the greatest forerunner of naturalistic drama, who inspired both Hauptmann and Brecht, was a physiologist, that Brecht was once a medical student, and that both

Chekhov and Schnitzler were practicing physicians. Arthur Schnitzler (1862-1931), another great dramatist who is far too little known in the English-speaking world, wrote in both a strictly naturalistic and a neo-romantic style and also used drama as a means of exploration—of depth psychology. His series of dialogues, *Reigen* (1900), was the first attempt to put the sexual act on the stage and to illustrate, with bitter irony and sparkling wit, the extent to which the purely physiological side of sex is overshadowed by social ambition, snobbery, and the struggle for domination. Sigmund Freud regarded Schnitzler as a kind of double of himself, a co-discoverer of the world of the subconscious. On the occasion of Schnitzler's sixtieth birthday he wrote to him:

> . . . again and again, in looking into your creations, I have thought to find, behind the make-believe of poetry, the same endeavors, interests, and results that I knew to have been my own. Your determination as well as your skepticism—what people call pessimism—your being captivated by the truths of the unconscious, of the instinctive nature of man, your disruption of the securities of cultural convention, your preoccupation with the polarity of love and death, all this has always struck me with an uncanny familiarity. . . . Thus I gained the impression that by intuition—but in fact by subtle self-observation—you know all that I have uncovered in painstaking work on other people. Yes, I believe that fundamentally you are a psychological depth explorer, as honestly unprejudiced as any . . . (letter to Schnitzler, May 14, 1922).

Among the explorations Schnitzler undertook was one of the earliest examples of a work of literature that consisted entirely of the thoughts and feelings of an individual—*monologue intérieur* (internal monologue). This was naturalism driven to its utmost consequence—nature as perceived through a single temperament, an attempt to encompass the totality of the existential process of a human being. Schnitzler's novella *Leutnant Gustl* (1901)—the thoughts of a young officer compelled to commit suicide by a ridiculous "affair of honor"—marks, among other things, a point of contact between the novel and the drama. (In his essay *Le Naturalisme au théâtre,* Zola had deplored the fact that "an increasingly deep gulf " had opened up between the novel and the drama.) The very fact of being couched in the form of a monologue—a soliloquy—turned the short story into a dramatic representation of reality: the reader was made to *witness* a sequence of events *as it happened* rather than being told about it as an event that had taken place in the past. Here again the naturalists' rejection of rigid categories and pre-ordained forms had led to a creative merging of ancient categories. The internal monologue was to become one of the main forms of the vast literature of introspection that arose in the twentieth century.

Leutnant Gustl was one of the earliest examples of internal monologue. The very first came from France: Edouard Dujardin's short novel, *Les Lauriers sont coupés* (1887), which James Joyce regarded as the model for his own use of internal monologue in *Ulysses* and *Finnegans Wake.* Here then is the direct link between the naturalists and the avant-garde literature of introspection, dream, and fantasy, which culminated in surrealism and the Theatre of the Absurd. Again, as in the case of the link between the naturalists and neo-romantics, the connection is narrow, organic, and initially so gradual as to amount to an imperceptible merging. Joyce started as an admirer of Ibsen; he learned Norwegian to read Ibsen in the original, and his first works of fiction were meticulously observed slices of life. The step from the careful description of external reality to the plan to encompass not only the outside but the inside of the hero's life was logical and inevitable. In the French novel, and in the wake of Dujardin, certainly by the same inner logic, Proust's monumental attempt to capture the process of time through his hero's consciousness also led to an *internalization* of the concept of reality: the same scenes, the same people, appear differently to an eager young and a disillusioned middle-aged Marcel. And this, again, is a process entirely analogous to the subjective vision behind Strindberg's *Ghost Sonata, A Dream Play,* and *To Damascus.*

Antonin Artaud directed Strindberg's *Dream Play* in 1928. Arthur Adamov derived his inspiration for his first absurdist plays from Strindberg as well as from Artaud himself; and Samuel Beckett's dramatic *oeuvre* forms part of a wider exploration of the inner world of the internal monologue closely related to the ideas and example of James Joyce. Thus we can observe the initial impulse behind the naturalist revolution spreading, and still active, in the manifold manifestations of contemporary theatre.

However revolutionary the ideas of the early naturalists may have been, they themselves saw themselves as part of a tradition. Zola proclaimed that "Naturalism is Diderot, Rousseau, Balzac, and twenty others." He even regarded Homer as a naturalist—in his own fashion—and consciously emulated passages from Homer. Taine, who admired English literature so much, derived many of the ideas that later inspired Zola from the English realistic social novel of the eighteenth and early nineteenth centuries. In Germany the dramatists of the *Sturm und Drang* period (Lenz, Zacharias Werner, Klinger) as well as the early Goethe and Schiller must clearly be regarded as forerunners of naturalism; and so must Kleist and Büchner, Grabbe and Hebbel. In Russia Gogol, Tolstoy, Dostoyevsky, and Ostrovsky exercised a powerful and decisive influence on Chekhov and Stanislavsky, Gorky and Leonid Andreyev. In the English-speaking theatre T. W. Robertson's *Caste* (1867) must be regarded as a trail-blazing forerunner of the realism of Shaw and Granville Barker.

The coming of the naturalist revolution was inevitable. It was an expression of the *Zeitgeist*—the rapid industrialization of Europe and North America, the growth of science, the impact of Darwinism, positivism, and the consequent collapse of old certainties and established faiths. What the early pioneers and theoreticians of naturalism achieved was no more than the systematization and clear, programmatic expression of the spirit of their age. Nevertheless, the effect was overwhelming—a feeling of excitement, of liberation. And it was this excitement that released the most valuable element in the naturalist revolu-

tion: by opening up a vast new field of subject matter, by removing age-old inhibitions and taboos, by destroying time-honored rules and recipes for writing dialogue and structuring plot, naturalism opened the floodgates for a vast stream of new poetic possibilities in the theatre.

Whatever their ideas, their social purpose, their political commitment may have been, the great naturalists Ibsen, Strindberg, Shaw, Hauptmann, Chekhov, Gorky, Schnitzler must ultimately be judged as great poets, poets of a new kind; they discovered the magic that lies behind the seemingly commonplace surface of ordinary life, the tragic greatness of simple people, the poetry of silences and reticences, the bitter ironies of unspoken thoughts: Mrs. Alving hearing the ghosts of the past in the next room, the old drunken doctor, Chebutikhin, washing his hands the night of the fire in *The Three Sisters,* the "Baron's" barely articulate account of his life in *The Lower Depths*—these are examples of a poetry *of* the stage with an intensity and poignancy that could not have been achieved with the rules and methods of an earlier theatre, a poetry arising out of, and entirely in tune with, an industrialized, urbanized society and the image of man that, for better or for worse, it had created. To have bridged the gulf between literature and the theatre, which had opened up so disastrously in the middle of the nineteenth century, to have restored the dignity of the stage not only as an art but also as an instrument of serious thought and inquiry, and to have created a new kind of poetry—these are the true achievements of the early naturalists. The contemporary theatre to a very large extent draws its impetus and energy from their ideas, their courage, their liberating influence.

Martin Esslin, "Naturalism in Perspective," in his Reflections: Essays on Modern Theatre, *Doubleday & Co., Inc., 1969, pp. 12-28.*

ORIGINS AND DEFINITIONS

Emile Zola

[*Zola was a nineteenth-century French novelist, short story writer, essayist, dramatist, and journalist. Perhaps the foremost theorist and proponent of literary naturalism, he argued that great literature must assume many of the features of the scientific and sociological document. Although Zola's ideas no longer have currency, his twenty-novel series* Les Rougon-Macquart *(1871-93) is considered the masterpiece of the French naturalist movement. In the following excerpt, he condemns highly conventionalized romantic plays and calls for a drama, that would be truer to real life.*]

No one contests the point that all the different forms of literary expression hold together and advance at the same time. When they have been stirred up, when the ball is once set rolling, there is a general push toward the same goal. The romantic insurrection is a striking example of this unity of movement under a definite influence. . . .

[The] current of the age is toward naturalism. To-day this force is making itself felt more and more; it is rushing on us, and everything must obey it. The novel and the stage are carried away by it. Only it has happened that the evolution has been much more rapid in the novel; it triumphs there while it is just beginning to put in an appearance on the stage. This was bound to be. The theater has always been the stronghold of convention for a multiplicity of reasons, which I will explain later. I simply wish, then, to come down to this: The naturalistic formula, however complete and defined in the novel, is very far from being so on the stage, and I conclude from that that it will be completed, that it will assume sooner or later there its scientific rigor, or else the stage will become flat, and more and more inferior.

Some people are very much irritated with me; they cry out: "But what do you ask? what evolution do you want? Is the evolution not an accomplished fact? Have not M. Émile Augier, M. Dumas, *fils,* and M. Victorien Sardou pushed the study and the painting of our society to the farthest possible lengths? Let us stop where we are. We have already too much of the realities of this world." In the first place, it is very naïve in these people to wish to stop; nothing is stable in a society, everything is borne along by a continuous movement. Things go in spite of everything where they ought to go. I contend that the evolution, far from being an accomplished fact on the stage, is hardly commenced. Up to the present time we have taken only the first steps. We must wait until certain ideas have wedged their way in, and until the public becomes accustomed to them, and until the force of things abolishes the obstacles one by one. . . . [I look upon] MM. Victorien Sardou, Dumas, *fils,* and Émile Augier . . . as simply laborers who are clearing the paths of *débris,* and not as creators, not as geniuses who are building a monument. Then after them I am waiting for something else.

This something else which arouses so much indignation and draws forth so many pleasantries is, however, very simple. We have only to read Balzac, M. Gustave Flaubert, and MM. de Goncourt again—in a word, the naturalistic novelists—to discover what it is. I am waiting for them, in the first place, to put a man of flesh and bones on the stage, taken from reality, scientifically analyzed, without one lie. I am waiting for them to rid us of fictitious characters, of conventional symbols of virtue and vice, which possess no value as human data. I am waiting for the surroundings to determine the characters, and for characters to act according to the logic of facts, combined with the logic of their own temperament. I am waiting until there is no more jugglery of any kind, no more strokes of a magical wand, changing in one minute persons and things. I am waiting for the time to come when they will tell us no more incredible stories, when they will no longer spoil the effects of just observations by romantic incidents, the result being to destroy even the good parts of a play. I am waiting for them to abandon the cut and dried rules, the worked-out formulas, the tears and cheap laughs. I am waiting until a dramatic work free from declamations, big words, and grand sentiments has the high morality of truth, teaches the terrible lesson that belongs to all sincere inquiry. I am waiting, finally, until the evolu-

tion accomplished in the novel takes place on the stage; until they return to the source of science and modern arts, to the study of nature, to the anatomy of man, to the painting of life, in an exact reproduction, more original and powerful than anyone has so far dared to place upon the boards.

This is what I am waiting for. They shrug their shoulders and reply to me that I shall wait forever. Their decisive argument is that you must not expect these things on the stage. The stage is not the novel. It has given us what it could give us. That ends it; we must be satisfied.

Now we are at the pith of the quarrel. I am trying to uproot the very conditions of existence on the stage. What I ask is impossible, which amounts to saying that fictions are necessary on the stage; a play must have some romantic corners, it must turn in equilibrium round certain situations, which must unravel themselves at the proper time. They take up the business side; first, any analysis is wearisome; the public demands facts, always facts; then there is the perspective of the stage; an act must be played in three hours, no matter what its length is; then the characters are endowed with a particular value, which necessitates setting up fictions. I will not put forth all the arguments. I arrive at the intervention of the public, which is really considerable; the public wishes this, the public will not have that; it will not tolerate too much truth; it exacts four attractive puppets to one real character taken from life. In a word, the stage is the domain of conventionality; everything is conventional, from the decorations to the footlights which illuminate the actors, even down to the characters, who are led by a string. Truth can only enter by little doses adroitly distributed. They even go so far as to swear that the theater will cease to exist the day that it ceases to be an amusing lie, destined to console the spectators in the evening for the sad realities of the day.

I know all these reasonings, and I shall try to respond to them presently, when I reach my conclusion. It is evident that each kind of literature has its own conditions of existence. A novel, which one reads alone in his room, with his feet on his andirons, is not a play which is acted before two thousand spectators. The novelist has time and space before him; all sorts of liberties are permitted him; he can use one hundred pages, if it pleases him, to analyze at his leisure a certain character; he can describe his surroundings as much as he pleases; he can cut his story short, can retrace his steps, changing places twenty times—in one word, he is absolute master of his matter. The dramatic author, on the contrary, is inclosed in a rigid frame; he must heed all sorts of necessities. He moves only in the midst of obstacles. Then, above all, there is the question of the isolated reader and the spectators taken *en masse;* the solitary reader tolerates everything, goes where he is led, even when he is disgusted; while the spectators, taken *en masse,* are seized with prudishness, with frights, with sensibilities of which the author must take notice under pain of a certain fall. All this is true, and it is precisely for this reason that the stage is the last citadel of conventionality. . . . If the naturalistic movement had not encountered on the boards a difficult ground, filled with obstacles, it would already have taken root there with the intensity and with the success which have attended the novel. The stage, under its conditions of existence, must be the last, the most laborious, and the most bitterly disputed conquest of the spirit of truth.

I will remark here that the evolution of each century is of necessity incarnated in a particular form of literature. Thus the seventeenth century evidently incarnated itself in the dramatic formula. Our theater threw forth then an incomparable glitter, to the detriment of lyrical poetry and the novel. The reason was that the stage then exactly responded to the spirit of the period. It abstracted man from nature, studied him with the philosophical tool of the time; it has the swing of a pompous rhetoric, the polite manners of a society which had reached perfect maturity. It is the fruit of the ground; its formula is written from that point where the then civilization flowed with the greatest ease and perfection. Compare our epoch to that, and you will understand the decisive reasons which made Balzac a great novelist instead of a great dramatist. The spirit of the nineteenth century, with its return to nature, with its need of exact inquiry, quitted the stage, where too much conventionality hampered it, in order to stamp itself indelibly on the novel, whose field is limitless. And thus it is that scientifically the novel has become the form, *par excellence,* of our age, the first path in which naturalism was to triumph. To-day it is the novelists who are the literary princes of the period; they possess the language, they hold the method, they walk in the front rank, side by side with science. If the seventeenth century was the century of the stage, the nineteenth will belong to the novel.

Let us admit for one moment that criticism has some show of reason when it asserts that naturalism is impossible on the stage. Here is what they assert. Conventionality is inevitable on the stage; there must always be lying there. We are condemned to a continuance of M. Sardou's juggling; to the theories and witticisms of M. Dumas, *fils;* to the sentimental characters of M. Émile Augier. We shall produce nothing finer than the genius of these authors; we must accept them as the glory of our time on the stage. They are what they are because the theater wishes them to be such. If they have not advanced further to the front, if they have not obeyed more implicitly the grand current of truth which is carrying us onward, it is the theater which forbids them. That is a wall which shuts the way, even to the strongest. Very well! But then it is the theater which you condemn; it is to the stage that you have given the mortal blow. You crush it under the novel, you assign it an inferior place, you make it despicable and useless in the eyes of future generations. What do you wish us to do with the stage, we other seekers after truth, anatomists, analysts, searchers of life, compilers of human data, if you prove to us that there we cannot make use of our tools and our methods? Really! The theater lives only on conventionalities; it must lie; it refuses our experimental literature! Oh, well, then, the century will put the stage to one side, it will abandon it to the hands of the public amusers, while it will perform elsewhere its great and glorious work. You yourselves pronounce the verdict and kill the stage. It is very evident that the naturalistic evolution will extend itself more and more, as it possesses the intelligence of the age. While the novelists are digging always further

forward, producing newer and more exact data, the stage will flounder deeper every day in the midst of its romantic fictions, its worn-out plots, and its skillfulness of handicraft. The situation will be the more sad because the public will certainly acquire a taste for reality in reading novels. The movement is making itself forcibly felt even now. There will come a time when the public will shrug its shoulders and demand an innovation. Either the theater will be naturalistic or it will not be at all; such is the formal conclusion.

And even now, to-day, is not this becoming the situation? All of the new literary generation turn their backs on the theater. Question the young men of twenty-five years—I speak of those who possess a real literary temperament; they will show great contempt for the theater; they will speak of its successful authors with such faint approval that you will become indignant. They look upon the stage as being of an inferior rank. That comes solely from the fact that it does not offer them the soil of which they have need; they find neither enough liberty nor enough truth there. They all veer toward the novel. Should the stage be conquered by a stroke of genius to-morrow you would see what an outpouring would take place. When I wrote elsewhere that the boards were empty I merely meant they had not yet produced a Balzac. You could not, in good faith, compare M. Sardou, Dumas, or Augier to Balzac; all the dramatic authors, put one on top of the other, do not equal him in stature. The boards will remain empty, from this point of view, so long as a master hand has not, by embodying the formula in a work of undying genius, drawn after him to-morrow's generations. . . .

I have perfect faith in the future of our stage. I will not admit that the critics are right in saying that naturalism is impossible on the stage, and I am going to explain under what conditions the movement will without question be brought about.

It is not true that the stage must remain stationary; it is not true that its actual conventionalities are the fundamental conditions of its existence.

Everything marches, I repeat; everything marches forward. The authors of to-day will be overridden; they cannot have the presumption to settle dramatic literature forever. What they have lisped forth others will cry from the house top; but the stage will not be shaken to its foundations on that account; it will enter, on the contrary, on a wider, straighter path. People have always denied the march forward; they have denied to the newcomers the power and the right to accomplish what has not been performed by their elders. The social and literary evolutions have an irresistible force; they traverse with a slight bound the enormous obstacles which were reputed impassable. The theater may well be what it is to-day; to-morrow it will be what it should be. And when the event takes place all the world will think it perfectly natural.

At this point I enter into mere probabilities, and I no longer pretend to the same scientific rigor. So long as I have reasoned on facts I have demonstrated the truth of my position. At present I am content to foretell. The evolution will take place, that is certain. But will it pass to the left?

will it pass to the right? I do not know. One can reason, and that is all.

In the first place, it is certain that the conditions existing on the stage will always be different. The novel, thanks to its freedom, will remain perhaps the tool, *par excellence,* of the century, while the stage will but follow it and complete the action. The wonderful power of the stage must not be forgotten, and its immediate effect on the spectators. There is no better instrument for propagating anything. If the novel, then, is read by the fireside, in several instances, with a patience tolerating the longest details, the naturalistic drama should proclaim before all else that it has no connection with this isolated reader, but with a crowd who cry out for clearness and conciseness. I do not see that the naturalistic formula is antagonistic to this conciseness and this clearness. It is simply a question of changing the composition and the body of the work. The novel analyzes at great length and with a minuteness of detail which overlooks nothing; the stage can analyze as briefly as it wishes by actions and words. A word, a cry, in Balzac's works is often sufficient to present the entire character. This cry belongs essentially to the stage. As to the acts, they are consistent with analysis in action, which is the most striking form of action one can make. When we have gotten rid of the child's play of a plot, the infantile game of tying up complicated threads in order to have the pleasure of untying them again; when a play shall be nothing more than a real and logical story—we shall then enter into perfect analysis; we shall analyze necessarily the double influence of characters over facts, of facts over characters. This is what has led me to say so often that the naturalistic formula carries us back to the source of our national stage, the classical formula. We find this continuous analysis of character, which I consider so necessary, in Corneille's tragedies and Molière's comedies; plot takes a secondary place, the work is a long dissertation in dialogue on man. Only instead of an abstract man I would make a natural man, put him in his proper surroundings, and analyze all the physical and social causes which make him what he is. In a word, the classical formula is to me a good one, on condition that the scientific method is employed in the study of actual society, in the same way that the chemist studies minerals and their properties.

As to the long descriptions of the novelist, they cannot be put upon the stage; that is evident. The naturalistic novelists describe a great deal, not for the pleasure of describing, as some reproach them with doing, but because it is part of their formula to be circumstantial, and to complete the character by means of his surroundings. Man is no longer an intellectual abstraction for them, as he was looked upon in the seventeenth century; he is a thinking beast, who forms part of nature, and who is subject to the multiplicity of influences of the soil on which he grows and where he lives. This is why a climate, a country, a horizon, a room, are often of decisive importance. The novelist no longer separates his character from the air which he breathes; he does not describe him in order to exercise his rhetorical powers, as the didactic poets did, as Delille does, for example; he simply notes the material conditions in which he finds his characters at each hour, and in which the facts are produced, in order to be absolutely thorough

in order that his inquiry may belong to the world's great whole and reproduce the reality in its entirety. But it is not necessary to carry descriptions to the stage; they are found there naturally. Are not the stage settings a continual description, which can be made much more exact and startling than the descriptions in a novel? It is only painted pasteboard, some say; that may be so, but in a novel it is less than painted pasteboard—it is but blackened paper, notwithstanding which the illusion is produced. After the scenery, so surprisingly true, that we have recently seen in our theaters, no one can deny the possibility of producing on the stage the reality of surroundings. It now remains for dramatic authors to utilize this reality, they furnishing the characters and the facts, the scene painters, under their directions, furnishing the descriptions, as exact as shall be necessary. It but remains for a dramatic author to make use of his surroundings as the novelists do, since the latter know how to introduce them and make them real.

> After the scenery, so surprisingly true, that we have recently seen in our theaters, no one can deny the possibility of producing on the stage the reality of surroundings. It now remains for dramatic authors to utilize this reality, they furnishing the characters and the facts, the scene painters, under their directions, furnishing the descriptions, as exact as shall be necessary.
>
> —*Émile Zola*

I will add that the theater, being a material reproduction of life, external surroundings have always been a necessity there. In the seventeenth century, however, as nature was not taken into consideration, as man was looked upon only as a purely intellectual being, the scenery was vague—a peristyle of a temple, any kind of a room, or a public place. To-day the naturalistic movement has brought about a more and more perfect exactness in the stage settings. This was produced little by little, almost inevitably. I even find here a proof of the secret work that naturalism has accomplished in the stage since the commencement of the century. I have not time to study any more deeply this question of decorations and accessories; I must content myself by stating that description is not only possible on the stage, but it is, moreover, a necessity which is imposed as an essential condition of existence.

There is no necessity for me to expatiate on the change of place. For a long time the unity of place has not been observed. The dramatic authors do not hesitate to cover an entire existence, to take the spectators to both ends of the world. Here conventionality remains mistress, as it is also in the novel. It is the same as to the question of time. It is necessary to cheat. A play which calls for fifteen days, for example, must be acted in the three hours which we set apart for reading a novel or seeing it played at the theater. We are not the creative force which governs the world; our power of creation is of a second-hand sort; we only analyze, sum up in a nearly always groping fashion, happy and proclaimed as geniuses when we can disengage one ray of the truth.

I now come to the language. They pretend to say that there is a special style for the stage. They want it to be a style altogether different from the ordinary style of speaking, more sonorous, more nervous, written in a higher key, cut in facets, no doubt to make the chandelier jets sparkle. In our time, for example, M. Dumas, *fils,* has the reputation of being a great dramatic author. His "mots" are famous. They go off like sky rockets, falling again in showers to the applause of the spectators. Besides, all his characters speak the same language, the language of witty Paris, cutting in its pardoxes, having a good hit always in view, and sharp and hard. I do not deny the sparkle of this language—not a very solid sparkle, it is true—but I deny its truth. Nothing is so fatiguing as these continual sneering sentences. I would rather see more elasticity, greater naturalness. They are at one and the same time too well and not well enough written. The true style-setters of the epoch are the novelists; to find the infallible, living, original style you must turn to M. Gustave Flaubert and to MM. de Goncourt. When you compare M. Dumas' style to that of these great prose writers you find it is no longer correct—it has no color, no movement. What I want to hear on the stage is the language as it is spoken every day; if we cannot produce on the stage a conversation with its repetitions, its length, and its useless words, at least the movement and the tone of the conversation could be kept; the particular turn of mind of each talker, the reality, in a word, reproduced to the necessary extent. MM. Goncourt have made a curious attempt at this in *Henriette Maréchal,* that play which no one would listen to, and which no one knows anything about. The Grecian actors spoke through a brass tube; under Louis XIV. the comedians sang their rôles in a chanting tone to give them more pomp; to-day we are content to say that there is a particular language belonging to the stage, more sonorous and explosive. You can see by this that we are progressing. One day they will perceive that the best style on the stage is that which best sets forth the spoken conversation, which puts the proper word in the right place, giving it its just value. The naturalistic novelists have already written excellent models of dialogue, reduced to strictly useful words.

There now remains but the question of sentimental characters. I do not disguise the fact that it is of prime importance. The public remain cold and irresponsive when their passion for an ideal character, for some combination of loyalty and honor, is not satisfied. A play which presents to them but living characters taken from real life looks black and austere to them, when it does not exasperate them. It is on this point that the battle of naturalism rages most fiercely. We must learn to be patient. At the present moment a secret change is taking place in the public feeling; people are coming little by little, urged onward by the spirit of the century, to admit the bold reproduction of real life, and are even beginning to acquire a taste for it. When

they can no longer stand certain falsehoods we shall very nearly have gained our point. Already the novelists' work is preparing the soil in accustoming them to the idea. An hour will strike when it will be sufficient for a master to reveal himself on the stage to find a public ready to become enthusiastic in favor of the truth. It will be a question of tact and strength. They will see then that the highest and most useful lessons will be taught by depicting what is, and not by oft-dinned generalities, nor by airs of bravado, which are chanted merely to tickle our ears.

The two formulas are before us: the naturalistic formula, which makes the stage a study and a picture of real life; and the conventional formula, which makes it purely an amusement for the mind, an intellectual speculation, an art of adjustment and symmetry regulated after a certain code. In fact, it all depends upon the idea one has of literature, and of dramatic literature in particular. If we admit that literature is but an inquiry about men and things entered into by original minds, we are naturalists; if we pretend that literature is a framework superimposed upon the truth, that a writer must make use of observation merely in order to exhibit his power of invention and arrangement, we are idealists, and proclaim the necessity of conventionality. I have just been very much struck by an example. They have just revived, at the Comédie Française, *Le Fils Naturel* of M. Dumas, *fils.* A critic immediately jumps into enthusiasm. Here is what he says: "*Mon Dieu!* but that is well put together! How polished, dove-tailed, and compact! Is not this machinery pretty? And this one, it comes just in time to work itself into this other trick, which sets all the machinery in motion." Then he becomes exhausted, he cannot find words eulogistic enough in which to speak of the pleasure he experiences in this piece of mechanism. Would you not think he was speaking of a plaything, of a puzzle, with which he amused himself by upsetting and then putting all the pieces in order again? As for me, *Le Fils Naturel* does not affect me in the least. And why is that? Am I a greater fool than the critic? I do not think so. Only I have no taste for clockwork, and I have a great deal for truth. Yes, truly, it is a pretty piece of mechanism. But I would rather it had been a picture of life, I yearn for life with its shiver, its breath, and its strength; I long for life as it is.

We shall yet have life on the stage as we already have it in the novel. This pretended logic of actual plays, this equality and symmetry obtained by processes of reasoning, which come from ancient metaphysics, will fall before the natural logic of facts and beings such as reality presents to us. Instead of a stage of fabrication we shall have a stage of observation. How will the evolution be brought about? Tomorrow will tell us. I have tried to foresee, but I leave to genius the realization. I have already given my conclusion: Our stage will be naturalistic, or it will cease to exist.

Émile Zola, "Naturalism on the Stage," in his The Experimental Novel and Other Essays, *translated by Belle M. Sherman, 1894. Reprint by Haskell House, 1964, pp. 109-57.*

W. L. Courtney

[*An English educator and scholar, Courtney was the author of several books on nineteenth-century philosophy. In the following excerpt he maintains that although realist drama derives from novel writing, novelistic techniques are inappropriate to plays, since they lack adequate scope for the development of themes, characters and situations.*]

I

The species of modern play whose origin I desire to discuss has no particular name, but can easily be defined by some of its characteristics. It professes to be a transcript of life, and is therefore a social drama, dealing with more or less fundamental traits, and including incidents which are ugly, tragic, or pathetic, as the case may be. This form of dramatic construction is at present nameless, because it cannot be put under any of the recognised formulæ. We know the well-worn classification of plays—tragedies, comedies, historical plays. A tragedy is a play, dealing for the most part with characters of distinction, involving a conflict between the characters and their fates, and ending with disaster to the persons concerned. A comedy, on the contrary, deals with the oddities, the humorous aspects of life. It laughs at follies, and sometimes at vices. The characters are a little artificial, or, at all events, exaggerated; the conclusion is a happy one. The plays we call historical explain themselves. They are occupied with a period of history, based on annals, dealing with actual personages, although a certain amount of latitude is allowed in recounting their careers. But what are we to say of the modern social dramas? They are intended to be a transcript from real life, and so far they may be called historical, but the characters are purely imaginary, and as a rule the story is intended to indicate, if not a moral, at least some social problem or difficulty. You cannot call them Comedies, because, as a rule, they have not a happy ending. You cannot call them Tragedies, but they undoubtedly include some very tragic events. Moreover—and that is a very distinctive feature—their *dramatis personæ* are not taken from those highly-placed or conspicuous heroes and heroines with whom Ancient Drama was concerned, but with the ordinary individual, the man whom you meet, the woman whom you meet, in the thoroughfares of life. Can we without offence call them Bourgeois Dramas? That, at least, would not be unjust with regard to the majority of Ibsen's social plays, and the title would serve to distinguish the characters from those familiar to us in Ancient Drama. Or shall we style them *Comédies Larmoyantes,* in order to show that, although they may seem in texture to belong to the comic Muse, in spirit and in intention, that is to say, in the range of pathetic incident, they have about them the scowl of the tragic Muse? Bourgeois Dramas or *Comédies Larmoyantes,* the name does not matter, so long as the variety indicated is understood. The great point is that they suggest a new type, a type which was utterly unknown to the earlier dramatic critic.

It is not difficult to find examples, for most of the contemporary work of Mr. Pinero and Mr. Henry Arthur Jones, Mr. Esmond, Captain Marshall, and others, illustrates in different ways the prevailing social type, either in accor-

A scene from the original production of Arthur Wing Pinero's The Second Mrs. Tanqueray, *1893.*

dance with the Robertsonian method or the psychological. It would be hardly unjust to say that some of the pieces of Mr. Pinero have reflected the influence of Ibsen, especially perhaps *The Notorious Mrs. Ebbsmith. Iris* illustrates a sort of joint influence of Ibsen and the French school of Alexandre Dumas. *The Second Mrs. Tanqueray* is decidedly modern French in its tendency, with such differences as are due to Germanic and Scandinavian examples. What, however, is perfectly plain is that Mr. Pinero has in studies like these accepted one form of the dramatic idea, the conception namely of Drama as analytic, psychological, dealing with social problems of the day. But now look at the opposite idea. No plays have recently been more successful than those of Captain Marshall. They are neither analytical nor psychological, nor do they deal with problems. Once, it is true, he made a hesitating experiment in this direction in *The Broad Road;* but if we take his best-known specimens, *His Excellency the Governor, The Royal Family, The Noble Lord, The Second in Command,* what are these but studies in the Robertsonian method, dealing not with social problems, but with all the bubbles that burst on the surface of social fashion, the chances and changes which now make us interested in Parliament and now in the Boer War? Mr. Esmond, who represents the most zealous and intelligent of the youthful contingent of dramatists, oscillates apparently between these two ideals. Mr. Henry Arthur Jones is more difficult to deal with, because in one sense he is more original than any of the others. That is to say he works more exclusively on his own lines; while no man of equal eminence has been guilty of such curious failures. Beginning with melodramas, he has gradually worked his way to the composition of comedy, sometimes admirable comedy as in *The Liars* and *The Case of Rebellious Susan,* sometimes ignoble comedy, as in *The Lackey's Carnival* and *The Princess's Nose,* sometimes paradoxical tragedy, as in *The Tempter.* But *Mrs. Dane's Defence* was a noteworthy production, because in a fashion it summed up some of the oddest of our contemporary dramatic views. It was a comedy—but was it indeed a comedy? It touched the fringes of a most serious question, the question whether there was any place of repentance for a woman who by her own fault or the fault of others had deviated from the recognised path. It attempted some psychology, but without much effect, for Mrs. Dane was by no means a complex character. Above all, it touched its subject sentimentally. Mrs. Dane was the heroine; Mrs. Dane was the sinner. Sir Daniel Carteret represented the voice of outraged Society, was the embodiment of the social conscience, so to speak. Nevertheless with whom were our sympathies supposed to lie? Assuredly with Mrs. Dane. Could it be described therefore as a comedy of revolt? No, for the heroine is conveniently got rid of, and the enamoured young man is sent, to effect his mental and moral cure, abroad. And in this uncertainty of touch it exactly summed up the vacillating temper of the modern audience. There must be a little psychological analysis, but not too much; there must be a little girding at social conventions, but the social conventions must ultimately prevail; there need not be much logic, but there must be romance and sentiment. The moral problems must be solved, not in terms of the head but of the heart.

II

How did such a variety of drama begin? It will be said that Shakespeare's comedies are not comedies in the ordinary sense of the term, and that he suggested this novel treatment of dramatic themes. Nevertheless there was a fanciful technique, a playful handling, about the Shakespearean Comedy, a delightful Arcadian atmosphere, of the Forest of Arden, of the enchanted isle, or of that midsummer night in the proximity of Athens, which take our great English dramatist's work in this department into quite another category. For the Bourgeois Drama, the *Comédie Larmoyante,* is in deadly earnest. There are no breezes about it of fairyland. The air is thick and heavy with northern fog, the spirit has some of the gloom, the meditative pessimism, which distinguish the art work of Northern Europe from that of the Southern races. We must go, I think, a little later than the seventeenth century to understand how this new phenomenon arose.

In the first quarter of the eighteenth century, there was developed a new department of literary effort, big with consequences for succeeding ages. It was the discovery of the novel. Of course there was a novel in Shakespeare's time, as M. Jusserand, amongst others, has shown, a sort of diffuse, amorphous, romantic story, full of incidents, the Picaresque novel. But that is not what we mean by novel. We mean a serious study of existing social aspects; an analytic study of certain kinds of character; the suggestion of a moral, the illustration at all events of the tendency and the

effect of certain moral laws, which so far as we can tell govern the Universe. And that was the capital invention of Samual Richardson, the odd, sympathetic little printer, always happy in the society of women, the man full of sensibility, the man also endowed with acutely perceptive instincts, the author who dared to tell the fortunes of a servant girl, one of the most extraordinary influences dominating European literature in the eighteenth century. What is the history of Pamela? Never mind what analogies we can find in contemporary work in France and elsewhere. Here is the man who set a definite stamp upon a particular kind of work. He wrote a romantic account of the temptations of a servant girl. He painted all her prudishness, all her resolute virtue, her absurd sentimentalities, her love for the master whom she yet feared. Or what is *Clarissa Harlowe?* Once more it is the analysis of a woman's mind, or the analysis of the mind of a seducer, infinitely protracted, yet never failing in a certain gift of reality and truth. The characters are of the middle class, more or less. One would hardly care to except even Sir Charles Grandison from this category. And what Richardson began, Rousseau carried on—the same passionate analysis, the same love of confession, the sorrows and agonies of sentimental souls, all the marks in short which characterise his *Nouvelle Héloïse,* and his *Confessions.* About the same time when Richardson was working, a man called George Lillo, born of a Dutch father and an English mother, produced a play, *George Barnwell, or The Merchant of London.* It was the story of an apprentice who falls into the hands of a courtesan, and is therefore led on to robbery and murder, written in a stilted style, full of rhetorical *gaucherie,* an admirable specimen of combined sentiment and fustian. This play had a great success in the Metropolis and possibly a still greater success abroad. It was precisely a Bourgeois Drama, the very prototype of some of the work of Ibsen, although infinitely more clumsy than any of the great Scandinavian's work. Now, Lillo, Richardson, Cumberland, Jean Jacques Rousseau were all engaged in precisely the same task; they were practically the inventors of new points of view for Literature and Art, deserting the classical thoroughfares and striking out modern paths of their own. The Germanic spirit in them was revolting against the Latin spirit which had hitherto dominated Europe. The Goths were once more sacking Rome.

Since that period Modern Drama has been more profoundly influenced by the extraordinary development of the novel than by any other single power or impulse in the modern world. Shakespeare, oddly enough, although wholly innocent of any classical upbringing, was almost remarkably true to Aristotelian canons of dramatic work. He knew nothing about the so-called dramatic unities. You can never compare him with Corneille or Racine, the men who were trained in classical schools. But the only unity which Aristotle probably cared about, the unity of action, Shakespeare faithfully illustrated in all his plays. And as Aristotle desired, he made his heroes and heroines conspicuous personages, to a large degree typical rather than individual. So have not worked his successors. The Bourgeois Drama has nothing Aristotelian about it. It is born of an antagonism, either expressed or implicit, to the whole of the classical tradition. When Richardson, chaperoned by Rousseau, gained his enormous ascendancy in France, those who strove to check the invasion were supporting the Latin spirit against the Germanic, the classical regularity and clear-cut formal outlines against the new irregularity, the want of form, the uncouth structures of the Bourgeois Drama.

Our occupation must be to dissect and analyse character, to watch the nuances, to delineate the motives, confused, contradictory, and vacillating, which govern the actions of the average individual.

—*W.L. Courtney*

III

What precisely is the influence of the novel upon Modern Drama? In what respects is it manifested? In the first place, the modern novel, as introduced by Richardson, deals with ordinary life and ordinary personages. There is no reason to look at Courts or at the chronicles of the nobility for human and moving themes. You will find such themes all round you, in the ranks of the *bourgeoisie,* among the merchants, among the clerks, in the drawing-rooms of struggling, ambitious, impecunious folk, in the ordinary experience of each twenty-four hours in each common-place life. In the second place, the subject or theme is to be a faithful transcript of existence as we know it, with little or no idealisation, including all the ugliness as well as all the prettiness, portraying meanness as well as nobility of temperament, a photograph of casual men and women with all their lines and freckles and pimples. In the third place, our occupation must be to dissect and analyse character, to watch the nuances, to delineate the motives, confused, contradictory, and vacillating, which govern the actions of the average individual. When Richardson commenced this sort of analysis, he hit upon the expedient of making his characters write voluminous letters to one another. Letters served the purpose of a public confessional, and in those times of self-abandonment, when sentimental men or sentimental women confide their secrets either to diaries or sympathetic correspondents, we undoubtedly reach some of the intricacies of a human personality. The letter form has never quite gone out of our modern literature, but its range has been fortunately curtailed. In the fourth place, the novel was the exposition of some given theme, or problem, social or moral. In Richardson the aim was avowedly didactic. Read his lengthy title pages. He explains to his reader that his Pamelas and Clarissas are to exemplify this, that, or the other about the excellency of virtue, the perils to which chastity is exposed, the unutterable excellence of modesty and a simple religiousness. Since then this didactic aim has not been so unblushingly avowed, yet in the greater part of Germanic literature it is there, implied, if not wholly revealed. Many analogies can be framed between the work of George Eliot

and that of Georges Sand. But what is the contrast, what is the great gulf fixed, between the French and the English novelist? Precisely this. Georges Sand was an idealist, and wrote in pursuit of purely artistic aims, whereas George Eliot faithfully and laboriously painted pictures of actual life, of which the moral, unutterably gloomy or moderately cheerful, was always near the surface. Ordinary people, ordinary life, a faithful transcript of reality, psychological analysis, a moral implicit or acknowledged—these are the characteristics of the novel which the Germanic peoples have invented for their own satisfaction. And because novels form a tremendously powerful department of literature, they have carried along with them Modern Drama, which in its turn illustrates precisely the same characteristics.

IV

The things which the novelist can do are, however, not necessarily easy for the dramatist. In a novel or romance of some length there is every opportunity for the author to carry out that serious analysis, that detailed investigation of motives, which render his personages vital and interesting. The novelist can build up his characters, piece after piece, brick after brick. He can show us his hero in chapter after chapter, developing slowly on predetermined lines, influenced by the various circumstances to which he is exposed, overpowered by one set of conditions, reacting against and overpowering another set of conditions. Such a study as this requires length, breadth and thickness, it needs some of those *longueurs* of narrative which the ordinary reader sometimes finds embarrassing in the case of Scott, of Thackeray, and even of Dickens. Or let us assume that the object in hand is the portrayal of a given phase of contemporary life with all its thousand and one incidents, with all those minutiæ whose infinitesimal differences distinguish one epoch of the world's history from another. The literary painter of such a period has got to take a big canvas. He has to be content to occupy a good deal of time in working out his details. Or, once more, he is thoroughly possessed by some lesson or moral he desires to inculcate. So far as he is an artist he will not make this too obvious. He will put it below the surface of his story with a hint here and a hint there, with a slow series of evolving incidents leading up to the end, the moral, the piece of didacticism which is in his mind. That I take it is how the novelist works, and the essence of his industry is that he should have elbow room. But now compare on the other hand the dramatist. The one thing he does not possess is time and space. He must make his effects sharply and clearly. He cannot afford to be dilatory. He must shorten processes, indicate, suggest the various steps and present broad and striking results which carry conviction to the eyes and mind of the spectator. His method, one would say, is the exact antithesis of that of the novelist. What the one can do slowly and gradually, the other must do summarily and rapidly. The effects which the one can produce by careful insistence on a series of details, the other must present to the eye with a certain sharp abruptness, with a certain concentrated clearness, in order to get his spectators in the right mood.

But if the dramatist is going to accept the influence of the novelist, if he is going to work with identical methods, is it not clear that he is essaying the extraordinarily difficult task of translating into colour for the eye what his brother artist portrays as ideas for the mind? The modern Social Drama has to give a picture of an ordinary life lived under ordinary conditions; it demands a careful psychological inquiry, the dissection of motives, the analysis of a social problem, the suggestion or the inculcation of a moral. Nine men out of ten if asked how all this is to be done, would answer without hesitation that it would require a book of 400 pages. And your modern dramatist says No, I will give it you in a series of pictures lasting two and a-half hours. Is it not inevitable that characters will be imperfectly designed, that events will happen for which we have not been properly prepared, that we shall suddenly find ourselves face to face with a crisis we did not anticipate, that we shall see the obvious external conditions of a given state or episode or conclusion, but be left wondering how the characters ever got there? The dramatist in endeavouring to imitate the procedure and aims of the novelist is from this point of view like a man trying to reproduce on a canvas seven feet by four an opera by Wagner.

No better illustration could be found than the latest specimen of the serious Drama, Mr. Pinero's play of *Iris*. The first three acts are occupied with the slow and careful elucidation of the heroine's character, a thing which would be done by a novelist, because he has got plenty of space and elbow room, in a series of elaborate chapters. But as a play *Iris* has to be brought to a conclusion, and suddenly in the last two acts we get to the very crisis of her fate. Iris the self-indulgent, the weak lover of luxury, the soft, charming, backboneless heroine is suddenly exchanged for Iris the betrayer, Iris the woman who has leapt over all social barriers, Iris the mistress of a man she loathes. And what has happened between the first three and the last two acts? Just what would be the most interesting part of the story as written in novel form; but it is absolutely omitted in the play. The heroine is given a rhetorical speech in the last act to explain her decline and fall. That is all. And this mixture of the methods of the novelist and the dramatist makes the first three acts of the drama somewhat tedious, and the last two startling and paradoxical.

Another reason might be suggested why our modern drama so often strikes one as moving like a blind man in unknown paths. The essential conditions of Art as such were fixed once and for all by the Greeks; but there are two forms of modern Art which have not got classical models. One is Music in all its later developments, the other is the modern novel. Think for a moment of the extremely divergent and contradictory views which are held as to the value and importance, or indeed justification, of Wagnerian music. It seems a region in which there are no signposts, and every man is bent on cutting out his own way. But observe how precisely the same thing happens also with regard to novels. There were some fugitive attempts at something like romances in Alexandrian times, just as there were Picaresque novels in the time of Shakespeare. But practically it would be true to say that the novel is a modern invention, born from a Teutonic or Germanic soil. To this day, however, we have no real canons of criticism

applicable to it. Nothing is clearer than that the novel, as understood by the Latin races, when they adopted this style of literature, is different from the novel as it was drawn and designed by that curiously self-introspective, gloomy, meditative spirit of the Northern races. Should the novel preach a moral? Can we judge a novel from the ethical standpoint, or ought we to think only of its artistic success or failure? In what form are the principles of æsthetics to be applied, for instance, to a novel like *Sir Richard Calmady?* Can you get to any positive, absolutely accepted verdict? And now, in contrast with music and the novel, observe how curious is the condition of the Modern Drama. For drama, at all events, had a classical model, a very clear, definite scheme of artistic principles, established precisely, unequivocally, by the genius of the Greek dramatists, and expressed in the criticisms of Aristotle. This classical tradition lasted for a great many centuries; only, in fact, for the last two and a-half centuries has it been seriously contested. The Latin races, naturally enough, adhered longer than any others to those classical traditions and rules out of which their own civilisation was born. The Northern races knew nothing of such schoolmasters. They attacked things in their own way. What is in succinct fashion the classical ideal of a play? It is this—a rounded and perfectly defined piece of art, an episode carried out to its logical conclusion, in which the characters are typical rather than individual, and in which, for the most part, poetic justice shall prevail. If a man dies, we know why. If a woman sins, we know the consequences. And neither the man nor the woman, neither hero or heroine, is a chance specimen of the human race, but a typical example, so that the lesson may be all the clearer. But the modern dramatist has chosen a perfectly different ideal; he has accepted the method, the procedure, the outlook of the novelist. The classical dramatist was, as Lessing said, a petty Providence, carefully seeing that the large ethical and natural laws should obtain in his selected province, just as they obtain in the world as a whole. But if we may judge from the work of Ibsen, of Sudermann, of Hauptmann, there is too much artificial completeness and smug symmetry in the older dramatic principles. A page is to be torn out of life, and you cannot judge of a whole book by a page. You must have a faithful transcript, a bit of realism; while the principle of classical Art is selection, not photography. You must take ordinary characters—not typical, but purely individual and accidental. And in this little corner of the world's great history which you are trying so painfully, so faithfully, to elucidate, you are not likely to find many indications of that higher justice, that consolatory solution of the problem, which only the widest outlook over centuries could hope to compass.

What is the result? Let a man or a woman, occupied with his own or her own immediate, pressing troubles and griefs, enunciate views about the world as a whole. Do we not know the lyrical cry, the *cri du cœur,* the passionate revolt? Is any sorrow like to my sorrow? Can there be a Providence? Is there an eternal Justice? So, too, in Modern Drama, the handling of social problems, as a rule, leads to an *impasse*. It is all mystery and discouragement. We can see no pattern, we hold no guiding clue. The baffling issues of life lead to the pessimistic temper, and problem plays are the reverse of cheerful. I have no desire to emphasise too much this modern spirit of querulous complaint. I am much more interested in the singular fact that drama, having an ancient prototype, has now fallen under a modern influence, and is for ever oscillating between the older ideals and the newer. The dramatic Muse has lost her first husband, and is trying to understand how to live with her second. Hence her confusion, her uncertainty, her tentative handling, her hesitating conclusions. While the ancient dramatist ended on a clear and unmistakeable note, it might be of disaster or of triumph, the modern, putting before the spectator all his own imperfect reasonings, finishes with a note of interrogation, does not reach an end at all. So long as a man is content to paint what he sees with faithful servility, he will always leave us in this quandary. He must bring something out of his own genius. For facts are the most useless things in the world. It is the ideas alone which by connecting them make them intelligible, the guiding ideas in the absence of which each of us in turn is only a blind leader of the blind.

> W. L. Courtney, *"Modern Social Drama as Influenced by the Novel,"* in The Fortnightly Review, *Vol. LXXVII, No. CCCCXXI, January 1, 1902, pp. 666-74.*

Thomas H. Dickinson

[*Dickinson charges that realist playwrights tailor their dramas to conform to their own social and psychological theories at the expense of artistic integrity.*]

[*Modern Dramatists* by Ashley Dukes] is a suggestive and thought compelling book. Here suddenly we have, after many random essays, a little volume that precipitates values. "Madam, I'm not arguing with you; I am telling you," Ruskin is said to have thundered to a contentious woman. That modern drama has reached the point at which one dares to be dogmatic about it is a significant thing. We might even say that it is a prophetic thing, for in arguing a certain completeness and settled quality in things present it promises change and another order of things to come. One is dogmatic when he has history on his side. He is not dogmatic in the midst of contending issues. So Mr. Dukes' dogmatism on the drama is both significant and prophetic.

"European drama has just reached the end of an odd and experimental, but stirring, period of artistic history," writes Mr. Dukes at the beginning of the book. The rest of the volume bears out the presumption of settled values and formulated standards. Standing with the author we see certain evidences of unity in the activities of recent drama which before have eluded our most careful searching. We are even able, through medium of Mr. Dukes' "polemical and intolerant" judgments, to pluck a little nearer to the heart of the mystery of one of the most puzzling periods in the records of the stage.

When men sought for a term by which to denominate the new drama of a generation or two ago they called it the drama of ideas. And this term served its purpose very well in calling attention to the particular concern of this type of play with ideas as such and with men as thinking beings.

Modern drama is concerned with ideas first and foremost. It has been created out of a world of thought, peopled by speculative mannikins, circumscribed in a technique prescribed by logic, and directed to the understanding. It may safely be said that every great modern play can be stated first in terms of abstract ideas, and only secondarily in terms of personal living. In modern drama life has been reduced to formulas. Now every great drama from Aeschylus to Synge has at its heart a modicum of ideas. It has been characteristic of modern drama to isolate and specify its ideas rather than submerge them and imply them.

This does not mean that modern drama is not artistic. As a matter of fact, this kind of writing is peculiarly appropriate to the spirit of the age. If one were asked what is the prevailing temper of the last fifty years he might fairly answer that it has been a keen and speculative interest in all the phenomena of living. Most of the real activity of this period has been toward the distribution of clear and independent thinking among the many. This intellectual interest in living has become so strong that it has had to be recognized as one of the factors of social existence. He who ignores it is a bad teacher, statesman, or artist. Along with the enfranchising of many minds there has gone forward another process, the separating off of a class who live all their lives in the circle of the mind, who value living not as a thing to be experienced, but as a thing of meanings and connotations. The discovery that men had minds as well as wills and passions was a rich one for all art, and especially rich for drama. These new minds, alert, skeptical, questioning, sometimes "sicklied over with the pale cast of thought," have provided the character material out of which modern drama has been made. The hero of the recent drama has been the man who is interested in life as a problem, or who lives his life in thoughts rather than in deeds. It is a significant thing that drama should have been among the first of the arts to reflect this modern intellectual temper.

The influence of the canons of thought in drama of recent times has been thorough and complete. It has governed the choice of themes, and made the stage the debating ground of social problems. It has stipulated the kind of characters to be introduced upon the stage, and has placed there the raisonneurs, the intellectuals, the introspectives, and those vexed with all the problems of mentality. In matters of form it has laid upon drama the control of an extraneous logic, and in the tenets of realism and naturalism has worked out a code of regulations as rigorous and as alien to the pure purposes of art as the rules of the classic French stage.

Characteristic modern drama begins and ends with a formula. It is said that Zola in writing his latest novels always began with a formula implicit in a word, sometimes the title of the book, as Truth, Justice, The Earth, Fecundity. If that is the case he was true to his code of an intellectually controlled and inspired art. Certainly the formula is the last thing left in the mind of the reader after the story is forgotten. In the same way modern drama is expanded from a formula. In the case of most great modern playwrights, from Dumas down, we are not left much room for question whether they are not rather thinkers using the medium of drama than dramatic artists implying an interpretation of life. Taking the titles of Dumas' plays—for instance, *The Money Question, The Ideas of Madame Aubray*—we must draw the conclusion that here it was the idea that came first in importance. So there can be no doubt that in *Pillars of Society* and in *Ghosts* the idea is the salient thing, the story but subordinant. In the old play ideas are implicit in the action. In the modern play action and life are but implicit in the formula. Often that formula is stated as a proposition. Ibsen takes the idea "the majority is always wrong," and *An Enemy of the People* expounds the thesis. Echegaray evolves a conception of society and writes a prologue to *The Great Galeoto* to show that the play is an exposition of that conception. Pinero's *The Profligate* and *The Second Mrs. Tanqueray* are expositions of Paula's formula "the future is but the past entered through another gate." In a word, the significant progress of dramatic art of the last fifty years has been toward making the drama a better expository medium for the expression of ideas.

It is this thing that Mr. Duke's book so adequately lays before us, and in its own right represents. His work represents the final word of the authority of ideas in art. Writing at the apex of a movement of dramatic positivism, in which the logic of fate may be summed up in Mrs. Gaskell's phrase made fifty years before, "Every deed, however remote, has its eternal consequences," Mr. Duke's book is the application to a dogmatic art of a dogmatic criticism. In this book we see represented the standards of the art that is limited to man as a thinking machine. And we see the cogent thinker evaluating his art. We see how this fetich of thought in art has drawn into drama some men who would by no possibility have been dramatists in other days, how it has made great poets turn into poor logicians, and has lifted craftsmen to eminences as leaders of thought. Nothing so clearly indicates the general artistic inadequacy of the drama of thought as this clear statement of its present standards and attainments. In showing what it is, Mr. Dukes has more significantly shown what it is not, and has pointed the way on which the more rounded human art of drama must come.

Realism came not so much from the application of the laws of logic to literature as from their application to life. Realism was a point of view and method of attack. So it was no accident that brought literary realism in at the same time as mental unrest. Every age has its own peculiar search, and it is usually the function of art to give voice to that search. The search that is typical of our time, as Dukes has said, is that of "honest men and women seeking for realities." This is the peculiar flavor of modernity, a search pursued with no less sacred fervor, instinct with no less personal tragedy, because pursued without prejudice and in a spirit of scientific doubt. The questions our age has asked are inner questions. Introspection has ceased to be abnormal in that it has come to be the normal pursuit of truth back to that only center of which we are credibly aware, the center of each searcher's inner consciousness.

Plays which deal with such a theme find their form prescribed within absolute limits. Ibsen's plays, more than being typical of his time, got their being from his time.

They would have been impossible in form and content in any other time. To make a play out of the inner motives of men we must provide characters who are themselves sufficiently interested in their inner motives to bring them to light. Not the character that completes itself in action, or diverts his own self-gropings to other activities, will provide the material of the play of thought. Imagine Rosmer not a dreamer, or Solness not a lonely visionary, and the inner drama of the mind of the reformer and the artist could not be written. In this respect an introspective era has provided for art the expedients that would make its inner meanings vocal.

One aspect of the domination of logic over art has been striking. Art has become the "handmaiden" of social causes. An art which has been constructed according to the close "logic of events" soon finds itself impressed by that same logic into social service. And then follows that mingling of the issues of art and practical life that has caused a heavy toll to be paid by the artists of the last fifty years. "How much worse for a man would it be were he not a citizen," wrote Dante out of the fulness of his love for Florence. The poets of our day have been led by easy stages from the first alluring logic of reality to the final offering of their art itself on the altar of their citizenship. Kingsley and Ruskin and Morris and Ibsen and Yeats have been honest men searching for reality. Their art pointed out reality for them and straightway as genuine men they tried to build their lives by the art, with what loss to the pure values of beauty no one can say. This is the price that art has paid to its passion for the realities of science, and this is the price our times have paid in insisting upon the interchangeable values of art and life.

We are coming to the time when we may again ask whether the values of art and life are after all interchangeable, whether art and life should not go their two ways side by side but separate. For there is a spiritual body and there is a temporal body. The white certainty of truth and beauty of the poet is not the logic of the scientist or the program of the reformer. What art needs, says Wilde, is not to study life, but to study art; not to imitate life but to imitate art. We have gone a long way from this thinking in these latter days of art for man's sake. Was it not with something of this feeling that Ibsen came back from his fifteen years of social propagandism to the weary disillusionment of *The Master Builder* and his frank repudiation of the commonplace world in *When We Dead Awaken?*

This mixing of values of art and logic is nowhere seen more clearly than in the case of Hauptmann. Like Morris, Hauptmann is a dreamer of dreams born out of his due time. As he was first of all an honest man, he felt called upon to set the crooked straight. Hauptmann was that pathetic combination, a poet and server of his time,—something different from time-server, though under the inexorable laws of art no less inconsistent with absolute greatness. If he had been more of poet he would have escaped the dangers of logic. If he had been a little more a thinker he would have hardened the delicate impractical edge of his art to definite social uses. But he was a little too much of both poet and thinker, so he falls between the stools of logic and dreams. Hauptmann appeared while the naturalists were asking Pilate's question, and each man staying long over his answer. His first works were written under their influence. The rest of his life seems to have been a struggle between what he thinks he ought to write to satisfy the call of his citizenship and what he wants to write to satisfy his soul. Often in his product the forms are mixed and we have in *Hannele, Elga, Und Pippa Tanzt* strains of poetry mingled with naturalism. Hauptmann comes out in his own person only once, and that is when the service of his citizenship is refused by his own time. In *The Sunken Bell* we have the poet soul freed from the trammels of a didactic thought, no longer the handmaiden of social causes, expressing in full abandon with all the clothing of color, of fancy and music the artist's reaction to reality. In the case of Hauptmann the "logic of events" seems likely to carry the artist on beyond the danger zone into a form of art that can be free and yet serviceable. The novel, the form which he has now undertaken, offers to Hauptmann a medium flexible enough for the contending claims of his didacticism and his artistry.

One of the chief influences of the code of systematic thinking has been the perfecting of the instrument of dramatic expression. On the side of pure technic, judged by our universal standards of efficiency and economy, it is safe to say there is little more to be done. The dramatic instrument has been tried and perfected. Yet, strange to say, criticism has always been grudging in its praise to the master craftsmen. Others get credit for their thoughts and ideals, but he who is master of his medium is ignored. This would not be the case in other arts. It is at this point that Mr. Dukes' hard and fast principle of modernity seems weakest. It may be asked whether the masters of technic in perfecting the art of the play to fit the temper of the time have not responded as closely to the orders of the day as have those others who have discovered new messages. Certainly, following the code of a refined logic, they have brought their art to a marvelous subtlety, truth and dexterity.

The expert man of the theatre is always alert to discover some new alignments in life which can be transmuted into theatrical conventions. The men who adapted to the theatre the intellectual problems of the nineteenth century were not necessarily thinkers. Those who did it best made no pretense to be thinkers at all, but skilled theatrical purveyors who knew how to get theatrical value out of the spirit of the age. Yet there is artistic value in this, and the man who can do it is a discoverer and a creator. The institutions of the stage are as a rule as nearly as possible correspondent with the institutions of society, but they are not identical with them, for they are more formalized. The implicit laws of social solidarity are made explicit on the stage to serve as the bases of clearly marked actions and divergences. For this reason dramatic ethics is more exact and concrete than the social ethics which it reflects. It is the province of the theatrical craftsman of each age to discover the theatrical correspondences of the vague social tempers of that time. The earliest statement of a new social point of view is usually made through the theatre. Even though he may not be a thinker at all in the absolute sense, the place of the theatrical craftsman should be considered high, for it is he who isolates the soul of the age. Dumas, in discovering the "demi monde," provided an expedient

of the highest theatrical usefulness. Though this class is more clean cut on the stage than it is in real life, and its ethics more of theatric than of social weight, the isolation of this class for technical purposes was by no means without social significance. In making *The Second Mrs. Tanqueray* very simple and bald, Pinero made good craftsmanship serve in the cause of social thinking, for the story is as true as life and a good deal easier to comprehend. Sudermann's *Magda* is theatrical with the kind of theatricalism that, cartoon-like, illustrates a modern theme in three or four swift strokes. And the technic of Schnitzler has served to epitomize into some very simple stage reactions the meaning of the vague "live your life" program that has been in the air. The craftsmen of naturalism have taken their place in the work of the drama of thought and have done their task so well that on this side there is little else to do. It would seem that as a logical thing the next step will be on some other path.

After revolution came the settling of values. Naturalism grew out of an uneasy romanticism through the operation of the logic of events. And this same logic which made art revolt and destroy is now directing art to the settling of issues and to social reconstruction. It remains to be seen whether constructive social thinking is any more consistent with art than destructive thinking, or indeed, whether it is as consistent. By a certain logic building-up must follow tearing down, but by the time this point is reached in an intellectual program art has ceased to listen to the dictates of logic. There is some kinship between the hot enthusiasms of intellectual revolt and the soul of art. There can be none between the calculating patience of science and the warm glow of artistic creation.

Nowhere is the price that art has to pay for an intellectual program more clear than in the case of those artists who pride themselves above all upon their intellects. Four of these come to mind, all treated in Mr. Dukes' book. These are Shaw, who is intellectual at the expense of sincerity; Barker, who is intellectual at the expense of warmth; Brieux, who is intellectual at the expense of charm; and Tchekhov, who is intellectual at the expense of vitality. A study of the plays of these men convinces one that after all and indubitably plays were never intended for expository documents, and that he who selects this medium is laying his thoughts under a heavy handicap. All the technical advance of the modern movement has been toward making the play a more efficient vehicle for the expression of thought, and it still remains inadequate compared with other forms of art. Those dramatists, like Ibsen, who value the play itself above everything, permit the play to speak for itself. Those writers, on the other hand, who use the play as an expository medium, are continually falling back upon other means of exposition, the preface, prologue, appendix, and expanded description of character and action. Dumas, the first of the intellectuals, introduced the long preface to aid him in the completer expounding of the theme inadequately treated in the play. Shaw, like Dryden, may in after times be better remembered for his prefaces, in which he expresses his thought well, than for his plays, in which he expounds his thoughts badly. Shaw and Barker stand as the latest striking examples of the influence of intellectualism in dramatic art. Both are thinkers, the one of a superficial brilliancy, the other of a tenacity and weight truly remarkable. Both reveal in their work the artistic shortcomings incident to a predominant intellectual intent. Shaw is the wielder of a lawless satire; Barker is inapproachable in a rarefied atmosphere of thought. Mr. Dukes hails Shaw as the greatest individual force in drama since Ibsen. We will not argue this assertion. But if Mr. Dukes means that Shaw is a representative modern, in the sense that he is a man abreast with or in advance of the thinking of his own times, we must take issue with him. Mr. Shaw never strikes a new note or discovers a new reaction. All his plays are based upon some current or some passing principle. He is a true satirist in that he is always facing the present and getting his text from that which is. The satirist is not the prophet, nor is he concerned with the discovery of coming meanings. Shaw dramatizes the discoveries of yesterday's scientists in a dozen sciences. The biologists, the social psychologists and philosophers, the Ferreros of history-writing, provide him his material. You may search through Shaw's plays, and not one will be found which could not be annotated from the text books of a generation of science and philosophy. How little Shaw is in fact a modern may be appreciated when he is compared with Ibsen. Twenty years after they were composed we pick up Ibsen's later plays with a feeling that now at last the world can understand what this man is talking about, for the world has grown up to him. Shaw's plays belong to yesterday, the day after they are written.

Where the drama of the intellectuals is not inadequate it is cold and almost ceases to be drama. Granville Barker's plays do not lack for a soul of intense feeling, but they are too controlled to be really significant of truth. The man who reacts to only one faculty is little more significant of humanity than the insane man would be. Let us quote from Dukes concerning the hero of the Barker play: "At present he appears something of an invalid; pallid, convalescent, bloodless, hobbling upon the crutches of intellect into the consulting room of wit." The men and women who in Ibsen so laboriously, drop by drop, unloaded their souls, have become with Barker easy and debonnair. "Know thyself" has become a commonplace. Interest in life is now becoming formulated into a set of automatic reactions, as certain as mathematics and all in perfect form. In taking much thought upon itself society is becoming a little smug. It would be hard to find greater intellectual feats than those performed by Barker as technician and thinker. But he has left drama naked.

In this clean cut little book of Mr. Dukes' we have a survey of a world of dramatic art that has become conscious of itself, conscious that it is naked and needs to be clothed. Whence is the clothing to come? Naturalism contains the germ of its own downfall, for naturalism pursues always the finer analyses of reality even to the isolation of the infinitesimal under the watchmaker's eye. When the ultimate of analysis has been reached there is still the mystery behind, and the mystery crowds most upon us when our methods have been most circumspect and logical. The exact processes of science carry the physicist to the point at which his science must give way to speculation. In the same way the processes of logic in art carry the artist to the point of mystery. Will not the drama of thought be brought to an end by the logic of its own thinking?

The first beginnings of the new movement are clear enough in this book. The Ibsen of the later plays and the young Maeterlinck had used the methods of the drama of thought to discover the unknowable. Unerringly Dukes sees in the younger Maeterlinck the notable discoverer in the region of unconscious mood and unrevealed truth. "He dramatized the subconscious, the subterranean and tremulous in man, called it forth and gave it life." He sat at the feet of the naturalists and confounded them with their own logic.

The strongest theme in the drama of the last few years has been the call for Life. Can it be that the keen minds of the dramatists have recognized the thing that is lacking in their art, and so they have made a theme out of that which should be a passionate experience? Has art followed life in reaching out for truth and beauty with the fingers of the mind, and so missed them? Certainly one who reads Ibsen, and Hauptmann, and Sudermann, and Schnitzler, is led to believe that this is so.

This call for Life which has been dominant as an intellectual thing in so much recent drama has been answered by some other artists in another way. During the last years of the naturalistic movement there have been two or three who have refused to join those who seek life with the mind. One of these, Hofmannsthal, in *Death and the Fool,* shows us an age which has lost its soul through much searching. Where Life is it is indivisible. That which is a law of life is also a law of art. It is only the inorganic that can be ultimately analysed. The microscope has not isolated life for the eye of science. Why should we expect it to do so for the eye of art? Hofmannsthal and D'Annunzio go back to the art of an indivisible life. They are joined by others, who by different avenues, some through a course of personal disillusion and defeat, have come to take their place with them. If Ibsen's latter plays mean anything, they mean that he, too, would be on the side of the life indivisible could the dead awaken. Maeterlinck and Hauptmann, at their best and truest, are there, each in his own character. Barrie has been there all along. Yeats and Synge are there. Through such an art as this festival can come back into drama, and ceremonial, and color, and music, and the old clothing of art in legend and tradition and myth.

It would be a mistake to suggest that art can ever again ignore the results of an era of industrious science. The chief glory of Hofmannsthal has been that he transmutes the facts of investigation into the larger life which we trust will constitute the coming order. We cannot expect the new art to be the same as the art of the days of our innocence. We have eaten of the tree of knowledge and the art will be a more sophisticated thing. But we believe it will be not less beautiful for that. For we will find the vivid imaginings of an ancient beauty taking on new meanings in the light of an understanding at once exact and reverent.

Thomas H. Dickinson, "The Drama of Intellectualism," in The Drama: A Quarterly Review, *No. 7, August, 1912, pp. 148-62.*

August Strindberg on his conception of drama:

If anyone asks what it is an intimate theater wants to achieve, . . . I can answer like this: in drama we seek the strong, highly significant motif, but with limitations. We try to avoid in the treatment all frivolity, all calculated effects, places for applause, star roles, solo numbers. No predetermined form is to limit the author, because the motif determines the form. Consequently: freedom in treatment, which is limited only by the unity of the concept and the feeling for style.

August Strindberg, in his Open Letters to the Intimate Theater, *translated by Walter Johnson, University of Washington Press, 1966.*

Stark Young

[*An American playwright, poet, and novelist, Young was, with Allen Tate, Robert Penn Warren, and several others, a prominent member of the Agrarian group of Southern poets. He also served for twenty years as drama critic for various publications. In the following essay Young maintains that because realist drama avoids music and poetry, it is incapable of covering "the full register of human experience."*]

To say that music is the most ideal of the arts, the only purely ideal art, were to say nothing new or original.

The other arts of painting and sculpture deal first with the external beauty of form, the beauty of a particular manifestation of existence. If one is to paint a picture of the emotion of fresh joy and gladness, one must present a phenomenon of it: nymphs dancing, rural sport, a spring landscape, young animals. In the art of words it is by expressing objects and concepts that one appeals to the intellectual and emotional faculties aimed at. The emotional effect is produced in part by the musical qualities of the word, but largely by the connotation, the association that surrounds the object or concept chosen; as, for instance, the effect of fresh joy and gladness that breathes in the word *spring*.

Music begins at the other end. Its method is wider and more elemental. Music expresses the beautiful eternity; it is the manifestation of the general, not of a particular phenomenon of beauty, not of a particular appearance out of the general existence. The lower forms of music are those that set out solely to imitate phenomena; to render battles, storms, cathedral bells. I tried on one occasion a theme of Beethoven's—from the Ninth Symphony—on some ten or twelve people. To each, when pushed to a definite concept, it furnished a suggestion in accord with his nature: spring fields, people at a fair, the happy heart, a festival, a dance of wood gods in Arcady. So we come again, from the opposite direction, to the idea of fresh joy and gladness.

Music taken with the word has a loosening effect that widens the word's meaning. The presence of the rhythm—which seems to be the primal force in music—brings us back to an elemental basis, the pulse, the heart-beat; and following the excitement of the rhythm, those other excitements of music appear, and bring to us a comprehensiveness that seems to take us beyond the mere word or concept and into the very life of the thing expressed. The music around the word loosens our emotional faculties to assist the intellectual in exhausting the content of the idea to be conveyed. The word behind the music defines the emotion, gives point to the general idea expressed.

The Greeks, in that large sanity and adaptation of theirs, employed music, as we know, very extensively in their theatres to reinforce the effect of the words. One might say, perhaps, that sometimes they used words to point the meaning of the music. At any rate there are times when, to my mind at least, the reserve, the marble-like surface of Greek tragic poetry is due partly to the fact that the poet could rely on the note following after the word to convey the full burden of his idea. One may speak quietly of one's desire so long as the flutes sing of passion and despair, "the woes of dying lovers."

Music indeed taken by itself tends to bring about a sort of tragic struggle. For each of us is filled with two spirits: one is the individual—the Apollonian, as Nietzsche would say—which strives to know, to master, to bound itself, to establish its identity in the universe; the other is that elemental impulse—the Dionysian—toward the universal, which would be boundless, *en rapport* with ecstasy, chaotic, free. Music tends to expand our elemental impulses, our emotional selves, and to appear to us in terms of our unsatisfied desires and longings; and thus to bring about a strife between the individual that tries to define itself and the instinct that longs for freedom. It is interesting to recall that, in our chaotic and unbounded century, this strife at the heart of man (to know oneself on the one hand, and on the other to be free) has found its most adequate expression in music. Wagner has reached thousands to whom Ibsen is still an alien.

In our great dramatic period the poetic style took the entire burden upon itself. The music of the Elizabethan verse must do the work that the Dionysian pipes and the stately verses shared between them.

Obviously poetry is the art most nearly akin to music. The regularity of rhythm—that fundamental distinction between poetry and prose—connects verse with that faithful register of our moods, the beating heart; and the audible harmonies of tone in the syllables chosen give the poetry a possible existence independent of its meaning; though music may not be, as Walter Pater claims, its first requirement. The poetic intention is to redeem the falsity of the prose fact. Perhaps it is true that for us, as vital beings, a fact loses its truth as it nears the prosaic. To say that there were crocuses in the grass is to tell but half the truth, which is that

> at their feet the crocus brake like fire.

The poetic intention is to say the truth in such a way that we may be aroused to receive it with all our faculties, imagination, enthusiasm, delight or despair, as well as with the bare reason. Thus to some extent the poetic vehicle does for the concept what music might do, in opening the way to its reception.

The Elizabethan drama, for all its faults of bombast and ranting and recurrent insularity, has in general the intention of universality, of widening the content and significance of the problem presented. It has that noble heart of Spencer's

> that harbors virtuous thought,
> And is with child of glorious great intent.

This ambitious intent is conveyed to us by means of the poetic style, which, with its imagery and ornamentation, its rhythm and harmony, is to insure in us a complete receptiveness. When Hamlet says:

> If thou didst ever hold me in thy heart,
> Absent thee from felicity awhile,
> And in this harsh world draw thy breath in pain,
> To tell my story,

we know that what Hamlet means is that Horatio should refrain from suicide, and live to tell the facts about Hamlet; but we have received more than the mere idea. We perceive the quality of the scholar and prince, what at this supreme moment he means and is. The fact of the physical incident of death is forgotten in the presence of the vital beauty and significance of the scene. We die indeed with Hamlet; but we glory in the range of understanding and the vision granted us, and thus achieve that metaphysical comfort of the philosophers.

Nowadays in our serious realistic drama all the people seem doomed to monosyllabic ends. A gasp, a word or two, a glance—and the art of suggestion, now in vogue, enters to do the rest. No doubt this expresses many deaths with perfect truth, but of some deaths surely it is but partially true. That inner tumult, that supreme significance that rise at the moment, must surely sometimes be of such a nature as to need a poetic heightening of style to make them wholly ours.

Unfortunately the English poetic drama of our time is more of a hindrance than a help in the development of a heightened medium of expression. The verse, if not archaic, imitative, scholarly, is apt to be narrative or lyrical, rarely dramatic. The poet learns his business of books and of his lyre. To write drama he must be, what they used to say of Aristippus, mother-taught, taught of life, the mother of all drama.

> Lyeth as quiet as mown grass at even

is an exquisite line, in harmony, in image and in rhythm; but it is lyrical, not dramatic, as Mr. Phillips himself must feel. Audiences, too, and actors, often, have come to regard verse as unnatural. Much of it is. But as a matter of fact, there is nothing that in vital moments is so deeply natural as verse. There is nothing that so fully expresses the mood, the idea, the emotion, that together compose and constitute the moment.

> My mother had a maid call'd Barbara;
> She was in love; and he she loved proved mad,
> And did forsake her: she had a song of *Willow,*
> An old thing 'twas, but it expressed her fortune,
> And she died singing it; that song, tonight,
> Will not go from my mind; I have much to do,
> But to go hang my head all at one side,

> And sing it, like poor Barbara.
> *Odi et amo. Quare id faciam, fortasse requiris.*
> *Nescio, sed fieri sentio et excrucior.*
> *Nessun maggior dolore*
> *Che ricordarsi del tempo felice*
> *Nella Miseria.*

Could anything be more natural, more deeply natural, than those verses?

And nothing can be more truly simple, more organically—to use a chemical term—simple, than verse when it wills so to be.

> *Parle-lui tous les jours des vertus de son père,*
> *Et quelquefois aussi parle-lui de sa mère.*
> *Natus parenti*
> *Oscula conprensis auribus eripiet,*
> And never lifted up a single stone.

Surely unnaturalness and complexity in verse are avoidable enough.

Realism professes to reproduce life as it is; by which it means to say that it photographs the exterior manifestations of life, and avoids portraying what ears and eyes alone may not experience. Realism is the scientific spirit treading the boards.

Realism professes to reproduce life as it is; by which it means to say that it photographs the exterior manifestations of life, and avoids portraying what ears and eyes alone may not experience. Realism is the scientific spirit treading the boards.

—Stark Young

The realistic drama, then, is forced to leave to the imagination all that in life is not expressed in words or acts. We are accustomed to think that the poetic drama requires of the audience more imagination. In reality though the poetic may require a higher flight at the time, the amount of imagination demanded for a true understanding of the theme is not so great as it is in the realistic. To take an example, it is easier to follow the closet scene with all the ecstasy of Hamlet's words to his mother, than it is to follow Oswald and Mrs. Alving. The torture, the tenderness, the ecstasy, the fantasy, that fill Hamlet's soul are there for anyone to see: in the case of Oswald we can only surmise, though his mood is perhaps as complex as Hamlet's. The average man does not greatly surmise; what is provided he takes, and goes no further.

In realistic drama the present medium of expression, the language put into the mouths of the characters, is tentative. William Vaughn Moody tried honorably, and failed; Henry Arthur Jones' talk is commonplace; Pinero's, except when his naughty people have the floor, is apt to be thin. The realistic method is to reproduce the very surface of what people say. But language at best mocks the meaning of our hearts. We are powerless behind the symbol that is supposed to express the living thought. Hence that frequent feeling of barrenness in these dramas; as in Ibsen, where there are times, even on the stage, when the characters seem to be smothering themselves, hiding the glow and stress of their experience behind a photographic life-mask of words.

The realistic drama—as the term is used at present—is limited in range. It has in fact two courses open. One is to confine itself to situations and problems that are easily perceptible through the medium of speech as we actually hear it and of acts that are fairly usual. Here realism is in its element. The other course is to risk undertaking situations and problems that the externals of actual life can but faintly reflect. Here realism is put to shifts; it eliminates, denies, psychologies, turns surgeon. It employs the scientific optimism which hopes to explain all things. The effect is often logical, scientific; but, in the rank and file of eternal values, barren and meager. The dislike for the realistic drama felt by many persons—and those not worshippers of the illusory—is due to this: this arrogant paucity, this assurance that whatever has been undertaken—remorse, longing for the sea, passion, idealism, for instance—has been expressed completely and conclusively. Such persons take these human tides—remorse, longing for the sea, passion, idealism, for instance—in good faith; and think them related widely and mysteriously to the eternal and universal as well as to hereditary impulses and nervous ganglia. They would feel certain that the appeal of *Oedipus Rex* is of more universal application and capacity than that of *Ghosts;* despite the myth of the oracle in Sophocles, and the plausible actuality of Ibsen's heredity.

Following this scientific bent, the realists have pursued a relentless technique that again sets limitations around their work. Surely the great and wise technique, the *architektone,* in drama has one end; which is to achieve the greatest result possible, of power and breadth of appeal and application. It vaunteth not itself. But in these technical exploits of our day one may often see a hand dressing and undressing the people, sorting essentials and unessentials, winding and unwinding—the Master of the Show is on the alert. And one knows that every breath to be uttered is to help blow up the bag that is to burst at the end. In Ibsen, and not rarely, we feel as if we were watching a game of chess with mortals for the chessmen. One may watch the game go forward with delight, but it is more often than not the delight of the specialist. No personage in the play finds time to stop a moment for an aimless folly or for some inconsequent pleasantry that has no bearing on the theme. All that the characters do and say is necessary; they live and they speak in line to one end. And they speak with a sort of uncanny inevitability; seeming to be possessed by devils who drive them to say precisely those words and to do precisely those deeds that will contribute to our theme and purpose. Hedda Gabler is stript and shorn for the surgeon. We are told from time to time by the other persons of the play that she is fascinating, alluring; we must take it on faith, for she has no time now to be so. In *Ghosts* one accepts more readily this obvious mission of every detail; concentration is necessary in this intensity of the final moment. But poor little Nora can eat only enough of the macaroons to show that she is a liar, and may dance only so many steps as at that moment the drama itself needs to advance. This is amazing mathematics, titanic architecture, if only one could be satisfied with problems and plans without the stars and spires. Such stripping to one purpose, such automatic certainty as is imposed upon them, may have its technical brilliance and its problematic function, but it limits necessarily the roundness of conception, the appeal, and the significance, of the characters.

Serious realism at this present stage seems again to have limited itself by marking out for its endeavor the darker paths of life. The scientific spirit seems helpless in the face of joy and faith. Alas, those darker paths are not the road to Rome! The deep power of joy that Wordsworth sang, is spread in commonalty wide enough to rule the world. Men still refuse to generalize upon the base, the hideous. Only the beautiful, the good, men feel, the *kalokagathon,* is creative, and enters into the universal and eternal. This beauty and good is inherent in all themes, tragic and comic; because the will to live, to taste experience, is our first and most buoyant instinct, whatever our lives may be. Its evidence in drama depends on the treatment. The law of heredity—the visitation of the father's sins upon the children—when given a wider treatment achieves its wider import: it safeguards the race, it is terrible, beautiful and wise. In the hands of the realist, it crushes one man, is hideous, appalling, unjust. Realism has taken too thoroughly that advice of Virgil's to the farmer—*laudato ingentia rura, exiguum colito*—and has cultivated small fields too thoroughly. The limitation of the method, then, comes partly from the fact that, by its scrupulous photography and scientific detail, it accents the particular manifestation rather than the idea, the phenomenon rather than its eternal content and significance. It tends to limit the application of its problem.

This is no arraignment of the realistic drama. All must recognize the serviceability of a patient and faithful realism to the world. The point here is, that the realistic method so far is tentative, experimental; and that to insist on its supremacy and its adoption, is to limit the drama in range and in that direct and universal ideality that may become almost musical.

The end of drama is to furnish us with exercise in living, to supply experiences, to patch out our lives as it were. In the manuscript of our lives it may fill a blank page sometimes, or right a passage for which we had lost the key. To come from the theatre with an analysis, a classification, is but to have piled the fagots; the imaginative life alone can light the fire.

Whatever, then, in drama tends to include the life of the spectator with the life of the play, to coax him into that desertion of himself, that collapse of his ego, as Nietzsche would say, which leads to the fullest sympathy and enjoyment; whatever sets free that infectious life in all vital things; all this is the dramatist's to use as best he may.

So far as methods go, ours is a transitional age. Music as a dramatic expedient, a reinforcement such as it was with the Greeks, is now another art, the opera. Its function with us has been assumed by the heightened poetic style. The poetic style as now developed seems adapted to plays that are of an ideal nature, and that are removed, to some extent at least, in time and place from the actual as it exists for us. The realistic methods have achieved a notable eminence only in fields more or less sordid or pessimistic; and have by no means as yet covered the full register of human experience. There are whole masses of experience which the realistic drama—the serious realistic drama of high and earnest purpose—has never found sufficiently plastic to its fingers. The medium of expression in this realistic method is unsatisfactory, meager, barren, photographic.

What is needed is some fusion of methods and styles that will give us a convincing and at the same time significant and elevating treatment of the life of which we are a part. The greatest drama, perhaps, must always have a certain remoteness. But the absence of the sublimity that comes from the awe and mystery of the remote, does not necessitate the squalor and depression of our present great realistic achievements. We need a language medium that will be more intimately true, more flexible, sympathetic and luminous. We want a means of portraying the outer fact that at the same time will not blur the inner significance. But always it must be remembered that, if either is to be sacrificed, it should be the outer, because the idea, the inner significance, is always more vital than the object or mere fact.

The *real* realism must include the ideal if it is to include life. And it must accept the ideal in good faith, not always as a pathological phenomenon to be recorded. The supreme instances of dramatic art in the world's repertory seem to be those scenes where realism and idealism meet to reinforce each other: as for examples, the churchyard scene in *Hamlet;* the storm in *King Lear;* or the entrance of Oedipus with his sightless and bloody eyes, his voice "floating in the invisible air," amid the ineffable dread and cloud of darkness. In such instances, the actual fidelity of the realistic gives point and convincingness: and the glow and flight of the poetry gives that loosening, that emotional, as well as intellectual, excitement that is necessary to the supreme effect.

The ideal method aimed at would be that there be no ideal method. There would be no reckoning of realistic or poetic; but a medium that would convey the whole to us as might a crystal around the delicate processes of an experiment. It is this adjustment of actuality, inner significance, and expression, which gives that effect of inevitability such as marks a summit in art.

Stark Young, "Music and the Poetic and Realistic Styles in Drama," in The Drama: A Quarterly Review, *No. 3, August, 1911, pp. 123-35.*

IMPACT AND INFLUENCE

W. L. Courtney

[*In the essay below, Courtney explores the development of realist drama in England, paying particular attention to Ibsen's influence on British playwrights.*]

[The] production of *The Profligate* at the Garrick Theatre in 1889 was a significant event, and, indeed, was prophetic of the much more important occasion—the production of *The Second Mrs. Tanqueray* in May, 1893. I shall be concerned in the present article with the progress of Realism in Drama, and with some of those pieces of Sir Arthur Pinero which were conceived and executed in a realistic vein. Those which are convenient for my purpose in this respect are *The Profligate, The Second Mrs. Tanqueray, The Benefit of the Doubt, the Notorious Mrs. Ebbsmith,* and *Iris.* These are all realistic plays in [a clearly defined sense]. . . . The dramatist writing about his own country and his own times desires to paint not flattering portraits but veracious likenesses. He does not want to ignore the ordinary conditions, the salient characteristics of the era in which he lives. He believes it to be his business to look steadily at the social fabric, to observe the different elements of which it is composed, to note the peculiar perils which surround and enfeeble its health, and to play the part, not indeed of a reformer, for that would be too didactic an aim for an artist—or, at all events, for some artists—but of a keen, quick-witted, and occasionally sympathetic observer. And in similar fashion with regard to the personages of this drama, the playwright will seek to draw men and women, not as viewed through the spectacles of a fantastic imagination, but in their habit as they live. If he does this with a certain remorselessness, he is a Realist.

Now it is exactly this remorselessness of his which gets him into trouble with a number of different sections of our world. He is unflinching in his portrayal, and men do not like unflinching portrait-painters. They want the picture touched up by some indulgent and benevolent philanthropist. The realist refuses to play with what he deems to be the truth. At the time when the younger Dumas was writing extremely interesting though not altogether persuasive prefaces to his plays, and was particularly occupied with some of the destructive activities of modern woman—a subject which, as we are aware, attracted him strongly—he made some remarks about the things we ought to laugh at and the things we ought not to laugh at. "It is our common habit in France," he wrote, "to laugh at serious things." We may, indeed, extend his observation and say that in England it is often our habit—especially in musical comedies—to laugh at serious things. But, according to Dumas, the only right attitude is to laugh at things which are not serious, and which have no pretension to be serious. When we are face to face with a grave social danger, it is a very curious sort of wisdom which dismisses such subjects with a laugh. There is, of course, a touch of pedantry in an observation like this, and there was certainly a good deal of pedantry in Dumas' didactic attitude. Nevertheless, there is solid truth beneath, which is very applicable to our modern audiences in England.

If we go back a certain number of years, to the time, for instance, when *The Profligate* was produced, or to the time when Ibsen's plays were first represented in our capital, we find that the common attitude of average people was one of shocked resentment. "The problem play" was looked at with open abhorrence, as though it were an accursed thing, revolutionary and immoral. Indeed, every serious effort made by the realist to represent life in plain, undisguised fashion was regarded, and is still regarded in many quarters, as savouring of impiety. Those who adopt such an attitude have certainly one justification. They point out that the playhouse is open to a very mixed public, of very different ages, and that it is wrong, or at all events highly injudicious to put on the stage problem plays which might be an offence to the youthful and immature. There is a further point also, which is somewhat open to controversy, but which is advanced by those who desire to keep serious discussion about life and morals away from the boards. There is all the difference, we are told, between what is read on the printed page and what is enacted before our eyes by living characters. The second is supposed to make a far deeper impression than the first, and therefore the enacted scene, if in any sense it is unpleasant, is likely to do more mischief in proportion to its vivid and lively character. It is difficult to dogmatise on a point like this, because it depends largely upon the individual whether a stronger impression is created by a story or a play. But the other point of objection proceeds on an assumption which no lover of drama can possibly concede. It assumes that a play is a mere entertainment, possessed of no serious dignity in itself, but only a sheer matter of amusement. In other words, it assumes that dramatic art is not art at all, because, directly we think of it, no art, whether painting, or sculpture, or literature, can be regulated in accordance with the age or immaturity of the public to whom it is presented. You do not ask your painter to remember that a child may look at his picture, nor do you ask your Hardys and Merediths to remember that their pages may be perused by young and sensitive persons.

The fact is that a good deal of ambiguity surrounds the use of such words as "the immoral," as applied to stage plays and the theatre. The very same critics who object to the problem play appear to have no objection when similar subjects are treated with easy wit and from a comical standpoint by the writers of musical comedy. What is it which should strictly be called "the immoral"? Immorality consists, obviously, in putting people wrong about the relations of virtue and vice. It consists in adorning vice with seductive colours, in hiding the ugliness of the corrupt, in adopting little affectations of worldliness or wit in the effort to screen from the public gaze the real misery of a decadent civilisation. Or, again, when we have to treat with the actual conditions which obtain in this world of ours, it is plainly immoral to ignore the law of cause and effect. To pretend, for instance, that vice has no consequences, that everything can be put right, that plenary forgiveness waits on repentance and remorse, is immoral. It is possible for human creatures to forgive, and in some rare cases it is even possible for them to forget. But Nature never forgives, and no tears can wipe out the social effects of crime. To confuse the public on points like these, to present them with a false theory, is, indeed, an immoral

thing. But how can it be called immoral to see some danger ahead and warn people of the enormous importance of avoiding it? How can it be immoral to observe men and women on the brink of a precipice, and to try to pull them back? The man who engages on a task like this cannot be called immoral, even though he may have to use very plain and ugly terms in acquitting himself of his disagreeable task.

This, I take it, is the defence of realism; its justification in the face of its numerous critics. There may be things to be said on the other side. Sometimes the realist may be like the satirist, and some satirists appear to have a predilection for ugly things. But that hardly touches the main centre of realism as we find it in drama. Its chief quality is to be absolutely fearless and ruthless in the exposure of all that is harmful, rotten, degrading, just as equally it should be its clear duty to set forth all that is helpful, stimulating, salutary. If realists are fonder of the first duty than the second, their excuse is that there is much necessary spadework to be done in removing the evil before we can even hope to see the good. Besides, it is a melancholy fact that the good is, from the dramatic standpoint, not rarely the uninteresting. The true apology of the realist, however, is to be found in his passionate desire for truth—truth at all costs, his equally passionate hatred of all hypocrisy and sham, his zeal to anchor himself on solid facts and to refuse to care whether he gives pain or discomfort to men and women who would rather live in a fool's paradise. The best part of the influence of Ibsen on the modern drama is to be found in his clear promulgation of the necessity for truth. This point we shall have an opportunity of observing presently.

In April, 1889, when *The Profligate* was produced, Ibsen's influence on English dramatists had not yet begun. Indeed, clear traces of its influence are only discoverable in 1895, when *The Notorious Mrs. Ebbsmith* was seen on the boards. But the impulse to veracity, the resolute desire to study human nature, and especially to discover the effects on that human nature of a certain course of conduct more or less deliberately and recklessly pursued—these are the signs which prove to us that Pinero's *The Profligate* was in truth a drama of realism. The real change can hardly be better seen than in the treatment of the principal character. That a human being is to a very large extent a slave of his habits is adequately recognised in the play. In other words, we see the first beginnings of the doctrine of determinism. If a man acts from motives, and if the motives are in their turn automatically suggested by a type of conduct deliberately pursued through several years, then in the case of human action we get as much certainty of sequence between cause and effect as we do in external nature. Given the antecedents, the consequents will follow. Given the motives supplied by the past life, and a man's action is inevitable. Or, to put the matter in a concrete case where its immediate pertinence is easily seen, given a vicious career, then the ordinary and habitual conduct of the man at each successive episode or incident in his life will be vicious. I lay stress on the point because here is the commencement of a scientific psychology quite as much as an illustration of realism on the stage.

Dunstan Renshaw is a profligate—not, observe, merely an ordinary "man of the world," as we call it, but one who has done definite acts which stamp his nature, especially in his relations with Janet Preece. Dunstan Renshaw falls in love with Leslie Brudenell, and in the first moments of emotional excitement and expansion he declares to his friend that the companionship of a pure woman is a revelation to him. "She seemed," he tells Murray, "to take me by the hand and to lead me out of darkness into the light." All his high-flown language is perfectly explicable in a man who had, apparently, lived on his nerves and who was capable of intense moments of feeling. But what does not follow—what, indeed, is in the highest sense improbable—is that any radical change in character can be thus effected. Let us even suppose that such a sudden conversion were possible—which is granting a good deal more than the scientific psychologist would allow—there is always the terrible past, which is never buried but is always starting into fresh and vivid reality. How can a man like Dunstan Renshaw, merely because he marries a pure woman, wipe out his past? The past has "overtaken him," he says in one excited utterance. "You know what my existence has been; I am in deadly fear; I dread the visit of a stranger or the sight of strange handwriting, and in my sleep I dream that I am muttering into Leslie's ear the truth against myself."

Of course, his past sins find him out, as his friend Murray had prophesied. The whole pitiful history of Janet Preece comes to the light, and looks all the uglier because by the use of the long arm of coincidence Leslie's brother Wilfrid has loved Janet. Ah, you say, but the woman can forgive: Leslie is a good woman! It is true that she can forgive, but she can hardly forget; and, even if she did, how does this help Dunstan Renshaw, who finds it impossible to forget? In other words, the past cannot be obliterated by a stroke of the pen, and it is the intimate and deadly quality of all sins that they leave permanent traces on the man and woman who have committed them.

> And having tasted stolen honey
> You can't buy innocence for money.

We can understand how new a thing in English drama was this ruthless treatment of a grave problem, when we discover that owing to the solicitations of John Hare, the only true, as well as artistic, end of this play was changed. John Hare was guided by the popular prejudice in favour of a happy ending, and he therefore besought the dramatist to soften down the terrible conclusion into something wholly unreal and artificial, which should send the spectators away in a happier frame of mind. Well, it is an old-established prejudice in theatrical audiences to desire happy endings. Even Aristotle recognised the fact. But such exhibitions of human weakness do not alter the stern facts of life; they only proclaim aloud the hopeless divergence between popular art and an art based on psychology and science. There are some problems that cannot be solved by tears or forgiveness. What sort of married life was possible for Dunstan Renshaw and Leslie? The dramatist cut the Gordian knot by making the hero kill himself, for in no other fashion probably can a dramatist bring home to those who see his plays the dreadful consequence of certain crimes. But if we want to see what is the result

of marriages of this kind, we cannot do better than turn to one of the works of the Norwegian dramatist, Ibsen. *Ghosts* is not a pleasant play, but it conveys a tremendous moral. In the course of the story we discover that Mrs. Alving's husband is a profligate of a type absolutely comparable with Dunstan Renshaw. For various reasons, including social and external decency, she determines to make the best of it and go on living with the man as if he were a sort of saint instead of a blackguard. Conventional morality requires that a wife should go on living with her husband whatever he may be guilty of—such is the moral of Pastor Manders. But it is exactly this worship of humbug and pretence which the true moralist reprobates in the severest terms. Ibsen's *Ghosts* is generally considered as a sort of sequel to Ibsen's *Doll's House*—it is equally a sequel to Pinero's *The Profligate*. Why Nora is justified in running away from her home is because in certain conditions life becomes impossible for a married pair. Why Dunstan Renshaw commits suicide is because certain sins are never forgiven or forgotten. If we choose to disregard these realities the next generation will suffer. "The fathers have eaten sour grapes, and the children's teeth are set on edge." The son of the profligate Councillor Alving ends by being a helpless idiot, crying for the sunshine.

It does not follow, of course, that *The Profligate* is in itself a good play, or even a good example of dramatic realism. It is worth while looking at this point for a moment, because it will throw light on our subject from another quarter. What are the obvious defects of *The Profligate*? We notice a certain crudeness in the composition and construction. If you look at the opening scene of *The Second Mrs. Tanqueray* you will find one of the most admirable examples that Sir Arthur Pinero has ever given us of what is technically called "exposition." The dinner party given by Aubrey Tanqueray to his friends reveals in the most natural way in the world the story in which we are to be interested, and the clever manner in which Paula is herself introduced at the end of the first act gives us a very necessary sight of the heroine who is to play so fatal a part in Aubrey Tanqueray's destiny. *The Profligate* commences with a conversation between Hugh Murray, Renshaw's friend, and Lord Dangars, which is by no means so happy. Moreover, in carrying out the intrigue there is a decided lack of naturalness, or rather of inevitableness. Every play of the sort must invoke the aid of coincidence, because in presenting a little picture, foreshortened and concentrated, of a complete and rounded-off story, the playwright must be permitted to use all the expedients which we recognise to be of the nature of accidents. But the use of coincidence in *The Profligate* goes beyond all bounds. It is necessary, of course, that Leslie, wife of Dunstan Renshaw, should come face to face with Janet Preece, who has been her husband's victim. But the mechanism which produces this result is decidedly arbitrary, if not far-fetched. Hazard and accident play an overwhelming part. Accident brings Janet to Paddington Station at the same time as Leslie and her brother; accident decides that Leslie's school friend, Miss Stonehay, should take Janet as a travelling companion; accident, once more, brings the Stonehay family precisely to the environs of Florence, and to the villa in which the Renshaws are living; and finally, there is not so much nature as artifice in the arrangement by which Janet stays with Leslie at the villa instead of going away as she naturally would—through feelings of sheer delicacy. There is another side on which *The Profligate* is open to criticism. The danger of all realistic plays is that they are apt to tumble unaware into melodrama. I mean by melodrama an exaggeration in the drawing of character, the sacrifice of a good deal of probability in order to accentuate the situation, and a noticeable want of connection between the motives and acts of the personages involved. The character of Dunstan Renshaw shows many signs of exaggeration. His *raison d' être* in the piece is to represent a profligate and a seducer, and a man who has lived the particular life that he is supposed to have lived, and who, even on the eve of his marriage, indulges in a stupid carouse, is hardly capable of those finer shades of feeling, of remorse and self-chastisement, which he betrays towards the end of the play. So, too, Leslie's evolution is decidedly abrupt from the innocence of the earlier stage to the knowledge of life after one month's *tête-à-tête* with her husband.

How different is the masterly treatment which we come across in *The Second Mrs. Tanqueray!* We understand the situation from the very beginning. The characters are not exaggerated, and we see them developing before our eyes on lines which we recognise as essentially probable and true. The personality of Aubrey Tanqueray may be a little obscure here and there, but Paula is an admirable creation, whose conduct throughout is what we might have expected of a woman in such circumstances and subject to such temptations; while, as in the case of Greek tragedy, we are dimly aware from the first scene to the last of a Fate hanging over all the characters and dooming them to their eventual ruin. There is, it is true, one coincidence which may strike some observers as strange. It is the accident which brings back Ardale, the accepted lover of Ellean, into the presence of the heroine, with whom he had such close relations in the past. Nevertheless here, as it seems to me, the coincidence is not in any sense surprising or unnatural, given the past circumstances of Paula's life and her numerous adventures before she became Mrs. Tanqueray. It is because of its fine theatrical execution, because it gives us living figures whose dispositions and character inevitably work up to the *dénouement,* and because it does not slide over into melodrama, that *The Second Mrs. Tanqueray* is, so far as I can judge, one of the masterpieces of the modern English stage.

For what is, or ought to be, the supreme excellence of a play which purports to deal with real events and real characters, true to the country in which they live and explicable on proper psychological grounds? I think the great test is this. Do we look upon the enacted drama as a mere spectacle, or do we find ourselves part of it? Are we merely sitting as spectators in a theatre divided from the stage by the footlights, living our own lives while the people on the boards live theirs? Or are we transported in very deed into the enacted scene, as though it were part of the life which for the time we ourselves are leading? A great play, which greatly deals with supreme issues, has the power to make us forget that we are in a theatre at all, or that there is any distinction between us and the actors. In other words, we live in the play, and do not merely look at it. But how rare-

ly do we undergo an experience like this! Assuredly, it is impossible in plays of romance; it is equally impossible in melodramas or farces. But the supreme virtue of a drama of realism is that now and again it has this strange power of transporting us out of ourselves. The audience becomes a part of the play. Every one, perhaps, will have his own instances to give of an experience of this kind: for myself I felt it when I first saw *The Second Mrs. Tanqueray,* and again, to take quite a modern instance, when I saw *Hindle Wakes.*

> A great play, which greatly deals with supreme issues, has the power to make us forget that we are in a theatre at all, or that there is any distinction between us and the actors. In other words, we live in the play, and do not merely look at it.
>
> —*W. L. Courtney*

This seems a fit opportunity for saying something of the predominant influence of Ibsen. I have called it predominant because it seems a mere matter of fact that since the vogue of the Norwegian dramatist most of the playwriters of England have either altered their methods or their style. But it is necessary to look at the matter a little closer, because the influence which a man exerts on the literature of another country is a somewhat intangible thing, and we are only too apt to go wrong as to its range and quality. The main influence of Ibsen has, undoubtedly, been in the direction of realism, defined in the sense in which I have all along tried to use it. Realism means above all else a devotion to the bare and explicit truth of human life and human character, and the avoidance of all romantic or poetic devices for obscuring the main issues. No sooner had Ibsen begun to compose his social dramas than he found himself immersed in a task—evidently congenial to him—of tearing down the social conventions, exposing the social hypocrisies which disguise the face of reality and truth. Nearly every one of his social plays is an exposure of humbug of some sort. Now it is the case of some shipowner, who recklessly sends a rotten old hulk to sea for reasons purely commercial; and now it is the more intimate relationship between men and women in the married state, which seems to the dramatist to require careful analysis and elucidation. Or, again, it is the fetish of mundane respectability at which Ibsen will gird. He will show us a Pastor Manders trying to persuade Mrs. Alving to go on living with her profligate husband for the sake of external decency; or else will paint for us the character of a sincere enthusiast for the truth who wishes to purify a town's water supply, together with all the fatal consequences in his case, the loss of personal prestige, the accusations of treachery, the desertion of all his friends. These are the various themes which Ibsen takes up in *The Pillars of Society,* in *A Doll's House,* in *Ghosts,* and in *An Enemy of the People.* And then, by a sudden change of outlook, in order to prove that he cares more for truth than for theory, Ibsen writes his strange play *The Wild Duck,* the whole purport of which is to show that a fanatical devotion to truth may cause just as much injury as the studious and calculated suppression of truth. What is wrong with society is the reign of conventional ethics, supported by such interested apostles of things as they are as clergymen and business men. There are many dark corners which ought to be looked into in this matter. Nevertheless, like everything else, truth is a difficult goddess to worship, and the intoxicated fanatic who devotes himself to her cause will often do her graver harm than even the conventional liar. Such seems to be the lesson of *The Wild Duck,* albeit that it is a play which has always caused a certain searching of heart among the disciples of Ibsen. But the general impulse of striving to attain to the exact and veritable fact remains as one of the chief heritages which Ibsen communicated to the dramatic world, and it is easy to see in this respect how great has been his influence amongst modern playwrights.

I pass to another point—the question of dramatic construction. Ibsen is a master of dramatic craftsmanship. He certainly learnt some lessons in the school of Scribe in Paris, but he applied and transformed the *pièce bien faite* in his own fashion, so that, externally at all events, an Ibsen play seems to differ *toto cœlo* from the ordinary pieces produced on the French stage. In some respects Ibsen has an almost classical severity and restraint of form. His *Ghosts* is, technically, like a Greek tragedy, so sure is the progression of its incidents, so close is the interaction between cause and effect. *A Doll's House* might possibly commend itself to Euripides, although, of course, the Greek dramatist would have solved the problem in his usual fashion by introducing some god or goddess to cut the Gordian knot. A method of which Ibsen was especially fond in his plays was what has been called the retrospective method. You start your plot on the very eve of a *dénouement,* as close as you can to the tragic issue. Then you make your characters expound the past in a series of animated dialogues, so that when the conclusion is reached you have become thoroughly acquainted with the personages who bring it about. Ibsen shows a wonderful skill in the fashion in which he makes the personages of the drama reveal their past actions and also themselves, to which we may add the obvious fact that his conversations themselves are conducted with a sense of actuality which makes them extraordinarily vivid. You can read a play by Ibsen with almost as much pleasurable interest as you can witness it on the stage, because there is not only something easy and natural in the sentences put into the mouths of the various characters, but there is also a distinct economy of effect. The sentences themselves have weight and importance because they so clearly lead up to the issue.

The only thing which interferes with this triumphant actuality is Ibsen's increasing tendency as he grew to his later years to use symbols and images, sometimes of a very vague and elusive character. The symbol of the Wild Duck is comparatively easy, for it very fairly indicates both the character and the fate of the girl heroine, Hedwig. In *The Lady from the Sea* we have advanced a step further in the symbolic direction. After all, the Wild Duck was a mere

symbol, subordinate to the plot itself, but in *The Lady from the Sea* the idea of the play itself is wholly symbolic. The problem of married life is not discussed as it had been, for instance, in *A Doll's House,* but is merged in a sort of allegory suggestive of the romance of love. Plays like *Rosmersholm* and *Hedda Gabler* belong to the earlier type, but when we come to *The Master Builder* and *Little Eyolf,* and especially to the last, *When We Dead Awaken,* symbolism is once more in full swing; and, indeed, in *When We Dead Awaken* it represents, or perhaps disguises, a definite weakening in dramatic power. According to the French critic, M. Filon, however, it is just this symbolism or allegorical element in Ibsen which makes him congenial to Anglo-Saxon and Teutonic tastes, while it renders it much more difficult for Parisian audiences and the Latin races to understand him. There is, undoubtedly, a strong strain of mysticism in all Northern peoples, Teutonic, Scandinavian, and Anglo-Saxon, but in the representations of Ibsen's plays in England I have never been able to detect that Ibsen owes such popularity as he has gained to his mystical elements. As a matter of fact, he never has been popular in the widest sense in England, and certainly the performance of plays like *A Master Builder* and *Little Eyolf* has not enabled English spectators to welcome Ibsen as akin to them in essence and spirit. Obviously, too, the symbolic tendency interferes in no slight measure with the realistic tendency which belongs to the best work of Ibsen. Symbolism may be valuable inasmuch as it suggests that realism is by no means the last word in dramatic art, but it is not a phase in the great Norwegian's work which has lent itself to much successful imitation on the part of his followers and admirers.

There is another aspect of Ibsen's work, however, which deserves attention, especially as connected with modern movements in social and intellectual life. I refer to the extraordinary prominence which he has given to women in his dramas, and especially to women as representing the individualistic idea as against State action or collectivism. Ibsen, undoubtedly, thought, as most of his social dramas prove, that all State action, as such, whether exercised through a compact majority or through police or other agencies, is entirely harmful and crippling because it puts chains upon the individual. As against society the individual is always right. Now, who are the great individualists? Women, undoubtedly, who not only attack problems in their own fashion, but instinctively resist the pressure of laws imposed upon them, as it seems to their intelligence, in an entirely arbitrary manner. Hence the importance of women in Ibsen's plays, and hence, too, the idea, for which, indeed, there is a good deal to be said, that Ibsen was the great feminist writer, doing more for the cause of women both as poet and artist than any thinker had done before him. It is not quite certain, however, whether the Norwegian dramatist really liked this identification of his views with those of the ordinary feminist platform. He certainly did not keenly support any women's movements, and, apparently, he was annoyed that his play *A Doll's House* should have been interpreted as a tract for feminism. But it remains true that to women he assigned all the virtues the possession of which he denied to men. The love of truth, a clear perception of what is reasonable, a fine dose of enthusiasm, immense energy, all these things

A scene from Henrik Ibsen's Ghosts, 1890.

are attributed to women in his plays, whereas, on the contrary, the men exhibit the mean vices—stupidity, selfishness, sometimes cowardice, sometimes also rascality and a reckless greed. There are exceptions, of course. Hedda Gabler is a woman entirely devoid of conscience, while Dr. Stockmann is a fine example of the well-meaning moralist who pursues his love of truth even though society be shattered. So, too, Dr. Wangel is a husband entirely praiseworthy, but I know of hardly any other husband in the Ibsenite drama of whom the same thing can be said. The women, I say, have all the virtues, or, at all events, all the virtues from the point of view of the Norwegian dramatist. Many examples occur. There is Nora, for instance, in *A Doll's House,* who cannot endure a married life which is not founded on respect for individual duties, as against her husband Torvald, who only desires to hush up scandal. Or there is Rebecca in *Rosmersholm,* a far finer character than the unhappy Rosmer, much braver and more resolute in her determination to save her soul through love. Or in *The Master Builder,* while Solness seems only inspired by the single idea that somehow or other he must keep back the advancing tide of the younger generation, Hilda is inspired by a much more healthy ambition in trying to restore to Solness his earlier dreams. Or, once more, in the last of the Ibsen plays, *When We Dead Awaken,* it is Irene who has truth and right on her side, as against the egotist Rubek, who only desires to make use of human personalities in the selfish pursuit of art for art's sake.

As we review these and many other instances we see that to Ibsen woman is not only the born anarchist, but that she is also justified in her anarchical views. The world is poisoned because every one is contented with outworn social and ethical conventions. Women refuse to be blinded by the dust of these antique superstitions; they are on the side of freedom, independence, self-realisation, the only ideals at which human life ought to aim, the only ideals which Ibsen, at all events, chooses to glorify. Of course, Ibsen was very one-sided in views of this kind. The progress of humanity depends on two movements which must go on side by side. One is the impulse towards change; the other is the steady drag towards stability. To prevent a given social state from petrification there must be constant revolts, a continuous series of fresh and lively efforts to strike out new paths. But in order that a social state may exist at all, the newer impulses must be harmonised with the older structure. Order is as necessary for the world as progress. Ibsen's ideal of self-realisation, if carried to its logical results, means the destruction of stability for the sake of a few hare-brained individuals. Nor yet is self-realisation to be distinguished in the last resort from a greedy and assertive selfishness.

In his influence on the world of drama, however, Ibsen's fondness not only for drawing women but for endowing them with energetic qualities has played no small part in the evolution of feminist ideas. In all modern realistic work whether you observe it in the plays of Pinero or of

George Bernard Shaw, the woman has attained a prominence and importance far removed from the older dramatic conception of women either as a toy or as a goddess or an idol to be worshipped in a shrine. None of us in this modern generation are likely to forget either Mr. Shaw's Candida or the same dramatist's Ann Whitefield. The first is to me, I confess, a somewhat enigmatic personage. You will remember what Candida, the excellent wife of an excellent clergyman, dared to do in the play bearing her name. She knows that she is loved by her clergyman husband; she is also aware that she is the object of a fantastic adoration on the part of a young poet, Eugene Marchbanks. She daringly puts lover and husband to the test, and says that whoever is the weaker and needs her most will have her for the future. She plays this cruel game, although she knows that her stupid common-place self-opinionated husband—who, by the way, is a very successful clergyman—adores her, and that her namby-pamby sentimental febrile lover puts her on a pinnacle as being much too great for her commonplace surroundings. Of course, the dramatist gets out of his difficulty by explaining to us that the Rev. James Morell was in reality the weaker man who needed Candida most of all, and so all comes right in the end. But whether we are for this reason to forgive the wife, or whether she is acting as all women act in similar circumstances, are questions which the mere man finds it difficult to answer. Mr. Shaw's heroines are not always pleasant people, with the exception, of course, of Lady Cecily Waynflete in *Captain Brassbound's Conversion*. Some of them are of the hard huntress type, like Ann Whitefield in *Man and Superman,* who runs down her quarry with magnificent persistence and success. Barbara is a subtle conception, subtle and interesting, but her creator does not improve her character as the play proceeds. To compare the women of Mr. Shaw with the women of Ibsen would be an interesting topic, but one for which, unfortunately, I have no space.

The women of Sir Arthur Pinero are very carefully drawn, and in this perhaps, once again, we can see the influence, consciously or unconsciously, exercised by Ibsen. I have already referred to Leslie Brudenell in *The Profligate,* and to Paula in *The Second Mrs. Tanqueray*. I have yet to deal with the heroine of *The Benefit of the Doubt,* with *The Notorious Mrs. Ebbsmith,* and with *Iris*. With regard to Agnes Ebbsmith, interesting character as she undoubtedly is, there is perhaps less to be said because the play in which she appears is not so carefully wrought, or at all events is not so successful as the others of which mention has been made. Still, the character of Agnes Ebbsmith raises several most curious problems which are worth studying, quite apart from the success or want of success of the play called by her name. There is a strange tragedy about the woman. She is full of independence and spirit, and without any doubt she wanted to be the companion, friend, and fellow-worker of Lucas Cleeve, with whom she had elected to live. Perhaps Lucas Cleeve himself thought at one time that life was possible both for him and for Agnes on the high platonic plane of companionship and *camaraderie*. But because Lucas is a half-baked creature, or rather because he is merely the ordinary man, *l'homme moyen sensuel,* the experiment is a failure. Agnes is forced, deliber-

ately, to appeal to his senses and lower nature in order to fortify his constancy.

I turn to *The Benefit of the Doubt* and to *Iris*. Both the heroines of these plays are, from an ordinary masculine standpoint, neither sincere nor praiseworthy. Yet, on the contrary, thanks to Pinero's art, we are only too ready to forgive them both. We make excuses for them; we say that circumstances were too strong, that their positions were unendurable, that their sins ought to be forgiven. Here is Theo Fraser in *The Benefit of the Doubt*. She is married to a hard, dour Scotsman, Fraser of Locheen, who will wear kilts at the dinner table, and insists on having his deplorable bagpipes played on every occasion. Well, it is not fair to a sensitive woman, on whose nerves these things act with terrible force. So she flies for refuge to Jack Allingham, and there is a scandal, an action for divorce, and the judge gives her the benefit of the doubt. Now, mark what ensued. Fraser, not being an absolute ass, says that they must go abroad in order to get over the malevolence of spiteful tongues. He wants to hush up scandal like Torvald in *A Doll's House*. Theo resolutely refuses to do anything of the kind, and says, on the contrary, that the situation must be faced, and that they must remain in town. She may have been right in principle, but the sequel proves that she was wrong in fact. Upset by her husband's arguments, she goes once more to Jack Allingham in a half-fainting condition; she drinks champagne on an empty stomach, and, not to put too fine a point on it, she gets intoxicated. In this condition she implores Jack Allingham to run away with her. Not a nice woman this, and yet, upon my soul, the dramatist makes us forgive her! Apparently he forgives her himself, for he lets her fall into the hands of the wife of a worthy bishop, who is going to spread her immaculate reputation over Theo's peccadilloes and gradually restore her in the public credit. I am always wondering why this fine play, *The Benefit of the Doubt,* has never been revived. I suppose we must wait until the National Theatre is established before we can hope to see it again. The first and second acts are masterpieces.

But let us continue with *Iris*. Iris Bellamy, according to her own account, is more sinned against than sinning. She is left a widow at a very early age, with a certain fortune, which she is to resign if she marries again. Round her are at least three men—Croker Harrington (who perhaps does not count, for he is a faithful, dog-like creature); Laurence Trenwith, an impecunious young man, with whom she is sincerely in love; and the Mephistopheles of the piece, Frederick Maldonado, a hard, wealthy, masterful financier. Now, Iris cannot be straight with any of these. She cannot make up her mind to live in poverty abroad with Laurence Trenwith. Poor Croker hardly enters into her calculations. Suddenly she is herself confronted with poverty, owing to the ill-doings of a rascally attorney; and this is Maldonado's chance. He leaves a cheque-book with her, and she makes use of it. He prepares a beautifully furnished flat for her, leaving the key with her, and eventually she drifts into accepting it. Then Trenwith returns, and she tells him the whole story, expecting him to forgive her. Immensely hurt at his refusal to have anything to do with her, both hurt and surprised, she is left to Maldonado's mercy: and because he has discovered the intrigue between Iris and Trenwith, she is finally driven out into the streets. You will say that she is punished, and terribly punished. It is quite true. The point is that we are genuinely sorry for her. And yet could there be a more worthless woman? Was she wicked, or merely weak? We really cannot say. Perhaps she was what Paula was originally before she commenced her career as a courtesan. But the case stands as it does with Sophy Fullgarney in *The Gay Lord Quex,* whom the hero very justly describes as a cat which scratches the hand that tries to pet it. Yet Sophy Fullgarney becomes in the sequel a quite estimable character, although she is a mean, despicable spy. And Iris, too, lives in our memory, although she is quite non-moral, perhaps even basely immoral. Need I add the instance of Paula Tanqueray? Did she ever love Aubrey Tanqueray? I think not. I think she only cared for comfort, for the satisfaction of living in a proper home, of being respected as a legitimate wife. She betrays her husband at every point. Capriciousness is the least of her vices. She asks her disreputable friends to stay with her. Even if she had won the love of her step-daughter, Ellean, it is doubtful if she would have known what to do with it. And yet—and yet—we are more than a little inclined to forgive Paula Tanqueray, although she had absolutely ruined a good man, and brought positive agony to his daughter. "There is a soul of goodness in things evil"; that is the dramatist's lesson. Or perhaps it is only an illustration of the famous text, "To know all is to pardon all." Pinero has made us understand his women, and though our judgment and our common sense rebel, we are sympathetically interested in them, and inclined to grant them plenary absolution.

We have yet to see how the progress of realism in drama has manifested itself among our latest contemporary writers, and especially among such dramatists as Mr. George Bernard Shaw—who is in some respects perhaps too fantastic to be called a realist—Mr. St. John Hankin, Mr. Granville Barker, Mr. Arnold Bennett, Mr. Galsworthy, and Mr. Stanley Houghton. I hope in a subsequent essay to find an opportunity of dealing with some of the most modern developments. In the present instance it seemed worth while to spend some little time over a period, which means more perhaps to the middle-aged man than it does to the more youthful of our contemporaries, and especially over the work of Sir Arthur Pinero, whom this present age, a little fickle and oblivious of what has been done in the past, has begun somewhat ungratefully to disparage. . . .

We have been living under the tyranny of realism for some years past, and in some respects I think the dominion of realistic modes of thought has become an obsession. If I confine myself to what realism means in drama, I should say that its tendency is to lead us straight to pessimism, to that characteristically sombre and gloomy pessimism which has invaded foreign literatures even more than our own, and of which the Russian literature affords us admirable specimens. Why should realism lead to pessimism? The answer is quite simple, and also instructive. The realistic treatment of human character lays stress on the individual, his rights, his claims, his sorrows, his passions, all that he demands of life and all that life seems to deny him.

Now, despite the teaching of Ibsen, the individual is not always right as against society, nor does ultimate wisdom reside with the minority as against the majority. The individual by himself is a weak and feeble thing, and the enumeration of his particular grievances distorts the proper perspective of human existence in general and depreciates the average health and sanity of the social state. Reflecting on his personal woes, the individual naturally becomes a pessimist; or, if we may put it in another way, selfishness, a narrow absorbing egotism, is the root of all evil. At all events our realists, both in literature and in drama, exhaust themselves in denouncing the injustice and the hopelessness of human life, because they persist in taking the standpoint of the acutely sensitive individual instead of regarding such matters from an objective or world standpoint.

One of the best ways of trying to discover the tendencies of a particular movement amongst ourselves is to see what is happening in foreign literatures. The Russian literature is very apt for this purpose, and, as we are aware, modern Russian literature has been not incorrectly described as "pessimism devoid of humour." I will not take such well-known writers as Tolstoy, Gorky, Dostoieffsky. I will only mention one of the modern novelists, Artzybascheff. A recent novel, entitled *At the Utmost Limit,* has no other theme than to portray the black night, the utter and irremediable senselessness of all earthly existence, and to suggest suicide as the only panacea for human ill. Nevertheless, what is happening even in Russia, the home of pessimism? There is a school of younger writers who, in reaction from this state of things, might almost be described as optimists. Something of the same sort has been happening among ourselves.

There are only two ways of waking from the nightmare of realism when pushed to its extreme of egotistic mania. One is the way of symbolism, the way of dreams. You may tell yourself that the only means to discover the mystery of the universe, and to reconcile the contradictions and disorders of life, is to shut your eyes to the ordinary world and throw the reins on the neck of imagination and fancy, living in the mystic's paradise, finding an ideal happiness in a world within the four walls of human consciousness. That is what Maeterlinck does in some of his plays. Many hints of the same kind of thing are to be found in Ibsen, who, as his life progressed, grew to be more and more fond of symbols. In a certain fashion also the Celtic mode of thought of Yeats and other writers of the Irish school affords another illustration. Mysticism then is one of the modes of reaction, which come easy to some dreaming minds, a mysticism which may be ascetic or may be sensuous, but which is at all events wholly imaginative. I am not sure that it is the more hopeful or the more effective path to lead us out of our swamp of despair.

There is another way. You may choose not to ignore the evils of life, but you may study them, just as the physician and the surgeon study all the morbid growths of mental and corporeal life. By a close study of the dreadful foe you may in the end master the secret of his destructive power, and, perchance, you may come upon this discovery, that the evils of life do not flow from the nature of things, but from human blindness, from human selfishness, from precisely that lack of cohesion amongst the various members of the human family which alone can raise them to higher levels of culture and happiness. If men were more sensitive to each other's feelings, if they could understand one another better, they would cease to deplore their own sufferings and find that life in the larger sense, a corporate life of consenting human individualities, contains within itself potentialities of real happiness. *La joie de vivre,* which is extinguished by narrow egotism, may burst out afresh in altruistic aims, in the efforts of a community to purge itself of its maladies, in its resolute concerted striving towards an exalted goal. Quite elementary and simple things like pity, and affection, and love, supply us with materials, not for wailing and misery, but for a rich contentment and a serene peace. And so from the realism of dreadful facts we get to the idealism of simple emotions, the discovery that man is not by nature depraved, but by nature good and filled with the joy of life, finding in love and human service the satisfaction alike of his heart and his head. Perhaps before that morrow dawns man must needs pass through the valley of the shadow of doubt and despair. But he may win the happy secret at last, and, if I may judge once more from the tendencies of Russian literature, and from the work especially of the young writer Alexis Remizoff, it is thus that we may find the path towards our future deliverance. We shall not be untrue to life; we shall not close our eyes to the existence of evil; but having once grappled with the malady of pessimistic selfishness we shall discover how the idealism of simple things can, as though by magic, make us healthful and sane.

> *W. L. Courtney, "Realistic Drama—II," in his* Old Saws and Modern Instances, *Chapman and Hall, Ltd., 1918, pp. 180-200.*

Negative characterizations of Ibsen's admirers:

Lovers of prurience and dabblers in impropriety who are eager to gratify their illicit tastes under the pretence of art.—*Evening Standard.*

Ninety-seven per cent. of the people who go to see *Ghosts* are nasty-minded people who find the discussion of nasty subjects to their taste in exact proportion to their nastiness.—*Sporting and Dramatic News.*

The sexless. . . . The unwomanly woman, the unsexed females, the whole army of unprepossessing cranks in petticoats. . . . Educated and muck-ferreting dogs. . . . Effeminate men and male women. . . . They all of them—men and women alike—know that they are doing not only a nasty but an illegal thing. . . . The Lord Chamberlain left them alone to wallow in *Ghosts.* . . . Outside a silly clique, there is not the slightest interest in the Scandinavian humbug or all his works. . . . A wave of human folly.—*Truth.*

> *Quoted by Bernard Shaw, in his* The Quintessence of Ibsenism, *Brentano's, 1908.*

J. L. Styan

[*Born and educated in England, Styan has taught at several American universities and published numerous books on drama, including* Drama, Stage and Audience *(1975), and* Chekhov in Performance: A Commentary on the Major Plays *(1971). In this essay he discusses the conflicts engendered by the introduction of dramatic realism into Ireland's somewhat isolated theatrical world.*]

Irish literary nationalism at the turn of the century was divided from the start. On the one hand was the loving desire to revive the heroic legends of Ireland's unhappy past, and on the other the need to represent the passionate purposes of the home-rule movement. The Dublin theatre became the centre of the literary awakening, a place where patriots could meet, and where the art of the drama could deal in folk-tales or politics, memories or prophecies. There the Gaelic League of Douglas Hyde, bent on reviving the Irish language and its culture, could quicken the imagination, and the nationalism of the Irish Literary Society could find a platform.

Irish dramatists writing for the London theatre have been the mainstay of English comedy since the seventeenth century: the distinguished company includes Congreve, Farquhar, Steele, Goldsmith, Sheridan, Boucicault, Wilde and Shaw. Their satirical wit, however, had done little or nothing for Irish drama itself. It fell to an Anglo-Irishman, William Butler Yeats (1865–1939), already an established poet, to promote a national Irish drama, this with the initial help of the writers Edward Martyn and George Moore. Yeats decided that the drama was the most likely form for stimulating a literary revival of wide appeal, and he was personally drawn to the folk imagination of the past—a factor which would have strange consequences. His lyrical verse play, *The Land of Heart's Desire,* had already been produced in London in 1894, but it was unknown in Ireland. A production of this rather sentimental piece at the Avenue Theatre, Dublin, in the same year could be said to mark the modest beginning of the Irish Dramatic Movement.

The journal of the Irish Literary Society, *Beltaine* (later, *Samhain*), at first urged those interested in the new cause to join in the advances being made in Europe. But at this time continental theatre was revolving round Ibsen and Ibsenism, and since Yeats did not much like Ibsen, the Irish movement did not follow the path of the Independent Theatres. Yeats had seen some of Ibsen's plays done in London by the Independent Theatre Society, and at first thought he had found the model for a theatre in Dublin. He could say at first that Ibsen was 'the one great master the modern stage has produced' and believed that 'we Irish' had 'far greater need of the severe discipline of French and Scandinavian drama than of Shakespeare's luxuriance' (*Plays and Controversies*). But he had seen only Ibsen's social plays, and found them insufficiently poetic for his idea of a national theatre.

After seeing *A Doll's House* in London, Yeats reported some years later on its first night:

> I was divided in mind, I hated the play . . . I re-

sented being invited to admire dialogue so close to modern educated speech that music and style were impossible . . . As time passed Ibsen became in my eyes the chosen author of very clever young journalists . . . and yet neither I nor my generation could escape him because, though we and he had not the same friends, we had the same enemies (*Autobiographies*).

Again on *A Doll's House*:

Ibsen has sincerity and logic beyond any writer of our time, and we are all seeking to learn them at his hands; but is he not a good deal less than the greatest of all times, because he lacks beautiful and vivid language? (*Plays and Controversies*).

And after seeing *Ghosts*:

At the first performance of *Ghosts* I could not escape from an illusion unaccountable to me at the time. All the characters seemed to me to be less than life-size; the stage, though it was but the little Royalty stage, seemed larger than I had ever seen it. Little whimpering puppets moved here and there in the middle of that great abyss (*Plays and Controversies*).

He recognized that *Rosmersholm* had touched symbolism, but complained of its 'stale odour of spilt poetry'. He also saw the danger in the second-rate problem plays that followed in Ibsen's wake, and was determined to avoid what he considered to be middle-class theatre: 'It is always Shakespeare or Sophocles, and not Ibsen, that makes us say, "How true, how often I have felt as that man feels".'

In his Preface to *The Playboy of the Western World* in 1907, Synge would echo Yeats in criticizing the drama of Ibsen and Zola as 'dealing with the reality of life in joyless and pallid words', and in his Preface to *The Tinker's Wedding* in the same year, he argued that the drama did not have to reproduce problems to be serious; it was enough that it gave 'the nourishment, not very easy to define, on which our imaginations live'. So it was that Europe's Ibsenite impulse was scarcely felt in Dublin. It was left to the Gate Theatre after 1928 to pursue continental experiments with expressionism and other modes neglected by the Irish National Theatre.

The Irish movement was exceptional in being run by writers and not by actors, which may account for the quarrels that followed, and, in Denis Johnston's view, for its remarkable survival. Yeats's dream was of a 'people's theatre', one in which artists could return to the 'sources of art', Ireland's primitive mythology and its native speech, in order to create on stage 'that life of poetry where every man can see his own image'. In his way, Yeats was for both the truth of reality and the ideal of the imagination at the same time. In the *Boston Evening Transcript,* he said he sought both to represent 'a real life where men talk picturesque and musical words', and to show that 'our theatre of folk art is . . . an expression of the Irish mind of today'.

The next step was to agree on a policy. Yeats met the influential landowner Lady Augusta Gregory (1852–1932) at her home in Coole, Galway, in 1898, and it was there in another historic meeting that they together conceived the idea of an Irish Literary Theatre based in Dublin. They drafted this manifesto:

We propose to have performed in Dublin, in the spring of every year, certain Celtic and Irish plays, which whatever be their degree of excellence will be written with a high ambition, and so to build up a Celtic and Irish school of dramatic literature. We hope to find in Ireland an uncorrupted and imaginative audience trained to listen by its passion for oratory, and believe that our desire to bring upon the stage the deeper thoughts and emotions of Ireland will ensure for us a tolerant welcome, and that freedom to experiment which is not found in theatres of England, and without which no new movement in art or literature can succeed. We will show that Ireland is not the home of buffoonery and of easy sentiment, as it has been represented, but the home of an ancient idealism. We are confident of the support of all Irish people, who are weary of misrepresentation, in carrying on a work that is outside all the political questions that divide us.

This document is reproduced in Lady Gregory's *Our Irish Theatre.*

The reference to buffoonery and easy sentiment is to that unreal image of the stage Irishman and his activities which plagued the drama of the nineteenth century in the need for quick laughter. Maurice Bourgeois has usefully described in Jonsonian terms this 'Pat' or 'Paddy' or 'Teague':

He has an atrocious Irish brogue, makes perpetual jokes, blunders and bulls in speaking, and never fails to utter, by way of Hibernian seasoning, some wild screech or oath of Gaelic origin at every third word; he has an unsurpassable gift of 'blarney' and cadges for tips and free drinks. His hair is of a fiery red; he is rosy-cheeked, massive and whiskey-loving. His face is one of simian bestiality, with an expression of diabolical archness written all over it. He wears a tall felt hat . . . with a cutty clay pipe stuck in front, an open shirt collar, a three-caped coat, knee-breeches, worsted stockings and cockaded brogue-shoes . . . His main characteristics . . . are his swagger, his boisterousness and his pugnacity.

In some of this we may recognize Sheridan's prototype for Sir Lucius O'Trigger of *The Rivals,* and may be sorry to lose him. But Yeats was taking a fundamental step in asking for a new degree of realism. It can be readily seen from the manifesto how different from the naturalistic theatre of Europe was the intention of the Irish movement, but it nevertheless aimed at comparable ideals of truth, and, like its European counterpart, wanted the chance to break new ground in opposition to the commercial theatre. In the event, the Abbey was the first successful English-speaking repertory company, even if run by writers and not by actors.

Yet, being run by writers, the new theatre was set about by rules. In its early years, Yeats prepared a further document entitled, 'Advice to Playwrights who are Sending Plays to the Abbey, Dublin'. This extract summarizes well enough Yeats's early ideas:

> The Abbey Theatre is a subsidized theatre with an educational object. It will, therefore, be useless as a rule to send it plays intended as popular entertainments and that alone, or originally written for performance by some popular actor at the popular theatres. A play to be suitable for performance at the Abbey should contain some criticism of life, founded on the experience or personal observation of the writer, or some vision of life, of Irish life by preference, important from its beauty or from some excellence of style; and this intellectual quality is not more necessary to tragedy than to the gayest comedy.
>
> We do not desire propagandist plays, nor plays written mainly to serve some obvious moral purpose; for art seldom concerns itself with those interests or opinions that can be defended by argument, but with realities of emotion and character that become self-evident when made vivid to the imagination . . . A work of art, though it must have the effect of nature, is art because it is not nature, as Goethe said: and it must possess a unity unlike the accidental profusion of nature.

Here again, Yeats clearly indicated the Society's rejection of the conventional fare of the popular theatre. Here, too, he sowed the seeds of dissent from naturalism.

In the 1904 issue of *Samhain,* Yeats went further, and declared his preference for tragedy over social drama:

> The arts are at their greatest when they seek for a life growing always more scornful of everything that is not itself and passing into its own fullness, as it were, even more completely as all that is created out of the passing mode of society slips from it; and attaining that fullness, perfectly it may be—and from this is tragic joy and the perfectness of tragedy—when the world itself has slipped away in death.

It is good that in principle the movement should be national without being nationalistic, but eventually Yeats's idealism, his desire for a drama composed without restrictions upon the imagination, will also eliminate character itself, and with it the human and social element that was the stock-in-trade of the realists.

The first productions of the Irish Literary Theatre were put on in the Ancient Concert Rooms, Dublin, in 1899. Yeats's *The Countess Cathleen,* written in the manner of a poetic fantasy by Maeterlinck, and Martyn's *The Heather Field,* an Ibsenite tragedy that had been refused in London, were chosen to launch the new movement. They were two plays which drew upon the Irish past and on the beauty of Irish speech, but which represented uncomfortably conflicting styles. *The Countess Cathleen* told the legendary story of a saint who sold her soul for Ireland, and it was quite unlike Martyn's play. *The Heather Field* reflected Strindberg as much as Ibsen, being about a poor wife who felt she had to commit her husband to an asylum, in spite of her need to support her children and herself. Realism and romance sat uneasily side by side, and Yeats

heard the first murmurings of distrust. Next year at the Gaiety Theatre the same contradiction was felt, with martyn's dreamlike *Maeve* set against his comedy of local politics, *The Bending of the Bough.* This precarious arrangement persisted, with Irish myth rubbing shoulders with plays of social commitment, until Martyn and Moore broke away to found the Irish Independent Theatre with the intention of producing despised European plays along with the native product. However, the Literary Theatre had at least begun to build itself an audience, if on somewhat parochial foundations.

These first productions were received with enthusiasm, although only English actors were to be had. As time passed, the Irish actors W. G. and Frank Fay greatly encouraged the submission of native plays when they reorganized the Literary Theatre as the Irish National Dramatic Company, employing only Irish actors. The year 1902 seemed to bring victory for Yeats's romantic theories when his own *Kathleen Ni Houlihan* and A. E.'s *Deirdre* appeared on the same bill. With Maude Gonne, the Irish patriot and beauty, playing the part of the lovely Kathleen who symbolized the spirit of Ireland, the direction of the Irish movement seemed assured. Then in 1904, an unexpected subsidy came from an English benefactor, Miss A. E. F. Horniman, a rich spinster, heiress to the family tea business. Annie Horniman guaranteed the company its own playhouse, which quickly became known as the Abbey Theatre. The Abbey was a tiny theatre, with a capacity of only 562 and a proscenium opening of only 18 feet, but in many ways it was just the right size to handle the intimate detail of realism and to excite those mutually patriotic feelings the movement wished to foster.

Certain other developments also offset the strongly poetic repertoire. Between 1903 and 1912, Lady Gregory herself for her own amusement wrote numerous one-act village comedies, including one or two tragedies. These little plays came closer to a realistic representation of Irish peasant life and speech than anything that had been written before. The best of them are *Spreading the News* (1904), *Hyacinth Halvey* (1906), *The Gaol Gate* (a patriotic tragedy, 1906), *The Rising of the Moon* (1907) and *The Workhouse Ward* (1908). She also translated several comedies of Molière and Goldoni, done into 'Kiltartan' Anglo-Irish. Lady Gregory said that she had never cared much for the theatre, but the delight with which, in her middle age, she discovered that she could write plays is to be felt in her book, *Our Irish Theatre.* She experimented eagerly with themes and techniques, happily working out her ideas in practice and not in theory. The limitations of the company and the small stage also compelled her to exercise extreme economy in her stage planning; for similar reasons the original first act of Synge's *Playboy,* depicting Christy and his father in the fields, was later jettisoned, to the immense advantage of the play as a whole. In her study *The Irish Dramatic Movement,* Una Ellis-Fermor considered the influence of the live theatre on the written drama to be 'astonishing', and described how *Spreading the News* was conceived as a tragedy, but was turned into a comedy simply because that was what the Abbey needed to balance Yeats's verse plays.

Of greater importance, the plays of John Millington Synge (1871–1909) were written for the Abbey in its early years, and directed the movement along paths that Yeats could not have anticipated. Synge's talent as a playwright overcame all theories and all arguments, and the new impulse he started was continued powerfully after the war by Sean O'Casey—to the point where Yeats and O'Casey came into direct conflict.

Like Yeats and Lady Gregory, Synge was an Anglo-Irish Protestant, and his writing on behalf of a largely Catholic audience was consequently suspect to begin with. Controversy over his plays began with his first one-act comedy of 1903, *The Shadow of the Glen,* and reached its peak in 1907 with the week of riots that accompanied *The Playboy of the Western World.* No doubt the Irish enjoy the fun of making a disturbance in the theatre, but in this case an incident became a cause. In the New York production of *The Playboy* in 1911, rioting broke out again, and in Philadelphia the following year the company was actually arrested and put in prison. In Dublin, night after night the actors struggled on through the noise of the crowd and the pelting of vegetables. But those who came to hiss and boo at least paid to go in, and the Abbey grew relatively prosperous. Moreover, Synge's fame spread abroad, and with it the reputation of the Irish drama.

As it happened, Synge was an apolitical man, and unconcerned with Irish nationalism, but the violent reaction to his drama was the immediate result of the overheated feelings which surround the birth of any patriotic revolution. He had his share of Irish mysticism and feeling for nature, but the important truth was that he was the first major realist of the Irish movement. He drew directly upon the peasant life he had observed among the Aran Islanders, and was Ireland's first playwright to insist upon a certain critical honesty. There is little in Synge's plays which resembles the work of Ibsen or Strindberg, but in spite of Yeats they had subtly encouraged the new Irish theatre away from its insularity, and Synge was seeing his countrymen with the frank eyes of a realist who stood, as it were, well apart from their heated interests. Of course, in its narrower concern for the honourable image of Ireland, its Church and its womanhood, the Dublin public at the time was unaware of the quality and stature of the drama it saw.

In 'The Cutting of an Agate', Yeats wrote that Synge seemed by nature unfitted to think a political thought: 'In Ireland he loved only what was wild in its people.' But by now every Abbey play was closely scrutinized by Arthur Griffith's *United Irishman* and subjected to its militant journalese. Synge's first play, *The Shadow of the Glen,* drew upon the ancient farce of the young wife and the old husband who pretends to die in order to test her and spy on her. Nora, the young wife, does indeed have a lover in the traditional way, and as a result Synge was considered to have 'attacked the sanctity of marriage'. When applied to farce, such a comment is totally irrelevant, but loveless marriages and faithless wives have no place in nationalist sentiment. Blinded by this slight against Irish women, few saw that the story of Nora was never intended as a social problem, but, if anything, as a spiritual one. Behind the

high spirits of the play lay Nora's fear of loneliness, as well as her desire to be free—a light view of the *Doll's House* situation. In vain did Synge protest in his Preface to *The Tinker's Wedding* that 'the drama, like the symphony, does not teach or prove anything', but the student of the Irish Dramatic Movement needs to study the political and religious assumptions of the Abbey audience to assess the truth of that.

The Playboy of the Western World tells the deceptively simple tale of Christy Mahon, a young farm lad of the Atlantic west coast. Christy has run away from home after he thinks he has killed his father with a loy in their potato field. He arrives at a shebeen run by Pegeen Mike, and there everyone assumes that he is running from the police. He soon becomes the hero of the village girls, and is delighted with his new reputation: 'Wasn't I a foolish fellow not to kill my father in the years gone by?', he asks innocently. His story of the loy swells with his glory, until his father, very much alive, arrives with a bandaged head and a foul temper. Now Christy is no hero at all, just the callow youth he always was, and the villagers turn on him viciously—they burn his leg—and throw him out. Dublin took this fantasy literally. How could patricide be so approved? Worse, how could a bachelor sleep under the roof of an unmarried Irish girl? The play was a travesty of both Irish womanhood and Irish manhood, nothing short of blasphemy against holy Ireland herself.

Judgment on the play's 'bestial depravity' and its 'malignant travesty of Irish character and of all that is sacred in Catholic life', as delivered by the Irish in Dublin, Boston and New York, strangely echoed the reception of *Ghosts.* Yeats's comment on the riots was that they were an outcry against the play's unsentimental way of seeing, 'a kind of sarcasm', as he put it. Synge had discovered his own mode of acid comedy by cutting down Pegeen's simple dream of 'a fine fiery fellow with great rages when his temper's roused' to the size of a simple-minded Christy Mahon, and placing at the centre the obvious but outrageous irony that the reality is not so impressive as the report. In fact, the reasons usually offered for the violence of the protest against *The Playboy* are not enough in themselves. No Irish audience could truly have believed that the oaths uttered by the characters constituted blasphemy—they were heard everywhere in Dublin. Nor did the city audiences really believe that the west coast peasantry was so noble, or so simple, that it would not provide cover for a murderer. The Dubliner may be an idealist, but he is not a fool. Yet no doubt he did perceive that Synge's manipulation of his fantasies was something of an insult, and we turn to the structure of the play itself, the way it works in performance, for clues to the real source of Irish indignation.

At the outset, Christy is a poor sort of creature and his deed is reprehensible by any code; yet he progresses to become 'a proven hero in the end of all'. Within this ironic framework, irony is piled upon irony as the audience rejects Christy, and then lends him grudging admiration, rejects and then approves the attitudes of those in the Mayo shebeen. By his mere presence, the snivelling coward Shawn Keogh constitutes a sarcastic comment on the situation, since for Pegeen's life partner he is the only alternative to a parricide. The miserable Shawn with his false piety is also apparently the Church's only answer in lieu of the presence of Father Reilly and the saints of God, all kept well offstage. When Pegeen's father, Michael James, tries to prompt Shawn to claim Pegeen for himself, Shawn can only whine that he is 'afeard to be jealous of a man did slay his da'. Which, for the audience, is reasonable enough, but no less vexing all the same.

Old Mahon himself is a second ironic presence lurking throughout the play, constantly undercutting Christy's heroic image by obstinately refusing to be dead. The audience is ready enough to grant the playboy some of the stage glory he has acquired by winning races on the beach, flaunting his colourful jockey silks and attracting all the young women in their bright red dresses (as authentically worn by the Aran peasant girls). He even pleases us by threatening Shawn's skull with another loy. But in the latter part of the play Old Mahon's sly presence is planted like a warning, threatening to thwart our pleasures. Nevertheless, Michael James himself accepts the idea that 'a daring fellow is the jewel of the world', even though he did 'split his father's middle with a single clout', and presumably may well do it again to a father-in-law; and so it seems, by dint of Synge's ironic stagecraft, that Christy's heroic image is solid and complete. When, therefore, Christy is finally chased off, threatening to kill his father a second time if necessary, the audience, as much as Pegeen herself, feels the pain and annoyance of self-deception.

Synge showed those on and off the stage how hollow is the fantasy of heroism upon which people feed, and not everyone who saw the first production was insensitive to the play's finely tuned comment on the Irish community. P. D. Kenny wrote in the *Irish Times* on 30 January 1907,

> I cannot but admire the moral courage of the man who has shot his dreadful searchlight into the cherished accumulation of social skeletons. He has led our vision through the Abbey-street stage into the heart of Connacht, and revealed to us there truly terrible truths, of our own making, which we dare not face for the present. The merciless accuracy of his revelation is more than we can bear. Our eyes tremble at it. The words chosen are, like the things they express, direct and dreadful, by themselves intolerable to conventional taste, yet full of vital beauty in their truth to the conditions of life, to the character they depict, and to the sympathies they suggest. It is as if we looked into a mirror for the first time, and found ourselves hideous. We fear to face the thing. We shrink at the word for it. We scream.

In other accounts of the production, there is little evidence of its quality, and perhaps we should assume that any element of farce or fantasy in the play was overlaid by the intimate realism of the Abbey performances.

Riders to the Sea (1904), Synge's little tragic masterpiece of Irish life and character, had been a safer play, the only work of his that the movement had accepted without question. *The Well of the Saints* (1905) was denounced, and the more anticlerical and inflammatory comedy *The Tinker's Wedding* (1907) was prudently never produced at the

Abbey. Man cannot stand very much reality, said T. S. Eliot, and even realism of Synge's ironic variety, with locations far away from cosmopolitan Dublin, must be adjusted to its audience. Compromise may have been the chief reason for the subsequent decline of the Irish National Theatre over several years, but it took on new life after the establishment of the Irish Free State. At that time the movement had thrown up the vital early plays of Sean O'Casey (1880–1964), in some eyes Ireland's greatest playwright.

O'Casey offered the Irish National Theatre and its audiences a new set of challenges in *The Shadow of a Gunman* (1923), *Juno and the Paycock* (1924) and *The Plough and the Stars* (1926). His next great play, *The Silver Tassie* (1928), was the cause of a divisive quarrel with Yeats over its use of expressionism . . . ; but his decision to go into exile in Devon was a double disaster for the Irish movement and for the playwright, who continued to write plays for the rest of his life without the use of a native theatre to test and nourish his art. It is easy to see why his work was in fundamental conflict with the original ideals of the movement. Born in an urban slum, O'Casey knew the life of the city poor as none of his predecessors had. Could Irish folk-tales also include such people? There is nothing mythical or heroic about the back streets of Dublin. Involved in the dock strike of 1913 and in the street fighting of the Easter Rebellion of 1916, O'Casey was a Communist and an anti-Catholic, a realist with a cause, a passionate Dubliner writing for real Dubliners. In his best work he achieved a Chekhovian objectivity, infusing a grim drama of real events with an irrepressible Irish humour, and mixing comic and tragic elements in new ways to catch the full flavour of Irish life as he knew it.

The Abbey lost its momentum after the war because the new generation of Irish playwrights, like T. C. Murray and Lennox Robinson, was writing a more sentimental realism in spite of Yeats's original precepts. And when O'Casey began to write plays, he knew almost nothing of the Abbey and its traditions, and was too poor to have seen anything of Synge's work there. If he found a model anywhere, it was in the popular drama of Dion Boucicault (1820–90), whose effectiveness in the theatre he has been witness to, and whose plays seemed to work well both in Dublin and London, and on either side of the Atlantic. O'Casey knew many of Boucicault's more than 150 plays, and was especially familiar with those with Irish subjects, like *The Colleen Bawn; or, The Brides of Garryowen* (1860), which opened in New York, *Arragh-na-Pogue; or, The Wicklow Wedding* (1864), which opened in Dublin, and *The Shaughraun* (1874), in New York again—plays which expertly mixed comedy and suspense, but which only marginally touched the real Ireland. Therefore, when O'Casey put on a naturalistic stage the Dublin working-class he knew so well, he too appeared to be slipping into sentimentality by borrowing too many of the conventions of domestic melodrama.

The Shadow of a Gunman was received indifferently, perhaps because the play whetted the appetite for melodrama without satisfying it. Seumas Shields and Donal Davoren are a pedlar and a poet who share a tenement room in a

Dublin slum, harassed by the typical landlord of melodrama. The beautiful patriot Minnie is in love with Davoren, and is shot in error by British soldiers. There is no heroic sacrifice in this story, and O'Casey's touch is present in making the patriotism seem hollow. *Juno and the Paycock* also draws on the stock situations of melodrama, this time the 'temperance' drama; his drunkard, Captain Boyle, is possibly modelled on Boucicault's character Conn in *The Shaughraun*. Melodrama dogs the family when his pathetic son Johnny is wounded in the hip and has an arm blown off in the fighting. Daughter Mary is an Irish beauty who attracts a sinister English lawyer named Bentham. She should have known better than to consort with the enemy, for in the last act we learn that she is pregnant and that Bentham has deserted her. No matter, Mary's loyal Irish boyfriend Jerry declares that his love for her is 'greater and deeper than ever'. Meanwhile, a legacy the family thought it had received turns out to be a mistake, and Johnny is marched off to a deserter's death at the hands of his former comrades-in-arms.

With such a plot, it might seem that nothing could redeem this play from a watery grave. Yet O'Casey perversely makes his drunkard a comedian and his heroine something of a shrew: Boyle and his wife Juno remarkably reflect the tough realities of Dublin life. Then, when Jerry discovers that Mary is pregnant, we discover that his charity does not extend to fathering another man's child. And the play ends in total irony as Boyle and his drinking partner Joxer turn Ireland's misery to ridicule. O'Casey has used the resources of the old melodrama to attract his audience, and then has the uncomfortable capacity for laughing at us before we can laugh at him. His sense of humour is unpredictable: when Mrs Tancred, one of the neighbours, is burying her son, others are throwing a party. This kind of irreverence was such that in the *Dublin Magazine* for March 1925 Andrew E. Malone complained that Barry Fitzgerald as Boyle and F. J. McCormick as Joxer had 'played for laughter' at the expense of the noble Sara Allgood as Juno. This was the O'Casey touch, a new, ironic kind of realism, and it worked. In fact, *Juno and the Paycock* was the greatest success in the twenty-year history of the Abbey Theatre; performances were extended for a second week and people were still turned away. In *Ireland's Abbey Theatre* (1951), Lennox Robinson considered that the play had rescued the Irish National Theatre from 'artistic as well as financial bankruptcy'.

O'Casey's first plays drew upon recent events in Ireland: the Easter uprising of 1916, the troubles brought about by the Sinn Fein in 1920 and the Civil War of 1922. So he was deliberately treading on thin ice to begin with. His comic irony appeared to go too far with *The Plough and the Stars,* which caused riots of the kind remembered from the great days of *The Playboy.* In his book on O'Casey, David Krause suggests that the play exposed 'the trinity of Irish taboos—religion, sex and patriotism', and certainly feelings about the sacrifices of Easter Week were too fresh. The play even dared to defend the victims of the fighting before the heroes, and bring the sacred flag of the Republic into a pub. Irish womanhood was again offended at Jennie Gogan's protest that each of her children 'was got between th' bordhers of th' Ten Commandments', and by the sight

of a prostitute on the stage: an Irish girl a whore? The actress Ria Mooney, who played Rosie Redmond, was warned that her career would be finished. And then to see the woman plying her trade at the same time as the patriot Joseph Plunkett proclaimed the Republic from the Post Office steps! The play shocked the would-be, sentimental patriots mercilessly, those, in Peter Kavanagh's view, 'who imagine Ireland to be as green and level as a lawn, where the girls go around with eyes cast down, green garlands in their hair, and Rosaries at their girdles, while the men, armed only with shillelaghs, beat heavily armed battalions of British soldiers' (Peter Kavanagh, *The Story of the Abbey Theatre,* 1946).

Vegetables, shoes and chairs were thrown and stink bombs exploded. Some of the audience climbed on to the stage and tried to set fire to the curtain; fights started with the actors. O'Casey collected the ladies who were flung off the stage and started a discussion group by the stage door. Heated speeches were delivered, and Yeats himself harangued the house with the immortal announcement, 'You have disgraced yourselves again!' And afterwards the *Catholic Bulletin* damned the play as 'sewage school' drama. According to his autobiography, it is from this time that O'Casey began to feel a certain revulsion for the Irish theatre; he wanted to avoid being suffocated in an atmosphere so nationalistic and narrow. 'Sean felt a surge of hatred for Kathleen ni Houlihan sweeping over him', he wrote in *Inishfallen Fare Thee Well.* 'He saw now that the one who had the walk of a queen could be a bitch at times'. The £100 award of the Hawthornden Prize for *Juno* at this time may have consoled him a little.

Nevertheless, the good old days of a realistic Irish drama seemed to have returned, even if as usual the heat of the occasion blurred the quality of production. Willie Fay and Maire Nic-Shiubhlaigh (Mary Walker), the Abbey's first leading lady, were the first to wrestle with the rhythms of the pseudo-Gaelic dialect Synge had invented after his visit to the west coast and transcribed without phonetic spelling. The importance of real dialect had never before been emphasized in a play to this extent, and now O'Casey was demanding authentic speech and behaviour. It was appreciated that the better the actors were, the more O'Casey's comic irony would hit home, and a first-rate Irish company was built up over the years. The Fays (William and Frank), Maire O'Neill (Polly Allgood), Sara Allgood, Arthur Sinclair, Barry Fitzgerald and F. J. McCormick were equal to the tones of a light, colloquial dialect, and could also catch the more sonorous notes heard occasionally. Even if isolation from the mainstream of European realistic experiment did not help to advance the Abbey's techniques, they had the virtue of simplicity, derived from the small size of the stage and Yeats's reaction against fussy business and the overelaboration of realistic detail. Writing in *Samhain* in 1902 of the production of A. E.'s *Deirdre,* he offered this advice:

> The background should be as of little importance as the background of a portrait-group, and it should, when possible, be of one colour or of one tint, that the persons on the stage, wherever they stand, may harmonize with it or contrast with it and preoccupy our attention. Their out-

line should be clear and not broken up into the outline of windows and wainscotting, or lost into the edges of colours.

At that time Yeats was thinking of a poetic stage, and arguing for a drama in which poetic language should be preeminent; his experiments in a symbolic mode would follow.

O'Casey's city realism was a far cry from Yeats's verse drama, yet he too would in time become a severe critic of realism. For neither Yeats nor O'Casey were Ibsenites, nor strictly romantics, and Yeats's limitations as a playwright were not such that he did not hold the art of drama well above the narrowness to which nationalism can reduce it. In the *Boston Evening Transcript* in 1911, George Moore wrote that while Yeats had 'no knowledge of the technique of the stage and no aptitude for learning it', and although he 'seemed the last man in the world who would succeed in running a theatre', he 'knew how to stoop to conquer, and he conquered, because he was possessed of an idea, and an idea is always sufficient to secure success'.

> *J. L. Styan, "Conflicts in Dublin: The Irish Dramatic Movement," in his* Modern Drama in Theory and Practice, Vol. 1: Realism and Naturalism, *Cambridge University Press, 1981, pp. 91-108.*

Stanley Kauffmann

[*Kauffmann is one of America's most well-known contemporary film and theater critics. A contributor of reviews to several magazines, he is currently the film critic for the* New Republic. *In the following essay, he examines the careers and artistic aims of Augustin Daly and David Belasco, directors who introduced realism into the scenery and acting styles of late-nineteenth-century American theatrical productions.*]

If we distinguish between drama and theater, a significant aspect of American cultural history becomes clear. Realism entered the American drama (playwriting) toward the end of the nineteenth century and reached full strength with the early work of Eugene O'Neill. This is widely known. What is less widely known is that, at least fifty years before O'Neill, realism entered the American theater (performance). The directing and acting and design of plays had begun to become realistic before O'Neill was born. Compared with Europe, American drama in the second half of the nineteenth century was laggard; compared with Europe, American theater was in the vanguard. Two men in particular, Augustin Daly and David Belasco, authors and producers of plays in the conservative modes popular at the time, directed those very plays with a progressivism that led to the theater of our day.

Content and style are rarely so discrete as they are in this matter. Almost every play mentioned hereafter, with the obvious exception of classics, is apparently well forgotten; but what was done with many of them is ill forgotten. Here, I will attempt to use a method familiar in film criticism, the auteur theory, in which execution is valued above the script. In film criticism, the auteur theory has severe limits if only because performance and script are not separable in any effective sense. But in the theater, where performance is ephemeral, the chief surviving element is the script; so judgment of the script—that is, literary judgment—often dominates our opinions of the theater's past. I attempt here to redress that dominance, to weigh in the performance elements, even to give them precedence. Reviews, memoirs, biographies, histories, and photographs help to provide contemporary production context.

In the history of all performance arts, this is the usual road to judgment, and here, as usual, it has risks. We can never really know whether a historian's description is wholly accurate or his judgment reliable. As our own experience confirms, we don't even know what the terms *accurate* and *reliable* mean. We have all seen performances that do not correspond with the descriptions we have read of them, let alone the appraisals. If this is true of performance that we can assay for ourselves, how much more flimsy it is to rely on reviews of past performances. Yet any historical discussion of performance art, with the exception of music since the advent of recording, depends on criticism in the past. This condition is sobering, even disturbing. Still that past comment, criticism and memoir, is all that we have. With portraits of bygone figures, we feel that if we see enough of them—even if they are idealized or crude or satirical—a reasonably reliable impression emerges. So with reviews of past performances.

Thus reliant, and aided by the writings of Daly and Belasco themselves, scholars have identified the years around 1875 as the era when realism entered American theater production, and all of them agree that Daly and Belasco were preeminent in the movement. I mean to explore why their two careers were amazing, why they help us to understand the American character, and what they signify to the theater of this century.

Fundamentally, their careers are amazing because they took place in America. Daly (1838-1899) is held to be the first American director, as we use the word today; Belasco (1853-1931) followed within a generation. Daly had no real native antecedents in his profession; Belasco had little more than Daly's example to go by. These facts become all the more impressive when we look at what was happening in Europe during their early lives. The profession of the director emerged in Europe toward the end of the eighteenth century, principally in Germany, and began to flourish in the nineteenth century. Between ancient Athens, where plays had been directed by their authors, and the end of the eighteenth century, the profession of the director did not exist. Managers of troupes and masters of revels are visible in history, but they do not correspond to directors—artists whose vision, taste, and authority determine performance. Until little more than a century ago, rehearsals were usually conducted by a stage-manager or a prompter with a promptbook (Peter Quince in *A Midsummer Night's Dream*). If it was an old play, he followed movement and "business" from earlier productions and allowed important actors to make changes. If it was a new play, he relied on his actors to supply movement and "business"; then he made suggestions, possibly aided by the author and manager of the theater.

Germany is the place where these practices first changed markedly. Many of the principalities that constituted the area now called Germany had state and court theaters: thus Germany had the most thoroughly articulated groundwork for theatrical progress. And even before it became a nation, Germany also had a unique national regard for the theater. Lessing's *Hamburg Dramaturgy* and Goethe's *Wilhelm Meister* both relate how necessary the improvement of the theater was held to be for the German spirit. This urgency, which increased through the next century, impelled the German theater to keep abreast of what was happening in all the arts; and what was happening was the rise of romanticism. The emergence of the artist who would make a production embody one individual's perception and experience seems to have been a response to the increasing subjectivity in other arts, which were becoming, in M. H. Abrams's terms, lamps instead of mirrors. Subjective expression was more immediately summoned by new plays, but once the director appeared, he took over the standard repertoire as well. Otherwise, the disjuncture between the new way and the old would have been too great.

This radical change in theater production was paralleled by what was happening at the same time in musical performance. Adam Carse says in *The Orchestra from Beethoven to Berlioz*:

> In the year 1800 it would have been difficult, or even impossible, to find any orchestra in which the playing was controlled by a musician who did nothing but beat the time and indicate by gesture how the music should be interpreted. By 1850 it would have been equally difficult to find any but small orchestras in which the playing was controlled by any other means than by a time-beating conductor. . . . The need for an interpretative conductor began . . . when the structure and texture of the music became less transparent and the rhythm was more irregular . . . when the dynamics changed more often, and the light and shade required more sensitive adjustment . . . when, in consequence of all these things, a good ensemble was more difficult to attain.

In short, when romanticism arrived. (As with the theater director, the conductor, once in place, did not step down for the older repertoire; the personal element, coherent and holistic, was applied to the classical pieces in order to bring them forward into the present.)

The late arrival of the theater director ought not to mislead us into thinking that all previous theater productions were bad, any more than all musical performance was bad before the conductor arrived. By current standards, a predirectorial theater production might now seem bizarre to the eye—scenery was often supplied from the warehouse, and each actor's costumes were usually supplied by himself or herself—and it might seem odd in its emphases; but it might well contain virtuoso acting in the principal roles that surpasses modern experience. (Comparable values must have prevailed in music before the conductor. Can we believe that composers before 1800 wrote for bad performance?) The earlier theater operated by its own standards; but they were different standards from those that apply under a director.

A company in the small German state of Saxe-Meiningen, assembled and inspired by its theater-loving duke, is recognized as the first true ensemble in Western theater. After almost a decade of preparation in the duke's sequestered small capital, the Meiningen company went to Berlin and made its debut there on 1 May 1874, a watershed date in theater history. For the next sixteen years the company toured Europe, from London to Moscow. Everywhere its work hugely influenced existing theaters and the formation of new ones. Konstantin Stanislavsky and André Antoine were only two of the pioneers who responded to the company's principles. By the end of the century, due in great measure to the example of the Meiningen troupe, the profession of the director had been well established in Europe.

These are the facts that make the careers of Augustin Daly and David Belasco amazing. The Meiningen company, its antecedents and successors, all grew out of a rich European culture that flowed around and through the theatrical arts and pressed them forward. But through the first half of the nineteenth century, the United States had little comparable cultural pressure to exert on even its best theater talents. American arts were in search of American identity, were struggling for selfhood in a belated cultural War of Independence. American romanticism existed, but it was no more indigenous than American classicism: both were derived from Europe. Virtually every American town and city from the eastern seaboard to wherever the frontier happened to be at the time—and then, with a continental leap, to the West Coast—had at least one theater. In most of these, until after the Civil War, a permanent company, occasionally visited by stars, played in repertory. But there was nothing in the United States like the state and court theaters of Germany. There were not even, until around 1830 with the rise of Edwin Forrest, any great American stars: most of the virtuosi were British. American playwrights were busy, generally with popular fare, though some of them tried to answer the call of Whitman and Poe for a native drama befitting the new republic; both the popular and the high-minded works are now almost impossible to read. For all these reasons, there was no great native cultural current in the American arts to carry the American theater with it, no exemplars to make the rise of the director as inevitable as it seemed in Europe. Insofar as any art can be said to be devoid of antecedents, Daly and Belasco started from scratch. Daly in particular, because he was first, seems to have summoned from within his own being the equivalent of the large cultural forces that had caused change in Europe.

John Augustin Daly was born in North Carolina in 1838, the son of Irish immigrants. His father died when he was three; his mother, after a stop in Virginia, took him and his younger brother to New York, a good place for an Irish family because the city had a large Irish immigrant population. It was an especially lucky move for Daly, as it turned out, because New York theaters were vigorous and the actors he saw as he grew up were among the best then on the stage. He left school in 1853, at the age of fiftteen, and had a series of clerical jobs. He got into amateur dramatics with some friends and was the manager of a modest production in a Brooklyn hall. In 1859 he joined a newspaper as a staff writer, then became its theater critic. Soon he was also writing theater criticism for four other newspapers (including the *New York Times*) simultaneously—apparently not an unusual practice in those teeming days. He had also begun to write and adapt plays with some success. *Leah the Forsaken,* his adaptation from the German, was produced in 1862 with the star Kate Bateman, and Daly subsequently went on tour with the production as manager and publicity man. In 1864 he performed the same duties for a star named Avonia Jones on a tour of the Union-held areas in the South. In 1867 came his first successful original play, *Under the Gaslight,* and by 1869 he resigned all his critical posts. He wanted to devote himself to playwriting and management.

In January of 1869 he married the daughter of a theatrical manager, and in August of that year, despite his father-in-law's headshakings, he rented the Fifth Avenue Theater for $25,000 a year. Translate that sum into our terms and you are in the millions. It is here that amazement about Daly begins. Up to this point his career, though hardly commonplace, had not been historically exceptional: a first-generation American, minimally educated, had plunged into the field of his choice and had done a prodigious amount of work. Now, at thirty-one, he launched a new career, independent management, at huge financial risk and thus with huge confidence; and that career was swiftly marked, according to one newspaper, "by lavish liberality, admirable taste, great boldness, and a general ardor for progress." The tribute was to his management, but the term patently included the functions of a director. Within two years another newspaper confirmed this:

> In this theater the prevailing feature is a naturalness in dialogue and action, and a finish which invests even the most commonplace scenes with interest, and takes away much of the stereotyped character of acting of the present day. . . . Such perfection of *ensemble* is the main secret of the success of the Fifth Avenue.

By the following year, 1872, Daly was already a municipal figure. A guidebook said of the Fifth Avenue:

> The manager is Mr. Augustin Daly, a well-known writer of successful plays. To his literary gifts Mr. Daly adds a high order of managerial talent, and it is to his efforts exclusively that the very marked success of the theater is due.

Daly had doubtless developed some skills in his previous sporadic managerial work, and he had been allowed some control over the production of *Under the Gaslight.* Also, his newspaper criticism during the 1860s displayed strong revisionist views of current production styles and methods. But this background—crafting popular plays, managing stars' tours, writing impatiently perceptive criticism—does not fully prepare us for the change in Daly in 1869. His work in the new field, directing, revealed genius.

For thirty years Daly was an intensively active manager-director. He was not the only manager in those days to show a directorial hand, but as Barnard Hewitt says,

"Daly is the first to stand forth clearly as a *régisseur.*" In his first six months at the Fifth Avenue, Daly produced twenty-one plays. He maintained a permanent company, and, as he did throughout his career, he scheduled plays from the repertory while he was rehearsing new ones. Subsequently he moved to other theaters in New York. He took his company on American tours. In 1884 he took his company to London on the first of several European tours that later included Berlin, Paris, and Dublin. In 1893 he opened a London theater that he had built. He died in Paris in June 1899, while on a business trip.

In his career he produced sixteen plays of Shakespeare. Almost all the rest—and there were many dozens—were new plays, and with few visible exceptions, the new plays were intended as entertainments, nothing more. Over ninety of those plays, originals and adaptations from the French and German, were credited to Daly, though it is now believed that many of the adaptations were written by his younger brother Joseph, a lawyer and a judge who was devoted to the theater and to Augustin. I underscore the light quality of most of the plays that Daly produced because it was precisely through fripperies and sentimentalities that he evolved what was then a modern view of theater art and won a reputation as a serious theater artist.

These achievements were noticed—but noticed only to be criticized—when Daly's company played in San Francisco in 1875. Daly wrote to his brother from California: "The press here still growl & call our acting tame and colorless—The fact is acting out here is all 15 yrs. behind the age. The thunder & lightning & absurd farce acting of our boyhood era." A San Francisco newspaper said:

> The 5th Avenue Theater Co. have a style of their own. . . . It is *quiet, elegant, languid,* making its points with a French shrug of the shoulders, little graceful gestures, and rapid play of features. The voice is soft, the tone low, and the manner at once subdued and expressive. It pleases a certain set of fashionables, but to the general public it is acting with the act of acting left out.

That "certain set of fashionables" increased through the years. A Philadelphia critic (1885): "There is an ease, a confidence, a perfect mastery of their art, in all that they do." A Boston critic (1888) compared Daly's troupe to the Meiningen company "in their rare intelligence, artistic fitness and perfect discipline." A Paris critic (1886):

> [The Daly company's] propensity for naturalism shows itself in a thousand details. The fashion of entering, sitting, taking a chair, talking, taking leave, going out, coming in—it is the usage of everyday life. With us, there is always a little conventionality in the movement of the characters. . . . If I may judge from what I see, the American stage is dominated exclusively by reality.

Daly had his detractors, of course, some of them notable. J. Ranken Towse, a veteran New York newspaper critic of discernible taste, wrote in *Sixty Years of the Theater*: "As a stage director [Daly] was brilliant, adventurous, prodigal, and catholic, but his knowledge was not universal nor his judgment always sound." Bernard Shaw slashed away regularly at Daly's London productions of Shakespeare. But the historical weight is heavily in Daly's favor. Shaw himself, in the middle of an adverse review of Daly's *As You Like It* in October 1897, conceded:

> . . . Mr. Daly was in his prime an advanced man relatively to his own time and place, and was a real manager, with definite artistic aims which he trained his company to accomplish. His Irish-American Yanko-German comedies, as played under his management . . . turned a page in theatrical history here. . . .

William Dean Howells seems to sum up the favorable consensus:

> Mr. Daly's Theater has been the nearest approach to a national school of acting we have had in America. His work in elevating the American Stage can scarcely be overestimated.

Throughout Daly's career, critics praised the way he produced plays rather than the plays themselves. Throughout his career, he cultivated with his production methods the "certain set of fashionables" that the San Francisco critic had sniffed at, and he helped to create that "fashion," which was coming to be called realism.

David Belasco, too, was the son of immigrants—Portuguese Jews who had settled in San Francisco, where Belasco was born in 1853, fifteen years after Daly. In 1858 the family moved to Vancouver. There Belasco had his first taste of the theater: Mr. and Mrs. Charles Kean were only two of the leading lights who passed through. In 1865 the Belasco family returned to San Francisco. After some schooling and some amateur theatricals, Belasco got his first professional engagement there in 1871, at the age of eighteen. He plunged into the busy theater life of the city as actor, stage-manager, prompter, and playwright. In 1873 he served as secretary to Dion Boucicault, the prolific British dramatist who spent much time in America and was himself a pioneer director. In 1875 Belasco tried, unsuccessfully, to join the visiting Daly company, whose work he studied. In 1879 he collaborated with James A. Herne (later in the forefront of American realistic playwriting) on a mystery drama that starred Eugene O'Neill's father, James. A second collaboration with Herne, says Lise-Lone Marker,

> evoked both the admiration and astonishment of his audience by employing real water, real beans, real boiled potatoes, and various other components of a real supper, as well as a real cat and a real, and apparently rather discontented, baby on the stage.

Simplistic though these devices may now seem as factors of realism, a reading of the plot synopsis and extant samples of the dialogue will show that Belasco's devices are much more realistic than the play itself.

In 1882 a play of Belasco's was produced successfully in New York. This led to his engagement by the Madison Square Theater as stage-manager, director, and playwright. (Theaters then sometimes employed playwrights as Hollywood studios later employed screenwriters.) He

insisted on taking the function of director seriously, and he wanted his views to prevail: this led to his departure from Madison Square. In 1887 he joined the Lyceum Theater as playwright and was also asked to teach acting there. Still in search of independence, he left the Lyceum in 1890, spent five years writing plays, and by 1895 established himself as a producer. By 1902 he acquired a theater of his own, and by 1907 he had built a second theater, the Belasco, which still stands.

A word about his dress because it relates to his histrionic sense. Throughout his life he wore the stand-up collar that was common in his youth, together with a black ascot. This collar, as time went on, came to suggest clerical garb, a suggestion he did not discourage although he never made false claims for himself. One biography of Belasco is subtitled *The Bishop of Broadway*.

Belasco's New York career extended for almost half a century. He directed more than ninety-five plays and was involved in the production of many more. Like Daly, he also wrote plays and adaptations—thirty-four in all—and he collaborated invisibly with many of the other authors he produced. He staged one Shakespeare play, *The Merchant of Venice*. Two plays of his own, *Madame Butterfly* (from a story by John Luther Long) and *The Girl of the Golden West,* were made into operas by Puccini. Very few of the other plays that he produced are in any way memorable. What is as vivid in Belasco as it is in Daly is the drive to improve theater practice, to bring it into accord with the growing general interest in realism outside the theater, yet to do it through the medium of old-fashioned plays. One frontier at a time.

How well Belasco knew Daly personally is not clear, though Joseph Daly, in his biography of his brother, lists Belasco as one of the friends who sent greetings when the Daly company opened in London in 1884. Certainly Belasco must have seen many Daly productions, beginning in San Francisco. It seems fair to assume that the younger man was warmed to his task by the Daly example. Belasco wrote later that he aimed in his productions at "a new style of acting which I felt was destined to take the place of the melodramatic method." This almost echoes Daly's letter from San Francisco to his brother.

Belasco left a detailed account of his producing and directing methods in *The Theater through Its Stage Door* (written with Louis V. Defoe), published in 1919. His "first step" in the production of a play was to study the scenic requirements and to work with the scenic artist in order to convince the audience of the reality of the setting. "For the completed play is impressive and fulfills its purpose only to the extent that it carries an audience back to its own experiences." He then proceeded to the "all-important factor in a dramatic production—the lighting of the scenes. . . . The greatest part of my success in the theater I attribute to my feeling for colors, translated into light." Belasco's priorities seem odd until we realize that he grounded his productions on the most accessible and dependable of realities, the physical aspects, and that the lighting he talked of was relatively new and limitlessly explorable. For centuries, lighting had been a problem in production, often ingeniously solved; but the introduction of electric light into American theaters, around 1880, turned a problem into an instrument. Belasco was the first in this country to realize that instrument's powers. He employed a staff electrician and built a workshop to develop new equipment, and he labored long to get the results he wanted: for instance, three months on a sunrise for *The Girl of the Golden West* and five months on the lighting of the protagonist, a revenant, in *The Return of Peter Grimm.*

Light is important, said Belasco, not just for its effect on the audience but for its effect on the actor. "Light has a psychological effect which perhaps he is not able to understand or explain, but he feels it instantly and responds to it, and then the audience quickly responds to him." Thus Belasco arrives at the subject of acting. "My explorations in search of stage equipment are really the most interesting parts of my work," he said, but he may have had strategic reasons for saying so at the time, because his record shows his sympathetic understanding of actors and his success with them. He developed a number of popular stars, such as Mrs. Leslie Carter and David Warfield, and was noted for the precision of his casting in general. Sometimes, in his quest for verism, he treated casting almost like shopping for props. "Should the characters be English or French or Italian, I try to engage actors of those nationalities to impersonate them."

Of his production of *The Merchant of Venice* in 1922 John Corbin wrote in the *New York Times* that "opulent good taste could not do more to provide a variety of form and color. . . . Seldom or never has pictorial Shakespeare been more beautiful." In this instance Belasco concentrated his passion for realism on the performance. Venetian street traffic occupied the stage for a few minutes before a word was spoken. As background for the scene in which the play's central bargain is struck, he introduced a synagogue, complete with rabbi, cantor, and congregation.

If these additions make us dubious, we can consider what Stanislavsky had to say of this production, which he saw during the Moscow Art Theater's first visit to New York. He wrote to his colleague Vladimir Nemirovitch-Danchenko:

> Such an actor as David Warfield, whom I saw in the part of Shylock, we have not got. And Belasco's production of *The Merchant of Venice* exceeds in sheer lavishness anything I ever saw, and as for its technical achievements, the Maly Theater could envy them. To tell you the truth, I have often wondered why the Americans praise us so much.

In 1927 Stanislavsky made Belasco an honorary member of the Moscow Art Theater.

Stark Young, reviewing that Shakespeare production, also reviewed what he knew of Belasco's career. He noted that Belasco's methods and aims had dated somewhat (it was 1922; Belasco had entered the theater in 1871) and also noted that Belasco was more of a showman than a connoisseur. Young continued:

> At least one kind of sincerity cannot be denied him, and that is theatrical sincerity. Events, peo-

ple, passions, the arts, his private and personal experience, his joys and sorrows, he can see in only one light; without footlights, in sum, without footlights he is blind. He trembles all through his being with a thousand echoes, despairing silences and warm applauding hands, invisibly awaited. And this in the theatrical faculty is a kind of genius.

Belasco, of course, had less generous critics. Young said, "Directors who could teach their companies very little could at least teach them to despise the Belasco spectacle and craft." George Jean Nathan, in the most frequently cited adverse article, attacked Belasco for the "show-shop piffle" he had produced throughout his career; Nathan even tried to deny Belasco originality in his stagecraft, contending that in comparison with Gordon Craig, Belasco faltered. (This may have rankled: Belasco disliked what he knew of Craig's work.)

Nathan's opinion contrasts directly with a comment by James Gibbon Huneker, a critic whose writings have weathered at least as well as Nathan's. After a trip abroad in 1921 Huneker said:

> I saw nothing that had not been foreshadowed by the genius of Belasco; not the startling lighting effects of Gordon Craig, nor the atmospheric innovations of Reinhardt, nor the resonant decorations of Bakst were novel to me, for I had watched the experiments at the several Belasco theaters, had heard the discoverer himself discourse his theme.

A comparison with Craig seems strange when we place the great plays that Craig produced (not many, in fact) alongside the "show-shop piffle" that occupied most of Belasco's professional life. But comparison with Craig becomes more apt when we remember what Craig wrote in *On the Art of the Theater* (1905):

> The theater must not forever rely upon having a play to perform, but must in time perform pieces of its own art. . . . When [the director] interprets the plays of the dramatists . . . he is a craftsman; . . . when he will have mastered the uses of actions, words, line, colour, and rhythm, then he may become an artist. Then we shall no longer need the assistance of the playwright—for our art will be self-reliant.

If we take Craig seriously, as many have done in this century, then he enables us to look through the "show-shop piffle" to see that Belasco was primarily interested in what the piffle helped him to create. He himself told us that the details of scenery and lighting were what interested him most—the "theater art." Craig had his own ideas about what he wanted that art to create. Belasco, under the same sway, wanted his theater to convey reality:

> The great thing, the essential thing . . . is to create *illusion* and *effect*. The supreme object in all my work has been to get near to nature; to make my atmosphere as real as possible. . . . Then, if the actors do their part, the audience forgets that it is not looking into a real place.

Realism was his aim, quite evidently, a realism that merely

used as a base—was almost independent of—the piffle of the literary element.

Along with the Daly-Belasco movement in the theater, a cognate movement stirred in American painting and sculpture. Such artists as Thomas Hovenden and Eastman Johnson and John Rogers were making works with utmost fidelity to physical detail while their subjects and intent came from the same popular sentimental sources as the plays of Daly and Belasco. The fact that the American visual arts, including theater production, moved toward realism some decades before American literature is grounds for a strong inference. Of all the familiar reasons for the rise of realism, including the social and political readjustments that followed the Industrial Revolution, one reason stands preeminent because of this American phenomenon: the invention of photography. The first photograph was made in France in 1826; technical improvement and the acceptance of the invention raced ahead from that date with forest-fire speed.

These events happened simultaneously with the rise of democratic hopes in Europe and South America, with the growth, in size and confidence and world importance, of the United States, the first and largest democracy of the age. It would be tenuous to assert that the rise of photography and of democracy were directly linked; it would be even more tenuous to assert that they had nothing to do with each other. At virtually the same time that political equality became the goal of millions, the camera was taking the privilege of representing the human face out of the hands of the rich and powerful, whose property it had exclusively been, and was making it available to many—in a short time, to all. All people, of whatever circumstances, were now material for pictorial record, as were the details of their lives; and realism, fixed and demonstrable, became a criterion with a public power it had not had before. Where would photography, with this inseparable public power, have been more warmly received than in a new nation founded on principles of equality?

The viewers who flocked to Hovenden's *Breaking Home Ties* at the World's Columbian Exposition of Chicago in 1893 were admiring a painting couched in domestic homily but executed with absolute fidelity to features and surfaces. Those viewers had been conditioned by photography. They were not ready to question the homilies involved, as the social protocols of the day attest; but the picture's popularity attests that they wanted physical detail to be accurate. Photography had given those viewers a new criterion, and it had given the painter new means for making old ideas effective by putting them in verifiable form. In her book *Realism* Linda Nochlin quotes Paul Valéry and then comments: " 'With photography . . . realism pronounces itself in our Literature,' and he might have said in our art as well." He might also have said in our theater practice, as far as the look of things went, not least in the American theater.

Of course audiences had always known that both easel painting and theater scenery did not correspond precisely to the observable world, but previous standards of realism had conformed to previous canons of art. In the post-camera theater new standards pressed harshly on the syl-

van glades and ruined castles, the mansions and humble cottages of the past. The old Italianate shape of stage settings—a backdrop with two sets of wing pieces downstage and parallel to it—gave way in contemporary plays to the box set, the walled set with one wall missing and with doors that worked. The theater historian William W. Appleton, noting that it is impossible to date precisely the first appearance of the box set, says: "It is surely more than a coincidence that the various dates suggested, bracketing the years 1829-33, coincide precisely with the years during which Louis Daguerre and Nicéphore Niépce experimented with 'heliographic pictures.' " The use of the box set quickly spread through Europe and America. By Belasco's time, "the audience forgets that it is not looking into a real place."

Within these new settings, acting in the old style, though a style with its own force and beauty, became dissonant. This change is signally dramatized in Pinero's *Trelawny of the "Wells"*, written in 1898 but set in the early 1860s. Rose Trelawny, who has been a successful actress at a London theater specializing in romances and melodramas, leaves the stage for personal reasons. When she returns, after some travail in love, she cannot repeat her earlier success. The theater is now doing a new kind of play, by a new young playwright, a play with real doors and real doorknobs, a play of surface realism; and it is not until Rose modernizes her acting style that she is once again successful. (The young playwright in *Trelawny* is patently based on T. W. Robertson, a mid-Victorian leader in realistic playwriting. It is hardly coincidence that Augustin Daly's first two productions at the Fifth Avenue Theater were Robertson plays.)

But, we can infer, the content of Trelawny's new play was not nearly as modernized as its settings and mode of performance. The new realism in scenery and acting style had little effect on the themes and values in new plays. Language became less rhetorical; structure became less episodic and more unified; principal characters now included persons other than the wealthy and grand; but few plays in the latter half of the nineteenth century questioned prevailing social and moral standards. Realism had arrived in the middle of an era of still-impregnable pietism, and the inroads of realism in the theater were confined to matters that would not disturb that pietism. Daly and Belasco, progressive in their producing methods, shunned the explosive new European drama and clung to ideationally conventional plays.

A distinction between acting and writing was rooted in the American temperament. Constance Rourke underscores this distinction in *American Humor*:

> Nothing can be clearer than the fact that the drama as a powerful native form did not appear in America . . . throughout the nineteenth century. But the theatrical seemed a native mode. . . . The American theater . . . was closely interwoven with the American character and the American experience.

Daly seemed to corroborate this view, this reliance on actors themselves for verity, in the criticism he wrote early in his career. In March 1863 he said: "The Nature we are given on our stage . . . is . . . the nature of the actor or actress who stalks before us." This distinction between acting and drama gave nineteenth-century America a means to exercise its vaunted belief in progress without upsetting snug social proprieties. What words would molest, action could imply. Modernity of view, the proud Yankee march to the horizon, was suggested by the daring new verism of movement and inflection, the replacement of large emotional gesture by vernacular emotional pattern. Americans prided themselves on their independence from Europe in many ways. The modernization of performance, compared with what they saw of visiting British and Continental actors, gave them a chance to support another kind of American independence. English actors, particularly those of T. W. Robertson's circle, had made some advance; but the effect of Daly's company on London and Berlin and Paris audiences indicates that, in this matter of realism, American acting was well in the fore.

In the European theater, the order of march was by and large exactly the reverse of America's. European drama advanced at a much greater rate than the American, but European acting styles (as Shaw's review suggests) advanced only some decades after Daly began and Belasco continued.

The literary tastes of these two men were naturally and congenially vulgar. We have not the slightest reason to suspect that they chafed at restraints in their writing. Both wrote prodigiously in the center of convention, and both produced conventional plays by others. But in theater performance they had insistent, courageous, ground-breaking genius; and that genius did much to clear the road for the completely realistic American theater after the turn of the century. True, realism has in our time become less a quest for truth than a refuge from imagination, but that is neither our subject nor their responsibility.

> *Stanley Kauffmann, "Two Vulgar Geniuses: Augustin Daly and David Belasco," in* The Yale Review, *Vol. 76, No. 4, September, 1987, pp. 496-513.*

J. L. Styan

[*In the following excerpt, Styan assesses the contribution to realist acting and production made by Vladimir Ivanovich Nemirovich-Danchenko, Konstantin Sergeyevich Stanislavsky, and their extremely influential Moscow Art Theatre.*]

It is ironic that the best answers to the practical challenges of the new realism—how the actor should match his art to the new dialogue, and how the writer should adapt his writing to the new techniques of the stage—did not come from Copenhagen or Paris or Berlin. It came from a city generally considered to be on the fringes of western theatre. Upon the creation of the Moscow Art Theatre by two giants of the modern stage, Nemirovich-Danchenko and Konstantin Stanislavsky, Moscow became the new centre of the naturalistic movement, and in the years that followed it was the fountainhead of the theory and method which nourished realistic acting and production everywhere. Where other companies succeeded only in imitating the surface of real life, the MAT realized its psychological depth.

Vladimir Ivanovich Nemirovich-Danchenko (1858–1943) was a respected playwright and novelist in his own right, and it was a literary and critical sensibility which enabled him to recognize the quality of a new play. He had also been a director and manager of the Moscow Imperial Dramatic Theatre, and it was his administrative ability which enabled the MAT to stay alive during the artistically demanding years of its beginning, and into the revolutionary years of the new Soviet state. These talents also combined to prepare him for the major theatrical upheaval which he and Stanislavsky were to cause. Danchenko was responsible for the planning of the world's leading repertory theatre, one which set such standards in professional discipline that it became the envy of every director.

Danchenko is known outside Russia only by his autobiography *My Life in the Russian Theatre;* inside Russia he was known as a great director and teacher of acting. He worked to create natural speech and behaviour in the actor, and what he called the actor's 'sincerity of experience'. Like Stanislavsky, he expected the actor to 'live' his part rather than merely present it, to feel and not merely 'act' an emotion, and on this basis Danchenko formulated a 'law of inner justification'. Like Stanislavsky again, he believed in the presence of a single will or spirit behind a production, that of the *régisseur,* whose 'intuition' should 'infect' everyone connected with the performance. Only then would the play assume a proper unity of style and atmosphere.

Konstantin Sergeyevich Stanislavsky (1863–1938) was born into a wealthy and influential family with artistic and theatrical leanings. Signs of his unusual dedication as an actor and director appeared early, when at twenty-four he urged his amateur cast to practise Japanese manners in preparation for a production of *The Mikado* of Gilbert and Sullivan; he even had the women tie their legs above the knee to remind them to walk with tiny steps. There was more than a touch of misplaced ingenuity in taking a burlesque comic opera so seriously. For ten years after its founding in 1888, he acted with the Society of Art and Literature, a group of enthusiastic amateurs, and during this time was inspired by the standards of realistic production he saw in the work of Chronegk and the Meiningen company. These standards Stanislavsky applied in Chronegk's own despotic way to productions of *Othello,* Hauptmann's *Hannele* and Tolstoy's *The Fruits of Enlightenment,* which owed to Stanislavsky its first production.

After this initiation, Stanislavsky was ready to form a permanent company, so that, as his work showed less of the trappings of external realism and more of the inner qualities of psychological honesty, the MAT had its beginnings in a more evolutionary than revolutionary way. In 1897, the famous meeting between Stanislavsky and Danchenko took place in a restaurant at the Slavyansky Bazaar in Moscow, where they found they had enough in common to talk for eighteen hours. At the end of that marathon, they had together drawn up the rules for a new kind of theatre. They determined to discard what was bad in the past, indeed everything that was characteristic of Moscow's leading commercial theatre, the Maly. Out would go the cheap repertoire of French and German farces, the star system that denied the possibility of ensemble work, and the declamatory manner of acting with all its stale theatrical tricks and habits. All of this had, of course, been heard before in Paris and Berlin, but never before was so stringent a set of rules drawn up for the members of a company. Any self-indulgence on the part of an actor was to be regarded as a crime, and any temperamental behaviour, lateness or laziness was to be forbidden: 'One must love art, and not oneself in art'. Actors were to be chosen for their devotion to work: 'There are no small parts; there are only small actors'. Thus did Stanislavsky's epigrams come into circulation. Rehearsals were to last as long as twelve hours a day, and would be conducted in an atmosphere of reverence for the drama. Dedication like this was good and necessary, provided it did not become bigotry.

The press at first found the new company something of a joke. Since it rehearsed in a barn some way out of Moscow, it was suggested, for example, that crickets had been brought in to add realism to the stagecraft. As it turned out, this was not far wrong, but in any case it was all good publicity. With the ardent support of his designer Victor A. Simov, Stanislavsky aimed at an historical authenticity on the stage never known before—not Charles Kean with his antiquarian Shakespeare, nor the Meiningens with all their visual detail of realistic illusion.

The first production of the Moscow Art Theatre in 1898 was a fair test of the new ideals: it was of Alexey Tolstoy's rambling historical piece, *Tsar Fyodor*. This play was given no less than seventy-four rehearsals, including five dress rehearsals. It became a sixteenth-century research project of the first magnitude, with the whole company going off on numerous field trips to museums, monasteries, palaces, bazaars and fairs, in order to recreate on the stage an authentic reproduction of life in old Russia, with its meals and manners, its clothing and jewelry, the correct weapons and furniture, and all the rest. The audience was treated to replicas of rooms in the Kremlin, the Cathedral and a bridge over the River Yaouza with barges passing beneath. For one device, the palace ceilings and doors were lowered to make the Boyars seem taller on their ritualistic entrance. The audience was dazzled, so much so that it was hardly aware of the natural speech, realistic acting and teamwork achieved by Ivan Moskvin and Olga Knipper as the Tsar and Tsarine, and by Vishnevsky as their strong minister Boris Godunov. The production established the new theatre overnight, and period plays in the realistic manner became a common feature of the repertoire for more than twenty-five years—indeed, they remain one of the strengths of modern Russian production on stage and screen generally.

It is of some interest that when the MAT brought *Tsar Fyodor* to New York in 1923, a generation later, certain doubts were expressed. The authenticity of the ensemble acting, costume and décor impressed everyone; but Stark Young, that most perceptive of theatre critics, nevertheless raised an objection which suggested that only certain features of the new style might survive. He declared that he had 'no interest in poetry taken as prose, and almost no interest in history taken . . . as contemporaneous human life'. He missed 'the magic of distance and scope, the conscious arrangement, the artifice and logic, that would create in my mind the idea'. And he deplored the loss of 'great style', which should remain in the mind 'like music, like great poetry, great abstractions'. For Stark Young, it seems, the realism of the MAT had already reached a limit.

If one wonders at the MAT's *Othello*, which involved the whole company in a research expedition to Cyprus, or at the pedantry of importing Norwegian furniture for *Hedda Gabler* and *The Enemy of the People*, or at the slavish requirement that the actors live in togas for several days before the opening of *Julius Caesar*, it was this quality of careful truth to life which also encouraged a new degree of psychology in the playing. The MAT's ability to embrace the subtleties of *contemporary* realism in all its aspects marked its difference from the Meiningen company. Without a complete commitment to an ideal of realism, the early successes of Chekhov's *The Seagull* in the production of 1898, *Uncle Vanya* (1899) and *The Lower Depths* (1902) by Maxim Gorky (1868–1936) would not have been possible. *The Lower Depths* was in fact the direct result of Gorky's seeing the kind of work the company could achieve with Chekhov. To these plays should be added Tolstoy's fierce indictment of human nature in his censored peasant play *The Power of Darkness*, which received its first production in Russian at the MAT in 1902. For this piece, Stanislavsky brought two old peasants as 'advisers' all the way from Tula, more than a hundred miles south of Moscow. We can imagine their bewilderment.

The success of *The Seagull* not only strengthened the uncertain finances of the company, but sent it on a greater quest: to find life in Chekhov's delicate nuances of atmosphere and mood, and to perfect an acting technique which would render his characters totally convincing. The play had failed miserably at the Alexandrinsky Theatre in St Petersburg in 1896, precisely because its actors had been unable to meet its psychological demands. The colloquial dialogue deceived them and the outlines of the characters seemed imperceptible. Even Vera Kommissarzhevskaya played Nina as the type of an abused maiden. Trained by the old professional rules and inadequately prepared, the players trusted that inspiration would come on the night. It did not, and the result was a disaster. The audience found Treplev's attempt at suicide a great joke, and the awkward symbolism of the property seagull quite ridiculous. Chekhov was crushed, and left the theatre swearing never to write another play. Danchenko, however, perceived the fresh qualities in *The Seagull;* it was written, he thought, in 'semitones' designed to capture a fragile mood of unhappiness. He also recognized that it was just the kind of play the new company needed to give it direction. Stanislavsky confessed that he had not understood 'its essence, its aroma, its beauty' at the time, but he agreed to let Danchenko try to persuade Chekhov to let them have the play.

With characteristic earnestness, Stanislavsky gave *The*

Seagull twenty-six rehearsals. The time was devoted to perfecting every detail of speech and gesture in order to capture the elusive tone of a scene, and Chekhov's genius for observed detail rewarded this kind of approach as few dramatists could have done. Moreover, Stanislavsky's respect for his author grew as he discovered how well every touch of character and action contributed to the whole, and by the first night, every member of the company was aware that a new mode of performance, a new kind of play, was to suffer its crucial test. The silence of the audience during the first act was nerve-wracking for the cast, but it was soon apparent that this indicated its total absorption. The audience had been caught up in the mesh of the play's details, and was responding to Stanislavsky's orchestration of its rhythms. At the final curtain the house broke into a roar of applause, and all the MAT's meticulous preparation seemed justified. *The Seagull* truly inaugurated a new era in Russian theatre, and the exultant company appropriately adopted a seagull as its emblem.

At this distance, we are in a position to make a balanced judgment. Set design still belonged to the age of the scene painter, and Simov's work would have pleased us less today. In his memoirs, he reported that the painting of the lake for act I was too photographic for Chekhov's liking, whose work in the last analysis is more impressionistic. Chekhov's dry comment on Simov's lake was, 'Well, it is wet', and one suspects that a hint of moonlight on water would have sufficed. Stanislavsky's request for a chill in the air during the last act, in order to convey the emptiness of the family's life, was better met by Simov, who hit upon the idea of placing the furniture on the stage in some disorder, so that its appearance suggested the indifference of those assumed to live with it.

Stanislavsky's 'score' for the play was recorded carefully in a notebook, and this has been conveniently edited by S. D. Balukhaty and translated by David Magarshack with the title *The Seagull Produced by Stanislavsky.* The concern for detail is apparent throughout, but the question remains, What kind of detail? Stanislavsky was not past using conventional ways of inducing emotion. At the end of the play, for example, Nina makes a last appearance to show how time has changed her into a more mature person, and Stanislavsky's pauses accordingly drew out the suspense—he created and groped his way through nineteen such pauses in this act alone. The repeated counterpoint of laughter in the next room, particularly from the apparent 'seducer' Trigorin, squeezed out the last drop of pathos. Stanislavsky knew he was using old stage trickery, and was not ashamed to say so: his jotting on the subject of this laughter is, 'It never misses with an audience', and we should know that Chekhov himself had first suggested it. However, such signs of Chekhov's weakness for the melodramatic in this scene, at this stage in his career as a playwright, might have been all the more reason why his director should have corrected the tendency.

Stanislavsky's Nina leaned towards the stereotype of the forsaken girl, although the author had written lines that belonged to a wiser, more decisive Nina, who, by choosing to leave Treplev, was telling him to grow up. More than this, Stanislavsky had the scene played against an obtrusive storm outside the house, and this was arranged to smash a pane of glass at the crisis. The tolling of a church bell afar off added to the tempestuous atmosphere, and Treplev even dropped a glass of water from lifeless fingers upon Nina's departure. In a letter to his friend Suvorin, Chekhov said that he had ended the play *pianissimo,* 'contrary to all the rules of dramatic art', but this infringement was evidently corrected by his director. It therefore remains in doubt who earned the roar of applause at the curtain of the first production of *The Seagull,* Chekhov or Stanislavsky.

The Lower Depths is not as demanding a play as *The Seagull,* but Gorky had written it in what he took to be a Chekhovian manner. In fact it was far more politically coloured than anything Moscow had seen on the stage before, and its portrait of human degradation in a doss-house in a provincial town on the Volga was a strong comment on social conditions in Tsarist Russia. Replete with grim realistic details of thievery, alcoholism, prostitution and violence, the play lent itself fully to the new methods, and the cast promptly went off to inspect some actual institutions of lower life in Moscow's notorious Khitrov Market. In performance, the actors wore real rags, so that some spectators feared they might catch lice from being too near the stage. But Gorky was not Chekhov, and the characters of *The Lower Depths* are more strident, less understated, than those of his friend. While remaining plotless and impressionistic in its realism, the play reverts to the pattern of the French thesis-play, driven by the need to preach. To avoid the theatricality of a propaganda piece, Stanislavsky worked for simplicity and sincerity in the speaking, and sought finally, as he said in *My Life in Art,* 'to enter into the springs of Gorky himself' (translated J. J. Robbins).

The production was an overwhelming success in Russia, but again an unusual objection was heard from Stark Young when he saw it in New York in 1923. He praised the scenes of 'pure theatre', like the scene of Luka the pilgrim when he ministers to the dying woman: this was 'poetic realism'. But, he added, 'character after character stood out to the eye, heavily accented, without a blur'. Stanislavsky himself, who played Satine the card-sharper, was the worst, he said, since his whole costume and appearance was of shreds and patches: 'everything insufferably scored—as his speeches, for all their great intelligence, were scored—like the work of a brilliant amateur'. We can sense this from the photographs of the time, with every character playing the part for all he is worth.

Many have commented with amusement on Stanislavsky's excesses in pursuit of surface realism, especially the sound effects he dearly loved: the crickets and frogs, the birds and dogs in *The Seagull, Uncle Vanya's* creaking swing, the insistent fire-alarms and fire-engines (not to mention the famous sound of a Stanislavsky mouse) in *Three Sisters,* and mosquitoes, frogs and corncrakes in *The Cherry Orchard,* together with a train passing in the distance, had Chekhov allowed it.

As both actor and director, Stanislavsky was also inclined to romanticize Chekhov's intentionally dry characters, so that his Trigorin was more of an elderly roué, his Astrov more of a passionate lover, his Vershinin too pathetic.

Stanislavsky's published notebooks on *The Seagull, The Lower Depths* and *Othello* reveal how his imagination as a director frequently led him right away from his author's play. These notebooks are highly detailed (act I of *The Lower Depths* includes thirty-nine diagrams alone), and were clearly composed in the study, with only what Stanislavsky called his 'inner eye and ear' on the stage. They suggest the approach of an enthusiastic director likely to impose his own ideas at the expense of the very actors who must discover their own answers. Stanislavsky later perceived his error as he began to work towards a greater psychological realism of character, and found it necessary for director and actor to 'grow together' in their work on a play.

None of these criticisms, however, should belittle Stanislavsky's unique achievement in uncovering the psychological attributes required of an actor to bring a literary creature to life on the stage. Over the years, Stanislavsky taught acting in the various studios of the MAT, and, prolific note-keeper and diarist that he was, constantly analysed everything he did. Thanks to this, he left us with a full account of how an actor might school himself to find a character's motives in his own mind. Indeed, Stanislavsky, and what he called his 'System', or what became known in America as 'The Method', have dominated schools of acting in this century. So far three books in English have collected his teachings: *An Actor Prepares* (1936), *Building a Character* (1949) and *Creating a Role* (1961).

The Stanislavsky System was intended to be as natural and organic, he said, as the growth of a tree, since it was based essentially on intuition and not on science or logic. Unhappily, a wealth of technical jargon associated with the System has grown up, and in the following outline of Stanislavsky's ideas, the terms that are current have been italicized for quick recognition.

1. The *super-objective* or *ruling idea* of a play often, though not necessarily, interprets the main direction of the plot: thus, Hamlet wishes to cleanse the world of evil, or, the three sisters wish to return to Moscow. All other dramatic elements subserve the superobjective which should help the actor find the *perspective of his role*, in order that he may relate his work to the whole. *Subtext* was a notion devised chiefly for the reform of nineteenth-century acting, after it was considered inadequate for a true performance merely to memorize the lines set down; the subtext, or *inner life*, of a part would supply the actor with clues to his hidden motives in the play.

2. Working from the 'facts' of the play, an actor's creativeness springs from his belief in the truth of the life on the stage in its *given circumstances*, the *magic if* behind the life to be created (*If* you were in love with Juliet, what would you do?). The actor seeks the feeling of *inner truth*, or *inner logic*, in his part, the *logic of the emotions*, and he begins to assume a character's psychological make-up by studying his *pre-text*, or what is suggested about his imaginary life before the curtain rises. The given circumstances at the beginning of *Hamlet* might be that the Prince had just returned from his father's graveside, and at the begin-

ning of *The Seagull* that Nina had just been quarrelling with her father.

3. With some sense of his part's inner truth, an actor can *motivate* all the details of his speech, gesture and movement on the stage. To facilitate this, he should divide the part into several minor *objectives* or *fragments,* which will then grow from one another when played in sequence. Imaginative exercises, loosely related to the play itself, can help place the actor in his *imaginary circle,* and help him recreate a living character by a personal effort of the will and memory. This *psycho-technique* compels him to evoke the appropriate *memory of emotions,* and to transfer to the stage his personal experience, his *inner images* from the past. This process is 'the conscious stimulation of the unconscious'. Thus, as an exercise, an actress might improvise a scene from Mme Ranevsky's life in Paris before she returned to the cherry orchard by recalling a party of her own that she did not fully enjoy.

4. The series of enacted objectives are finally strung together in the actor's *through line of action,* or *through action,* which retains the sincerity of his emotional state while simultaneously exercising the detached control necessary to achieve the teamwork and unity of a play's performance. Olga Knipper as Masha in *Three Sisters* could say a dry-eyed 'Goodbye' to her lover, but the impact of her total performance would bring tears to the eyes of those who watched her.

This kind of preparation for acting is hard and slow work, as patient and disciplined a way of life as that required of a musician, a singer or a dancer. There are those who believe uncritically that Stanislavsky's teaching has a universal validity, off the stage as well as on, and it is no doubt true that genuine emotions in the actor will result from the quality of his effort of understanding or feeling. However, Elizabeth Hapgood has reminded us in *Stanislavsky's Legacy* that the master suggested the actor ask himself only '*If* I were Hamlet, or a tree, or a grand piano, how would I react?', and never to believe 'I *am*' Hamlet, or a tree, or a grand piano, unless he wished disaster upon himself.

> *J. L. Styan, "Realism in Russia: Nemirovich-Danchenko, Stanislavsky and the Moscow Art Theatre," in his* Modern Drama in Theory and Practice, Vol. 1: Realism and Naturalism, *Cambridge University Press, 1981, pp. 70-81.*

Bernard Beckerman

[*Beckerman is an American scholar and educator who has published numerous books and articles, including* Dynamics of Drama: Theory and Method of Analysis *(1970). Here, Beckerman contrasts the dramatic techniques of Anton Chekhov and Harold Pinter in order to illustrate two different forms of realism: one concerning the actions of the characters and the other focusing on the context and background against which the action occurs.*]

"Reality" is one of those elusive words that we can not do without. It can mean virtually anything, and so it often comes to mean nothing. And yet, it does suggest notions of concreteness, actuality, and relevance that are central to drama. Whether we like it or not, we are bound to use this word, though, at best perhaps, we can only acknowledge its import without being able to define its limits.

For my purposes, I should like to distinguish two main sources of that elusive "reality" in the drama. First, there is the impress of reality which comes from our habit of relating a play or a scene to some broader context. The slice of life, after all, comes from a whole loaf, and our awareness of that whole loaf lends a sense of "reality" to the stage event. Even a non-naturalistic drama, such as Jean Genet's *The Balcony,* derives a powerful sense of actuality from the fact that we see the ritualized and deliberately antiquated charade against the background of our revolutionary age. In drama, then, one effect of "reality" is produced when the context within which the stage action occurs carries intense associational resonance. We can speak of this contextual envelope as the background or ground of the action.

The second source of "reality" is the act of presentation itself, or to be more precise, the structure of the action scene by scene. There is a raw reality which the actor projects by the sheer expenditure of energy in an organized manner. This organized manner takes the form of recurrent activities. Whereas this observation is true about all drama, it can be most easily illustrated by reference to the *commedia dell'Arte.* In *commedia dell'Arte* each character type had a repertory of speeches and stage routines out of which a play could be put together. The *inamoroso* had his declarations of love and despair, the *zanni* had their routines of cheating and being cheated. These set pieces in themselves strike a chord of "reality," albeit a theatricalized "reality." That is why they have survived and survive even to this day. And because such set pieces have a distinct structure—that is, they provide a proven path for the expression of the actor's energy—they appear to us as figures in the foreground set against the background of association already mentioned.

The impress of "reality" that we gain from these "figures of action," as I shall call them, comes in part from the contextual ground against which they are set. For instance, the poignancy of Romeo's duel with Tybalt is in large measure stimulated by the fact that as we watch the fight, we bear in mind the consequences it is having for the two lovers. At the same time, the fight engages our attention on a primal plane. It is exciting in and of itself, as a physical contest, and so we experience a sense of "reality" through the interplay of energies between the two actors. Indeed, this "reality" is double-sided, the "reality" of the convincing life-illusion of battle, and the "reality" of the actual skill displayed by the actors as duellists. We want and expect both kinds of "reality."

Our impressions of "reality" thus have different origins. First, as I have said, they come from the nature of the subject matter and the relation of the subject to the audience's own frame of reference, thus producing a ground of association. Second, they come from the artful structures writers and actors jointly compose to engage our interest, and thereby form "figures of action." Impressions from both these sources overlap and mingle, conflating the provinces of art and truth in the theatre. Since "reality" became synonymous with "realism" in the course of the nineteenth century, we find it exceptionally difficult to dissociate the idea of "reality" from that of versimilitude. That is why we insist on reading and seeing such work as Harold Pinter's associationally. We cannot help asking ourselves what really happened to his characters before we meet them in his plays. In *The Birthday Party,* was the phantom concert that Stanley remembers ever a fact? Indeed, was Stanley ever a pianist? And in *No Man's Land,* have Spooner and Hirst known each other before the play begins? Theatre reviewers of *No Man's Land* were particularly frustrated by not being able to answer this question. The urge to give contextual logic to Pinter's plays or, in fact, to any play is natural enough. To give that logic, however, only in terms of versimilitude—of how life appears to be lived in actuality—betrays a cultural limitation.

The problem of "reality" is further complicated by the fact that an audience has its own code of acceptance to which it expects the dramatic image to conform. A fascinating example of the clash between an audience's ground and a dramatist's "figure of action" can be seen in the history of the Abbey Theatre. Irish playgoers at the turn of the century rejected the images of peasant life that Synge and others brought from rural Ireland. To these playgoers, the fresh images could not be accurate since they did not satisfy the idealized conception of what was noble and true in the Irish character. What was real for the average playgoer then and there, and what is real for most audiences, is not the way the stage image matches the actual experience of the audience in life, but the way the stage image matches what the audience thinks its experience has been and should be.

Obviously, if a dramatist's possibilities were limited by the audience's ground, a play could not express anything that lay beyond the audience's imagination. Fortunately, the dramatist and the performers can produce "figures of action" so artfully that they either challenge the audience's expectations or expand the audience's perceptions. Such a challenge or such an expansion may take time to influence audiences, as we can see in the case of Chekhov. What presented an impediment to the performance and the reception of Chekhov, at least in the United States as I have observed developments in the last generation, was not the confusion about the background of the action. Critics and audiences recognized immediately that the decay of the old landed families, the indolence of every class in society, and the unfulfilled longings of most individuals were the subjects of the plays. Instead, American audiences had difficulty with the artistic scale of Chekhov's dramaturgy. Raised on melodrama and intrigue, they could not discriminate the more subtle dramatic movements of Chekhov, and therefore assumed that nothing happened, that the characters merely talked and talked, and that Chekhov's works were only mood pieces. With repeated exposure and in the wake of other changes in theatrical style, though, successive generations of playgoers have been better prepared to see what is happening in the plays. With time, the "figures of action" became more readily apparent; they could be differentiated from the background of forlornness and decay. Thus, one came to depend less upon the generalized "reality" of the subject and mood, more on the "reality" of the subtle shifts of energy from moment to moment.

What I have been describing is a symbiosis between figure and ground. As a play unfolds, the ground of the action, whether arising from the audience's expectation, the topicality of the text, or even the particular style of a production, becomes assimilated by the audience into a prevailing attitude. Features of the early scenes become absorbed into the later groundwork. What we learn from an episode in the first act becomes the ground for the second act.

In the course of a play, then, the ground of action is increasingly activated, vitalized, made responsive to successive episodes. Later "figures of action" become more highly charged because there are more points where they can interact with the activated ground of association as they form these "figures of action," to that extent they create an impression of "reality" for us. Such an impression of "reality," it goes without saying, may or may not have very much to do with verisimilitude.

In particular, Chekhov and Pinter illuminate this process of creating "reality" in drama. They overlap and diverge from each other in many interesting ways. Some people have seen connections in subject matter. John Lahr [in his "Pinter and Chekhov: The Bond of Naturalism," *Tulane Drama Review,* 1968], for one, has noted similarities in their treatment of nature. But I am interested in comparing Chekhov and Pinter not so much in terms of theme or subject matter as in terms of how each uses the figure-ground symbiosis to spark his own image of "reality."

It is notorious that early productions equated Chekhov's plays with naturalism. In his stage management, Stanislavsky initially tried to create an atmosphere of actuality by multiplying off-stage sounds of birds and other natural phenomena. He thus raised the question of exactly what kind of ground Chekhov had created for his action. Was it symbolic, or was it illustrative? Was the mood unified and impressionistic, or was it the manifestation of many distinct impulses? It is significant, of course, that all of Chekhov's full-length plays are set in or around country homes, and even more, in and around country homes that are not part of productive enterprises. Life in these homes is undergoing constant change: the residents depart, or they are ousted, or they are left behind. That is all part of the background. In the foreground, the people of these houses seek love, affection, intimacy. In none of his four major works does Chekhov show a single enduring love. Trigorin meekly accepts Arkadina's possessiveness; Astrov lacks the resolution to pursue Elena's fascination; the one deep passion of Masha for Vershinin is transitory; and the childlike infatuation of Anya for Trofimov remains unrealized. What is particularly notable is the number of love affairs that occur in Chekhov's plays: five or six in *The Sea Gull,* three in *Uncle Vanya,* five or six in *The Three Sisters,* and five in *The Cherry Orchard.* Nor is it merely the number of love affairs that is significant. Equally tantalizing is the central position that these affairs occupy in the various plays. For despite all the emphasis that critics have placed on social and historical issues in Chekhov's works, the overwhelming number of scenes re-

volves about matters of love. The decay of aristocratic society, the indolence of people in the face of disaster, all that is part of the background against which the figures of unfulfilled, thwarted, or hopeless love-making are played out.

As I have remarked, there is a symbiotic relationship between figure and ground. The inadequacy of efforts to achieve love, evident with so many of Chekhov's characters, is paralleled by the general inadequacy that pervades the surrounding world. And the nonfulfillment of love that is so hopelessly or tentatively pursued is only a more obvious example of the more minute instance when an individual seeks response or sympathy, usually futilely, so that he or she is left to say, like Madame Ranevsky [in *The Cherry Orchard*], "But that should be said differently, differently." With Chekhov, it is only by looking at the fine shifts of thought and feeling that one perceives the plane of action on which his play is operating. And since he is always tracing a continually shifting state of sentiment or mind, one cannot resort to individual lines to capture Chekhov's "reality," but one must follow his action from word to word, impulse to impulse.

Because he reveals a character's state obliquely, Chekhov relies upon the interplay between a suggestive, half-articulate figure and an explicit ground to generate audience response. This is easily seen in the case of Masha and Vershinin's love affair in *The Three Sisters.* Masha is married to the kindly pedant Kuligin, Vershinin to an unbalanced woman periodically prone to suicide attempts. The two unhappy people are drawn to each other. Yet only once are they alone in the play, in the second act. At that time she for the most part chats about her husband, he about his wife. Suddenly Vershinin declares his admiration for Masha. She, confused and troubled, laughs, tells him, "Don't do it again, I beg you. . . . "; then, in a low voice, "But talk, though, it's all the same to me (*Covering her face with her hands*) It's all the same to me." These are the very same words that run as a refrain through the act and are spoken by the nihilistic doctor at the end of the play. Thus, in the midst of her budding love, Masha expresses apparent indifference. In fact, the only complete exchange of love between Vershinin and Masha comes in the form of a hummed code in Act Three. She signals to him: "Tram-tam-tam. . . . " He answers: "Tam-tam. . . . " She inquires: "Tra-ra-ra?" And he confirms: "Tra-ta-ta." They laugh. That is their love song, elusive, oblique, suggestive, pathetic. What Chekhov has done is to provide an evident ground of circumstances in relation to which the love affair takes place. It is a familiar, almost trite set of circumstances of the dull husband, the mad wife, and the provincial town choking the life out of sensitive people. But then, by eschewing direct confrontation between the lovers, and instead intimating how tenuous the link is between them, Chekhov leaves it to the audience to complete the "figure of action," and so to feel the "reality" of their passion for each other.

How different is Pinter's method! By contrast, Pinter deliberately obscures or confuses the ground of action. He does little to elaborate the off-stage worlds of his plays. Even when there is such a world, the world of the boardwalk in *The Birthday Party* or of Hampstead Heath in *No Man's Land,* it lacks sensory substance. But it is particularly in the narrative background that Pinter is puzzling or, if one prefers, exasperating. We can rarely say with any confidence who did what when. Things did or did not happen to people. In *The Homecoming,* Lenny did or did not slug the woman under the archway. Pinter indicates that the truth as such is not important. What is important is that Lenny tells the story to intimidate Ruth-as-woman. In short, Pinter seeks to separate the figure from the ground, to de-familiarize the ground so that we do not lose the figure in the swirl of attendant circumstances and can see the constituent parts of the figure freshly and vividly. He forces us to attend to the motions and not the meanings. As Ruth says, "The action is simple . . . My lips move. Why don't you restrict . . . your observations to that? Perhaps the fact that they move is more significant . . . than the words which come through them."

The trouble is that we are not used to seeing motion without context. We become disoriented. We have to put the foreground into some relationship with a background. And this Pinter does not permit us. Thus, our problem with him is the reverse of what we noted with Chekhov. With Chekhov, the ground was apparent; it was the foreground to which we had to adjust our vision. With Pinter, the foreground is clear; we do not have difficulty following the sequence of action. But how to relate that action to a context? In *The Homecoming,* are we to take Pinter's presentation of wife-turned-whore as a serious comment on family life? Hardly. No wonder we are puzzled. We are not used to seeking the context through the self-contained action of a sealed world.

There are other contrasts in the craftsmanship of each dramatist. Chekhov links events through narration and association; Pinter builds actions architectonically on a few ruthless confrontations. Chekhov unfolds a number of parallel actions, such as yearning for love; Pinter ties all the characters to a central action, often showing the relentless imposition of one will upon another. Indeed, in this respect Pinter is quite a classical dramatist.

Yet both men, in the way they shape their "figures of action," recognize and dramatize the failure of direct encounters. Character A makes a demand, Character B neither yields nor quite confronts the challenge. Anya invites a declaration of love, Trofimov talks of working for the future; Max insists on knowing who has been making noise in the night, Lenny responds by demanding that Max talk about the night when Lenny was conceived. For both writers, the dislocation between energy expended and resistance encountered produces the strange effect of events skidding along rather than rising to crescendos.

Parallel examples of dislocation between demand and response can be found in *The Three Sisters* and *No Man's Land.* I refer to the third act of Chekhov's play and the ending of Pinter's. Throughout the third act of *The Three Sisters,* all the Prozorovs—that is, the three sisters and their brother, as well as their tenant, the old army doctor—make a series of confessions. Yet no one wants to hear any of them. The doctor, who speaks first, is alone

on the stage when he goes through a drunken babbling. Irina and Olga in part, but only in part, speak to each other. When Masha confesses her love for Vershinin, Olga refuses to listen, and finally, the last to speak, Andrey, the brother, is forced to address Olga and Irina as they hide behind a screen in their bedroom. In this "figure of action," Chekhov emphasizes the gap between Andrey's longing to assert his worth and their faceless resistance to that attempt. He starts out by trying to defend his wife, and then gradually admits his responsibility for deceiving his sisters. Finally, because they make no reply, he cannot help but hear his own words and the lie they contain. He breaks down, crying out that they should not believe him. It is this combination of strong assertion with lack of response that produces the effect of hollow words ringing out an ineffectual pathos.

Something similar occurs at the end of *No Man's Land.* Spooner, a self-acclaimed litterateur, at first sought to intimidate Hirst into letting him stay in Hirst's home. Now, near the end, he tries persuasion. He tells Hirst about all the things he can do for Hirst. Hirst does not reply. As Spooner goes through his long plea, Hirst sits absolutely silent. Spooner's words become more and more hollow, and the result more and more pathetic. The effort of voluble desperation striking against absolute indifference engenders, as it did in Chekhov, the feeling that life is draining out of the speaker.

By pitting desperate yet futile men against others who refuse to acknowledge their existence, Chekhov and Pinter focus our attention on the impossibility that either man will ever cross the chasm that lies between himself and his would-be listener or listeners. The more each asserts himself, the weaker he seems, and therefore the more vast the chasm between him and others. Our impression of "reality" comes from experiencing, kinesthetically and emotionally, that widening chasm.

Chekhov and Pinter induce that experience of the widening chasm in analogous yet somewhat different ways. Ultimately Andrey breaks down, and we are swept up by his plaintive outburst of the truth. In that outburst is something painful, but also something human. Spooner, however, has no outburst. Instead, he coldly accepts Hirst's rejection. He is forced to realize that he is in "no man's land. Which never moves, which never changes, which never grows older, but which remains forever, icy and silent."

In both plays, it is the artful composition of the "figures of action" and the artful manipulation of these figures in respect to a ground that create the peculiar impression of "reality" which belongs to each author. Both writers are oblique in their methods, both are aware of the life of silence. At the same time, they create very different kinds of "reality," because ultimately Chekhov wrote at a time when there was still a context to which he could relate his "figures of action." No matter how despairing his characters are, they sense an affinity to some larger force in human existence. Pinter, on the other hand, has abandoned context and created an autonomous "reality." He has fully accepted the implications of contemporary fragmentation. His "figures of action," adrift amidst the flotsam and jetsam of circumstance, produce a bleak and fearful impression of inevitability. In both instances, it matters very little whether the dramatist adheres to the world of objective fact. Each has created a "reality" of his own that becomes objective for us every time one of his plays is staged.

Bernard Beckerman, "The Artifice of 'Reality' in Chekhov and Pinter," in Modern Drama, Vol. XXI, No. 2, June, 1978, pp. 153-61.

REALIST DRAMA AND TRAGEDY

Alfred Schwarz

[*Born in Vienna, Schwarz was educated in the United States, where he has taught for many years. A prolific scholar, he includes* From Büchner to Beckett: Dramatic Theory and Modes of Tragic Drama *(1978) among his many publications. In this essay, Schwarz analyzes the redefinition of tragedy that occurs in realist drama as the protagonist engages in struggle against a particularized social milieu rather than the unchanging natural forces that oppose classical heroes. Such a conflict, he argues, evokes a sense of "tragic paradox" rather than the "tragic irony" of traditional drama.*]

The great traditional examples of dramatic theory, Aristotle's *Poetics,* Dryden's *Essay of Dramatic Poesy,* Coleridge's Shakespearean criticism, were written after the fact; that is, they looked back upon a body of dramatic work which had proved its power to move and had stood up to the test of experience. In the view of these critics the tragic poet was primarily an artist, a maker, who had the skill (or even the God-given gift) to express the human comedy or tragedy in dramatic form. Therefore, the traditional poetic was largely formal in nature; it was a critical rationale of that skill or, as in Coleridge's case, an adoration of that imaginative gift.

During the nineteenth century there emerged another poetic which was the composite work of a number of thoughtful theorists of the drama; the most articulate among them were Hettner, Hebbel, Zola, Strindberg, and their eloquent exponent early in this century, Georg Lukács. They were critics and playwrights who reflected the emerging modern conceptions of man's fate in the world and who helped shape the development of modern realistic tragedy. The difference between the new poetic and those of the past was that it did not analyze established forms of drama in order to determine their excellence; on the contrary, the aim of the new theorists was to abandon set forms which were no longer expressive of modern philosophical views and modern dramatic subjects. The desirability of a post-Aristotelian and a post-Shakespearean poetic became explicit in their writings. The new dramatic theory was prophetic of things to come. It regarded the playwright not merely as a skilled and inspired artist, but as the purveyor of new knowledge.

Aside from the revolt against romanticism and idealism in the theater and the contempt felt for the pseudo-realism of the French school, the modern theorists sought to determine the major features of the new drama on the basis of a changed outlook on life. A new tragic theater would have to come into being, cognizant of modern theories of history, sociology, psychology, and biology. The modern tragedy itself would become a form of inquiry or reexamination of man's estate in the world and thus possess cognitive value. It would extend the range of our perceptions and understanding. And indeed, perhaps the outstanding characteristic of the new drama is that it directs our attention inquisitively and exclusively to the *phenomenal* world. The plot, as medium of imitation, no longer reenacts an archetypal action, like the Greek legends or the moral allegories which Shakespeare fashioned out of historical and fictional sources; on the contrary, the new drama attempts an artistic conquest of external reality, in an effort to understand the natural and social forces, the ineluctable fate, to which the modern individual is exposed. From this basic shift in the function of the drama we can derive a number of general characteristics of modern tragedy as the realists and naturalists conceived it. [For my present purpose, I ignore the philosophical and technical quarrels between the two schools. As René Wellek says, "the distinction between 'realism' and 'naturalism' was not stabilized for a long time. . . . The separation of the terms is only a work of modern literary scholarship" ("The Concept of Realism in Literary Scholarship," *Neophilologus* [Groningen, 1960], XLV, 6; reprinted in *Concepts of Criticism,* ed. Stephen G. Nichols, Jr. [New Haven, 1963], p. 233). —Author's note.]

But we should be clear at the outset that it is realism and naturalism understood as an intellectual point of view or attitude toward human existence which determine the characteristic forms of modern tragedy; realism as a technique of faithful imitation has for the moment little bearing on the questions with which we are concerned. The distinction is important. It was self-evident to the architects of the poetic of realistic drama in the nineteenth century. And it allows us for example to understand the difference between two modern plays like Tolstoy's *The Power of Darkness* and Miller's *Death of a Salesman.* Mr. Miller writes in the realistic tradition, although in the staging of his play there was no attempt at giving a lifelike illusion; the setting, the lighting, the music, the evocation of Loman's hallucinations were far removed from the conventional practice of realistic production. On the other hand, Tolstoy's imitation of the daily life of the Russian peasant is deceptively realistic. He delineates the bestial conduct of his characters in meticulous detail; few naturalistic plays can match the shocking presentation of Nikita's murder of the newborn baby. Yet by the time the last curtain comes down, it is clear that Tolstoy wrote a modern morality play. Nikita's confession before God and the community testifies to the truth of a religious conviction; and the play as a whole exemplifies the traditional pattern of temptation, sin, the turning from the good angel (father Akim), deeper sin, despair, and finally the act of contrition. Tolstoy reenacts the allegory of the fall and redemption in keeping with a Christian conception of the human condition and in the manner of the old drama, but his *technique* is scrupulously realistic, except that Nikita's sudden illumination of spirit cannot have a rational motivation.

The main impulse of the realistic drama is to see things as they are, to gain a rational understanding of the causes for human suffering in a given situation. Hence the typical role which the realist playwright assumes is that of the historian who dramatizes the significant moment of conflict between the individual and his social milieu. "The dramatic poet is in my view nothing but an historian," said Büchner in 1835; and in a pointed rejection of idealism in art he continued, "His highest task is to come as close as possible to the historical event as it really happened. His work should not be any more nor any less moral than *history itself.*" [*George Büchners Werke und Briefe,* ed. Fritz Bergemann (Leipzig: Inselverlag, n.d.), pp. 383-384. —Author's note.] Hettner and Hebbel were convinced that the highest form of drama was that which mirrored the dialectic process of history. More recently, Hauptmann maintained the same point of view of the realist with even greater conviction: "Every drama is an historical drama; there is no other." ["Einsichten und Ausblicke," *Das Gesammelte Werk* (Berlin: Suhrkamp Verlag), XVII (1943), 433. —Author's note.] And among our contemporary playwrights, Arthur Miller [in his *Collected Plays,* 1957] puts himself squarely in this realistic tradition. He cites the cognitive function of the new drama: "Drama is akin to the other inventions of man in that it ought to help us to know more, and not merely to spend our feelings." Every genuine new form of the drama makes possible a "new and heightened consciousness . . . of causation in the light of known but hitherto inexplicable effects." And he too rediscovers the historical function of the modern dramatist: "A new poem on the stage is a new concept of relationships between the one and the many and the many and history, and to create it requires greater attention, not less, to the inexorable, common, pervasive conditions of existence in this time and this hour."

The dramatist as historian perceives the social situation, and more narrowly the physical milieu, as the condition of a tragic action. He is as much interested in the role of the determining historical circumstances as he is in the role of the suffering individual; and he attempts to present the resultant conflict or the inescapable dilemma as a concrete instance of modern man's subjection to time conceived as history or to natural forces beyond his power. The tragic conception need not, however, be fully deterministic, though the purely naturalistic play tends to view the individual as a victim of environmental and hereditary, i.e., psychological or biological, forces. From Hebbel to Miller, there is a distinct tradition of realistic tragic writing which conceives of the individual as a protagonist with a will of his own, which, in other words, allows for the interplay between historical necessity and individual freedom. Yet also in this respect the difference remains absolute between the old drama and the new; for the hero of the new drama is the representative of a moment in history and a distinct stratum of society whereas the Greek or Shakespearean hero symbolizes the human condition in a timeless context of universal powers. ["Classicism, like realism, wants to be objective, wants to arrive at the typi-

cal, and it is certainly didactic. But obviously realism rejects the 'ideality' of classicism: it interprets 'type' as a social type and not as universally human." Wellek, *Concepts of Criticism,* p. 253. —Author's note.] The free act of self-assertion or challenge may appear to be the same, yet in one instance the necessity lies in the way of the world so that the tragedy is the result of conditions at a given time, whereas in the other instance the necessity lies in the inexorable consequences of a moral commitment, where the momentary circumstances do not function as an independent fatalistic power, but only as an instrument of supernatural agencies.

The modern tragic hero, as Hebbel perceived, is the meeting point of clashing ideas. He is witness and victim of a dynamic social or historical change. This is as true of Danton, Saint Joan, and John Proctor as it is of figures in plays on non-historical subjects, like Mrs. Alving, Miss Julie, and Willy Loman. Consequently, as George Lukács has pointed out, a new form of the conflict between generations comes into being; the scene of the new drama is in this case the meeting point between two worlds separated in time, and with the end of each tragedy a whole world collapses since the difference between the generations is a radical ethical difference. The conflict has to do with the relative claims of different values at a given moment of confrontation. [Georg von Lukács, "Zur Soziologie des modernen Dramas," *Archiv für Sozialwissenschaft und Sozialpolitik,* XXXVIII (1914). 334-337. —Author's note.] Thus, the contrast between a family tragedy like *Maria Magdalene* and *King Lear.* In Shakespeare the fathers' errors unleash evil in the children, causing the destruction of both generations, but every action, whether for evil or good, derives its meaning from the unalterable moral framework which embraces both generations. Therefore the world of Edgar and Albany and Kent stands firm at the end; it is the timeless norm of love, allegiance, and patience in suffering. And the convulsive clash between the generations turns out to be an episode of individual error and sin *sub specie aeternitatis.* But in the modern play Hebbel views the strict morality of the older generation as an historical phenomenon, subject to the pressures of a changing world. He questions its validity in the contemporary social circumstances; and it is precisely because the father raises his fundamentalist convictions to the status of iron law in his household that the conflict between the generations must end tragically.

What interests the modern dramatist is not the tragic change of the hero (*quantum mutatus ab illo:* "O, woe is me / T'have seen what I have seen, see what I see!") within an accepted frame of ideal moral order, but the tragic role of the individual either as victim of an inflexible, institutionalized social order or as agent and sacrificial victim at the point of collision between old and new ideologies. A thoroughly modern aphorism reads, "In a war of ideas it is people who get killed." [Quoted in a review of Stanislaw J. Lec, *Unkempt Thoughts* (Macmillan), in *TLS,* May 31, 1963, p. 394. —Author's note.] Since the fate of the modern hero can be understood only in the context of an historical moment of change or a compelling social milieu, his role is partially defined by factors external to his personality. He suffers before he acts, or as Hebbel

A scene from August Strindberg's Comrades, *produced by the author at the Intimate Theatre, Stockholm, in 1910.*

put it more precisely, the suffering gives birth to action. Therefore, the modern protagonist, like Hamlet, seems to have lost the cue to independent action or at best tries to escape his dilemma in a desperate final act. He is a passive figure compared with the traditional heroes who suffer in consequence of a free act of commitment, right or wrong; whatever motives for action he has, they are not alone derived from his individual character or from a moral conviction or a specific passion, but are in part given by the situation in which he finds himself. Hebbel had accurately predicted that Shakespeare's dialectic of characters would be replaced by a dialectic of ideas in the new drama, thus reducing the modern protagonist to the role of agent and victim of forces beyond him; he would have to *re*act to circumstances not of his own making.

In their determined rejection of all forms of romantic idealism, the realists and naturalists of the latter part of the 19th century embraced this bleak view of the human condition as the only honest one. They refused to grant their protagonists resources of energy and inspiration to shape and suffer their own destiny since that would have been a falsification of the actual conditions of existence in modern society. The typical conception of the hero's role in the new drama was an inevitable result of the task which the realists and naturalists set themselves: to mirror the contemporary world with scrupulous attention to historical, sociological and psychological facts. Hence, on the one hand we have Strindberg's claim that the characterization in his drama is both a more faithful rendering of life and much more complex than that of the older drama. But on the other hand such a conception of character as being the product of multiple external and internal forces also re-

duces the hero's autonomy; thus it calls into question the possibility of a tragic act and, beyond that, even the possibility of dramatic action and dialogue, which was Brunetière's criticism of the new drama.

Not long after the first flush of excitement over the renascence of the modern drama had worn off, Georg Lukács worked out the sociological implications and their formal consequences in the development of this new social drama, recognizing the crucial shift of focus in the modern conception of tragedy. If the tragic act is no longer a matter of free moral choice, if, on the contrary, the human agent is so inextricably connected with his background, his time, the ideological atmosphere, and a given social situation that his will cannot be considered autonomous, the relation of the doer to his deed must be called into question. If he is not responsible for his deed, since the motivation has been largely determined by social forces and circumstances around him, can we still speak of tragedy? Lukács clearly saw the risk that naturalism might reduce the human actor to the position of a figure on a chessboard and thus become altogether non-dramatic. But in answering this question, he took his cue from Hebbel who faced the same dilemma in his critical speculations half a century earlier. From a realistic, historical point of view, the domination of the character by his situation, of the actor by his act, is undeniable. The problem, then, is "to build a bridge between the deed and the doer," to find another point of view by which, all "scientific" facts to the contrary, the autonomy of the tragic actor can be saved. [Lukács, pp. 338-342. —Author's note.] Hebbel had found it in his conception of tragic guilt, which was for him not merely a "way out" in order to preserve the genre in modern times, but a moral and an artistic insight showing the personal cost of the dialectic war of ideas. Guilt, in Hebbel's view, accompanies all human action insofar as individual self-assertion, representing a single ethical claim, comes in conflict with the general will. In *Maria Magdalene,* for example, he had set himself the task of deriving the idea of guilt without resorting to positively evil motives. Ibsen shared this tragic vision in his social plays, but in his late work, in an effort to overcome the ambiguous motivation inherent in the naturalistic outlook, he resorted to the idea of the daemonic, returning to his heroes a measure of autonomy and moral presumption reminiscent of the tragic aura of the older drama.

But Lukács, though he writes incisively about the dilemma of the realistic social drama and the naturalistic milieu drama, was evidently so intent upon defending them as new forms of tragedy that he minimized, quite unnecessarily, the difference between two distinct tragic experiences. It makes no difference, he says, whether the will which resists fate originates entirely inside the human actor or not, whether it is free or determined by circumstances. The conflict of forces in the latter instance is, in fact, more complex and more interesting so long as the inner power of resistance lasts. But what of the dramatic quality of such a conflict? Again Hebbel clarified the problem for him by his perception that in the modern situation suffering is equivalent to an inwardly directed action and that every act, in opposition to one's fate, assumes the form of suffering. Lukács makes an excellent case for the tragic stature of the modern hero: his will is not his own, he is driven to defend himself, he acts from desperation and necessity—yet the intensity of his commitment is such that he symbolizes the fate of the modern individual in a conflict of essentially abstract forces. The new drama demonstrated that an idea or a social value can serve as a powerful motive, and if it is made palpable dramatically as a passionate tenacity in suffering and action, it can assume tragic proportions. [Lukács, pp. 340, 342-345. —Author's note.]

Obviously, the nature of the tragic experience is altered in the modern social drama. In the classic tragic theaters, whether Greek, Elizabethan, or French, where the moral order of the universe was predetermined, the hero lost his autonomy only as a consequence of his freely chosen course of action. In contrast, the modern drama must first delineate the complex social order which is to be the arena of the hero's possible actions; it must each time create a rational structure of ideas, events, and psychological motives which defines the protagonist and at the same time foreshadows his sealed fate. Thus it embraces a wider and more analytic consciousness of the forces outside the human character which initially formulate his tragic dilemma; this consciousness becomes part of the tragic experience, as, for example, the dialectic scene between Warwick and Cauchon in *Saint Joan.* The tragic necessity is given at once in the situation as it unfolds rather than surmised in the moral consequences of an act disruptive of a universally accepted order. Thus, Strindberg's remark that the naturalists have abolished guilt with God in their dramas is not to be taken as testimony of widespread unbelief; it only shows that the basis of tragic guilt in the new

drama is not necessarily ethical. The fourth scene of *Saint Joan* in effect seals the Maid's tragic fate since she cannot swerve from an idea which she embodies, yet neither Warwick nor Cauchon, and least of all Joan herself can be considered guilty in the moral sense.

These new premises of the realistic and naturalistic drama have so changed the conception and the aesthetic form of tragedy that not only our intellectual but also our emotional response must be different. Tragic irony in the traditional sense has disappeared. In the Aristotelian view it depended on *peripeteia,* a "good" intention reversed. And since the fate of the legendary heroes was a matter of public knowledge, even the first entrance of Oedipus was a powerful stroke of irony; beneath the royal robes of the self-confident king the audience must have seen the beggar in exile, groping in the darkness. In the Shakespearean tragedy the audience could recognize the fatal error long before the hero did—an ironic distancing from the hero. But significantly this is not the case in *Hamlet,* the most "modern" of Shakespeare's tragedies, where from the start the hero is placed in a complex and baffling situation to which he must *react.* Under these circumstances tragic irony in the classic sense is impossible because, as the Romantic critics indicated, we *are* the oppressed hero. Similarly, as an audience of common men, we instinctively recognize the reality of modern life in the caged existence of Woyzeck or Mrs. Alving or Willy Loman. With the loss of tragic irony, however, we also experience the loss of a sense of pity. Since the modern playwrights typically assume the role of advocate or executioner, and not the role of judge, and since we therefore tend to identify ourselves with the realistically portrayed characters, the emotional effect of the new tragic drama is sometimes terror, but more often self-pity.

Of course, different forms of incidental irony are still possible in the new drama, but the pervasive sense of tragic irony predicated on the blindness of the hero is gone. In its stead the modern drama often produces a sense of tragic paradox predicated on the guiltless guilt of the modern hero; the world cannot tolerate his momentary inspirations, his dreams, his gestures of independence, in short his attempts at asserting his individual being, however good his intentions may be. But not only a personal idea transformed into purpose may clash with the impersonal laws of nature or society, sometimes his very being, the fact of human existence, can become a tragic motive. At this point the feeling of helplessness gives way to the feeling of despondency; the best of these dramas, from *Woyzeck* to *Death of a Salesman* elicit a response which is necessarily distinct from the classic formulation, pity and terror.

Helplessness and despondency are typically private feelings. They are possible because in the modern drama, unlike the traditional theaters, the community has no stake in the tragic action. In fact, the community as the determinant of social values and the ground of moral judgment has disappeared; so has the community as a central consciousness or a body capable of suffering misfortune, as expressed by the theatrical device of the chorus or choric characters. The modern concept of *society,* though it may presuppose the quality of cohesiveness as well as diversity, does not carry the meaning of common weal in the sense that the audience as a whole responds to the hero's fate; what happens to him may happen to the individual spectator, but his action and suffering makes no difference to the society as a whole. That is to say, he is never an object of danger and revulsion or of celebration and pity. He is never expelled from the community or sacrificed for the common weal.

"The time will demand a social drama," said the nineteenth-century critics. They were correct, and what they meant was that society itself would become an object of analysis. Dramatically it would become one of the chief actors in a tragic struggle put on view for the modern audience. A great historic struggle may signal a modification in social values, but in general the social structure survives unaffected. Thus society has become a dramatic agent, a stage concept, a given set of imperturbable powers, and our response as single spectators is directed to the private motives, the suffering and the destruction of the individual protagonist. From this point of view, Eliot's *Murder in the Cathedral* is an instructive compromise between the old drama and the new. It manages to resemble both *Samson Agonistes* and *Saint Joan* in that the society, the temporal power, serves as antagonist, making Becket's martyrdom possible, yet the action and the suffering of the hero is at the same time a communal matter—the women of Canterbury suffer and in their suffering get to know the meaning of Becket's action. Eliot attempts to recreate the fusion of audience and chorus in communal consciousness.

The developing concept of the social drama, as well as the novel relationship between hero and spectator, brings with it characteristic formal changes. In particular, the function and, therefore, the form of the plot in the new drama adapt themselves to altered purposes. If by plot in its most general sense we mean the arrangement of incidents amounting to an intention (i.e., giving direction to a complex experience), the ends which the playwright has in view will determine his means. If the end of a tragic action is to arouse pity and fear, Aristotle's law of probability or necessity is a reasonable deduction to make as to the best formal arrangement of the incidents; in a "complex" plot it insures the effects of inevitability and surprise. Shakespeare's mixed logical and analogical plot structures serve in turn his view of the drama as *exemplum* or as analogue of the fall of man; thus Cassio's temptation and subsequent loss of reputation in the second act prefigure Othello's greater temptation and fall. On the other hand, the end of the modern social drama is to render, not Everyman's disruption of the moral law and his consequent destruction, but every man's potentially fatal involvement with the external and internal forces that shape his life; the end is to explore and, as Otto Mann has said, to *interpret* reality. But the pattern of such an analytic and mimetic rendering of life need not be logical, nor is it prefigured in myth or any known symbolic action.

The classical conviction that poetry (i.e. tragedy) is more philosophical than history and the Christian humanist corollary that it is morally preferable eventually give way to the notion of the modern realistic writer that the serious drama should be a faithful interpretation of history. For to him the historical or sociological event is inescapable fact which needs to be understood in itself as a determinant of the human condition; it is the sum of reality. Thus plot in the traditional sense, which is the imposition of a symbolic pattern upon the recognizable events of life or the logical ordering of moral consequences, is liable to disappear. That is why the "well-made" plot, a pale vestige of the law of probability or necessity, when it is used for serious purposes in the social drama, leaves the impression of disingenuousness. For the explicit aim of realistic drama is to imitate history in the making; consequently, the devices of an irrelevant logic betray the intention of demonstrating a moral lesson or a sociological thesis. Therefore, the realistic and naturalistic playwrights who looked to the possibility of a modern tragic drama avoided this exercise in form without substance. They preferred to analyze inductively the significant relation of character to milieu and the course of a human passion as it would naturally develop.

Ibsen, who was attracted both by temperament and training to the logical plot, converted the formula of the well-made plot to usefulness in his tragic drama by placing the center of gravity in the moral choice of his characters rather than the fatal play of misstep and accidental discovery. He became, in effect, a classical dramatist, increasingly devoted to the moral and symbolical representation of human failure rather than the strictly analytic and historical representation of reality. The possibility of abandoning the traditional plot structures presented itself to the less conservative dramatists as a result of their new conception of the function of the drama and the example of the novel as a flourishing art form. Hence the tendency toward epic form in the drama which was due to the effort to trace the process of historical change and the evolution of ideas. Zola tried to reproduce on stage the effect of the physical and social milieu upon the lives of individuals. And Strindberg noted with interest that *Hamlet* was "novellenartig." On the assumption that the suffering and the defeat of the modern hero was due to a multiplicity of causes which could be explained in their cumulative effect, the traditional logical plot lost its relevance to this new view of tragic necessity. The modern dramatist as historian, sociologist, and psychologist tends to present his case in its devious, concrete, and intellectual ramifications; he lets the intellectual perception of a tragic dilemma emerge from a sequence of scenes which is no less compelling than the dramatically logical operation of Nemesis.

Once the tragic focus shifted from the moral and psychological interplay between human agents within a known framework of natural order to the interplay between the protagonist and the forces to which he is exposed in a specific political and social milieu, the drama was bound to break out of its traditional forms. But the power of tradition is strong, and the theater has always been a conservative institution. Therefore, though a great number of plays produced in the last hundred years display the characteristic outlook of realism and naturalism, they yet limit their range of perception by adhering to the classic dramatic forms. The landmarks in the history of the modern drama are those plays which experimentally tried to find an adequate form to embody new premises of thought (for example, Büchner's *Dantons Tod*) and those plays which represent the triumph of the experiment. As we have seen, the more or less radical formal changes in the new drama, which account for a response that is necessarily different from that elicited by the traditional drama, are principally due to the changed conception of the tragic hero. As Ronald Peacock says [in his "Public and Private Problems in Modern Drama," *TDR,* III, 1959], we ought to be aware of "distinct dramatic forms for distinct visions of man in society and amidst historical change." Related to the altered view of man's potentially tragic condition is the question of the hero's capacity and motive for action in a realistically conceived dramatic world, and ultimately the question of the relation between agent and action in a situation shaped by forces other than the hero's will.

Alfred Schwarz, "Toward a Poetic of Modern Realistic Tragedy," in Modern Drama, *Vol. 9, No. 2, September, 1966, pp. 136-46.*

Jovan Hristić

[*A Serbian dramatist, poet and scholar, Hristić has won awards in his country for his stage and radio plays. In the following essay, he asserts that realism rather than tragedy dominates the modern stage because it corresponds "almost perfectly with our time, which rejects any idea of the possible existence of the transcendental." If the techniques of realism do not produce great drama, he claims, they nevertheless effectively articulate the loneliness of the modern individual.*]

We could begin with a number of possible definitions of realism, and then observe the ways in which they can be applied to the modern drama. But it seems to me that there is an approach which is far more relevant to the problem of realism in modern drama. We should not forget that literary movements do not take the form of more or less abstract theoretical definitions: they are closely connected to certain literary genres, and we can scarcely think about them without considering these genres at the same time. Romanticism represents the absolute domination of lyric poetry, and when we say "realism," there immediately comes to mind the novel, "the major vehicle of literary realism," as Harry Levin has called it. The novel is certainly the genre in which the ideals of realism are best and most adequately realized—to be more precise, in order that they be realized at all, the novel was needed, the only literary genre equipped to recreate observed and everyday life in a way which would satisfy our instinct for imitation and the desire for recognition.

That is why the problem of realism in modern drama should first of all be treated as a problem of the relationship between the drama and the novel. It is not at all accidental that the beginnings of naturalistic theater are connected with the dramatization of one novel in particular, Zola's *Thérèse Raquin.* In this manner realist theater (the expressions *realism* and *naturalism* can for now be considered synonymous) already at the very outset emphasized the close tie with the art of the novel, which had become a certain type of model for observing and representing life. Nor can we forget that Ibsen's realist plays—the first real-

ist plays in the history of modern theater—are often considered final chapters of unwritten novels. It is for this reason that Lukács says that *Rosmersholm* is in fact a novel, whose last chapter Ibsen "dressed in the exterior form of the drama," and Raymond Williams says that *The Wild Duck* "involves a degree of detail which cannot fully be realized in the explicit, spoken framework of the play. The refinement of the characters, one might say, is a fictional refinement; the degree of attention to motive and behavior is that of the psychological drama." In the jargon of the theatrical world, realist drama is often called "the art of the novel on the stage."

What does all this mean? Ibsen is a writer who initiated the modern period in the history of drama, and when at the very beginning of this period we find that the drama is in such close proximity to the novel, something is revealed about the nature not only of realist drama, but also of modern drama in general. Ibsen wanted to return to drama its lost literary and intellectual dignity and—consciously or unconsciously—he found himself close to the art of the novel, the central literary genre of the second half of the nineteenth century. The novel was—and still remains—a genre which speaks in the most adequate fashion possible about problems which we consider the most relevant for man, and Ibsen wanted, without doubt, to show how the drama could also deal with them. He wished to show how the drama could be serious literature, and to accomplish this, he had to write drama which would speak about things which the novel spoke of, in a way which the novel spoke about them: that was one proof of seriousness, just as in seventeenth-century France taking subjects from classical mythology and history was proof that the drama could be a serious literary genre, and not just a dubious form of amusement. For drama is a genre which is in constant danger of being degraded, and this is why dramatists, when they wish to emphasize the dignity of their work, turn most often to others for help. When Racine, in his introductions, refers to Tacitus or Livy, it is not only an exhibition of classical erudition but also a direct proof that writing for the theater can be as serious as any historical work. And in the nineteenth century, when sociology and psychology did not yet exist in the form in which we know them today, the novel was a scientific exploration of life, expressing certain ultimate and important truths about life.

That is why Ibsen leaned on the novel: to be more exact, he had to lean on the novel because it was a guarantee of literary and intellectual seriousness. It is even possible to show who his model is: Balzac. Plays of Ibsen's realist period were meant to be studies of society and human character equally as serious as *La Comédie humaine.* Admittedly, Balzac is great, while Ibsen remains only a great second-rate writer, but both of them want to explore man and society, man in the various relationships in which we find him in society. We can read *La Comédie humaine*—if we have the time—from the very beginning to the end, without interruptions; we cannot see productions of separate plays one after another. But if it were possible, in some imaginary theatrical festival, to see all of Ibsen's thirteen realist plays one after another, a magnificent panorama of personalities would appear in front of our eyes, just as in Balzac: of families, great capitalist firms, public life in all its forms, personalities who adapt themselves, and those who do not, success and failure, and so on.

This relationship with the novel is not only the mark of Ibsen's drama, nor is it only the beginning of modern theater; the entire history of modern drama develops within its framework. There are writers who accepted the challenge of the novel: for example, Chekhov, a great writer of short stories who did not write novels. Drama was his greatest literary form. He undertook minute psychological analysis of characters, which is a privileged area of the novel; he accepted temporal extension, which also belongs to the novel. But we cannot say that we discover behind his plays the skeleton of a novel. He extended the frontiers of drama—as all great writers extend frontiers of the genre in which they write—in the direction of the novel in the same way that Shakespeare succeeded in incorporating into drama the greatest poetry written in the English language. On the other hand we find in Chekhov's plays a violent antinaturalistic reaction which in fact signifies a revolt not only against naturalism, or realism, but also an effort to separate the drama from the novel, an effort to create, in our time, a specific dramatic form.

But what is this specific dramatic form? What certainly strikes one immediately are the limitations of the drama in relationship to the novel. The drama, says Una Ellis-Fermor in her brilliant book *The Frontiers of Drama,* demands "strong passions, a brief, shapely series of related deeds, grand simplicity of idea, directness, rapidity and shapeliness of presentation. Essentials of dramatic form are: brevity, concentration and immediacy, clear, firm lines, strict artistic form, concentration of emotion and tempo, rapidity of pace." But, in return, from this spring "heavy liabilities inherent in its form: danger of poverty of implication or detail, thinness of character, absence of suggestive comment." In contrast to drama, the novel is an endlessly expansive genre, a genre that can assimilate practically everything; it is, as Marthe Robert calls it in her study *Roman des origines et origines du roman*—"le genre indefini": "de la littérature, le roman fait rigoureusement ce qu'il veut: rien ne l'empêche d'utiliser à ses propres fins la description, la narration, le drame, l'essai, le commentaire, le monologue, le discours . . . le roman est sans règles ni frein, ouvert a tous les possibles, en quelque sorte indéfini de tous côtés." The novel is a genre which can support a mixture of genres, and this seems to suit us especially in these times; drama, by its very nature, must be a far purer genre because it is performed on the stage. If it can be said in this fashion, it is a genre destined for purity, and that is one of the reasons why poets have been much more tempted to write drama than have novelists.

Yet this formal purity is far from being the only relevant characteristic of dramatic form. There are several far more evident features with which we must begin. In his *The Historical Novel* Lukács suggests that drama is a basically public art:

> As soon as the absent fourth wall of the theatre became only a transparent attic from Lesage's "Le Diable briteux," drama ceased to become really dramatic. For the individual viewing

drama does not accidentally participate in some sort of accidental event taken from life, does not observe through some key-hole the private life of his fellow-men, but on the contrary that which is presented to him, in its most profound content and in its essential form, must be a public event. The difficulty of a modern dramatic writer's work lies just in finding such topics in life and in subjecting these topics to an internal dramatic transformation so that, in their entirety, and in the sense previously referred to, they can satisfy the public. And here a modern dramatic writer must fight against not only the live material of modern society in the external sense, but also against his own living feelings which originate in the roots of that society.

Only what is meant by "public"? Is it only an event which is not private, that is to say, which does not limit itself to the space of one room in a house into which only those are allowed who are invited? No doubt we live in times of privacy, when everything most important in man's life takes place in his house or in his room, out of reach of those who are not directly involved in the events in question. On the other hand, the idea of what is public has degenerated to what we read in newspapers or see on television. And just because of that degeneration, drama finds itself in a rather paradoxical situation: by its most profound nature, drama is a public art, but an ever smaller circle of truly serious and meaningful events is public today. That which is public is in fact only the visible result of what is to us an inaccessible and concealed *mise-en-scène;* what is important takes place—as in Greek or classicist tragedy—behind the props, and we see only the results of certain invisible causes, ones to which we ourselves do not have access, so that which is public is in fact no longer public but actually only a decorative facade. There no longer exists the spontaneous public realm of the *polis* which, according to Hannah Arendt, is "the space where I appear to others and others appear to me, where men exist not merely like other living or inanimate things but make their appearance explicitly." Only in the private realm is man still the one who acts, who is responsible for his actions and their consequences; in the public realm man's actions and their consequences have significance for which he alone is no longer responsible, in respect to which he is not the one who acts, but is the one who is acted upon.

However, this concept of the public realm does not mean only that an event is not private, that it is limited in its consequences and significant only to a few persons who participate directly in it. For Lukács, the dramatic hero is similar to Hegel's "universal-historical individual," that is, he is a personality whose "particular goals contain what is essential in the will of the universal spirit": "a completely developed, dramatically formed plastic personality of the 'universal-historical individual' is presented in such a way that this personality, in that behavior to which he is driven by conflict, finds not only a form of direct and complete expression, but that expression at the same time comes to represent the general social, historical, and human balance of the struggle." This formation may appear quite abstract and indefinite, especially for those who do not have great sympathy for Hegel's philosophical jargon. In fact, Lukács wants to say the same thing that Northrop Frye says about the tragic hero: "The tragic hero is very great as compared with us, but there is something else, something on the side of him opposite the audience, compared to which he is small. This something else may be called God, gods, fate, accident, fortune, necessity, circumstance, or any combination of these, but whatever it is the tragic hero is our mediator with it." In other words, conflict between two persons in a play is not only a conflict between two individuals, but something larger and more embracing is at stake, something that is projected on a more universal plane. "L'essential, pour le tragique, est de mettre en présence transcendence et liberté," says the philosopher Henri Gouhier, and this observation does not refer only to tragedies, but to great drama in general insofar as we consider that "tragedy" and "great drama" are synonymous, as in fact they are. In contrast to the novel, which does not require that universal and transcendental plane on which conflicts and events are projected in the drama, the drama is always focused on something which is beyond and above life. The novel is a form of gossip, says Virginia Woolf, and this clearly expresses the basic direction taken by the novel: towards personality, towards personal history and psychology. Drama is turned away from personality, towards something which surpasses it. "Le théâtre ne s'occupe pas de la réalité, mais seulement de la vérité," says Sartre. In contrast to the novel, which is a layman's form, drama is a religious genre par excellence: from man, it always turns toward the Other, toward a broader context in which human actions acquire a meaning. That context we can call by various names, but what is important is its continual presence.

The presence of this transcendental plane on which all events are projected means that drama is not a picture of life, as is the realistic novel, but a formula of life. Of course, it is extremely difficult to define precisely what is understood by "picture" and "formula," and for this reason we must begin by following a roundabout path. Instead of a definition, let us consider—if we can call it that—a negative example: O'Neill's drama, *Mourning Becomes Electra.* O'Neill has tried to create from the classical tragedy, Aeschylus' *Oresteia,* a modern realistic psychological drama, and the result is a psychology which has no way out but to turn into the pathological. In *Oresteia,* meanwhile, there is nothing pathological, because the motives which drive Clytemnestra to murder Agamemnon, and Orestes and Electra to murder Clytemnestra and Aegisthus, are different from those everyday psychological motives which we encounter in a courtroom. We cannot be completely convinced by the oedipal hatred of Lavinia (Electra) toward Christine (Clytemnestra), nor the oedipal relationship of Orin (Orestes) toward Christine: they are only crutches which have to make psychologically convincing and recognizable a set of circumstances which is basically nonpsychological. But the relationships in the family of Atrides cannot be translated into the language of our psychology, because psychology plays hardly any role in them. They relate to our lives in a completely different way, not as an extension of our psychological and empirical life, but indirectly, in the way that mathematical formulae express certain relationships in the perceived world, translating them into a completely different language. In O'Neill's plays that transcendental level where events achieve their full dramatic meaning does not exist; in its place, he uses psychological causal relationships, which necessarily lead us to the pathological, in the same way in which Zeno's proofs against motion—which can be considered as an attempt to translate mathematical concepts directly into the language of perception—end in a paradox.

Now we can see more clearly where the problem of realism lies in modern drama. The demands of realism that events which we see in drama be immediately recognizable are in fact contrary to demands which drama must make of events about which it speaks. To be more exact, drama by its nature is a nonrealistic genre. It is hardly accidental that the idea of "realism," when applied to drama, has come to have pejorative connotations. Thus T. S. Eliot speaks about the "desert of absolute likeness to reality," and Francis Fergusson finds that "modern realism is a lingua franca, a pigeon-English of the imagination which everyone in our time can understand . . . If we have lost our bearings, if we automatically reject any stable picture of the human condition, we can still gossip about the neighbors and eavesdrop on other lives." And a man of the theater, the director Branko Gavella, concludes: "realism is too limited, and too narrow to fill the large spiritual space which the stage presents." What is more, we hardly speak about realistic drama; most often we speak about "naturalistic" theater or drama, in this way tacitly assuming that naturalism is an expression which does not flatter drama, but quite the opposite.

In any case, the problem is not only that realistic drama—as T. S. Eliot thinks—lacks firm conventions which would hold it "within the limitations of art," or (as Fergusson says) that realistic drama is "paradoxical theater, which pretends to be not art, but life itself." The problem is much broader. Conventions come later; they are something that is a consequence, and not a cause. That which is basic for Greek tragedy—which is still for us the model of drama which is "within the limitations of art"—are not conventions, but a way of looking at people, for which conventions are a totally natural expression. Without this manner of observing man, conventions lose all their meaning and become an empty form, which can best be seen in plays which attempt to resurrect for our time conventions suited to a totally different period: the plays of W. B. Yeats could serve as an example. The question of conventions is not only a question of aesthetics, but also of metaphysics, something that philosophers call a world view, and this is why it might happen that the conventions of realism, with their demand that life be directly recognizable and there be a fidelity to our perceived world, correspond almost perfectly to our time, which rejects any idea of the possible existence of the transcendental.

For, can we say that a great dramatic form has been created in our age? And next to the brilliant creations of which we are aware, the answer to this question cannot be given with certainty. First of all, for one very general reason, which relates not only to drama. Our age is not an age which has created forms capable of a long and fruitful life; it is an age of individual efforts pushed to their extremes, which demonstrate to us the existence of certain problems, but whose solution is valid only for one writer, and no one else. Those who follow in the footsteps of these writers always appear a bit comical, and end up revealing more about their origins than becoming associated with the elaboration of a fruitful program. What Eliot said for Joyce's *Ulysses*—one is enough—applies here also. In that respect, Pirandello is a challenging example. With his "theater within the theater" it appears that he was on the track of creating a great dramatic form for our time, a dramatic form of an age which rejects everything that is transcendental as far as man is concerned; yet the plays which Pirandello wrote after *Six Characters in Search of an Author* fall far short of this first effort. Neither *Each in His Own Way* nor *Tonight We Improvise* is the elaboration of a fruitful discovery, but both are rather a marking time, repeating in a somewhat monotonous fashion an idea in such a way that it turns into a cliché. The dramatic metaphors of the "theater of the absurd" have been too quickly transformed into clichés; Brecht's epic theater is somewhat more fruitful—his followers at least look less comical—but its inherent limitations lie in the fact that Brecht's view of man is too narrow: he thought, mistakenly, that society is the court of final judgment before which all questions of man's fate are decided. Thus we return to what has been said before: to be created, a great dramatic form demands a method of observation of man which is directly contrary to our own.

That is why, no matter how many efforts are made to break with realism, it is characteristic that modern drama returns to realism. Three of the most recent plays by playwrights whom we usually place among the avant-garde, or nonrealistic, demonstrate this unambiguously. I am thinking of *Not I* by Beckett, *All Over* by Albee, and *Old Times* by Pinter. After the great dramatic metaphors in *Waiting for Godot* and *Endgame,* Beckett has more and more begun to approximate a special version of psychological realism. In fact, his most recent plays are almost all realistic, with one bizarre *tour de force* which cleverly hides their realistic basis. *Play* is, in fact, a naturalistic drama broken up into fragments by a complex theatrical apparatus—persons up to their necks in large earthenware jugs, lights which illuminate their heads one by one—and by remembrances of which only fragments are left. *Eh, Joe* is also almost a totally realistic drama of the Ibsen type clothed in a bizarre theatrical form: we do not see the woman who speaks, but only the reactions of the man to whom she is addressing herself. *Not I* is also very close to psychological realism, except for the fact that the theatrical presentation is unusual. This is a long stream-of-consciousness monologue by an enormous mouth above the stage (whose obvious model is the monologue of Molly Bloom at the end of *Ulysses*) which a man listens to, from time to time lifting his hands or shrugging his shoulders. From the theatrical point of view, this is a brilliant *tour de force* in which the avant-garde achieves an almost classical purity and simplicity. But fundamentally, *Not I* is a psychological and realistic play, not only because the monologue which the listener listens to is a realistic story broken into fragments, but also because—and this is still more important—in this play Beckett is exploring a theme which is typically psychological and realistic: the theme

of man's loneliness. At first glance this may sound conventional, but the problem of loneliness is not, as we often think, that of the difficulty of communication among people (that is banal) but that some of our most important communications are picked up by those for whom they were not intended. In Beckett's play, the Listener is listening to that which, clearly, is not intended for him; to be more exact, that which is not directed toward anyone. And we all, like the Mouth, would like for someone to hear and understand that which, in essence, is not meant for anyone, and which no one can understand. Here Beckett appears to have found an adequate dramatic form for the basic human situation of our age: privacy. Similarly, both in the case of Albee and Pinter—who are writers inferior to Beckett—characters speak in monologues, which their collocutors overhear rather than listen to. If the form of the psychological realistic drama were not today overworked, *Old Times* would be such a play; but for Pinter the play of psychological causes and consequences is not necessary—today we no longer believe in causality in the unswerving way in which Ibsen did—but rather events, words, sentences, memories, associations, which seem to come from nowhere, as though they fall before us like stars from a black sky. But these events and these memories belong absolutely in the circle of realistic psychological drama.

We must be clear about one thing: art never renounces a territory it has conquered. Psychological realism—no matter how much it owes to the novel and represents, in fact, the novel on the stage—is something which exists for us as a fact; it can be the "lingua franca of the imagination" but we have not created any other. We have not created either a public language—the public language today is a caricature of language—or a great language of embracing visions of the human situation; we have created the language of privacy and loneliness, and we have nourished it, regardless of how small an area it expresses. And it is for this reason that the real discovery of modern drama lies not in the discovery of great dramatic forms modeled after the Greeks, but rather in the manner in which on the stage, which is a public place, human loneliness has been portrayed.

Jovan Hristić, "The Problem of Realism in Modern Drama," translated by Maria Shoup, in New Literary History, *Vol. VIII, No. 2, Winter, 1977, pp. 311-18.*

FURTHER READING

Brockett, Oscar G. and Findlay, Robert R. "The Independent Theatre Movement." In their *Century of Innovation: A History of European and American Theatre and Drama Since 1870,* pp. 86-119. Englewood Cliffs, N. J.: Prentice-Hall, 1973.

Delineates the effect that realism had on staging and acting in the late nineteenth century through the influence of André Antoine's *Théâtre Libre*.

Elsom, John. "Realism Revisited." *Contemporary Review* 255, No. 1482 (July 1989): 31-4.

Recounts an argument with a student in Moscow about the difference between realism and a mere accumulation of factual data.

Figgis, Darrell. "Reality in Drama." *The Living Age* LIX, No. 3595 (31 May 1913): 571-73.

Asserts that the permanent moods of humankind are best expressed in poetry, not realist prose.

Gassner, John. *Form and Idea in Modern Theatre.* New York: Holt, Rinehart and Winston, 1956, 290 p.

Discusses how realism came to dominate the modern stage and chronicles the reaction against it.

Hubbs, Clayton A. "Chekhov and the Contemporary Theatre." *Modern Drama* XXIV, No. 3 (September 1981): 357-66.

Examines the realist elements in Chekhov's *Three Sisters,* finding them characteristic of the playwright's work as a whole and an important source of his continuing sense of modernity and relevance.

Klein, John W. "Plausibility in the Theatre." *Drama,* No. 90 (Autumn 1968): 41-4.

Maintains that a slavish attention to realism degrades drama.

Leamon, Warren. "Yeats, Synge, Realism, and 'The Tragic Theatre'." *The Southern Review* IX, No. 1 (January 1975): 129-38.

Argues that William Butler Yeats's hatred of realism led him to dismiss any theory that places the roots of tragedy in the terrestrial world, and thus caused him to misunderstand the plays of John Millington Synge.

Motley, Warren. "Hamlin Garland's *Under the Wheel*: Regionalism Unmasking America." *Modern Drama* XXVI, No. 4 (December 1983): 477-85.

Demonstrates the influence of Henrik Ibsen on Garland's pessimistic social drama, *Under the Wheel.*

Nicoll, Allardyce. *A History of Late Nineteenth Century Drama, 1850-1900,* Volume I. Cambridge: Cambridge University Press, 1946, 228 p.

Surveys the history of the theater in the second half of the nineteenth century and stresses the impact of realism on drama.

Valency, Maurice. *The Flower and the Castle.* New York: The Macmillan Company, 1963, 460 p.

Presents an analysis of modern drama with an emphasis on the contribution of realism. Contains chapters on Henrik Ibsen and August Strindberg.

Irish Nationalism and Literature

INTRODUCTION

In the second half of the nineteenth century, nationalist sentiment in Ireland became increasingly widespread as the Irish people sought to free themselves from British control. The independence movement was led by the Irish Republican Brotherhood, or Fenians, a militant group of partisans who actively confronted England with the demands of the Irish cause. The most famous Fenian leader was Charles Stewart Parnell, who led the political struggle as an Irish nationalist in the British Parliament; he also amassed large public support for the Irish home rule initiative (which would have granted Ireland limited autonomy), and led the Irish Land League, an organization founded by peasant advocate and agitator Michael Davitt in 1879. Despite his parliamentary successes and extreme popularity, Parnell's credibility was severely weakened by the revelation of his adulterous affair with Katherine O'Shea in 1890, leaving the nationalist movement without an acknowledged leader. The political struggle had also been complicated by the terrorist activity of the Fenian Irish Invincibles, led by Jeremiah O'Donovan Rossa, whose exploits included the infamous 1882 Phoenix Park murders of two British ministers in Dublin. Another Fenian leader, John O'Leary, objected to both the diplomacy of Parnell and the terrorism of O'Donovan Rossa and patiently worked to organize the insurrection he viewed as inevitable; he edited the revolutionary *Irish People* newspaper, and was convicted of treason for using the publication to call the Irish people to arms against Britain. Passionate about literature as well, O'Leary believed that an artistic movement was essential to the revolutionary cause; according to scholar Malcolm Brown, O'Leary "believed that Irish poetry must be national, and Irish nationalism poetic." In the mid-1880s, O'Leary recruited William Butler Yeats to the nationalist cause; Yeats has been described as "the fertile . . . father" of the nationalist movement in literature.

While motivated by political events, the nationalist literary movement was essentially cultural rather than political. Building on the themes presented by the Young Ireland group of the 1840s (which included Thomas Davis, John Mitchel, and Charles Gavan Duffy), the literary nationalists advocated an Irish literary revival—a return to Irish mythology, culture, and history. According to Brown, Yeats and fellow revivalist George Moore frequently related Turgenev's comment that "Russia can do without everyone of us, but not one of us can do without her" in order to emphasize the importance of Ireland in their writing. The movement, however, was far from being ideologically homogeneous. Yeats, A. E. (George Russell), and John Eglinton conducted a public debate in Dublin's *Daily Express* on the forms and consequences of nationalism and isolationism. Douglas Hyde (who wrote under the Irish pseudonym An Craoibhín Aoibhinn, meaning "the fair branch") advocated the de-anglicization of Irish literature and language, while Lady Isabella Augusta Gregory's nationalism was entirely steeped in the English language. At the same time, writers such as James Joyce and Bernard Shaw were living abroad, advocating Irish independence but rejecting the revivalists' stipulation of a nationalist literature. In addition to its concentration on Irish themes, the movement was concerned with renouncing the racist histories put forth by English scholars such as James Anthony Froude and W. E. H. Lecky, as well as combatting the stereotyped and over-simplified analyses of Irish writing (such as Matthew Arnold's hugely influential 1866 study) which had thus far shaped world reaction to the literature of Ireland.

THE CELTIC ELEMENT IN LITERATURE

Matthew Arnold

[*One of the leading English critics of the nineteenth century, Arnold advocated a disinterested approach to criticism which demanded that a work of art be evaluated according to its own qualities, apart from the influence of history and the limitations of subjective experience. In late 1865 and early 1866, he delivered a series of lectures at Oxford under the title "The Study of Celtic Literature" that became the definitive analysis of the subject. In the following excerpt from those lectures, Arnold assesses the nature of the Celtic genius and its impact on the style of English poetry.*]

Let me repeat what I have often said of the characteristics which mark the English spirit, the English genius. This spirit, this genius, judged, to be sure, rather from a friend's than an enemy's point of view, yet judged on the whole fairly, is characterised, I have repeatedly said, by *energy with honesty.* Take away some of the energy which comes to us, as I believe, in part from Celtic and Roman sources; instead of energy, say rather *steadiness;* and you have the Germanic genius: *steadiness with honesty.* It is evident how nearly the two characterisations approach one another; and yet they leave, as we shall see, a great deal of room for difference. Steadiness with honesty; the danger for a national spirit thus composed is the humdrum, the plain and ugly, the ignoble: in a word, *das Gemeine, die Gemeinheit,* that curse of Germany, against which Goethe was all his life fighting. The excellence of a national spirit thus composed is freedom from whim, flightiness, perverseness; patient fidelity to Nature,—in a word, *science,*—leading it at last, though slowly, and not by the most brilliant road, out of the bondage of the humdrum and common, into the better life. The universal dead-level of plainness and homeliness, the lack of all beauty and distinction in form and feature, the slowness and clumsiness of the language, the eternal beer, sausages, and bad tobacco, the blank commonness everywhere, pressing at last like a weight on the spirits of the traveller in Northern Germany, and making him impatient to be gone,—this is the weak side; the industry, the well-doing, the patient steady elaboration of things, the idea of science governing all departments of human activity,—this is the strong side; and through this side of her genius, Germany has already obtained excellent results, and is destined, we may depend upon it, however her pedantry, her slowness, her fumbling, her ineffectiveness, her bad government, may at times make us cry out, to an immense development.

For dulness, the creeping Saxons,—says an old Irish poem, assigning the characteristics for which different nations are celebrated:—

> For acuteness and valour, the Greeks,
> For excessive pride, the Romans,
> For dulness, the creeping Saxons;
> For beauty and amorousness, the Gaedhils.

We have seen in what sense, and with what explanation, this characterisation of the German may be allowed to stand; now let us come to the beautiful and amorous Gaedhil. Or rather, let us find a definition which may suit both branches of the Celtic family, the Cymri as well as the Gael. It is clear that special circumstances may have developed some one side in the national character of Cymri or Gael, Welshman or Irishman, so that the observer's notice shall be readily caught by this side, and yet it may be impossible to adopt it as characteristic of the Celtic nature generally. For instance, in his beautiful essay on the poetry of the Celtic races, M. Renan, with his eyes fixed on the Bretons and the Welsh, is struck with the timidity, the shyness, the delicacy of the Celtic nature, its preference for a retired life, its embarrassment at having to deal with the great world. He talks of his *douce petite race naturellement chrétienne,* his *race fière et timide, à l'extérieur gauche et embarrassée.* But it is evident that this description, however well it may do for the Cymri, will never do for the Gael, never do for the typical Irishman of Donnybrook fair. Again, M. Renan's *infinie délicatesse de sentiment qui caractérise la race Celtique,* how little that accords with the popular conception of an Irishman who wants to borrow money! *Sentiment* is, however, the word which marks where the Celtic races really touch and are one; sentimental, if the Celtic nature is to be characterised by a single term, is the best term to take. An organisation quick to feel impressions, and feeling them very strongly; a lively personality therefore, keenly sensitive to joy and to sorrow; this is the main point. If the downs of life too much outnumber the ups, this temperament, just because it is so quickly and nearly conscious of all impressions, may no doubt be seen shy and wounded; it may be seen in wistful regret, it may be seen in passionate, penetrating melancholy; but its essence is to aspire ardently after life, light, and emotion, to be expansive, adventurous, and gay. Our word *gay,* it is said, is itself Celtic. It is not from *gaudium,* but from the Celtic *gair,* to laugh; and the im-

pressionable Celt, soon up and soon down, is the more down because it is so his nature to be up—to be sociable, hospitable, eloquent, admired, figuring away brilliantly. He loves bright colours, he easily becomes audacious, overcrowding, full of fanfaronade. The German, say the physiologists, has the larger volume of intestines (and who that has ever seen a German at a table-d'hôte will not readily believe this?), the Frenchman has the more developed organs of respiration. That is just the expansive, eager Celtic nature; the head in the air, snuffing and snorting; *a proud look and a high stomach,* as the Psalmist says, but without any such settled savage temper as the Psalmist seems to impute by those words. For good and for bad, the Celtic genius is more airy and unsubstantial, goes less near the ground, than the German. The Celt is often called sensual; but it is not so much the vulgar satisfactions of sense that attract him as emotion and excitement; he is truly, as I began by saying, sentimental.

Sentimental,—*always ready to react against the despotism of fact;* that is the description a great friend of the Celt gives of him; and it is not a bad description of the sentimental temperament; it lets us into the secret of its dangers and of its habitual want of success. Balance, measure, and patience, these are the eternal conditions, even supposing the happiest temperament to start with, of high success; and balance, measure, and patience are just what the Celt

Charles Stewart Parnell.

has never had. Even in the world of spiritual creation, he has never, in spite of his admirable gifts of quick perception and warm emotion, succeeded perfectly, because he never has had steadiness, patience, sanity enough to comply with the conditions under which alone can expression be perfectly given to the finest perceptions and emotions. The Greek has the same perceptive, emotional temperament as the Celt; but he adds to this temperament the sense of *measure;* hence his admirable success in the plastic arts, in which the Celtic genius, with its chafing against the despotism of fact, its perpetual straining after mere emotion, has accomplished nothing. In the comparatively petty art of ornamentation, in rings, brooches, crosiers, relic-cases, and so on, he has done just enough to show his delicacy of taste, his happy temperament; but the grand difficulties of painting and sculpture, the prolonged dealings of spirit with matter, he has never had patience for. Take the more spiritual arts of music and poetry. All that emotion alone can do in music the Celt has done; the very soul of emotion breathes in the Scotch and Irish airs; but with all this power of musical feeling, what has the Celt, so eager for emotion that he has not patience for science, effected in music, to be compared with what the less emotional German, steadily developing his musical feeling with the science of a Sebastian Bach or a Beethoven, has effected? In poetry, again,—poetry which the Celt has so passionately, so nobly loved; poetry where emotion counts for so much, but where reason, too, reason, measure, sanity, also count for so much,—the Celt has shown genius, indeed, splendid genius; but even here his faults have clung to him, and hindered him from producing great works, such as other nations with a genius for poetry,— the Greeks, say, or the Italians,—have produced. The Celt has not produced great poetical works, he has only produced poetry with an air of greatness investing it all, and sometimes giving, moreover, to short pieces, or to passages, lines, and snatches of long pieces, singular beauty and power. And yet he loved poetry so much that he grudged no pains to it; but the true art, the *architectonicé* which shapes great works, such as the *Agamemnon* or the *Divine Comedy,* comes only after a steady, deep-searching survey, a firm conception of the facts of human life, which the Celt has not patience for. So he runs off into technic, where he employs the utmost elaboration, and attains astonishing skill; but in the contents of his poetry you have only so much interpretation of the world as the first dash of a quick, strong perception, and then sentiment, infinite sentiment, can bring you. Here, too, his want of sanity and steadfastness has kept the Celt back from the highest success.

If his rebellion against fact has thus lamed the Celt even in spiritual work, how much more must it have lamed him in the world of business and politics! The skilful and resolute appliance of means to ends which is needed both to make progress in material civilisation, and also to form powerful states, is just what the Celt has least turn for. He is sensual, as I have said, or at least sensuous; loves bright colours, company, and pleasure; and here he is like the Greek and Latin races; but compare the talent the Greek and Latin (or Latinised) races have shown for gratifying their senses, for procuring an outward life, rich, luxurious, splendid, with the Celt's failure to reach any material

civilisation sound and satisfying, and not out at elbows, poor, slovenly, and half-barbarous. The sensuousness of the Greek made Sybaris and Corinth, the sensuousness of the Latin made Rome and Baiæ, the sensuousness of the Latinised Frenchman makes Paris; the sensuousness of the Celt proper has made Ireland. Even in his ideal heroic times, his gay and sensuous nature cannot carry him, in the appliances of his favourite life of sociability and pleasure, beyond the gross and creeping Saxon whom he despises; the regent Breas, we are told in the *Battle of Moytura of the Fomorians,* became unpopular because "the knives of his people were not greased at his table, nor did their breath smell of ale at the banquet." In its grossness and barbarousness is not that Saxon, as Saxon as it can be? just what the Latinised Norman, sensuous and sociable like the Celt, but with the talent to make this bent of his serve to a practical embellishment of his mode of living, found so disgusting in the Saxon.

And as in material civilisation he has been ineffectual, so has the Celt been ineffectual in politics. This colossal, impetuous, adventurous wanderer, the Titan of the early world, who in primitive times fills so large a place on earth's scene, dwindles and dwindles as history goes on, and at last is shrunk to what we now see him. For ages and ages the world has been constantly slipping, ever more and more, out of the Celt's grasp. "They went forth to the war," Ossian says most truly, *"but they always fell."*

And yet, if one sets about constituting an ideal genius, what a great deal of the Celt does one find oneself drawn to put into it! Of an ideal genius one does not want the elements, any of them, to be in a state of weakness; on the contrary, one wants all of them to be in the highest state of power; but with a law of measure, of harmony, presiding over the whole. So the sensibility of the Celt, if everything else were not sacrificed to it, is a beautiful and admirable force. For sensibility, the power of quick and strong perception and emotion, is one of the very prime constituents of genius, perhaps its most positive constituent; it is to the soul what good senses are to the body, the grand natural condition of successful activity. Sensibility gives genius its materials; one cannot have too much of it, if one can but keep its master and not be its slave. Do not let us wish that the Celt had had less sensibility, but that he had been more master of it. Even as it is, if his sensibility has been a source of weakness to him, it has been a source of power too, and a source of happiness. Some people have found in the Celtic nature and its sensibility the main root out of which chivalry and romance and the glorification of a feminine ideal spring; this is a great question, with which I cannot deal here. Let me notice in passing, however, that there is, in truth, a Celtic air about the extravagance of chivalry, its reaction against the despotism of fact, its straining human nature further than it will stand. But putting all this question of chivalry and its origin on one side, no doubt the sensibility of the Celtic nature, its nervous exaltation, have something feminine in them, and the Celt is thus peculiarly disposed to feel the spell of the feminine idiosyncrasy; he has an affinity to it; he is not far from its secret. Again, his sensibility gives him a peculiarly near and intimate feeling of nature and the life of nature; here, too, he seems in a special way attracted by the secret before him, the secret of natural beauty and natural magic, and to be close to it, to half-divine it. In the productions of the Celtic genius, nothing, perhaps, is so interesting as the evidences of this power: I shall have occasion to give specimens of them by and by. The same sensibility made the Celts full of reverence and enthusiasm for genius, learning, and the things of the mind; *to be a bard, freed a man,*—that is a characteristic stroke of this generous and ennobling ardour of theirs, which no race has ever shown more strongly. Even the extravagance and exaggeration of the sentimental Celtic nature has often something romantic and attractive about it, something which has a sort of smack of misdirected good. The Celt, undisciplinable, anarchical, and turbulent by nature, but out of affection and admiration giving himself body and soul to some leader, that is not a promising political temperament, it is just the opposite of the Anglo-Saxon temperament, disciplinable and steadily obedient within certain limits, but retaining an inalienable part of freedom and self-dependence; but it is a temperament for which one has a kind of sympathy notwithstanding. And very often, for the gay defiant reaction against fact of the lively Celtic nature one has more than sympathy; one feels, in spite of the extravagance, in spite of good sense disapproving, magnetised and exhilarated by it. The Gauls had a rule inflicting a fine on every warrior who, when he appeared on parade, was found to stick out too much in front,—to be corpulent, in short. Such a rule is surely the maddest article of war ever framed, and to people to whom nature has assigned a large volume of intestines, must appear, no doubt, horrible; but yet has it not an audacious, sparkling, immaterial manner with it, which lifts one out of routine, and sets one's spirits in a glow?

All tendencies of human nature are in themselves vital and profitable; when they are blamed, they are only to be blamed relatively, not absolutely. This holds true of the Saxon's phlegm as well as of the Celt's sentiment. Out of the steady humdrum habit of the creeping Saxon, as the Celt calls him,—out of his way of going near the ground,—has come, no doubt, Philistinism, that plant of essentially Germanic growth, flourishing with its genuine marks only in the German fatherland, Great Britain and her colonies, and the United States of America; but what a soul of goodness there is in Philistinism itself! and this soul of goodness I, who am often supposed to be Philistinism's mortal enemy merely because I do not wish it to have things all its own way, cherish as much as anybody. This steady-going habit leads at last, as I have said, up to science, up to the comprehension and interpretation of the world. With us in Great Britain, it is true, it does not seem to lead so far as that; it is in Germany, where the habit is more unmixed, that it can lead to science. Here with us it seems at a certain point to meet with a conflicting force, which checks it and prevents its pushing on to science; but before reaching this point what conquests has it not won! and all the more, perhaps, for stopping short at this point, for spending its exertions within a bounded field, the field of plain sense, of direct practical utility. How it has augmented the comforts and conveniences of life for us! Doors that open, windows that shut, locks that turn, razors that shave, coats that wear, watches that go, and a thousand more such good things, are the invention of the Philistines.

. . . . .

If I were asked where English poetry got these three things, its turn for style, its turn for melancholy, and its turn for natural magic, for catching and rendering the charm of nature in a wonderfully near and vivid way,—I should answer, with some doubt, that it got much of its turn for style from a Celtic source; with less doubt, that it got much of its melancholy from a Celtic source; with no doubt at all, that from a Celtic source it got nearly all its natural magic. . . .

[The] Celts certainly have [*style*] in a wonderful measure. Style is the most striking quality of their poetry. Celtic poetry seems to make up to itself for being unable to master the world and give an adequate interpretation of it, by throwing all its force into style, by bending language at any rate to its will, and expressing the ideas it has with unsurpassable intensity, elevation, and effect. It has all through it a sort of intoxication of style,—a *Pindarism,* to use a word formed from the name of the poet, on whom, above all other poets, the power of style seems to have exercised an inspiring and intoxicating effect; and not in its great poets only, in Taliesin, or Llywarch Hen, or Ossian, does the Celtic genius show this Pindarism, but in all its productions:—

> The grave of March is this, and this the grave of
>   Gwythyr;
> Here is the grave of Gwgawn Gleddyfrudd;
> But unknown is the grave of Arthur.

That comes from the Welsh *Memorials of the Graves of the Warriors,* and if we compare it with the familiar memorial inscriptions of an English churchyard (for we English have so much Germanism in us that our productions offer abundant examples of German want of style as well as of its opposite):—

> Afflictions sore long time I bore,
> Physicians were in vain,
> Till God did please Death should me seize
> And ease me of my pain—

if, I say, we compare the Welsh memorial lines with the English, which in their *Gemeinheit* of style are truly Germanic, we shall get a clear sense of what that Celtic talent for style I have been speaking of is.

Or take this epitaph of an Irish Celt, Angus the Culdee, [creator of the] *Félire,* or festology, . . . in which, at the end of the eighth or beginning of the ninth century, he collected from "the countless hosts of the illuminated books of Erin" (to use his own words) the festivals of the Irish saints, his poem having a stanza for every day in the year. The epitaph on Angus, who died at Cluain Eidhnech, in Queen's County, runs thus:—

> Angus in the assembly of Heaven,
> Here are his tomb and his bed;
> It is from hence he went to death,
> In the Friday, to holy Heaven.
>
> It was in Cluain Eidhnech he was rear'd;
> It was in Cluain Eidhnech he was buried;
> In Cluain Eidhnech, of many crosses,
> He first read his psalms.

That is by no eminent hand; and yet a Greek epitaph could not show a finer perception of what constitutes propriety and felicity of style in compositions of this nature. Take the well-known Welsh prophecy about the fate of the Britons:—

> Their Lord they will praise,
> Their speech they will keep,
> Their land they will lose,
> Except wild Wales.

To however late an epoch that prophecy belongs, what a feeling for style, at any rate, it manifests! And the same thing may be said of the famous Welsh triads. We may put aside all the vexed questions as to their greater or less antiquity, and still what important witness they bear to the genius for literary style of the people who produced them! . . .

The Celt's quick feeling for what is noble and distinguished gave his poetry style; his indomitable personality gave it pride and passion; his sensibility and nervous exaltation gave it a better gift still, the gift of rendering with wonderful felicity the magical charm of nature. The forest solitude, the bubbling spring, the wild flowers, are everywhere in romance. They have a mysterious life and grace there; they are Nature's own children, and utter her secret in a way which makes them something quite different from the woods, waters, and plants of Greek and Latin poetry. Now of this delicate magic, Celtic romance is so pre-eminent a mistress, that it seems impossible to believe the power did not come into romance from the Celts. Magic is just the word for it,—the magic of nature; not merely the beauty of nature,—that the Greeks and Latins had; not merely an honest smack of the soil, a faithful realism,—that the Germans had; but the intimate life of Nature, her weird power and her fairy charm. As the Saxon names of places, with the pleasant wholesome smack of the soil in them,—Weathersfield, Thaxted, Shalford,—are to the Celtic names of places, with their penetrating, lofty beauty,—Velindra, Tyntagel, Caernarvon,—so is the homely realism of German and Norse nature to the fairy-like loveliness of Celtic nature. Gwydion wants a wife for his pupil: " 'Well,' says Math, 'we will seek, I and thou, by charms and illusions, to form a wife for him out of flowers.' So they took the blossoms of the oak, and the blossoms of the broom, and the blossoms of the meadow-sweet, and produced from them a maiden, the fairest and most graceful that man ever saw. And they baptized her, and gave her the name of Flower-Aspect." Celtic romance is full of exquisite touches like that, showing the delicacy of the Celt's feeling in these matters, and how deeply Nature lets him come into her secrets. The quick dropping of blood is called "faster than the fall of the dewdrop from the blade of reed-grass upon the earth, when the dew of June is at the heaviest." And thus is Olwen described: "More yellow was her hair than the flower of the broom, and her skin was whiter than the foam of the wave, and fairer were her hands and her fingers than the blossoms of the wood-anemone amidst the spray of the meadow fountain." For loveliness it would be hard to beat that; and for magical clearness and nearness take the following:—

> And in the evening Peredur entered a valley, and

at the head of the valley he came to a hermit's cell, and the hermit welcomed him gladly, and there he spent the night. And in the morning he arose, and when he went forth, behold, a shower of snow had fallen the night before, and a hawk had killed a wild-fowl in front of the cell. And the noise of the horse scared the hawk away, and a raven alighted upon the bird. And Peredur stood and compared the blackness of the raven, and the whiteness of the snow, and the redness of the blood, to the hair of the lady whom best he loved, which was blacker than the raven, and to her skin, which was whiter than the snow, and to her two cheeks, which were redder than the blood upon the snow appeared to be.

And this, which is perhaps less striking, is not less beautiful:—

> And early in the day Geraint and Enid left the wood, and they came to an open country, with meadows on one hand and mowers mowing the meadows. And there was a river before them, and the horses bent down and drank the water. And they went up out of the river by a steep bank, and there they met a slender stripling with a satchel about his neck; and he had a small blue pitcher in his hand, and a bowl on the mouth of the pitcher.

And here the landscape, up to this point so Greek in its clear beauty, is suddenly magicalised by the romance touch:—

> And they saw a tall tree by the side of the river, one-half of which was in flames from the root to the top, and the other half was green and in full leaf.

Magic is the word to insist upon,—a magically vivid and near interpretation of nature; since it is this which constitutes the special charm and power of the effect I am calling attention to, and it is for this that the Celt's sensibility gives him a peculiar aptitude. . . .

Matthew Arnold, "On the Study of Celtic Literature," in Lectures and Essays in Criticism, *Vol. III, edited by R. H. Super, 1962. Reprint by The University of Michigan Press, 1973, pp. 291-386.*

John V. Kelleher

[*In the following essay, Kelleher portrays Matthew Arnold's* On the Study of Celtic Literature *as a misrepresentation of earlier Irish literature, but argues that it marked a turning point in the critical reception of Irish literature and was strongly influential in the subsequent Celtic literary revival.*]

I

When Matthew Arnold set out to describe the characteristics of Celtic literature and to analyze its effects, he paid the Celtic world the first valuable compliment it had received from an English source in several hundred years. However, the compliment, though enthusiastic, was guarded. Arnold noted this literature as the source of much of the lightness and brightness that rescued English literature from the heavy dullness of its Teutonic origin. He did not suggest that it rivaled English or classical literature in stature, or that any attempt should be made to revive it as a living mode. He took care, too, to be modest in his praise of its excellencies, to claim no more for it than could easily be justified—and this perhaps was his greatest service to the Celtic cause; for if he had shown too much enthusiasm, the audience he addressed would likely have dismissed his entire essay as another example of crackpot philo-Celticism. So carefully did he seem to measure and balance his thesis that the lectures became a contemporary classic of criticism, and in another generation had become the accepted doctrine, not only on Celtic literature, but on the literature of the Celtic Revival which Arnold had not contemplated. For all practical purposes it is the doctrine commonly accepted today.

The influence of Arnold's praise can be judged from the ease with which the Celtic Revival won popular critical support. As a literary movement the Revival began to be prominent in the early nineties. At about the turn of the century it became a large movement with a great many writers working within its boundaries; and nearly all, late or early, who were identified with it had a remarkably easy time getting themselves accepted. Even at the beginning, when its language and themes were awkward or unfamiliar, its authors obscure young people, it got unusually good notices and sympathetic handling in the English press. This cordiality lasted the life of the Revival—that is to say, for the quarter century between 1890 and the outbreak of the Irish Revolution—and it was expressed in almost exactly the same terms at the end as at the beginning. In other words, the critics had come by what they considered a satisfactory estimate of the movement as soon as it appeared, and later saw no reason to alter their decision substantially. As might be suspected from so general an agreement, no one of the contemporary critics had laid down the terms of the appraisal himself. Rather they were accepting in this, as in so much else, a commentary of Arnold's. And let it be noted, Arnold's commentary has gone virtually uncontradicted since it was made, in 1866.

This long immunity from criticism is one of the strangest things about the essay. From the start it must have been plain to Celtic scholars that Arnold, though a sympathetic partisan of their work, was not very well qualified to discuss it, at least in such sweepingly general terms. Then, too, not content with discussing literature, he had gone on to describe and pass judgment on the Celtic character in terms more kindly than complimentary. Though he assessed his own qualifications very modestly indeed, his modesty was not reflected in the way he cut up or retouched the passages he quoted to prove his points. And there was much that must have been plain irritating at any time about his calm assumption that the Anglo-Saxon, for all his faults, was head and shoulders above the Celt in any trait or talent that really counted in this world. Since most of the Celtic scholars were Celts themselves—or Germans, and in this essay Arnold seemed insultingly patronizing to the German character, or lack of it—it is really surprising that the publication of the essay, in 1867, was not followed at once by a series of competent rebuttals. As

it was, no one did fire the shot at him. Apart from a polite footnote of Whitley Stokes's modifying one of Arnold's statements and Alfred Nutt's mild strictures in his critical edition of the essay, published in 1910, no one seems to have called Arnold to question for anything he said on the subject. Indeed, till this day, though it probably would be hard to find anyone to support Arnold's thesis, the only plain opposition to it is contained in *John Bull's Other Island,* where Shaw proves that every characteristic Arnold thought of as typically Celtic is typically English, and, of course, vice versa. And Shaw does not mention Arnold either in the introduction or the play.

There are plenty of reasons for this hands-off attitude, any of which might be sufficient to account for it. The most obvious is that those competent to criticize the essay at the time it appeared were not impressed by it or thought it too wide of the mark to discuss. Afterwards, it would be thought of as out of date and forgotten. There is, too, the fact that Arnold was sympathetic, which for the time made him unique of his kind and generation and one to be treated gently. But I think the most likely explanation is that the Celts and their few friends saw him only as one more of those perennial British reformers, kindly, innocent, and slightly foolish, who have always been ready to take a shot at solving the Anglo-Celtic question or some aspect of it without hurting anybody. Such Englishmen are always given free run in the Celtic provinces. It is well known that they don't bite.

Arnold was particularly that sort of Englishman. Besides *On the Study of Celtic Literature* (1867) he published, in the early eighties, two essays on Irish problems, one dealing with Gladstone's Land Act of 1881, the other with a subject he knew a good deal more about: the educational system in Ireland. He was always cautious—one never knew in those years when the latest round of concession and coercion would be punctuated with a blast of Fenian dynamite—but it is plain that he felt the basic question could be solved by sound British sense, a little fair give-and-take, and hands clasped all round. Maybe he was right. Those ideas were never fully tried. But the trouble with all those who thought like Arnold, and it is to England's credit that they were very many, is that they seem never to have considered seriously the third alternative to the kiss or the kick, that of letting the Irish have the limited independence and national recognition they were fighting for. Arnold really meant what he said about the Celts; and as we shall see, that meant no separation from England, no throwback from the millennial advance of British progress. Present circumstances aside, it was for the Celts' own good that they should be absorbed by the Anglo-Saxon society that ruled them. Arnold could be sympathetic, particularly to that which touched his poetic sensibilities; but as a trueborn Englishman he would stand for no damned foolishness.

To the Irish, who were less inclined to ignore the present circumstances, Arnold's political and racial ideas could only seem a weary staleness. Well-intentioned Englishmen had been saying the same things about reason and light for a long time now, but they did not seem to affect the government of Ireland. Every concession the Irish won had to be fought for, no matter who agreed that it was obviously justified. The number of necessary concessions yet to be won was immense. And who in Ireland could take seriously the man who, in 1866, had come up with this whopper:

> The sensuousness of the Greek made Sybaris
> and Corinth, the sensuousness of the Latin made
> Rome and Baiae, the sensuousness of the Lati-
> nised Frenchman makes Paris; the sensuousness
> of the Celt proper has made Ireland.

The Irishman proper of 1866, sensuously tightening his belt after a meal of sour milk and potatoes, could only reply that he hadn't quite made this Ireland all by himself, and turn his thoughts back to landlordism, rents, potatoes, rents, and landlords.

The chances are that, until 1892 or after, nobody in Ireland paid any serious attention to what Arnold had to say on any Celtic or Irish subject. After 1892 a great many young men did; but then the circumstances of Irish life were much changed; and Arnold was dead and not likely to contradict the young men's interpretation of his ideas. That the Celtic Revival and Arnold's plain influence on it came then shows, if you like, that in 1866 Arnold had been far in advance of his time. More likely it shows that he had been talking without any realistic observation in mind. Certainly he had neither predicted nor advocated a Celtic Revival: quite the contrary. Certainly it is plain that he had no notion of the circumstances under which literature of the type he described could prosper and become influential in the modern world. Very likely he would have been annoyed by the whole thing, at least until it had proved its merits, when his fair mind would have brought him to praise it as he praised all fine things. But he died in 1888.

II

The Celtic Revival expressed the mood of its time, and in Ireland that mood was established by the Parnellite disaster and by the double failure of the Fenian movement, first in its attempt at open rebellion, culminating in 1867, then in the involvement of the Fenian rank and file in the collapse of Parnell's party in 1891. The Fenian failure meant the end for a long time of effective revolutionary action. Parnell's fall, after he had brought the country so near to Home Rule, took away all real hope that the constitutional movement would get to its goal of a separate legislature for Ireland at any time in the near future. At least as important was the fact that the political split, coupled with the very substantial and continuing land reforms won in the eighties, had changed the spirit of the peasantry from the most radical in Europe to the caution of newly established or anticipant petty proprietors. There would be no further serious action in Ireland until these new gains had been consolidated, and until a new generation, brought up to a large share of political freedom, would declare for more. That it would so declare was by no means certain.

The advance of Irish prosperity from the 1880's onward was real and tangible. Rackrenting, pauperism, recurrent famine had at last come to an end. For the first time in centuries the Irish peasant and small farmer could look beyond this year's crop and plan for security. The economic basis of freedom was being established, which meant that if another bout of rebellion came Ireland would have some staying power, would not have to depend solely on the hope that a sudden fierce blow might catch England involved in greater difficulties and compel her to let Ireland go by default.

For all that, the mood of the strictly orthodox Nationalists was low. The older Fenians, those who like John O'Leary had refused to go along with Davitt and Parnell in combining land agitation with the political movement, had always insisted that to solve the land question before achieving the political solution would be to destroy the fighting spirit of the peasantry. Now it seemed as if they had been right. There was plenty of passion in Ireland in the years immediately following the Parnellite disaster, but it was no longer pure—it had been infected by materialistic motives. Truly the golden age of '98 and '48 and the silver age of '67 had passed, and the iron age had come. While Redmond and Dillon and Healy and O'Brien squabbled and fought for the leadership none could fill, the romance of Irish patriotism seemed to dim and wink out. Year followed dull prosperous year, each adding new thousands to the lists of small holders, and with every year the response to the old slogans became feebler and more prosaic, till at last Yeats would write,

> Romantic Ireland's dead and gone,
> It's with O'Leary in the grave,

mourning at once the greatest Fenian spirit and the apparent loss of all that that spirit had coveted.

What no one seemed to reflect upon was the plain truth that Irish romanticism had always been a middle-class notion, and that this iron age was establishing a middle-class Ireland. With the rise of prosperity from the eighties on, and the spread of education, the audience receptive to romantic nationalism was greatly increased. This was apparent enough in 1916 when a few hundred men could rise "in the name of God and of the dead generations," taking on the armed might of England in what they knew was a blood sacrifice; and when, in the same year, after the leaders had been executed, most of the country took up the challenge and accepted the consequences of revolution. Among the leaders of that rising were schoolteachers, minor poets, Gaelic enthusiasts, their heads full of Yeats's poetry and all the heroic antiquity his school had evoked. Yet Yeats himself was the last to recover from the shock of the Rising. He wrote the O'Leary poem in 1913.

The question of his responsibility for Easter Week, 1916, dogged him to the end of his life, cropping up more and more insistently in his verse till the *Last Poems* are full of it.

> Did that play of mine send out
> Certain men the English shot?

It had; and not only the play *Cathleen ni Houlihan,* but his poetry, and all that he had preached in his earlier years. That he conceived of the poet's role as that of patriot and creative nationalist was clear enough, in 1892, when he had written:

> May not we men of the pen hope to move some

Irish hearts and make them beat true to manhood and to Ireland? Will not the day come when we shall have again in Ireland . . . men like the men of '48, who lived by the light of noble books and the great traditions of the past? Amidst the clash of party against party we have tried to put forward a nationality that is above party.

For many reasons—among them its date—that is a most important statement in regard to the Celtic Revival. It shows how soon Yeats had recognized what the character of Irish literature must be after Parnell. The poet's nationalism is henceforth "above party." He is to be like the men of '48, like Thomas Davis who had founded the Young Ireland school that still dominated Irish writing, and like them he is to appeal to Irish hearts through the "great traditions of the past."

Yet the poet would no longer be bound by Young Ireland's forms, however much he hoped to stand within their tradition. In the same year Yeats got the provisional committee of the Irish Literary Society to issue an appeal that amounted to a declaration of independence from Young Ireland:

> In recent years we have heard much of the material needs of Ireland, and little or nothing of her intellectual and literary . . . Without an intellectual life of some kind we cannot long preserve our nationality. Every Irish national movement of recent years has drawn a great portion of its power from the literary movement started by Davis, but that movement is over, and it is not possible to live forever upon the past. A living Ireland must have a living literature.

That once firmly stated—though the older writers shortly afterwards tried to retract it—the new movement was begun. All that remained was to determine the style of the new literature and what it should be about.

That had practically determined itself. After the double defeat of the constitutional and revolutionary movements, to go on writing the sort of balladry in which Young Ireland had specialized for fifty years was so impossible that it could be taken for granted the new poetry would be almost diametrically opposite in tone, if not in purpose. If Irish nationalism was not to lose heart, too many failures had to be explained and justified for poetry to go on appealing to long past victories that had never seemed to win anything, anyway, no matter how enthusiastically one remembered them now. Irish self-confidence had received a terrible jolt. It could not restore itself with stale assurances—assurances that amounted to hearty repetition of the belief that one good Irishman could lick any ten Englishmen, providing only that he were fighting in the good cause and was not hamstrung by treachery. A more subtle rationale than this was needed to hearten a nation that was now used to defeating itself. Poetry in Ireland would have to accept the atmosphere of defeat as its first ingredient; and out of defeat and melancholy it must somehow make the ultimate victory not only credible but expected.

III

With that we return to Arnold and his description of the

Celts, their literature, and their character. Twenty-six years had passed since he had lectured at Oxford on the study of Celtic literature; twenty-five, since he had published the lectures. They were now well known to everyone interested in the subject, and certainly no Irish writer would be ignorant of them. At the same time, it is useless to look for significant statistics on Arnold's influence in Ireland. It would be too painful for an evangelizing Celt to admit, even to himself, that he had got any substantial share of his gospel from an Englishman—even a good Englishman, now dead. Yeats in his essay, "The Celtic Element in Literature," first published in 1897, does "not think any of us who write about Ireland have built any argument upon [Arnold's ideas]." We may still have our suspicions about it. Of course, it may have been entirely accidental that the Celtic Revival reproduced, element for element, Arnold's picture of Celtic literature, with the difference that every weakness Arnold deplored in the Celt and his works has now become a strange characteristic strength. Or it may be that the Revival did revive the true qualities of Celtic literature, and that Arnold had been uncannily right in his estimate of those qualities. Neither is very likely. That the resemblance between Arnold's idea and the ideas of the Revival was accidental might possibly be true. The second possibility is certainly wrong. Celtic Revival literature does not resemble Celtic literature very much at all; and Arnold's knowledge of the subject was neither wide nor trustworthy. For that matter, with the exception of Douglas Hyde—and his work was only adjunct to the Revival—Yeats and his followers did not know much about Celtic literature, either. And there is the real connection.

There would likely be little to choose between Arnold's Celtic knowledge in 1866 and Yeats's knowledge in the 1890's. Yeats had collected folk stories in the Irish-speaking west; he had spent much of his youth in Sligo; he had read most Anglo-Irish literature and knew the principal heroic tales in one English redaction or another. And he was an Irishman. Arnold had none of these advantages, but he had read many of the best books and apparently all the worst books on Celtic literature and history, and he had a pretty fair nose for what was ridiculous or unsound. He appreciated good scholarship. He could recognize from a distance the worth of a great scholar like Eugene O'Curry. Better still, though he felt that the era of genuine Celtic studies had just dawned, he could give intelligent praise, across sixty or a hundred and sixty years, to great collectors like Owen Jones and Edward Lhuyd. In the *Study* the range of his learning is unobtrusively apparent: he quoted from or referred to some thirty books, covering nearly every branch of the subject then studied and including the works of French and German Celticists. (His firsthand knowledge of several of these books is not certain, since his quotations from them can also be found in others on the list.) Few English or American critics who have dealt with a Celtic topic have been so well prepared to speak—which is still not much of a compliment.

Examination of his sources gives us another significant fact. With very few exceptions the books are all *about* Celtic literature or culture. As nearly as one can make out from his references and remarks, he seems to have read—in translation, of course, for he knew no Celtic language—very little of the literature itself. Of Welsh he had read Lady Guest's *Mabinogion* and possibly Williams ap Ithel's translation of *Brut y Tywysogion,* though he only quotes from the preface to that; for Breton he had Villemarqué's French translations and Tom Taylor's English translation from Villemarqué. The rest of his quotations are from selections given in critical or descriptive works, that chiefly used being D. W. Nash's *Taliesin; or, The Bards and Druids of Britain* (1858), and as a distant second and the source of nearly every Irish passage, O'Curry's *Lectures on the Manuscript Materials of Ancient Irish History* (1861). In all, a singularly small foundation for comment on the native literatures of three countries and several provinces.

Next most remarkable is his free handling of what he had read. Take, for instance, that string of passages from the *Mabinogion,* through which, in the fifth lecture, he leads up to his illustration of Celtic "magic." The last two passages and Arnold's comment may be given here. I indicate in parentheses Lady Guest's words where Arnold has changed them; his wordings are italicized.

> "And early in the day *Geraint and Enid* (they) left the wood, and they came to an open country, with meadows on one hand and mowers mowing the meadows. And there was a river before them, and the horses bent down and drank the water. And they went up out of the river by a *steep bank* (lofty steep), and there they met a slender stripling with a satchel about his neck, (but they knew not what it was); and he had a small blue pitcher in his hand, and a bowl on the mouth of the pitcher."

> And here the landscape, up to this point so Greek in its clear beauty, is suddenly magicalised by the romance touch:—

> "And *they* (he) saw a tall tree by the side of the river, one half of which was in flames from the root to the top, and the other half was green and in full leaf."

The fault with Arnold's comment and the point he is making here is that the landscape is not thus "magicalised" for Enid and Geraint. The first passage is from the story of "Geraint the Son of Erbin," and the second is from the preceding story in the collection, "Peredur the Son of Evrawc." There are many pages in between the passages. It is also interesting that Yeats, in the "Celtic Element in Literature," quoted twice from the same string of passages, emphasizing the one about the burning tree, and in both instances with Arnold's wording. To be sure, he acknowledged his source, but may we guess that, in 1897, he knew no more about Welsh literature than Arnold had known, or knew it chiefly from Arnold?

This is by no means a unique example of how Arnold stacked his cards. When he was convinced that a "Celt-lover" had written nonsense, he was not above embellishing the nonsense on his own, to make the poor man more ridiculous than he was. He certainly did it to Algernon Herbert, to whom he credits a worse translation than Her-

bert had actually used; and there is in the first lecture a passage ascribed to Sharon Turner which conflicts with what Turner had to say and which I have not been able to find in Turner's book, *A Vindication of the Genuineness of the Ancient British Poems* (1803). Indeed, after an examination of the *Study,* it seems fairly reasonable to conclude that Arnold had made up his mind about Celtic literature before he consulted most of his material on it. How else can one explain his bland insistence that Macpherson's *Ossian,* for all that it was a fraud, still had "a residue with the very soul of Celtic genius in it"? Alfred Nutt pointed out that if Arnold had known any of the genuine Gaelic poems attributed to Oisin he would have noticed—and presumably have admitted—the utter difference in tone. Oisin, as Nutt truly said, does not weep about going forth interminably to battle and as consistently falling; rather, he does the knocking down and he enjoys it very much. Nutt, however, underestimated Arnold's resistance to what conflicted with the criteria he had himself established. At the end of the third lecture, quoting from Henry Morley's *English Writers,* where Morley spoke of "Oisin's dialogues with St. Patrick," Arnold changed the spelling to "Ossian."

His reasons for preferring Macpherson are, I think, easy enough to understand. Macpherson gave him what he wanted and what he felt ought to be right. *Ossian* fits Arnold's formula for Celticity far better than any authentic Celtic poetry would—as in turn Arnold's formula fitted the needs of the Celtic Revivalists better than did the history of any Irish period since the coming of Christianity. And once more we are indebted to Nutt for reminding us that *Ossian* reflects, through Macpherson's mind, the atmosphere of melancholy and defeat that pervaded the Scotch Highlands after 1745. We have then a reasonably clear recurrence of a similar emotional tone, first in Scotland in the mid-eighteenth century, thereafter in Macpherson, then in that part of Arnold's temperament which sensed the world as

> a darkling plain
> Swept with confused alarms of struggle and
>   flight
> Where ignorant armies clash by night,

and at last in the general feeling of disheartenment in Ireland after Parnell. And at no point in the series is real Celtic literature brought in for the primary effect. The concern is always with the present emotion and the conception it leads to. The emotions are similar and decisive.

IV

Before we come to Arnold's formula, it is but fair that we consider his motives in writing the *Study of Celtic Literature.* In his recent *Matthew Arnold: A Study in Conflict,* E. K. Brown has shown very clearly that the motives were generous and sincere: his strictures on Celtic weaknesses, part of the "strategy of disinterestedness."

> There is no doubt that he does dispel distrust, that he does preserve the appearance of disinterestedness; but, on the other hand, he does clutch at every shred of evidence he can find to sustain his argument—his dependence on current theories of race must now appear astonishingly un-

critical—he is in his heart an advocate for the Celt and not a dispassionate judge. The disinterestedness is one of strategy rather than of essential disposition. He wishes to know the Celt; he wishes no less to exalt him.

To all of which we can agree, except for his clutching at "every shred of evidence." If one means only such evidence as would bolster the Celtic claim to greatness, it is true. If one means evidence concerning Celtic literature, it is not true. Arnold took astonishingly little pains about that, and by no means for lack of evidence. For Irish literature alone the amount of recent, scholarly translation available in the 1860's was very considerable. Yet all his Irish references can be traced to four sources, two of which are more grammatical than literary. I refer to O'Curry's *Manuscript Materials,* mentioned before as the chief Irish source; to Whitley Stokes's *Three Irish Glossaries* (1862), from which he took the etymology of *triath,* "the sea," which he misspells as *traith;* and to Johann Kaspar Zeuss's *Grammatica Celtica* (1853), from which he quoted two prefatory footnotes and Zeuss's discussion of the *destitutio tenuium* as a measure for the age of linguistic forms. The fourth is probably Stokes's early edition of the "Félire of Angus the Culdee," published in India in 1863, which is likely the source of the two stanzas from the "Leabhar Breac" poem on Angus quoted in the fifth lecture. It must readily be admitted that, as an argument for recognition of Celtic worth, the *Study of Celtic Literature* is a fine, large-hearted plea. More the pity that the title is so irrelevant.

The formula, when we get to it, is not so distinctively Arnold's own as one might expect from the very Arnoldesque approach to it. As most of the illustrations of Celtic poetry in the *Study* are from Nash's *Taliesin,* so many of the touchstones are from Renan's "La Poésie des races celtiques" (1859). The mixture is Arnold's, mixed at his common-sensical British best. Renan had observed the Celts in Brittany and on a flying trip to Wales, and Arnold, plainly without an eye to the Irish vote, reminded his audience that Renan had not seen the Celt at his least tamed.

> M. Renan, with his eyes fixed on the Bretons and the Welsh is struck with the timidity, the shyness, the delicacy of the Celtic nature . . . He talks of the *douce petite race naturellement chrétienne,* his *race fière et timide, à la extérieur gauche et embarrassée.* But it is evident that this description, however well it may do for the Cymri, will never do for the typical Irishman of Donnybrook fair. Again, M. Renan's *infinie délicatesse de sentiment qui caractérise la race Celtique,* how little that accords with the popular conception of an Irishman who wants to borrow money!

But at once he adds that "sentiment" is the key word for the Celtic nature, the word "which marks where the Celtic races really touch and are one." And with that, he is off—without, however, quite warning his audience that he uses "sentimentality" in a double sense, both as the French *sentimentalité* and in a special meaning of his own: "Sentimental,—*always ready to react against the despotism of fact,*" a phrase taken from Henri Martin's chapter on the

Celts in his *Histoire de France* (1855-1860). Its effect, too, was as double as its meaning. It gave the Celt an "organisation quick to feel impressions, and feeling them very strongly; a lively personality . . . keenly sensitive to joy and sorrow," but at the same time it deprived him of "balance, measure, and patience . . . the eternal conditions . . . of high success."

"The Celtic genius," Arnold thought, had "sentiment as its main basis, with love of beauty, charm, and spirituality for its excellence, ineffectualness and self-will for its defect." It contrasted sharply and, one must admit, not altogether favorably against German "steadiness with honesty" and English "energy with honesty." Much as Arnold appreciated Celtic passion, he did not think the Celts could do much with it, for in business and politics it became evident that "the skillful and resolute appliance of means to end which is needed both to make progress in material civilisation, and also to form powerful states, is just what the Celt has least turn for." "Sensuousness" betrayed them: the sensuousness of the Celt proper that had made Ireland. Even in the realm of art failure dogged them for the same reasons.

> In . . . poetry which the Celt has so passionately, so nobly loved; poetry where emotion counts for so much, but where reason, too, reason, measure, sanity, also count for so much,—the Celt has shown genius, indeed, splendid genius; but even here his faults have clung to him, and hindered him from producing great works . . . he has only produced poetry with an air of greatness investing it all, and sometimes giving . . . to short pieces, or to passages . . . singular beauty and power.

The Celt had not patience for the "steady, deep-searching survey," the "firm conception of the facts of human life," on which true art was based.

> So he runs off into technic, where he employs the utmost elaboration, and attains astonishing skill; but in the contents of his poetry you have only so much interpretation of the world as the first dash of a quick, strong perception, and then sentiment, infinite sentiment, can bring you.

So much then for the deficiencies of Celtic poetry. They were hardly what must have attracted Arnold's interest. He had as much again to say of its excellencies; and though he may have annoyed patriotic Celts by appropriating all these virtues for English verse, he was charmingly particular about acknowledging where they had come from.

"Celtic poetry," he said, "seems to make up to itself for being unable to master the world and give an adequate interpretation of it, by throwing all its force into style, by bending language at any rate to its will, and expressing the ideas it has with unsurpassable intensity, elevation and effect." And this style was itself induced by what it had to control: the penetrating passion and melancholy bred into the Celts by their "sensuous nature, their manifold striving, their adverse destiny, their immense calamities," and issuing in what Arnold could only call *Titanism.* There was still more, for this Titanism might have created a deep and deeper gloom ending in a depression too compacted for poetical release; and this, Arnold pointed out, had not happened. Celtic literature had a "lightness and brightness" as native as its gloom: a radiance magical in its effect. "Magic is the word to insist upon,—a vivid and near interpretation of nature," an observation that went beyond faithful description of observed fact, beyond even the Greek interpretation where clarity of vision is implemented by an additional human radiance, to a perception of an interior and wayward life in the object itself, so that Celtic interpretation became as much a venture into magical revelation as into description.

V

Here, then, was a thoughtful analysis of Celtic literature, made with sympathy and good will—though with notably insufficient evidence—and published twenty-five years before the appearance of the Celtic school in English. It provided even the dullest critic with a set of tools guaranteed to give the measurements of any work called "Celtic"; and the critics used it gratefully when the need and opportunity came. So did the young Irish and Scottish authors whose work, the critics noticed, could thus be measured. The writers did not use it, however, precisely in its original form: they had to reinterpret and get rid of Arnold's strategical qualifications. The virtues he praised could be accepted at face value; the faults and weaknesses he deplored had to be explained, and, in the explanation, be shown as hidden but distinctive merits. After all, it was hardly fair that the English should wreck Celtic life and then complain of its lack of wholeness. More than a thousand years of steady, energetic Teutonic mayhem stood between the unbroken Celtic world and modernity. It would be enough, therefore, for Arnold to note the grace and indestructible vitality of the Celtic spirit—Celtic competence was not his proper concern.

It might be, as he said, that the steady Teuton or energetic Anglo-Saxon, blessed with balance, measure, and patience, was responsible for "doors that open, windows that shut, razors that shave, coats that wear, and a thousand more such good things." What had the Celt to do with these or these to do with the Celt while Ireland remained unfree? The intense spirituality of the Celt could not be shackled to such material concerns: magic and mechanics do not go together. (Besides, as Sinn Fein began presently to argue, Ireland had only to be free, and then the world would see such watches, razors, coats, and household appliances as were never seen before.)

As for Arnold's queer suggestion (it was really a remarkable insight, considering how little he knew of it) that Celtic poetry was wanting *architectonicé,* what did he expect? Was there—as any indignant patriot could ask—but one structure for great poetry, one manner of indicating that the poet's survey and conception of the facts of human life were steady, deep searching, and firm? It was quite true that the Celtic poet did not imitate the heavy didacticism of the English. He didn't need to. His audience preferred the thing "half-said," their quick response completing his subtly sketched allusion. Or so the neo-Celt of 1890 might argue, forgetting, if he had ever known, the tedious acres of bardic verse stretching out to a gray garrulous infinity.

At the same time, it is significant that those who essayed the "Celtic mode" did not often attempt any of the larger forms. Irish poetry has till now remained pretty much content with the lyric, the shorter poem of any type, satisfied apparently to depend for its effects, as Arnold said it did, on "quick, strong perception," style, and intensity.

Besides these, there was his charge of "ineffectualness and self-will." The latter seemed to require little apology. If the Celt was self-willed, he had a right to be; it was not for the humdrum Saxon to pass on that. Ineffectualness was a more pointed indictment, for it could not, on the fact of it, be easily denied—particularly by a people who had just wrecked the most powerful political movement they had ever had. It was, as a matter of fact, never really disposed of by the Celtic Revivalists. About as close as they got to a satisfactory answer was the romanticized paradoxical statement of Celtic wisdom and spirit, a way of hinting that the Celt was defeated by his own superiority. That device was, as we shall see, a favorite with the lesser poets and poetesses.

Of course, in speaking of formulas and conventions, we must understand that the convention of the Celtic school was not an elaborate, well-defined set of rules for the sure and easy production of "Celtic" literature. Rather, such a convention is a sort of lowest common denominator, made up of those elements most frequently to be found in the work of a group of writers who are related in a general

Matthew Arnold, by H. Weigall.

213

way by elements of style and choice of subject. And since those authors who begin such a convention and contribute most to it are usually those most independent of it, it is not among the works of the best Irish writers that we must look for the most complete and indicative examples. It is the minor bards, the imitators, who may write little individually, but whose numbers are as the sands of the sea or the stars on a winter's night, who can give us the convention entire in a sigh. Yeats, for instance, though he created most of the elements of the convention, never wrote a perfect Celtic Revival poem or play—though some of his early things come pretty close to it. AE's opalescent language of vision and his hazy pantheon of Celtic divinities were widely borrowed: his concern with spiritual discipline and human liberty and decency did not fit into any nationalistic school. Lady Gregory had too much common sense and humor. Synge had too much reserve. They could not, in any case, be bothered with exploiting a particular literary mode beyond the point of diminishing returns, and what was good in the Revival was very soon worked out. In 1904 Yeats discovered Padraic Colum, and the new generation began to speak, to the surprise of all, in terms of "peasant realism." After that the Celtic mode was the property of the third-string writers.

There are many reasons why we do not find the pure convention in Yeats's work at any period of his life. The most obvious, of course, is that he was too big to be contained by it. As important is that he disagreed with Arnold on perhaps the most important detail of Arnold's description of Celtic literature. He held [in *Ideas of Good and Evil*] that the "mystery and magic charm" Arnold had so praised was not simply the product of the Celtic imagination, with its "passionate, turbulent, indomitable reaction against the despotism of fact"—it was not even specifically Celtic.

> When Matthew Arnold wrote it was not easy to know as much as we know now of folk song and folk belief, and I do not think he understood that our "natural magic" is but the ancient religion of the world, the ancient worship of nature and the troubled ecstacy before her, that certainty of all beautiful places being haunted, which it brought into men's minds.

That being so, the magic and mystery could not be evoked, the obscurely preserved fragments of the ancient belief recovered, by any vague Celticism. They could be interpreted and understood only by analogy with European and Oriental occult lore, derived presumably from the same antiquity. And only when they had thus been given meaning could they be used again for sure poetical effect. That belief and the laborious practice it called for gave Yeats's poetry the discipline and intensity of symbolistic suggestion that increasingly distinguished it, a richness that could not be imitated without equal skill and labor.

It was not successfully imitated, but it could be counterfeited—and the counterfeiting resulted in the fanciest hogwash ever manufactured in Ireland. In scores of slim green volumes the discovery of popular Celtic mysticism was celebrated. It was a great time for the feeble-minded: never before had it been so easy and practicable to be wise without wisdom, visionary without visions, acutely sensitive

without feeling. As mentioned before, the romanticized paradox was the secret means. Equipped with it, the common or garden Irish poet began to hear the inaudible, see the invisible, comprehend the unintelligible, apparently with no more elaborate qualification for all this than his presumably Celtic paternity. (Scotsmen could do all this, too, as "Fiona Macleod" demonstrated.) And presently it began to be done on a grand scale, for about this time the last of Arnold's Celtic touchstones was brought up and set in place. That was *Titanism,* which Arnold had defined as that "vein of piercing regret and passion . . . [which] Macpherson's *Ossian* carried in the last century . . . like a flood of lava through Europe." Most of the lesser poets seem to have mistaken it, however, as an appellation for sheer size. The nine-foot Gaelic hero came into vogue [as in Seosamh MacCathmhaoil's "The Fighting Man"]:

> A fighting man he was,
> Guts and soul;
> His blood as hot and red
> As that on Cain's hand-towel.
>
> . . . . .
>
> I've seen him swing an anvil
> Fifty feet,
> Break a bough in two,
> And tear a twisted sheet.
>
> And the music of his roar—
> Like oaks in thunder cleaving;
> Lips foaming red froth,
> And flanks heaving.
>
> God! a goodly man,
> A Gael, the last
> Of those that stood with Dan
> On Mullach-Maist!

That, incidentally, is by a poet who wrote some of the loveliest and most tender lyrics in the literature, when he eschewed the convention and worked his own vein.

By this time, the convention had become so elaborate and so embarrassingly empty that it was beyond even the salutary aid of parody. One cannot parody the funny; and despite the fierce patriotism that undoubtedly justified this poetry in the minds of its creators, it could no longer be taken seriously by those not drunk on the same brew.

Or could it? There is one really skillful poem of this mode which still survives as an established anthology piece— used to illustrate the Celtic Revival, though it was written, not by one of the Dublin group, but by a young New Yorker. I refer to Shaemas O'Sheel's "They Went Forth to Battle But They Always Fell," a poem published in 1911 and written in a style and with a smooth facility Yeats might have envied twenty years before. In three stanzas it reproduces practically the entire formula. All of Arnold's Celtic touchstones are there: Titanism and magic and piercing melancholy and doomed bravery and ineffectualness and verbal sensuality and splendid dream-haunted failure and the exquisite spiritual sensitivity of the Celt. And there is sentiment, "infinite sentiment," too, though perhaps not of the sort Arnold meant. The title is that quotation from *Ossian* with which Arnold had headed his lectures. For the meaning it will probably be enough to quote the second stanza:

It was a secret music that they heard,
A sad sweet plea for pity and for peace;
And that which pierced the heart was but a
  word,
Though the white breast was red-lipped where
  the sword
Pressed a fierce cruel kiss, to put surcease
On its hot thirst, but drank a hot increase.
Ah, they by some strange troubling doubt were
  stirred,
And died for hearing what no foeman heard.

Here then is the new view of Irish history which explains defeat and removes its sting. It suggests that Irish were beaten not because they were divided, or badly led, or armed with obsolete weapons, or even seriously outnumbered, but because they were distracted by more important, if less pressing, matters: matters indeed so profound that only a Celt could understand them or even be aware of them, and then only when he was not attending to business. They were beaten because, in other words, they were *fey*, doomed by their own spiritual sensitivity. One notes that the music or the word that did the dirty work was inaudible to the crass but competent enemy. Yet there was nothing weak or cowardly about the fallen. The poem goes on to imply that once they got over being doomed, by, for instance, being dead, they could conquer even the powers of darkness:

Yet they will scatter the red hordes of Hell,
Who went to battle forth and always fell.

A heartening statement for those who were now preparing themselves for the last revolt. And considering the odds these rebels faced, and the bravery with which they faced them, it would be a poor thing for outraged sense to begrudge them what comfort such poetry may have given. We need note it here only as the ultimate expression of the train of ideas Arnold had so carefully, so moderately, set going, in a different age, on a different theme. Except of course as a theological problem, moral responsibility in the chain of cause and effect, it has almost nothing whatever to do with what Arnold had said or thought—as Arnold certainly would have had nothing to do with it.

VI

One can only repeat that he had not predicted or desired a Celtic literary revival. He had wanted the Celts fully to enter the Anglo-Saxon cultural and political system, bringing with them their great spiritual and artistic gifts. His lectures were in large part a plea that they be welcomed as coequal citizens, valued for the qualities they alone possessed and without which, he felt, English literature and English life would lack savor. It was a noble intent. It did not, however, have much to do with the literature which was his ostensible subject, or induce him to go beyond a cursory inspection of that literature. What he saw of it, he probably saw steadily and saw whole; but he saw only fragments, and the picture he drew, while distantly recognizable, lacks depth and outline. He seems, for instance, totally unaware of that quality of reserved emotion that gives the best Gaelic poetry a whiplash sting, particularly when, as in so many of the poems translated by Frank O'Connor, it is set down in language so severely objective as to seem at first impassive. On the other hand, one would never gather from what he says of it that much Celtic poetry is very dull stuff indeed. He saw the technical intricacy of standard Celtic verse, without, however, seeing that inspiration could be killed by the tradition that required this mathematical intricacy, or rather, be smothered by it before birth. But then Celtic dullness was not part of his argument. Since the argument came first, one may question whether he would have cared for, or used, fuller information. He did not, at any rate, seek it out.

And yet, in the *Study of Celtic Literature* we are dealing with the observations of a great critic. The book can never be unconsidered by anyone dealing with the subject, or be taken lightly, or—in the end—be read with anything but recurrent admiration. Whether or not one agrees with his estimate of Celtic literature, one's own estimate is bound to be affected by his, as it is affected also by Yeats's. When the great critic or the great writer speaks on literature, we must listen with avid attention. It does not matter how much or how little he knows. We do not listen to him, hoping for information. We listen for insight. If he knew more, he would probably see into more, and that would be better; but we are grateful for what we can get. It is thus with Joyce in the *Portrait of the Artist* when he explains why he, as a young man, rejected what the Celtic Revival admired: "the broken lights of Irish myth . . . the myth upon which no individual mind had ever drawn out a line of beauty . . . its unwieldy tales that divided against themselves as they moved down the cycles." It is thus with Arnold. Does it matter, in the end, how much they knew? Certainly, all the scholarly interpretation in the world, so long as it is uncombined with the genuine critical faculty, can never by itself give us the insights we need for an artistic valuation. The field of Celtic studies has not been particularly blessed with the critical gift. Arnold's book is still unique—a fact which he would undoubtedly have deplored.

As for the Celtic Revival, the period it spans brought about an enormous improvement in the quality of Irish writing. It saw, too, the secure establishment of an Irish literature in English. This, however, was not an effect of the Celtic convention: it was the result of Yeats's insistence on that care and finish and economy which had been conspicuously missing from Irish writing up until that time. By precept and example he forced the Irish writers to learn the tools of their trade, to respect their words and emotions, to say what they had to say and no more. For the first time in English, Irish poetry could lay a general claim to "intensity, elevation, and effect."

There were two great writers, Yeats and Synge, and a dozen fine ones associated with the Revival in the years when it won international respect. When its convention withered and grew stale, the withering did not affect the tradition of excellent workmanship that they had created. At its peak—and the peak came early—the Celtic convention was embodied in a great deal of fine writing. The inanity we have examined was the later phase, when nearly every writer worth his salt had outgrown it or deserted it. One thing was sure. No longer would there be one or two good Irish writers in each generation, working alone, without sympathy or a sound native canon of style, doomed to idiosyncracy, wasting their sweetness in a howling desert of rhetoric and easy tears. If the Celtic convention played any part in ending that over-prolonged condition, it justified itself a thousand times.

John V. Kelleher, "Matthew Arnold and the Celtic Revival," in Perspectives of Criticism, *edited by Harry Levin, Cambridge, Mass.: Harvard University Press, 1950, pp. 197-222.*

William Butler Yeats

[*The leading figure of the Irish literary revival, Yeats has been lauded for his sincerity, passion, and vital imagination. In the following essay, Yeats responds to Arnold's assessment of Celtic literature by providing his own account of the salient characteristics of Irish writing, the influence of folklore on Irish literature, and the revival movement of the 1890s.*]

Ernest Renan described what he held to be Celtic characteristics in *The Poetry of the Celtic Races*. I must repeat the well-known sentences: 'No race communed so intimately as the Celtic race with the lower creation, or believed it to have so big a share of moral life.' The Celtic race had 'a realistic naturalism,' 'a love of nature for herself, a vivid feeling for her magic, commingled with the melancholy a man knows when he is face to face with her, and thinks he hears her communing with him about his origin and his destiny.' 'It has worn itself out in mistaking dreams for realities,' and 'compared with the classical imagination the Celtic imagination is indeed the infinite contrasted with the finite.' 'Its history is one long lament, it still recalls its exiles, its flights across the seas.' 'If at times it seems to be cheerful, its tear is not slow to glisten behind the smile. Its songs of joy end as elegies; there is nothing to equal the delightful sadness of its national melodies.' Matthew Arnold, in *The Study of Celtic Literature*, has accepted this passion for nature, this imaginativeness, this melancholy, as Celtic characteristics, but has described them more elaborately. The Celtic passion for nature comes almost more from a sense of her 'mystery' than of her 'beauty,' and it adds 'charm and magic' to nature, and the Celtic imaginativeness and melancholy are alike 'a passionate, turbulent, indomitable reaction against the despotism of fact.' The Celt is not melancholy, as Faust or Werther are melancholy, from 'a perfectly definite motive,' but because of something about him 'unaccountable, defiant and titanic.' How well one knows these sentences, better even than Renan's, and how well one knows the passages of prose and verse which he uses to prove that wherever English literature has the qualities these sentences describe, it has them from a Celtic source. Though I do not think any of us who write about Ireland have built any argument upon them, it is well to consider them a little, and see where they are helpful and where they are hurtful. If we do not, we may go mad some day, and the enemy root up our rose-garden and plant a cabbage-garden instead. Perhaps we must restate a little, Renan's and Arnold's argument.

Once every people in the world believed that trees were divine, and could take a human or grotesque shape and dance among the shadows; and that deer, and ravens and foxes, and wolves and bears, and clouds and pools, almost all things under the sun and moon, and the sun and moon, were not less divine and changeable. They saw in the rainbow the still bent bow of a god thrown down in his negligence; they heard in the thunder the sound of his beaten water-jar, or the tumult of his chariot wheels; and when a sudden flight of wild duck, or of crows, passed over their heads, they thought they were gazing at the dead hastening to their rest; while they dreamed of so great a mystery in little things that they believed the waving of a hand, or of a sacred bough, enough to trouble far-off hearts, or hood the moon with darkness. All old literatures are full of these or of like imaginations, and all the poets of races, who have not lost this way of looking at things, could have said of themselves, as the poet of the *Kalevala* said of himself, 'I have learned my songs from the music of many birds, and from the music of many waters.' When a mother in the *Kalevala* weeps for a daughter, who was drowned flying from an old suitor, she weeps so greatly that her tears become three rivers, and cast up three rocks, on which grow three birch-trees, where three cuckoos sit and sing, the one 'love, love,' the one 'suitor, suitor,' the one 'consolation, consolation.' And the makers of the Sagas made the squirrel run up and down the sacred ashtree carrying words of hatred from the eagle to the worm, and from the worm to the eagle; although they had less of the old way than the makers of the *Kalavala*, for they lived in a more crowded and complicated world, and were learning the abstract meditation which lures men from visible beauty, and were unlearning, it may be, the impassioned meditation which brings men beyond the edge of trance and makes trees, and beasts, and dead things talk with human voices.

The old Irish and the old Welsh, though they had less of the old way than the makers of the *Kalavala*, had more of it than the makers of the Sagas, and it is this that distinguishes the examples Matthew Arnold quotes of their 'natural magic,' of their sense of 'the mystery' more than of 'the beauty' of nature. When Matthew Arnold wrote it was not easy to know as much as we know now of folk song and folk belief, and I do not think he understood that our 'natural magic' is but the ancient religion of the world, the ancient worship of nature and that troubled ecstasy before her, that certainty of all beautiful places being haunted, which it brought into men's minds. The ancient religion is in that passage of the *Mabinogion* about the making of 'Flower Aspect.' Gwydion and Math made her 'by charms and illusions' 'out of flowers.' 'They took the blossoms of the oak, and the blossoms of the broom, and the blossoms of the meadow-sweet, and produced from them a maiden the fairest and most graceful that man ever saw; and they baptized her, and called her Flower Aspect'; and one finds it in the not less beautiful passage about the burning Tree, that has half its beauty from calling up a fancy of leaves so living and beautiful, they can be of no less living and beautiful a thing than flame: 'They saw a tall tree by the side of the river, one half of which was in flames from the root to the top, and the other half was green and in full leaf.' And one finds it very certainly in the quotations he makes from English poets to prove a Celtic influence in English poetry; in Keats's 'magic casements opening on the foam of perilous seas in faery lands forlorn'; in his 'moving waters at their priest-like task of pure ablution round earth's human shore'; in Shakespeare's 'floor of heaven,' 'inlaid with patens of bright gold'; and in his Dido standing 'on the wild sea banks,' 'a willow in her hand,' and waving it in the ritual of the old worship of nature and the spirits of nature, to wave 'her love to come again to Carthage.' And his other examples have the delight and wonder of devout worshippers among the haunts of their divinities. Is there not such delight and wonder in the description of Olwen in the *Mabinogion:* 'More yellow was her hair than the flower of the broom, and her skin was whiter than the foam of the wave, and fairer were her hands and her fingers than the blossoms of the wood-anemone amidst the spray of the meadow fountains.' And is there not such delight and wonder in—

> Meet we on hill, in dale, forest, or mead,
> By paved fountain or by rushy brook,
> Or on the beached margent of the sea?

If men had never dreamed that fair women could be made out of flowers, or rise up out of meadow fountains and paved fountains, neither passage could have been written. Certainly, the descriptions of nature made in what Matthew Arnold calls 'the faithful way,' or in what he calls 'the Greek way,' would have lost nothing if all the meadow fountains or paved fountains were meadow fountains and paved fountains and nothing more. When Keats wrote, in the Greek way, which adds lightness and brightness to nature—

> What little town by river or sea-shore
> Or mountain built with quiet citadel,
> Is emptied of its folk, this pious morn;

when Shakespeare wrote in the Greek way—

> I know a bank where the wild thyme blows,
> Where oxlips and the nodding violet grows;

when Virgil wrote in the Greek way—

> Muscosi fontes et somno mollior herba,

and

> Pallentes violas et summa papavera carpens
> Narcissum et florem jungit bene olentis anethi

they looked at nature without ecstasy, but with the affection a man feels for the garden where he has walked daily and thought pleasant thoughts. They looked at nature in the modern way, the way of people who are poetical, but are more interested in one another than in a nature which has faded to be but friendly and pleasant, the way of people who have forgotten the ancient religion.

Men who lived in a world where anything might flow and change, and become any other thing; and among great gods whose passions were in the flaming sunset, and in the thunder and the thunder-shower, had not our thoughts of weight and measure. They worshipped nature and the abundance of nature, and had always, as it seems, for a supreme ritual that tumultuous dance among the hills or in the depths of the woods, where unearthly ecstasy fell upon the dancers, until they seemed the gods or the godlike beasts, and felt their souls overtopping the moon; and, as some think, imagined for the first time in the world the

blessed country of the gods and of the happy dead. They had imaginative passions because they did not live within our own strait limits, and were nearer to ancient chaos, every man's desire, and had immortal models about them. The hare that ran by among the dew might have sat upon his haunches when the first man was made, and the poor bunch of rushes under their feet might have been a goddess laughing among the stars; and with but a little magic, a little waving of the hands, a little murmuring of the lips, they too could become a hare or a bunch of rushes, and know immortal love and immortal hatred.

All folk literature, and all literature that keeps the folk tradition, delights in unbounded and immortal things. The *Kalevala* delights in the seven hundred years that Luonaton wanders in the depths of the sea with Wäinämöinen in her womb, and the Mahomedan king in the Song of Roland, pondering upon the greatness of Charlemagne, repeats over and over, 'He is three hundred years old, when will he weary of war?' Cuchulain in the Irish folk tale had the passion of victory, and he overcame all men, and died warring upon the waves, because they alone had the strength to overcome him. The lover in the Irish folk song bids his beloved come with him into the woods, and see the salmon leap in the rivers, and hear the cuckoo sing, because death will never find them in the heart of the woods. Oisin, new come from his three hundred years of faeryland, and of the love that is in faeryland, bids St. Patrick cease his prayers a while and listen to the blackbird, because it is the blackbird of Darrycarn that Finn brought from Norway, three hundred years before, and set its nest upon the oak-tree with his own hands. Surely if one goes far enough into the woods, one will find there all that one is seeking? Who knows how many centuries the birds of the woods have been singing?

All folk literature has indeed a passion whose like is not in modern literature and music and art, except where it has come by some straight or crooked way out of ancient times. Love was held to be a fatal sickness in ancient Ireland, and there is a love-poem in *The Songs of Connacht* that is like a death cry:

> My love, O she is my love, the woman who is most for destroying me, dearer is she for making me ill than the woman who would be for making me well. She is my treasure, O she is my treasure, the woman of the grey eyes . . . a woman who would not lay a hand under my head. . . . She is my love, O she is my love, the woman who left no strength in me; a woman who would not breathe a sigh after me, a woman who would not raise a stone at my tomb. . . . She is my secret love, O she is my secret love. A woman who tells me nothing, . . . a woman who does not remember me to be out. . . . She is my choice, O she is my choice, the woman who would not look back at me, the woman who would not make peace with me. . . . She is my desire, O she is my desire: a woman dearest to me under the sun, a woman who would not pay me heed, if I were to sit by her side. It is she ruined my heart and left a sigh for ever in me.

There is another song that ends, 'The Erne shall be in strong flood, the hills shall be torn down, and the sea shall have red waves, and blood shall be spilled, and every mountain valley and every moor shall be on high, before you shall perish, my little black rose.' Nor do the old Irish weigh and measure their hatred. The nurse of O'Sullivan Bere in the folk song prays that the bed of his betrayer may be the red hearth-stone of hell for ever. And an Elizabethan Irish poet cries: 'Three things are waiting for my death. The devil, who is waiting for my soul and cares nothing for my body or my wealth; the worms, who are waiting for my body but care nothing for my soul or my wealth; my children, who are waiting for my wealth and care nothing for my body or my soul. O Christ, hang all three in the one noose.' Such love and hatred seek no mortal thing but their own infinity, and such love and hatred soon become love and hatred of the idea. The lover who loves so passionately can soon sing to his beloved like the lover in the poem by 'A. E.,' 'A vast desire awakes and grows into forgetfulness of thee.'

When an early Irish poet calls the Irishman famous for much loving, and a proverb, a friend has heard in the Highlands of Scotland, talks of the lovelessness of the Irishman, they may say but the same thing, for if your passion is but great enough it leads you to a country where there are many cloisters. The hater who hates with too good a heart soon comes also to hate the idea only; and from this idealism in love and hatred comes, as I think, a certain power of saying and forgetting things, especially a power of saying and forgetting things in politics, which others do not say and forget. The ancient farmers and herdsmen were full of love and hatred, and made their friends gods, and their enemies the enemies of gods, and those who keep their tradition are not less mythological. From this 'mistaking dreams,' which are perhaps essences, for 'realities' which are perhaps accidents, from this 'passionate, turbulent reaction against the despotism of fact,' comes, it may be, that melancholy which made all ancient peoples delight in tales that end in death and parting, as modern peoples delight in tales that end in marriage bells; and made all ancient peoples, who like the old Irish had a nature more lyrical than dramatic, delight in wild and beautiful lamentations. Life was so weighed down by the emptiness of the great forests and by the mystery of all things, and by the greatness of its own desires, and, as I think, by the loneliness of much beauty; and seemed so little and so fragile and so brief, that nothing could be more sweet in the memory than a tale that ended in death and parting, and than a wild and beautiful lamentation. Men did not mourn merely because their beloved was married to another, or because learning was bitter in the mouth, for such mourning believes that life might be happy were it different, and is therefore the less mourning; but because they had been born and must die with their great thirst unslaked. And so it is that all the august sorrowful persons of literature, Cassandra and Helen and Deirdre, and Lear and Tristan, have come out of legends and are indeed but the images of the primitive imagination mirrored in the little looking-glass of the modern and classic imagination. This is that 'melancholy a man knows when he is face to face' with nature, and thinks 'he hears her communing with him about' the mournfulness of being born and of dying; and how can it do otherwise than call into his mind 'its exiles, its flights across the seas,' that it may stir the

ever-smouldering ashes? No Gaelic poetry is so popular in Gaelic-speaking places as the lamentations of Oisin, old and miserable, remembering the companions and the loves of his youth, and his three hundred years in faeryland, and his faery love: all dreams withering in the winds of time lament in his lamentations:

> The clouds are long above me this night; last night was a long night to me; although I find this day long, yesterday was still longer. Every day that comes to me is long. . . . No one in this great world is like me—a poor old man dragging stones. The clouds are long above me this night. I am the last man of the Fianna, the great Oisin, the son of Finn, listening to the sound of bells. The clouds are long above me this night.

Matthew Arnold quotes the lamentation of Leyrach Hen as a type of the Celtic melancholy, but I prefer to quote it as a type of the primitive melancholy;

> O my crutch, is it not autumn when the fern is red and the water flag yellow? Have I not hated that which I love? . . . Behold, old age, which makes sport of me, from the hair of my head and my teeth, to my eyes which women loved. The four things I have all my life most hated fall upon me together—coughing and old age, sickness and sorrow. I am old, I am alone, shapeliness and warmth are gone from me, the couch of honour shall be no more mine; I am miserable, I am bent on my crutch. How evil was the lot allotted to Leyrach, the night he was brought forth! Sorrows without end and no deliverance from his burden.

An Elizabethan writer describes extravagant sorrow by calling it 'to weep Irish'; and Oisin and Leyrach Hen are, I think, a little nearer even to us modern Irish than they are to most people. That is why our poetry and much of our thought is melancholy. 'The same man,' writes Dr. Hyde in the beautiful prose which he first writes in Gaelic, 'who will to-day be dancing, sporting, drinking, and shouting, will be soliloquizing by himself to-morrow, heavy and sick and sad in his own lonely little hut, making a croon over departed hopes, lost life, the vanity of this world, and the coming of death.'

Matthew Arnold asks how much of the Celt must one imagine in the ideal man of genius. I prefer to say, how much of the ancient hunters and fishers and of the ecstatic dancers among hills and woods must one imagine in the ideal man of genius. Certainly a thirst for unbounded emotion and a wild melancholy are troublesome things in the world, and do not make its life more easy or orderly, but it may be the arts are founded on the life beyond the world, and that they must cry in the ears of our penury until the world has been consumed and become a vision. Certainly, as Samuel Palmer wrote, 'Excess is the vivifying spirit of the finest art, and we must always seek to make excess more abundantly excessive.' Matthew Arnold has said that if he were asked 'where English got its turn for melancholy and its turn for natural magic,' he 'would answer with little doubt that it got much of its melancholy from a Celtic source, with no doubt at all that from a Celtic source is got nearly all its natural magic.'

I will put this differently and say that literature dwindles to a mere chronicle of circumstance, or passionless phantasies, and passionless meditations, unless it is constantly flooded with the passions and beliefs of ancient times, and that of all the fountains of the passions and beliefs of ancient times in Europe, the Sclavonic, the Finnish, the Scandinavian, and the Celtic, the Celtic alone has been for centuries close to the main river of European literature. It has again and again brought 'the vivifying spirit' 'of excess' into the arts of Europe. Ernest Renan has told how the visions of purgatory seen by pilgrims to Lough Derg—once visions of the pagan under-world, as the boat made out of a hollow tree that bore the pilgrim to the holy island were alone enough to prove—gave European thought new symbols of a more abundant penitence; and had so great an influence that he has written, 'It cannot be doubted for a moment that to the number of poetical themes Europe owes to the genius of the Celt is to be added the framework of the divine comedy.'

A little later the legends of Arthur and his table, and of the Holy Grail, once it seems the cauldron of an Irish God, changed the literature of Europe, and it may be changed, as it were, the very roots of man's emotions by their influence on the spirit of chivalry and on the spirit of romance; and later still Shakespeare found his Mab, and probably his Puck, and one knows not how much else of his faery kingdom, in Celtic legend; while at the beginning of our own day Sir Walter Scott gave Highland legends and Highland excitability so great a mastery over all romance that they seem romance herself.

In our own time Scandinavian tradition, because of the imagination of Richard Wagner and of William Morris and of the earlier and, as I think, greater Heinrich Ibsen, has created a new romance, and through the imagination of Richard Wagner, become all but the most passionate element in the arts of the modern world. There is indeed but one other element as passionate, the still unfaded legends of Arthur and of the Holy Grail; and now a new fountain of legends, and, as I think, a more abundant fountain than any in Europe, is being opened, the great fountain of Gaelic legends; the tale of Deirdre, who alone among the women who have set men mad was at once the white flame and the red flame, wisdom and loveliness; the tale of the Sons of Tuireann, with its unintelligible mysteries, an old Grail Quest as I think; the tale of the four children changed into four swans, and lamenting over many waters; the tale of the love of Cuchulain for an immortal goddess, and his coming home to a mortal woman in the end; the tale of his many battles at the ford with that dear friend he kissed before the battles, and over whose dead body he wept when he had killed him; the tale of his death and of the lamentations of Emer; the tale of the flight of Grainne with Diarmuid, strangest of all tales of the fickleness of woman, and the tale of the coming of Oisin out of faeryland, and of his memories and lamentations. 'The Celtic movement,' as I understand it, is principally the opening of this fountain, and none can measure of how great importance it may be to coming times, for every new fountain of legends is a new intoxication for the imagination of the world. It comes at a time when the imagination of the world is as ready, as it was at the coming of the tales of Arthur and of the Grail, for a new intoxication. The reaction against the rationalism of the eighteenth century has mingled with a reaction against the materialism of the nineteenth century, and the symbolical movement, which has come to perfection in Germany in Wagner, in England in the Pre-Raphaelites, and in France in Villiers De l'Isle Adam, and Mallarmé, and Maeterlinck, and has stirred the imagination of Ibsen and D'Annunzio, is certainly the only movement that is saying new things. The arts by brooding upon their own intensity have become religious, and are seeking, as I think Verhaeren has said, to create a sacred book. They must, as religious thought has always done, utter themselves through legends; and the Sclavonic and Finnish legends tell of strange woods and seas, and the Scandinavian legends are held by a great master, and tell also of strange woods and seas, and the Welsh legends are held by almost as many great masters as the Greek legends, while the Irish legends move among known woods and seas, and have so much of a new beauty, that they may well give the opening century its most memorable symbols.

> *William Butler Yeats, "The Celtic Element in Literature," in his* Ideas of Good and Evil, *A. H. Bullen, 1903, pp. 270-95.*

ANTI-IRISH SENTIMENT AND THE CELTIC RESPONSE

John Mackinnon Robertson

[*In the following excerpt from an article originally published in 1889, sociologist Robertson discusses James Anthony Froude's* Two Chiefs of Dunboy and The English in Ireland *as examples of anti-Irish sentiment in literature, assailing Froude for his hypocrisy and lack of clear thinking.*]

A more interesting question for a literary plebiscitum than a good many that have been propounded would be this, Who is the most mischievous English writer of the day? I cannot pretend to guess how the decision of the majority would be likely to go, but I should have little hesitation in casting my own vote for Mr James Anthony Froude. . . .

Now comes *The Two Chiefs of Dunboy, or An Irish Romance of the Last Century,* in which Mr Froude essays to write at once a novel and a homily on Irish affairs, combining the art-methods of the literary generation before last with a temper and a sociology all his own. This is not the place to discuss the book as a work of fiction. Suffice it to say, on that head, that Mr Froude does not appear to recognise any progress in the art of novel-writing since Scott; that his power of character-drawing is very limited, though he sketches some good old conventional types with considerable vigour; and that quite the best passages in the book are those describing fights, particularly the sea chase of a privateer by a British frigate. He has founded his hero, apparently, on the historic Colonel Eyre, and has drawn some quasi-humorous local colour from the Memoirs of Sir Jonah Barrington. His vacillating and valueless doctrine concerning Ireland and the Irish problem he drew from his own perturbed and capricious judgment.

"Colonel Goring," he says of his murdered hero at the close, "belonged to an order of men who, if they had been allowed fair play, would have made the sorrows of Ireland the memory of an evil dream; but he had come too late, the spirit of the Cromwellians had died out of the land, and was not to be revived by a single enthusiast." That is to say, Colonel Goring was too late, but yet was not too late if only he had been allowed fair play and had not been otherwise too late. What then was the late Colonel Goring's policy? Let his fluent creator tell:

> He had studied Ireland anxiously. He had observed with disgust the growing weakness of the Protestant settlement and the reviving energy of the Catholics. To him, *an Englishman of the old Puritan School,* the Pope was anti-Christ. He absolutely disbelieved that Irish Popery could be brought *either by connivance or toleration* into loyal relations with the English Crown. *He did not like penal laws.* He knew that the relations of his own country with the Catholic Powers of Europe *made the enforcement of such laws impossible,* except spasmodically and uncertainly, and he thought that laws which were not meant to be obeyed were *better off the Statute Book. But he was convinced also* that Ireland could only be permanently attached to the British Crown if the Protestants were there *in strength enough to hold their own ground.* Cromwell's policy of establishing Protestant settlements South as well as North was the only rational one.

I would call attention to this as a compendious illustration of Mr Froude's habits of political thought. Written with every appearance of confidence, the passage is but a string of self-stultifications. First we are told in Colonel Goring's scheme that there is to be *no tolerance whatever* of Catholicism (as there was none in Colonel Eyre's practice); and it is obvious that not to tolerate Catholicism means to enforce penal laws. In the next breath we learn that Colonel Goring did not like penal laws because they could not be enforced in the face of the protests of Catholic States which had it in their power similarly to oppress Protestants. Finally we are told that Goring's idea was to make all over Ireland, on Cromwell's principle, Protestant plantations which should be able to "hold their own"; and we are left to imagine how Catholicism is to be suppressed as Anti-Christ without penal laws. It would be difficult to cite from the writings of any man who ever claimed to speak with authority on matters of conduct, such another display of irrelevance and inconsequence. But the confusion of the passage, I take it, will surprise nobody who has sought to extract from Mr Froude's *English in Ireland* any coherent doctrine as to the Irish problem; and as little will the student of Mr Froude's earlier works be astonished at the primitive barbarism, the pre-Burkean blindness, of the political prescription he lays down in his novel.

The Two Chiefs of Dunboy, as a whole, serves chiefly to raise afresh the question raised formerly by its author's

books and by his lectures in the United States, namely, What is his real opinion about the Irish? It might have been supposed that, conscious as he must be that his *English in Ireland* said nothing, or rather said everything by turns, on that head, he would have seen in his novel a useful means of expressing an intelligible opinion, the more so as his book is no dispassionate Shaksperean presentiment of life, but as explicitly didactic as *Robert Elsmere.* But the novel is, if possible, more self-contradictory, more vacillating, more distracted in its doctrine than the historic treatise. The truth is that Mr Froude never did and never will hold to a consistent opinion on any subject whatever.

We have seen how he gives to his hero his own distraction of doctrine in sum: let us see how the confusion fulfils itself in detail. Again and again do we have the cheap and commonplace assumption of a "double dose of original sin" in the Irish or "Celtic" race. "So far as accurate knowledge goes," he makes a shrewd character say as against a crotchetty one, "the Irish race have always been noisy, useless, and ineffectual. They draw their picture in their own annals. They have produced nothing, they have done nothing, which it is possible to admire. What they are they have always been, and the only hope for them is that their ridiculous Irish nationality should be buried and forgotten." Then we have Mr Froude's own allusion, in a description of the villain, to "the abject manner under which *every Irishman* knows so well how to conceal his real feeling"—this though he introduces many Irishmen who show no trace of abjectness. If this be not enough, we have the leading Irish patriot and hero in the story made to say of his race: "What were we when we had the island to ourselves? If you can believe those glorious ballad singers and annalists of ours, we were no better than the cannibals of the Pacific. If we were again free, we should cut one another's throats in the old style." There is no hint in any of these or similar passages that the barbarism of the Irish was much the same sort of thing as the barbarism of the Saxon Heptarchy. There is no reminder that England had her Wars of the Roses. There is not a word of reflection as to how Ireland might conceivably have developed if England had left her alone. There is no question as to how far Welsh development has been a success under different auspices. It is just taken for granted that the Irish are an unimproveable race.

And yet, as of old, we have the *per contra.* Colonel Goring is made to say: "I have heard others say that the faults of the Irish are the faults of a noble nature, which has been wrenched out of its proper shape. I believe it now; for in no race in this world could I have found man or woman who would have risked what you [a girl who saved his life] have risked to save one whom you have been told to look on as the enemy of your country." And we have the old admission that the Normans settled in Ireland became more Irish than the Irish themselves; Teutons being thus confessed to develop Irish characteristics under Irish circumstances. The upshot of which is—? This or nothing— that the way to settle the Irish problem is (or once was) to flood Ireland with English Protestants, refusing to tolerate Catholicism but making no law to put it down.

James Anthony Froude.

The grotesque nugatoriness of all this, I repeat, does not come of any artistic impartiality of Mr Froude the novelist, but from the incurable intellectual instability of Mr Froude the thinker and publicist. He is repeating in the form of a novel the see saw of his former explicit argumentations. It is worth while going back on the old medley, if it were only to show more fully how worthless is the counsel which does so much to inspire English policy at the present moment. At the beginning of *The English in Ireland* Mr Froude appears to lay down a tolerably positive if ill-digested doctrine:

> In a world in which we are made to depend so largely for our well-being on the conduct of our neighbours, and yet are created infinitely unequal in ability and worthiness of character, the superior part has a natural right to govern; the inferior part has a natural right to be governed; and a rude but adequate test of superiority and inferiority is provided in the relative strength of the different orders of human beings. Among wild beasts and savages might constitutes right. Among reasonable beings right is for ever tending to create might. Inferiority of numbers is compensated by superior cohesiveness, intelligence, and daring. The *better sort* of men submit willingly to be governed by those who are *wiser and nobler* than themselves,

—*i.e.,* by those who are better than the better sort.

Yet even in the opening section the fatal infirmity of the writer's mind destructively asserts itself.

> When resistance has been tried and failed—when the inequality has been proved beyond dispute by long and painful experience—the wisdom, and *ultimately the duty,* of the weaker party is to accept the benefits that are offered in exchange for submission: and a nation which at once will not defend its liberties in the field, nor yet allow itself to be governed, but struggles to preserve the independence which it wants the spirit to uphold in arms, by insubordination and anarchy and secret crime, may bewail its wrongs in wild and weeping eloquence in the ears of mankind—may at length, in a time when the methods by which sterner ages repressed this kind of conduct are unpermitted, make itself so intolerable as to be cast off and bidden go upon its own bad way: but it will not go for its own benefit; it will have established no principle and vindicated no natural right; liberty profits only those who can govern themselves better than others can govern them, and those who are able to govern themselves wisely have no need to petition for a privilege which they can keep or take for themselves.

I doubt whether a more aimless and pointless piece of mock reasoning was ever concocted by a serious historian. It is the declamation of a hysterical weakling. Evidently enough Mr Froude does not feel the slightest confidence in his preaching as to the "duty" of the Irish or the natural tendency of things. And the same vacillation comes out still more ruinously at the close of the book. We have, of course, some positive doctrine:

> As the Asiatics are, so are the Irish. An Englishman would revolt against a despotism, however just the despotism might be. The Irishman is instinctively loyal to an authority which is not afraid to assert itself. He respects courage; he despises cowardice. Rule him resolutely, and he will not rebel; rule him justly, and he will follow you to the world's end.

It is quite needless to rebut this happy stroke of sociology, of which the whole basis is the assumption that the political ideals of Irishmen in the nineteenth century are those of barbarian Irishmen in the fourteenth. Mr Froude himself makes it abundantly clear that his generalisation amounts to nothing:

> England will never touch Ireland except under pressure of agitation: she then finds something must be done; she does the 'something' in a hurry to get rid of the subject, and she finds she has created more harm than she has cured. . . . The English people do not see that to remove even just grounds of complaint is made useless by the form in which the concession is made. They never legislate beforehand with a desire to be just; they wait for rebellion or danger of it, and then they yield without dignity and without deliberation. What they give is accepted without gratitude, and is regarded only as a victory won in the campaign which is being fought for the in-

dependence of Ireland. If there was a hope that anything which we could give would make the Irish contented and loyal subjects of the British Empire, no sacrifice would be too great for such an object. But there is no such hope. The land tenure is not the real grievance. It is merely a pretext. The real grievance is our presence in Ireland at all. . . . Mr Gladstone is a statesman. . . . He has perhaps recognised that from the date of the Conquest we have neglected every duty which a ruling power owes to its subjects.

Of course these sweeping admissions are sweepingly contradicted in other parts of the book, where it occurs to Mr Froude to assert that "England" as a whole is naturally just in her disposition towards weaker States in her grasp:

> Everything which she [England] most valued for herself—her laws, and liberties, her orderly and settled government, the most ample security for person and property—England's first desire was to give to Ireland in fullest measure. The temper in which she was met exasperated her into hardness and cruelty . . . till it seemed at last as if no solution of the problem were possible save the destruction or expulsion of a race which appeared incurable.

Against this it is sufficient to place the previous quotations, with, say, Mr Froude's admission in his novel as to the insane iniquity of "England" towards the *English* planted in Ireland:

> When the last rebellion was crushed, Ireland was a sheet of paper on which England might have written what character she pleased. Like a wanton child with a toy, she had no sooner accomplished her long task than she set herself to work to spoil it again. *She destroyed the industries of her colonists by her trade laws.* She set her Bishops to rob them of their religion.

So that Mr Froude, the most destructive opponent of Mr Froude, recognises with his usual versatility that England, even in recent centuries, has seemed more incapable of rational justice to affiliated communities outside of her own borders than any State since the time of Carthage. Still the see-saw goes on:

> Were England, even now at this eleventh hour, to say that she recognised the state of Ireland to be a disgrace to her, that . . . the constitution would be suspended, and that the three southern provinces would for half a century be governed by the Crown, the committee of the Land League are well aware that without a shot being fired in the field their functions would be at an end.

Much virtue in an "if." We are seeing at present how it serves to *half* suspend the constitution; and the effect on Irish discontent is not hard to discover. It does not tend to satisfy Mr Froude. The prescription is that "England," the hypothetical national unit of one mind, bent on acting towards outsiders as a master or officer towards his subordinates, is simply to forget that she is herself the scene of a struggle of the poor against the rich, and of a progressive democratism, and is to make believe to be a good healthy

Oriental despotism. Of course the accommodating Mr Froude admits that there is no more practical meaning in this than in his other generalisations; so we get this final double somersault;

> But I am told that it is impossible. . . . Despotism is out of date. We can govern India; we cannot govern Ireland. Be it so. [*Weeps.*] Then let Ireland be free. [After all these volumes.] She is miserable because she is unruled. We might rule her, but we will not [wilful "we," "thirty millions, mostly fools"], lest our arrangements at home might be interfered with. In an independent Ireland the ablest and strongest would come to the front, and the baser elements be crushed. The state of things which would ensue would not be satisfactory to us [strange to say, "we" don't want the best in Ireland to get uppermost, and the worst undermost!] but at least there would be no longer the inversion of the natural order which is maintained by the English connection, and the compelled slavery of education and intelligence [*alias,* absentee landlords] to the numerical majority. This too is called impossible—yet if we will neither rule Ireland nor allow the Irish to rule themselves, nature and fact may tell us that whether we will or no, an experiment which has lasted for seven hundred years shall be tried no longer.

—World without end, Amen! It is a free country, and you may hold about Ireland whatever opinion you please, even as Mr Froude thinks everything he pleases, that is to say, everything by turns and nothing long.

Is it possible, one asks, to regard with any respect an empiric of this kind? One says once more that there was never a more flagrant case of saddling the wrong horse than the proceeding of holding up as Mr Froude's principal literary misdeed his publication of the Carlyle documents. There, with of course his usual frailty in detail, he was helping the world to some truth: in his own books, expressing his own message, he is a perpetual influence for moral darkness. Any reader who peruses Mr Froude without arriving at a clear view of his mischievousness is either demoralised by his contagious confusion or hardened by him in similar empiricism and prejudice. It was truly said of him long ago that his historic researches on Ireland only opened up an old wound, for he went to work with a view, not to calmly showing that in the past both sides had been brutal, wicked, and mad, but to showing contemporaries how much reason they had to harbour old grudges. A man of his temper, whose convictions are sentiments and whose sentiments are moods, could only work on mood and sentiment, zealously reminding Protestants of the massacre of 1641, and anon reminding Catholics of Protestant tyranny, and leaving them recriminating, without a hint that the true lesson of the past was that we should turn our back on it and bring cool reason to bear on the present. His own leading quality is just that which he is always condemning in the Irish race, infirmity of purpose; and he covers it with just the bluster that he attributes to them as constitutional. Condemning their racial vanity, he displays his own in claptrap worthy of a schoolboy, intimating that "Englishmen are not easily frightened at the sound of danger," and so forth.

And withal, when challenged, as he was by Father Burke in New York in 1872, he affects the *bon enfant* and claims to be himself a warm friend of Ireland. As thus:

> I have been accused of having nothing practical to propose for Ireland. I have something extremely practical. *I want to see the peasants taken from under the power of their landlords, and made answerable to no authority but the law.* It would not be difficult to define for what offence a tenant might be legally deprived of his holding. He ought not to be dependent on the caprice of any individual man. If Father Burke and his friends will help in that way, instead of agitating for a separation from England, I would sooner find myself working with him than against him.

That was sixteen years ago. And in the interval Mr Froude's whole pernicious influence has gone to inflame the dogged and stupid English obstinacy that has at length made Home Rule a necessity and a certainty; Liberal and Tory leaders equally leading up to the issue, and the Liberal only saving appearances at the last moment by suddenly turning a somersault without a warning to the bewildered multitude.

John Mackinnon Robertson, "Mr. Froude on Ireland," in his The Saxon and the Celt: A Study in Sociology, *University Press, Limited, 1897, pp. 294-304.*

Dr. Goldwin Smith on the Irish character:

That the Irish Celt has gifts and graces, or that under a good master or commander he makes a good worker or soldier, nobody who knows anything of him denies. Nobody who knows how Irish emigrants have been assisted by their kinsmen in America will deny that the Irishman has strong domestic affections and a generous heart. But nobody who is not angling for his vote will affirm that in Cork, in Liverpool or Glasgow, in New York or the Australian colonies, or anywhere, he has as yet become a good citizen under free institutions. Nobody who is not angling for his vote will affirm that he is by nature law-abiding, or that when his passions are excited, whether his victims be his agrarian enemies in Ireland or the hapless negroes in New York, he is not capable of dreadful crimes. The Anglo-Saxon, when he takes to rioting may be brutal: in the Lord George Gordon riots (!) he was brutal enough; but he does not card or hough, nor does he cut off the udders of kine. The Phœnix Park murders were a Celtic, not an Anglo-Saxon deed.

Quoted by John Mackinnon Robertson, in his The Saxon and the Celt, *1897.*

L. P. Curtis, Jr.

[*In the following excerpt, Curtis examines the racist historiography of English writers such as J. A. Froude and W. E. H. Lecky. Discussing the Irish response to these negative portrayals, Curtis claims that such biased accounts acted as a stimulus for both the literary and political movements of Celtic Ireland.*]

More than any of his fellow historians James Anthony Froude exemplified the Celtophobia which underlay so much of the Unionist campaign against Home Rule as well as the writing of Irish history in England. Froude's researches into that history were animated by his desire to discover why it was that the Irish people had achieved so little of value in comparison with their English neighbors and rulers. As in the case of so many of his contemporaries, Froude found the answer he wanted in race and national character. One of the curious things about Froude is that he had spent more time in Ireland than any other English historian of his day. On his first trip to that country in 1840 the contrast between the serenity of Anglo-Irish civilization and the misery of Celtic Ireland had fascinated him, and he returned to Ireland in 1845, 1848, and again in the years 1867 to 1870 when he spent the summers writing in a house rented from Lord Lansdowne at Derreen. His love of the country itself remained undimmed by the famine and by the lowly estimate he had formed of Irish character.

It would be an understatement to call Froude's portrait of Paddy unflattering. In his autobiographical fragment he once described the Irish as "the most superstitious, the most imaginative and inflammable people in Europe." On a drive from Bandon to Killarney in 1845 he had encountered people who seemed "more like tribes of squalid apes than human beings." In Catholic Ireland, he wrote, nothing thrived except the Church; the truth was that an "evil genius" hung over the country [quoted in W. H. Dunn's *James Anthony Froude*, 1961]. Froude never denied the great kindness and charm of the Irish people, and he had rather a soft spot for the Paddies. Unfortunately they suffered from incurable faults in their political and social organization and they required the presence of a superior race in order to keep them up to the mark. Such prejudices about Celtic Ireland not only informed his study of *The English in Ireland* but they inspired his novel, the *Two Chiefs of Dunboy*, wherein the theme of racial conflict between Saxon and Celt predominates. Froude embodied that struggle in the persons of Colonel Goring, the English evangelical and improving landlord—a composite figure resembling both Cromwell and Joseph Chamberlain—and Morty Sullivan, patterned on many an Irish rebel leader, fiercely proud, daring and desperate. Froude depicted the Irish people as being "unstable as water," and as synonymous with anarchy and unbridled passion, whereas the English stood for order and self-control. Froude's tale of violent conflict between two races and cultures ended, not surprisingly, with the deaths of both heroes, as though their demise symbolized the fatal collision of the two islands.

In his historical works Froude played on the theme of a prolonged struggle between two races for ascendancy in Ireland; the mightier English had been unable to subdue the weaker Irish for centuries largely because they had misunderstood Irish character. What the Irish respected was brute force and steady, unyielding government. The antithesis of Protestant Saxon and Catholic Celt runs throughout the *History of England*. According to Froude, the "fatal fascination" of the Anglo-Norman conquerors with the Irish spirit had caused most of the trouble in Ireland; and he described that spirit as "an impatience of control, a deliberate preference for disorder, a determination in each individual man to go his own way, whether it was a good way or a bad, and a reckless hatred of industry." Only one form of government could ever have succeeded in Ireland and that was an "efficient military despotism," because the "wild Irish" understood only force. It is hardly necessary to add that Froude prescribed the same remedy for Irish troubles in the 1880's.

The apologist of the Protestant reformation and the English occupation of Ireland soon turned to a full-length study of Anglo-Irish relations in the eighteenth century, and in 1872 the first volume of *The English in Ireland* appeared. Froude dedicated this important work to that stern champion of Anglo-Irish culture, Sir Garnet Wolseley, whom he called "the most distinguished living representative of the English in Ireland." This highly ethnocentric study emphasized the inability of the Irish to show the courage and resolution of the Scottish people and the inability of the English to conciliate the Irish or to prevent them from rebelling. Mindful of the intimate connection between might and right, as befitted the leading disciple of Carlyle, Froude ventured to declare that had the Irish been successful in their struggle for freedom, they would then have acquired the qualities which would have made them worthy of that freedom.

Like [Charles] Dilke, Froude noted a similarity between the Irish and Asians: both had to be governed with firmness, otherwise they would begin to cut throats. Whereas an Englishman would revolt against any kind of despotism, [Froude wrote in his *The English in Ireland in the Eighteenth Century* that] an Irishman was "instinctively loyal to an authority which is not afraid to assert itself. He respects courage; he despises cowardice. Rule him resolutely, and he will not rebel; rule him justly and he will follow you to the world's end." Only a few references to Parnellism needed to be added to this passage to make it read like an excerpt from a Unionist speech or pamphlet in the 1880's or 1890's. Even before the completion of this book in 1874, the young Anglo-Irish historian William Lecky had set to work to demolish the foundations of Froude's thesis in two long reviews in *Macmillan's Magazine* in which he accused the author of trying to defame the Irish people by means of distorted evidence and extreme partiality.

The various scathing reviews which *The English in Ireland* provoked did little to chasten Froude; and in 1879 he wrote a long and unrepentant article in the *North American Review*, entitled "Romanism and the Irish Race," which was nothing more than a frontal assault on the Roman Catholic Church in America as well as on the hordes of Irishmen who made that Church such a menace to Anglo-Saxon and Protestant civilization. Froude argued here that the Irish Celts could no more be absorbed by American than by British society because they were a "nation separate in blood, separate in religion." In their mixture of racial, religious, and social prejudices against the Irish people, Froude's writings continue to provide rare insights into that mélange of Anglo-Saxonist attitudes which characterized so many members of the English governing classes in the second half of the century.

The most trenchant criticism of Froude's *The English in Ireland* came from the pen of W. E. H. Lecky, who fits less comfortably into the Anglo-Saxonist mold than his adversary in Irish historiography. Unlike Stubbs, Freeman, Green, and Froude, Lecky managed to stay clear of the heady Anglo-Saxonist atmosphere of Oxford except for the award of an honorary degree in 1888. But after 1885, he joined in the campaign against Home Rule with all the resources at his command. Lecky was too perceptive and cosmopolitan an historian to subscribe to a purely racial explanation of human behavior, but he had made up his mind in the 1860's that the Irish people were utterly unfit for self-government, and he never budged from that position in later years. A strong defender of property rights in Ireland and a man who thought the Irish needed firm government "on the Indian model," Lecky once wrote to his old friend, W. J. O'Neill Daunt that Home Rule would be "the most perfect of all earthly realisations of Pandemonium" [quoted in Elisabeth Lecky's *Memoir of the Rt. Hon. William E. H. Lecky,* 1910].

The precocious historian of European rationalism and morals assigned a large role in human affairs to fictions, myths, and ideas; at the same time he did not neglect national character. Referring to the absence of an industrial spirit in Ireland, Lecky observed in his *History of European Morals:*

> The usual characteristic of the latter nation is a certain laxity or instability of character, a proneness to exaggeration, a want of truthfulness in little things, an infidelity to engagements from which an Englishman, educated in the habits of industrial life, readily infers a complete absence of moral principle. But a deeper experience and a larger philosophy soon dispel this error.

Lecky's Irish volumes in his *History of England* were based on several years of painstaking research among the state papers in Dublin and London, and the message he conveyed was that Irish nationhood had flourished in the later eighteenth century because of its intimate connection with an enlightened natural aristocracy made up of Anglo-Irish landowners and graduates of Trinity College, Dublin, whose background and principles he shared. Lecky's Irish patriotism was thus patrician and moderate in the tradition of Henry Grattan. The only Irish nation he recognized as worthy of emulation was that produced by Anglo-Irish, not Celtic, genius, by the likes of Grattan, Flood, Burke, and Charlemont. Having no real sympathy for Catholic, Celtic, and working class Ireland, Lecky identified himself with those leaders of public opinion who had made possible Ireland's finest hour. If the Parnellite agitation really did succeed in driving out the descendants of that Anglo-Irish governing class, then the country would disintegrate into political, social, and economic chaos. Froude's history of Ireland impugned Irish Celtic character; Lecky's history virtually ignored Celtic Ireland, and focused instead on Anglo-Irish Ireland because it contained "the intellect, the property, the respectability of the country."

Lecky's work in Irish history was, of course, far more balanced, judicious, and accurate than Froude's, but he did not, or could not, detach himself from the political realities of his own day while writing about the Ireland of Grattan and Burke; and it was his basic agreement with Froude about the evil workings of democratic nationalism in the country that helped to preserve their friendship from any rift over their conflicting interpretation of Irish history. Lecky not only wrote weighty articles as well as letters to newspapers about the iniquity of Home Rule, but he championed the Unionist cause in Parliament as the member for Dublin University from 1895 to 1902. In his last lengthy book, *Democracy and Liberty* (1896), which was the expression of an embittered conservative rather than a disinterested historian, he fulminated against Irish clericalism and Parnellism in a manner Froude would have approved. "It is curious," Lecky had once written to a close friend, "how Irish affairs turn us all into Tories." . . .

. . . . .

The impact of strident Anglo-Saxonism upon Irish literature and Irish nationalism in the late nineteenth and early twentieth centuries deserves much more thorough treatment than can be provided here; but a brief outline of the counter current which English images of Ireland stimulated in that country and, indeed, in all parts of what might be called, *pace* Dilke, Greater Ireland, may serve to illustrate the contrapuntal nature of Anglo-Irish cultural relations. The dominant Irish response to Anglo-Saxonism, which is called here Celticism, but which might equally well be labeled Gaelicism, had many antecedents before the 1880's and 1890's when it began to blossom into an exotic flower of lasting significance. To quote Yeats, who did much to fertilize that flower with his own brand of Celticism:

> Come near; I would, before my time to go,
> Sing of old Eire and the ancient ways:
> Red Rose, proud Rose, sad Rose of all my days.
> ["To the Rose upon the Rood of Time"]

In the late Victorian and Edwardian period many Irish men and women sang of old, proud, and sad Celtic Ireland, and they sang as ardently and nostalgically of Cuchulain, Oisin, and Brian Boru as had Thomas Moore when celebrating "The Coming of the Milesians" and Thomas D'Arcy McGee when praising that mighty race in "The Celts." The songs of these modern Irish bards grew ever louder and more replete with myths and folklore, mystical and nationalistic allusions as the century came to a close with the cause of Home Rule still stymied. The repetition in this neo-bardic literature of such themes as war, rebellion, and heroic death made it dramatically clear to some nationalists just which examples of conduct they were supposed to follow. If the popular heroes of Victorian Englishmen were military figures like Wolseley, Roberts, Gordon, and Kitchener, the heroes of Irish men and women in the same period were either legendary figures like Cuchulain, Queen Maev, Finn Mac Cumhal, and Grania, or fighting rebels like Shane O'Neill, Wolfe Tone, and Robert Emmet.

Celticism was an ethnocentric form of nationalism with a strong measure of race consciousness which many Irishmen used to arm themselves against Anglo-Saxonist claims of cultural and racial superiority. Celticism refers to that body of assumptions, beliefs, and myths, which emphasized not only the uniqueness but the sophistication of early Irish culture, and in particular the virtue of ancient Irish political, legal, and social institutions. Celticists also attached much importance to the continuity of Irish blood from the time of the alleged arrival of the Milesians around 1000 B.C. down to the present day. This antithesis or antidote to Anglo-Saxonism provided Irish political leaders with some of the inspiration needed in order to sustain Ireland's claim to be an ancient nation eminently deserving of the independence which the Sassenach had seized centuries ago. There was a good deal of ancestor worship and racial mythology in Celticism, just as much, in fact, as in Anglo-Saxonism. Rare was the meeting of a branch of the Gaelic League, the Gaelic Athletic Association, or the Ancient Order of Hibernians at which there was no allusion to the purity and the antiquity of the Irish race. Whether labeled Celtic, Gaelic, Goidelic, Milesian, or plain Irish, that race possessed qualities and virtues far superior to those of Anglo-Saxons. According to the Celticist authorities, the high and holy culture of ancient Ireland had been crushed by ruthless, barbarous invaders from Britain and northern Europe, and the most barbarous of them all had been the rapacious Anglo-Saxons and Anglo-Normans, better known in Ireland as "bloody brutal Sassenachs."

In its ethnology and historiography Celticism was essentially separatist and exclusive, refusing to admit that anything good had come from England, except perhaps coal. Lacking so many of the tangible outlets of Anglo-Saxonists in the form of worldwide economic and imperial assets as well as great power status and lacking, too, the quintessential fact of sovereign national independence, the champions of Celticism kept up a much steadier flow of ethnocentric sentiments through the media of books, articles, newspapers, journals, plays, and lectures as well as clubs and associations. Dozens of organizations were launched in the nineteenth century throughout Greater Ireland which were dedicated to the preservation and promotion of Gaelic, Celtic, or Irish culture. The most important difference between English and Irish forms of ethnocentrism was that Anglo-Saxonism represented the mythology of a people who were largely self-fulfilled in a nationalist as well as material and imperial sense. England was a nation, no matter how deep the divisions of class, party, and sect might be. Celticism, on the one hand, was the ethnocentric expression of a people still in the throes of a profound nationalist struggle who were determined to achieve the kind of independence from Westminster which Anglo-Saxonism explicitly denied them. Celticism thus flowed into the main political channel of Irish nationalism, and it sustained the agitation for the return of Ireland's ancient Celtic liberties. Anglo-Saxonism, on the other hand, served the useful function of transferring the more personal and immediate anxieties of Englishmen about their own well-being onto the more abstract and impersonal plane of assumed threats to their ancient liberties and Anglo-Saxon culture. The absence from the Irish scene of a stereotype of English character as rigid and elaborate as Paddy shows that projection played a smaller role in Celticist thinking. For most Celticists the real enemy was as much that impersonal force "English rule" as it was John Bull.

The varieties and extent of Celticism in Ireland, England, and America, not to mention Pan-Celticism in Western Europe, have yet to be explored in depth, and here it is possible only to sketch the outlines of a movement that was as rich in talent as it was in mythology. Like all revivals, whether classical, Gothic, romantic, or otherwise, the Celtic revival of the late nineteenth century had no sharply defined beginning, middle, or end. George Moore, in his caustic reminiscences, *Hail and Farewell,* quoted his friend Edward Martyn as saying: "Ninety-nine is the beginning of the Celtic Renaissance." To this Moore replied: "I am glad to hear it; the Celt wants a renaissance and badly; he has been going down in the world for the last two thousand years." Now Martyn might be excused for trying to connect the Irish renaissance with the acceptance of his own play for production by Yeats' new Irish Literary Theater; but what he ignored was the number of Celtic revivals which had occurred in the three centuries before the performance of *The Heather Field* and Yeats' *The Countess Cathleen* in the Antient Concert Rooms, Dublin, in 1899. The sources of the last great revival, which was made memorable by Yeats, Lady Gregory, AE, Synge, Hyde, Martyn, O'Grady, Sigerson—to mention only the most obvious—reach far back into Irish history, back to those bards, poets, and holy story tellers who were responsible for such classics as the *Táin Bo Cuailgne* and the *Annals of the Four Masters.* Geoffrey Keating's eloquent *History of Ireland,* which was written in Irish in the early seventeenth century, also provided the Celticists of the 1890's and after with much the same kind of evidence about the remote Irish past which Anglo-Saxonists had extracted from Tacitus, Bede, and Giraldus Cambrensis in order to support their own foregone conclusions.

The most important source of Celticism in the eighteenth century was the Celtic or 'Celtic-English' revival which began in the 1750's and 1760's with the poems of Thomas Gray, William Mason, James Macpherson, and Evan Evans who specialized in creating a mood of noble melancholy out of Celtic druids, bards, and warriors. That revival was almost entirely couched in the English language, and judged by the standards of *Ossian,* it was distinguished by a specious style and content. The revival had relatively little to do with Ireland and Irish myths, being heavily Scottish and Welsh in its orientation, not least because of the powerful stimulus provided by Macpherson, Scott, and Burns.

By contrast, the Celtic revival of the late nineteenth century was far more Irish in content, authorship, and language—although English continued to be the dominant medium—and it was much more nationalist in tone than its predecessor. It was also more indebted to the work of Celtic folklorists, philologists, and archaeologists as well as to political writers like the men of Young Ireland. This climactic Celtic revival owed a great deal of its thrust to the organization of Irishmen and women—poets, publicists, journalists, popular historians, and dreamers—into

countless societies and associations which flourished in the second half of the century. The founding of the Ossianic Society in Dublin in 1853, the Irish Literary Society of London in 1891, the National Literary Society of Dublin in 1892, the Royal Society of Antiquaries of Ireland in 1890, and the Gaelic League in 1893, to mention but a few examples, reflected in part the trend toward increasing political organization in both England and Ireland in this period. But the immediate inspiration of these new societies was literary and scholarly, and among their patrons could be found aristocrats like the Marquis of Ormonde and the 2nd Earl of Dunraven as well as scrupulous Irish scholars of a more middle class hue like Eugene O'Curry, John O'Donovan, and George Petrie. In France the *Revue Celtique* founded in 1870, and later edited by the noted Celticist D'Arbois de Jubainville, and in Germany the *Zeitschrift für Celtische Philologie* founded in 1896 by Kuno Meyer and L. C. Stern provided a foundation of impressive and cosmopolitan scholarship on which less erudite Celticists could build their raths, dolmens, and castles. All of these societies and journals helped to put together that synthesis of philology, history, mythology, folklore, and fantasy which is called here Celticism.

The Celticist response to Anglo-Saxonism in the late Victorian period drew some of its historical inspiration from the topographical sections of the famous Irish Ordnance Survey, launched by Sir Thomas Larcom in the 1830's and aborted by the British government in the early 1840's. It derived some of its vigor and lyrical quality from the poetry and prose of Thomas Davis, Thomas D'Arcy McGee, and Clarence Mangan which contained among other derivatives a hard core of Gaelic or Celtic legend. Along with Charles Gavan Duffy these fervent young nationalists wished to provoke the readers of their weekly journal *The Nation* into equal fervor by making it "racy of the soil."

Young Ireland was not as exclusive in its ethnocentrism as were the more militant nationalists of the early twentieth century because, as Davis declared in his poem "Celts and Saxons," it was time for Irish Celts and Irish Saxons to unite and make common cause against English Saxons. Celticism also owed something to the Fenians of the 1860's, whose choice of name revealed an awareness of Irish mythology and whose nationalist views were animated by a strong note of ethnocentrism. Above all, Celticism depended for much of its content and inspiration on the growing body of folklore, myth, legend, and superstition which was being collected and published in Dublin and London in the last decades of the century. Such were some of the roots of that 'wild rose' which blossomed in the 1890's with the coming together of those gifted, indeed inspired, men and women who made the Irish literary renaissance what it was. Theirs was the supreme expression of Celticism. Apart from the early poems and plays of Yeats as well as his *Celtic Twilight* (1893), one may cite such examples of this "racy" ethnocentrism as Lady Gregory's *Gods and Fighting Men* (1904) and the collection of Celticist essays she edited, *Ideals in Ireland* (1901), George Sigerson's *Bards of the Gael and Gall* (1897), Sophie Bryant's *The Genius of the Gael* (1913), Douglas Hyde's *A Literary History of Ireland* (1898), Alice Stopford Green's *The Making of Ireland and its Undoing* (1908), and Edmund Hogan's *The Irish People* (1899). Heavy deposits of Celticism may also be found in *The Leader,* edited by that apostle of Irish Ireland, D. P. Moran, in the files of the *Irish Peasant* once it had fallen into the editorial hands of W. P. Ryan, in the pages of *The New Ireland Review,* and also in the 'Ossianized' poetry of Fiona Macleod, otherwise known as William Sharp. The official organs of the Gaelic League and the Irish Literary Theater shared with *The Gaelic Journal* and Arthur Griffith's *United Irishman* a distinctly Celticist flavor.

One of the most forceful statements of the Celticist position was Hyde's lecture "The Necessity for De-Anglicising Ireland," delivered in Dublin in 1892. In the course of his address Hyde implored the sons of the noble Gaelic race to throw off the insidious culture of the Saxon and to return to a pure Irish culture by learning "our once great national tongue." Hyde was preaching the same kind of cultural purity that Freeman had done in his Anglo-Saxonist way twenty or thirty years earlier. Both men were equally sensitive to the corrupting influences they saw at work in their respective cultures, and both were equally absolutist in the remedies they prescribed. The Irish and Anglo-Irishmen who made possible this cultural revival were convinced that in order to create a new Ireland and to animate it with a new Celtic spirit they had to rediscover the old Ireland of pre-conquest times through both folklore and history. To some extent they found an escape from such paraphernalia of modernity as Dublin Castle bureaucrats, land judges, Congested Districts Board officials, school inspectors, and scientific agriculturists in ancient bards and heroic warriors. In their enthusiasm for uncovering 'hidden' Gaelic Ireland, they underestimated the difficulties of the Irish language, and, uninhibited by the learning of Zeuss or Meyer, they plunged ahead into the thickets of that language often insensible to the errors in grammar, spelling, meaning, and pronunciation which they left in their wake.

In spite of their denials of political intent Hyde and his associates in the Gaelic League were far more 'political' than they cared to admit. That is to say, they were politicized intellectuals rather than partisan nationalists. The Celticism of their writings and speeches furnished their more politically active contemporaries with many of the materials of a separatist movement. Nothing was easier than for a militant nationalist—and there were many degrees of militancy in Ireland after the fall of Parnell—to interpret Hyde's arguments about "de-Anglicising" Ireland in a purely political context.

Like the Anglo-Saxonists, the Celticists also had their fictional historians or historical myth-makers who spun out of a few thin threads an elaborate tapestry depicting a social and political Arcadia in Ireland before the coming of the Sassenach. Alice Green carried forward her late husband's Home Rule sympathies, but she betrayed the Anglo-Saxonist legacy of *The Short History* repeatedly in her writings on Irish history. Ancient Ireland, she once asserted [in her *Irish Nationality*], was a "true democracy—a society in which ever broadening masses of the peo-

ple are made intelligent sharers in the national life, and conscious guardians of its tradition." The theory of the Milesian origins of the Irish accomplished for Celticist historians what the Teutonic origins theory had done for Anglo-Saxonists. Irish historians found in the sept and communal property rights in ancient Ireland their equivalent of the mark system; and in gavelkind they saw a practice superior to English laws of primogeniture. If Celticist ethnology was much less scientific than its Anglo-Saxonist counterpart, it contained the same emphasis on tracing the distinct as well as distinctly superior qualities of the Irish or Celtic race. Despite the painful invasions, plantations, and migrations in Irish history, despite all of Ireland's vaunted contacts with the Continent before the twelfth century, the so-called native Irish were still held to be pure of blood. Genealogists like John O'Hart traced the pedigree of Irish kings and chieftains straight back in an unbroken line to Adam. Both Celticist poetry and history carried the message that a rich mixture of Milesian, Firbolgian, Tuatha de Danann and Gaelic blood flowed in Irish veins, unblemished by Saxon, Norman, Danish or any other non-Celtic blood.

Needless to say the Celticists, too, had their lunatic fringe made up of patriots who insisted on racial purity or who declared that America had been discovered in the year 545 by that great Christian missionary, St. Brendan, Bishop of Clonfert. But these myths were innocuous by comparison with those of Gobineau, Knox, and H. S. Chamberlain. By means of associations and meetings as different in tone and patronage as the Pan-Celtic Society (1888), the Irish Race Convention (1897), and the Pan Celtic Congress (1901) the Celticists assembled a self-image of the Irish people that was as flattering to the believer as the one put together by Anglo-Saxonists a generation or so earlier. The so-called genius of the Gael or Celt was as emotionally satisfying to many Irishmen as the genius of the Anglo-Saxon had been and continued to be for many of their English contemporaries.

If the Celticists in Ireland lacked historians of the eminence of Freeman, Stubbs, Green, and Froude, they could boast of many more journals and societies specifically dedicated to the promotion of all things Celtic, Gaelic, or Irish. Hyde's agitation of the language question was fully exploited by Arthur Griffith, Padraic Pearse, and many other nationalists of the post-Parnellite generation; and Eoin MacNeill carried the cause forward from his position in the new National University of Ireland. Sinn Fein was in some respects the political expression of this Celticist revival: its name, its emphasis on self-reliance and pride in race, and its increasing resort to proclamations, titles of address, and names in Irish showed that its leaders were not insensitive to the work of Hyde and his Gaelic Leaguers. The Celticist message of pride in race and culture was not only heard but repeated endlessly in Irish-American communities across the Atlantic; and societies for preserving and promoting the Irish language sprang up in the major cities of the eastern seaboard, notably in New York and Boston. After the fall of Parnell, and throughout the period of constant feuding within the Irish parliamentary party, more and more young Irishmen succumbed to the Celticist attractions of the G.A.A., the A.O.H., the

I.R.B., and, eventually, Sinn Fein wherein Irish history and mythology were inseparable. Irish nationalism had, indeed, become "racy of the soil," or, rather, 'racy of the race.'

Celticism thus helped many Irishmen to defend themselves against Anglo-Saxonist slurs and to arm themselves with a form of cultural self-respect on the strength of which they sought to oppose or defy the imperial authority at Westminster. Patterns of ethnocentric thinking, and especially pride in the Irish race, could be found in all the more extreme organizations from the Gaelic Athletic Association and the Irish Republican Brotherhood, to the Dungannon Clubs, Cumann na nGaedheal, and, after 1907, the Sinn Fein movement led by Griffith. Modern Irish nationalism was, of course, a mosaic made up of many beliefs and goals, a number of which conflicted with one another, but the Celticism of the late nineteenth century helps to explain not only the decline in prestige and effectiveness of the Irish parliamentary party, but the increasingly separatist trend of nationalist thought, especially after the new Liberal government of 1906 had made it clear that Home Rule was not the first item on its agenda. The repudiation by Sinn Fein and other immoderate groups of the constitutional agitation carried on by Redmond and his party was as much a condemnation of the policy of playing the English game of parliamentary process under English rules as it was a rebuke to Redmond and his lieutenants for becoming too 'Anglicised' at Westminster. It is significant that Padraic Pearse found the finest embodiment of the Irish race in Wolfe Tone, not O'Connell or Parnell, and he did so because Tone had been willing to sacrifice his life for the principles in which he believed. Celticism was an expression of both nationalist frustration and cultural striving. It stimulated as well as nourished the appetite of many Irishmen for a sense of cultural and racial solidarity; and by so doing it enabled a few of them, a mere handful in fact, to fight more boldly not only for their country but their race. The belief of many 'physical force' men in the purity and nobility of their Celtic blood made the 'blood sacrifice' of Easter, 1916, all the more an act of racial pride and all the less a gesture of political despair.

> *L. P. Curtis, Jr., "Anglo-Saxonist Historiography" and "Celticism: The Irish Response," in his* Anglo-Saxons and Celts: A Study of Anti-Irish Prejudice in Victorian England, *Conference on British Studies, 1968, pp. 74-89, 108-16.*

Douglas Hyde (An Craoibhín Aoibhinn)

[*Renowned as a translator of Irish literature into English, Hyde is recognized as an important member of the Irish nationalist movement; his influence is seen in the works of Yeats, Gregory, and Synge. In the following excerpt from a speech delivered before the Irish National Literary Society in Dublin, Hyde laments the anglicising of Ireland, speaking with pride of his nation's history and culture.*]

When we speak of "The Necessity for De-Anglicising the Irish Nation," we mean it, not as a protest against imitating what is *best* in the English people, for that would be absurd, but rather to show the folly of neglecting what is Irish, and hastening to adopt, pell-mell, and indiscriminately, everything that is English, simply because it *is* English.

This is a question which most Irishmen will naturally look at from a National point of view, but it is one which ought also to claim the sympathies of every intelligent Unionist, and which, as I know, does claim the sympathy of many.

If we take a bird's-eye view of our island to-day, and compare it with what it used to be, we must be struck by the extraordinary fact that the nation which was once, as every one admits, one of the most classically learned and cultured nations in Europe, is now one of the least so; how one of the most reading and literary peoples has become one of the *least* studious and most *un*-literary, and how the present art products of one of the quickest, most sensitive, and most artistic races on earth are now only distinguished for their hideousness.

I shall endeavour to show that this failure of the Irish people in recent times has been largely brought about by the race diverging during this century from the right path, and ceasing to be Irish without becoming English. I shall attempt to show that with the bulk of the people this change took place quite recently, much more recently than most people imagine, and is, in fact, still going on. I should also like to call attention to the illogical position of men who drop their own language to speak English, of men who translate their euphonious Irish names into English monosyllables, of men who read English books, and know nothing about Gaelic literature, nevertheless protesting as a matter of sentiment that they hate the country which at every hand's turn they rush to imitate.

I wish to show you that in Anglicising ourselves wholesale we have thrown away with a light heart the best claim which we have upon the world's recognition of us as a separate nationality. What did Mazzini say? What is Goldwin Smith never tired of declaiming? What do the *Spectator* and *Saturday Review* harp on? That we ought to be content as an integral part of the United Kingdom because we have lost the notes of nationality, our language and customs.

It has always been very curious to me how Irish sentiment sticks in this half-way house—how it continues to apparently hate the English, and at the same time continues to imitate them; how it continues to clamour for recognition as a distinct nationality, and at the same time throws away with both hands what would make it so. If Irishmen only went a little farther they would become good Englishmen in sentiment also. But—illogical as it appears—there seems not the slightest sign or probability of their taking that step. It is the curious certainty that come what may Irishmen will continue to resist English rule, even though it should be for their good, which prevents many of our nation from becoming Unionists upon the spot. It is a fact, and we must face it as a fact, that although they adopt English habits and copy England in every way, the great bulk of Irishmen and Irishwomen over the whole world are known to be filled with a dull, ever-abiding animosity against her, and—right or wrong—to grieve when she prospers, and joy when she is hurt. Such movements as Young Irelandism, Fenianism, Land Leagueism, and Parliamentary obstruction seem always to gain their sympathy and support. It is just because there appears no earthly chance of their becoming good members of the Empire that I urge that they should not remain in the anomalous position they are in, but since they absolutely refuse to become the one thing, that they become the other; cultivate what they have rejected, and build up an Irish nation on Irish lines.

But you ask, why should we wish to make Ireland more Celtic than it is—why should we de-Anglicise it at all?

I answer because the Irish race is at present in a most anomalous position, imitating England and yet apparently hating it. How can it produce anything good in literature, art, or institutions as long as it is actuated by motives so contradictory? Besides, I believe it is our Gaelic past which, though the Irish race does not recognise it just at present, is really at the bottom of the Irish heart, and prevents us becoming citizens of the Empire, as, I think, can be easily proved.

To say that Ireland has not prospered under English rule is simply a truism; all the world admits it, England does not deny it. But the English retort is ready. You have not prospered, they say, because you would not settle down contentedly, like the Scotch, and form part of the Empire. "Twenty years of good, resolute, grandfatherly government," said a well-known Englishman, will solve the Irish

Douglas Hyde.

question. He possibly made the period too short, but let us suppose this. Let us suppose for a moment—which is impossible—that there were to arise a series of Cromwells in England for the space of one hundred years, able administrators of the Empire, careful rulers of Ireland, developing to the utmost our national resources, whilst they unremittingly stamped out every spark of national feeling, making Ireland a land of wealth and factories, whilst they extinguished every thought and every idea that was Irish, and left us, at last, after a hundred years of good government, fat, wealthy, and populous, but with all our characteristics gone, with every external that at present differentiates us from the English lost or dropped; all our Irish names of places and people turned into English names; the Irish language completely extinct; the O's and the Macs dropped; our Irish intonation changed, as far as possible by English schoolmasters into something English; our history no longer remembered or taught; the names of our rebels and martyrs blotted out; our battlefields and traditions forgotten; the fact that we were not of Saxon origin dropped out of sight and memory, and let me now put the question—How many Irishmen are there who would purchase material prosperity at such a price? It is exactly such a question as this and the answer to it that shows the difference between the English and Irish race. Nine Englishmen out of ten would jump to make the exchange, and I as firmly believe that nine Irishmen out of ten would indignantly refuse it.

And yet this awful idea of complete Anglicisation, which I have here put before you in all its crudity, is, and has been, making silent inroads upon us for nearly a century.

Its inroads have been silent, because, had the Gaelic race perceived what was being done, or had they been once warned of what was taking place in their own midst, they would, I think, never have allowed it. When the picture of complete Anglicisation is drawn for them in all its nakedness Irish sentimentality becomes suddenly a power and refuses to surrender its birthright.

What lies at the back of the sentiments of nationality with which the Irish millions seem so strongly leavened, what can prompt them to applaud such sentiments as:

> They say the British empire owes much to Irish
>   hands,
> That Irish valour fixed her flag o'er many con-
>   quered lands;
> And ask if Erin takes no pride in these her gal-
>   lant sons,
> Her Wolseleys and her Lawrences, her Wolfes
>   and Wellingtons.
>
> Ah! these were of the Empire—we yield them to
>   her fame,
> And ne'er in Erin's orisons are heard their alien
>   name;
> But those for whom her heart beats high and
>   benedictions swell,
> They died upon the scaffold and they pined with-
>   in the cell.

Of course it is a very composite feeling which prompts them; but I believe that what is largely behind it is the half unconscious feeling that the race which at one time held possession of more than half Europe, which established itself in Greece, and burned infant Rome, is now—almost extirpated and absorbed elsewhere—making its last stand for independence in this island of Ireland; and do what they may the race of to-day cannot wholly divest itself from the mantle of its own past. Through early Irish literature, for instance, can we best form some conception of what that race really was, which, after overthrowing and trampling on the primitive peoples of half Europe, was itself forced in turn to yield its speech, manners, and independence to the victorious eagles of Rome. We alone of the nations of Western Europe escaped the claws of those birds of prey; we alone developed ourselves naturally upon our own lines outside of and free from all Roman influence; we alone were thus able to produce an early art and literature, *our* antiquities can best throw light upon the pre-Romanised inhabitants of half Europe, and—we are our father's sons.

There is really no exaggeration in all this, although Irishmen are sometimes prone to overstating as well as to forgetting. Westwood himself declares that, were it not for Irishmen, these islands would possess no primitive works of art worth the mentioning; Jubainville asserts that early Irish literature is that which best throws light upon the manners and customs of his own ancestors the Gauls; and Zimmer, who has done so much for Celtic philology, has declared that only a spurious criticism can make an attempt to doubt about the historical character of the chief persons of our two epic cycles, that of Cuchullain and of Finn. It is useless elaborating this point; and Dr. Sigerson has already shown in his opening lecture the debt of gratitude which in many respects Europe owes to ancient Ireland. The dim consciousness of this is one of those things which are at the back of Irish national sentiment, and our business, whether we be Unionists or Nationalists, should be to make this dim consciousness an active and potent feeling, and thus increase our sense of self-respect and of honour.

The present writer recently heard the teacher of a school in an Irish-speaking district of Connemara describing the process of dealing with the mind of a little child: "The first thing we have to do is to wring the Irish out of them," and making a motion with the hands as if twisting a cloth,—"we wring the Irish out of them, and then they can begin to understand what we teach them." "And how long does it take to wring the Irish out?" "About two years," was the reply.

—*From an article in* All Ireland Review, *3 November, 1900.*

What we must endeavour to never forget is this, that the Ireland of to-day is the descendant of the Ireland of the seventh century, then the school of Europe and the torch of learning. It is true that Northmen made some minor settlements in it in the ninth and tenth centuries, it is true that the Normans made extensive settlements during the succeeding centuries, but none of those broke the continuity of the social life of the island. Dane and Norman drawn to the kindly Irish breast issued forth in a generation or two fully Irishised, and more Hibernian than the Hibernians themselves, and even after the Cromwellian plantation the children of numbers of the English soldiers who settled in the south and midlands, were, after forty years' residence, and after marrying Irish wives, turned into good Irishmen, and unable to speak a word of English, while several Gaelic poets of the last century have, like Father English, the most unmistakably English names. In two points only was the continuity of the Irishism of Ireland damaged. First, in the north-east of Ulster, where the Gaelic race was expelled and the land planted with aliens, whom our dear mother Erin, assimilative as she is, has hitherto found it difficult to absorb, and in the ownership of the land, eight-ninths of which belongs to people many of whom always lived, or live, abroad, and not half of whom Ireland can be said to have assimilated.

During all this time the continuation of Erin's national life centred, according to our way of looking at it, not so much in the Cromwellian or Williamite landholders who sat in College Green, and governed the country, as in the mass of the people whom Dean Swift considered might be entirely neglected, and looked upon as hewers of wood and drawers of water; the men who, nevertheless, constituted the real working population, and who were living on in the hopes of better days; the men who have since made America, and have within the last ten years proved what an important factor they may be in wrecking or in building the British Empire. These are the men of whom our merchants, artisans, and farmers mostly consist, and in whose hands is to-day the making or marring of an Irish nation. But, alas, *quantum mutatus ab illo!* What the battleaxe of the Dane, the sword of the Norman, the wile of the Saxon were unable to perform, we have accomplished ourselves. We have at last broken the continuity of Irish life, and just at the moment when the Celtic race is presumably about to largely recover possession of its own country, it finds itself deprived and stript of its Celtic characteristics, cut off from the past, yet scarcely in touch with the present. It has lost since the beginning of this century almost all that connected it with the era of Cuchullain and of Ossian, that connected it with the Christianisers of Europe, that connected it with Brian Boru and the heroes of Clontarf, with the O'Neills and O'Donnells, with Rory O'More, with the Wild Geese, and even to some extent with the men of '98. It has lost all that they had—language, traditions, music, genius, and ideas. Just when we should be starting to build up anew the Irish race and the Gaelic nation—as within our own recollection Greece has been built up anew—we find ourselves despoiled of the bricks of nationality. The old bricks that lasted eighteen hundred years are destroyed; we must now set to, to bake new ones, if we can, on other ground and of other clay. Imagine for a moment the restoration of a German-speaking Greece.

The bulk of the Irish race really lived in the closest contact with the traditions of the past and the national life of nearly eighteen hundred years, until the beginning of this century. Not only so, but during the whole of the dark Penal times they produced amongst themselves a most vigorous literary development. Their schoolmasters and wealthy farmers, unwearied scribes, produced innumerable manuscripts in beautiful writing, each letter separated from another as in Greek, transcripts both of the ancient literature of their sires and of the more modern literature produced by themselves. Until the beginning of the present century there was no county, no barony, and, I may almost say, no townland which did not boast of an Irish poet, the people's representative of those ancient bards who died out with the extirpation of the great Milesian families. The literary activity of even the eighteenth century among the Gaels was very great, not in the South alone, but also in Ulster—the number of poets it produced was something astonishing. It did not, however, produce many works in Gaelic prose, but it propagated translations of many pieces from the French, Latin, Spanish, and English. Every well-to-do farmer could read and write Irish, and many of them could understand even archaic Irish. I have myself heard persons reciting the poems of Donogha More O'Daly, Abbot of Boyle, in Roscommon, who died sixty years before Chaucer was born. To this very day the people have a word for archaic Irish, which is much the same as though Chaucer's poems were handed down amongst the English peasantry, but required a special training to understand. This training, however, nearly every one of fair education during the Penal times possessed, nor did they begin to lose their Irish training and knowledge until after the establishment of Maynooth and the rise of O'Connell. These two events made an end of the Gaelicism of the Gaelic race, although a great number of poets and scribes existed even down to the forties and fifties of the present century, and a few may linger on yet in remote localities. But it may be said, roughly speaking, that the ancient Gaelic civilisation died with O'Connell, largely, I am afraid, owing to his example and his neglect of inculcating the necessity of keeping alive racial customs, language, and traditions, in which with the one notable exception of our scholarly idealist, Smith O'Brien, he has been followed until a year ago by almost every leader of the Irish race.

Thomas Davis and his brilliant band of Young Irelanders came just at the dividing of the line, and tried to give to Ireland a new literature in English to replace the literature which was just being discarded. It succeeded and it did not succeed. It was a most brilliant effort, but the old bark had been too recently stripped off the Irish tree, and the trunk could not take as it might have done to a fresh one. It was a new departure, and at first produced a violent effect. Yet in the long run it failed to properly leaven our peasantry who might, perhaps, have been reached upon other lines. I say they *might* have been reached upon other lines because it is quite certain that even well on into the beginning of this century, Irish poor scholars and schoolmasters used to gain the greatest favour and applause by reading out manuscripts in the people's houses at night, some of which manuscripts had an antiquity of a couple of hundred years or more behind them, and which, when they got illegible from age, were always recopied. The Irish

peasantry at that time were all to some extent cultured men, and many of the better off ones were scholars and poets. What have we now left of all that? Scarcely a trace. Many of them read newspapers indeed, but who reads, much less recites, an epic poem, or chants an elegiac or even a hymn?

Wherever Irish throughout Ireland continued to be spoken, there the ancient MSS. continued to be read, there the epics of Cuchullain, Conor MacNessa, Déirdre, Finn, Oscar, and Ossian continued to be told, and there poetry and music held sway. Some people may think I am exaggerating in asserting that such a state of things existed down to the present century, but it is no exaggeration. I have myself spoken with men from Cavan and Tyrone who spoke excellent Irish. Carleton's stories bear witness to the prevalence of the Irish language and traditions in Ulster when he began to write. My friend Mr. Lloyd has found numbers in Antrim who spoke good Irish. And, as for Leinster, my friend Mr. Cleaver informed me that when he lived in Wicklow a man came by from the County Carlow in search of work who could not speak a word of English. Old labourers from Connacht, who used to go to reap the harvest in England and take shipping at Drogheda, told me that at that time, fifty years ago, Irish was spoken by every one round that town. I have met an old man in Wicklow, not twenty miles from Dublin, whose parents always repeated the Rosary in Irish. My friend Father O'Growny, who has done and is doing so much for the Irish language and literature at Maynooth, tells me that there, within twenty miles of Dublin, are three old people who still speak Irish. O'Curry found people within seven miles of Dublin city who had never heard English in their youth at all, except from the car-drivers of the great town. I gave an old man in the street who begged from me, a penny, only a few days ago, saying, *"Sin pighin agad,"* and when he answered in Irish I asked him where he was from, and he said from *Newna (n' Eamhain)*, *i.e.,* Navan. Last year I was in Canada and out hunting with some Red Indians, and we spent a night in the last white man's house in the last settlement on the brink of the primeval forest; and judging from a peculiarly Hibernian physiognomy that the man was Irish, I addressed him in Gaelic, and to the intense astonishment both of whites and Indians we entered into a conversation which none of them understood; and it turned out that he was from within three miles of Kilkenny, and had been forty years in that country without forgetting the language he had spoken as a child, and I, although from the centre of Connacht, understood him perfectly. When my father was a young boy in the county Leitrim, not far from Longford, he seldom heard the farm labourers and tenants speak anything but Irish amongst themselves. So much for Ulster and Leinster, but Connacht and Munster were until quite recently completely Gaelic. In fact, I may venture to say, that, up to the beginning of the present century, neither man, woman, nor child of the Gaelic race, either of high blood or low blood, existed in Ireland who did not either speak Irish or understand it. But within the last ninety years we have, with an unparalleled frivolity, deliberately thrown away our birthright and Anglicised ourselves. None of the children of those people of whom I have spoken know Irish, and the race will from henceforth be changed; for as Monsieur Jubainville says of the influence of Rome upon Gaul, England "has definitely conquered us, she has even imposed upon us her language, that is to say, the form of our thoughts during every instant of our existence." It is curious that those who most fear West Britainism have so eagerly consented to imposing upon the Irish race what, according to Jubainville, who in common with all the great scholars of the continent, seems to regret it very much, is "the form of our thoughts during every instant of our existence."

So much for the greatest stroke of all in our Anglicisation, the loss of our language. I have often heard people thank God that if the English gave us nothing else they gave us at least their language. In this way they put a bold face upon the matter, and pretend that the Irish language is not worth knowing, and has no literature. But the Irish language *is* worth knowing, or why would the greatest philologists of Germany, France, and Italy be emulously studying it, and it *does* possess a literature, or why would a German savant have made the calculation that the books written in Irish between the eleventh and seventeenth centuries, and still extant, would fill a thousand octavo volumes.

I have no hesitation at all in saying that every Irish-feeling Irishman, who hates the reproach of West-Britonism, should set himself to encourage the efforts which are being made to keep alive our once great national tongue. The losing of it is our greatest blow, and the sorest stroke that the rapid Anglicisation of Ireland has inflicted upon us. In order to de-Anglicise ourselves we must at once arrest the decay of the language. We must bring pressure upon our politicians not to snuff it out by their tacit discouragement merely because they do not happen themselves to understand it. We must arouse some spark of patriotic inspiration among the peasantry who still use the language, and put an end to the shameful state of feeling—a thousand-tongued reproach to our leaders and statesmen—which makes young men and women blush and hang their heads when overheard speaking their own language. Maynooth has at last come splendidly to the front, and it is now incumbent upon every clerical student to attend lectures in the Irish language and history during the first three years of his course. But in order to keep the Irish language alive where it is still spoken—which is the utmost we can at present aspire to—nothing less than a house-to-house visitation and exhortation of the people themselves will do, something—though with a very different purpose—analogous to the procedure that James Stephens adopted throughout Ireland when he found her like a corpse on the dissecting table. This and some system of giving medals or badges of honour to every family who will guarantee that they have always spoken Irish amongst themselves during the year. But, unfortunately, distracted as we are and torn by contending factions, it is impossible to find either men or money to carry out this simple remedy, although to a dispassionate foreigner—to a Zeuss, Jubainville, Zimmer, Kuno Meyer, Windisch, or Ascoli, and the rest—this is of greater importance than whether Mr. Redmond or Mr. MacCarthy lead the largest wing of the Irish party for the moment, or Mr. So-and-So succeed with his election petition. To a person taking a bird's-eye view of the situation a hundred or five hundred years

hence, believe me, it will also appear of greater importance than any mere temporary wrangle, but, unhappily, our countrymen cannot be brought to see this.

We can, however, insist, and we *shall* insist if Home Rule be carried, that the Irish language, which so many foreign scholars of the first calibre find so worthy of study, shall be placed on a par with—or even above—Greek, Latin, and modern languages, in all examinations held under the Irish Government. We can also insist, and we *shall* insist, that in those baronies where the children speak Irish, Irish shall be taught, and that Irish-speaking schoolmasters, petty sessions clerks, and even magistrates be appointed in Irish-speaking districts. If all this were done, it should not be very difficult, with the aid of the foremost foreign scholars, to bring about a tone of thought which would make it disgraceful for an educated Irishman—especially of the old Celtic race, MacDermotts, O'Conors, O'Sullivans, MacCarthys, O'Neills—to be ignorant of his own language—would make it at least as disgraceful as for an educated Jew to be quite ignorant of Hebrew.

> Douglas Hyde, "The Necessity for De-Anglicising Ireland," in The Revival of Irish Literature *by Charles Gavan Duffy, George Sigerson and Douglas Hyde, 1894. Reprint by Lemma Publishing Corporation, 1973, pp. 115-61.*

William Patrick Ryan

[*Ryan was an Anglo-Irish critic and historian who was involved in the nationalist movement as well as literary societies in Dublin and London. In the following excerpt, he champions the cause of the revival, encouraging Irish writers to "teach Ireland to see herself, to be herself, to set her in her true place."*]

[The origin of the Irish literary revival movement] was simple and humble enough. Like the Druid rocking-stone, a gentle touch set it in motion—a few young men made it possible. Their work, as it widened, touched that educational and literary instinct in the Irish nature which, however dormant or unnoted, is never wholly dead. The first workers were of that cultured and studious force in the Land League, who saw in the agitation at first a real national upheaval, a picturesque popular revolution, or who hoped to make it such, but who, as time went on, were somewhat disillusioned. Others came who had taken their lessons from Young Ireland, others who had looked deep into Celtic legend, others yet who had drunk at the old founts of Gaelic bardic poetry. Later still, the advisings of Sir Charles Gavan Duffy made an impression without as well as within the movement. The political strife of the past few years, which some believed would check or kill the revival, became in reality a strong source of help. Thoughtful Irish sections, aloof before, now paused and rallied to it. Here was a national path, apart from odium and obloquy, along which those who believed in Ireland could travel with safety and with hope. Men of letters, whose pens had been sold to an alien market, were attracted to it. Irish students were taught how rich and gracious, if we only see, is our Ireland of the past and of the present. Some young Irishmen were taught how ignoble it was that in their hours of leisure they should stand idly by our street-corners, adding to the useless and clamorous elements in Ireland, while foreign *savants* were pouring with enthusiasm over our ancient manuscripts, while a few devotees were gathering up the dying lore of Gaelic Ireland, while a few, with seeing eyes, were declaring that Ireland at heart was her old self, with vigour and virility enough for a bright life yet amongst the nations. The movement has not yet made new men of such idlers, but it has caused some profitable searchings of heart amongst the best of them. . . .

[The] movement is far from being confined to Dublin or London. A weakness at present is that there is little cohesion amongst its different bodies. They have hardly a common programme; they have not a common organ. Literary Ireland is a thing of many fragments, very far apart, and even yet very strange to one another. Till they have a common system, with a spirit of real brotherhood pervading them all, some of the strength of this movement will be wasted, will be spent in isolated or even in contrary efforts.

It must be said of too many of the younger men who ought to be its real strength that although their work proves them to be stronger intellectually than their predecessors of Young Ireland, yet it is probable as things stand that in ten years they would not stir Ireland as effectually or render as noble an account of themselves as the Young Ireland coterie could in a twelvemonth. For many of them, able as they are, there is one thing needful before they can be forces as well as units. It is a missionary spirit. Irish sections here and there throughout Ireland and Great Britain now look up to them with hope, await their light and leading. Let them look to it that those who so watch and wait will not be in the smallest measure disappointed.

A nation that numbers amongst its younger school such writers as W. B. Yeats, William O'Brien, Miss Barlow, Standish O'Grady, T. W. Rolleston, Edmund Downey, Frank Mathew, Francis Fahy, Dr. Hyde, Katherine Tynan, Miss Sigerson, Miss Milligan and Lionel Johnson, stands in no need of ministering spirits. They and their brethren have been scattered so much, have worked in so many different channels, home and foreign, have mixed among, and been lost among so many foreign schools, that we have no idea of their number, their capacities till we slowly and patiently separate them from the crowd and call them to ourselves. It is our misfortune furthermore that in London and Boston, New York and Melbourne, writers of ours are "units merely of the undistinguished mass" of minor poets and novelists, who at home amid more congenial ways and audiences might be the delight of a nation. As Ireland grows more herself, more alive, more intellectual, the more will these misplaced children of song and story be drawn to her shores and her ideals. To help towards so devoutly to be wished a consummation is another hope of our movement.

Certain it is that as the revival of Irish ideas grows apace, and the literary spirit blossoms into promising life in so many quarters, more cohesion, more fraternity, more of a missionary spirit are amongst our needs, in order that the two great objects of the movement—influence as an educating and teaching force, and literary creativeness—may go on and widen. In the educational direction we can all labour, continuing and perfecting the work which will be handed over at a future day to a real National Board of Education. We can carry out Sir Gavan Duffy's wise purpose and desire of bringing technical lore to our peasants, showing them the riches of the soil, the homely world about them. They will learn that true nationhood presupposes a people thoroughly conversant with their own characteristics and powers, keenly conscious of their industrial and other resources, proud of their rights and their home institutions, manly, dignified, self-supporting, but in sympathy with the human and spiritual interests of outer humanity; loving their own artistic and intellectual creations, and finding in them something spiritually noble to rally to; distinctive but not insular. As yet, the unfortunate truth is that three-fourths of our people are as strangers in their own land; strangers to her capacities, strangers to her traditions and her proudest associations. There is an appealing legend of ours which tells that in a cave under Aileach, in Donegal, a band of the old Fenian heroes lie sleeping through the ages, awaiting the day of Ireland's successful uprising for independence, when they will come forth to take their places in the ranks beside their living kindred. Dim and mysterious as these forms in the gloom of the mountain cave appear to our minds are too many of the first figures of Irish history even yet. They are apart, unreal, or all but lost—theirs is a legend-life at the best. Yet in a vivid-living, a studious, a creative Ireland, the dramatist, the artist, the ballad-writer, would find material for their live's best work in those heroes and those ways we have allowed to grow dim. The study would vivify our national life. As for our legendary riches and our little-known Gaelic fields, they are fascinating. Fine work has been done of late years for Irish folk-lore, but higher matters of Irish mythology are, strangely enough, neglected. We have taken our notions of the old gods from peasant stories; we have, as it were, surveyed the Irish Olympus through cabin-smoke. Some of us, perhaps, never gave it a glance or a thought. To many, with whom Jove and Diana and Pan are abiding figures, Dagda Mor and Mananan are the merest shadows. Afar in the western ocean in the bygone ages the Celtic fancy saw the beautiful islands of light and youth. There the gods and the great spirits had abode. Time and sorrow were strangers by those mystic waves in the West. There Oisin sang of the Fenii; there Mananan, the great god of the sea, had his home; there the three queen-sisters—Eire, Fohla, and Banba—lived in immortal peace. There were the mystic bell-branches, which to all who listened brought glorious sleep under the enchanted trees. In fine, the lore of that western world is almost an epic in itself, and one which in these days, when so much materialism invades us from the East, it were well we studied somewhat more than we do. Immortal itself, as the old bards deemed, it might be also the instrument of immortality to many an Irish writer. We must try to make it familar by Irish firesides.

As the Irish revival expands in new directions, will not some one take heart and attempt something for Irish dramatic literature? The real Irish drama is a thing unknown. Why it is so is to me something of a marvel; for in our tastes, ideas, and lives we are essentially dramatic. And surely the materials for the national drama are wasting in profusion before us. We may see in our day in Dublin genuine Irish plays, of truth and talent, written for the people, prized by the people, moving and moulding the people. Otherwise I fear that the city will not half deserve to be the capital of a nation.

Leaving the question of the revival of Irish ideas generally, which every day becomes more palpable and hopeful, and examining the possibility which is the most important of all—the possibility of a new, characteristic, and original Irish literature—there are signs that thrill and cheer. Our writers, for one thing, are becoming more sensible of the dignity of literature, more devoted to it for its own sake. With some of their forerunners literature was now and then a spasmodic or half-hearted affair, neither an art nor a passion nor even a great pursuit. They stood within the sanctuary, but gave no sign which told that they had the sacred "vocation." Now a higher order of things is arising. Life, humanity, imagination, are taking the place of polemics and abstractions in Irish prose and verse.

Our writers will not want materials after their own hearts. Some there are who will find their highest inspiration in their own inner lives; others will seek it in the complex, strenuous life of our new Ireland. Others in the olden legends, stories, life-ways, will have fresh and fruitful ground, as yet only partially broken. Leaving England, where so much of latter-day thought and song is suggestive of decay, decrepitude and dying impulse, and landing on Celtic shores, is like passing from a worn old world to the rich vistas and the exultant life of a new, to feel

> Like stout Cortez, when with eagle eyes
> He stared at the Pacific, and all his men
> Looked at each other with a wild surmise,
> Silent, upon a peak in Darien.

So much are these possibilities being taken advantage of that a critic recently declared that latter-day English literature is fast becoming an Irish literature. In the most eloquent words that Sir Gavan Duffy used of late years he expressed the conviction that in Ireland "there is place for a great experiment for humanity." Perhaps it can be said, with even greater truth, that in Ireland there is place for a great experiment for literature.

As the leading writers . . . gave us their typical books— Standish O'Grady, William O'Brien, W. B. Yeats, and the rest—had not each book an interest outside and beyond itself? Was it not as a light rising out of a dark country, showing us charms and possibilities of which we had been entirely oblivious? "Spread the Light"—such light as this—we well may say to these writers. And well may we advise our younger authors to seek that dark country of charms and beauties unexplored.

We will aim to promote in new quarters that enlightened nationality which studies the past, prizes the best in it, keeps it as a meet background to lives of noble action in the present; whose intelligent aim through the years is the development of all that is worthy and distinctive in the nation. Ireland's best will never have a fair field until a great system of National Education, framed on a Celtic basis, meeting at every turn the requirements and characteristics

of the people, has had time to become, as it were, part and parcel of the nation. Our movement is doing something to supply the want; and there are splendid possibilities before it in the same direction. When it has found an organ or a press of its own, the course will be surer. Meanwhile, and after, our authors, with their more subtle graces, will be drawing brighter native ideals around the masses. They will illustrate life after our own hearts, and bring more hallowed associations around our Irish scenery. They will, if true to their genius, create characters that will enrich our lives, that will touch our Celtic sympathies, stir our latent or living worthiness; characters to which we will rally, and be the better men and women for so doing.

Such then is the movement—literary in essence, social and national in some of its purposes and effects. Its aim is to teach Ireland to see herself, to be herself, to set her in her true place, realising her nature and her mission. It is an effort to bring knowledge, books, brave hopes, Celtic idealism as her ministering spirits. Its pioneers have it in their power to touch, to thrill, to weld together for the noblest national purposes all that is thoughtful, strenuous, and original in their own land. But their mission must not be a mere transient, recreative, after-dinner idea—it must be a constant plan and passion. Most interesting of all are the efforts of the *littèrateurs* in the heart of the movement. Should they tend, as they promise, to keener interpretation than hitherto of Ireland's life, to brighter developments of Ireland's genius, the gain will be not only hers but humanity's.

> *William Patrick Ryan, "Needs and Possibilities," in his* The Irish Literary Revival: Its History, Pioneers and Possibilities, *1894. Reprint by Lemma Publishing Corporation, 1970, pp. 176-84.*

LITERARY IDEALS IN IRELAND

William Butler Yeats

[In 1901, Lady Gregory, who co-founded the Irish Literary Theater with Yeats and was an instrumental figure in the establishment of Irish national drama, published a collection of essays under the title Ideals in Ireland *for the purpose of showing "in what direction thought is moving in Ireland." In the following excerpt from his contribution to that volume, Yeats discusses the state of the literary movement in Ireland and its possibilities for the future.]*

I have just come to a quiet Connaught house from seeing a little movement, in a great movement of thought which is fashioning the dreams of the next generation in Ireland, grow to a sudden maturity. Certain plays, which are an expression of the most characteristic ideals of what is sometimes called the "Celtic movement," have been acted in Dublin before audiences drawn from all classes and all political sections, and described at great length in every Nationalist newspaper. Whatever be the merit of these plays, and that must be left to the judgment of time, their success means, as I think, that the "Celtic movement," which has hitherto interested but a few cultivated people, is about to become a part of the thought of Ireland.

Before 1891, Unionists and Nationalists were too busy keeping one or two simple beliefs at their fullest intensity for any complexity of thought or emotion; and the national imagination uttered itself, with a somewhat broken energy, in a few stories and in many ballads about the need of unity against England, about the martyrs who had died at the hand of England, or about the greatness of Ireland before the coming of England. They built up Ireland's dream of Ireland, of an ideal country weighed down by immemorial sorrows and served by heroes and saints, and they taught generations of young men to love their country with a love that was the deepest emotion they were ever to know; but they built with the virtues and beauties and sorrows and hopes that would move to tears the greatest number of those eyes before whom the modern world is but beginning to unroll itself; and, except when some rare, personal impulse shaped the song according to its will, they built to the formal and conventional rhythm which would give the most immediate pleasure to ears that had forgotten Gaelic poetry and not learned the subtleties of English poetry. The writers who made this literature or who shaped its ideals, in the years before the great famine, lived at the moment when the middle class had brought to perfection its ideal of the good citizen, and of a politics and a philosophy and a literature which would help him upon his way; and they made a literature full of the civic virtues and, in all but its unbounded patriotism, without inconvenient ardours. They took their style from Scott and Campbell and Macaulay, and that "universally popular" poetry which is really the poetry of the middle class, and from Beranger and that "peasant poetry" which looks for its models to the Burns of "Highland Mary" and "The Cottar's Saturday Night." Here and there a poet or a story-writer found an older dream among the common people or in his own mind, and made a personality for himself, and was forgotten; for it was the desire of everybody to be moved by the same emotions as everybody else, and certainly one cannot blame a desire which has thrown so great a shadow of self-sacrifice.

The fall of Parnell and the wreck of his party and of the organisations that supported it were the symbols, if not the causes, of a sudden change. They were followed by movements and organisations that brought the ideas and the ideals which are the expression of personalities alike into politics, economics, and literature. Those who looked for the old energies, which were the utterance of the common will and hope, were unable to see that a new kind of Ireland, as full of energy as a boiling pot, was rising up amid the wreck of the old kind, and that the national life was finding a new utterance. This utterance was so necessary that it seems as if the hand that broke the ball of glass, that now lies in fragments full of a new iridescent life, obeyed some impulse from beyond its wild and capricious will. More books about Irish subjects have been published in these last eight years than in the thirty years that went before them, and these books have the care for scholarship

and the precision of speech which had been notoriously lacking in books on Irish subjects. An appeal to the will, a habit of thought which measures all beliefs by their intensity, is content with a strenuous rhetoric; but an appeal to the intellect needs an always more perfect knowledge, an always more malleable speech. The new writers and the new organisations they work through—for organisations of various kinds take the place held by the critical press in other countries—have awakened Irish affections among many from whom the old rhetoric could never have got a hearing, but they have been decried for weakening the national faith by lovers of the old rhetoric. I have seen an obscure Irish member of Parliament rise at one of those monthly meetings of the Irish Literary Society, when the members of the society read sometimes their poems to one another, and ask their leave to read a poem. He did not belong to the society, but leave was given him, and he read a poem in the old manner, blaming the new critics and praising the old poems which had made him patriotic and filled his imagination with the images of the martyrs, and, as he numbered over their names, Wolfe Tone, Emmet, Owen Roe, Sarsfield, his voice shook, and many were angry with the new critics.

The organisations that are making this change are the Irish Literary Society in London, the National Literary Society in Dublin, which has founded, or rather sheltered with its influence, the Irish Literary Theatre, and the Feis Ceoil Committee in Dublin, at whose annual series of concerts of Irish music singers and pipers from all parts of Ireland compete; and more important than all, the Gaelic League, which has worked for the revival of the Gaelic language with such success that it has sold fifty thousand of its Gaelic text-books in a year. All these organisations have been founded since the fall of Parnell; and all are busy in preserving, or in moulding anew and without any thought of the politics of the hour, some utterance of the national life, and in opposing the vulgar books and vulgarer songs that come to us from England. We are preparing, as we hope, for a day when Ireland will speak in Gaelic, as much as Wales speaks in Welsh, within her borders, but speak, it may be, in English to other nations of those truths which were committed to her when "He set the borders of the nations according to His angels"; as Dionysius the Areopagite has written. Already, as I think, a new kind of romance, a new element in thought, is being moulded out of Irish life and traditions, and this element may have an importance for criticism, even should criticism forget the writers who are trying to embody it in their work, while looking each one through his own colour in the dome of many-coloured glass.

Contemporary English literature takes delight in praising England and her Empire, the master-work and dream of the middle class; and, though it may escape from this delight, it must long continue to utter the ideals of the strong and wealthy. Irish intellect has always been preoccupied with the weak and with the poor, and now it has begun to collect and describe their music and stories, and to utter anew the beliefs and hopes which they alone remember. It may never make a literature preoccupied with the circumstance of their lives, like the "peasant poetry," whose half deliberate triviality, passionless virtue, and passionless vice has helped so many orderly lives; for a writer who wishes to write with his whole mind must knead the beliefs and hopes, which he has made his own, with the circumstance of his own life. Burns had this preoccupation, and nobody will deny that he was a great poet; but even he had the poverty of emotions and ideas of a peasantry that had lost, like the middle class into which it would have its children absorbed, the imagination that is in tradition without finding the imagination that is in books. Irish literature may prolong its first inspiration without renouncing the complexity of ideas and emotions which is the inheritance of cultivated men, for it will have learned from the discoveries of modern learning that the common people, wherever civilization has not driven its plough too deep, keep a watch over the roots of all religion and all romance. Their poetry trembles upon the verge of incoherence with a passion all but unknown among modern poets, and their sense of beauty exhausts itself in countless legends and in metaphors that seem to mirror the energies of nature.

Dr. Hyde has collected many old Irish peasant love-songs, and, like all primitive poetry, they foreshadow a poetry whose intensity of emotion, or strangeness of language, has made it the poetry of little coteries. His peasant lover cries—

> It is happy for you, O blind man, who do not see
>   much of women.
> O! if you were to see what I see, you would be
>   sick even as I am.
> It is a pity, O God, that it was not blind I was
>   before I saw her twisted hair.
> I always thought the blind were pitiable, until
>   my calamity grew beyond the grief of all,
> Then though it is a pity I turned my pity into
>   envy.
> In a loop of the loops in a loop am I.
> It is sorrow for whoever has seen her, and it is
>   sorrow for him who does not see her every
>   day.
> It is sorrow for him who is tied in the knot of her
>   love, and it is sorrow for him who is loosed out
>   of it.
> It is sorrow for him who is near her, and it is sor-
>   row for him who is not near her.

Or he cries—

> O Maurya! you are my love, and the love of my
>   heart is your love—
> Love that is without littleness, without weak-
>   ness,
> Love from age till death,
> Love growing out of folly,
> Love that will send me close beneath the clay,
> Love without a hope of the world,
> Love without envy of fortune,
> Love that has left me withered in captivity,
> Love of my heart beyond women;
> And a love such as that, it is seldom to be got
>   from any man.

And Lady Gregory has translated a lament, that Raftery the wandering fiddler made for a fiddler some sixty years ago, into the simple English of the country people of to-day—

> The swans on the water are nine times blacker

> than a blackberry, since the man died from us
>   that had pleasantness on the top of his fingers;
> His two grey eyes were like the dew of the morn-
>   ing that lies on the grass;
> And since he was laid in the grave, the cold is
>   getting the upper hand.
> There are young women, and not without rea-
>   son, sorry and heart-broken and withered,
>   since he was left at the church;
> Their hair, thrown down and hanging, turned
>   grey on their head.
> No flower in any garden, and the leaves of the
>   trees have leave to cry, and they falling on the
>   ground;
> There are no green flowers on the tops of the
>   tufts since there did a boarded coffin go on
>   Daly.

All are not like this, but the most inspired and, as I think, the most characteristic are like this. There is a square stone tower called Ballylee Castle, a couple of miles from where I am writing. A farmer called Hynes, who had a beautiful daughter, Mary Hynes, lived near it some sixty years ago; and all over the countryside old men and old women still talk of her beauty, and the young and old praise her with a song made by Raftery—

> O star of light, and O sun in harvest,
> O amber hair, O my share of the world;
> There is no good to deny it or to try and hide it,
> She is the sun in the heavens who wounded my
>   heart.
>
> There was no part of Ireland I did not travel,
> From the rivers to the tops of the mountains,
> To the edge of Lough Greine, whose mouth is
>   hidden,
> And I saw no beauty but was behind hers.
>
> It is Mary Hynes, the calm and easy woman,
> Has beauty in her mind and in her face;
> If a hundred clerks were gathered together
> They could not write down a half of her ways.

This song, though Gaelic poetry has fallen from its old greatness, has come out of the same dreams as the songs and legends, as vague, it may be, as the clouds of evening and of dawn, that became in Homer's mind the memory and the prophecy of all the sorrows that have beset and shall beset the journey of beauty in the world. A very old woman who remembers Mary Hynes said to me, and to a friend who was with me: "I never saw one so handsome as she was, and I never will until I die. There were people coming from all parts to look at her, and maybe some of them forgot to say, 'God bless her' [so that their admiration might not give the fairies power over her]. Any way, she was young when she died, and my mother was at her funeral, and as to whether she was taken, well, there's others have been taken that were not handsome at all, and so it's likely enough she might have been, for there is no one to be seen at all that is handsome like she was." The spirit of Helen moves indeed among the legends that are told about turf-fires, and among the legends of the poor and simple everywhere. A friend of mine was told a while ago, in a remote part of Donegal, of a young man who saw a light before him on the road, and found when he came near that it was from a lock of hair in an open box. The hair was so bright that, when he went into the stable where he slept, he put the box into a hole in the wall and had no need of a candle. After many wanderings he found her from whose head it had been taken, and after many adventures married her and reigned over a kingdom.

The peasant remembers such songs and legends, all the more, it may be, because he has thought of little but cows and sheep and the like in his own marriage, for his dream has never been entangled by reality. The beauty of women is mirrored in his mind, as the excitement of the world is mirrored in the minds of children, and like them he thinks nothing but the best worth remembering. The child William Blake said to somebody who had told him of a fine city, that he thought no city fine that had not walls of gold and silver. It may be that poetry is the utterance of desires that we can only satisfy in dreams, and that if all our dreams were satisfied there would be no more poetry. Dreams pass from us with childhood, because we are so often told they can never come true, and because we are taught with so much labour to admire the paler beauty of the world. The children of the poor and simple learn from their unbroken religious faith, and from their traditional beliefs, and from the hardness of their lives, that this world is nothing, and that a spiritual world, where all dreams come true, is everything; and therefore the poor and simple are that imperfection whose perfection is genius.

The most of us think that all things, when imagined in their perfection, that all images which emotion desires in its intensity, are among the things nobody has ever seen or shall ever see; and so we are always reminding one another not to go too far from the moderation of reality. But the Irish peasant believes that the utmost he can dream was once or still is a reality by his own door. He will point to some mountain and tell you that some famous hero or beauty lived and sorrowed there, or he will tell you that Tir-nan-og, the country of the young, the old Celtic paradise,—the Land of the Living Heart, as it used to be called,—is all about him. An old woman close by Ballylee Castle said to a friend of mine the other day, when someone had finished a story of the poet Usheen's return from Tir-nan-og, where he had lived with his fairy mistress: "Tir-nan-og? That place is not far from us. One time I was in the chapel of Labane, and there was a tall thin man sitting next to me, and he dressed in grey; and after the mass I asked him where he came from. 'From Tir-nan-og,' he said. 'And where is that?' I asked him. 'It's not far from you,' he said. 'It's near the place where you live.' I remember well the look of him, and he telling me that. The priest was looking at us while we were talking together."

There are many grotesque things near at hand, the dead doing their penance in strange shapes, and evil spirits with terrible and ugly shapes, but people of a perfect beauty are never far off; and this beauty is often, I know not how often, that heroic beauty "which changes least from youth to age," and which has faded from modern painting and poetry before a fleeting voluptuous beauty. One old Mayo woman, who can neither read nor write, described it to me, though with grotesque comparisons. She has been long in service, and her language has not the simplicity of those who live among fields. She was standing in the window of her master's house looking out toward a mountain where Queen Maeve, the Queen of the Western Spirits, is said to have been buried, when she saw "the finest woman she ever saw" travelling right across from the mountain and straight to her. The woman had a sword by her side and a dagger lifted up in her hand, and was dressed in white, with bare arms and feet. She looked "very strong and warry and fierce, but not wicked"; that is, not cruel, at all. The old woman had seen the Irish giant, and "though he was a fine man, he was nothing to this woman, for he was round, and could not have stepped out so soldierly." She told me that she was like a certain stately lady of the neighbourhood, "but she had no stomach on her, and was slight and broad in the shoulders, and was handsomer than anyone you ever saw now; she looked about thirty." The old woman covered her eyes with her hands, and when she uncovered them the apparition had vanished. The neighbours were "wild" with her for not waiting to see if there was a message, for they are sure it was Queen Maeve, who often shows herself to the pilots. I asked the old woman if she had seen others like Queen Maeve, and she said: "Some of them have their hair down, but they look quite different, like the sleepy-looking ladies you see in the papers. Those with their hair up are like this one. The others have long white dresses, but those with their hair up have short dresses, so that you can see their legs right up to the calf." After some careful questioning I found that they wore what appeared to be buskins. She went on: "They are fine and dashing-looking, like the men one sees riding their horses in twos and threes on the slopes of the mountains, with their swords swinging." She repeated over and over: "There is no such race living now, none so fine proportioned," or the like, and then said: "The present queen is a nice, pleasant-looking woman, but she is not like her. What makes me think so little of the ladies is that I see none as they be," meaning the spirits; "when I think of her and of the ladies now, they are like little children running about, without being able to put their clothes on right. Is it the ladies? Why, I would not call them women at all!"

There are many old heroical tales about Queen Maeve, and before she was a queen she was a goddess and had her temples, and she is still the most beautiful of the beautiful. A young man among the Burren Hills of Clare told me, a couple of years ago, that he remembered an old poet who had made his poems in Irish, and had met in his youth one who had called herself Queen Maeve, and asked him if he would have money or pleasure. He said he would have pleasure, and she gave him her love for a time, and then went from him and ever after he was very sad. The young man had often heard him sing a lamentation he had made, but could only remember that it was "very mournful," and called her "Beauty of all Beauty." The song may have been but a resinging of a traditional theme, but the young man believed it.

Many, perhaps most, of those that I have talked with of these things have all their earthly senses, but those who have most knowledge of these things, so much indeed that they are permitted, it is thought, to speak but broken words, are those from whom the earthly senses have fallen away. "In every household" of the spirits even, there is "a

queen and a fool, and, maybe, the fool is the wisest of all."
This fool, who is held to wander in lonely places and to
bewitch men out of the world,—for the touch of the queen
and of the fool give death,—is the type of that old wisdom
from which the good citizen and the new wisdom have led
the world away, forgetting that "the ruins of time build
mansions in eternity." The poetry that comes out of the
old wisdom must turn always to religion and to the law
of the hidden world, while the poetry of the new wisdom
must not forget politics and the law of the visible world;
and between these poetries there cannot be any lasting
peace. Those that follow the old wisdom must not shrink
too greatly from the journey described in some verses Miss
Hopper, a poet of our school, has put into the mouth of
Dalua, the fairy fool—

> The world wears on to sundown, and love is lost
>   or won,
> But he recks not of loss or gain, the King of Ire-
>   land's son.
> He follows on for ever when all your chase is
>   done,
> He follows after shadows, the King of Ireland's
>   son.

Alone among nations, Ireland has in her written Gaelic
literature, in her old love tales and battle tales, the forms
in which the imagination of Europe uttered itself before
Greece shaped a tumult of legend into her music of the
arts; and she can discover, from the beliefs and emotions
of her common people, the habit of mind that created the
religion of the muses. The legends of other European
countries are less numerous, and not so full of the energies
from which the arts and our understanding of their sanctity arose, and the best of them have already been shaped
into plays and poems. "The Celt," as it seems, created romance, when his stories of Arthur and of the Grail became
for a time almost the only inspiration of European literature, and it would not be wonderful if he should remould
romance after its oldest image, now that he is recovering
his possessions.

The movement of thought which has made the good citizen, or has been made by him, has surrounded us with
comfort and safety, and with vulgarity and insincerity.
One finds alike its energy and its weariness in churches
which have substituted a system of morals for spiritual ardour; in pictures which have substituted conventionally
pretty faces for the disquieting revelations of sincerity; in
poets who have set the praises of those things good citizens
think praiseworthy above a dangerous delight in beauty
for the sake of beauty. The Romantic movement, from the
times of Blake and Shelley and Keats, when it took a new
form, has been battling with the thoughts of the good citizen, as moss and ivy and grass battle with some old building, crumbling its dead stone and mortar into the living
greenery of earth. The disorders of a Shelley or of a Heine
in their art, and in their lives that mirror their art, are but
a too impetuous ardour of battle, a too swift leaping of ivy
or of grass to window ledge or gable end; and the intensity
and strangeness of a picture by Rossetti or of an early picture by Watts are but a sudden falling of stones. Moss and
ivy and grass gather against stone and mortar in unceasing
enmity, for while the old is crumbling the new is building;

William Butler Yeats.

and the Romantic movement will never have perfect victory unless, as mystics have thought, the golden age is to
come again, and men's hearts and the weather to grow
gentle as time fades into eternity. Blake said that all art
was a labour to bring that golden age, and we call romantic art romantic because it has made that age's light dwell
in the imaginations of a little company of studious persons.

Because the greater number of persons are too busy with
the work of the world to forget the light of the sun, romantic art is, as I think, about to change its manner and become more like the art of the old poets, who saw the golden age and their own age side by side like substance and
shadow. Ever since Christianity turned men's minds to
Judea, and learning turned them to Greece and Rome, the
sanctity has dwindled from their own hills and valleys,
which the legends and beliefs of fifty centuries had filled
so full of it that a man could hardly plough his fields or
follow his sheep upon the hillside without remembering
some august story, or walking softly lest he had divine
companions. When the valleys and the hills had almost become clay and stone, the good citizens plucked up their
heart and took possession of the world and filled it with
their little compact thoughts; and romance fled to more
and more remote fairylands, and forgot that it was ever
more than an old tale which nobody believes. But now we
are growing interested in our own countries, and discovering that the common people in all countries that have not
given themselves up to the improvements and devices of
good citizens, which we call civilization, still half under-

stand the sanctity of their hills and valleys; and at the same time a change of thought is making us half ready to believe with Ecclesiasticus, that "all things are made double one above another," and that the forms of nature may be temporal shadows of realities.

In a little time places may begin to seem the only hieroglyphs that cannot be forgotten, and poets to remember that they will come the nearer the old poets, who had a seat at every hearth, if they mingle their own dream with a story told for centuries of some mountain that casts its shadows upon many doors, and if they understand that the beauty they celebrate is a part of the paradise men's eyes shall look upon when they close upon the world. The paradise of the Christian, as those who think more of the order of communities than of the nature of things have shaped it, is but the fulfilment of one dream; but the paradise that the common people tell of about the fire, and still half understand, is the fulfilment of all dreams, and opens its gates as gladly to the perfect lover as to the perfect saint, and only he who understands it can lift romance into prophecy and make beauty holy. Their paradise, Tir-nan-og, the Land of the Living Heart, the Grass Green Island of Apples, call it what you will, created that religion of the muses which gave the arts to the world; and those countries whose traditions are fullest of it, and of the sanctity of places, may yet remould romance till it has become a covenant between intellectual beauty and the beauty of the world. We cannot know how many these countries are until the new science of folklore and the almost new science of mythology have done their work; but Ireland, if she can awake again the but half-forgotten legends of Slieve Gullion, or of Cruachmagh, or of the hill where Maeve is buried, and make them an utterance of that desire to be at rest amid ideal perfection which is becoming conscious in the minds of poets as the good citizen wins the priests over to his side; or if she can make us believe that the beautiful things that move us to awe, white lilies among dim shadows, windy twilights over grey sands, dewy and silent places among hazel trees by still waters, are in truth, and not in phantasy alone, the symbols, or the dwellings, of immortal presences, she will have begun a change that, whether it is begun in our time or not for centuries, will some day make all lands holy lands again.

Ireland has no great wealth, no preoccupation with successful persons to turn her writers' eyes to any lesser destiny. Even the poetry which had its form and much of its matter from alien thought dwelt, as the Gaelic ballads had done before it, on ideas living in the perfection of hope, on visions of unfulfilled desire, and not on the sordid compromise of success. The popular poetry of England celebrates her victories, but the popular poetry of Ireland remembers only defeats and defeated persons. A ballad that is in every little threepenny and sixpenny ballad book asks if Ireland has no pride in her Lawrences and Wellingtons, and answers that these belong to the Empire and not to Ireland, whose "heart beats high" for men who died in exile or in prison; and this ballad is a type of all. The popular poetry, too, has made love of the earth of Ireland so much a part of her literature that it should not be a hard thing to fill it with the holiness of places. Politics are, indeed, the forge in which nations are made, and the smith has been so long

busy making Ireland according to His will that she may well have some important destiny. But whether this is so or not, whether this destiny is to make her in the arts, as she is in politics, a voice of the idealism of the common people, who still remember the dawn of the world, or to give her an unforeseen history, it can but express the accidents and energies of her past, and criticism does its natural work in trying to prophesy this expression; and, even if it is mistaken, a prophecy is not always made all untrue by being unfulfilled. A few years will decide if the writers of Ireland are to shape themselves in our time for the fulfilment of this prophecy, for need and much discussion will bring a new national agreement, and the political tumult awake again.

> *William Butler Yeats, "The Literary Movement in Ireland," in* Ideals in Ireland, *by A. E. and others, 1901. Reprint by AMS Press, 1978, pp. 87-104.*

John Eglinton

[*Eglinton was a nationalist social critic who engaged in a lively debate concerning the ideology of the revival movement with W. B. Yeats in Dublin's* Daily Express. *In the following essay, taken from the pages of that publication, Eglinton argues that without "a native interest in life and its problems," Irish literature risks being absorbed by the French and British literary movements.*]

Supposing a writer of dramatic genius were to appear in Ireland, where would he look for the subject of a national drama? This question might serve as a test of what nationality really amounts to in Ireland—a somewhat trying one, perhaps, yet it is scarcely unfair to put the question to those who speak of our national literature with hardly less satisfaction in the present than confidence in the future. Would he look for it in the Irish legends, or in the life of the peasantry and folk-lore, or in Irish history and patriotism, or in life at large as reflected in his own consciousness? There are several reasons for thinking that the growing hopes of something in store for national life in this country are likely to come to something. In the great countries of Europe, although literature is apparently as prosperous as ever and is maintained with a circumstance which would seem to ensure it eternal honour, yet the springs from which the modern literary movements have been fed are probably dried up—the springs of simplicity, hope, belief, and an absolute originality like that of Wordsworth. If also, as seems likely, the approaching ages on the Continent are to be filled with great social and political questions and events which can hardly have immediate expression in literature, it is quite conceivable that literature, as it did once before, would migrate to a quiet country like Ireland, where there is no great tradition to be upset or much social sediment to be stirred up, and where the spectacle of such changes might afford a purely intellectual impulse. More important, of course, and certain than any such chances from without is the positive feeling of encouragement which is now taking the place of the hatreds and despondencies of the past. We may think that the peasantry are outside the reach of culture, that the gentry exhaust their function in contributing able officers to the British army, and that, frankly, there is nothing going on in the political or ecclesiastical or social life of Ireland on which to rest any but the most sober hopes for the future, still no one can say that political feebleness or stagnation might not be actually favourable to some original manifestation in the world of ideas. What Renan says, in speaking of the Jews, that "a nation whose mission it is to revolve in its bosom spiritual truths is often weak politically," may be used with regard to Ireland as an argument that at least nothing stands in its way in this direction.

The ancient legends of Ireland undoubtedly contain situations and characters as well suited for drama as most of those used in the Greek tragedies which have come down to us. It is, nevertheless, a question whether the mere fact of Ireland having been the scene of these stories is enough to give an Irish writer much advantage over anyone else who is attracted by them, or whether anything but belles lettres, as distinguished from a national literature, is likely to spring from a determined pre-occupation with them. Belles lettres seek a subject outside experience, while a national literature, or any literature of a genuine kind, is simply the outcome and expression of a strong interest in life itself. The truth is, these subjects, much as we may admire them and regret that we have nothing equivalent to them in the modern world, obstinately refuse to be taken up out of their old environment and be transplanted into the world of modern sympathies. The proper mode of treating them is a secret lost with the subjects themselves. It is clear that if Celtic traditions are to be an active influence in future Irish literature they must seem to us worthy of the same compliment as that paid by Europe to the Greeks; we must go to them rather than expect them to come to us, studying them as closely as possible, and allowing them to influence us as they may. The significance of that interest in folk-lore and antiquities, which is so strong in this country, can hardly be different from that of the writings of Herder and others in German literature, and may lie in this, that some hint is caught in such studies of the forgotten mythopœic secret.

As to Irish history and the subjects which it offers—a well-known Scotch Professor once said that Ireland was not a nation because it had never had a Burns nor a Bannockburn. It is, however, as reasonable to think that these glorious memories of Scottish nationality will form a drag on its further evolution as that the want of a peasant poet, or of a recollection of having at least once given the Saxons a drubbing, will be fatal to an attempt to raise people above themselves in this country by giving expression to latent ideals. Ireland must exchange the patriotism which looks back for the patriotism which looks forward. The Jews had this kind of patriotism, and it came to something, and the Celtic peoples have been remarkable for it. The Saxon believes in the present, and, indeed, it belongs to him. The Romance nations, from whose hold the world has been slipping, can hardly be expected just yet to give up the consolations of history.

In short, we need to realise in Ireland that a national drama or literature must spring from a native interest in life and its problems and a strong capacity for life among the people. If these do not, or cannot exist, there cannot exist a national drama or literature. In London and Paris they seem to believe in theories and "movements," and to regard individuality as a noble but "impossible" savage; and we are in some danger of being absorbed into their error. Some of our disadvantages are our safeguards. In all ages poets and thinkers have owed far less to their countries than their countries have owed to them.

> John Eglinton, "What Should be the Subjects of National Drama?" in Literary Ideals in Ireland by John Eglinton and others, T. Fisher Unwin, 1899, pp. 9-13.

A. E.

[*A key figure in the literary revival, A. E. (the pen name of George William Russell) was a gifted conversationalist and a popular lecturer who, with Yeats, Gregory, and Synge, was instrumental in the development of the Irish Literary Theatre. In the following essay, taken from the* Daily Express *of Dublin, A. E. expresses his desire for a national literature, but remains skeptical that art produced from the perspective of unabashed nationalism can be valuable in a broader context.*]

As one of those who believe that the literature of a country is for ever creating a new soul among its people, I do not like to think that literature with us must follow an inexorable law of sequence, and gain a spiritual character only after the bodily passions have grown weary and exhausted themselves. Whether the art of any of the writers of the decadence does really express spiritual things is open to doubt. The mood in which their work is conceived, a sad and distempered emotion through which no new joy quivers, seems too often to tell rather of exhausted vitality than of the ecstacy of a new life. However much, too, their art refines itself, choosing ever rarer and more exquisite forms of expression, underneath it all an intuition seems to disclose only the old wolfish lust hiding itself beneath the golden fleece of the spirit. It is not the spirit breaking through corruption, but the life of the senses longing to shine with the light which makes saintly things beautiful; and it would put on the jewelled raiment of seraphim, retaining still a heart of clay smitten through and through with the unappeasable desire of the flesh: so Rossetti's women, who have around them all the circumstances of poetry and romantic beauty, seem through their sucked-in lips to express a thirst which could be allayed in no spiritual paradise. Art in the decadence in our times might be symbolized as a crimson figure undergoing a dark crucifixion; the hosts of light are overcoming it, and it is dying filled with anguish and despair at a beauty it cannot attain. All these strange emotions have a profound psychological interest. I do not think because a spiritual flaw can be urged against a certain phase of life that it should remain unexpressed. The psychic maladies which attack all races when their civilization grows old must needs be understood to be dealt with; and they cannot be understood without being revealed in literature or art. But in Ireland we are not yet sick with this sickness. As psychology it concerns only the curious. As expressing a literary ideal, I think a consideration of it was a mere side-issue in the discussion. . . .

The discussion on the one side was really a plea for nationality in our literature, and on the other a protest on behalf of individualism. It is true that nationality may express itself in many ways; it may not be at all evident in the subject matter, but may be very evident in the sentiment. But a literature loosely held together by some emotional characteristics common to the writers, however great it may be, does not fulfil the purpose of a literature or art created by a number of men who have a common aim in building up an overwhelming ideal—who create, in a sense, a soul for their country, and who have a common pride in the achievement of all. The world has not seen this since the great antique civilizations of Egypt and Greece passed away. We cannot imagine an Egyptian artist daring enough to set aside the majestic attainment of many centuries. An Egyptian boy as he grew up must have been overawed by the national tradition and have felt that it was not to be set aside; it was beyond his individual rivalry. The soul of Egypt incarnated in him, and, using its immemorial language and its mysterious lines, the efforts of the least workman who decorated a tomb seem to have been directed by the same hand that carved the Sphinx. This adherence to a traditional form is true of Greece, though to a less extent. The little Tanagra terra-cottas might have been done by Phidias, and in literature Ulysses and Agamemnon were not the heroes of one epic, but appeared endlessly in epic and drama. Since the Greek civilization no European nation has had an intellectual literature which was genuinely national. In the present century, leaving aside a few things in outward circumstance, there is little to distinguish the work of the best English writers or artists from that of their Continental contemporaries. Millais, Leighton, Rossetti, Turner—how different from each other, and yet they might have painted the same pictures as born Frenchmen and it would not have excited any great surprise as a marked divergence from French art. The cosmopolitan spirit, whether for good or for evil, is hastily obliterating distinctions. What is distinctly national in these countries is less valuable than the immense wealth of universal ideas; and the writers who use this wealth appeal to no narrow circle: the foremost writers, the Tolstois and Ibsens, are conscious of addressing a European audience.

If nationality is to justify itself in the face of all this, it must be because the country which preserves its individuality does so with the profound conviction that its peculiar ideal is nobler than that which the cosmopolitan spirit suggests—that this ideal is so precious to it that its loss would be as the loss of the soul, and that it could not be realised without an aloofness from, if not an actual indifference to, the ideals which are spreading so rapidly over Europe. Is it possible for any nationality to make such a defence of its isolation? If not, let us read Goethe, Balzac, Tolstoi, men so much greater than any we can show, try to absorb their universal wisdom and no longer confine ourselves to local traditions. But nationality was never so strong in Ireland as at the present time. It is beginning to be felt, less as a political movement than as a spiritual force. It seems to be gathering itself together, joining men, who were hostile before, in a new intellectual fellowship; and if all these could unite on fundamentals it would be possible in a generation to create a national ideal in Ireland, or rather to

let that spirit incarnate fully which began among the ancient peoples, which has haunted the hearts and whispered a dim revelation of itself through the lips of the bards and peasant story-tellers.

Every Irishman forms some vague ideal of his country, born from his reading of history, or from contemporary politics, or from an imaginative intuition; and this Ireland in the mind it is, not the actual Ireland, which kindles his enthusiasm. For this he works and makes sacrifices; but because it has never had any philosophical definition, or a supremely beautiful statement in literature which gathered all aspirations about it, the ideal remains vague. This passionate love cannot explain itself; it cannot make another understand its devotion. To reveal Ireland in clear and beautiful light, to create the Ireland in the heart, is the province of a national literature. Other arts would add to this ideal hereafter, and social life and politics must in the end be in harmony. We are yet before our dawn, in a period comparable to Egypt before the first of her solemn temples constrained its people to an equal mystery, or to Greece before the first perfect statue had fixed an ideal of beauty which mothers dreamed of to mould their yet unborn children. We can see, however, as the ideal of Ireland grows from mind to mind it tends to assume the character of a sacred land. The Dark Rosaleen of Mangan expresses an almost religious adoration, and to a later writer it seems to be nigher to the Spiritual Beauty than other lands:—

And still the thoughts of Ireland brood

AE (George W. Russell).

Upon her holy quietude.

The faculty of abstracting from the land their eyes behold, another Ireland through which they wandered in dream, has always been a characteristic of the Celtic poets. This inner Ireland which the visionary eye saw, was the Tir-na-noge, the country of immortal youth, for they peopled it only with the young and beautiful. It was the Land of the Living Heart, a tender name which showed that it had become dearer than the heart of woman, and overtopped all other hopes as the last dream of the spirit, the bosom where it would rest after it had passed from the fading shelter of the world. And sure a strange and beautiful land this Ireland is, with a mystic beauty which closes the eyes of the body as in sleep, and opens the eyes of the spirit as in dreams; and never a poet has lain on our hillsides but gentle, stately figures, with hearts shining like the sun, move through his dreams, over radiant grasses, in an enchanted world of their own; and it has become alive through every haunted rath and wood and mountain and lake, so that we can hardly think of it otherwise than as the shadow of the thought of God. The last Celtic poet who has appeared shows the spiritual qualities of the first, when he writes of the grey rivers in their "enraptured" wanderings, and when he sees in the jewelled bow which arches the heavens

> The Lord's seven spirits that shine through the
> rain.

This mystical view of nature, peculiar to but one English poet, Wordsworth, is a national characteristic; and much in the creation of the Ireland in the mind is already done, and only needs retelling by the new writers. More important, however, for the literature we are imagining as an offset to the cosmopolitan ideal, would be the creation of heroic figures, types, whether legendary or taken from history, and enlarged to epic proportions by our writers, who would use them in common, as Cuculain, Fionn, Oseian, and Oscar, were used by the generations of poets who have left us the bardic history of Ireland, wherein one would write of the battle fury of a hero, and another of a moment when his fire would turn to gentleness, and another of his love for some beauty of his time, and yet another tell how the rivalry of a spiritual beauty made him tire of love; and so from iteration and persistent dwelling on a few heroes their imaginative images found echoes in life, and other heroes arose continuing their tradition of chivalry.

That such types are of the highest importance and have the most ennobling influence on a country, cannot be denied. It was this idea led Whitman to "exploit" himself as the typical American. He felt that what he termed a "stock personality" was needed to elevate and harmonise the incongruous human elements in the States. English literature has always been more sympathetic with actual beings than with ideal types, and cannot help us much. A man who loves Dickens, for example, may grow to have a great tolerance for the grotesque characters which are the outcome of the social order in England, but he will not be assisted in the conception of a higher humanity; and this is true of very many English writers who lack a fundamental philosophy, and are content to take man, as he seems to be for the moment, rather than as the pilgrim of eternity—

as one who is flesh to-day but who may hereafter grow divine, and who may shine at last like the stars of the morning, triumphant among the sons of God.

Mr. Standish O'Grady, in his notable epic of Cuculain, was the first in our time to treat the Celtic traditions worthily. He has contributed one hero who awaits equal comrades; if, indeed, the tales of the Red Branch chivalry do not absorb the thoughts of many imaginative writers, and Cuculain remain the typical hero of the Gael, becoming to every boy who reads the story a revelation of what his own spirit is.

I have written at some length on the two paths which lie before us, for we have arrived at a parting of ways. One path leads, and has already led many Irishmen, of whom Professor Dowden is a type, to obliterate all nationality from their work. The other path winds spirally upwards to a mountaintop of our own, which may be in the future the Meru to which many worshippers will turn. To remain where we are as a people, indifferent to literature, to art, to ideas, wasting the precious gift of public spirit we possess so abundantly in the sordid political rivalries, without practical or ideal ends, is to justify those who have chosen the other path and followed another star than ours. I do not wish anyone to infer from this a contempt for those who, for the last hundred years or so, have guided public opinion in Ireland. If they failed in one respect, it was out of a passionate sympathy for wrongs of which many are memories, thanks to them. And to them is due the creation of a force which may be turned in other directions, not without a memory of those pale sleepers to whom we may turn in thought, placing

> A kiss of fire on the dim brow of failure,
> A crown upon her uncrowned head.

> *A. E., "Nationality and Cosmopolitanism in Literature," in* Literary Ideals in Ireland *by John Eglinton and others, T. Fisher Unwin, 1899, pp. 79-88.*

A. E.

[*In the following essay from Lady Gregory's* Ideals in Ireland, *A. E. urges the Irish population to rebel against British materialism, which he views as a threat to both the physical and spiritual lives of the Irish people.*]

The idea of the national being emerged at no recognisable point in our history. It is older than any name we know. It is not earth born, but the synthesis of many heroic and beautiful moments, and these, it must be remembered, are divine in their origin. Every heroic deed is an act of the spirit, and every perception of beauty is vision with the divine eye, and not with the mortal sense. The spirit was subtly intermingled with the shining of old romance, and it was no mere phantasy which shows Ireland at its dawn in a misty light thronged with divine figures, and beneath and nearer to us, demigods and heroes fading into recognisable men. The bards took cognisance only of the most notable personalities who preceded them; and of these only the acts which had a symbolic or spiritual significance; and these grew thrice refined as generations of poets in enraptured musings along by the mountains or in the woods, brooded upon their heritage of story until, as it passed from age to age, the accumulated beauty grew greater than the beauty of the hour, the dream began to enter into the children of our race, and their thoughts turned from earth to that world in which it had its inception.

[And] we who would keep the Gaelic tongue and Gaelic memories and Gaelic habits of mind would keep them, as I think, that we may some day spread a tradition of life that makes neither great wealth nor great poverty, that makes the arts a natural expression of life, that permits even common men to understand good art and high thinking, and to have the fine manners these things can give.

—*William Butler Yeats*

It was a common belief among the ancient peoples that each had a national genius or deity who presided over them, in whose all-embracing mind they were enclosed, and by whom their destinies were shaped. We can conceive of the national spirit in Ireland as first manifesting itself through individual heroes or kings; and, as the history of famous warriors laid hold upon the people, extending its influence through the sentiment engendered in the popular mind until it created therein the germs of a kindred nature.

An aristocracy of lordly and chivalrous heroes is bound in time to create a great democracy by the reflection of their character in the mass, and the idea of the divine right of kings is succeeded by the idea of the divine right of the people. If this sequence cannot be traced in any one respect with historical regularity, it is because of the complexity of national life, its varied needs, and its infinite changes of sentiment; but the threads are all taken up in the end, and ideas which were forgotten and absent from the voices of men will be found, when recurred to, to have grown to a rarer and more spiritual beauty in their quiet abode in the heart. The seeds which are sown at the beginning of a race bear their flowers and fruits towards its close; and those antique names which already begin to stir us with their power, Angus, Lu, Deirdre, Finn, Ossian, and the rest, will be found to be each one the symbol of enduring qualities, and their story a trumpet through which will be blown the music of an eternal joy, the sentiment of an inexorable justice, the melting power of beauty in sorrow, the wisdom of age, and the longings of the spirit.

The question arises how this race inheritance can best be preserved and developed. To some it is of no value, but these are voices of dust. To some the natural outcome is coalition with another power, and a frank and full acceptance of the imperial ideal. To some the solution lies in a self-centred national life. I will not touch here upon the material advantages of one or other course, which can best be left to economists to discuss. The literary man, who is, or ought to be, concerned mainly with intellectual interests, should only intervene in politics when principles affecting the spiritual life of his country are involved. To me the imperial ideal seems to threaten the destruction of that national being which has been growing through centuries, and I ask myself, What can it profit my race if it gain the empire of the world and yet lose its own soul—a soul which is only now growing to self-consciousness, and this to be lost simply that we may help to build up a sordid trade federation between England and her Colonies? Was our divine origin for this end? Did the bards drop in song the seed of heroic virtues, and beget the mystic chivalry of the past, and flood our being with spiritual longings, that we might at last sink to clay and seek only to inherit the earth? The mere area of the empire bewitches the commonplace mind, and turns it from its own land; yet the State of Athens was not so large as the Province of Munster, and, though dead, the memory of it is brighter than the living light of any people on earth to-day. Some, to whom I would be the last to deny nobility of thought and sincere conviction, would lead us from ourselves through the belief that the moral purification of the empire could be accomplished by us. I wish I could believe it. I am afraid our own political and social ethics demand all the attention we can give. There is a reservoir of spiritual life in the land, but it is hardly strong enough to repel English materialism, while we are nominally hostile to English ideas; and shall it be triumphant when we have given over our hopes of a separate national existence, and merged our dreams and longings with a nation which has become a by-word for materialism? Under no rule are people so free,— we are told. A little physical freedom more or less matters nothing. Men are as happy and as upright as we, in countries where a passport is necessary to travel from one town to another. No form of government we know is perfect, and none will be permanent. The federation of the world and its typical humanity, exists in germ in the spiritual and intellectual outcasts of our time, who can find no place in the present social order. A nation is sacred as it holds few or many of those to whom spiritual ideals are alone worth having; the mode of life, prosperous or unfortunate, which brings them to birth and enables them to live is the best of any; and the genius of our country has acted wisely in refusing any alliance offering only material prosperity and power. Every race must work out its own destiny. England and the Colonies will, as is fit and right, work out theirs without our moral guidance. They would resent it if offered, just as we resent it from them. It may be affirmed that the English form of government is, on the whole, a good one, but it does not matter. It may be good for Englishmen, but it is not the expression of our national life and ideas. I express my ideals in literature; you, perhaps, in social reform. Both may be good; yours, indeed, may be best, but I would feel it a bitter injustice if I was compelled to order my life in accordance with your aims. I would do poorly what you shine in. We ask the liberty of shaping the social order in Ireland to reflect our own ideals, and to embody that national soul which has been slowly incarnating in our race from its cloudy dawn. The twentieth century may carry us far from Finn and Oscar and the stately chieftains and heroes of their time, far even from the ideals of Tone, Mitchell, and Davis, but I hope it will not carry us into contented acceptance of the deadness, the dulness, the commonplace of English national sentiment, or what idealism remains in us, bequeathed from the past, range itself willingly under a banner which is regarded chiefly as a commercial asset by the most famous exponent of the imperial idea.

I feel that the idea expressed by several writers lately, that with many people in Ireland patriotism and nationality are only other names for race hatred, must be combated. It may be so with a few, but the charge has been levelled not at isolated individuals here and there, but at a much larger class who seriously think about their country.

We are told our attitude towards England and English things is a departure from the divine law of love. Let us look into the circumstances: a number of our rapidly dwindling race have their backs to a wall, they are making an appeal for freedom, for the right to choose their own ideals, to make their own laws, to govern their own lives according to the God-implanted law within them; seeing everywhere, too, the wreck of their hopes, the supremacy of an alien will,—to such people, striving desperately for a principle which is sacred and eternal, these moral platitudes are addressed. Is not freedom as necessary as love to my human soul or to any people? Can there be any real brotherhood without it? If we are debarred from the freedom we would have, how narrow is the range for human effort! We in Ireland would keep in mind our language, teach our children our history, the story of our heroes, and the long traditions of our race which stretch back to God. But we are everywhere thwarted. A blockhead of a professor drawn from the intellectual obscurity of Trinity, and appointed as commissioner to train the national mind according to British ideas, meets us with an ultimatum: "I will always discourage the speaking of Gaelic wherever I can." We feel poignantly it is not merely Gaelic which is being suppressed, but the spiritual life of our race. A few ignoramuses have it in their power, and are trying their utmost, to obliterate the mark of God upon a nation. It is not from Shelley or Keats our peasantry derive their mental nourishment, now that they are being cut off from their own past. We see everywhere a moral leprosy, a vulgarity of mind creeping over them. The Police Gazettes, the penny novels, the hideous comic journals, replace the once familiar poems and the beautiful and moving memoirs of classic Ireland. The music that breathed Tir-nan-og and overcame men's hearts with all gentle and soft emotions is heard more faintly, and the songs of the London music halls may be heard in places where the music of fairy enchanted the elder generations. The shout of the cockney tourist sounds in the cyclopean crypts and mounds once sanctified by druid mysteries, and divine visitations, and passings from the mortal to the immortal. Ireland Limited is being run by English syndicates. It is the descent of a nation into hell, not nobly, not as a sacrifice made for a great end, but ignobly and without hope of resurrection. If we who watch protest bitterly at the racial degradation—for we have none of us attained all the moral perfections—we are assured that we are departing from the law of love. We can have such a noble destiny

if we will only accept it. When we have lost everything we hoped for, lost our souls even, we can proceed to spiritualise the English, and improve the moral tone of the empire. Some, even those who are Celts, protest against our movements as forlorn hopes. Yet what does it matter whether every Celt perished in the land, so that our wills, inviolate to the last, make obeisance only to the light which God has set for guidance in our souls? Would not that be spiritual victory and the greatest success? What would be the success we are assured of if we lay aside our hopes? What could we have or what could we give to humanity if our mental integrity is broken? God gives no second gift to a nation if it flings aside its birthright. We cannot put on the ideals of another people as a garment. We cannot, with every higher instinct of our nature shocked and violated, express ourselves as lovers of the law that rules us. We would be slaves if we did. The incarnate love came not with peace but a sword. It does not speak only with the Holy Breath, but has in its armoury death and the strong weapons of the other immortals. It is better to remain unbroken to the last, and I count it as noble to fight God's battles as to keep His peace.

I confess I do not love England. Love is a spirit which will not, with me at least, come at all. It bestows itself, and will not be commanded, having laws and an end of its own. But for that myriad humanity which throngs the cities of England I feel a profound pity; for it seems to me that in factory, in mine, in warehouse, the life they have chosen to live in the past, the lives those born into that country must almost inevitably lead now, is farther off from beauty, more remote from spirit, more alien from deity, than that led by any people hitherto in the memory of the world. I have no hatred for them. I do not think any of my countrymen have, however they may phrase the feeling in their hearts. I think it is a spiritual antagonism they feel which they translate into terms of the more limited conscious mind. I think their struggle is in reality not against flesh and blood, but is a portion of the everlasting battle against principalities and powers and spiritual wickedness in high places, which underlies every other battle which has been or will be fought by men. I do not say that everything English is stupid, invariably and inevitably wrong. But I do say that every act by which England would make our people other than they would be themselves, is stupid, invariably and inevitably wrong. Not invariably wrong, perhaps, when judged from the external point of view, but invariably wrong when judged from the interior spiritual standpoint. How terrible a thing it is to hinder the soul in its freedom, let the wild upheavals and the madness of protest bear witness.

Though we are old, ethnologically considered, yet as a nation, a collective unit, we are young or yet unborn. If the stupefying influence of foreign control were removed, if we had charge of our own national affairs, it would mean the starting up into sudden life of a thousand dormant energies, spiritual, intellectual, artistic, social, economic, and human. The national spirit, like a beautiful woman, cannot or will not reveal itself wholly while a coarse presence is near, an unwelcome stranger in possession of the home. It is shy, hiding itself away in remote valleys, or in haunted mountains, or deep in the quiet of hearts that do not reveal themselves. Only to its own will it come and sing its hopes and dreams; not selfishly for itself alone, but sharing in the universal human hopes, and desirous of solving some of the eternal problems. Being still so young as a nation, and before the true starting of our career, we might say of ourselves as the great American poet of his race [Walt Whitman], with which so many of our own have mingled—

> Have the elder races halted?
> Do they droop and end their lesson, wearied,
>   over there beyond the seas?
> We take up the task eternal, and the burden, and
>   the lesson,
> Pioneers! Oh, pioneers!

> *A. E., "Nationality and Imperialism," in* Ideals in Ireland *by A. E. and others, edited by Lady Gregory, 1901. Reprint by AMS Press, 1978, pp. 15-24.*

LITERARY EXPRESSIONS

Roibeárd O'Faracháin

[*In the following excerpt, O'Faracháin discusses Yeats and A. E. as Irish poets writing in English. He calls the former "the fertile but careless father" and the latter "the careful midwife" of the Celtic nationalist movement in literature.*]

Yeats: who of all Irish poets since Thomas Moore has had widest fame and influence. Coming to him here in this scrutiny of Irish poetry we see that there lay to his hand a cumulus of hints and examples, most of them given by men already dead or directly to die, but some by men who like him were starting for fame. Poets had already been patriots; they already had written upon Irish themes:—land, legend, myth; country, religion, history: already they had translated Gaelic poetry, echoing some of its distinctive music and seizing some of its intensity; while a man here and there had suffused some stanzas with a moment of Irish atmosphere. What was there left, after these, for a Yeats to do?

An immensity, we know. To write with manifest genius and illumination, and with multiform development, for nearly five decades. To gather many scatterings. To resolve with deliberation, in response to a vocational urge, to be first and last and all the time an *Irish* poet; and, being this, to be the leader of a literature.

Yeats had deficiencies. By birth, environment and temperament; by philosophic and religious turn of mind; by intellectual bent and custom, he was disposed rather to halt and to counter than to continue and round-off the work of Ferguson and Mangan. (And of course he did so counter as well as round-off their work.)

Yeats was of middle-class Protestant breed; in himself he was fastidious, aloof, subjective, aristocratic rather than not, in fact arrogant; his youth was largely lived away from Ireland, and his schooling within it was shaky; most of his life he "sat loose" to Christianity, being best described perhaps as a latter-day gnostic—as one, that is, who hungered for the arcana of all the cults and the disciplines; coveting more keenly to be mage than saint; a Simon Magus whose purchase-money was poetry. None of these attributes were such as would make him seek to be, or succeed in being, the leader of the Irish as a poet. To the end of his days he lacked Irish; and this was retrogression, and a special fetter in his lifetime; for he lived when the movement for revival began and bore ample fruits.

He had, of course, to counter his deficiencies, many and powerful advantages: genius, the incomparable advantage for whatsoever task, being first.

Were I asked what was special in his genius I should say two things.

This: that there was in him a power, many times shown, to detect in a realm of knowledge wherein he was himself but a dabbler that precise thought, conclusion, illustration or hypothesis, or whatever else it might be, which held some enrichment for his poetry. "He had" Austin Clarke said once to me, though not in exactly this connection, "the forceps."

And this (I would say secondly): his mind had many sides. As a first example I would remark his adaptability, by which—notwithstanding his *hauteur* and aloofness—it was put in his power to be led in his early years to the common people. As a second example I would demonstrate his power to make friendships of spiritual profit to himself. Balancing this power, and killing what was mere self-seeking, he had fires of imagination, a fountain's play of ideas, and a crystalline artistic honour which, between them, repaid his friends; by their virtue he renewed himself, and in doing so renewed them also.

He read himself, talked himself, thought, imagined and befriended himself out of most of his defects; thereby he did what he planned.

Consider him in terms of people—to take one point. Ferguson died when Yeats was two years old, Larminie when he was nineteen, Allingham when he was twenty-five, de Vere when he was eight-and-twenty; Sigerson and Standish James O Grady were vigorous in Yeats's twenties and thirties, while Hyde was his elder contemporary. He knew and learned from most of them, and besides these George Moore, A.E., York Powell, Lionel Johnson, John O Leary and more. The saturnine Synge broke briefly but sharply across his forties; and one might name them continuously up to his death: Augusta Gregory, Maud Gonne, F. R. Higgins and all the others. They enabled him to learn things—sometimes things they knew, sometimes things they did *not* know, or at least did not know that they knew till he learned them from them.

We might even make out what it was he learned from each: from O Grady the myths, from Gregory and Hyde that there were country tales and that country talk could make poetry, from Synge that a hard, sharp, salty zest is inbred in Irish writing. But more to the point than what he learned is what he did with it all.

For one thing, he tweaked the ear of the world and made it turn towards Ireland, to listen to himself, and in some degree to his company. That day when Robert Louis Stevenson praised *Innisfree* was possibly the day when the "sweet, wild twist of Irish song" first charmed our neighbours. Moore pleased them hugely, but seldom with a native style; Rossetti praised Allingham, and other Englishmen other Irishmen; but little long-term attention followed. Yeats first got such attention, and he gets it still; so decidedly does he get it that attack—sure sign that a writer is mattering—has begun among English critics quite lately.

Yeats wrote of Irish myth and country tale, of our history and of our life as he watched it; and others wrote with him; the upshot of which, among other things, is, that matters such as these are well-known to some cultivated persons whose language is English; while those who read creative literature at all in that language are aware that Irish things have been, and have the force to be, the concern of good writers. He mixed un-Irish things with Irish things? Very well, he mixed them. What creative writer of power has ever done otherwise?

But I quote himself on these affairs:

> I thought one day—I can remember the very day when I thought it—'If somebody could make a style which would not be an English style and yet would be musical and full of colour, many others would catch fire from him, and we would have a really great school of ballad poetry in Ireland.'

> I had a conviction, which indeed I have still, that one's verses should hold, as in a mirror, the colours of one's own climate and scenery in their right proportion; and when I found my verses too full of the reds and yellows Shelley gathered in Italy, I thought for two days of setting things right, not as I should now by making my rhythms faint and nervous and filling my images with a certain coldness, a certain wintry wildness, but by eating little and sleeping upon a board . . .

> From that day to this I have been busy among the verses and stories that the people make for themselves.
> Essay on "What is popular poetry?" 1901

> . . . and now a fountain of legends, and, as I think, a more abundant fountain than any in Europe, is being opened, the fountain of Gaelic legends.
> *The Celtic element in literature,* 1897

> I would have our writers and craftsmen of many kinds master this history and these legends, and fix upon their memory the appearance of mountains and rivers and make all visible again in their arts, so that Irishmen, even though they had gone thousands of miles away, would still be in their own country.

> I could not now write of any other country but

Ireland, for my style has been shaped by the subjects I have worked on . . .
> *Ireland and the arts,* 1901

> When Lionel Johnson and Katharine Tynan . . . and I, myself, began to reform Irish poetry . . . we sought to make a more subtle rhythm, a more organic form, than that of the older Irish poets who wrote in English, but always to remember certain ardent ideas and high attitudes of mind which were the nation itself, so far as a nation can be summarized in the intellect . . .

> I . . . took from Allingham and Walsh their passion for country spiritism, and from Ferguson his pleasure in heroic legend, and while seeing all in the light of European literature, found my symbols of expression in Ireland . . . Here were unwasted passion and precedents in the popular memory for every needed thought and action . . .

> It was our criticism, I think, that set Clarence Mangan at the head of the Young Ireland poets in the place of Davis, and put Sir Samuel Ferguson, who had died with but little fame as a poet, next in the succession.
> *Poetry and Tradition,* 1907

None before him in Ireland, of those who wrote English, pondered and harped upon style as he did; on style which arises "out of a deliberate shaping of all things, and from never being swept away, whatever the emotion, into confusion or dullness," on style "which is but high breeding in words and in argument."

Perhaps it was unlikely that any before him should do so. Perhaps it was the Francophil Nineties, bringing over at last from France the zeal of Flaubert, perhaps it was Pater or George Moore or old John Butler Yeats—or all these men and currents going one way—which made it likely that an Irish poet, professedly and in set terms, should worship style.

"Professedly and in set terms" is a needed qualification. There is no native word for "style" in Irish, but if any one thing lasts out through every aberration, through every deformity or lack in Gaelic poetry, that thing is style. Yet Mangan, the best before Yeats of the English-writing poets, was without it. Style as an unsheddable skin was never Mangan's. Wads of his verse were as bad as Gavan Duffy's and fell as entirely out of the climate of literature into that of journalism. This is true of the best we had had, in English. But Yeats is different. Yeats at his worst, Yeats below his own average or that of his inferiors, is still palpably Yeats: style is the skin of his words. "Sometimes" (to quote himself) "it may be, he is permitted the licence of cap and bell, or even the madman's bunch of straws, but he never forgets or leaves at home the seal and the signature."

I may be allowed, perhaps, to gloss one or two of the *dicta* contained in the above quotations.

"One's verses should hold, as in a mirror, the colours of one's own climate and scenery in the right proportion."

This is not simply a striking principle; it is almost a discovery, so far as verse in English is concerned. One tends to take it figuratively, and no doubt it will bear a figurative interpretation, but Yeats meant it first in the simple meaning of his words. He speaks of Shelley's reds and yellows; and his own poems, as everyone knows, shimmer with greys, pearl-pales, cloud-pales, and wan half-lights. When he names colours they are outward as well as inward colours; for was he not son and brother to painters, and schooled for a time himself to palette and brush?

A moment ago I quoted Austin Clarke. I quote him again on this matter. Poets in English, according to Clarke, did not until the Celtic Twilight cease to see about them the hues and the climate of Italy, that country from which they borrowed so lavishly, starting with Chaucer, continuing with Spenser, Wyatt, Shakespeare, the Elizabethans and Dryden, and finding in Rossetti a poet with a title to full borrowing, a title based upon Italian blood. English poetry, says Clarke in effect, sings of a rain-drenched, hazy, greyish corner of creation as though suns drenched it and lent it Italianate light; while the movement called The Celtic Twilight washed its verse in the regions' rainfalls, dimmed it with its mists, and made its rhymes weatherwise. For that, he says, it has been dubbed romantic, when properly its realism should have been admired.

Yeats dilates upon the ancient legends, and with truth, for they served him in every way: as stories, as symbols and as wells of allusion. Whatever other arsenals he raided, in Byzantium or India or England or Egypt or Greece, or even in his cavernous, glowing heart, the powders of his charges had in them grains of old legend; and his last brief play brings once more on the man Cuchulainn.

"A more subtle rhythm," he says, "a more organic form" . . . Style . . . But style defined; style which had in it inherited things, but things as well superadded by himself—the exquisite senses and the spirit of Yeats; his genius for cadence, euphony, wit, and resinous emotion; his skill in ordering and appointing words; his control and submission to control; his antennae always feeling for thought, figure, tale and creative impulse . . . Style which is personal and racial, and each because the other. He was an Irish poet.

Thinking of the doubters I had chosen a sheaf of verses to show his Irishry, but revising my words and my argument I leave them aside. Everyone knows them, and those who want to doubt him would doubt him despite them. I am discussing here the ways in which he was an Irish poet, rather than striving to prove him one; the indignity of proof would exceed that of doubt, with such a one as Yeats.

He was Irish, betimes, in a "rebelly" way. I remember that when in 1941 we in the Abbey Theatre commemorated the second anniversary of his death by staging two of his plays and having some of his poems spoken, a woman who came to the performance, and whose feelings one supposes were strongly engaged by the war, charged us with choosing only his "rebelly" poems. We had not done so consciously; indeed we had chosen from every period of his work, and chosen many poems; yet a number really were "rebelly",

among them *Easter 1916,* and *The Ballad of Roger Casement,* the one which jibes at John Bull and declares that

> The ghost of Roger Casement is beating on the
> door.

But of course Yeats was Irish at other times than when he was baiting John Bull, or lighting lamps to Pearse and Casement. He was Irish when he foamed about "the daily spite of this unmannerly town" or stigmatized some Irishmen as "Paudeen fumbling in the greasy till"; and still Irish when he made current the unfounded rumour that

> Romantic Ireland's dead and gone:
> It's with O Leary in the grave.

I do not mean simply that this was an angry lover's talk—though it *was* that, of course: only a lover could be struck so hurtfully or could smart aloud so wrathfully. But I mean more than that. I mean that he drew the common, current wrangles and collisions of Irish affairs deep within his poetry, and that instead of sinking his poetry he raised these affairs.

Furthermore the tempest of his scorn was Irish; and his being so vulnerable to calumnious tongues. If often there were on the one side the mass of the Irish, and he himself only or few beside him on the other, then the words of Thomas MacDonagh to his court-martial judges in 1916 might have helped him:

"We do not claim," MacDonagh said, "to represent the people of Ireland; we claim to represent the intellect and the immortal soul of Ireland."

A man may differ from millions of his own, and, in the very act and moment of differing, show common blood and ultimate community of cause with them. This was sometimes Yeats's act. But then too he spoke *for* the Irish, in the simpler sense. To Pearse he was the man "who in our time (in *Cathleen Ni Houlihan*) has best given expression to Irish Nationalism"; and apart from opinions he brought the Irishman's *voice*—its inflexions, cadences and idioms—into verse. The wavering, unemphasized rhythms, and the half-hushed, murmuring music, have been most remarked; but MacDonagh judged that even the line of seven syllables came through. In his last years what he most desired to make was a balladry akin to that which Higgins had found in Mayo.

Again one must remember this, that despite his early love for Verlaine's *dictum* about strangling rhetoric, he saw that the Irish loved eloquence, and became the only good Irish poet except Mangan to make eloquent lyrical poetry. His *Red Hanrahan's Song about Ireland* is consummate eloquence in lyric; I surmise that it was made to the verbal tune of Mangan's *Kathaleen Ny Houlihan,* which again was got from O Heffernan, who got it from O Bruadair.

If religious care for finesse in one's craft be Irish—and Gaelic metric suggests it is—then Yeats was Irish. His last poem begins (to the fury of poets in Ireland, and this again is witness): *Irish poets learn your trade.* One of the first he ever wrote begins: *Words alone are certain good.*

If what the world, or anyhow the English world, avers of us is true: that we vary swiftly in mood: then Yeats is Irish.

He has tenderness, quietness, pity; rage, love and lust; gaiety, fantasy, indignation; robustness, delicacy, arrogance . . . how many more passions and spiritual weathers? Mockery and reverence surely.

Since I am not disputing politics, I do not set down these notions from the motive some might find in them, the motive of silencing those Irish critics who would hand Yeats over to the English, who indeed very frequently speak as though they owned him and who seldom know we have other poets in Ireland. I set them down to show that, after many decades, an abundant and grandly-achieving poet had come who was certainly Irish, and Irish in subtle as well as in evident ways, "shaking his scourges" over us, as well as tilling our fields.

One matter more I must speak of: the theatre which Yeats and others gave us. They were like surgeons who, by making a tiny correction in the action of a gland, free the body for some necessary and hitherto-impeded function. That the Irish made no Gaelic drama suggests an aberrant gland in the race; for they strike all observers, and themselves equally, as made for drama. They sense and relish it hourly, they are dramatic in speech and often in act. Yet they hardly can be said to have given a playwright to the world before the eighteenth century. In that century the Dublin theatres were busy, but the playwrights we remember best wrote not for them but for England. In the nineteenth century the fact was unchanged; hence Goldsmith, Sheridan, Congreve, Wilde and Shaw are more England's than ours. England needed them almost as badly as we; but this was small comfort to us.

But then at the start of the present century Yeats, A. E., George Moore, Hyde, Lady Gregory, the Fays and others provided the beginnings of an Irish drama. It was in part universal as well; but the Universe needed less to rejoice than we: we had nothing of our own before.

One after another the arts were entering our ambit. There was science before, scholarship in letters and history; and then came the art of translation. There were scholars of folk-music, Bunting and others; and original poets followed, translating first and afterwards repeating the designs of the poems they brought over, composing poems to the tunes the Buntings saved, and transferring the verbal tunes to poems not made for music. Statuary followed some way; at least such a sculptor as Hogan made living stone of Davis and Daniel O Connell. Novelists attempted to get into the swim, though not for some decades did they catch the stroke. And now in the first of the nineteen-hundreds the mesmeric, popular art of the theatre fell into line . . . As we know, painting, with a story like that of the Irish theatre, followed; and stained-glass-making; and finally story-telling found its stroke and swam . . . And into the theatre flowed all the comminglings which Ireland was and was grasping to be.

Poetry got into that theatre, because Yeats was in it; and genius in acting got in because the Fays joined him.

The English theatre just then was empty of poetry; it was empty of everything, to speak quite justly: people talked nothings on the stage and people heard nothings on their benches. Shakespeare survived, as a "vehicle" for actor-managers; but that was all, till Shaw, Granville-Barker and some more set to. That is why this Irish literary theatre made Ireland important at the time.

Irish letters, with Yeats, became a movement. Not that he was a demi-urge setting everyone else on the move. Hyde, for instance, had his own electric turbines, and was pressing-down the switches in many a house in Ireland. Neither do I mean to credit Yeats with all the attributes and plaudits of a leader; there are signs he was divided between the wish to lead, and the wish to leave behind, other writers. What I do mean is this: that, partly willy and partly nilly, Yeats gave cohesion; around about him writers had a common aim, and though often at issue as persons they were generally grouped as artists.

No one reason will ever explain a human fact, and a full explanation of this relative community would take us far. But Yeats was one prime cause of it. First because his keel was sharp, and cut such a trough in our literary sea that the waves around flowed into it. Second because among his endowments was that of discerning and stating aims; for all his talk of dreams he was the broad-awake kind of artist, the Ronsard, the Ibsen, the Wagner, the Eliot, the one who is interiorly compelled not only to innovate but beyond innovation to say what it is he innovates; to find and to promulgate the luminous and fructifying formulae. This sort of artist needs others; his work must be buttressed, spread and prolonged. Therefore he unified our letters and made a movement.

. . . . .

We know the men and women who made the movement with him, and the names which follow after theirs. Among the first class A. E. (George Russell) has a special place.

He knew Yeats when both were youths, and admired and lauded him for forty years, while for most of that time in addition he supplied to younger men that kindly, generous, personal aid (so essential in a movement) which Yeats was by temperament hardly fitted to give so continuously and copiously. All remember that about A. E. . . . . Doubtless his art was less than that of Yeats; but he had his individual facets, and diversified the total achievement. If we think of Yeats as, in some way, the fertile but careless father of some of these writers, then A. E. may be called the careful midwife who delivered them alive, and the wet-nurse who suckled them to strength. He even had by him the sheets on which to lay them: the sheets of his *Irish Statesman,* which he edited for years.

Distinct and rich personality is affluence, in any kind of work whatsoever, but more in the arts than in most; and this red-faced, bulky, bespectacled, hairy Armagh-man, an assemblage of shrewdness, mysticism, poetry, and economic and political inquisitiveness, was a godsend. He tended in ways to deflect the prevailing winds of the Irish tradition; but winds are not easy to change, and we need not be fearful; the signs are we shall choose and reject from what he offered, according to its healthfulness or noxiousness.

Thus A. E.'s pantheistic Earth-worship on the one hand, and on the other the voracity for land of the Irish peasant,

Yeats and AE sketching, drawn by AE.

are both comprehensible phenomena in Ireland, being each a deformation of the passionate and reverent regard of the Christian as he looks on the "proliferating mould", the creature and the limited manifestation of a God transcendent yet immanent.

Thus again in A. E.'s words and work, through the whole of his life, the spirit's primacy meant much more than art. He was ascetic, devout and charitable, and insistent upon the fact and the value of mystical experience; hence a predominantly Catholic people may honour him and gain by his example, shedding his exotic and erroneous tenets, and remembering as part of the greater wisdom of their teachers a cardinal truth A. E. did not know: that mystical experience is pure gift of God, and not to be induced at will by drill for the spirit. Thus corrected, his life is a noble witness. The religious sense abides in Irish poetry, and A. E. is Irish in possessing it.

Un-Irish indeed he was in suffering through his spiritual perception a dimming of the sensuous world. Few wrote poetry less earthy than he, the Earth-worshipper; for among the major wants of his verse is want of sensuousness. His poems are never tactile; the ear finds them thin, on the whole; and even the eye, though A. E. was a painter, finds lack of particularity and of variousness of colour. Besides he is hardly concerned in his verse with the hues of human character, or, save in *The Dark Lady,* which is a "sport" in his work, with the chameleon passions of men.

In all these lacks, which are really one, he was un-Irish. Add to them this, to conclude our catalogue, that A. E. the poet was incurious in matters of craft; his technical armature was simple, the same, you might say, at the end as it was at the start. He was no experimenter.

It remains true that his verse has Irish lineaments, other than spirituality and mystical glow. At perhaps his nearest approach to particularity he seconds Yeats in picturing our skies and weathers: and then his lines shimmer, dissolve and slide like our secret half-lights and our brief, multiple minglings of sun and vapour and rain. He absorbed our mythology and employed, insubstantially, suggestions from our fairy lore; and he played those slurring spinet-rhythms begun by Callanan in English.

A. E. lost more than Yeats through ignorance of Irish: it might have humanised his too rarefied verse, and mixed in humour or the rich by-products of humour with it; it might too have made his tunes more plangent when they needed be; perhaps sharpened also his blunted dramatic sense. Some say his use of mythology was poor, because he knew the myths at second hand; but this seems to me illegitimate criticism. A poet is not bound to take any material as he finds it, nor is he less Irish for passing old tales through his personal spectrum. Whether one prefers the older or newer versions is quite beside the point.

We remark in these two, in Yeats and A. E., an additional talent, one not to be found before them in an Irish writer, unless we count Davis as such. I mean the talent of the bellman, the billposter, the advertising agent; and do not mistake me, I count this addition among the gains of Irish letters: every Irish writer, if no other Irishman, is keenly aware how distinctly its absence can confine the effect of their art.

It was not just Yeats's genius as a poet which threw new shadows on the screens of the world, but his way of persuading the world that they must be thrown. He was fortunate in looking like a poet: they tell us few poets do: he was lucky in talking like a poet—not all of them do; moreover, through his father, he had enviable friendships with most of those who dictated the arts in England. But it may be that these were secondary helps, and he just had a genius for gospelling. Gospel he did to advantage anyhow: through him the Americans and English attended to our writing as never before or since. If Shaw played *Cornet-di-Bassetto*, Yeats played the trumpet, an instrument a little more refined but sounding as far.

A. E.'s propaganda was simpler, and even more unselfish. He displayed an improbable capacity for journalism, for writing, that is, upon current subjects in a manner at once rapid, varied and quickly-understood. His writing in this mode had, as journalism has, the object of instant effect; but of course he evaded the journalist's penalty, slapdashness. For years his subsidised weekly, *The Irish Statesman*, dinned into readers the excellence of Irish writing; its bankruptcy was a disaster, and its place has not been taken.

Because A. E. is only ten years dead, and because most of his poems which look like lasting have all for decades been current in anthologies, those which are quotable here will be very familiar. I will quote very few for that reason.

The wavering rhythm and religious mood are in *Immortality*:

> We must pass like smoke or live within the spirit's fire;
> For we can no more than smoke unto the flame return
> If our thought has changed to dream, our will unto desire,
> As smoke we vanish though the fire may burn.

And in *Remembrance*:

> There were many burning hours on the heart-sweet tide,
> And we passed away from ourselves, forgetting all
> The immortal moods that faded, the god who died,
> Hastening away to the King on a distant call.

In *Carrowmore* the sing-song of an older English metre is made to carry the interpenetration of the visible world and the Land of Youth, in a typical Celtic Twilight poem:

> It's a lonely road through bogland to the lake at Carrowmore,
> And a sleeper there lies dreaming where the water laps the shore;
> Though the moth-wings of the twilight in their purples are unfurled,
> Yet his sleep is filled with music by the masters of the world.
>
> There's a hand is white as silver that is fondling with his hair:
> There are glimmering feet of sunshine that are dancing by him there:
> And half-open lips of faery that were dyed a faery red
> In their revels where the Hazel Tree its holy clusters shed.

> Oh, the great gates of the mountain have opened once again,
> And the sound of song and dancing, falls upon the ears of men,
> And the Land of Youth lies gleaming, quick with rainbow light and mirth,
> And the old enchantment lingers in the honey-heart of earth.

Typical also is *A Call of the Sidhe,* where the rhythm combines with the other factors, and where A. E. signs his fairies more certainly with his own mark, seeing them, not as casual, disconnected "sports" of the spiritual world, but as one more kind of elementals:

> Drink: the immortal waters quench the spirit's longing.
> Art thou not, bright one, all sorrow past, in elation,
> Made young with joy, grown brother-hearted with the vast,
> Whither thy spirit wending flits the dim stars past
> Unto the Light of Lights in burning adoration.

A. E. did not work with Yeats's thoroughness on all that made up his poems. He is capable, in his third book, of inversions which Yeats rejected soon after *Innisfree,* and of a well-rubbed diction ("in elation"); there are hints as well that he shared some phrases with the better poet. Better poets sometimes appropriate casts of phrasing from poets less good, so we cannot say for certain who first made images like "moth-wings of the twilight" or thought of the fairies as dancers; but Yeats seems generally to have had them earlier in print.

But A. E., I say it again, has his personal accent. It is in *Reconciliation*:

> I begin through the grass once again to be bound to the Lord;
> I can see, through a face that has faded, the face full of rest
> Of the earth, of the mother, my heart with her heart in accord,
> As I lie mid the cool, green tresses that mantle her breast
> I begin with the grass once again to be bound to the Lord.

And it is, somehow, notwithstanding the English cast of the diction, in his sonnet on Terence MacSwiney; for a soul's force to downface its enemies, among them the clamours of its own protesting flesh, was something A. E. with the whole of his being revered. He was transported by this incontestable demonstration that

> There is that within us can conquer the dragon pain,
> And go to death alone, slowly and unafraid.

Spirit responded to spirit, and the dying hunger-striker and the gladdened poet gave double expression to the Irishman's passion for spiritual gold.

Roibeárd O'Faracháin, "Yeats" and " 'A.E.' (George Russell)," in his The Course of Irish Verse in English, *Sheed & Ward, 1947, pp. 64-78, 79-85.*

Frank O'Connor

[*An Irish historian, translator, and writer of short stories, O'Connor (the pen name of Michael John O'Donovan) contributed to the* Irish Statesman, *edited by A. E., and was co-director of the Abbey Theatre Company in Dublin with Yeats, who once declared that "O'Connor is doing for Ireland what Chekhov did for Russia." In the following excerpt, O'Connor discusses the work of two leading revival figures besides Yeats—J. M. Synge and Lady Gregory—arguing that the three must be considered together in the context of the literary movement.*]

Nobody will ever understand much about modern Irish literature who does not grasp the fact that one cannot really deal with any of its three great writers [William Butler Yeats, John Millington Synge, and Isabella Augusta Gregory] in isolation. Synge and Lady Gregory are as much part of Yeats' life-work as are his plays, and until his death he proudly linked their names with his own. They are converts, not imitators, and what they share with him is a religion as much as an aesthetic. The death of Synge came very close to being the end of the others as writers: Yeats' work between 1909 and his marriage is the least important part of his work, and all Lady Gregory's best work was written during Synge's lifetime. In many ways she was temperamentally closer to him than she was to Yeats, and in a peculiar way he seems to have acted as a challenge to her.

It is because the relationship of the three was a conversion rather than a conspiracy that it does not really affect the originality of Synge and Lady Gregory. That it was a true conversion we can see if we consider what they were like about the year 1895. Lady Gregory was a London literary hostess who seemed to model herself on Queen Victoria. In 1886 the English poet Scawen Blunt [in his *Land War in Ireland*] wrote of her:

> It is curious that she, who could see so clearly in Egypt when it was a case between the Circassian pashas and the Arab fellahin, should be blind now that the case is between English landlords and Irish tenants in Galway. But property blinds all eyes, and it is easier for a camel to pass through the eye of a needle, than for an Irish landlord to enter the kingdom of Home Rule. She comes of a family, too, who are 'bitter Protestants', and has surrounded herself with people of her class from Ireland, so that there is no longer room for me in her house.

Synge was a shy and sickly young man who was quietly starving in a Paris attic, producing badly written little articles which editors fought shy of. A couple of years later the London hostess was hard at work learning Irish, writing down folk-stories in the cottages of the poor peasants she had cut Blunt for trying to assist, and indeed was being restrained only by Yeats himself from turning Catholic as well. Synge, dressed in homespuns, was living a comfortless life on a barren island on the edge of Europe. The conversion was complete, but within, both remained very much what they had always been.

Not that I find Synge very easy to understand either before

John Millington Synge.

or after conversion. Yeats' autobiography, Lady Gregory's journals, George Moore's gossip, Professor D. H. Greene's *Life*, Dr. Henn's criticism all leave him completely opaque to me. The only passage I can think of that suggests a real man is in Miss Walker's reminiscences [*The Splendid Years*].

> At the first opportunity, he would lever his huge frame out of a chair and come up on the stage, a half-rolled cigarette in each hand. Then he would look enquiringly round and thrust the little paper cylinders forward towards whoever was going to smoke them. In later years he became the terror of fire-conscious Abbey stage managers. He used to sit timidly in the wings during plays, rolling cigarettes and handing them to the players as they made their exits.

At least the shy man in that little sketch is alive, even if one cannot exactly see him as author of *The Playboy of the Western World.*

So one must fall back on the work, and even here I find myself mystified. In every writer there are certain key words that give you some clue to what he is about. Words like 'friend' and 'friendship' are valuable when one is reading Yeats, but in Synge all I can find are words that suggest carrion.

> Yet these are rotten—I ask their pardon—
> And we've the sun on rock and garden;
> These are rotten, so you're the Queen
> Of all are living, or have been.

If this is how he usually addressed girls it is hardly surprising that he had to spend so much time rolling cigarettes. When he escaped for a while from this carrion view of life it was into a sort of Wordsworthian pantheism. Clearly he was deeply influenced by Wordsworth, and Wordsworth need hardly have been ashamed of signing some of his poems.

> Still south I went and west and south again,
> Through Wicklow from the morning till the
> 　　night,
> And far from cities, and the sites of men,
> Lived with the sunshine, and the moon's delight.
>
> I knew the stars, the flowers, and the birds,
> The grey and wintry sides of many glens,
> And did but half remember human words,
> In converse with the mountains, moors, and
> 　　fens.

How Yeats managed to persuade him at all is a mystery. Yeats had not a glimmer of carrion consciousness. I get the feeling that he carefully avoided the whole subject as being exaggerated, dull, and totally irrelevant. Where he may have managed to communicate with Synge is through Wordsworthianism. Not that Yeats had much time for Wordsworth—'the only great poet who was cut down and used for timber'—but when he preached about the Aran Islands, the necessity for writing about peasants and for adopting peasant speech, a student of Wordsworth could easily have caught what seemed to be echoes of the English poet.

> Low and rustic life was generally chosen because in that situation the essential passions of the heart find a better soil in which they can attain their maturity, are less under restraint, and speak a plainer and more emphatic language; because in that situation our elementary feelings exist in a state of greater simplicity and consequently may be more accurately contemplated and more forcibly communicated; because the manners of rural life germinate from those elementary feelings; and from the necessary character of rural occupations are more easily comprehended and are more durable; and lastly, because in that situation the passions of men are incorporated with the beautiful and permanent forms of nature. The language, too, of these men is adopted (purified indeed from what appear to be its real defects from all lasting and rational causes of dislike or disgust) because such men hourly communicate with the best objects from which the best part of language is originally derived; and because from their rank in society and the sameness and narrow circle of their intercourse, being less under the action of social vanity they convey their feelings and notions in simple and unelaborated expressions.
>
> [Wordsworth, Preface to *Lyrical Ballads*]

It seems to me possible that when we read Synge's prefaces, which so often seem to echo Yeats, we may find that they are really—saving the syntax—echoing Wordsworth.

The material of Synge's plays is slight, and, for the most part, according to Yeats' formula. What is extraordinary is the impact the plays themselves made by comparison with Yeats' and Lady Gregory's. *In the Shadow of the Glen,* for instance, is a folk-story about a flighty wife whose husband pretends to be dead so as to expose her. At the end of the play she goes off with a tramp who, as so often in these plays, represents the Wordsworthian compromise. It is a harmless little play that barely holds interest on the stage, but Arthur Griffith screamed his head off about it as about everything else Synge wrote. 'His play is not a work of genius, Irish or otherwise. It is a foul echo from degenerate Greece.'

It is hard to understand the ferocity of the Catholic reaction to Synge, so much fiercer than the reaction to Joyce. Though it is doubtful if Yeats himself understood it, instinct seems to have warned him that his theories stood or fell by Synge's work.

It must have been instinct too that warned Arthur Griffith what to attack. Essentially Synge seems to have been, as everyone describes him, gentle, and I should say with little self-confidence. He was willing to write folk plays, mystery plays, or mythological plays to order, though they always turned out to be much the same play. Yeats describes him somewhere as the most 'unpolitical' man who ever lived, but he was 'anti-political' rather than 'unpolitical'.

Isabella Augusta Gregory, by John Butler Yeats.

Once some group of patriotic people persuaded him to write a really patriotic play about the heroes of 1798 and the wickedness of the English soldiery. In his obliging way Synge came back with a most extraordinary scenario. The characters were two girls, one Protestant, the other Catholic, who in fear of being raped took shelter in a mountain cave. During the play they discuss the cruel and immoral behaviour of both sides, the Catholic girl defending the rebels and the Protestant the military, till they begin to pull one another's hair out. Finally they separate, the Catholic declaring that she would prefer to be raped by an Englishman than listen to further heresy; and the Protestant that she would prefer to be raped by a rebel than listen to Catholic lies.

Much chance there was that a man like that would write a play to reunite everybody!

In the Shadow of the Glen fails because the story on which it is based is farcical, while the play itself is serious. *Riders to the Sea* succeeds brilliantly because, though it is a Yeatsian miracle, one can watch it without even being aware that a miracle is involved. We can perceive its originality best if we study Lawrence's imitation of it in 'Odour of Chrysanthemums'. A fisherman's death, a miner's death represent the whole of life concentrated in a limited society. Both are anti-political, and in neither is there any reference to the price of fish or coal, or any demand for safety regulations. In these two worlds there is no safety except a clean burial. 'What more can we want than that? No man at all can be living for ever, and we must be satisfied.'

The Tinker's Wedding fails as a play because it has no Synge in it; *The Well of the Saints* because it has too much. The truth is that neither Yeats himself nor any of his followers ever really mastered the problems of extended form, and once they went beyond the one-act play they made the most extraordinary mistakes. . . . In a one-act play dealing with a miracle, it is the miracle which automatically establishes itself as the crisis, the point towards which a playwright must build and then work away from; but in *The Well of the Saints* there are two miracles, neither of which is the real crisis.

The Playboy of the Western World is Synge's masterpiece because it contains more of the real Synge than anything else he wrote, and naturally, it created a greater storm. Synge himself is the shy and sickly young man who scandalizes the world by a crime he has not committed at all, but he remains a hero even when he is shown up, because he has at last learned to live with his image of himself. Unfortunately he discovered what life was like only as death caught up with him. When the *Playboy* appeared he was world-famous and dying.

His greatest achievement as a writer was his elaboration of a style. It was he who really came to grips with the problems posed by Hyde in *Beside the Fire*—the problems of adapting folk speech to literary ends. Yet Synge's own ear for folk speech cannot have been very good. Though he describes himself recording the conversation in the kitchen below his bedroom in Wicklow he never seems to have studied Hyde's introduction to *Beside the Fire*, where he points out the most obvious fact about English spoken in

Ireland: the absence of the pluperfect. In Modern Irish, unlike Old Irish, there are no perfect tenses, so they rarely occur in spoken English. We do not normally say 'He had been there an hour' or 'I shall have discussed it with him.' If we need to supply the missing tense we use the adverb 'after' with the verbal noun: 'He was after being there an hour' or 'I'll be after discussing it with him.'

Synge could never get this quite straight. He dropped the relative pronoun, as in the lines I quoted earlier, 'Of all are living or have been', a construction that in my experience does not occur at all, and rounded it off with a past perfect; and twice at the climax of *Riders to the Sea* he uses improbable tenses: 'It isn't that I haven't prayed for you, Bartley, to the Almighty God. It isn't that I haven't said prayers in the dark night till you wouldn't know what I'd be saying.' Even in the very opening scene he gives us the English use of 'shall' in 'Shall I open it now?'

What he did succeed in was giving Anglo-Irish speech a strong cadence structure. The dialogue in Lady Gregory's *Spreading the News* is enchanting, but it is prose, and in the passionate moments of real drama there is no reserve of language upon which to draw. Lady Gregory herself must have been keenly aware of what he had achieved because in a play that she obviously intended as a rival to *Riders to the Sea, The Gaol Gate,* she used an irregular ballad metre, which she then concealed by writing it as prose; but this is a clumsy device because if the actor becomes aware of the metre he can scarcely avoid falling into singsong, while if he is not, he is just as liable to break up the cadences as though they were nothing but prose. Hyde had given Irish prose writers a medium by which they could keep their distance from English writers; Synge went one better and invented a medium which enabled them to keep the whole modern prose theatre at a distance.

Nobody that I know of has analysed this cadence structure. One obvious cadence fades out on an unimportant word like 'only' or 'surely'. Another of the same sort ends on a temporal clause, which in modern English would be placed at the beginning of the phrase, and this is emphasized by the modern Irish use of the conjunction 'and' as an adverb. Thus, where an English speaker would be inclined to say, 'When I was coming home it was dark', we tend to say, 'It was dark and I coming home', and Synge tends to use it for its slightly melancholy colour.

> MAURYA: Isn't it a hard and cruel man won't hear a word from an old woman, and she holding him from the sea?
>
> CATHLEEN: It's the life of a young man to be going on the sea, and who would listen to an old woman with one thing and she saying it over?

A notable cadence seems to end on a single accented long vowel, often a monosyllable which is preceded by another long and a short—cretics alternating with choriambs is perhaps how it might be described. Synge makes very effective use of it in the great love scene in the *Playboy*—'in the heat of noon', 'when our banns is called', 'in four months or five', and 'in his golden chair'.

If Synge remains a mysterious figure, there is nothing

whatever mysterious about Lady Gregory. If there is one word that sums her up it is complacency—Victorian complacency at that. To please Yeats she rewrote the early sagas and romances that had been edited by famous scholars in English, French and German, but when she came to a line such as 'Will we ask her to sleep with you?' in 'The Voyage of Mael Dúin', Lady Gregory, remembering what the Dear Queen would have felt, turned it into 'Will we ask her would she maybe be your wife?'

Yet I think the critic in the *Times Literary Supplement* who not so long ago told us that there would be no Lady Gregory revival was probably wrong. If ever we get a national theatre again I should expect more revivals of *Spreading the News, The Rising of the Moon, The Travelling Man,* and *The Gaol Gate* than of *Riders to the Sea* or *On Baile's Strand.* We have to learn to appreciate the work of Yeats and Synge, and in doing so lose something of its original freshness, but anyone can appreciate a Lady Gregory play just as anyone can enjoy watching a children's game. Under the Victorian complacency is the Victorian innocence, and this is a quality that does not easily date.

I do not mean that she is unsophisticated. If Yeats had his Corneille for master and Synge his Racine, she has her Molière, and anyone who knows Molière will notice his little tricks in her comedies; as for instance the slow passages of elaborate exposition that suddenly give place to the slapstick stichomythia.

MR. QUIRKE: The man that preserved me!

HYACINTH: That preserved you?

MR. QUIRKE: That kept me from ruin!

HYACINTH: From ruin?

MR. QUIRKE: That saved me from disgrace!

HYACINTH: (*To Mrs. Delane.*) What is he saying at all?

MR. QUIRKE: From the Inspector!

HYANCINTH: What is he talking about?

But in spite of the Victorian complacency she had a genuine tragic sense. Naturally it was a very limited one. She had a tendency to repeat a phrase of Yeats': 'Tragedy must be a joy to the man that dies.' Even as stated it is a very doubtful critical principle, because we do not go to the theatre to see Oedipus enjoy himself, but as she applied it it was even more restricting because it tended to turn into 'Tragedy must be a *pleasure* to the man who dies', which is a very Victorian notion indeed and somewhat reminiscent of the Father of All putting his creatures across his knee and saying, 'This hurts me more than it hurts you.'

But within that Victorian framework she achieves remarkable results, as she does for instance in *The Gaol Gate.* When the play opens we see two poor countrywomen, mother and daughter-in-law, at the gate of Galway Gaol, waiting for the release of a young man who is supposed to have betrayed his comrades in some agrarian outrage. Instead, when the gaol gate opens, they are informed that his comrades have been released and that he has been

hanged; and as they walk back through the streets of the town the old mother bursts into a great song of praise. Lady Gregory had been studying *Riders to the Sea* and old Maurya's great tragic tirade at the curtain, and to make certain of a poetic effect has deliberately chosen to write in a loose and ungainly metre. But even more striking is the contrast between the two climaxes, Synge's haunted by the imminence of death, Lady Gregory's by the triumph of life.

> MARY CAHEL: (*Holding out her hands.*) Are there any people in the streets at all till I call on them to come hither? Did they ever hear in Galway such a thing to be done, a man to die for his neighbour?
>
> Tell it out in the streets for the people to hear, Denis Cahel from Slieve Echtge is dead. It was Denis Cahel from Daire-caol that died in the place of his neighbour! . . .
>
> Gather up, Mary Cushin, the clothes for your child; they'll be wanted by this one and that one. The boys crossing the sea in the springtime will be craving a thread for a memory. . . .
>
> The child he left in the house that is shook, it is great will be his boast of his father! All Ireland will have a welcome before him, and all the people in Boston.
>
> I to stoop on a stick through half a hundred years, I will never be tired with praising! Come hither, Mary Cushin, till we'll shout it through the roads, Denis Cahel died for his neighbour!

Apart from the fact that this is as great as anything in classical tragedy, it is also one of the most astonishing things in the Irish Literary Revival, for it is the work of a Protestant landowner, whose own son would die as an officer in the British Air Force and who had broken off an old friendship with Scawen Blunt because he himself had occupied a cell in Galway Gaol with the Denis Cahels of his day. It makes everything else written in Ireland in our time seem like the work of a foreigner.

There is an even more haunting tragic climax in *Dervorgilla* of the following year, 1908. Dervorgilla keeps on attracting romantic writers since Thomas Moore called her 'falsest of women', and in *The Dreaming of the Bones* even Yeats denies her forgiveness for her imaginary crime. According to the chestnut, which is served up even in the most recent histories and guide-books, she was the wife of O'Rourke of Breany and eloped with MacMurrough of Leinster, thus precipitating the Norman invasion. The writers have most peculiar notions of Irish dynastic marriages: Dervorgilla was a woman famous for her piety, whose 'marriages' to two unmitigated ruffians like O'Rourke and MacMurrough she had nothing whatever to say to.

But what we are dealing with in Lady Gregory's play is the legend of the unfaithful woman who sacrificed Ireland to her passions, and we see her in retirement and repentance at Mellifont Abbey, acting Lady Bountiful to the young people of the countryside till her identity comes to light. Her last great speech is as noble as anything in Irish literature; in a sense we may, I think, read it as Lady Gregory's own apology for her withdrawal from Kiltartan Cross.

> DERVORGILLA: Since you were born and before you were born I have been here, kneeling and praying, kneeling and praying, fasting and asking forgiveness of God. I think my father God has forgiven me. They tell me my mother the Church has forgiven me. That old man had forgiven me, and he had suffered by the Gall. The old—the old—that old woman, even in her grief, she called out no word against me. You are young. You will surely forgive me, for you are young. (*They are all silent. Then Owens comes over and lays down his cup at her feet, then turns and walks slowly away.*) It is not your hand that has done this, but the righteous hand of God that has moved your hand. (*Other lads lay down their gifts.*) I take this shame for the shame in the west I put on O'Rourke of Breffny, and the death I brought upon him by the hand of the Gall. (*The youngest boy, who has hesitated, comes and lays down his hurl and silver ball, and goes away, his head drooping.*) I take this reproach for the reproach in the east I brought upon Diarmuid, King of Leinster, thrusting upon him wars and attacks and battles, till for his defence and to defend Leinster he called in the strangers that have devoured Ireland. (*The young men have gone. Mamie comes as if to lay down her gift, but draws back. Dervorgilla turns to her.*) Do not be afraid to give back my gifts, do not separate yourself from your companions for my sake. For there is little of my life but is spent, and there has come upon me this day all the pain of the world and its anguish, seeing and knowing that a deed once done has no undoing, and the lasting trouble my unfaithfulness has brought upon you and your children for ever. (*Mamie lays down her necklace and goes away sadly.*) There is kindness in your unkindness, not leaving me to go and face Michael and the scales of judgement wrapped in comfortable words, and the praises of the poor, and the lulling of psalms, but from the swift, unflinching, terrible judgement of the young.

I have quoted that great speech, partly that you may understand why the first play I insisted on reviving when I became a director of the Abbey Theatre was *Dervorgilla*, partly to pass on the terrible lesson I learned from it. The play was produced by a young English producer I admired, and the part of Dervorgilla acted by an exceptionally intelligent young actress, and I did not attend the theatre until the dress rehearsal. I listened in bewilderment and horror, and it was only in the last few minutes that I could bring myself to moan, 'For God's sake, stop that infernal snivelling!' It was that evening that I asked Yeats if it was ever permissible for an actor to weep at the curtain of a play and he wrote his answer into 'Lapis Lazuli'.

But my mistake, of course, went deeper than production or acting. It was that in post-Civil War Ireland I expected the atmosphere of that whole dazzling decade; a decade in which Kuno Meyer could casually edit 'King and Hermit' and 'Liadan and Cuirithir' and George Moore in the same year produce the Irish version of *The Untilled Field;* when people acted superbly who had never acted before and in a single year one might have joined in the *Playboy* riots and seen *The Rising of the Moon* and *Dervorgilla* itself, while English and American critics wondered what would happen next.

Only a literary historian will ever be able to capture again anything of that magic—'All the Olympians, a thing never known again.'

> *Frank O'Connor, "All the Olympians," in his* A Short History of Irish Literature: A Backward Look, *G. P. Putnam's Sons, 1967, pp. 183-93.*

Maureen S. G. Hawkins

[*In the following essay, Hawkins addresses the two versions of Lady Gregory's historical drama* Kincora, *examining in particular the social, religious, and political aspects of the characters. She also comments extensively on Gregory's role in the nationalist movement and in the Irish literary revival.*]

The Anglo-Irish were progressively deprived of political hegemony by the passage of such bills as the Act of Union, the Catholic Emancipation Act of 1829, the disestablishment of the Church of Ireland in 1869, and the land acts which culminated in the Ashbourne Act of 1885 and its successors, all of which empowered the mere Irish Catholic majority at their expense. As a result they turned to cultural hegemony to retain their socio-political position within a changing Ireland which, influenced by the tenets of Romantic nationalism, increasingly defined its identity in cultural terms. By teaching the Anglicized middle-class native Catholics the language, history, and culture of Ireland on which the Romantic nationalist claim to Irish nationhood rested, as well as by expressing that claim in art and politics, they not only asserted their right to inclusion within an Irish nation from which the Romantic nationalist definition excluded them on the grounds of natal language, ethnic origin, class, and religion, but also asserted their right to continue to lead the nation. Not all were political nationalists, but of those who were, many, especially in the early twentieth century, were women.

As women of the Ascendancy class, they were doubly disenfranchised—and not merely because women did not have the vote. The increasing misogyny which marked late nineteenth and early twentieth century Western culture was exacerbated within the Irish nationalist movement by the popular reaction to Mrs. O'Shea's role in Parnell's downfall; many regarded his destruction and that of Ireland's hope for Home Rule as being the result of his, as W. R. Fearon picturesquely puts it in his preface to *Parnell of Avondale*, 'turning from the outstretched arms of Kathleen ni Houlihan to the warmer endearments of Kate O'Shea'. Women came to be seen, not as revolutionary helpmeets and political inspirations to nationalist heroes, as Sarah Curran is usually portrayed in relation to Robert Emmet in early nineteenth-century treatments of his life, but as *femmes fatales* who, even if dedicated to Irish freedom, could dangerously distract their men from the cause.

The model nationalist hero became a rebel like Padraic Pearse, who eschewed all women save his mother, rather than Emmet, who lingered for Sarah's sake until he was captured, or Joseph Plunkett, who married Grace Gifford before his execution. Though (usually Anglo-Irish) women such as Anna Parnell, Maud Gonne, Constance Markievicz, Mary Spring Rice, Mary MacSwiney, Alice Stopford Green, Anna Isabel Johnston (Ethna Carbery), Alice Milligan, and Lady Gregory played prominent roles in the political and cultural nationalist movements, they and their efforts were marginalized: sometimes suppressed, like Anna Parnell's Ladies Land League and her history of the Land League; sometimes ridiculed, as O'Casey ridicules Countess Markievicz in *Drums Under the Windows,* or criticized for a lack of femininity, as Yeats frequently criticizes Maud Gonne; most often simply taken less seriously than their male counterparts.

The predominance of the Anglo-Irish among female nationalists must be at least partly a reflection of the greater freedom, leisure, education, and opportunity allowed to women of their class. However, nineteenth-century colonial discourse, which conjoined what Cairns and Richards [in their *Writing Ireland: Colonialism, Nationalism and Culture,* 1988] call 'the mutually supportive discourses of gender, race and politics', especially in the form given it by Matthew Arnold, may also have played a role.

Drawing on Renan, Arnold typed 'the Celt' as an essentially 'feminine' race in terms which, as Cairns and Richards demonstrate, 'flattered [the Irish] into accepting a subsidiary position for themselves vis-à-vis the English' even as he utilized the patriarchialist discourse of the period to justify the continued hegemony of the 'masculine' Teutonic English over them; because this image 'offered [the Anglo-Irish] the position of Ireland's resident Teutons', it was particularly appealing to them. However, the Ascendancy had also, since the early eighteenth century, identified with the ruling class of pre-Norman Gaelic Ireland, regarding themselves as the legitimate heirs of Ireland's ancient kings, whom they saw as serving the same function in Irish society as their own: to preserve Ireland from foreign invasion and the Irish from themselves. Nineteenth-century Celticism, which emphasized the martial virtues of the Irish Heroic Age, reinforced the appeal of this identification. As a result, the Anglo-Irish identity was hyphenated in all particulars: English-Irish, Teutonic-Celtic, and masculine-feminine.

When early twentieth-century, often bourgeois Catholic, nationalists began to reject the feminine image of the Irish as Celts in favour of what Cairns and Richards call ' "the Gael" who, in contradistinction to the Celt, was masculine and antagonistic to the Anglo-Saxon, "the Gall" ', many Anglo-Irish nationalists followed their lead. But they did not completely give up their identification with the martial Celt, whose image remained especially popular with Anglo-Irish women nationalists like Alice Stopford Green, Alice Milligan and Lady Gregory, perhaps because, by conjoining martial valour with femininity, it empowered them as women at the same time that it justified the Ascendancy's inclusion within and hegemony over the Irish nation.

Among Lady Gregory's earliest celebrations of this image are the two versions of her play about Brian Boru, *Kincora,* one produced in 1905 and the other in 1909. *Kincora* I was The National Theatre Society's first historical drama, as well as the first expression of Lady Gregory's dream of creating plays through which to teach Irish history in the schools. As an avowed nationalist, her purpose was, through such plays, to influence the formation of the national dream which was then taking shape; as an Anglo-Irish woman nationalist, it was to ensure that that dream would include both women and her class as active, powerful participants.

A vital issue for such a project is defining the nature of the national identity. One major way in which Lady Gregory does so is through her characterization of Gormleith who, as a war-loving woman, embodies and justifies the paradoxical image of the martial, feminine (and hence Anglo-Irish) Celt. Lady Gregory reinforces this image by subtly identifying Gormleith with the Ascendancy and thus re-establishing their right to pre-eminence within the Irish Nation. The pagan, aristocratic Gormleith, like the Anglo-Irish, is of a different religion and class than her subjects, Brian's Christian servants. Especially in the first version, she is strongly linked with Celticism's ideal of pre-Christian Heroic Ireland, espousing its war-like ideals against what she considers the weakening influence of Christianity.

Lady Gregory further endorses the Anglo-Irish claim to hegemony by casting Gormleith in a role which is rooted in the mythical Celtic Goddess of the Sovereignty of Ireland and which had been conventional in Anglo-Irish historical drama since the early eighteenth century: that of the heroine who embodies Ireland and conveys its kingship in marriage. But, unlike such previous heroines, she is neither dedicated to a native-born king nor opposed to the invading Danes. She has married one Viking, has married and divorced two Irish rulers, and now willingly offers her hand and the sovereignty of Ireland to either of the leaders of the latest Danish invasion.

Her apparent fickleness, however, reflects the will of the nation she embodies. She divorced Malachi and married Brian, taking the High Kingship with her, because Malachi had become too old to rule effectively and the people had called for his removal. Even in inviting the Danes to invade, she expresses the will of Irish rebels who are waiting to welcome them.

Her love of strife, which she stimulates in the kings and their servants, is also innately Irish, as Malachi stresses by calling her 'Crow of Battle', a title of the ancient Irish war-goddess, the Morrigu. It further reflects her role as the embodiment of the mythical Goddess of the Sovereignty of Ireland because it stems from her concern for the well-being of the nation. Gormleith despises Brian's peaceful Christian values because, as a social Darwinist who equates conflict with light, life, and growth, and peace with darkness, degeneration, and death, she fears that peace will destroy heroism in Ireland.

This love of dissension, a characteristic long attributed to the mere Irish by the Ascendancy, has both positive and negative aspects. Lady Gregory sees Ireland as, in Ann Saddlemyer's words [in her *In Defence of Lady Gregory, Playwright,* 1966], 'pursued by [what Yeats called] "an ungovernable heroic emotion" which in its strength gives Ireland her greatness and in its weakness subsides into petty hatred'. Uncontrolled, this emotion leads to the disunity which the eighteenth century Anglo-Irish regarded as the major Irish failing. The quarrelling of the kings' servants and Murrough's baiting of Maelmora over the chess game or of Sitric at the treaty-signing demonstrate this emotion in its weakest, uncontrolled aspect. But, controlled, it is a source of greatness and Ireland's only hope for freedom. Gormleith's exultant love of battle motivates Brian in his final struggle as much as it motivates his servants in their petty squabbling; he dies a hero because of it, just as his weaker subordinates instigate his, and Ireland's, destruction because of it. It is not the 'heroic emotion' which is at fault, but the 'petty hatred' which arises from the weakness of most of those who express it. The Irish, Lady Gregory suggests, do not necessarily want peace and will not accept it unless it is imposed on them by a strong, aristocratic ruler like Parnell.

Gormleith's characterization, especially in the first version, has feminist as well as nationalist aspects. Malachi views her as the turn of the century misogynist's feared 'emancipated woman' who, he says, has 'left a woman's work' to make trouble. But in *Kincora* making trouble *is* 'a woman's work', whether the woman be Gormleith, one of the 'witches of the air', or one of the women whom, Brian says, his ancestors loved and were betrayed by. Far from being the mark of an unsexed, ambitious virago, Gormleith's martial temperament is the sign of a devoted wife. Her warlike urgings and eventual betrayal of Brian are necessary to lead him to the death of a true hero-king rather than, as she puts it, 'the death of a man that is lessening and stiffening, the time he grows attentive to his bed'; 'I was maybe,' she crows, 'a right wife for him. . . in spite of all.'

But Gormleith is not the sole embodiment of Ireland; her rival for Brian's attention also represents aspects of the Irish character, though she does not grant sovereignty. This rival is split into two figures in the first version of *Kincora*: Aoibhell, the *Ban Sídhe*, and Maire, the Christian servant. Though Aoibhell is a pagan spirit and Maire a Christian mortal, they are linked by the promise of peace, by pastoral and Christian imagery, and by association with old age and death. The two women are aspects of the same figure: Aoibhell offers Brian personal peace while Maire offers national peace, but either peace is permanently attainable only in death, and its price is a withdrawal from the conflict of life, which Gormleith regards as dishonest, dishonourable, debilitating, and destructive. Both women, whose function and temptations are economically subsumed in the character of the Beggar Girl, Gormleith's rival in the second version of *Kincora,* represent an idealistic, yet pietistic and death-oriented, element of the Irish character which constantly strives for supremacy over the more earthy, heroically warlike Ireland which Gormleith embodies.

The association of these rival figures with Christianity, the

servant's religion, and with pastoral imagery suggests their identification with Catholic, peasant Ireland in distinction to Gormleith's Ascendancy Ireland, thus implying that, though the Romantic nationalist definition of Irish identity may be at least partly valid, to grant its embodiments hegemony would lead to the degeneration and death of all that is vital and heroic in Irish culture. Like the pagan, though crypto-Christian, Aoibhell, Gormleith recognizes the essential facetiousness of the Irish character, while Maire and the Beggar Girl, blinded by devotion to Brian and Christ, do not. This division would seem to imply that the Anglo-Irish are, as the eighteenth-century Ascendancy conceived themselves to be, the true descendants of the ancient, heroic Irish, and that they are more closely in touch with the reality of Ireland than the Catholic mere Irish—a reflection of the Ascendancy contention that the native Irish are 'priest-ridden' and hence incapable of governing themselves.

However, the characterization of the rival women also suggests a repudiation of the conventional roles of women. Aoibhell, Maire, and the Beggar Girl are all, literally, *femmes fatales* in that the temptations they offer Brian will lead to his death and that of his nation, though only Aoibhell fits the stereotypical image of sexual seductress which the term evokes. Maire and the Beggar Girl embody the religiosity and self-abnegation expected of more respectable women, and all three women, by valuing peace over conflict, privilege the conventional feminine virtue of passivity. Yet their influence on Brian is shown to be detrimental both to his masculinity and to Ireland's heroic culture; all three encourage him to become similarly passive, and therefore 'feminine'. The true helpmeet of the national hero is not the passive, 'feminine' woman who saps his masculine strength and lures him to a meaningless death, but the active, 'masculine' Gormleith who forces him to live up to (or, failing that, to at least die up to) his potential.

Another major way in which Lady Gregory defines the Irish identity and the right to hegemony within the Irish state in favour of the Ascendancy is through her characterization of the Vikings, whom she subtly identifies with the Anglo-Irish. Though, in the first version of *Kincora,* Brian, in traditional nationalist rhetoric, declares that the Danes are guilty of robbery and oppression against the people of Ireland, Lady Gregory, in both versions, grants the Vikings grievances as valid against the native Irish—such as the Irish enslavement of them after the Battle of Glen Mama—as the Irish grievances against them.

Though they are presented as having robbed Ireland, they see themselves as having a legitimate place in Irish society and a legitimate claim to their estates, which they refuse to surrender. Others acknowledge the validity of their claims, especially in the second version, in which Brian treats them as Irish rather than as foreigners: after the Battle of Glen Mama, he castigates Maelmora and Sitric equally for disturbing the peace rather than, as in the first version, treating Maelmora as a native rebel and Sitric as a foreign invader. Most important, Gormleith not only accepts and reiterates the Danes' claims to own their estates, but boasts of her own part-Viking ancestry, and, though she at first insists that they should not be allowed to return, in the end, rejected by Brian, she goes to welcome them in person.

Much of what Sitric and Gormleith say about Viking injuries and claims applies equally to contemporary Anglo-Irish fears and claims. The formations of the Independent Orange Order in 1903 and the Ulster Unionist Council in 1905 were intended to meet the threat of a Home Rule Bill which many feared would totally disenfranchise them. Furthermore, the passage in 1903 of Wyndham's land act, establishing a massive, government-sponsored scheme of land purchase, and in 1909 of Birrell's land act, authorizing compulsory purchase by the Congested Districts Board, inflamed lingering Ascendancy resentment against the Ashbourne and Balfour acts of 1885 and 1891, which many Anglo-Irish landlords viewed as depriving them of their estates. By presenting the Vikings sympathetically and as parallel figures to the Anglo-Irish, Lady Gregory puts the Ascendancy's case for at least parity within the nationalist movement.

Lady Gregory's treatment of the Danes further develops her contentions that the Irish are ruled by Yeats's 'ungovernable heroic emotion' and that the Ascendancy are as 'Irish' as their Catholic compatriots. By presenting Danes as rebellious Irishmen, rather than as foreign invaders, she alters the traditional presentation of the battles of Glen Mama and Clontarf from wars to expel an invader to wars to unify a quarrelsome nation. Early in the play, Maelmora stresses the Danes' relationship by marriage with the mere Irish. Though his hot temper, like Sitric's, links him to Gormleith, his pettiness suggests that the more noble half-Irish, half-Danish Sitric is a truer scion of the Irish Heroic Age than the mere Irish Maelmora—and that ethnicity is a less reliable index of nationality than spirit. Having settled in Ireland, the acculturated Danes are no less Irish than their mere Irish neighbours; they share their character flaws as well as their good points.

Despite her estimation of the Irish, whatever their origin, Lady Gregory remains a nationalist, determined to free a united Ireland from British rule. She writes, in *Our Irish Theatre,* that it is impossible to 'study Irish History without getting a dislike and distrust of England' and, whatever her differences with the Romantic nationalists on the roles of the mere Irish and the Anglo-Irish in an independent Ireland, she agrees with them that Ireland must become unified and free of England.

One reason, in her estimation, that the English must be expelled is that they rule by playing the Orange Card—directing Irish pugnacity into the internal squabbling that the Ascendancy have always deplored, but which she sees her culturally assimilated co-religionists as equally ready to engage in. Though she argues for the acceptance of the Anglo-Irish as true Irish and for a position of power for them within a free Irish state, she will not accept their separation from the rest of Ireland as the price of their power. Brian's refusal to cede Leinster to Sitric and Maelmora on the grounds that he refuses to 'make [any] settlement that leaves any one of the provinces a nest and a breeding ground for the enemies and the ill-wishers of the rest of Ireland' is a clear rejection of partition as a solution to the Ulster problem.

Lady Gregory's conception of Brian's final heroism owes much to the Parnellite perception of the true hero as, above all, a noble, solitary warrior, betrayed by a cowardly, materialistic society. He rises to greatness and confers its possibility upon his nation not by dying for his treacherous, squabbling compatriots, but by recognizing their nature and the well-springs of heroism in it, which may be tapped by fearlessly accepting the death that their treachery imposes. By so doing, he shows them how they too can control and direct the national character that drives them and thus render it a national strength, while warning them against the consequences of letting it, and through it, external enemies, manipulate them into divisive quarrelling.

Brian's desire for peace is partly a manifestation of a pietistic streak, which leads him to turn to the Christian rival, even though that means turning away from Gormleith, Ireland and life itself. It associates him with the spirit of Christianity and death as opposed to the spirit of Heroic Ireland, and life and blinds him both to the realities of the Irish temperament and to the origin of his kingship, which is not bequeathed to him by God, as he thinks, but by the Irish people embodied in Gormleith. By rejecting his queen's values in favour of those of her rival and by attempting to force her to submit to Christian governance and embrace the virtue of passivity, he loses her and, with her, his right to rule an Ireland which he does not fully understand. Lady Gregory uses his folly to comment metaphorically on the foolishness of the nationalist movement's rejection of Ascendancy hegemony in favour of submitting the newly forming Irish nation to the power of the Catholic Church, but it also comments on the folly of forcing women into passive subjection. Both actions, Lady Gregory suggests, will destroy the Irish nation by rendering it prey both to petty materialism and to the self-destructive, uncontrolled aspects of its 'ungovernable heroic emotion'.

In revising *Kincora,* Lady Gregory eschews poetic diction and characterization in favour of the more realistic style she developed in her comedies as well as by freeing herself from some of the constraints historicity imposes on her dramatic imagination. She also follows a pattern which Ann Saddlemyer says is typical of her revision process, that is to:

> throw the characters into relief against the situation and each other by reducing [their] number and by a corresponding simplification of action and motive [leading to]. . . . greater clarity[,] . . . a strengthening of characterization [and] balance.

As a result, the 1909 version is both dramatically and psychologically superior to the 1905 version, as well as politically more explicit. The characters are better developed and more complexly motivated; the structure is more balanced, unified, and coherent, and the pro-Ascendancy, pro-feminist message is harder to ignore. A major example of the effect of this technique is the conflation of the two rival figures of the first version, Aoibhell and Maire, into the single rival of the second, the Beggar Girl, and the corresponding changes in the characterization of Gormleith. The rivalry between Gormleith and the Beggar Girl, one of a long line of mad messengers who carry ideals from the world beyond to the denizens of this world in Lady Gregory's plays, is clearer cut than that between Gormleith and Maire and is emphasized by Lady Gregory's non-realistic treatment of the Beggar Girl, who often speaks in verse. Her characterization points up her symbolic function, while the more sharply delineated conflict between her and Gormleith, who is more realistically characterized than in the first version, allows Gormleith to function on a symbolic level without undercutting her portrayal on the realistic level.

In the first version, Gormleith is not only the embodiment of the fractious Irish temperament, she is also the prime instigator of its expression. But in the second version she no longer embodies it in its entirety, nor is she at the root of all strife, which is seen as being imminent in the very air of Ireland. Although, as in the first version, her comments incite the kings' servants into squabbling over their masters' precedence, the quarrel requires far less provocation from her, nor does she take such a gleeful delight in it. Though she rebuts the Beggar Girl's insistence that Ireland is at peace, she is less eager to instigate war. Even her motivation for joining Sitric's conspiracy is no longer an excited anticipation of battle over herself, but fear for the safety of her son and brother and jealousy over Brian's neglect. One effect of these changes is to transfer the responsibility for internal dissension from the representative of the Irish people to the Irish people themselves. Their contentiousness can no longer be seen as an externalized characteristic over which they have no control, but is an intrinsic characteristic which needs little prompting from the embodiment of their race—or from anyone else—to manifest itself.

The conventional Romantic nationalist characterization of the national hero was as a sacrificial victim and folk-hero who represents the best qualities of his people and willingly fights and dies for their emancipation. In his unceasing opposition to 'the Gall', he embodies the 'Gael' rather than the 'Celt'; in his self-sacrificing devotion, he embodies the Christ-like martyr-hero whose redemptive death ensures the eventual physical as well as spiritual salvation of his long-suffering people. Many aspects of the first version of *Kincora,* misleadingly fit this mould. The Prologue and the last two scenes, for example, emphasize Brian's role as Ireland's self-sacrificing, martyred defender who surrenders his own life and that of his beloved son in Ireland's service; the dominant impression these scenes create is that of a play designed to glorify the efforts of the Irish, led by their noble hero-king, to free Ireland from foreign oppression.

These scenes, however, are eliminated in the second version. One effect of this excision is more clearly to focus the action of the play, which in the first version revolves around a double conflict: one between the Irish and the invading Danes, and one between Gormleith and her rivals for Brian's heart and mind. The revision satisfies Aristotle's requirement of a single action by centering on the sec-

ond conflict, but it also renders much clearer Lady Gregory's rejection of conventional Catholic Romantic nationalist definitions of the Irish identity and the Irish national hero.

In the first version Brian is linked to legendary ancient Ireland by Aoibhell's first temptation and by Gormleith's exhortation to behave like his heroic ancestors. The effect is apparently to validate Brian's death-oriented pietism as an authentic expression of the Irish heroic character and to privilege equally the Catholic Gael and the Ascendancy Celt. However in the second version, both Aoibhell and these allusions are absent. Brian repudiates the example of his fighting forefathers in favour of that of peacemaking foreign kings, not recognizing that his models, Charlemagne, Harold of Norway and Alfred the Great, did not have the contentious, treacherous Irish to deal with. It is only at the end of the play, after Gormleith has left him and he realizes that he must fight, that he chooses to associate himself with his heroic Irish ancestors and take his place among them by fighting as they did, though betrayed as they were.

Though concerned with historical accuracy, Lady Gregory is a dramatist first, and, as such, she chooses her development of theme, plot or character over historical verisimilitude whenever the two come too strongly into conflict. Her confidence in doing so, however, grows between the first version of *Kincora,* which she faults in her 'Notes' to the published version for 'having kept too close to history', and the second version. Her revision increases the subordination of the demands of historicity to those of art by ignoring historical chronology wherever it opposes her dramatic purpose. For example, she alters the date of Brian's marriage to Gormleith, which she gives accurately in the first version, in order to stress from the outset the conflict between Brian's desire for peace and Gormleith's desire for heroic action and between their opposed understandings of the nature of the Irish people. Thus she establishes the Beggar Girl and Gormleith as the opposite poles, not only of the play's dynamic, but also of Irish society. Their contention for Brian's heart transforms the play into a *psychomachia* which allows her to develop his character more complexly and critically, as well as to project her political message more forcefully and explicitly.

The nationalist press loved the first version of *Kincora,* which they regarded, in [commentator Joseph] Holloway's words, as 'written on purely Irish lines and laden with patriotic sentiment' but, despite its dramatic superiority, they hated the second version. [The Irish nationalist journal] *Sinn Fein* objected vehemently to the 'jabbering and snarling' that rendered the revision, in its reviewer's eyes, 'the national and artistic degradation of a great subject'. Presumably the conventional Romantic nationalism of the first version's frame, the Prologue and the final two scenes, blinded the nationalists to the presence of the traditional Ascendancy criticism of the Irish character, which had long been used as an argument against self-government, to the justification of Ascendancy hegemony, and to the feminist defence of the active role of women. With the second version's excision of the frame, naturalization of the Vikings and more clearly delineated conflict between the values of Gormleith and the Beggar Girl, the play became unacceptable. The *Sinn Fein* reviewer's insistence 'that historical subjects cannot be handled by dramatists who have narrow conceptions' may suggest that Lady Gregory's gender and Ascendancy affiliation, whatever her nationalist credentials, rendered the message of her dramatized history lesson even less acceptable.

Some events between 1905 and 1909, such as the *Playboy* riots, strengthened Lady Gregory's Ascendancy convictions, while others, such as the formation of *Sinn Fein,* strengthened her commitment to a free, united Ireland. The result is a more extreme set of paradoxical tensions in the second version of *Kincora* than in the first. But her theatre work during this period also strengthened her mastery of stagecraft and focused her vision, allowing her to control these tensions. She learned, for example, to sharpen her oppositions, as she does by eliminating the character of Aoibhell. Her playwriting and staging experience gave her the confidence to alter any historical chronology that does not serve her dramatic purpose and to eliminate scenes, such as Brian's death, which a patriotic audience would expect, if those scenes would obscure that purpose. At the same time, she gained experience in characterization, allowing her to create characters like Gormleith who could be both more realistic in motivation and expression, yet also more symbolic in function than those she created in 1905. The result is that, though the first version sometimes displays more bravura theatricality and poetic intensity, the second displays a more certain control of more difficult, more complex tensions and a surer thematic focus, as well as richer character development.

Both versions, however, demonstrate a major advance in the dramatic treatment of Irish historical figures. By melding the Parnellite hero of Irish Renaissance mythological poetic drama with 'Kiltartanese' diction and her own talent for realistic characterization, and comic scenes with the conventional matter of historical dramaturgy, she transmutes the form, opening new possibilities of linguistic, thematic, and characterizational treatment of Irish historical material on the stage.

The tensions which vitalize both versions of the play result, at least in part, from Lady Gregory's position as a female Ascendancy nationalist in a movement that, by its very nature, tends to exclude her, her people, and her sex from its ranks. Through paradoxical hybridizations and inversions of established conventions, she successfully honours service to and death for an Ireland which inevitably repays such service with betrayal and rejection, justifies the inclusion of the Anglo-Irish in the Irish nation and their continued hegemony over it, and celebrates the active role of women in an increasingly misogynic movement which views even the most devoted female patriot as a danger to the dedication and success of male revolutionaries. That her more explicit revision proved politically unpopular is not surprising, but that it is so dramatically superior as to constitute a welcome landmark in the subgenre of Irish historical drama is unquestionable.

> *Maureen S. G. Hawkins, "Ascendency Nationalism, Feminist Nationalism, and Stagecraft in Lady Gregory's Revision of 'Kincora'," in*

Irish Writers and Politics, *edited by Okifumi Komesu and Masaru Sekine, Colin Smythe, 1989, pp. 94-108.*

John Stuart Mill on resolving the Irish Question:

Matters of affronted feeling, and of minor or distant pecuniary interest, will occupy men's minds when the primary interests of subsistence and security have been cared for, and not before. Let our statesmen be assured that now, when the long deferred day of Fenianism has come, nothing which is not accepted by the Irish tenantry as a permanent solution of the land difficulty, will prevent Fenianism, or something equivalent to it, from being the standing torment of the English Government and people. If without removing this difficulty, we attempt to hold Ireland by force, it will be at the expense of all the character we possess as lovers and maintainers of free government, or respecters of any rights except our own; it will most dangerously aggravate all our chances of misunderstandings with any of the great powers of the world, culminating in war; we shall be in a state of open revolt against the universal conscience of Europe and Christendom, and more and more against our own. And we shall in the end be shamed, or, if not shamed, coerced, into releasing Ireland from the connexion; or we shall avert the necessity only by conceding with the worst grace, and when it will not prevent some generations of ill blood, that which if done at present may still be in time permanently to reconcile the two countries.

John Stuart Mill, in his "England and Ireland," 1868. Reprinted in Essays on England, Ireland, and the Empire, *University of Toronto Press, 1982.*

Herbert Howarth

[In the following excerpt, American scholar Howarth discusses the nationalist movement's anti-materialist position as well as the influence of political leader Charles Parnell as a messianic figure for writers such as A. E. and Yeats.]

Irish writers slowly recognised [political leader Charles] Parnell's death as the source of the creation of the Irish Republic. Out of the public passions and the ignominy that caused his death a myth flared up that produced the Rising of 1916 and the quick subsequent events: revolution, civil war, and the Republic. There had been a superiority in Parnell that is not easy to grasp when, so many years later, one reads the biographies. His aloofness, his very despotism, had made men ready to worship him. His followers invested him with the status of a prophet. Those who hated him most after the divorce proceedings hated him because they could not bear their prophet to be less than immaculate. The Irish committed the crucial act of killing their prophet, and the guilt, the desire to purify the guilt, the belief that his sacrifice sanctified, the belief that sacrifice assures rebirth, gave them irresistible vigour in the next generation.

The Irish Parliamentary Party which had thrown him over in order to survive, survived pointlessly when it had thrown him over. It ceased to matter, because it no longer had a man of stature directing it, because it despised itself for having abandoned him, because the ardent young despised it. The young gradually integrated his memory into their hopes of an ancient, powerfully imaginative, physically powerful and audacious Ireland. A literary movement found symbols and a language for their dream. The literary movement thereby inflamed—half-consciously, for it doubted the value of dynamite—the militant movement. Events proved, as always, that, much as one might wish otherwise, militancy prevails and obtains what words and wisdom alone do not. Parnell was reborn in the intransigent underground from which he had, by class, temperament, and policy, stood apart.

MESSIANISM

Yeats had published the *Wanderings of Oisin,* in which the Fenians are contrasted with the priests, in 1889. Celtic legend, and a challengingly militant voice, are present in it. The new literary movement pre-dated the Parnell crash. Yeats and his friends, poets and painters and sculptors of his own age, were conscious in the 'eighties that an earlier generation of Irish writers had made it their business to support the Irish nationalist movement with poetry and with a social and political philosophy. By 1889 they had already set out to continue the work of Davies, Mangan, and Ferguson—to continue and to deepen it, for they felt that, Mangan's best poetry apart, it had been too superficial a reflection of the political movement, and that it must establish more subtle values and humanise the political movement. What Parnell's death immediately did for the writers and artists, besides raising their passions, was to raise their sense of responsibility, indicate emphatically the necessity for Irish self-criticism; and because there were men and women looking for guidance in the perplexity that followed the 1891 schism, it multiplied their audience.

The beliefs and the myths that consolidated in Irish imagining and Irish writing after Parnell's death, were not new. They had been eddying among the people for at least a century. But the fall and death and portentous burial of the Chief pulled them to a focus. They had been filtering into literature as something attractive but scarcely understood. Now the poets seized on them deliberately.

The essence of these beliefs was Messianic. Among the oppressed, Messianism is always strong. Ireland had been an occupied land, a land exploited, for 700 years. Its peasants were among the poorest in Western Europe. For a point of comparison we have to think of Portugal and Spain, perhaps of Morocco or pre-Kemalist Turkey, or Egypt. In these countries the poor had long been enfolded within the close organisation of Catholicism or Islam. They were faithfully orthodox, but beneath the orthodoxy they moved to the rhythm of more primitive convictions, which lived in their stories, proverbs and parables, and songs. The oppressed wait for a Messiah to come to redeem them—literally to bring them food and raiment and consolation. The Irish oppressed were more than once ready to identify a political leader with Him. How quickly they gave the nineteenth-century leaders such names as the Counsellor, the Agitator, the Liberator.

There was a period when they seemed to recognise Him in [nationalist leader Daniel] O'Connell. While compiling *Mr. Gregory's Letter-Box,* Lady Gregory met an old peasant on a mountain pass, fell into talk with him about politics. He told her this story, which she included in the book, about O'Connell's father:

> O'Connell was a grand man, and whatever cause he took in hand it was as good as won. But what wonder. He was the gift of God.
>
> His father was a rich man, and one day he was out walking he took notice of a house that was being built. Well, a week later he passed by the same place, and he saw the walls of the house were no higher than before. So he asked the reason, and he was told it was a priest that was building it, and he hadn't the money to go on with.
>
> So a few days after, he went to the priest's house, and he asked was this true, and the priest said it was. So, says O'Connell, "Would you pay the money back to the man that 'ud lend it to you?" "I would", said the priest. So with that O'Connell gave him the money that was wanting, *500 l.,* for it was a very grand house.
>
> Well, after some time the priest came to O'Connell's house, and he found only the wife at home. So, says he, "I have some money that Himself lent me". But he never had told his wife of what he had done, so she knew nothing about it; and says she, "Don't be troubling yourself about it, he'll bestow it on you." "Well", says the priest, "I'll go away now, and I'll come back again."
>
> So when O'Connell came in, the wife told him all that had happened, and how a priest had come, saying he owed him money, and how she said he'd bestow it on him. "Well," said O'Connell, "if you said I'd bestow it, I'll bestow it." And so he did. Then the priest said "Have you any children?" "Ne'er a child", said O'Connell. "Well, then, you'll have one", said he, and that day nine months their young son was born. So what wonder if he was inspired, being as he was the gift of God.

As a young Catholic lawyer defending the poor, O'Connell worked with inspiration and inspired the watching public. The hopes that he attracted were never wholly forgotten, not even after his failure of 1843. In that year it seemed to the younger men that he declined the opportunity to lead a rebellion against England—declined, that means, the violence which must precede the millennium. After that his power ebbed away from him. New leaders were sought, new Messianic candidates; but even a false Messiah is never forgotten, if his moment has been radiant. Half a century after O'Connell's best days, Yeats read of him . . . and responded to the story with emulation. More than half a century later Lady Gregory transcribed the legend of his birth from the old peasant.

Only a few years after that she was transcribing evidence of the incorporation of Parnell into the popular mythology. At Spiddal on Galway Bay she listened to an old man addressing a crowd with urgent gestures. " 'Tha se beo, tha se beo'—'he is living, he is living', I heard him say over and over again. I asked what he was saying and was told: 'He says that Parnell is alive yet'." The Irish imagination was hungry for a leader like Christ or Charlemagne or Barbarossa—a hero whose death is only similitude, who rises again, who will come, a Golem, from his covert when his people need him. Joyce, objectively recording the mind of Dublin, said as much:

> Somewhere imperceptibly he would hear and somehow reluctantly, suncompelled, obey the summons of recall. Whence, disappearing from the constellation of the Northern Crown he would somehow reappear reborn above delta in the constellation of Cassiopeia and after incalculable eons of peregrination return an estranged avenger, a wreaker of justice on malefactors, a dark crusader, a sleeper awakened, with financial resources (by supposition) surpassing those of Rothschild or of the silver king.

The hopes and torments of Ireland, and the legends that promised a metamorphosis, belonged to the poor. They took effect, were translated into action, when they seeped to the better-off and the educated. They filtered into sheltered homes through the servants, with whom the education of the children lay. The nurses had the greatest advantage. Perhaps no single influence ate so deep into the minds of the politicians and writers of Ireland as the stories of their nurses, told them at the most impressionable age. Lady Gregory's old Catholic nurse, Mary Sheridan, brought the traditions of '98 and the anecdotes and language of the people, their passion and insight, to the Protestant home at Roxborough. Bernard Shaw had an old nurse, who equally stimulated his sense of justice though not equally successfully his national sentiment. At Parnell's home, Avondale, Ireland's history penetrated through the housekeeper and her husband who served at the gate. Katharine Tynan writes:

> Old Gaffney at the gate lodge at Avondale was old enough to remember the Rebellion. He used to tell how a rebel named Byrne was flogged from the mill to the old sentry-box in Rathdrum by the orders of a savage named Colonel Yeo. How this gallant gentleman ordered the lashes to be inflicted on the front part of the body instead of the back; how the bowels protruded as the man ran stumbling and shrieking, "For the love of God have mercy on me, Colonel Yeo"; how the savagery was not abated till he died.
>
> In this story told by old Gaffney, the gatekeeper at Avondale, to the growing boy—Mr. Parnell used to tell it without apparent emotion—lay the genesis of a great Irish rebel.

These atrocious or hungry memories ferment with the antique underground religion of the peasants, and the result is, obviously, hatred of the oppressor, but also a readiness to endure the chaos of revolution, and a sharp vision of a sheer Utopia that the revolution supposedly will confer. While it is recognised that a military struggle will be destructive, the temper with which it is faced is sanguine. The Messiah seems to walk ahead: on him the agony centres, through him the obstacles drop apart. By a natural development the most urgently-dedicated men and women have hours when they dream that they may be chosen for the Messianic sacrifice.

As they listened to their nurses, those mid-nineteenth-century children glimpsed, through the window or between the bars of a gate or peering from a swaying carriage, certain typical characters and scenes, which, printed on their minds, became inseparable from their sense of their land and its problems and destiny. Such was the image of the duelling landlords, that craggy and violent image shared by Yeats and Moore. A man who has killed all his opponents, whose appetite for fighting is still insatiable, gallops down a road. The country-folk are shocked by his history and are determined to have no more of it. They block his passage with the priest at their head. It seems they have him coralled, but he knows their passions better than the Father, and with a rough joke he topples their patriotism on to his side—"Now lads, which will ye choose, the Mayo cock or the Galway cock?" and they break ranks with a cheer and he rides past to the kill. Such, again, is the image of the Irish tinkers and their promiscuous marriages. Lady Gregory was struck by the reminiscence of an old lady who, years earlier, had sat on a wall at Kilkenny and had seen the tinkers at their annual rally bartering wives with one another—"yes, they did so, it was their custom . . . and the children went away with the women."

The minds that made the Irish literary movement, the Irish Risorgimento, were shaped at the earliest age by the tradition of the rebellion and the hopes of a Messiah and interpenetrated by images like these. When they grew older, they consciously acquired cognate material and grafted it on to the original stem. At first they gathered it because they undertook activities that brought them into touch with the people, like Lady Gregory undertaking her charitable round among her tenantry. Then, beginning with Yeats, they acquired it by deliberate seeking.

LITERARY MESSIANISM

The outburst of theosophical discussion among the Dublin art students in 1885 has become a commonplace of literary history. Enquiring into esoterica as part of their search for a differentiating power, Yeats and AE learned to connect the legends of rural Ireland with a central body of underground tradition.

It seemed to AE in retrospect that one of the most influential books they met in their explorations of the next five years was Madame Blavatsky's *Secret Doctrine*. However crude the presentation, they found there that the drifting hopes of Ireland were part of a widespread faith. The promise of a Messiah; the revolutionary context of His coming; the belief, which Fenians like John Mitchel and James Stephens had held, that oppressed peoples become free during an international conflagration—these hopes of the Irish could be traced in esoteric literature. Let us see Yeats making the discovery in one among the curious books he opened. George Rodway of London was publishing titles concerned with theosophy and the antiquarianism which was the forerunner of anthropology. His 1887 list included *The Real History of the Rosicrucians* by Arthur Edward Waite. The trend of the book was not particularly favourable to the devotees of secret cults, but Yeats' eye picked out the passages that suited his inclinations. At the beginning of Chapter II he found a short account of the expectation of a Messiah early in the seventeenth century and of the earlier prophecies of Paracelsus, notably his declaration that the comet of 1572 was "the sign and harbinger of the approaching revolution", and his promise in his *Treatise of Metals* that a discovery would be opened to the world by "a marvellous being . . . who as yet lives not". These passages stimulated his memories of childhood hearsay and traditional patter noted during his wanderings or when gathering folk-lore in libraries.

At the same date AE was saying in correspondence with Carrie Rea: "I think the world is striding greatly into the light, let us go with it". It is a theosophical transcription of the nineteenth-century belief in progress, but it is more, a first vague translation of the peasant legends of the Messiah into the international prophecy of the millennium.

By 1889 Yeats was studying Blake with Edwin Ellis in preparation for their work of 1893. In the Prophetic Books he found the New Jerusalem, the dramatic image which the Reformation adopts, whom he had already met in Waite, had handed down from the Middle Ages, and which Blake, on receiving it from them, had transformed. Writing from the excitement of the American war of liberation and the French tumult, Blake had sharpened religious prophecy with the accents of the revolutionary; on the ancient tradition that the Messiah or Golem will walk to accomplishment through ruin he had impressed the interpretation of freedom through militant insurrection. So satisfied with this doctrine and its poetry that he convinced himself Blake was Irish, Yeats began to think of Ireland's freedom coming as part of the rebirth of all the nations in a violent conflict. He hastened his study of Irish folk-lore with an enhanced sensitivity to the Messianic suggestions in it. He came across a prediction ("all over Ireland", he says in his unreliable, blarneying way) "of a coming rout of the enemies of Ireland, in a certain Valley of the Black Pig". This he understood both as a promise for Ireland—she will scatter her enemies and be free—and as a promise to the world—the battle will be the world conflagration anciently foretold.

The rational and humane side of the Irish thinkers sometimes blenched at the Armageddon image, but they overcame their doubts by reminding themselves of the sufferings of Ireland unliberated. When John Mitchel, a generation earlier, had been rebuked by his Doppelgänger: "And, for the *chance* of getting Ireland severed from Britain in the dreadful *melée,* do you desire to see all Europe and America plunged in desperate war?" he had replied that he would rather war than a repetition of the Irish famine of the 'forties and had cited an Armageddon image from the Old Testament. Richard Ellmann has shown in *Yeats: the Man and the Masks* that between 1893 and 1896 Yeats was talking a great deal about the war in which the world would fall apart. The first reference in the *Letters,* edited by Allan Wade, shows a tinge of the ambivalence of Mitchel's inner colloquy. Dated December 1895, it is an enquiry to the actress Florence Farr—in her capacity as a higher member of the Order of the Golden Dawn—

whether the Venezuelan crisis, over which the Press speculated that America might go to war, means that "the magical armageddon has begun at last". If so, he goes on, "The war would fulfil the prophets and especially the prophetic vision I had long ago with the Mathers's, and so would be for the glory of God, but what a dusk of the nations it would be!" He assimilated the problem into a poem, *The Valley of the Black Pig,* published in the *Savoy,* April, 1896:

> The dews drop slowly and dreams gather: unknown spears
> Suddenly hurtle before my dream awakened eyes,
> And then the clash of fallen horsemen and the cries
> Of unknown perishing armies beat about my ears. . . .

Yeats was less sure than AE that the outcome of the conflagration must be light and a universal settlement. Sometimes he was content to see the final battle as the consecration of darkness. In 1902 he was talking to a poor woman of Sligo, a soldier's widow: "And presently our talk of war shifted, as it had a way of doing, to the battle of the Black Pig, which seems to her a battle between Ireland and England, but to me an Armageddon which shall quench all things in the Ancestral Darkness again."

Ellmann has shown how the expectation of the Messiah flared up in 1896. In June that year AE wrote to Yeats: "You remember my writing to you about the awakening of the ancient fires which I knew about. Well it has been confirmed and we are told to publish it. *The Gods have returned to Eri* and have centred themselves in the sacred mountains and blow the fires through the Country. They have been seen by several in a vision . . . I believe profoundly that a new Avatar is about to appear and in all spheres the forerunners go before him to prepare. . . . " Undeterred by the cacophonous prose of this announcement, Yeats, who received it in London, was enthusiastic. It became a matter of urgency for him to share the revelation. He travelled to Ireland with Arthur Symons that summer. One night at Edward Martyn's estate, Tillyra, he had a vision. Having invoked the spirits of the moon, he saw, between sleeping and waking, "a beautiful woman firing an arrow among the stars". The same woman, a "symbolic Diana", appeared that same night to Symons, his fellow-guest. William Sharp, a letter soon told him, had also about that time seen an arrow shot into the sky, piercing a faun's heart. Also, a stranger's child had dreamed of a man shooting at a star with a gun and bringing it down, whereupon it lay in a cradle.

The barb transfixed Yeats' imagination and remained embedded there for the rest of his life. He published the evidence of the coincidental visions and dreams a generation later in *The Trembling of the Veil.* By then he was conscious of what he wanted to prove by it. Certain modifications crept in, as compared with the above account (which is based on a letter to William Sharp, August 1896). He no longer said that the woman fired her arrow "among the stars", but at a star, and reported the presence of a galloping centaur: "I saw between sleeping and waking, as in a kinematograph, a galloping centaur, and a moment later a naked woman of incredible beauty, standing upon a pedestal and shooting an arrow at a star." . . . The immediate point is that three elements are configured with it in the vision: the star of Bethlehem; the comet of 1572 on which Paracelsus had hinged his prophecy of a modern Messiah; the lights that flamed over Parnell's grave. We know that this last element is involved, because Yeats says so in a poem of the 'thirties, *Parnell's Funeral,* using there the vision of 1896 and the comparative material as presented in *The Trembling of the Veil:*

> Under the Great Comedian's tomb the crowd.
> A bundle of tempestuous cloud is blown
> About the sky; where that is clear of cloud
> Brightness remains; a brighter star shoots down;
> What shudders run through all that animal
>   blood?
> What is this sacrifice? Can someone there
> Recall the Cretan barb that pierced a star?
>
> Rich foliage that the starlight glittered through,
> A frenzied crowd, and where the branches
>   sprang
> A beautiful seated boy; a sacred bow;
> A woman, and an arrow on a string;
> A pierced boy, image of a star laid low.
> That woman, the Great Mother imaging,
> Cut out his heart. Some master of design
> Stamped boy and tree upon Sicilian coin.

The imagery and the matted anthropological references of the second stanza are clarified by the notes to *The Trembling of the Veil.* There we find that, advised by "a man learned in East-Mediterranean Antiquities" (whose name he, typically, can no longer remember or trace), Yeats understands the salient images of his vision as follows: the shot star is the sun with its annual death and rebirth (and we know from other work of his that he regards the sun as symbol of the kingly mind); it is also Balder "who is shot to death that is life by means of a sprig or arrow of mistletoe"; the woman who shot the arrow is "the Mother-Goddess, whose representative priestess shot the arrow at the child whose sacrificial death symbolised the death and resurrection of the Tree-spirit, or Apollo"; the heart is taken, in an ancient festival, from the body of the sacrificed child and placed in the chest-cavity of the figure that is to be the child reborn; the arrow is "a sign of Initiation and Rebirth".

This is Yeats' reading in old age of the lights in the Dublin sky in the fall of 1891. The dropping meteor over Parnell's grave had been shot down by the Mother-Goddess. The third stanza of the poem unequivocally identifies Parnell's fate in Ireland with the archetypal situation. The Irish political martyrs of a century earlier, Emmet, Fitzgerald, Wolfe Tone, had been murdered by "strangers", the occupying British—

>   But popular rage,
> *Hysterica passio* dragged this quarry down.
> None shared our guilt; nor did we play a part
> Upon a painted stage when we devoured his
>   heart.

Three statements are hurled by Irish poet at Irish reader (that is the meaning of "we"): the death of Parnell was an Irish act, an all-impassioned Irish act; it was the sacrifice

of the leader in his role as Balder the beautiful; the sacrifice postulates rebirth, or in the Irish context a national rejuvenation, when the heart of the sacrificed hero is eaten. Then comes a terrible last verse disowning these very statements. . . . The immediate point is this: enquiry into Irish history and legend and into analogues, endless spiritual exercises, endless involvement in the rough fury of Irish living, led Yeats to collate the scattered drifting prophecies of a Messiah and believe that they could be, or should have been, fulfilled in a birth linked with the national sacrifice of Parnell. He had worked slowly—it is striking how very slowly—to that conclusion. But it was clear to him in old age that the thinking of his early and middle years had already presupposed it.

WRITERS AS FORERUNNERS—THE SACRED BOOK

Ellmann and Jeffares have described how Yeats set himself, after the exchange with AE in 1896, to inaugurate a cult and a ritual for the "forerunners". The Irish writers were to be evangelists. In fact, the image of John the Baptist became a favourite among all the writers. George Moore had a natural bent to the imitation of the Evangelist. At the warmest point of his relations with Yeats, after they had collaborated for only a short time, he professed himself unworthy to unlatch his shoes. Later his view modified, and for him, as for each of the writers in turn, there came a moment when he wondered whether Parnell's spirit had passed into his own person. There is, in fact, a double character to the prophesying (the endless prophesying that makes the record of Irish nationalism in these years as hectic as the Old Testament). Sometimes literature and journalism prophesy a leader of the State, and often enough writers seem willing to take on this practical role. Sometimes they more modestly write as if an unknown man will appear as leader, and they, favoured scribes who prepared the way for him, will recognise him, interpret him, and write his scriptures. . . . For the moment it may be useful to show how the writers talked about the writing of a sacred book. A conversation recorded by Moore in *Hail and Farewell* allows us to hear some of them speculating. The occasion is one of their evening gatherings in Dublin in the first years of this century:

> Then we began to talk, as all Irishmen do, of what Ireland was, what she is, and what she is becoming.
>
> There is no becoming in Ireland, I answered; she is always the same—a great inert mass of superstition.
>
> Home Rule, said AE, will set free a flood of intelligence.
>
> And perhaps the parish priest will drown in this flood.
>
> AE did not think this necessary.
>
> Do you think the flood of intelligence will penetrate into the convents and release the poor women wasting their lives?
>
> I'm not thinking of nuns, John Eglinton said; those who have gone into the convents had better remain in them; and Home Rule will be of

no avail unless somebody comes with it, like Fox
or like Bunyan, bringing the Bible or writing a
book like the *Pilgrim's Progress.* . . .

These sentences are to be accepted, not perhaps as a replica of a conversation but at least as a condensation of sayings in vogue, and it is significant that the decisive pronouncement on the need for the Bible of the independent nation is put into the mouth of Eglinton. He is the man of taste, the non-fanatic, prejudiced if anything against Gaelism and separation from England. If he says that the task of the literary movement is to produce a sacred book, he says it soberly.

Yeats expected to be the author of that book. He defined it to himself originally as an exposition of psychic lore, familiar to the country people of Ireland. In the preface to the new edition of *The Celtic Twilight,* 1902, he promised: "I shall publish in a little while a big book about the commonwealth of faery, and shall try to make it systematical and learned enough to buy pardon for this handful of dreams." He and Lady Gregory busied themselves with that system for the next fourteen years and more. . . . Yeats recognised that the book was her work—recognised it because he also recognised that it was not the sacred book he had dreamed of. The sacred book would still be his occupation; it would be a philosophy of history. With the help of the spirits who communicated with him through his wife's automatic writing he began the slow preparation of *A Vision.* While engaged on that he reminded the public of the imminence of a sacred book, by choosing as title of his autobiographical essays *The Trembling of the Veil,* the preface to which narrates how he had discovered in an "old diary"—the kind of source he loves to quote, because it implies that he had already divined as a young man what maturity confirmed—his note of a saying of Mallarmé: "Is it true", he asks, "that our air is disturbed, as Mallarmé said, by 'the trembling of the veil of the Temple', or 'that our whole age is seeking to bring forth a sacred book'?"

Towards the end of his life he ceased to insist that *A Vision* was a holy book, or that any Irish writer had written one. His thoughts blackened by the angry view that all that had been said in Ireland was a lie, he conjectured that the scriptures of the age were probably not of Irish provenance, but had been written earlier in continental Europe. Perhaps they consisted of the quadrivium: *Faust, Louis Lambert, Seraphita, Axel.*

Lady Gregory, an admirer of Shaw, who was after all nearly her own age, thought *he* might be both the sacred writer and the political, Messianic leader, and this though he had largely kept apart from Irish affairs. When she was meditating *The Jester,* Shaw was in her mind, and in her note to the play she comments: "looking now at the story of that Great Jester, in the history of the ancient gods, I see that for all his quips and mischief and 'tricks and wonders', he came when he was needed to the help of Finn and the Fianna, and gave good teaching to the boy-hero, Cuchulain." She liked Shaw and trusted him, perhaps hoped with these remarks to coax him; but although he occasionally made a gesture for Ireland, his bent, ambition, hatred of childhood memories, were too much

against a full response. Yet though he wrote neither in Ireland nor for Ireland, the Irish pattern of thinking was engrained in him. The Irish passion for a sacred book drove him. He attempted three: *Man and Superman; Back to Methuselah;* and *Saint Joan.* The second was his most serious offer, the primitive scriptures of "Creative Evolution . . . the religion of the twentieth century". The third was less a sacred book than an Irishman reporting, in the light of his country's experience, on the nature and techniques of a nationalist Messiah, and how a Messiah is thrown to the wolves.

Although delighted with himself, delighted with his success in seizing the international pulpit and mesmerising world attention, Shaw knew that his art was defective and its durability uncertain. In 1912 he added to the current predictions of a greater writer coming: "I am", he said to an interviewer, "only one of the first attempts of the new Ireland. She will do better—probably has done better already—though the product is not yet grown up enough to be interviewed". A decade later he thought he had found the younger man, the half-Irish T. E. Lawrence, and made a protegé of him. Lawrence transposed the dream of freeing a people from Ireland to the Near East, and wrote the story of his struggle in a book to which he gave a title which seemed to promise a sacred book. Many Englishmen who have not had time to open *Seven Pillars of Wisdom* think it is a key to the supreme oriental knowledge. Whereas it is a study of political aspirations and political cynicism which perhaps only a man with mixed Anglo-Irish blood could have written. Discontented with it, he tried again, with the documentary compiled in the light of Joyce's achievement, *The Mint;* and by willing a long delay before its publication he invested it with an apocryphal aura, so that again, as with *Seven Pillars,* the book radiates a legend which its text cannot match. Lawrence had an instinct for all the devices which impress the public with the sacred status of a book, but he never succeeded in making a book which could live up to the impression. Yet his books have their minor merit, and a place on the margin of the Irish achievement—and also on the margin of the English romantic achievement.

Of all the prophets of the Messiah AE was the most persistent. He can be heard foretelling the man of destiny again and again. Here he is, for example, in 1917, advising John Quinn about young Irish poets: "if they are not great, like Yeats, still they all have contributed genuine poetry, and I feel that this confluence of poets means that a great man is going to arise and that we are forerunners or disciples or torch-bearers. I am convinced that in the next few years you will hear of a very big man in Ireland doing great things".

Joyce's *Ulysses* was almost immediately heard of, but AE did not see Joyce as the man he had promised. The Irish were always talking about each other—but jealously and captiously. They jostled each other, all candidates for the role of Messiah or evangelist or leading organiser, whatever exactly it was to be. It has been said that Yeats showed his transcendence from the outset: Katharine Tynan remembered so in 1913; and there is an essay of AE dated 1896 that calls him great. Yet in the 'nineties Yeats was apprehensive that AE might outstrip him. In 1894 the publication of *Homeward* established that poet's claim to equality or near-equality. Lady Gregory summoned both men to take a look at them before making her decision that Yeats was the right candidate for the national laureate and adopting him and devising a programme of special nourishment to power him for the work. It took some years before Yeats was sure that he was safely ahead. After the turn of the century a coldness came between the two poets diminishing what had been their helpfulness to one another. Yeats had by then, it is true, reasons to assail the nature of AE's influence on the younger poets, but that was not the sole condition of his attitude. He was jealous of any near rival. Of a talent at the opposite pole to AE's he was equally jealous and critical: of Shaw's. He was jealous of Moore, and Moore was jealous of him.

ANTI-MATERIALISM

The rivalries in the Irish movement are worth noting, because they illustrate how the men concerned felt they were doing more than writing verse: they were prescribing a course for Ireland, perhaps for the world. So they elevated the jealousies of any literary coterie into the nailing of each other's heresies. But the views they shared, the common stock of thinking from which they developed their different results, are as important as their differences.

It would have been sufficient justification of the Irish struggle for political freedom from England simply to say "We want to be free". The literary movement was curiously uncontent with that. It elaborated a social case as well: England stood for commerce and "materialism", whereas Ireland stood for "imagination and spirituality". The world must support Ireland's freedom-movement, and the Irish must fight the harder for it, because the purity of the imagination, its preservation from the world's slow stain—visibly symbolised in the creeping of industry over the once pretty English rural Midlands—was at stake.

Yeats and AE inherited this argument from the Young Ireland group of the mid-nineteenth century. Davis had been its exponent, and his version of it Yeats and his contemporaries found in Charles Gavan Duffy's *Young Ireland.* That book is a piece of Irish nationalist history remembered and reported after nearly thirty years (thirty years of absence which the extraordinary author had spent in rising to the premiership of Victoria and a British knighthood). "When I was twenty years old", Yeats said, "we all read Gavan Duffy's *Young Ireland,* and then read the Young Ireland poets it had introduced to us." The book had appeared in London in 1880, and in Ireland in 1883. Duffy quoted lengthy passages from Davis, the burthen of which was that Ireland, physically and politically oppressed by Britain, would be finally and irrevocably conquered if she gave up her imaginative integrity by imitating British commercialism.

It is clear that Davis emphasised this thesis as a last stand. He might save the last shred of Irish individuality that way—to save political freedom seemed a remote prospect. When Yeats and AE read him in the 'eighties and took up the cry, they altered its character. They made it a weapon in a renewed Irish drive for liberation. Conditions were propitious to it. First Matthew Arnold and then William Morris had been criticising British materialism from within, had demanded a new scrutiny of the purposes of living and accordingly of the proper way of living, and had detected in the Celtic ethos a principle of spiritual health akin to what they were recommending. Yeats and AE began their work under the immediate influence of Arnold and Morris. AE regarded Arnold as a fount of "vitality and wisdom". Yeats had met Morris in Dublin when he was a boy (Morris had come there to lecture on the Celtic legends, but was disturbed at the unpreparedness of the Irish audience), then gravitated towards him in London. Their authority, and authoritative phrasing, assisted the restatement of the Young Ireland doctrine. Professor John V. Kelleher, who has dealt brilliantly with this subject [in his *Perspectives of Criticism,* 1950], has argued that the whole Irish literary mythos is mainly a borrowing from Arnold's intuitive presentation of the Celtic mind; but in fact, as the material in *Young Ireland* shows, the foundations of the mythos had been laid in the 'forties; the importance of the work of Arnold was to give the young Irishmen the courage to build on them and to make the non-Irish world appreciative of the developments.

It became a convention of the Irish movement that Ireland had kept her spirituality, her contact with the soil and thus her contact with the archetypes, because she had been spared the Roman invasion. There is a typical passage in AE's introduction to *The Wild Bird's Nest, Poems from*

Bernard Shaw.

the Irish, by Frank O'Connor. He argues that the Romans were great builders, but also great destroyers: in England, France, and Spain they obliterated "almost all traces" of the culture which preceded their own; but in Ireland, which they never made part of their empire, "there are rich survivals of . . . the primaeval culture of the imagination". AE wrote that passage as late as 1932, still using the ideas and language of 1900. Their currency in Dublin in 1904 gave Joyce one of his serio-farcical rollicks: measuring the Romans and the English, materialist manufacturers of water-closets, against the Jews and the Irish, builders of altars to Jehovah. Joyce hooted derisively at the Irish claim to spirituality, and yet shared it too. In the early pages of *Ulysses* there is a hint that, before he thought of carrying Europe into Irish literature for the purpose of civilising Ireland, he had imagined himself as carrying Ireland into Europe. He had seen himself as a new St. Columba. Every Irish writer had felt like that. While the French neo-classicists were developing the thesis, later to be taken up by T. S. Eliot, that the tradition which had grown from Attica through Rome into Western Europe was the world's highest achievement and that its continuation was the world's best hope, the Irish were claiming that that tradition was limited and barren, and could only be fertilised by the uncontaminated Irish fancy.

The problem about claims as lofty as the Irish made is that they have to be at least within beckoning distance of reality. Real Ireland contrasted sharply with the spiritual Ireland of the nationalist thesis. It is part of the merit of Anglo-Irish literature, seen as a whole, that it takes account of the contrast and includes a refutation of the "spirituality" claims as well as a statement of them. Side by side with the early imagination-praising pages of Yeats, there are the realistic pages of George Moore describing the peasants brutalised by insecurity and starvation, and Joyce's mockery of the much-vaunted chastity of Ireland, and Sean O'Casey's tenement scenes. These acts of self-criticism were essential, or the Irish would have died of complacency. But there had been, it should be added, a kernel of truth in the myth of spirituality and in the consequent attack on English materialism (an attack which never gave credit to the forces in English literature fighting that materialism). Rural Ireland *did* secrete energy under its filth, for race memories are kept alive by contact with the soil. Literary nationalism got hold of this energy and activated it.

> *Herbert Howarth, "A Myth and a Movement," in his* The Irish Writers, 1880-1940: Literature Under Parnell's Star, *Rockliff, 1958, pp. 1-31.*

Peter Archer

[*Archer is an English barrister who has served as a member of Parliament and has written extensively on socialist themes. In the following essay, Archer discusses Bernard Shaw's political position on Irish independence as expressed in his 1904 play* John Bull's Other Island *and his 1906 "Preface for Politicians."*]

Whatever the respective merits of Shaw and Shakespeare,

the wisdom of the Englishman was manifested by his decision not to write prefaces to his plays, explaining what he meant and enlarging on the implications. If we are looking for a timeless quality, we are more likely to find it in a play than in a preface. *Richard III* may be set firmly in its own period, but it is about ambition and self-delusion, about hubris and nemesis, abstractions which we have with us always.

John Bull's Other Island is Shaw's only systematic treatise on the relations between the respective patrimonies of St. George and St. Patrick, and while the incidents belong to 1904, the themes are timeless. That is not to say that the characters still typify contemporary attitudes. The insensitive arrogance of the upper-middle-class Englishman is now replaced by a bewildered renunciation of any claim to economic or technical preeminence. The assumption of an imperial destiny, held in 1904 even by those who, like Broadbent, ostentatiously renounced it, has been overtaken by a less ambitious resolve to be internationally competitive. The condescension toward foreigners is now simply a characteristic of the Alf Garnetts of this world, the Cockney counterparts of Archie Bunker.

But the self-centered and opinionated complacency of Broadbent is as apparent in the contemporary English yuppie as in the Edwardian man of affairs. The mutually uncomprehending encounter of cultures, the erecting into universal importance of what is merely local and transient, and the seeing in part and prophesying in part are all aspects of the human condition which transcend period.

It is when Shaw composed his 1906 "Preface for Politicians," and wrote expressly of political matters, that he was most obviously a child of his time. It is not that his diagnosis no longer applies. Ireland's condition is depressingly persistent. What has been falsified is his expectation that there could be a simple solution.

He is right in denouncing England's deliberate and repeated sabotage of the Irish economy in order to benefit its own, although more usually the English attitude was one of indifference to distress which was far enough away to be forgotten. The example most frequently cited, the blight of the Irish potato crop in the years from 1845 to 1848, was not brought about by the English government. Indeed, Peel sent a scientific mission to ascertain the causes of the infection, and (of more immediate use) he imported Indian corn. The Whig administration which succeeded him initiated a program of relief work, and even many of the despised landlords contributed to the assistance. But the wheat grown on the best land continued to be exported to England.

Of course, governments in London showed scarcely greater compassion for the sufferings of the poor in England. The outburst of the valet, Hodson, against English landlordism and Irish immigrant labor (evils which for him are inseparably intertwined) is a restrained expression of the bitterness among the underprivileged in the larger island. The difference is that while the English victims had to find a conceptual framework of class politics into which to channel their indignation, the Irish found a ready-made vehicle in the national resentment against the exploiters from over the water.

But the roots of that resentment were not economic. Nor did Shaw pretend that the departure of the last Englishman from Irish soil would ring the death knell of exploitation. Patsy Farrell will be no better off when his Irish neighbors have the ordering of affairs.

Shaw did not identify nationalism with an economic or social program. Indeed, it acted as an antidote to any such program. Nationalism for Shaw is not a crusade for social justice. It is a stage through which a people which perceives itself as enslaved must pass. And all other issues will remain in abeyance until the nationalist aspiration is satisfied.

"A conquered nation," he wrote [in "Preface for Politicians"], "is like a man with cancer: he can think of nothing else, and is forced to place himself, to the exclusion of all better company, in the hands of quacks who profess to treat or cure cancer."

It may be replied that the concept of the conquered nation is flexible. The Welsh do not perceive themselves as a conquered nation. They prefer to see their future as part of Britain and have used their considerable energies to procure for themselves a predominant voice in British politics. They are well represented in the House of Commons, in the Civil Service, and on the High Court Bench. And they have secured what most of them regard as the appropriate measure of regional autonomy, conscious that if they wish to vary the degree, they are in a strong position to do so, provided they themselves are broadly in agreement.

The Scots are largely content to maintain their identity within the United Kingdom, and their periods of doubt are inspired by the severely practical circumstance that they differ politically from the governments repeatedly chosen by the electors of southeast England. The people of Cornwall do not perceive themselves as a nation at all, despite a strong local pride in their ancestry and in their traditions.

Irish nationalism is different. It is reenforced by a number of factors. First is the physical separation of the island from what the English regard as the mainland. Second is the trick of history which, in the sixteenth century, caused the Irish to cling to the old faith while England was led by the sexual proclivities of Henry VIII to the Protestant side of the dispute. It is possible to argue that this was no accident. Most European peoples (or at least their rulers) were choosing between a Mass recited in Latin and one declaimed in their own tongue. For the Irish, the choice was between Latin and English.

It does not follow that, 250 years later, every Irish patriot (even excluding Protestant freethinkers like Shaw) was a submissive child of the Church. Anticlericalism was as widespread as in most other Catholic countries. Financially exploited, intellectually straitjacketed, and socially enthralled, many Irish recognized the Church of Father Dempsey as the Church of Pius IX and Cardinal Cullen. But that is a quarrel within the family. It does not dimin-

ish the gulf which separates even mystics, romantics, and rebels like Keegan from the Protestant ethic.

Of all this Shaw is fully aware, and it is portrayed with an ample measure of Shavian wit. But he saw Irish nationalism as an ephemeral obstacle which, once satisfied, would make way for real political debate in Ireland. When the nationalist aspirations were fulfilled, the Irish would turn their attention to the questions which, for other peoples, constitute the stuff of politics. And Shaw assumed that fulfillment would come with the achievement of home rule.

In his 1906 "Preface for Politicians," he accepted that home rule was the ultimate aspiration of Irish nationalism. He did not envisage that this demand would be overtaken by an insistence on total separation. Sinn Fein did not take the stage until the following year. And there is little doubt that an unconditional offer of home rule would have settled the issue for at least a generation. True, the Irish Republican Brotherhood had other ideas, but such vitality as it possessed was located in America, and its relationship with events or opinions in Ireland was similar to that of Trotsky in exile with everyday life and politics in the Soviet Union. It was the failure to achieve home rule in 1913 that finally discredited the constitutional nationalists, persuaded the new generation of Irish nationalists that the issue must be resolved outside Westminster, and increased the stake to total severance. Even in 1917, Shaw was seeking to warn the Irish that independence was a dangerous snare: "If the English had a pennyworth of political sagacity," he wrote [in his *How to Settle the Irish Question*, 1917], "instead of being, as they are, incorrigible Sinn Feiners almost to the last man, they would long ago have brought the Irish to their senses by threatening them with independence."

Even more significantly, Shaw was no more percipient than any of his contemporaries in foreseeing a divided Ireland. Consequently, he failed to appreciate that when Irish electors gained control of four-fifths of the island, they would not then proceed to debate the issues of social justice, but would simply continue to dispute who was the most implacable enemy of English colonialism. Still less was it predictable that this situation would continue long after the great majority of Irish people ceased to visit, to understand, or to care about the Six Counties.

Shaw was right in insisting that nationalism is not a prescription for paradise. It may or may not be associated with any other aspirations. Irish nationalism has shared few visions with its counterparts in other areas of Europe. Cavour condemned it on the ground that Ireland would be economically better off as part of the United Kingdom. Mazzini rejected it because it expressed no sense of mission or moral purpose for the Irish nation.

Rosa Luxemburg referred to nation-states and nationalism as "empty vessels into which each epoch and the class relations in each particular country pour their particular material content." The tragedy of Ireland is that no one poured in anything. The vessel remains empty. Of course, there are those in Ireland who are anxious to debate real politics. But as the class politics of Connolly and Larkin were never more than minor themes in a symphony about home rule, so the advocates of social justice still remain electorally on the fringe. And in Northern Ireland the energy and passion of political debate are channeled into sterile arguments about constitutional solutions, and those who seek to raise other issues are eventually pressed to declare themselves on the side of Pope or Queen. Conversely, there are those who are primarily nationalist but who sometimes speak the language of class politics. There are elements within Sinn Fein that claim to be Marxist, but the Marxism amounts to little beyond the hijacking of useful economic issues and the insertion as an afterthought of a few buzzwords.

The running sore is of course the existence of the border. And in 1904 it did not occur to anyone that the result of the conflict between an irresistible campaign for home rule and an immovable attachment to the Union Jack would be a divided Ireland which would sterilize the politics of the new freedom and destroy the attachment of the English to the Union.

At the time, the advocates of home rule, encouraged by the active commitment of the Liberal party, saw no reason to compromise. English Unionists were concerned for the integrity of the empire, and they spoke of playing the Orange card not to share the kitty, but to win the game. Ulster Unionists were determined to resist separation not merely for themselves, but for any part of Ireland. When introducing the first Home Rule Bill in 1886, Gladstone had offered to consider whether "Ulster itself, or, perhaps with more appearance of reason, a portion of Ulster, should be excluded from the operation of the Bill," but the offer was not pursued by any of the principal groups concerned.

After 1921, expectations had changed, with the paradoxical consequence that attitudes remained frozen. It was inevitable that when Ireland (or even four-fifths of it) was free, the dreamlike quality of the new age would pass. Throughout the long years of the struggle, the Irish people had been upheld by the belief that with independence would come the solution to all their problems. Whether a free Ireland would return to the romantic world of the past, as the writers of Young Ireland appeared to assume, or whether it would apply an unencumbered mind to resolving economic and social questions, as Shaw hoped, there had appeared little need to consider in advance the solution of practical problems in the golden age. A measure of disillusionment was bound to follow when daily life under the new dispensation was found to be scarcely less pedestrian than before. But while there remained fuel to support the nationalist dream, while it was possible to relegate utopia yet further into the future, the facing of reality could wait.

Of course, Shaw was conscious of the ingredients which were to interact with such fateful consequences. As a part of the Protestant Ascendancy with nationalist sympathies, he delighted in the paradox which associated Catholicism, the creed of authority, of tradition and submission, with revolt, while the Protestants, whose spiritual ancestors had emphasized individualism and the right of protest, supported the establishment.

He was well aware, too, of the importance of mutual caricature in perpetuating a quarrel. He may even have appreciated, though he did not emphasize, that an effective caricature must contain a germ of truth. The Irish Protestant's picture of himself as honest, hardworking, realistic, practical, and successful becomes his rival's caricature of a dour, humorless, unimaginative grafter with no time for the better things of life. The Irish Catholic's self-portrait as an artistic, community-loving, unselfish, and lovably untidy dreamer becomes in the eye of the Prod the exposure of a lazy, feckless, unsuccessful, and untrustworthy good-for-nothing.

This mutual distortion is facilitated by segregation within the educational process. The Catholic church prefers to educate its future generations in Catholic schools. Protestants have no complaint, since this leaves them with a virtual monopoly of the state system. And many young people in Northern Ireland have reached adulthood without once in their lives actually meeting anyone from the other tradition. Shaw spoke of education in Ireland as a hellish training which prolongs "the separation of the Irish people into two hostile camps." At once a consequence and a cause of segregation is the drawing of the "battle lines" which followed the renewal of violence in 1969, when Belfast families living in areas dominated by the other tradition moved away to the safety of homogeneous housing areas.

The natural distortion within Northern Ireland is true to a lesser degree between Irish and English. The misapprehensions between Doyle and Broadbent in *John Bull's Other Island* are amusing and instructive not, as Shaw would persuade us in the Preface, because they represent total self-delusion, but because enshrined within them is a germ, though only a germ, of truth.

Sometimes it is necessary to invent a caricature in order to explain away what would otherwise spoil the argument. Those who seek to understand why Irish Protestants have been so reluctant to accept rule from a Catholic-dominated south are fobbed off with accounts of Catholic social teaching. What Protestant, it is asked, shares the Catholic view of divorce, or contraception, or a national health service? The answer is "most Irish Protestants." The Presbyterians of Ulster have been in total agreement with Catholic teaching on all these subjects, at least throughout most of the period when they have resisted incorporation. Recently, indeed, there has emerged a generation which has questioned such teaching. But equally there have been nationalists who reject it. The issue in Northern Ireland is not individual liberation.

And Shaw was aware of the importance of history in Irish discourse, and specifically of the history which is taught in the respective traditions. The English, who, with an effort, can recall from schooldays the year of the Battle of Hastings, fail totally to understand the number of events of which the least scholarly Irishman can recall the precise dates, and which accordingly are celebrated each year, reviving afresh the passions which were evoked by the original deed.

Of course, the history is sometimes edited, as it is in most educational systems, to exemplify what is required of it. The Battle of the Boyne (1690), celebrated annually by Ulster Protestants, may have been won by predominantly Protestant mercenaries over Catholic ones, but it occasioned great joy to the Pope, who gave thanks for the discomfiture of James's patron, Louis XIV. The tragic Battle of the Somme in 1916 may have cost the lives of virtually an entire Protestant division, but there were as many bereaved Catholic families in Ireland.

Shaw must have known that the events thus remembered are not thought of as history. For the participants, the massacres of Drogheda or of Scullabogue are eternally reenacted. And it is hard for the English, whose island has been relatively free from bloodshed for three centuries, to appreciate how, for the Irish, political violence has rarely been far away, and how martyrdom is a perpetual recognition of the tragedy in the very substance of the Godhead.

But it is not the spoils that matter. It is the waste, the sterilization, the perversion of fruitful brain power into flatulent protest against unnecessary evil, the use of our very entrails to tie our own hands and seal our own lips in the name of our honor and patriotism.

—*Bernard Shaw*

But Shaw had little to say about all this because when he wrote *John Bull's Other Island* in 1904, the dispute appeared to be between Irish and English, not between Taig and Prod. And he believed, rightly, that English Unionism was a temporary phenomenon. Even in 1929, when he wrote a sequel to the 1906 Preface, he failed to appreciate the paralyzing pervasiveness of the sectarian division within Ireland. He argued that by cutting off the industrial economy of the northeast from the conservative influence of the agricultural areas, the employers in Ulster had deprived themselves of their allies against the growing power of the working class. And he concluded that they would be driven to seek a federal government embracing the two parts of Ireland.

This is a thesis which he first set out in *How to Settle the Irish Question* in 1917, and he was still arguing it in 1950 when, six months before his death, he wrote to Sean O'Casey,

> Now we are an insignificant cabbage garden in a little islet quite out of the headlines; and our Fianna Fail Party is now The Unionist Party and doesn't know it. I have nothing to tell them except that the Ulster capitalists will themselves abolish the Partition when the Labor [*sic*] Party is strong enough to threaten them with an Irish 1945 at the polls, and they must have the support of the Catholic agricultural south to avert it.

What still eluded him was the persistent stranglehold of the rival nationalisms upon the industrial workers to whom he looked for a political initiative. The employers of Ulster still sleep easy in their beds, or at least their anxieties are not evoked by any demand among their workforce for a more substantial share of the profits. The trade unions are too busy coping with potentially divisive cultural conflict, and the electorate continues to listen to sectarian rallying cries.

Perhaps Shaw's greatest contribution to the discussion is his exposure of the uncomprehending, flat-footed, hazily indignant reaction of the English to Irish affairs. In 1904 he was devastatingly derisive of the clumsy devices adopted by the English to maintain their colonial rule. And even before Protestant nationalism became a coherent political force, he had stripped away the claim of the English to serve as an honest broker.

In other parts of the world, they had rejoiced in the role of arbitrator between bickering factions. But the English were dealing with peoples who, at that time, had few aspirations to democracy. In a country which aspired not only to self-government but to representative government, the uninvited umpire was a nonstarter.

Shaw dismissed the suggestion on two distinct grounds. First, the roles of judge and governor are inconsistent: "For there is only one condition on which a man can do justice between two litigants, and that is that he shall have no interest in common with either of them, whereas it is only by having every interest in common with both of them that he can govern them tolerably." The very lack of sympathetic understanding of, or interest in, Irish affairs which might have qualified the English to help negotiate a final settlement of the dispute was their gravest disqualification from governing any part of Ireland in a continuing situation.

But, second, England had hardly presented itself as just and principled in its dealings with Ireland. And the more complicated the situation has become since 1904, the more tragic its consequences, the less consistent have become the turns and twists of the English as they grab at any solution. The one theme on which the people of both traditions in Northern Ireland are in complete agreement is that it is pointless to address to the English a principled argument relating to the merits. Ultimately, they insist, the English will opt for the line of least resistance. They will succumb to the most troublesome and most immediate threat.

In the 1929 Postscript Shaw returned to the theme of English ineptitude with the additional ammunition provided by the Government's response to the Easter Rising. But he failed to foresee where it would lead. With only one other party to the dialogue, there remained hope that more rational voices in England would prevail, and that a little goodwill and tolerance might resolve the problem. But confronted by two deeply entrenched and internecine forces, each dedicated to resisting any concession to the other, the English were out of their depth.

The purpose of English policy in Ireland has changed since 1904. The hope then was that, by being granted home rule, Ireland would be satisfied to remain politically a part of the British Isles and content to be shown as red on the map. Today, England's most fervent hope is to find a way of abdicating further involvement with the quarrels of Ireland. It is a policy of disengagement. The debate about the border is perceived as a dialogue of the deaf, and the search for a peaceful solution as a quest for an illusion. Northern Ireland is seen largely as a security problem, and England's policy has become an exercise in crisis management.

The difficulty is how to leave without unleashing a bloodbath and how to disengage without being seen to back away in the face of violence, and so encourage terrorism. It would be unfair not to add that the English pride themselves still on their sense of justice and their real compassion for the Irish people, and that they would be reluctant to admit that they had departed with no heed for the consequences for all the people of Northern Ireland. The Irish perception of England's unprincipled convolutions, like every other aspect of the relationship, is a mixture of truth and caricature.

But what Shaw could not be expected to foresee are the consequences of the subsequent troubles for the three generations in Ireland who have known little else. Their experiences have changed the very nature of Ireland. No one purporting to write about the country in the last decade of the twentieth century would have written *John Bull's Other Island,* nor yet a treatise like the 1906 "Preface for Politicians," even together with its Postscripts.

Shaw recorded in the 1906 Preface that the play was produced in London rather than at the Irish Literary Theatre, for which it was written, because "It was uncongenial to the whole spirit of the neo-Gaelic movement, which is bent on creating a new Ireland after its own ideal, whereas my play is a very uncompromising presentment of the real old Ireland."

Yeats and O'Leary, Davis and Hyde undoubtedly altered the course of Irish history. The old Ireland was destined to change. But they were not to foresee the Ireland which they helped to conjure. Ideas change reality, but the changes are not necessarily reflections of the ideas, for the ideas need to activate the men of deeds, and they are by definition different from the scholars.

Even of them it can be said that they knew not what they did. Those who seek political aims by violence fail all too often to realize that bloodshed easily becomes an end in itself. It is a way of life which gradually loses its relationship with the original objective. And even where it is successful, it changes and distorts its own purpose. The analogy is not of a destination with violence as only one option among the various routes. The destination itself is destroyed.

A peaceful, free, and united Ireland cannot be achieved by violence, repression, and division. Violence leads only to further violence. An outrage is requited with a further outrage, and that in turn with the next. For the patriot, the original vision is lost. For the community, life becomes a nightmare of perpetual anxiety and fear.

The violence discourages economic investment, and the distortion of political debate perpetuates the deprivation. The result is to provide paramilitaries with a source of resentful, frustrated, and frequently unemployed potential recruits. And there has evolved a class of godfathers whose power, prestige, and prosperity depend upon perpetuating the rival paramilitary systems, and therefore the divisions, the myths, and the hatred which nourish them.

Only those who see bloodshed from a safe distance can long entertain illusions about its romance or its purifying qualities. Shaw in a cynical mood had replied to those who warned of bloodshed if the English withdrew from Ireland that "civil war is one of the privileges of a nation." He added, "if hatred, calumny and terror have so possessed men that they cannot live in peace as other nations do, they had better fight it out and get rid of their bad blood that way."

It is doubtful whether this was ever more than an exercise in shocking the English. As early as 1903, when he wrote his Preface to "The Revolutionist's Handbook" (added as an appendix to the text of *Man and Superman*), he dismissed political violence as futile. Having conceded that improvement was unlikely to come about through persuasion, he continued:

> I make a present of all these admissions to the Fenian who collects money from thoughtless Irishmen in America to blow up Dublin Castle; to the detective who persuades foolish young workmen to order bombs from the nearest ironmonger and then delivers them up to penal servitude. . . . But of what use is it to substitute the way of the reckless and bloodyminded for the way of the cautious and humane? . . .
>
> No: what Caesar, Cromwell and Napoleon could not do with all the physical force and moral prestige of the State in their mighty hands, cannot be done by enthusiastic criminals and lunatics.

It has to be admitted that this denunciation of political violence stemmed (ostensibly at least) from a developing conviction that eugenics was more helpful than politics as a method of improving the world. Already in 1903 Shaw was beginning to despair of the human material with which politicians have of necessity to work. His contribution to the debate might have been more effective had he used his dramatic genius to expose the tragedy and ugliness of political violence.

In *Saint Joan,* he tore away the euphemisms from physical suffering. After de Stogumber, who had called throughout for the burning of Joan and had been driven mad by the reality when he saw it, indicates in the Epilogue that he has become a different man as a result, Cauchon asks, "Must then a Christ perish in torment in every age to save those that have no imagination?" It is a question which he might well have asked of Ireland in the twentieth century.

But perhaps it would have been demanding too much to expect that Shaw should have appreciated the reality of the continuing, apparently endless conflict in Northern Ireland. If he could have done so, would he have resigned himself to the belief that nothing can improve the world except the gradual evolution of a superior race? Fortunately, there are those who believe that hope still lies in the real human beings whose actions will determine the foreseeable future. Shortsighted, prejudiced, arrogant, and aggressive as we are, we may yet not be past redeeming. And if there is a suffering remnant to whom there may be vouchsafed a redeeming insight into the human condition, it may well be the Irish.

Peter Archer, "Shaw and the Irish Question," in SHAW, Vol. 11, 1991, pp. 119-30.

Bernard Shaw

[*Generally considered the greatest and best-known dramatist to write in the English language since Shakespeare, Shaw determined that the theater was to be a "moral institution" and an "elucidator of social conduct," whose themes would reflect society as it is, and provide suggestions for what it should be. In the following excerpt from his treatise on Irish independence, "Preface for Politicians," Shaw, an ardent socialist, argues against the "curse of nationalism," but claims that Ireland has simply a natural right to govern itself.*]

A conquered nation is like a man with cancer: he can think of nothing else, and is forced to place himself, to the exclusion of all better company, in the hands of quacks who profess to treat or cure cancer. The windbags of the two rival platforms are the most insufferable of all windbags. It requires neither knowledge, character, conscience, diligence in public affairs, nor any virtue, private or communal, to thump the Nationalist or Orange tub: nay, it puts a premium on the rancor or callousness that has given rise to the proverb that if you put an Irishman on a spit you can always get another Irishman to baste him. Jingo oratory in England is sickening enough to serious people: indeed one evening's mafficking in London produced a determined call for the police. Well, in Ireland all political oratory is Jingo oratory; and all political demonstrations are maffickings. English rule is such an intolerable abomination that no other subject can reach the people. Nationalism stands between Ireland and the light of the world. Nobody in Ireland of any intelligence likes Nationalism any more than a man with a broken arm likes having it set. A healthy nation is as unconscious of its nationality as a healthy man of his bones. But if you break a nation's nationality it will think of nothing else but getting it set again. It will listen to no reformer, to no philosopher, to no preacher, until the demand of the Nationalist is granted. It will attend to no business, however vital, except the business of unification and liberation.

That is why everything is in abeyance in Ireland pending the achievement of Home Rule. The great movements of the human spirit which sweep in waves over Europe are stopped on the Irish coast by the English guns of the Pigeon House Fort. Only a quaint little offshoot of English pre-Raphaelitism called the Gaelic movement has got a footing by using Nationalism as a stalking-horse, and popularizing itself as an attack on the native language of the Irish people, which is most fortunately also the native language of half the world, including England. Every election is fought on nationalist grounds; every appointment is made on nationalist grounds; every judge is a partisan in the nationalist conflict; every speech is a dreary recapitulation of nationalist twaddle; every lecture is a corruption of history to flatter nationalism or defame it; every school is a recruiting station; every church is a barrack; and every Irishman is unspeakably tired of the whole miserable business, which nevertheless is and perforce must remain his first business until Home Rule makes an end of it, and sweeps the nationalist and the garrison back together into the dustbin.

There is indeed no greater curse to a nation than a nationalist movement, which is only the agonizing symptom of a suppressed natural function. Conquered nations lose their place in the world's march because they can do nothing but strive to get rid of their nationalist movements by recovering their national liberty. All demonstrations of the virtues of a foreign government, though often conclusive, are as useless as demonstrations of the superiority of artificial teeth, glass eyes, silver windpipes, and patent wooden legs to the natural products. Like Democracy, national self-government is not for the good of the people: it is for the satisfaction of the people. One Antonine emperor, one St Louis, one Richelieu, may be worth ten democracies in point of what is called good government; but there is no satisfaction for the people in them. To deprive a dyspeptic of his dinner and hand it over to a man who can digest it better is a highly logical proceeding; but it is not a sensible one. To take the government of Ireland away from the Irish and hand it over to the English on the ground that they can govern better would be a precisely parallel case if the English had managed their own affairs so well as to place their superior faculty for governing beyond question. But as the English are avowed muddlers—rather proud of it, in fact—even the logic of that case against Home Rule is not complete. Read Mr Charles Booth's account of London, Mr Rowntree's account of York, and the latest official report on Dundee; and then pretend, if you can, that Englishmen and Scotchmen have not more cause to hand over their affairs to an Irish parliament than to clamor for another nation's cities to devastate and another people's business to mismanage.

The question is not one of logic at all, but of natural right. English universities have for some time past encouraged an extremely foolish academic exercise which consists in disproving the existence of natural rights on the ground that they cannot be deduced from the principles of any known political system. If they could, they would not be natural rights but acquired ones. Acquired rights are deduced from political constitutions; but political constitutions are deduced from natural rights. When a man insists on certain liberties without the slightest regard to demonstrations that they are not for his own good, nor for the public good, nor moral, nor reasonable, nor decent, nor compatible with the existing constitution of society, then he is said to claim a natural right to that liberty. When, for instance, he insists on living, in spite of the irrefutable demonstrations of many able pessimists, from the author of the book of Ecclesiastes to Schopenhauer, that life is an evil, he is asserting a natural right to live. When he insists on a vote in order that his country may be governed according to his ignorance instead of the wisdom of the

Privy Council, he is asserting a natural right to self-government. When he insists on guiding himself at 21 by his own inexperience and folly and immaturity instead of by the experience and sagacity of his father, or the well-stored mind of his grandmother, he is asserting a natural right to independence. Even if Home Rule were as unhealthy as an Englishman's eating, as intemperate as his drinking, as filthy as his smoking, as licentious as his domesticity, as corrupt as his elections, as murderously greedy as his commerce, as cruel as his prisons, and as merciless as his streets, Ireland's claim to self-government would still be as good as England's. King James the First proved so cleverly and conclusively that the satisfaction of natural rights was incompatible with good government that his courtiers called him Solomon. We, more enlightened, call him Fool, solely because we have learnt that nations insist on being governed by their own consent—or, as they put it, by themselves and for themselves—and that they will finally upset a good government which denies them this even if the alternative be a bad government which at least creates and maintains an illusion of democracy. America, as far as one can ascertain, is much worse governed, and has a much more disgraceful political history than England under Charles I; but the American Republic is the stabler government because it starts from a formal concession of natural rights, and keeps up an illusion of safeguarding them by an elaborate machinery of democratic election. And the final reason why Ireland must have Home Rule is that she has a natural right to it.

Bernard Shaw, " 'John Bull's Other Island': Preface for Politicians," in his Complete Plays with Prefaces, Vol. II, *Dodd, Mead & Company, 1962, pp. 443-502.*

FURTHER READING

Arnold, Matthew. "The Incompatibles." In his *English Literature and Irish Politics,* pp. 238-85. Ann Arbor: The University of Michigan Press, 1973.

    Presents Arnold's thoughts on the issue of Irish independence.

Corkery, Daniel. "On Anglo-Irish Literature." In his *Synge and Anglo-Irish Literature,* pp. 1-27. 1931. Reprint. New York: Russell & Russell Inc., 1965.

    Examines Anglo-Irish writing, suggesting that it is neither a "normal" nor a national literature.

Deane, Seamus. *Celtic Revivals: Essays in Modern Irish Literature, 1880-1980.* London: Faber and Faber, 1985, 199 p.

    Contains numerous essays regarding elements of nationalism and Celticism in Irish literature.

Duffy, Charles Gavan. "The Revival of Irish Literature." In *The Revival of Irish Literature: Addresses by Sir Charles Gavan Duffy, K.C.M.G., Dr. George Sigerson, and Dr. Douglas Hyde,* pp. 9-60. 1894. Reprint. New York: Lemma Publishing Corporation, 1973.

    Comprises two lectures given before the Irish Literary Society in 1892 and 1893. Duffy advocates embracing Irish culture, as well as a formal Irish education for the people of Ireland.

Flanagan, Thomas. "Nationalism: The Literary Tradition." In *Perspectives on Irish Nationalism,* edited by Thomas E. Hachey and Lawrence J. McCaffrey, pp. 61-78. Lexington: The University Press of Kentucky, 1989.

    Discusses Irish nationalism as it was embodied in the literary tradition, particularly in the histories of the Abbe MacGeoghegan and John Mitchel and the poetry of Samuel Ferguson and W. B. Yeats.

Hyde, Douglas. *A Literary History of Ireland.* London: T. Fisher Unwin, 1899, 654 p.

    Presents "a general view of the literature produced by the Irish-speaking Irish," and discusses some salient features of that body of work.

———. "What Ireland Is Asking For." In *Ideals in Ireland,* edited by Lady Gregory, pp. 53-61. 1901. Reprint. New York: AMS Press, 1978.

    Criticizes the English school system established in nineteenth-century Ireland, contending that the schools "killed the mind of the country."

Krans, Horatio Sheafe. *William Butler Yeats and the Irish Literary Revival.* New York: McClure, Phillips & Co., 1904, 196 p.

    Discusses the works of W. B. Yeats, specifically in regards to the revival movement in Irish literature.

Lee, Joseph. *The Modernisation of Irish Society, 1848-1918.* Dublin: Gill and Macmillan, 1973, 180 p.

    Includes a discussion of the Celtic revival movement.

McCaffrey, Lawrence J. *The Irish Question, 1800-1922.* Lexington: University of Kentucky Press, 1968, 202 p.

    A broad study of Anglo-Irish relations throughout the nineteenth century. McCaffrey asserts that "rural Ireland contained the necessary spiritual energy" to drive the Celtic movement both politically and artistically.

Raine, Kathleen. Introduction to *The Celtic Twilight,* by William Butler Yeats, pp. 7-29. Gerrards Cross, England: Colin Smythe Limited, 1981.

    Discusses the role of Irish myth and folklore in Yeats's early works.

Snyder, Thomas S. "Matthew Arnold and the Irish Question." *The Arnoldian* 4, No. 2 (Winter 1977): 12-20.

    Details Arnold's opinions of and involvement in Ireland's attempt to establish a national identity.

Travel Writing in the Nineteenth Century

INTRODUCTION

The nineteenth century is recognized as the great era of travel literature. British imperial expansion in the East, the New World in the West, and archaeological discoveries in Italy and elsewhere summoned visitors to foreign sites in ever increasing numbers. Seeking to appease the demands of curious readers hungry for adventure and escape, publishers printed hundreds of diaries and other narratives recording the journeys of both prominent and relatively unknown travelers alongside the more ambitious chronicles of scientists, explorers, and journalists. These personal accounts commonly feature an intimate, first-person narrative and informal, nostalgic style that greatly appealed to nineteenth-century readers. Travel journals have therefore been compared with the autobiography as forms of reflective testimonial. Modern historians and students of literature presently value these writings as works of social history, exploring in particular their manifestations of nationalist and imperialist thought.

The most noteworthy of nineteenth-century travel accounts are those describing journeys in the Orient and in North America. The British, the French, and, to a lesser extent, the Germans, had historically been great colonial powers in Africa, the Near East, India, and Southeast Asia. During the nineteenth century educated upper- and middle-class Europeans were visiting these colonial possessions in swelling numbers, frequently remaining for many years. Avant-garde artists and writers rejected European cultural values, seeking to immerse themselves in an exotic culture outside the Western tradition. The more numerous travelers, however, were the European colonials, many of whom took up residence, usually with their entire households, in the arid climates of Egypt or the Near East for health reasons. The written perceptions of these colonials vividly reveal the simultaneous attraction and repulsion that many nineteenth-century Europeans felt for the East, and commentators have noted the dynamics of dominance and submission revealed in the confrontation of the two highly developed cultures. The accounts of North American travel, by contrast, take the reader into a realm of territorial exploration and expansion within a continent that was still largely wilderness and unsettled prairie, focusing on the magnitude and sublimity of the North American landscape.

Some of the greatest writers of the nineteenth century, including Stendhal, John Ruskin, and Henry James, crafted travel works that manipulated the traditional touring descriptions in innovative ways, using a third-person narrator, for example, or fictionalizing their accounts to create deliberate, thought-provoking ambiguity. These, along with the many compelling accounts written by less well-known figures, are recognized as uniquely enriching to nineteenth-century studies, elucidating the social and cultural values of those who participated in European colonialism and the expansion of the American frontier.

REPRESENTATIVE WORKS

Birkbeck, Morris
  Notes of a Journey in America 1817
Burton, Sir Richard Francis
  Pilgrimage to El-Medinah and Mecca 1855-56
  First Footsteps in East Africa 1856
Byron, George Gordon, Lord
  Childe Harold's Pilgrimage 1812
Dickens, Charles
  American Notes for General Circulation 1842
  Pictures from Italy 1846
Doughty, Charles
  Travels in Arabia Deserta 1888
Gautier, Théophile
  Voyage en Espagne 1845
  Voyage en Italie 1852
Howe, Julia Ward
  A Trip to Cuba 1860
  From the Oak to the Olive: Records of a Pleasant Journey 1868
Irving, Washington
  The Sketch Book of Geoffrey Crayon, Gent. 1819-20
James, Henry
  A Little Tour in France 1884
Jameson, Anna Brownell
  The Diary of an Ennuyée 1826
  Winter Studies and Summer Rambles in Canada 1838
Kinglake, Alexander W.
  Eothen; or, Traces of Travel Brought Home from the East 1844
Murray, John
  Handbook for Travellers in the Ionian Isles, Greece, etc. 1840
Nerval, Gérard de
  Voyage en Orient 1851
Ruskin, John
  Ruskin's Letters from Venice, 1851-52 1955
  Ruskin in Italy: Letters to His Parents, 1845 1972
  A Tour to the Lakes in Cumberland: John Ruskin's Diary for 1830 1990
Stendhal
  Rome, Naples et Florence en 1817 1826
  Promenades dans Rome 1829
  Mémoires d'un touriste 1838

Stevenson, Robert Louis
  An Inland Voyage   1878
  Travels with a Donkey in the Cévennes   1879
Stowe, Harriet Beecher
  Sunny Memories of Foreign Lands   1854
Thackeray, William Makepeace
  *Notes of a Journey from Cornhill to Grand Cairo
  by Michel Angelo Titmarsh*   1846
Trollope, Anthony
  North America   1862
Trollope, Frances Milton
  Domestic Manners of the Americans   1832
Twain, Mark
  The Innocents Abroad; or, The New Pilgrim's Progress
  1869

THE EUROPEAN GRAND TOUR

Ahmed M. Metwalli

[*In the following excerpt, Metwalli discusses reasons for the popularity of nineteenth-century American travel writing about Europe.*]

Almost every prominent American literary figure of the nineteenth century has written one type or another of travel book or based some of his literary output on his experiences of travel in foreign lands. And yet the travel literature of the century has not been adequately studied and, so far, books of travel have never been universally accepted as a literary genre. More than twenty years ago, Thomas H. Johnson underscored the undeserved neglect that was and still is the lot of this genre: "And discussion of the literature written to interpret foreign countries," said Johnson, "must at present be very incomplete, for few investigations of the subject have been undertaken" [quoted in *The Literary History of the United States,* 1963]. Yet the value of this literature in interpreting the Old World to America in the nineteenth century, especially on the level of popular interest, the vital role it played in mass culture, and the impact it had on some cultural trends of the century cannot be overestimated.

The "cultural" orientation of the age was responsible for the increased production and dissemination of books of travel. During the nineteenth century, almost every literate and zealous traveler managed to avail himself of one or more, and sometimes all, public media, to excite, entertain, or instruct the masses with his own experiences in foreign lands. Public lectures in the increasingly popular Lyceums, serialized travel letters, serialized articles, and books were available organs of expression. The romantic adventurer, the explorer, the missionary, the merchant or mercantile agent, the diplomatic and military envoy, as well as the man of letters, were all able to reach and influence the public in one way or another.

The interest and avidity of a reading public aware of its deficiency in knowledge and information encouraged this kind of composition. The cultural milieu was certainly ripe. Moreover, since it was the fashionable thing to do and also the most lucrative financially, almost every individual who left home—even for a hike in the mountains—committed his impressions and experiences to paper and inflicted them on the reading public. Most of these producers of travel yarns lacked what Matthew Arnold calls "the power of the man," which, combined with "the power of the moment," produces a work of literary merit. The very few nineteenth-century travelers who possessed this "power" and who concern us here, were submerged in an interminable sea of mediocrity. And though their travel books were instrumental in the ultimate shaping and vitality of their literary artistic lives, these books were engulfed in oblivion—the oblivion which is almost always the destiny of whatever is written for the level of popular rather than intellectual interest—by the indiscriminate and uncritical taste of the contemporary reading public which made an instant success of almost every travel book.

All kinds of books of travel, a large number of which were mere hasty collections of unedited letters or article serials, sold by the tens of thousands. Many ran into tens of reprints and were in constant demand for decades after their first publication. Because they almost always succeeded in satisfying the immediate cultural and nationalistic needs of the reading public, they were among the best sellers of the day. Publishers encouraged authors to write accounts of their travel experiences at home and abroad; they knew well that travel narratives needed very little promotion and almost no puffing. Six editions of Bayard Taylor's first book of travels, *Views Afoot,* plublished in 1846 when he was barely twenty years old, were sold in the first year; and in less than a decade twenty editions were printed. His royalties from *Journey to Central Africa* (August, 1854) and *The Lands of the Saracens* (October, 1858), had mounted to $2,650 by the first of the new year. He must have anticipated the success of his volumes of travel and the sums that would accrue from their immediate sale. Attuned to the needs and demands of the reading public, Taylor, in a casual and business-like manner, stated in the preface to the first edition of his second volume of travel, *Journey to Central Africa,* that his "reasons for offering this volume to the public are, simply, that there is room for it." Indeed, there was "room" enough not only for his personal accounts, but for a *Cyclopedia of Modern Travel* and a whole *Illustrated Library of Travel,* both of which he edited.

Nor was this instant success and popular favor Bayard Taylor's lot alone. The travel books of other literary figures were similarly, if not as spectacularly, blessed. The first edition of 2,500 copies of George William Curtis's book, *Nile Notes of Howadji* (1851) was exhausted within six months. His second book, *Howadji in Syria* (1852), met with the same success. Significantly, the sale of Melville's books declined as he moved away from the domain of popular travel literature which he had considered at the onset of his career to be his literary field. The first edition of some 3,000 copies of *Omoo* (1847), which is a melange of fact and fiction based on Melville's travel adventures in the South Seas, was selling out so rapidly in its first week of publication that a new printing was immediately planned. On the other hand, the more intellectual and subtle *Moby Dick* (1851) sold only 2,500 copies in its first five years, and only 2,965 in its first twenty.

Emerson was also graced by this same popular favor. The first printing of 3,000 copies of his *English Traits* (1856), which is actually more an essay in cultural anthropology dealing with ideas and institutions than a travel book of intinerant wanderings and recorded experiences, sold immediately. Within a month, a second edition of 2,000 copies was printed. Mark Twain's *The Innocents Abroad* (1869) established his fame as a popular author. A little over thirty thousand copies were sold during the first five months after publication, and by the end of the first year 67,000 copies were bought at $3.50 each.

The demand for travel literature was not restricted to the printed word. Lyceums and the popular lectures which grew out of the Lyceum system were other media used by travelers to entertain, instruct and satisfy the curiosity of the public about ancient and faraway places. Enterprising lecture booking-agents, such as James Redpath and his successor, James B. Pond, guided and catered to the needs and tastes of the new national audience; and travelers and travel writers were their most profitable assets. Much could be learned about the popularity of travel literature from the fact that while Emerson could earn as much as $2,000 for a season of lecturing after a considerable effort, Bayard Taylor often made $5,000 from his travel lectures. These travel lectures were derived mostly from the lecturer's own travel journal or book; sometimes, the lecture room functioned as a useful proving ground for materials intended for publication. In either case, the lecture podium was utilized by the travelers to promote their already available or forthcoming travel books, augmenting their sales considerably.

These figures provide us with ample evidence of the phenomenal popularity of travel literature. But the question that needs to be answered is why were nineteenth-century books of travel the best sellers of their time?

Geared for the masses, popular literature in all its infinite variety—and American popular literature included such diverse types as travel books, tall tales of the Near and Far East and the American West, sea-lore adventures, popular journals and magazines, almanacs, dime or best-selling novels—mirrors the intellectual complex of an age, reflecting its ideas, activities, and motivations to action; in short, it sums up its culture. It also reveals the "cultural dialects" which may exist side by side in the writings of representative men in any given period, and which may appear, especially if divested of their historical and intellectual contexts, as puzzling or paradoxical. Arthur E. Christy aptly described popular literature as the "weathercock which points the direction of all winds of opinion that blow" [*The Asian Legacy and American Life*, 1945]. An understanding of these "winds of opinion" is essential in comprehending the *raison d'etre* of the bulk and popularity of books of travel in the nineteenth century. It was the remarkable increase in the number of travel books as the century progressed that prompted James Grant Wilson to note in 1886 that "American books of Old World travel" were appearing in "battalions." Stanley

Williams [in his *Spanish Background of American Literature*, 1955] pointed out the necessity of tracing the real roots of this phenomenal growth and popularity of travel books, which rivaled those of history and fiction, when he observed:

> To ascribe the increase of travel books, expanding from a rivulet at the beginning of the century to a gigantic river at its close, to the growing number of travelers and these to the enlarged facilities of transportation is too simple a logic.

The not too simple logic behind the phenomenal growth and popularity of travel books could be traced to two seemingly opposed traits in the American temperament, which were markedly reflected in the American literary scene. The one was the conscious need for a past with its established values, institutional continuity, and stable traditions. The other was a similarly strong conscious need for national identity and the establishment of the definable American "Self," the creation of the "New Adam" entirely based on the exclusively American vistas of democratic experience. The pull of the past and the push of the present formed the nucleus of this double consciousness, and most travel books of the nineteenth century did indeed embody it.

Culturally, America was still an unhistorical land, a land which had neither a childhood replete with romantically lovable experiences nor a youth confirmed in exemplary patterns. The short historical past that the Americans possessed was not yet crystallized in terms of popular "traditions" or "myths," which are needed psychologically for man's sense of stability. A large number of Americans who were entering upon the life of the mind for the first time during the first half of the nineteenth century had a strong romantic bent. This bent expressed itself in a serious interest in the past, in faraway places, and in the vast treasures of knowledge that they contained. The strong obsession with the past was partially, yet vehemently, stirred by the public's acute consciousness of the wide chasm that separated it from old stable traditions. A large segment of the new reading public was aware of what it lacked and also was concerned about the danger of both intellectual and cultural insularity that 3,000 miles of ocean could lead to. The measure of the awareness and concern of this new class evinced itself in the response of the literary figures. American men of letters were obliged to satisfy the needs of increasing millions of new readers. Lacking a past, the literary figures in the United States had to look to the other side of the Atlantic and more often than not cross the Atlantic itself in their endeavor to meet their obligations. Inevitably, the development and growth of an indigenous literature were hampered in proportion to the success of the literary figures in their attempts to satisfy these needs; for the outcome was largely a derivative literature.

The strong need for national identity and the desire to trace and establish an identifiable American "Self" was the other facet of this double consciousness. It had its roots in the political experiment of the new nation, which demanded a break with the past and an assertion of the sovereignty of the present. Such sentiment was forcibly conveyed in the declamation of the *Democratic Review* in 1839: "Our national birth was the beginning of a new history . . . which separates us from the past and connects us with the future only." Declamations like this had their repercussions in the literary scene; and as R.W.B. Lewis has pointed out [in his *American Adam: Innocence, Tragedy, and Tradition in the Nineteenth Century,* 1965], such "a manifesto of liberation from the past" meant a more vigorous demand "for an independent literature to communicate the novelty of experience in the New World."

Furthermore, since the beginning of the century, the question of a native literature was constantly confused with the issue of patriotism; and patriotism was rampant in a nation that had won its political independence only a few decades earlier, and whose viability was further tested in the War of 1812. In the eighteen twenties and early thirties the British reviews, the *Quarterly* and *Blackwood's,* carried on a campaign of invective in which they "decried and insulted America as a barbarous land," intending, as Van Wyck Brooks remarked, to "discourage emigration and arouse a republicanism in the rising English masses." Accounts written by English travelers who visited America in the eighteen thirties and forties contributed to igniting the patriotic zeal of Americans, for a goodly number of these accounts depicted the new nation as uncouth and vulgar. Americans were hypersensitive to criticisms leveled against them in such books as Mrs. Frances Trollope's *Domestic Manners of the Americans* (1832), Harriet Martineau's *Society in America* (1837), Captain Marryat's *A Diary in America* (1837), and, the unkindest of them all, Charles Dickens' *American Notes* (1842). These and various other accounts of travelers nurtured what Washington Irving termed "the literary animosity daily growing up between England and America." To him, as to most of his contemporaries, these accounts seemed "intended to diffuse error rather than knowledge" [*The Sketch Book,* 1893]. Such unfair treatment of the new nation by the British reviews and travelers confirmed patriotic Americans in their detestation of the imitative quality of their literature, and in their rejection of what they regarded as toadying to the Old World, and especially to England.

But despite Emerson's teachings, particularly in "The American Scholar," and the zeal of such representative Americans as Bryant, Thoreau and Whitman, most men of letters persisted in relying on European ideas, literary traditions and intellectual habits as sources of inspiration. They realized that the total American experience had no rich local accumulation of character, legend or lore, sufficient to ignite originality or sustain the creative imagination. To be sure, such figures as Irving, Cooper and Hawthorne were indubitably successful in their determination to grasp the "usable truth" defined by F. L. Matthiessen as "the actual meaning of civilization as it had existed in America"; yet they were nonetheless aware of the scantiness of native sources and frequently voiced their concern.

Nineteenth-century authors' awareness of the lack in America of what Henry James called "the items of high civilization" was rendered much more acute by their sense of obligation to satisfy the need of the growing reading public for knowledge and for a romantic past with all its traditions. Since the past could not be invented, most of the authors persisted in facing eastward, in borrowing and recreating. Similarly, since "items of civilization" could not be imported, most men of letters crossed the Atlantic to plunder the riches of old-world cultures.

Almost all of the well-known American authors of the nineteenth century traveled extensively: Irving, Bryant, Cooper, Hawthorne, Dana, Melville, Emerson, Longfellow, Howells, DeForest, Lowell, Mark Twain, Bret Harte, Henry Adams, James, Crane—and this is only a partial list of major writers. It does not include authors who were well known and influential during their lifetime but who are regarded now as minor: N. P. Willis, John Lloyd Stephens, George William Curtis, Bayard Taylor, Charles Dudley Warner, Charles Warren Stoddard—to mention only a few. As travelers they were all in a sense pilgrims on a quest—a quest for both knowledge and experience.

However, there was the other facet of the double consciousness that characterized the American temperament throughout the century, namely, the patriotic, the conscious need for national identity and the assertion of the rising American "Self," which paradoxically enough regarded dependence on Europe and the Old World as sycophantic and unpatriotic, and demanded dispensing with the past and all that it connoted. The American men of letters found themselves caught in a dilemma. On the intellectual and literary level the dilemma emanated from this double consciousness could not be resolved. Despite the growing utilization of native materials, literary traditions and forms remained largely foreign. It was on the popular level and most notably in the multifarious forms of the travel book that the American author was able to resolve the dilemma. No other literary genre was as successful as the travel book in providing the author with a medium by means of which he could fulfill some of his literary and personal aspirations, and, most importantly, the conflicting demands of this double consciousness.

Written chiefly for those who, in Bayard Taylor's words, "can only travel by their fireside"—and most Americans, especially in the years before and during the Civil War, were unable to enjoy the pleasure of foreign travel—the travel book, in its fluid, undefined shape enabled its author to give the growing reading masses what they needed, when they needed it. Everything that was old enchanted Americans. They shared this romantic bent with their European counterparts of the first half of the nineteenth century; yet the enchantment of Americans was more poignant and lasted longer because their country was all so new. They cherished the relics of the European past, the memories and culture of their "Old Home." The newness of their country was an underlying factor in the persistence, almost permanence, of an important ingredient of the romantic movement throughout the century, namely the craving for remoteness both in space and time. The hunger of the reading public for every crumb of knowledge about the lands of the oldest civilizations was satisfied by the vicarious tours of these lands. To the average American the words of the travelers who had beheld with their own eyes the ancient sites of London, Paris, Rome,

Constantinople, the Holy Land or Cairo were more authentic than the words of the poets, historians or translators which were secondhand and remote. And as Willard Thorp has pointed out, even amateur travelers "often returned home better instructed than the scholars and critics whose profession it was to interpret European civilization" [quoted in *Literary History of the United States*].

The authentic element in books of foreign travel was largely engendered from the desire to convey information and communicate firsthand personal experiences and impressions. This authenticity was further enhanced by the personal approach employed by most travel writers in the retelling of their experiences. The reader is almost always addressed in the second person. He is often called upon to join the traveler in touring a famous monument or exploring an ancient site. Nonetheless, when carried to an extreme, this personal approach rendered the travel writer more of a tourist guide in the modern sense of the term; and his account can be legitimately described as not written but told. Moreover, the emphasis on authenticity caused most of these travel accounts to become anecdotal rather than analytical, and hence not very demanding intellectually. They were easy reading material for the new literate class. Dry information, whether historical, geographical, cultural or statistical, was often made alive and palatable by the inclusion of vignettes of native exoticism. The fact that they conveyed information of various kinds in an entertaining context gave travel books much prominence and popularity in an age which was not only thirsty for knowledge but intent on disseminating it.

Travel books also satisfied vicariously the general readers' craving for the romantic associations of adventure. Some of the actual experiences of the travelers were exaggerated in the retelling to make them assume the dimensions of real adventure. Even the sophisticated travelers who criticized this bent among some of their predecessors and made fun of the anticipated adventure that never came did not tone down accounts of incidents involving encounters with danger. A touch of adventure, factual or fanciful, gave the vicarious experience of the general reader an added measure of charm.

Similarly, the reading public found in books of foreign travel a gratification of their patriotic zeal, and an assertion of their national identity. In spite of all the interest in the Old World and its culture, many Americans still considered the vogue of foreign travel unpatriotic. Traveling abroad was declared unhealthy for all young men. It was even thought that travel corrupted them and weakened their patriotism; that the experience of visiting or staying in foreign countries made Americans worse instead of better, for it led them not only to praise but to adopt some foreign manners and habits. Washington Irving, for instance, was frequently chided for his long sojourns abroad. Howells, in later years, spoke contemptuously of those American romancers who tried to be "little Londoners." For this reason, many authors did not spare the chance when it offered itself on the pages of their accounts of travel to reveal to their readers the great value of foreign travel to the American national character. They constantly reassured their countrymen that their stay abroad had increased their faith in their country, and strengthened rather than weakened their patriotism and loyalty to America. They demonstrated that in addition to the acquisition of the knowledge and culture which the Old World offered them—and which were essential to the gradual education of the American masses themselves— they were also able to gain new insights into the traditions and institutions of the Old World. By contrasting the traditions and institutions of the Old World societies with those of the New, the travelers contributed significantly toward fulfilling the need for national as well as cultural identity. They exhibited and interpreted the American way, its republicanism and the virtue of its free institutions in the light of European and Eastern history. In this juxtaposition the readers were made to perceive the intrinsic values of the democratic traditions of their nation and the salutary effects they had on the ultimate betterment and happiness of the individual. It was repeatedly pointed out in books of foreign travel that if the Old World excelled in the cultural and historical riches of the past, America had a better present and certainly a more promising future.

The appeal to the patriotic and national impulses of the reading public was often sentimental and in some instances verged on the chauvinistic. The sight of the Stars and Stripes flying from the tallest of poles in some remote corner of the world was always declared to be a source of unexpected delight to the traveler. On learning that Bayard Taylor was ready to leave the town of Berber in the Sudan, the Governor sent word to him that he would bring a company of his soldiers down to the banks of the Nile and salute his flag; and, Taylor wrote [in his *Journey to Central Africa*],

> Truly enough, when we were all embarked and I had given the Stars and Stripes of the Ethiopian winds, a company of about fifty soldiers ranged themselves on the high bank, and saluted the flag with a dozen rattling volleys.

The flag was much more than a mere symbol in books of travel. There was always the satisfaction of identifying with it. Physically, its presence was an assertion of the eminent place the young nation occupied in the world community and an evidence that other peoples recognized and respected that place. Psychologically, the flag was a source of inner security; the American's sense of his personal value and importance was largely derived from his feeling of belonging to America, the favored land, rather than from an inner conviction of his worth as a well-rounded individual. He was acutely conscious of what he lacked: culture, experience, and cosmopolitanism—the qualities that his European counterparts possessed. He could not vie with them on those grounds. But by posing as a representative of America, which he believed to be morally and politically superior to the Old World, he could bolster his own ego and extract a deep sense of pride in his identity. Simultaneously, the loyalty of the traveler was assured; and the reader, by experiencing the vicarious thrill, could identify with the writer and share his feelings.

In the same patriotic vein, the travel book was frequently used as a weapon of retaliation. American authors found in books of travel a conveniently fitted platform for rebutting the criticisms and misrepresentations of European, especially English, travelers in the United States. (Cooper's *Notions of the Americans* [1828] is a good case in point.) The virtue of American traditions and free institutions was reiterated vis-a-vis the current evils and injustice inherent in the European and Eastern societies. Patriotic Americans who were incensed by the condescending attitude of European and English observers read with great approbation the pages of the travel books that vindicated their country. Some American authors went so far as to give European and English travelers a taste of their own medicine. Usually assuming an air of superiority, they singled out and conspicuously framed the vulgarities of the European and English travelers, especially those who made claims to nobility, whom they encountered on neutral grounds—for example, in the Levant. With a streak of sarcastic glee, in *My Winter on the Nile* (1876) Charles Dudley Warner gibed:

> I hear the natives complain that almost all the English men of rank who came to Egypt, beg, or shall we say accept? substantial favors of the Khedive. The nobility appear to have a new rendering of *noblesse oblige.* This is rather humiliating to us Americans, who are, after all, almost blood-relations of the English; and besides, we are often taken for *Inglese,* in villages where few strangers go.

Inwardly, readers must have revelled in sharing Warner's conscious snobbery, and relished the connotations of such words as "complain," "beg" and "substantial favors"; and the more so because these words were used in direct reference to English nobility—the standard-bearers of tradition with all their civilized embellishments—in an attempt to mark a low ebb in their values and codes of moral behavior. Self-righteously and with an added degree of pride, they must also have winced at being often branded in faraway lands as *"Inglese"* and thus suffering what they considered an undeserved humiliation.

Significantly then, the travel book gave the growing reading masses all they needed when they needed it. The two poles of nineteenth-century American temperament, the conscious need of the public for knowledge, specifically that of its ancestral heritage and of the stable traditions and institutions of old civilizations, and its conscious need for national identity, inspiring confidence and pride in being American, were reconciled in books of foreign travel. Knowledge of European and Eastern civilizations was disseminated in America to satisfy the insatiable appetite of the reading public. Yet the travelers never portrayed the Old World as the exemplary or redeemed society to the American Man. This Old World was seen and criticized from a peculiarly American point of view. Furthermore, by seeing in juxtaposition the structures and textures of both the Old and the New societies, the American reader was able to perceive the intrinsic value and virtues of the democratic traditions and free institutions of his society. This was ultimately the logic behind the phenomenal growth and popularity of travel books in the nineteenth century. They were triumphantly American, written by Americans exclusively for Americans.

Ahmed M. Metwalli, "Americans Abroad: The Popular Art of Travel Writing in the Nineteenth Century," in America: Exploration and Travel, *edited by Steven E. Kagle, Bowling Green State University Popular Press, 1979, pp. 68-82.*

American Civil War General Ulysses S. Grant witnesses an excavation at Pompeii:

The Italian Authorities did General Grant special honor on his visit to Pompeii by directing that a house be excavated. It is one of the special compliments paid to visitors of renown. . . . [When] the director of excavations led the way to the proposed work, there were the General and his party and a group of our gallant and courteous friends from the "Vandalia." The quarter selected was near the Forum. Chairs were arranged for the General, Mrs. Grant, and some of us, and there quietly, in a room that had known Pompeian life seventeen centuries ago, we awaited the signal that was to dig up ashes that had fallen from Vesuvius that terrible night in August. . . . We formed a group about the General, while the director gave the signal to the workmen. The spades dived into the ashes while with eager eyes we looked on. . . . Nothing came of any startling import. There were two or three bronze ornaments, a loaf of bread wrapped in cloth, the grain of the bread and the fiber of the cloth as clearly marked as when this probable remnant of a humble meal was put aside by the careful housewife's hands. Beyond this, and some fragments which we could not understand, this was all. . . . The director was evidently disappointed. He expected a skeleton at the very least to come out of the cruel ashes and welcome our renowned guest, who had come so many thousand miles to this Roman entertainment.

J. R. Young, quoted in The Golden Age of Travel: Literary Impressions of the Grand Tour, *edited by Helen Barber Morrison, Twayne Publishers, 1951.*

Willard Thorp

[*In the following essay, Thorp discusses the travel accounts of several American writers who visited Europe in the latter half of the nineteenth century, including those of Ralph Waldo Emerson, Nathaniel Hawthorne, Mark Twain, and Henry James.*]

The historians have had much to say about the influence of the idea of the West on the American mind and imagination. They have neglected an equally powerful force operative during the years between 1850 and 1900, a force which, incidentally, helped to maintain the dominion of the "defenders of Ideality" in poetry and criticism. During this half-century Americans discovered Europe, with results which were culturally quite as significant as the discovery of the West.

In ever increasing numbers travelers returned home to record what they had seen and felt in the Old World. From this migration came a superlative travel literature and a new type of fiction, the "international novel." Ultimately this exodus was also responsible for a shift in attitude which, on the eastern seaboard and with the more literate classes, transformed the chauvinism of the forties into the cosmopolitanism of the 1900's.

The causes of this great exodus are not obscure. There was, of course, more money and more leisure for travel. After the *Great Western,* marvel of the age, made its first voyage in 1838, the terrors of the Atlantic were converted into pleasures, even for the invalids on their way to European spas. The revolutions of 1848 drew patriotic Americans to Italy and France that they might be on hand when monarchical Europe was republicanized. Though their hopes were betrayed, liberals continued to arrive in order to learn why the revolutions had been abortive. The various European countries wooed American tourists by providing them with special objectives for their holiday, such as the Great Exhibition at the Crystal Palace in 1851 and the Paris exhibitions of 1855 and 1867.

More powerful than any other persuasive were the books written by the pioneer generation of travelers. Irving's *Sketch Book* (1819) and *Bracebridge Hall* (1822), though they imaged an England which scarcely existed in actuality, inspired his countrymen to search for it. N. P. Willis' *Pencillings by the Way* (1844), his collected travel letters contributed to the New York *Mirror,* enchanted the subscribers to the five hundred newspapers which made excerpts from them. Longfellow's *Hyperion* (1839), Irving's *Conquest of Granada* (1829), and more factual but equally influential books, such as Silliman's *A Journal of Travels in England, Holland and Scotland* (1810), induced thousands of Americans to go in quest of the holy places of Europe these pioneers had so eloquently described. In the time of Irving and Willis the casual tourist, who was abroad chiefly to absorb as much as he could in a short time, was the exception. After 1850 he is the type.

2

Few Americans in the fifties went to Europe without a sense of the momentousness of their journey. They often apologized for leaving home, knowing that many of their countrymen believed that one's Americanism could be corrupted by foreign travel. It was possible to enjoy Europe too well, and a good American had to be on his guard. W. W. Story, an early expatriate, spent the winter of 1849-1850 in Berlin, which seemed to many Americans the most nearly like Boston of European cities, as a kind of expiation for his excessive enjoyment of Italy. As Henry James says of this visit, he had not yet burnt his ships; "he was to saturate himself . . . but he was somehow, by the same stroke, and in some interest to be felt better than named, to be protected against that saturation." Few of the apologists were so philosophical as C. A. Bartol in *Pictures of Europe, Framed in Ideas* (1855), which is more a transcendentalist treatise on the theory of travel than a book about Europe, but invariably, at some point in his narrative, the traveler in these earlier years reassured his readers that he had come home undamaged.

There was much to disapprove of in Europe: the power of the Roman Church, the beggars, the indifference to social reform of the British upper-classes, the evils of the land system in the Papal states, the lax morals of Parisians and Florentines, the absence of a "go-ahead" spirit. Some patriotic travelers were so disturbed by what they saw that they considered it their duty to indict Europe. Julia Ward Howe, for instance, decided that even art study hardly justified a prolonged residence abroad. "The Prometheus of the present day is needed rather to animate statues than to make them."

The professional humorists warned their countrymen against losing their native common sense among the ruins and becoming monarchists or aesthetes. The devotees of Artemus Ward, Petroleum V. Nasby, and Samantha Allen, of J. M. Bailey (the Danbury News Man) and Mr. Dunn Browne (of the Springfield *Republican*) were eager to hear such undeludable Americans inform against Europe. Unfortunately the calculated candor of the humorists seldom goes beyond a scornful paragraph on the battered noses of the Elgin Marbles or a tempered insult aimed at the British royal family. Their books are, on the whole, as mild as milk, possibly because they had a profitable public in England. Two or three, Locke's *Nasby in Exile* (1882) for example, comment shrewdly on European manners and morals, but the only masterpiece of this genre is Mark Twain's *The Innocents Abroad.*

After the failure of the revolutions in the mid-century made Americans less sure that democracy was predestined to triumph everywhere and after our own Civil War had sobered their chauvinism, they were more open to the persuasions of travelers like E. C. Benedict, who asked them to believe, in his *A Run Through Europe* (1860), that an acquaintance with the Old World "must be of great value to our national character . . . letting some of the gas out of our conceit, and some of the hyperbole out of our vanity." Readers of G. S. Hillard's *Six Months in Italy* (1853), the most widely quoted of all the travel books, were at length ready to submit to his advice that they must leave notions of progress behind, and "learn to look on churchmen and church rites as a pageant."

The gradual aesthetic education of Americans during these earlier years is fascinating to watch. What they knew of European art they had learned from line drawings, engravings, bad copies in oil of Raphael and Guido, plaster casts of statuary in a few sepulchral galleries. Ruskin had taught them to admire Gothic art and to despise that of the High Renaissance. Some of them debated whether a preoccupation with aesthetic matters was not debilitating. There was always a searching of the conscience when the tourist confronted the nudity of the Venus of the Tribune in the Uffizi and turned to gaze on her even more unabashed sister smiling from Titian's canvas across the room. This cabinet, remarked one traveler, might be called a public boudoir.

No one worked harder to diffuse artistic knowledge in America than James Jackson Jarves, world traveler, editor of the first paper published in Honolulu, art critic, connoisseur, and collector. Jarves is remembered now because he was forced in 1871, because of poverty, to relinquish his magnificent collection of Italian primitives to Yale; but he should be known also as the author of four delightful European travel books (which will be discussed later in this [essay]) and for *Art Hints* (1855) and three other pioneer works of this sort notable for their acuteness. In all these books his announced purpose was to convince Americans that their moral and utilitarian prejudices blinded them to what they had gone to Europe to see.

Equally independent are the aesthetic theories and judgments advanced by a Philadelphia amateur, Horace Binney Wallace, whose *Art, Scenery and Philosophy in Europe* was issued posthumously in 1855. One of the first to propose a functional theory of architecture, Wallace discusses in "The Law of the Development of Gothic Architecture," one of the best essays in his book, ideas which are far in advance of his time. In another chapter he describes with great perspicuity the aesthetic effect produced by various European cathedrals, an achievement which is not a little remarkable when one considers how firmly he held to the requirement of functionalism in architecture.

One is likewise interested to watch the progress in aesthetics of certain better known Americans. In all three of his travel books Edward Everett Hale shows an extraordinary open-mindedness. Possessing the usual prejudices in favor of the later Gothic style, he worked his way back, by study and contemplation, until he could enjoy primitive painting and Romanesque and Byzantine art. Hawthorne struggled with art while he was in Italy even though he was often weary and sometimes disgusted. He went back to certain pictures and statues time after time, trying to find—not what his friend Powers, the sculptor, told him was to be found in them—but what he might experience by himself. His *Italian Note Books* show him "improving" day by day. His persistence bore fruit in *The Marble Faun,* whole pages of which are observations from the *Note Books* transformed for the purposes of fiction.

These amateurs, indeed, often returned home better instructed than the scholars and critics whose profession it was to interpret European civilization. Charles Eliot Norton, Harvard's Professor of the History of Art from 1875 to 1898, was, for example, strangely limited by his American prejudices. As friend and disciple of Ruskin, a founder of the Archaeological Institute of America, the School of Classical Studies at Rome, and the *American Journal of Archaeology,* Norton might have been expected to comprehend and treat sympathetically various schools of painting and styles of architecture. Actually few American travelers in Europe were so narrow. His lifelong hatred of Catholic institutions—he once wrote Lowell that he thought he could roast a Franciscan with pleasure and that he would only need a tolerable opportunity to make him stab a Cardinal in the dark—constantly interfered with his aesthetic judgments. With a zeal worthy of a member of the Know-Nothing party (whose principles he approved) he sets forth his detestation of the Roman Church in his early *Notes of Travel and Study in Italy* (1860) and permits it to intrude on his observations about art.

3

There was scarcely a professional writer of this period who did not furnish his public with his impressions of Europe. Grace Greenwood (Sara Jane Lippincott) in *Haps and Mishaps of a Tour in Europe* (1854) satisfied her readers, for whom she was the arbiter in matters of sentiment, with long meditations inspired by famous paintings or historical scenes. Mrs. Stowe, celebrated as the author of *Uncle Tom's Cabin,* described in *Sunny Memories of Foreign Lands* (1854) her royal progress through the drawing rooms of England and the Continent. Bayard Taylor's fate was settled when his *Views A-Foot* (1846), the naïve raptures of a twenty-year-old boy, captivated the nation. Twenty editions were required in the next ten years. Taylor would be fifty before he could cease traveling up and down in the world as a professional weigher and gauger of culture for his countrymen. Year by year he pushed into new lands: Africa, Asia Minor, India, and Japan, the Scandinavian countries, Iceland. "I am led," he wrote, "into these wanderings without my will; it seems to be my destiny."

The less imaginative of the professional writers soon evolved a sort of standard pattern for the travel book. The author must begin with the excitements of the ocean voyage itself and devote at least a portion of a chapter to the thrill, so long anticipated, of setting foot on foreign soil. From this point on he should mix architecture and scenery with comment on philanthropies, skillfully work in a little history cribbed from Murray's guides, taking care to add a touch of sentiment or eloquence when the occasion permitted. If the essay or book required a little padding, it was always possible to retell an old legend or slip in an account of dangers surmounted in crossing the Alps.

Soon there would be interesting deviations from this pattern, but in the fifties and sixties the reader wanted a series of variations on a theme. It did not matter to him that he had read forty descriptions of the hallowed places—Shakespeare's tomb, the Burns country, Warwick Castle, and the Tower of London, the vale of Chamonix, and the Roman Campagna. He listened with delight to any new variations which Edward Everett Hale or Helen Hunt Jackson could compose.

In the sixties this predominantly sentimental approach begins to yield to the kind of book which offers chiefly information and advice. Tourists were in a hurry and they wanted to know how to get over the ground without wasting any time in unprofitable expeditions. The books such determined travelers found most useful were those represented by J. H. B. Latrobe's *Hints for Six Months in Europe* (1869) and C. C. Fulton's *Europe Viewed Through American Spectacles* (1874) which supplied, in addition to 310 double-columned pages of fact, an appendix of "Hints to European Tourists."

Soon the more sophisticated began to shun the spots where their meditations might be disturbed by the rushing hordes to whom such books appealed and fled to haunts whose charms had not yet been defiled. As early as 1852 W. W. Story complained to Lowell, "We must take some untravelled paths which the English have not spoiled, and go into the wildest fastnesses of the Abruzzi, perhaps to Sora." Eugene Benson, whose *Art and Nature in Italy* (1882) is caviar for the élite, traveled to Ferrara not for the sake of Tasso and Lucrezia Borgia whom the vulgar pursued there, but to seek out the work of an obscure painter named Scarscinello [sic]. It was a mistake to let such secrets out. Henry James knew well enough what always happened. Writing in 1903 of W. W. Story's *Vallombrosa* (1881), he lamented that the dense Etrurian coverts to whose secluded beauty Story had unwisely given publicity, would by then be "scarred and dishonoured by the various new contrivances for access without contact and acquaintance without knowledge."

These books unlocking the secret charms of particular regions are sufficiently numerous to constitute a subdivision of travel literature, but the sophisticates who produced them were also responsible for another kind of book. This is the detailed study of some city already repeatedly described but never so minutely nor by a traveler so devoted and so learned. W. W. Story, for example, knew Rome as few Americans have ever known it, and he found in Italy, and in Rome especially, an antidote to the ugliness of the rest of the world. It is not surprising therefore that some of the chapters in his *Roba di Roma* (1862)—on *villeggiature,* on games, ceremonies, and holidays—are unexcelled.

One book of this type, F. Marion Crawford's *Ave Roma Immortalis* (1898), possesses a distinction which almost makes it great. Son of the Italian-trained sculptor Thomas Crawford, convert to Catholicism, after 1883 a resident of Italy, Crawford was in every way fitted to write the perfect book about Rome. Accurate, swift, adroitly planned, heightened in the right places by a careful rhetoric, his *Ave Roma Immortalis* achieves the totality of impression which eluded scores of novices. Crawford's Rome is not the Rome of Garibaldi or of Pio Nono, but his description fulfills the ideal toward which many writers, baffled by the beauty and mystery of the city, had struggled. Here at last the glories of the fourteen "regions" and the immensities of St. Peter's are adequately reduced to words.

Before the century ended, the travel writers had devised yet another sort of book designed for tourists who went to Europe to escape. Too sophisticated to ration their days to the Blue Grotto at Capri and the castle at Heidelberg, and too well traveled to need hints and helps, they were in Europe in search of the picturesque. Stevenson's *Travels with a Donkey in the Cévennes* (1879) had delighted them, and for them the Pennells drew and wrote the series of "pilgrimages" beginning with *A Canterbury Pilgrimage* in 1885. F. Hopkinson Smith in *Gondola Days* (1897) describes the mood of these latter-day travelers.

> In this selfish, materialistic, money-getting age, it is a joy to live, if only for a day . . . in a city the relics of whose past are the lessons of our future; whose every canvas, stone, and bronze bear witness to a grandeur, luxury, and taste that took a thousand years to perfect, and will take a thousand years of neglect to destroy.

All that had vexed the first generation of European visitors—ecclesiastical corruption, feudal survivals, filth, indolence—was now dissolved in a glow generated by acceptance. Smith, noting the toppling of jamb and lintel in Venice, is full of thanks to the little devils of rot and decay. They are, he says, really "the guardians of the picturesque."

Among the hundreds of Americans who attempted travel books, at least a dozen theorize about what they are doing and strive to give shape and character to their observations. In "Leaves from My Journal in Italy and Elsewhere" Lowell wrote at length on modern travelers. They see nothing out of sight, are skeptics and doubters, materialists reporting things for other skeptics to doubt still further upon. With every step of the modern tourist "our inheritance of the wonderful is diminished," and year by year more and more of the world gets disenchanted. Lowell's own travel book was written in emulation of the elder navigators to whom the world was a huge wonder born.

The young George William Curtis, returning from abroad in 1850, sought in his *Nile Notes of a Howadji* (1851) to re-create for his readers—and he soon had a host of them—the "essentially *sensuous,* luxurious, languid and sense-satisfied spirit of Eastern life." No one, he noted, had ever sought to do this. He accomplished his aim so successfully that his family was terribly shocked, especially by his voluptuous description of an Oriental dancer whose style descended from Salome's. The spirit of this book, Curtis wrote to his aggrieved father, is "precisely what I wish it. I would not have it toned down, for I toned it up intentionally."

Several later writers, determined to do more than furnish guidebook information colored intermittently a deep purple, throw a challenge to their readers. John Hay ironical-

Watercolor and ink drawing of Santa Maria della Spina at Pisa, by John Ruskin, c. 1846-7.

4

ly warns in *Castilian Days* (1871) that he does not belong to the "praiseworthy class of travelers who feel a certain moral necessity impelling them to visit every royal abode within reach." Charles Dudley Warner in *Saunterings* (1872), the first of ten travel books, suggests to his audience that, as a compromise, "we shall go somewhere and not learn anything about it." Thomas Bailey Aldrich in *From Ponkapog to Pesth* (1883) complains of another restriction on the freedom of the travel writer. He is not vexed, like Hay and Warner, by the requirement that he be informative, but he does reject the convention which decrees that he may be "aesthetic, or historic, or scientific, or analytic, or didactic, or any kind of ic, except enthusiastic."

Aldrich indulged in nostalgia rather than enthusiasm, but his chapters have a characteristic quality. This is compounded partly from his humorous picture of himself as a provincial American, awed though not cowed by Europe; partly from his conveyance of that disturbing desire which American travelers have always experienced, a longing to possess Europe, to stave off disenchantment, to carry home, in Signor Alinari's sepia photographs or by act of memory, some of the age and beauty of the Old World.

Because these authors took care to organize their impressions and to infect their readers with their discoveries, the travel books of Lowell, Curtis, Hay, Warner, and Aldrich are still alive. But they do not reach the level attained in the records left by Emerson, Hawthorne, Jarves, Twain, Howells, De Forest, and Henry James. The difference is not explained by simply noting that the men in the second group are better writers. The point is that they were more concerned to find a valid answer to the question which was, in some degree, in the consciousness of all traveling Americans: What shall I, as an American, do about Europe?

The first of these records, in point of time as well as in absolute excellence, is Emerson's *English Traits* (1856). The book gave him much trouble and did not appear until nearly ten years after his second visit to England. In his anxiety to make it deep and accurate, he invited the young Clough to stay with him for two or three months at Concord to "answer a catechism of details touching England, revise my notes on that country, and sponge out my blunders." This plan did not go through; but Emerson expended an unusual amount of labor on his book, and it was much on his conscience before the printers finally got the first chapter in October, 1855.

The first printing of 3,000 copies sold quickly, and a second printing of 2,000 was required within a month. Emerson's countrymen sensed that here, at last, was the true and perfect answer to the British travelers who for a half-century had sneered at the nascent American civilization. The liberal British reviews gave the book serious attention; the conservative journals conjured it away by ignoring its existence.

English Traits is less a travel book in the ordinary sense of the word than an essay in cultural anthropology, undertaken years before the science was named. Only a civi-

lized man like Emerson who understands the interaction between ideas and institutions can judge wisely the faults and achievements of a civilization alien to his own. He had little to say about architecture and scenery, but much to say about the English character. He did not admire it with a whole heart, and though, as Richard Garnett observed, there is not a sneer in the book it is full of a wonderful irony. England lacked, for Emerson, what the best civilization must have, spirituality; but England was a success, and he wished to know why. His proposition is stated in the first paragraph of the chapter called "Result."

> England is the best of actual nations. It is no ideal framework, it is an old pile built in different ages, with repairs, additions, and makeshifts; but you see the poor best you have got. London is the epitome of our times, and the Rome of today.

A fact of such importance for the nineteenth century needed to be explained, and so Emerson probed his way through chapters on Land, Race, Ability, Manners, Truth, Character, Wealth, and pondered the influence exerted by the aristocracy, the universities, the Anglican Church, and the *Times*.

The marvel of the book is how much of it is still true, a tribute both to Emerson's penetration and to the unchanging characteristics of the English people. Page after page could be reprinted as the record of an observer living in our time. Admirers of English unity and courage during the desperate nights of 1940 understand what he means in saying, "In politics and in war, they hold together as by hooks of steel." Though it is now less true than it was in the fifties that "man in England submits to be a product of political economy," England's rivals, as Emerson noted, are still irritated because the English have found out how to unite success with honesty. What he has to say about England's dealings with other nations, particularly those she rules, still needs no amendment.

> They assimilate other races to themselves, and are not assimilated. . . . The English sway of their colonies has no root of kindness. They govern by their arts and ability; they are more just than kind; and, whenever an abatement of their power is left, they have not conciliated the affection on which to rely.

Such is their tenacity, and such their practical turn, that they hold all they gain. Of these memorable judgments, none goes so far in explaining the equipoised character of English civilization as Emerson's conclusion to his chapter on "Literature." There are, he says, two nations in England, not Norman and Saxon, or Celt and Goth, but the perceptive class, and the practical finality class. These

> are ever in counterpoise, interacting mutually; one, in hopeless minorities; the other, in huge masses; one studious, contemplative, experimenting; the other, the ungrateful pupil, scornful of the source, whilst availing itself of the knowledge for gain; these two nations, of genius and of animal force, though the first consist of only a dozen souls, and the second of twenty millions, forever by their discord and their accord yield the power of the English State.

While Emerson labored at the composition of *English Traits,* Hawthorne, his Concord neighbor, serving as our consult at Liverpool, was keeping a 300,000-word record of his impressions. The experiences of these years between 1853 and 1857 affected him profoundly. If his health had not failed, he would have transmuted them into a novel. It was mainly for this purpose that the *English Notebooks* (completely published in 1941) were compiled. In two abortive romances, *Dr. Grimshaw's Secret* and *The Ancestral Footstep,* he attempted to tell his story, the theme of which was the symbolic return to England of an American whose ancestor in Cromwellian times had violently broken his ties with the homeland. Fortunately, before his creative powers weakened, Hawthorne distilled the more significant passages from the *Notebooks* into *Our Old Home* (1863).

To one who knows something of Hawthorne's state of mind in his last years, his apprehension over the imminence of civil war in America, his struggle to find himself at home in England, the shift in his thinking from the belief that England and America might complement each other, the one supplying the deficiencies the other lacked, to the view, which was also Emerson's, that the two civilizations could not be reconciled and that the future lay with America; to one who perceives how these and related themes return again and again in the pages of *Our Old Home,* the book becomes the most moving autobiographical record left by any of the travelers.

His best chapters are built from the themes related to the all-engrossing question: How shall an American come to terms with England? In the chapter on Leamington Spa these themes emerge most insistently. The little resort city evidently attracted him because it is a "home to the homeless all the year round," though no man has reared a house there wherein to bring up his children. From this theme Hawthorne moves on to his disquiet in trying to picture the influence of hoar antiquity lingering into the present daylight; then to the theme of the illusion to which Americans are constantly subject in England, of having been there before, the result of the print of a recollection in some ancestral mind, transmitted with fainter and fainter impress, through several generations, to the descendant who returns to our old home.

5

James Jackson Jarves resembles Emerson as a travel writer in at least one respect: both men were concerned to describe only those particulars which illustrate general propositions. Because, either unconsciously or by intent, Jarves usually succeeded in going to the heart of the matter in his books about France and Italy, the modern reader who discovers them will be impressed with the significance as well as the prodigality of the details of life in Paris, Florence, and Rome which pour from his pages. His four books are valuable "documentaries."

Parisian Sights and French Principles Seen Through American Spectacles (1852) takes us, in the fashion of the earlier travel books, to the favorite tourist haunts—the Morgue, Père-Lachaise, the Madeleine; but already Jarves evinces the wit and the independence of judgment which make his books the most amusing of the group now under discussion. He likes to begin a chapter with an informing idea, often epitomized by a symbolic building or a Parisian type, and then to describe the ceremony or process or institution or social class about which he has generalized. Occasionally the details swamp the generalization; but the reader is none the poorer, for he is permitted to see Paris as it was in 1852, recovering from the coup d'état by which Louis Napoleon undid the Second Republic, gay and splendid in its new boulevards, squalid in its attics and slums. Jarves has already begun to discuss freely subjects hinted at by other travelers. What, one wonders, did the family circle think of Chapter VIII, "Something Curious for Moralists"—an unsentimental account of prostitution in Paris and of the French code of extramarital behavior? In the second series of *Parisian Sights* (1855) Jarves even more consistently follows his own bent, poking his nose into dubious alleys and hitherto unvisited places.

In *Italian Sights and Papal Principles Seen Through American Spectacles* (1856) Jarves was again under the necessity of reporting on the usual tourist places. But he saw in his rounds so much more than any of his contemporaries that the reader's interest never diminishes. His incomparable chapter on Pompeii is a tour de force of historical reconstruction. As he went deeper into his subject, Jarves became increasingly reflective. Few Americans meditated with such profit, for instance, on the comparative influence of Romanism and Protestantism on the societies in which each predominated. He ridiculed the mummeries of Holy Week in Rome; but he was no bigot, and, as always, he told his fellow Americans what it was good for them to hear. In this early book, as in the later and mellower *Italian Rambles* (1883), he warned them against the false and meretricious, and encouraged them to carry home a desire to make a civilization in which the artist could exercise his function freely and fully.

Mark Twain's *The Innocents Abroad* (1869) was, in its day, the most famous of American travel books. At last his fellow countrymen, long deceived by the sentimentalities of the guidebooks, were to have the truth about the Old World fraud. He would convince them that the pictures they had rhapsodized over were now too dingy to be deciphered, and the tales of chivalry were actually records of cruelty and avarice. Some of his impieties were shrewdly calculated, but most of them sprang from a deep suspicion of Europe. A success Europe could never be, Italy least of all, for it is the "heart and home of degradation, poverty, indolence, and everlasting unaspiring worthlessness."

Everything Mark saw on his first trip abroad affected him too immediately to permit any historical or aesthetic detachment. Napoleon III, bowing to the plaudits of the crowd and watching everybody with cat's-eyes to discover incipient treason, was no nearer to him in time than the Medicis who required their hireling artists to drag pride and manhood in the dirt for bread. In funereal Venice thoughts of its hidden trials and sudden assassinations crowded out the splendor of St. Mark's. He hurried past frescoes and altarpieces because his anger was still hot from the sight of the gold hoard in the *trésor.*

In these satiric attacks on the easy, un-American acceptance of what is esteemed to be culture we find the Mark Twain we know in his other books; the hater of pretense, resentful of all forms of tyranny, defender of the Jews and other oppressed minorities, tender toward women, the extravagant admirer of what is new and progressive. One enjoys this book, chiefly perhaps, as one does *A Tramp Abroad* (1880), for these sudden fires kindled by the ardor of his prejudices. For the sake of them we indulge him in the crudities of his humor—his fondness for burlesquing venerable legends (a hint here of *A Connecticut Yankee in King Arthur's Court*), his tiresome fun with the intricacies of foreign languages, his set pieces of comic meditation, such as the doing-up of a spectacle in the Coliseum as a Barnum might have produced it.

As compensation for these barbarisms we receive passages which move us strangely, for Mark was not always without reverence. The monuments of Greece and of Rome (before it became Peter's seat) could stir him to write descriptive prose of an unexpected quality. His unlawful visit to the Acropolis by moonlight, the silence of the streets of Pompeii, which he peoples with the oblivious workaday citizens soon to be stricken, Damascus as the type of immortality, such sights and moments impelled him to drop his clown's false face.

The chapters on the new pilgrims in the Holy Land are the best of the book, though they must have pained many churchgoers in the seventies. This climactic episode in the *Quaker City* excursion was Mark Twain's meat. Ill at ease when confronted by a cathedral, he was specially created to satirize the grim willingness with which his pious countrymen endured heat and risked filthy diseases in order that they might follow in His steps. One gets more than delight from these chapters. In no other book is the psychology of the modern pilgrim so clearly exposed, his determination to find a Presbyterian or Baptist Palestine, his ruthless lugging off what of Judaea was not trampled into mud. As for Mark himself, if he had met the Queen of Sheba on the way to Solomon, he would have said to himself, "You look fine, madam, but your feet are not clean and you smell like a camel."

6

Remembering William Dean Howells as the novelist of social change in America, *Atlantic* editor, and convert to Socialism, we forget that he was from 1861 to 1865 our consul at Venice and that out of this experience came some of his first work in prose, *Venetian Life* (1866) and *Italian Journeys* (1867). Nor do these and his other travel books, *Tuscan Cities* (1886) and *A Little Swiss Sojourn* (1892), contain the sum of his impressions of Europe. In his early years he was as much an "international novelist" as his friend Henry James, delighting in contrasts between the fresh innocence of young American girls and the deviousness of Europeans. His first novel, *Their Wedding Journey* (1872), is more travel book than novel, and *A Chance Acquaintance* (1873) furnishes a better portrait of Quebec than of its heroine. He saw Europe as a novelist might be expected to see it. The life of Lucca in the past, the life of Venice in his years there—this is what he has his eye on. We notice before we have read far how frequently these

sketches turn into fiction. The patriarch of Capri is as engagingly introduced as if he were to be the leading character in a novel; episodes blossom inevitably into dialogue. Passages from these travel books turn up, only a little transformed, in the novels themselves. (In the twentieth century Howells wrote six travel books.)

No travel writer of these years gives us a fuller sense of how it felt to be in Pisa in 1883, in Vevey in 1887. His attention soon loses its grip on church and statue, but, to our profit, it fixes on what the average tourist, nose down in Hare, would have thought trivial: the little steam tram snuffling through the Piazza Santa Maria Novella; his Holiness hawking into his handkerchief during Mass; the guide in the Baptistry at Pisa who could howl so ably that he has to perform twenty times a day for the tourists who have read about him in the guidebooks.

Howells' observations on architecture and painting are prejudiced, but at any spot where men have been moved to great actions, he was willing to be entranced. "At home," he says, "one may read history, but one can realize it, as if it were something personally experienced, only on the spot where it was lived." To effect this realization, Howells believed, was the prime use of travel. Henry James, the perfect travel writer, saw that the problem for the artist in this genre was to fuse the past and present, the monuments of unaging intellect and the politics of the moment. This fusion Howells could not effect; and he admits that he cannot. For him there was a "sweet confusion" in travel. When we try to lose ourselves in the past, our modern dreariness intrudes. Yet if we were less modern we should be the more indifferent to the antique charm. He cannot bring the two worlds together.

This division of interest between the present and the past is everywhere apparent in his books. *Venetian Life* concentrates on the present. Howells had resolved to tell as much as possible about the everyday life of the Venetians and to develop a just notion of their character. He studied the social structure of Venice and the effect of the weight of the past on its inhabitants. He penetrated every quarter of the city, festival, and gathering place where he might observe them advantageously. In the end he thought he took on a little of the Venetian tone himself, the dispiritedness and the sense of loss and helplessness. His method in *Tuscan Cities* accords with his equally compelling purpose as a traveler: the "experiencing" of history. He lounges in some memorable square or court until the thought of its great moment drives out all other impressions, and the story follows. In telling it he strives for the circumstantial minuteness, the air of simple truth he so much admired in the old Florentine gossipers, in whose tales "the passions are as living, the characters as distinct, as if the thing happened yesterday."

Howells' predilections as a traveler changed, as did those of his countrymen, between the sixties and the nineties. Beneath the ingratiating manner of *Venetian Life* one detects the seriousness of the generation of Americans for whom Europe was a problem to be solved. The tone of *A Little Swiss Sojourn* is very different. Howells is content now to escape for a time, imagining how pleasant life might be in a certain noble *château meublé à louer* by the

Rhone. If one had daughters to educate or were wearing out a heavy disappointment, this great house would suit very well. For many Americans, as for Howells, Europe was becoming a château to be rented for a season of self-indulgence.

Like Howells, who was his admiring critic and sponsor, John W. De Forest first practiced the art of the novelist in his travel books. His *Oriental Acquaintance* (1856) is lifted above the usual accounts of the tour to the Holy Land by its descriptions of the antics of the enraptured tourists. An even better book is his *European Acquaintance* (1858). In his conversation De Forest, so he would have us believe, indulged in the usual banalities of tourists who felt it was their duty to compare the canvases of the Venetian painters to gorgeous sunsets; but his book is almost entirely about the wonderful eccentrics he met by the way. Twelve chapters are devoted to those who endured with him the savage water cure at Gräfenberg and the more effeminate wettings and purgings and freezings at Divonne, near the Swiss border. More valuable than Norton on Orvieto cathedral is his account of the horrors of the Curd Cure, and the Straw Cure, and, most terrible of all, the Wine Cure, so barbaric that patients and doctors, when the prescribed tortures were relaxed each Saturday, all got drunk together.

In the travel essays of Henry James, collected in three volumes—*Transatlantic Sketches* (1875), *Portraits of Places* (1883), and *A Little Tour in France* (1884)—the genre attains its highest development. One thinks regretfully in reading these neglected books of the misfortune of the hundreds of James' countrymen who carried their prejudices abroad in their baggage. And not Americans only. In a devastating attack on Ruskin's inadequate perceptions (*Portraits of Places*), James defines by implication his own qualifications for this sort of writing. "Instead of a garden of delight, [Ruskin] finds a sort of assize-court, in perpetual session. Instead of a place in which human responsibilities are lightened and suspended, he finds a region governed by a kind of Draconic legislation." For James travel was an immense pleasure. Perpetually going a journey, he was willing to permit the scene to take hold of him and "speak"—to use the word he often uses himself.

For each experience he returns a picture which is harmonious and complete. Having sorted out and related the multitude of separate impressions, he builds his essay around a dominant idea or object or mood, so that the reader may grasp the essence of the scene. At Lichfield his theme is the commonplaceness of the little city looked down on by the wonderful cathedral whose great towers overtake in mid-air the conditions of perfect symmetry; at Wells it is the perpetual savor of a Sunday afternoon. In Venice what most impresses one is the way one lives "in a certain sort of knowledge as in a rosy cloud," which "certain sort of knowledge" James exquisitely defines.

What moves him least is scenery. There is a limit to the satisfaction with which one can sit staring at a mountain. Even the liquid sapphire and emerald of Leman and Lucerne suffer when compared with firm palace floors of lapis and verd-antique. He retreats in haste from literary shrines too much possessed by tourists. What pleases most is a great English country house like Haddon Hall, where the incommunicable spirit of the ghost-haunted scene strikes with almost painful intensity; or the brooding villas of Florence whose extraordinary largeness and massiveness are a satire on their present fate. For him a great building is the greatest conceivable work of art, because it represents difficulties annulled, resources combined, labor, courage, and patience. A great building has been, and still may be, inhabited by men and women, and James relishes above all a human flavor in his pleasure.

These essays fascinate for another reason than their superb art. Whether James is contemplating the façade of Rheims cathedral from his stage-box window at the Lion d'Or or abstracting the French character from the display of bathing manners on the *plage* at Etretat, the scene is always, to him, a drama. "To travel," he says, is "to go to the play, to attend a spectacle." Sometimes the gestures and murmured conversation of actual persons supply the plot; sometimes it rises from the contrast between past and present, as when he is struck with the insufferable patronage of the culture-seeking tourists toward Young Italy, preoccupied with its economical and political future and heartily tired of being admired for its eyelashes and its pose. Often it is the conflict of ideas implicit in the scene before him which transforms it into a psychomachia. Thus, in the midst of his enjoyment of the tranquil grandeur of Rheims he is overwhelmed with the realization that the hierarchy which erected this magnificent structure is now the go-between of Bonapartism. "How far should a lover of old cathedrals let his hands be tied by the sanctity of their traditions? How far should he let his imagination bribe him, as it were, from action?"

If the modern world obtrudes in these sketches more insistently than one might have expected, the past is always there as a continuous present, made palpable by the endless devices of James' art. He hated the restorers of the nineteenth century, professional vandals like Sir George Gilbert Scott and Viollet-le-Duc, the more, perhaps, because their licensed depredations deprived him of his chance to evoke and reconstruct. To James a great ruin was a great opportunity. Mark Twain fled from ruins because he did not have the skill to make them speak. James was impelled to them by a kind of aesthetic hunger. Though only a beautiful shadow remain (as he said of Leonardo's "Last Supper" and of the hoary relics of Glastonbury), that "shadow is the artist's thought." This thought was James' quest; it gave him each time new proof of that most pertinent lesson of art, "that there is no limit to the amount of substance an artist may put into his work."

Willard Thorp, "Pilgrims' Return," in Literary History of the United States, *edited by Robert E. Spiller and others, revised edition, The Macmillan Company, 1953, pp. 827-42.*

Herbert Barrows

[In the excerpt below, Barrows examines the responses of the English poets Shelley and Byron to Italian landscape and culture, concluding that the Italian experi-

ences of these two writers were not uniformly positive and fulfilling, as they are commonly portrayed in discussions of Romanticism.]

The word in my title ["Convention and Novelty in the Romantic Generation's Experience of Italy"] which I wish to emphasize is "experience." My point, and I shall try to illustrate it with reference to the Italian experience of Shelley and Byron, is that the study of the English literary traveler's interest in Italy ought to be focussed, more sharply than it has been in the past, on the exact nature and quality of each individual experience. Certainly the individual tour or sojourn has to be seen against the background of the experience of Italy that was generally available at the time. But it must also be seen in the context of the individual life, with its specific motivations and needs, and we should always try to study it in the light of a sympathetic awareness of what it means to be a traveler.

Foreign travel has been a possibility for the English private citizen since the very beginning of the eighteenth century, and the records of his travels—letters, diaries, and travel books as well as poems and novels—, even when we limit our attention to a single country such as Italy, constitute an almost overwhelming amount of material. Some of the most valuable studies of the English traveler's response to Italy have undertaken to reduce this mass of material to order by establishing a pattern of the growth, peak, and decline of the English enthusiasm for Italy and Italian values. A recent book, C. P. Brand's *Italy and the English Romantics,* reaches a conclusion not very different from that reached by Roderick Marshall in the pioneer study of the subject, *Italy in English Literature 1755-1815,* that the peak of the "Italianate fashion" came in the ten or twenty years immediately following the Napoleonic Wars, with the generation of Byron and Shelley, after which the pitch of enthusiasm suddenly declined. The standard here is the number of works of Italian literature published in England, the number of writers who made use of Italian forms or subject-matter, and the sheer volume of enthusiasm with which spokesmen of this generation claimed to know and love Italy.

Seen in the perspective afforded by such studies, there are three readily distinguishable periods of English travel in Italy. First, there is the eighteenth century as a whole, under the sign of the Grand Tour as a recognized institution. Second, there are the years from 1815 to 1830 when the Romantics were coloring the experience of Italy with the legend of their lives and their personalities. And third, there are the years from 1830 or 1840 right through the end of the century and even into our own time (though this third period is capable of further subdivision, especially in its latter stretches). In each of these periods, the English traveler's experience of Italy had its characteristic modes and qualities, its characteristic features of content. And it might be possible to place the peak in any one of the three, depending on the criteria we use.

The eighteenth-century traveler, from Addison to Mrs Piozzi, was sometimes diffident about what he saw and sometimes downright grouchy. He focussed on a narrow range of elements from the vast complex of elements which later travelers have found in Italy, but he focussed

on them with great singleness of purpose. When we look back on the consistency with which he pursued his vision of Italy—in a tour which lasted a year or two years and was often extremely difficult—, we may wonder if he did not reach a certain climax of functional perfection. At least he knew what he expected from his tour, and most of his aims were realizable: later aims, beginning with those of the Romantics, were not always to be so. The Romantic experience was based to a much greater extent than is generally recognized on the content of the eighteenth-century experience, to which it added a new brand of enthusiasm, vehemence, and style: the Romantics certainly succeeded in dramatizing the idea of English devotion to Italy. Nevertheless, for the kind of travel experience which is based on the sober, appreciative knowledge of a very widely inclusive range of Italian values and achievements, we have to wait for the successive generations of Victorians.

It is a rare traveler who is able to move outside the limits of the pattern of experience common to his time, but on the other hand it is only by close scrutiny of the individual experience and not at all by statistics that we can know what that pattern really was. The Romantic poets themselves—Byron in the Fourth Canto of *Childe Harold,* for example—helped to create the image according to which we see their generation as passionately enthusiastic in its response to Italy, and the enthusiasm really did exist, really did give a coloring, a direction to the works in which they wrote about Italy. But it is only an element, for any one of these travelers, in the totality of his day to day experience of Italy. If we go behind the accepted image to examine the actual experience, in even one or two instances, we gain a valuable corrective to some of our notions as to the exact place occupied by the Romantic generation in the development of this important cultural relationship.

The Italian experience of Shelley and Byron has been the subject of many special studies; and of course it has figured prominently in the general biographical and critical treatments of each poet and in the panoramic studies of the English in Italy. While there has not been unanimity as to just what Italy meant to each of them, the abiding impression, always invoked when a biographer or critic wishes to make a point on the basis of common assumptions, is that in their attitudes towards Italy, in the personal and literary values they derived from their Italian experience, the pattern of English response to Italy was at last fully realized.

And yet when this experience is scrutinized, it wears a certain equivocal air. It is neither so entirely new, so positive, or so completely and happily absorbed in Italian values as it has often been thought to be. All of which is, in many important respects, nothing against it. The critic can make himself ridiculous by seeming to prescribe, with such personalities as Shelley and Byron, what their experience *should* have been, what it might have been if they had been wiser, or better informed, or interested in this rather than that, or perhaps just more docile and ordinary.

But if it is foolish to prescribe after the fact, it is not foolish to wish to keep the record straight. To tell the story of the Italian experience of either of the two poets in full detail, and with adequate reference to the points on which there is agreement or disagreement among previous investigators, is not possible here, where our purpose is illustrative. In outline, however, their two stories are somewhat as follows.

With Shelley, the full story would begin with an attempt to distinguish the real motives that prompted him to leave England for Italy in the early spring of 1818, from the various declared motives. As early as the previous summer his letters begin to detail the symptoms of bad health which, as he no doubt believed and as he was especially anxious to convince Godwin, made it imperative to leave England for a warmer climate; finally he is declaring, "It is not health, but life, that I should seek in Italy" [*The Letters of Percy Bysshe Shelley,* 1909]. The word "life" here bears a double sense, which it would not have borne for earlier travelers, and the fuller sense involves a psychological urgency which produced the physical symptoms. It is reasonably clear that while Shelley himself believed that he had gone to Italy solely because his health forced him to do so, the particular symptoms of ill health which he noted in crescendo during these months were the results of his unconscious attempt to find a reason for leaving England which would be acceptable not only to Godwin but to himself. Among the real reasons for going were the pleasurable excitement he always found in travel and the delight with which he looked forward to seeing Italy. But a more important one was his anxiety to escape from the persecution and oppression which had gradually become inescapable in England. None of these reasons could be admitted either to himself or to others; and his health was instinctively enlisted as an excuse for the journey. (It is significant that in a letter to Keats urging him to come to Italy he said: "You ought, at all events, to see Italy, and your health which I suggest as a motive, may be an excuse for you.") In the first letter to Peacock from Italy, Shelley gives a more realistic explanation of the sense in which Italy meant the difference between life and death to him:

> . . . No sooner had we arrived at Italy, than the loveliness of the earth and the serenity of the sky made the greatest difference in my sensations. I depend on these things for life; for in the smoke of cities, and the tumult of human kind, and the chilling fogs and rain of our own country, I can hardly be said to live.

Shelley was not typical of his generation, or of later generations, but the fact is that with him, as with Byron, we see the beginning of a pattern of connections between the Italian journey on the one hand and very complex life-motives on the other which had not existed for the eighteenth-century traveler. The Grand Tourist, going over an itinerary that was prescribed in all its details, expected to receive a measureable accretion of knowledge from his visits to the best-known sites, monuments, and works of art, from his observation of men and manners. This knowledge he took back to England with him and applied it to the life in which the Grand Tour had been only an interlude. With Byron and Shelley, though they are not to be seen as sole instigators of the phenomenon, travel has become something more than a means for adding certain elements to an existing life-pattern. It has become a means for trans-

forming the previous life, for remedying anything that was amiss with it (and not only economically or in terms of health), for challenging the old life. Given the right conditions in the traveler's relations to his own country, there is produced something that might be termed the "exile's complex"; and both Byron and Shelley were, as it happens, exiles. The words "life" and "live" in Shelley's letter to Peacock are symbolic of the expanded or heightened aims with which the Romantic generation began to undertake the sojourn in Italy.

With the other sentence from the same letter, about the loveliness of the earth and the serenity of the sky, we have an indication of what was to be the most important single element in Shelley's Italian experience. It was in the nature of his perceptive and imaginative processes to subject the world to an analysis which reduced it, in his experience, to its elements of earth, air, and water. The letters from Italy abound in evocations of "the green earth," in descriptions of the atmosphere, capable, for all its tenuous shifting and changing, of being fixed in exact notation; in descriptions of water, as the source of endless pleasures of sight and touch and motion. In his brief description of "the first things we met in Italy"—

> a ruined arch of magnificent proportions in the Greek taste, standing in a kind of road of green lawn, overgrown with violets and primroses, and in the midst of stupendous mountains, and a *blonde* woman of light and graceful manners, something in the style of Fuseli's Eve—

both woman and monumental arch are accessories which serve to point up the beauty of the landscape, a landscape which seems a fitter setting for a myth than for the incidents of real life. At its most positive, at the times when it reached its highest level of exhilaration, Shelley's response to Italy was a response to its natural elements, especially when they were seen as the surroundings for images and vestiges of the life of ancient Rome and, better still, of Greece

One of the most powerful imaginative responses that Shelley made during his years in Italy was that called forth at Pompeii by the beauty of its site and surroundings. As he and his companions sat under the colonnade of the temple of Jupiter he was moved to a vision of what life had been, in such places as this, for the Greeks who had inhabited them: for

> they lived in harmony with nature; and the interstices of their incomparable columns were portals, as it were, to admit the spirit of beauty which animates this glorious universe to visit those whom it inspired. If such is Pompeii, what was Athens? What scene was exhibited from the Acropolis, the Parthenon, and the temples of Hercules, and Theseus, and the Winds. The islands and the Aegean sea, the mountains of Argolis, and the peaks of Pindus and Olympus, and the darkness of the Boeotian forests interspersed.

At such moments Shelley's experience of Italy reached its greatest intensity: and at such moments, it is easy to see, his experience was composed of two elements: first, the

Shelleyan response to the beauty of nature; and second, his response to the stimulus afforded by the remains of classical antiquity. For Shelley, Italy sometimes seems to have been a substitute for Greece.

In the areas of specifically Italian life and achievement, Shelley's responses were either negative or conventional or both. The contemplation of man and society in Italy afforded him no pleasure at all. His total impression, by July 25, was that "the modern Italians seem a miserable people, without sensibility, or imagination, or understanding." Although this impression referred to members of the upper classes whom he had met at the Casino at Bagni di Lucca, a letter he wrote to Peacock from Ferrara on November 6, although it contains a minute description of the farms he had seen on the journey from Este, shows that he had been unable to make a sympathetic penetration of the lives of the peasants he talked to. The few Italians who became members of the Shelley's circle of friends at Pisa a few years later were regarded as exceptions to the rule that all Italians were uninteresting and unsympathetic, until further acquaintance revealed that they, too, had, their weaknesses. "There are *two* Italies," he declared in a letter to Leigh Hunt in December 1818—

> one composed of the green earth and transparent sea, and the mighty ruins of ancient time, and aërial mountains, and the warm and radiant atmosphere which is interfused through all things. The other consists of the Italians of the present day, their works and ways. The one is the most sublime and lovely contemplation that can be conceived by the imagination of man; the other is the most degraded, disgusting and odious.

Nothing in Shelley's later letters suggests that he ever revised the judgment which he here expresses on the basis of nine or ten months' travel in Italy. This failure to find anything commendable or interesting in the Italian people, while we encounter it regularly in the eighteenth century, had already begun by the time Shelley was in Italy to give way to more receptive attitudes.

One broad aspect of the national life did, however, make a strong impression on him. He saw the lower orders as a race of slaves whose lives presented symbols of oppression and despair more lurid than any he had seen in England or Ireland. In Rome for the second time in the spring of 1819, after the journey to Naples, he was shocked by seeing a band of fettered criminals, about three hundred in number, at work in the Square of St Peter's.

> The iron discord of those innumerable chains clanks up into the sonorous air, and produces, contrasted with the musical dashing of the fountains, and the deep azure beauty of the sky, and the magnificence of the architecture around, a conflict of sensations allied to madness. It is the emblem of Italy—moral degradation contrasted with the glory of the arts.

As for the glory of the arts, Shelley was pretty well content to follow the lead of his predecessors, certainly in the objects he chose to look at and often even in his responses to them. In the long letters to Peacock describing what he had seen in Rome we meet the same descriptions of the

Forum and the Colosseum that we can find in the letters of almost any eighteenth-century traveler. Like his predecessors, he is far more interested in Roman than in post-Roman achievement; and like them, too, he was seeing according to a convention which set very narrow limits on what he was able to see. After describing his disappointment in St Peter's—"internally it exhibits littleness on a large scale, and is in every respect opposed to antique taste"—he is led back, by force of contrast, to the Pantheon. He then returns to modern times to describe the fountains of the Piazza Navona and the Piazza di Trevi; of the latter he says:

> The whole is not ill conceived nor executed; but you know not how delicate the imagination becomes by dieting with antiquity day after day! The only things that sustain the comparison are Raffael, Guido, and Salvator Rosa.

Shelley was a free spirit, if ever there was one, but these are not free judgments. (And far from rousing in us any sentiments of superiority, they may well remind us of the likelihood that our own personal tastes and judgments have been largely created by the judgments of our time.) The rigid exclusion of all post-classical achievement, only to allow Salvator Rosa to march in as one of three possible modern claims to glory, is evidence of the automatic acceptance of a convention that was well over a hundred years old and all but doomed in Shelley's own day. A good deal has been written about Shelley's response to the visual arts; but while a close study of the subject can be rewarding for what it tells us about Shelley, it offers us very little that we can regard as negotiable, or even interestingly suggestive, as accounts of the works themselves. The painters he mentions are Raphael, Guido Reni, Correggio, Salvator Rosa, Guercino, Domenichino, the Caracci, Albani, Franceschini, Elisabetta Sirani, Titian, Michelangelo, and (in the belief that the Medusa in the Uffizi was his work) Leonardo. All of Michelangelo's chief virtues, as Sir Herbert Read has pointed out, struck him as defects; and any pictures painted before the fifteenth century—probably even before the sixteenth—he would have lumped together under some such heading as one guide-book reserved for them: "curious old pictures."

Tastes change, and once again we look with interest and admiration at the Carracci, at Guido Reni and Guercino, at Domenichino and Sassoferrato. Even so, it is a good deal less interesting than one might have hoped to look at pictures in Bologna with Shelley's descriptions of them in hand. His response to pictures is always literary; he does not view them as the result of specific choices of form and technique, but rather as absolute achievements, capable of being interpreted as directly as life itself. Of Raphael's St Cecilia he says, "You forget that it is a picture as you look at it." But that is not an unusual experience for him, since the saint's or madonna's smile was always the object of the same sort of attempt to penetrate its meaning, with its implications of a past and a future, as would appropriately be directed to the reading of a smile on a living countenance.

Shelley himself made no claims to connoisseurship in painting, and there is little evidence that his interest in

Italian painting was not perfunctory as well as conventional. What drew him to the galleries in Rome and Florence was the works of classical sculpture they contained. Reaching Florence in the autumn of 1819, he announced his purpose of "studying the gallery piecemeal," one of his chief objects in Italy being, as he said, "the observing in statuary and painting the degree in which, and the rules according to which, that ideal beauty, of which we have so intense yet so obscure an apprehension, is realized in external forms." But the notes he made there, as in Rome, dealt entirely with sculpture. His experience of sculpture seems to have been more intense than his experience of painting, and its importance in the development of his mind and art has received careful attention. That importance, it seems to me, is primarily a philosophical one. He viewed the works of sculpture he saw in Italy, whether Greek or Roman, as a means for achieving an understanding of the Greek approach to the problem of expressing ideal beauty. In fact, he approached painting and sculpture at the point at which, the technical part of the artist's work having been done, they resembled rather than differed from one another. At this point they also resembled poetry, at least for Shelley, so that the poet could turn to them for lessons which could be directly applied to his task of rendering ideal truth and beauty in humanly apprehensible forms.

All this constitutes an aesthetic, to be sure, and that for Shelley it was a valid aesthetic is demonstrated by his success in transmuting motifs from his experience of the arts into the characteristically rarefied element of his poetry, where they indeed play their occasionally traceable part in the creation of "beautiful idealisms of moral excellence." But it should be noted that at the beginning of this process which ended in such splendid metamorphosis, there was an experience of works of art which relied entirely on convention and which, whatever its validity and richness for Shelley, does nothing to enhance our sense of the presence or significance either of the works he mentions or of art in general.

Back in Florence in 1821, he writes to Mary at Pisa,

> I spent three hours this morning principally in the contemplation of the Niobe, and of a favorite Apollo; all worldly thoughts and cares seem to vanish from before the sublime emotions such spectacles create; and I am deeply impressed with the great difference of happiness enjoyed by those who live at a distance from these incarnations of all that the finest minds have conceived of beauty, and those who can resort to their company at pleasure.

I do not suggest that the delight in contemplation was not genuine, or that the Niobe and the favorite Apollo were not worthy of being contemplated with delight, but merely that we see here an instance of the traveler abandoning himself uncritically to values guaranteed by the received opinion of his time, so that the response is very highly subjective. It is Shelley's idealizing power which gave value to this experience, and unless we possess the same power there is nothing in it for us to emulate. This, it seems to me, is the typical distribution of values in Shelley's experience of Italy. At such times as he was happy there, the

light and air, the ancient monuments, certain works of art, produced a lifting of the spirit which carried him into the realm of his most fruitful contemplation and creativity. In a sense, the influence behind all this was Italy, but Shelley's experience of more specifically Italian values, Italian achievement, was restricted enough, even commonplace. What he made of it—and not only in the sense of something that he put into his poetry, but in the sense of the élan of the day-to-day experience itself, when it was at its best—we should certainly call distinguished and are kept from doing so only by the thought that we probably ought to call it sublime.

He was certainly not always happy in Italy, and in the darker side of his years there we recognize an element that will occasionally figure in the post-Romantic experience of Italy, as a potential if not inevitable concomitant of the traveler's desire to make a complete substitution of the new life for the old. Expatriates there had been even in the eighteenth century, for reasons of health or economy, and we need not point out how often in Victorian biography we encounter the pattern of a prolonged domesticity in Italy. Shelley and Byron, however, were not expatriates but exiles. Writing to Thomas Medwin in January 1820, and urging him to come to Italy for its climate and its art, Shelley calls Italy "the Paradise of exiles, the retreat of pariahs." "But," he adds, "I am thinking of myself rather than of you."

The circumstances under which both poets had left England were, to say the least, special; and there were actual legal obstacles to their returning which make it not strictly necessary to look for metaphysical ones. Granted these harsh facts, however, we see in the two poets' varied and characteristic reactions to their expatriation an illustration of attitudes that occur fairly frequently in the annals and the experience of the post-Romantic traveler, down to and including our own time.

It all begins when we see the word "life" figuring in a writer's proclamation of his travel aims, when the idea starts to take shape that essential rewards can be obtained by going to the new country to live, or at any rate to settle down for a prolonged stay. A new ideal comes in, with its virtues and its values no doubt, but also with its own vices and its own possibilities for foolishness: the ideal of entering the life of the new country from the inside, of penetrating it with complete sympathy and knowledge. It should be noted that even while he entertains this ideal the traveler remains English or American in certain important respects, for he usually has no intention of taking up work or citizenship in the country in question. Right here there enters the possibility of a confusion of aim, the possibility that the traveler is making demands of himself and his experience that he will ultimately be unable to fulfill. Perhaps the hidden principle that underlies these claims may be seen as the traveler's willingness to give absolute, rather than contingent, value to the exotic.

When the traveler has undergone some deeply painful experience in his own country, when it has rejected him or failed to treat him as he thinks he should be treated, then there may come into being the emotional pattern of opposing tensions which we have already described as the exile's complex. Under less crucial circumstances, the new post-Romantic ideal results in the pursuit of a mystique which, while it has certainly thickened and intensified and subtilized the traveler's potential experience, has also added many a spiritual burden to his lot. Attendant on this mystique is a host of typically modern snobbisms: the cult of the undiscovered, the pursuit of the truly native and characteristic, the dread (in James's phrase) of "the foot-fall of the detested fellow-pilgrim." Attendant on it also is a certain amount of inevitable disappointment, and the likelihood that when things go wrong the eager, uncritical enthusiasm will turn to bitterness and contempt.

Not all of this is the fault of Shelley and Byron, to be sure, but they do afford early, premonitory instances of what may happen to the modern traveler who is prompted to substitute *life* in the new country for life in the old, to set one up in opposition to the other. Shelley in particular, with his aristocrat's aloofness and his eclecticism, can scarcely be said to have sought too deep a penetration of life around him in Italy. But intermingled with the many passages in his letters which describe the delights of the new life, his satisfaction with the bargain, there are also many, beginning early and recurring up to the end, which describe a homesickness whose bitterness was compounded by the sense that he had willingly rejected what he now missed.

> All that I see in Italy—and from my tower window I now see the magnificent peaks of the Apennines half enclosing the plain—is nothing; it dwindles into smoke in the mind, when I think of some familiar forms of scenery, little perhaps in themselves, over which old remembrances have thrown a delightful colour. How we prize what we despised when present! So the ghosts of our dead associations rise and haunt us, in revenge for our having let them starve, and abandoned them to perish.

These are the realities of Shelley's Italian experience, too, just as much as "the Praxitelean shapes that throng the Vatican, the Capitol, and the palaces of Rome," or the happiness of the last summer at Lerici—"this divine bay"—reading Calderon, sailing, listening to "the most enchanting music," regretting only that "the summer must ever pass." To ignore them, or to ignore the comparative narrowness of it all, is to give an account of Shelley's Italian experience that is both naive and false and that will sooner or later break down when it is pressed into service for critical or biographical purposes.

Byron's sojourn in Italy was longer than Shelley's and the records of it, in the *Letters and Journals* as well as in contemporary memoirs, are full and detailed. Like Shelley's, Byron's Italian experience was in many areas the conventional experience of his time and, hence, of the preceding century; like Shelley, Byron made on the basis of such experiences something new and highly personal that transposed the English traveler's potential response into a new and higher key. The fourth canto of *Childe Harold* was at once the apotheosis and the swan-song of the Grand Tour. A reader accustomed to jogging up and down the peninsula with the eighteenth-century tourist will always know what is coming next in this poem, and yet everything is

new, not merely altered by being used as a backdrop for the dramatic figure of Byron himself, but transfigured by style and energy of treatment. The poem's basis in first-hand experience was the rudimentary and fairly blasé version of the Grand Tour in which Byron was engaged off and on from the fall of 1816 to the spring of 1817, helped out by Hobhouse's notes and by Byron's reading in such works as Dr John Moore's *Italy* and Mrs Hemans' *Restoration of the Works of Art to Italy.* Considered from the point of view of the materials that went into it, of what it was in any objective sense about, the poem is a *tour de force* in which Byron succeeds in giving a remarkably new kind of life to an old experience about which he was sometimes cynical—"all that time-tax of travel," in the phrase he used for the sights of Verona—but which at most times he saw from an entirely traditional point of view. Nothing needs to be said about the role played by Byron's familiarity with Italian literature (whatever the debt to Whistlecraft in the entire transaction) in creating the form and spirit of *Don Juan*. It is customary to point out that in *Beppo,* based as it was on Byron's familiarity with Venetian domestic life, Byron widened the range and altered the tone of Italian subject matter that was available for treatment by English writers. Here too, in a way, something new was being made from something old. The figure of the cicisbeo had fascinated the eighteenth-century commentators, but they never felt that they knew the whole story of his functions: perhaps Byron was a little late, but he felt that at last he had the answers to their questions.

These and other aspects of Byron's demonstrable literary debt to Italy have been explored in detail, though often with too naive an approach to the questions of what constitutes indebtedness and of the way a writer's personal experience enters the fabric of his work. At the moment, however, if the record is to be kept accurate it ought to be corrected by an analytic reading of the personal side of Byron's Italian experience. C. P. Brand, in the work mentioned earlier, pointing out that there were English travelers who remained aloof from Italian life and others who entered into it closely, cites Byron as being among the few Englishmen who, in his own words, had lived "in their houses and in the heart of their families . . . long enough . . . to feel more for them as a nation than for any other in existence." Comparatively speaking, Byron's claim was just, but if we come to it after having traced his experience and his attitudes as they shifted and developed during his years in Italy, it will be seen to mean both more and less than it means when we encounter it out of context.

Byron's attitudes towards Italy—among them the affection which he often proclaimed and no doubt sincerely felt, the desire to think of himself as having been completely assimilated into Italian life, as well as the negative attitudes, the contempt and disgust which sometimes assailed him—must all be seen primarily as functions of his attitude towards England. He was there in the first place because life had become impossible in England, and the psychological mechanism by which he set Italy, the richness and exclusiveness of his Italian experience, up against the country which had rejected him, is perfectly obvious. For example in 1819, in a letter to Murray, he says,

Besides, I mean to write my best work in *Italian,* and it will take me nine years more thoroughly to master the language; and then if my fancy exist, and I exist too, I will try what I *can* do *really.* As to the Estimation of the English which you talk of, let them calculate what it is worth, before they insult me with their insolent condescension.

Italy, and his Italian interests, offered him the possibility of feeling, and of announcing as fact whenever it seemed necessary, that he had loftily withdrawn himself from further competition for glory in English letters. Meanwhile, the life he was leading in Italy must be made to seem, at least, to exceed in charm and ease, in freedom from stupid constraint, the life he might have led in England.

Often it did seem to do so, and no doubt his years in Italy offered him as much happiness as he could have found anywhere. But at other times the happiness must have seemed to him, as it seems to us, to be built up from frail, pinchbeck materials. The Venetian family life into which he had gained an entrée gradually came to seem not only corrupt but endlessly boring. Later, for about a year beginning in the spring of 1820, the activities of the insurgents around Ravenna promised excitement and a chance for serious action; but the insurrection refused to come to a boil. At such times, when the charm or interest failed, all Byron saw about him was a country that was not his own. He could pretend, as he does for example in a letter to Francis Hodgson, written from Ravenna in December 1820, to have become almost more Italian than English:

> . . . What I have been doing would but little interest you, as it regards another country and another people, and would be almost speaking another language, for my own is not quite so familiar to me as it used to be.

But ten days later, he is recording in his journal his disappointment at receiving no letters from England: "Very sulky in consequence (for there ought to have been letters), and ate in consequence a copious dinner; for which I am vexed, it makes me swallow quicker—but drank very little." He could be as vehement as any traveler has ever been in his distaste for the figure cut by his compatriots abroad—"a parcel of staring boobies, who go about gaping and wish to be at once cheap and magnificent," but Trelawny, speaking of Byron's prolonged absence from England, said that "it had not effaced the mark John Bull brands his children with; the instant he loomed above the horizon, on foot or horseback, you saw at a glance he was a Britisher." And Trelawny (not always a trustworthy witness, to be sure) adds, "He did not understand foreigners, nor they him; and, during the time I knew him, he associated with no Italians except the family of Count Gamba" [Edward John Trelawny, *Records of Byron, Shelley, and the Author,* 1887].

I hope it is clear that I am not trying to reduce Byron's experience, ultimately, to the commonplace. Again I would merely suggest, as with Shelley, that his Italian experience is not the uniformly positive, glowing, happy affair that it has sometimes thoughtlessly been described as being, and that we should not take Byron's own assessment of it, at his most enthusiastic or most wishful mo-

ments, as the whole story. Distinction there certainly is, and a truly creative originality, but these qualities can be rightly appraised only if we see them as they emerge from a total experience which was not exempt from the laws, and the all too human impulses, which operate whenever it is a question of the travel experience.

One cannot have been in Italy very long before becoming aware, if only from the commemorative plaques on palace walls, that one has had remarkable predecessors, writers especially, who might be expected to have interesting things to say about all that one is seeing. Gradually, with the requisite humility, one develops the habit of comparing their responses with one's own—and although it is true that some see better than others, that less has been lost on some individual travelers than on others, on some generations than on others, still all the responses are interesting, so long as they are genuine, all have something to add to our understanding of the most inexhaustibly interesting of countries. But if what they saw helps us, if the very *way* they saw often gives us a capacity of vision which we could not have attained without them, it might also be remembered that when we undertake to study their responses, to analyze them and make comparisons among them, something will be gained if we bring to bear on our study anything we may have learned at first hand about the traveler's lot: if in reading travel literature we will try not to forget what it is to be a traveler.

> *Herbert Barrows, "Convention and Novelty in the Romantic Generation's Experience of Italy," in* Literature as a Mode of Travel: Five Essays and a Postscript, *The New York Public Library, 1963, pp. 69-84.*

Victor Hugo, on a trip from Geneva to the Mediterranean in 1830, describes the Rhone River:

I reached the Mediterranean by the Rhone. I have seen the Rhone enter the Mediterranean two leagues wide, yellow, muddy, magnificent, filthy. Six days before, I had seen it rush out of Lake Leman, under the old mill-bridge of Geneva, clear, transparent, limpid, blue as sapphire. At Lake Leman, the Rhone is like a young man; at the Mediterranean it is like an old man. Above, it has seen as yet only its mountains; here it has passed through cities. God gives it snow; men give it sewage.

This is what it means to have lived and run. After living, roaring, swallowing up torrents and rivers, shattering rocks, washing bridges, bearing burdens, nourishing cities, reflecting skies and clouds, the river which departed from the lake narrow and tumultuous, arrives, immense and calm, at the sea and buries itself there. . . .

> *Victor Hugo, quoted in* The Golden Age of Travel: Literary Impressions of the Grand Tour, *edited by Helen Barber Morrison, Twayne Publishers, 1951.*

Pierina Carcich

[*In the following excerpt, Carcich explores Stendhal's*

narrative devices in his travelogue, Rome, Naples and Florence in 1817, *showing how Stendhal rearranged the chronology of his journey in order to highlight the emotional significance of his experiences.*]

Rome, Naples and Florence in 1817 can be read as a simple account of Stendhal's journey undertaken in 1816, just one year prior to its publication, as the author would like us to believe. However, this travelogue, based on Stendhal's earlier stays in Italy, offers a critical view not only of Italy, but of France, Europe and even the United States. Privileged by his direct participation in the historical events of his times, Stendhal gives his viewpoint on politics; he probes into the historical and artistic heritage of Italy, shedding light indirectly on France's past, and reaches a global, yet close, understanding of these countries which enables him to prophesy about their future.

Rome, Naples and Florence in 1817 lends itself to multiple readings and interpretations: a vivid description of travel experiences, criticisms and up-to-date evaluations of the state of fine arts, political, social and philosophical speculations, contemporary chronicle, autobiography, or a theory on the pursuit of happiness, and, somewhat less readily, a fictional narrative. It is the literary aspect of this text, its narrative devices rather than Stendhal's ideological pronouncements, that deserve to be examined, for the other aspects have already received the critics' attention.

In this respect, a distinction between our use of the terms "narrative devices" and "style" may be necessary. An avowal about style made by the narrator in the Preface to *Rome, Naples and Florence in 1817* could be misleading or even puzzling at first reading. He assures us that he merely "notes" things as they were, not in a book but in a "sketch . . . [which] is a *natural work.*" Each evening, he explains, "I used to write down what had made the greatest impression on me. I was often so tired that I had barely the courage to pick up my papers. I've hardly made any changes in these sentences, but, inspired by the objects they describe, many expressions doubtless lack in measure." Stendhal's traveler-narrator does indeed write with naturalness. Writing, he seems to be speaking. His typical, as well as his finest, passages sound like selections of conversations held by or with various characters met on his journey, or with the reader himself: "Today, Sunday, I was about to die of hunger. I had let myself be taken to the Colosseum to look at St. Gregory's chapel and the charming frescos by Guido, especially *Angel's Concert.* I came back into the inhabited Rome dying of hunger; I get to the great café Ruspoli, closed because it is vespers time. 'When does it open?—At five o'clock'."

He strews each entry with subjective, incisive though often self-righteous, remarks and a myriad of anecdotes. He alternates lengthy entries with short ones. Only a few times, the informal talk turns into a lecture, often consisting of a long quotation on literature, government or the arts, borrowed from a contemporary journal. In general, however, the tone is infused with a living presence.

The traveler-narrator's spontaneity, ebullience and impulsiveness fit the unstructured and disjointed paragraphs, as well as the discursiveness, the many repetitions and even contradictions therein. The flat syntax leaves the impression of improvisation. There is a nearly total absence of imagery. The style is direct, often terse, but overblown in descriptive passages of tableaux where the narrator is self-conscious as an artist or a very sensitive individual or a traveler idealizing Italy.

In fact, Stendhal mistrusts the art of language, suspects it of affectation and insincerity. There is a real difficulty in discussing his travelogue in terms of style understood as art of language. To Stendhal, the word is but an instrument. He gives merit to what one is saying, rather than to words themselves. This is evident in his frequent criticism of Chateaubriand, whose elaborate language is a source of irritation to him: "In vain do I try to put myself in his place, I cannot stand him; it always seems ridiculous to me." Mme de Staël, another traveler-author to precede him to Italy, is equally not trusted for her style: "That tense style whose least fault is to exact ceaseless admiration . . . That mind which pretends to be recognized as a genius, and fails to see that the most striking quality (naturalness) is lacking in her, this comedy, which makes fun of what I like most, hurt me greatly. . . . Putting her sentences into natural style, I noticed they were hiding only common ideas, and feelings obviously exaggerated . . ." [Stendhal, *Journal* in *Œuvres intimes,* 1955].

To these style-conscious travelogue authors, Stendhal prefers Duclos, Young, Forsyth, Spon, and de Brosses whom he describes as "natural" or as "being themselves in their work." In regard to the last one, he writes specifically: "In de Brosses' style, depth and naiveté that become Dominique's character." [The author adds in a footnote that Dominique was Stendhal's pseudonymn for the intimate and vulnerable self as opposed to the public one.] "The style I like most is de Brosses', a style that says a lot of things, in a few words and very clearly, with grace, without pedantry . . . I believe this taste is even more true to myself in as much as it agrees with my taste for comedy and my dislike for tragedy." Indeed, Stendhal creates a familiar tone that reminds one of epistolary travelogues like de Brosses' *Lettres d'Italie,* whose quizzing smile at the expense of Italian customs distinguishes this author from his more serious English contemporaries. Among these, let us look at a typical passage from Young's travelogue, (one among the most widely translated ones in Stendhal's, as well as in our time); we find that his descriptions are rare and limited to remarks like: "The scene is sublime . . . delicious . . . beautiful . . . interesting" [Arthur Young, *Travels to Italy,* 1942].

One will not fail to notice that Stendhal equates a stark, even naive language, with sincerity, and an elaborate style with affectation of feeling. Like the Ideologues, whose influence he had felt especially in the years immediately prior to his trip to Italy, Stendhal sees in language the feeling and the thought itself.

In contrast with the pervasive improvisation of style, there is a carefully premeditated form, that of an idealized archetypal voyage. This becomes apparent by examining the various sources and components of the narrative matter and the organizational stratagems which the final structure reveals.

Detail of the Baptistry of Florence Cathedral, in a watercolor by John Ruskin, 1872.

The content of *Rome, Naples and Florence in 1817* consists of numerous notes and memories gathered by Stendhal in 1800, during his first visit to Italy, of his *Journal* of 1811 covering his trips to different points in Italy, and of his fresh memories of his stay in Milan from 1814 to 1817, and finally, of secondhand documents such as Vallardi's *Italian Itinerary,* Bianconi's *New Guide to Milan,* de Brosses' *Lettres d'Italie,* and *The Edinburgh Review.*

A comparison with the *Journal* of 1811, from which Stendhal extracts the largest portion of his subject matter, will be instructive on the fictional stratagems used in the final published account. There is no "pure" journal for this segment of Stendhal's life, as the extant Journal of 1813 is a result of rehandling of the 1811 *Journal* or Mr. Léry's notebook ("Cahier de M. de Léry," as the author had first called it), made in view of some publication projects which never materialized. Nevertheless, this document enables one to see the contributions of the literary imagination to the basic subject matter of *Rome, Naples and Florence in 1817.* The mere choice of the 1811 journey, rather than the 1800-1801 one (which merely by its duration, if not by the space covered, surpasses the earlier one), is revealing of the author's awareness of the public. "The year 1811 is one

of Beyle's most brilliant years," writes Pierre Martineau; Stendhal leads a life of leisure and experiences considerable success in the salons, especially among women. He is twenty-eight years old and knows how to enjoy life; whereas in 1800, he was but a provincial young man, painfully conscious of his awkwardness in the Italian social circles.

He keeps the overall linear or progressive itinerary (north-south-north), but he adds some detours to less known places, thus creating "buckles" that are inconceivable not only to the expert Italian traveler but to any discriminate reader. Through this device, however, he obtains, first of all, the effect of the unknown in a land directly or indirectly known to some of his readers; besides, he affirms his individuality as a traveler in a classical country. He also changes the original chronology but keeps the approximate length of his stays in the visited places, as it is not temporality but geography that affects this traveler. Moreover, he keeps the order of events, except for the opening and the conclusion of the travel account. In 1811, for example he had reached Milan via Geneva and not via Munich and Berlin, visited last in 1808. In fact, he had gone back to Paris directly from Milan, via Geneva.

By reorganizing the structure of the beginning and the end, Stendhal mounts Italy between two Nordic countries in order to better set off his idealized vision of Italy. This sets the ground for a real narrative, having a beginning, a middle and an end, where a certain logic can now be detected, which was absent in the *Journal.* One can distinguish sections imitating the rhythm of a journey that progresses according to the model of the archetypal voyage. Stendhal's traveler, too, goes from the known to the unknown, in the sense that he leaves from a personal image of Italy to arrive at the real one, and, simultaneously, from ignorance or uncertainty of himself to not only identity, but consciousness and affirmation of self. The evolution of the traveler's consciousness and his progressive experience of the land of dreams make up the plot of Stendhal's narrative. This can be observed in the division of the text into two main parts. The first third of the travelogue is enthusiastic and praiseful in tone. Then an encounter with reality occurs which engenders sharp remarks. Italian customs, institutions, heritage are criticized: Rome's society is "without attraction," its people are "the least civilized." In conclusion, "Rome and Naples are barbarian places dressed up in the European fashion."

About two thirds of the way through, a turning point occurs. The traveler's experiences, which transcend the traditional itinerary, bring about a change of heart and enable him to assert his former view, without denying reality but integrating it with his original vision. Like Proust's narrator in *Remembrance of Things Past,* Stendhal's traveler fuses dream and experience in the final representation of his reality.

By choosing for his plot the evolution of the traveler's consciousness, Stendhal undermines the intimate and sentimental matter of his journal and accentuates the effects of the foreign experience on him. The introspective analysis made by the traveler of 1811 (who compares himself with the one of 1800) which constitutes one third of the whole journal is eliminated. Also, the relationship with Angela Pietragrua, whose detailed account makes up half of the journal, disappears totally from the published travelogue. The suppression of the confessional autobiography, we believe, is dictated less by the embarrassment before the reader than by the effort to focus the reader's attention on only one character set in as many situations of Italian life as possible. To this end, the traveling companions, M. Lechi and M. Crozet, are also sacrificed.

In the travelogue (in contrast with the journal) the tourist's attention is directed toward the exterior. Rubriques of general interest are added: politics, habits and customs, descriptions of urban and country landscape. The original enthusiasm of Milan spreads to the whole nation. But Lombardy still remains the eminent region both for the traveler and in the division of the travelogue, in spite of the title which excludes it totally.

The traveler in the journal is but a thin silhouette of the fully delineated portrait in the published text. He is ceaselessly preoccupied and occupied by women. Determined but awkward, he imagines amorous strategies whose results he notes scrupulously in his journal. In the published version, however, he wins effortlessly the women's attention and admiration, without attaching himself to any one in particular, as a worldly man would. Fine arts, landscape, history are some of his favorite distractions; in the 1817 version of *Rome, Naples and Florence* (and even more visibly so in the 1826 version) they become interests pursued in a systematic and exhaustive way. The introvert life of 1811 had left little place for observation of customs and none for political questions. The few judgments passed were either prudent or impersonal and conformist, echoing those of the author's predecessors.

Stendhal develops the sketch of the 1811 travel account primarily by extending the consciousness and the social experiences of his traveler. He raises him to a distinguished social rank by adding "de" to his recent German pseudonym, Stendhal, and conferring on him the title of cavalry officer who fought in the Russian Campaign. His abundant knowledge of military, political and historical Europe gives him a considerable authority in his reader's eye, even though his assurance at times reaches a somewhat pedantic and pretentious tone. At thirty-four, the narrator-traveler gives the impression of being a little young man, "plain-spoken, self-assertive about everything" [according to Roland Beyer in his Introduction to *Rome, Naples et Florence*, 1964].

The narrator-hero's exuberance, spontaneity, sensual and artistic personality are in distinct opposition to the materialistic values of the Louis XVIII society that he denounces most symbolically by choosing Germany as his place of residence from 1814 on, at the very outset of the Bourbon restoration. The discriminating reader or one of the "happy few," to whom Stendhal dedicates the first in a series of his Italian works, will readily recognize himself in the tourist. Thus Stendhal rejoins the archetypal hero of the Renaissance romance which represents the ideals and aspirations in all spheres of activities—philosophical, social and sentimental—of his society.

The tripartite structure (departure, adventure, return) gives unity to the narrative. Although departure and arrival do not constitute the main moments of the travelogue as in *Pilgrim's Progress* or the *Odyssey,* they are remarkable for the imaginative reversal or the theme variation *vis-à-vis* romance. The hero in *Rome, Naples and Florence in 1817* does not set out on his trip from his fatherland, but from Germany:

> Berlin, October 4, 1816.-[. . .] How crazy am I still at the age of thirty-four! So I will see this beautiful land of Italy. But I hide carefully from the minister; the eunuques are permanently cross with the libertines. But this trip gives me too much pleasure and *who knows where the world may be in three weeks from now.*

This is the opening entry in *Rome, Naples and Florence in 1817.* The season in which the journey starts is not a negligible detail. In October, the cold weather has already done its damage; from the outset Germany stands out as the land of dying life and emotional sterility ("nothing here for the heart: the cold weather does not allow me to find pleasure"). The situation is completely reversed in "this beautiful Italy" where the musical genius restores immediately the "worn out . . . organs that were no longer susceptible to pleasure." Almost instantly, the traveler goes from non-existence to existence.

The image of the North, hostile to Stendhal's narrator, evokes by contrast the romance hero who is always associated with the warm season, fertility, vigor, youth. And, if one pursues the characterization of the land of adventure according to the dialectical structure proper to this type of narrative, one can have a fairly clear image of the country which the hero is about to discover. Since the reader has already seen the traveler's immediate enthusiasm and exaltation of Italy, he cannot fail to wonder what really constitutes the quest of this journey.

Frye's analysis of romance can shed light on this point. The main quest for the Stendhalian hero seems to correspond to the fourth phase of romance, that is "maintaining the integrity of the innocent world against the assault of experience" [*Anatomy of Criticism,* 1967]. In search of the ideal land and of oneself, the Stendhalian hero will have to defend and preserve his mythical or "innocent" vision of Italy, unadulterated by the adjustment to or conciliation with the deceiving reality. Unlike the Renaissance romance, Stendhal's travelogue does not end with the hero's reintegration into his original society, but with the confirmation of its refusal and with the affirmation of the newly discovered land. The traveler in *Rome, Naples and Florence* returns to Germany via Switzerland, which allows the reader to make, by contrast, a final evaluation of Italy. Stendhal's image of Geneva is indeed sad: the Swiss woman lacks naturalness, vivacity, and passion, the qualities exalted in the Italian woman:

> Women's prudery is an incredible article by dint of ridicule and boredom. I noticed that they say exactly the same thing about the foreigners they are introduced to. To be lovable for them means to repeat the formula of amiability that their maid taught them.

For Stendhal, the Swiss customs revolve around "what will people say," a worry unknown in Italy where everyone follows his own inclination. The narrator's scorn goes as far as to demythify Swiss "freedom" or political independence:

> I would like to know who is the traveler who was the first to say there is freedom in Switzerland. In Geneva, in Berne, there are four hundred supervisors of which every one wants to show off his power. If you choose them by the way you put your tie on, they persecute you.

The open criticism and complaints against the North, met in the prelude, change into irony here. The return to the "dark North" with the "veiled sun" that makes the traveler regret "the land of genius" and "the land of voluptuousness" is "one of the unhappiest moments in [his] life."

Whereas the hero of the archetypal voyage upon his return to his fatherland enriches his society by sharing his experiences and wisdom, Stendhal's hero delights in taking stock of his personal gain. After substantiating his immediate love for Italy with his subsequent experiences, he can recount with certainty its beneficent effects, knowing however that he will be unable to influence the majority of his society (those "eunuques [who] are permanently cross with the libertines") among whom he is a despised and despising stranger. But the hero has acquired a new self-knowledge that enables him to affirm himself against those who do not resemble him: "it is not that I gained intellectually; it is the soul that has gained. Moral old age for me is postponed by ten years. . . . 'Dry' people will have no more influence on me; I know the land where one breathes this celestial air whose existence they deny; I am made of iron for them." The foreign experience reinforces in him the sensitive man who has won over the analytical one. Traveling for Stendhal is, therefore, not a chance to lose or evade one's self, but to find an identity and the self. However, this identity will prove to be a temporary discovery of the self, since Stendhal's subsequent travelers in Italy will continue to oscillate between the analytical and the sensuous inclination of their temperament.

The trip has been a movement in several directions. The acquisition of an ethnological knowledge, set as the primary goal in his *Journal* was only fortuitously important. It is the exploration of the self, or the internal voyage, that forms the essence of the adventure. Psychologically, the narrator has freed himself from the embarrassment of being eccentric by becoming fully aware of his differences by identifying himself with the foreign, in reality kindred, people. He has accepted or become more tolerant of himself: he is stronger and more serene. This ensuing tranquillity makes him see the French and the German in a more benevolent light, his feeling of social alienation has been attenuated. Biographically, from a French civil servant, stationed in Germany, the narrator-hero has become the author of his book. The final point of the journey is not the return, but the narration to the sensitive souls, to the elite society of the happy few who are the equivalent of the Faerie Queene for whom Spenser's hero undertakes his quest.

The epilogue of *Rome, Naples and Florence*—the passing through a Northern country—contains, in fact, the last two phases of romance. After the action, the hero reflects, glances at a distance from an elevated point, at his experience. He contemplates his adventure: he keeps intact his original myth of Italy (beauty, passion, naturalness, kindness, creativity, exuberance), a reflexion of his intimate self that he now has the generosity to confide and entrust to his reader-brother.

Unlike the archetypal voyage, *Rome, Naples and Florence* is narrated chronologically in the present, without following the order in which Stendhal lived the events he presents. The itinerary of his travelogues is often imagined and many of the events are invented. This carelessness about the chronological order must not make one suspect Stendhal of total fabrication. By paradox, it is a warranty of the authenticity of his feelings: he does not try to recreate the event or the facts of his travelogue. In writing *La Vie de Henry Brulard,* he explains that he is looking for the effect produced by the thing, not the thing itself, the brutal emotion, not the image or the physiognomy of the thing: "I do not know the details . . . I can only describe my feelings . . ."

The application of this process can easily be imagined in the writing of the travelogue. Writing not being simultaneous with traveling, the travelogue becomes by necessity a collection of memories. Not only have eight years passed between Stendhal's first long journey to Italy and the writing of *Rome, Naples and Florence,* but in the regular experience of the traveler, it is paradoxical to be a traveler and a writer at the same time. In writing the travelogue, Stendhal makes the past and present memories coincide. Memory, or the relived sensation, may bring about yet another sensation of the same kind or of the same intensity (or even its opposite), which in real life took place at an earlier or later time than the first one. Sacrificing the order of lived events to the benefits of the relived ones by the act of writing makes it possible to keep the intensity of the sensation that could otherwise be lost. It is the involuntary memory that guides Stendhal in the writing of his travelogues; it is not surprising, therefore, that later in his career he will use the epithet "mémoires" for his account of travel experiences in France (*Mémoires d'un Touriste*).

By submitting to his affective rather than voluntary memory, Stendhal hopes to find the meaning of his experiences and thus reach self-knowledge. The travelogue lends itself to this egotistical quest by the unique importance it grants the narrator. Only the autobiography or the journal can surpass it in this respect. (Stendhal's need of and compatibility with this type of genre is best seen in his use and exploitation in *La Vie de Henry Brulard.*) On the contrary, the travelogue offers very few possibilities in the disposition of event sequences: flashback and flash-forward (or foreknowledge of the future) are made impossible; only a concatenation of events is allowed; juxtaposition is limited only in the progressive direction. (For example, one can join June 13 and 14, but, unlike in the novel, one will never be able to fuse June 14 with any other but the immediately preceding or following day.) The mercurial properties of memory being incompatible with the rigidity of temporal or linear sequence of the travelogue, Stendhal has no choice but to feign progressive linearity when in reality he is advancing only by association of feeling or memories.

The tense of narration thus becomes true in so far as it is not the present of the event that it pretends to depict, but the present of the narrator's memory at the moment of writing. Therefore the present remains fictional in so far as it revives or re-presents the past.

The narrative devices in *Rome, Naples and Florence in 1817* aim as a whole at affirming the narrator-traveler as a man of feeling, a man of heart, who is looking for happiness; they contribute to the making of Italy as the land where one knows and practices the art of being happy.

> Pierina Carcich, "The Idealized Voyage in Stendhal's 'Rome, Naples and Florence'," in Essays in Arts and Sciences, *Vol. XIV, May, 1985, pp. 13-22.*

Henry James on the sixteenth-century French château of Chenonceaux:

The pale yellow front of the château, the small scale of which is at first a surprise, rises beyond a considerable court, at the entrance of which a massive and detached round tower, with a turret on its brow (a relic of the building that preceded the actual villa), appears to keep guard. This court is not inclosed—or is inclosed at least only by the gardens, portions of which are at present in process of radical readjustment. Therefore, though Chenonceaux has no great height, its delicate façade stands up boldly enough. This façade, one of the most finished things in Touraine, consists of two stories, surmounted by an attic which, as so often in the buildings of the French Renaissance, is the richest part of the house. The high-pitched roof contains three windows of beautiful design, covered with embroidered caps and flowering into crocketed spires. The window above the door is deeply niched; it opens upon a balcony made in the form of a double pulpit—one of the most charming features of the front. Chenonceaux is not large, as I say, but into its delicate compass is packed a great deal of history,—history which differs from that of Amboise and Blois in being of the private and sentimental kind. The echoes of the place, faint and far as they are to-day, are not political, but personal.

> *Henry James, in* A Little Tour in France, *Houghton, Mifflin, 1900.*

Bonney MacDonald

[*In the following excerpt, MacDonald argues that Henry James's travel essays "not only offer 'portraits of places' and accounts of travel, but also exhibit a theoretical probing of aesthetic experience" that was later to inform James's fiction.*]

In the early life of Henry James, the 1860s are unique for marking a decade of domestic calm and stasis in an otherwise well-traveled and cosmopolitan youth. By 1860, James had toured Europe three times, lived in Manhattan twice, attended numerous European and American academies, and had, after a fascinating but peripatetic "sensuous education," taken up a quieter residence in Newport, Rhode Island. In 1864 the James family moved from Newport to Boston and, in 1866, made their permanent home in nearby Cambridge. From 1860 to 1869 James lived with his family in New England—in Newport and the Boston area—for a longer period of time than he had yet remained in any one place. In these formative and relatively peaceful years, James followed the path of many Eastern men of letters. He was known and published by James T. Fields at the *Atlantic,* by James Russell Lowell and Charles Norton at the *North American Review,* and by E. L. Godkin at the *Nation.* In short, during the 1860s, Henry James displayed the talent, social finesse, and, seemingly, the ambition of a future Boston man of letters.

Toward the end of this successful decade at home, however, James became constructively restless. Despite impressive literary success and social ease, he longed for more stimulating company and unfamiliar landscapes. James had outgrown his surroundings and was ready to move on. "You may imagine," as he wrote to T. S. Perry during a hot New England August, "that existence here has not been thrilling or exciting. I have seen no one and done nothing— . . . I like Cambridge very well, but at the end of another year, I'm sure I shall have had enough of it" [*Henry James Letters*].

Eighteen months later the prediction was realized when, on 17 February 1869, James sailed to England to begin his first unaccompanied tour of Europe. The departure marked, for the rest of James's life, a fully saturated and determining event, a moment to which he would return repeatedly in his essays, letters, and fiction. As he recalled years later in the autobiography, his long-awaited and foggy arrival in Liverpool teemed with a sense of promise, youthful ecstasy, and personal destiny:

> I found myself, from the first day in March 1869, in the face of an opportunity that affected me then and there as the happiest, the most interesting, the most alluring and beguiling, that could ever have opened before a somewhat disabled young man who was about to complete his twenty-sixth year.

During these first days in England, James reveled in his "exposure to appearances, aspects, images, [and] every protrusive item almost, in the great beheld sum of things." Receptive, eager, and in search of revelatory impressions, James submerged himself in British details. "Wherever I looked . . . I sank in up to my nose. . . . Recognition . . . remained, through the adventure of the months to come, the liveliest principle at work."

However, if in the early spring of 1869, James "uncapped his throbbing brow in the wild dimness of [Oxford's] courts," revered the verdant splendor of England's countryside, and explored the "dusky vistas" of Dickensian London, his senses were overwhelmed when, in September of the same year, he descended the alpine slopes of Switzerland into northern Italy. If his responses to England were stately, reverent, and appreciative, his reactions to Italy were filled with runaway enthusiasm and energetic rapture. England, as he wrote back to Cambridge, was a "good matron," and Switzerland, where he had traveled that summer, was a "magnificent man"; but Italy, as he reported in newly impassioned prose, was a "beautiful dishevelled nymph." James's five-month Italian tour carried him through the northern Alps to Lake Como, and then on to Milan, Venice, Florence, and, by November, to Rome. His journey, as he wrote of his memorable descent down the Simplon Pass into Isella, was a "rapturous progress thro' a wild luxuriance of corn and vines and olives and figs and mulberries and chestnuts and frescoed villages."

In near-Whitmanian relish for listing the seen and felt objects of the world, James significantly could not total the sum of his Italian pleasure, name enough sights, nor find the words to convey his newfound delights. "If I might talk of these things," he wrote to [his brother] William, "I would talk of *more* and tell you in glowing accents how beautiful this month in Italy has been and how my brain swarms with pictures and my bosom aches with memories. I should like in some neat formula to give [you] the 'Italian feeling' . . ." As the travel essays and letters attest, however, James's love of Italy remained *beyond* the reach of words, lending the Italian writings—for James as well as his readers—much of their magic. As implied in the fiction and stated in the preface to *Roderick Hudson*, "the loved Italy was the scene of my fiction—so much more loved than one has ever been able, even after fifty efforts, to say!"

These travel works of the early 1870s are part of James's growing fascination with European travel and the international theme. But, while critics have explored the theme of Americans abroad in the fiction, and while biographers have agreed on the importance of European travel in James's formative years, few have closely examined the travel essays. Perhaps this gap in criticism is generated by the form itself, since travel writing generally constitutes a genre which is difficult to define. The travel essay, after all, is neither biography, nor fiction, nor wholly factual account, but some combination of the three. It constitutes, as Paul Fussell has remarked in his work on twentieth-century travel, a "sub-species of memoir in which autobiographical narrative arises from the speaker's encounter with . . . unfamiliar data, and in which the narrative—unlike that in a novel or a romance—claims literal validity by constant reference to actuality" [*Abroad: British Literary Traveling Between the Wars,* 1980]. Moreover, literary accomplishment is not always expected from travel writing. We may "know" that travel literature is rich in content but, as H. M. Tomilson rightly notes, we too often relegate it to the territory of light or "background reading."

James's early travel essays, then, offer a valuable tool for readers of James. Combining narrative structure with attention to visual and factual detail, they illuminate artistic as well as epistemological concerns which culminate in the later fiction. They are, as Carl Smith claims, "tales of a sort" which underscore James's interest in the "traveler as perceiver" ["James' Travels, Travel Writing and the Development of His Art," *Modern Language Quarterly,* 1977]. In addition to portraying scenes of travel, these essays reveal James's developing ideas on perception and the artistic process. They not only offer "portraits of places" and accounts of travel, but also exhibit a theoretical probing of aesthetic experience—an exploration of visual perception and thought, as well as the related issues of seeing and knowing which inform the later novels.

That James explores such issues in his fiction is well established; that he does so in the travel writings, and that he accomplishes the task so directly is not as widely recognized. The travel essay, according to Fussell, traditionally incorporates a "gross physicality [and] a tie to the actual"—characteristics often attributed to travel writing but rarely associated with James's work itself. In contrast to the abstraction of the late style, James's early travel essays focus on direct impressions and "felt" experience in the Italian landscape. Their point of view, as Edel has suggested, "is empirical; its interest lies in places and persons." James is concerned "with things his eyes can rest upon, . . . [and] [a]t every turn [he] invites us to look; and through sight we are asked to charge our other senses" [Leon Edel, *Henry James, The Conquest of London: 1870-1881,* 1962]. Unlike much of James's early fiction, and certainly unlike many of the late works, James's travel pieces *directly* display the texture of the seen and felt world which structures James's Italian experience. Through their attention to receptive sight, tactile vision, and picturesque impressions, these essays chart James's developing visual and artistic stance, and trace the revelatory force of the visible world as it reveals itself during James's early years in Italy.

Depicting a scene to which James would return in memory and fiction, "The Old Saint-Gothard" recounts James's cherished descent into northern Italy. The journey begins at dawn in Lucerne where James boards a steamer to Flüelen. Here in the Alps—watching the porters load the south-bound coaches—James describes the receptive and wondrous mood that characterizes his travel essays. Finding himself "on the threshold of Italy" before the Simplon Pass, James "surrender[s] to the gaping traveller's mood, which," he tellingly adds, "surely isn't the unwisest the heart knows":

> I don't envy people . . . who have outlived or outworn the simple sweetness of feeling settled to go somewhere with bag and umbrella. . . . In this matter wise people are content to become children again. We don't turn about on our knees to look out of the omnibus-window, but we [do] indulge in very much the same round-eyed contemplation of visible objects.

Bound for Italy by coach, James thus begins his descent and engages in the pleasures of the innocent and receptive eye, "sucking in the gladness of gaping," and taking delight in the surrounding landscape. In the visual drama which follows, his "traveller's mood" remains one of receptivity and leisurely pleasure. He must "ignore the very dream of haste," and proceed slowly and "very much at random."

Along with this unhurried pace, James's emerging portrait of the traveler incorporates an overall receptive stance. The Italian essays abound with portraits of the *flâneur* who, in hours of receptive delight, "roam[s] and ram-ble[s]" through Italian cities. James "*stroll*[*s*] among Florentine lanes; *sit*[*s*] on parapets . . . [and] *look*[*s*] across at the Fiesole or down the rich-hued valley of the Arno." Continuing with the receptive verbs that characterize these essays, he finds himself "*pausing* at the open gates of villas, and *wondering* at the height of the cypresses and the depth of the loggias." At Arezzo he "*lounges* away the half-hours . . . under a spell," and in Perugia his stance is nearly Whitmanian as he relishes the chance to

> lie aloft there in the grass with silver-grey ramparts at one's back and the warm rushing wind in one's ears, and watch the beautiful plain mellow into the tones of twilight. . . .

With an affection for lounging and loafing not often associated with the upright and meticulous observer, James immerses himself in the pleasures of "aimless contemplation." He is never weary, he reports, of "*staring* into gateways, of *lingering* by . . . half-barbaric farm-yards, [or] of feasting a foolish gaze on sun-cracked plaster and unctuous indoor shadows." In contrast to the focused and appropriative vision often associated with James's artistry, the author of these sketches is an unhurried and "musing wanderer" who enjoys his impressions as he finds them. In Rome he rides on the Campagna, and takes in the "strong sense of *wandering* over boundless space, . . . hardly knowing whether it is better to gallop far and drink deep of air and grassy distance . . . or to *walk* and *pause* and *linger,* and try and grasp some ineffaceable memory of sky and color and outline."

Whether in the open air of the Campagna or the hushed atmosphere of a gallery, James frequently finds himself exhausted by the sheer multiplicity of sight, sound, and sense, claiming that he has "received more impressions than [he] knows what to do with," and that Italian sights and "details overwhelm" him. These protests, however, are short-lived. For if Italy abounds with an unmanageable number of pictures and impressions, it is that very undefined multiplicity and uncontained grandeur of place that James also treasures. Every observed detail, in this "ever suggestive part of the world," not only holds *specific* meaning, but also resonates with the unseen beauty of its context. Thus, when walking outside the Villa Borghese on a sunny March afternoon, James is struck by the immediately visible scene of Italian schoolboys playing in the sun while a young priest looks on, but he is also carried away by larger, unseen, and undiscovered reverberations as well. The specific scene, he notes, may "sound like nothing, but the *force behind* it, . . . the setting, the air, the chord struck, make it a *hundred* wonderful things."

These "hundred" reverberations and relations, however, remain unnamed in James's early sketches. The penumbra of relations resonates with the undefined and *undefinable* nature of Italy's magic. Thus, a moment's impression is not merely singular, but informed by a host of surrounding details, associations, and what William James calls "vague," "fringe," or relational meanings. The observed scenes of Italy, to recall Henry's term, are thus "eversuggestive" because they resonate, like overtones in music, with unseen but present meanings and associations. After the initial impression, the drama of any one observation

becomes saturated with a fund of associations, impressions, and expectations which—like William James's famous "stream of thought"—are multiple and continuous. The "unbroken continuity of impressions," Henry thus writes, is an

> example of the intellectual background of all enjoyment in Rome. . . . [Y]our sensation rarely begins and ends with itself; it reverberates, commemorates, [and] resuscitates something else.

This multiplity of impressions influences not only the way in which James *sees* Italy, but the style of his Italian essays as well. Throughout, James expands his vision to meet the magnitude of his surroundings. Italy's multiplicity of sound and sense prompts not only perpetual delight but an enthusiastic and consciously nonhierarchical vision reminiscent of Whitman. Without attention to an ordered or selected progression, James takes in as much as his senses will allow, and "pray[s] *not* to grow in discrimination."

The multiplicity of Italian impressions generates a nonhierarchical catalog of the visible landscape and inspires a Whitmanian rapture in cataloging the objects viewed. James attempts to name the objects of his impressions as they come to him, without selection and without "discrimination." The magic of the northern lakes, as he writes of his journey from Bellinzona to Como, "lay before me for a whole perfect day":

> [it gleams] in the shimmering melting azure of the southern slopes and masses; in the luxurious tangle of nature and the familiar amenity of man; in the lawn-like inclinations, where the great grouped chestnuts make so cool a shadow in the warm light; in the rusty vineyards, [and in] the littered cornfields and the tawdry wayside shrines. But most of all it's the deep yellow light that enchants you and tells you where you are.

In this account of the drive to Como, James is unable to name or list all of the delights of the land, and his catalog—like that in "Song of Myself"—seems at once to note the limitations of language when faced with the rapturous multiplicity of experience, as well as to take simple delight in the passing scenes of life and landscape.

James's catalog passage, however, evokes not only a delight in multiplicity but an overall reverence for the seen and "accessible" world as well. The Italian landscape, as James wrote of Perugia, "continually solicits his wonder and praise," prompts "worshipful gazing" and "helpless wonderment," and indulges him in countless hours of "romantic *flânerie.*" Sheer joy in perception permeates his descriptive accounts of Italian cities, so that visual experience becomes a full-time pursuit. "The mere use of one's eyes" as James wrote of Venice, "is happiness enough."

If much of Italy became a delight to James's receptive vision, it was in Rome that this instinctive and consciously embraced reverence was most pronounced. Under what Nathalia Wright has called "unpremeditated rapture," James wandered through the city "at random," visiting galleries and back streets and, in the following passage, St. Peter's basilica. James's account of the church not only registers his receptive stance and the multiplicity of his impressions, but an overall reverence for the sheer magnitude of St. Peter's grandeur and Italy's splendor.

Walking across the threshold, James is brought to "an immediate gasping pause" by the overwhelming size and beauty of the church. Describing his receptive glance, he insists that no projection of the imagination is needed, and adds that "[he] only ha[s] to stroll and stroll and gaze and gaze" at the vaulted interior for its magic to take hold. Continuing his exploration, James lingers as the beauty of the basilica transcends his conscious attention. And in the midst of this magnitude he records not only the receptivity of his vision and the multiplicity of his impressions, but a distinctly Jamesian reverence for a grandeur that is larger than himself. Watching

> the glorious altar-canopy lift its bronze architecture . . . [and] its collossal embroidered contortions, like a temple within a temple, [you] feel yourself, at the bottom of the abysmal shaft of the dome, dwindle to a crawling dot.

Responding to the magnitude of the church, here, James instinctively and consciously reveres the vast interior which overwhelms his vision. Reverence in this passage (as elsewhere in the essays) is less a religious stance than an aesthetic experience charged and structured by religious emotion. In the receptive and reverent vision inspired by Italy, James treasures and records those visual moments during which the grandeur and multiplicity of the tangible Italian world not only delight the senses but also lead the viewer (as in religious experience) to a reality which transcends the present moment and stands larger than the self.

If James delights in the multiple and suggestive sights of Italy, he also stands in awe of the tangible and tactile nature of those Italian impressions. Visual impressions, in these early Italian essays, seem to carry substance and weight, and *present themselves* to the viewer as if animated from within. In James's flights of descriptive reverie there reigns an implied insistence on the physical impact of visual experience so that "every glance is a *sensation.*" A sensuousness of place and impression shapes the Italian essays and suggests that visual perception—as William James knew well—is not limited to the mind; rather, it is tactile in nature, and evokes sensation as well as thought.

This tangible nature of impressions first emerges with Henry James's 1869 arrival in Rome, when Italy leaves the realm of preconception and imagination to become a fully actualized presence and reality. Italy's atmosphere, James wants to suggest and confirm, carries substance, and its "tone . . . lies richly on my soul and gathers increasing *weight.*" "Languishing beneath the weight of Rome's impressions," James makes a phenomenological observation on the *tangible* nature of imaginative and visual experience: "The aesthetic," as he writes in an essay on Rome, "is so intense that you should live on the taste of it, should extract the nutritive essence of the atmosphere."

Visual perception, in this comment, becomes imbued with the warmth and immediacy of sensorial experience. Gazing, looking, and glancing at Italy, Henry James bears witness to William James's claim that acts of perception and imagination are "more like a process of sensation than like a thought." And although mental association may later take over, all acts of imagination and cognition, William suggests, begin in "sensorial vividness." Before the mind grasps an object or scene in its larger or relational context, vision is stunned into a moment of pre-associative receptivity in which the object of vision is revealed in its tactile immanence. Sensations, as William thus writes in the *Principles,* are the

> starting point of cognition, thoughts the developed tree. . . . [T]he objective presence of reality known about, [and] the mere beginning of knowledge [are most often] named by the word which says the least. Such a word is the interjection, as lo! there! ecco! [or] *voilà!*

Together, William's account of perception and Henry's narrated experience suggest that "knowledge about" an object (a cathedral, for instance) begins in a receptive moment of visual awe. Acknowledging the distinct beauty or "thisness" inherent in an object or scene, the viewer awakens, as the *Principles* suggests, "to the consciousness of something there [which] has [an] objectivity, unity [and] substantiality" independent of the viewer's mind or imagination. In opposition to the Berkeleyan idea that the realities of visual perception (such as spatiality, density, or depth) are a result of intellectual association and projection, William and Henry James each suggest that perception of substance, depth, and beauty is rooted in primary experience in the seen and tactile world.

In addition to having substance and weight, the objects of James's receptive vision seem to take on, as it were, a life of their own. Throughout the early Italian essays, they vibrate with a seemingly independent force and with what Merleau-Ponty has called "internal animation." Italy functions, then, not only as a tangible presence, but as an active agency which solicits response and commands attention. "At every step," as James wrote of Rome's "weighty" historical presence, it "*confronts* you, and the mind must make some response." It speaks to the viewer, solicits a response, and invites him into an exchange. Florentine scenes, as James thus writes, do not merely await the interested gaze, they actively recruit the viewer's attention and "*force*" themselves into view. In Florence, James continues, "the scene *itself,* the mere scene, shares with you such a wealth of consciousness" that you feel the unmistakable "genius of the place" in all its substantial and active presence.

Thus, when Henry James is brought to an "immediate gasping pause" on the threshold of St. Peter's, or when he "surrenders to the gaping traveler's mood [in] . . . round-eyed contemplation of accessible objects," he not only absorbs the scenery with pleasure and delight, but also engages in a phenomenologically structured visual moment. Viewing the wide open space of the Campagna, or the grandeur of St. Peter's, James immerses himself in all that Italy has to offer. In addition, that is, to seeking out scenic beauty, he allows the actualized splendor of Italy to *reveal itself* to him. The object of vision, as Pierre Thévanez has written in "What Is Phenomenology?" is not "constructed by consciousness, [but] gives itself" to the viewer.

A phenomenological reading of James's travel sketches, then, highlights what James himself suggests: that Italian scenes actively *impress themselves* upon the viewer with a vividness that surpasses the mind's ability to create and project images, and that the seen world of Italy comes to the viewer with a distinct and animated presence. A visual phenomenon, Thévanez claims, is "that which gives itself and [stands] immanent to consciousness." It is not a matter of simple realism or of "making an object appear in its factual reality," Thévanez continues, but of rendering it "in its immanent reality to the [viewing] consciousness."

With an emphasis on receptive vision, multiplicity of impressions, tactile experience, and the "gestalt of the picturesque," Henry James gives voice to the concrete and tactile nature of full consciousness—to the "worldliness," as William James wrote, "of thought." James's Italian sketches suggest that the sensorial world actively participates in acts of imagination and thought, and that the whole felt and lived world generates meaning and artistry. Focusing on moments of direct experience and perception (as in the above accounts of St. Peter's, a Florentine afternoon, or Italian schoolboys at play), phenomenological consideration of the travel sketches highlights James's seldom-noted reverence for the felt life in its "total and concrete density" [Thévanez, "Phenomenology"].

Through this reverence for the seen, felt, and tactile world, Henry James implicitly concurs with what Bruce Wilshire calls a central doctrine of phenomenology. All states of consciousness, Wilshire claims, "are intrinsically referential and worldly, [and] cannot be specified in isolation" from the material and sense world. Phenomenology, he continues, is an "exercise in seeing" and offers, moreover, the insight that all acts of thought and imagination are rooted in the concreteness of the seen and felt world. With their repeated reference to "locatable" scenes and local textures, James's Italian essays reveal the "intrinsic referentialness of mind" central to a phenomenological account of visual experience. Consciousness is "referential" or "intentional," and does not operate in isolation from lived experience. Consciousness, as phenomenology suggests, is always *of* something—it refers, points, or "intends" toward some object.

With these premises in mind, the reader approaches a fuller understanding of William James's explicit claim that cognitive and mental acts begin in primary "sensorial vividness"; but more important, he also approaches a better understanding of Henry James's implicit suggestion that acts of imagination similarly engage the world of seen and tactile experience. In this light, moments of visual impression in the Italian essays can be seen to illustrate what Merleau-Ponty has called "primary perception." By the words, the "primacy of perception," he explains,

> we mean the experience of perception . . . at the moment when things, truths, values are constituted for us. . . . It is not a question of *reducing* human knowledge to sensation, but of assisting at the birth of this knowledge to make it as sensi-

ble as the sensible and . . . to define a method for getting closer to present and living reality.

Gazing at the glory of Roman ruins, at the beauty of the Arno, or at the magnitude of St. Peter's, Henry James is brought by the *"scene itself"* to an "immediate, gasping pause" (see above). During these moments of receptive vision and direct impression, James not only retraces the rapture of travelers before him, he seizes it as his own, and in so doing evokes Merleau-Ponty's account of visual wonder. Rather, consciousness is also structured by primary visual experience and thus remains eternally open to the actual and the visible.

From an exploration of James's receptive stance and the tactile nature of his visual experience in Italy, a pattern begins to emerge. James's Italian essays not only convey his visual stance and the character of his impressions, but the *structure* of those impressions as well. In addition to being sensorial and tactile, James's Italian perceptions are structured by his understanding of the "picturesque." Visual impressions of Italy—whether of St. Peter's or of a work by Tintoretto—are received by the eye as fully formed, unified, and self-contained. As William James and phenomenologists have claimed, we "see in wholes." Thus the beauty of a cathedral or painting does not enter our vision through an association of separately perceived images, but—as Henry James wrote of Sargent's paintings—as a "whole, . . . a scene, and a *comprehensive* impression." Arriving in Rome, Henry James happily reported to William that "for the first time I know what the picturesque is"; it means, as he defined it elsewhere, "simply the presentation of a picture, *self-informed* and *complete.*"

If Henry James first comprehended the picturesque upon his arrival in Rome, he had nonetheless come across the concept before: first, through William Morris Hunt's teachings in Newport and, among others, through those of William James. Studying art with Hunt in 1861 along with William, Henry James learned a great deal about *seeing* as well as about painting and drawing. He came to learn how a painting can, as it were, speak for itself. During his "hours of Art" in the Newport studio, James pored over Hunt's collection and listened to instruction on drawing and painting. And although James does not record the specifics of this instruction, Hunt's *Talks on Art* offers a reliable source for understanding the lessons that James must have received from this "genial and admirable master." A painting, Hunt claims, must "instantly *seize* and hold the attention." For this reason, as he advised young painters, a picture must "keep the first impression . . . [and] seize you as forcibly as if a man has seized you by the shoulder! It should impress you," Hunt insists, "like *reality.*" In order to achieve this forceful impression of reality, Hunt further claims, a painting must be perceived and offered as *unified* impression. While drawing, he advises his students, "see what the shape of the whole thing is [and] establish the fact of the *whole,* [for] it is [that first] impression of the thing that you want to get."

Like Hunt, William James also claims that visual impressions are structured by an initial unity. Although the visible world is multiple and filled with unrelated phenomena, thought and perception are nonetheless "sensibly continuous." And though, after an initial sensation, we do associate images and meanings in order to comprehend an object in all its relational or "fringe meanings," our initial impression is structured by a unified and "single pulse of consciousness." No matter how complex, William thus writes, an object "is at any moment thought in one idea." Perception, he thus insists, "is one state of mind or nothing," so that our impressions of the world, no matter how complicated, always arrive in consciousness—as in Henry's definition of the picturesque—self-informed and unified. They "vibrate," William explains, not as a series of separately perceived details, but as a "systematic whole."

With this definition of visual impressions in mind, the reader can now find new meaning in James's remarks on Italian art. Sitting amidst the glories of St. Peter's, for instance, James notes that the "constituted beauty" cannot be defined simply by describing the beauty of Michelangelo's *Pietà* of the rich interior of the cathedral. Similarly, as James claims in "Venice: An Early Impression," Tintoretto had an unequaled distinctness of vision for his ability to convey the whole pictorial unity of a scene. When Tintoretto conceived a painting, he did not compose a scene solely from his imagination. Instead, "it *defined itself* to his imagination with an intensity [and] amplitude . . . which [make] one's observation of his pictures seem less an operation of the mind than a kind of supplementary experience of life." Tintoretto's work does not merely give the viewer a visually interesting display of separate colors and images. Visual scenes in his works are the product of unified impressions, so that "you get from [Tintoretto] the impression that he *felt,* pictorially, the great, beautiful and terrible spectacle of human life":

> It was the whole scene that [Tintoretto] seemed to have beheld in a flash of inspiration intense enough to stamp it ineffaceably on his perception; and it was the *whole scene, complete,* peculiar, individual [and] unprecedented that he committed to canvas with all the vehemence of his talent.

In painting, then, James admired an artist's ability to capture that fleeting moment when the visible world reveals itself in its pictorial unity—when the painter's artistry conveys what Merleau-Ponty has called the "coming-to-itself of the visible." But if James admired a painter's ability to convey the picturesque, he was equally impressed by a writer's ability to capture that same pictorial unity. "I'd give a great deal," he thus proclaimed after viewing Tintoretto in Venice, "to be able to fling down a dozen of his pictures into prose of corresponding force and color."

These comments on visual perception offer clues to the way in which James organized visual experience. In recording his impressions in the Italian sketches, James *shapes* visual experience according to a consistent aesthetic of perception by which visual impressions become a source of revelatory knowledge and transformation. Visual perception in James's Italian essays—whether of a cathedral or a painting—is not only receptive in its stance and tactile in effect, but unified and self-informed in structure. As James wrote of a Tintoretto canvas, it "*defines itself* to the imagination" and makes a "stamp" or impress

on perception. Indeed, as it emerges in James's Italian essays, visual experience resonates with the physicality and force associated with the words "impress" or "impression."

As "impress" describes a characteristic stamp or mark (as in printing), so the act of "impressing" suggests some application of pressure to produce that mark. But in addition to describing this physical action, "impress" carries a military connotation. To "impress," in this definition, is to "enlist, force or press into duty"—or, as the *O.E.D.* notes, "to take or *seize*" a person for military or public service. Similarly, "impression" connotes transactions of force and power. It describes an influence or pressure from an external force, a "charge," as the *O.E.D.* continues, "in some *passive* subject by the operation of an external cause." As in the military account which suggests a "charge, attack, or assault," a perceptual definition includes a similar physical pressure. Impressions are those "perceptions which enter with [the] most *force* and violence."

As James's travel essays indicate, impressions arrive in the senses not only with the charm of local scenes, the tactile nature of vision, and the unity of the picturesque, but with a full physical "force." The act of perception thus reveals the artist, as the phenomenologist Herbert Speigelberg notes, as "not only projecting the world, but as having been *taken over* by the world" [*The Phenomenological Movement,* 1960]. In James's essays, the visible world of Italy is sufficiently forceful to overtake and "enlist" its viewer. It not only delights the eye but, in bringing the viewer to an "immediate gasping pause," impresses and—to recall Hunt's term—"seizes" him with the force of reality. Thus, whether viewing a church or a canvas, James is not only drawn to beauty, but compelled by its power as well. The impact of Italy's beauty in the essays is thus not so different from a dramatic "charge" or "onset." Italy makes its colorful, tactile, and picturesque stamp or impress on its receptive viewer at every turn. The scenes and objects of the visible world are often beyond and more forceful than the descriptive power of language—as, indeed, James had hoped they would be.

For these reasons, James's Italian sketches often insist that the glory of Italy is "more lovely than words can tell," and that the whole, picturesque impression of Italy's splendor surpasses description. The "charm of certain grassy surfaces in Italy, overfrowned by masses of brickwork that are honeycombed by the suns of centuries," as James is eager to discover, "is something that I hereby renounce once for all the attempt to express." And the grandeur of the Colosseum, he continues, "is a thing about which it is useless to talk, [although] as a piece of the picturesque . . . it is thoroughly and simply delightful." Under the "spell" of the surrounding landscape, James—in keeping with his understanding of the picturesque as internally animated and self-informed—attempts to discover and confirm the possibility that the power of Italy is greater than that of his emerging craft. "Do what we will," he thus announces and projects, "there remains in all these deeply agreeable impressions a charming something we can't analyze" or define.

With its colorful, picturesque, and impressive force, James's Italy remains—to cite Bernard Berenson's term—"life enhancing" because it generates not only beauty but revelatory force as well. The seen world of landscape, architecture, and art impels its viewer into a state of enchantment and rapture; the visible world, as Berenson knew, can convert or change its viewer, and enlist him, as it were, in a newly heightened state of perceptual consciousness. For years, as Berenson recalled, he had known this feeling of being transformed by visible beauty, but had not been able to identify it. But, as he writes in *Aesthetics and History in the Visual Arts,*

> then one morning as I was gazing at the leafy scrolls carved on the door jambs of St. Pietro outside Spoleto, suddenly [the] stem, tendril and foliage became alive [and] . . . made me feel as if I had emerged into the light after long groping in the darkness of initiation. I felt as one illumined, and beheld a world where every surface was in living relation to me and not, as hitherto, in a merely cognitive one. Since that morning, nothing visible has been indifferent or even dull.

On his Italian travels, as the essays and early letters attest, Henry James experienced a similar discovery of the picturesque and the "radiation of the visible world." James associates visual impressions of Italy with an experience of conversion, joy, and revelatory power similar to that described by Berenson. In a passage worth quoting in full for its uncontained enthusiasm and sense of revelatory conversion, Henry James writes to William of his first day in Rome and the "excitement of [his] first hour[s]." His delight in the surroundings speaks for itself:

> At last—for the first time—I live! . . . I went reeling and moaning thro' the streets, in a fever of enjoyment. In the course of four or five hours I traversed almost the whole of Rome and got a glimpse of everything—the Forum, the Coliseum (stupendissimo!), the Pantheon . . . [and] all the Piazzas and ruins and monuments. The effect is something indescribable. For the first time I know what the picturesque is. . . . Even if I should leave Rome tonight I should feel that I have caught the keynote of its operation and the senses. . . . In fine, I've seen Rome, and I shall go to bed a wiser man than I last rose—yesterday morning.

In 1869 James left America in search of inspiration, drama, and the picturesque sights of Italy, with a desire to be "deeply impressed by some *given* aspect of life." What he sought and found was material for a lifetime's work—an "arrangement of things hanging together," as he recalled of his arrival in Europe, "that had the force of revelation." On his Italian tour, James learned to recognize and receive what he would later call a "direct impression of life," and learned to utilize the impact and structure of that impression—learned to employ an uncanny union of perception and thought, of seeing and knowing, which would inform his writing in the years to come. On his Italian travels James discovered the joy of receptive vision, and the sheer pleasure and force of visual impression. And, by returning to these visual moments again and again in his work, as well as to the Italian setting which

generated them, he would later demonstrate how the moment of visual "revelation" itself could become an implicit and powerful source for his art.

Describing the sights of Italy on this first "passionate pilgrimage," Henry James began to work with a creative tension between receptive sight on the one hand and the power of the creative imagination on the other. The essays that grew out of these early Italian travels suggest that while art may well "make life," the opposite may also be true. Life, to reverse James's famous claim, may also "make art." The early Italian travel writings display moments of this very transformation. Here, the seen and felt world of Italy generates sufficient "romantic rightness" and revelatory "force" to overtake its young and receptive observer, so that when the artist, as Rilke has written, has "the right eyes . . . the sight transforms the seer." Although James would indeed go on to transform much of his world through the power of his remarkable craft, the early Italian essays record those resonant and influential moments in which the world transforms its viewer. In these moments of vivid impression, James has the "right eyes" and thus stands expectant, receptive, and willingly transformed by the wondrous sights and felt life of the surrounding Italian landscape.

> *Bonney MacDonald, "The Force of Revelation: Receptive Vision in Henry James's Early Italian Travel Essays," in* The Sweetest Impression of Life: The James Family and Italy, *edited by James W. Tuttleton and Agostino Lombardo, New York University Press, 1990, pp. 128-48.*

THE ORIENT

Wallace Cable Brown

[*In the following essay, Brown discusses the wealth of travel literature about the Near East published between 1775 and 1825 as a reflection of the English public's burgeoning interest in exotic cultures.*]

The place of the Near East in English commercial and political activities constitutes one of the most significant chapters in the overseas history of Great Britain, and the influence of this relationship on the literature and social life in England is widely recognized. The most important era of English interest in the Near East began about the middle of the eighteenth century, and not until then did this region become generally known to the people at home through accurate first-hand accounts by Englishmen. Before 1750 relatively few British travellers—whose interests were mainly in trade or religion—had invaded the Near East; and it is clear from their reports that most of them had taken full advantage of the poetic license of a prescientific age, and of the privilege of the pioneer traveller, to mingle inextricably fact and fiction. Even as late as 1738 a traveller in northeastern Africa felt obliged to disillusion his English readers about the traditional ideas of monsters supposed to exist there:

> . . . some persons perhaps may be surprized that they have been so little, if at all, entertained with an Account of such strange and wonderful Objects, as might be expected from This Country. Now, in Answer to this, it may be observed that the natural and ordinary Course of Things is much the same in Barbary as in other Places; each Species . . . keeping inviolably to Itself . . . few, I presume, if any . . . Instances can be fairly urged in favour of the old observation that Africa is always producing some new Monster.
>
> [Thomas Shaw, *Travels to . . . Several Parts of Barbary and the Levant,* 1738]

Although in the first half of the eighteenth century the English reading public showed considerable interest in the Near East, particularly in the oriental tale, yet this interest was almost wholly the product of French accounts of the Near East or of French translations of the *Arabian Nights.* It was not until the last quarter of the century that new developments brought

> the Orient much nearer to England than ever before . . . In letters, this modern spirit was first expressed by the increased number of travelers' accounts, and by the accompanying activity of orientalists under the guidance of Sir William Jones.
>
> [Martha P. Conant, *The Oriental Tale in England in the Eighteenth Century,* 1908]

Throughout the eighteenth century, however, several important conditions contributed to the growth of a *direct* interest in the Near East, and provided new and powerful incentives to travel there. It is well known that this century witnessed an increase of travelling to all parts of the world. It was the great period of English colonial expansion; it was the hey-day of the Grand Tour; and by the end of the century the newly enriched middle classes, who earlier would never have dreamt of crossing the channel, began touring abroad, many of them with their entire families. Three important factors directed this stream of travellers eastward. One was the growing interest in scientific archaeology, which by the middle of the century had caused many Englishmen on the Grand Tour to extend their itinerary to Greece, Asia Minor, and Egypt. A second factor was the focusing of English colonial interests on India; and a third was the effect upon travelling of the continental wars, which, during the latter part of the century, closed western Europe to sight-seers.

As a result of these conditions, throngs of English travellers toured the countries of the Near East in the early nineteenth century, if we are to believe the abundant testimony of contemporary writers. One of these in the *Quarterly Review* [July 1814], for example, declares that,

> No man is now accounted a traveller who has not bathed in the Eurotas and tasted the olives of Attica; while, on the other hand, it is an introduction to the best company, and a passport to literary distinction, to be a member of the 'Athe-

nian Club,' and to have scratched one's name upon a fragment of the Parthenon.

And another, in the *Eclectic Review* [April 1824] observes:

> How times are altered since the tour of Europe, the grand tour, was the *ne plus ultra* of gentlemen travellers! No one can now pretend to have seen the world who has not made one of a party of pleasure up the Nile or taken a ride on camel-back across the Syrian desert. As for France and Flanders and Switzerland, our next-door neighbors, they may serve John Bull very well for a country-house; but to have seen those countries is no longer worth speaking of.

William Macmichael, in his biography of famous English physicians, *The Gold-Headed Cane* [1828], makes the following startling comparison between the extent of travelling to the Near East in the mid-eighteenth and the early nineteenth century:

> Dr. Askew had been in his youth a great traveller; at least he was so considered in those days, for he had been absent from England three years [1746-9], and had, during that time, visited Hungary, and had, during that time, visited Hungary, and resided at Athens and Constantinople. . . . In consequence of these peregrinations, he was regarded on his return . . . as no ordinary person, but one who had enjoyed most unusual advantages . . . This will perhaps hardly be credited at the present moment [1826], when it is scarcely possible to turn the corner of a street without meeting an Englishman recently arrived, either from the borders of the Red Sea, the cataracts of the Nile, or the ruins of Palmyra. Interviews with the Beys and Pashas of the empire of Mohamet have now-a-days succeeded to the usual presentations at the courts of the Continent; and the camel, the firman, and the Tartar, have been substituted for the ordinary facilities of the poste, the passports, and the couriers of the beaten roads of civilized Europe.

It is natural that, with hundreds of people visiting a distant region, many of them should feel impelled to publish accounts of their travels; and, because of the strangeness and glamor of the Near East, this region offered to Englishmen an especially rich field for comment and description. The half century between 1775 and 1825 witnessed the publication of an almost uninterrupted stream of Near East travel books, which as a group have been completely overlooked by students of English literary history. In fact, the whole subject of travel literature in this period has been inadequately studied. This indifference is curious in the light of the facts (1) that philosophical speculation about the nature of man had at that time excited such a deep interest in the habits of people living in distant parts of the world, and (2) that before 1825 the travel book had assumed an important place as a popular type of literature.

There are at least three important reasons why the Near East travel books in particular should not be ignored. First, the unusually large number and great popularity of these books alone give them significance. Second, the travellers emphasized in their accounts many of the dominant ideas which were then current at home, the popularity of the travel books in turn reinforcing the vogue of these ideas. And third, the materials and interpretations of the Near East which appear in the travel books captured the imagination of numerous writers in England, and created a large body of literature of which the Near East is the theme or background. It would be impracticable to deal adequately with all three of these subjects in the scope of a single article. I shall therefore limit myself, in the remainder of this paper, to the demonstration of the popularity of the travel books, and reserve the other two subjects for later treatment.

The great popularity of this group of books in the period, 1775-1825, is clearly indicated by the continuous attention given them in contemporary magazines. It is hardly possible to open a single issue of a periodical of the time without encountering a review or a listing of some new travel account of the Near East. In the *Eclectic Review* alone, for example, forty-six extensive reviews of Near East travel books, some of them continuing through several issues, appeared between 1805 and 1825.

Although most of these contemporary reviews, particularly the ones before 1800, give little more than a detailed resumé of the contents of the travel books, some of them comment specifically on the great number of Near East travel accounts and the popular enthusiasm for them. Two significant comments appear at the beginning of the period, in the *Critical Review* for 1775 and 1776, in connection with two extensive reviews of Richard Chandler's *Travels in Asia Minor* and *Travels in Greece*. In the first one the writer remarks: "It was not without some anxiety for the favourable attention of our readers, that we found ourselves obliged to extend the account of these Travels through the extraordinary number of five successive Reviews." And in the second review the following comment proves that the writer's anxiety, with regard to the favorable reception of his article on a Near East travel book was groundless: "As many of our readers were pleased to approve of the circumstantial account we gave of the former work [*Travels in Asia Minor*], we shall adopt the same method in reviewing the present volume [*Travels in Greece*]."

But the most conclusive magazine evidence of the popularity of Near East travel books appears after 1800, when this popularity was well established and when book-reviewing had become more fully developed. Thus the *Eclectic Review* remarks in 1806 that "the present circumstances of the Ottoman dominions in general, but particularly of European Turkey, have long excited, in an uncommon degree, the attention and expectation of the public." And in 1809 the same magazine explains what it fears is a premature review of Lord Valentia's *Voyages and Travels to India, Ceylon, the Red Sea, Abyssinia, and Egypt* on the grounds of the impatience of the public:

> Though time has hardly yet permitted us to read more than the first volume of this magnificent work, we presume the avidity of the public curiosity, respecting a performance so splendidly announced, will warrant us to give an abstract of this first portion of it, before we proceed any further.

Also the *Edinburgh Review* notes, about the same time [1814] that the attention of all Englishmen had been turned to the Near East because the activities of Napoleon there had made it the strategic region between England and India:

> At that period . . . young gentlemen and old ladies were almost as curious about the best road to India as about the pleasantest route to the Lakes of Cumberland . . . The glorious march of Alexander—the humble path of Tom Coryat—the bloody track of Nadir Shah and the Journal of Foster—were all, in their turn, examined with minute attention.

In 1812 the *Eclectic Review,* after commenting on "that inquisitiveness which has of late years so eagerly and indiscriminately caught at information concerning any country and all countries, as appears from the reception given to such an unprecedented multitude of books of travels," refers to Greece in particular as,

> one of the selected countries composing that world in the imagination, which is the scene of enthusiastically affecting historical recollections; which scene in the imagination becomes more strongly pictured and defined, by means of accounts given of those real tracts of the earth, to which the mind has its corresponding territories of the same name.

And in 1813 the *Quarterly Review* leaves no room for doubt when it states emphatically that "the last and present year have been abundant . . . in accounts of the countries bordering upon the Mediterranean."

By 1815 even such a relatively inaccessible part of the Near East as Albania had been so well reported in travel books like those of J. C. Hobhouse and Henry Holland, and these books had had such a vogue, that the *Edinburgh* could remark in a review of the latter's work:

> It is but a few years since Mr. Gibbon could say with truth, that the country which is the principal theatre of these travels was as little known to the civilized world as the wilds of North America. There is, however, no longer the same room for this reproach.

And the following statement, in the same magazine for 1816, apropos of Thomas Legh's *Journey in Egypt,* is an index of the high favor in which an enthusiasm for the countries of the Near East was held by even the most captious critics of that period:

> The interest which the geography of Africa, and the condition of its population, have excited amongst us of late years, is still not extinct; and we are desirous of contributing all in our power to maintain this spirit; convinced that the object is one well worthy to engage the curiosity and feelings of a cultivated people.

It is clear from the contemporary reviews of travel books that by the 1820's the most famous parts of the Near East had been thoroughly explored, and the materials amply recorded for the benefit of the great host of arm-chair adventurers at home. Concerning Egypt, for example, the *Eclectic Review* declares in 1822 that "in every point of view . . . Egypt is an object of the highest interest, and is likely to become increasingly such"; and in the same year the *Quarterly* [*Review*] notes: "If the old 'Land of Egypt' be not thoroughly known, it is not from any want of travellers and travel-writers." According to the *Eclectic* [1822], Palestine was equally well known by this time: "All that learned speculation and research could do to illustrate the topography of Palestine has been accomplished." And *Blackwood's Magazine* [1822] emphasizes "the most ample information," which was then available about Greece:

> Of the physiognomy of the landscape, of the ruins, and of the scenes, hallowed by the exploits of patriotism, the literary portion of the public possess the most ample information, in the myriads of costly volumes with which the artists and scholars of every European nation have so industriously furnished their libraries.

The great number and popularity of travel books about the Near East is indicated not only by the testimony of contemporary magazines, but also by the existing evidence of the actual number of such books published and the number of editions through which the most popular of them went. I have thus far compiled a bibliography of seventy separate titles of these books published in England between 1775 and 1825, comprising in all eighty-seven substantial volumes. There are doubtless additional Near East travel accounts in private libraries, particularly in England, which have not yet been catalogued, and many others which have disappeared in the intervening years. Of these seventy books, at least fifteen appeared in more than one edition, many of which were also translated into foreign languages, before 1830. . . .

The great vogue for the writing and reading of Near East travel books between 1775 and 1825 naturally had a marked influence on contemporary thought and activity. This influence appears clearly in English social life and the arts, of which, for example, the popularity of Greek and Turkish fashions in dress and household decoration is an unmistakable indication. In the literature of the period the vogue of Near East travel books exerted an even stronger influence. First, by providing the necessary knowledge of the Near East, these travel books helped to create at home a large body of poetry and prose of which this region is the theme or background. Second, the interest in the travel-book material explains why certain ideas recur throughout the minor poetry about the Near East. And finally, the contemporary English reader's familiarity with the Near East, through the travel books, partly accounts for the instantaneous popularity of such works as Byron's *Childe Harold* (Canto II), his Turkish verse tales, Moore's *Lalla Rookh*, Thomas Hope's *Anastatius*, and James Morier's *Hajji Baba*. Because of the wide popularity and general influence of this group of travel books, a study of their contents and of their relationship to the other writings of the time will necessarily be of some significance in the literary history of the age of romanticism.

Wallace Cable Brown, "The Popularity of English Travel Books About the Near East, 1775-1825," in Philological Quarterly, *Vol. XV, No. 4, October, 1936, pp. 70-80.*

Anita Damiani

[*In the following excerpt, Damiani differentiates the writings of nineteenth-century travelers from those of their eighteenth-century predecessors.*]

Although many eighteenth-century travelogues are now considered archaic, their information outdated and their speculations dubious, none of the later narratives rival them in either scope or content. This is mainly due to the objective and enlightened approach of the earlier travellers, reinforced by the awe and respect they felt for cultures of the East. The special importance that was attributed to travel by philosophers such as Locke, Tucker and other writers of the Enlightenment, was largely to acquire that enlarged and impartial view of Men and Things, which no one single country can afford. As a result, the libraries and museums of the West became inundated with books, manuscripts, marble sculptures, and a wide variety of coins, medals, fossils and ancient relics from various parts of the world. This made the gathering of more data redundant, and the shift from a classical towards a romantic attitude was welcomed by a public which never ceased to be interested in all information that emanated from the various countries of the East.

Nineteenth and twentieth century travellers sought richer, and more subtle currents of thought and feeling than their predecessors. Supporting the revolution in England which, in accordance with the precepts of Rousseau, had moved from logic and sophistication towards feeling and simplicity, these voyagers viewed all previous methods of accumulating data as too ambitious and often irrelevant to a developing society. Together with the Romantic poets they regarded man's source of creativity as lying within his innermost mind, while the external world was merely a mirror reflecting and making visible that which was within. More than at any time in history, and in accordance with the teachings of Kant and Coleridge, voyagers had "a faith in *á priori*, deductive, geometric principles", which, together with a sentimental belief in a kind of 'inner light' within the human heart, would in their opinion allow them to grasp, during their travels, simple, inexorable and axiomatic truths.

Prominent among nineteenth and early twentieth century travellers to the East were William Kinglake, Bartholomew Eliot George Warburton, Lady Hester Stanhope, William Makepeace Thackeray, Charles Doughty, T. E. Lawrence and Richard Burton. Kinglake, who was the first to break with the traditional method of acquiring information, considered an account of a journey as being a deeply personal experience, and addressed *Eothen* directly to Warburton. In this work, published ten years after his journey to the Ottoman dominions in 1833-34, Kinglake preferred to present his own deductions and reflections on the regions of the East rather than compile "those impressions which *ought to have been* produced upon any 'well constituted mind' ". "As I have felt, so I have written," he states in the preface to his narrative, and thus started a journey for Kinglake, which, with its insistence on 'sentimental truth', echoed Sterne's *Sentimental Journey*.

The advantages of the personal approach towards travel

were many. By addressing his narrative to Warburton, Kinglake revealed to him his various impressions of the East, a technique which Warburton, in turn, was to emulate in his *The Crescent and the Cross* (1845). Both narratives, shorn of much of the massive amount of detail that characterized the works of their predecessors, readily attracted the majority of their readers. Consequently, Warburton's work went through 17 editions in ten years, while *Eothen's* portraits of the Levantine Turk, the Levantine European and the Levantine Jew, presented pictures which, according to D. G. Hogarth [in his Introduction to *Eothen,* 1931], "would be less true today for a single added touch".

Unfortunately, however, the more appealing these modern narratives became to the public, the further away they drifted from truth. Increasingly aware of the growing importance of the British nation at home and abroad, travellers became less inclined to find merit in civilizations which were either 'dead or dying'. Thus Kinglake described his situation at the end of his trip to the East as follows:

> My place upon this dividing barrier was as a man's puzzling station in eternity, between the birthless Past, and the Future that has no end. Behind me I left an old and decrepit World—Religions dead and dying—calm tyrannies expiring in silence—women hushed, and swathed, and turned into waxen dolls—Love flown, and in its stead mere Royal, and 'Paradise', pleasures.—Before me there waited glad bustle and strife—Love itself, an emulous game—Religion a Cause and a Controversy, well smitten and well-defended—men governed by reasons and suasion of speech—wheels going—steam buzzing—a mortal race, and a slashing pace, and the Devil taking the hindmost—taking *me,* by Jove (for that was my inner care), if I lingered too long, upon the difficult Pass that leads from Thought to Action. I descended, and went towards the West.

Unlike his predecessors' narratives, Kinglake's account took on a heroic character, one in which he was determined to show the superiority of Western character. The Bedouin, to whom Robert Wood had looked for a portrayal of some of the ancient Homeric traits which would ennoble 'natural' man, ceased to interest Kinglake. Too aware of his "ascendancy as a European", he was only willing to explore the life of the nomad within the possibilities of *Sturm und Drang,* the more sentimental and fanciful currents of thought and feeling.

His journeys in the deserts of Palestine and Egypt gave Kinglake, as well as later travellers the chance to test their endurance and match their wits against those of the native inhabitants. Finding himself separated from his retinue on several occasions, Kinglake was afforded the opportunity of capturing those moments of truth for which he yearned, and was able to refresh those parched sensibilities, of which, in the manner of Childe Harold, he had complained. But, mainly, when faced with the majesty of the elements, Kinglake was more than ever aware of his frailty, prompting him to write: "There were these two pitted together, and face to face,—the mighty sun for one, and

for the other—this poor, pale, solitary Self of mine that I always carry about with me". It was this feeling, he decided, which had caused men of old to succumb to the "fiery sceptre" of the sun and to create their mythologies in order to bridge the gap between the greatness of nature and their own mortality.

In the early twentieth century, Doughty, sincere, humane and brave, failed to find his holy grail in the deserts of Arabia; while Burton, who juxtaposed the "vigorous, passionate life of Europe" with that of Arab bravery and freedom, also decided, finally, that he preferred European life, since the "Bedouin daring was usually practised from necessity" [Michael Foss, "Dangerous Guides; English Writers and the Desert", *The New Middle East,* June 1969]. Thus, wrote Burton, taking Kinglake's position still further: "In the desert, even more than upon the ocean, there is present death: hardship is there, and piracies, and shipwreck, solitary, not in the crowds when, as the Persians say, 'Death is a Festival' ". The reward for this toughness was the Arab *Kayf:* "The savouring of animal existence; the passive enjoyment of mere sense; the pleasant languor, the dream of tranquility, the airy castle-building, which in Asia stand in lieu of the vigorous, intensive, passionate life of Europe".

The divergent methods of viewing primitive people in the eighteenth and nineteenth centuries, and onwards, is best illustrated by Hazlitt's comments on Wordsworth's poem 'Gipsies'. In it Wordsworth criticised a band of gypsies who had remained in the 'self-same spot', for the last twelve hours while he had spent them as a 'traveller under open sky,/Much witnessing of change and cheer'. Scornfully, and much in the manner of many nineteenth century travellers to the East, Wordsworth labelled them 'Wild outcasts of society'; Hazlitt questioned Wordsworth ironically on how he had himself been spending his time: "Had he been admiring a flower, writing a sonnet?" He then took him to task, for he, as the "prince of poetical idlers," and patron of the 'philosophy of indolence', had little right to preach the doctrine of utility. Such an attitude, as that adopted by Wordsworth, would be tantamount to taking up the proposal to make Stonehenge useful, by building houses with it. Hazlitt added: "Mr. W's quarrel with the gypsies is an improvement on this extravagance, for the gypsies are the only living monuments of the first ages of society. They are an everlasting source of thought and reflection on the advantages and disadvantages of the progress of civilization: they are a better answer to the cotton manufactories than Mr. W. has given in the *Excursion.* 'They are a grotesque ornament to the civil order'." In conclusion, Hazlitt wrote:

> We should be sorry to part with Mr. Wordsworth's poetry, because it amuses and interests us: we should be still sorrier to part with the tents of our old friends, the Bohemian philosophers, because they amuse and interest us more. If any one goes a journey, the principal event in it is his meeting with a party of gipsies. The pleasantest trait in the character of Sir Roger de Coverley, is his interview with the gipsy fortuneteller. This is enough.

Kinglake's pride in British prowess abroad was echoed by

Warburton. After writing of his superior powers as a Westerner which always made him "swell with fresh pride of race", Kinglake hinted of the good relations his own compatriots could enjoy with the inhabitants of the East. He noted that "the merit of the English, especially, was so great that a good Mussulman flying from conscription or any other persecution, would come to seek from the formerly despised hat that protection which the turban could no longer afford". Warburton, who echoed Kinglake's sentiments about the bigotry and confining influence of the Muslim religion, and the necessity for Christianity to escape from its influence, concluded that Britain actually had a mission in the East, and wrote: "England is expected in the East" [Bartholomew Eliot George Warburton, *The Crescent and the Cross,* 1845]. Thus nineteenth century travellers were not content merely to comment, as Thackeray did, that "the much-maligned Orient, I am confident, has not been maligned near enough; for the good reason that none of us can tell the amount of horrible sensuality practised there" [William Makepeace Thackeray, *Notes of a Journey from Cornhill to Grand Cairo,* 1846], but were convinced of their mission to mould the destiny of the area in a manner commensurate with Western interests.

Warburton's remarks about the British role in the East

Engraved view of the Tunis Market at Cairo in the nineteenth century.

proved to be clairvoyant and met with the approval of public officials and politicians of his day. His astute remark that "Gold wins its way where angels might despair, and the interests of India may obtain what the Sepulchre of Christ has been denied" almost paved the way for Britain's prime minister, Benjamin Disraeli, to obtain the Suez Canal for Britain some years later. A Jew by birth, Disraeli would have echoed Warburton's belief that the Jewish inhabitant of the East personified a Destiny incarnate. "That fierce, dark eye, the noble brow; that medallic profile, that has been transmitted unimpaired through a thousand generations and a thousand climates", Warburton wrote, "these are Nature's own illustrations, and vindicate old history". Both East and West, in their opinion, in view of their common Judaic Christian traditions, must necessarily share the same religious and economic future. Thus that sublime language of the Hebrew faith which had so captured the interest of Lowth and Herder, in view of its poetically elevated style and sublime imagery, finally found pure political expression in Laurence Oliphant's *The Land of Gilead: With Excursions in the Lebanon* (1850). In his book Oliphant painstakingly surveys the various regions of Palestine, Jordan and Lebanon in order to make it attractive for Jewish immigrants, an attitude which was to have ominous consequences in the twentieth century.

In conclusion, we can see that although many of the travel trends continued into the nineteenth and twentieth centuries, yet travel during this last period sounded a very aggressive and imperialistic note, which had been muted in earlier centuries. We also find missing from these later accounts, the spirit of eager inquiry and open-mindedness

---

British historian and adventurer Alexander W. Kinglake describes his crossing of the Jordan River:

The Arabs now went to work in right earnest to effect the passage of the river. They had brought with them a great number of the skins which they use for carrying water in the desert; these they filled with air, and fastened several of them to small boughs which they cut from the banks of the river. In this way they constructed a raft not more than about four or five feet square, but rendered buoyant by the inflated skins which supported it. On this a portion of my baggage was placed, and was firmly tied to it by the cords used on my pack-saddles. . . .

At length the raft entered upon the difficult part of its course; the whirling stream seized and twisted it about, and then bore it rapidly downwards; the swimmers flagged, and seemed to be beaten in the struggle. But now the old men on the bank, with their rigid arms uplifted straight, sent forth a cry and a shout that tore the wide air into tatters, and then to make their urging yet more strong they shrieked out the dreadful syllables, " 'Brahim Pasha!" The swimmers, one moment before so blown and so weary, found lungs to answer the cry, and shouting back the name of their great destroyer, they dashed on through the torrent, and bore the raft in safety to the western bank.

A.W. Kinglake, in his Eothen, *1844.*

which characterized the works of earlier travellers. . . .
As a result, we find Thackeray's dandified remarks at the
end of a three-month journey from Portugal to Egypt not
too strange. "If it be but to read the Arabian Nights again
on getting home", he wrote, "it is good to have made this
little voyage and seen these strange places and faces"
[*Notes of a Journey*]. Thus, at the end, we find much of the
dignity and dedication of earlier travellers swept away,
being replaced by journeys which are undertaken at whim
or to satisfy a passing fancy.

> Anita Damiani, "The Romantic Perspective,"
> *in her* Enlightened Observers: British Travel-
> lers to the Near East, 1715-1850, *American
> University of Beirut, 1979, pp. 171-78.*

Charisse Gendron

[*In the following excerpt, Gendron examines the representation of Middle-Eastern women in the works of several prominent Victorian travel writers.*]

Nearly all Victorian travelers to Egypt, Turkey, and Arabia addressed the issue of the condition of Middle-Eastern
women. As Eliot Warburton put it in *The Crescent and the
Cross* (1844), foreign women are the first item of interest
"to the moralist as well as the epicurean" abroad. Some
Western travelers—Lamartine, Flaubert, Warburton himself—were indeed epicureans, and today must face the
charges of those who see the history of "Orientalism" as
one in which the West attempted to recreate the East as
a fantasy of the exotic Other. According to this analysis,
announced in Edward Said's *Orientalism,* the male traveler's sense of boundless adventure in journeying to the
Middle East, where he sheds his inhibitions and tests his
will, is epitomized in his freedom to consider as sex objects
women towards whom he bears no social responsibility.
In any case, he encounters in the Middle-Eastern woman
one whom he has already possessed, erotically and culturally, through Western appropriation of the tales of the
Arabian Nights. As Algerian writer Malek Alloula suggests, however, the epicurean's gaze meets resistance in
the practices of the harem and the veil, a resistance that
generates in him an obsession to penetrate the obstacles
to his desire.

This analysis implies that the Victorian traveler's view of
Middle-Eastern women will be colored by both his nation's sense of manifest destiny in the East and by his own
sexuality, unleashed by the encounter with the exotic
Other and by the opportunity in writing to refashion the
encounter according to the requirements of his fantasy. In
general terms, I accept this analysis; as I hope to show,
however, from a literary point of view the analysis becomes most interesting when we look at travel books by
women as well as men and see that no absolute national
ideology and no single personal sexuality exist, but rather
variations that produce significantly different images of
women.

And what of the other category of travelers for whom
women are the primary item of interest, according to Warburton? These are the moralists, whose concerns in the
Middle East are with the institutions of slavery and polyg-

amy. Florence Nightingale and Harriet Martineau are
clear examples of this category, although the categories do
not always remain distinct. The Victorian interest in the
Woman Question at home and slavery in America lead
even such epicureans as Warburton to make judgments
about the harem system. Travelers with a moral agenda
difficult to separate from a political agenda, particularly
missionaries and colonial administrators, have of course
received their share of anti-orientalist criticism. Barbara
Harlow, for example, writes of colonial European efforts
to discourage the practices of suttee in India, female cir-
cumcision in Kenya, and veiling in Algeria and Iran as attempts "to collaborate with the women under the pretext
of liberating them from oppression by their own men."
And, since critics tend to argue that "professional Orientalism" is inseparable from "personal" or literary descriptions of the Middle east, I am not surprised to find Leila
Ahmed, in a recent article in *Feminist Studies,* categorizing people who disapprove of harems, from the seventeenth-century traveler George Sandys to American feminists of the 1980's, as Western ethnocentrists.

Although neither Alloula, Harlow, Said, nor Ahmed re-
proves Harriet Martineau specifically, their arguments
might easily include her. Ahmed, for instance, insists that
enthnocentrism prevents Westerners from seeing that the
segregation of women from the world of men may oppress
women less than the integration of women in a man's
world. Martineau, who worked for women's education
and against slavery and prostitution, did not see the harem
as a space defined by women for women, and Ahmed herself admits that for Middle-Eastern women "it is . . . impossible, in an environment already so negatively primed
against us, to be freely critical—a task no less urgent for
us than for Western feminists—of our own societies." Her
defense of traditional Islamic social structure is implicitly
refuted by turn-of-the-century Egyptian feminist and nationalist Huda Shaarawi, who, according to her memoir
Harem Years, incorporated Western thinking into her political campaigns to abolish the veil as well as to achieve
for Egypt autonomy from Western Europe.

Rather than to reject Victorian moralists out of hand as
culturely prejudiced or worse, I believe that the more interesting endeavor is to see how they contribute to an on-
going dialogue among Western and Eastern writers over
the sometimes competing claims of feminism and nationalism. As with the epicureans', the moralists' judgments
are not monolithic; they depend, not only on a writer's national ideology and personal sexuality, but upon his or her
sexual politics—what he or she considers to be the proper
role of women. Although sometimes these determining
factors only can be inferred, let us attempt to analyze how
they shape images of women in the books of four Victorians in the Middle East: Alexander Kinglake, Eliot Warburton, Harriet Martineau, and Lucie Duff Gordon.

As a young man recently down from Cambridge in 1834,
Alexander Kinglake toured the Middle East. Ten years
later, he published an account of his experiences in a travel
book that is, as the preface boasts, "quite superficial in its
character," "thoroughly free" "from all display of 'sound
learning and religious knowledge.' " *Eothen* made a sensa-

tion, and is still classed with Lady Mary Wortley Montagu's letters from Turkey and Sterne's *A Sentimental Journey* as a gem among travel books. Also in 1844, Kinglake published "The Rights of Women," an ironical review of Richard Monckton Milnes's poetic defense of the harem, *Palm Leaves.* Kinglake's familiar tone in this review, in which he teases the poet about his mustachios, suggests that he knew Milnes as a member of the London literary world where Kinglake was welcomed for his conversation. Among his personal friends were Lucie Duff Gordon, the poet Bryan Procter and his wife Anne (known for her wit as "Our Lady of Bitterness"), and Caroline Norton, a writer who used her scandalous separation from her husband to publicize the injustice to women of England's marriage and property laws. Kinglake himself never married. In *Eothen,* he brings to his description of Middle-Eastern women a taste for the company of intelligent women with liberal views, as well as a bachelor's playful gallantry, quite another thing from desire.

To understand fully Kinglake's attitude towards the harem system, which puts women at an intellectual and moral disadvantage by denying them knowledge and freedom of choice, we must consider his ideal of social intercourse between men and women. This ideal is a battle of wits. In "The Rights of Women," for instance, where he proceeds from the harem to women at home, he encourages his countrywomen to abandon the pursuit of "Nothing" as a topic of conversation in favor of literary debate, which he envisions as an intellectual skirmish with erotic overtones: "how good for the taste and judgment, how stimulative of the intellect, how favourable for the love of fairness and fair play, is the gentle strife thus provoked!" Kinglake, in this respect typical of the men who built the British empire, loves a challenge: in *Eothen* he tells us that he traveled to the East to strengthen his will. The desert tests his will, but Eastern society, particularly intercourse with women, provides no challenge. "Behind me I left . . . women hushed, and swathed, and turned into waxen dolls—love flown, and in its stead mere royal, and 'Paradise' pleasures," he writes at the close of his journey, when he again faces the West. "Before me there waited glad bustle and strife—love itself, an emulous game— religion a cause and a controversy, well smitten and well defended . . . wheels going—steam buzzing—a mortal race, and a slashing pace, and the devil take the hindmost." Kinglake prizes the "emulous game" of love, with no insistence that it lead on to paradisal pleasures. The harem system of sequestration and surveillance, by eliminating a woman's choice as to whether she will remain faithful to her spouse, puts an end to the game. "Now it is not of course by establishing a rivalry between husbands and lovers that domestic happiness is to be secured," Kinglake concedes in the review of *Palm Leaves,* "but still, when the wholesome *possibility* of rousing emulation is excluded by brutal force, the subjection and humiliation of woman are complete" ["The Rights of Women," *The Quarterly Review* 75 (Dec. 1844-Mar. 1845)]. Subjected and humiliated, Kinglake opines, women are no fun.

Kinglake earns the modern reader's admiration by standing up to the demand by Mrs. Sarah Stickney Ellis, author of Victorian conduct books, that women practice self-abnegation in the service of husband and children. "We are made up of our foibles and faults," he writes in a section of "The Rights of Women" devoted to Ellis's tracts *The Women of England . . .* and *The Wives of England . . . ,* "and to destroy all these one after the other is to extinguish sweet human nature—to efface us from out of the earth." Kinglake's equal disapprobation of the Victorian angel and the Oriental odalisque reminds us that the first has merely consented to internalize the suppression externalized in the harem system. He reserves his approval for women who resist being turned into wax dolls, for instance the "romping girls of Bethlehem" described in *Eothen.* In this perhaps fictionalized account, the Christian girls are free of both the modest veil that paradoxically marks the Moslem woman as a sex object and of the unnaturally confined manners of the English drawing room. "[I]f you will only look virtuous enough to prevent alarm, and vicious enough to avoid looking silly," Kinglake writes,

> the blithe maidens will draw nearer and nearer to you. . . . And if they catch a glimpse of your ungloved fingers, then . . . will they make the air ring with their sweet screams of delight and amazement, as they compare the fairness of your hand with the hues of your sunburnt face, or with their own warmer tints. . . . And when they see you, even then, still sage and gentle the joyous girls will suddenly, and screamingly, and all at once, explain to each other that you are surely quite harmless and innocent—a lion that makes no spring—a bear that never hugs. . . . But the one—the fairest and the sweetest of all, is yet the most timid: she shrinks from the daring deeds of her playmates. . . . But her laughing sisters will have none of this cowardice; . . . they seize her small wrist and drag her forward by force, and at last . . . they vanquish her utmost modesty, and marry her hand to yours. The quick pulse springs from her fingers and throbs like a whisper upon your listening palm.

Of course, while praising the innocently bold girls of Bethlehem, Kinglake mildly satirizes them; they are *farouche,* not quite rational creatures. Even so, the passage celebrates gentle strife between near-equals, in which man, with his advantages of physique, education, and worldly experience, agrees to be "a bear that never hugs," and woman, though compelled to join hands, retains a certain wildness, a "quick pulse" indicative of independent life.

Similar to the game here described between man and woman is the game Kinglake plays with his audience, in which he again acts the part of the bear, although he never hugs. His irreverent approach to sacred Victorian topics, including womanhood and religion, raised eyebrows. John Murray refused to publish the manuscript, and Eliot Warburton, to whom the book is dedicated, warned in a review of it that the author goes rather far. Yet while Kinglake makes use of a rhetoric of wickedness, of seduction and betrayal, he actually insinuates nothing base. The description of the romping girls of Bethlehem, for instance, sports with the notion of sexual compromise in the tradition of *The Rape of the Lock* and *A Sentimental Journey,* a tradition appreciated by women like Lucie Duff Gordon, sophisticated and virtuous, who had nothing but praise for *Eothen.*

His love of the game assures that Kinglake will endorse freedom for women; it also assures that he will never be completely serious. In "The Rights of Women," sounding very much like John Stuart Mill, Kinglake asserts that "[m]en may have in their helpmate the virtues enforced by compulsion, or the virtues that spring from free will, but they cannot have both." But he gives a skeptical twist to the distinction between freely willed and compulsory virtue in *Eothen,* where he plays on the cliché of the veiled woman's increased opportunities to sin:

> She turns, and turns again, and carefully glances around her on all sides, to see that she is safe from the eyes of Mussulmans, and then suddenly withdrawing the *yashmak,* she shines upon your heart and soul with all the pomp and might of her beauty. . . . She sees, and exults in your giddiness—she sees and smiles; then, presently, with a sudden movement, she lays her blushing fingers upon your arm, and cries "Yumourd-jak!" (Plague! meaning, "There is a present of the plague for you!")

This *femme fatale* seems to embody the fear of death Kinglake confesses to have suppressed while sojourning in plague-ridden Cairo. His more overt intention is comically to defame the image, perpetrated by Milnes's poem *Palm Leaves,* of the Middle Eastern woman as the cloistered beloved, source of solace and inspiration for her world-weary husband. The poem goes wrong from the start, as Kinglake points out in his review, by taking the "audacious poetical licence" of occupying its harem with but a single wife. By "importing into Mahometan countries a system of strict monogamy," Milnes sentimentalizes the harem and, implicitly, the subjection of women. Although the description of the hypocritical, malicious veiled woman in *Eothen* seems less flattering than that of Milnes's wife, Kinglake, in his review, assumes the Middle-Eastern woman's perspective sufficiently to see that, as one of several wives or concubines, she could hardly enjoy the crucial position in the home afforded her by Milnes. He prefers the hard-headed account of another traveler to the region, Mrs. Poole, who, "[a]t the very time that our bard was wandering on the banks of the Nile, as blind as Homer . . . was visiting many a hareem, and carefully counting the wives."

The test of a traveler's attitude towards women is his or her description of those who make no attempt to charm: old or work-worn women; women who dress or act like men; savage women whose arts, if any, are alien to the traveler. While Kinglake advocates a kind of equality in social interactions between men and women, he—like most Victorians, notably Ruskin—prefers that women remain different from men, that they be traditionally feminine. In unveiled Bedouin women, for instance, who work like pack animals but carry themselves like free beings, he finds that

> [t]he awful haggardness that gave something of character to the faces of the men was sheer ugliness in the poor women. It is a great shame, but the truth is, that except when we refer to the beautiful devotion of the mother to her child, all the fine things we say and think about women apply only to those who are tolerably good-looking or graceful. These Arab women . . . may have been good women enough . . . but they had so grossly neglected the prime duty of looking pretty in this transitory life that I could not at all forgive them.

I, for one, forgive Kinglake for attending to the prime duty in this transitory life of being amusing and self-ironic, even while confessing his gravest sins. Among male Victorian travelers to the Middle East, I can think of only one—Charles Doughty—who does not display a double standard which makes women whom the writer considers unattractive less human than men. Curiously, this reaction seems to have less to do with sex than with ideology, since writers express it when sex would not seem to be in question. The homosexual Edward Lear, for instance, in the wilds of Albania, describes a group of women who dress and work like men as "unfeminine and disagreeable," even though their eyes express "something pensive and pleasing." And the feminist Florence Nightingale, sailing up the Nile in 1849, associates the unfeminine—nakedness, indecorum—with the demonic: "Four Ethiopian women, perfectly black, were washing in the river, dancing on the clothes like imps, not with movements like human creatures." Kinglake does not go so far as Nightingale in expressing the fear of chaos underlying the double standard; he simply admits, in his role of "man about town" in the Middle East, that he is prejudiced against plain women. Yet this role itself seems to mask anxieties about the nature of women, glimpsed in Kinglake's comment that the confinement of women in harems was a logical outcome of "forty centuries experience of the married state" in the Middle East.

If part of my argument is that art, as represented by Kinglake's persona, can absorb a certain amount of political incorrectness, I shall attempt to prove it further by Eliot Warburton's negative example. His *The Crescent and the Cross* was published the same year as *Eothen,* imitates *Eothen* in content and style, and yet offends where *Eothen* delights. Warburton, whose cautious review of *Eothen* strikes me as hypocritical, lacks Kinglake's distancing irony, and manages in *The Crescent and the Cross* to be heavy-handed as both epicurean and moralist. Describing slaves in the market he echoes Kinglake's phrase about wax dolls to compliment English women at the expense of Georgians and Circassians: "The sunny hair and heaven-blue eyes, that in England produce such an angel-like and intellectual effect, seemed to me here mere flax and beads; and I left them to the 'turbaned Turk' without a sigh." Warburton's fondness for English angels, compared to Kinglake's zest for "love . . . an emulous game," blunts the point of the comparison between free women and slaves, and sounds sanctimonious. But he reveals his latent cynicism towards both Western and Middle-Eastern women—a grosser form of Kinglake's sexual skepticism—in the further comment: "As for the Georgian and Circassian beauties . . . their only ambition, like that of many fair maidens in happier lands, is to fetch a high price; and their only hope is to be first favorite in the hareem—*whose* hareem they care not."

Warburton seems to conflate two episodes from *Eothen* in his description of the young Christian women of Damascus who come to the Franciscan convent to confess, "which," Warburton says with a leer, "if their tongue be as candid as their eloquent eyes, must be rather a protracted business." His flock of "fair penitents" recalls Kinglake's romping girls of Bethlehem, while his insinuation that the women use their veils to entice men "while wandering about these cloisters, waiting till the little confessional is vacant, or, perchance, until they have more to say to its cowled occupant," suggests Kinglake's Cairene *femme fatale*. Warburton, however, imagines wickedness only in terms of sexual license, and parades his fair penitents like prostitutes. Posing as a satirist, Warburton reveals himself as a sensualist, never more so than when he broaches the topic of the unfeminine woman. He describes the typical Arab woman in the market place as "an ugly, old, sun-scorched hag, with a skin like a hippopotamus, and a veil-snout like an elephant's trunk; her scanty robe scarcely serving the purpose of a girdle; her hands, feet, and forehead tattooed of a smoke color; and there is scarcely a more hideous spectacle on earth." This seems an elaboration of Kinglake's description of the Bedouin woman but, where Kinglake then disarms the reader by admitting the injustice of judging women according to sexual criteria, Warburton aggravates the offense by continuing: "But the Lady of the Hareem, on the other hand—couched gracefully on a rich Persian carpet strewn with soft pillowy cushions—is as rich a picture as admiration ever gazed on."

If Kinglake's art neutralizes much of the nationalist and sexist aggression of which Victorian travelers stand accused, and which are more clearly exposed in Warburton, we cannot defend Harriet Martineau's *Eastern Life, Present and Past,* published in 1848 when she was forty-six, on the grounds of art. Martineau wrote to inform and persuade rather than to entertain, although she sometimes used fiction to illustrate a point. The sister of Unitarian minister James Martineau, her early interest in religion survives as moral fervor in her travel books condemning slavery in America and the harem system in Cairo and Damascus. Her feminism, which derived force from her moral training but which also sprang from her own wide interests and achievements, made her question the acquiescence of other women in the assumption that their sex should be concerned exclusively with love and marriage. She questioned this assumption in the novels of Charlotte Brontë as she did in the lives of women in the harem. Her contemporary Lucie Duff Gordon suggests in *Letters from Egypt* (1865) that Martineau's opinions blinded her to the humanity of the Egyptians, so that "the difference of manners is a sort of impassable gulf, the truth being that their feelings and passions are just like our own. . . . [H]er attack upon hareems [is] outrageous; she implies that they are brothels." Undeniably, Martineau's puritanical streak jaundiced her view of the harems so invitingly depicted by her worldly eighteenth-century predecessor, Lady Mary Wortley Montagu. At the same time, I disagree with Duff Gordon that Martineau failed to see an important reality of women's lives in the Middle East of the last century. Her analysis of the relationship between slavery, polygamy, and the harem is acute. She never implies that a harem

is literally a brothel, but Duff Gordon is correct if she means that to Martineau the distinction between concubinage and prostitution would be slight.

Martineau's prudery seems to mark her as an insular traveler, as when she dismisses Egyptian female dancing as a "disagreeable and foolish wriggle." Such remarks seem less arbitrary, however, if we see them as part of a larger reaction against what she saw as the over-sexualization of women's lives under the harem system. By any account, the structure of the harem defines women as sexual property and discourages them from the pursuit of learning that might allow them to redefine themselves. "[T]he only idea of their whole lives," Martineau complains, "is that which, with all our interests and engagements, we consider too prominent with us. . . . There cannot be a woman of them all who is not dwarfed and withered in mind and soul by being kept wholly engrossed with that one interest." Not all readers will share Martineau's apparent lack of interest in sex, but some will pause thoughtfully over her assertion that the master's eunuchs, who are both his slaves and surrogates, not only bully the women of the harem but frequently establish emotional and physical intimacy with them. If this is true—and Huda Shaarawi attests to the bullying part at least—harem women are rehearsed endlessly in their role as sexual possessions, and to think of the harem as separate female space becomes impossible.

Engraved portrait of Harriet Martineau.

Sex aside, one sees how the intrepid Martineau, who wrote books on economics, traveled in barbarous America, and ironed her clothes in the desert, would suffer under the passivity of harem life. She writes of a visit among women who assume that, like themselves, she has nothing but time: "To sit hour after hour on the deewán, without any exchange of ideas, having our clothes examined . . . and being gazed at by a half-circle of girls in brocade and shawls . . . is as wearisome an experience as one meets with in foreign lands." To make matters worse, Martineau, like Florence Nightingale after her, must put up with the condescension of harem women who fail to understand that her unmarried, independent status is voluntary: "Everywhere they pitied us European women heartily, that we had to go about traveling, and appearing in the streets without being properly taken care of,—that is, watched." If Martineau seems sensitive on this point, she had probably been similarly pitied at home, where even most Englishwomen were not as self-reliant as she. When she defends women's interests, however, she is thinking not only of herself; one of my favorite passages, expressing concern with Middle-Eastern women's digestions, calls for the introduction of jump ropes into the harem. More important, and this argues against the insularity of her views, Martineau contrasts "the cheerful, modest countenance of the Nubian girl busy about her household tasks" in primitive Upper Egypt with "the dull and gross face of the handmaid of the hareem" in civilized Cairo. What matters to Martineau, in contrast to Warburton, Kinglake, Nightingale, and Lear, is the practical freedom and social usefulness the woman enjoys, rather than her physical attractiveness or conventional femininity. That Martineau describes as modest a woman who was probably half-naked is significant.

In spite of claiming to find Milnes's *Palm Leaves* to be a beautiful poem, Martineau effectively challenges the assumptions of Western supporters of the harem. Watching the antics of eunuchs, wives, and concubines who might have been monogamous and free in Nubia, she realizes that two systems of oppression can support each other, that "slavery and polygamy . . . can clearly never be separated." She follows up the implications of Montesquieu's defense of polygamy, that Middle-Eastern men must be allowed amiable companions in addition to child brides, by suggesting that society think of marriage in terms of companionship to begin with and that women be educated appropriately. She answers those "cosmopolitan" philosophers who view the harem system as intrinsic to Middle-Eastern culture that "[i]t is as pure a conventionalism as our representative monarchy, or German heraldry, or Hindoo caste," and so not above reform. Her most irrefutable argument, however, may be implicit in her description of a visit to a Damascus harem:

> But the great amusement was my ear trumpet. The eldest widow . . . put it to her ear; when I said "Bo!" When she had done laughing, she put it into her next neighbor's ear, and said "Bo!" and in this way it came round to me again. But in two minutes, it was asked for again, and went round a second time—everybody laughing as loud as ever at each "Bo!"—and then a third time!

Seclusion in the harem has not liberated these women from patriarchal structures; it has infantalized them.

Martineau is a moralist rather than an epicurean, not only in her response to the condition of Middle-Eastern women, but also in her approach to writing, which is journalistic rather than artistic. Her counterpart, Lucie Duff Gordon, more subtly blends an ability to entertain not unlike Kinglake's with a desire to inform the English people about the situation in Egypt, where in the 1860's a corrupt government was starving and conscripting the peasants in order to support French projects. Duff Gordon, once described by Kinglake as "so intellectual, so keen, so autocratic, sometimes even so impassioned in speech, that nobody feeling her powers could go on feebly comparing her to a . . . mere Queen or Empress" [Janet Ross, "Memoir" in *Lady Duff Gordon's Letters from Egypt,* 1902], wields in *Letters from Egypt* the aristocratic tolerance of one whose London house was open to writers and parliamentarians and who, as a German translator, helped to support her noble but poor husband. She values the forms of courtesy, but overlooks infractions of puritanical religious and sexual codes. Her comment on traditional Egyptian dancing, rather unusual for a Victorian, is that the dancer "moved her breasts by some extraordinary muscular effort, first one and then the other; they were just like pomegranates and gloriously independent of stays or any support."

If her worldliness helps Duff Gordon cross the gap between Western and Eastern manners, however, she is not merely one of Martineau's fashionable cosmopolitans. Tuberculosis impelled her to live in sun-baked Nubia from 1862 until her death in 1869. She makes a cross-cultural passage, in the Forsterian sense, living among her Egyptian servants in Luxor, nursing the people, and vindicating Islamic customs in the letters collected and published in 1865. Although she remains Christian and faithful to her absent husband, her identification with Egyptian culture and irritation with Western prejudices prevent her from judging the harem system according to external standards. She tells the story of a Turkish man who, when teased by an Englishman for having several wives, replies

> "Pray, how many women have you, who are quite young, seen (that is the Eastern phrase) in your whole life?" The Englishman could not count—of course not. "Well, young man, I am old, and was married at twelve, and I have seen in all my life seven women; four are dead, and three are happy and comfortable in my house. *Where are all yours?*"

Candidly admitting the polygamous behavior of men in both West and East, Duff Gordon here prefers the Islamic system as more responsible and less hypocritical.

This judgment, however, does not address the consequences of the harem system, beyond physical security, for women. Duff Gordon's privileged position in rural Egyptian society may partly account for her distance from this question, especially during the earlier part of her sojourn, before she had visited a harem in Cairo. Although she lived very simply, she held a position of respect in local society. The villagers accepted that, as a foreigner, she would go unveiled and associate with the most learned men, sheiks and magistrates. She confesses her attitude towards the women's society when she writes of a French journalist's visit as "a very agreeable interlude to the Arab prosiness, or rather *enfantillage,* on the part of the women." Even in England male society lauded Duff Gordon as the exception, the "manfully-minded" woman, in George Meredith's phrase. Such a progressive woman, however, could not remain unmindful of the difficulties facing all women in the nineteenth century, and Duff Gordon, having made clear her advocacy of Egyptian culture, shows in later passages her concern for the victims of its sexual double standard. When the crew finds a woman's body off her houseboat on the Nile, the pilot explains, " 'most likely she has blackened her father's face, and he has been forced to strangle her, poor man.' I said 'Alas!' and the Reis continued, 'ah, yes, it is a heavy thing, but a man must whiten his face.' " When she finally visits a Turkish harem in Cairo, she concedes that the first wife must find it "rather a bore to have to educate little girls for her husband's use." "Alas" and "rather a bore" do not sound like harsh condemnations—she saves those for French-Egyptian politics—but given her urbane view of foreign marital customs, the phrases carry weight.

Duff Gordon knows how to praise when she sees another woman who has lifted herself above social expectations. She says of a Cairene widow:

> I am filled with admiration at her good sense and courage. She has determined to carry on her husband's business of letting boats herself, and to educate her children to the best of her power in habits of independence. I hope she will be successful, and receive the respect such rare conduct in a Turkish woman deserves from the English.

Fascinating to compare with previously mentioned passages describing traditionally unfeminine Middle-Eastern women is Duff Gordon's account of an "eccentric" Arab woman traveling through a Nile village

> dressed like a young man, but small and feminine and rather pretty, except that one eye was blind. . . . I was told—indeed, I could hear—that her language was beautiful, a thing much esteemed among Arabs. She is a virgin and fond of travelling and of men's society, being very clever, so she has her dromedary and goes about quite alone. No one seemed surprised, no one stared, and when I asked if it was *proper,* our captain was surprised. "Why not? If she does not wish to marry, she can go alone; if she does, she can marry—what harm? She is a virgin and free."

Duff Gordon's account of this wealthy, militant, and free virgin transcends the sexual criteria that underlie Kinglake's gallantry, Warburton's cynicism, and Nightingale's horror of the unfeminine. Most characteristic of all, she takes the opportunity to compliment the Egyptians for accepting one who has escaped the harem system.

In an article admitting how poorly the English can behave in the East, E. M. Forster salutes Duff Gordon for transcending race prejudice ["Salute to the Orient," in *Abinger Harvest,* 1955]. She is not discussed by the anti-orientalist critics mentioned above. Obviously, neither Duff Gordon's cultural openness, Kinglake's irony, nor Martineau's abolitionist commitment provides a rationale for Victorian England's imperialist activities in the Middle East. Perhaps, even, by traveling to and writing critically about the region these writers contributed to that British sense of ascendancy so advantageous to imperial ventures. I feel, however, now that critics of imperialism and Orientalism have established the connections between Victorian politics and travel literature, that politics and literature may be separated somewhat again. Our political analysis continuously evolves, and from where I sit Martineau's *Eastern Life* addresses the global issue of the oppression of women, whereas Said's *Orientalism* and Alloula's *The Harem* exhibit a male bias; in Said's discussion of Arab sexuality as a revolutionary force, his representative Arab is male; Alloula worries about how Western men, by gazing at forbidden Algerian women, displace Algerian male society. The point is that, dangerous as Victorian travel books may seem in the mass, the best of them contribute individual versions of cultural history that may be read in numerous ways. Kinglake's *Eothen* and Duff Gordon's *Letters from Egypt* even may be read, with a clear conscience, for pleasure.

> Charisse Gendron, "Images of Middle-Eastern Women in Victorian Travel Books," in The Victorian Newsletter, *No. 79, Spring, 1991, pp. 18-23.*

Susan Morgan

[*Co-founder of the Women's Studies Program at Cornell University, Morgan is a South African-born American educator and critic who has written extensively on representations of gender in nineteenth-century literature. In the following essay, she examines travel literature written by English women in Southeast Asia.*]

> I am content to sympathize with common mortals, no matter where they live; in houses or in tents, in the streets under a fog, or in the forests behind the dark line of distant mangroves that fringe the vast solitude of the sea.
> —Joseph Conrad, "Preface" to *Almayer's Folly*

> Then he asked me in a solemn voice: "You know Stambul, Monsieur?"
>
> "Yes."
>
> "I lived in Stambul a year, and I tell you, Monsieur, it is a hell from which there is no way out."
> —Robert Byron, *The Road to Oxiana*

During the last three decades of the nineteenth century a wealth of travel books written by women were published in England. Many of these travel books share distinctive features. They were focussed on countries geographically far removed from England which were non-Western and non-white: in Africa, in the Middle East, in India, in Southeast Asia, and in the Far East. They were often the products of long stays in and substantial familiarity with the countries that were their subjects. The authors did not present themselves, and may not even have thought of themselves, as particularly adventuresome or somehow different from other women. They declared their books to have specific, practical aims which were usually political and economic. Although often implicitly, the books also addressed other, more philosophic questions, about the future of England, the meaning of progress, and the definition of human nature. These books enjoyed a large reading audience in their own era. And, finally, they have all but been forgotten in ours.

Traditional Victorian scholars in the twentieth century focussed on fiction, poetry, and the essays that as a graduate student I was taught to call nonfiction prose. In their critical writings about the period they reconstructed a kind of cultural fantasyland in which every Victorian who was anybody read or was influenced by such wise patriarchs as Carlyle, Newman, Ruskin, and Arnold, the classic Victorian sages. But a great many Victorians were reading, and admiring, the travel writings of Annie Brassey, Anna Forbes, and Margaret Brooke. Yet there is no published study of Victorian women's travel writings about the East, and the potentially major role of these writings in shaping the cultural currents of their age has never been considered. The initial reason, then, why these writings are so significant must simply be that they were so significant.

That significance has an aesthetic as well as a factual dimension. The central charm of these writings, and where both their literary and their historical value should be placed, is in their sensitive acuteness to and complex relations with Eastern cultures. The quality of their prose is inseparable from the moral, emotional, and intellectual sophistication of their insights about what for many readers were, and are, imaginatively remote worlds. That sophistication is based on a particular notion of the value of human sympathy, of the truths of the heart, which spoke to many Victorian readers with powerful eloquence.

There are two distinct but interdependent issues that these travel books raise for a critic today. First, what can their presence as a salient element of Victorian culture tell us about their own time? Second, what can their absence—and, hopefully, their renewed presence—tell us about ours? I want to begin this brief, and necessarily introductory, discussion by turning first to the question of the meaning of these works in their own time.

It may be that the West has always been fascinated with the East—and if not quite always, then certainly long enough. Just as certainly, "to believe that such things happen as a necessity of the imagination, is to be disingenuous" [Edward W. Said, *Orientalism*, 1978]. In nineteenth-century England the passion for the faraway first appears as a major literary event with Byron's grand tour of the mid-East, and the huge success during the second decade of the century of such poems as *The Turkish Tales* and the Eastern cantos of *Don Juan*. But the long-term British love affair with the exotic expanded throughout the century and functioned in many ways. Any attempt to understand some of the dimensions of that expansion must begin with Edward Said's brilliant insight that "the Orient was Orientalized not because it was discovered to be 'Oriental' in all those ways considered commonplace by the average

nineteenth-century European, but also because it *could be*—that is, submitted to being—*made* Oriental."

If Byron's work was popular due both to the general charm of its eastern topics for the British public and to its author's particular ability to make those topics "Oriental," his poems are still rather different phenomena from the prose accounts of journeys that long have captured the attention of the British public. Byron himself certainly knew other travel accounts, at least in poetry. He dedicated *The Giaour* to his friend, Samuel Rogers, the author of that forgettable 1810 fragment, *The Voyage of Columbus*. After Byron, the most notable prose account in the first decades of the nineteenth century of a voyage of discovery was Charles Darwin's 1839 *Journal of Researches into the Geology and Natural History of the Various Countries Visited by H.M.S. Beagle*.

The difference between the subject of Roger's failed poem and of Darwin's popular book highlights the special qualities of the latter. *The Voyage of Columbus* tried to recreate a discovery that was fundamentally a discovery of a place. It was a great physical adventure, a journey into the literal unknown. The larger significance of that journey, its power to change the ways people view the world, had been reverberating for three centuries before Rogers wrote his account. Darwin's *Journal of Researches* was also an account of physical discoveries; of the birds, beetles, and fossil mammals of South America. Yet those discoveries, in themselves minute and cumulative, only carry significance as traces of a meaning that no one, including the author, could know with any confidence at the time the *Journal* was published. This was writing to the moment, and it would take Darwin another twenty years of research to publish the book that limned the significance of that moment. After *The Origin of the Species* was published in 1859 it would take his readers the rest of the nineteenth century, and arguably the twentieth and perhaps the twenty-first century as well, to follow the implications of his insights. Darwin's *Journal*, though written during what often must have been a daring physical adventure, is really an account of the adventures of the scientific mind. Its exciting moments have to do with bone structures and barnacles, with uncovering patterns in the natural world.

There are many accounts of how Darwin spent twenty years tabulating and adding to his findings from the journey of the Beagle in order to write *The Origin of the Species*, only to find his central ideas suddenly and fairly completely anticipated by Alfred Russel Wallace. In May or June of 1858 Wallace, who had conducted his own researches in South America, the Malay Archipelago, and Indonesia, sent Darwin a paper from Southeast Asia with a theory that Wallace said had come to him in "a flash of insight." Wallace was generous in acknowledging that Darwin's years of commitment to the subject took precedence over his "flash." For his part, Darwin was prodded by Wallace's achievement to start writing his own book rapidly enough to have it ready for publication the following year.

What Wallace and Darwin shared, and what made their mutual discoveries and the sorting out of the question of precedence amicable (apart from decency of character), was a commitment to the process of personal observation and fact-collecting that could make a theory stand or fall. That is why Wallace, though publishing the theory first, would concede Darwin's prior claim. It is also why Darwin, absorbed in accumulating and categorizing evidence, took so long to get around to writing out his explanatory conclusions. It is fair to say that Darwin's voyage of discovery lasted from 1831, when Darwin first boarded the Beagle, to 1859, when he directly spelled out the scientific conclusions of that voyage.

Implicit in the unfolding of this publishing event, arguably the most important intellectual event in nineteenth-century history, is the belief that knowledge is a matter of personal involvement, of long, attentive experience. What made Darwin's work truer than Wallace's was not the objective fact, the right answer, the theory of evolution of species through natural selection that both of them had more or less independently arrived at. Darwin's work was seen as truer because of his enormous accumulation of details in five years on the Beagle and twenty more years in England. Thus, Darwin's theory was truer not merely because it was backed by more factual evidence but also substantially because it had evolved from virtually a lifetime of committed involvement. The process gave substance, and value, to the product.

The history of Darwin's researches demonstrates a basic principle of scientific investigation: that what is most essential is not the abstract theory but the concrete evidence that can prove or disprove it. But the publication history of Darwin's discovery demonstrates a great deal more. The value that the various players in that history placed on the research process, far from reflecting just a rule for objective procedure, is part of a familiar and frequent belief among all sorts of writers in nineteenth-century England that what is of value is process. The lived experience matters; out of it come truths that take their quality as truths exactly from the fact of their having emerged from experience. George Eliot, a famous proponent of this organic view, wrote [in *The Lifted Veil*] that "we learn *words* by rote, but not their meanings; *that* must be paid for with our life-blood, and printed in the subtler fibres of our nerves." Whether it be a matter of objectivity or emotion, of science or philosophy, of economics or art, wisdom is to be gleaned from the living whole.

The sense that truth comes out of lived experience has long been cited as a defining quality of the intellectual history written by the male Victorian sages. Their most famous critical chronicler, John Holloway, explaining Newman's idea of Real Assent, described it [in his *The Victorian Sage: Studies in Argument,* 1953] as "directed towards assertions based on the whole trend of our experience." Yet this idea, in tandem with the sages' belief that the purpose of their writing is to modify "the reader's perceptiveness," also constitutes the defining quality of Victorian women's travel writings about Southeast Asia.

The commitment to a wisdom that comes out of lived experience recurs in women's travel writings. Anna Forbes, who travelled with her husband on his naturalist expedition to Java in the early 1880s, wrote her own account [*Insulinde: Experiences of a Naturalist's Wife in the Eastern Archipelago,* 1887]. Her direct explanation for the differences in their versions of the journey is that "we shared for the most part the same experiences; but we looked upon them from an entirely different standpoint." Part of the difference in standpoint was not just the matter of their being different people but also of their being a different sex. This was a fact of culture rather than of biology. English women in the East, whatever their number of servants, still attended to such domestic matters as laundry, shopping, cooking, and particularly children, matters that they shared with their foreign counterparts. Their perspectives on Southeast Asia reflect this sense of having a connection to other women that they did not share with English men. And one of the most common ways in which these women writers assert their bonds with women of another country is through motherhood.

The pervasive Victorian belief that truth comes from perceptions felt along the bone, far from providing an exclusive blessing for the oracular writings of Victorian men, also functioned to validate a woman's voice and special experience. Within the genre of travel literature of the period, the organic principle served to distinguish between women's and men's writings about the same country. Finally, it also served to distinguish views between women. One of the most dramatically negative accounts of British station life in Malaya is Emily Innes's *The Chersonese with the Gilding Off* (1885). Innes wrote her exposé explicitly to contrast with Isabella Bird's celebration of the Malay peninsula, *The Golden Chersonese* (1883). Yet, in her conclusion, Innes praises Bird's "delightful" book and goes on to claim that "notwithstanding the brilliancy and attractiveness of her descriptions, and the dullness and gloom of mine, I can honestly say that her account is perfectly and literally true. So is mine. The explanation is that she and I saw the Malayan country under totally different circumstances."

[According to Khoo Kay Kim, in the introduction to Innes' work], Innes was "a nonentity compared to Isabella Bird." Bird already had a substantial reputation as a travel writer before writing her Malay account and it gave her real power: "Government officers did their best to make themselves agreeable, knowing that she wielded in her right hand a little instrument that might chastise or reward them." One clear measure of the difference between the two women's experiences is that it never occurred to Innes "in those days that I might write an account of it all." Eventually, she realized the power of a public voice. She took up "the little instrument" for the practical power she hoped it would give her as well, in her case to arouse public opinion against the corrupt Colonial Office, which had refused her husband six years of back pay.

Two specific implications of the extensive nineteenth-century commitment to the organic nature of truth are immediately relevant to the question of women and wisdom. First, as Holloway lucidly pointed out over thirty-five years ago, the commitment to finding truth through an observation of and an involvement in concrete life lends itself to novels or, to put it more generally, to the truth-value of ideas embodied in characters and narrative. The distance may not be so great after all between Darwin poring over his barnacles and a literary critic poring over *Middle-march.* Certainly, there are important similarities between a novel and *The Origin of the Species.* Many readers have noted *The Origin*'s narrative qualities, and have attributed part of its early success, extensive popularity, and impact on a nonscientific audience to its readable personal style.

Second, there is a significant tie in nineteenth-century intellectual history between the influence of Darwinism and the popularity of travel books, and thus between scientific and what I would loosely describe as nonscientific explorations. The journeys of the naturalists in the 1830s, 1840s, and 1850s and the resulting travel accounts—of Darwin in South America, of Wallace in the Malay Archipelago, of Sir Joseph Dalton Hooker in Antarctica, New Zealand and Tasmania—may well form the enabling intellectual context for such travel accounts of the 1870s, 1880s, and 1890s as those by Anna Leonowens about Siam and India, by Brassey about Tahiti and the South Seas, and by Bird, Innes, and Emily Richings about the Malay Archipelago. These women travellers saw their journeys as crucial experiences, most expressing a view similar to Darwin's that the voyage was "by far the most important event in my life." All the writers, male and female, were searching for truth. If the men looked for it in the immediacy of their field experiences, the women hoped to find it in the daily act of living the life that they also observed. Like their naturalist counterparts, the women believed that this truth, once recorded in its organic and concrete form, could cause a public, and important, change in the perspective of their readers.

Apart from the historical accuracy of pointing out critical connections between the accounts of travelling naturalists and the accounts of nonscientific travellers, there is another important advantage. The scientific journey offers a much-needed alternative context to that of the novel through which to approach nineteenth-century travel writings. There are, roughly speaking, three different nineteenth-century genres which need to be distinguished here: scientific writings, often cast in the narrative form of voyage accounts or of journal accounts recording the process of discovery; travel writings, which are usually but not inevitably in narrative form; and novels. All three genres share certain elements. Readers have long been attentive to the connections between science writings and literature, from T. H. Huxley's *Science and Culture* and Edward Dowden's "The Scientific Movement and Literature" to such present works as Gillian Beer's *Darwin's Plots,* George Levine's *Darwin and The Novelists,* and Peter Morton's *The Vital Science.* The much more limited work on travel writings has attended to their fictional qualities, as in Percy Adams's *Travel Literature and the Origin of the Novel.* Yet the links between scientific and travel writings have been almost completely ignored.

All three kinds of work aim to depict in a concrete form the truths of life. To say this highlights immediately the limitations as well as the advantages of using a fictional model to discuss travel writings. The working fiction about travel writings is that they are about real people and real places, that they are factual as well as true. Quite simply, when the critical models are taken from fiction, what

are actual journeys take on the dimensions of generic events, as what Marilyn Butler [in "Voyages in Metaland," *Times Literary Supplement,* 22 June 1984] has called "surrogates for the modern reader's psychic journeys, or symbolic representations of the whole of life." They lose their specific personal and historical status. This is not to say that critics should not read travel accounts in terms of the pattern of fiction, "so intimately are literature and travel implicated with each other" [according to Paul Fussell, in his *Abroad: British Literary Traveling Between the Wars,* 1980]. The story (if it is a story) that a traveller tells can be read as either true or false. But it should not lose its dimension as a history.

Working from the example of Victorian scientific journeys immediately suggests distinctions among kinds of nineteenth-century travel writings. One of the most famous versions of the genre is the gentleman's grand tour. There were hundreds of accounts of the grand tour, usually to Europe but sometimes farther, published in the first half of the nineteenth century. Byron's idiosyncratic tours formed the basis for much of his poetry. Alexander Kinglake's 1844 *Eothen,* one of the most popular travel books in Victorian England, is an account to a friend of his grand tour of the Middle East. The charm—and the horror—of *Eothen* lie in its witty style; Kinglake [according to Jan Gordon in an introduction to that work] "was one of God's Englishmen, . . . a convinced advocate of the theory that all things English were, on the whole, best." If it weren't for the enormous number of accounts by young English gentlemen with the same attitude, though perhaps with less verbal grace, I could convincingly name Kinglake's book as the direct source for George Meredith's account in his 1879 *The Egoist* of Sir Willoughby Patterne's letters home from his grand tour. As the narrator in *The Egoist* characterizes the hero's travel accounts, a "word, a turn of the pen, or a word unsaid, offered the picture of him in America, Japan, China, Australia, nay, the continent of Europe, holding an English review of his Maker's grotesques."

Meredith's description captures a key element of Kinglake's account, that it contained "a picture of him," with the various places he visited functioning as a sort of backdrop for his virtues and charms. As Kinglake wrote in his "Preface" while arguing for the truth of his little book, "as I have felt, so have I written," thus "refusing to dwell upon matters which failed to interest my own feelings." Darwin, and many other travel writers, could make the same claim. But the important difference is that Kinglake is interested in himself, in part because, as an Englishman, he assumes that he is of superior interest to anything or anyone around him. As Said argues, "Orientalism depends for its strategy on this flexible *positional* superiority, which puts the Westerner in a whole series of possible relationships with the Orient without ever losing him the relative upper hand."

The outrageous point of Kinglake's travels is that in a fundamental sense they are pointless. His travels are not really experiences that can change, affect, or somehow alter his understanding of his life. Instead, they are experiences that do not matter, or that matter precisely because they do not matter, that demonstrate Kinglake's superiority on the very grounds that the rest of the world, even if new, strange, and interesting, can add nothing to what, as an Englishman, he already is. The kind of travel writing exemplified by *Eothen,* ostensibly based on a presumed interest in other places, is finally and essentially about a lack of interest in them. The tremendously flattering and reassuring point for the reader, after having been delightfully entertained, is that by not taking such a journey he has really missed nothing, for there is nothing much out there after all. He already has the essential experience of being English, he already knows all he needs to know by staying at home. And that is the ultimate fact that a record of the grand tour can provide.

The entertainment of this sort of travel writing, what there is for the reader to enjoy, is the narrator himself—the feelings, the wit, the intelligence of a fellow Englishman. If the external world is not of particular interest, the internal world that carries within it all the preestablished criteria of value for Victorian masculine culture is. All the world is a stage, but the play and the characters are always English, and the lead character is always an Englishman. In *Eothen* we are to be intrigued not by what Kinglake sees but by how, and to what, he responds. In contrast to the premise of the scientific voyages of discovery, the premise of this sort of travel writing is that experience does not matter, and that truth does not emerge from experience but is already intrinsically felt and known. The result is a record of encounters with other, radically different cultures that reassures rather than unsettles its readers, and bolsters rather than challenges their most basic national and cultural and masculine chauvinism.

Separating out those travel writings that, under the forms of romance or essay, guidebook or memoir, are really exercises in the superiority of the travelling Englishmen to whatever wonders he may survey is fairly easy. It is more difficult to approach those travel writings that seem to be doing something else. In his fascinating study of twentieth-century British travel writings between the two World Wars, Paul Fussell is able to suggest patterns of meaning precisely because of his attention to the historical moment, that period following the Great War and continuing until the ominous rumblings that signalled the beginning of the Second World War. Fussell's admirable sense of history also reveals, perhaps inadvertently, that there are limits to what even a properly historical-critical approach can explain. Thus, Fussell argues that the fondness these travel writings show for the tropics, for palm trees, and sunny oranges, is a "celebration of freedom" and a reaction to the freezing barrenness of the trenches. Yet that explanation hardly will account for the fondness for the tropical exhibited in women's travel writings well before the First World War. One example among a multitude is Brassey's rhapsodic account of her first visit to Tahiti [*Tahiti, a Series of Photographs taken by Colonel Stuart-Wortley with Letterpress by Lady Brassey,* 1882]: "I look on that voyage now as one long dream of azure seas, and purple, gold, and crimson sunrises." Fussell's account is startling in its blithe assumption that the genre is a male phenomenon (perhaps because no women were in the trenches?). Nonetheless, in its commitment to historical specificity, if not

in its apparently unconscious masculine bias, Fussell's work is an apt reminder that a critical approach to Englishwomen's travel writings in the latter half of the nineteenth century requires attention to time and place as well as to the conventions of other contemporary modes of writing.

The 1870s, 1880s, and 1890s were a time of increased travel for Englishwomen, in part because they were a time of increased travel for Englishmen. The long stays in India had always meant that it was commonplace for men to bring their women and children along and for family members from England to visit relatives in India. But during the nineteenth century there were radical changes in the length and safety of the route. The trip around the Cape of Good Hope, even after the end of the Napoleonic wars, took several months and was dangerous enough that many ships did not complete the journey. The overland route across the Suez isthmus was about the same until the opening of the Suez railway in 1858. The Suez Canal opening in 1869 again shortened the trip considerably. From Eliza Fay's *Original Letters From India, 1779-1815* to Harriet Tytler's *An Englishwoman in India: Memoirs, 1828-1858* to Isabel Burton's 1879 *Arabia, Egypt, and India,* the routes to the East were increasingly travelled and written about by Englishwomen.

Not only India but many places in the East became more accessible for Englishwomen in the latter half of the century. First, many originally drawn to India continued on to other parts. [Anna] Leonowens, who went to live with her mother and stepfather in India as a young girl fresh out of school, married an English officer there who was then transferred to Singapore. Her 1884 memoir of the early 1850s in India subtitled *Recollections of a Journey Before the Days of Railroads* emphasizes the important changes in forms of travel. British commercial interest in the Far East was firmly established with the consolidation of the British areas of Penang, Malacca, and Singapore as the Straits Settlements in 1826 and, after the unease throughout the East that followed the 1857 Indian Mutiny, their transfer in 1867 from the India office to the Colonial Office. By the middle of the century travel between India and the Straits Settlements took a mere eight days. Starting in 1845, steamships replaced sailing ships from England to Singapore, Penang, and Hong Kong, and established a regular biweekly service. A journey that had taken, with luck, four months, now took only four weeks. The result was increased economic growth, particularly in the tin trade, and increased social as well as commercial contact with England.

Two other significant political events need to be mentioned in this overview of the historical context of Victorian women's travel writings. The first was the American Civil War. Regardless of the range of specific English responses, the slavery question generally was elevated to an issue of major public importance that concerned people everywhere. Leonowens's next-door neighbor in Singapore lent her a copy of *Uncle Tom's Cabin* in the early 1860s. Leonowens took her own concern about the evil of slavery to Siam, and much of the private sympathy for the harem women that infuses her writing finds public expression through that concern.

Entwined with the matter of slavery is the matter of women's rights, an increasingly visible and powerful political issue in Victorian England. Travel writings by women continually discuss the situation of women in strange lands, often in comparison with the situation of women in England. While some find the English situation better and some find other situations better, almost all express an admiration for as well as an empathy with the women of Southeast Asia. As Leonowens put it [in her *Siamese Harem Life*], in a chapter entitled " 'Muang Thai,' or the Kingdom of the Free," among the "poor, doomed women" of the royal harem she has known some that accepted their fate with a "sweet resignation that told how dead must be the heart under that still exterior; and it is here, too, that I have witnessed a fortitude under suffering of which history furnishes no parallel."

Frequently, these women's travel writings testify to the validity and the importance of the experience of Southeast Asian women. Again and again, the writers see themselves as witnesses who have the special qualifications to describe the lives of these foreign women, to make their English readers really see. Their accounts commonly emphasize the similarities they notice and the connections they feel with these other women who lead what culturally seem to be deeply different lives. There are such occasional horrors as Florence Caddy's comment [in her *To Siam and Malaya,* 1889] on visiting Siam: "how like the 'Arabian Nights' it is to see these three slaves in white garments approach our party with refreshments, and kneel and prostrate themselves in offering the huge silver trays." Caddy is also capable of claiming that "it is another popular fallacy that tropical fruits are delicious; they are not to be compared with ours." Both of these amazing remarks function to mediate, and thereby to denigrate, Caddy's actual experience, one through literature and the other presumably through memory. Clearly, her readers can forget about Siam. They need only read *The Arabian Nights* while eating English pears.

Caddy's commentary directly invokes the chauvinistic authorial posture of *Eothen.* Yet if Caddy and Kinglake are similar in their jingoism and blindness, this is only to say that her work must be classed with his. Such cultural snobbery, so common in the books by male authors about the grand tour, is rare among women's travel books about Southeast Asia. Perhaps because the authors were Englishwomen rather than Englishmen, their books tended to exhibit only occasionally what functioned as a typical convention of the literature of the grand tour: the fundamental assumption that the British traveler was superior to all he surveyed.

There are certainly psychological and cultural explanations for this difference. I want to emphasize here a literary explanation as well. These travel books by women are a different genre, with conventions and perspectives more in keeping with the published accounts of journeys by male scientists than of journeys by gentlemen tourists. Moreover, the mere act of writing about journeys in Southeast Asia appears to have been self-selecting. The

women who did not like what they saw, and there must surely have been many, apparently did not bother to write about it. And there are simply many fewer instances of women being ready to view their travels as the occasion to write about themselves.

Their books about Southeast Asia do share a notion of the truth, though not always with the same intensity or clarity. To paraphrase Little Bilham's words in *The Ambassadors,* the truth they wanted their readers really to see is the identity and the value of human nature, of women as well as men, of nonwhite races as well as white, in Borneo as well as in Bournemouth. Thus, Leonowens, at one of her first dinner parties in India, is acutely aware of the "dark restless eyes" of the servants, while the rest of the company discusses British supremacy in India. "I did comprehend, and that very painfully, that no one seemed to mind those dark, silent, stationary figures any more than if they had been hewn out of stone." Within the Victorian debate about human nature, the kindred sense that many British women felt with other peoples, most often with other women, functioned within these travel writings, and thus for their readers, as an argument for the universality of the human condition and the relativity of its cultural manifestations.

Cultural relativity also meant the possibility of comparing British institutions unfavorably with foreign institutions, implying that when the British travel they do have something to learn. One of the features of nineteenth-century European Orientalism was a view of the Orient as primitive, as [according to Edward Said in *Race and Class* 27, 1985] "ceding its historical preeminence and importance to the world spirit moving westwards away from Asia and towards Europe." Many women's accounts, specifically those that emerged from the experience of living for a time in countries in the East, speak to the real superiority of particular Eastern ways. These views range from Leslie Milne's practical preference for the Burmese Shan's habit of buying shoddy but affordable goods over the English habit of requiring well-made but expensive ones to Leonowens's startlingly impassioned testimonial that in the harem she knew a woman who "helped to enrich my life and to render fairer and more beautiful every lovely woman I have since chanced to meet."

The question of imperial attitudes points to another area in which the specific historical facts of time, place, and person must guide our reading. Nineteenth-century Western travel writings about the East are hardly monolithic. If the gender of the author mattered, so did his or her nationality and activities. A simple example is that the American women (and men) who wrote about Southeast Asia in the 1800s were most often fervent missionaries. Authored by missionaries or not, the genre in its American form typically expresses some version of E. R. Skidmore's horrified and eloquent view of her travel in the East [*Java, The Garden of the East,* 1899] as a matter of "landing in small boats among the screaming heathen." The very zeal that took Americans East allowed them to be particularly sure that the visions they brought with them were superior to the visions they beheld while there.

At least as important as gender and nationality is the actual country the book is about. As Victorian colonialists may have understand better than twentieth-critics, the distinctive qualities of various countries shaped the experience of being there. Those local qualities involved not only the political and economic history of a place but also the history of its relations to Europe, particularly to England. It must have felt notably different to be English in India, even before the 1858 Great Mutiny, than it did to be English in the more peaceable and in many ways less colonially violated areas of Sarawak or Singapore. Southeast Asia was, and is, quite a different region from the Middle East or the Far East. Critical approaches to Victorian travel writings must take into account the countries or regions that are being written about at least as much as the gender and nationality of the author.

Victorian women travelers who wrote about Southeast Asia were looking for truth in their exploration of different cultures in much the same way as were many of the scientists who explored the organisms and geology of strange lands. Neither kind of exploration can be understood, or its contributions to human knowledge evaluated, without taking into account the question of intent, at least to the extent that it appears in the written record. Is the language of discovery a matter of conquest or a matter of engagement? Evelyn Fox-Keller [in *The 'Signs' Reader: Women, Gender, and Scholarship,* edited by Elizabeth Abel and Emily K. Abel] has observed that "to see the emphasis on power and control so prevalent in the rhetoric of Western science as a projection of a specifically male consciousness requires no great leap of the imagination. But she goes on to make the central point that "control and domination are intrinsic neither to selfhood (i.e., autonomy) nor to scientific knowledge." Nor, I would add, are they intrinsic to the literature of travel, even nineteenth-century Western travel to the East.

Fox-Keller's useful distinction in scientific rhetoric between mastery over and union with nature can also help to describe and to evaluate accounts of Western explorations in other cultures. Many Victorian travel writings by women allow for, and even insist on, a sense of identification with other people as the truth of a travel experience. That sense of identification, made to an extensive reading public back home, carried political and social implications for Victorian definitions of truth, human nature, and progress. We cannot begin to chart those implications as long as we read this genre in relation to that other major narrative genre in Victorian England, the novel. Relying on the more sophisticated tools we have developed for discussing fiction to guide explanations of this nonfictional mode of writing, we can too easily term travel literature as the less effective genre, the little sister of its big brother, the novel. This would have the political effect of helping to conserve and even to bolster that familiar but highly dubious truism of cultural history: that Victorian women did not participate in the public history of their nation.

Travel writings about Southeast Asia indicate that Victorian women had audible, and often extremely popular, voices outside the novel. Brassey, who published several travel books during the later decades of the century, was perhaps the most widely read. Her account of eleven months of touring the East on her yacht, *A Voyage in the 'Sunbeam,'* went to at least eleven editions. Whether her works, or books written by other travel writers, both women and men, had any impact on the changing political, economic, and social conditions in England will have to emerge from a fuller study of the genre than any single article, or even single book, can provide.

It has been a truism of Victorian studies in the twentieth-century that women are more liberated in our century than they were in the nineteenth, and that the dominant ideology of the Victorian period was the notion of the separation of private and public spheres, with women belonging in the private and men in the public. We have been assured almost as often in scholarly journals as in television commercials that "you've come a long way, baby." Connected with this truism is another: that notions of wisdom in the Victorian intellectual context were defined by men, were "masculine," and even when "feminine" were embodied in men (like Pater). Men—and by "men" traditional critics usually mean Carlyle, Ruskin, Arnold, and Eliot in her role as the woman with the masculine mind—were the sages of Victorian culture. These cultural elites decided what wisdom was. They were the prophetic voices, the keepers and feeders of the ethical flame, and were publicly recognized as such.

Can we take Carlyle, Ruskin, Arnold, or any of their modern apologists' word for what defined wisdom for a whole culture? At least one reason why we must cease to write about these familiar sages as if they were the representative sages for all Victorians is not so much because we cannot trust these nineteenth-century purveyors of wisdom as because we cannot trust ourselves. After all, academics have been studying Victorian culture for several generations, but until the explosion of feminist studies in the 1970s had smoothly left out an enormous section of Victorian culture. What I would point out here is that this selectivity was possible in part because of the sheer convenience for twentieth-century critics of the notion of separate spheres. It may well have been twentieth-century academics who fulfilled the fantasies of Victorian masculinist writers by inflating a wishful (prescriptive) ideological principle into a full-fledged general truth of actual history. If Victorian women did operate only in the private world, then a responsible scholar could justifiably talk about cultural activities like defining wisdom and behaving as a prophet as occurring in the general, public realm, and not have to consider even published works by women.

There is no doubt that the notion of separate spheres was a significant ideology in Victorian England. There is also no doubt that it has become a most useful ideology about Victorian England in twentieth-century America. But how dominant was it? How many of the lives of real nineteenth-century women fit into it? I would argue that many women put the notion of separate spheres to public use by defining it as incomplete and therefore as an empowering rather than a disabling paradigm. Through the very ideology of truth as organic, they brought the wisdom to which they had special access in the private sphere to bear on philosophic as well as on social issues in the public domain. The question for critics now is how many exceptions we need to gather before the weight of accumulated facts will finally deflate to its proper, and modest, size this long-favored phallic truism.

A substantial number of those ever-accumulating facts are the travel writings of Victorian women. While traditional critics of Victorian culture never mentioned them and almost certainly did not know they existed, the number of editions of such travel books suggests that Victorian readers knew very well that they existed. These works, telling again and again of women living far away from England, well out of the private enclosures of English family life, offer literal proof that Victorian women could, and did, leave home. Further, the kind of detail these books offer about Southeast Asia—ranging from the export price of hemp on a Borneo plantation to the history of the Dyak wars in Sarawak and the diplomatic intrigues between England and France in Siam—makes it impossible for readers to place their female authors in the private sphere, with that sphere somehow transported intact to a distant shore. Moreover, the declared political aims of many of the books, from Brooke's wish [in her *My Life in Sarawak*] to keep Sarawak "from the devastating grasp of money-grabbing syndicates" to Leonowens's ceaseless arguments against slavery, make it clear that the authors saw their words as operating, even powerfully operating, within the sphere of public discourse.

Finally, I suggest that this genre of travel writing by women compels twentieth-century critics to redefine their understanding of the Victorian notion of the sage. The rhetorical strategies of Carlyle, Newman, or Arnold, oracular and prophetic, offer a vision of wisdom that is as assertive in spirit as it is reformist in intent. Nonetheless, regardless of such individual strategies, this vision rests on the firm foundation of the belief in the experiential quality of truth. And that foundation, refusing by its very nature to be exclusive, not only justifies Victorian men's cultural criticism but also justifies Victorian men's scientific accounts and Victorian women's travel writings. All of these kinds of writing lay claim to a wisdom that bases its truth on the extent to which it has emerged as lived experience. That pervasively held Victorian belief, perhaps in connection with the notion of women's emotional powers, may well have provided the cultural context that enabled so many women to write so confidently and sympathetically about their experiences in Southeast Asia.

> *Susan Morgan, "Victorian Women, Wisdom, and Southeast Asia," in* Victorian Sages and Cultural Discourse: Renegotiating Gender and Power, *edited by Thaïs E. Morgan, Rutgers University Press, 1990, pp. 207-24.*

Eva-Marie Kröller

[*Kröller is a German-born Canadian scholar and critic. In the following essay, she investigates the multi-voiced personas of two Victorian women travel writers, contending that both are at once accomplices and critics of British imperialism.*]

One recurrent feature in the as yet sketchily developed systematic study of Victorian travel narrative is an insistence on the author's multiple persona, which allows him or her to be both accomplice in, and critic of, the business of imperialism. Jonathan Bishop, in "The Identities of Sir Richard Burton: The Explorer as Actor," presents a parody of the

> image of the typical Victorian explorer, forcing his way through wild nature and wilder men, reaching his goal by willpower, guns, and money, a worthy representative of the audience his *Travels* [1893] would subsequently entertain. Morally, as well as politically, he is an imperialist; his achievement is the extension of home values to alien contexts. He may have his eccentricities, but his didactic effectiveness depends on his essential anonymity. His prose style is as simple as his function.

Bishop then proceeds to demonstrate various aspects of Burton's complex role playing, in a "life . . . putative and rhetorical, a theatrical gesture exploiting the attitudes it rejects," and in a body of writing in which an obsession with sexual and geographical domination reflects a deep sense of personal inadequacy. Although his subject's motivations are different from Burton's, John Tallmadge's analysis of Charles Darwin's *The Voyage of the Beagle* (1839) also recognizes the "different sets of demands" which Darwin attempted to reconcile in his narrative, namely his father's expectations, his own professional reputation, and his clerical career. *The Voyage of the Beagle* constitutes an extensive re-shaping of the original diary; the result is symptomatic of the dialogic interaction of various forms of discourse in several Victorian travel-books: although some authors, like Darwin, kept log-book and narrative separate, leaving it for a later critic to unravel the complicated personal agenda of *The Voyage,* others integrated the two, creating twice-told tales following Defoe's model in *Robinson Crusoe.* The theoretically most urgent plea to date for the multiplicity of the traveller-researcher's persona and his/her conflicting rhetorical voices comes from Mary-Louise Pratt. In "Fieldwork in Common Places," her contribution to James Clifford and George Marcus' seminal *Writing Culture: The Poetics and Politics of Ethnography,* Pratt insists that "anthropologists stand to gain from looking at themselves as writing inside as well as outside the discursive traditions that precede them," and that "a first step . . . is to recognize that one's tropes are neither natural nor, in many cases, native to the discipline."

Within the study of the Victorian travel narrative, the writing of women assumes a special role. Not only may the tropes they share with their male colleagues be used with different intention and to different effect, but the rhetorical complexities outlined above may be heightened to the embarrassment of critics eager to co-opt these women for one ideological discourse or another. Thus, critics bent on demonstrating the independence, vigour, and sensuality of women, even at a time when public ideology discouraged such qualities, mine the accomplishments of Isabella Bird, Mary Kingsley, Marianne North, Anna Jameson, and Kathleen Coleman for all they are worth but are dismayed at some of the women's insistence on propriety, their conservative politics and sense of racial superiority, and, perhaps most of all, their apparent lack of pride in their own achievements. Good examples of this approach are two otherwise very fine books, Barbara M. Freeman's *Kit's Kingdom: The Journalism of Kathleen Blake Coleman* and Katherine Frank's *A Voyager Out: The Life of Mary Kingsley.* Freeman scolds Coleman for not providing contemporary feminists with a less ambivalent role model, while Frank, clearly in despair over Kingsley's determined prudishness amidst a voluptuous African environment, conflates the epistemic and the deontic mode of the modal perfect when she wistfully (or grimly) affirms that

> [d]aily observing such things [circumcision, menstruation, sexual intercourse, and childbirth] *must* have transformed Mary's awareness of her own body, its impulses, changes, even desires. Her monthly periods came and went; she bathed naked and washed her long hair in streams and rivers. (emphasis mine)

I would like to take a closer look at the rhetorical strategies of two books by Victorian women travellers, Isabella Bird's *Unbeaten Tracks in Japan: An Account of Travels in the Interior Including Visits to the Aborigines of Yezo and the Shrine of Nikko* (1880) and Mary Kingsley's *Travels in West Africa: Congo Français, Corisco and Cameroons* (1897), not to join in the frustration of the critics whose argument I outlined above, but to insist that a more fruitful way to deal with such texts is to acknowledge their metonymic specificity and, above all, to suspend the tyranny of "the pattern of an idealized circumnavigation, [the presumably] archetypal plot structure of developing consciousness" [John Tallmadge, in *Victorian Studies* 23, 1980]. This tyranny may be exerted by genres such as the *bildungsroman* or the picaresque novel, which have long been found to be gender-specific and in need of revision to accommodate the life stories of women. But monologism may also be imposed by the opposite perspective, which is determined to rework Victorian narratives to tell a very specific feminist success story, whose components may be equally prescriptive and conducive to canon-building. Self-assertion in a Victorian traveller did not automatically imply that she extended the same privilege to others. Nor should diffidence and self-consciousness necessarily earn a narrator pity rather than respect.

The more worrisome of the two texts under scrutiny here is Isabella Bird's *Unbeaten Tracks in Japan.* Published after she had already made a name for herself with *The Englishwoman in America* (1856), *Six Months in The Sandwich Islands* (1875), and *A Lady's Life in the Rocky Mountains* (1879), *Unbeaten Tracks* is the first in a series of books on her travels in the East, which earned her election to the Royal Geographical Society as its first woman member: *The Golden Chersonese* (1883), *Journeys in Persia and Kurdistan* (1891), *Among the Tibetans* (1894), *Korea and Her Neighbours* (1898), *The Yangtze Valley and Beyond* (1899), and *Chinese Pictures* (1900) followed in rapid succession. Terrence Barrow, editor of the Tuttle edition, praises *Unbeaten Tracks* as "both poetic and objective" and, because of its "factual reporting," confirms its distinction "as an ethnographical document" of some value. Yet, from the first page it becomes clear that the

"poetic" and the "objective" cannot be as clearly separated as the correlative conjunctions suggest. Instead, the two are frequently used to shore each other up and to compensate for each other's inconsistencies, only to create additional ambivalence. The latter even affects the relationship of text and scholarly apparatus: if other travel books imply a dialogic interaction between log-book and continuous narrative, then the most startling tensions in *Unbeaten Tracks,* as we shall see, are between text and index. The genre of the letter of which the book is composed allows for a certain amount of discursiveness, redundancy, and the *non-sequiturs* of spontaneous response, and Bird's readers must have been prepared to accept minor inconsistencies. But it was essential to Bird's sense of personal identity that the underlying imperialist ideology not be seriously undermined. Bird's persistent efforts to keep the balance between the "poetic" and the "objective" intact indicates just how strong the demands of that programme must have been.

Bird's arrival by boat demonstrates typical features of the arrival scene which Pratt has persuasively identified as a crucial episode in ethnographic discourse. Bird opens with one of several picturesque or sublime set-pieces scattered throughout the book:

> Broken wooded ridges, deeply cleft, rise from the water's edge, gray, deep-roofed villages cluster about the mouths of the ravines, and terraces of rice cultivation, bright with the greenness of English lawns, run up to a great height among dark masses of upland forest.

The comparison, "bright with the greenness of English lawns," and others, such as a perceived similarity between Fujisan and "the cone of Tristan d'Acunha," help to naturalize an unfamiliar environment, as does a sketch of Fujisan remodelling it to look like the Matterhorn. There is also an approving nod toward the "American nomenclature which perpetuates the successes of American diplomacy," when the ship passes by "Reception Bay, Perry Island, Webster Island, Cape Saratoga, and Mississippi Bay" and "a red lightship with the words 'Treaty Point' in large letters upon her." Self-confident as this inscription of a familiar discourse, aesthetic and literal, on an unknown environment may appear, the description acquires some urgency from "the grayness and dumbness" of the early morning, which conflicts sharply with the sublime scenery evoked in the first paragraph. The first three pages obsessively return to the word "pale," often coupled with adjectives such as "phantom," "ghastly," and "wan." Nor is it fully clear whether "the grayness and dumbness" applies to the environment only or also to the traveller, and equally ambiguous is Bird's summary of her arrival as a form of penetration both aggressive and dazed: "it was all so pale, wan, and ghastly, that the turbulence of crumpled foam which we left behind us and our noisy throbbing progress seemed a boisterous intrusion upon sleeping Asia." The trope of arrival in a foreign land as an act of sexual penetration (and subsequent domination) may seem startling considering that Bird and other women travellers went abroad precisely to escape the demands of their families in general, and their fathers, brothers, suitors, and husbands in particular. Bird's lack of self-consciousness in using her erotic metaphor suggests that her insistence on her own freedom did not necessarily imply a refusal to collude in the oppressive business of imperialism.

Dea Birkett has described how such ambivalence sometimes extended to the women's treatment of their servants whom they deliberately kept in a state of infantile dependency, styling themselves mothers of their "babies" and "child-people." A latter-day version of Man Friday, the servant, guide, or interpreter may be chosen in a ritual involving several applicants of increasing objectionability, and the interviewer may pretend to make his decision in an act of defiant despair. *Unbeaten Tracks* provides an excellent example of the process: after surveying a number of candidates who are either too European or too Japanese, Bird settles on Ito, "a creature [who] appeared without any recommendation at all," and her description of him bears similarities with her description of her arrival in Japan: "First View of Japan" and "First Impression of Ito" are especially marked in the brief synopses prefacing each letter and in the index:

> [Ito] is only eighteen, but this is equivalent to twenty-three or twenty-four with us, and only 4 feet 10 inches in height, but, though bandy-legged, is well proportioned and strong-looking. He has a round and singularly plain face, good teeth, much elongated eyes, and the heavy droop of his eyelids almost caricatures the usual Japanese peculiarity. He is the most stupid-looking Japanese that I have seen, but, from a rapid, furtive glance in his eyes now and then, I think that the stolidity is partly assumed.

Bird then recounts the list of qualifications which Ito claims to bring to the job, repeating that he "had no recommendations" and affirming that she "suspected and disliked the boy." Still, as "he understood my English and I his . . . I engaged him for twelve dollars a month." In her description, Bird aggressively naturalizes the unknown "creature" by placing his height and age within a European context, applying her knowledge of phrenology to his features to diagnose his likely degree of intelligence, and assessing his physical strength to determine his usefulness to her. Although now more kindly disposed towards Ito, Bird later affirms his role as a go-between when she describes "a strangely picturesque sight" in an Aino hut where "the yellow-skinned Ito" serves as "the connecting link between [eastern savagery and western civilization]."

Unlike the opium-dazed Hadji whom Bird acquired on her travels through Persia and Kurdistan, however, or Kaluna, "a half-tamed creature from the woods" (*Six Months*), who served her in Hawaii, Ito refuses to be completely naturalized into Bird's stereotype of who he ought to be. On several occasions Bird allows herself to be criticized or corrected by him for her gauche western ways, always claiming that she remains in full control of the situation: "I take his suggestions as to what I ought to do and avoid in very good part, and my bows are getting more profound every day!" The exclamation mark at the end of this statement suggests irony, hence detachment, but the latter is a quality Bird increasingly loses in her dealings with Ito. In answering his probing questions about the eti-

quette of her language, Bird teaches him idiomatic English; at the same time, she is introduced to a foreign epistemology, an unsettling process signalled in her sometimes abrupt wavering between one response and another. For page 101, for instance, the index notes a discussion of "freedom from insult and incivility in [Japan]," followed by "barbarism and ignorance in [Japan]" only six pages later.

Ito's significance is reflected in the long entry in the index, equalled (and surpassed) only by the entries on "Japan," "Japanese," and the major sights. In this entry, Bird (or her editor, with whose decisions she would have had to agree) sets accents and tells a plot which belie the actual events, and the whole passage may be read as an attempt to rectify her undue impressionability and "straighten" the record. In the narrative, Bird parts from Ito "with great regret . . . I miss him already." An earlier revelation that Ito "ran away [from an earlier master] and entered [Bird's] service with a lie" creates a brief flurry, but Ito clearly comes out victorious when he responds to Bird's reproaches that his are "just missionary manners!" By contrast, the entry in the index tells the following tale about Bird and Ito's relationship:

> Ito, first impression of, 17, 18; taking a "squeeze," 65; personal vanity, 78; ashamed, 86, 125; cleverness and intelligence, 87; a zealous student, 87; intensely Japanese, 87; a Shintoist, 161; keeps a diary, 161; characteristics, 162; prophesy, 162; patriotism, 162; an apt pupil, 163; fairly honest, 164; surliness, 175; delinquency, 214; selfishness, 236; smitten, 287; cruelty, 307; parting, 321.

Here, Ito has become a classifiable specimen, on a par with temples and geographical curiosities. Pages 161 to 162 are given the most detailed sub-entries, but none of them draws attention to his considerable influence over his employer. Instead, he falls suddenly from grace, with an abrupt transition from "fairly honest" to "surliness" and a rapid decline through the remaining entries. The "cruelty" which Bird perceives in Ito's condescending dealings with aboriginal Japanese remains unspecified in the index and seems to result directly in his dismissal.

In contrast to Isabella Bird's three-page arrival scene and her briskly indexed dealings with her servant, Mary Kingsley's arrival in West Africa in 1894 seems to extend over the entire *Travels in West Africa* (1897) as she describes attempted entries into, and bare escapes from, treacherous mangrove swamps, muddy rivers, unpredictable roads, and slippery bridges. She proceeded in the company of constantly changing "personnel," none of whom ever comes as close to Kingsley as Ito did to Bird, and none of whom is as easily dismissed. It would be wrong to idealize Kingsley. She too "believed that England . . . had every right to extend trade across the globe and to protect it by the English flag, emblem of the highest form of justice" ([Elizabeth] Claridge [in her introduction to Kingsley's work]), and her text contains the familiar tropes of imperialism: Africans are "teachable and tractable," "sweet unsophisticated children of nature" and "black, naked savages" who, at their physical best, shine "like polished bronze" but, at their intellectual worst, feature a "lamblike calfheadedness" or perennial "mind muddle." The agents of imperialism, Kingsley agrees, make extraordinary sacrifices in training such a deficient people; deft vignettes in her book outline educational success. Describing a particularly well-kept plantation, she affirms that "[t]he whole is kept as perfectly as a garden, amazing as the work of one white man with only a staff of unskilled native labourers—at present only eighty of them." As well as supporting the business of imperialism, however, *Travels in West Africa* presents an extensive critique of its practices, including Kingsley's own place in it. Her honest assessment of her limitations often leads her to remarkable insight, including the admission "that there is nothing really 'child-like' in [the Africans'] form of mind at all," and that their "mind muddle" constitutes a different epistemology *tout court*.

Kingsley's arrival scene has none of the "poetic" features so notable in Bird's first letter; instead, Kingsley presents an "objective" description in the style of a guidebook:

> We reached Sierra Leone at 9 A.M. on the 7th of January. . . . The harbour is formed by the long low strip of land to the north called the Bullam shore, and to the south by the peninsula terminating in Cape Sierra Leone, a sandy promontory at the end of which is situated a lighthouse of irregular habits. Low hills covered with tropical forest growth rise from the sandy shores of the Cape, and along its face are three creeks or bays, deep inlets showing through their narrow entrances smooth beaches of yellow sand, fenced inland by the forest of cotton-woods and palms, with here and there an elephantine baobab.

Guidebook descriptions of the geography and flora of a place are of course also an act of possession; a detailed description of a coastline, especially if presented in "detached" language, mimics the process of reconnoitring a terrain prior to its military and economic occupation. But Kingsley undercuts the effect with a number of ironic strategies. Instead of the "red lightship with the words 'Treaty Point' in large letters upon her" which welcomed Bird in Japan, Kingsley is impressed by "a lighthouse of irregular habits," a phrase quite out of tune with the remainder of the passage, because it is both anthropomorphic and comic, and because it acknowledges from the first a resistance of the land to be efficiently or thoroughly conquered. In fact, such resistance seems to have been present from the moment of departure: the *Batanga* is unable to leave the Mersey "for the dock gates that shut her in could not be opened, so fierce was the gale"; furthermore, she must forego the cannon salute with which she customarily announces her arrival at her ports of call because the weather is too fierce to take powder on board. The reader is led to interpret these episodes as the classic signals of foreboding with which travel fictions, *Robinson Crusoe* foremost among them, prepare a tale of adversity finally to be overcome by the protagonist. But Kingsley thwarts the reader's "sense of an ending" and anticipates the departure scene, not as a conclusion to victorious deeds, but as a hasty flight from an obstreperous environment. By using the second-person pronoun, Kingsley includes the reader in the fall from any missionary pretension that she or he may have harboured: "It is the general opinion, indeed, of those who ought to know that Sierra Leone appears at its best when seen from the sea, particularly when you are leaving the harbour homeward bound." Under these circumstances, the naturalization of Free Town as "the Liverpool of West Africa" loses much of its comfort, especially since it comes accompanied by the footnote that "Lagos also likes to bear this flattering appellation, and has now-a-days more right to the title."

Most significantly, however, the arrival scene is *preceded* by fourteen pages giving a detailed account of Kingsley's bumbling preparations for the journey, all presented in her typically self-deprecatory style. As if to prove, from the beginning, that "thinking is not [her] strong point" and that her work will best produce a "varied tangled rag-bag of facts" that needs the intervention of "some great thinker" to make sense, Kingsley conflates her 1893 and 1894 arrivals in Africa such that she must remind her reader at the end of chapter I that the long episode recounted last "was not on the *Batanga*, but in the days before I was an honourary aide-de-camp, remember." From a feminist perspective, Kingsley's befuddled pose may at times be exasperating, but it does make for the kind of deconstructionist narrator whom virtually all of the contributors to *Writing Culture* posit as a solution to the *impasse* of ethnographical discourse. Thus, [James] Clifford [in *Writing Culture: The Poetics and Politics of Ethnography*, 1986] praises Richard Price's *First-Time: The Historical Vision of an Afro-American People* (1983) for clearly stating "external and self-imposed limits to the research, about individual informants, and about the construction of the final written artifact." The many false starts forming part of Kingsley's departure place her undertaking in ironic brackets from the start, without questioning its sincerity or undermining its usefulness.

Price's *First-Time* translates its epistemological self-consciousness into a collage narrative, "literally pieced together, full of holes" (Clifford and Marcus [in *Writing Culture*]). Kingsley pursues a similar approach by inserting extracts from her journal into her narrative; this technique aligns with the defence she made of her dialogic approach against a "great thinker," editor Henry Guillemard, who was determined to rework her *Travels* into a more "scientific" discourse. Kingsley explains that in the diary "the reader gets . . . notice of things that, although unimportant in themselves, yet go to make up the conditions of life under which men and things exist." The diary upsets the hierarchy of "important" events, and suggests a sequence almost as random as the alphabetical order to which Roland Barthes subjected his autobiography in an attempt to break the tyranny of cultural ideas embodied in the *bildungsroman*. Precise botanical and zoological information, adventurer's tale, missionary story, and cooking recipe cohabit without apology in Kingsley's diary, and, lest the reader conclude that her physical progress automatically implies teleological progress in her acquisition of knowledge, Kingsley recounts at some length her experience with a wayward path which, like the lighthouse on Cape Sierra Leone, appears to have a life of its own:

> The path goes on through grass, and then makes for a hollow—wish it didn't, for hollows are horrid at times, and evidently this road has got

something against it somewhere, and is not popular, for the grass falls across it like unkempt hair. Road becomes damp and goes into a belt of trees, in the middle of which runs a broad stream with a log laid across it. Congratulating myself on absence of companions, ignominiously crawl across on to the road, which then and there turns round and goes back to the stream again higher up—evidently a joke, "thought-you-were-going-to-get-home-dry-did-you" sort of thing.

The scene is virtuoso comedy. At the same time it is one of many in *Travels* in which Kingsley dramatizes her ineffectual efforts to make way, geographically and linguistically. From the beginning, language is as independent and wayward as African paths and rivers. In the traditional apologia prefacing the book, Kingsley (somewhat disingenuously) commends Guillemard for "lassoing prepositions which were straying outside their sentence stockade"; as well, there are many circular conversations in which dialogue is reduced to an inexorable mechanism of question and answer. Examples include a hilarious exchange, set to musical notation, beginning and ending with "You should have been here last week when we had the races," the merciless recital of the virtues of the paw-paw, or Joseph's testimony before the Directeur de l'Administration de l'Intérieur. Not infrequently, communication breaks down altogether, either because the surf is deafening or Kingsley's linguistic skills are insufficient and she is reduced to "smil[ing] wildly." On such occasions in particular, the narrative of *Travels* slides rapidly in and out of various forms of discourse, often seeking to establish a slippery footing by referring to outside authority. "As X. would call it" is one of the most recurrent phrases in the book. In her celebrated encounter with a crocodile, the author grasps for two different discourses to help describe the incident, as if they were paddles held out to pull her out of "the black batter-like, stinking slime":

> Twice this chatty little incident, as Lady Mac-Donald would call it, has happened to me, but never again if I can help it. On one occasion, the last, a mighty Silurian, as the *Daily Telegraph* would call him, chose to get his front paws over the stern of my canoe, and endeavoured to improve our acquaintance.

But the phrase "As X. would call it," together with more impressive ammunition, such as long footnotes and quotations in German, are not fully trustworthy either because Kingsley gently mocks their authors as well: "Great as the protection to the mind is, to keep it, as Hans Breitmann says, 'still skebdical,' I warn you that . . . the study of African metaphysics is bad for the brain."

Sometimes Kingsley's pervasive self-mockery is poignantly counterpointed by experiences of desolation and pantheistic elation. Thus, she does sketch a hilarious picture of herself "tide-trapped away in the swamps [and] . . . cheered by the thought of the terrific sensation [she] will produce 20,000 years hence," but she also evokes scenes in which all sense of self appears obliterated, whether it be a truly terrifying, and rhetorically carefully crafted, vision of "the malarial mud . . . creeping and crawling and

gliding out from the side creeks and between the mangrove-roots," or an epiphany as she gazes on the river, "los[ing] all sense of human individuality, all memory of human life . . . and becom[ing] part of the atmosphere." Always wary of settling down to a cliché, Kingsley brings each scene to an abrupt conclusion with a rapid change in tone and by refusing to mark the change with a paragraph ending. The skilful alliterative patterns which mark these passages also recur in burlesque scenes, such as the story of the man-eating paw-paw, "pepsine, . . . papaine, . . . purloining pagan," and all. The principle of the collage is to relativize each one of these experiences and its attendant discourse while at the same time paradoxically endowing it with greater authenticity; in this sense, Kingsley's narrative is [according to Donald B. Kuspit in *Collage: Critical Views*, 1989] "an experiment in ordering reality, rather than a way of decisively determining it."

Both Isabella Bird and Mary Kingsley then speak with multiple voices. Bird's register is more limited: an opinionated, bigoted travel writer if ever there was one when she described her impressions of America in her first book, she found her ethnocentricity increasingly sabotaged by the cultures and individuals she encountered in subsequent expeditions. In *Unbeaten Tracks*, her self-assured imperialist persona loses ground before an assertive representative of the culture she has come to investigate, and seeks refuge in the folds of the index. Kingsley, by contrast, cultivates her fragmented persona so determinedly that it seems insufficient to assume that she was permanently overcome by a sense of personal inadequacy. Rather, her self-consciousness reveals a respect for her subject matter and a narratological sophistication that place her ahead of many of her contemporaries, both male and female. Travel writing by Victorian women remains to be fully charted, but now that the deconstructive tools to deal with it have been developed, it is high time that it be given the place in a diversified history of feminism that it deserves.

Eva-Marie Kröller, "First Impressions: Rhetorical Strategies in Travel Writing by Victorian Women," in Ariel: A Review of International English Literature, *Vol. 21, No. 4, October, 1990, pp. 87-99.*

Charisse Gendron

[*In the excerpt below, Gendron discusses Lucie Duff Gordon's* Letters from Egypt *as the correspondence of a well-educated and aristocratic British woman who developed a strong sympathy for Egyptian and Islamic culture during her residence in Egypt from 1861 to 1869.*]

Lucie Duff Gordon's *Letters from Egypt* was one of a number of lively, personal books of travel to the East that delighted Victorian readers. If it is now largely unread, this is less because the writing is stale or unskilled than because the subject, nineteenth-century Egypt, is no longer topical. Yet picking up the book today, we find that as a travel account it embodies certain recurrent themes—or rather, certain ways of looking at the archetypal theme of the journey that belong particularly to writers of the British empire.

Letters from Egypt, containing letters Duff Gordon wrote to her family in England when she was forced by ill health to emigrate, was sufficiently popular in its day to go into three printings in the first year of its publication, 1865. It owed its success in part to the Victorian fascination with anything concerning the Orient, which then meant not only India and beyond but also Greece, Turkey, North Africa, the Arabian Peninsula, and Persia. These regions, it was becoming increasingly clear to British observers, would form the path of empire from the Mediterranean to India, and from this point of view public curiosity was natural.

But an equal incitement to curiosity was that the East formed a link to the classical past: the Greece and Troy of Homer; the Persia and Arabia of the *Arabian Nights;* the Egypt of Herodotus; and, chiefly, the lands of the Bible. Throughout the nineteenth century, the British looked to history to explain and dignify their own rapidly expanding civilization. Those who doubted the direction of material progress sought the lesson of history and a steadier view of truth by reading the ancient authors or by travelling to the very scenes of ancient life, such as Egypt and the Holy Lands. They found in the East a place where time, in terms of European knowledge and progress, had stopped and where the ancient life went on in field, court, and bazaar. Though many Britons viewed the modern Eastern countries as graveyard civilizations where ignorant peoples lived unconscious of the former glories of their race, other British travellers thought that in the modern inhabitants they glimpsed human nature at a stage closer to its origins, before society strayed into new-fangledness. As the Victorian traveller Charles Doughty writes in a preface to his prose epic, *Travels in Arabia Deserta* (1888):

> As for the nomad Arabs . . . we may see in them that desert life, which was followed by their ancestors, in the Bible tents of Kedar. . . . While the like phrases of their . . . speech, are sounding in our ears, and their like customs, come down from antiquity, are continued before our eyes; we almost feel ourselves carried back to the days of the nomad Hebrew Patriarchs. . . .

In rapidly changing times, many Victorians felt the need to re-establish contact with that patriarchal world.

Fascinated by the East, then, British readers welcomed not only the scholarly tomes of great Orientalists like Sir Edward Lane and Sir Richard Burton but also the light-hearted memoirs of writers such as Alexander Kinglake, who made himself a name with the dashing travel book *Eothen* (1844), and even William Makepeace Thackeray, who did rather less well with *Notes of a Journey from Cornhill to Grand Cairo* (1845). These writers, both friends of Lucie Duff Gordon, helped to prepare an audience for her intimate views of Egyptian life. Further, *Letters from Egypt* had an advantage in Duff Gordon's own popularity among certain circles in England. As a girl she had been ably educated by her parents, friends of the radical philosophers James Mill and Jeremy Bentham. In the natural course of things she became a translator of German works, including the histories of Leopold von Ranke—a talent that came in handy when she married the

charming but indigent aristocrat Alexander Duff Gordon. The Duff Gordons collected a large circle of friends, people in literature and parliament, who cherished Lucie's easy hospitality and good talk.

Lucie Duff Gordon, in fact, was a classic Victorian grand woman, one who powerfully impressed those around her by seeming to rise, almost supernaturally, above what was then the frankly limited intellectual condition of women. The powers Duff Gordon wielded were beauty, a sympathetic nature, and possession of what was admiringly known as "masculine" reason. She was the inspiration, Tennyson claimed, for *The Princess,* his long poem on the education of women. George Meredith, in turn, modelled the sage Lady Jocelyn in *Evan Harrington* on "this most manfully-minded of women." And Alexander Kinglake, with characteristic teasing wit, described Duff Gordon as "so intellectual, so keen, so autocratic, sometimes even so impassioned in speech, that nobody feeling her powers could go on feebly comparing her to a . . . mere Queen or Empress." Such friends, no doubt, helped to launch *Letters from Egypt.*

Our pleasure in the letters today will be less topical, more purely literary; and part of that pleasure will derive from the very form of the book. A collection of letters imposes

Portrait sketch of Lucie Duff Gordon.

a pattern on a life, especially if the letters are from abroad. Travel itself implies a motivation: an urge to escape, to seek, or to connect. But in tracing the pattern of Duff Gordon's travels we need to note that their original cause was a matter of circumstance. She went to Egypt to try to slow the consumption of which she in fact died after eight years' struggle. She began her self-exile at the age of thirty-nine on the aptly named Cape of Good Hope, but when she realized that she would never again be able to live in cold, damp England, she joined a daughter and son-in-law in Alexandria. There she took up the regimen that lasted until her death in Cairo in 1869: wintering in sunbaked Nubia, as the upper Nile was then called, and summering with members of her family in lower Egypt or, occasionally, England.

Yet Duff Gordon's consumption, seemingly a practical enough reason to travel, in fact places her among an almost symbolic category of British writers, those forced by the disease to flee bone-chilling England for a place nearer the sun. Often this wasting but feverish illness has impelled its victims to seek not only physical ease but spiritual peace. We see the pattern in Laurence Sterne, Keats, and Katherine Mansfield embarking for southern Europe; Robert Louis Stevenson for the South Seas; D. H. Lawrence for the American Southwest. The reprieve in a sunny climate seems to offer a last chance to live simply and pleasurably, to re-enter an earthly Eden bounded by the consciousness of death.

What makes this category of writers symbolic is that, from the industrial revolution to the Second World War, dozens of other British writers sought the same remedy for spiritual rather than physical malaise. Shelley, Byron, Samuel Butler, W. H. Hudson, E. M. Forster, Christopher Isherwood—all took various routes south to escape what they saw as England's cold, inhibited social and emotional climate for a supposedly more whole and spontaneous life in the sun. That myth informs Duff Gordon's journey as it evolves from a mere search for health to the embrace of a new life, simpler but in the end more aesthetic and perhaps even more humane than that she had known in England.

Duff Gordon spent her first year in Egypt moving up and down the Nile in inverse relation to the temperature. In her second year she took a house, the old French consulate built over the ruined temple of Thebes in the village of Luxor on the upper Nile. The beauty of this situation was such that Gustave Flaubert, regarding it by moonlight some years earlier, complained of the "wretched poverty of language" to describe it. Duff Gordon lived there with her English maid, Sally Naldrett, her Alexandrian servant, Omar Abu Halawy, and assorted houseboys. Besides these, her society comprised the local elders and their wives, the peasants she doctored for cholera and other ailments, and occasional European travellers. The heat of upper Egypt was the only remedy for her cough, and much as she missed her family she soon dreaded the trip to meet them in Cairo, where she hacked and shivered in the damp.

From Esneh in upper Egypt, where she has escorted a visiting cousin, she writes:

Yesterday we had the thermometer at 110; I was the only person awake all day in the boat. Omar, after cooking, lay panting at my feet on the deck. Arthur went fairly to bed in the cabin; ditto Sally. All the crew slept on the deck. Omar cooked amphibiously, bathing between every meal. The silence of noon with the *white heat* glowing on the river which flowed like liquid tin, and the silent Nubian rough boats floating down without a ripple, was magnificent and really awful.

Here as in so many European descriptions of the East, the sheer heat seems to reveal a mysterious presence, a *genus loci* nearly inexplicable to people in the remote North, consumed with the busy round of their affairs.

The heat dictates an entirely foreign way of life, which Duff Gordon describes at first as an outsider:

Can you imagine a house without beds, chairs, tables, cups, glasses, knives—in short, with nothing but an oven, a few pipkins, and water-jars, and a couple of wooden spoons, and some mats to sleep on? And yet people are happy and quite civilized who live so. An Arab cook, with his fingers and one cooking-pot, will serve you an excellent dinner quite miraculously. The simplification of life possible in such a climate is not conceivable unless one has seen it.

But it is not long before the climate and a restricted income convert Duff Gordon to this same simplicity. She writes to her husband from her sparsely-furnished, half-open "Theban palace":

I am now writing in the kitchen, which is the coolest place where there is any light at all. Omar is diligently spelling words of six letters, with the wooden spoon in his hand and a cigarette in his mouth, and Sally is lying on her back on the floor. I won't describe our costume. It is now two months since I have worn stockings, and I think you would wonder at the fellaha who "owns you," so deep a brown are my face, hands and feet. One of the sailors in Arthur's boat said: "See how the sun of the Arabs loves her; he has kissed her so hotly that she can't go home among English people."

Here Duff Gordon has come far from the London life of bowler hats and stays, and far too from Victorian assumptions about the proper distance between a lady and her servant, especially a male servant of colour. From the British point of view, of course, the Egyptian, with few exceptions, was a "native," a racial inferior to be kept in his place, ultimately to be ruled. This distinction, like the need for stockings, ceased to have meaning for Duff Gordon as the Arab sun and simple, direct mode of existence claimed her for their own.

In Egypt, in fact, Duff Gordon attained the privileged perspective of being able to see two cultures—the complicated European and the pastoral Egyptian—with detached amusement. Thus she is able to appreciate the astonishment of a villager who watches her prepare her houseboat to rent to English tourists. She writes:

I settled all accounts with my men, and made an

inventory in Arabic, which Shaikh Yussuf wrote for me, which we laughed over hugely. How to express a sauce-boat, a pie-dish, etc. in Arabic, was a poser. A genteel Effendi, who sat by, at last burst out in uncontrollable amazement; "There is no God but God: is it possible that four or five Franks can use all these things to eat, drink and sleep on a journey?" (n.b. I fear the Franks will think the stock very scanty.) Whereupon master Ahmad, with the swagger of one who has seen cities and men, held forth. "Oh Effendim, that is nothing: Our lady is almost like the children of the Arabs. One dish or two, a piece of bread, a few dates, and Peace (as we say, there is an end of it). But thou shouldst see the merchants of Alexandria, three tablecloths, forty dishes, to each soul seven plates of all sorts, seven knives and seven forks and seven spoons, large and small, and seven different glasses for wine and beer and water." "It is the will of God," ' replied the Effendi, rather put down: "but," he added, "it must be a dreadful fatigue to them to eat their dinner."

In leaving England for the upper Nile, at least Duff Gordon escaped the fatigue, common to cosmopolites of London and Cairo, of using multiple forks to dine.

On that magnificent location on the Nile, with the props of material progress removed, Duff Gordon glimpsed the paradisal life, simple yet aesthetically and spiritually complete, for which her compatriots so often crossed continents. She writes to Alick Duff Gordon:

> If I find Thebes too hot as summer advances I must drop down and return to Cairo. . . . But it is very tempting to stay here—a splendid cool house, food extremely cheap . . . no trouble, rest and civil neighbors. I feel very disinclined to move unless I am baked out, and it takes a good deal to bake me. . . . The weather has set in since five or six days quite like paradise. I sit on my lofty balcony and drink the sweet northerly breeze, and look at the glorious mountain opposite, and think if only you and the chicks were here it would be "the best o' life."

Of course it would be foolish to suggest that in Egypt Duff Gordon attained the unattainable—complete harmony of being. She missed her family and she knew that she was dying. Yet the beauty she found there, in both the landscape and the people, was a gift—one that others in her family, she sometimes suggests, would be incapable of receiving even if they had come to live with her. Thoroughly creatures of European civilization, pursuing social and business interests, they had neither her motivations nor her resources to re-envision life.

Finding herself, then, an exile in paradise, Duff Gordon strove to fill the hollowness by reclaiming a cultural past which she had thus far known only through literature. This nineteenth-century search for roots, incidentally, did not cease with Victoria's reign; it merely shifted its definition. Where Doughty and Duff Gordon quested after the universals of human nature revealed in the great books, British travellers between the world wars sought a transfusion of psychic vitality: recall, for example, D. H. Lawrence's quest for "blood" knowledge among the

Sardinians and Graham Greene's "journey without maps" through West Africa on the trail of the truly seedy, the pit of the Freudian self. Certainly Duff Gordon is on no such trail of risky initiations, but her recovery of the past does finally engage her in criticisms of British culture similar to those underlying the primitive journeys of Lawrence and Greene.

According to contemporary accounts, Duff Gordon's nature was extraordinarily sympathetic, and perhaps that is why, in Egypt, she was so able to comprehend the truth to life of classical literature. She writes of the rural life of upper Egypt:

> Nothing is more striking to me than the way in which one is constantly reminded of Herodotus. The Christianity and the Islam of this country are full of the ancient worship, and the sacred animals have all taken service with Muslim saints. . . . This country is a palimpsest, in which the Bible is written over Herodotus, and the Koran over that.

Yet her experience of Egypt is never coldly literary. She enters her new life—which is also the most ancient life—with her whole imagination. "Last evening," she writes,

> I went out to the threshing-floor to see the stately oxen treading out the corn . . . and saw the reapers take their wages, each a bundle of wheat according to the work he had done—the most lovely sight. The graceful, half-naked, brown figures loaded with sheaves; some had earned so much that their mothers or wives had to help to carry it, and little fawn-like, stark-naked boys trudged off, so proud of their little bundles of wheat. . . . The *sakka* (water-carrier), who has brought water for the men, gets a handful from each, and drives home his donkey with empty water-skins and a heavy load of wheat, and the barber who had shaved all these brown heads on credit this year past gets his pay, and everyone is cheerful and happy in their gentle, quiet way; here is no beer to make men sweaty and noisy and vulgar; the harvest is the most exquisite pastoral you can conceive.
>
> As I sat with Abdurrachman on the threshing-floor and ate roasted corn, I felt quite puzzled as to whether I were really alive or only existing in imagination in the Book of Ruth.

Such an apprehension of oneself in the human continuum is what many travellers seek but probably few find.

From the point of view of her own Christian upbringing, Duff Gordon's rediscovery of history is revisionist. Not that she is ever disappointed by the truthfulness of the Bible, but that she is disillusioned with the use made of the Bible to teach dogma and, worse, intolerance of other faiths, particularly Islam. "Every act of life here is exactly like the early parts of the Bible and it seems totally new when one reads it here," she writes.

> Old Jacob's speech to Pharoah really made me laugh (don't be shocked), because it is so exactly what a fellah says to a Pasha: "Few and evil have been the days," etc. (Jacob being a most prosperous man); but it is manners to say all that, and

> I feel quite kindly to Jacob, whom I used to think ungrateful and discontented. . . . All the vulgarized associations with Puritanism and abominable little "Scripture tales and pictures" peel off here, and the inimitably truthful representation of life and character—not a flattering one certainly—comes out, and it feels like Homer.

The European reverence for the Bible and ironical contempt for the modern peoples that still live the Biblical life confront Duff Gordon with the hypocrisies of her own race. Her wider experience radicalizes her; her letters become filled with the defence of Moslem ways, pleas for customs to be understood in their cultural context. An example is the anecdote of the elderly Moslem who, having been teased for marrying more than one wife, asks a young Englishman how many women he has "seen" in his life, in the Eastern phrase. "The Englishmen could not count—of course not," Duff Gordon comments; but of the old Moslem's mistresses, those still living are comfortably installed in his house. The purpose of the anecdote is not to advocate harems, but to insist, more in the manner of a modern anthropologist than of an imperial Briton abroad, on the integrity of a culture removed from the mainstream of the West.

Duff Gordon, then, shifts from a historical interest in Egypt to a deep involvement with present life. Seeing villagers brutally exploited by an arbitrary government playing into the hands of Europeans, she writes to her mother:

> You will think me a complete rebel—but I may say to you what most people would think "like my nonsense"—that one's pity becomes a perfect passion, when one *sits among the people*—as I do, and sees it all; least of all can I forgive those among Europeans and Christians who can help to "break these bruised reeds."

She urged her family to publish her letters in order to inform the British of the bad conditions in Egypt, where they had rosy hopes of expanding trade. (Her own son-in-law, Henry Ross, was a director of a company that exported "ostrich feathers, bees-wax, oxhides and gold-dust." It collapsed when the Egyptian government went bankrupt.) Gradually, the greed and arrogance of Westerners who came to Egypt alienated Duff Gordon from her native culture and bound her to her adoptive one. In Cairo, having been insulted by Englishmen who see her exchanging courtesies in the street with a black Nubian, she writes, "I hate the sight of a hat here now."

One of Duff Gordon's twentieth-century appreciators was the novelist E. M. Forster, and it is interesting to think that she may have subtly influenced his ideas. It was Forster who encapsulated the ethos of the Bloomsbury group of writers, artists, and philosophers in his prescription, "only connect"; only connect, that is, to what is fundamentally decent and loving in others, regardless of apparent barriers of class and race. To make that connection, though, Forster realized, is more difficult than it sounds. It requires a deliberate passage, a journey across the borders prescribed by one's culture. Such is the theme of his greatest novel, *A Passage to India* (1924), where the gulf between would-be friends is specifically that between West and East. Forster's protagonist, Fielding, falls short: he retreats from Oriental muddle to European order, while his counterpart, Aziz, warns that it is too soon for an Indian to trust an Englishman. Yet it is a revolution that they come as close as they do.

Lucie Duff Gordon's passage is more complete than Fielding's: she gives up more of England and takes more of Egypt. In many letters she tries to prepare her family for this change. She describes, for example, a visit to provide medical care to the Shaikh Mohammed:

> There he lay in a dark little den with bare mud walls, worse off, to our ideas, than any pauper; but these people do not feel the want of comforts, and one learns to think it quite natural to sit with perfect gentlemen in places inferior to our cattle-sheds. I pulled some blankets up against the wall, and put my arm behind Shaikh Mohammed's back to make him rest while the poultices were on him, whereupon he laid his green turban on my shoulder, and presently held up his delicate brown face for a kiss like an affectionate child. As I kissed him, a very pious old moollah said, *"Bismillah"* (In the name of God), with an approving nod, and Shaikh Mohammed's old father, a splendid old man in a green turban, thanked me with effusion, and prayed that my children might always find help and kindness.
>
> I suppose if I confessed to kissing a "dirty Arab" in a "hovel" the English travellers would execrate me; but it shows how much there is in "Mussulman bigotry, unconquerable hatred, etc.," for this family are Seyyids (descendents of the Prophet) and very pious.

Duff Gordon usually addressed letters like this to her mother, whom she trusted to understand that she was bound by human laws deeper than those of English propriety and religious dogma.

One incident particularly tried Duff Gordon's loyalties, divided between her British past and Egyptian present. While the episode might have disillusioned her with her new life, however, it had the opposite effect of more firmly attaching her to an Egyptian friend while further straining old ties. The Egyptian friend was her servant Omar, with whom she had formed an almost filial bond. She writes to her husband of a night at Aswan:

> . . .Omar woke, and came and sat at my feet, and rubbed them, and sang a song of a Turkish slave. I said, "Do not rub my feet, oh brother— that is not fit for thee" (because it is below the dignity of a free Muslim altogether to touch shoes or feet), but he sang in his song, "The slave of the Turk may be set free by money, but how shall one be ransomed who has been paid for by kind actions and sweet words?"

This intimacy is threatened when, to Duff Gordon's consternation, Omar and her maid Sally produce a baby. One can understand her anger and sense of betrayal. Throughout her seven lonely years in Egypt, and despite plausible offers, she stuck to the Christian law against adultery; while here was Sally doing what she pleased. For it was

Sally, not Omar, whom Duff Gordon blamed. "I find that these disasters are wonderfully common here," she writes acidly; "—is it the climate or the costume I wonder that makes the English maids ravish the Arab men so continually?" Her harsh treatment of Sally, as her great-grandson Gordon Waterfield has pointed out, might have at least two causes: jealousy of Omar, both friend and nurse; and a suspicion that her family would toe the color line and blame Omar, which they did. She herself was too proud, having begun the passage across cultural boundaries, to turn back.

Duff Gordon lost much in the course of her exile—family and friends and ultimately even the pastoral Egypt that had first consoled her. Lamenting the enforced labour that depopulated villages to construct railroads and canals, she writes, "When I remember the lovely smiling landscape which I first beheld from my windows, swarming with beasts and men, and look at the dreary waste now, I feel the 'foot of the Turk' heavy indeed." Yet she managed in exile to create a new life. The social ease and aristocratic independence that made her a grand woman in Victorian drawing rooms made her an Emeereh in Egypt. She seemed instinctively to know when to condescend by sitting on the carpet and eating with her fingers, when to conquer with eloquent speech. The people of Luxor, whom she doctored through an epidemic, named her Noor-ala-Noor, or "light from the light." Her daughter Janet Ross writes of how, on a journey to visit her mother at Luxor, the Ross party had difficulty obtaining food until the Egyptian ship's captain "proclaimed aloud that the daughter of the Sitt-el-Kebir (the Great Lady) was on board," whereupon the people brought out milk, fowls, and lambs. Arrived at Luxor, Ross continues:

> Our procession to dinner was quite Biblical. Mamma on her donkey, which I led, while Henry walked by her side. Two boys in front had lanterns, and Omar in his best clothes walked behind carrying some sweet dish for which he is famous, followed by more lantern bearers. As we went through the little village the people came out of their mud huts and called on Allah to bless us, the men throwing down their poor cloaks for my mother to ride over and the women kissing the hem of her dress.

One hears again echoes of *A Passage to India* and the spontaneous cult of the sympathetic Englishwoman Mrs. Moore—or "Emiss Esmoor," as her name is chanted through the streets.

Back in England and America, the letters of Lucie Duff Gordon did help to create sympathy for the Egyptian people. And to future readers, the letters proved that at the height of imperial progress, the ability of the British to connect did not entirely fail. Forster pays tribute to the few travellers to the East who transcended that maddening British insularity: "Kinglake, Doughty, Blunt, Lucie Duff-Gordon, discovered more than Dagoland: they found gravity and mirth here, also health, friendship, peace . . . " [E. M. Forster, "Salute to the Oriental!" *Abinger Harvest*, 1955].

Charisse Gendron, "Lucie Duff Gordon's 'Letters from Egypt'," in Ariel: A Review of International English Literature, *Vol. 17, No. 2, April, 1986, pp. 49-61.*

British traveler Amelia Edwards, describing vandalism to the Great Temple at Abu Simbel, Egypt:

The tourist carves it all over with names and dates, and in some instances with caricatures. The student of Egyptology, by taking wet paper "squeezes," sponges away every vestige of the original colour. The "collector" buys and carries off everything of value that he can get; and the Arab steals for him. The work of destruction, meanwhile, goes on apace. There is no one to prevent it; there is no one to discourage it. Every day, more inscriptions are mutilated—more tombs are rifled—more paintings and sculptures are defaced. The Louvre contains a full-length portrait of Seti I, cut out bodily from the walls of his sepulchre in the Valley of the Tombs of the Kings. The Museums of Berlin, of Turin, of Florence, are rich in spoils which tell their own lamentable tale. When science leads the way, is it wonderful that ignorance should follow?

Amelia Edwards, quoted in Lifting the Veil: British Society in Egypt 1768-1956 *by Anthony Sattin, J. M. Dent & Sons, 1988.*

John Barrell

[In the following excerpt from a lecture delivered in 1991, Barrell suggests that Western travelers' fears of Oriental peoples were embodied in sexual and genocidal fantasies, as revealed in the mid-nineteenth-century literature of tourism in Egypt.]

I

The mid-nineteenth century, say from the early 1830s to 1860, has been represented as a missing link in the history of Egyptology. In terms of general enthusiasm and interest, however, as distinct from scholarly research, the same period is probably the high point of admiration in Europe and the United States of the culture of the Ancient Egyptians. With the decipherment of the hieroglyphics, the extraordinary age of Egyptian civilization was becoming increasingly clear, and so were the questions it raised about the chronology of world history and especially of ethnology. It was then still possible to believe that what was best in Greek civilization had been learned from Egypt. More crucially, it was still possible to believe that the religion of Ancient Egypt, in whatever vulgar forms it had been propagated to the populace at large, had been at its best moments a monotheism: the forerunner of Judaism and therefore of Christianity. It is as if the true test of a civilization was that it should be based on a monotheist religion, a test failed even by the Greeks, except in the opinion of those few who believed that they too were closet monotheists. It may seem odd, then, that so often in the tourist literature of the period, admiration of the Ancient Egyptians seems to grow at the expense of any respect for the civilization of modern Egypt. In the confrontation of western tourists and the Arabs, the Turks, and the Nubians they encountered between Alexandria and Abu Simbel, it is not often this test that is used to judge the degree of civilization attained by the modern Egyptians; quite other criteria are used, ethnological and anthropological rather than theological.

A case in point is Harriet Martineau's *Eastern Life,* the narrative of her tour in Egypt first published in 1848. As we shall see, the book is remarkable for the liberal position it takes up in relation to the politics of Egyptology. Martineau held what to many in the mid-nineteenth century had become incompatible beliefs: that the Ancient Egyptians were black, and that they had created one of the great civilizations of the world. Her account of the religion of Ancient Egypt—an account evidently directed against an Evangelical fear and contempt of 'idolatry'—is a model for the mid-nineteenth century of how to conduct the discussion of cultural difference. But what are we to make of passages such as this, a parting reflection as she takes leave of Karnac after a final, moonlit visit?

> Here was enthroned the human intellect when humanity was elsewhere scarcely emerging from chaos. And how was it now? That morning I had seen the Governor of Thebes, crouching on his haunches on the filthy shore among the dung heaps, feeding himself with his fingers among a circle of apish creatures like himself.

Here as so often in the tourist literature I shall be talking about, a distinction between the modern and the ancient Egyptian seems to do duty also as a distinction between East and West. And it takes the form of denying, sometimes in tones of elaborate disgust, sometimes with a casualness hardly less disturbing, that the Muslim inhabitants of modern Egypt, whether Arab, Nubian, Turkish or Albanian, are human at all. This vision of the Governor of Thebes as an ape who does not hold himself upright but crouches on his haunches, who has insufficient manual dexterity to use tools and so feeds himself with his fingers, is evidently offered in terms which evoke and question the anatomical distinctions made, most notably by [anthropologist Johann Friedrich] Blumenbach, between human beings and apes. And the fact that he is represented, not as eating but as feeding himself, in a place of filth, among dung heaps, and in that offensive crouching posture, suggests that for Martineau the question about where the line is drawn, between human and animal, is calling up distinctions and confusions between the mouth and the anus, between eating and excreting. The Governor of Thebes has become an extraordinary emblem for what Freud described as the formation of judgment, expressed in the language of the oral impulse, about what belongs to the ego and what it rejects or projects as alien to itself.

All the recent work on what is called colonial discourse and on the relations of the West and East has started from the binary distinction, however much it may come to be complicated, between the western self and its exotic or oriental other, in which the other is conceived in terms of the projection of whatever in the western psyche is an object of disgust and terror: the East as the embodiment of western fears. Beyond that common starting point, however, this work seems to take one of two main directions, though sometimes (as in the work of Gayatri Spivak or

Homi Bhabha for instance) it may take both at once. There has been the attempt to produce an account of the relations of western imperialism and the East in the terms of hegemony and of power; of the discourses by which the West positions itself as subject and the East as object, and of the practices by which that distinction is established as a matter of established academic or administrative fact. There has also been an attempt—I associate it particularly with Sander Gilman—to focus more closely on the operations of fantasy and projection, and to talk about that attitude of disgust towards the Other which is always a self-disgust, about the western fear of the Oriental, including the Jew, as a fear of something inside the western psyche, something which is imperfectly repressed or is even produced by the civilizing process. . . .

It is in these terms that I have become interested in the literature of tourism, and specifically of tourism in Egypt, as one of the genres in which the mid-nineteenth-century fear and loathing of the East may find its most articulate and most violent expression. The literature of tourism in Egypt is only one of several genres of western writing in which the British, in particular, were reinventing the western image of Egypt and the East. There was also a literature of exploration, for example—of the search for the hidden source of the Nile, eventually 'discovered' by John Hanning Speke in 1858; there was a literature of social anthropology, though the term is of course an anachronism, represented most famously by E. W. Lane; there was an expanding literature of archaeology, in which Sir John Gardner Wilkinson was the most famous name. The variety of writings in which Egypt was being described and constructed in the mid-nineteenth-century makes it easier here than elsewhere to attempt to define a genre of tourist literature.

I shall not spend much time on that attempt today, except to remark that although there is no clear line between these genres and what I think of as tourist-literature, there is an obvious difference of emphasis. Authors like Lane and Wilkinson think of themselves as engaged to some degree or another in the practice of a science, and as obliged to attempt to write with some degree of impersonality. Whatever notions of occidental superiority are encoded in that attempted impersonality, and whatever eludes its vigilance, such writers are in a very different position from tourists, whose accounts of the country seem often to have been judged in terms of the degree of personality displayed in what are always represented as 'personal impressions' of the country. The geography of Egypt ensured that everyone made more or less the same tour, and the idiosyncratic variety of the tourist literature should probably be thought of as an essential commercial response to the sameness of the itinerary.

This is not to say that a writer like Martineau, in particular, does not aspire to provide useful knowledge of the antiquities, the ancient religion, the history, the geography and the political economy of Egypt. Other tourists, one of whom I will talk about, attempted to represent their treasure-hunting and grave-robbing as responsible archaeology. In spite of all that, however, the generic obligation of the writers of tourist literature, that they should describe the impression Egypt has made upon them, how deeply or otherwise it has imprinted itself into their personality, encourages or requires the use of a language especially hospitable to fantasy, to that virus of interiority which seems to break out in the imaginative literature of the 1820s, which spreads so insidiously and so unchecked through Victorian writing, and which enables the unguarded utterance of sentiments such as Martineau's in her description of the Governor of Thebes.

Tourist accounts of Egypt are of special interest, too, because they are so much a part and an effect of imperialism. The growth of British tourism in Egypt after about 1840 was partly an effect of 'agreements' imposed on Egypt, largely by the British, with the aim of reversing its progress towards economic as well as political independence. In particular, it was an effect of the development of the overland route to India. In 1841, the Peninsular and Oriental Steamship Company was granted the concession to land at Suez; by the following year there was a regular P & O service on both sides of the isthmus; and though earlier in the century there had been travellers to Egypt whom we can think of as tourists, it was only now that Egypt began to become a convenient and fashionable tourist destination. The tourists arrived in Alexandria usually in November or December, when the weather was at its most bearable and when the conditions were right for a voyage on the Nile; they travelled by canal and river to Cairo; hired their house-boat and crew; sailed and were towed directly up-river, taking advantage of the north wind and virtually ignoring the sights until they reached the second cataract; and then, turning round, they began a leisurely inspection of the monuments, beginning at Abu Simbel.

In the 1840s and 50s dozens of narratives of tourism in Egypt were published in Britain, as well as in the United States, France and Germany. In this lecture I shall be mainly concerned with Martineau's *Eastern Life,* with Florence Nightingale's *Letters from Egypt,* privately printed in 1854, and William C. Prime's *Boat Life in Egypt and Nubia,* published in 1857: Prime was a lawyer from New York City. Pressure of time will not permit me to discuss more than these, which of course I have chosen because they contain passages that enable me to make my points fairly economically; in different ways they are not at all untypical, however, of the dozen or so tours from this period which I have read so far.

II

I want to look at just one more incident from Martineau's narrative, her last glimpse of the antiquities of Egypt, when on their return journey her party stopped to inspect the Pyramids and the Sphinx. She was disappointed by the Pyramids themselves, which were somehow less, or at any rate no more, than she expected; as for the Sphinx, at first she could not see it at all. It is only when her party has passed it by, and someone refers to the Sphinx as something they have already seen, that Martineau realises that, unaccountably enough, she has simply missed it. I should explain that in the mid-nineteenth century little more than the head of the Sphinx was visible above the sand—though that was over 20 feet high, and very hard to miss, as Martineau herself acknowledges. The whole account of the visit

turns on and returns to this moment of non-recognition: Martineau is 'utterly bewildered', as she puts it, by the incident, and cannot leave it unexplained. In fact, she writes, when her party returns to examine the Sphinx, 'I found I had seen it;' intent on looking at the Pyramids, she had taken the Sphinx only for 'a capriciously-formed rock'. 'I rather doubt,' she writes, 'whether any traveller would take the Sphinx for anything but a rock unless he was looking for it, or had his eye caught by some casual light', though this hardly explains why she had forgotten to look for it in the first place.

Her description of the Sphinx itself is extraordinary: it seems to carry the weight of an intense anxiety about the boundaries of western self and eastern other, which once again compels her to reflect upon that moment of nonrecognition. 'What a monstrous idea was it from which this monster sprang! . . . I feel that a stranger either does not see the Sphinx at all, or he sees it as a nightmare.'

> When we first passed it, I saw it only as a strange-looking rock; an oversight which could not have occurred in the olden time, when the head bore the royal helmet or the ram's horns. Now, I was half-afraid of it. The full serene gaze of its round face, rendered ugly by the loss of the nose, which was a very handsome feature of the old Egyptian face;—this full gaze, and the stony calm of its attitude almost turn one to stone. So lifelike,—so huge,—so monstrous,—it is really a fearful spectacle.

The inability to *see* the Sphinx, and the terror it inspires, are both explained in terms of the lack of some identifying projection. She *would* have recognised it if the helmet or the ram's horns had been there; it would have been handsome if the nose had been there. We are positively invited, it seems, to discuss the Sphinx—a new Medusa's Head, the sign of an absence which can petrify—in terms of the crudest version of an anxiety about sexual difference. For the purposes of this lecture, however, I want to suggest that it speaks just as emphatically of an anxiety about the difference between human and animal as between male and female. Each of course may involve, may be a figure for, the other, by the convention which attributes to the 'other woman', including the exotic and/or oriental woman, an 'animal' sensuality. Appropriately, perhaps, Martineau's description of the 'fearful spectacle' of the Sphinx is recalled a few chapters later, when, in Cairo, she encounters an Egyptian 'dancing girl'—a 'horrid sight', 'so hideous a creature . . . I never saw', her movements just a 'disagreeable and foolish wriggle'.

The Sphinx of course is part human, part animal, and Martineau's visit to the Pyramids occurs between a discussion of the mummification of animals and a series of anecdotes about cannibalism in Egypt consequent upon the failure of the inundation. Dead animals treated as humans, dead humans treated as animals, humans behaving as animals: the boundary between the two is especially unstable in this part of Martineau's narrative. Earlier in the book, the Sphinx as idea is understood by Martineau in the conventional terms of a union of mind and body, wisdom and strength, human and animal. But when she finally encounters the Sphinx itself, it appears not as the union but as the confusion of all those binaries.

Martineau's anxiety about the humanity of the Sphinx needs to be understood within a specific historical and discursive context, ethnological and Egyptological. 'We have here,' she writes,

> a record of the Egyptian complexion, or of the Egyptians' own notion of it, as well as of the characteristic features of the race. . . . The face is (supposing the nose restored) much like the Berber countenance. The long, mild eye, the thick, but not protuberant lips, . . . and the projecting jaw, with the intelligent, gentle expression of the whole face, are very like what one sees in Nubia at every village.

This description, which gives clear indications of Martineau's familiarity with ethnological debate, is the last of her many declarations that she believes the Ancient Egyptians were black. In this she shows her allegiance to a number of French Enlightenment thinkers from Volney on who stressed the importance of Upper Egypt or even Ethiopia as the sources of Egyptian civilization. The most influential British ethnologist, James Cowles Prichard, had pronounced that, though their racial character was considerably modified in later ages, the Egyptians had originally been 'nearly' Negro [*Researchers into the Physical History of Man*, 1813]. I use the word 'negro', here and elsewhere, in its pseudo-technical sense, which refers to one of the races or families which for nineteenth-century ethnologists made up the 'Ethiopian' variety of mankind, the black Africans. The notion that the Ancient Egyptians had been black was, however, regularly denounced; most recently by Samuel George Morton, the Philadelphia craniologist, whose research—even as Martineau was writing—was giving a new scientific justification for slavery in the Southern USA. Prichard himself came to accept Morton's view, and by 1848 Martineau's belief in the blackness of the Egyptians was becoming increasingly hard to sustain. What was at stake, of course, was more than the identity of the Ancient Egyptians; it was the humanity of the blacks. The 'Negro race' wrote Cuvier, is marked by 'the projecting muzzle and thick lips'. The same characteristics that Martineau sees in the Sphinx are those which, according to Cuvier, 'approximate' the negro 'to the Apes' [*Cuvier's Animal Kingdom, Arranged According to its Organization,* 1840].

What may be showing through, then, in Martineau's reaction to the Sphinx—the fear, the racial typing—is the anxiety caused by her belief in the blackness of the Ancient Egyptians, an anxiety no doubt especially severe at a time when that belief was generally thought to have been discredited. It is as if the strain of that belief, in opposition not only to science but to her own inner doubts about the humanity of non-European peoples, is at last finding expression, at the end of her Nile journey, at her last sight of the civilization of Ancient Egypt. The description of the Sphinx, and the description of the Governor of Thebes, may reveal the price she pays for that belief, as well as the price to be paid by the modern Egyptians. Like every tourist in Egypt I have read, but more frequently and much more inventively, Martineau represents the inhabitants of

Egypt as animals: in her narrative the modern Egyptians or individuals among them are described as or associated with frogs, camels, bees, ants, beavers, sheep, birds, pigs, deer, rabbits, and apes. To insist, as Martineau does, that the Ancient Egyptians were black, is to acknowledge that blacks, and *a fortiori* the modern Egyptians, are human, are like us Europeans. It may be this acknowledgement that is withheld in Martineau's original failure to recognise the Sphinx; or it may be the acknowledgement that she too is animal as well as human, or female as well as human, a sexual as well as an intellectual being. But however we understand that curious moment of non-recognition, of negation, what the Sphinx tells Martineau, and what at first she will not hear, is that she is kin with all those—Turks, Arabs, Copts, Nubians, and women of the East of whatever 'race'—with whom she also denies all kindred.

III

Two pages or so after William Prime's party disembarked at Alexandria, they went to inspect Pompey's pillar. 'Shall I confess it?' he writes:

> There was an Arab girl, who came from a mud village close by, . . . whose face attracted more of my attention than this mysterious column, in whose shade I sat. She was tall, slender, graceful as a deer, and her face exceedingly beautiful. She was not more than fourteen. She was dressed in the style of the country; a single blue cotton shirt . . . It was open from the neck to the waist, exposing the bust, and it reached but to her knees. She stood erect, with a proud uplifted head, and to my imagination she answered well for a personification of the degraded country in which I found myself. The ancient glory was there, but, clothed in the garb of poverty, she was reduced to be an outcast among the nations of the earth.
>
> As I sat on the sand and looked at her, I put out my hand to support myself, and it fell on a skull. Bones, whether of ancient or modern Egyptians I knew not then, lay scattered round.
>
> When I would have apostrophised the brown angel, she started, in affright, and vanished in a hut built of most unromantic materials, such, indeed, as lay sun-drying all around us. It was gathered in the streets, and dried in cakes, which served the purpose of fuel, and occasionally of house building.
>
> *(Boat Life)*

The passage is a convenient anthology of many of the clichés of nineteenth-century western attitudes to the Middle East. I am thinking in particular of the expression of simultaneous desire and disgust for the Arab woman; the habit of personifying the East itself, or individual countries of the East, as a woman who is to be seen unveiled if the true East, or the true Egypt, is to be discovered; the representation of the landscape of Egypt, especially, as a place of death.

I am quoting the passage now, though, to point out two things in particular. First, there is the description of the Egyptians as a degraded nation, which is obscurely reinforced by the skull that lies so oddly to hand. This may well be a submerged memory of, or reference to Samuel Morton's *Crania Aegyptiaca,* published in 1844, and sumptuously illustrated with hundreds of engraved Egyptian skulls, which had identified the *fallāhín* as the nearest descendants of the Ancient Egyptians, though degraded almost beyond recognition. Morton's work was probably, by the mid-century, the most influential element in ethnological accounts of the Ancient Egyptians as well as of the black slaves in America, and it would almost certainly have been known, by reputation at least, by all three of the tourists I am discussing. Secondly, I want to point out once more the association between the modern inhabitants of Egypt, in this case a peasant girl, and the earth, itself associated with excrement. This 'brown angel' is said to live in a hut built at first of mud, then of dung; she 'vanishes' into it, as if entirely camouflaged by it, as if she has rejoined her natural element. It is a continuous theme of this tourist literature to associate, or rather to identify 'the sordid mud and clay of human nature and human life'—the phrase is Florence Nightingale's—with earth and with their habitations.

Of Asyût, Nightingale wrote that it looked like 'the sort of city the animals might have built . . . a collection of mud heaps' [*Letters from Egypt*]. The remark makes it clear that the most vulnerable element in the association between the mud of human nature and mud huts is the adjective 'human'. It is as if the belief that mankind is made of dust has given rise to a notion that a civilization is to be measured by the degree of distance a people has managed to put between itself and its earthy origins, or between its mouth and its anus. This notion is reinforced not only by the distinction made in comparative anatomy between ape and human, in terms of which is best at standing upright, but by the similar distinction, imposed after the Fall, between human and reptile.

Nightingale represents Luxor as overrun, as infested, as crawling with intrusive Arabs who are figured as reptiles. She was particularly shocked by the village which had grown up in the great temple itself. What offended her was not just the intrusion of the sordid modern into the grandeur of the past. It was also the fact that the houses of the village were built with doorways only four feet high. Nightingale does not pause to wonder if there might be a good reason for this design-feature in a windy and sandy desert where the temperature dropped rapidly at night. She exclaims against 'the moral degradation, the voluntary debasement'

> to see human beings . . . choosing to crawl upon the ground like reptiles, to live in a place where they could not stand upright, when the temple roof above their heads was all they needed! . . . If they had been deserted, you would have thought it was the dwelling-place of some wild animal. I never before saw any of my fellow creatures degraded (thieves, bad men, women and children), but I longed to have intercourse with them, to stay with them, and make plans for them; but here, one gathered one's clothes about one, and felt as if one had trodden in a nest of reptiles . . . these seem voluntarily to have abdicated their privilege as men. The thieves in Lon-

> don, the ragged scholars in Edinburgh, are still human beings; but the horror which the misery of Egypt excites cannot be expressed, for these are beasts.
>
> [*Letters from Egypt*]

The progression by which these *fallāhín* are progressively dehumanised as the passage proceeds could hardly be clearer. They begin as humans with free will, who choose to degrade themselves, to be *like* animals: 'it seemed as if they did it on purpose,' writes Nightingale, 'to be as like beasts as they could'. By the end, emphatically, they *are* beasts; and it is the comparison and contrast between the poor of Egypt and the poor of Britain—even they are human—which finally tears the veil of humanity from the villagers of Luxor, and reveals them as inhuman, as entirely alien to Nightingale. In the essay entitled 'Vision of Temples' which concludes her volume, Nightingale images Amunoph II returning to his temple in the nineteenth century, and finding it 'full of unclean beasts and creeping things; and of the unclean things, of all the dogs, and goats, and asses, the most unclean was man; and vilest of the creeping things and most abject was man'.

In the essay on Florence Nightingale in her book *Uneven Developments* [1988], Mary Poovey has discussed the strategies of representation by which the working class and the colonial subject could be made available as the objects of the middle-class career nurse. 'When she displaced class,' writes Poovey,

> so as to transform the brute soldier into a tractable, infantilized patient, she provided a strategy that could also displace race by transforming the Indian from a dirty foreigner into a sickly child. In . . . England's imperial dream, conquest and colonial rule could . . . be rewritten as the government of love.

In Nightingale's account of the temple at Luxor, however, the point of evoking the children of the poor in Britain is that they fail to provide the terms on which the foreign, colonised subject could be drawn within the pale of the human. The passage was written, of course, before Nightingale had begun her professional career, and long before her concern with the Indian hospitals. Nevertheless, it seems to demonstrate either the limits of the strategy that Poovey has described, or the resistance that had to be overcome before that strategy could develop. Throughout her tour of Egypt Nightingale is troubled by the impossibility of deciding whether the modern Egyptians are human or animal. The villages around Cairo, for example, are similarly populated with 'crawling creatures', creatures who bend and crouch and cannot walk upright. 'They do not strike one,' she says, 'as half-formed beings, who will grow up and grow more complete, but as evil degraded creatures', evil because they have chosen their own degradation. 'Oh, if one could either forget, or believe, that the people here were one's fellow creatures, what a country this would be!'

IV

That flesh is dust, and that burial is the return of dust to dust, is the organising metaphor of Prime's *Boat Life in Egypt*. The mummified bodies which, as a result of the new market in antiquities, are now exhumed and strewn across the desert, and which collapse into dust when trodden upon or merely touched, are among the most conspicuous instances of this figure. So are the jackals which haunt the cemeteries, exhuming the corpses of the dead, eating them, and ejecting them as excrement. The figure allows the fantasy that the whole desert is composed of the decomposed bodies of 4000 years of its oriental inhabitants, of all races, from the Ancient Egyptians to the modern Turks. The dust is scattered and mixed by the wind so that the bodies of individuals and races become horrifyingly undifferentiated; it is carried away by the river, to the sea, to unknown worlds.

Prime's account of his own excavations, and those carried out on his behalf, returns continually to this figure and the anxiety it gives rise to, an anxiety which is apparently associated with a sexual guilt. This is perhaps especially clear when he describes an encounter at Isna with 'one of the noblest specimens of feminine beauty that I remember'. The passage recapitulates the meeting with the silent and beautiful Arab girl Prime had seen at Alexandria; and as is usual in descriptions of encounters between male tourists and beautiful peasant women, the wind blows back this woman's garment to reveal 'the outlines of a perfect form, one that Praxiteles might have dreamed, one such as it is seldom permitted human eyes to see.' There follows a detailed account of her appearance, offered in the apparent belief that the invocation of Praxiteles will guarantee the purely aesthetic character of Prime's gaze. The woman returns that gaze with 'cold curiousity, and eyes devoid of interest, but dark, lustrous eyes withal, that had fire in them which might be made to flame'. She is wearing a necklace of antiques, mainly scarabs. 'I walked up to her and took hold of them. She stood like a statue, motionless, with her black eyes fixed on mine, but was silent, and allowed my examination without fear or objection.' He asks her how much she wants for the necklace: she makes no reply, but lifts up her jar, places it on her head, and walks off without looking back. Was she deaf? Prime wonders; was she an idiot? how else could her behaviour possibly be explained?

A few pages later Prime takes an elaborate revenge for his rejection, in an extended fantasy about the practice of grave-robbing, in which the association in the waking encounter, between the desire to possess the peasant woman and the desire to possess her necklace, is now refigured as the violation of a tomb by Arabs, and the robbery, rape and destruction of a mummified woman. Prime invites us to imagine a young, beautiful and (unaccountably) golden-haired woman who lived in Egypt 3000 years ago, and whose tomb is opened by Arab grave-robbers. Outraged by what is, after all, his own fantasy, Prime demands to know

> What fingers tore the coverings from her delicate arms! What rude hands were around her neck, that was once white and beautiful! What sacrilegious wretches wrested the jeweled amulet from its holy place between those breasts, once white and heaving full of love and life, and bared her limbs to the winds, and cast them out on the desert sand!

One answer to that question is clear enough: at Alexandria and elsewhere, Prime had done his own grave-robbing, which he had described in a language elaborately poeticised and eroticised: 'it was a strange sensation that of crawling into these resting-places of the dead of long ago on my hands and knees, feeling the soft and moss-like crush of the bones under me, and digging with my fingers in the dust for memorials of its life and activity'. What fingers?—his fingers. And the point can be made more generally: grave-robbing in the mid-nineteenth century was the main means of supplying the tourist demand for antiques, and was often carried out at the direct instigation of tourists. Prime himself encourages those he describes, wittily, as 'resurrectionists', to open tombs and to bring him the antiquities they discover.

But just as grave-robbing is represented as an Arab crime in that earlier fantasy of the violation of an Egyptian tomb, so Prime's desire to possess the Egyptian woman is fantasised as another Arab violation of a Europeanised victim, white, golden-haired. It is an unambiguously Caucasian body that is pulverised and scattered to the winds. 'I have,' he writes, on discovering that one grave he has rifled was the grave of an early Christian, 'a more than Roman veneration for the dead; and, though I felt no compunctions of conscience in scattering the dust of the Arabs . . . yet I did not like the opening of that quiet place in which a Christian of the early days was buried'. There is an issue of boundaries at stake here: violation must be by Arabs on westerners; only Arab bodies must be scattered to the winds. But the image and fear of decomposition that runs through Prime's book makes it only too clear that, at the most intimate level of the body, boundaries are impossible to secure. This is most apparent in Prime's fear that instead of being decently and separately interred in a New England burying ground, he might die and be buried in Egypt; that his own Christian dust might be mixed with the dust of all those dead Egyptians; that he would be absorbed into the terrifying masses of the Orient, lose his western identity, and with it all individuality. He writes repeatedly of his desire to be buried

> under green sods, whereon violets may grow, and . . . this vile dust of humanity may have a resurrection in roses or myrtle blossoms . . . No grave in Egypt has turf on it . . . I do not think I could sleep here at all. I do not think that my dust would consent to mingle with this soil.

> God forbid that I die here! to be laid, coffinless, three feet deep in the dry sand, and to-night disentombed by the jackals, or to-morrow by the wind. Such burial . . . who would not abhor?

Sometimes, however, the fantasy works as it were in reverse: instead of dying and being dispersed in the dust, Prime's exploration and excavation of the tombs of humans and of mummified crocodiles leave him covered in dust, which enters his mouth, as if he is ingesting the oriental dead, with all the danger that involves that he will become them. The most extreme instance of his fear of dying and being buried in Egypt, among orientals—of becoming dust with their dust—is his visit to the crocodile caves at Manfalût, where, as Prime reminds us, at least one earlier explorer had died of suffocation. 'I found that

I was actually crawling over mummies'; the caverns 'were piled full of mummied crocodiles to the very ceiling', and among the crocodiles were the mummies of men. 'If I thought that I were to be laid in that horrible company—I would—I would—if they did lay me there I would rise up and walk from very horror and find another grave for myself'. But though he avoids becoming part of the dust of the Orient, the dust of the Orient becomes part of him. After this exploration, everything tastes of mummy; there is an 'impalpable dust' of mummy in his mouth, on his moustache; on emerging from the pits, 'my complexion was dead crocodile, my odor was dead crocodile, my clothes were dead crocodile . . . I was but little removed from being a dead crocodile myself'. In eating the dust he is eating the dead of the Orient, as the jackals do; he is ingesting the Orient; he is becoming an animal, which is how he so often describes the modern Egyptians.

Alongside the notion of Egyptians as animals, or as mere dust, the terror of losing one's identity as human, as western, among these unindividualised orientals, there are also fantasies in Prime's narrative which attempt to make Egypt a safe place. The most elaborate of these is reserved for the final pages of the book, where Prime makes an attempt to appropriate the dust of Egypt, to represent it as a hospitable medium in which to bury Christians. Egypt, he now argues, is a holy land. It is sanctified not by those who have walked the earth of Egypt—Abraham, Jacob, Solon, Plato, Aristotle, Herodotus, Mary, even Christ—but by those who have become the earth itself. Joseph, his brethren and his sons are buried here: 'This that I hold in my hand, this grain of dust, may have been part and parcel of the clay that throbbed against the heart of Joseph. . . .' Not only these men, but 'their' women also are buried in Egypt: and here as elsewhere in the narrative the corpses of these women are eroticised, and they are visualised in prurient detail (some of them are blonde), lying in the arms of their dead husbands.

The fantasy ends as a religio-imperialist dream of Christian or Judaic ownership of Egypt. At the day of judgment there will be 'no spot on all the surface of the earth where the scene will be like this'. At various occasions through the narrative, Prime has expressed a fear that 'the dust of all the earth' will suddenly be reanimated and start back into life: 'what strange, wild countenances of affright and horror would men see staring at them from the earth beneath their feet in every land!' In the final pages of the book that fear is enlisted into an optimistic vision of the last day as it will be in Egypt. The present inhabitants, 'followers of the prophet', will rise in their millions and 'start in horror' to find the land crowded with Ancient Egyptians. But among them there will be 'a few tall forms and calm faces uplifted to the heavens', and all 'will be awed to silence by the majestic appearance of the men they trampled on and despised. The very sand of the desert will spring to life. If it could but now do so! If the lips that are dust here now under my feet would but syllable words!' These are the saved; all the others will be resurrected, as if by the grave-robbers, but only to perish again.

V

It is in the context of the anxieties I have been charting,

about whether the modern inhabitants of Egypt are animals or humans, that we should situate another no less disturbing aspect of much of this tourist-literature, the death-wish so often directed at the modern Egyptians, which amounts to a fantasy of their extinction, a kind of imaginative mass-murder, even genocide. At Luxor Nightingale decides that 'Egypt should have no sun and no day, no human beings. It should always be seen in solitude and by night' [*Letters from Egypt*]. At Qena she compares America with the East: in America, 'there is no Past, an ugly and prosperous Present, but such a Future!' In the East, 'there is a such a Past, no Present, and, for a Future, one can only hope for extinction!' At the island of Elephantine, the silence of the river is broken by the yells of 'troops of South Sea savages'. These Nubian children are a disappointment: they are 'not shiny as savages *ought* to be,' and were quite without the glossiness attributed by various ethnologists to the inhabitants of the banks of the Upper Nile. Instead, their 'black skins [were] all dim and grimed with sand . . . their naked hair plaited in rats' tails'. 'I heard some stones fall into the river,' writes Nightingale, 'and hoped it was they, and that that debased life had finished'. There are occasions in Prime's narrative, too, where the strategy used to make the East safe is a kind of imaginary genocide. At Aswan, contemplating the journey over the first cataract south to Abu Simbel, he writes that if all that lies beyond here—the men, the buildings, the trees, the river—'were blotted out of existence, swept off from the chart of the world and the page of history, who would miss any thing? Verily the world ends just here'. At Cairo, too, he composes this night-time meditation on the populousness of the city.

> Two hundred thousand people were lying around me, and I asked who and what they were, and what part they formed in the grand sum of human valuation? Literally nothing. They are not worth the counting among the races of men. They are the curse of one of the fairest lands on this earth's surface.

At this point I am reminded of Freud's first example of 'negation', in his essay of that name: ' "Now you'll think I mean to say something insulting, but really I've no such intention" '. At some level, perhaps, these exclamations and meditations do not mean what they say: though the expected extinction of degraded races was certainly established as a topic of civilized conversation in the 1850s, the modern Egyptians were not generally regarded as destined for early extinction, and I shall say more about this in a moment. I want to leave open, therefore, the possibility that Prime and Nightingale would have been unfeignedly horrified by a reading of these passages as fantasies of mass-murder. This wishing the inhabitants of Egypt dead, it might be argued, is no more than an ill-considered hyperbole, a way of putting what is only a wish for silence and space, away from the incessant demands for *baksheesh,* in which to contemplate the sublime of Ancient Egypt. It is a wish for a kind of contemplative *lebensraum,* and the hyperbole should be taken simply as an index of how urgent that wish is. On the other hand, one might argue that a desire for the extinction of the modern Egyptians is indeed in the minds of Prime and Nightingale, and can find expression in their writings only as a figurative, a hyperbolic expression of some more acceptable desire. If these passages are taken as hyperbole, that hyperbole may be operating here as what Freud describes as a 'symbol' of negation, which frees the mind from the restrictions of repression by marking its utterances with an asterisk, as if spurious, as if not participating in the authority of the author. But it is impossible to imagine the wish for peace and silence taking the violent and uncensored form it does except in relation to a people who are not recognised as human; whose death can so casually be wished precisely because it will not be like real death, like human death. The claim that this death wish does not mean what it says can be sustained only insofar as it also means *exactly* what it says—that these people do not, *should* not, belong in the world of the human.

It is important to understand that these fantasies of the modern inhabitants of Egypt as less than human, as animals of one kind or another, and as destined, hopefully, to disappear from the face of the earth, do not all have the same weight, or rather would not all have been weighed equally by readers in Britain and the United States in the mid-nineteenth century. Historians of nineteenth-century ethnology and anthropology are familiar enough with the claim that blacks are less human than others, and with debates about the degree to which they can be humanised or made more human, especially in the writings of militant polygenists, those who denied that human beings shared a common origin and who allowed the possibility therefore that they could be classified by type or species. It is perfectly clear that Nightingale in particular harbours some such notions of those she classifies as blacks. The distance, she suggests, between Europeans and Nubians is about the same as between 'men and animals'. She has clear doubts about whether the 'Ethiopian' slaves she sees are human or not, and she does not seem to expect them to be treated as humans.

All British or American tourists on the Nile seem to have been well-enough up in ethnological science to know that at the first cataract on the Nile or thereabouts, they were entering what most ethnologists regarded as a new racial division of the globe, a new ethnic territory: behind them were Arabs, ahead of them were blacks—Barabras or Nubians, often classified as Ethiopians and identified as belonging to the same variety of mankind as those who were classified as 'negroes'. These are the people that Nightingale wishes drowned at Elephantine; whom she describes, at Aswan, as not men but 'monsters'; these are the people, together with all the peoples to the south of Nubia, that Prime wishes into extinction, also at Aswan. It is certainly shocking, but it is not especially surprising to find Nightingale fantasising as she does about those she classifies as blacks, and it is still less surprising to find Prime doing so, for when he was writing there were more American than British ethnologists prepared to hint that the humanity of blacks might be in question. It is odder, and in the context of this lecture it may demand more comment, that in their anxiety to distinguish themselves as Franks from these oriental others, Nightingale and Prime should be harbouring similar fantasies about Arabs, who did not usually figure on the ethnological hit-list.

'Oh, if one could either forget, or believe, that the people here were one's fellow creatures, what a country this would be!' Are the modern Egyptians white or black? human or animal? food or excrement? the same or different? These questions were not questions in Nightingale's mind alone: in the early and mid-nineteenth century the ethnology of the modern Egyptians was the subject of widespread uncertainty and disagreement. There was disagreement, to begin with, about whether the *falláhín* were of the same race as the other Arab groups in Egypt. Then there was argument and uncertainty about whether the Arabs of Egypt were racially the same as the inhabitants of peninsular Arabia. More urgent, however, was the question whether the Arabs and/or the modern Egyptians were of the same variety of mankind as northern Europeans. The question took two forms, philological and anatomical. Were the Semitic and the Indo-European languages unrelated?—and if so were Semitic languages, as some suggested, of African origin? were they human languages, in Schlegel's terms, or animal languages? Or were the Semitic and the Indo-European languages consanguineous?—and if so, should Hebrew and Arabic nevertheless be seen as stunted growths on a degraded, somehow inorganic branch of the Indo-European? Were the Arabs, including the inhabitants of Lower Egypt at least, Caucasians, as Blumenbach and Cuvier and Prichard believed? or were they black, as R. G. Latham believed? Or had they become, by conquest, polygamy and slavery, an entirely hybrid or mongrel race?

More complicated still, did the modern inhabitants of Egypt put in question the very possibility of combining the conclusions of physical anthropology and of comparative philology in a unified science of ethnology? Were they anatomically Japetic and philologically Semitic? Or, still more confusing, were they fair of face and black of tongue—a white race speaking a language of Africa? Writers about Egypt in the years around 1850 were confronted with all these various versions of the question 'who are the modern Egyptians?', and with all the various answers they imply, for the science of ethnology itself, confronted with the Egyptians, collapsed into an untidy heap of borrowed opinions, hearsay evidence, prejudice and self-contradiction. There was as little agreement about their ethnic identity as there was about the ethnic identity of the Ancient Egyptians, and no doubt for the same reasons. For both peoples, ancient and modern, had been manoeuvred into occupying a borderline, a liminal, facing-both-ways position between white and black; and there was no comfort to be had either by acknowledging one's racial kinship with the Bedouin and the *falláhín,* or by crediting a black race with the invention of algebra, chemistry and whatever else.

At about the same time as Florence Nightingale was despairing of finding the solution to this new riddle of the Sphinx, the anatomist Robert Knox—till this point famous mainly as the man who had employed the Edinburgh resurrectionists Burke and Hare to furnish him with a supply of 'fresh' corpses—was preparing for the press his notorious 'fragment' *The Races of Men,* first published in 1850. Contemplating the *falláhín,* Knox asks, 'what race constitutes the present labourers of Egypt? No one that I know has condescended to clear up this question'. And just as Nightingale appeals by implication to the ethnologist to resolve her doubts about the humanity of the Arabs, so Knox appeals in vain to the tourist for a solution: why is it, he asks, that all the 'silly books of travels' written about Egypt had not managed to clear up this question? In the end, Knox answers it by a figurative chain of similes and substitutions which is entirely out of control and which ends, as we might expect, in a fantasy of genocide. It is not clear from Knox's excitable prose whether he decides that the *fallàhín* are the same as the Copts, or like the Copts, or whether he simply confuses them with the Copts. Either way, he appears to identify the two, and he goes on to explain that the Copts are like Jews but are not 'precisely Jews' but that the Jews, when racially pure, are 'Egyptian—that is African', and are like the Copts in that both belong 'to the dark races of men', and like all the dark races are destined for 'extinction'. As if to make sure that this inevitable fate applies to all the Egyptians, of whatever supposed race, Knox announces his further belief that *all* the inhabitants of Egypt, whether Copt, Arab, Turk or negro, will prove unable to hold their ground against the twin incursions of the Saxon race and the desert. 'Thus,' he writes, 'may the whole motley population of Egypt perish.' The fate which Nightingale devoutly wishes on the modern Egyptians is in Knox's view the inevitable fate that awaits so impure, so degraded, so motley and so unclassifiable a people.

It goes without saying that all forms of racism depend upon a denial of similarity as well as of difference: on a refusal to recognise the self in the other, as well as a refusal to acknowledge or to come to terms with otherness. The evident similarities between Europeans and blacks were easy to ignore, because of the evident differences between them, which could easily be made the basis of theories about the supposed physical, cultural, and intellectual inferiority of blacks, an inferiority so great—it could be alleged—as to call into question the right of blacks to be thought of as humans at all, or to be treated with humanity. The extermination of native Africans, native Australians, native Americans, could be imagined in part because it was believed they could be shown to be members, if not of other species, at least of other, inferior varieties of mankind. In the case of the Arabs, however, the sciences of philology and ethnology could give no unambiguous and quasi-objective justification to the desire of the West to deny its kinship with the East. It is in the affront, I am suggesting, of that uncertainty, as unbearable in its way as the affront of absolute otherness, that we can understand the genocidal fantasy I have been pointing out; for it produces an uncertainty about the identity and even the humanity of the European, too, and so about the very grounds of similarity and difference. The failures of recognition; the fantasmatic logic which defines Arabs as black in all but colour, as it also defines Jews in just the same way; the figurative negation of the humanity of the Egyptians; the deniable genocidal fantasy by which they are wished away; the chain of comparisons and substitutions which has no reason to end and so can end only in extinction—these are all ways of wishing away that uncertainty, by wishing away the Egyptians themselves. They are forms of a final

solution to the Egyptian, the Arab, the Semitic question, to the uncertainty of its answers.

I have said that tourist accounts of Egypt are of special interest because they are so much a part and an effect of imperialism. In the minds of all the tourists from Britain, especially, but from elsewhere too, the visible importance of the overland route to the future of the Empire means that they all arrive in Cairo with the same question in their minds: will the British annex Egypt, and if so, how can its annexation be justified, in terms of the process and progress of civilization? The subsequent history of Anglo-Egyptian relations suggests that the structure of feeling I have been looking at may be understood, in part, as an unofficial answer to that question. The official answer, of course, offered everywhere in this tourist-literature, is very different: the inhabitants of Egypt, it is argued, the slaves, the women of the harem, the over-taxed *fallàhín,* are indeed humans—and look how they are brutalised, degraded to the level of animals, by their own masters, their own husbands, their own governors. The structure of feeling I have been tracing in this lecture should perhaps be thought of as the repressed of this official argument. I do not believe for a moment that it is simply in the service of imperialism. But it may have been as serviceable as the official argument, in enabling imperialism to be thought; in permitting a general disregard for the interests of the colonised, under cover of the claim that it is primarily in their interests that their country is to be invaded and occupied.

> *John Barrell, "Death on the Nile: Fantasy and the Literature of Tourism 1840-1860," in Es-says in Criticism, Vol. XLI, No. 2, April 2, 1991, pp. 97-128.*

Dennis Porter

> [*In the following excerpt, Porter provides a psychoanalytic examination of Gustave Flaubert's Romantic travel work* Voyage en Orient.]

In his travel writings, from *Rome, Naples et Florence en 1817* to *Promenades dans Rome,* Stendhal made it very clear that he had no interest in traveling outside Europe. If the Italian peninsula was the source and center of Western civilization since the Renaissance, then he saw no necessity to emulate Byron's Childe Harold in this respect, at least, by pursuing his travels into the Eastern Mediterranean and the Near East. The purpose of travel for Stendhal, as for the grand tourists in general, was to move up on the scale of civilization, not down, to go from a land where artistic creativity and the arts of social living were less developed to one where they were more so. To travel in the opposite direction would certainly have struck him as perverse.

Yet, by the late 1820s Stendhal appears to have been something of an exception in his homeland, since it was precisely that kind of travel which a great many travelers with literary and artistic ambitions began to seek out. It was non-Europe that interested them, mostly for reasons that were very different from those of the emergent anthropology of the eighteenth century; they were drawn to otherness for its own sake, the otherness of "the uncivilized" or of lands at least uncontaminated by the Christian religion, Enlightenment humanism, democratic politics, or industrial progress. Nowhere is this more apparent than in the vogue of the so-called Orient, a vogue that largely overlaps with the romantic movement in French art, literature, and music, and whose most familiar icons are Victor Hugo's collection of poems, *Les Orientales* (1829), the sketches and paintings of Delacroix that were inspired by his official visit to Algeria in 1832, and Gustave Flaubert's own *Salammbô* (1862).

At least since Napoleon's incursions into Egypt, the French state under various regimes down through the nineteenth century sought to assert political hegemony of one kind or another over a number of countries in North Africa and the Middle East, often in competition with Britain. The subjugation of Algeria began in earnest in 1827, as a response to a perceived provocation, but was not completed until 1847; and in 1836 the erection of the obelisk of Sesostris on the Place de la Concorde was in itself a grand hegemonic gesture, designed to affirm the kind of homage the French imperial state expected from tributary nations.

Furthermore, French artists, writers, and scholars were

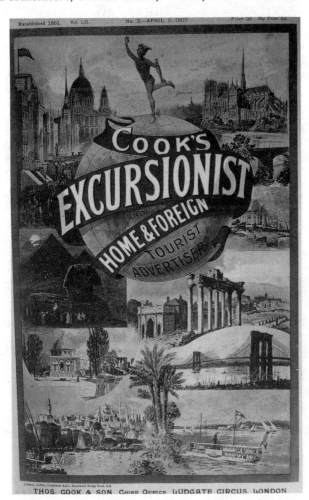

Illustrated cover of Cook's Excursionist, *a travel newsletter issued by the famous agency of Thomas Cook & Son in London.*

not loath to follow the flag, especially in exploring North African and Middle Eastern countries and their cultures, for purposes that were frequently in conformity with the discourse of French public life but often were not. In fact, as far as writers were concerned, from Chateaubriand—whose *Itinéraire de Paris à Jerusalem* of 1811 became something of a model—to Lamartine, Théophile Gautier, Gérard de Nerval, Pierre Loti, and Maurice Barrès, the *voyage en Orient* came to assume the character of an obligatory journey, a challenge to one's imagination and a test of one's powers as a writer—although, as notably with Lamartine, that did not necessarily prevent such writers from asserting French geopolitical rights and civilizing duties.

By the time Flaubert set out on his journey south on 29 October 1849, in the company of his friend Maxime du Camp, the literary and artistic avant-garde already associated the Orient with the emancipation of all the senses that Rimbaud was to pursue barely two decades later and that found its most memorable formulation in his poetic narrative of an hallucinatory voyage, "The Drunken Boat." Flaubert as traveler is situated somewhere between the early-nineteenth-century Bohemian and the *poète maudit* of its closing decades. The account of his journey is, in fact, such that it calls for the addition of yet another type to Laurence Sterne's catalogue of travelers: namely, the Perverse Traveler, a type that emerges in its fullness only with the late romantic moment.

The Stendhal of *Promenades dans Rome* still belongs to the eighteenth-century, sentimental tradition in travel writing that Sterne inaugurated; he shares his predecessor's propensity "to overestimate" a feminine love object, and the sites and cities associated with it. The Perverse Traveler of Flaubert's *Voyage en Orient,* on the other hand, indulges in no such fantasies. He expresses none of the celebratory Enlightenment attitude of the grand tourist toward Western civilization. Nor does he show the combination of tenderness and sensuality for a partner of the opposite sex that the Freud of *Three Essays on Sexuality* (1905) associated with the sex drive of the normal adult and the traditional idea of "love"—a combination that has a prominent place in Nerval's *Voyage en Orient,* for example. In Flaubert's oriental journey one finds instead a symptomatic fondness for forms of sexual deviance, including scenarios of voyeurism and sadism.

The importance of Freud's *Essays* for the understanding of perversity was, of course, that they insisted on the extraordinarily polymorphous character of human sexuality and on the fact that the sexual drive of the mature adult is not a simple given. On the contrary, it is constructed out of a number of component drives that are precariously integrated in the course of the complex process of physiological maturation and the assumption of human subjecthood under the aegis of a genital sexuality that identifies a partner of the opposite sex as its object and genital satisfaction as its aim. Freud concludes the *Three Essays on Sexuality* with the summarizing comment that "a disposition to perversions is an original and universal disposition of the human sexual instinct," and "normal sexual behavior is developed out of it as a result of organic changes and psychical inhibitions occuring in the course of maturation."

Given that the various drives are born separately and develop relatively independently, the potential for deviation from the object and aim that Freud defines as the norm is great—for the dissociation of the component instincts, regression, and fixation on pregenital modes of satisfaction. Further, Freud interprets perversion as a pathological structure of the adult human being that results from the unsatisfactory overcoming of the Oedipus complex under the threat of castration. Preliminary acts are preferred to the normal sexual act, and the choice of object is sometimes a person of the same sex (homosexuality) or a detached part of the partner's body (fetishism).

Finally, for the purpose of my argument, it is important to remember two more points in Freud's discussion of the perversions. First, the drive as such—looking or offering oneself to the other's look, sexual aggression or passivity—is not in itself a perversion. It becomes so only if it turns out to be the principal source of sexual satisfaction for the adult libido and if it has the kind of psychic fixity for which psychoanalysis invented the categories of voyeurism and exhibitionism, sadism and masochism. Thus, the scopophilia that is the drive classically associated with travel assumes a perverse form only exceptionally, and it does so increasingly in travel writings from the romantic age on. Second, as Freud notes in the "Summary" of the *Essays,* "neurosis is, as it were, the negative of perversion." The opposition between the two pathological structures consists in whether perverse fantasms are consciously acknowledged or are repressed by the subject, are directly narratable or emerge only as symptoms. In a carefully argued discussion of the issue, Patrick Valas summarizes the distinction as follows: "the *unconscious* fantasms of the neuroses (witnesses of the original perverse impulses) are identical in their smallest details to the conscious fantasms of perversion." Just how "conscious" such fantasms may become in the self-conscious elaborations of a travel narrative is apparent in Flaubert's *Voyage en Orient.*

For Freud, then, looking was a perversion if it ceased to be a component instinct of genital sexuality and became an end in itself; it was present wherever the eroticized curiosity found all the satisfaction it required in the intensity of a look. Moreover, an extra charge is attached when it is not just a matter of looking, but of "over-looking"; voyeurism is an eavesdropping of the eyes. The voyeur is mostly, but not invariably, an unseen seer. Thus, it is no accident if that phrase calls up Michel Foucault's discussion of the panopticon. The pleasures of voyeurism are commonly related to the exercise of power in one form or another. That is why, in Flaubert's *Voyage* as elsewhere, it is frequently associated with sadism. The powerful curiosity to see the body of a potential sexual partner is joined to the desire to overpower and to despoil it. In the end, this whole complex of more or less potent impulses are written into the text of Flaubert's journey to the Middle East as an orientation toward destruction and death.

Studies of Flaubert's adolescent literary taste, his letters, and his posthumously published *œuvres de jeunesse* have amply demonstrated his enthusiasm for the clamorous and flamboyantly iconoclastic writings of the so-called *petits romantiques,* for the imperial decadence of ancient Rome, or for the extravagant lives of saints and sinners in general. The other face of Flaubert's famous withdrawal from active life in the solitary cult of his craft was, in fact, his occasional excursions into the Bohemian world of Parisian artistic circles. Long periods of denial of the senses in Normandy were interrupted by more or less brief interludes of sensual indulgence in the capital.

Moreover, from early on the young Flaubert contrived to *épater le bourgeois* in his own way. He took, in particular, a special pleasure in inventing ways to shock his putative readers. Thus, there is an obvious continuity between the enthusiastic overwriting of the early, more or less gothic tales, with their grotesque twists and macabre detailing, and the Middle Eastern travel book itself. On one level, the *Voyage en Orient* reminds us how single-minded its author was from the beginning to the end of his career. "If ever I play an active role in the world," Flaubert wrote when he was still an adolescent, "it will be as a thinker and demoralizer. I will simply tell the truth, but it will be horrible, cruel, and naked" [*Correspondance,* 1926-33]. Not surprisingly, therefore, the truth he discovers in the lands bordering the Mediterranean is his kind of "truth," one associated precisely with a laying bare that shocks and unsettles beliefs.

That Flaubert was single-minded throughout the course of his artistic life does not, of course, imply that his works are monotonously repetitive or even unified. The *Voyage* is no exception to this general rule. Although there are a great many passages in which Flaubert turns himself into a kind of underground guide to forbidden, disturbing, and even horrifying spectacles or activities, at other times he evokes episodes that belong to the register of heroic adventure or describes sites and natural scenes with the painterly precision of the picturesque tradition.

Nevertheless, if . . . Sartre was accurate in enumerating the major themes of the nineteenth-century *déclassé* writer as, after art itself, love, travel, and war, Flaubert's career in letters can be seen to have marked a decisively new and more disturbing stage in the way such themes are developed compared with Stendhal's. Art, of course, had become preeminent. Love comes to be sacrilegiously reconnected to a scandalously corrupt body. Travel is embraced as a form of *voyage maudit.* War, finally, is uncoupled from the heroics of *la grande armée* and survives in the *Voyage* in the frenzies of the hunt. Sartre glossed the situation of the nineteenth-century French writer in general as a form of destructive parasitism: "That discredit with which military, aristocratic societies regarded the professions is taken over by the writer. But it is not enough for him to be useless, like the *ancien régime* courtiers; he seeks to trample underfoot utilitarian work, to smash, burn, and destroy things, thus imitating the carelessness of feudal lords who led their hunt across fields of ripe grain" [*Qu'est-ce que la Littérature?* 1948].

. . . . .

The journey south that began in October 1849 in a mood of depression was completed some eighteen months later when, in June 1851, Flaubert returned to his home at Croisset. The journal that gives an account of Flaubert's journey was first published in something like its entirety under the title *Notes de Voyage en Orient* in the Conard edition of 1910. Like the subsequent editions, this one retains the disparate and fragmentary character of a work that the author himself never recast for the purpose of publication.

In spite of frequent *longueurs* and whole pages where the author merely reproduces the kind of shorthand catalog of artifacts or perfunctory guidebook descriptions that are of little interest to a modern reader, Flaubert's *Voyage en Orient* is a disturbing and symptomatic text on a number of levels. On the one hand, like the systematic apologists for empire whose writings were analyzed in Said's *Orientalism,* Flaubert underwrites throughout the inherited binary opposition between an Occident associated with European civilization and an Orient that begins in Alexandria or Beirut. On the other hand, he more often than not reverses the traditional Eurocentric hierarchy in order to contrast Oriental wisdom with Western cultural smugness. For him, the East frequently reveals the very "truths" of existence that Western sentimentality and Western hypocrisy have made it their task to conceal in the bourgeois century. Thus, the writing of Flaubert's travel book—like that of the version of *The Temptation of Saint Anthony* he completed just before setting out on his journey or that of the subsequent *Salammbô*—belongs at least as much to what Mario Praz first called "the romantic agony" as to what Said calls "Orientalism." It speaks to the discontents of a repressive civilization whose values it goes out of its way to subvert.

The Flaubertian self is no more homogeneous or consistently self-present than any other. There are, therefore, a great many passages in the text that express indirectly the peculiarly overdetermined character of any encounter with foreign places and peoples. The themes raised in the opening pages of the *Voyage* as well as the odd chronology of the presentation make this immediately apparent. Right after the leave-taking of October 1849, there follows a section written on a boat on the Nile in February 1850; and that section itself begins with the recall of the author's first voyage to Corsica ten years previously, when he was eighteen years old. Further, interspersed with a few references to the Nile and a description of the scene, are longer passages that call up memories of other journeys, including the one south to Marseilles from which he had embarked for Egypt just three months before but which, to the writer on the Nile, now seems so long ago—"My God, how distant it all is." In short, not too far into his Eastern journey, Flaubert scrambles memories of the immediate and remoter past along with more generalized cultural reminiscences of the significance of travel as psychic loss and recovery.

The point to note is that, in Flaubert's novels as in the *Voyage,* when travel is at issue the present opens effortlessly onto the past or fantasizes a future somewhere else, memory becomes reverie and vice versa. As a result, it is sometimes difficult to disentangle real events from their representation *après coup.* The *déjà vu* of travel is "locat-

ed" in the sense that the countries one is passing through for the first time are part of a complex transferential network; they belong to one's own intimate geography as lands already desired or feared.

In this connection, a stretch of Flaubert's journey from Paris by that older mode of locomotion beloved of the German romantics, the stagecoach, inspires a suggestive question: "In the corner of your memory doesn't there exist the still vivid reminiscence of some hill dominating a desired land?" That reference to "a desired land" remembered—"in the corner of your memory"—may serve as a reminder that human psychic activity is such that no approach to a foreign country is ever wholly unprepared. On his Oriental journey, Nerval, like Baudelaire after him, even speculated about the persistence of memories from *une vie antérieure.*

It is no accident, then, that Flaubert's travel book begins where, at their deepest level, all travel books begin, whether or not that fact is acknowledged in the text: at home. Yet, among such books not written under external duress, few give a greater emphasis to the pain of departure. It is a pain that is associated chiefly with separation from the author's mother but, in part, also with the phobia of travel—our late-twentieth-century fear of flying had a nineteenth-century counterpart, most notably in the traumas associated with journeys by rail.

The narrator opens his story by describing the day he took leave of his mother as "an atrocious day, the worst I have ever lived through." And he goes on to evoke the scene in his mother's little garden and house at Nogent with a sharpness that recalls the peculiarly wrenching emotions of significant departures. After having mentioned the kisses and caresses he gave her seated in her armchair, he concludes the episode with a reference to the memorable last sound he heard her make: "What a cry she uttered when I closed the living room door! It reminded me of the one I heard her emit at the death of my father, when she took his hand." It is a cry that suggests at least two important and incompatible ideas. On the one hand, Flaubert hears in it a recognition of the fact that he now occupies the place of his dead father; on the other, there is also the implication that his decision to leave signifies his own death as far as his mother is concerned. The narrator's reaction is characteristically ambivalent. The guilt he apparently felt at the demand for love spurned cohabits with a sense of power. There is pleasure as well as displeasure in his mother's pain.

It is thus characteristic that, like such celebrated travelers as Byron and Stendhal before him, Flaubert rejects the path of familial duty. In a symptomatic sentence that follows immediately the one just quoted, the devoted son refers to his other life in the capital, a life in which the apparent overestimation of a mother gives way to the systematic underestimation of women of another kind: "The next two days I lived in the grand style, feasting, drinking, and whoring; the senses are not far from tenderness, and my poor nerves had been so cruelly twisted, they needed to relax." This nineteenth-century neurasthenic recognized his depressive symptoms and prescribed his own treatment through a form of emancipation in which the perversions of voyeurism and sadism were frequently engaged in. Flaubert's text demonstrates the validity of Valas's comment that "perversion is a subjective position (and not a manifestation of instinct) that is sustained by a conscious fantasm, a fantasm that the subject may be led to realize in modes of behavior which are organized in terms of this fantasm."

In any case, as Freud makes clear in the *Three Essays on Sexuality* and elsewhere, psychoanalysis relates perverse behavior in an adult to an early sexual history in which a strong fear of castration plays a prominent role. As a result, love for the mother is repressed but, for a variety of reasons, does not reemerge as love for a substitute female love object. In Flaubert's case, one finds instead a form of homoeroticism that narcissistically celebrates maleness by repeatedly exposing and calling attention to the signs of imperfection on female bodies. His apparent mother-love disguises a depreciation of the mother that is nevertheless displaced onto other women in his fantasms.

The fact that Flaubert celebrates travel as transgression more systematically than any of his predecessors is confirmed, in part, by the fact that throughout the whole *Voyage* he only once mentions the possibility that a traveler might have responsibilities to home and country that transcend the pursuit of individual pleasure or self-cultivation. He mentions the possibility precisely in order to reject it mockingly, when he suddenly realizes how bored he is by Egyptian temples: "Doing what one is supposed to do! Being always, as circumstances require (however repugnant you happen to find it), like a proper young man, a traveler, an artist, a son, a citizen, etc. is supposed to be." Flaubert's Orient exists for the traveler's personal use or, in other words, his pleasure.

Even before leaving France, Flaubert's narrator makes clear two of the major motifs of the travel book as a whole; they have nothing to do with the notion of dutifulness. The first concerns the different degrees of pleasure associated with travel and registered in the body as one moves at different speeds through space. A little later in the text, with the description of the traveler's first sight of Marseilles, the pleasures of the journey become sharper. He wakes up and suddenly finds himself looking down on the Mediterannean city in the early morning light. The pleasure here is in the look itself: "I had a sensation of virile pleasure (*volupté virile*) such as I have never felt since. I fell immediately in love with this ancient sea that I had so often dreamed about!" One recognizes in the discourse of the passage that *romantisme flamboyant* which associated the south with sensuality and vibrancy of local color. The narrator finds himself stirred by the warm air to an anticipatory "Oriental indolence (*mollesses orientales*)," and he concludes the paragraph with a future conditional that was to be the characteristic tense of Emma Bovary's reveries: "the large paving stones of the Canebière, which warmed the soles of my pumps, made my calves stiffen at the idea of the burning beaches on which I would have liked to walk." One hardly needs the adjective "virile" at the beginning of the passage to be alerted to the erotic metonymic displacements down to the passionate surrender of self implied by the "burning beaches" of the end.

The second major motif of this early section is connected to the first, because it involves an active kind of looking animated by a more obvious, sexually charged curiosity. Curiosity may, of course, be associated with a sublimated form of looking, the kind associated with cognition and socially useful discovery in Darwin's *Voyage*. But in Flaubert's journal it is conflated with a scopic drive that associates knowing with a laying bare. Thus, an illuminating passage connects the narcissistic satisfaction in the rise of virility contingent on a proffered sight to a form of looking that is a progressive unveiling or, in the context, undisguised sexual aggression. The object in this case is not a city but a woman, a fellow passenger on a boat on the Saône.

The circumstances of the meeting, along with elements of the portrait Flaubert presents, anticipate the celebrated opening chapter of *Sentimental Education.* In both cases, the narrator begins with a characteristically precise description of a woman's clothes and the outlines of a body they simultaneously hide and reveal. The fetishistic circumstantiality displayed is, of course, an expression of that preoccupation with "fashion" which is a typical feature of nineteenth-century French literature. It is also, in Flaubert's fiction at least, the preliminary tableau that fixes a certain image of woman as the fullness of an ideal, before that image is progressively "disrobed" in the course of the narrative.

The difference between Flaubert's novel and his travel book is that whereas in the former he distances himself from his material in order to allow his narrative to unfold, in the latter he theorizes the curiosity he feels as a writer. The inquisitiveness he expresses about the woman is at the same time the curiosity of a man and of a novelist; the desire to know here is, on the one hand, a desire to see and possess and, on the other, a desire to expose what has been seen and possessed through the act of writing: "For I have that mania of constructing books on the people that I meet. In spite of myself, an ungovernable curiosity makes me wonder what kind of life a passerby might lead. I would like to know his profession, his country, his name. . . . And if a woman is involved, especially a middle-aged woman, then the itch becomes unbearable. Admit how you would like straightaway to see her naked, naked to her very heart."

Such a passage connects the activity of the novelist with an aggressive male voyeurism—"naked to her very heart"—that finds in travel a wonderful variety of exciting new objects for its look. The violence done involves a form of forbidden seeing that is exercised on an unwitting victim. And such a visual pursuit of nakedness of and beyond the unclothed body is a recurrent motif in the *Voyage.* The perverse scenario of this and other passages anticipates in a more explicit way Frédéric Moreau's experience of women. It even suggests that that wayward hero's famous "N'est-ce que ça?" (Is that all there is to it?) is less the lament of a disabused idealist than that of an embittered fetishist who compulsively repeats in disgust and anger his encounter with nonphallic woman.

Furthermore, the force of the scopic drive that is here directed at the female body focuses with a symptomatic re-

petitiveness at other moments in the text on precise evocations of eroticism and death that embody the grotesque
and the macabre. In the same way that clothes hide that
nakedness which is the "reality" of the flesh, so the flesh
in its turn hides the profounder nakedness of what lies beneath. In the *Voyage,* as throughout Flaubert's work, to
go to the end of a significant experience is to experience
the *néant* in a beyond of pleasure. One is reminded that
in his fiction Flaubert is an especially acute observer of
decay. His narrators typically find satisfaction in recording scenarios of loss and even of dismemberment.

Yet, before exploring these themes further, it is worth recalling that all is not "romantic agony" in Flaubert's *Voyage.* The nineteenth-century Bohemian-cum-*poète maudit*
is different from the eighteenth-century rake, in part because his rebellion against society's moral codes and values is informed by the cult of art. And throughout his travel book Flaubert attempts to do justice to the sights and
scenes in a self-consciously literary prose that, like
Byron's verse, takes up the challenge of its object and of
the sensations inspired. There are, therefore, numerous
more or less short descriptive passages that would not be
out of place in a contemporary novel. There are set-piece
descriptions of landscapes, village or urban scenes, evocations of architectural monuments, palaces, temples, ruins,
celebrated sites, and pictures of crowds or memorable individuals. There is also the more than usual number of
those incidents and strange encounters which are the
stock in trade of travel writing.

At the same time, anyone who is habituated to the idea of
Flaubert as a prototypical nineteenth-century aesthete is
likely to be surprised by the elements of heroic adventure
in the *Voyage.* In his late twenties at least, Flaubert often
appears very different from the aesthete or *fin-de-siècle*
decadent with which he is sometimes associated. Much of
the time in Egypt and the Near East, making full use of
France's network of colonial relations, he and his companions traveled on horseback or occasionally by ass. They
passed through the desert and were exposed to the risks
and hardships—from fleas and bedbugs to extreme cold—
of travel in that region at the time. Not only do they often
camp out and enjoy the traditional male camaraderie of
campfire scenes by night, they also go armed and carry
swords, frequently hunt with the characteristic wantonness of nineteenth-century European hunters, and on at
least one occasion are pursued by brigands, who shoot at
them from their horses.

The sentiments expressed on such occasions are consistent
with the homoerotic excitement that the narrator reveals
from time to time for the fierce primitivism of the desert
Arabs. In the swift sketches he draws of one of contemporary European man's most radical Others, the narrator is
clearly attracted not by languor but by instinctive directness and male pride. "Fierceness of manner and laughter"—he notes of an Arab and a Negro passing by together, beating their camels as they go—"Accents guttural and
harsh, and with large gestures of their arms." Moreover,
such and similar praise of male attributes and beauty is not
subsequently undermined, as it is in the case of women,
by means of a scenario of disrobing.

If all is not "romantic agony" in the text of Flaubert's Oriental journey, its most memorable moments nevertheless
concern perversely charged, erotic encounters—not "heroic" but "sexual adventures" that are pornographic in
kind—and experiences at the limit in confrontations with
death, ecstatic religion, or hallucination. At its extreme,
adventure of such an order is less an assertion of the self-
regarding, self-preserving ego than the kind of swooning
annihilation of ego for which Jacques Lacan reinvented
the word *jouissance.* Flaubert's Near Eastern journey afforded him opportunities not available in the same way in
Europe to push beyond the limits of the pleasure principle.
The writer who was preoccupied both before and after he
left France with the appropriate means to represent the
temptations of Saint Anthony in the desert, was peculiarly
open to the traditional expressions of the anguish and
transcendence of the flesh.

There are, then, a number of moments in the *Voyage*
where the narrator finds himself deeply stirred in ways
that are incompatible with the functioning of the pleasure
principle. One such concerns the approach to Thebes
along the Nile, and another, also near the Nile, the encounter of Flaubert's party with a passing caravan in a
sandstorm. In the former case, the whole spectacle inspires in him an unusual, if not unprecedented, response
of quasi-religious awe, an "oceanic feeling": "It was while
I was enjoying (*jouissais*) these things . . . that I felt rise
within me a sense of solemn happiness which went forward to meet the spectacle, and I thanked God in my heart
for having made me capable of taking pleasure (*jouir*) in
such a way. . . . I experienced an inner joy (*volupté*) of
my whole being."

The second occasion concerns one of the moments where
adventure in the heroic sense is transformed into something that is both more exciting and more disturbing. The
camels with their hooded drivers and veiled women
emerge out of the swirling, reddish-brown sand like spirits
immersed up to their bellies in clouds. The image strikes
the narrator with all the power of an hallucination that
leaves him beside himself: "I felt something like a sensation of terror and of furious admiration run along my
spine; I sneered nervously; I must have been very pale, and
I felt a rush of pleasure (*jouissais*) that was extraordinary."

The motivation for Flaubert's journey to the Middle East
is to be found in the pursuit of such experiences. The continuity with Byronic romanticism resides in a similar
flight from the *ennui* of the well-regulated, bourgeois Europe of the emergent Industrial Revolution into a world
that offered powerful, novel sensations. It is, therefore, no
surprise if the young traveler was especially drawn to what
the Middle East offered in the way of exotic sexual experiences, for it is in that sphere above all that the lure of Europe's Orient and of Oriental difference has proved the
most potent. And it is in this connection that his text gives
a special emphasis to the scopic drive.

Probably no writer more than Flaubert has managed to
suggest so well throughout his works the way in which the
look is drawn by the play of highlights against a muted
background or through a veil; it is the intermittence of
light that attracts, in a titillating game of revelation and

concealment, of now you see it, now you don't. Thus, women seen in Constantinople fix his attention precisely because their dress reveals a brilliance that it simultaneously conceals: "Women in golden carriages, a natural palor beneath their veil or created by the veil itself; through their veils, the rings of their fingers, the diamonds of their foreheads. How brilliant their eyes are! When you look at them for a long time, it doesn't excite so much as impress; they end up looking like spirits stretched out on divans. The divan follows the Oriental everywhere." The brief notation is typical, not least for the way in which desire is arrested by the spectacle itself; not only is seeing enough here, it also disincarnates the women involved and leads into a characteristic Orientalist generalization, concerning the celebrated signifier of Oriental indolence and sensuality, the divan.

The most famous sexual adventure of the *Voyage* concerns Flaubert's visit to the celebrated courtesan Kuchak Hanem. And what is most apparent in the episode is the power of the look that fixes the images in that act of recall which is narration. In this case, however, seeing does not stop desire but stimulates the protagonist to seek genital satisfaction. But it turns out that such satisfaction is characteristically located between two looks.

The narrator dramatizes the scene with great care, from the first impression of Kuchak Hanem standing on the stairs of her apartment—with pink trousers and a violent gauze wrap covering her otherwise-naked upper body, smelling of sweet-scented turpentine—to the moment when, the act of sex complete, he watches her sleeping next to him and recalls the sensations he had felt. The voyeur's pleasure resides in observing with detached attention a sleeping woman unaware that she is observed.

As with the woman seen on the boat on the Saône, the narrator records details of clothing and body with a fetishistic precision that is even more marked here, apparently because of the fascination exercised by a Middle Eastern woman in her difference and by the fashion that helps constitute that difference. The way every detail of her hair is recorded in a verbless, pedantically punctuated sentence is typical—"Her black hair, curly, resistant to the brush, separated in two bands by a part on the forehead, small tresses caught up at the nape of the neck." Even more characteristic is the decisive notation of the smallest sign of physical decline: "The upper incisor on the right is beginning to decay." That decayed tooth is, in the context, another of those signifiers of female imperfection which are scattered throughout Flaubert's writings, the mark of a mutilation that recalls the constitutive mutilation of femininity: castration.

Perhaps the most fully developed of Flaubert's perverse scenarios in the *Voyage* is, however, that which concerns Kuchak Hanem's "dance of the bee." It is a dance that is also a striptease and, in order to heighten the voyeuristic charge, it was performed for "the eyes" of the two visiting European males only—her musicians are blindfolded. The climactic moment of the performance is precisely the point at which the play of show and hide is brought to an end by the throwing aside of the scarf that is the dancer's last garment and that apparently gave the dance its name.

Once the bee has flown away, for the pleasure of the voyeur and the pain of the fetishist, sexual difference can no longer be disavowed.

Flaubert goes on to savor narcissistically the satisfaction of his own genital potency in the crude language he characteristically has recourse to in his more or less private papers: "After the most brutal of f—s, she falls asleep with her folded hand in mine, and snores . . . Her little dog slept on my silk jacket on the divan . . . I gave myself up to the nervous intensity of feelings rich in reminiscences. The sensations produced by her belly on my —s, her—, even hotter than her belly warmed me like a hot iron."

That the narrator reports on the sensations experienced after the fact is also characteristic. In the kind of striptease Flaubert practiced as both male traveler and author, the relative passivity of voyeurism sooner or later gives way to action; the looking turns into an unveiling and an exposure. If there are references to Kuchak Hanem's decaying tooth, to her snores, or to the heat of her sexual organs, and if a traditional male slang is used to describe sexual activity, it is because to see and to know all there is to know about a woman is to see the "reality" of mutilation and future decay beneath the lure of the flesh. The ironist's "N'est-ce que ça?"—the "N'est-ce que ça" of Frédéric Moreau in the *Sentimental Education*—masks behind its melancholy the satisfaction of the sadistic as well as the scopic drive.

It is, therefore, consistent with such an attitude if throughout the *Voyage* the narrator seems to take a particular pleasure in noting both the fascination of women's bodies clothed in novel and richly various, regional, or ethnic fashions and the frequent grotesqueness or ugliness of those same bodies once exposed. That most visible icon of femininity as mother or as desired sexual other, the breast, is a particular focus of the desecrating look. Misshapen breasts draw an eye that enjoys lingering with cruel relish over the female grotesque: "A Negress's tit—it certainly hung down at least as far as her navel, and it was so flaccid that there was scarcely more than the thickness of the two skins; when she goes on all fours, it must certainly touch the ground."

Given the importance accorded the scopic drive in Flaubert's text as well as a more generalized openness to exotic sexual experiences, it would be surprising indeed if the topos of the harem did not figure there. The harem had long been a peculiarly charged signifier to the extent that, for the Western fantasy at least, it signified an inaccessible space in which the omnipotence of a master male over compliant women is juxtaposed both with the powerlessness of the excluded males and with the physical impotence of those mutilated males who serve the master's women, the eunuchs. The harem is thus the site of a threat as well as of a promise; the despotic power of the sultan comes closer than anything in modern Western man's experience to the mythic concept of the primal father. And to a traveler such as Flaubert, it is the threat embodied in that power which is the most visible.

Thus, like others before and after him, Flaubert is both fascinated and disturbed in the Old Seraglio of Constantinople at the sight of the eunuchs, not least because they are white. After having evoked their wrinkled, old women's faces, and their elaborate costumes, he goes on: "The sight of a white eunuch makes a disagreeable impression, as far as one's nerves are concerned; it's a strange product, one difficult to take one's eyes off; the sight of black eunuchs never caused a similar reaction in me." In effect, Flaubert is acknowledging here the shock—"one's nerves"—of the spectacle of castration in a male with whom he can identify: namely, a white male.

The closest the narrator comes in this section to evoking the promise of the harem is in a brief reference to "the stolen odalisque (*l'odalisque ravie*)": "It is in such a place that one could live with a stolen odalisque. This crowd of veiled women with their large eyes that look straight at you, this whole unknown world . . . arouses a dreamy sadness that seizes hold of you." It is characteristic that the narrator should fantasize possession of a sexual object not from the point of view of the master of the harem, but from that of the oedipal son as the theft of a woman. Flaubert's Oriental journey is lived as the flight of two young bachelors and aesthetes from the paternal Law, from duty and responsibility. Thus, along with the displaced aggression that the *Voyage* expresses relative to the mother figure, one finds throughout an implied refusal to identify with the father. The passage that concerns the motif of "the stolen odalisque" seems, in fact, to embody the regressive desire for a return to the original duality of the imaginary register. The smoking of a narghile and the drinking of raki are conducive to the pursuit of formerly forbidden pleasures in the forever-closed space of one's private harem. In any case, it is apparent that, far from being associated with the reproductive function of genital sex, the properly paternal function, Middle Eastern eroticism is associated in Flaubert, as in the discourse of his European contemporaries, with a voluptuous retreat from life.

The reference to "a dreamy sadness that seizes hold of you" points to another aspect of the Middle East that appealed to Flaubert's late-romantic sensibility. His particular *mal du siècle* enjoyed evoking all the evidence of death and decay in the midst of life and discovering true Oriental wisdom in a kind of languorous embrace of death. On the one hand, this gives rise to his fondness for that form of grotesque associated with death: namely, the macabre. And, on the other, it leads to reflections on the extinction of self achieved either through quietistic reverie or ecstatic experience.

Representations of the macabre abound throughout the *Voyage*. The traveler visits pyramids, tombs, charnel houses, leper colonies, and hospitals. Everywhere he discovers the openness with which the distressing facts of physical existence are displayed in the Middle East. The narrator comments frequently on the ubiquity of human and animal remains, on the piles of bones and detritus, or on the bloody and mutilated carcasses around which circle such predators as vultures, wild dogs, and jackals. The same precision he gave to the description of women's fashions is, in fact, expended on the effects of disease upon a human body.

The portrait of a leper next to a fountain is typical—"His lips, all eaten away, reveal the bottom of his throat; he is hideous with purulence and sores; in place of his fingers green rags hang, it's his skin; before I put my lorgnette on, I thought it was cloth." Equally typical is the exhibition the narrator witnessed at a hospital near the Nile: "At a sign from the doctor, they all stood up on their beds, unbuttoned the belt of their trousers (it was like a military exercise) and opened their anuses with their fingers to show us their cankers." The reference to the lorgnette is, of course, calculated. It draws attention to the self-conscious voyeurism of the pose and to the provocative coolness the aesthete is able to bring to the horrors of the flesh, "paring his fingernails."

In the end, the scene that presents in its most concentrated form the combination of voyeurism and sadism that invests the *Voyage* concerns a hunting expedition alongside an aqueduct near Cairo. Having finished hunting eagles and kites, the narrator and du Camp start shooting with reckless indifference at the wild dogs that swarm around a kind of open-air slaughterhouse: "The hot sun makes the carcasses stink, the dogs doze as they digest or peacefully rip up the remains." But there is more to this particular day's sport than the simple sadism of hunting.

Beneath the aqueduct, soldiers' whores are plying their trade and Flaubert decides to indulge the hired help: "I treated to Venus our three donkey-drivers for the small sum of 60 paras (one and a half piasters, about six sous)." And the expense was apparently worth it, since it afforded Flaubert a particularly memorable, voyeuristic shock: "I shall never forget the brutal movement of my old donkey-driver as he seized the whore, taking her with his right hand, stroking her breasts with his left, and dragging her away in a single gesture, laughing through his big white teeth, with his little black wooden chibouk slung over his shoulders, and his rags wrapped around the bottom of his diseased legs." This long sentence reads like a peculiarly harsh allegory, a kind of sadistic parody of "Death and the Maiden" that was to recur with the leitmotiv of the blind beggar in *Madame Bovary;* it captures the oppositions of youth and age, female and male, aggression and passivity, sex and death in a single complex image. The observer typically takes his pleasure in witnessing the peculiar ferocity of the sexual assault. In the precision and energy of his writing in such passages, in any case, Flaubert outdoes that literary hero of his youth, Sade himself.

It is, then, no accident if one of the great masters of fictional prose ends his vignette with a resonant reference to poverty and disease. Played out against the particularly sinister Egyptian background referred to, the passage contains in its way the demoralizer's last debunking word on romantic love and the virtues of femininity implied by the tradition of chivalry. This consciously elaborated fantasm of a *Liebestod* is not designed to satisfy the genital drive for heterosexual union that classical psychoanalysis posited as the adult norm; it speaks instead to those component drives which, once they become fixated as perversions, we know as voyeurism and sadism.

There are other episodes in the *Voyage* in which the narrator evokes the startling proximity of eros and death that attracted the Perverse Traveler, episodes in which sex in a cemetery is substituted for sex near a slaughterhouse. At other times still, however, Flaubert's peculiar "necrophilia" has a less lurid, though equally destructive, aspect. It frequently takes the more common form of a desire for extinction of self, or death wish. Thus, the narrator describes enthusiastically on more than one occasion the ecstatic dances of the whirling dervishes. What he finds there is a "volupté mystique," which in the context is also synonymous with *jouissance.*

Finally, the narrator reveals that he, too, was open to that enchantment which European travelers have traditionally associated with the Orient since the pre-romantic period: namely, the enchantment of slow-paced, ritualized movement, of mythic landscapes as old as Homer or the bible, and of the spaciousness and silence of the desert: "that's the true Orient, a melancholy effect that makes you feel sleepy; you sense right away something immense and implacable in the midst of which you are lost." The pleasure for this particular Western traveler is in that loss, in the tranquil submission of self to a force more powerful than that which animates the self-assertive ego. In short, the Middle East caters wonderfully to that *hantise du néant,* or seduction of the void, first celebrated by the romantics. And Flaubert in his travel book showed himself to be peculiarly receptive to such seduction.

. . . . .

Whatever their quarrels with their fatherlands, both Byron and Stendhal remain firm in their commitment to "Western civilization" as embodied in the tradition of Greece, Rome, and Renaissance Italy. Moreover, they both sympathized with the cause of liberal reform and national emancipation in their time. It is characteristic of the attitudes embodied in Flaubert's *Voyage,* on the other hand, that the part which concerns his return journey through Italy is the most perfunctory. The section is limited almost entirely to enumeration and the driest of descriptions of museum artifacts.

In effect, it turns out that Flaubert is . . . [among the earliest of travel writers to] express that central motif of the early-twentieth-century, European avant-garde from *fauvisme* to Futurism and Dada: *delenda est Roma.* In an important sense, Flaubert never outlived the fiercely iconoclastic fantasy of his youth to storm Rome as a barbarian. In the *Voyage,* as elsewhere, the demoralizer's destructive energies take the form of the death wish not simply on the individual level but also on that of Western civilization. Flaubert expresses neither reverence for the past nor faith in the future, which is also a way of saying that he was as contemptuous of traditional Western religion as he was of its substitute in the postrevolutionary, secular age: the politics of emancipation. The brief notation on his first entry into Jerusalem is typical of a generalized apostasy vis-à-vis all that the West has held sacred: "We enter by the gate of Jaffa and I emit a fart beneath it as I cross the threshold, but not on purpose; I was even, in fact, a little angry at the Voltaireanism of my anus." The denial is, of course, undermined by the fact that he chooses to narrate the incident nevertheless.

On the level of belief, the testimony of the *Voyage* is that the only thing left following the death of faith is the pursuit of experience for its own sake and the consequent transformation of life into spectacle. From such a perspective, travel becomes a particularly privileged activity. On foreign territory one is apparently without any responsibilities whatsoever except to the savoring of fresh encounters with the new and, if one is a writer, to the precision of its representation. Where all has become spectacle, one's only commitment is to one's art; the only morality, a morality of composition, perspective and color combinations. The goal of the romantic colorist, in prose as in painting, was to promote powerful, dissonant sensations. And Flaubert found the Middle East peculiarly rich in the raw materials of such a colorist's art. The extraordinary contrasts the region offered between great power and powerlessness, luxury and squalor, refined pleasure and deprivation were central to its appeal for him. That is why poverty, leprosy, prostitution, and death are grist to Flaubert's aesthetic mill, equally as much as landscapes, pyramids, mosques, and ruins. The only thing that shocks the aesthete on his travels is bad taste, and in the Middle East of the nineteenth century that tended to be supplied by fellow tourists from Europe.

On another level, what Flaubert also touches on is the melancholy of travel made manifest in particular in the phenomenon of tourism. That there never was a golden age of travel is confirmed, if confirmation were needed, in Flaubert's comments on the evidence left by his predecessors at certain hallowed sites. The name "Thompson of Sunderland," written in letters three feet high on the base of Pompey's column, is only the most glaring example of the futile gestures made by countless travelers from numerous countries over the centuries to record that they came, saw and, in the eyes of their own narcissistic egos at least, conquered. The effort "to make one's mark" by defacing a monument with one's name is a kind of poor man's claim to fame and immortality. It is also, in a sense, a pastiche of the gesture of those more sophisticated travelers who prefer to record their journey by means of a narrative.

The peculiar form of the anxiety of influence to which the latter are subject is touched on by Flaubert as he surveys the writings on the colossi of Memnon: "Stones that have interested so many, that so many men have come to see, are a pleasure to look at. How many bourgeois eyes have looked up there! Everyone had his little word to say and then left." The pleasure, it seems, is mitigated for the traveling aesthete by the very fact that he risks repeating the absurd gestures of those bourgeois for whom he professed the utmost contempt. The simultaneous fascination and horror Flaubert felt for the cliché and the *idée recue* make him peculiarly sensitive to the risks of falling into similar traps on his own Oriental journey.

It is finally at Baalbek that he succumbs fully, less to that eighteenth-century melancholy of ruins than to the melancholy of tourism of the kind that has become virtually ubiquitous in the late twentieth century. The sight of ancient inscriptions on the gutted temples at Baalbek written over with endless graffiti in English, French, Turkish, and

Arabic, leaves Flaubert profoundly chastened: "This testimony to so many unknown lives, read in silence while the wind blows and all is quiet, has a more chilling effect than the names of the dead on the tombs of a cemetery." The lesson of the world's tourist monuments is not, in the end, one's heroic self-importance at having come so far, but one's insignificance.

In short, whereas the religious pilgrim prostrates himself at a hallowed shrine and happily acknowledges his nothingness in the presence of the divine principle, and whereas the cultural pilgrim is uplifted at the spectacle of artistic greatness, this particular nineteenth-century aesthete on his travels is conscious of nothing so much as his belatedness. Moreover, like the layered graffiti, the travel narrative that will be the final test of his sensibility on tour is also, in its way, a form of "writing over," a redefacing of already defaced monuments in the futile endeavor "to make one's mark." In the resonant silence of Baalbek, Flaubert acknowledges the ultimate nakedness of the void against which no writing is proof.

> Dennis Porter, "The Perverse Traveler: Flaubert in the Orient," in his Haunted Journeys: Desire and Transgression in European Travel Writing, *Princeton University Press, 1991, pp. 164-83.*

NORTH AMERICA

Christopher Mulvey

[*In the following excerpt, Mulvey discusses the popular travel accounts of English and American writers who traveled abroad during the nineteenth century, focusing especially on the expectations and preconceptions that colored each group's view of the other's country.*]

In the nineteenth century, some hundreds of Britons and Americans travelled to each other's country and then published accounts of their journeys in the form of travel books. There are hundreds of English titles and almost as many American. There are more travel accounts in the form of journals and diaries that remained unpublished during the writers' lifetimes but which have been published by descendants and scholars, and there are further accounts to be found in the letters sent home by travellers. These often formed the basis of a travel book; sometimes they are a source of information additional to a travel book; sometimes they are the only record of any kind that the traveller left of his journey. Among the most interesting and complex of these records, it is not surprising that the most prominent are those by men and women otherwise famous as leading literary figures of the day, both English and American. It may well be surprising, however, to discover quite how many famous literary figures did in fact write travel books or leave journals, diaries, or letters as a record of a transatlantic journey.

The traveller, especially the American traveller, might make a deliberate artefact out of the record of his journey. This sometimes involved the consciousness of the writer that he was himself an artist, and the most obvious and interesting instances arose with those travellers who were professional authors. Some presented their material under pseudonyms—Geoffrey Crayon (a name invented for the occasion), Artemus Ward, Petroleum V. Nasby, Mark Twain—but these were not necessarily indications of any greater distance between narrator and author than was the case with writers like Nathaniel Hawthorne and Henry James who did not conceal their identity. The work might in special instances become more of a novel than a travel book, as did Washington Irving's *Bracebridge Hall,* and the peculiar example of *Notions of the Americans,* which purported to be an Englishman's view of America, but it was in fact a creation of James Fenimore Cooper. Similarly, in authors like Dickens, Marryat, Anthony Trollope, Stevenson, and Kipling, the reader encountered a highly organised individuality that might speak intimately or publicly but was at all points recognisable, conveying in the tones of its voice a strong impression of the man that saw, heard, and experienced.

This kind of distinctiveness was in contrast to an unindividualised *persona* cultivated by less imaginatively capable writers. They adopted a voice that was insistent in its self-assurance, unawed by any society that it encountered (whether in Boston or in London), only to be surprised by gross violations of taste, expecting the same standards of its auditors that it set for itself. Despite a wide variety in the social backgrounds of authors, the voice was adopted with great uniformity and by many writers. At its best it reverberated with an almost Augustan wit, taking the traditional stance of the satirist whose moral fervour raised him above those he criticised. This tone of condescension was particularly re-enforced by the Englishman's automatic assumption of superiority to the social values and cultural life of America. The hierarchical attitude, however, could be perceived in American writers also, for America preserved class as a social and cultural formulation long after it had abandoned it as a political and commercial structure. A special modification of the voice was made by those writers, British and American, who saw themselves as men of learning, political scientists, or professional observers. Here some form of scholarly, scientific, or reportorial standard re-enforced, even replaced, the judgement based on taste, gentlemanly instinct, or good breeding.

Travellers are said to be great liars. The prefaces of nineteenth-century travel books abound with noble reasons for crossing the Atlantic though in fact their authors were often motivated by rather meaner considerations. Such discrepancies, however, were not necessarily the result of lies. Washington Irving came to the mouth of the Mersey in 1815 to lend a hand with the Liverpool end of his brothers' hardware business. Fanny Trollope came to the mouth of the Mississippi in 1827 to find a way of supporting husband, self, and children. Both ventures ended in bankruptcy. But *The Sketch-Book of Geoffrey Crayon, Gent.* and *Domestic Manners of the Americans* breathed not a word that might betray the gentility of their authors.

Both writers presented a picture of men, manners, and society as they would have them to be and a picture of themselves as they would have others believe them to be. To do so, they both adopted a social voice that presumed equality with a gentlemanly reader. And why not?

Travellers who wrote travel books crossed the Atlantic for all manner of reasons. They were going to do business, they were accompanying other more wealthy travellers, appearing on stage and taking exhibitions on tour, writing for newspapers, out-manoeuvring copyright pirates, even emigrating. Travellers went simply for holidays (though few admit to no higher purpose), to visit friends and relatives, to recuperate from illnesses. Richard Burton, having just discovered the source of the Nile, took six months off from travelling in Africa to visit the holy city of the Great Salt Lake. J. Bayard Taylor took two years off from the printing trade to go abroad, *"at the cost of only $500, and this sum earned on the road",* to show that the poor as well as the rich man could travel to Europe. All he needed was a knapsack (and strong feet). Higher and lower motives merged.

Men who wrote travel books crossed the Atlantic to teach, to improve, to proselytise, and to reform one another. Frederick Douglass fled America to escape slave takers and to speak out for abolition. William Cobbett fled England to escape the "tyrants" of his native country (and to teach Long Island farmers how to cultivate the rutaba-

Frontispiece to Bayard Taylor's Picturesque Europe, *one of the luxury publications directed to would-be American travelers in the nineteenth century.*

ga). Travellers came to England to establish international peace and travellers came to America to fight civil war. In a class all his own, Robert Louis Stevenson travelled as cheap as he dared—second cabin and emigrant train—from London to Monterey to marry another man's wife. He waited out her divorce on the Californian beaches and took her to honeymoon in the Californian hills. (Beyond a sly pun in its title—*The Amateur Emigrant*—Stevenson's account of his journey made no mention of the woman; *The Silverado Squatters,* his account of the honeymoon, made no mention of the divorce.)

English lecturers went to America for fame and for money. In the letters sent home by Thackeray during his tours of 1852 and 1855 the only topic more frequent than dollars was Dickens. Boz's lecture tour of 1842 set the standard by which not only Thackeray but Charles Kingsley, Oscar Wilde, Matthew Arnold and Edmund Gosse judged themselves. When he was asked by the ladies of Plymouth, Massachusetts for a lock of his hair, Dickens had had to refuse on the grounds that if he were to grant all such requests it were "likely to terminate before long in [his] total baldness." Arnold had no such problems but in return for his lecture fees undertook no less than the civilisation of America. He acknowledged that "our dissenting ministers think themselves in paradise when they visit America," but thought it a very different place himself [Matthew Arnold, *Civilisation in the United States: First and Last Impressions of America,* 1889].

American clergymen went to Europe for rest and recuperation. Should they be so worthy, ministers would find themselves offered a passage to England by a congregation grateful for their labours and eager to reinvigorate their preaching. Duty and pleasure combined nicely here. A published account of the journey seemed only a proper return. Henry Ward Beecher's first tour of Europe in 1850 was made by way of recreation after three energetic years on the platform of the Plymouth Congregational Church in Brooklyn. The English essays in his *Star Papers* were evidence of his renewed spirits. A. Cleveland Coxe, one day to be a bishop, and like Beecher a recuperative clergyman, found his tonic in 1851 by taking possession of England in the name of his Anglican faith, his Saxon race, and his English tongue. Some years before he set sail, he had brought himself nearer to his motherland by abandoning Presbyterianism and changing the spelling of his name, allegedly believing that the addition of an "e" gave it an earlier, more English, form.

Americans of all dispositions made reference to their childhood as they approached and as they first explored England. The sense of impending excitement as a ship closed on the Mersey estuary was always intense, sometimes painful. For Coxe in 1851, the realisation that he would have to exchange the England of fancy for the England of fact was too much and he had had to retire to his stateroom. Even for Henry James, who had, by 1869, been to England many times, the excitement of re-arrival was "almost intolerably strong." The Englishman's arrival at Halifax, Boston, or New York was by no means unexciting. Dickens spoke of his indescribable interest as the "first patches of American soil peeped like molehills from the green sea," but there is no record of an Englishman's being overcome. The Englishman was more likely to speak of his or his reader's ignorance of America than to indulge childhood reminiscence. When Fanny Trollope's eldest sons had finished their schooling at Harrow and joined her to help run the bazaar she had set up in Cincinnati, she found them as knowledgeable about America as they were about Fairyland. To dispel this kind of ignorance and to make the two peoples better known to each other were the declared aims of many English travel books.

The Englishman, imaginative or otherwise, was turned into something of a fact-finder when he landed in America. Whether what he found were facts or fictions, polemics took hold of him and put a curb on the romantic impulse. The Englishman's preconceptions about America were strong but they were not deep. They were not usually positive nor were they usually precise. Henry James said that the American mind had a "latent preparedness" for English life. The reverse held true for the English mind and American life. There were no rooted childhood ties. Few had been fed tales of America by their mothers though some may have heard adventure stories from their fathers. John Lambert, Charles Kingsley, and Robert Louis Stevenson had had boyhood romances with the excitements of pioneer danger and the glories of Indian war. Arthur Hugh Clough had actually spent part of his childhood in Charleston but this seemed to have left no sentimental ties whatsoever. Because of England's imperial power, because of the actual wars of 1776 and 1812, and because of the recurrent threats of war until as late as 1865 (indeed, rumours of war occured as late as 1898), attitudes could be distinctly hostile. War and the rumour of war made the American traveller unhappy; war and the rumour of war made the English traveller indignant. The American may have had all kinds of artificial and fanciful notions about England before he arrived, but as often as not England proved to be what he expected it to be. With all the information available to the American about England and Europe and the cultural and social value attached to this knowledge by other Americans, it was likely that the American had a more lively and more accurate perception of England than the Englishman had of America. The Englishman had usually read little about the United States and came from a society that prided itself, if anything, on its ignorance of its ex-colony. When the American arrived in England, his emotional needs conspired to make him feel an identity with what he saw. The American's preconceptions became accurate because he wanted them to have been accurate.

The Englishman was, then, more bewildered by America than the American by England. The Englishman's latent unpreparedness began to show itself as soon as he landed. He had known it was a rude country but his body felt the affront of hard roads, benches, and beds with a force that intellectual anticipation did little to mollify. The Englishman knew he had come to and had known he was going to a democracy but his dignity felt the affront of bold coachmen, landlords, and steamship captains with a misery that intellectual anticipation did little to assuage. All these men addressed him as "Sir", but it was a democratic "Sir" from men who believed themselves to be his equal, not a reverential "Sir" from men who knew themselves to be his inferior. (Caught between admiration for self-improvement and anger at bad manners, Anthony Trollope had wanted to weep.) So it was with spitting, and smoking, and sprawling. It was much harder to go from a country that did not spit to one that did than *vice versa.*

The Englishman in America was on the look out for England. When he found a deferential servant, he recorded it as a sign of improvement; when he found a rude one, he recorded it as a sign of progressive decay. This attitude led to stress. An American did not look for America in England; he (like the Englishman) was looking for England, and was more likely to find it. With his ill-conceived images of America, the Englishman did not know what he was looking for and this led from stress to boredom, to Matthew Arnold's complaint that America was not "interesting," that American life lacked "savour." With no perceptual scheme ready to receive and to organise impressions, the English suffered from a kind of perceptual impoverishment that was quite the reverse of the enriched, imaginatively organised vision that the American brought to his looking at England.

Those who came to the American landscape with a professional purpose—the army officer, the botanist, the geologist, the hunter, the illustrator—did not complain of that landscape's lack of interest. But the American wilderness filled most other travellers with a sense of threat and oppression. It contrasted so absolutely with the garden-like appearance of England that so impressed American travellers. A repeated source of complaint from the English traveller was the condition of American farms and the absence of any garden around the American home. The ragged fences, tree-stumped fields, and unkempt property made the Englishman miserable.

The most positive emotional response of the English traveller faced with the American landscape was awe in the presence of the sublime—an element for which the American looked in vain in the English landscape. The Hudson River and its great glacial valley through the Catskills never failed to excite an interested response. It became an occasion for a set piece in landscape description and always evoked comparison with the Rhine Valley or the Scottish Highlands. A European model was available as an aid and response was immediate. A greater challenge was set by Niagara Falls. Here the travellers found no European equivalent. But this did not make them turn from the sight. Niagara Falls was a great stimulant to the Romantic imagination; it provided an example of divine sublimity found elsewhere only in the sea. It became a crucial test of the sensibility of writer and reader. Both felt relief when this portion of the journal or travel book had been written up. But the trial of sensibility set by the Mississippi River proved too much. With the Hudson, the travellers felt comfortable; with Niagara, they felt tested; with the Mississippi, they felt overcome. Many more turned from it with disgust and anxiety than turned to it with reverence and awe. The river, still more the valley, was too huge for Romantic reverie. Only in its upper reaches where the river is more "European" did the Mississippi excite the pleasant responses triggered so readily by the Hudson.

The Mississippi, like the forest at the beginning of the century and the prairie in the middle, overwhelmed most travellers, leaving them depressed and exhausted by what they could *not* see as much as by what they could see. Wordsworth had set no pattern for response to Nature on this scale.

But the Americans had found a way and some Englishmen could follow them. Puritan iconography had provided a pattern for response to natural phenomena too great to be seen, too great for sensual apprehension. A universal, cosmological scheme focused upon America, represented by the Great Forest, the Great Valley, or the Great Prairie, could generate a religious and millennial awe as it excited a personal and patriotic identity. The corresponding outflow of emotion could give an energising value to the very boundlessness of the landscape and at the same time aggrandise the viewer with a daemonic activity. The landscape did not, then, diminish the viewer into a depressive passivity.

The English obviously had real difficulties adapting to this millennial and patriotic pattern. It was not their religion and it was not their country. The resistance to all the elements in this emotional mix was especially marked in the English reaction to 4 July rhetoric. Most agreed with William Russell of *The Times*. He described the holiday as an occasion when the nation became as drunk on words as on liquor. This annual, national, and colossal bacchanalia gave pyrotechnic release to emotions that the English found difficult enough to tolerate in the modest, quotidian form of the American's boast that his was a great country. Englishmen found 4 July celebrations ludicrously disproportionate. They could allow themselves no part in the emotions released and judged those emotions to be an over-reaction, a typical manifestation of the superficial excitability of the Americans, to which many English travellers objected.

But the English worshipped the same God and were members of the same race, and a diffused version of the American topological emotion was possible. It grew increasingly more so as the two peoples admitted and permitted closer identity towards the end of the century. The more that the English were able to acknowledge the Americans as partners, or at least potential partners, in the business of world shaping and world power, the more the English could begin to rejoice in the notion of the resources and prospects of the Mississippi Valley. Some English travellers fastened on to the numerical expression of the American religious and patriotic vision. Romantic nature took on a statistical appearance. With this statistical Romanticism, the willing Englishman was able to project himself across the void between the Alleghenies and the Rockies and join in the hymn of praise to Numbers, the number of acres to be filled and the number of people that would be called forth and was being called forth to fill them.

But numbers and boundlessness continued to appal the Englishman and he often gave the impression that he had crossed the Atlantic to confront his fears; the American often gave the impression that he had crossed the Atlantic to take possession of things long dreamt about. It was the strong conviction of the American who loved England to believe that he loved it more than did Englishmen. "To enjoy England one must be an American and a hearty and earnest member of the Anglican Church" [declared Arthur Cleveland Coxe in *Impressions of England; or Sketches of English Scenery and Society,* 1863]. And if, like the Reverend Coxe, you were so lucky, you need ask permission of no Englishman to walk the land, enjoying all that was best while the Englishman filled his head with details of trade and taxes. Coxe could put the land of his forefathers to better use than that. He had not gone to England to watch a people engaged in a political process but to gaze at a land that was the stuff of history. The English could be wished elsewhere and the imagination could be allowed to take flight. America without people would be a wilderness; England without people might be a paradise.

The American landing in nineteenth-century England was invariably impressed by the tame quality of the landscape. He began to see England as a series of gardens revealing a perfection of domesticity from the small plots of the cottager to the great grounds of Blenheim Palace. For Hawthorne and for James, the cathedral close added a spiritual to a vegetative peace to make paradisal spots. In London itself, the gardens of the Inns of Court, the Royal Parks, and of individual homes became oases, repose in pandemonium. They spoke to the American like Richard Rush, Washington Irving, James Russell Lowell, of an English life that had its roots in the country and not in the city. In this gentle landscape there was no wilderness and no sublimity. The American found neither in the Lake District or in Wales. Some few found both in Scotland, but only the sea itself could remind them of the immense wilderness they had left at home. The great wealth of England (though anticipated) took traveller after traveller by surprise, but a world of desolation—in itself a wilderness—was found by these same travellers in the blasted industrial landscape and the desperate populations of the great cities.

The English landscape was for all Americans interesting because of its variety and associations. Two great views, that from Richmond Hill and that from Warwick Castle, contained every kind of association, and called upon each traveller to test to the limits his expressive power. Above all other kinds, literary memories enhanced a view for the American traveller and the prospect of Richmond and the view from Warwick looked upon the valleys of two rivers, the Thames and the Avon, that contained more literary reference for the speaker of English than all other rivers in the world. Their literary relationship to the landscape of England was the source of the most frequent and deepfelt satisfactions for these American men and women.

This kind of response might be expected from a group of travellers among whom were so many professional writers. This, of course, accounted for the fact that among these particular travellers nearly half met and talked with professional English writers. They made acquaintance with Scott, Wordsworth, Coleridge, Southey, Byron, Hazlitt, Lamb, Landor, Campbell, Moore, Hunt and De Quincey; with Sydney Smith, Francis Jeffrey, Lockhart, Brougham, Macaulay, and Harriet Martineau; with Tennyson, the Brownings, and Matthew Arnold; with Newman, Mill, Ruskin, and Carlyle; with Dickens, Disraeli, Bulwer Lytton, Thackeray, Trollope, George Eliot, Meredith, Stevenson, and Hardy; with Swinburne, Rossetti, Morris, Patmore, Wilde, and Yeats. Meeting these writers in their homes and at meals, going for walks and taking holidays with them, the American traveller experienced a special instance of the ideal becoming real—the results were sometimes amusing, sometimes moving, always intense.

But meeting the living poets and writers of England in England was only one way of establishing the relationship of literature and landscape. More important, and a way open to all travellers, obscure as well as distinguished, was to visit those houses and towns made sacred as the birthplaces and homes of dead writers. The journey that Hawthorne said all Americans had to make was to Stratford, and he, like others, made it. The journey to Stratford became for many Americans a matter not simply of personal pleasure but of cultural pilgrimage and something more than that yet, an occasion of patriotic duty, an insistence that this poet was as much America's as he was England's. Shakespeare and Stratford were the most potent combination of place and writer, but it was a formula that was repeated in journey after journey throughout England. A third way of realising the relationship of literature and landscape was achieved by visitation to those places and buildings that figured in poem, play, and novel and were the scenes of great moments in literature themselves. The journey to Kenilworth was undertaken not to see a place where the acts of history had really happened long ago but to see a place where the deeds of fancy were fictionally recurring forever.

The experience of the literature that he counted his own shaped the search of the American traveller for the spot "most sacred" in his ancestral soil. The time-and-space journey became a mythological and psychic one in which the traveller might reconstruct his childhood of tales, books, pictures, legends, and dreams. A passionate moment when England might most be England was continuously sought. The travellers anticipated what Henry James called the "rare emotion" when they might "feel England." They expected it at landfall, at landing, at the first sight of an ancient city. Two places above all others inspired a sense that the traveller had finally reached his goal—Poets' Corner in Westminster Abbey and a narrow triangle of Warwickshire bounded by Kenilworth, Warwick, and Stratford. This might be midmost England.

In their moments of enriched perception, the travellers saw far more than was presented to the senses; what they saw was shaped by their deepest needs and values. It was the repeated experience of American travellers to feel that all they were now seeing for the first time they had already seen before. Travellers most susceptible to the "rare emotion" were those who felt a strong religious identity with England, those who felt a strong racial identity with England, those whose parents or grandparents had been born in England, those who were willing to admit the social superiority of the English and were eager to gain acceptance among them. The travellers predisposed to appreciate what they saw intensified experience by selective perception. The American in England in his moment of excitation simply did not see what would destroy his preconceived image, and cause him distress. The visual ugliness of industrialisation, urban squalor, and rural degeneration were not permitted to impose upon the "rare emotion," though the traveller might be very distressed by these things in more sober moments. The perceptual defence gave no meaning to what was offensive and the traveller took only limited notice of it.

The picture of England created by the sentimental American traveller was the reverse of Matthew Arnold's description of America. For Arnold, America was England minus its castles, churches, cathedrals, and palaces. America, that is, was a place of industry, railroads, new towns, and huge populations. For the sentimental traveller, England was exclusively the England of castles, churches, cathedrals, and palaces. He filtered out of his vision industry, railways, new towns, and did his best to overlook the population. Perceived England was England minus America. The image of England that the traveller had brought from America was little modified by any contradictions that experience presented, whereas every castle or cathedral reinforced preconception. From the sketchiest outline of his image of England, the traveller could make up his reality. His consciousness was poised to seize upon and to enjoy the prize and so could make all it needed out of a ruin or a cottage garden. The more highly susceptible, like Washington Irving, Harriet Beecher Stowe, or A. Cleveland Coxe, actually peopled their scenes with visionary figures from history and literature. Henry James spoke of the landscapes as compositions and undertook to rearrange them with strokes of his pen.

Travellers who had good reason to be hostile to the United States but had diminished racial ties with England—escaped slaves like Frederick Douglass and William Wells Brown—were quite capable of the sentimental impulse that was usually found in those who identified strongly with England. This suggested that the emotional openness to "England" involved some rejection of "America." Correspondingly those American travellers who had identified themselves very closely with America or who had special cause to dislike England vigorously resisted the sentimental impulse. (The same traveller, however, might be capable of both sets of emotions at different times and in different moods.) The classically republican figures of the early nineteenth century, men like William Austin and James Fenimore Cooper, countered any impulse to the sentimental by their stern disapproval of monarchical rule and aristocratic luxury (plus their unremitting anxiety that the English might show them condescension). These postures hardly outlived the Jacksonian Republic but another source of resistance to sentimentality was found in the disposition of the intellectuals of the mid and later nineteenth century. The historian John Motley was quite unsentimental about historical evidence; Henry Adams, the writer of *The Education,* was severe on Henry Adams, the subject of *The Education,* for his lapses into the softer mood; Charles Eliot Norton showed tense caution in the face of temptation, and William James showed disdain for his brother's enthusiasm. Any American like Horace Greeley, David Locke, or Henry James's sister, Alice, who felt sympathy for the Irish was more likely to be made angry than to be seduced by the "English effects." This did not, however, preclude fascination by them.

The sentimental American could and did dream about an England that he had all to himself, or at least one that he shared with the men and women of history and literature only; the Englishmen did not indulge dreams of solitary possession of America. (With the exception of a few like Richard Burton or Laurence Oliphant, most English travellers were not explorers, and were there no whitemen in America, they would not have gone there.) Moreover, the English spent a good deal of their time justifying to their readers the fact that they were burdening them with an account of a journey that they were not always certain themselves had a purpose beyond curiosity. The American seldom questioned why he had gone to Europe, did not expect his readers to do so, and could, when he needed to, give simple, lofty, and convincing arguments in his own support. The American did however apologise to the reader for doing once again what so many had done before. The great number of travel accounts of Europe that had already been published were at once an inducement and a deterrent.

All travel writers who thought of themselves as such suffered from a kind of generic insecurity. This made them turn on their craft, on themselves, or on their readers at the least provocation. Richard Burton protested that he had no less right to go into the details of "his bed, his meat, and his drink" than had the novelist "to elaborate, in the 'domestic epic,' the most trivial scenes of household routine." To strengthen his case, Burton reminded his readers that Dr Johnson himself had written a travel book. The Lady Emmeline Stuart Wortley explained that she had only resorted to publication at the earnest entreaties of friends to whose "better judgement" she felt bound to defer. Isabella Bird apparently found herself in the same dilemma, and Mrs Sarah Maury published only because of a promise impulsively given to Mr (later President) Buchanan of Washington. Thomas Hamilton, officer and gentleman, published a travel book only because the political exigence of the times—the Reformed Parliament—demanded that the English be made aware of the outcome of popular government. Protestations of this kind were so frequent that they became conventional, like those of novelists in the previous century. (In Sarah Maury's case though, there was a reason to take her literally. *An Englishwoman in America* was so misshapen and chaotic that some apology to the reader was in order.)

Though American authors were more confident about the overall justification of their journeys, they could become as diffident as the English about the business of publication. Professor Benjamin Silliman, like Lady Emmeline and Miss Bird, explained himself by appeal to the importunities of friends. Washington Irving told the readers of the revised edition of *The Sketch-Book* that his reluctance to publish had extended only to Great Britain; he had believed his subject one of interest to Americans alone. He had at the same time been "distressed by the severity with which American productions had been treated by the British press." (He wept when he learnt that his was the first

to be treated kindly.) The Reverend John Freeman Clarke justified his contribution to a glutted market by the excuse that "every new pair of eyes sees something new" and he liked to think that his friends and acquaintances would be glad to know how Europe affected his mind. Since his congregation paid for his trip, he might well have been right. It was refreshing to learn that one travel book at least was "not issued in compliance with any demand for it . . . The volume is a purely mercantile speculation, which may or may not be successful." Its author, David Locke, obviously felt that by 1881 some debunking of the reluctant travel writer was in order.

In a highly competitive market and with an insecure literary identity, it was not surprising that the most frequent object of attack was other authors. William Austin, an American resident in London at the beginning of the nineteenth century, cursed the whole tribe indiscriminately: "Of two men," he said, "in all respects equal, one of whom is not an author, I prefer the company of him who has not written a book." This may have been a paradoxical way of establishing Austin's own social standing. Other travellers were more selective and singled out their own kind for special insult. Near the end of her lively, lengthy, and highly unreliable book, *The Englishwoman in America* (1854), Isabella Bird wrote that "it has been truly observed that a reliable book on the United States yet remains to be written." Her contribution did not alter the situation, but writing it seemed to have made her alive to the requirements of one who would do the job properly. He must not, she said, be a tourist or a temporary resident; he must examine every state for years; he must be a discriminating student of republican politics and racial groups; not least, he must be able to distinguish the real from the false.

Isabella Bird's specification of such demanding qualifications reflected her own apprehensions that her readers would see that she fell very short of fulfilling them. Like others, she anticipated criticism of her craft by making the criticism herself. Travel writers feared that travel writing was socially inferior to other occupations. It was too close to a trade, too easily identified with commercialised forms of writing like journalism—and indeed many travel writers, both English and American, were journalists. Travel writers feared that travel writing was artistically inferior to other genres. It was not given serious consideration by literary critics. Travel writers feared that travel writing was academically inferior to other sciences. It was not clearly an art or a science. It could be either, which was suspicious; it was frequently neither, which was shameful. The self-defensive postures adopted in prefaces and introductions, in first and last chapters, tried to counter charges that were anticipated on all these grounds. Like the novelists of a previous age, the travel writers needed to justify themselves to a silent but possibly accusing readership.

The hostility of travel writers to their craft and to each other was an expression of self-contempt, and this dislike of their own reflection was pronounced in the travellers' reactions to other travellers whom they found touring the country innocent of the ambition of writing a travel book perhaps, but otherwise not unlike the travel writers themselves. Richard Burton, English gentleman, traveller, and sportsman took special exception to other English gentle-men-traveller-sportsmen that he ran into in America. In New York, Burton was disgusted to find, there were so many that the Americans had "learned to look upon this Albionic eccentricity as 'the thing.' " Rudyard Kipling had similar reactions. In Montana, he met up with "a young English idiot . . . knocking about inside his high collars, attended by his valet." When the idiot Englishman began to criticise America and Americans, Kipling rushed to their defence: "Now that man was a barbarian (I took occasion to tell him so.)" Up to this point in his narrative, *From Sea to Sea* [1899], Kipling had been cheerfully slang-ing everything from Boss Buckley in San Francisco to Old Faithful in Yellowstone.

The response of American travel writers to Americans in England was very similar to that of their English counter-parts. Henry James was one of the few travel writers who had the self-confidence to identify himself with the sorry being, the tourist. Occasionally in *English Hours,* James spoke of the "American tourist" as if both he and the read-er might be such a one. The device had curious effects of irony. Applied to others the term "tourist" could be nasty, and it was used by most travel writers in the nineteenth century to separate the serious traveller from the frivolous and the serious writer from the superficial. Democratic manners did not allow the American to criticise his fellow countrymen with the condescension that came so easily to Englishmen, and American writers who were living in En-gland became sensitive not only to the behaviour of tour-ists but to their own reaction to that behaviour.

James subtly insulted and slyly appeased his American readership by saying in one of his *Transatlantic Sketches* (later to be republished as one of the *English Hours*) that "Haddon Hall lies among the Derbyshire Hills, in a region infested, I was about to write, by Americans." Bret Harte wrote to an English friend that he found Henry James, "nervous, in a nice, ladylike way, at the spectacle" of the unconventional behaviour of Americans abroad, but Harte had not been in Europe long himself then. Three years later, in 1882, he had had enough. He wrote sorrow-fully to his wife that "every American who comes to En-gland helps to swell the inordinate conceit of the English." A few years earlier, a junior member of the American Le-gation in London, had published an essay entitled, "Americans Abroad." He pointed to those things that Americans might and might not do to avoid ridicule when they were in Europe. It was painfully clear that the Ameri-can-in-residence suffered more than the American-on-vacation from this ridicule.

A painful sense of self-identity marked these encounters with compatriots in foreign lands. The hostility of the traveller to his own kind was to some extent an expression of a curiously displaced sense of territoriality that over-took men outside their own country. This arose in large part from the traveller's conviction that he *understood.* The tourist was, by contrast, an "idiot." The traveller saw into things. He could distinguish between the real and the false. He might criticise, or praise; others might not. If the traveller could establish the worthlessness of the tourist's

response, he could confirm the value of his own; if that traveller wrote a book about his journey, he could by the same show of contempt for the tourist increase his, the writer's, stature in his readers' eyes.

There was a correspondence here between authenticity of statement and authenticity of feeling. The English travel writer was preoccupied with the first; the American with the second. English travel literature was primarily direct-ed at the intellect and the political imagination. American travel literature was primarily concerned with the sensibil-ity and the cultural memory. The American travel book was likely to be, at its best, intense where the English was, at its best, comprehensive. Periodically the English pro-duced a work of great scale and reach, minute in its de-scription and lofty in its conception, attempting to match its continental subject. The grand ambition of this litera-ture was "the aim of portraying the whole political system of the country in its practice as well as its theory"—the aim that James Bryce set himself in *The American Com-monwealth.* The result was a book that created widespread admiration and debate on both sides of the Atlantic. Para-doxically, the paradigm was the work of a foreigner to both lands, Alexis de Tocqueville. The great studies of the American people made by Harriet Martineau, Alexander Mackay, and James Bryce must be judged against the achievement of *Democracy in America.*

The British went to America as to a laboratory in which democracy was under investigation; the Americans went to England in a different frame of mind. The greatest studies of England were done not by men of theory but by men of feeling, by men like Ralph Waldo Emerson, Na-thaniel Hawthorne, and Henry James. At an intellectual and spiritual level, two great and complementary drives impelled one group of writers east and one group west. Travellers repeatedly made the point that to go to Ameri-ca was to look at a Europe of the future. It is, wrote An-thony Trollope, "the best means of prophesying, if I may say so, what the world will next be, and what we will next do." Travellers repeatedly made the point that to go to Eu-rope was to look at a world of the past. "My ancestors left England in 1635," wrote Nathaniel Hawthorne, "I return in 1853. I feel sometimes as if I myself had been absent these two hundred and eighteen years." Even if he did get the date wrong (his ancestors left in 1630), the point was made. There was a time dimension to these space journeys.

Christopher Mulvey, "Transatlantic Eyes," in his Anglo-American Landscapes: A Study of Nineteenth-Century Anglo-American Travel Literature, *Cambridge University Press, 1983, pp. 3-25.*

Janet Giltrow

[*In the following excerpt, Giltrow addresses the social es-trangement that prompts many travelers to write letters, diaries, and travel narratives, citing the experiences of two well-known English women travelers to North America.*]

Paradoxical as it might sound, the cause of nationalism is often best furthered through "international" means. Thus one of the best ways of highlighting what is distinctly Canadian in a given Canadian literary work is to examine it in the context of the genre to which it belongs and to contrast it with other works of its kind written by non-Canadians. Employing such an approach, I will in this essay attempt to come to terms with a work which is regarded as central to the Canadian literary heritage: Susanna Moodie's *Roughing It in the Bush* (1852). After delineating the major features of travel narrative, I will then go on to consider how Moodie's work differs from a comparable travel narrative by Frances Trollope, *Domestic Manners of the Americans* (1832).

Travel narrative comes about as a result of the writer's separation from his cultural habitat and his term abroad in a place where he is an alien and a stranger. On his return home, the narrator addresses the community of which he is a member on the subject of places and societies foreign to him and his audience, comparing what he found abroad with what he had known at home. His narration is the verbal signal of his reincorporation into his native mileu; it repairs the breach which occurs when one group member is estranged from his community, and the publication of details of the writer's whereabouts during his absence compensates for the alienation he has experienced.

Collections of letters-home are the mode of travel commentary which most clearly demonstrate the social function of the genre. Letters reserve the absentee's place at home, simulating the face-to-face connections that have been temporarily ruptured. As they reconstruct the writer's alien experience, they reintroduce him into the familiar world he left behind. Many travel books are cast in the form of a series of letters to actual or fictive recipients. Other travel books are logs or journals composed with minute regularity for the benefit of home readers. In travel narrative where these structures are not explicit—where the chapter or the sketch rather than the letter or the day is the organizational unit of prose—exposition nevertheless performs the same rhetorical purpose of accounting for the writer's absence.

While the traveler is abroad, his accustomed social relationships are interrupted. To replenish this void, he may resort to letter-writing, to journalizing, or, ambitiously, to narration. Written language then stands in for every other form of social relatedness. Cut off from this supportive network of connections he is used to at home, the traveler is on his own—except for this connecting verbal strand. Often, the foreign community will not recognize his social status: his cultural assets are discounted, his idiom misunderstood, his identity mistaken. To counteract feelings of anonymity and alienation, the travel narrator can reassure himself of his continued membership in the community he left behind by becoming very pronounced indeed in his expression of native cultural attitudes and habits. Away from home, we perhaps most emphatically declare our national provenance and identity.

The travel narrator is alone, detached from the scenes he describes and unassimilated by the foreign community. At their most extreme, the conditions of travel lead to social disorientation, anomie, feelings of being dépaysé. But the traveler's isolation has a counterpoise in the affinity he feels with the culture he addresses—an affinity amounting sometimes to homesickness. Even at the most remote quarters of the earth, home exerts an irresistible attraction and travel narrative advances toward a denouement of homecoming. Having embarked, some travelers and travel writers never get home again. Nevertheless, the idea of getting home continues to structure and inspire narrative. In its circularity—its obedience to the round-trip—travel narrative differs from literature posed on a quest theme, for its goal is its point of departure. When the one-way journey of permanent emigration is the actual experience of the writer, but round-trip travel remains his ideal of a due course, his consequent art is often poignant with disappointment and unresolvable alienation.

Frances Trollope's *Domestic Manners of the Americans* is clearly a travel book: it begins with the writer's embarkation from England; it includes large, discursive, informational units comparing life in the New World to life in the Old; it concludes with the writer's departure from the foreign scene. Susanna Moodie's *Roughing It in the Bush* also begins with her departure from home; it includes substantial information on Canadian life, organized for the benefit of European readers. In contrast to Trollope, however, Moodie never made the return trip: her book ends with the family's move from the bush to Belleville, which was a more congenial site but still no asylum on this cheerless continent. But although Moodie's book thus fails to conform to the classic structure of the genre, *Roughing It* is a travel book and the generic values of the text are those of travel narrative. In her rhetorical stance, Moodie is a travel writer; in Canada, she is a watchful visitor—a tourist and sightseer—and her observations are directed toward a European audience.

She arrives in the New World with a ready command of the expressive sentiments of nature description, bringing with her a diction and perspective in tune with the literary habits of eighteenth- and nineteenth-century Grand Tourists. At Québec, the sublimities she witnesses overwhelm her: "The mellow and serene glow of the autumnal day harmonized perfectly with the solemn grandeur of the scene around me, and sank so silently and deeply into my soul, that my spirit fell prostrate before it, and I melted involuntarily into tears. . . . my soul at that moment was alone with God."

Moodie's pious pleasure in landscape does not easily anticipate her own incorporation into the scene. In contrast, Catharine Parr Traill's more analytic observations in *The Backwoods of Canada* (1836) do look forward to settling down. Where Traill's prose stops at small particulars, Moodie's rides on, along an abstract plane of diffuse enthusiasm. Her high excitement at panoramic vistas and her neglect of concrete details belong to genteel sightseeing—and a quick, unimplicating view of foreign sites.

The ruling conflict in *Roughing It* lies between this travel esthetic and the settler's destiny. In this book and its sequel, *Life in the Clearings,* it seems that Moodie never learned, temperamentally, that the journey was done and travel concluded. She expects, at least unconsciously, that there has been some mistake and that she must finally turn back and resume her route. Obviously, she was pinioned

Thomas Cole's View from Mount Holyoke, Northampton, Massachusetts, after a Thunderstorm (The Oxbow). *Oil on canvas, 1836.*

by manifest evidence to the contrary, and the distance between these two poles of mind—the imagination of travel and the realization of stasis—is sometimes resolved in *Roughing It* by the idea of death. Morbidity alleviates the emotional stress of homesickness by suggesting a mystic return-trip, a homing of the spirit to an earthly paradise. Thus Moodie addresses "dear, dear England": "Oh that I might be permitted to return and die upon your wave-encircled shores, and rest my weary head and heart beneath your daisy-covered sod at last!" After a residence of nearly twenty years in Canada, Moodie uses the exclamatory present tense to express the anguish and helplessness of a newcomer.

Her reflections on letters from home, and on the gradual diminishment of their numbers, suggest that for a long while she did not believe she was here to stay: "After seven years' exile, the hope of return grows feeble, the means are still less in our power, and our friends give up all hope of our return; their letters grow fewer and colder. . . . Double those years, and it is as if the grave had closed over you, and the hearts that once knew and loved you know you no more."

The "hope of return" is a durable one, on both sides of the breach, but its dissolution is finally inevitable, and emigration is a type of death for the settler. Return and home-

coming are privileges of the traveler but not of the emigrant, and in Moodie's view the anticipation of homecoming is the basis for communication between the New World and the Old. To give up hope of return is to suffer the exchange of letters to dwindle and end: a grievous silence marks the irrevocable separation. Communication from the New World to the Old sustains the emigrant in her foreign exile, and maintains her attachment, however attenuated or unrealistic, to the society where she is "known" and from which she derives her identity. The interruption of this vital communication cuts a life-line and sentences the settler to fatal anonymity: "it is as if the grave had closed over you, and the hearts that once knew and loved you know you no more." If we can see this connecting, epistolary current as a survival mechanism, we can see the importance of the larger verbal enterprise— *Roughing It* or *Life in the Clearings*—in maintaining overseas connections. That "hope of return" may disappear in reality, but it can be renewed rhetorically by a literary communication with an Old World audience. By taking up travel narrative, Moodie revives the conceit of travel.

In dispatching a successful communication to English readers, the writer cultivates her original cultural and social values, and resists the New World attitudes which might dispossess her of these imported assets. Only a peculiar strength of mind can assure the emigrant's successful resistance. In her introduction to *Roughing It,* Moodie describes the determination with which the settlers depart: "they gird up the loins of the mind, and arm themselves with fortitude to meet and dare the heart-breaking conflict." Refusing to capitulate to Canadian society, the displaced Englishwoman internalizes all those native institutions which had once supported her. She thus remains a traveler, never adopting the ways of the foreign place.

But this is only one view of the "heart-breaking conflict." There are alternatives to it which permit the immobilized traveler some relief from traumatic restlessness and death-wishing. Moodie suggests that the settler give up making comparisons between the New World and the Old, and get rid of one aspect of the traveler's mentality: "But, oh! beware of drawing disparaging contrasts between the colony and its illustrious parent." With this warning she temporarily modifies her rhetorical stance to address "British mothers of Canadian sons" and instruct them in the process of settling down and learning to love Canada. Although Moodie is herself never innocent of suggesting contrasts which disparage the colony, she does at least reach a position where she no longer wants to die. Expressions of Canadian nationalism help her a little in this, but much more helpful and vivifying is her satire. Her comic vision effaces some of her morbidity, but without rupturing her essential connection with her English audience. The laugh is on the North American, even when Moodie is the apparent victim of the incidents she reports. The objects of her wit are patently too ignorant and morally inexperienced to see the joke, which is told for the entertainment of a European reader who shares her sense of humor.

In *Roughing It in the Bush* life is most hilarious when it is most dreadful. At Cobourg the Moodies find themselves in an insanely inhospitable neighborhood. Moodie is surrounded by unregenerate "savages"—Yankee squatters who harass her with outrageous rudeness. So exaggerated are these characters in their outlandish greed and unscrupulousness that the Cobourg episodes create a lunatic, lawless world at the center of which is the sane, astonished Moodie. She is culturally and economically disoriented; all social and moral principles are inverted in an antic parody of the life she has known. As she was respected and regarded in England, here she is reviled and loathed. In an alien land where she is "the stranger whom they hated and despised," she is powerless to alter her circumstances, and can only laugh and submit. Rebuke is futile in this desert of "ignorance and sin" where the moral voice echoes emptily. So Susanna Moodie learns to be quiet at Cobourg but vociferous in her literary life. Particularly vexing to her is the local practice of addressing genteel settlers as "man" and "woman," and "bare-legged Irish servants" as "mem" and " 'sir,' " but she comes to see it philosophically: "it is very irksome until you think more deeply upon it; and then it serves to amuse rather than irritate." Reproach is profitless; amusement at least produces a humorous critique of a barbarous custom when she does have a chance to speak out and be heard.

Moodie's comedy is social comedy, arising from the serious travel issue of social insubordination and disorientation. Comedy defends the insulted immigrant and her of-

fended values by ridiculing the hostile society which discounts her. Without the perpetual comparison of the New World to the Old there would be no joke, for the fun lies in the application of a superior intelligence which knows both the true shape of society and its ludicrous mutation in Upper Canada. The narrative voice of *Life in the Clearings* speaks, for the most part, in this knowing, wry tone.

Moodie wrote *Life in the Clearings* in 1852, when she had been in Canada twenty years, most of which she had spent not in the bush but at Belleville. Although the occasion of *Clearings* is a pleasure trip to Niagara, much more of the narrative focuses on Belleville, Moodie's home, than on sights *en route.* Belleville, in spite of her long residence there, is as curious and foreign a phenomenon as the less familiar scenes encountered along the way.

In *Life in the Clearings* Moodie is especially concerned, as many European travelers in North America were, with analysis of class and of distribution of power and status in this new society. She identifies the materialism of colonial culture as the most influential factor in the corruption of traditional values, and she complains that the "educated man" belongs to a socially disenfranchised minority in the colony. But Moodie is convinced that a universal cultural hierarchy underlies even the most adverse conditions: "There is no mistaking the superiority that mental cultivation bestows," even when the local economic structure promotes illiterate, unrefined citizens.

Armed with this conviction, Moodie can withstand even the most blatant disparagements conferred on a woman of letters by an illiterate society: "The idea that some country people form of an author is highly amusing. One of my boys was tauntingly told by another lad at school, 'that his ma' said that Mrs. M— invented lies and got money for them.' This was her estimation of works of mere fiction."

But, even if she can shrug off such taunts, Moodie's art cannot address such a population and must revert to an audience which shares her own idea of literature and her own vision of society. Fortunately, she has recourse to another public.

Other authors in Moodie's Canada are less fortunate. For want of sympathy, and for want of membership in a cultural community, some writers are driven to despair, drink and suicide. She tells of a talented but unappreciated poet whose cultural alienation moved him to retire to a wilderness hut and there, with a like-minded companion, drink himself to death. With the artist's physical as well as psychological survival at issue, Moodie chooses to ignore the philistine and materialistic Canadians and go abroad for her audience.

The travel structure of *Life in the Clearings* permits a type of social satire which expresses its author's estrangement from the country through which she journeys and from the community where she resides. When she attends the performance of an itinerant circus, in her own town, she goes to watch not the show but the audience: "Persons of all ranks are there; and the variety of faces and characters that nature exhibits gratis are far more interesting to watch than the feats of the athletes." Moodie is an unimplicated sightseer, observing the exotic assortment of curiosities which comprises Upper Canadian society, and her narrative form is so elastic as to accommodate the social observations of other, similarly detached reporters. These reporters are outsiders—travelers or guests—who witness instances of cultural depravity and then tell their stories in such a way as to recover a sense of their own station and perspective. Always, this recovery involves a satiric exaggeration of North American folly. Chapters 5 and 6 purport to be the memoirs of a traveling musician, dictated to Moodie and published posthumously. They are thematically and stylistically indistinguishable from the rest of the text, and they give Moodie a narrative opportunity to travel farther imaginatively than she did actually, through the western states of the American union. "Few people have a better opportunity of becoming acquainted with the world than the travelling musician," and this extended range introduces a nation of counterfeit poets, idiot vocalists and pretentious, ignorant audiences—a cultural wasteland that gives no quarter to the serious artist. The singer-narrator conducts himself demurely even in the face of devasting rudeness and retaliates only when he tells his story, which he does with annihilating ridicule. Here again is Moodie's own smug condescension when her narrator responds to insult to his art with wicked affability: "I was very much amused at his comparing me to a bantam cock, and felt almost inclined to clap my wings and crow."

The musician's memoirs extend the geographical reference of *Life in the Clearings* and corroborate Moodie's generalizations about North American life. Sometimes whole chapters are necessary to formalize anecdotal or digressive impulses, but *Clearings* always, sooner or later, recovers its direction. At the conclusion of the book stands the tourist's destination—Niagara. Early in the narrative Moodie justifies natural spectacle as a proper object of sightseeing: "Next to love of God, the love of nature may be regarded as the purest and holiest feeling of the human breast. In the outward beauty of His creation, we catch a reflection of the divine image of the Creator, which refines the intellect, and lifts the soul upward to Him." Moodie's "love" of natural forms is violently consummated when she finally arrives at Niagara. At her first view of the falls she is assaulted, bruised, driven nearly wild by the sight: "the great cataract burst on my sight without any intervening screen, producing an overwhelming sensation in my mind, which amounted to pain in its intensity." North Americans are less excitable, and less accomplished as sightseers. Rapturously contemplating the falls from the hotel verandah, Moodie overhears "a lady remarking to another, who was standing beside her, 'that she considered the Falls a great humbug; that there was more fuss made about them than they deserved; that she was satisfied with having seen them once; and that she never wished to see them again.' "

Frances Trollope also went to Niagara, and she was as deeply impressed as Susanna Moodie: "To say that I was not disappointed is but a weak expression to convey the surprise and astonishment which the long dreamed of scene produced. It has to me something beyond its vastness; there is a shadowy mystery that hangs about it. . . . " Her account of the falls and of her whole term

abroad appeared in *Domestic Manners of the Americans,* which was published in London in 1832, the year of the Moodies' departure. Moodie may have known the book, for it had an extremely successful publication, but that possibility has less to do with the similarities between *Domestic Manners* and *Roughing It* than coincidences in the authors' social and economic situations. The Moodies came to Canada to avoid the ignominy of a moderate but, to them, intolerable poverty; they expected to enhance magically their meager assets. When Trollope sailed in 1827 she left behind a horrendous tangle of debts and financial disappointments which she hoped to sort out in short order by investing a small capital on the American frontier. Both families were nearly obliterated financially by the North American economic structure.

Both Moodie and Trollope were, in a sense, exceptionally bad travelers: every detail of their existence reminded them that they were abroad and not at home. But if their disgruntlement made them bad travelers, it made them very good travel writers, giving them a profound sense of relocation, of having been radically transported and set down elsewhere. On a superficial level, the occasion of *Domestic Manners* can be compared to that of *Roughing It in the Bush* and *Life in the Clearings*. Both writers saw something of the wilderness: Trollope spent a few weeks on the Tennessee frontier; Moodie lived six years in the Canadian bush. Both women knew town life, too: Trollope passed two years in Cincinnati, and by the early 1850s, when *Roughing It* and *Life in the Clearings* were published, Moodie had been more than ten years at Belleville. The pleasure tour described in *Life in the Clearings* corresponds to the more extensive tourism which concluded Trollope's sojourn in the United States. But the most profitable basis for comparing *Domestic Manners* to *Roughing It* and its sequel lies in the fact of each writer's cultural alienation from the site of her economic project.

For brilliant recklessness, the Trollopes' scheme for financial recovery far surpasses the Moodies' drab attempts at homesteading. Donald Smalley's introduction to the 1949 edition of *Domestic Manners* provides a background to which Trollope herself never directly refers: the enterprise which occupied her during her two years at Cincinnati was the construction of an enormous, arabesque emporium known as "The Bazaar," to house all the social and cultural business Trollope believed the city lacked and desired. Imported "fancy goods" were to be displayed for sale; an "Exchange" would be a setting for coffee-house conviviality; a ballroom, theater and gallery would host important events. The edifice was architecturally eclectic, supplying at once *all* the design deficiencies of a frontier town. Strangest of all, the building actually was constructed, the "fancy goods" arrived, and a few evenings of dramatic recitations did occur. Unfortunately, the people of Cincinnati did not appreciate the opportunity offered them, and ignored this facsimile of European culture—as far as this was possible, given the dimensions and singularity of the thing. Irony lies in the fact that Trollope, creator of this prominent public fantasy, isolates bad taste and "want of refinement" as distinguishing characteristics of Americans.

Frances Trollope left England in 1827; three years and nine months later she was back. Just less than half of *Domestic Manners* deals with her arrival in America and her residence in Cincinnati. The remainder of the book follows her to Baltimore, Washington, Philadelphia, New York, Niagara and through the terrains which intervene. During this second phase she industriously collected material for the travel book that represented her only hope of recouping some of the devastating losses incurred by the unfortunate voyage. The greatest part of her memoirs refers to the social landscape, but she looked at nature, too.

For both Trollope and Moodie, nature and wilderness are separate quantities. Although neither can establish any firm esthetic connection with wilderness and neither comes near Traill's ability to discover structure in organic forms, both women were schooled in nature description. They responded fluently and easily to sites like Niagara, for Niagara was a familiar text, existing within a received verbal tradition. It demanded only marginal innovation to renew it, and nothing like the profound revisions of esthetic and rhetorical convention required by the infinite vacuity of unpeopled forests and plains.

But Trollope was not absolutely silent about wilderness. Faced with elemental nature at the mouth of the Mississippi, she declares the scene uninteresting: "Only one object rears itself above the eddying waters; this is the mast of a vessel long since wrecked in attempting to cross the bar, and it still stands, a dismal witness of the destruction that has been, and boding prophet of that which is to come." This introduction to the continent has at least its forlorn relic with which to construe a meaning; when Trollope truly penetrates to the wilderness, an undelineated blankness and unutterable meaninglessness confront her. This is certainly all she finds at Nashoba, an experimental settlement in Tennessee founded on libertarian principles and intended for the education of emancipated slaves. Even the highly civilized *raison d'être* of Nashoba cannot make up for the negative environment in which it exists, and for its lack of familiar, humane objects: "Desolation was the only feeling—the only word that presented itself. . . ." when Trollope arrived. Unnerved by this indescribable emptiness, she decamps after ten days and flees Nashoba.

She is better pleased by the views along the Ohio, as she makes her way to Cincinnati, but even those are regrettably limited in esthetic reference: "were there occasionally a ruined abbey, or feudal castle, to mix the romance of real life with that of nature, the Ohio would be perfect." Trollope's sentiments are typical: many other travelers in America, Washington Irving and Henry James among them, lament the esthetic incompleteness of even the most exquisite scenery when it is unassimilated by an historical tradition.

As early as Frances Brooke's *History of Emily Montague* (1769) European travelers were critical of the North American's lack of interest in celebrated scenery. At Niagara Trollope describes the American tourist as ignorantly nonchalant "before the god of nature," as indifferent and irreverent as Moodie's fellow guest. At Cincinnati the Trollopes were unique among the populace for the pleasure they took in nature: "A row upon the Ohio was another of our favourite amusements; but in this I believe, we were also very singular, for often, when enjoying it, we were shouted at, by the young free-borns on the banks, as if we had been so many monsters." However, in spite of regular picnics and excursions, Trollope cannot love her location: "On first arriving, I though the many tree-covered hills around very beautiful, but long before my departure, I felt so weary of the confined view that Salisbury Plain would have been an agreeable variety."

Cincinnati may be an interesting place to visit, but it is no place to live, Trollope observes: "The more unlike a country through which we travel is to all we have left, the more we are likely to be amused; everything in Cincinnati had this newness, and I should have though it a place delightful to visit, but to tarry there was not to feel at home." Trollope is arrested and impatient in an inhospitable environment. And however distasteful the scenery becomes, it is a minor problem compared with the difficulties of living in a society hostile to her own values and ambitions. Throughout her residence at Cincinnati Trollope remains in a state of nervous irritation over every feature of frontier society. Her hypersensitivity distinguishes her from the community around her, isolating her as a person habituated to the refinements of civilization. Where every delicate pleasure and subtle amenity are missing, the individual accustomed to them is at a loss: "where the whole machine of the human frame is in full activity, where every sense brings home to consciousness its touch of pleasure or pain, then every object that meets the sense is important as a vehicle of happiness or misery. But let no frame so tempered visit the United States, or if they do, let it be with no longer pausing than will store the memory with images, which, by the force of the contrast, shall sweeten the future."

Trollope pauses much longer than the brief interval she recommends. Rather than enjoy the traveler's pleasure in notable differences and the opportunity for discursive comparison-making, she has to live through the profundity of the abysmal contrast.

Like Susanna Moodie, Frances Trollope is intensely concerned with social insubordination and class order in a society which does not acknowledge her claims to station and status. Like Moodie, she finds the behavior of her servants a sign of the corruption of traditional social values. Until she finds a deferential English servant-girl, she is abused and exploited by "free-born" servants who come and go as they please and boldly declare their own terms.

Moodie puts up with being called "woman"; Trollope endures worse, for she is referred to as "old woman." She is forced into social relations with those she regards as her inferiors, and even invited to the home of a greengrocer. These humiliations do not go unaccounted. In her writing, to redress the offense, Trollope adopts a tone of amused disdain remarkably like Moodie's. She goes to the grocer's house, but only to observe and "report" and flesh out the irony of her social predicament. Like Moodie at Belleville, she is an aloof spectator, a social sightseer. Trollope describes her "amusement": "Had I not become heartily tired of my prolonged residence in a place I cordially disliked, and which moreover I began to fear would not be attended with the favourable results we had anticipated, I should have found an almost inexhaustible source of amusement in the notions and opinions of the people I conversed with; and as it was, I often did enjoy this in a considerable degree." Again, comedy and social satire serve the hapless alien stationed in a foreign habitat.

This foreign place is not merely incompatible with the social assumptions of the European visitor; it openly announces its hatred and contempt for her: "We received, as I have mentioned, much personal kindness; but this by no means interferred with the national feeling of, I believe, unconquerable dislike, which evidently lives at the bottom of every truly American heart against the English. This shows itself in a thousand little ways, even in the midst of the most kind and friendly intercourse, but often in a manner more comic than offensive." Trollope says she was neither disappointed nor injured by this popular loathing for her kind. Once she finds that she cannot be loved in America, that she will be only misunderstood and reviled, she becomes stoical, feeling the same "amusement" Moodie felt at insults to her art and dignity:

> One lady asked me very gravely, if we had left home in order to get rid of the vermin with which the English of all ranks were afflicted? "I have heard from unquestionable authority," she added, "that it is quite impossible to walk through the streets of London without having the head filled."
>
> I laughed a little, but spoke not a word.

Like Moodie, who spoke out when she found an audience but kept quiet at Cobourg, Trollope dispenses her opinions generously at home but hoards them here, for she finds it impossible to communicate with citizens of the Republic: "I have conversed in London and in Paris with foreigners of many nations, and often through the misty medium of an idiom imperfectly understood, but I remember no instance in which I found the same difficulty in conveying my sentiments, my impressions, and my opinions to those around me, as I did in America." One need hardly wonder at the length and fluency of her memoirs when one learns that she was virtually incommunicado for almost four years—all those sensations and opinions stopped-up, pressing to flood forth and inundate a receptive audience.

Upon one occasion, however, Trollope does find a sympathetic interlocutor. At Philadelphia, in a grassy square, she spies an interesting-looking woman playing with a child: "There was something in her manner of looking at me, and exchanging a smile when her young charge performed some extraordinary feat of activity on the grass, that persuaded me she was not an American. I do not remember who spoke first, but we were presently in a full flow of conversation." This young woman is a homesick European, a German who is disdainful of Americans. " 'They do not love music,' " she complains. " 'Oh no! and they never amuse themselves—no; and their hearts are not warm, at least they seem not so to a stranger. . . . But I will not stay long, I think, for I should not live.' " Trollope

admires the German, with her languishing spirit and her negative analysis of American manners.

Trollope despises the artificiality of those manners. When some ceremony or social procedure comes to her attention, she finds it silly or pretentious. But when the matrix of social conventions is missing, she deplores its absence, for she finds the idea of social and economic independence "unnatural." Mournfully, she describes the existence of a backwoods family, and then offers her interpretation of the meaning of such a life: "These people were indeed independent . . . but yet it seemed to me that there was something awful and almost unnatural in their loneliness. No village bell ever summoned them to prayer, where they might meet the friendly greeting of their fellow-men. When they die, no spot sacred by ancient reverence will receive their bones. . . . " Trollope turns to the idea of lonely death as the best way of registering her emotional response.

After four years of "attentive observation" Trollope can unconditionally assert that in America "the moral sense is on every point blunter than with us." A society so lacking in moral equipment is a society incapable of comprehending Trollope's values and certainly incapable of endorsing her art. The popular uproar in America which followed news of the London publication of *Domestic Manners* could only have confirmed her opinions on the impossibility of communication between the European traveler and Americans.

Had Trollope's North American journey not included a two-year residence in the West, she might have kept an objective interest in novelty—for, as she says, the more novel the scene the more valuable it is to the traveler. But as it was, comparisons and contrasts were of no mere academic, instructive interest; they were personal crises to be endured. For every social and cultural asset—class, capital, sensibility—to be discounted and for the traveler to be left bankrupt and socially demoralized required some quick action to recuperate the loss. Like Moodie, Trollope saw that the best way to recover a personal investment was to make a literary inquiry into the very foreignness of the manners so alien to her own interests. Trollope, rather than waste her experiences in regret and dismay, husbanded them to retail in a better market. One of her few happy social experiences in America was her half-hour of intense conversation with the homesick German. *Domestic Manners* expands the measure of that moment, telling the whole story and getting home again.

Susanna Moodie did not get home again. Her only way of retraversing her route lay in dispatching an appeal to her distant audience. She asks for commiseration. Frances Trollope, on the other hand, was sure that her course would restore her eventually to her home; her appeal to her audience satisfies her need to redress the offenses she suffered at the hands of a society which demeaned her. She expresses her outrage through denunciation.

Frances Trollope is only an interesting footnote to American literary history. Samuel Clemens refers to her appreciatively in *Life on the Mississippi* (1883), but she is less an inspiration to him than a source of historical background for his documentation of his own journey. She belongs in the British tradition, voicing esthetic, political and social attitudes which were familiar and attractive to her English audience. Susanna Moodie, however, with her melancholy lament for what she had lost and her sly satire of colonial manners, is central to the Canadian literary tradition. In the structure and expression of her attitudes—her reference to a distant point of origin, her homing tendencies and her feelings of literary and cultural isolation—are patterns recognizable to Canadian readers and artists. For Susanna Moodie, the true audience is elsewhere.

With their passage across the Atlantic, Moodie and Trollope felt themselves vanishing anonymously into a social and cultural void. Travel was at best disorienting; at worst, it was an existential threat. For both women, the idea of death expressed the loss they felt and the danger they faced. In Trollope's book, it is the backwoods settler who is destined for a remote grave, and the homesick German who will die for lack of sympathy; she herself is finally secure in the round-trip itinerary which will restore her to England. In *Roughing It,* Moodie imagines her own death; in *Life in the Clearings,* it is the neglected artist who dies in a wilderness hut. Less fortunate than Moodie, he has established no rhetorical connection with a receptive audience, and he does not survive.

> Janet Giltrow, " 'Painful Experience in a Distant Land': Mrs. Moodie in Canada and Mrs. Trollope in America," in Mosaic: A Journal for the Interdisciplinary Study of Literature, Vol. XIV, No. 2, Spring, 1981, pp. 131-44.

Philip G. Terrie

[*In the following excerpt, Terrie discusses the romanticized travel writings of mid-nineteenth-century Americans inspired by the Adirondack mountain region. He notes that "to the romantic traveler the notion of actual or imagined scenic vistas was more important than the reality of the wilderness itself."*]

Sometime in the 1840s Joel T. Headley—Protestant minister, popular historian, journalist, author of biographies of Napoleon and George Washington and a guide to Italy—took the first of several camping trips in the Adirondack wilderness. He later wrote that an "attack on the brain . . . drove me from the haunts of men to seek mental repose and physical strength in the woods," thus affirming the romantic faith in the redemptive powers of nature. In 1849, he published *The Adirondack, Or Life in the Woods,* a book which was reissued, reprinted, expanded and plagiarized in numerous editions over the next thirty years: it was a prime example of one of the nineteenth century's most popular genres, the illustrated volume of romantic travel literature. More exactly, Headley's *Adirondack* typified a distinct type of romantic writing, books and magazine and journal articles devoted exclusively to the American wilderness. Headley's book included all the standard apparatus of the Adirondack sporting and touring narrative—instructions on how to reach the woods and how to prepare for a camping trip, exciting descriptions of hunting and fishing, meditations on the meaning of life in the wilderness, stock responses to scenery, discoveries of the deity in nature and detailed accounts of day-to-day life in the woods with guides.

Expeditions like Headley's and the many narratives they inspired were part of a cultural phenomenon. During the three or four decades before the Civil War, comfortably affluent, educated Easterners were fascinated with the wilderness. The intellectual climate of the day promoted nature as the place where modern man invigorated body and soul, where he restored his physical, mental and moral fortitude. And when educated men sat in their drawing rooms on Washington Square and Beacon Hill and pondered nature, they apparently saw little distinction between nature and wilderness, assuming that wilderness was but the most natural of nature's possibilities. When the same men, however, sought the answer to their physical and spiritual needs in the wilderness—as many of them did—they found that wilderness as an actual place was far less appealing than the wild landscapes so glowingly depicted in romantic literature and art.

In this article I focus on the romantic response to a particular wilderness—the Adirondacks, one of the most popular camping grounds of the antebellum era; I am interested in seeing how a particular group of people—literate, Eastern men, who actually camped in and achieved intimacy with a wild landscape of mountains, forests, lakes and rivers—responded to the wilderness they encountered. My emphasis is on the experience of traveling in the wilderness for reasons other than exploration or emigration. How did the wilderness affect those men (before the Civil War, very few women went camping in the Adirondacks for recreation) who left their comfortable homes in New York or Philadelphia and spent a few weeks roughing it in the Adirondacks? Certainly there were romantics to whom nature was important and whose thinking was affected by the notion of the wilderness, but who did not see fit to sleep on the ground and risk the unpleasantness of wet blankets and annoying insects. I will not address their approach to the wilderness.

For the most part, I will deal with popular romanticism and its written response to a specific wilderness. By popular romanticism I mean the loose collection of assumptions, ideas and values of culturally aware but not extraordinary men and women. Popular romanticism contains much that reminds us of the more complex thinking of men like Emerson or Thoreau, but it is not the same thing. I propose that environmental and cultural historians may have overemphasized the importance of the truly deep thinkers like Thoreau at the expense of writers like Headley whose response to nature was less complex than Thoreau's, but perhaps more representative of his day. To understand the development of American attitudes to all of nature, we must study the views of both the Thoreaus and the Headleys.

In studying the romantic response to the Adirondack wilderness we can examine both the popular romanticism of Headley and the high or complex romanticism of no less a figure than Ralph Waldo Emerson, who camped there for a few weeks in 1858. In both cases we find a profound ambivalence about the existence and the future value of wilderness. Although the depth of the negative side of the ambivalence in Emerson's reaction seems less pronounced than that of Headley and his ilk, Emerson was nonetheless unsure of the meaning of the wilderness and reluctant to extend his ostensible predilection for all of nature to an actual wilderness actually encountered. When Emerson came to the Adirondacks, he arrived, as did his romantic brethren, with preconceptions about the positive features of intimacy with nature in any form. While he was there, he began to reassess this view, and thus concluded that the proper response to wilderness had to consider more than wild scenery and the redemptive powers of nature.

The scores of romantic travel narratives written about the Adirondacks before the Civil War are loaded with predictable ecstasies about the glories of nature, the invigorating pleasures of shooting deer and catching trout, the immanence of God in nature and the pictorial magnificence of the scenery. Leafing through the pages of any of the documents quoted or cited in this article, one will find endless and eventually tedious examples of the romantic appreciation of nature, but these positive responses surround and to a large extent disguise a less affirmative attitude, ranging from occasional outright fear and hostility to Emerson's detached irony. The romantic response to wilderness was far from an unqualified appreciation of untrammeled nature; virtually all romantic travelers, from kneejerk romantics like Headley to Emerson himself, felt constrained to erect some sort of mediating buffer between themselves and the stark reality of the wilderness. From nature where man's cultivating and taming influence was not apparent, romantic travelers, once they actually saw it, often recoiled in horror. Men persuaded by their culture's insistence that all of nature was physically and spiritually edifying became alarmed by the wilderness they personally encountered and thus faced a perplexing psychological dilemma. To reconcile conflicting impulses they needed an imaginative construct to protect them psychologically. Torn between the facile assumptions of popular romanticism and a deeper antipathy to the wilderness, most romantic travelers in the Adirondacks employed a variety of strategies to reconcile mutually antagonistic responses to this particular form of nature. The need to discover some way to tolerate the wilderness, of course, suggests that the hatred of wilderness displayed by earlier generations was dissipating, but it also emphasizes how this hostility persisted in the romantic mind.

Beginning in the 1830s the Adirondack region of upstate New York attracted increasing numbers of Eastern men, who traveled for a spell in the summer wilderness and returned to their homes to write books and articles describing their experiences. The typical Adirondack camping trip of this period usually involved several weeks spent in the woods. Generally, a party consisted of a group of about three or four city sportsmen and the same number of guides, who were hired at the small settlements on the edge of the wilderness. The intricate system of connecting rivers and lakes provided easy access to the heart of the wilderness; romantic travelers seldom hiked. Arriving by boat at a pleasant spot on a lake or river, the party would establish a more or less permanent campsite. This involved the construction of a lean-to or shanty out of poles and spruce or hemlock bark. Once this base camp was ready, the sportsmen could spend their time hunting, fishing, meditating and admiring the scenery.

The reactions of romantic travelers to Adirondack scenery constituted an ostensibly lavish and enthusiastic appreciation of one of the more obvious features of the wilderness—its visual magnificence. They fill page after page of Adirondack travel narratives and suggest a genuine love of wild scenery. And in a sense that love is there, but the descriptions of scenery also contain the most significant strategy whereby romantic travelers could accept the wilderness itself. The essential ingredient of this strategy was the conversion of the landscape from topographical, biological and geological reality into an object of aesthetic appreciation. Romantic travelers characteristically invoked the aesthetic vocabulary of Edmund Burke; they acknowledged Burke's definitions of the sublime and the beautiful, and they imposed Burke's response to nature on their descriptions of the Adirondacks. The Burkean aesthetic of the sublime and beautiful was a significant factor in the renewed interest in nature of the eighteenth century, and Burke's vocabulary and definitions continued to affect the romantic response to nature. But the Burkean aesthetic, in its emphasis on the scenic and pictorial, encouraged a distinction between scenery and wilderness, and we must not confuse repeated and eloquent appreciations of wild scenery with a positive response to wilderness as such. For when romantic travelers encountered landscapes which failed to fit the Burkean scheme, their disgust at discovering thick woods, dead trees and the ubiquitous Adirondack swamp emphasizes how the appeal of the cult of the sublime and beautiful was its usefulness in mediating between the romantic consciousness and the reality of nature.

Testimonials to the grandeur of Adirondack scenery appear in virtually every account of visits to the region. While these descriptions typically reflect stock Burkean attitudes and while they often seem tediously similar, they nonetheless reveal an honest effort to address a magnificent landscape. Even from the otherwise skeptical pen of Thomas Bangs Thorpe, the Southwestern humorist, the Adirondacks elicited praise: after a camping trip that took him up the Fulton Chain in John Brown's Tract, Thorpe wrote [in *Harper's New Monthly Magazine,* 19], "I question if there is in the wide world a place where the natural scenery so strongly combines every possible variety of expression to gratify the eye and call forth admiration." And John Todd, a minister from Massachusetts who paid several visits to Long Lake and the central Adirondacks in the 1840s, predicted [in his *Long Lake*] that the marvels of the Adirondack landscape would soon make the region a popular resort:

> The scenery on these lakes is grand and beautiful beyond any thing of which I ever conceived. The lakes of Scotland have been celebrated of old in story and song; but the time will come, I doubt not, when these lakes will become the most interesting resort to be found in the country, for the great, the rich, the curious and the fashionable.

After the Civil War, Todd's prediction that the Adiron-

In Asher B. Durand's Kindred Spirits, *poet William Cullen Bryant and painter Thomas Cole survey a Catskills landscape. Oil on canvas, 1849.*

dacks would become a playground of the wealthy would prove prescient.

Although many of the writers who visited the Adirondacks in this period saw only the lake country accessible to boats, those who did make their way to the high peaks and Indian Pass responded to the scenery there in terms emphasizing the influence of the cult of the sublime. The great cliffs on Wallface at Indian Pass, which Headley called "the most remarkable gorge in the country, if not in the world," particularly excited a consciousness of sublimity in the souls of those who saw it. Charles Fenno Hoffman wrote [in his *Wild Scenes in the Forest and Prairie*] that Indian Pass "was one of the most savage and stupendous among the many wild and imposing scenes at the sources of the Hudson. . . . It is a tremendous ravine, cloven through the summit of a mountain." Headley's reaction was similar: "Majestic, solemn and silent, with the daylight from above pouring all over its dread form, it stood the impersonation of strength and grandeur." Standing at the height of the pass, Headley felt that "there was something fearful in that mysterious, profound silence." Likewise, Jervis McEntee, an artist who visited Indian Pass in 1851, explicitly underscored Burke's observation that one of the features of the sublime was its capacity to remind the viewer of the omnipotence of God: "It is one of those wild scenes so full of majesty and sublimity which the Creator has formed for us to look upon that we may the better comprehend his boundless power." In a description of the view from Mount Marcy, Headley emphasized another of Burke's points, that the response to a sublime scene is "founded on pain"; standing on the summit, Headley found himself

> in the centre of a chaos of mountains, the like of which I never saw before. It was wholly different from the Alps. There were no snow peaks and shining glaciers; but all was grey, or green, or black, as far as the vision could extend . . . grand and gloomy . . . a background of mountains, and with nothing but the most savage scenery between—how mysterious—how awful it seemed!
>
> Mount Colden, with its terrific precipices—Mount McIntyre with its bold, black, barren, monster-like head.

In the less imposing, more gentle scenery around the lakes of the central Adirondacks romantic travelers discovered Burke's second landscape category—the beautiful. Headley's description of the scene at Forked Lake provides a revealing contrast to his account of the view from Marcy; from his boat

> . . . all was wild but beautiful. The sun was stooping to the western mountains, whose sea of summits were calmly sleeping against the golden heavens: the cool breeze stirred a world of foliage on our right—green islands, beautiful as Elysian fields, rose out of the water as we advanced; the sparkling waves rolled as merrily under as bright a sky as ever bent over the earth, and for a moment I seemed to have been transported into a new world. I never was more struck by a scene in my life: its utter wildness,

> spread out there where the axe of civilization had never struck a blow—the evening—the sunset—the deep purple of the mountains—the silence and solitude of the shores, and the cry of birds in the distance, combined to render it one of enchantment to me.

In this passage Headley emphasized the serenity of the scene in an explicit counter to the menacing violence dormant in the high peaks. Amid the wilderness of Forked Lake Headley felt safe and peaceful. As he was rowed across the lake, Headley enjoyed the openness of the scene, having felt threatened by the closeness of the cliffs of Indian Pass or the peaks surrounding Marcy. Indeed, one of the features of the lake country which appealed to Headley and others was the absence of the sense of claustrophobia they experienced in the high peaks. When the wilderness was too close, it seemed oppressive. When, on the other hand, Headley was able to view the high peaks from a distance, he could integrate their hard lines into a more pleasant perception; for example, from Owl's Head, a low mountain on the shore of Long Lake, he observed that, "to the left, shoot up into the heavens the massive peaks of the Adirondack chain, mellowed here, by the distance, into beauty."

Although both sublime and beautiful landscapes evoked rapturous responses from romantic travelers, the beautiful was clearly preferred. Comparing the relative attributes of sublime and beautiful scenery, Headley wrote,

> The gloomy gorge and savage precipice, or the sudden storm, seem to excite the surface only of one's feelings, while the sweet value, with its cottages and herds and evening bells, blends itself in with our very thoughts and emotions, forming a part of our after existence. Such a scene sinks away into the heart like a gentle rain into the earth, while a rougher, nay, sublimer one, comes and goes like a sudden shower.

This response suggests an important source of the preference for the beautiful. Although Headley elsewhere responded positively to the absence of marks of civilization and the opportunity to settle into a reverie of introspective solitude, here he indicates his faith in the likelihood or at least the possibility that the beautiful landscape—gentle, rolling, peaceful—could be turned into a cultivated middle landscape, thus eliminating the implicitly useless wilderness.

Romantic writers repeatedly suggested that a huge improvement in the Adirondacks would be effected by the emergence of a scene of farms and fields—a change seen as inevitable and positive. Todd explicitly stated that it was a sin against God's grand design for man's occupation of the earth not to subject the wilderness to the plow:

> It is God's plan and will that the earth should be tilled and thus yield food for man and beast. Any people who fall in with this plan, and till the earth shall prosper. Any people who will not, shall perish.

Although Todd admired certain of the characteristics of the woodsmen he encountered in the Adirondacks, he eagerly predicted their disappearance as the region became more settled. Another observer [Henry J. Raymond in the *New York Times*] echoing Crèvecoeur, was less kind to the backwoodsmen who did not live by agriculture; finding a few homesteads at Raquette Lake, this man was appalled to learn that the inhabitants did not till their land but led lives characterized by "hunting and fishing rather than . . . farming."

The predictions of the appearance of a middle landscape in the Adirondacks confirm the mythic quality of the middle-landscape ideal in the American consciousness. The elimination of the wilderness was clearly part of the American mission to establish, even in "these glorious mountains" of the Adirondacks, "a virtuous, industrious and Christian population." Then, according to S. H. Hammond [in his *Hills, Lakes and Forest Streams*], the Adirondacks would be a land of "beautiful and productive farms. Where meadows and green fields would stretch away from the river towards the hills, and where fine farm-houses and barns would be seen, and flocks and herds would be grazing in rich pastures." In addition to reflecting the mythic significance of the middle landscape, Hammond's prediction also suggests that a chief virtue of the evolution from wild to georgic was the scenic, visual change. When writers like Hammond imagined this alteration in the land, they commonly dwelt on its scenic elements. To the romantic traveler the notion of actual or imagined scenic vistas was more important than the reality of the wilderness itself, and the exercise of the visual imagination emerged as one of the critical strategies for taming the threatening character of the wilderness.

This is more than simply deeming the landscape picturesque. It involves the imposition of cultural, aesthetically defined standards on nature and reflects the need of the romantic traveler to reconcile his fear of the wilderness with his predisposition to love all of nature. It allowed him to isolate or at least distance himself from the physical reality of the wilderness. Romantic travelers often expressed a genuine appreciation of the wild scenery of the Adirondacks, but they were responding to *scenes,* to certain arrangements of natural elements—trees, rocks, mountains, water. As Burke's popularizer, William Gilpin wrote [in his *Observations on the Western Parts of England . . .*] "*Picturesque beauty* is a phrase but little understood. We precisely mean by it that kind of beauty which *would look well in a picture.*"

In the responses of some travelers this absorption in the visual led to accepting nature as more or less perfect according to the extent that it satisfied the criteria of landscape painting. Thomas Cole, the most important artist to visit the Adirondacks before the Civil War, wrote [in his journal] of the terrain in the Schroon Lake vicinity, "I do not remember to have seen in Italy a composition of mountains so beautiful or pictorial as this glorious range of the Adirondack." Cole, despite the glowing tone of his description, was judging the landscape in a rather mechanical fashion, criticizing the "composition" of the peaks according to how well they would fit onto a canvas. Eventually it became possible for writers to judge the scenery according to the precise canons of the then current aesthetic school. A writer [A. B. Street in *Woods and Wa-*

ters] thus described a scene along the Saranac River: "One view particularly pleased us, soon after our departure from the Lake House: A graceful curve of the stream, lost at either end in woods with one dry jagged tree slanting athwart, the only sign of decay amid the overflowing life." The curving river and the blasted tree are common elements in the paintings of romantic American landscape artists. . . .

These writers often suggested, moreover, that the wilderness was in fact an impediment to the observer of fine vistas. Thomas Cole, wandering through the woods near Schroon Lake, looking for a good spot from which to paint Schroon Mountain, wished that the forest had been lumbered so that his view could be unobstructed. Likewise, Headley, on Owl's Head, "wanted to set fire to the trees on the summit of the mountain, so as to present an unobstructed view, but the foliage was too green to burn." Jervis McEntee observed [in his diary] that reaching Indian Pass required an arduous hike: "They who look upon it must endure no little toil for the privilege for its gateway is of the rugged rock and the tangled forest and the feet that pass through it are few as the hardly discernable path will attest." "He who sketches Indian Pass," further remarked McEntee, "will have to work for it[,] for it is a toilsome work to it." The solution to this difficulty, as proposed by T. A. Richards [in *Harper's,* 19], author of an account of an Adirondack camping trip published in 1859, was to build a road through the pass, from which "the traveler may be able to see the wonders which now, in the denseness of the forest, he can only infer." Louis Noble, Cole's first biographer, who accompanied the artist on an 1846 trip to the Adirondacks, suggested that it was scenery not wilderness which attracted him and Cole:

> It is not, perhaps, generally known that, to this day, a jaunt through the region of the State of New York will ordinarily subject the tourist to more privation and fatigue than almost any other he can take in the United States, this side of the Mississippi. The wilderness, haunted by the great moose, the wolf, the bear, the panther, seems almost interminable, and nearly houseless: the mountains, some of them reaching into the sky, ragged, rocky pinacles, and robed with savage grandeur, are pathless and inaccessible without a guide: the lakes, which are every where, and often strikingly beautiful, repel by the oppressive loneliness in which they slumber.

Noble undoubtedly exaggerated the hardships of Adirondack camping in order to show what perils his friend Cole was willing to endure in the name of art, but at the same time he clearly showed that he thought of wilderness itself as an irrelevant distraction or an actual peril.

The growing taste evinced for wild scenery by Cole and others was, to be sure, a critical element in what eventually developed as the modern appreciation for wilderness itself, but it was most certainly not the same thing. The modern concept of wilderness promotes the appreciation of any area where the signs of human activity are substantially absent. While natural beauty is almost invariably associated with such an area, it is not the *sine qua non*. To the modern wilderness purist, natural beauty often derives simply from nature itself, from the fact that the elements of the natural environment appear unaffected by any human activity.

When romantic travelers found themselves in parts of the Adirondacks which conformed to neither the sublime nor the beautiful, they were unable to employ any mediating strategy and responded with nearly unqualified hostility. In the swamps and thick forests away from the lakes and high peaks they discovered landscapes for which the Burkean aesthetic did not provide a ready-made vocabulary, and their descriptions of this part of the region are thus not couched in derivative words and phrases. The reactions of several romantic travelers to the area around the head of the Bog River, where they went searching for the even then rapidly disappearing moose, show particularly well how raw, untouched nature, when it failed the aesthetic test, horrified the romantic traveler. Because this region was accessible by boat from Tupper Lake, travelers were willing to visit it; but once there, they discovered a dark and forbidding terrain of thick timber and many marshes. The presence of dead and decaying trees particularly offended the senses of these men. S. H. Hammond noted [in his *Hills, Lakes and Forest Streams*] both the absence of appealing scenery and the (to him) oppressive presence of process:

> Of all the lakes I have visited in these northern wilds, this [Mud Lake] is the most gloomy . . . no tall mountain peaks, reaching their heads toward the clouds, overlooking the water, no ranges stretching away. . . . It is in truth, a gloomy place, typical of desolation . . . [with] so sepulchral an air of desolation all around, that it brings over the mind a strong feeling of sadness and gloom.

A. B. Street [in his *Woods and Waters*] responded to this region in a similar way; it had, wrote Street, a "lonely and funereal aspect. In every direction, also, dead pines and hemlocks thrust up their pallid, rough raggedness, dripping with grey moss. . . . Over the whole brooded an air of utter loneliness, which, aided by the dull, heavy sky, rested with a depressing weight upon my spirits."

Street reacted similarly to a cluster of small, isolated lakes west of Upper Saranac: "The scene . . . was as utterly lonely and desolate and wild as could be imagined. The shores, unlike those of the other lakes and ponds in this alpine region, were low, belted with swamp and disfigured with dead, ghastly trees." Finally, wrote Street, "as this profoundly desolate scene smote my sight, I felt a weight deeper than I had ever experienced in the forest." Not only was the absence of conventionally approved scenery repugnant to the romantic traveler, but the ubiquity of natural processes, wherein new life depended on death and decay, reminded mid-nineteenth-century man too much of his own mortality.

Thoughts of the deep woods, away from the comforting shores of the larger central lakes, also evoked a terror of getting lost. Most people, of course, avoid losing their way in the wilderness, but the fears expressed by travelers of this period approach hysteria and show, beyond a reasonable apprehension about losing one's way, the horror of

the wilderness itself and an attribution to it of actively malicious powers. Meditating on the more isolated parts of the Adirondacks, Street wrote, "I was more and more impressed with the utter savageness of the scene, and my entire helplessness should I be left alone. The few paths, if not of deer, could only be of bear, wolf, or panther, and tended doubtless toward their fearful haunts." John Todd [in *Long Lake*] displayed a similarly high-pitched fear of being alone in the woods: "The sensation of being lost in this vast forest is horrific beyond description. No imagination can paint the bewilderment and terrific sensations which you feel when you are alone and fairly lost. . . . It is probably as near derangement as can be, if there is any difference."

In one sense, the notion that the Adirondack wilderness was a place where a man could actually get lost and disappear was part of the attractiveness of the region. It was a function of the wilderness similar to the sublimity of mountain scenery, fascinating in its very terribleness. But the source of this fascination and of the fears expressed by writers like Street and Todd lay in the conviction that in the wilderness a man would be particularly likely to lose his mind, that the wilderness was a hostile environment where man's rationality might desert him in the face of irrational forces. Such suspicions reflect a vestigial subscription to the old Puritan fear that life in the wilderness can lead to mental or moral degeneration. With enthusiastic trust in its veracity Todd recounted a story told him at Long Lake about a man "of liberal education, and fine promise" who became lost in the woods and went insane. Todd offered this tale as proof of the pernicious effects of being alone in the woods without the protection of comrades against the wilderness's inherent malignity. Nor did a man have to be lost to suffer the loss of rationality. The artist William James Stillman, whose feelings toward the wilderness were generally far more positive than those of most of his contemporaries, observed [in his *The Autobiography of a Journalist*] that he could easily imagine a solitary life in the forest "leading to insanity."

But romantic travelers did not venture into the wilderness alone, nor did they stay long enough to lose their sanity. And the brevity of the traveler's stay suggests the irrelevance of the wilderness to the progressive world which waited back home. The romantic traveler needed to remind himself of the permanence of the civilized, urban world beyond the wilderness, and he satisfied this need by surrounding himself with civilized artifacts like neckties and champagne. Such mementos of what he considered the real world supplied physical evidence that the traveler's important pursuits were those of his office in the city—the same world which produced fine wine and insisted on decorous clothing. Although travelers commonly rehearsed the familiar arguments about how an urban society demands the redemptive powers of nature, they also implied that they did not feel altogether comfortable with having abandoned, if only temporarily, the progressive reality of American life. Behind the pleasures of being away from ordinary responsibilities lies a reluctance to be too long away from the exciting world of politics, technology and all civilized activity. Headley described the unmasked enthusiasm with which he devoured a recent newspaper after a long trek through the wilderness: it put "into my hands again the links of the great chain of human events I had lost—rebinding me to my race and replacing me in the mighty movement that bears all things onward."

The paradox inherent in a man's repairing to the wilderness for spiritual regeneration but simultaneously admiring the material and scientific achievements of nineteenth-century technology apparently escaped Headley. But Emerson, who camped for several weeks on Follensby Pond near Long Lake in 1858, did not fail to note the ambivalence suggested by such a contradictory set of responses. Emerson's party, organized by the painter and journalist William James Stillman, also included the scientist Louis Agassiz, James Russell Lowell and others from the Concord-Cambridge axis. After returning home, Emerson wrote a long blank-verse poem describing his reactions to the Adirondack wilderness and to a startling event which took place while he was in the woods; the laying of the first trans-Atlantic cable, one of the premier achievements, in Emerson's view, of nineteenth-century American technology. Receiving this news, Emerson found himself in a situation analogous—but not identical—to that of other romantic travelers; although aware of the irony implicit in his reaction, he too needed some sort of imaginative mediation to reconcile antagonistic yet attractive impulses.

Emerson's response to the Adirondack wilderness is particularly important because he was, on the one hand, one of the purveyors of the romantic sensibility which so clearly influenced less creative men like Headley and other romantic travelers. On the other hand, Emerson's trip to the Adirondacks constituted the only extended experience of his life with genuine wilderness, and his reaction to what he saw and felt made him a romantic traveler in the wilderness for the first and only time in his life. Assessing Emerson's reaction to the Adirondack wilderness, we see that nature as concept and nature as place are not necessarily the same thing. To confuse them is to misinterpret Emerson, who uses the terms *nature* and *wilderness* interchangeably as philosophical concepts in his efforts to find meaning in the world—both material and ideal—around him: this he does in *Nature,* probably the most quoted, best known and most comprehensive of American transcendentalist manifestos.

In *Nature,* immediately after the famous "transparent eyeball" passage, Emerson writes, "In the wilderness, I find something more dear and connate than in streets and villages." He thus advances the familiar romantic distinction between the country and the city, affirming the romantic inclination to find virtue and meaning in the rural while deprecating the ostensible degradation of the urban. Emerson seems further to be insisting that a particular kind of natural setting—the wilderness, that landscape where man's impact is either nonexistent or at least unnoticeable—is most likely to possess the truths inherent in all of nature. But when he composed these words, he had never seen a wilderness; the word *wilderness* was to Emerson a philosophical abstraction, not a term denoting geographical reality. His experience with nature was limited to the tame woods around Concord—until he camped in the Adirondacks.

In 1858 Follensby Pond was as isolated and untouched as nearly any spot east of the Mississippi River. Accessible only by boat or a tortuous hike across many miles of unmapped territory, it was surrounded by a vast tract of virgin timber and showed absolutely no trace of human activity. Like nearly all sporting parties of the day, Emerson and his comrades reached their campsite by boat, rowing from Saranac Lake via the Raquette River. After describing their journey and the construction of their crude shelter, Emerson proceeded to run through the characteristic romantic litany of the virtues of nature and a life close to it. He and his friends adopted the rigorous regimen of farmers, rising with the dawn and dining on hearty, simple fare. Beyond the reach of letters, visitors, advertisements and all of the commercial intrusions of urban life, they "were made freemen of the forest laws." Observing the woodcraft of the Saranac Lake guides, Emerson concluded (perhaps ironically) [in his "The Adirondacs (sic): A Journal Dedicated to My Fellow Travellers in August, 1858"] that his own intellectual prowess was inferior to the practical knowledge of men who lived in the bosom of nature:

> Look to yourselves, ye polished gentlemen!
> No city airs or arts pass current here.
> Your rank is all reversed; let men of cloth
> Bow to the stalwart churls in overalls:
> *They* are the doctors of the wilderness,
> And we the low-prized laymen.

As his stay in the wilderness lengthened, Emerson reacted more and more positively to it, finding there a peace and freedom which his life back home denied him:

> Bounded by dawn and sunset, and the day
> Rounded by hours where each outdid the last
> In miracles of pomp, we must be proud,
> As if associates of the sylvan gods.
> We seemed the dwellers of the zodiac,
> So pure the Alpine element we breathed,
> So light, so lofty pictures came and went.
> We trode on air, contemned the distant town,
> Its timorous ways, big trifles. . . .

Sinking into a reverie of introspection prompted by nature's "visitings of graver thought," Emerson found spiritual truths in the wilderness:

> Nature spoke
> To each apart, lifting her lovely shows
> To spiritual lessons pointed home,
> And as through dreams in watches of the night,
> So through all creatures in their form and ways
> Some mystic hint accosts the vigilant,
> Not clearly voiced, but waking a new sense
> Inviting to new knowledge, one with old.

But one day some of his party rowed to Tupper Lake to examine the scenery and encountered another group of men, who had word of a remarkable event. Thus was the news of the transatlantic cable relayed to Emerson, who suddenly waxed ecstatic about the powers of technological society to control nature. From the entire party a great shout arose to celebrate this most recent evidence of man's continuing triumph over nature. The announcement of this accomplishment had a profound impact on Emerson: "We have a few moments in the longest life / Of such delight and wonder." The news of such a triumph of civilization suggested that his earlier musings on the spirituality of the wilderness were insignificant in the grand scheme of American progress. The mission of American civilization was to subdue nature:

> The lightning has run masterless too long;
> He must to school and learn his verb and noun
> And teach his nimbleness to earn his wage,
> Spelling with guided tongue man's messages
> Shot through the weltering pit of the salt sea.

Emerson began to rethink his earlier response to the wilderness; the guides do well enough in their element, but the men truly important are scientists like Agassiz:

> We flee away from cities, but we bring
> The best of cities with us, these learned classifi
> ers,
> Men knowing what they seek, armed eyes of ex
> perts.
> We praise the guide, we praise the forest life:
> But will we sacrifice our dear-bought lore
> Of books and art and trained experiment,
> Or count the Sioux a match for Agassiz?
> O no, not we!

Emerson thus found himself faced with the same dilemma which confronted other romantic travelers. Preconceptions emphasized the positive features of the wilderness experience, and Emerson himself initially adhered to a conventional response. Then, though for reasons different from those of ordinary romantic travelers, he subsequently discovered some reason for deprecating the wilderness. In order to deal with these conflicting demands Emerson too employed a mediating strategy. The nature of his strategy, though, shows that he was not repelled by wilderness to the extent that other romantic travelers often were. Indeed, when he saw the flat, visually unexciting marshes surrounding the route into Follensby Pond, he described the scene in relatively neutral terms quite different from the responses of romantic travelers to similar terrain: the outlet of Follensby was

> a small tortuous pass
> Winding through grassy shallows in and out,
> Two creeping miles of rushes, pads, and sponge.

Nonetheless Emerson needed to reconcile ostensibly contradictory attitudes toward the wilderness. His solution was the conceit that the wilderness understood the joyous shout which greeted the news of man's technological achievement, that such exultation was not "unsuited to that solitude." The wilderness itself, according to this strategy, acknowledged man's accomplishment and conceived its own

> burst of joy, as if we told the fact
> To ears intelligent; as if gray rock
> And cedar grove and cliff and lake should know
> This feat of wit, this triumph of mankind;
> As if we men were talking in a vein
> Of sympathy so large, that ours was theirs,
> And a prime end of the most subtle element
> Were fairly reached at last. Wake, echoing caves!
> Bend nearer, faint day-moon! Yon thundertops,
> Let them hear well! 'tis theirs as much as ours.

The news of the transatlantic cable was only one of the reminders of the relative virtues of civilization compared with the wilderness; on another day Emerson was rowing with his guide on the Raquette River and was startled to hear the wilderness silence broken by the strains of a Beethoven composition. Near the river was a log cabin inhabited by a man of evident education and other genteel attributes, who had managed to drag a piano to his wilderness retreat. The sound of the music was similar to the news of the cable: both confirmed man's need to employ art, science or whatever mediation was effective in eliminating those features of nature which seemed menacing or irrelevant to a progressive age. On hearing the Beethoven, the listener cries,

> Well done! . . . the bear is kept at bay,
> The lynx, the rattlesnake, the flood, the fire;
> All our fierce enemies, ague, hunger, cold. . . .

Science and art—these are the truly significant discoveries of man, not spirituality in the wilderness.

After suggesting that the wilderness approves of human accomplishments which continuously diminish both its power and extent, Emerson retreated further from his earlier sense of transcendence. He too invoked the notion that camping in the wilderness is somehow failing to participate in the momentous achievements of modern life. On the one hand, Emerson's description of his departure from the wilderness seems to affirm the traditional view that urban life is antagonistic to the peace of nature. But at the same time, since he has just written so eloquently about technology and progress, he implies a need to get back home before something else important happens:

> The holidays were fruitful, but must end;
> One August evening had a cooler breath;
> Into each mind intruding duties crept;
> Under the cinders burned the fires of home;
> Nay, letters found us in our paradise.

Stillman too [in his *The Old Rome and the New, and Other Studies*] noted the transient nature of the idyll on Follensby Pond and observed that Emerson particularly perceived the need to return to the pressing demands of Concord:

> Our paradise was no Eden. The world that
> played bo-peep with us across the mountains
> came for us when the play-spell was over; this
> summer dream, unique in the record of poesy,
> melted like a cloud-castle, and Emerson was one
> of the first to turn back to the sterner use of time.

Although Emerson was less hostile to the wilderness than were most of his contemporaries, his reluctance to extend the romantic love of nature to an acceptance of the wilderness as such is useful to our understanding of modern attitudes. All the romantic travelers invoked one strategy or another to disguise or alter the reality of untrammeled nature. Behind their occasional distaste for wilderness as such was the assumption, which Emerson suggests, that it had no future in a bustling, modern, progressive, technological nation. The popular belief in the therapeutic or redemptive powers of all of nature notwithstanding, the romantic traveler foresaw the disappearance of the wilderness—in the East, anyway—as inevitable. The suspicion that wilderness was irrelevant, an engaging (when not outright threatening) entity one might as well see while it lasted, informs the response to the Adirondacks of both Emerson and popular writers like Headley.

Although I have emphasized the more or less negative features of the romantic response to wilderness, I recognize that these are but one side of a dual response, an ambivalence. Both Emerson and Headley were representatives of a busy, progressive age; to discover their participation in the enthusiastic anticipation of a technologically oriented future should come as no surprise. Likewise, to discover that an American romantic shared his ancestors' fears of the malignant or depriving aspects of wilderness is no shock. In the long run, what is remarkable is that men like Headley kept returning—and he did, throughout the 1840s and '50s. Compromised as his attitude was, it nonetheless contains a perception of the power of the wilderness. The response to scenery may have been a meticulously constructed strategy for making the wilderness tolerable, but the very necessity for effecting the strategy in the first place shows that the romantic traveler did suspect that God actually dwelt in the landscape. Hammond and Street may have been repulsed by the swampy terrain around the Bog River, but they both returned to the Adirondacks on many subsequent camping trips. The failure of one particular part of the landscape to satisfy their overall expectations did not eliminate the inherent capacity of the wilderness to work its mystical medicine.

Although neither Headley nor Emerson, despite the romantic predisposition to see virtue in all of nature, could fully accept the imposing reality of wilderness as such, both did perceive positive values there. In describing their efforts to maintain their cultural equilibrium, I have thus stressed the strategies which they established in response to features of the wilderness which seemed threatening; I have done this because I think that cultural historians have not paid sufficient attention to this aspect of both popular and complex romanticism. But I conclude, as have others, that the chief characteristic of the romantic response to wilderness is its ambivalence, an endlessly interesting mixture of sympathy and fear, of love and hostility, of the impulse to embrace and the equally powerful urge to flee. The whole elaborate effort to make the wilderness tolerable helped lay the foundation for the later, more consistently positive response to wilderness of men like John Muir and Aldo Leopold.

> *Philip G. Terrie, "Romantic Travelers in the Adirondack Wilderness," in* American Studies, *Vol. XXIV, No. 2, Fall, 1983, pp. 59-75.*

Kris Lackey

[*In the following excerpt, Lackey argues that the major influences for nineteenth-century writers who described the vast wilderness landscapes west of the Alleghenies were the values of Romanticism and eighteenth-century aesthetics.*]

In addition to their trunks or saddlebags, many travelers in trans-Allegheny America in the early and middle nineteenth century brought with them on their journeys very particular criteria for judging the landscape they encountered from the Ohio Valley to the Rockies. The vogue of western travel during this period coincided with the rise of Romantic consciousness and followed closely upon late eighteenth- and early nineteenth-century debates over the nature of aesthetic perception of landscape. Romantic awareness provided a range of expression for the projective subject and a means of connecting landscape and emotion; and, as a number of studies have demonstrated, the descriptive taxonomy and vocabulary of aesthetic theorists such as Edmund Burke, Uvedale Price, William Gilpin and Richard Payne Knight often shaped the traveler's impressions of "discovered" territory. Together these influences educated the traveler's eye. They taught him or her what qualities and effects to look for in a landscape, how to look for them, how to arrange them, and what to call them. Moreover, this alliance of Romanticism and aesthetic terminology often figured in the political agendas of travelers who bestowed symbolic value on American landscape.

Readers of travel works by Frances Trollope, Washington Irving, Francis Parkman and Charles Dickens will find in these authors' evocations of western landscape the Romantic interplay of nature and spirit (in Trollope somewhat subdued), but the terminology all save Dickens employed to discriminate among various types of visual effects derives from pre-Romantic aesthetic theory concerned with the content and form of garden landscaping and landscape painting. Late-eighteenth-century debates about "painterly" vision, while they often addressed the problem of subjective participation, concentrated on objective qualities. But the terms they produced to describe visual effects—"beautiful," "sublime," "picturesque"— when employed by later writers usually bore the Romantic tension between the inherent and projected qualities of perceived objects. Building upon the established vitality of both Romantic sensibility and eighteenth-century aesthetic theory in nineteenth-century travel writing about America, this essay examines how both influences operate (in some cases conditioning cultural judgment) in four widely-read travel books published between 1832 and 1849: Trollope's *Domestic Manners of the Americans* (1832), Irving's *A Tour on the Prairies* (1835), Dickens' *American Notes for General Circulation* (1842) and Parkman's *Oregon Trail* (1849). Dickens' and Irving's books were American bestsellers, the *Notes* selling 50,000 copies in three days. *Domestic Manners* provoked a storm of criticism and inspired the colloquial term "trollope"—an aspersion on America. And *The Oregon Trail* is of course a classic personal vision of the westward expansion. These four works, all of which remain in print, have since their appearance provided for both popular and academic readers a fascinating spectrum of responses, by highly literate observers, to the exploration and/or early settlement of trans-Allegheny America.

When Meriwether Lewis came upon the Great Falls of the Missouri in the late spring of 1805 he was moved to reach beyond the typically dispassionate and empirical voice in which he and his companion recorded information for Jefferson's great Enlightenment undertaking. Lewis chafed at the restrictions of objective, statistical description that robbed the spectacle of wonder; his initial effort in this vein left him "so much disgusted with the imperfect idea which it conveyed of the scene" that he "determined to draw [his] pen across it and begin again," this time recording his first *impressions;* he "wished for the pencil of Salvator Rosa . . . or the pen of [James] Thomson" in order to recreate the scene adequately. Acknowledging his lack of such skills, Lewis in the end resorted to the critical vocabulary of Edmund Burke (whom he might have read in Jefferson's library) to distinguish between the visual effects of the lesser and greater falls: "At length I determined between these two great rivals for glory, that this was *pleasingly beautifull,* while the other was *sublimely grand.*" The smaller, "beautifull," cataract "pitches over a shelving rock, with an edge as regular and as streight as if formed by art"; the "sublime" cascade falls onto "irregular and somewhat projecting rocks below," where "large roling bodies of the same beaten and foaming water is thrown over . . . the water after descending strikes against the butment . . . on which I stand, and seems to reverberate and being met by the more impetuous courant, they roll and swell into half formed billows of great hight."

Lewis' struggle to find a satisfactory means of conveying both a correct image and its emotional impact is in fact a search for the happy descriptive paradigm. The ingenuous anxiety revealed in Lewis' journal de-naturalizes this selective process, exposing its subjective arbitration and erasing, with each rejected approach, still more of the landscape's inherent qualities. Writing of the proposed Indian Territory two decades later, Washington Irving possessed literary skills that allowed him to conceal such anxiety in the interest of creating the illusion that sublimity and beauty, while apprehended by a human mind, also inhere in the forests and prairies of the West: he naturalized the Romantic correspondence.

But the example of Meriwether Lewis, who tried clumsily to be for the nonce what Parkman (echoing Gilpin) would later call a "picturesque tourist," serves to make us sensitive to the textual conditioning of vision in sophisticated popular travel books about the American West. When thousands of nineteenth-century British and American readers first glimpsed trans-Allegheny America in the pages of Trollope, Irving and Parkman, its topography usually appeared as a sequence of vistas, framed, described and evaluated (both objectively and subjectively) in terms borrowed from criticism in the visual arts. Like painters, sculptors and photographers who treated western subjects—Catlin, Remington, Curtis—these writers adapted convention to place and in the bargain transformed place with convention. In the course of composing a landscape, Parkman, for instance, replaced the picturesque banditti of Salvator Rosa with frontiersmen, and Irving transmogrified a heap of sandstone into a Moorish castle. Both Americans, like Trollope, brought to their western travels an aesthetic sense informed by transatlantic art and theory: the *phenomenal* landscape of western America as depicted in travel literature owed its form to imported principles of organization. Dickens differs from the other three writers in his comparatively slight attention to formal

Worthington Whittredge's Twilight on Shawangunk Mountain. *Oil on canvas, 1865.*

criteria for appraising landscape. He relies more fully on imaginative projection, which enables him to reconfigure the landscape in accordance with his cultural prejudices.

The reputation of Frances Trollope as an American traveler does not rest on her landscapes. We remember chiefly the bluff Tory persona of *Domestic Manners* (1832), her lively encounters with the republicans, her witty and derisive estimates of American egalitarianism, and of course her diatribes against tobacco juice. Yet she plays the incisive comparatist of landscape with the same sprightly dogmatism that won the admiration of Twain. The terrain of America, no less than its citizens, had to take its place before the Trollopian bar.

While she admitted that America was a land of much rural beauty and that its "clearness and brightness" of atmosphere gave its landscapes an aesthetic advantage over those of England, Trollope often complained that the absence of ruins damped interest in the landscape. As she steamed up the Ohio after taking leave of the Nashua colony, she celebrated the varying riparian scenery and the cheering effects it produced by distracting her from brutish riverboat society.

> I imagine that this river presents almost every variety of river scenery; sometimes its clear wave waters a meadow of level turf; sometimes it is bounded by perpendicular rocks; pretty dwellings, with their gay porticos are seen, alternately with wild intervals of forest, where the tangled bear-brake plainly enough indicates what inhabitants are native there.

Notwithstanding this pleasant composition, "were there occasionally a ruined abbey, or feudal castle, to mix the romance of real life with that of nature, the Ohio would be perfect."

Later, as she traversed the "Allegheny Alps" on the National Road, Trollope once again praised the "beautiful succession of wild and domestic scenery":

> we were again cheered by abundance of evergreens, reflected in the stream, with fantastic piles of rock, half visible through the pines and cedars above, giving the idea of a vast gothic castle. It was folly, I confess, but I often lamented they were not such; the travelling for thousands of miles, without meeting any nobler trace of the ages that are passed, than a mass of rotten leaves, or a fragment of fallen rock, produces a heavy, earthly, matter-of-fact effect on the imagination, which can hardly be described, and for which the greatest beauty of scenery can furnish only an occasional and transitory remedy.

We can note several parallels between Trollope's remarks on American landscape and eighteenth-century debates over the nature of aesthetic vision. Although the word "picturesque" has a long and complex history (which has been traced by Walter Hipple, Jr.), the technical aesthetic phrase "Picturesque Beauty" was defined and illustrated by William Gilpin in his 1792 work *Three Essays: On Picturesque Beauty; On Picturesque Travel; and on Sketching Landscape: to Which is Added a Poem, On Landscape Painting.* Gilpin, who devoted less attention to the psycho-

logical bases of aesthetic perception than did Burke, undertook to explain the texture and composition of picturesque scenes—gardens or unimproved landscapes that satisfied the painter's eye. He singled out *roughness* as the essential quality that distinguished the picturesque from the beautiful, which is smooth and regular. His advice to "improvers" (as landscape gardeners were called) was to replace flowering shrubs with rugged oaks, break up smooth walks and mark them with wagon ruts, and "scatter around a few stones and brushwood" in order to produce a picturesque scene. As for natural formations that resemble bold architecture, "The spiry pinnacles of the mountains, and the castle-like arrangement of the rock, give no particular pleasures to the picturesque eye. It is fond of the simplicity of nature . . . in her *most usual* forms." However, if, as Trollope found, natural forms suggestive of human architecture disappoint the eye and the imagination, human architecture itself, Gilpin argued, inspires both: "among the objects of art, the picturesque eye is perhaps most inquisitive after the elegant relics of ancient architecture; the ruined towers, the Gothic arch, the remains of castles, and abbeys." In a subsequent edition of *Domestic Manners* Trollope responded to American critics of her aesthetic bias on this point by arguing that human art, however meager in comparison with the grandeur of unimproved nature, exerts a greater power on the eye because it links us with a vast history of human endeavor.

Despite the renewed political gibe implicit in Trollope's response, her appended argument echoes the aesthetic theory of Richard Payne Knight, who located the origin of aesthetic response in the viewer's associations, and not, like Burke, Gilpin and other theorists, in the landscape itself. In *An Analytical Inquiry into the Principles of Taste* (1805), Knight subordinated the role of "sensual" delight to that of subjective association in his perceptual model of landscape appreciation. In the "pleasing train of ideas" excited by "the venerable ruin, the retired cottage" lies the genesis of picturesqueness, according to Knight. Such associations might include not only memories of landscape paintings (which formalize vision) but also historical musings or fond remembrances of other landscapes. If Trollope was denied a ruined abbey, she found some recompense, as she crossed the Allegheny plateau, in another "pleasing train of ideas":

> I little expected that the first stop which should recall the garden scenery of our beautiful England would be found among the mountains. . . . Often on descending the narrow valleys we found a little pot of cultivation, a garden or a field, hedged round. . . . These valleys are spots of great beauty.

In this passage traits of "the beautiful," as defined by Burke and Gilpin—smoothness, regularity, smallness of scope—enter the associative process described by Knight to render an "English" landscape in America. As Peter Conrad notes [in his *Imagining America*, 1980], Trollope's "criteria of beauty and interest are genteel and domestic." By extension, Trollope generally missed in American landscape what she missed in the citizenry—evidence of cultivation, tradition and educated taste—and she typically made these qualities conditions of her aesthetic approval, as she had made them conditions of her cultural approval.

But it is not quite accurate to claim, as Conrad does, that Trollope "objects . . . to nature's unmannerliness." For all her reservations, Trollope generally relished the sublime experiences a relatively untamed America could offer. As distinct from a "beautiful" or "picturesque" scene, a sublime scene depends less, or not at all, on human artifice in the landscape. Unaided nature can terrify, and according to Burke "Whatever therefore is terrible, with regard to sight, is sublime." Writing of the Great Falls of the Potomac, Trollope makes use of Burke's familiar distinction:

> To call this scene beautiful would be a strange abuse of terms, for it is altogether composed of sights and sounds of terror. The falls of the Potomac are awfully sublime: the dark deep gulf which yawns before you, the foaming, roaring cataract, the eddying whirlpool, and the giddy precipice, all seem to threaten life, and to appal the senses. Yet it was a great delight to sit upon a high and jutting crag, and look and listen.

She follows Burke closely here, emphasizing one after another of his criteria for sublimity: power, loudness, obscurity (the dark deep gulf), extent, terror, the excited instinct for self-preservation, and delight made possible by removal from the source of danger. In an earlier and somewhat less touristly passage treating the sublime, she describes the effect of Ohio thunderstorms:

> Every thing seems colossal on this great continent; if it rains, if it blows, if it thunders, it is all done *fortissimo:* but I often felt terror yield to wonder and delight; so grand, so glorious were the scenes a storm exhibited.

The metaphor of "exhibited scenes"—a succession of framed vistas whose composition and subject matter effect the sublime—reveals the conventionality and structure even of Trollope's most exuberant descriptions of the American landscape. Like Gilpin's "picturesque traveler" she moved through the countryside in pursuit of "new scenes" that would inspire the painterly eye. Her descriptions of these scenes, as well as her expressions of delight or disappointment with them, owe their words and manner to a relatively new kind of landscape appreciation, one that both intensified and formalized human interaction with nature during the latter half of the eighteenth century. The forms this interaction might take, as we have seen, were various; its essence could be instinctual, associational, painterly—or any combination of the three. While the Romantic impulse may be discerned in the sublime moments of Trollope's narrative, she confines subjective expression to an established vocabulary of responses, resisting extreme fashions of spontaneous emotion or imaginative projection.

The American nature passages in Charles Dickens' *American Notes* (1842) are by contrast much more deliberately projective—the products of what Conrad calls his "malign magic." Like Trollope, Dickens usually endows his landscapes with cultural criticism. Trollope locates the basis for parallels between landscape and culture in a codified body of aesthetic desiderata. For her, the advantages and shortcomings of the culture may be registered (with reference to conventional aesthetic criteria) in the aesthetic felicities or disappointments afforded by framed vistas. Dickens, on the other hand, transforms western American landscape with the projective imagination that marks his fiction. Freely employing personification, hyperbole and patterns of imagery, he fashions an impressionistic landscape that accords with his cultural judgment of the western extremity of settlement as a region of isolation, deprivation and decay.

As representatives of western society, Dickens' steamboat company fared little better than Trollope's. He found that "nothing could have made head against the depressing influence of the general body. There was a magnetism of dulness in them. . . . Such deadly leaden people; such systematic plodding weary insupportable heaviness." The landscape description succeeding this complaint intensifies the prevailing mood, compounding particulars into a satisfactory novelistic whole:

> Nor was the scenery, as we approached the junction of the Ohio and Mississippi rivers, at all inspiriting in its influence. The trees were stunted in their growth; the banks were low and flat; the settlements and log cabins fewer in number: their inhabitants more wan and wretched than any we had encountered yet. . . . Hour after hour, the changeless glare of the hot, unwinking sky, shone upon the same monotonous objects. . . . But what words shall describe the Mississippi, great father of rivers. . . . An enormous ditch . . . running liquid mud . . . choked and obstructed everywhere by huge logs and whole forest trees . . . now rolling past like monstrous bodies, their tangled roots showing like matted hair; now glancing by like giant leeches; now writhing round and round in a vortex of some small whirlpool, like wounded snakes . . . mud and slime on everything.

A "gorgeous" sunset mitigates the ugliness for a short time, but then the scene becomes "a thousand times more lonesome and more dreary than before." The genii of Dickens' animated landscape are the deadly leaden steamboat passengers: boorish, aloof, preoccupied by "tremendous concealments," they roll like social corpses down the father of rivers. The more he saw of America, especially the West, the more Dickens shared Tocqueville's misgivings about the social effects of individualism in America. While American manners, according to the French critic, were "moulded upon the feelings and notions of each individual," the strange issue of this independence was an apparent uniformity of manners. "The people are all alike," Dickens complained of the passengers. "There is no diversity of character."

As the westernmost point of his 1842 tour, the Looking-Glass Prairie outside St. Louis offered Dickens a long-anticipated vista of the spacious frontier. Whether his expectations were too steep (as he thought) or his recent sojourn in western society too stultifying, the prairie revealed itself a cipher:

It would be difficult to say why, or how—though it was possibly from having heard and read so much about it—but the effect on me was disappointment. Looking out towards the setting sun, there lay, stretched out before my view, a vast expanse of level ground; unbroken, save by one thin line of trees, which scarcely amounted to a scratch upon the great blank; until it met the glowing sky, wherein it seemed to dip: mingling with its rich colours, and mellowing in its distant blue. There it lay, a tranquil sea or lake without water, if such a simile be admissible, with the day going down upon it: a few birds wheeling here and there: and solitude and silence reigning paramount around. . . . Great as the picture was, its very flatness and extent, which left nothing to the imagination, tamed it down and cramped its interest. I felt little of that sense of freedom and exhilaration which a Scottish heath inspires, or even our English downs awaken. It was lonely and wild, but oppressive in its barren monotony. I felt that in traversing the Prairies, I could never abandon myself to the scene, forgetful of all else; as I should do instinctively, were the heather underneath my feet . . . but should often gaze toward the distant and frequently-receding line of the horizon, and wish it gained and passed.

In purely aesthetic terms, the scene, as a picture, lacks variety. In locating a picturesque scene, Gilpin argued, the painter seeks a "happy union of simplicity and variety" that allows for massing. "An extended plain," he continued, "is a simple object. It is the cultivation of only one uniform idea. . . . the mere *simplicity* of a plain produces no beauty." But Dickens cared less about such criteria than did Trollope. He viewed the landscape in its imaginative potential—its susceptibility to projection and transformation. The Looking-Glass Prairie inhibited rather than excited his imagination. It seemed to him a dead and deadening thing because, I think, it mirrored his growing dissatisfaction with the culture that would overrun it. Several years before Dickens' visit, Washington Irving had hit on similar descriptive terms for the western prairie of Indian Territory—"vastness and simplicity"—yet for Irving, who was vaunting his patriotism in order to quell suspicions that he had become a European man, the effect was sublime. Irving found in the open plains a natural corollary for the exhilarating spirit of individualism and self-reliance that a young American could develop there, but Dickens, who had begun to feel the social oppressiveness engendered by democracy, found just so much space, barren of spiritual promise and romantic inspiration alike.

En route to St. Louis Dickens had steamed past the Big Grave Indian mound in what is now West Virginia. Though not the ruined abbey Frances Trollope had wished for, the mound was indeed a "nobler trace of the ages that are passed" than were geological formations. Salient among the surrounding natural hills, it furnished what was for Dickens one of very few bright vistas along the Ohio. In Dickensian fashion the scene bears the excesses of interpretive projection: it is a labored emblematic contrast between the "hoarse, sullen" machine transporting similar cargo, and the placid Ohio, which, "as though it shared one's feelings of compassion for the extinct tribes who lived so pleasantly here, in their blessed ignorance of white existence . . . steals out of its way to ripple near this mound." As Dickens' meditation extends, in subsequent pages, to the general deforestation of Ohio, he fondly imagines a distant era when American civilization will have vanished and the primordial forests reclaimed the land. At bottom these fantasies reverse Trollope's aesthetic logic while they partake of her cultural judgments. She shared the common view that ruins added human resonance to the landscape: they nurtured historical reflection by connecting nature with art, and they inspired a racial kinship with the improvers of nature through the ages. Dickens viewed the Big Grave mound as a memento of a primitive society, harmoniously involved with the land, which had given place to the occupation of a narrow and rapacious culture of empty expansionism. The mound's beauty was, for Dickens, largely the product of association, but in his case the "pleasing train of ideas" does not link modern American civilization with the past; instead, the associations lead backward to a time when it didn't exist and forward to a time when it won't. The Looking-Glass Prairie and the Mississippi at Cairo suggested only the bleak course of emigration, whereas the Big Grave mound represented the comforting ephemerality of American culture.

It was only coincidence, I think, that Dickens gave himself over completely to an American landscape only after he had crossed into Canada and found a civilization more to his liking. The Canadian vantage of Niagara Falls offered him solitude, and he wished to "shun strange company" while he viewed the falls for ten days. His description of the spectacle commences in good Romantic fashion with a sequence of subjective responses: he is "stunned, and unable to comprehend the vastness of the scene. . . . the first effect, the enduring one—instant and lasting—of the tremendous spectacle, was Peace. Peace of Mind, Tranquility." As if to emphasize the peculiarity of such a reaction, Dickens takes pains to distinguish it from a conventional sublime experience: he feels "nothing of gloom or terror." The Boz sublime admits of no theoretical prescription. It arises spontaneously from imaginative absorption in the landscape, it obliterates care, and it manifests itself in a compound of physical description and sentimental fantasy. The play of light and shadow on the falls, summoning images of angels' tears, speaking visages, and ghosts, restores that sense of exhilarating self-abandonment Dickens had felt on the heath and missed at the Looking-Glass Prairie. "Oh how the strife and troubled daily life receded from my view," he says of his Niagara sojourn, and he clearly means the burden of his western experience. The mound at Big Grave had freed Dickens' imagination from immediate historical involvement by inspiring a reverie that contracted and displaced history, leaving the Romantic self in an untenanted paradise. The conclusion of Dickens' passage on Niagara Falls leaves him pondering the moment when "Darkness brooded on the deep, and that first flood before the Deluge—Light—came rushing on Creation at the word of God." For Dickens, it would seem, the American landscape served a radically Romantic function, assuming the fantastic shapes of his disappointments and desires. If it overpowered ugly historical circumstances, it was a version of paradise; if it evoked them, it was a kind of hell.

Preceding Dickens' *Notes* by only a few years, Washington Irving's *A Tour on the Prairies* (1835) recounts his rambling in 1832 over what was to be Indian Territory, and later Oklahoma. Irving's book poses more rhetorical difficulties than *American Notes* because its narrator is more clearly a persona, in this case designed to effect Irving's rapprochement with his readers in the United States. In creating this persona Irving had to tread a fine line, for while his readers expected a genteel, cosmopolitan narrator who could draw upon his European experience to embellish his writing and draw contrasts between Continental and American scenery, they wanted proof of his commitment to American experience. Irving's self-portrait in the pages of *A Tour* is thus fashioned to garner maximum political capital from what he knew was the most American of enterprises—a journey to the frontier. His readers understood that when Irving advocated sending young men out west—to toughen them and instill in them the individualism and self-reliance demanded by American political institutions—instead of to Europe, where they might be effeminized, he was describing his own regimen in reverse.

The persona of *A Tour,* in short, obscures the author's uneasiness with home as found (not to mention his improvidence, haughtiness and nervousness on the trail, as noted by his companions). Although Irving's reservations about the American society he returned to coincided with some of Dickens' objections, he took care to avoid sensitive ideological issues in *A Tour,* instead endowing this persona with the sort of bland, floating patriotism evident in the remark about western acculturation. Irving's sophisticated and enthusiastic treatment of western landscape fits nicely into such a program in two respects. First, Romantic impressions of the landscape in *A Tour* arise from the sensibility of a genial and nearly ahistorical persona. Second, the objective landscape is translated as a picture, with some reference to the theoretical criteria (especially those relating to the sublime) that we have discussed in connection with Trollope. Both features set Irving's book apart from Dickens' *Notes,* in which the perceiving mind bristles with historical prejudices and creates its own aesthetic.

There is little need to reexamine Irving's debt to aesthetic theory throughout *A Tour.* However, a brief recapitulation of his treatment of the prairie as a symbolic landscape provides a helpful contrast for both Dickens' and Parkman's prairie extracts. Like Dickens, Irving stood on the verge of the open prairie at the most western point of his tour. The term "prairie," of course, is a relative one, for Irving looked out over a larger, emptier expanse than did Dickens at the Looking-Glass Prairie outside St. Louis—and neither of them saw the high plains traversed by Parkman in 1846. Yet in both *American Notes* and *A Tour* the prairie appears, in its palpable difference, a uniquely American landscape, and in a fashion reminiscent of the Alps in *The Prelude* it marks the topographical climax in both books. The extreme and divergent responses to the prairie recorded by Dickens and Irving thus chart their respective political agendas when these programs are

brought to bear on a symbolic place—a place full as much in the mind as on the continent. Dickens relies on the fiction of spontaneous impression to naturalize the prairie—that is, to affirm its essence as discrete from his prejudices. Irving takes a different tack, though his goal is the same. He creates the illusion of objectivity by identifying the prairie's physical features with those features of landscape Burke claimed would produce the sublime. (Unlike Richard Payne Knight, who contended that aesthetic responses grow purely out of association, Burke held that the object itself engenders the sublime effect.) Rhetorically, Irving operates on the basis of informed judgment among fixed aesthetic alternatives rather than by simple ingenuousness, and with this strategy he gains the cogent fiction of a seamless and inherent identity of the object, its aesthetic qualities, and the subject's response.

After a tedious march through gullied and difficult country, Irving's party

> emerged upon a grand prairie. Here one of the characteristic scenes of the Far West broke upon us. An immense extent of grassy, undulating, or, as it is termed, rolling country, with here and there a clump of trees, dimly seen in the distance like a ship at sea; the landscape deriving sublimity from its vastness and simplicity.

He had earlier observed that a "thunderstorm on the prairie, as upon the ocean, derives grandeur and sublimity from the wild and boundless waste over which it rages and bellows." And during a subsequent pause on the prairie he notes that "there is something inexpressibly lonely in the solitude of a prairie."

Irving's prairie occupies and divides space differently than Trollope's Potomac Falls, but the subliminity of each scene arises from a visual impetus expressly characterized by Burke, whose *Enquiry* Irving prescribed for himself in 1810. The falls inspire awe with noise, power, a "rugged or broken surface," and a perpendicular orientation. The prairie excites similar emotions, but it does so in an apparently opposite manner—through "*general* privations" such as vacuity, solitude and silence, and through "succession and *uniformity* of parts" that "constitute the artificial infinite":

> Infinity has a tendency to fill the mind with that sort of delightful horror, which is the most genuine effect, and truest test of the sublime. . . . the eye not being able to perceive the bounds of many things, they seem to be infinite, and they produce the same effects as if they were really so.

Recapitulating Burke on the artificial infinite, Uvedale Price says that "Infinity is one of the most efficient causes of the sublime; the boundless ocean, for that reason, inspires awful sensations." The illustration also belongs to Burke, who cites the sea as a more terrible example of infinity than the only other horizontal scape that can produce it—"A level plain of a vast extent on land."

Irving did not, of course, borrow the parallel from Burke: the sea metaphor in literature about the prairie was conventional before the mid-point of the century. Rather, like Melville, who compared the sperm whale's brow to the prairie in its power to awaken "dread powers," Irving found in Burke's criteria the path to an objective correlative for the awe he wanted his readers to share as he beheld the grand prairie of the American West.

With a fresh Harvard law degree, Francis Parkman set out from his Beacon Hill home in the spring of 1846 to see the West. He had two primary motives for undertaking this adventure: he wanted a rest from his studies, and he wanted to get some first-hand experience of the emigration with an eye toward beginning a history of the English and French in America. In the end, the recuperation he sought complicated his neurotic ailments, and the emigrants he encountered along the Oregon Trail disgusted him. Bernard De Voto has argued that Parkman's Brahmin snobbery, manifested in his rejection of the "coarse, crude folk who were the movement he traveled with . . . denied our culture a study of the American empire at the moment of its birth." But if the emigrants disappointed Parkman, the emigration itself—and the vast canvas on which it was enacted—did not. Despite misgivings about democracy and the bent of the common people, he celebrated the westward expansion as a testament to Anglo-Saxon perseverance in the American wilderness. In *The Oregon Trail* (1849) Parkman records these varied responses in the context of adjusting his readers' notions (and his own) about the conditions and terrain faced by emigrants. The romantic West—one resembling Irving's Cimarron valley, apparently laid out by the hand of taste—did indeed exist, and Parkman paid it its due, but he discovered another West as well—a bleak, violent desert beyond Irving's gardens, starker than his sublime prairie. In other words, he is at pains to describe an uncanny environment, one that will explain both the prevailing "fear and dissension" of wagon train members struggling over the prairie and intermontane "deserts," and the perplexity of some former backwoodsmen who are "totally out of their element" on the prairie. In so doing he can at once mitigate the unsavory or pitiable conduct of the emigrants he encounters and blend them into the grand setting of his relatively unfettered individual adventure.

As a "spectator" of western landscape, Parkman shows that he is well versed in the argot of eighteenth-century aesthetic theory. He handles its distinctions in a conventional manner, making greater use of them than Irving. Parkman does share with the *Sketch-Book* author the ability to naturalize the interplay of subject and object by creating detailed, painterly vistas from which the Romantic response seems to develop organically. In this respect both authors place a degree of emphasis on the object, with regard to its composition and aesthetic type, that is consistent with the concerns of Gilpin or Burke, while engaging the feeling self in typically Romantic fashion. In certain passages of *The Oregon Trail,* however, Parkman stakes a special claim outside the purview of both Romantic and picturesque travelers. Adjusting his readers' conception of the West sometimes requires a new traveling posture—that of the realist who can put aside conventional visions of the West and attest to the desolation of some stretches of the Rockies and the ugliness of the high plains.

These instances of ekphrasis (assertions of verity, based on

contrasts with "less-than-realistic" expressions) appear at the passings into and out of a band of undulating prairie east of the high plains. The rolling prairie, "a wide and fertile belt," meets all the requirements of the "beautiful": a "land of gardens" that needs no improvement, no "foreign aid," it has "all the softened and polished beauty of a region that has been for centuries under the hand of man." According to Parkman the landscapes of this band

> will probably answer tolerably well to [a traveler's] preconceived ideas of the prairie; for this it is from which picturesque tourists, painters, poets, and novelists, who have seldom penetrated farther, have derived their conceptions of the entire region. If he has a painter's eye, he may find his period of probation [before entering the high plains] not wholly void of interest. The scenery, though tame, is graceful and pleasing.

And upon regaining the area in-bound, Parkman repeats that "These are the prairies of the poet and the novelist." West of this region, however, a traveler following the Platte valley must relinquish for a time the "paradise of his imagination" as he encounters not only the climatic violence and formidable terrain of the great plains—double bane of the emigrants—but a distinctly *un*paradisiacal landscape: "it had not one picturesque or beautiful feature; nor had it any of the features of grandeur, other than its vast extent, its solitude, and its wildness. . . . a barren, trackless waste." Parkman follows Irving in his strategy of emphasizing the aesthetic uniqueness of the plains with the help of a conventional critical vocabulary. But in accordance with his realist's posture, he does so by rejecting all three aesthetic categories (though hedging some on the sublime) as insufficient to describe the Platte valley. Instead, he recounts his odd reaction: "It was right welcome; strange, too, and striking to the imagination." "The naked landscape," he continues, is "monstrous enough; and yet the wild beasts and wild men . . . make it a scene of interest and excitement."

Parkman, I think, is trying to shed artifice in his rendering of the Platte valley. To get at the stark but haunting essence of the place, he eschews the painterly mode (in which he elsewhere demonstrates talent) because it subdues and conventionalizes the landscape; he shuns effusive expressions of the sublime for the same reason—the formulaic sublime smacks of hyperbole, insincerity and, worst, effeteness. The high plains desert being traversed by weary emigrants calls for a vocabulary of studiously candid descriptive terms, and it demands as well a peculiarly understated response: it is barren and monstrous, strange and right welcome.

Parkman repeats this ekphrastic gesture only once, in his description of a stretch of mountains, near Ft. Laramie, which he passed with a band of Ogillallah (P's spelling): "On the next morning we entered again among the mountains. There was nothing in their appearance either grand or picturesque, *though* they were desolate to the last degree, being mere piles of black and broken rocks, without trees or vegetation of any kind" (my ital.). In other words, the barrenness and desolation of this landscape do not add up to a sublime effect; there is neither painterly interest nor anything that might awaken the delightful fear Burke associates with the sublime.

As if to bolster the authority of his discrimination, Parkman characterizes the landscape through which his party marches the very next day as "a sublime waste, a wilderness of mountains and pine-forests, over which the spirit of loneliness and silence seemed brooding." The privative sublime, it would seem, can be found in the mountains as well as on Irving's prairie, but both require some pictoral stimulant of the proper emotion.

In the course of extracting from *Domestic Manners, American Notes, A Tour on the Prairies* and *The Oregon Trail* a variety of interpretive paradigms and strategies for dealing with western landscape, I have necessarily overlooked and simplified some issues. For example, Parkman and Irving often blur the distinction between the beautiful and the sublime. Moreover, the focus on passages that contain aesthetic terminology exaggerates somewhat the role of these terms in the profusion of descriptive passages in Trollope, Irving and Parkman. Such are the hazards of emphasis. Nonetheless, the vocabulary of eighteenth-century aesthetic theory, in addition to supplying the taxonomy of vistas, establishes a common ground of aesthetic judgment between the traveler and the sophisticated reader. As we have seen, this terminology does not always have description as its end. In various ways, it serves Trollope, Irving and Parkman as a conduit for cultural and political judgment—a vehicle for connecting landscape with social enterprise. The "objectivity" that is supposed to inhere in these terms bestows a rhetorical authority on such judgment, while further naturalizing the identity of terrain and culture. In *American Notes* Dickens makes small use of the vocabulary of aesthetic theory while delivering his cultural appraisals by way of a thoroughly projective and symbolic landscape. The most fully Romantic of the four travelers, Dickens internalizes the landscape and so gains authority from a different quarter—the rhetorical "ingenuous" self—by concealing epistemological system.

Meriwether Lewis threw down his pencil at the falls of the Missouri because his descriptive paradigms had failed him. A second try yielded somewhat more satisfactory results in the form of Burke's categories, yet Lewis keenly missed the powers of the poet and painter in his desire to capture the wonderful force of the Missouri as it fell toward the high plains. His hermeneutic deliberation, recounted with the immediacy and candor characteristic of a journal entry, lays bare the process—and limitations—of choosing a handle for western landscape. If some of the literary travelers in the half century after his trek effectively obscured such arbitration in the interest of naturalizing their descriptions of landscape, we can, by tracing both the influence of aesthetic theory and the motives behind their cultural judgments, detect in their books patterns of choice masquerading as seamless perception.

> *Kris Lackey, "Eighteenth-Century Aesthetic Theory and the Nineteenth-Century Traveler in Trans-Allegheny America: F. Trollope, Dickens, Irving and Parkman," in* American Studies, *Vol. 32, No. 1, Spring, 1991, pp. 33-48.*

Sharon Rogers Brown

[*In the following excerpt, Brown contrasts American author Washington Irving's accounts of his travels through the Oklahoma prairies with those of a foreign writer and a government official, both of whom were his traveling companions.*]

[Scientists and explorers were] by no means the most famous contributors to the [travel literature] genre during the nineteeth century. Professional American writers capitalized upon the renewed spirit of nationalism by writing of their travels in their homeland. In 1832, Washington Irving wrote *A Tour on the Prairies,* the first travel narrative about America by an established author of American literature. The book glows with the creativity and rhetorical skill of a professional writer; at the same time it also displays the characteristics of a fine American travel narrative.

A Tour on the Prairies records Irving's excursion through the wilderness prairie land of Oklahoma in the company of friends and a unit of the United States Cavalry. The trip came about as a result of propitious circumstances. In 1832 President Jackson assigned Commissioner Henry Leavitt Ellsworth an important mission; in order to keep peace between the United States and the Cherokee and Creek Indian nations, Ellsworth was to "study the country, to mark the boundaries, to pacify the warring Indians, and, in general, to establish order and justice" [Henry Leavitt Ellsworth, *Washington Irving on the Prairie or A Narrative of a Tour of the Southwest in the Year 1832,* 1937]. Ellsworth traveled by steamer from Buffalo to meet his cavalry unit and begin his overland journey in Detroit. Fortunately for the genre of American travel literature, Washington Irving established a friendship with him on the steamer, and after hearing Ellsworth's plans, Irving asked permission to join him.

As Ellsworth writes, "After some acquaintance we discoursed upon the nature of my mission, and discovering a desire to accompany me, I invited them all to go with me even to the Buffalo range, promising them the protection of the Government and my individual exertions to make their excursion pleasant" [quoted in *Mississippi Valley Historical Review,* Vol. XXIX, No. 3]. Ellsworth's remark that he "invited them all" refers to Irving and two other travelers, one of whom, Charles Joseph Latrobe, produced a journal that may be compared to Irving's narrative. Latrobe was an English travel writer and Irving's friend. Along with his charge, a young Swiss Count, he was touring the United States to experience the West and to write of his observations. When Ellsworth invited Irving and the others to accompany the cavalry on a tour of duty, the excursion resulted in four narratives, one by Ellsworth, one by Latrobe and two by Irving (a rough journal written on the trail and *A Tour on the Prairies,* the revised, published manuscript). How fortunate that Irving's book, *A Tour on the Prairies,* was written under circumstances that provide an opportunity to recognize the differences between the travel narratives of a professional American writer (Irving), a foreign writer (Latrobe), and an American traveling on official business (Ellsworth).

The narratives differ from each other in many ways. Although they all describe the same journey, they do not all attend to the same details of the trip. In addition to differences in content, a variation exists in the authors' tones. In *A Tour* Irving romanticizes events, whereas Latrobe and Ellsworth present them realistically and impersonally. Irving makes scenes vivid, memorable and meaningful. When John Francis McDermott writes an introduction to [a 1956 edition of] *A Tour* he says,

> In *A Tour on the Prairies,* then, we have the zestful response of a man to his first experience beyond the Western Frontier. But Irving has a great deal more to offer than a readable account of personal experience. His book is a document, for in it he has preserved a segment of society. Its scenes and activities are original and unique because, perceiving them as an artist, he captured life rather than merely recorded information. The historian searching for facts who finds none in the *Tour* is gravely limited in his concept of the word. Facts are not limited to scientific, military, topographical, ethnological, or commercial data: Whatever "fixes" a scene of human activity or a person is a fact.

McDermott correctly recognizes Irving's "zestful response" and the narrative's inclusion of "personal experience." Irving creates an Edenic Western frontier decorated with wild flowers and prancing stallions. He presents himself as a refined gentleman who takes his dandelion, prairie tea sweetened with wild honey. McDermott describes Irving "as an artist . . . [who] captured life rather than merely recorded information"; one needs only to be familiar with the other accounts of this trip to know exactly what McDermott means. Latrobe and Ellsworth may record the number of buffalos they chase in a hunt; Irving imagines what each buffalo thinks as he outruns his captors.

In comparison to *A Tour,* Latrobe's and Ellsworth's records of the journey lack Irving's personal tone and enthusiasm. Latrobe wrote two volumes about his travels in North America, one hundred pages of which tell of his journey with Irving. Describing the prairie and the Indians, Latrobe uses a terse objectivity. When he invests himself in his writing, he uses his creative energies to be critical of America and express his disappointments in the country. Perhaps his European patrons expected a scornful description of the uncivilized American prairie.

Ellsworth, on the other hand, is also objective but far less negative about his experiences. He does not criticize anyone or anything; rather he formally and scientifically reports facts. He composed his narrative as a letter to his wife, but only occasionally does it approach the friendly, informal tone of a matrimonial epistle, and it totally lacks sentimentality and always maintains a narrative distance. When the editors of the most recent publication of Ellsworth's journal introduce it, they comment that "students of this particular period of American history will read the journal to the end" [Stanley T. Williams and Barbara D. Simison, "Introduction" in *Washington Irving on the Prairie* by Henry Leavitt Ellsworth, 1937]. The statement suggests a major difference between Ellsworth's and Irving's narratives: Ellsworth's work pleases students

of American history. Irving's *A Tour on the Prairies* pleases students of American literature.

Compared to Latrobe's fault finding and Ellsworth's scientific objectivity, *A Tour on the Prairies* glows with heartfelt enthusiasm. Irving describes his trip in an exhilarating, subjective voice. His excitement becomes a unifying factor that enables him to transform each individual experience into a meaningful component of the total narrative; all incidents develop his love of Nature on America's Western frontier. He writes with a definite purpose—to express his passion for the prairies—and when necessary he glorifies events to underline this theme. By comparing passages from *A Tour* to their counterparts in the narratives of Latrobe and Ellsworth, the reader recognizes Irving's artistic presentation of his experiences. For example, a passage in which Irving describes the party's first sighting of a wild horse demonstrates the differences in content, tone and style among the three narratives.

The selection from Irving's *Tour* shows his admiration for the wild horse:

> After a time, the horse suddenly made his appearance to our right, just ahead of the line, emerging out of a small valley, on a brisk trot; having evidently taken the alarm. At sight of us he stopped short, gazed at us for an instant with surprise, then tossing up his head, trotted off in fine style, glancing at us first over one shoulder, then over the other, his ample mane and tail streaming in the wind. Having dashed through a skirt of thicket, that looked like a hedge-row, he paused in the open field beyond, glanced back at us again, with a beautiful bend of the neck, snuffed the air, then tossing his head again broke into a gallop, and took refuge in a wood.
>
> It was the first time I had ever seen a horse scouring his native wilderness in all the pride and freedom of his nature.

Irving animates the horse's "brisk trot," his "tossing" head "glancing" over shoulders and his "streaming" mane. Along with these vivid descriptions, Irving communicates his thrill at seeing the horse and produces an immediacy that allows his readers to share that excitement. When Irving uses the pronoun "I" in the last paragraph, the scene becomes a personal epiphany that he invites his audience to witness. He closes with his description of the "horse scouring his native wilderness in all the pride and freedom of his nature." These words express the overall theme of his book: all that is natural on the American frontier abounds with glory, pride and freedom.

In comparison to Irving's meaningful and personal passage, Ellsworth's description offers an objective explanation of events. To begin with, Ellsworth places the incident after an account of the methods used for capturing wild horses on the prairie. He then writes,

> We had not advanced far, before we descried an elegant horse, feeding at some distance—The Capt and his Lieutenant and one more, went in pursuit, hoping to get near enough to crease him, as neither of them had a Lariat or knew how to use one—We saw them advance upon the ani-

Thomas Moran's The Grand Canyon of the Yellowstone. *Oil on canvas, 1872.*

mal, still unconscious that an enemy was approaching—When near the steed the Capt dismounted, and creeping along to make sure of his horse the animal spied him, and ran towards us—we saw it coming, he took our troops to be a kindred gang of wild colts—he came with elegant motions very near Mr Irving & myself, and neighing, was answered by the Doct's horse, who stood by the side of ours—the Wild horse was a beautiful iron grey—well made and had a most lofty carriage—As soon as he discovered our true character, he cut the acquaintance and ran with surprising speed through brush & Mire until his escape was effected—he might easily have been shot down but none wished to destroy so fine an animal, but Mr Brialy who regretted he did not shoot him, to see how he looked—We were all delighted with our view of a wild horse—the Capt soon joined us, and we went on our course.

This excerpt is one of the more informal passages in Ellsworth's Journal, with a chatty, relaxed tone rather than a scientific one; but still, Ellsworth seems more an observer than a participant in the scene. Whereas Irving's description suggests that the incident stirred emotions within him, Ellsworth does not indicate that the horse had any special effect on him.

While Ellsworth agrees with Irving about the horse's beauty writing that the "beautiful iron grey" horse was "well made and had a most lofty carriage," he never transforms that beauty into any kind of symbol. When Irving associates the horse with "pride and freedom," it suggests the glory of the American wilderness; Irving layers descriptive images until, in the conclusion, the horse represents his theme, the marvels of the prairies. Ellsworth simply concludes with the bland, impersonal remarks, "We were all delighted" and "we went on our course." He does not interpret the meaning of the encounter, nor does he create a private scene; instead he leaves with the other travelers while the horse runs away from them all. The reader feels that Ellsworth did not witness anything important, as if Ellsworth viewed the wild horse as a pleasant but meaningless diversion that distracted from the important "course" of business. Considering that Ellsworth traveled through the prairies on a mission to scout the territory for the United States government and to pacify the Indians, his sighting of a wild horse must not have been momentous. Irving, on the other hand, traveled on vacation and as a way to gather material for his book. Of course Irving and Ellsworth interpreted and presented their experiences differently—Ellsworth wrote as a professional statesman traveling on business, Irving as a professional writer traveling for pleasure.

But Charles Latrobe was also a professional writer traveling to gather material for a book. Nonetheless, a major difference exists between the Englishman's book and Irving's in their descriptions of America. Latrobe traveled in America as a British tourist, and though half a century had passed since the Revolution, Latrobe's criticism of

America makes it seem as if the British still hold a grudge. Here is his account of the wild horse scene:

> Just before we descended to covert from the higher grounds, we had seen a wild horse dashing across our line of march. It was the first we had met with, but, however its appearance seemed to excite general attention at the time, after getting to camp, no more was thought of it. The breed of horses which are scattered in numbers over these plains, is a cross between those introduced by the Spaniards and French, but are, with single exceptions, rather a degenerate race both in appearance and power.
> [*The Rambler in North America,* 1835]

Latrobe reduces the noble steed of Irving's description to a member of "a degenerate race." Irving's pleasure trip and Ellsworth's "course" of business are a "march" for Latrobe, and the horse incident has no place in it. For Irving the horse represents the grandeur of wild America; for Ellsworth the horse provides a pleasant diversion from the "course"; but Latrobe sees only a "degenerate" animal that cuts across the "line of march."

Latrobe finds fault with most aspects of his trip. He has little admiration for the American natives, and his descriptions of them comprise one of the notable differences between his book and *A Tour on the Prairies.* Irving describes the "Osages: stately fellows; stern and simple in garb and aspect. . . . They had fine Roman countenances, and broad deep chests." In Latrobe's *The Rambler,* they become "the rude tribes and inhabitants of the West." If Irving is to be faulted, as he occasionally is, for romantically idealizing the West, Latrobe should be faulted for unfairly denouncing it.

Irving optimistically presents the West in all its glory and then some; like the angler who tells the great fish story about the one that got away, Irving has been accused of exaggerating the wonders of the prairies in his effort to immortalize them before they drown in the wake of farms, shops, homes and graveled roads. McDermott calls Irving's *Tour* a work that reveals "the magnificence of his imagination," but is faulted by "conventionalized romantic elements. . . . As a historian and a travel reporter his method is questionable." These comments, taken in context, criticize Irving for his elaboration of incidents. They appear in McDermott's introduction to *The Western Journals* that Irving wrote on the trail. McDermott praises the journals in comparison to *A Tour on the Prairies,* saying that they are more factual. Irving kept the journals to aid his memory; they are objective records, not literary accounts. When Irving writes with an audience in mind, he transforms objective records into belles lettres, a transformation that can be seen by comparing Irving's original accounts in *The Journals* with his revised versions in *A Tour on the Prairies.*

Irving's journal entry dated October 13, for example, includes a passage of approximately 250 words about a bee hunt. Chapter Nine of *A Tour on the Prairies* contains four and a half pages, almost 1500 words, entitled a "A Bee Hunt." On the simplest level, the original journal methodically tells of finding the hive, chopping down the tree on which it sits, smoking out the bees, and taking the honey; Irving does not include any reaction to the incidents. In *A Tour,* Irving elaborates on the same information and includes additional facts and personal reactions.

Irving begins chapter nine of *A Tour* with an explanation about bee migration. He then offers a detailed exposition of the axing of the bee tree. He follows the action with a lengthy description of the bees' reactions to the devastation of their hive. With wit and satire, Irving makes part of this section an extended metaphor of the fall of a state. While the defeated bees "contemplate the prostrate ruin, and buzz forth doleful lamentation over the downfall of their republic," their neighbors practice the "habits" of "laborious and gainful man." Irving "beheld numbers from rival hives, arriving on eager wing, to enrich themselves with the ruins of their neighbors." None of this material appears in the journal.

As for stylistic changes, Irving turns choppy fragments from the journal into complete sentences for *A Tour.* He embellishes the descriptions and brings excitement to the sentences by adding vivid phrases such as the bees "wheeled about in the air" and the forests are "teeming with ambrosial sweets." While the journal only contains dull statements that tell briefly of cutting the honey out of the hives, "A Bee Hunt" in *A Tour* includes distinctive images of the honey-rich combs and the sweet-toothed cavalry men. In the journals, the men find "combs much broken—some white, clean & new, others old—take out flakes in a pail—everyone with spoon & knife helps himself to the rich honey." In *A Tour,*

> every one of the party now fell to, with spoon and hunting-knife, to scoop out the flakes of honey-comb with which the hollow trunk was stored. Some of them were of old date and a deep brown color, others were beautifully white, and the honey in their cells was almost limpid. Such of the combs as were entire were placed in camp-kettles to be conveyed to the encampment; those which had been shivered in the fall were devoured upon the spot. Every stark bee-hunter was to be seen with a rich morsel in his hand, dripping about his fingers, and disappearing as rapidly as a cream tart before the holiday appetite of a schoolboy.

Irving has taken his lifeless journal entry and, in *A Tour,* has animated it with active, eager participants in the harvest. Phrases such as "the party now fell to" each with "a rich morsel in his hand, dripping about his fingers" create vivid images of "schoolboy" joy. The bee hunters' enthusiasm vibrates with the energy of bees hovering around honey. Not a drop goes to waste—what is not carried back to camp is "devoured upon the spot" by the men; what they can not reach "will be cleared off by varmint . . . bears, and skunks, and racoons, and 'possums." A hollow tree offers this sweet treasure to the hunters if they know how to harvest it. Likewise, the American prairies offer unique beauty to the traveler if he knows how to recognize it. Latrobe sees only the hollow trees; Irving sees the treasures they offer. The passage is a perfect example of what McDermott means when he suggests that Irving observes and writes "as an artist" who "captures life rather than merely recorded information."

By glorifying the bee hunt Irving turns it into a spectacle that typifies life: the Western expanse becomes

> the land of promise, "a land flowing with milk and honey"; for the rich pasturage of the prairies is calculated to sustain herds of cattle as countless as the sands upon the sea-shore, while the flowers with which they are enamelled render them a very paradise for the nectar-seeking bee.

Throughout the book, Irving turns every phenomenon into evidence that the prairies are "the land of promise." The same sort of comparisons can be made between most entries in Irving's journals and their corresponding chapters in *A Tour*. Skillfully transforming each minor incident into a major one, whether it is the sighting of a wild horse, a bee hive, a buffalo hunt, a prairie fire, or an Indian, Irving proclaims his excitement, wonder, and optimism.

Even though in his introduction to the journals, McDermott criticizes *A Tour,* he correctly states that "Irving [in *A Tour*] is not a traveler reporting what he sees; he is ever the self-conscious literary man, the feature-story writer who, by the ready use of his imagination, makes a little go a long way." McDermott implies that Irving romanticizes the facts; *A Tour on the Prairies* is more aptly described as Irving's creative response to America's need for a national literature at a time when American romanticism was setting its buds. In keeping with eighteenth-century, neoclassical tradition, Sarah Kemble Knight embellished her narrative with heroic couplets and classical allusion. In keeping with nineteenth-century, American romantic tradition, Irving transforms reality into myth and nature into symbol. By the nineteenth century, the literature of travel has evolved in America to the point where it welcomes such imagination.

Irving imagined the kind of book he wanted to write during the journey, and it begins to take shape in letters to his family. Soon after the trip he described how it came about to his brother [in a letter on 18 December 1832]:

> The offer [to travel with Ellsworth] was too tempting to be resisted: I should have an opportunity of seeing the remnants of those great Indian tribes, which are now about to disappear as independent nations, or to be amalgamated under some new form of government. I should see those fine countries of the "far west," while still in a state of pristine wildness, and behold herds of buffaloes scouring their native prairies, before they are driven beyond the reach of a civilized tourist.

Irving recognized an opportunity to witness and record American scenes that were fast becoming history. During the same period, James Fenimore Cooper used historical legends to create romantic novels about Indians and American heroes. Irving would use actual observations for his travel book, but he too would write in the romantic style and would offer images that could add to the composite of an American identity as expressed in a national literature.

Yet McDermott praises the realistic journals and criticizes the romantic travel narrative. Instead, *A Tour on the Prairies* should be praised because it represents Irving's accomplishment as a professional writer and an American mythmaker. Irving is well known for creating legends about the history of New York out of German folklore. In *A Tour on the Prairies* he constructs a legend of the wonderful last days of the prairie, and the source for the legend is his own frontier experience. The folklore he uses in *A Tour* comes from native Americans, stories of the Flower of the Prairie, of the Indian brave and the moccasins of thunder, of the Delaware Chief rescued by the American eagle. The enthusiasm that unifies the whole book comes from within Irving, from the spirit of patriotism that imbued Americans in the early nineteenth century, and from the beauty of the prairies.

Irving begins his book with an apology to his readers for being an expatriate from 1815 to 1832. In "Author's Introduction" Irving discusses "his long absence and the doubts and suggestions to which it had given rise." After his trip he can write,

> I make no boast of my patriotism; I can only say, that, as far as it goes, it is no blind attachment. I have sojourned in various countries; have been treated in them above my deserts; and the remembrance of them is grateful and pleasant to me. I have seen what is brightest and best in foreign lands, and have found, in every nation, enough love and honor; yet, with all these recollections living in my imagination and kindling in my heart, I look round with delightful exultation upon my native land, and feel that, after all my ramblings about the world, I can be happiest at home.

Irving's exuberance in *A Tour on the Prairies* regenerated the love of those American readers who had begun to wonder why he left America to live in and write of Europe for seventeen years.

> *Sharon Rogers Brown, "Professional Travelers and a Professional Travel Narrator: Fact and Fancy in Early Nineteenth-Century Narratives," in her* American Travel Narratives as a Literary Genre from 1542 to 1832: The Art of a Perpetual Journey, *The Edwin Mellen Press, 1993, pp. 107-24.*

Franklin R. Rogers

[*Rogers, an American critic, has published several studies of Mark Twain's nonfiction and humorous writings and has served as editor of* The Mark Twain Papers: Satires and Burlesques. *In the following excerpt, he places two of Twain's works,* The Innocents Abroad *and* Roughing It, *in the context of traditional burlesque travel literature, showing how Twain introduced fundamental changes into the genre.*]

In July, 1870, Elisha Bliss of the American Publishing Company completed a contract with Samuel L. Clemens, the latest arrival among the ranks of the American comic writers, which called for the delivery by January 1 1871 of sufficient manuscript to make a 600-page book. Bliss, of course, expected the author to furnish something which would repeat the success of *The Innocents Abroad,* which had been published the previous year, and Clemens proposed to outdo himself, if possible, this time with a tale based upon his trip across the Plains in 1861 and his six years' sojourn in Nevada and California. The six months allotted by the contract proved entirely too short for the completion of the projected book. The protracted illness and finally the death of Clemens' father-in-law, Jervis Langdon, and the illness and death of a house-guest, Emma Nye, consumed much of the author's time, and progress on the manuscript was further retarded by a dissatisfaction with the product of his labors which led to extensive revisions. Even an additional six months did not free him from the sense of pressure. As a result, the book which he finally produced exhibits at least two major flaws. One is the awkward break in tone, structure, and point of view evident in the last eighteen chapters, the consequence of his hasty incorporation at the last moment of the series of letters written from Hawaii for the Sacramento *Union* in 1866. The other is the padding of the text with statistics and quotations, principally from his newspaper clippings, which characterizes a number of the earlier chapters. But despite its imperfections the book proved quite acceptable to Bliss, and its subsequent success apparently stilled any misgivings Twain himself may have had on the score of his patchwork. Interested as he no doubt was in securing another comic best-seller, Bliss ignored its faults; he probably also failed to appreciate the essential importance of the manuscript which Clemens sent him in batches during the first months of 1871. For while *Roughing It* marks the culmination of a seventy-year-old tradition in burlesque travel literature, it also represents the successful transformation of burlesque travel literature conventions into the means for significant literary expression.

The tradition to which *Roughing It* owes a substantial debt begins with William Combe's *The Tour of Dr. Syntax in Search of the Picturesque* which first appeared serially in the *Poetical Magazine,* 1809-1811. Written in a pseudo-Hudibrastic verse which "may wel be rym dogerel," the tour proved a popular success. Combe exploited its popularity with an edition in book form in 1812 and two sequels, *The Second Tour of Dr. Syntax in Search of Consolation* (1820) and *The Third Tour of Dr. Syntax in Search of a Wife* (1821); during the next half-century several British publishers managed to keep the three tours before the reading public. As the title of the first poem suggests, it is a burlesque of the popular late eighteenth-century literature of picturesque travel to which Wordsworth's *An Evening Walk* and *Descriptive Sketches* are closely related. In its general conception Combe's poem reflects the work of such writers of picturesque travel poetry as Anthony Champion, Thomas Maude, and George Cumberland; the central figure, Dr Syntax, is a caricature of William Gilpin, Rector of Boldre, who has been fittingly called [by Christopher Hussey in *The Picturesque*] "the high priest of the picturesque." George Crabbe reacted to this literature with a grim realism which a hundred years later won Edwin Arlington Robinson's admiration; Combe reacted with a satire conveyed primarily through his character, Dr Syntax, whose excessive fastidiousness and sublimity of

taste cause him to reject and suppress the disturbing truths which Crabbe fastened upon. Dr Syntax is the very quintessence of the artist in search of the picturesque, the artist who, in order to achieve the picturesque, must take liberties with the actuality before him, blinding himself to that which offends his taste and freely substituting from his imagination that which will heighten his gratification, thus forcing the observed reality into a preconceived ideal pattern of the picturesque. "What man of taste," Dr Syntax asks,

> my right will doubt,
> To put things in, or leave them out?
> 'Tis more than right, it is a duty,
> If we consider landscape beauty:
> He ne'er will as an artist shine,
> Who copies Nature line by line.

According to Combe, this character stems from the mock-heroic tradition: in Canto XII of the first tour, he wrote:

> You'll see, at once, in this Divine,
> Quixote and Parson Adams shine:
> An hero well combin'd you'll view
> For FIELDING and CERVANTES too.

Certainly in structure, the Dr Syntax poems are a derivative of the knight-errant tradition on which *Don Quixote* is built, but, despite the doctor's encounter with highwaymen which is in the same vein as the battle with the huntsman's hounds in *Joseph Andrews,* very little of the mock-heroic actually appears in the series. An important difference between Don Quixote and Dr Syntax is that Cervantes' character is deranged, totally dissociated from the actuality through which he moves; the doctor perceives the actuality, but for reasons of taste ignores some aspects of it and, ignorant of worldly matters, fails to understand others. Instead, in his extreme sentimentality and his frequent soliloquies upon picturesque or melancholy scenes, he is much closer to Mr Yorick of Sterne's *Sentimental Journey.*

The popularity of Dr Syntax and his adventures is demonstrated not only by the frequent editions and reprints but also by the extent to which subsequent humorists resorted to them for guidance in shaping their own burlesques of travel literature. Apparently it was not so much the doctor's pretense to refined taste and sentiment which attracted the later humorists as it was the comic possibilities inherent in the coupling of this attitude with his artistic and scientific aspirations. Armed with sketchbook and notebook, the doctor traveled about England ever ready to preserve the picturesque scene which fluttered his pulse or the "curious" information which excited his mind. As a result of this combination, a third dimension, as it were, could be added to the burlesque. Not only is the reader moved to laughter by the contrast between the traveler's expectations and the actuality encountered; he is also moved to laughter by the traveler's subsequent interpretations in the form of wretched poetry, crude drawings, or fantastic scientific theories. A host of similar travelers, each equipped with sketchbook or notebook or both and eager to present the results of his travels to the reading public, crowd the pages of the British comic magazines down through the first twenty years of *Punch,* that is, from the 1840s to the

1860s, and appear in such less well-known humor magazines as *Fun, Judy,* and *Punch and Judy.* But only two of Dr Syntax's progeny, Thackeray's Michael Angelo Titmarsh and Dickens' Mr Samuel Pickwick, P.C., have won a permanent place in literature.

Imitative of the British periodicals, the American humor magazines also afford several examples of the type. Generally, the American humorists appear to have modelled their work after the current British burlesques, without any direct reference to the original tours of Dr Syntax, but in at least one instance the American by-passed the contemporary British examples and returned directly to Combe's work. In the first issue of his *Illustrated California Magazine* (1856), J. M. Hutchings began a burlesque entitled "Dr. Dotitdown in Search of the Picturesque, Arabesque, Grotesque, and Burlesque." The title contains, of course, references to Combe's *Tour of Dr. Syntax in Search of the Picturesque* and to Poe's *Tales of the Grotesque and Arabesque.*

By the 1860s Combe's conception had undergone several mutations. One was the very early abandonment of his doggerel verse in favor of prose; another was the addition of a traveling companion who bears a distant relationship to Sancho Panza, a more immediate one to Sam Weller. A vernacular character, this companion, usually a servant or a young relative or family friend, serves a function slightly different from Sancho Panza's. As far as the reader is concerned, one of Sancho's major services is to report the actuality which the Knight, because of his delusions, cannot see. The companion of the nineteenth-century burlesque constantly reminds the reader and the traveler himself of those unpicturesque elements of the actuality which the traveler has chosen to ignore, and contributes a knowledge, sometimes surprisingly full for one of his years, in those fields where the traveler, in his innocence, is totally uninitiated: the properties of a wide variety of strong beverages, the wiles of worldly women, the art of gambling, and the devices of a wide variety of tricksters, swindlers, and other petty criminals. With predilections for such activities as those indicated by his knowledge, the companion is the major source of conflict for the traveler. With the emergence of the companion, this type of burlesque, some fifty years after Dr Syntax first set out on his swaybacked mare, had become fairly conventional: the traveler is a refined and sophisticated gentleman bent upon studying art, discovering sources for other ponds of Hampstead, or devising further theories of tittlebats; his companion is his antithesis in taste, sentiments, and interests; their itinerary takes the pair to scientific wonders, monuments of antiquity, or paintings of the Masters; and a series of arguments and mishaps, precipitated by the companion, disappoint or deflate the gentleman's expectations.

The conventional character of these burlesques is suggested not only by the frequent reappearance of the same elements but also by the failure of the British magazines to keep pace with developments in travel literature. Long after the focus of interest in travel books had shifted from the haunts of the Romantics in Italy, France, and Germany, to scenes of intrepid adventure in the Near East, the Orient, Africa, and the western United States, the travel-

ers in the burlesques still studied their art in the Louvre and the Capitol and sought the picturesque in the Lake District, the Rhine Valley, the Black Forest, and the Harz Mountains. The result, in the British magazines of the 1860s, was a dissociation of the burlesques from the literature upon which they should have fed, with a consequent loss of vitality which is reflected in the mutation of the central character, who is reduced from a caricature of the sentimental traveler to a simple straightman. No longer mad, not even north-north-west, he has become to a great degree merely the center from which we measure the antics of his ebullient companion and others. The mutation is quite visible in one of the longest of such burlesques, "Our Roving Correspondent," which began in the first issue of *Punch* for 1860. In the July 27 1861 issue, the refined traveler, Jack Easel, comments upon young female tourists at the Italian art galleries:

> The ease and rapidity with which these charming critics form acquaintance with and discuss the merits of the Old Masters is truly astonishing. I once heard a young lady . . . remark, that she had "done" the Capitol between the hours of breakfast and lunch, adding that she would be able to give me a full description of the Borghese Collection by the time we met at dinner. "*Per Bacco!* Ma'am," I exclaimed—you know we were in Italy, and I always ejaculate, if possible in the language of the country where I am residing—"*per Bacco!* What a muff is your humble servant. Here have I been spending months in the study of a single gallery and am half inclined to throw up my profession in despair, at my ignorance."

Although the comment about ejaculations suggests the exaggerated sophistication of earlier travelers who did things "by the book," the passage in general demands that the reader regard Jack Easel as the standard against which the charming critics are measured and found wanting.

In the United States the type retained a great deal of its vitality simply because, while British readers were exploring the mysteries of the Middle East in such books as Warburton's *The Crescent and the Cross,* Curzon's *Monasteries of the Levant,* and Burton's *A Pilgrimage to Al-Medinah and Meccah,* the Americans were re-discovering a picturesque Europe in such books as Sara Jane Lippincott's *Haps and Mishaps of a Tour in Europe,* Harriet Beecher Stowe's *Sunny Memories of Foreign Lands,* and Bayard Taylor's *Views A-Foot.* As Professor Willard Thorp has noted in his study of such American travel books:

> The less imaginative of the professional writers soon evolved a sort of standard pattern for the travel book. The author must begin with the excitements of the ocean voyage itself and devote at least a portion of a chapter to the thrill, so long anticipated, of setting foot on foreign soil. From this point on he should mix architecture and scenery . . . , skillfully work in a little history . . . , taking care to add a touch of sentiment or eloquence when the occasion permitted. If the essay or book required a little padding, it was always possible to retell an old legend or slip in an account of dangers surmounted in crossing

the Alps. ["Pilgrim's Return" in *Literary History of the United States,* 1953]

That is, the travel books which American writers were producing lent themselves well to the sort of burlesque treatment we have been considering; it is not surprising to find them getting such treatment from Artemus Ward, Petroleum V. Nasby, J. Ross Browne, and, of course, Mark Twain.

In *The Innocents Abroad,* the most famous burlesque product of this spate of American travel books, we find Mark Twain building upon the pattern which Thorp has noted. The first paragraph contains a passage which is, with its alliterations, rhythms, hyperboles, and clichés, at once a revelation of the delusions of the passengers and a parody of the effusive statements of anticipatory thrills in the books upon which it is modelled:

> [The passengers] were to sail for months over the breezy Atlantic and the sunny Mediterranean; they were to scamper about the decks by day, filling the ship with shouts and laughter—or read novels and poetry in the shade of the smoke-stacks, or watch for the jelly-fish and the nautilus, over the side, and the shark, the whale, and other strange monsters of the deep; and at night they were to dance in the open air, on the upper deck, in the midst of a ballroom that stretched from horizon to horizon, and was domed by the bending heavens and lighted by no meaner lamps than the stars and the magnificent moon—dance, and promenade, and smoke, and sing, and make love, and search the skies for constellations that never associate with the "Big Dipper" they were so tired of: and they were to see the ships of twenty navies—the customs and costumes of twenty curious peoples—the great cities of half a world—they were to hobnob with nobility and hold friendly converse with kings and princes, Grand Moguls, and the anointed lords of mighty empires!

But although *The Innocents Abroad* is a burlesque of travel literature, the controlling fiction of the conventional Dr Syntax type of burlesque, the conflict between a sentimental traveler and his irrepressible companion, is missing, or rather is subordinated to such an extent that it appears only in occasional episodes.

The Innocents Abroad is actually an intermediate stage in a series of experiments through which Twain gradually shaped the burlesque conventions to his own artistic purposes. The first stage in the sequence dates from 1866, when Twain built the controlling fiction of his Sandwich Islands letters directly upon the conventional traveler-companion conflict. Adopting for these letters the pose of Mr Twain, a traveler with all the sensibilities and most of the aspirations of Dr Syntax, and creating a companion, Mr Brown, as bitter an enemy to sentiment as any of his predecessors, Twain tried to fulfill the two major conditions of his contract with the Sacramento *Union,* that he write a humorous travel sketch and that he furnish factual information about the Hawaiian Islands for the *Union* readers. The attempt to fulfill these two conditions involved Twain directly in a problem inherent in this type of burlesque from its beginnings: how to convey to the reader a clear concept of the actuality which moves the sophisticated traveler to sentimental tears or his companion to snorts of derision. As long as the burlesque is written in the third person, there is no problem. The author, on his own authority, presents the actuality and then permits the two characters to give their interpretations of it. But when, as in the greater portion of the burlesques of this type, the author chooses the first person form of narration, the problem becomes central. Whether he adopts for himself the pose of the traveler or the companion, he must accept as the price a blindness to and ignorance of certain elements in the actuality before him. Of course, he may very easily work in the reactions and interpretations of his associate as, from his point of view, shocking examples of blindness or ignorance, but the reader must discern the actuality for himself somewhere between the two extremes resulting from the traveler's exaggerated sentimentality and the companion's exaggerated skepticism and unregeneracy.

Here we can perceive what may well have been the reason for the failure of the British burlesques to keep pace with the mid-century developments in travel literature. As long as the books being burlesqued dealt with countries which the anticipated audience knew with a fair degree of intimacy, the humorist could depend upon the reader's knowledge to supply the information which his chosen pose prevented him from presenting in the burlesque. But when British travelers pushed on into new and relatively unknown regions, the humorist could not follow unless he forged new tools for his art. Mark Twain faced exactly the same problem, but one cannot say he solved it; he merely ignored the demands of consistency, slipping easily out of his pose to the role of reporter as frequently as he wished, apparently without even asking himself whether such a course indicated Emersonian greatness or artistic weakness.

The letters written for the *Alta Californian* describing Twain's journey from San Francisco to New York by way of the Isthmus in 1866-67 and the *Quaker City* excursion retain the same controlling fiction and exhibit the same disregard for consistency, but in the reworking of these letters for *The Innocents Abroad* Twain took the first major step toward the achievement of *Roughing It* when he attempted to fuse the characteristics of the traveler and his companion in one narrator. The fusion involved him in further difficulties, for this new narrator must exhibit on the one hand the sophistication and sentimentality of the traveler, on the other the uncouthness and insensitivity of the companion, and as necessary the judiciousness of the reporter. Once again he ignored the demands of consistency and let the contradictions stand. For example, his narrator is disdainful of sentimental tears after weeping over the graves of Abelard and Heloise and then learning their history, but he weeps as copiously as either Dr Syntax or Mr Yorick when he views Adam's tomb. Then, in order to justify his denunciation of William C. Prime's sentimental tears on the shores of Galilee, Twain must cast his narrator in the role of a clear-eyed and judicious reporter of the observed reality.

In that portion of *Roughing It* which concludes with the

departure for the Sandwich Islands, Twain devised a method of reconciling the opposed points of view. *Roughing It* opens with a passage which is both similar to and subtly and significantly different from the statement of anticipatory thrills in the first pages of *The Innocents Abroad*:

> I was young and ignorant, and I envied my brother. I coveted his distinction and his financial splendor, but particularly and especially the long, strange journey he was going to make, and the curious new world he was going to explore. He was going to travel! I never had been away from home, and that word "travel" had a seductive charm for me. Pretty soon he would be hundreds and hundreds of miles away on the great plains and deserts, and among the mountains of the Far West, and would see buffaloes and Indians, and prairie dogs, and antelopes, and have all kinds of adventures, and maybe get hanged or scalped, and have ever such a fine time, and write home and tell us all about it, and be a hero. And he would see the gold mines and the silver mines, and maybe go about of an afternoon when his work was done, and pick up two or three pailfuls of shining slugs, and nuggets of gold and silver on the hillside. And by and by he would become very rich, and return home by sea, and be able to talk as calmly about San Francisco and the ocean, and "the isthmus" as if it was nothing of any consequence to have seen those marvels face to face.

The significant difference is in the pronoun used in each instance. The pronoun *they* in the earlier passage directs the ridicule toward the other *Quaker City* passengers and to travelers who write travel books. It implicitly exempts the narrator himself. The shift in point of view to the first person in the *Roughing It* passage focuses the ridicule upon the narrator himself and tends to remove travelers as a class to the background, if not out of the picture.

A change of plan during the composition of *Roughing It* reveals Twain's struggle with the problem of the point of view. On March 4 1871 he wrote to his brother, Orion, that "right in the first chapter I have got to alter the whole style of one of my characters and re-write him clear through to where I am now." Since the narrator himself is the only character who appears with sufficient frequency to require the sort of extensive revision suggested by this comment, the letter reflects some important discovery Twain had made relative to the point of view to be used, and his determination to act upon it. The discovery was made as Twain pored over several letters he had written to the Keokuk *Gate City* in 1861 and '62 describing his adventures in Nevada, and therefore was apparently connected with them. In these letters, Twain had adopted the pose of an unsophisticated, unregenerate "bitter enemy to sentiment" whose letters home were designed primarily to shatter the illusions of a pious, genteel, and excessively sentimental mother. That is, the relationship between the fictive mother and son in these letters prefigures the Mr Twain-Mr Brown relationship of the Sandwich Islands letters.

No evidence exists to indicate clearly the details of Twain's first draft of *Roughing It*, but a logical deduction from the available evidence is that, after the difficulties encountered with the point of view in *The Innocents Abroad*, he had returned to the Mr Twain-Mr Brown conflict of the Sandwich Islands and *Alta Californian* letters, patterning his narrator after Mr Twain and his companion, renamed Bemis, after Mr Brown. In the finished text, the narrator's gullibility, revealed in his prevision of the journey, and his sentimentality, his predisposition to view things through the "mellow moonshine of romance," are indications of his kinship with Mr Twain and ultimately with Dr Syntax. And certainly Bemis exhibits in his infrequent appearances most of the characteristics of Mr Brown not only when he climaxes the "noble sport" of buffalo hunting ignobly treed by the bull but also when he launches out on his own in Salt Lake City and experiments with a local concoction known as "valley tan" with predictable results. Such traces of the burlesque conventions in the finished text strongly suggest a more fully developed traveler-companion relationship in the first draft, that is, before the revision which Twain described to his brother.

Apparently, then, the *Gate City* letters taught Twain how he could dispense with such a character as Bemis and how he could link the contradictory points of view of a Mr Twain and a Mr Brown in the one character. As Professor Henry Nash Smith has demonstrated [in his "Mark Twain as an Interpreter of the Far West: The Structure of *Roughing It*," in *The Frontier in Perspective,* 1958], in the prevision of the journey and in much of the subsequent text "the pronoun 'I' links two quite different personae: the tenderfoot setting out across the Plains, and the old-timer, the veteran, who has seen the elephant and now looks back upon his own callow days of inexperience." Sophisticated and sentimental at the outset, the narrator's romantic expectations are shattered by the experiences of his journey and residence in the mining districts of Nevada. Envisioned at first as a character analogous to Mr Twain, the narrator is transformed by his experiences into a character analogous to Mr Brown.

Such a manipulation of the point of view, in itself a relatively simple affair, has enormous consequences for the art of that fiction which strives to build the illusion of objective reality. Stendhal's contribution to the development of literary realism, according to Erich Auerbach, is the technique of placing fictive characters in an externally real historical and social continuum: "Insofar as the serious realism of modern times," he declares, "cannot represent man otherwise than as embedded in a total reality, political, social, and economic, which is concrete and constantly evolving . . . Stendhal is its founder" [*Mimesis: The Representation of Reality in Western Literature,* 1957]. To the sort of time-perspective exploited by Stendhal, Twain added an internal time-perspective gained by the evolution of his narrator from tenderfoot to old-timer, an evolution which is implicit in the point of view from the very beginning of the narrative when, in introducing the tenderfoot's prevision of the journey, the old-timer comments, "I was young and ignorant." A great deal of the verisimilitude in the subsequent narrative derives from this manipulation of the point of view. By presenting the tenderfoot's prevision in a burlesque tone and coupling with it the old-timer's explicit disdain of his youthful folly, Twain predisposes the reader to a willing suspension of disbelief when the reader encounters the fictive reality which has transformed the tenderfoot into the old-timer and upon which the old-timer bases his judgment. As far as the reader is concerned, the technique contributes materially to the obscuring of the distinctions between the fictive world in which the narrator moves and the external reality of travel across the Plains and life in the silver-mining regions of Nevada in the early 1860s.

The internal time-perspective, the movement from youthful delusion to mature skepticism, is not the only important consequence of the change in point of view. The movement is one in space as well as in time, almost literally a journey along a road to reality, and the wisdom of the old-timer results not so much from the time elapsed since he started out on his journey as it does from his removal from one geographical region to another and his consequent initiation, as Professor Smith has noted, into a new society, the society of the mining regions. The shift in the point of view has produced a shift in the nature of the conflict which now becomes an internal one based on the differences between the mores of the East and those of the West. Bearing with him on his journey not only the heritage of his youth in the eastern United States but also highly erroneous concepts gleaned from his readings about the West, the tenderfoot must learn to adjust to the mores of the new society before he can become the old-timer. The insecurity, the humiliation, and occasionally the danger attendant upon actions performed and attitudes revealed while one is ignorant of the basic rules of the "curious new world" in which he finds himself are at the heart of the first thirty-three chapters, that is, to that point where the introduction of a new tenderfoot, General Buncombe, signals the narrator's own emergence into the community of old-timers. One humorous illustration of this inner conflict is the narrator's encounter with the desperado Slade:

> The coffee ran out. At last it was reduced to one tincupful, and Slade was about to take it when he saw that my cup was empty. He politely offered to fill it, but although I wanted it, I politely declined. I was afraid he had not killed anybody that morning, and might be needing diversion. But still with firm politeness he insisted on filling my cup, and said I had traveled all night and better deserved it than he—and while he talked placidly poured the fluid, to the last drop. I thanked him and drank it, but it gave me no comfort, for I could not feel sure that he would not be sorry, presently, that he had given it away, and proceed to kill me to distract his thoughts from the loss.

As a further consequence of the shift in point of view, Twain transformed burlesque into a remarkably effective fictive representation of the experience of those sensitive Americans whose adult lives spanned the Civil War years. With basic convictions, often excessively optimistic, formed in the pre-Civil War era, such Americans suffered a most intense disillusionment in the post-war era while at the same time they gained the sobered maturity of, say, the Walt Whitman of "Out of the Cradle Endlessly Rock-

ing." Vernon L. Parrington was correct when, in opening his discussion of Mark Twain in the third volume of his *Main Currents,* he identified the narrator of *Roughing It* as the image of the post-Civil War American. Certainly Twain's old-timer is as powerful an image for this period as Cooper's Natty Bumppo is for the former. But Parrington was quite wrong when he chose the tenderfoot's brief spree in stock speculation to epitomize the American of the Gilded Age. The American whom Twain epitomized with the narrator of *Roughing It* is one who, nurtured in one culture, suddenly finds himself faced with the necessity of adjusting to another, or succumbing. One indication of the accuracy of Twain's image appears in the parallel between the narrator of *Roughing It* and the Henry Adams of *The Education.* What Twain achieved with the two personae merged in the pronoun "I," Adams achieved by writing his autobiography in the third person: the detachment and distance of the educated Adams from the Henry Adams who was undergoing the painful and seemingly fruitless education. Like Twain's old-timer, the Henry Adams of the twentieth century looks back with disdain upon what it pleased him to call his deluded "eighteenth-century youth," chronicles the events which produced the maturity, and reveals what is implicit in Twain's narrative, the loss as well as the gain of education. Although we can perceive it in the book, Twain did not make much of the point that the gaining of maturity necessarily involves a loss of that freedom from reality upon which the romantic imagination is based. The point is, nevertheless, implicit in the *Weekly Occidental* episode which occupies a rather prominent place toward the end of the adventures in Nevada. In this episode, the narrator and several fellow old-timers attempt to write a "sensation" novel in instalments for their literary weekly. But the narrator and his fellow novelists are totally unable to produce such flights of the imagination as those upon which the tenderfoot's preconception of the Far West had been based. Later, in *Old Times on the Mississippi,* Twain was more explicit. Commenting upon the results of the cub's education as a river pilot, he wrote,

> Now when I had mastered the language of this water and had come to know every trifling feature that bordered the great river as familiarly as I knew the letters of the alphabet, I had made a valuable acquisition. But I had lost something, too. I had lost something which could never be restored to me while I lived. All the grace, the beauty, the poetry, had gone out of the majestic river!

The hero which Twain thus developed differs somewhat from the Young Man from the Provinces, whom Professor Lionel Trilling discerned as the defining hero in "a great line of novels" running "through the nineteenth-century as . . . the very backbone of its fiction." Professor Trilling describes the Young Man as one who "need not come from the provinces in literal fact, his social class may constitute his province. But a provincial birth and rearing suggest the simplicity and the high hopes he begins with—he starts with a great demand upon life and a great wonder about its complexity and promise. He may be of good family but he must be poor. He is intelligent, or at least aware, but not at all shrewd in worldly matters. He must have acquired a certain amount of education, should have learned something about life from books, although not the truth" [Lionel Trilling, "The Princess Casamassima," *The Liberal Imagination,* 1950]. Twain's hero differs primarily in the assurance which is his as a result of his illusions. Confident of his superiority, or at least of his equality, in ability, social station, and sophistication, he eagerly embarks upon a penetration into a strange society, only to be exposed by his very illusions in a series of experiences to the painful truth that he has been deluded, that he must discard his previous self-conception. The successful learning of this lesson, although it involves the loss of youthful ebullience, brings mature self-knowledge.

All this is to say that the conflict which Twain developed from the mutation of the burlesque conventions anticipates that of the international novel later developed by Henry James, which Professor Oscar Cargill has defined [in "The First International Novel," *PMLA* LXXIII (September 1958)] as a novel "in which a character, usually guided in his actions by the mores of one environment, is set down in another, where his learned reflexes are of no use to him, where he must employ all his individual resources to meet successive situations, and where he must intelligently accommodate himself to the new mores, or, in one way or another, be destroyed." The anticipation suggests a relatively close bond between Twain and James. But the closeness is obscured by Professor Cargill's failure to stress in his definition two essential elements: the initial illusory self-conception which precipitates a course of action leading toward an anticipated conquest in the new society, and the self-discovery resulting from the disappointment of his hopes.

Twain took the comic view; James, the tragic, first in *The American.* In doing so James created a character, Christopher Newman, whose attitudes, background, and even physical appearance are close enough to those of Twain or his fictive counterparts in *The Innocents Abroad* and *Roughing It* to cause the reader to suspect a direct indebtedness. James, of course, gave to the theme perhaps its most embracing significance when almost as if he were retelling the story of Hawthorne's Miriam, he took another American innocent, Isabel Archer, along the road that led to Rome. "Rome was actual," Henry Adams discovered on the eve of the Civil War: to him Rome meant the first painful realization of the enchainment, the confinement of the romantic imagination, the anchoring of a soaring idealism to the hard and heavy facts of actuality. To Isabel, Rome finally signifies substantially the same thing. Envisioning happiness, at the outset of her European adventures, as dashing over a strange road in a coach and four on a dark night, so self-confident and assured of a special destiny that she refuses Lord Warburton with but little trepidation, she discovers herself in Rome married to Gilbert Osmond, confined to a "dark narrow alley with a blind wall at the end." Rome is indeed the actual for her when she turns away from Caspar Goodwood's impassioned embrace to follow the "very straight path" back to Osmond.

When we recall the differences between the two writers, the fact that James was impelled to express in his fiction

a theme almost identical with Twain's attests to the accuracy and, one might almost say, the universality of the image of the American evoked by the mutation of the burlesque conventions in Twain's *Roughing It.*

> Franklin R. Rogers, "The Road to Reality: Burlesque Travel Literature and Mark Twain's 'Roughing It'," in Literature as a Mode of Travel: Five Essays and a Postscript, The New York Public Library, 1963, pp. 85-98.

Paul Goetsch

[*In the following essay, Goetsch discusses the representation of Canada in nineteenth-century German travel literature.*]

In the nineteenth century it was the United States rather than Canada that fascinated German-speaking travellers. Because of its rapid growth and the increasing numbers of immigrants from Central Europe, the United States prompted travel writers to take a stand on such different issues as emigration, national identity and German ethnicity, democracy, material progress and urbanization. It challenged them to weigh the pros and cons of the American dream, to criticize the American way of life as a paradigm of modern civilization, and to see Europe from new perspectives. The titles of two novels, *Der Europamüde* ("Tired of Europe," 1893) by Ernst Willkomm and *Der Amerikamüde* ("Tired of America," 1856) by Ferdinand Kürnberger, mark the poles between which typical reactions to the New World in German travel literature oscillated.

Canada attracted fewer travellers from Austria, Germany, and Switzerland and elicited fewer literary responses than the United States. Nevertheless, it too played a role, though a minor one, in the contemporary debate on the character of North America. Besides, it was considered interesting in its own right—as a country with a number of striking sights and places, with peculiar, if not anomalous, ties to Europe, and with an untapped potential for future development, also as a country shaped and dominated by the British, divided in itself, beleaguered by the U.S., with or without political future of its own. In the following survey I am going to characterize the different kinds of travel literature available in the German language and then concentrate on the image of Canada which emerges from them.

Johann Wolfgang von Goethe dutifully subscribed to the opinionated travel report of Duke Bernhard of Weimar, but also informed himself about Canada by reading articles in *Fraser's Magazine,* for instance. To those readers who had no access to foreign language periodicals and books, the German book market regularly offered translations of English and French works. As in the eighteenth century, accounts of explorers and expeditions stood high in public favour. Among others, the books by Alexander Mackenzie and John Franklin appeared in translation soon after they had first come out in England. In addition, translations of conventional travel books compensated for the relative dearth of comprehensive first-hand accounts by German travellers, at least in the first half of the nineteenth century. Here, the German editions of works by Edward Allen Talbot, Charles Lyell, Isaac Weld, Catherine Parr Traill, and Anna Jameson perhaps deserve special mention. What was popular with publishers and readers were anthologies of travel reports and sketches of life in the U.S. and Canada. Sometimes expressly designed and edited for younger readers, they reprinted exciting and eventful travel episodes and tended to see Canada, to borrow Patrick Anderson's phrase, as America's empty attic and cold kingdom. One of them, for example, contained excerpts from two accounts of Arctic expeditions, a chapter of Labrador and a sketch, by Audubon, of the life of squatters in that region. The rest of the book was reserved for contributions about the United States. More balanced anthologies usually included a description of the falls at Niagara and sketches of Upper and Lower Canada, using diverse travel books as sources.

For the reader Canada was put on the map not only by such translations and compilations but also by Austrian, German and Swiss scholars, explorers and travellers. In the course of the nineteenth century a number of handbooks dealing with North America appeared. If one leaves aside the guide books for immigrants published by the Canadian Government or by Germans, the handbooks with a historical and political orientation usually focused on the United States. In his *Statistik von Amerika* (1828) Alexander Lips dismissed Canada in three pages. Similarily, the Berlin historian Friedrich von Raumer [in his *Die Vereinigten Staaten von Nordamerika*, 1845] devoted only a couple of pages of his survey to Canada, although he had gone there and reprinted letters about his journey in the appendix of his book. Canada was much better represented, it seems, in handbooks with geographical bias. In 1851 Karl Andree [in his *Nord-Amerika in geographischen . . .*, 1854] put his extensive readings in older travel books to good use when discussing the North, the role of the Hudson's Bay Company, the life of the Eskimos and Indians. That, in addition, he reserved almost forty pages for the British colonies in North America is remarkable for the period. For a book-length treatment of Canada (again aside from guide books) German readers had to wait till Ernst von Hesse-Wartegg's *Kanada und Neufundland* (1888). Wartegg claims to have travelled to most of the places he describes and gives a systematic survey of Upper and Lower Canada, the Hudson Bay area, the prairie territories, British Columbia and Newfoundland. He also deals with such diverse topics as the lumbermen, the *voyageurs,* the Indians, polite society in Montreal and seal-hunting in Labrador and Newfoundland.

Among German contributions to the literature of exploration and discovery, Franz Boas' account of an expedition to Baffin Island in 1883 and 1884 [*Baffin Land*, 1885] stands out for its vivid descriptions of the hardships endured and for its manifold observations about the Eskimos. Another rich mine of information is Johann Georg Kohl's study of the Ojibwa Indians [*Kitschi-Gami oder Erzzählungen von Obern See*] which the author made during a stay near Lake Superior in 1855. Some light on important phases of the settlement of Canada is shed by the travel reports of Friedrich von Graffenried and Ignatz

Hülswitt. Graffenried, an ex-soldier, went to the Selkirk settlement in the Red River area and remained there from 1813 to 1819 as a sort of military supervisor. His narration of his voyage from Toronto to the Red River by boat and canoe ["Sechs Jahr in Canada, 1813-1819" in *X. Jahresbericht der Geographischen Gesellschaft . . . ,* 1891] still makes interesting rading. So do his accounts of various winter journeys in the Red River region. His comments on the competition between the North West Company and the Hudson's Bay Company are rather superficial, though. Hülswitt, another ex-soldier, offers accounts of a number of exciting events [in his *Tagebuch einer Reise. . . ,* 1828], including his kidnapping by Indians in the Nootka area in present-day British Columbia. He is, however, too impatient to be a good observer and narrator.

It is not adventures but occasional misadventures (usually on the boat trip) that are characteristic of the travel books and sketches in the narrow sense. Since an excursion to the falls at Niagara was a must for North American travellers, many Austrian, German and Swiss visitors to the United States submitted to the trend and crossed over to the Canadian side only to be able to see the Horseshoe Falls better. Their lack of first-hand knowledge did not always prevent them from playing the game of comparing the United States and Canada. Other travellers used Niagara Falls as a point of departure for a journey, usually by boat, to Montreal and sometimes Quebec. The typical nineteenth-century travel book in the German language reflects this practice. It alots a greater part for the journey through the United States, then describes the marvels of the falls, and proceeds to record the voyage to Montreal. Toronto and Kingston may or may not be stopovers. Among the sights and places along the way, which regularly excited comment, were the Thousand Isles, Mount Royal and the cathedral in Montreal, the French Canadian villages along the St. Lawrence River, the citadel of Quebec, the Plains of Abraham and the falls at Montmorency.

In the early nineteenth-century travel books the conditions of the boat trip and the accommodation on the shore frequently came in for criticism, which is not surprising if one reads what the German travellers had to say against Edwin C. Guillet's scholarly study of *Pioneer Travel in Upper Canada* (1966). Though travel facilities improved in the course of the century, the standard practice, a journey from Niagara Falls to Montreal or Quebec, prevailed till the 1890s. Apart from a few exceptions to, and modifications of, the basic route the ordinary travel writer stuck to the well-known and most highly developed areas of Canada. He did not go west like the geographers Penck and Hesse-Wartegg or the farmer Wiedersheim, who, at the invitation of the Canadian government, visited Manitoba in 1882. Nor was he interested in the North. In this sense the travel books convey a far more limited image of Canada than the handbooks or the guides for immigrants. To put it simply, for the ordinary travel writers from Austria, Germany or Switzerland the journey to Canada was an excursion made during a tour of the United States, a diversion welcome to most of them because it promised not only different sights but also either a respite from the task of generalizing about the United States or an opportunity of comparing the States to a different kind of society.

In a recent study of travel literature [*Abroad: British Literary Tourists Between the Wars,* 1980] Paul Fussell has made the following distinction between the explorer, the tourist, and the traveller:

> . . . the explorer seeks the undiscovered, the traveller that which has been discovered by the mind working in history, the tourist that which has been discovered by entrepreneurship and prepared for him by the arts of mass publicity. The genuine traveller is, or used to be, in the middle between the two extremes.

Of the writers under discussion here, everyone felt like a tourist during his visit to the falls at Niagara and commented about the difficulty of observing and describing what had been described a hundred times before. During the later stages of their journey in Canada most of them behaved like tourists in that they moved "toward the security of pure cliché." The time set aside for the visit to Canada was too short for leaving the beaten track. So the genuine traveller, who is informed and observant, goes to the well-known places, like a tourist, but retains "all he can of the excitement of the unpredictable attaching to exploration," was a rare bird among nineteenth-century visitors from Central Europe. Johann Georg Kohl no doubt qualifies. Perhaps Hesse-Wartegg would be the second on a short list. Rather than concentrate on such exceptions to the general rule, I shall describe the leitmotifs running through some of the travel books, handbooks, and guides. Focusing on those themes and clichés which concern Canadian society and its development in general, I hope to indicate how the German image of Canada developed in the nineteenth century and where it is closely related to what English and French Canadians thought about themselves.

One point of interest to the travel writers was the character of English Canada. For some this character manifested itself in Toronto. While de Wette described Toronto in 1838 [in *Reise in den Vereinigten Staaten und Canada im Jahre 1837,* 1838] as poorer and dirtier than the towns in the U.S., Löher in 1855 [in *Land und Leute . . . ,* 1885] stressed the fact that the town had developed rapidly. He called it the centre of trade in the Lake Ontario region, praised the good harbour and the huge market hall, and noted that British and American influences existed side by side. According to him, the upper classes of Toronto, while consisting of social climbers and self-made men to some extent, were superior in education and manners to the elites in the large American towns. On the whole they tried to imitate polite society in Great Britain, although the ladies would ride and drive much more wildly than their British counterparts. The British influence also made itself felt, Löher believed, in the solidly built houses, the well-regulated traffic, the quiet business life, and the cooperation between the Anglo-Catholic church and leading families. And yet Löher detected many signs that—to use his imagery—the British foundation was being eroded by the wild American stream, for example, the fast development of the economy, American investments, the Americanization of the common people, that is the coming-into-

existence of a more egalitarian society, and last but not least the inclination of the younger generation to favour a union with the United States.

Later German visitors to Toronto confirmed Löher's observations in part. In 1856 Müller [in *Reisen in den Vereinigten Staaten, Canada und Mexico,* 1864] emphasized the importance of the harbour and of the city as a business centre. He complained about the absence of interesting sights apart from the rich stores of King Street, and he was shocked at the tumultuous behaviour of politicians at a meeting of the provincial parliament. In the same year Kohl [in *Reisen in Canada und durch die Staaten von New-York und Pennsylvannien,* 1856] mentioned the rising costs of apartments as a result of the rapid development of Toronto and praised Egerton Ryerson and the educational system of Toronto and Ontario highly. He criticized the Puritan mood of anti-Popery in the province and regretted the founding of denominational colleges at the University of Toronto because he feared intolerance and narrow-mindedness. The complaint that Toronto had hardly any attractions for the sightseer was reiterated by Hesse-Wartegg and Zschokke in 1880 and 1881, respectively. In 1887 Lemcke [in *Canada, das Land und Seine Leute*] with his usual guide book enthusiasm, called Toronto the Athens of Canada, compared its parks to those of London, and praised its clean and fine streets. Five years later Deckert [in *Die Neue Welt,* 1892] more or less returned to descriptions from the mid-century but denied that the Americanization predicted by Löher had actually taken place. He insisted on the differences between Toronto and American cities such as Milwaukee, Detroit and Buffalo. While the citizens of Toronto were busy and active, the town lacked the feverish tempo and drive of American life. It was developing more slowly and quietly, which Deckert explained with its British character. Architectural symbols of the British influence were for him St. James Cathedral, Osgoode Hall and the buildings of the University. Deckert also regarded the solidly constructed houses and homes as a distinctive feature of Toronto: they were an illustration of the British motto "My home is my castle" as opposed to the American concept "My wigwam is my house." Toronto seemed to be an incarnation of the British spirit not only to Deckert but also to Lamprecht [in *Americana,* 1906]. Having recourse to a primitive environmental biology, Lamprecht, in 1904, discovered many English types in Toronto but only the gradual emergence of a new Canadian type with long face and long bony hands. Vancouver was ahead of Toronto in this respect because there the girls, like the local trees, were growing tall.

Apart from such dubious hypotheses, the generalization about Toronto conveys a fairly accurate impression of the way English Canada was seen in travel books, handbooks, and guides. Since the travellers usually moved quickly from Niagara Falls to Montreal, they had not much to say about interesting sights and places in Ontario. They felt the urge, however, to define English Canada by contrasting it with the United States.

This usually involved observations about the slow economic growth in Ontario and the progress made in the country to the South. Duke Bernhard of Weimar said in 1828:

> Generally the towns in Canada look impover-
> ished in comparison with towns in the U.S. and
> will probably never achieve as good an estate as
> the latter; for the settlers in Canada are mostly
> poor Scots or Irishmen who came out at the ex-
> pense of the government, obtained land and are
> then placed under the pressure of the feudal sys-
> tem which keeps down everybody who tries to
> rise in the world; emigrants, on the other hand,
> with some means and possessing any enterpris-
> ing spirit rather settle in the U.S. where nothing
> keeps them down and where everything rather
> contributes to their improvement.

The reasons given for the time lag varies. To admirers and critics of the United States alike, the Americans were more dynamic, mobile, and active than the Canadians. From one perspective, however, the Americans were characterized as brash, given over to money speculation and to materialism while the English Canadians were said to play it safe and reflect before acting. For example, Löher was persuaded that the Americans were much more self-reliant and aggressive than the Canadians, filled with the spirit of manifest destiny and the wish to conquer the world, if possible. Lemcke traced the English Canadian reserve and modesty back to the British influence and argued that Canada offered the immigrant a more solid kind of happiness than the United States. Lamprecht saw the Canadians grounded in European culture and believed that therefore Canada might achieve a high level of civilization sooner than the States. As Hesse-Wartegg asserted in 1888, Ontario had been Americanized only on the surface. Because of the close ties to Great Britain the English Canadians still managed to resist the uniformity of American life. Half-jokingly, Hesse-Wartegg envisioned the English Canadian as a cross between a reticent English gentleman and a straightforward masculine type, in short, as a man of whom Victorian advocates of muscular Christianity might have been proud:

> The differences between Canada and the neigh-
> bouring States express themselves in a great
> number of features which are not very striking
> in themselves but can easily be detected by the
> patient observer of Yankees in Canada and Ca-
> nadians in America. The Canadian is more dig-
> nified in behaviour and slower in his movements,
> his clothes are simpler and follow British fash-
> ions; he prefers the short English pipe to Ameri-
> can cigars and cigarettes; he carries a walking-
> stick and uses gloves more often than the Yan-
> kee; his face is usually more tanned, his beard
> less well groomed than that of the American; he
> dislikes the American stove-pipe hat, and he
> avoids—this fact speaks for him—drinking
> mixed drinks, cocktails, lemonades and iced
> water, but prefers his liquor undiluted and usu-
> ally has whiskey pure. Given a choice between
> the weak and badly tasting lager beer and ale or
> porter, in nine out of ten cases he takes the
> stronger beer.

Within Hesse-Wartegg's Darwinian approach the masculine qualities are assets indeed. The author has, however,

difficulties in explaining how they came into existence and why the Yankees and the English Canadians had developed in different directions even though they were of the same origin and shared a similar geographical environment and climate.

From another perspective such differences were easily accounted for. As some travel and handbook writers assumed, the American system of government and the American way of life were superior. Lips, in 1828, and de Wette, in 1838, mentioned the relative lack of freedom in Canada. Raumer argued in 1845 that the Canadian system should never be regarded as a model for the United States. According to the Social Darwinist Deckert the colonial status of Canada encouraged unhealthy developments, for example the existence of parasites such as lazy Irish whiskey drinkers and sectarian ministers. Other writers explained the differences between the U.S.A. and Canada with the lack of capital in English Canada, the general neglect of the colony by Great Britain, and with the stagnation of economic and social life in French Canada. While Andree's assumption of 1851 that at least English Canada had caught up economically with the State of New York, was exceptional, his praise of the energy and inventiveness of the Yankees was shared by several observers. Even Kohl, who abstained from a comparison of the different political and social systems, wrote that Americans were often the pacesetters of progress and the conquerors of the wilderness, not only in the United States but also in Canada.

Of course many of the generalizations about English Canada and the United States can be traced back to the European background of the writers. Some authors preferred the United States over English Canada because they were against colonialism and for republicanism. Men like Andree and Versen, who wrote in the second half of the century, were distrustful of British imperialism. A few writers were either so disillusioned with the United States or so much rooted in Central European assumptions about the polarity between culture and civilization that they appreciated the slower development of Canada as a healthy sign.

Though many of the observations and judgments originated in German wishes, fears, and prejudices, it is necessary to point out that the contradictory image of English Canada emerging from the books under discussion resembles the image Canadians made of themselves. Time and again, British travellers and emigrants commented on the advances made in the United States and illustrated the differences by comparing Canadian and American towns. Thomas Chandler Haliburton recommended some of the virtues of the Yankee to his fellow-countrymen. Catherine Parr Traill [in *The Backwoods of Canada*] noted in 1836:

> . . . of all people the Yankees . . . are the most
> industrious and ingenious; they are never at a
> loss for an expedient: if one thing fails them they
> adopt another, with a quickness of thought that
> surprises me, while to them it seems only a mat-
> ter of course. They seem to possess a sort of in-
> nate presence of mind, and instead of wasting
> their energies in words, they *act*.

On the other hand many English Canadian commentators were, naturally enough, frightened at what the development of the United States might mean for Canada. Genteel visitors and immigrants from Great Britain, for example, John Howison, Edward Talbot, and Susanna Moodie, described the lack of respect and the egalitarian spirit in lower-class arrivals from Europe as a sign of Americanization. Others turned against American materialism, lamented the lack of freedom in the slavery-ridden States, and praised the more solid attractions of English Canada. John Galt's *Bogle Corbet* (1831) is perhaps the best literary expression of the more conservative English Canadian attitudes toward the settlement of the new country: it opposes American individualism, materialism, and reckless speculation with the cautions proceeding of a group of settlers mutually supporting each other and following the advice of their leaders. Since other Canadians were in favour of competing with the United States on its own terms or even toyed with the idea of annexation, the general evaluation of the development in the two countries was contradictory both in the English Canadian debate and in the German books.

Similar parallels between English Canadian and Central European views can be discovered as soon as one turns to the contemporary image of French Canada. One difference should, however, be noted at the outset. The image of French Canada developed by the European writers was far more uniform than that of English Canadians. Besides, in German travel books French Canada received much more attention than English Canada and yet provoked less controversy. This paradox can easily be explained. Because of the importance of the St. Lawrence for the standard journey, French Canada offered more interesting sights to the tourist. Moreover, it came much closer to what Fussell has called the implicit aim of travelling, the "quest for anomaly."

French Canada struck those who had recently visited the United States, as an anachronism, as an old country in the New World. According to Hesse-Wartegg in 1888, going to the city of Quebec was like making a journey into the past after coming from the country of the future. Like Hesse-Wartegg, a number of writers expressed their admiration of the villages along the St. Lawrence river and of Montreal and Quebec as beautiful and interesting cities; but this admiration was usually tempered with the belief that French Canada, if not actually doomed, was an anomaly in North America.

As far as material progress, industrialization, and modern habits and attitudes were concerned, French Canada was often compared disadvantageously with English Canada. For those who marvelled at the fast development in the United States, it was far less acceptable than English Canada; for the critics of the United States French Canadian society had not made the unavoidable adjustments to the New World. Correspondingly, the British influence in Montreal was usually mentioned as an explanation for the economic importance of the town, though observers like Raumer believed that of course Montreal lagged behind comparable American cities.

The backwardness of Lower Canada or Quebec encour-

aged some writers to characterize the French Canadians in terms of pastoral literature. In 1855 Löher, for instance, sketched rural Quebec in a way only too familiar to the reader of English and French Canadian literature. After commenting on the "medieval" villages and the seigneurial system, he discribed the *habitants* as uneducated, kindhearted, modest, and hospitable, as people resisting innovations, enjoying festivities, and living happily from day to day under the guidance of priest and landlord. By emphasizing the idyllic traits of life in rural Quebec, Löther, like other writers, made it clear that the French Canadians were incapable of competing with their more energic neighbours of English or American origin.

When trying to account for the disparity between French Canada and either English Canada or the United States, the authors fell back upon prejudices acquired in their home countries. One of the first German travellers to rely on anti-Catholic arguments was Duke Bernhard of Weimar. Though chiefly interested in reviewing military parades in Montreal and Quebec, the Duke quickly branded the French Canadians as bigoted and was carried away by his anti-Catholicism, it seems, to a critique of feudalism in Quebec which was hardly to be expected of a German duke. He did point out, however, that the French Canadian clergy was loyal to the British Crown. For Lips, another anti-Catholic, the French Canadians were steeped in superstition and stupidity. Andree blamed the clergy for the lack of education and social mobility in Quebec, while Deckert held the separation of French Canada from the advances made in post-enlightenment France responsible for the backwardness of Laval University in comparison with McGill. Similarly, Hesse-Wartegg used arguments from the German debate about the modern school system when he called French Canadian education far too impractical for the demands of the New World.

Anti-French prejudices made Raumer argue that the failure of French Canada was owing to the lack of talent in the Latin races for the tasks of imperialism. Weichhardt repeated this argument in his compilation. Löher took it up in 1855 and, like Hesse-Wartegg, believed that the French had gone to the wrong country and climate anyway. Not surprisingly, several authors predicted that the French Canadians would ultimately disappear (de Wette, Hesse-Wartegg) or would be pushed into a corner like the Pennsylvania Dutch (Löher) and the Germans in Milwaukee (Deckert) or like the lower classes in general (de Wette). Zschokke, a Catholic traveller, turned against such prophecies in 1881; Lamprecht, who had many good things to say about farming in Quebec and about Montreal as a business centre, was too cautious to indulge in generalizations about the French Canadians and their future. Most writers, however, regarded French Canadian society as charmingly old-fashioned and doomed and thus came close of the image of French Canada developed in the English Canadian historical novel, which tended to treat the French Canadians in the way Scott dealt with the Highlanders.

A noteworthy exception to the general rule was Kohl's discussion of the situation in French Canada. Kohl was familiar with the works of Talbot, Hall, Buckingham,

Henry, Bouchette, and others and came into personal contact with Garneau and other French Canadian leaders. Aware of the many prejudices about Lower Canada, he tried to present a more balanced view by opposing the arguments of Scotsmen and English Canadians with the statements of real or fictitious French Canadians and his own observations. For instance, he makes a Scotsman call the French Canadians effeminate and then reminds his readers of the courage of the *voyageurs*. Or he quotes standard English Canadian opinions about the lack of business acumen among French Canadian farmers and counters them implicitly with remarks about the positive work ethic to be found in rural Quebec. While admitting the threat of economic competition for Quebec, he points out that one group of French Canadians has begun to take an active part in the economy so long dominated by the British.

At times, Kohl's wish to defend French Canada against unfair labels and charges, involves him in contradictions. He turns against prejudices about rural Canada being an impediment to progress, and yet he goes on to praise and idyllicize the life of the *habitants,* mentioning Virgil and the commonplace of the golden Age. What seems to lie behind such contradictions is a longing for life and traditional communities coupled with the insight that a certain degree of Americanization may be necessary for the survival of Quebec. From a similar aversion to progress for its own sake Kohl expresses his deep respect for the educational system in Quebec and yet makes a French Canadian acquaintance criticize it as old-fashioned. Here as elsewhere Kohl probably came very close to echoing the temperate views of some of the French Canadian leaders he had met in Montreal and Quebec. Perhaps it was this contact with Garneau and others that made him first mention the past ill-treatment of French Canadians by their conquerors, and then stress the harmonious coexistence of the English and the French in Canada.

Other writers were less sure whether the two-nation problem could be solved. To Müller the French Canadians appeared to be anti-English when he went there in 1856. According to Raumer it was doubtful whether national unity could ever be achieved in Canada. Others, as mentioned before, believed that any kind of national unity would imply either the subjugation or the disappearance of French Canada.

Contradictory and cliché-like as such statements are, they indicate at least the awareness of, and some interest in, specifically Canadian problems. The same holds true for what Austrian, German, and Swiss writers had to say about Canada as a whole and its relationship with the United States. Because of their knowledge of the Canadian situation, the authors approached the question of the future development of Canada with great caution. Early commentators had doubts about the survival of Upper and Lower Canada as British colonies; later observers were usually convinced that the new nation would continue to survive. None of the early travel and handbook writers was enthusiastic about the idea of emigrating to Canada rather than to the U.S.A. On the other hand, none of them was so repelled by what he saw in Canada that he reacted like contemporary Central European critics of the States. While the American and European dreams seemed to force any visitor of the U.S.A. to make up his mind about the country and its way of life, Canada as a sort of halfway house between Europe and the States challenged European expectations and hopes to a far lesser degree.

In a way this is confirmed by the early guides for immigrants which I have seen. Like William Catermole's famous book *Emigration: The Advantages of Emigration to Canada* (1831), they are on the whole rather sober and instructive. It is clear that the authors of the guides felt on the defensive when addressing the would-be immigrant. In any case, they attempt time and again to refute their reader's negative assumptions about Canada, especially opinions concerning the climate of the country, the degree of political freedom found there, the income of workers as compared to the United States, and the economic development of the two neighbouring nations. Rather than promise easy riches, adventures, and a stirring national myth, they wrote about hard work, stressed the support given by the government to the immigrants, or mentioned that Germans were better liked in Canada than in the States. Traugott Bromme, whose guide of 1834 and 1835 [*Reisen durch die Vereinigten Staaten und Ober-Canada*] in part imitates a travel book, compared emigration to the United States and Canada and said:

> For Europeans from the lower classes emigration to Upper Canada has a number of advantages. Upper Canada is the country for the poor of Europe. Though no reasonable man will say that the Canadians are better off than the citizens of the United States, most Canadians have more than enough to live on and can look forward to further improvements; this is something of which more than half of the population of Europe would be envious.

Guides published in the last third of the century expressed greater confidence. The Canadian government issued a guide in 1882 announcing that the country would soon be the home of one of the largest and most powerful nations on earth. In 1887 Lemcke misled his German readers about the winter temperatures, wrote a long chapter on winter enjoyments in Montreal, called Canada almost a republic, described it as the land of opportunity, and held out the lure of the unsettled prairie territories to prospective immigrants. At least in Hesse-Wartegg's and Lamprecht's handbooks of 1888 and 1904, respectively, the optimism of the guides is confirmed, for instance by observations about the rapid development of the West, the advantages of the railway system, and the enormous natural resources of the country. Although Hesse-Wartegg echoed, among other things, the comparison between Siberia and Canada which the guidebooks were turning against, he shared their optimistic predictions about future development. Already in his compilation of 1880, and again in his handbook of 1888, he foretold a great future for Canada because it had space enough for a population of 100,000,000 people. This optimism no doubt reflected the mood of public opinions and leaders in Canada and anticipated Sir Wilfrid Laurier's famous statement that the twentieth century would be Canada's century. At any rate, it was a product of the astounding development which Canada, though lagging behind the States, had gone through and which hardly any of the earlier travellers from Central Europe had dared to predict.

As the German writer Börne once asserted, travelling does not change anybody; whether one goes to Canada, Paris or any other place one will only discover and meet oneself. This scepticism seems justified if we think of the prejudices the visitors from Central Europe brought with them to Canada. On the other hand, many of their other observations and judgments had some foundation in real life. Taken together, the handbooks, guides, and travel sketches conveyed not only a fairly accurate picture of the development of Canada in the nineteenth century but also an awareness of specifically Canadian problems which are still important today. If, as Hermann Boeschenstein has argued ["Is There a Canadian Image in German Literature?" in *Seminar*, 1967], "German awareness of Canada arose in the late 18th century," it certainly widened and deepened in the nineteenth century.

> *Paul Goetsch, "The Image of Canada in 19th Century German Travel Literature," in* German-Canadian Yearbook, *Vol. VII, 1983, pp. 121-35.*

FURTHER READING

Berben, Jacqueline. "The Romantic Traveler as Questing Hero: Théophile Gautier's *Voyage en Espagne.*" *Texas Studies in Literature and Language* 25, No. 3 (Fall 1983): 367-89.

Contends that Gautier's account of a journey to Spain in 1840 functions on two distinct levels: "One is a physical tour from Paris to Andalusia and back while the other is a psychological or spiritual venture into the unknown."

Briggs, Asa. "Trollope the Traveller." In *Trollope Centenary Essays,* edited by John Halperin, pp. 24-52. New York: St. Martin's Press, 1982.

Describes Trollope's numerous travel volumes and sketches, focusing on his awareness of the demands of his reading audience.

Buzard, James. *The Beaten Track: European Tourism, Literature, and the Ways to Culture, 1800-1918.* Oxford: Clarendon Press, 1993, 357 p.

Analyzes a wide range of travel writings to define "tourism" as a cultural phenomenon having its origin in the modern industrial nations of northern Europe and America.

Edel, Leon, and Lind, Ilse Dusoir. Introduction to *Parisian Sketches: Letters to the 'New York Tribune' 1875-1876,* by Henry James, pp. ix-xxxvii. New York: New York University Press, 1957.

Discusses the topics and literary style of the letters written from Paris by the young Henry James.

Hurt, James. "Reality and the Picture of Imagination: The Literature of the English Prairie." *The Great Lakes Review* 7, No. 2 (Summer 1981): 1-24.

Discusses the literature of the founding of an English settlement on the Illinois prairie, emphasizing the writings of Morris Birkbeck and George Flowers.

Lueck, Beth L. "James Kirke Paulding and the Picturesque Tour: 'Banqueting on the Picturesque' in the 1820s and '30s." *The University of Mississippi Studies in English* 9 (1991): 167-88.

Examines the travel narratives of American James Kirke Paulding, maintaining that "Paulding contributed in an important way to the development of the picturesque tour in America by transforming it into a vehicle for nationalism."

Mickel, Emanuel J., Jr. "Pilgrimage in Memory: Gerard de Nerval, Barbey D'Aurevilly and Eugene Fromentin." In *Travel, Quest and Pilgrimage as a Literary Theme,* edited by Frans C. Amelinckx and Joyce N. Megay, pp. 179-89. Boulder, Colo.: Society of Spanish and Spanish-American Studies, 1978.

Examines the works of three French Romantic writers, noting that "travel plays an important role in the lives and literature of all three authors and each one uses memory in a vital effort to establish for himself a sense of reality which escapes the corrosive, destructive change wrought by the passage of time."

Monkman, Leslie. "Primitivism and a Parasol: Anna Jameson's Indians." *Essays on Canadian Writing* No. 29 (Summer 1984): 85-95.

Considers Jameson's *Winter Studies and Summer Rambles* a major work of literary anthropology for its illumination of tensions between aboriginal and European cultures in Upper Canada.

Peters, Bernard C. "Revolt from the Wilderness: Romantic Travellers on Lake Superior." *Michigan Academician* 13, No. 4 (Spring 1981): 491-501.

Demonstrates the impact of Romanticism on early American wilderness writing, as represented by descriptions of Michigan's Lake Superior shoreline between 1820 and 1840.

Schick, Constance Gosselin. "A Case Study of Descriptive Perversion: Théophile Gautier's Travel Literature." *Romanic Review* LXXVIII, No. 3 (May 1987): 359-67.

Discusses subjectivity and fictionalization in Gautier's descriptive travel writings.

Schriber, Mary Suzanne. "Julia Ward Howe and the Travel Book." *New England Quarterly* LXII, No. 2 (June 1989): 264-79.

Discusses Julia Ward Howe's *From the Oak to the Olive* in the context of barriers to women's travel writing.

Steinbrink, Jeffrey. "Why the Innocents Went Abroad: Mark Twain and American Tourism in the Late Nineteenth Century." *American Literary Realism* 16, No. 2 (Autumn 1983): 278-86.

Describes the popularity of American travel in Europe after the Civil War and Mark Twain's humorous satire of middle-class behavior abroad.

Stowe, William W. "Conventions and Voices in Margaret Fuller's Travel Writing." *American Literature: A Journal of*

Literary History, Criticism, and Bibliography 63, No. 2 (June 1991): 242-62.

Situates Fuller's travel writings in the context of influential American writers who employed the polyphonic model of the travel narrative.

Thompson, C. W. "French Romantic Travel and the Quest for Energy." *The Modern Language Review* 87, No. 2 (April 1992): 307-19.

Compares travel works by three French Romantic writers—Stendhal, Victor Hugo, and Gerard de Nerval—highlighting common themes and techniques.

Watt, Helga Schutte. "Ida Pfeiffer: A Nineteenth-Century Woman Travel Writer." *The German Quarterly* 64, No. 3 (Summer 1991): 339-52.

Discusses the travelogues of an Austrian woman who earned international recognition as a pioneering woman traveler with two solo journeys around the world.

Worley, Linda Kraus. "Through Others' Eyes: Narratives of German Women Travelling in Nineteenth-Century America." *Yearbook of German-American Studies* 21 (1986): 39-50.

Examines the narratives of several German women travelers in America, exploring their "complex subjectivity," while highlighting their revelations about nineteenth-century American domestic life and mores.

Nineteenth-Century Literature Criticism

Topics Volume

Cumulative Indexes

Volumes 1-44

How to Use This Index

The main references

Calvino, Italo
1923-1985.....CLC 5, 8, 11, 22, 33, 39,
73; SSC 3

list all author entries in the following Gale Literary Criticism series:

BLC = *Black Literature Criticism*
CLC = *Contemporary Literary Criticism*
CLR = *Children's Literature Review*
CMLC = *Classical and Medieval Literature Criticism*
DA = *DISCovering Authors*
DC = *Drama Criticism*
HLC = *Hispanic Literature Criticism*
LC = *Literature Criticism from 1400 to 1800*
NCLC = *Nineteenth-Century Literature Criticism*
PC = *Poetry Criticism*
SSC = *Short Story Criticism*
TCLC = *Twentieth-Century Literary Criticism*
WLC = *World Literature Criticism, 1500 to the Present*

The cross-references

See also CANR 23; CA 85-88;
obituary CA 116

list all author entries in the following Gale biographical and literary sources:

AAYA = *Authors & Artists for Young Adults*
AITN = *Authors in the News*
BEST = *Bestsellers*
BW = *Black Writers*
CA = *Contemporary Authors*
CAAS = *Contemporary Authors Autobiography Series*
CABS = *Contemporary Authors Bibliographical Series*
CANR = *Contemporary Authors New Revision Series*
CAP = *Contemporary Authors Permanent Series*
CDALB = *Concise Dictionary of American Literary Biography*
CDBLB = *Concise Dictionary of British Literary Biography*
DLB = *Dictionary of Literary Biography*
DLBD = *Dictionary of Literary Biography Documentary Series*
DLBY = *Dictionary of Literary Biography Yearbook*
HW = *Hispanic Writers*
JRDA = *Junior DISCovering Authors*
MAICYA = *Major Authors and Illustrators for Children and Young Adults*
MTCW = *Major 20th-Century Writers*
SAAS = *Something about the Author Autobiography Series*
SATA = *Something about the Author*
YABC = *Yesterday's Authors of Books for Children*

Literary Criticism Series
Cumulative Author Index

Antoine, Marc
See Proust, (Valentin-Louis-George-Eugene-) Marcel

Antoninus, Brother
See Everson, William (Oliver)

Antonioni, Michelangelo 1912- . . . . . **CLC 20**
See also CA 73-76

Antschel, Paul 1920-1970. . . . . . **CLC 10, 19**
See also Celan, Paul
See also CA 85-88; CANR 33; MTCW

Anwar, Chairil 1922-1949 . . . . **TCLC 22**
See also CA 121

Apollinaire, Guillaume . . **TCLC 3, 8, 51; PC 7**
See also Kostrowitzki, Wilhelm Apollinaris de

Appelfeld, Aharon 1932- . . . . **CLC 23, 47**
See also CA 112; 133

Apple, Max (Isaac) 1941-. . . . . **CLC 9, 33**
See also CA 81-84; CANR 19; DLB 130

Appleman, Philip (Dean) 1926- . . . . . **CLC 51**
See also CA 13-16R; CAAS 18; CANR 6, 29

Appleton, Lawrence
See Lovecraft, H(oward) P(hillips)

Apteryx
See Eliot, T(homas) S(tearns)

Apuleius, (Lucius Madaurensis)
125(?)-175(?) . . . . **CMLC 1**

Aquin, Hubert 1929-1977. . . . . **CLC 15**
See also CA 105; DLB 53

Aragon, Louis 1897-1982. . . . . . . **CLC 3, 22**
See also CA 69-72; 108; CANR 28; DLB 72; MTCW

Arany, Janos 1817-1882. . . . . **NCLC 34**

Arbuthnot, John 1667-1735 . . . . **LC 1**
See also DLB 101

Archer, Herbert Winslow
See Mencken, H(enry) L(ouis)

Archer, Jeffrey (Howard) 1940- . . . . **CLC 28**
See also BEST 89:3; CA 77-80; CANR 22

Archer, Jules 1915- . . . . **CLC 12**
See also CA 9-12R; CANR 6; SAAS 5; SATA 4

Archer, Lee
See Ellison, Harlan

Arden, John 1930- . . . . **CLC 6, 13, 15**
See also CA 13-16R; CAAS 4; CANR 31; DLB 13; MTCW

Arenas, Reinaldo
1943-1990 . . . . **CLC 41; HLC**
See also CA 124; 128; 133; HW

Arendt, Hannah 1906-1975 . . . . **CLC 66**
See also CA 17-20R; 61-64; CANR 26; MTCW

Aretino, Pietro 1492-1556 . . . . **LC 12**

Arghezi, Tudor. . . . . **CLC 80**
See also Theodorescu, Ion N.

Arguedas, Jose Maria
1911-1969 . . . . **CLC 10, 18**
See also CA 89-92; DLB 113; HW

Argueta, Manlio 1936- . . . . **CLC 31**
See also CA 131; HW

Ariosto, Ludovico 1474-1533 . . . . **LC 6**

Aristides
See Epstein, Joseph

Aristophanes
450B.C.-385B.C. . . . . **CMLC 4; DA; DC 2**

Arlt, Roberto (Godofredo Christophersen)
1900-1942 . . . . **TCLC 29; HLC**
See also CA 123; 131; HW

Armah, Ayi Kwei 1939- . . . . **CLC 5, 33; BLC**
See also BW; CA 61-64; CANR 21; DLB 117; MTCW

Armatrading, Joan 1950- . . . . **CLC 17**
See also CA 114

Arnette, Robert
See Silverberg, Robert

Arnim, Achim von (Ludwig Joachim von Arnim) 1781-1831 . . . . **NCLC 5**
See also DLB 90

Arnim, Bettina von 1785-1859. . . . **NCLC 38**
See also DLB 90

Arnold, Matthew
1822-1888 . . . . . **NCLC 6, 29; DA; PC 5; WLC**
See also CDBLB 1832-1890; DLB 32, 57

Arnold, Thomas 1795-1842 . . . . . . **NCLC 18**
See also DLB 55

Arnow, Harriette (Louisa) Simpson
1908-1986 . . . . **CLC 2, 7, 18**
See also CA 9-12R; 118; CANR 14; DLB 6; MTCW; SATA 42, 47

Arp, Hans
See Arp, Jean

Arp, Jean 1887-1966. . . . . **CLC 5**
See also CA 81-84; 25-28R; CANR 42

Arrabal
See Arrabal, Fernando

Arrabal, Fernando 1932- . . . **CLC 2, 9, 18, 58**
See also CA 9-12R; CANR 15

Arrick, Fran. . . . . **CLC 30**

Artaud, Antonin 1896-1948 . . . . . **TCLC 3, 36**
See also CA 104

Arthur, Ruth M(abel) 1905-1979. . . . **CLC 12**
See also CA 9-12R; 85-88; CANR 4; SATA 7, 26

Artsybashev, Mikhail (Petrovich)
1878-1927 . . . . **TCLC 31**

Arundel, Honor (Morfydd)
1919-1973 . . . . **CLC 17**
See also CA 21-22; 41-44R; CAP 2; SATA 4, 24

Asch, Sholem 1880-1957 . . . . **TCLC 3**
See also CA 105

Ash, Shalom
See Asch, Sholem

Ashbery, John (Lawrence)
1927- . . . . . . **CLC 2, 3, 4, 6, 9, 13, 15, 25, 41, 77**
See also CA 5-8R; CANR 9, 37; DLB 5; DLBY 81; MTCW

Ashdown, Clifford
See Freeman, R(ichard) Austin

Ashe, Gordon
See Creasey, John

Ashton-Warner, Sylvia (Constance)
1908-1984 . . . . **CLC 19**
See also CA 69-72; 112; CANR 29; MTCW

Asimov, Isaac
1920-1992 . . . . . . **CLC 1, 3, 9, 19, 26, 76**
See also BEST 90:2; CA 1-4R; 137; CANR 2, 19, 36; CLR 12; DLB 8; DLBY 92; JRDA; MAICYA; MTCW; SATA 1, 26, 74

Astley, Thea (Beatrice May)
1925- . . . . **CLC 41**
See also CA 65-68; CANR 11, 43

Aston, James
See White, T(erence) H(anbury)

Asturias, Miguel Angel
1899-1974 . . . . **CLC 3, 8, 13; HLC**
See also CA 25-28; 49-52; CANR 32; CAP 2; DLB 113; HW; MTCW

Atares, Carlos Saura
See Saura (Atares), Carlos

Atheling, William
See Pound, Ezra (Weston Loomis)

Atheling, William, Jr.
See Blish, James (Benjamin)

Atherton, Gertrude (Franklin Horn)
1857-1948 . . . . **TCLC 2**
See also CA 104; DLB 9, 78

Atherton, Lucius
See Masters, Edgar Lee

Atkins, Jack
See Harris, Mark

Atticus
See Fleming, Ian (Lancaster)

Atwood, Margaret (Eleanor)
1939- . . . . . **CLC 2, 3, 4, 8, 13, 15, 25, 44; DA; PC 8; SSC 2; WLC**
See also BEST 89:2; CA 49-52; CANR 3, 24, 33; DLB 53; MTCW; SATA 50

Aubigny, Pierre d'
See Mencken, H(enry) L(ouis)

Aubin, Penelope 1685-1731(?). . . . . **LC 9**
See also DLB 39

Auchincloss, Louis (Stanton)
1917- . . . . **CLC 4, 6, 9, 18, 45**
See also CA 1-4R; CANR 6, 29; DLB 2; DLBY 80; MTCW

Auden, W(ystan) H(ugh)
1907-1973 . . . . . . **CLC 1, 2, 3, 4, 6, 9, 11, 14, 43; DA; PC 1; WLC**
See also CA 9-12R; 45-48; CANR 5; CDBLB 1914-1945; DLB 10, 20; MTCW

Audiberti, Jacques 1900-1965 . . . . . . **CLC 38**
See also CA 25-28R

Auel, Jean M(arie) 1936-. . . . . **CLC 31**
See also AAYA 7; BEST 90:4; CA 103; CANR 21

Auerbach, Erich 1892-1957 . . . . **TCLC 43**
See also CA 118

Augier, Emile 1820-1889 . . . . **NCLC 31**

August, John
See De Voto, Bernard (Augustine)

Augustine, St. 354-430 . . . . **CMLC 6**

Aurelius
See Bourne, Randolph S(illiman)

Austen, Jane
1775-1817 .... **NCLC 1, 13, 19, 33; DA; WLC**
See also CDBLB 1789-1832; DLB 116

Auster, Paul 1947- .... **CLC 47**
See also CA 69-72; CANR 23

Austin, Frank
See Faust, Frederick (Schiller)

Austin, Mary (Hunter)
1868-1934 .... **TCLC 25**
See also CA 109; DLB 9, 78

Autran Dourado, Waldomiro
See Dourado, (Waldomiro Freitas) Autran

Averroes 1126-1198 .... **CMLC 7**
See also DLB 115

Avison, Margaret 1918- .... **CLC 2, 4**
See also CA 17-20R; DLB 53; MTCW

Axton, David
See Koontz, Dean R(ay)

Ayckbourn, Alan
1939- .... **CLC 5, 8, 18, 33, 74**
See also CA 21-24R; CANR 31; DLB 13;
MTCW

Aydy, Catherine
See Tennant, Emma (Christina)

Ayme, Marcel (Andre) 1902-1967... **CLC 11**
See also CA 89-92; CLR 25; DLB 72

Ayrton, Michael 1921-1975........ **CLC 7**
See also CA 5-8R; 61-64; CANR 9, 21

Azorin........................... **CLC 11**
See also Martinez Ruiz, Jose

Azuela, Mariano
1873-1952 .... **TCLC 3; HLC**
See also CA 104; 131; HW; MTCW

Baastad, Babbis Friis
See Friis-Baastad, Babbis Ellinor

Bab
See Gilbert, W(illiam) S(chwenck)

Babbis, Eleanor
See Friis-Baastad, Babbis Ellinor

Babel, Isaak (Emmanuilovich)
1894-1941(?) .... **TCLC 2, 13**
See also CA 104

Babits, Mihaly 1883-1941 .... **TCLC 14**
See also CA 114

Babur 1483-1530................. **LC 18**

Bacchelli, Riccardo 1891-1985 ..... **CLC 19**
See also CA 29-32R; 117

Bach, Richard (David) 1936-....... **CLC 14**
See also AITN 1; BEST 89:2; CA 9-12R;
CANR 18; MTCW; SATA 13

Bachman, Richard
See King, Stephen (Edwin)

Bachmann, Ingeborg 1926-1973..... **CLC 69**
See also CA 93-96; 45-48; DLB 85

Bacon, Francis 1561-1626 .... **LC 18**
See also CDBLB Before 1660

Bacovia, George................. **TCLC 24**
See also Vasiliu, Gheorghe

Badanes, Jerome 1937-........... **CLC 59**

Bagehot, Walter 1826-1877 ...... **NCLC 10**
See also DLB 55

Bagnold, Enid 1889-1981 .... **CLC 25**
See also CA 5-8R; 103; CANR 5, 40;
DLB 13; MAICYA; SATA 1, 25

Bagrjana, Elisaveta
See Belcheva, Elisaveta

Bagryana, Elisaveta
See Belcheva, Elisaveta

Bailey, Paul 1937- .... **CLC 45**
See also CA 21-24R; CANR 16; DLB 14

Baillie, Joanna 1762-1851 .... **NCLC 2**
See also DLB 93

Bainbridge, Beryl (Margaret)
1933- .... **CLC 4, 5, 8, 10, 14, 18, 22, 62**
See also CA 21-24R; CANR 24; DLB 14;
MTCW

Baker, Elliott 1922- .... **CLC 8**
See also CA 45-48; CANR 2

Baker, Nicholson 1957- .... **CLC 61**
See also CA 135

Baker, Ray Stannard 1870-1946 ... **TCLC 47**
See also CA 118

Baker, Russell (Wayne) 1925-...... **CLC 31**
See also BEST 89:4; CA 57-60; CANR 11,
41; MTCW

Bakshi, Ralph 1938(?)-........... **CLC 26**
See also CA 112; 138

Bakunin, Mikhail (Alexandrovich)
1814-1876 .... **NCLC 25**

Baldwin, James (Arthur)
1924-1987 ...... **CLC 1, 2, 3, 4, 5, 8, 13,
15, 17, 42, 50, 67; BLC; DA; DC 1;
SSC 10; WLC**
See also AAYA 4; BW; CA 1-4R; 124;
CABS 1; CANR 3, 24;
CDALB 1941-1968; DLB 2, 7, 33;
DLBY 87; MTCW; SATA 9, 54

Ballard, J(ames) G(raham)
1930- .... **CLC 3, 6, 14, 36; SSC 1**
See also AAYA 3; CA 5-8R; CANR 15, 39;
DLB 14; MTCW

Balmont, Konstantin (Dmitriyevich)
1867-1943 .... **TCLC 11**
See also CA 109

Balzac, Honore de
1799-1850 .... **NCLC 5, 35; DA; SSC 5;
WLC**
See also DLB 119

Bambara, Toni Cade
1939- .... **CLC 19; BLC; DA**
See also AAYA 5; BW; CA 29-32R;
CANR 24; DLB 38; MTCW

Bamdad, A.
See Shamlu, Ahmad

Banat, D. R.
See Bradbury, Ray (Douglas)

Bancroft, Laura
See Baum, L(yman) Frank

Banim, John 1798-1842 .... **NCLC 13**
See also DLB 116

Banim, Michael 1796-1874 ...... **NCLC 13**

Banks, Iain
See Banks, Iain M(enzies)

Banks, Iain M(enzies) 1954- .... **CLC 34**
See also CA 123; 128

Banks, Lynne Reid .... **CLC 23**
See also Reid Banks, Lynne
See also AAYA 6

Banks, Russell 1940- .... **CLC 37, 72**
See also CA 65-68; CAAS 15; CANR 19;
DLB 130

Banville, John 1945-.............. **CLC 46**
See also CA 117; 128; DLB 14

Banville, Theodore (Faullain) de
1832-1891 .... **NCLC 9**

Baraka, Amiri
1934- .... **CLC 1, 2, 3, 5, 10, 14, 33;
BLC; DA; PC 4**
See also Jones, LeRoi
See also BW; CA 21-24R; CABS 3;
CANR 27, 38; CDALB 1941-1968;
DLB 5, 7, 16, 38; DLBD 8; MTCW

Barbellion, W. N. P............... **TCLC 24**
See also Cummings, Bruce F(rederick)

Barbera, Jack 1945-.............. **CLC 44**
See also CA 110

Barbey d'Aurevilly, Jules Amedee
1808-1889 .... **NCLC 1**
See also DLB 119

Barbusse, Henri 1873-1935 .... **TCLC 5**
See also CA 105; DLB 65

Barclay, Bill
See Moorcock, Michael (John)

Barclay, William Ewert
See Moorcock, Michael (John)

Barea, Arturo 1897-1957 .... **TCLC 14**
See also CA 111

Barfoot, Joan 1946-.............. **CLC 18**
See also CA 105

Baring, Maurice 1874-1945 .... **TCLC 8**
See also CA 105; DLB 34

Barker, Clive 1952- .... **CLC 52**
See also AAYA 10; BEST 90:3; CA 121;
129; MTCW

Barker, George Granville
1913-1991 .... **CLC 8, 48**
See also CA 9-12R; 135; CANR 7, 38;
DLB 20; MTCW

Barker, Harley Granville
See Granville-Barker, Harley
See also DLB 10

Barker, Howard 1946-............ **CLC 37**
See also CA 102; DLB 13

Barker, Pat 1943-............... **CLC 32**
See also CA 117; 122

Barlow, Joel 1754-1812 .... **NCLC 23**
See also DLB 37

Barnard, Mary (Ethel) 1909-....... **CLC 48**
See also CA 21-22; CAP 2

Barnes, Djuna
1892-1982 ... **CLC 3, 4, 8, 11, 29; SSC 3**
See also CA 9-12R; 107; CANR 16; DLB 4,
9, 45; MTCW

Barnes, Julian 1946-.............. **CLC 42**
See also CA 102; CANR 19

Barnes, Peter 1931- .... **CLC 5, 56**
See also CA 65-68; CAAS 12; CANR 33,
34; DLB 13; MTCW

Baroja (y Nessi), Pio
    1872-1956 . . . . **TCLC 8; HLC**
    See also CA 104

Baron, David
    See Pinter, Harold

Baron Corvo
    See Rolfe, Frederick (William Serafino
    Austin Lewis Mary)

Barondess, Sue K(aufman)
    1926-1977 . . . . **CLC 8**
    See also Kaufman, Sue
    See also CA 1-4R; 69-72; CANR 1

Baron de Teive
    See Pessoa, Fernando (Antonio Nogueira)

Barres, Maurice 1862-1923 . . . . **TCLC 47**
    See also DLB 123

Barreto, Afonso Henrique de Lima
    See Lima Barreto, Afonso Henrique de

Barrett, (Roger) Syd 1946- . . . . **CLC 35**
    See also Pink Floyd

Barrett, William (Christopher)
    1913-1992 . . . . **CLC 27**
    See also CA 13-16R; 139; CANR 11

Barrie, J(ames) M(atthew)
    1860-1937 . . . . **TCLC 2**
    See also CA 104; 136; CDBLB 1890-1914;
    CLR 16; DLB 10; MAICYA; YABC 1

Barrington, Michael
    See Moorcock, Michael (John)

Barrol, Grady
    See Bograd, Larry

Barry, Mike
    See Malzberg, Barry N(athaniel)

Barry, Philip 1896-1949 . . . . **TCLC 11**
    See also CA 109; DLB 7

Bart, Andre Schwarz
    See Schwarz-Bart, Andre

Barth, John (Simmons)
    1930- . . . . . . **CLC 1, 2, 3, 5, 7, 9, 10, 14,
                        27, 51; SSC 10**
    See also AITN 1, 2; CA 1-4R; CABS 1;
    CANR 5, 23; DLB 2; MTCW

Barthelme, Donald
    1931-1989 . . . . . . **CLC 1, 2, 3, 5, 6, 8, 13,
                            23, 46, 59; SSC 2**
    See also CA 21-24R; 129; CANR 20;
    DLB 2; DLBY 80, 89; MTCW; SATA 7,
    62

Barthelme, Frederick 1943- . . . . **CLC 36**
    See also CA 114; 122; DLBY 85

Barthes, Roland (Gerard)
    1915-1980 . . . . **CLC 24**
    See also CA 130; 97-100; MTCW

Barzun, Jacques (Martin) 1907- . . . . **CLC 51**
    See also CA 61-64; CANR 22

Bashevis, Isaac
    See Singer, Isaac Bashevis

Bashkirtseff, Marie 1859-1884 . . . **NCLC 27**

Basho
    See Matsuo Basho

Bass, Kingsley B., Jr.
    See Bullins, Ed

Bass, Rick 1958- . . . . **CLC 79**
    See also CA 126

Bassani, Giorgio 1916- . . . . **CLC 9**
    See also CA 65-68; CANR 33; DLB 128;
    MTCW

Bastos, Augusto (Antonio) Roa
    See Roa Bastos, Augusto (Antonio)

Bataille, Georges 1897-1962 . . . . **CLC 29**
    See also CA 101; 89-92

Bates, H(erbert) E(rnest)
    1905-1974 . . . . **CLC 46; SSC 10**
    See also CA 93-96; 45-48; CANR 34;
    MTCW

Bauchart
    See Camus, Albert

Baudelaire, Charles
    1821-1867 . . . . . **NCLC 6, 29; DA; PC 1;
                        WLC**

Baudrillard, Jean 1929- . . . . **CLC 60**

Baum, L(yman) Frank 1856-1919 . . . **TCLC 7**
    See also CA 108; 133; CLR 15; DLB 22;
    JRDA; MAICYA; MTCW; SATA 18

Baum, Louis F.
    See Baum, L(yman) Frank

Baumbach, Jonathan 1933- . . . . . . **CLC 6, 23**
    See also CA 13-16R; CAAS 5; CANR 12;
    DLBY 80; MTCW

Bausch, Richard (Carl) 1945- . . . . . . **CLC 51**
    See also CA 101; CAAS 14; CANR 43;
    DLB 130

Baxter, Charles 1947- . . . . **CLC 45, 78**
    See also CA 57-60; CANR 40; DLB 130

Baxter, George Owen
    See Faust, Frederick (Schiller)

Baxter, James K(eir) 1926-1972 . . . . **CLC 14**
    See also CA 77-80

Baxter, John
    See Hunt, E(verette) Howard, Jr.

Bayer, Sylvia
    See Glassco, John

Beagle, Peter S(oyer) 1939- . . . . **CLC 7**
    See also CA 9-12R; CANR 4; DLBY 80;
    SATA 60

Bean, Normal
    See Burroughs, Edgar Rice

Beard, Charles A(ustin)
    1874-1948 . . . . **TCLC 15**
    See also CA 115; DLB 17; SATA 18

Beardsley, Aubrey 1872-1898 . . . . . **NCLC 6**

Beattie, Ann
    1947- . . . . **CLC 8, 13, 18, 40, 63; SSC 11**
    See also BEST 90:2; CA 81-84; DLBY 82;
    MTCW

Beattie, James 1735-1803 . . . . **NCLC 25**
    See also DLB 109

Beauchamp, Kathleen Mansfield 1888-1923
    See Mansfield, Katherine
    See also CA 104; 134; DA

Beaumarchais, Pierre-Augustin Caron de
    1732-1799 . . . . **DC 4**

**Beauvoir, Simone (Lucie Ernestine Marie
    Bertrand) de**
    1908-1986 . . . . **CLC 1, 2, 4, 8, 14, 31, 44,
                        50, 71; DA; WLC**
    See also CA 9-12R; 118; CANR 28;
    DLB 72; DLBY 86; MTCW

Becker, Jurek 1937- . . . . **CLC 7, 19**
    See also CA 85-88; DLB 75

Becker, Walter 1950- . . . . **CLC 26**

Beckett, Samuel (Barclay)
    1906-1989 . . . . . **CLC 1, 2, 3, 4, 6, 9, 10,
                        11, 14, 18, 29, 57, 59; DA; WLC**
    See also CA 5-8R; 130; CANR 33;
    CDBLB 1945-1960; DLB 13, 15;
    DLBY 90; MTCW

Beckford, William 1760-1844 . . . . **NCLC 16**
    See also DLB 39

Beckman, Gunnel 1910- . . . . **CLC 26**
    See also CA 33-36R; CANR 15; CLR 25;
    MAICYA; SAAS 9; SATA 6

Becque, Henri 1837-1899 . . . . **NCLC 3**

Beddoes, Thomas Lovell
    1803-1849 . . . . **NCLC 3**
    See also DLB 96

Bedford, Donald F.
    See Fearing, Kenneth (Flexner)

Beecher, Catharine Esther
    1800-1878 . . . . **NCLC 30**
    See also DLB 1

Beecher, John 1904-1980 . . . . **CLC 6**
    See also AITN 1; CA 5-8R; 105; CANR 8

Beer, Johann 1655-1700 . . . . **LC 5**

Beer, Patricia 1924- . . . . **CLC 58**
    See also CA 61-64; CANR 13; DLB 40

Beerbohm, Henry Maximilian
    1872-1956 . . . . **TCLC 1, 24**
    See also CA 104; DLB 34, 100

Begiebing, Robert J(ohn) 1946- . . . . . **CLC 70**
    See also CA 122; CANR 40

Behan, Brendan
    1923-1964 . . . . **CLC 1, 8, 11, 15, 79**
    See also CA 73-76; CANR 33;
    CDBLB 1945-1960; DLB 13; MTCW

Behn, Aphra
    1640(?)-1689 . . . . **LC 1; DA; DC 4; WLC**
    See also DLB 39, 80, 131

Behrman, S(amuel) N(athaniel)
    1893-1973 . . . . **CLC 40**
    See also CA 13-16; 45-48; CAP 1; DLB 7,
    44

Belasco, David 1853-1931 . . . . **TCLC 3**
    See also CA 104; DLB 7

Belcheva, Elisaveta 1893- . . . . **CLC 10**

Beldone, Phil "Cheech"
    See Ellison, Harlan

Beleno
    See Azuela, Mariano

Belinski, Vissarion Grigoryevich
    1811-1848 . . . . **NCLC 5**

Belitt, Ben 1911- . . . . **CLC 22**
    See also CA 13-16R; CAAS 4; CANR 7;
    DLB 5

Bell, James Madison
    1826-1902 . . . . **TCLC 43; BLC**
    See also BW; CA 122; 124; DLB 50

Bell, Madison (Smartt) 1957- . . . . . . **CLC 41**
    See also CA 111; CANR 28

Bell, Marvin (Hartley) 1937- . . . . . **CLC 8, 31**
    See also CA 21-24R; CAAS 14; DLB 5;
    MTCW

Bell, W. L. D.
See Mencken, H(enry) L(ouis)

Bellamy, Atwood C.
See Mencken, H(enry) L(ouis)

Bellamy, Edward 1850-1898 ...... **NCLC 4**
See also DLB 12

Bellin, Edward J.
See Kuttner, Henry

Belloc, (Joseph) Hilaire (Pierre)
1870-1953 .... **TCLC 7, 18**
See also CA 106; DLB 19, 100; YABC 1

Belloc, Joseph Peter Rene Hilaire
See Belloc, (Joseph) Hilaire (Pierre)

Belloc, Joseph Pierre Hilaire
See Belloc, (Joseph) Hilaire (Pierre)

Belloc, M. A.
See Lowndes, Marie Adelaide (Belloc)

Bellow, Saul
1915- ...... **CLC 1, 2, 3, 6, 8, 10, 13, 15,
25, 33, 34, 63, 79; DA; SSC 14; WLC**
See also AITN 2; BEST 89:3; CA 5-8R;
CABS 1; CANR 29; CDALB 1941-1968;
DLB 2, 28; DLBD 3; DLBY 82; MTCW

Belser, Reimond Karel Maria de
1929- .... **CLC 14**

Bely, Andrey .... **TCLC 7**
See also Bugayev, Boris Nikolayevich

Benary, Margot
See Benary-Isbert, Margot

Benary-Isbert, Margot 1889-1979... **CLC 12**
See also CA 5-8R; 89-92; CANR 4;
CLR 12; MAICYA; SATA 2, 21

Benavente (y Martinez), Jacinto
1866-1954 .... **TCLC 3**
See also CA 106; 131; HW; MTCW

Benchley, Peter (Bradford)
1940- .... **CLC 4, 8**
See also AITN 2; CA 17-20R; CANR 12,
35; MTCW; SATA 3

Benchley, Robert (Charles)
1889-1945 .... **TCLC 1**
See also CA 105; DLB 11

Benedikt, Michael 1935- .... **CLC 4, 14**
See also CA 13-16R; CANR 7; DLB 5

Benet, Juan 1927-................ **CLC 28**
See also CA 143

Benet, Stephen Vincent
1898-1943 .... **TCLC 7; SSC 10**
See also CA 104; DLB 4, 48, 102; YABC 1

Benet, William Rose 1886-1950 ... **TCLC 28**
See also CA 118; DLB 45

Benford, Gregory (Albert) 1941-.... **CLC 52**
See also CA 69-72; CANR 12, 24;
DLBY 82

Bengtsson, Frans (Gunnar)
1894-1954 .... **TCLC 48**

Benjamin, David
See Slavitt, David R(ytman)

Benjamin, Lois
See Gould, Lois

Benjamin, Walter 1892-1940...... **TCLC 39**

Benn, Gottfried 1886-1956........ **TCLC 3**
See also CA 106; DLB 56

Bennett, Alan 1934-........... **CLC 45, 77**
See also CA 103; CANR 35; MTCW

Bennett, (Enoch) Arnold
1867-1931 .... **TCLC 5, 20**
See also CA 106; CDBLB 1890-1914;
DLB 10, 34, 98

Bennett, Elizabeth
See Mitchell, Margaret (Munnerlyn)

Bennett, George Harold 1930-
See Bennett, Hal
See also BW; CA 97-100

Bennett, Hal .... **CLC 5**
See also Bennett, George Harold
See also DLB 33

Bennett, Jay 1912-............... **CLC 35**
See also AAYA 10; CA 69-72; CANR 11,
42; JRDA; SAAS 4; SATA 27, 41

Bennett, Louise (Simone)
1919- .... **CLC 28; BLC**
See also DLB 117

Benson, E(dward) F(rederic)
1867-1940 .... **TCLC 27**
See also CA 114; DLB 135

Benson, Jackson J. 1930-......... **CLC 34**
See also CA 25-28R; DLB 111

Benson, Sally 1900-1972 .... **CLC 17**
See also CA 19-20; 37-40R; CAP 1;
SATA 1, 27, 35

Benson, Stella 1892-1933......... **TCLC 17**
See also CA 117; DLB 36

Bentham, Jeremy 1748-1832 ..... **NCLC 38**
See also DLB 107

Bentley, E(dmund) C(lerihew)
1875-1956 .... **TCLC 12**
See also CA 108; DLB 70

Bentley, Eric (Russell) 1916-...... **CLC 24**
See also CA 5-8R; CANR 6

Beranger, Pierre Jean de
1780-1857 .... **NCLC 34**

Berger, Colonel
See Malraux, (Georges-)Andre

Berger, John (Peter) 1926- ...... **CLC 2, 19**
See also CA 81-84; DLB 14

Berger, Melvin H. 1927-.......... **CLC 12**
See also CA 5-8R; CANR 4; CLR 32;
SAAS 2; SATA 5

Berger, Thomas (Louis)
1924-.......... **CLC 3, 5, 8, 11, 18, 38**
See also CA 1-4R; CANR 5, 28; DLB 2;
DLBY 80; MTCW

Bergman, (Ernst) Ingmar
1918- .... **CLC 16, 72**
See also CA 81-84; CANR 33

Bergson, Henri 1859-1941........ **TCLC 32**

Bergstein, Eleanor 1938-.......... **CLC 4**
See also CA 53-56; CANR 5

Berkoff, Steven 1937-............ **CLC 56**
See also CA 104

Bermant, Chaim (Icyk) 1929- ...... **CLC 40**
See also CA 57-60; CANR 6, 31

Bern, Victoria
See Fisher, M(ary) F(rances) K(ennedy)

Bernanos, (Paul Louis) Georges
1888-1948 .... **TCLC 3**
See also CA 104; 130; DLB 72

Bernard, April 1956- .... **CLC 59**
See also CA 131

Bernhard, Thomas
1931-1989 .... **CLC 3, 32, 61**
See also CA 85-88; 127; CANR 32;
DLB 85, 124; MTCW

Berrigan, Daniel 1921-............ **CLC 4**
See also CA 33-36R; CAAS 1; CANR 11,
43; DLB 5

Berrigan, Edmund Joseph Michael, Jr.
1934-1983
See Berrigan, Ted
See also CA 61-64; 110; CANR 14

Berrigan, Ted..................... **CLC 37**
See also Berrigan, Edmund Joseph Michael,
Jr.
See also DLB 5

Berry, Charles Edward Anderson 1931-
See Berry, Chuck
See also CA 115

Berry, Chuck..................... **CLC 17**
See also Berry, Charles Edward Anderson

Berry, Jonas
See Ashbery, John (Lawrence)

Berry, Wendell (Erdman)
1934- .... **CLC 4, 6, 8, 27, 46**
See also AITN 1; CA 73-76; DLB 5, 6

Berryman, John
1914-1972 ...... **CLC 1, 2, 3, 4, 6, 8, 10,
13, 25, 62**
See also CA 13-16; 33-36R; CABS 2;
CANR 35; CAP 1; CDALB 1941-1968;
DLB 48; MTCW

Bertolucci, Bernardo 1940-........ **CLC 16**
See also CA 106

Bertrand, Aloysius 1807-1841 .... **NCLC 31**

Bertran de Born c. 1140-1215..... **CMLC 5**

Besant, Annie (Wood) 1847-1933 ... **TCLC 9**
See also CA 105

Bessie, Alvah 1904-1985......... **CLC 23**
See also CA 5-8R; 116; CANR 2; DLB 26

Bethlen, T. D.
See Silverberg, Robert

Beti, Mongo................ **CLC 27; BLC**
See also Biyidi, Alexandre

Betjeman, John
1906-1984 .... **CLC 2, 6, 10, 34, 43**
See also CA 9-12R; 112; CANR 33;
CDBLB 1945-1960; DLB 20; DLBY 84;
MTCW

Bettelheim, Bruno 1903-1990 ...... **CLC 79**
See also CA 81-84; 131; CANR 23; MTCW

Betti, Ugo 1892-1953 .... **TCLC 5**
See also CA 104

Betts, Doris (Waugh) 1932-.... **CLC 3, 6, 28**
See also CA 13-16R; CANR 9; DLBY 82

Bevan, Alistair
See Roberts, Keith (John Kingston)

Beynon, John
See Harris, John (Wyndham Parkes Lucas)
Beynon

Bialik, Chaim Nachman
    1873-1934 .... **TCLC 25**

Bickerstaff, Isaac
    See Swift, Jonathan

Bidart, Frank   1939- .... **CLC 33**
    See also CA 140

Bienek, Horst   1930- .... **CLC 7, 11**
    See also CA 73-76; DLB 75

Bierce, Ambrose (Gwinett)
    1842-1914(?) ...... **TCLC 1, 7, 44; DA;**
                               SSC 9; WLC
    See also CA 104; 139; CDALB 1865-1917;
      DLB 11, 12, 23, 71, 74

Billings, Josh
    See Shaw, Henry Wheeler

Billington, Rachel   1942- .... **CLC 43**
    See also AITN 2; CA 33-36R

Binyon, T(imothy) J(ohn)   1936- .... **CLC 34**
    See also CA 111; CANR 28

Bioy Casares, Adolfo
    1914- .... **CLC 4, 8, 13; HLC**
    See also CA 29-32R; CANR 19, 43;
      DLB 113; HW; MTCW

Bird, C.
    See Ellison, Harlan

Bird, Cordwainer
    See Ellison, Harlan

Bird, Robert Montgomery
    1806-1854 .... **NCLC 1**

Birney, (Alfred) Earle
    1904- .... **CLC 1, 4, 6, 11**
    See also CA 1-4R; CANR 5, 20; DLB 88;
      MTCW

Bishop, Elizabeth
    1911-1979 ...... **CLC 1, 4, 9, 13, 15, 32;**
                               DA; PC 3
    See also CA 5-8R; 89-92; CABS 2;
      CANR 26; CDALB 1968-1988; DLB 5;
      MTCW; SATA 24

Bishop, John   1935- .... **CLC 10**
    See also CA 105

Bissett, Bill   1939- .... **CLC 18**
    See also CA 69-72; CANR 15; DLB 53;
      MTCW

Bitov, Andrei (Georgievich)   1937-... **CLC 57**
    See also CA 142

Biyidi, Alexandre   1932-
    See Beti, Mongo
    See also BW; CA 114; 124; MTCW

Bjarme, Brynjolf
    See Ibsen, Henrik (Johan)

Bjornson, Bjornstjerne (Martinius)
    1832-1910 .... **TCLC 7, 37**
    See also CA 104

Black, Robert
    See Holdstock, Robert P.

Blackburn, Paul   1926-1971 ...... **CLC 9, 43**
    See also CA 81-84; 33-36R; CANR 34;
      DLB 16; DLBY 81

Black Elk   1863-1950 .... **TCLC 33**

Black Hobart
    See Sanders, (James) Ed(ward)

Blacklin, Malcolm
    See Chambers, Aidan

Blackmore, R(ichard) D(oddridge)
    1825-1900 .... **TCLC 27**
    See also CA 120; DLB 18

Blackmur, R(ichard) P(almer)
    1904-1965 .... **CLC 2, 24**
    See also CA 11-12; 25-28R; CAP 1; DLB 63

Black Tarantula, The
    See Acker, Kathy

Blackwood, Algernon (Henry)
    1869-1951 .... **TCLC 5**
    See also CA 105

Blackwood, Caroline   1931- .... **CLC 6, 9**
    See also CA 85-88; CANR 32; DLB 14;
      MTCW

Blade, Alexander
    See Hamilton, Edmond; Silverberg, Robert

Blaga, Lucian   1895-1961 .... **CLC 75**

Blair, Eric (Arthur)   1903-1950
    See Orwell, George
    See also CA 104; 132; DA; MTCW;
      SATA 29

Blais, Marie-Claire
    1939- .... **CLC 2, 4, 6, 13, 22**
    See also CA 21-24R; CAAS 4; CANR 38;
      DLB 53; MTCW

Blaise, Clark   1940- .... **CLC 29**
    See also AITN 2; CA 53-56; CAAS 3;
      CANR 5; DLB 53

Blake, Nicholas
    See Day Lewis, C(ecil)
    See also DLB 77

Blake, William
    1757-1827 ..... **NCLC 13, 37; DA; WLC**
    See also CDBLB 1789-1832; DLB 93;
      MAICYA; SATA 30

Blasco Ibanez, Vicente
    1867-1928 .... **TCLC 12**
    See also CA 110; 131; HW; MTCW

Blatty, William Peter   1928- .... **CLC 2**
    See also CA 5-8R; CANR 9

Bleeck, Oliver
    See Thomas, Ross (Elmore)

Blessing, Lee   1949- .... **CLC 54**

Blish, James (Benjamin)
    1921-1975 .... **CLC 14**
    See also CA 1-4R; 57-60; CANR 3; DLB 8;
      MTCW; SATA 66

Bliss, Reginald
    See Wells, H(erbert) G(eorge)

Blixen, Karen (Christentze Dinesen)
    1885-1962
    See Dinesen, Isak
    See also CA 25-28; CANR 22; CAP 2;
      MTCW; SATA 44

Bloch, Robert (Albert)   1917- .... **CLC 33**
    See also CA 5-8R; CANR 5; DLB 44;
      SATA 12

Blok, Alexander (Alexandrovich)
    1880-1921 .... **TCLC 5**
    See also CA 104

Blom, Jan
    See Breytenbach, Breyten

Bloom, Harold   1930- .... **CLC 24**
    See also CA 13-16R; CANR 39; DLB 67

Bloomfield, Aurelius
    See Bourne, Randolph S(illiman)

Blount, Roy (Alton), Jr.   1941- ..... **CLC 38**
    See also CA 53-56; CANR 10, 28; MTCW

Bloy, Leon   1846-1917 .... **TCLC 22**
    See also CA 121; DLB 123

Blume, Judy (Sussman)   1938-... **CLC 12, 30**
    See also AAYA 3; CA 29-32R; CANR 13,
      37; CLR 2, 15; DLB 52; JRDA;
      MAICYA; MTCW; SATA 2, 31

Blunden, Edmund (Charles)
    1896-1974 .... **CLC 2, 56**
    See also CA 17-18; 45-48; CAP 2; DLB 20,
      100; MTCW

Bly, Robert (Elwood)
    1926- .... **CLC 1, 2, 5, 10, 15, 38**
    See also CA 5-8R; CANR 41; DLB 5;
      MTCW

Bobette
    See Simenon, Georges (Jacques Christian)

Boccaccio, Giovanni   1313-1375
    See also SSC 10

Bochco, Steven   1943- .... **CLC 35**
    See also CA 124; 138

Bodenheim, Maxwell   1892-1954 ... **TCLC 44**
    See also CA 110; DLB 9, 45

Bodker, Cecil   1927- .... **CLC 21**
    See also CA 73-76; CANR 13; CLR 23;
      MAICYA; SATA 14

Boell, Heinrich (Theodor)   1917-1985
    See Boll, Heinrich (Theodor)
    See also CA 21-24R; 116; CANR 24; DA;
      DLB 69; DLBY 85; MTCW

Boerne, Alfred
    See Doeblin, Alfred

Bogan, Louise   1897-1970 ..... **CLC 4, 39, 46**
    See also CA 73-76; 25-28R; CANR 33;
      DLB 45; MTCW

Bogarde, Dirk .... **CLC 19**
    See also Van Den Bogarde, Derek Jules
      Gaspard Ulric Niven
    See also DLB 14

Bogosian, Eric   1953- .... **CLC 45**
    See also CA 138

Bograd, Larry   1953- .... **CLC 35**
    See also CA 93-96; SATA 33

Boiardo, Matteo Maria   1441-1494 .... **LC 6**

Boileau-Despreaux, Nicolas
    1636-1711 .... **LC 3**

Boland, Eavan (Aisling)   1944-... **CLC 40, 67**
    See also CA 143; DLB 40

Boll, Heinrich (Theodor)
    1917-1985 .... **CLC 2, 3, 6, 9, 11, 15, 27,**
                               39, 72; WLC
    See also Boell, Heinrich (Theodor)
    See also DLB 69; DLBY 85

Bolt, Lee
    See Faust, Frederick (Schiller)

Bolt, Robert (Oxton)   1924- .... **CLC 14**
    See also CA 17-20R; CANR 35; DLB 13;
      MTCW

Bomkauf
    See Kaufman, Bob (Garnell)

Breslin, Jimmy .... CLC **4, 43**
See also Breslin, James
See also AITN 1

Bresson, Robert 1907- .... CLC **16**
See also CA 110

Breton, Andre 1896-1966... CLC **2, 9, 15, 54**
See also CA 19-20; 25-28R;
CAP 2; DLB 65; MTCW

Breytenbach, Breyten 1939(?)- .. CLC **23, 37**
See also CA 113; 129

Bridgers, Sue Ellen 1942- .... CLC **26**
See also AAYA 8; CA 65-68; CANR 11,
36; CLR 18; DLB 52; JRDA; MAICYA;
SAAS 1; SATA 22

Bridges, Robert (Seymour)
1844-1930 .... TCLC **1**
See also CA 104; CDBLB 1890-1914;
DLB 19, 98

Bridie, James.................... TCLC **3**
See also Mavor, Osborne Henry
See also DLB 10

Brin, David 1950-................ CLC **34**
See also CA 102; CANR 24; SATA 65

Brink, Andre (Philippus)
1935- .... CLC **18, 36**
See also CA 104; CANR 39; MTCW

Brinsmead, H(esba) F(ay) 1922- .... CLC **21**
See also CA 21-24R; CANR 10; MAICYA;
SAAS 5; SATA 18

Brittain, Vera (Mary)
1893(?)-1970 .... CLC **23**
See also CA 13-16; 25-28R; CAP 1; MTCW

Broch, Hermann 1886-1951....... TCLC **20**
See also CA 117; DLB 85, 124

Brock, Rose
See Hansen, Joseph

Brodkey, Harold 1930-........... CLC **56**
See also CA 111; DLB 130

Brodsky, Iosif Alexandrovich 1940-
See Brodsky, Joseph
See also AITN 1; CA 41-44R; CANR 37;
MTCW

Brodsky, Joseph .... CLC **4, 6, 13, 36, 50**
See also Brodsky, Iosif Alexandrovich

Brodsky, Michael Mark 1948- ..... CLC **19**
See also CA 102; CANR 18, 41

Bromell, Henry 1947-............. CLC **5**
See also CA 53-56; CANR 9

Bromfield, Louis (Brucker)
1896-1956 .... TCLC **11**
See also CA 107; DLB 4, 9, 86

Broner, E(sther) M(asserman)
1930- .... CLC **19**
See also CA 17-20R; CANR 8, 25; DLB 28

Bronk, William 1918-............. CLC **10**
See also CA 89-92; CANR 23

Bronstein, Lev Davidovich
See Trotsky, Leon

Bronte, Anne 1820-1849......... NCLC **4**
See also DLB 21

Bronte, Charlotte
1816-1855 ... NCLC **3, 8, 33; DA; WLC**
See also CDBLB 1832-1890; DLB 21

Bronte, (Jane) Emily
1818-1848 .... NCLC **16, 35; DA; PC 8;
WLC**
See also CDBLB 1832-1890; DLB 21, 32

Brooke, Frances 1724-1789 .... LC **6**
See also DLB 39, 99

Brooke, Henry 1703(?)-1783 .... LC **1**
See also DLB 39

Brooke, Rupert (Chawner)
1887-1915 .... TCLC **2, 7; DA; WLC**
See also CA 104; 132; CDBLB 1914-1945;
DLB 19; MTCW

Brooke-Haven, P.
See Wodehouse, P(elham) G(renville)

Brooke-Rose, Christine 1926- ...... CLC **40**
See also CA 13-16R; DLB 14

Brookner, Anita 1928- ...... CLC **32, 34, 51**
See also CA 114; 120; CANR 37; DLBY 87;
MTCW

Brooks, Cleanth 1906- .... CLC **24**
See also CA 17-20R; CANR 33, 35;
DLB 63; MTCW

Brooks, George
See Baum, L(yman) Frank

Brooks, Gwendolyn
1917- ...... CLC **1, 2, 4, 5, 15, 49; BLC;
DA; PC 7; WLC**
See also AITN 1; BW; CA 1-4R; CANR 1,
27; CDALB 1941-1968; CLR 27; DLB 5,
76; MTCW; SATA 6

Brooks, Mel..................... CLC **12**
See also Kaminsky, Melvin
See also DLB 26

Brooks, Peter 1938- .... CLC **34**
See also CA 45-48; CANR 1

Brooks, Van Wyck 1886-1963...... CLC **29**
See also CA 1-4R; CANR 6; DLB 45, 63,
103

Brophy, Brigid (Antonia)
1929- .... CLC **6, 11, 29**
See also CA 5-8R; CAAS 4; CANR 25;
DLB 14; MTCW

Brosman, Catharine Savage 1934-.... CLC **9**
See also CA 61-64; CANR 21

Brother Antoninus
See Everson, William (Oliver)

Broughton, T(homas) Alan 1936- ... CLC **19**
See also CA 45-48; CANR 2, 23

Broumas, Olga 1949- .... CLC **10, 73**
See also CA 85-88; CANR 20

Brown, Charles Brockden
1771-1810 .... NCLC **22**
See also CDALB 1640-1865; DLB 37, 59,
73

Brown, Christy 1932-1981........ CLC **63**
See also CA 105; 104; DLB 14

Brown, Claude 1937- .... CLC **30; BLC**
See also AAYA 7; BW; CA 73-76

Brown, Dee (Alexander) 1908- .. CLC **18, 47**
See also CA 13-16R; CAAS 6; CANR 11;
DLBY 80; MTCW; SATA 5

Brown, George
See Wertmueller, Lina

Brown, George Douglas
1869-1902 .... TCLC **28**

Brown, George Mackay 1921-.... CLC **5, 48**
See also CA 21-24R; CAAS 6; CANR 12,
37; DLB 14, 27; MTCW; SATA 35

Brown, (William) Larry 1951-...... CLC **73**
See also CA 130; 134

Brown, Moses
See Barrett, William (Christopher)

Brown, Rita Mae 1944- ..... CLC **18, 43, 79**
See also CA 45-48; CANR 2, 11, 35;
MTCW

Brown, Roderick (Langmere) Haig-
See Haig-Brown, Roderick (Langmere)

Brown, Rosellen 1939-........... CLC **32**
See also CA 77-80; CAAS 10; CANR 14

Brown, Sterling Allen
1901-1989 .... CLC **1, 23, 59; BLC**
See also BW; CA 85-88; 127; CANR 26;
DLB 48, 51, 63; MTCW

Brown, Will
See Ainsworth, William Harrison

Brown, William Wells
1813-1884 .... NCLC **2; BLC; DC 1**
See also DLB 3, 50

Browne, (Clyde) Jackson 1948(?)-... CLC **21**
See also CA 120

Browning, Elizabeth Barrett
1806-1861 ..... NCLC **1, 16; DA; PC 6;
WLC**
See also CDBLB 1832-1890; DLB 32

Browning, Robert
1812-1889 .... NCLC **19; DA; PC 2**
See also CDBLB 1832-1890; DLB 32;
YABC 1

Browning, Tod 1882-1962 .... CLC **16**
See also CA 141; 117

Bruccoli, Matthew J(oseph) 1931- .. CLC **34**
See also CA 9-12R; CANR 7; DLB 103

Bruce, Lenny.................... CLC **21**
See also Schneider, Leonard Alfred

Bruin, John
See Brutus, Dennis

Brulls, Christian
See Simenon, Georges (Jacques Christian)

Brunner, John (Kilian Houston)
1934- .... CLC **8, 10**
See also CA 1-4R; CAAS 8; CANR 2, 37;
MTCW

Brutus, Dennis 1924- .... CLC **43; BLC**
See also BW; CA 49-52; CAAS 14;
CANR 2, 27, 42; DLB 117

Bryan, C(ourtlandt) D(ixon) B(arnes)
1936- .... CLC **29**
See also CA 73-76; CANR 13

Bryan, Michael
See Moore, Brian

Bryant, William Cullen
1794-1878 .... NCLC **6; DA**
See also CDALB 1640-1865; DLB 3, 43, 59

Bryusov, Valery Yakovlevich
1873-1924 .... TCLC **10**
See also CA 107

Buchan, John 1875-1940 .... TCLC **41**
See also CA 108; DLB 34, 70; YABC 2

Buchanan, George 1506-1582 .... LC **4**

Buchheim, Lothar-Guenther 1918- ... **CLC 6**
See also CA 85-88

Buchner, (Karl) Georg
1813-1837 .... **NCLC 26**

Buchwald, Art(hur) 1925-......... **CLC 33**
See also AITN 1; CA 5-8R; CANR 21;
MTCW; SATA 10

Buck, Pearl S(ydenstricker)
1892-1973 .... **CLC 7, 11, 18; DA**
See also AITN 1; CA 1-4R; 41-44R;
CANR 1, 34; DLB 9, 102; MTCW;
SATA 1, 25

Buckler, Ernest 1908-1984........ **CLC 13**
See also CA 11-12; 114; CAP 1; DLB 68;
SATA 47

Buckley, Vincent (Thomas)
1925-1988 .... **CLC 57**
See also CA 101

Buckley, William F(rank), Jr.
1925- .... **CLC 7, 18, 37**
See also AITN 1; CA 1-4R; CANR 1, 24;
DLBY 80; MTCW

Buechner, (Carl) Frederick
1926- .... **CLC 2, 4, 6, 9**
See also CA 13-16R; CANR 11, 39;
DLBY 80; MTCW

Buell, John (Edward) 1927-....... **CLC 10**
See also CA 1-4R; DLB 53

Buero Vallejo, Antonio 1916- ... **CLC 15, 46**
See also CA 106; CANR 24; HW; MTCW

Bufalino, Gesualdo 1920(?)-....... **CLC 74**

Bugayev, Boris Nikolayevich 1880-1934
See Bely, Andrey
See also CA 104

Bukowski, Charles
1920-1994 .... **CLC 2, 5, 9, 41, 82**
See also CA 17-20R; CANR 40; DLB 5,
130; MTCW

Bulgakov, Mikhail (Afanas'evich)
1891-1940 .... **TCLC 2, 16**
See also CA 105

Bulgya, Alexander Alexandrovich
1901-1956 .... **TCLC 53**
See also Fadeyev, Alexander
See also CA 117

Bullins, Ed 1935- .... **CLC 1, 5, 7; BLC**
See also BW; CA 49-52; CAAS 16;
CANR 24; DLB 7, 38; MTCW

Bulwer-Lytton, Edward (George Earle Lytton)
1803-1873 .... **NCLC 1**
See also DLB 21

Bunin, Ivan Alexeyevich
1870-1953 .... **TCLC 6; SSC 5**
See also CA 104

Bunting, Basil 1900-1985.... **CLC 10, 39, 47**
See also CA 53-56; 115; CANR 7; DLB 20

Bunuel, Luis 1900-1983 .. **CLC 16, 80; HLC**
See also CA 101; 110; CANR 32; HW

Bunyan, John 1628-1688 .. **LC 4; DA; WLC**
See also CDBLB 1660-1789; DLB 39

Burford, Eleanor
See Hibbert, Eleanor Alice Burford

Burgess, Anthony
. **CLC 1, 2, 4, 5, 8, 10, 13, 15, 22, 40, 62, 81**
See also Wilson, John (Anthony) Burgess
See also AITN 1; CDBLB 1960 to Present;
DLB 14

Burke, Edmund
1729(?)-1797 .... **LC 7; DA; WLC**
See also DLB 104

Burke, Kenneth (Duva)
1897-1993 .... **CLC 2, 24**
See also CA 5-8R; 143; CANR 39; DLB 45,
63; MTCW

Burke, Leda
See Garnett, David

Burke, Ralph
See Silverberg, Robert

Burney, Fanny 1752-1840 .... **NCLC 12**
See also DLB 39

Burns, Robert
1759-1796 ...... **LC 3; DA; PC 6; WLC**
See also CDBLB 1789-1832; DLB 109

Burns, Tex
See L'Amour, Louis (Dearborn)

Burnshaw, Stanley 1906-..... **CLC 3, 13, 44**
See also CA 9-12R; DLB 48

Burr, Anne 1937- .... **CLC 6**
See also CA 25-28R

Burroughs, Edgar Rice
1875-1950 .... **TCLC 2, 32**
See also CA 104; 132; DLB 8; MTCW;
SATA 41

Burroughs, William S(eward)
1914- .... **CLC 1, 2, 5, 15, 22, 42, 75; DA; WLC**
See also AITN 2; CA 9-12R; CANR 20;
DLB 2, 8, 16; DLBY 81; MTCW

Burton, Richard F. 1821-1890.... **NCLC 42**
See also DLB 55

Busch, Frederick 1941- ... **CLC 7, 10, 18, 47**
See also CA 33-36R; CAAS 1; DLB 6

Bush, Ronald 1946- .... **CLC 34**
See also CA 136

Bustos, F(rancisco)
See Borges, Jorge Luis

Bustos Domecq, H(onorio)
See Bioy Casares, Adolfo; Borges, Jorge
Luis

Butler, Octavia E(stelle) 1947- ..... **CLC 38**
See also BW; CA 73-76; CANR 12, 24, 38;
DLB 33; MTCW

Butler, Robert Olen (Jr.) 1945-..... **CLC 81**
See also CA 112

Butler, Samuel 1612-1680 .... **LC 16**
See also DLB 101, 126

Butler, Samuel
1835-1902 ...... **TCLC 1, 33; DA; WLC**
See also CA 104; CDBLB 1890-1914;
DLB 18, 57

Butler, Walter C.
See Faust, Frederick (Schiller)

Butor, Michel (Marie Francois)
1926- .... **CLC 1, 3, 8, 11, 15**
See also CA 9-12R; CANR 33; DLB 83;
MTCW

Buzo, Alexander (John) 1944-...... **CLC 61**
See also CA 97-100; CANR 17, 39

Buzzati, Dino 1906-1972 .... **CLC 36**
See also CA 33-36R

Byars, Betsy (Cromer) 1928-....... **CLC 35**
See also CA 33-36R; CANR 18, 36; CLR 1,
16; DLB 52; JRDA; MAICYA; MTCW;
SAAS 1; SATA 4, 46

Byatt, A(ntonia) S(usan Drabble)
1936- .... **CLC 19, 65**
See also CA 13-16R; CANR 13, 33;
DLB 14; MTCW

Byrne, David 1952-................. **CLC 26**
See also CA 127

Byrne, John Keyes 1926-......... **CLC 19**
See also Leonard, Hugh
See also CA 102

Byron, George Gordon (Noel)
1788-1824 ...... **NCLC 2, 12; DA; WLC**
See also CDBLB 1789-1832; DLB 96, 110

C.3.3.
See Wilde, Oscar (Fingal O'Flahertie Wills)

Caballero, Fernan 1796-1877..... **NCLC 10**

Cabell, James Branch 1879-1958 ... **TCLC 6**
See also CA 105; DLB 9, 78

Cable, George Washington
1844-1925 .... **TCLC 4; SSC 4**
See also CA 104; DLB 12, 74

Cabral de Melo Neto, Joao 1920-... **CLC 76**

Cabrera Infante, G(uillermo)
1929- .... **CLC 5, 25, 45; HLC**
See also CA 85-88; CANR 29; DLB 113;
HW; MTCW

Cade, Toni
See Bambara, Toni Cade

Cadmus
See Buchan, John

Caedmon fl. 658-680............. **CMLC 7**

Caeiro, Alberto
See Pessoa, Fernando (Antonio Nogueira)

Cage, John (Milton, Jr.) 1912-..... **CLC 41**
See also CA 13-16R; CANR 9

Cain, G.
See Cabrera Infante, G(uillermo)

Cain, Guillermo
See Cabrera Infante, G(uillermo)

Cain, James M(allahan)
1892-1977 .... **CLC 3, 11, 28**
See also AITN 1; CA 17-20R; 73-76;
CANR 8, 34; MTCW

Caine, Mark
See Raphael, Frederic (Michael)

Calasso, Roberto 1941- .... **CLC 81**
See also CA 143

Calderon de la Barca, Pedro
1600-1681 .... **LC 23; DC 3**

Caldwell, Erskine (Preston)
1903-1987 .... **CLC 1, 8, 14, 50, 60**
See also AITN 1; CA 1-4R; 121; CAAS 1;
CANR 2, 33; DLB 9, 86; MTCW

Caldwell, (Janet Miriam) Taylor (Holland)
1900-1985 .... **CLC 2, 28, 39**
See also CA 5-8R; 116; CANR 5

Calhoun, John Caldwell
1782-1850 .... **NCLC 15**
See also DLB 3

Calisher, Hortense
1911- .... **CLC 2, 4, 8, 38; SSC 15**
See also CA 1-4R; CANR 1, 22; DLB 2;
MTCW

Callaghan, Morley Edward
1903-1990 .... **CLC 3, 14, 41, 65**
See also CA 9-12R; 132; CANR 33;
DLB 68; MTCW

Calvino, Italo
1923Cameron, Peter. . 1959-. . . . **CLC 44**
See also CA 125

Campana, Dino 1885-1932....... **TCLC 20**
See also CA 117; DLB 114

Campbell, John W(ood, Jr.)
1910-1971 .... **CLC 32**
See also CA 21-22; 29-32R; CANR 34;
CAP 2; DLB 8; MTCW

Campbell, Joseph 1904-1987 .... **CLC 69**
See also AAYA 3; BEST 89:2; CA 1-4R;
124; CANR 3, 28; MTCW

Campbell, (John) Ramsey 1946- . . . . **CLC 42**
See also CA 57-60; CANR 7

Campbell, (Ignatius) Roy (Dunnachie)
1901-1957 .... **TCLC 5**
See also CA 104; DLB 20

Campbell, Thomas 1777-1844 .... **NCLC 19**
See also DLB 93

Campbell, Wilfred .... **TCLC 9**
See also Campbell, William

Campbell, William 1858(?)-1918
See Campbell, Wilfred
See also CA 106; DLB 92

Campos, Alvaro de
See Pessoa, Fernando (Antonio Nogueira)

Camus, Albert
1913-1960 .... **CLC 1, 2, 4, 9, 11, 14, 32,**
63, 69; DA; DC 2; SSC 9; WLC
See also CA 89-92; DLB 72; MTCW

Canby, Vincent 1924-............. **CLC 13**
See also CA 81-84

Cancale
See Desnos, Robert

Canetti, Elias 1905- ...... **CLC 3, 14, 25, 75**
See also CA 21-24R; CANR 23; DLB 85,
124; MTCW

Canin, Ethan 1960-............... **CLC 55**
See also CA 131; 135

Cannon, Curt
See Hunter, Evan

Cape, Judith
See Page, P(atricia) K(athleen)

Capek, Karel
1890-1938 ..... **TCLC 6, 37; DA; DC 1;**
WLC
See also CA 104; 140

Capote, Truman
1924-1984 ..... **CLC 1, 3, 8, 13, 19, 34,**
38, 58; DA; SSC 2; WLC
See also CA 5-8R; 113; CANR 18;
CDALB 1941-1968; DLB 2; DLBY 80,
84; MTCW

Capra, Frank 1897-1991.......... **CLC 16**
See also CA 61-64; 135

Caputo, Philip 1941-.............. **CLC 32**
See also CA 73-76; CANR 40

Card, Orson Scott 1951- .... **CLC 44, 47, 50**
See also CA 102; CANR 27; MTCW

Cardenal (Martinez), Ernesto
1925- .... **CLC 31; HLC**
See also CA 49-52; CANR 2, 32; HW;
MTCW

Carducci, Giosue 1835-1907....... **TCLC 32**

Carew, Thomas 1595(?)-1640........ **LC 13**
See also DLB 126

Carey, Ernestine Gilbreth 1908-.... **CLC 17**
See also CA 5-8R; SATA 2

Carey, Peter 1943-............ **CLC 40, 55**
See also CA 123; 127; MTCW

Carleton, William 1794-1869...... **NCLC 3**

Carlisle, Henry (Coffin) 1926-...... **CLC 33**
See also CA 13-16R; CANR 15

Carlsen, Chris
See Holdstock, Robert P.

Carlson, Ron(ald F.) 1947-........ **CLC 54**
See also CA 105; CANR 27

Carlyle, Thomas 1795-1881 .. **NCLC 22; DA**
See also CDBLB 1789-1832; DLB 55

Carman, (William) Bliss
1861-1929 .... **TCLC 7**
See also CA 104; DLB 92

Carnegie, Dale 1888-1955 .... **TCLC 53**

Carossa, Hans 1878-1956........ **TCLC 48**
See also DLB 66

Carpenter, Don(ald Richard)
1931- .... **CLC 41**
See also CA 45-48; CANR 1

Carpentier (y Valmont), Alejo
1904-1980 .... **CLC 8, 11, 38; HLC**
See also CA 65-68; 97-100; CANR 11;
DLB 113; HW

Carr, Emily 1871-1945........... **TCLC 32**
See also DLB 68

Carr, John Dickson 1906-1977 ...... **CLC 3**
See also CA 49-52; 69-72; CANR 3, 33;
MTCW

Carr, Philippa
See Hibbert, Eleanor Alice Burford

Carr, Virginia Spencer 1929-....... **CLC 34**
See also CA 61-64; DLB 111

Carrier, Roch 1937-........... **CLC 13, 78**
See also CA 130; DLB 53

Carroll, James P. 1943(?)-......... **CLC 38**
See also CA 81-84

Carroll, Jim 1951- .... **CLC 35**
See also CA 45-48; CANR 42

Carroll, Lewis .... **NCLC 2; WLC**
See also Dodgson, Charles Lutwidge
See also CDBLB 1832-1890; CLR 2, 18;
DLB 18; JRDA

Carroll, Paul Vincent 1900-1968.... **CLC 10**
See also CA 9-12R; 25-28R; DLB 10

Carruth, Hayden 1921- .... **CLC 4, 7, 10, 18**
See also CA 9-12R; CANR 4, 38; DLB 5;
MTCW; SATA 47

Carson, Rachel Louise 1907-1964... **CLC 71**
See also CA 77-80; CANR 35; MTCW;
SATA 23

Carter, Angela (Olive)
1940-1992 ...... **CLC 5, 41, 76; SSC 13**
See also CA 53-56; 136; CANR 12, 36;
DLB 14; MTCW; SATA 66;
SATA-Obit 70

Carter, Nick
See Smith, Martin Cruz

Carver, Raymond
1938-1988 ... **CLC 22, 36, 53, 55; SSC 8**
See also CA 33-36R; 126; CANR 17, 34;
DLB 130; DLBY 84, 88; MTCW

Cary, (Arthur) Joyce (Lunel)
1888-1957 .... **TCLC 1, 29**
See also CA 104; CDBLB 1914-1945;
DLB 15, 100

Casanova de Seingalt, Giovanni Jacopo
1725-1798 .... **LC 13**

Casares, Adolfo Bioy
See Bioy Casares, Adolfo

Casely-Hayford, J(oseph) E(phraim)
1866-1930 .... **TCLC 24; BLC**
See also CA 123

Casey, John (Dudley) 1939-........ **CLC 59**
See also BEST 90:2; CA 69-72; CANR 23

Casey, Michael 1947-.............. **CLC 2**
See also CA 65-68; DLB 5

Casey, Patrick
See Thurman, Wallace (Henry)

Casey, Warren (Peter) 1935-1988... **CLC 12**
See also CA 101; 127

Casona, Alejandro................. **CLC 49**
See also Alvarez, Alejandro Rodriguez

Cassavetes, John 1929-1989........ **CLC 20**
See also CA 85-88; 127

Cassill, R(onald) V(erlin) 1919-... **CLC 4, 23**
See also CA 9-12R; CAAS 1; CANR 7;
DLB 6

Cassity, (Allen) Turner 1929- .... **CLC 6, 42**
See also CA 17-20R; CAAS 8; CANR 11;
DLB 105

Castaneda, Carlos 1931(?)-......... **CLC 12**
See also CA 25-28R; CANR 32; HW;
MTCW

Castedo, Elena 1937- .... **CLC 65**
See also CA 132

Castedo-Ellerman, Elena
See Castedo, Elena

Castellanos, Rosario
1925-1974 .... **CLC 66; HLC**
See also CA 131; 53-56; DLB 113; HW

Castelvetro, Lodovico 1505-1571..... **LC 12**

Castiglione, Baldassare 1478-1529 ... **LC 12**

Castle, Robert
See Hamilton, Edmond

Castro, Guillen de 1569-1631........ **LC 19**

Castro, Rosalia de 1837-1885 ..... **NCLC 3**

Cather, Willa
See Cather, Willa Sibert

Cather, Willa Sibert
1873-1947 . . . . **TCLC 1, 11, 31; DA;**
SSC 2; WLC
See also CA 104; 128; CDALB 1865-1917;
DLB 9, 54, 78; DLBD 1; MTCW;
SATA 30

Catton, (Charles) Bruce
1899-1978 . . . . **CLC 35**
See also AITN 1; CA 5-8R; 81-84;
CANR 7; DLB 17; SATA 2, 24

Cauldwell, Frank
See King, Francis (Henry)

Caunitz, William J. 1933- . . . . **CLC 34**
See also BEST 89:3; CA 125; 130

Causley, Charles (Stanley) 1917- . . . . . **CLC 7**
See also CA 9-12R; CANR 5, 35; CLR 30;
DLB 27; MTCW; SATA 3, 66

Caute, David 1936- . . . . **CLC 29**
See also CA 1-4R; CAAS 4; CANR 1, 33;
DLB 14

Cavafy, C(onstantine) P(eter) . . . . . . **TCLC 2, 7**
See also Kavafis, Konstantinos Petrou

Cavallo, Evelyn
See Spark, Muriel (Sarah)

Cavanna, Betty . . . . **CLC 12**
See also Harrison, Elizabeth Cavanna
See also JRDA; MAICYA; SAAS 4;
SATA 1, 30

Caxton, William 1421(?)-1491(?) . . . . . **LC 17**

Cayrol, Jean 1911- . . . . **CLC 11**
See also CA 89-92; DLB 83

Cela, Camilo Jose
1916- . . . . **CLC 4, 13, 59; HLC**
See also BEST 90:2; CA 21-24R; CAAS 10;
CANR 21, 32; DLBY 89; HW; MTCW

Celan, Paul . . . . **CLC 53, 82**
See also Antschel, Paul
See also DLB 69

Celine, Louis-Ferdinand
. . . . **CLC 1, 3, 4, 7, 9, 15, 47**
See also Destouches, Louis-Ferdinand
See also DLB 72

Cellini, Benvenuto 1500-1571 . . . . **LC 7**

Cendrars, Blaise
See Sauser-Hall, Frederic

Cernuda (y Bidon), Luis
1902-1963 . . . . **CLC 54**
See also CA 131; 89-92; DLB 134; HW

Cervantes (Saavedra), Miguel de
1547-1616 . . . . . **LC 6, 23; DA; SSC 12;**
WLC

Cesaire, Aime (Fernand)
1913- . . . . **CLC 19, 32; BLC**
See also BW; CA 65-68; CANR 24, 43;
MTCW

Chabon, Michael 1965(?)- . . . . **CLC 55**
See also CA 139

Chabrol, Claude 1930- . . . . **CLC 16**
See also CA 110

Challans, Mary 1905-1983
See Renault, Mary
See also CA 81-84; 111; SATA 23, 36

Challis, George
See Faust, Frederick (Schiller)

Chambers, Aidan 1934- . . . . **CLC 35**
See also CA 25-28R; CANR 12, 31; JRDA;
MAICYA; SAAS 12; SATA 1, 69

Chambers, James 1948-
See Cliff, Jimmy
See also CA 124

Chambers, Jessie
See Lawrence, D(avid) H(erbert Richards)

Chambers, Robert W. 1865-1933 . . . **TCLC 41**

Chandler, Raymond (Thornton)
1888-1959 . . . . **TCLC 1, 7**
See also CA 104; 129; CDALB 1929-1941;
DLBD 6; MTCW

Chang, Jung 1952- . . . . **CLC 71**
See also CA 142

Channing, William Ellery
1780-1842 . . . . **NCLC 17**
See also DLB 1, 59

Chaplin, Charles Spencer
1889-1977 . . . . **CLC 16**
See also Chaplin, Charlie
See also CA 81-84; 73-76

Chaplin, Charlie
See Chaplin, Charles Spencer
See also DLB 44

Chapman, George 1559(?)-1634 . . . . . . **LC 22**
See also DLB 62, 121

Chapman, Graham 1941-1989 . . . . . . **CLC 21**
See also Monty Python
See also CA 116; 129; CANR 35

Chapman, John Jay 1862-1933 . . . . . **TCLC 7**
See also CA 104

Chapman, Walker
See Silverberg, Robert

Chappell, Fred (Davis) 1936- . . . . **CLC 40, 78**
See also CA 5-8R; CAAS 4; CANR 8, 33;
DLB 6, 105

Char, Rene(-Emile)
1907-1988 . . . . **CLC 9, 11, 14, 55**
See also CA 13-16R; 124; CANR 32;
MTCW

Charby, Jay
See Ellison, Harlan

Chardin, Pierre Teilhard de
See Teilhard de Chardin, (Marie Joseph)
Pierre

Charles I 1600-1649 . . . . **LC 13**

Charyn, Jerome 1937- . . . . **CLC 5, 8, 18**
See also CA 5-8R; CAAS 1; CANR 7;
DLBY 83; MTCW

Chase, Mary (Coyle) 1907-1981 . . . . . . **DC 1**
See also CA 77-80; 105; SATA 17, 29

Chase, Mary Ellen 1887-1973 . . . . **CLC 2**
See also CA 13-16; 41-44R; CAP 1;
SATA 10

Chase, Nicholas
See Hyde, Anthony

Chateaubriand, Francois Rene de
1768-1848 . . . . **NCLC 3**
See also DLB 119

Chatterje, Sarat Chandra 1876-1936(?)
See Chatterji, Saratchandra
See also CA 109

Chatterji, Bankim Chandra
1838-1894 . . . . **NCLC 19**

Chatterji, Saratchandra . . . . **TCLC 13**
See also Chatterje, Sarat Chandra

Chatterton, Thomas 1752-1770 . . . . . . **LC 3**
See also DLB 109

Chatwin, (Charles) Bruce
1940-1989 . . . . **CLC 28, 57, 59**
See also AAYA 4; BEST 90:1; CA 85-88;
127

Chaucer, Daniel
See Ford, Ford Madox

Chaucer, Geoffrey
1340(?)-1400 . . . . **LC 17; DA**
See also CDBLB Before 1660

Chaviaras, Strates 1935-
See Haviaras, Stratis
See also CA 105

Chayefsky, Paddy . . . . **CLC 23**
See also Chayefsky, Sidney
See also DLB 7, 44; DLBY 81

Chayefsky, Sidney 1923-1981
See Chayefsky, Paddy
See also CA 9-12R; 104; CANR 18

Chedid, Andree 1920- . . . . **CLC 47**

Cheever, John
1912-1982 . . . . . . **CLC 3, 7, 8, 11, 15, 25,**
64; DA; SSC 1; WLC
See also CA 5-8R; 106; CABS 1; CANR 5,
27; CDALB 1941-1968; DLB 2, 102;
DLBY 80, 82; MTCW

Cheever, Susan 1943- . . . . **CLC 18, 48**
See also CA 103; CANR 27; DLBY 82

Chekhonte, Antosha
See Chekhov, Anton (Pavlovich)

Chekhov, Anton (Pavlovich)
1860-1904 . . . . **TCLC 3, 10, 31; DA;**
SSC 2; WLC
See also CA 104; 124

Chernyshevsky, Nikolay Gavrilovich
1828-1889 . . . . **NCLC 1**

Cherry, Carolyn Janice 1942-
See Cherryh, C. J.
See also CA 65-68; CANR 10

Cherryh, C. J. . . . . **CLC 35**
See also Cherry, Carolyn Janice
See also DLBY 80

Chesnutt, Charles W(addell)
1858-1932 . . . . **TCLC 5, 39; BLC; SSC 7**
See also BW; CA 106; 125; DLB 12, 50, 78;
MTCW

Chester, Alfred 1929(?)-1971 . . . . **CLC 49**
See also CA 33-36R; DLB 130

Chesterton, G(ilbert) K(eith)
1874-1936 . . . . **TCLC 1, 6; SSC 1**
See also CA 104; 132; CDBLB 1914-1945;
DLB 10, 19, 34, 70, 98; MTCW;
SATA 27

Chiang Pin-chin 1904-1986
See Ding Ling
See also CA 118

Ch'ien Chung-shu 1910- .... **CLC 22**
See also CA 130; MTCW

Child, L. Maria
See Child, Lydia Maria

Child, Lydia Maria 1802-1880 .... **NCLC 6**
See also DLB 1, 74; SATA 67

Child, Mrs.
See Child, Lydia Maria

Child, Philip 1898-1978 .... **CLC 19, 68**
See also CA 13-14; CAP 1; SATA 47

Childress, Alice
1920- .... **CLC 12, 15; BLC; DC 4**
See also AAYA 8; BW; CA 45-48;
CANR 3, 27; CLR 14; DLB 7, 38; JRDA;
MAICYA; MTCW; SATA 7, 48

Chislett, (Margaret) Anne 1943- .... **CLC 34**

Chitty, Thomas Willes 1926- .... **CLC 11**
See also Hinde, Thomas
See also CA 5-8R

Chomette, Rene Lucien 1898-1981 .. **CLC 20**
See also Clair, Rene
See also CA 103

Chopin, Kate .... **TCLC 5, 14; DA; SSC 8**
See also Chopin, Katherine
See also CDALB 1865-1917; DLB 12, 78

Chopin, Katherine 1851-1904
See Chopin, Kate
See also CA 104; 122

Chretien de Troyes
c. 12th cent. - .... **CMLC 10**

Christie
See Ichikawa, Kon

Christie, Agatha (Mary Clarissa)
1890-1976 ...... **CLC 1, 6, 8, 12, 39, 48**
See also AAYA 9; AITN 1, 2; CA 17-20R;
61-64; CANR 10, 37; CDBLB 1914-1945;
DLB 13, 77; MTCW; SATA 36

Christie, (Ann) Philippa
See Pearce, Philippa
See also CA 5-8R; CANR 4

Christine de Pizan 1365(?)-1431(?) .... **LC 9**

Chubb, Elmer
See Masters, Edgar Lee

Chulkov, Mikhail Dmitrievich
1743-1792 .... **LC 2**

Churchill, Caryl 1938- .... **CLC 31, 55**
See also CA 102; CANR 22; DLB 13;
MTCW

Churchill, Charles 1731-1764 .... **LC 3**
See also DLB 109

Chute, Carolyn 1947- .... **CLC 39**
See also CA 123

Ciardi, John (Anthony)
1916-1986 .... **CLC 10, 40, 44**
See also CA 5-8R; 118; CAAS 2; CANR 5,
33; CLR 19; DLB 5; DLBY 86;
MAICYA; MTCW; SATA 1, 46, 65

Cicero, Marcus Tullius
106B.C.-43B.C. .... **CMLC 3**

Cimino, Michael 1943- .... **CLC 16**
See also CA 105

Cioran, E(mil) M. 1911- .... **CLC 64**
See also CA 25-28R

Cisneros, Sandra 1954- ...... **CLC 69; HLC**
See also AAYA 9; CA 131; DLB 122; HW

Clair, Rene .... **CLC 20**
See also Chomette, Rene Lucien

Clampitt, Amy 1920- .... **CLC 32**
See also CA 110; CANR 29; DLB 105

Clancy, Thomas L., Jr. 1947-
See Clancy, Tom
See also CA 125; 131; MTCW

Clancy, Tom .... **CLC 45**
See also Clancy, Thomas L., Jr.
See also AAYA 9; BEST 89:1, 90:1

Clare, John 1793-1864 .... **NCLC 9**
See also DLB 55, 96

Clarin
See Alas (y Urena), Leopoldo (Enrique
Garcia)

Clark, Al C.
See Goines, Donald

Clark, (Robert) Brian 1932- .... **CLC 29**
See also CA 41-44R

Clark, Eleanor 1913- .... **CLC 5, 19**
See also CA 9-12R; CANR 41; DLB 6

Clark, J. P.
See Clark, John Pepper
See also DLB 117

Clark, John Pepper 1935- .... **CLC 38; BLC**
See also Clark, J. P.
See also BW; CA 65-68; CANR 16

Clark, M. R.
See Clark, Mavis Thorpe

Clark, Mavis Thorpe 1909- .... **CLC 12**
See also CA 57-60; CANR 8, 37; CLR 30;
MAICYA; SAAS 5; SATA 8, 74

Clark, Walter Van Tilburg
1909-1971 .... **CLC 28**
See also CA 9-12R; 33-36R; DLB 9;
SATA 8

Clarke, Arthur C(harles)
1917- ...... **CLC 1, 4, 13, 18, 35; SSC 3**
See also AAYA 4; CA 1-4R; CANR 2, 28;
JRDA; MAICYA; MTCW; SATA 13, 70

Clarke, Austin 1896-1974 .... **CLC 6, 9**
See also CA 29-32; 49-52; CAP 2; DLB 10,
20

Clarke, Austin C(hesterfield)
1934- .... **CLC 8, 53; BLC**
See also BW; CA 25-28R; CAAS 16;
CANR 14, 32; DLB 53, 125

Clarke, Gillian 1937- .... **CLC 61**
See also CA 106; DLB 40

Clarke, Marcus (Andrew Hislop)
1846-1881 .... **NCLC 19**

Clarke, Shirley 1925- .... **CLC 16**

Clash, The .... **CLC 30**
See also Headon, (Nicky) Topper; Jones,
Mick; Simonon, Paul; Strummer, Joe

Claudel, Paul (Louis Charles Marie)
1868-1955 .... **TCLC 2, 10**
See also CA 104

Clavell, James (duMaresq)
1925- .... **CLC 6, 25**
See also CA 25-28R; CANR 26; MTCW

Cleaver, (Leroy) Eldridge
1935- .... **CLC 30; BLC**
See also BW; CA 21-24R; CANR 16

Cleese, John (Marwood) 1939- ..... **CLC 21**
See also Monty Python
See also CA 112; 116; CANR 35; MTCW

Cleishbotham, Jebediah
See Scott, Walter

Cleland, John 1710-1789 .... **LC 2**
See also DLB 39

Clemens, Samuel Langhorne 1835-1910
See Twain, Mark
See also CA 104; 135; CDALB 1865-1917;
DA; DLB 11, 12, 23, 64, 74; JRDA;
MAICYA; YABC 2

Cleophil
See Congreve, William

Clerihew, E.
See Bentley, E(dmund) C(lerihew)

Clerk, N. W.
See Lewis, C(live) S(taples)

Cliff, Jimmy .... **CLC 21**
See also Chambers, James

Clifton, (Thelma) Lucille
1936- .... **CLC 19, 66; BLC**
See also BW; CA 49-52; CANR 2, 24, 42;
CLR 5; DLB 5, 41; MAICYA; MTCW;
SATA 20, 69

Clinton, Dirk
See Silverberg, Robert

Clough, Arthur Hugh 1819-1861 .. **NCLC 27**
See also DLB 32

Clutha, Janet Paterson Frame 1924-
See Frame, Janet
See also CA 1-4R; CANR 2, 36; MTCW

Clyne, Terence
See Blatty, William Peter

Cobalt, Martin
See Mayne, William (James Carter)

Coburn, D(onald) L(ee) 1938- ...... **CLC 10**
See also CA 89-92

Cocteau, Jean (Maurice Eugene Clement)
1889-1963 .... **CLC 1, 8, 15, 16, 43; DA;
WLC**
See also CA 25-28; CANR 40; CAP 2;
DLB 65; MTCW

Codrescu, Andrei 1946- .... **CLC 46**
See also CA 33-36R; CANR 13, 34

Coe, Max
See Bourne, Randolph S(illiman)

Coe, Tucker
See Westlake, Donald E(dwin)

Coetzee, J(ohn) M(ichael)
1940- .... **CLC 23, 33, 66**
See also CA 77-80; CANR 41; MTCW

Coffey, Brian
See Koontz, Dean R(ay)

Cohen, Arthur A(llen)
1928-1986 .... **CLC 7, 31**
See also CA 1-4R; 120; CANR 1, 17, 42;
DLB 28

Cohen, Leonard (Norman)
1934- .... **CLC 3, 38**
See also CA 21-24R; CANR 14; DLB 53;
MTCW

de la Roche, Mazo　1879-1961 . . . . . . **CLC 14**
See also CA 85-88; CANR 30; DLB 68;
SATA 64

Delbanco, Nicholas (Franklin)
1942- . . . . **CLC 6, 13**
See also CA 17-20R; CAAS 2; CANR 29;
DLB 6

del Castillo, Michel　1933- . . . . **CLC 38**
See also CA 109

Deledda, Grazia (Cosima)
1875(?)-1936 . . . . **TCLC 23**
See also CA 123

Delibes, Miguel . . . . **CLC 8, 18**
See also Delibes Setien, Miguel

Delibes Setien, Miguel　1920-
See Delibes, Miguel
See also CA 45-48; CANR 1, 32; HW;
MTCW

DeLillo, Don
1936- . . . . . **CLC 8, 10, 13, 27, 39, 54, 76**
See also BEST 89:1; CA 81-84; CANR 21;
DLB 6; MTCW

de Lisser, H. G.
See De Lisser, Herbert George
See also DLB 117

De Lisser, Herbert George
1878-1944 . . . . **TCLC 12**
See also de Lisser, H. G.
See also CA 109

Deloria, Vine (Victor), Jr.　1933- . . . . **CLC 21**
See also CA 53-56; CANR 5, 20; MTCW;
SATA 21

Del Vecchio, John M(ichael)
1947- . . . . **CLC 29**
See also CA 110; DLBD 9

de Man, Paul (Adolph Michel)
1919-1983 . . . . **CLC 55**
See also CA 128; 111; DLB 67; MTCW

De Marinis, Rick　1934- . . . . **CLC 54**
See also CA 57-60; CANR 9, 25

Demby, William　1922- . . . . **CLC 53; BLC**
See also BW; CA 81-84; DLB 33

Demijohn, Thom
See Disch, Thomas M(ichael)

de Montherlant, Henry (Milon)
See Montherlant, Henry (Milon) de

de Natale, Francine
See Malzberg, Barry N(athaniel)

Denby, Edwin (Orr)　1903-1983 . . . . . **CLC 48**
See also CA 138; 110

Denis, Julio
See Cortazar, Julio

Denmark, Harrison
See Zelazny, Roger (Joseph)

Dennis, John　1658-1734 . . . . **LC 11**
See also DLB 101

Dennis, Nigel (Forbes)　1912-1989 . . . . **CLC 8**
See also CA 25-28R; 129; DLB 13, 15;
MTCW

De Palma, Brian (Russell)　1940- . . . . **CLC 20**
See also CA 109

De Quincey, Thomas　1785-1859 . . . **NCLC 4**
See also CDBLB 1789-1832; DLB 110

Deren, Eleanora　1908(?)-1961
See Deren, Maya
See also CA 111

Deren, Maya . . . . **CLC 16**
See also Deren, Eleanora

Derleth, August (William)
1909-1971 . . . . **CLC 31**
See also CA 1-4R; 29-32R; CANR 4;
DLB 9; SATA 5

de Routisie, Albert
See Aragon, Louis

Derrida, Jacques　1930- . . . . **CLC 24**
See also CA 124; 127

Derry Down Derry
See Lear, Edward

Dersonnes, Jacques
See Simenon, Georges (Jacques Christian)

Desai, Anita　1937- . . . . **CLC 19, 37**
See also CA 81-84; CANR 33; MTCW;
SATA 63

de Saint-Luc, Jean
See Glassco, John

de Saint Roman, Arnaud
See Aragon, Louis

Descartes, Rene　1596-1650 . . . . **LC 20**

De Sica, Vittorio　1901(?)-1974 . . . . . **CLC 20**
See also CA 117

Desnos, Robert　1900-1945 . . . . **TCLC 22**
See also CA 121

Destouches, Louis-Ferdinand
1894-1961 . . . . **CLC 9, 15**
See also Celine, Louis-Ferdinand
See also CA 85-88; CANR 28; MTCW

Deutsch, Babette　1895-1982 . . . . **CLC 18**
See also CA 1-4R; 108; CANR 4; DLB 45;
SATA 1, 33

Devenant, William　1606-1649 . . . . **LC 13**

Devkota, Laxmiprasad
1909-1959 . . . . **TCLC 23**
See also CA 123

De Voto, Bernard (Augustine)
1897-1955 . . . . **TCLC 29**
See also CA 113; DLB 9

De Vries, Peter
1910-1993 . . . . **CLC 1, 2, 3, 7, 10, 28, 46**
See also CA 17-20R; 142; CANR 41;
DLB 6; DLBY 82; MTCW

Dexter, Martin
See Faust, Frederick (Schiller)

Dexter, Pete　1943- . . . . **CLC 34, 55**
See also BEST 89:2; CA 127; 131; MTCW

Diamano, Silmang
See Senghor, Leopold Sedar

Diamond, Neil　1941- . . . . **CLC 30**
See also CA 108

di Bassetto, Corno
See Shaw, George Bernard

Dick, Philip K(indred)
1928-1982 . . . . **CLC 10, 30, 72**
See also CA 49-52; 106; CANR 2, 16;
DLB 8; MTCW

Dickens, Charles (John Huffam)
1812-1870 . . . . . **NCLC 3, 8, 18, 26; DA;**
WLC
See also CDBLB 1832-1890; DLB 21, 55,
70; JRDA; MAICYA; SATA 15

Dickey, James (Lafayette)
1923- . . . . **CLC 1, 2, 4, 7, 10, 15, 47**
See also AITN 1, 2; CA 9-12R; CABS 2;
CANR 10; CDALB 1968-1988; DLB 5;
DLBD 7; DLBY 82; MTCW

Dickey, William　1928- . . . . **CLC 3, 28**
See also CA 9-12R; CANR 24; DLB 5

Dickinson, Charles　1951- . . . . **CLC 49**
See also CA 128

Dickinson, Emily (Elizabeth)
1830-1886 . . **NCLC 21; DA; PC 1; WLC**
See also CDALB 1865-1917; DLB 1;
SATA 29

Dickinson, Peter (Malcolm)
1927- . . . . **CLC 12, 35**
See also AAYA 9; CA 41-44R; CANR 31;
CLR 29; DLB 87; JRDA; MAICYA;
SATA 5, 62

Dickson, Carr
See Carr, John Dickson

Dickson, Carter
See Carr, John Dickson

Didion, Joan　1934- . . . . . **CLC 1, 3, 8, 14, 32**
See also AITN 1; CA 5-8R; CANR 14;
CDALB 1968-1988; DLB 2; DLBY 81,
86; MTCW

Dietrich, Robert
See Hunt, E(verette) Howard, Jr.

Dillard, Annie　1945- . . . . **CLC 9, 60**
See also AAYA 6; CA 49-52; CANR 3, 43;
DLBY 80; MTCW; SATA 10

Dillard, R(ichard) H(enry) W(ilde)
1937- . . . . **CLC 5**
See also CA 21-24R; CAAS 7; CANR 10;
DLB 5

Dillon, Eilis　1920- . . . . **CLC 17**
See also CA 9-12R; CAAS 3; CANR 4, 38;
CLR 26; MAICYA; SATA 2, 74

Dimont, Penelope
See Mortimer, Penelope (Ruth)

Dinesen, Isak . . . . **CLC 10, 29; SSC 7**
See also Blixen, Karen (Christentze
Dinesen)

Ding Ling . . . . **CLC 68**
See also Chiang Pin-chin

Disch, Thomas M(ichael)　1940- . . . **CLC 7, 36**
See also CA 21-24R; CAAS 4; CANR 17,
36; CLR 18; DLB 8; MAICYA; MTCW;
SAAS 15; SATA 54

Disch, Tom
See Disch, Thomas M(ichael)

d'Isly, Georges
See Simenon, Georges (Jacques Christian)

Disraeli, Benjamin　1804-1881 . . **NCLC 2, 39**
See also DLB 21, 55

Ditcum, Steve
See Crumb, R(obert)

Dixon, Paige
See Corcoran, Barbara

Dixon, Stephen 1936-............ **CLC 52**
See also CA 89-92; CANR 17, 40; DLB 130

Dobell, Sydney Thompson
1824-1874 .... **NCLC 43**
See also DLB 32

Doblin, Alfred .... **TCLC 13**
See also Doeblin, Alfred

Dobrolyubov, Nikolai Alexandrovich
1836-1861 .... **NCLC 5**

Dobyns, Stephen 1941-............ **CLC 37**
See also CA 45-48; CANR 2, 18

Doctorow, E(dgar) L(aurence)
1931- ..... **CLC 6, 11, 15, 18, 37, 44, 65**
See also AITN 2; BEST 89:3; CA 45-48;
CANR 2, 33; CDALB 1968-1988; DLB 2,
28; DLBY 80; MTCW

Dodgson, Charles Lutwidge 1832-1898
See Carroll, Lewis
See also CLR 2; DA; MAICYA; YABC 2

Dodson, Owen (Vincent)
1914-1983 .... **CLC 79; BLC**
See also BW; CA 65-68; 110; CANR 24;
DLB 76

Doeblin, Alfred 1878-1957....... **TCLC 13**
See also Doblin, Alfred
See also CA 110; 141; DLB 66

Doerr, Harriet 1910- .... **CLC 34**
See also CA 117; 122

Domecq, H(onorio) Bustos
See Bioy Casares, Adolfo; Borges, Jorge
Luis

Domini, Rey
See Lorde, Audre (Geraldine)

Dominique
See Proust, (Valentin-Louis-George-Eugene-)
Marcel

Don, A
See Stephen, Leslie

Donaldson, Stephen R. 1947-....... **CLC 46**
See also CA 89-92; CANR 13

Donleavy, J(ames) P(atrick)
1926- .... **CLC 1, 4, 6, 10, 45**
See also AITN 2; CA 9-12R; CANR 24;
DLB 6; MTCW

Donne, John
1572-1631 .... **LC 10, 24; DA; PC 1**
See also CDBLB Before 1660; DLB 121

Donnell, David 1939(?)-........... **CLC 34**

Donoso (Yanez), Jose
1924- .... **CLC 4, 8, 11, 32; HLC**
See also CA 81-84; CANR 32; DLB 113;
HW; MTCW

Donovan, John 1928-1992 .... **CLC 35**
See also CA 97-100; 137; CLR 3;
MAICYA; SATA 29

Don Roberto
See Cunninghame Graham, R(obert)
B(ontine)

Doolittle, Hilda
1886-1961 ..... **CLC 3, 8, 14, 31, 34, 73;**
DA; PC 5; WLC
See also H. D.
See also CA 97-100; CANR 35; DLB 4, 45;
MTCW

Dorfman, Ariel 1942-.... **CLC 48, 77; HLC**
See also CA 124; 130; HW

Dorn, Edward (Merton) 1929-... **CLC 10, 18**
See also CA 93-96; CANR 42; DLB 5

Dorsan, Luc
See Simenon, Georges (Jacques Christian)

Dorsange, Jean
See Simenon, Georges (Jacques Christian)

Dos Passos, John (Roderigo)
1896-1970 ...... **CLC 1, 4, 8, 11, 15, 25,**
34, 82; DA; WLC
See also CA 1-4R; 29-32R; CANR 3;
CDALB 1929-1941; DLB 4, 9; DLBD 1;
MTCW

Dossage, Jean
See Simenon, Georges (Jacques Christian)

Dostoevsky, Fedor Mikhailovich
1821-1881 ...... **NCLC 2, 7, 21, 33, 43;**
DA; SSC 2; WLC

Doughty, Charles M(ontagu)
1843-1926 .... **TCLC 27**
See also CA 115; DLB 19, 57

Douglas, Ellen
See Haxton, Josephine Ayres

Douglas, Gavin 1475(?)-1522........ **LC 20**

Douglas, Keith 1920-1944 .... **TCLC 40**
See also DLB 27

Douglas, Leonard
See Bradbury, Ray (Douglas)

Douglas, Michael
See Crichton, (John) Michael

Douglass, Frederick
1817(?)-1895 ...... **NCLC 7; BLC; DA;**
WLC
See also CDALB 1640-1865; DLB 1, 43, 50,
79; SATA 29

Dourado, (Waldomiro Freitas) Autran
1926- .... **CLC 23, 60**
See also CA 25-28R; CANR 34

Dourado, Waldomiro Autran
See Dourado, (Waldomiro Freitas) Autran

Dove, Rita (Frances)
1952- .... **CLC 50, 81; PC 6**
See also BW; CA 109; CANR 27, 42;
DLB 120

Dowell, Coleman 1925-1985........ **CLC 60**
See also CA 25-28R; 117; CANR 10;
DLB 130

Dowson, Ernest Christopher
1867-1900 .... **TCLC 4**
See also CA 105; DLB 19, 135

Doyle, A. Conan
See Doyle, Arthur Conan

Doyle, Arthur Conan
1859-1930 .... **TCLC 7; DA; SSC 12;**
WLC
See also CA 104; 122; CDBLB 1890-1914;
DLB 18, 70; MTCW; SATA 24

Doyle, Conan 1859-1930
See Doyle, Arthur Conan

Doyle, John
See Graves, Robert (von Ranke)

Doyle, Roddy 1958(?)-............ **CLC 81**
See also CA 143

Doyle, Sir A. Conan
See Doyle, Arthur Conan

Doyle, Sir Arthur Conan
See Doyle, Arthur Conan

Dr. A
See Asimov, Isaac; Silverstein, Alvin

Drabble, Margaret
1939- .... **CLC 2, 3, 5, 8, 10, 22, 53**
See also CA 13-16R; CANR 18, 35;
CDBLB 1960 to Present; DLB 14;
MTCW; SATA 48

Drapier, M. B.
See Swift, Jonathan

Drayham, James
See Mencken, H(enry) L(ouis)

Drayton, Michael 1563-1631........ **LC 8**

Dreadstone, Carl
See Campbell, (John) Ramsey

Dreiser, Theodore (Herman Albert)
1871-1945 .... **TCLC 10, 18, 35; DA;**
WLC
See also CA 106; 132; CDALB 1865-1917;
DLB 9, 12, 102; DLBD 1; MTCW

Drexler, Rosalyn 1926- .... **CLC 2, 6**
See also CA 81-84

Dreyer, Carl Theodor 1889-1968.... **CLC 16**
See also CA 116

Drieu la Rochelle, Pierre(-Eugene)
1893-1945 .... **TCLC 21**
See also CA 117; DLB 72

Drop Shot
See Cable, George Washington

Droste-Hulshoff, Annette Freiin von
1797-1848 .... **NCLC 3**
See also DLB 133

Drummond, Walter
See Silverberg, Robert

Drummond, William Henry
1854-1907 .... **TCLC 25**
See also DLB 92

Drummond de Andrade, Carlos
1902-1987 .... **CLC 18**
See also Andrade, Carlos Drummond de
See also CA 132; 123

Drury, Allen (Stuart) 1918-........ **CLC 37**
See also CA 57-60; CANR 18

Dryden, John
1631-1700 ... **LC 3, 21; DA; DC 3; WLC**
See also CDBLB 1660-1789; DLB 80, 101,
131

Duberman, Martin 1930-.......... **CLC 8**
See also CA 1-4R; CANR 2

Dubie, Norman (Evans) 1945-...... **CLC 36**
See also CA 69-72; CANR 12; DLB 120

Du Bois, W(illiam) E(dward) B(urghardt)
1868-1963 ...... **CLC 1, 2, 13, 64; BLC;**
DA; WLC
See also BW; CA 85-88; CANR 34;
CDALB 1865-1917; DLB 47, 50, 91;
MTCW; SATA 42

Dubus, Andre 1936-... **CLC 13, 36; SSC 15**
See also CA 21-24R; CANR 17; DLB 130

Duca Minimo
See D'Annunzio, Gabriele

Ducharme, Rejean 1941- .... **CLC 74**
See also DLB 60

Duclos, Charles Pinot 1704-1772 ..... **LC 1**

Dudek, Louis 1918- .... **CLC 11, 19**
See also CA 45-48; CAAS 14; CANR 1;
DLB 88

Duerrenmatt, Friedrich
.... **CLC 1, 4, 8, 11, 15, 43**
See also Duerrenmatt, Friedrich
See also DLB 69, 124

Duerrenmatt, Friedrich
1921-1990 ...... **CLC 1, 4, 8, 11, 15, 43**
See also Duerrenmatt, Friedrich
See also CA 17-20R; CANR 33; DLB 69,
124; MTCW

Duffy, Bruce (?)- .... **CLC 50**

Duffy, Maureen 1933- .... **CLC 37**
See also CA 25-28R; CANR 33; DLB 14;
MTCW

Dugan, Alan 1923- .... **CLC 2, 6**
See also CA 81-84; DLB 5

du Gard, Roger Martin
See Martin du Gard, Roger

Duhamel, Georges 1884-1966 .... **CLC 8**
See also CA 81-84; 25-28R; CANR 35;
DLB 65; MTCW

Dujardin, Edouard (Emile Louis)
1861-1949 .... **TCLC 13**
See also CA 109; DLB 123

Dumas, Alexandre (Davy de la Pailleterie)
1802-1870 .... **NCLC 11; DA; WLC**
See also DLB 119; SATA 18

Dumas, Alexandre
1824-1895 .... **NCLC 9; DC 1**

Dumas, Claudine
See Malzberg, Barry N(athaniel)

Dumas, Henry L. 1934-1968 ..... **CLC 6, 62**
See also BW; CA 85-88; DLB 41

du Maurier, Daphne
1907-1989 .... **CLC 6, 11, 59**
See also CA 5-8R; 128; CANR 6; MTCW;
SATA 27, 60

Dunbar, Paul Laurence
1872-1906 ...... **TCLC 2, 12; BLC; DA;
PC 5; SSC 8; WLC**
See also BW; CA 104; 124;
CDALB 1865-1917; DLB 50, 54, 78;
SATA 34

Dunbar, William 1460(?)-1530(?) .... **LC 20**

Duncan, Lois 1934- .... **CLC 26**
See also AAYA 4; CA 1-4R; CANR 2, 23,
36; CLR 29; JRDA; MAICYA; SAAS 2;
SATA 1, 36, 75

Duncan, Robert (Edward)
1919-1988 .... **CLC 1, 2, 4, 7, 15, 41, 55;
PC 2**
See also CA 9-12R; 124; CANR 28; DLB 5,
16; MTCW

Dunlap, William 1766-1839 .... **NCLC 2**
See also DLB 30, 37, 59

Dunn, Douglas (Eaglesham)
1942- .... **CLC 6, 40**
See also CA 45-48; CANR 2, 33; DLB 40;
MTCW

Dunn, Katherine (Karen) 1945- ..... **CLC 71**
See also CA 33-36R

Dunn, Stephen 1939- .... **CLC 36**
See also CA 33-36R; CANR 12; DLB 105

Dunne, Finley Peter 1867-1936 .... **TCLC 28**
See also CA 108; DLB 11, 23

Dunne, John Gregory 1932- .... **CLC 28**
See also CA 25-28R; CANR 14; DLBY 80

**Dunsany, Edward John Moreton Drax
Plunkett** 1878-1957
See Dunsany, Lord; Lord Dunsany
See also CA 104; DLB 10

Dunsany, Lord .... **TCLC 2**
See also Dunsany, Edward John Moreton
Drax Plunkett
See also DLB 77

du Perry, Jean
See Simenon, Georges (Jacques Christian)

Durang, Christopher (Ferdinand)
1949- .... **CLC 27, 38**
See also CA 105

Duras, Marguerite
1914- ...... **CLC 3, 6, 11, 20, 34, 40, 68**
See also CA 25-28R; DLB 83; MTCW

Durban, (Rosa) Pam 1947- .... **CLC 39**
See also CA 123

Durcan, Paul 1944- .... **CLC 43, 70**
See also CA 134

Durrell, Lawrence (George)
1912-1990 .... **CLC 1, 4, 6, 8, 13, 27, 41**
See also CA 9-12R; 132; CANR 40;
CDBLB 1945-1960; DLB 15, 27;
DLBY 90; MTCW

Dutt, Toru 1856-1877 .... **NCLC 29**

Dwight, Timothy 1752-1817 ...... **NCLC 13**
See also DLB 37

Dworkin, Andrea 1946- .... **CLC 43**
See also CA 77-80; CANR 16, 39; MTCW

Dwyer, Deanna
See Koontz, Dean R(ay)

Dwyer, K. R.
See Koontz, Dean R(ay)

Dylan, Bob 1941- ...... **CLC 3, 4, 6, 12, 77**
See also CA 41-44R; DLB 16

Eagleton, Terence (Francis) 1943-
See Eagleton, Terry
See also CA 57-60; CANR 7, 23; MTCW

Eagleton, Terry .... **CLC 63**
See also Eagleton, Terence (Francis)

Early, Jack
See Scoppettone, Sandra

East, Michael
See West, Morris L(anglo)

Eastaway, Edward
See Thomas, (Philip) Edward

Eastlake, William (Derry) 1917- ..... **CLC 8**
See also CA 5-8R; CAAS 1; CANR 5;
DLB 6

Eberhart, Richard (Ghormley)
1904- .... **CLC 3, 11, 19, 56**
See also CA 1-4R; CANR 2;
CDALB 1941-1968; DLB 48; MTCW

Eberstadt, Fernanda 1960- .... **CLC 39**
See also CA 136

Echegaray (y Eizaguirre), Jose (Maria Waldo)
1832-1916 .... **TCLC 4**
See also CA 104; CANR 32; HW; MTCW

Echeverria, (Jose) Esteban (Antonino)
1805-1851 .... **NCLC 18**

Echo
See Proust, (Valentin-Louis-George-Eugene-)
Marcel

Eckert, Allan W. 1931- .... **CLC 17**
See also CA 13-16R; CANR 14; SATA 27,
29

Eckhart, Meister 1260(?)-1328(?) .. **CMLC 9**
See also DLB 115

Eckmar, F. R.
See de Hartog, Jan

Eco, Umberto 1932- .... **CLC 28, 60**
See also BEST 90:1; CA 77-80; CANR 12,
33; MTCW

Eddison, E(ric) R(ucker)
1882-1945 .... **TCLC 15**
See also CA 109

Edel, (Joseph) Leon 1907- ...... **CLC 29, 34**
See also CA 1-4R; CANR 1, 22; DLB 103

Eden, Emily 1797-1869 .... **NCLC 10**

Edgar, David 1948- .... **CLC 42**
See also CA 57-60; CANR 12; DLB 13;
MTCW

Edgerton, Clyde (Carlyle) 1944- .... **CLC 39**
See also CA 118; 134

Edgeworth, Maria 1767-1849 ...... **NCLC 1**
See also DLB 116; SATA 21

Edmonds, Paul
See Kuttner, Henry

Edmonds, Walter D(umaux) 1903- .. **CLC 35**
See also CA 5-8R; CANR 2; DLB 9;
MAICYA; SAAS 4; SATA 1, 27

Edmondson, Wallace
See Ellison, Harlan

Edson, Russell .... **CLC 13**
See also CA 33-36R

Edwards, G(erald) B(asil)
1899-1976 .... **CLC 25**
See also CA 110

Edwards, Gus 1939- .... **CLC 43**
See also CA 108

Edwards, Jonathan 1703-1758 .... **LC 7; DA**
See also DLB 24

Efron, Marina Ivanovna Tsvetaeva
See Tsvetaeva (Efron), Marina (Ivanovna)

Ehle, John (Marsden, Jr.) 1925- .... **CLC 27**
See also CA 9-12R

Ehrenbourg, Ilya (Grigoryevich)
See Ehrenburg, Ilya (Grigoryevich)

Ehrenburg, Ilya (Grigoryevich)
1891-1967 .... **CLC 18, 34, 62**
See also CA 102; 25-28R

Ehrenburg, Ilyo (Grigoryevich)
See Ehrenburg, Ilya (Grigoryevich)

Eich, Guenter 1907-1972 .... **CLC 15**
See also CA 111; 93-96; DLB 69, 124

Eichendorff, Joseph Freiherr von
1788-1857 .... **NCLC 8**
See also DLB 90

Eigner, Larry . . . . CLC 9
See also Eigner, Laurence (Joel)
See also DLB 5

Eigner, Laurence (Joel) 1927-
See Eigner, Larry
See also CA 9-12R; CANR 6

Eiseley, Loren Corey 1907-1977 . . . . . CLC 7
See also AAYA 5; CA 1-4R; 73-76;
CANR 6

Eisenstadt, Jill 1963- . . . . CLC 50
See also CA 140

Eisner, Simon
See Kornbluth, C(yril) M.

Ekeloef, (Bengt) Gunnar
1907-1968 . . . . CLC 27
See also Ekelof, (Bengt) Gunnar
See also CA 123; 25-28R

Ekelof, (Bengt) Gunnar . . . . CLC 27
See also Ekeloef, (Bengt) Gunnar

Ekwensi, C. O. D.
See Ekwensi, Cyprian (Odiatu Duaka)

Ekwensi, Cyprian (Odiatu Duaka)
1921- . . . . CLC 4; BLC
See also BW; CA 29-32R; CANR 18, 42;
DLB 117; MTCW; SATA 66

Elaine . . . . TCLC 18
See also Leverson, Ada

El Crummo
See Crumb, R(obert)

Elia
See Lamb, Charles

Eliade, Mircea 1907-1986 . . . . CLC 19
See also CA 65-68; 119; CANR 30; MTCW

Eliot, A. D.
See Jewett, (Theodora) Sarah Orne

Eliot, Alice
See Jewett, (Theodora) Sarah Orne

Eliot, Dan
See Silverberg, Robert

Eliot, George
1819-1880 . . . . NCLC 4, 13, 23, 41; DA;
WLC
See also CDBLB 1832-1890; DLB 21, 35, 55

Eliot, John 1604-1690 . . . . LC 5
See also DLB 24

Eliot, T(homas) S(tearns)
1888-1965 . . . . . CLC 1, 2, 3, 6, 9, 10, 13,
15, 24, 34, 41, 55, 57; DA; PC 5; WLC 2
See also CA 5-8R; 25-28R; CANR 41;
CDALB 1929-1941; DLB 7, 10, 45, 63;
DLBY 88; MTCW

Elizabeth 1866-1941 . . . . TCLC 41

Elkin, Stanley L(awrence)
1930- . . . CLC 4, 6, 9, 14, 27, 51; SSC 12
See also CA 9-12R; CANR 8; DLB 2, 28;
DLBY 80; MTCW

Elledge, Scott . . . . CLC 34

Elliott, Don
See Silverberg, Robert

Elliott, George P(aul) 1918-1980 . . . . . CLC 2
See also CA 1-4R; 97-100; CANR 2

Elliott, Janice 1931- . . . . CLC 47
See also CA 13-16R; CANR 8, 29; DLB 14

Elliott, Sumner Locke 1917-1991 . . . CLC 38
See also CA 5-8R; 134; CANR 2, 21

Elliott, William
See Bradbury, Ray (Douglas)

Ellis, A. E. . . . . CLC 7

Ellis, Alice Thomas . . . . CLC 40
See also Haycraft, Anna

Ellis, Bret Easton 1964- . . . . CLC 39, 71
See also AAYA 2; CA 118; 123

Ellis, (Henry) Havelock
1859-1939 . . . . TCLC 14
See also CA 109

Ellis, Landon
See Ellison, Harlan

Ellis, Trey 1962- . . . . CLC 55

Ellison, Harlan
1934- . . . . CLC 1, 13, 42; SSC 14
See also CA 5-8R; CANR 5; DLB 8;
MTCW

Ellison, Ralph (Waldo)
1914- . . . . . . CLC 1, 3, 11, 54; BLC; DA;
WLC
See also BW; CA 9-12R; CANR 24;
CDALB 1941-1968; DLB 2, 76; MTCW

Ellmann, Lucy (Elizabeth) 1956- . . . . CLC 61
See also CA 128

Ellmann, Richard (David)
1918-1987 . . . . CLC 50
See also BEST 89:2; CA 1-4R; 122;
CANR 2, 28; DLB 103; DLBY 87;
MTCW

Elman, Richard 1934- . . . . CLC 19
See also CA 17-20R; CAAS 3

Elron
See Hubbard, L(afayette) Ron(ald)

Eluard, Paul . . . . TCLC 7, 41
See also Grindel, Eugene

Elyot, Sir Thomas 1490(?)-1546 . . . . . LC 11

Elytis, Odysseus 1911- . . . . CLC 15, 49
See also CA 102; MTCW

Emecheta, (Florence Onye) Buchi
1944- . . . . CLC 14, 48; BLC
See also BW; CA 81-84; CANR 27;
DLB 117; MTCW; SATA 66

Emerson, Ralph Waldo
1803-1882 . . . . . . NCLC 1, 38; DA; WLC
See also CDALB 1640-1865; DLB 1, 59, 73

Eminescu, Mihail 1850-1889 . . . . . NCLC 33

Empson, William
1906-1984 . . . . CLC 3, 8, 19, 33, 34
See also CA 17-20R; 112; CANR 31;
DLB 20; MTCW

Enchi Fumiko (Ueda) 1905-1986 . . . . CLC 31
See also CA 129; 121

Ende, Michael (Andreas Helmuth)
1929- . . . . CLC 31
See also CA 118; 124; CANR 36; CLR 14;
DLB 75; MAICYA; SATA 42, 61

Endo, Shusaku 1923- . . . . . CLC 7, 14, 19, 54
See also CA 29-32R; CANR 21; MTCW

Engel, Marian 1933-1985 . . . . CLC 36
See also CA 25-28R; CANR 12; DLB 53

Engelhardt, Frederick
See Hubbard, L(afayette) Ron(ald)

Enright, D(ennis) J(oseph)
1920- . . . . CLC 4, 8, 31
See also CA 1-4R; CANR 1, 42; DLB 27;
SATA 25

Enzensberger, Hans Magnus
1929- . . . . CLC 43
See also CA 116; 119

Ephron, Nora 1941- . . . . CLC 17, 31
See also AITN 2; CA 65-68; CANR 12, 39

Epsilon
See Betjeman, John

Epstein, Daniel Mark 1948- . . . . CLC 7
See also CA 49-52; CANR 2

Epstein, Jacob 1956- . . . . CLC 19
See also CA 114

Epstein, Joseph 1937- . . . . CLC 39
See also CA 112; 119

Epstein, Leslie 1938- . . . . CLC 27
See also CA 73-76; CAAS 12; CANR 23

Equiano, Olaudah
1745(?)-1797 . . . . LC 16; BLC
See also DLB 37, 50

Erasmus, Desiderius 1469(?)-1536 . . . . LC 16

Erdman, Paul E(mil) 1932- . . . . CLC 25
See also AITN 1; CA 61-64; CANR 13, 43

Erdrich, Louise 1954- . . . . CLC 39, 54
See also AAYA 10; BEST 89:1; CA 114;
CANR 41; MTCW

Erenburg, Ilya (Grigoryevich)
See Ehrenburg, Ilya (Grigoryevich)

Erickson, Stephen Michael 1950-
See Erickson, Steve
See also CA 129

Erickson, Steve . . . . CLC 64
See also Erickson, Stephen Michael

Ericson, Walter
See Fast, Howard (Melvin)

Eriksson, Buntel
See Bergman, (Ernst) Ingmar

Eschenbach, Wolfram von
See Wolfram von Eschenbach

Eseki, Bruno
See Mphahlele, Ezekiel

Esenin, Sergei (Alexandrovich)
1895-1925 . . . . TCLC 4
See also CA 104

Eshleman, Clayton 1935- . . . . CLC 7
See also CA 33-36R; CAAS 6; DLB 5

Espriella, Don Manuel Alvarez
See Southey, Robert

Espriu, Salvador 1913-1985 . . . . CLC 9
See also CA 115; DLB 134

Espronceda, Jose de 1808-1842 . . . NCLC 39

Esse, James
See Stephens, James

Esterbrook, Tom
See Hubbard, L(afayette) Ron(ald)

Estleman, Loren D. 1952- . . . . CLC 48
See also CA 85-88; CANR 27; MTCW

Eugenides, Jeffrey 1960(?)- . . . . CLC 81

Euripides c. 485B.C.-406B.C. . . . . DC 4
See also DA

Evan, Evin
See Faust, Frederick (Schiller)

Evans, Evan
See Faust, Frederick (Schiller)

Evans, Marian
See Eliot, George

Evans, Mary Ann
See Eliot, George

Evarts, Esther
See Benson, Sally

Everett, Percival
See Everett, Percival L.

Everett, Percival L.   1956-........ **CLC 57**
See also CA 129

Everson, R(onald) G(ilmour)
1903-....................... **CLC 27**
See also CA 17-20R; DLB 88

Everson, William (Oliver)
1912-................... **CLC 1, 5, 14**
See also CA 9-12R; CANR 20; DLB 5, 16;
MTCW

Evtushenko, Evgenii Aleksandrovich
See Yevtushenko, Yevgeny (Alexandrovich)

Ewart, Gavin (Buchanan)
1916-.................... **CLC 13, 46**
See also CA 89-92; CANR 17; DLB 40;
MTCW

Ewers, Hanns Heinz   1871-1943 ... **TCLC 12**
See also CA 109

Ewing, Frederick R.
See Sturgeon, Theodore (Hamilton)

Exley, Frederick (Earl)
1929-1992 .... **CLC 6, 11**
See also AITN 2; CA 81-84; 138; DLBY 81

Eynhardt, Guillermo
See Quiroga, Horacio (Sylvestre)

Ezekiel, Nissim   1924-............. **CLC 61**
See also CA 61-64

Ezekiel, Tish O'Dowd   1943-....... **CLC 34**
See also CA 129

Fadeyev, A.
See Bulgya, Alexander Alexandrovich

Fadeyev, Alexander............... **TCLC 53**
See also Bulgya, Alexander Alexandrovich

Fagen, Donald   1948-............. **CLC 26**

Fainzilberg, Ilya Arnoldovich   1897-1937
See Ilf, Ilya
See also CA 120

Fair, Ronald L.   1932-............. **CLC 18**
See also BW; CA 69-72; CANR 25; DLB 33

Fairbairns, Zoe (Ann)   1948- .... **CLC 32**
See also CA 103; CANR 21

Falco, Gian
See Papini, Giovanni

Falconer, James
See Kirkup, James

Falconer, Kenneth
See Kornbluth, C(yril) M.

Falkland, Samuel
See Heijermans, Herman

Fallaci, Oriana   1930-............. **CLC 11**
See also CA 77-80; CANR 15; MTCW

Faludy, George   1913-............. **CLC 42**
See also CA 21-24R

Faludy, Gyoergy
See Faludy, George

Fanon, Frantz   1925-1961..... **CLC 74; BLC**
See also BW; CA 116; 89-92

Fanshawe, Ann .... **LC 11**

Fante, John (Thomas)   1911-1983 ... **CLC 60**
See also CA 69-72; 109; CANR 23;
DLB 130; DLBY 83

Farah, Nuruddin   1945-....... **CLC 53; BLC**
See also CA 106; DLB 125

Fargue, Leon-Paul   1876(?)-1947 ... **TCLC 11**
See also CA 109

Farigoule, Louis
See Romains, Jules

Farina, Richard   1936(?)-1966 .... **CLC 9**
See also CA 81-84; 25-28R

Farley, Walter (Lorimer)
1915-1989 .... **CLC 17**
See also CA 17-20R; CANR 8, 29; DLB 22;
JRDA; MAICYA; SATA 2, 43

Farmer, Philip Jose   1918-....... **CLC 1, 19**
See also CA 1-4R; CANR 4, 35; DLB 8;
MTCW

Farquhar, George   1677-1707........ **LC 21**
See also DLB 84

Farrell, J(ames) G(ordon)
1935-1979 .... **CLC 6**
See also CA 73-76; 89-92; CANR 36;
DLB 14; MTCW

Farrell, James T(homas)
1904-1979 .... **CLC 1, 4, 8, 11, 66**
See also CA 5-8R; 89-92; CANR 9; DLB 4,
9, 86; DLBD 2; MTCW

Farren, Richard J.
See Betjeman, John

Farren, Richard M.
See Betjeman, John

Fassbinder, Rainer Werner
1946-1982 .... **CLC 20**
See also CA 93-96; 106; CANR 31

Fast, Howard (Melvin)   1914- ...... **CLC 23**
See also CA 1-4R; CAAS 18; CANR 1, 33;
DLB 9; SATA 7

Faulcon, Robert
See Holdstock, Robert P.

Faulkner, William (Cuthbert)
1897-1962 ..... **CLC 1, 3, 6, 8, 9, 11, 14,
18, 28, 52, 68; DA; SSC 1; WLC**
See also AAYA 7; CA 81-84; CANR 33;
CDALB 1929-1941; DLB 9, 11, 44, 102;
DLBD 2; DLBY 86; MTCW

Fauset, Jessie Redmon
1884(?)-1961 .... **CLC 19, 54; BLC**
See also BW; CA 109; DLB 51

Faust, Frederick (Schiller)
1892-1944(?) .... **TCLC 49**
See also CA 108

Faust, Irvin   1924-................. **CLC 8**
See also CA 33-36R; CANR 28; DLB 2, 28;
DLBY 80

Fawkes, Guy
See Benchley, Robert (Charles)

Fearing, Kenneth (Flexner)
1902-1961 .... **CLC 51**
See also CA 93-96; DLB 9

Fecamps, Elise
See Creasey, John

Federman, Raymond   1928- ...... **CLC 6, 47**
See also CA 17-20R; CAAS 8; CANR 10,
43; DLBY 80

Federspiel, J(uerg) F.   1931-........ **CLC 42**

Feiffer, Jules (Ralph)   1929-.... **CLC 2, 8, 64**
See also AAYA 3; CA 17-20R; CANR 30;
DLB 7, 44; MTCW; SATA 8, 61

Feige, Hermann Albert Otto Maximilian
See Traven, B.

Fei-Kan, Li
See Li Fei-kan

Feinberg, David B.   1956-.......... **CLC 59**
See also CA 135

Feinstein, Elaine   1930-............ **CLC 36**
See also CA 69-72; CAAS 1; CANR 31;
DLB 14, 40; MTCW

Feldman, Irving (Mordecai)   1928-.... **CLC 7**
See also CA 1-4R; CANR 1

Fellini, Federico   1920-1993........ **CLC 16**
See also CA 65-68; 143; CANR 33

Felsen, Henry Gregor   1916- .... **CLC 17**
See also CA 1-4R; CANR 1; SAAS 2;
SATA 1

Fenton, James Martin   1949-....... **CLC 32**
See also CA 102; DLB 40

Ferber, Edna   1887-1968........... **CLC 18**
See also AITN 1; CA 5-8R; 25-28R; DLB 9,
28, 86; MTCW; SATA 7

Ferguson, Helen
See Kavan, Anna

Ferguson, Samuel   1810-1886..... **NCLC 33**
See also DLB 32

Ferling, Lawrence
See Ferlinghetti, Lawrence (Monsanto)

Ferlinghetti, Lawrence (Monsanto)
1919(?)- .... **CLC 2, 6, 10, 27; PC 1**
See also CA 5-8R; CANR 3, 41;
CDALB 1941-1968; DLB 5, 16; MTCW

Fernandez, Vicente Garcia Huidobro
See Huidobro Fernandez, Vicente Garcia

Ferrer, Gabriel (Francisco Victor) Miro
See Miro (Ferrer), Gabriel (Francisco
Victor)

Ferrier, Susan (Edmonstone)
1782-1854 .... **NCLC 8**
See also DLB 116

Ferrigno, Robert   1948(?)-.......... **CLC 65**
See also CA 140

Feuchtwanger, Lion   1884-1958 ..... **TCLC 3**
See also CA 104; DLB 66

Feydeau, Georges (Leon Jules Marie)
1862-1921 .... **TCLC 22**
See also CA 113

Ficino, Marsilio   1433-1499 .... **LC 12**

Fiedeler, Hans
See Doeblin, Alfred

Gill, Patrick
See Creasey, John

Gilliam, Terry (Vance) 1940-........ **CLC 21**
See also Monty Python
See also CA 108; 113; CANR 35

Gillian, Jerry
See Gilliam, Terry (Vance)

Gilliatt, Penelope (Ann Douglass)
1932-1993 .... **CLC 2, 10, 13, 53**
See also AITN 2; CA 13-16R; 141; DLB 14

Gilman, Charlotte (Anna) Perkins (Stetson)
1860-1935 .... **TCLC 9, 37; SSC 13**
See also CA 106

Gilmour, David 1949-............ **CLC 35**
See also Pink Floyd
See also CA 138

Gilpin, William 1724-1804....... **NCLC 30**

Gilray, J. D.
See Mencken, H(enry) L(ouis)

Gilroy, Frank D(aniel) 1925-........ **CLC 2**
See also CA 81-84; CANR 32; DLB 7

Ginsberg, Allen
1926- ...... **CLC 1, 2, 3, 4, 6, 13, 36, 69;**
DA; PC 4; WLC 3
See also AITN 1; CA 1-4R; CANR 2, 41;
CDALB 1941-1968; DLB 5, 16; MTCW

Ginzburg, Natalia
1916-1991 .... **CLC 5, 11, 54, 70**
See also CA 85-88; 135; CANR 33; MTCW

Giono, Jean 1895-1970......... **CLC 4, 11**
See also CA 45-48; 29-32R; CANR 2, 35;
DLB 72; MTCW

Giovanni, Nikki
1943- ...... **CLC 2, 4, 19, 64; BLC; DA**
See also AITN 1; BW; CA 29-32R;
CAAS 6; CANR 18, 41; CLR 6; DLB 5,
41; MAICYA; MTCW; SATA 24

Giovene, Andrea 1904-............ **CLC 7**
See also CA 85-88

Gippius, Zinaida (Nikolayevna) 1869-1945
See Hippius, Zinaida
See also CA 106

Giraudoux, (Hippolyte) Jean
1882-1944 .... **TCLC 2, 7**
See also CA 104; DLB 65

Gironella, Jose Maria 1917-....... **CLC 11**
See also CA 101

Gissing, George (Robert)
1857-1903 .... **TCLC 3, 24, 47**
See also CA 105; DLB 18, 135

Giurlani, Aldo
See Palazzeschi, Aldo

Gladkov, Fyodor (Vasilyevich)
1883-1958 .... **TCLC 27**

Glanville, Brian (Lester) 1931-...... **CLC 6**
See also CA 5-8R; CAAS 9; CANR 3;
DLB 15; SATA 42

Glasgow, Ellen (Anderson Gholson)
1873(?)-1945 .... **TCLC 2, 7**
See also CA 104; DLB 9, 12

Glassco, John 1909-1981 .... **CLC 9**
See also CA 13-16R; 102; CANR 15;
DLB 68

Glasscock, Amnesia
See Steinbeck, John (Ernst)

Glasser, Ronald J. 1940(?)-........ **CLC 37**

Glassman, Joyce
See Johnson, Joyce

Glendinning, Victoria 1937-........ **CLC 50**
See also CA 120; 127

Glissant, Edouard 1928-........ **CLC 10, 68**

Gloag, Julian 1930- .... **CLC 40**
See also AITN 1; CA 65-68; CANR 10

Gluck, Louise (Elisabeth)
1943- .... **CLC 7, 22, 44, 81**
See also Glueck, Louise
See also CA 33-36R; CANR 40; DLB 5

Glueck, Louise.................. CLC 7, 22
See also Gluck, Louise (Elisabeth)
See also DLB 5

Gobineau, Joseph Arthur (Comte) de
1816-1882 .... **NCLC 17**
See also DLB 123

Godard, Jean-Luc 1930-........... **CLC 20**
See also CA 93-96

Godden, (Margaret) Rumer 1907-... **CLC 53**
See also AAYA 6; CA 5-8R; CANR 4, 27,
36; CLR 20; MAICYA; SAAS 12;
SATA 3, 36

Godoy Alcayaga, Lucila 1889-1957
See Mistral, Gabriela
See also CA 104; 131; HW; MTCW

Godwin, Gail (Kathleen)
1937-............ **CLC 5, 8, 22, 31, 69**
See also CA 29-32R; CANR 15, 43; DLB 6;
MTCW

Godwin, William 1756-1836...... **NCLC 14**
See also CDBLB 1789-1832; DLB 39, 104

Goethe, Johann Wolfgang von
1749-1832 .... **NCLC 4, 22, 34; DA;**
PC 5; WLC 3
See also DLB 94

Gogarty, Oliver St. John
1878-1957................ **TCLC 15**
See also CA 109; DLB 15, 19

Gogol, Nikolai (Vasilyevich)
1809-1852 .... **NCLC 5, 15, 31; DA;**
DC 1; SSC 4; WLC

Goines, Donald
1937(?)-1974 .... **CLC 80; BLC**
See also AITN 1; BW; CA 124; 114;
DLB 33

Gold, Herbert 1924-....... **CLC 4, 7, 14, 42**
See also CA 9-12R; CANR 17; DLB 2;
DLBY 81

Goldbarth, Albert 1948-........ **CLC 5, 38**
See also CA 53-56; CANR 6, 40; DLB 120

Goldberg, Anatol 1910-1982 .... **CLC 34**
See also CA 131; 117

Goldemberg, Isaac 1945-.......... **CLC 52**
See also CA 69-72; CAAS 12; CANR 11,
32; HW

Golden Silver
See Storm, Hyemeyohsts

Golding, William (Gerald)
1911-1993 .... **CLC 1, 2, 3, 8, 10, 17, 27,**
58, 81; DA; WLC
See also AAYA 5; CA 5-8R; 141;
CANR 13, 33; CDBLB 1945-1960;
DLB 15, 100; MTCW

Goldman, Emma 1869-1940...... **TCLC 13**
See also CA 110

Goldman, Francisco 1955-......... **CLC 76**

Goldman, William (W.) 1931-.... **CLC 1, 48**
See also CA 9-12R; CANR 29; DLB 44

Goldmann, Lucien 1913-1970 ...... **CLC 24**
See also CA 25-28; CAP 2

Goldoni, Carlo 1707-1793 .... **LC 4**

Goldsberry, Steven 1949-......... **CLC 34**
See also CA 131

Goldsmith, Oliver
1728-1774 .... **LC 2; DA; WLC**
See also CDBLB 1660-1789; DLB 39, 89,
104, 109; SATA 26

Goldsmith, Peter
See Priestley, J(ohn) B(oynton)

Gombrowicz, Witold
1904-1969 .... **CLC 4, 7, 11, 49**
See also CA 19-20; 25-28R; CAP 2

Gomez de la Serna, Ramon
1888-1963 .... **CLC 9**
See also CA 116; HW

Goncharov, Ivan Alexandrovich
1812-1891 .... **NCLC 1**

Goncourt, Edmond (Louis Antoine Huot) de
1822-1896 .... **NCLC 7**
See also DLB 123

Goncourt, Jules (Alfred Huot) de
1830-1870 .... **NCLC 7**
See also DLB 123

Gontier, Fernande 19(?)- .... **CLC 50**

Goodman, Paul 1911-1972.... **CLC 1, 2, 4, 7**
See also CA 19-20; 37-40R; CANR 34;
CAP 2; DLB 130; MTCW

Gordimer, Nadine
1923- .... **CLC 3, 5, 7, 10, 18, 33, 51, 70;**
DA
See also CA 5-8R; CANR 3, 28; MTCW

Gordon, Adam Lindsay
1833-1870 .... **NCLC 21**

Gordon, Caroline
1895-1981 ...... **CLC 6, 13, 29; SSC 15**
See also CA 11-12; 103; CANR 36; CAP 1;
DLB 4, 9, 102; DLBY 81; MTCW

Gordon, Charles William 1860-1937
See Connor, Ralph
See also CA 109

Gordon, Mary (Catherine)
1949-.................... **CLC 13, 22**
See also CA 102; DLB 6; DLBY 81;
MTCW

Gordon, Sol 1923-................ **CLC 26**
See also CA 53-56; CANR 4; SATA 11

Gordone, Charles 1925-.......... **CLC 1, 4**
See also BW; CA 93-96; DLB 7; MTCW

Gorenko, Anna Andreevna
See Akhmatova, Anna

Gorky, Maxim............. TCLC 8; WLC
See also Peshkov, Alexei Maximovich

Goryan, Sirak
See Saroyan, William

Gosse, Edmund (William)
1849-1928 .... **TCLC 28**
See also CA 117; DLB 57

Gotlieb, Phyllis Fay (Bloom)
  1926- . . . . **CLC 18**
  See also CA 13-16R; CANR 7; DLB 88

Gottesman, S. D.
  See Kornbluth, C(yril) M.; Pohl, Frederik

Gottfried von Strassburg
  fl. c. 1210- . . . . **CMLC 10**

Gould, Lois . . . . **CLC 4, 10**
  See also CA 77-80; CANR 29; MTCW

Gourmont, Remy de 1858-1915. . . . **TCLC 17**
  See also CA 109

Govier, Katherine 1948- . . . . **CLC 51**
  See also CA 101; CANR 18, 40

Goyen, (Charles) William
  1915-1983 . . . . **CLC 5, 8, 14, 40**
  See also AITN 2; CA 5-8R; 110; CANR 6;
  DLB 2; DLBY 83

Goytisolo, Juan
  1931- . . . . **CLC 5, 10, 23; HLC**
  See also CA 85-88; CANR 32; HW; MTCW

Gozzi, (Conte) Carlo 1720-1806 . . **NCLC 23**

Grabbe, Christian Dietrich
  1801-1836 . . . . **NCLC 2**
  See also DLB 133

Grace, Patricia 1937- . . . . **CLC 56**

Gracian y Morales, Baltasar
  1601-1658 . . . . **LC 15**

Gracq, Julien . . . . **CLC 11, 48**
  See also Poirier, Louis
  See also DLB 83

Grade, Chaim 1910-1982 . . . . **CLC 10**
  See also CA 93-96; 107

Graduate of Oxford, A
  See Ruskin, John

Graham, John
  See Phillips, David Graham

Graham, Jorie 1951- . . . . **CLC 48**
  See also CA 111; DLB 120

Graham, R(obert) B(ontine) Cunninghame
  See Cunninghame Graham, R(obert)
    B(ontine)
  See also DLB 98, 135

Graham, Robert
  See Haldeman, Joe (William)

Graham, Tom
  See Lewis, (Harry) Sinclair

Graham, W(illiam) S(ydney)
  1918-1986 . . . . **CLC 29**
  See also CA 73-76; 118; DLB 20

Graham, Winston (Mawdsley)
  1910- . . . . **CLC 23**
  See also CA 49-52; CANR 2, 22; DLB 77

Grant, Skeeter
  See Spiegelman, Art

Granville-Barker, Harley
  1877-1946 . . . . **TCLC 2**
  See also Barker, Harley Granville
  See also CA 104

Grass, Guenter (Wilhelm)
  1927- . . . . . **CLC 1, 2, 4, 6, 11, 15, 22, 32,**
                          49; DA; WLC
  See also CA 13-16R; CANR 20; DLB 75,
  124; MTCW

Gratton, Thomas
  See Hulme, T(homas) E(rnest)

Grau, Shirley Ann
  1929- . . . . **CLC 4, 9; SSC 15**
  See also CA 89-92; CANR 22; DLB 2;
  MTCW

Gravel, Fern
  See Hall, James Norman

Graver, Elizabeth 1964- . . . . **CLC 70**
  See also CA 135

Graves, Richard Perceval 1945- . . . . **CLC 44**
  See also CA 65-68; CANR 9, 26

Graves, Robert (von Ranke)
  1895-1985 . . . . . . **CLC 1, 2, 6, 11, 39, 44,**
                              45; PC 6
  See also CA 5-8R; 117; CANR 5, 36;
  CDBLB 1914-1945; DLB 20, 100;
  DLBY 85; MTCW; SATA 45

Gray, Alasdair 1934- . . . . **CLC 41**
  See also CA 126; MTCW

Gray, Amlin 1946- . . . . **CLC 29**
  See also CA 138

Gray, Francine du Plessix 1930- . . . . **CLC 22**
  See also BEST 90:3; CA 61-64; CAAS 2;
  CANR 11, 33; MTCW

Gray, John (Henry) 1866-1934 . . . . **TCLC 19**
  See also CA 119

Gray, Simon (James Holliday)
  1936- . . . . **CLC 9, 14, 36**
  See also AITN 1; CA 21-24R; CAAS 3;
  CANR 32; DLB 13; MTCW

Gray, Spalding 1941- . . . . **CLC 49**
  See also CA 128

Gray, Thomas
  1716-1771 . . . . . . **LC 4; DA; PC 2; WLC**
  See also CDBLB 1660-1789; DLB 109

Grayson, David
  See Baker, Ray Stannard

Grayson, Richard (A.) 1951- . . . . **CLC 38**
  See also CA 85-88; CANR 14, 31

Greeley, Andrew M(oran) 1928- . . . . **CLC 28**
  See also CA 5-8R; CAAS 7; CANR 7, 43;
  MTCW

Green, Brian
  See Card, Orson Scott

Green, Hannah
  See Greenberg, Joanne (Goldenberg)

Green, Hannah . . . . **CLC 3**
  See also CA 73-76

Green, Henry . . . . **CLC 2, 13**
  See also Yorke, Henry Vincent
  See also DLB 15

Green, Julian (Hartridge) 1900-
  See Green, Julien
  See also CA 21-24R; CANR 33; DLB 4, 72;
  MTCW

Green, Julien . . . . **CLC 3, 11, 77**
  See also Green, Julian (Hartridge)

Green, Paul (Eliot) 1894-1981 . . . . . . **CLC 25**
  See also AITN 1; CA 5-8R; 103; CANR 3;
  DLB 7, 9; DLBY 81

Greenberg, Ivan 1908-1973
  See Rahv, Philip
  See also CA 85-88

Greenberg, Joanne (Goldenberg)
  1932- . . . . **CLC 7, 30**
  See also CA 5-8R; CANR 14, 32; SATA 25

Greenberg, Richard 1959(?)- . . . . **CLC 57**
  See also CA 138

Greene, Bette 1934- . . . . **CLC 30**
  See also AAYA 7; CA 53-56; CANR 4;
  CLR 2; JRDA; MAICYA; SAAS 16;
  SATA 8

Greene, Gael . . . . **CLC 8**
  See also CA 13-16R; CANR 10

Greene, Graham
  1904-1991 . . . . **CLC 1, 3, 6, 9, 14, 18, 27,**
                          37, 70, 72; DA; WLC
  See also AITN 2; CA 13-16R; 133;
  CANR 35; CDBLB 1945-1960; DLB 13,
  15, 77, 100; DLBY 91; MTCW; SATA 20

Greer, Richard
  See Silverberg, Robert

Greer, Richard
  See Silverberg, Robert

Gregor, Arthur 1923- . . . . **CLC 9**
  See also CA 25-28R; CAAS 10; CANR 11;
  SATA 36

Gregor, Lee
  See Pohl, Frederik

Gregory, Isabella Augusta (Persse)
  1852-1932 . . . . **TCLC 1**
  See also CA 104; DLB 10

Gregory, J. Dennis
  See Williams, John A(lfred)

Grendon, Stephen
  See Derleth, August (William)

Grenville, Kate 1950- . . . . **CLC 61**
  See also CA 118

Grenville, Pelham
  See Wodehouse, P(elham) G(renville)

Greve, Felix Paul (Berthold Friedrich)
  1879-1948
  See Grove, Frederick Philip
  See also CA 104; 141

Grey, Zane 1872-1939 . . . . **TCLC 6**
  See also CA 104; 132; DLB 9; MTCW

Grieg, (Johan) Nordahl (Brun)
  1902-1943 . . . . **TCLC 10**
  See also CA 107

Grieve, C(hristopher) M(urray)
  1892-1978 . . . . **CLC 11, 19**
  See also MacDiarmid, Hugh
  See also CA 5-8R; 85-88; CANR 33;
  MTCW

Griffin, Gerald 1803-1840 . . . . **NCLC 7**

Griffin, John Howard 1920-1980. . . . **CLC 68**
  See also AITN 1; CA 1-4R; 101; CANR 2

Griffin, Peter . . . . **CLC 39**

Griffiths, Trevor 1935- . . . . **CLC 13, 52**
  See also CA 97-100; DLB 13

Grigson, Geoffrey (Edward Harvey)
  1905-1985 . . . . **CLC 7, 39**
  See also CA 25-28R; 118; CANR 20, 33;
  DLB 27; MTCW

Grillparzer, Franz 1791-1872 . . . . . . **NCLC 1**
  See also DLB 133

Grimble, Reverend Charles James
See Eliot, T(homas) S(tearns)

Grimke, Charlotte L(ottie) Forten
1837(?)-1914
See Forten, Charlotte L.
See also BW; CA 117; 124

Grimm, Jacob Ludwig Karl
1785-1863 .... **NCLC 3**
See also DLB 90; MAICYA; SATA 22

Grimm, Wilhelm Karl 1786-1859 .. **NCLC 3**
See also DLB 90; MAICYA; SATA 22

Grimmelshausen, Johann Jakob Christoffel
von 1621-1676 .... **LC 6**

Grindel, Eugene 1895-1952
See Eluard, Paul
See also CA 104

Grossman, David 1954- .... **CLC 67**
See also CA 138

Grossman, Vasily (Semenovich)
1905-1964 .... **CLC 41**
See also CA 124; 130; MTCW

Grove, Frederick Philip .... **TCLC 4**
See also Greve, Felix Paul (Berthold
Friedrich)
See also DLB 92

Grubb
See Crumb, R(obert)

Grumbach, Doris (Isaac)
1918- .... **CLC 13, 22, 64**
See also CA 5-8R; CAAS 2; CANR 9, 42

Grundtvig, Nicolai Frederik Severin
1783-1872 .... **NCLC 1**

Grunge
See Crumb, R(obert)

Grunwald, Lisa 1959- .... **CLC 44**
See also CA 120

Guare, John 1938- .... **CLC 8, 14, 29, 67**
See also CA 73-76; CANR 21; DLB 7;
MTCW

Gudjonsson, Halldor Kiljan 1902-
See Laxness, Halldor
See also CA 103

Guenter, Erich
See Eich, Guenter

Guest, Barbara 1920- .... **CLC 34**
See also CA 25-28R; CANR 11; DLB 5

Guest, Judith (Ann) 1936- .... **CLC 8, 30**
See also AAYA 7; CA 77-80; CANR 15;
MTCW

Guild, Nicholas M. 1944- .... **CLC 33**
See also CA 93-96

Guillemin, Jacques
See Sartre, Jean-Paul

Guillen, Jorge 1893-1984 .... **CLC 11**
See also CA 89-92; 112; DLB 108; HW

Guillen (y Batista), Nicolas (Cristobal)
1902-1989 ..... **CLC 48, 79; BLC; HLC**
See also BW; CA 116; 125; 129; HW

Guillevic, (Eugene) 1907- .... **CLC 33**
See also CA 93-96

Guillois
See Desnos, Robert

Guiney, Louise Imogen
1861-1920 .... **TCLC 41**
See also DLB 54

Guiraldes, Ricardo (Guillermo)
1886-1927 .... **TCLC 39**
See also CA 131; HW; MTCW

Gunn, Bill .... **CLC 5**
See also Gunn, William Harrison
See also DLB 38

Gunn, Thom(son William)
1929- .... **CLC 3, 6, 18, 32, 81**
See also CA 17-20R; CANR 9, 33;
CDBLB 1960 to Present; DLB 27;
MTCW

Gunn, William Harrison 1934(?)-1989
See Gunn, Bill
See also AITN 1; BW; CA 13-16R; 128;
CANR 12, 25

Gunnars, Kristjana 1948- .... **CLC 69**
See also CA 113; DLB 60

Gurganus, Allan 1947- .... **CLC 70**
See also BEST 90:1; CA 135

Gurney, A(lbert) R(amsdell), Jr.
1930- .... **CLC 32, 50, 54**
See also CA 77-80; CANR 32

Gurney, Ivor (Bertie) 1890-1937 ... **TCLC 33**

Gurney, Peter
See Gurney, A(lbert) R(amsdell), Jr.

Gustafson, Ralph (Barker) 1909- .... **CLC 36**
See also CA 21-24R; CANR 8; DLB 88

Gut, Gom
See Simenon, Georges (Jacques Christian)

Guthrie, A(lfred) B(ertram), Jr.
1901-1991 .... **CLC 23**
See also CA 57-60; 134; CANR 24; DLB 6;
SATA 62; SATA-Obit 67

Guthrie, Isobel
See Grieve, C(hristopher) M(urray)

Guthrie, Woodrow Wilson 1912-1967
See Guthrie, Woody
See also CA 113; 93-96

Guthrie, Woody .... **CLC 35**
See also Guthrie, Woodrow Wilson

Guy, Rosa (Cuthbert) 1928- .... **CLC 26**
See also AAYA 4; BW; CA 17-20R;
CANR 14, 34; CLR 13; DLB 33; JRDA;
MAICYA; SATA 14, 62

Gwendolyn
See Bennett, (Enoch) Arnold

H. D. .... **CLC 3, 8, 14, 31, 34, 73; PC 5**
See also Doolittle, Hilda

Haavikko, Paavo Juhani
1931- .... **CLC 18, 34**
See also CA 106

Habbema, Koos
See Heijermans, Herman

Hacker, Marilyn 1942- .... **CLC 5, 9, 23, 72**
See also CA 77-80; DLB 120

Haggard, H(enry) Rider
1856-1925 .... **TCLC 11**
See also CA 108; DLB 70; SATA 16

Haig, Fenil
See Ford, Ford Madox

Haig-Brown, Roderick (Langmere)
1908-1976 .... **CLC 21**
See also CA 5-8R; 69-72; CANR 4, 38;
CLR 31; DLB 88; MAICYA; SATA 12

Hailey, Arthur 1920- .... **CLC 5**
See also AITN 2; BEST 90:3; CA 1-4R;
CANR 2, 36; DLB 88; DLBY 82; MTCW

Hailey, Elizabeth Forsythe 1938-... **CLC 40**
See also CA 93-96; CAAS 1; CANR 15

Haines, John (Meade) 1924- .... **CLC 58**
See also CA 17-20R; CANR 13, 34; DLB 5

Haldeman, Joe (William) 1943-..... **CLC 61**
See also CA 53-56; CANR 6; DLB 8

Haley, Alex(ander Murray Palmer)
1921-1992 .... **CLC 8, 12, 76; BLC; DA**
See also BW; CA 77-80; 136; DLB 38;
MTCW

Haliburton, Thomas Chandler
1796-1865 .... **NCLC 15**
See also DLB 11, 99

Hall, Donald (Andrew, Jr.)
1928- .... **CLC 1, 13, 37, 59**
See also CA 5-8R; CAAS 7; CANR 2;
DLB 5; SATA 23

Hall, Frederic Sauser
See Sauser-Hall, Frederic

Hall, James
See Kuttner, Henry

Hall, James Norman 1887-1951 ... **TCLC 23**
See also CA 123; SATA 21

Hall, (Marguerite) Radclyffe
1886(?)-1943 .... **TCLC 12**
See also CA 110

Hall, Rodney 1935- .... **CLC 51**
See also CA 109

Halliday, Michael
See Creasey, John

Halpern, Daniel 1945- .... **CLC 14**
See also CA 33-36R

Hamburger, Michael (Peter Leopold)
1924- .... **CLC 5, 14**
See also CA 5-8R; CAAS 4; CANR 2;
DLB 27

Hamill, Pete 1935- .... **CLC 10**
See also CA 25-28R; CANR 18

Hamilton, Clive
See Lewis, C(live) S(taples)

Hamilton, Edmond 1904-1977 .... **CLC 1**
See also CA 1-4R; CANR 3; DLB 8

Hamilton, Eugene (Jacob) Lee
See Lee-Hamilton, Eugene (Jacob)

Hamilton, Franklin
See Silverberg, Robert

Hamilton, Gail
See Corcoran, Barbara

Hamilton, Mollie
See Kaye, M(ary) M(argaret)

Hamilton, (Anthony Walter) Patrick
1904-1962 .... **CLC 51**
See also CA 113; DLB 10

Hamilton, Virginia 1936-.......... **CLC 26**
See also AAYA 2; BW; CA 25-28R;
CANR 20, 37; CLR 1, 11; DLB 33, 52;
JRDA; MAICYA; MTCW; SATA 4, 56

Hammett, (Samuel) Dashiell
1894-1961 . . . . **CLC 3, 5, 10, 19, 47**
See also AITN 1; CA 81-84; CANR 42;
CDALB 1929-1941; DLBD 6; MTCW

Hammon, Jupiter
1711(?)-1800(?) . . . . **NCLC 5; BLC**
See also DLB 31, 50

Hammond, Keith
See Kuttner, Henry

Hamner, Earl (Henry), Jr. 1923- . . . **CLC 12**
See also AITN 2; CA 73-76; DLB 6

Hampton, Christopher (James)
1946- . . . . **CLC 4**
See also CA 25-28R; DLB 13; MTCW

Hamsun, Knut . . . . **TCLC 2, 14, 49**
See also Pedersen, Knut

Handke, Peter 1942- . . **CLC 5, 8, 10, 15, 38**
See also CA 77-80; CANR 33; DLB 85,
124; MTCW

Hanley, James 1901-1985 . . . **CLC 3, 5, 8, 13**
See also CA 73-76; 117; CANR 36; MTCW

Hannah, Barry 1942- . . . . **CLC 23, 38**
See also CA 108; 110; CANR 43; DLB 6;
MTCW

Hannon, Ezra
See Hunter, Evan

Hansberry, Lorraine (Vivian)
1930-1965 . . . . . . **CLC 17, 62; BLC; DA;
DC 2**
See also BW; CA 109; 25-28R; CABS 3;
CDALB 1941-1968; DLB 7, 38; MTCW

Hansen, Joseph 1923- . . . . **CLC 38**
See also CA 29-32R; CAAS 17; CANR 16

Hansen, Martin A. 1909-1955 . . . . . **TCLC 32**

Hanson, Kenneth O(stlin) 1922- . . . . **CLC 13**
See also CA 53-56; CANR 7

Hardwick, Elizabeth 1916- . . . . **CLC 13**
See also CA 5-8R; CANR 3, 32; DLB 6;
MTCW

Hardy, Thomas
1840-1928 . . . . . . **TCLC 4, 10, 18, 32, 48,
53; DA; PC 8; SSC 2; WLC**
See also CA 104; 123; CDBLB 1890-1914;
DLB 18, 19, 135; MTCW

Hare, David 1947- . . . . **CLC 29, 58**
See also CA 97-100; CANR 39; DLB 13;
MTCW

Harford, Henry
See Hudson, W(illiam) H(enry)

Hargrave, Leonie
See Disch, Thomas M(ichael)

Harlan, Louis R(udolph) 1922- . . . . . **CLC 34**
See also CA 21-24R; CANR 25

Harling, Robert 1951(?)- . . . . **CLC 53**

Harmon, William (Ruth) 1938- . . . . . **CLC 38**
See also CA 33-36R; CANR 14, 32, 35;
SATA 65

Harper, F. E. W.
See Harper, Frances Ellen Watkins

Harper, Frances E. W.
See Harper, Frances Ellen Watkins

Harper, Frances E. Watkins
See Harper, Frances Ellen Watkins

Harper, Frances Ellen
See Harper, Frances Ellen Watkins

Harper, Frances Ellen Watkins
1825-1911 . . . . **TCLC 14; BLC**
See also BW; CA 111; 125; DLB 50

Harper, Michael S(teven) 1938- . . **CLC 7, 22**
See also BW; CA 33-36R; CANR 24;
DLB 41

Harper, Mrs. F. E. W.
See Harper, Frances Ellen Watkins

Harris, Christie (Lucy) Irwin
1907- . . . . **CLC 12**
See also CA 5-8R; CANR 6; DLB 88;
JRDA; MAICYA; SAAS 10; SATA 6, 74

Harris, Frank 1856(?)-1931 . . . . . . **TCLC 24**
See also CA 109

Harris, George Washington
1814-1869 . . . . **NCLC 23**
See also DLB 3, 11

Harris, Joel Chandler 1848-1908 . . . **TCLC 2**
See also CA 104; 137; DLB 11, 23, 42, 78,
91; MAICYA; YABC 1

**Harris, John (Wyndham Parkes Lucas)
Beynon** 1903-1969 . . . . **CLC 19**
See also CA 102; 89-92

Harris, MacDonald
See Heiney, Donald (William)

Harris, Mark 1922- . . . . **CLC 19**
See also CA 5-8R; CAAS 3; CANR 2;
DLB 2; DLBY 80

Harris, (Theodore) Wilson 1921- . . . . **CLC 25**
See also BW; CA 65-68; CAAS 16;
CANR 11, 27; DLB 117; MTCW

Harrison, Elizabeth Cavanna 1909-
See Cavanna, Betty
See also CA 9-12R; CANR 6, 27

Harrison, Harry (Max) 1925- . . . . **CLC 42**
See also CA 1-4R; CANR 5, 21; DLB 8;
SATA 4

Harrison, James (Thomas)
1937- . . . . **CLC 6, 14, 33, 66**
See also CA 13-16R; CANR 8; DLBY 82

Harrison, Kathryn 1961- . . . . **CLC 70**

Harrison, Tony 1937- . . . . **CLC 43**
See also CA 65-68; DLB 40; MTCW

Harriss, Will(ard Irvin) 1922- . . . . . . **CLC 34**
See also CA 111

Harson, Sley
See Ellison, Harlan

Hart, Ellis
See Ellison, Harlan

Hart, Josephine 1942(?)- . . . . **CLC 70**
See also CA 138

Hart, Moss 1904-1961 . . . . **CLC 66**
See also CA 109; 89-92; DLB 7

Harte, (Francis) Bret(t)
1836(?)-1902 . . . . **TCLC 1, 25; DA;
SSC 8; WLC**
See also CA 104; 140; CDALB 1865-1917;
DLB 12, 64, 74, 79; SATA 26

Hartley, L(eslie) P(oles)
1895-1972 . . . . **CLC 2, 22**
See also CA 45-48; 37-40R; CANR 33;
DLB 15; MTCW

Hartman, Geoffrey H. 1929- . . . . **CLC 27**
See also CA 117; 125; DLB 67

Haruf, Kent 19(?)- . . . . **CLC 34**

Harwood, Ronald 1934- . . . . **CLC 32**
See also CA 1-4R; CANR 4; DLB 13

Hasek, Jaroslav (Matej Frantisek)
1883-1923 . . . . **TCLC 4**
See also CA 104; 129; MTCW

Hass, Robert 1941- . . . . **CLC 18, 39**
See also CA 111; CANR 30; DLB 105

Hastings, Hudson
See Kuttner, Henry

Hastings, Selina . . . . **CLC 44**

Hatteras, Amelia
See Mencken, H(enry) L(ouis)

Hatteras, Owen . . . . **TCLC 18**
See also Mencken, H(enry) L(ouis); Nathan,
George Jean

Hauptmann, Gerhart (Johann Robert)
1862-1946 . . . . **TCLC 4**
See also CA 104; DLB 66, 118

Havel, Vaclav 1936- . . . . **CLC 25, 58, 65**
See also CA 104; CANR 36; MTCW

Haviaras, Stratis . . . . **CLC 33**
See also Chaviaras, Strates

Hawes, Stephen 1475(?)-1523(?) . . . . . **LC 17**

Hawkes, John (Clendennin Burne, Jr.)
1925- . . . . . . **CLC 1, 2, 3, 4, 7, 9, 14, 15,
27, 49**
See also CA 1-4R; CANR 2; DLB 2, 7;
DLBY 80; MTCW

Hawking, S. W.
See Hawking, Stephen W(illiam)

Hawking, Stephen W(illiam)
1942- . . . . **CLC 63**
See also BEST 89:1; CA 126; 129

Hawthorne, Julian 1846-1934 . . . . . **TCLC 25**

Hawthorne, Nathaniel
1804-1864 . . . . . . **NCLC 39; DA; SSC 3;
WLC**
See also CDALB 1640-1865; DLB 1, 74;
YABC 2

Haxton, Josephine Ayres 1921- . . . . **CLC 73**
See also CA 115; CANR 41

Hayaseca y Eizaguirre, Jorge
See Echegaray (y Eizaguirre), Jose (Maria
Waldo)

Hayashi Fumiko 1904-1951 . . . . **TCLC 27**

Haycraft, Anna
See Ellis, Alice Thomas
See also CA 122

Hayden, Robert E(arl)
1913-1980 . . . . . . **CLC 5, 9, 14, 37; BLC;
DA; PC 6**
See also BW; CA 69-72; 97-100; CABS 2;
CANR 24; CDALB 1941-1968; DLB 5,
76; MTCW; SATA 19, 26

Hayford, J(oseph) E(phraim) Casely
See Casely-Hayford, J(oseph) E(phraim)

Hayman, Ronald 1932- . . . . **CLC 44**
See also CA 25-28R; CANR 18

Haywood, Eliza (Fowler)
1693(?)-1756 . . . . **LC 1**

Hazlitt, William 1778-1830 . . . . . . **NCLC 29**
See also DLB 110

Hazzard, Shirley 1931- . . . . **CLC 18**
See also CA 9-12R; CANR 4; DLBY 82;
MTCW

Head, Bessie 1937-1986 . . . **CLC 25, 67; BLC**
See also BW; CA 29-32R; 119; CANR 25;
DLB 117; MTCW

Headon, (Nicky) Topper 1956(?)- . . . **CLC 30**
See also Clash, The

Heaney, Seamus (Justin)
1939- . . . . **CLC 5, 7, 14, 25, 37, 74**
See also CA 85-88; CANR 25;
CDBLB 1960 to Present; DLB 40;
MTCW

Hearn, (Patricio) Lafcadio (Tessima Carlos)
1850-1904 . . . . **TCLC 9**
See also CA 105; DLB 12, 78

Hearne, Vicki 1946- . . . . **CLC 56**
See also CA 139

Hearon, Shelby 1931- . . . . **CLC 63**
See also AITN 2; CA 25-28R; CANR 18

Heat-Moon, William Least . . . . **CLC 29**
See also Trogdon, William (Lewis)
See also AAYA 9

Hebbel, Friedrich 1813-1863 . . . . . **NCLC 43**
See also DLB 129

Hebert, Anne 1916- . . . . **CLC 4, 13, 29**
See also CA 85-88; DLB 68; MTCW

Hecht, Anthony (Evan)
1923- . . . . **CLC 8, 13, 19**
See also CA 9-12R; CANR 6; DLB 5

Hecht, Ben 1894-1964 . . . . **CLC 8**
See also CA 85-88; DLB 7, 9, 25, 26, 28, 86

Hedayat, Sadeq 1903-1951 . . . . **TCLC 21**
See also CA 120

Heidegger, Martin 1889-1976 . . . . . . **CLC 24**
See also CA 81-84; 65-68; CANR 34;
MTCW

Heidenstam, (Carl Gustaf) Verner von
1859-1940 . . . . **TCLC 5**
See also CA 104

Heifner, Jack 1946- . . . . **CLC 11**
See also CA 105

Heijermans, Herman 1864-1924 . . . **TCLC 24**
See also CA 123

Heilbrun, Carolyn G(old) 1926- . . . . . **CLC 25**
See also CA 45-48; CANR 1, 28

Heine, Heinrich 1797-1856 . . . . **NCLC 4**
See also DLB 90

Heinemann, Larry (Curtiss) 1944- . . **CLC 50**
See also CA 110; CANR 31; DLBD 9

Heiney, Donald (William)
1921-1993 . . . . **CLC 9**
See also CA 1-4R; 142; CANR 3

Heinlein, Robert A(nson)
1907-1988 . . . . . . **CLC 1, 3, 8, 14, 26, 55**
See also CA 1-4R; 125; CANR 1, 20;
DLB 8; JRDA; MAICYA; MTCW;
SATA 9, 56, 69

Helforth, John
See Doolittle, Hilda

Hellenhofferu, Vojtech Kapristian z
See Hasek, Jaroslav (Matej Frantisek)

Heller, Joseph
1923- . . . . **CLC 1, 3, 5, 8, 11, 36, 63; DA;**
WLC
See also AITN 1; CA 5-8R; CABS 1;
CANR 8, 42; DLB 2, 28; DLBY 80;
MTCW

Hellman, Lillian (Florence)
1906-1984 . . . . . . **CLC 2, 4, 8, 14, 18, 34,**
44, 52; DC 1
See also AITN 1, 2; CA 13-16R; 112;
CANR 33; DLB 7; DLBY 84; MTCW

Helprin, Mark 1947- . . . . . **CLC 7, 10, 22, 32**
See also CA 81-84; DLBY 85; MTCW

Helyar, Jane Penelope Josephine 1933-
See Poole, Josephine
See also CA 21-24R; CANR 10, 26

Hemans, Felicia 1793-1835 . . . . . . **NCLC 29**
See also DLB 96

Hemingway, Ernest (Miller)
1899-1961 . . . . **CLC 1, 3, 6, 8, 10, 13, 19,**
30, 34, 39, 41, 44, 50, 61, 80; DA; SSC 1;
WLC
See also CA 77-80; CANR 34;
CDALB 1917-1929; DLB 4, 9, 102;
DLBD 1; DLBY 81, 87; MTCW

Hempel, Amy 1951- . . . . **CLC 39**
See also CA 118; 137

Henderson, F. C.
See Mencken, H(enry) L(ouis)

Henderson, Sylvia
See Ashton-Warner, Sylvia (Constance)

Henley, Beth . . . . **CLC 23**
See also Henley, Elizabeth Becker
See also CABS 3; DLBY 86

Henley, Elizabeth Becker 1952-
See Henley, Beth
See also CA 107; CANR 32; MTCW

Henley, William Ernest
1849-1903 . . . . **TCLC 8**
See also CA 105; DLB 19

Hennissart, Martha
See Lathen, Emma
See also CA 85-88

Henry, O. . . . . **TCLC 1, 19; SSC 5; WLC**
See also Porter, William Sydney

Henry, Patrick 1736-1799 . . . . **LC 25**

Henryson, Robert 1430(?)-1506(?) . . . . **LC 20**

Henry VIII 1491-1547 . . . . **LC 10**

Henschke, Alfred
See Klabund

Hentoff, Nat(han Irving) 1925- . . . . . **CLC 26**
See also AAYA 4; CA 1-4R; CAAS 6;
CANR 5, 25; CLR 1; JRDA; MAICYA;
SATA 27, 42, 69

Heppenstall, (John) Rayner
1911-1981 . . . . **CLC 10**
See also CA 1-4R; 103; CANR 29

Herbert, Frank (Patrick)
1920-1986 . . . . **CLC 12, 23, 35, 44**
See also CA 53-56; 118; CANR 5, 43;
DLB 8; MTCW; SATA 9, 37, 47

Herbert, George 1593-1633 . . . . **LC 24; PC 4**
See also CDBLB Before 1660; DLB 126

Herbert, Zbigniew 1924- . . . . **CLC 9, 43**
See also CA 89-92; CANR 36; MTCW

Herbst, Josephine (Frey)
1897-1969 . . . . **CLC 34**
See also CA 5-8R; 25-28R; DLB 9

Hergesheimer, Joseph
1880-1954 . . . . **TCLC 11**
See also CA 109; DLB 102, 9

Herlihy, James Leo 1927-1993 . . . . . . **CLC 6**
See also CA 1-4R; 143; CANR 2

Hermogenes fl. c. 175- . . . . **CMLC 6**

Hernandez, Jose 1834-1886 . . . . . . **NCLC 17**

Herrick, Robert 1591-1674 . . . . . **LC 13; DA**
See also DLB 126

Herring, Guilles
See Somerville, Edith

Herriot, James 1916- . . . . **CLC 12**
See also Wight, James Alfred
See also AAYA 1; CANR 40

Herrmann, Dorothy 1941- . . . . **CLC 44**
See also CA 107

Herrmann, Taffy
See Herrmann, Dorothy

Hersey, John (Richard)
1914-1993 . . . . **CLC 1, 2, 7, 9, 40, 81**
See also CA 17-20R; 140; CANR 33;
DLB 6; MTCW; SATA 25;
SATA-Obit 76

Herzen, Aleksandr Ivanovich
1812-1870 . . . . **NCLC 10**

Herzl, Theodor 1860-1904 . . . . **TCLC 36**

Herzog, Werner 1942- . . . . **CLC 16**
See also CA 89-92

Hesiod c. 8th cent. B.C.- . . . . **CMLC 5**

Hesse, Hermann
1877-1962 . . . . **CLC 1, 2, 3, 6, 11, 17, 25,**
69; DA; SSC 9; WLC
See also CA 17-18; CAP 2; DLB 66;
MTCW; SATA 50

Hewes, Cady
See De Voto, Bernard (Augustine)

Heyen, William 1940- . . . . **CLC 13, 18**
See also CA 33-36R; CAAS 9; DLB 5

Heyerdahl, Thor 1914- . . . . **CLC 26**
See also CA 5-8R; CANR 5, 22; MTCW;
SATA 2, 52

Heym, Georg (Theodor Franz Arthur)
1887-1912 . . . . **TCLC 9**
See also CA 106

Heym, Stefan 1913- . . . . **CLC 41**
See also CA 9-12R; CANR 4; DLB 69

Heyse, Paul (Johann Ludwig von)
1830-1914 . . . . **TCLC 8**
See also CA 104; DLB 129

Hibbert, Eleanor Alice Burford
1906-1993 . . . . **CLC 7**
See also BEST 90:4; CA 17-20R; 140;
CANR 9, 28; SATA 2; SATA-Obit 74

Higgins, George V(incent)
1939- . . . . **CLC 4, 7, 10, 18**
See also CA 77-80; CAAS 5; CANR 17;
DLB 2; DLBY 81; MTCW

Higginson, Thomas Wentworth
1823-1911 . . . . **TCLC 36**
See also DLB 1, 64

Highet, Helen
See MacInnes, Helen (Clark)

Highsmith, (Mary) Patricia
1921- . . . . CLC 2, 4, 14, 42
See also CA 1-4R; CANR 1, 20; MTCW

Highwater, Jamake (Mamake)
1942(?)- . . . . CLC 12
See also AAYA 7; CA 65-68; CAAS 7;
CANR 10, 34; CLR 17; DLB 52;
DLBY 85; JRDA; MAICYA; SATA 30,
32, 69

Hijuelos, Oscar 1951- . . . . . . CLC 65; HLC
See also BEST 90:1; CA 123; HW

Hikmet, Nazim 1902(?)-1963. . . . . . CLC 40
See also CA 141; 93-96

Hildesheimer, Wolfgang
1916-1991 . . . . CLC 49
See also CA 101; 135; DLB 69, 124

Hill, Geoffrey (William)
1932- . . . . CLC 5, 8, 18, 45
See also CA 81-84; CANR 21;
CDBLB 1960 to Present; DLB 40;
MTCW

Hill, George Roy 1921- . . . . CLC 26
See also CA 110; 122

Hill, John
See Koontz, Dean R(ay)

Hill, Susan (Elizabeth) 1942- . . . . CLC 4
See also CA 33-36R; CANR 29; DLB 14;
MTCW

Hillerman, Tony 1925- . . . . CLC 62
See also AAYA 6; BEST 89:1; CA 29-32R;
CANR 21, 42; SATA 6

Hillesum, Etty 1914-1943 . . . . TCLC 49
See also CA 137

Hilliard, Noel (Harvey) 1929- . . . . . . CLC 15
See also CA 9-12R; CANR 7

Hillis, Rick 1956- . . . . CLC 66
See also CA 134

Hilton, James 1900-1954 . . . . TCLC 21
See also CA 108; DLB 34, 77; SATA 34

Himes, Chester (Bomar)
1909-1984 . . . . CLC 2, 4, 7, 18, 58; BLC
See also BW; CA 25-28R; 114; CANR 22;
DLB 2, 76; MTCW

Hinde, Thomas . . . . CLC 6, 11
See also Chitty, Thomas Willes

Hindin, Nathan
See Bloch, Robert (Albert)

Hine, (William) Daryl 1936- . . . . CLC 15
See also CA 1-4R; CAAS 15; CANR 1, 20;
DLB 60

Hinkson, Katharine Tynan
See Tynan, Katharine

Hinton, S(usan) E(loise)
1950- . . . . CLC 30; DA
See also AAYA 2; CA 81-84; CANR 32;
CLR 3, 23; JRDA; MAICYA; MTCW;
SATA 19, 58

Hippius, Zinaida . . . . TCLC 9
See also Gippius, Zinaida (Nikolayevna)

Hiraoka, Kimitake 1925-1970
See Mishima, Yukio
See also CA 97-100; 29-32R; MTCW

Hirsch, E(ric) D(onald), Jr. 1928-. . . CLC 79
See also CA 25-28R; CANR 27; DLB 67;
MTCW

Hirsch, Edward 1950- . . . . CLC 31, 50
See also CA 104; CANR 20, 42; DLB 120

Hitchcock, Alfred (Joseph)
1899-1980 . . . . CLC 16
See also CA 97-100; SATA 24, 27

Hitler, Adolf 1889-1945 . . . . TCLC 53
See also CA 117

Hoagland, Edward 1932- . . . . CLC 28
See also CA 1-4R; CANR 2, 31; DLB 6;
SATA 51

Hoban, Russell (Conwell) 1925- . . CLC 7, 25
See also CA 5-8R; CANR 23, 37; CLR 3;
DLB 52; MAICYA; MTCW; SATA 1, 40

Hobbs, Perry
See Blackmur, R(ichard) P(almer)

Hobson, Laura Z(ametkin)
1900-1986 . . . . CLC 7, 25
See also CA 17-20R; 118; DLB 28;
SATA 52

Hochhuth, Rolf 1931-. . . . . . . CLC 4, 11, 18
See also CA 5-8R; CANR 33; DLB 124;
MTCW

Hochman, Sandra 1936- . . . . CLC 3, 8
See also CA 5-8R; DLB 5

Hochwaelder, Fritz 1911-1986. . . . . . CLC 36
See also CA 29-32R; 120; CANR 42;
MTCW

Hochwalder, Fritz
See Hochwaelder, Fritz

Hocking, Mary (Eunice) 1921- . . . . . CLC 13
See also CA 101; CANR 18, 40

Hodgins, Jack 1938-. . . . . CLC 23
See also CA 93-96; DLB 60

Hodgson, William Hope
1877(?)-1918 . . . . TCLC 13
See also CA 111; DLB 70

Hoffman, Alice 1952-. . . . . CLC 51
See also CA 77-80; CANR 34; MTCW

Hoffman, Daniel (Gerard)
1923- . . . . CLC 6, 13, 23
See also CA 1-4R; CANR 4; DLB 5

Hoffman, Stanley 1944-. . . . . CLC 5
See also CA 77-80

Hoffman, William M(oses) 1939- . . . CLC 40
See also CA 57-60; CANR 11

Hoffmann, E(rnst) T(heodor) A(madeus)
1776-1822 . . . . NCLC 2; SSC 13
See also DLB 90; SATA 27

Hofmann, Gert 1931-. . . . . CLC 54
See also CA 128

Hofmannsthal, Hugo von
1874-1929 . . . . TCLC 11; DC 4
See also CA 106; DLB 81, 118

Hogan, Linda 1947- . . . . CLC 73
See also CA 120

Hogarth, Charles
See Creasey, John

Hogg, James 1770-1835. . . . . NCLC 4
See also DLB 93, 116

Holbach, Paul Henri Thiry Baron
1723-1789 . . . . LC 14

Holberg, Ludvig 1684-1754 . . . . LC 6

Holden, Ursula 1921-. . . . . CLC 18
See also CA 101; CAAS 8; CANR 22

Holderlin, (Johann Christian) Friedrich
1770-1843 . . . . NCLC 16; PC 4

Holdstock, Robert
See Holdstock, Robert P.

Holdstock, Robert P. 1948-. . . . . . . CLC 39
See also CA 131

Holland, Isabelle 1920- . . . . CLC 21
See also CA 21-24R; CANR 10, 25; JRDA;
MAICYA; SATA 8, 70

Holland, Marcus
See Caldwell, (Janet Miriam) Taylor
(Holland)

Hollander, John 1929-. . . . . . CLC 2, 5, 8, 14
See also CA 1-4R; CANR 1; DLB 5;
SATA 13

Hollander, Paul
See Silverberg, Robert

Holleran, Andrew 1943(?)-. . . . . CLC 38

Hollinghurst, Alan 1954-. . . . . CLC 55
See also CA 114

Hollis, Jim
See Summers, Hollis (Spurgeon, Jr.)

Holmes, John
See Souster, (Holmes) Raymond

Holmes, John Clellon 1926-1988. . . . CLC 56
See also CA 9-12R; 125; CANR 4; DLB 16

Holmes, Oliver Wendell
1809-1894 . . . . NCLC 14
See also CDALB 1640-1865; DLB 1;
SATA 34

Holmes, Raymond
See Souster, (Holmes) Raymond

Holt, Victoria
See Hibbert, Eleanor Alice Burford

Holub, Miroslav 1923-. . . . . CLC 4
See also CA 21-24R; CANR 10

Homer c. 8th cent. B.C.- . . . . . . CMLC 1; DA

Honig, Edwin 1919- . . . . CLC 33
See also CA 5-8R; CAAS 8; CANR 4;
DLB 5

Hood, Hugh (John Blagdon)
1928- . . . . CLC 15, 28
See also CA 49-52; CAAS 17; CANR 1, 33;
DLB 53

Hood, Thomas 1799-1845. . . . . NCLC 16
See also DLB 96

Hooker, (Peter) Jeremy 1941-. . . . . . CLC 43
See also CA 77-80; CANR 22; DLB 40

Hope, A(lec) D(erwent) 1907- . . . . CLC 3, 51
See also CA 21-24R; CANR 33; MTCW

Hope, Brian
See Creasey, John

Hope, Christopher (David Tully)
1944- . . . . CLC 52
See also CA 106; SATA 62

Hopkins, Gerard Manley
1844-1889 . . . . NCLC 17; DA; WLC
See also CDBLB 1890-1914; DLB 35, 57

Hopkins, John (Richard) 1931-. . . . . . CLC 4
See also CA 85-88

Hopkins, Pauline Elizabeth
1859-1930 . . . . **TCLC 28; BLC**
See also CA 141; DLB 50

Hopkinson, Francis 1737-1791 . . . . . . **LC 25**
See also DLB 31

Hopley-Woolrich, Cornell George 1903-1968
See Woolrich, Cornell
See also CA 13-14; CAP 1

Horatio
See Proust, (Valentin-Louis-George-Eugene-)
Marcel

Horgan, Paul 1903- . . . . **CLC 9, 53**
See also CA 13-16R; CANR 9, 35;
DLB 102; DLBY 85; MTCW; SATA 13

Horn, Peter
See Kuttner, Henry

Hornem, Horace Esq.
See Byron, George Gordon (Noel)

Horovitz, Israel 1939- . . . . **CLC 56**
See also CA 33-36R; DLB 7

Horvath, Odon von
See Horvath, Oedoen von
See also DLB 85, 124

Horvath, Oedoen von 1901-1938 . . . **TCLC 45**
See also Horvath, Odon von
See also CA 118

Horwitz, Julius 1920-1986 . . . . **CLC 14**
See also CA 9-12R; 119; CANR 12

Hospital, Janette Turner 1942- . . . . . **CLC 42**
See also CA 108

Hostos, E. M. de
See Hostos (y Bonilla), Eugenio Maria de

Hostos, Eugenio M. de
See Hostos (y Bonilla), Eugenio Maria de

Hostos, Eugenio Maria
See Hostos (y Bonilla), Eugenio Maria de

Hostos (y Bonilla), Eugenio Maria de
1839-1903 . . . . **TCLC 24**
See also CA 123; 131; HW

Houdini
See Lovecraft, H(oward) P(hillips)

Hougan, Carolyn 1943- . . . . **CLC 34**
See also CA 139

Household, Geoffrey (Edward West)
1900-1988 . . . . **CLC 11**
See also CA 77-80; 126; DLB 87; SATA 14,
59

Housman, A(lfred) E(dward)
1859-1936 . . . . . . **TCLC 1, 10; DA; PC 2**
See also CA 104; 125; DLB 19; MTCW

Housman, Laurence 1865-1959 . . . . . **TCLC 7**
See also CA 106; DLB 10; SATA 25

Howard, Elizabeth Jane 1923- . . . **CLC 7, 29**
See also CA 5-8R; CANR 8

Howard, Maureen 1930- . . . . . **CLC 5, 14, 46**
See also CA 53-56; CANR 31; DLBY 83;
MTCW

Howard, Richard 1929- . . . . . . **CLC 7, 10, 47**
See also AITN 1; CA 85-88; CANR 25;
DLB 5

Howard, Robert Ervin 1906-1936 . . . **TCLC 8**
See also CA 105

Howard, Warren F.
See Pohl, Frederik

Howe, Fanny 1940- . . . . **CLC 47**
See also CA 117; SATA 52

Howe, Julia Ward 1819-1910 . . . . . **TCLC 21**
See also CA 117; DLB 1

Howe, Susan 1937- . . . . **CLC 72**
See also DLB 120

Howe, Tina 1937- . . . . **CLC 48**
See also CA 109

Howell, James 1594(?)-1666 . . . . **LC 13**

Howells, W. D.
See Howells, William Dean

Howells, William D.
See Howells, William Dean

Howells, William Dean
1837-1920 . . . . **TCLC 7, 17, 41**
See also CA 104; 134; CDALB 1865-1917;
DLB 12, 64, 74, 79

Howes, Barbara 1914- . . . . **CLC 15**
See also CA 9-12R; CAAS 3; SATA 5

Hrabal, Bohumil 1914- . . . . **CLC 13, 67**
See also CA 106; CAAS 12

Hsun, Lu . . . . **TCLC 3**
See also Shu-Jen, Chou

Hubbard, L(afayette) Ron(ald)
1911-1986 . . . . **CLC 43**
See also CA 77-80; 118; CANR 22

Huch, Ricarda (Octavia)
1864-1947 . . . . **TCLC 13**
See also CA 111; DLB 66

Huddle, David 1942- . . . . **CLC 49**
See also CA 57-60; DLB 130

Hudson, Jeffrey
See Crichton, (John) Michael

Hudson, W(illiam) H(enry)
1841-1922 . . . . **TCLC 29**
See also CA 115; DLB 98; SATA 35

Hueffer, Ford Madox
See Ford, Ford Madox

Hughart, Barry 1934- . . . . **CLC 39**
See also CA 137

Hughes, Colin
See Creasey, John

Hughes, David (John) 1930- . . . . **CLC 48**
See also CA 116; 129; DLB 14

Hughes, (James) Langston
1902-1967 . . . . . **CLC 1, 5, 10, 15, 35, 44;**
BLC; DA; DC 3; PC 1; SSC 6; WLC
See also BW; CA 1-4R; 25-28R; CANR 1,
34; CDALB 1929-1941; CLR 17; DLB 4,
7, 48, 51, 86; JRDA; MAICYA; MTCW;
SATA 4, 33

Hughes, Richard (Arthur Warren)
1900-1976 . . . . **CLC 1, 11**
See also CA 5-8R; 65-68; CANR 4;
DLB 15; MTCW; SATA 8, 25

Hughes, Ted
1930- . . . . **CLC 2, 4, 9, 14, 37; PC 7**
See also CA 1-4R; CANR 1, 33; CLR 3;
DLB 40; MAICYA; MTCW; SATA 27,
49

Hugo, Richard F(ranklin)
1923-1982 . . . . **CLC 6, 18, 32**
See also CA 49-52; 108; CANR 3; DLB 5

Hugo, Victor (Marie)
1802-1885 . . **NCLC 3, 10, 21; DA; WLC**
See also DLB 119; SATA 47

Huidobro, Vicente
See Huidobro Fernandez, Vicente Garcia

Huidobro Fernandez, Vicente Garcia
1893-1948 . . . . **TCLC 31**
See also CA 131; HW

Hulme, Keri 1947- . . . . **CLC 39**
See also CA 125

Hulme, T(homas) E(rnest)
1883-1917 . . . . **TCLC 21**
See also CA 117; DLB 19

Hume, David 1711-1776 . . . . **LC 7**
See also DLB 104

Humphrey, William 1924- . . . . **CLC 45**
See also CA 77-80; DLB 6

Humphreys, Emyr Owen 1919- . . . . . **CLC 47**
See also CA 5-8R; CANR 3, 24; DLB 15

Humphreys, Josephine 1945- . . . . **CLC 34, 57**
See also CA 121; 127

Hungerford, Pixie
See Brinsmead, H(esba) F(ay)

Hunt, E(verette) Howard, Jr.
1918- . . . . **CLC 3**
See also AITN 1; CA 45-48; CANR 2

Hunt, Kyle
See Creasey, John

Hunt, (James Henry) Leigh
1784-1859 . . . . **NCLC 1**

Hunt, Marsha 1946- . . . . **CLC 70**
See also CA 143

Hunt, Violet 1866-1942 . . . . **TCLC 53**

Hunter, E. Waldo
See Sturgeon, Theodore (Hamilton)

Hunter, Evan 1926- . . . . **CLC 11, 31**
See also CA 5-8R; CANR 5, 38; DLBY 82;
MTCW; SATA 25

Hunter, Kristin (Eggleston) 1931- . . . **CLC 35**
See also AITN 1; BW; CA 13-16R;
CANR 13; CLR 3; DLB 33; MAICYA;
SAAS 10; SATA 12

Hunter, Mollie 1922- . . . . **CLC 21**
See also McIlwraith, Maureen Mollie
Hunter
See also CANR 37; CLR 25; JRDA;
MAICYA; SAAS 7; SATA 54

Hunter, Robert (?)-1734 . . . . **LC 7**

Hurston, Zora Neale
1903-1960 . . . . **CLC 7, 30, 61; BLC; DA;**
SSC 4
See also BW; CA 85-88; DLB 51, 86;
MTCW

Huston, John (Marcellus)
1906-1987 . . . . **CLC 20**
See also CA 73-76; 123; CANR 34; DLB 26

Hustvedt, Siri 1955- . . . . **CLC 76**
See also CA 137

Hutten, Ulrich von 1488-1523 . . . . . . **LC 16**

Huxley, Aldous (Leonard)
1894-1963 . . . . . **CLC 1, 3, 4, 5, 8, 11, 18,**
35, 79; DA; WLC
See also CA 85-88; CDBLB 1914-1945;
DLB 36, 100; MTCW; SATA 63

Huysmans, Charles Marie Georges
1848-1907
See Huysmans, Joris-Karl
See also CA 104

Huysmans, Joris-Karl . . . . TCLC 7
See also Huysmans, Charles Marie Georges
See also DLB 123

Hwang, David Henry
1957- . . . . CLC 55; DC 4
See also CA 127; 132

Hyde, Anthony 1946- . . . . CLC 42
See also CA 136

Hyde, Margaret O(ldroyd) 1917- . . . CLC 21
See also CA 1-4R; CANR 1, 36; CLR 23;
JRDA; MAICYA; SAAS 8; SATA 1, 42,
76

Hynes, James 1956(?)- . . . . CLC 65

Ian, Janis 1951- . . . . CLC 21
See also CA 105

Ibanez, Vicente Blasco
See Blasco Ibanez, Vicente

Ibarguengoitia, Jorge 1928-1983 . . . . CLC 37
See also CA 124; 113; HW

Ibsen, Henrik (Johan)
1828-1906 . . . . TCLC 2, 8, 16, 37, 52;
DA; DC 2; WLC
See also CA 104; 141

Ibuse Masuji 1898-1993 . . . . CLC 22
See also CA 127; 141

Ichikawa, Kon 1915- . . . . CLC 20
See also CA 121

Idle, Eric 1943- . . . . CLC 21
See also Monty Python
See also CA 116; CANR 35

Ignatow, David 1914- . . . . . . CLC 4, 7, 14, 40
See also CA 9-12R; CAAS 3; CANR 31;
DLB 5

Ihimaera, Witi 1944- . . . . CLC 46
See also CA 77-80

Ilf, Ilya . . . . TCLC 21
See also Fainzilberg, Ilya Arnoldovich

Immermann, Karl (Lebrecht)
1796-1840 . . . . NCLC 4
See also DLB 133

Inclan, Ramon (Maria) del Valle
See Valle-Inclan, Ramon (Maria) del

Infante, G(uillermo) Cabrera
See Cabrera Infante, G(uillermo)

Ingalls, Rachel (Holmes) 1940- . . . . . CLC 42
See also CA 123; 127

Ingamells, Rex 1913-1955 . . . . TCLC 35

Inge, William Motter
1913-1973 . . . . CLC 1, 8, 19
See also CA 9-12R; CDALB 1941-1968;
DLB 7; MTCW

Ingelow, Jean 1820-1897 . . . . NCLC 39
See also DLB 35; SATA 33

Ingram, Willis J.
See Harris, Mark

Innaurato, Albert (F.) 1948(?)- . . CLC 21, 60
See also CA 115; 122

Innes, Michael
See Stewart, J(ohn) I(nnes) M(ackintosh)

Ionesco, Eugene
1912- . . . . CLC 1, 4, 6, 9, 11, 15, 41; DA;
WLC
See also CA 9-12R; MTCW; SATA 7

Iqbal, Muhammad 1873-1938 . . . . . TCLC 28

Ireland, Patrick
See O'Doherty, Brian

Iron, Ralph
See Schreiner, Olive (Emilie Albertina)

Irving, John (Winslow)
1942- . . . . CLC 13, 23, 38
See also AAYA 8; BEST 89:3; CA 25-28R;
CANR 28; DLB 6; DLBY 82; MTCW

Irving, Washington
1783-1859 . . . . NCLC 2, 19; DA; SSC 2;
WLC
See also CDALB 1640-1865; DLB 3, 11, 30,
59, 73, 74; YABC 2

Irwin, P. K.
See Page, P(atricia) K(athleen)

Isaacs, Susan 1943- . . . . CLC 32
See also BEST 89:1; CA 89-92; CANR 20,
41; MTCW

Isherwood, Christopher (William Bradshaw)
1904-1986 . . . . CLC 1, 9, 11, 14, 44
See also CA 13-16R; 117; CANR 35;
DLB 15; DLBY 86; MTCW

Ishiguro, Kazuo 1954- . . . . . . CLC 27, 56, 59
See also BEST 90:2; CA 120; MTCW

Ishikawa Takuboku
1886(?)-1912 . . . . TCLC 15
See also CA 113

Iskander, Fazil 1929- . . . . CLC 47
See also CA 102

Ivan IV 1530-1584 . . . . LC 17

Ivanov, Vyacheslav Ivanovich
1866-1949 . . . . TCLC 33
See also CA 122

Ivask, Ivar Vidrik 1927-1992 . . . . . . CLC 14
See also CA 37-40R; 139; CANR 24

Jackson, Daniel
See Wingrove, David (John)

Jackson, Jesse 1908-1983 . . . . CLC 12
See also BW; CA 25-28R; 109; CANR 27;
CLR 28; MAICYA; SATA 2, 29, 48

Jackson, Laura (Riding) 1901-1991
See Riding, Laura
See also CA 65-68; 135; CANR 28; DLB 48

Jackson, Sam
See Trumbo, Dalton

Jackson, Sara
See Wingrove, David (John)

Jackson, Shirley
1919-1965 . . . . . CLC 11, 60; DA; SSC 9;
WLC
See also AAYA 9; CA 1-4R; 25-28R;
CANR 4; CDALB 1941-1968; DLB 6;
SATA 2

Jacob, (Cyprien-)Max 1876-1944 . . . TCLC 6
See also CA 104

Jacobs, Jim 1942- . . . . CLC 12
See also CA 97-100

Jacobs, W(illiam) W(ymark)
1863-1943 . . . . TCLC 22
See also CA 121; DLB 135

Jacobsen, Jens Peter 1847-1885 . . NCLC 34

Jacobsen, Josephine 1908- . . . . CLC 48
See also CA 33-36R; CAAS 18; CANR 23

Jacobson, Dan 1929- . . . . CLC 4, 14
See also CA 1-4R; CANR 2, 25; DLB 14;
MTCW

Jacqueline
See Carpentier (y Valmont), Alejo

Jagger, Mick 1944- . . . . CLC 17

Jakes, John (William) 1932- . . . . CLC 29
See also BEST 89:4; CA 57-60; CANR 10,
43; DLBY 83; MTCW; SATA 62

James, Andrew
See Kirkup, James

James, C(yril) L(ionel) R(obert)
1901-1989 . . . . CLC 33
See also BW; CA 117; 125; 128; DLB 125;
MTCW

James, Daniel (Lewis) 1911-1988
See Santiago, Danny
See also CA 125

James, Dynely
See Mayne, William (James Carter)

James, Henry
1843-1916 . . . . . . TCLC 2, 11, 24, 40, 47;
DA; SSC 8; WLC
See also CA 104; 132; CDALB 1865-1917;
DLB 12, 71, 74; MTCW

James, Montague (Rhodes)
1862-1936 . . . . TCLC 6
See also CA 104

James, P. D. . . . . CLC 18, 46
See also White, Phyllis Dorothy James
See also BEST 90:2; CDBLB 1960 to
Present; DLB 87

James, Philip
See Moorcock, Michael (John)

James, William 1842-1910 . . . . . TCLC 15, 32
See also CA 109

James I 1394-1437 . . . . LC 20

Jameson, Anna 1794-1860 . . . . NCLC 43
See also DLB 99

Jami, Nur al-Din 'Abd al-Rahman
1414-1492 . . . . LC 9

Jandl, Ernst 1925- . . . . CLC 34

Janowitz, Tama 1957- . . . . CLC 43
See also CA 106

Jarrell, Randall
1914-1965 . . . . CLC 1, 2, 6, 9, 13, 49
See also CA 5-8R; 25-28R; CABS 2;
CANR 6, 34; CDALB 1941-1968; CLR 6;
DLB 48, 52; MAICYA; MTCW; SATA 7

Jarry, Alfred 1873-1907 . . . . TCLC 2, 14
See also CA 104

Jarvis, E. K.
See Bloch, Robert (Albert); Ellison, Harlan;
Silverberg, Robert

Jeake, Samuel, Jr.
See Aiken, Conrad (Potter)

Jean Paul 1763-1825 . . . . NCLC 7

Joyce, James (Augustine Aloysius)
 1882-1941 ..... **TCLC 3, 8, 16, 35; DA;
 SSC 3; WLC**
 See also CA 104; 126; CDBLB 1914-1945;
 DLB 10, 19, 36; MTCW

Jozsef, Attila 1905-1937......... **TCLC 22**
 See also CA 116

Juana Ines de la Cruz 1651(?)-1695 ... **LC 5**

Judd, Cyril
 See Kornbluth, C(yril) M.; Pohl, Frederik

Julian of Norwich 1342(?)-1416(?) .... **LC 6**

Just, Ward (Swift) 1935- .... **CLC 4, 27**
 See also CA 25-28R; CANR 32

Justice, Donald (Rodney) 1925- .. **CLC 6, 19**
 See also CA 5-8R; CANR 26; DLBY 83

Juvenal c. 55-c. 127 .... **CMLC 8**

Juvenis
 See Bourne, Randolph S(illiman)

Kacew, Romain 1914-1980
 See Gary, Romain
 See also CA 108; 102

Kadare, Ismail 1936- .... **CLC 52**

Kadohata, Cynthia................. **CLC 59**
 See also CA 140

Kafka, Franz
 1883-1924 .... **TCLC 2, 6, 13, 29, 47, 53;
 DA; SSC 5; WLC**
 See also CA 105; 126; DLB 81; MTCW

Kahn, Roger 1927-............... **CLC 30**
 See also CA 25-28R; SATA 37

Kain, Saul
 See Sassoon, Siegfried (Lorraine)

Kaiser, Georg 1878-1945 .... **TCLC 9**
 See also CA 106; DLB 124

Kaletski, Alexander 1946-......... **CLC 39**
 See also CA 118; 143

Kalidasa fl. c. 400- .... **CMLC 9**

Kallman, Chester (Simon)
 1921-1975 .... **CLC 2**
 See also CA 45-48; 53-56; CANR 3

Kaminsky, Melvin 1926-
 See Brooks, Mel
 See also CA 65-68; CANR 16

Kaminsky, Stuart M(elvin) 1934- ... **CLC 59**
 See also CA 73-76; CANR 29

Kane, Paul
 See Simon, Paul

Kane, Wilson
 See Bloch, Robert (Albert)

Kanin, Garson 1912-.............. **CLC 22**
 See also AITN 1; CA 5-8R; CANR 7;
 DLB 7

Kaniuk, Yoram 1930-............. **CLC 19**
 See also CA 134

Kant, Immanuel 1724-1804 ...... **NCLC 27**
 See also DLB 94

Kantor, MacKinlay 1904-1977 ...... **CLC 7**
 See also CA 61-64; 73-76; DLB 9, 102

Kaplan, David Michael 1946- ...... **CLC 50**

Kaplan, James 1951- .... **CLC 59**
 See also CA 135

Karageorge, Michael
 See Anderson, Poul (William)

Karamzin, Nikolai Mikhailovich
 1766-1826 .... **NCLC 3**

Karapanou, Margarita 1946-....... **CLC 13**
 See also CA 101

Karinthy, Frigyes 1887-1938..... **TCLC 47**

Karl, Frederick R(obert) 1927- ..... **CLC 34**
 See also CA 5-8R; CANR 3

Kastel, Warren
 See Silverberg, Robert

Kataev, Evgeny Petrovich 1903-1942
 See Petrov, Evgeny
 See also CA 120

Kataphusin
 See Ruskin, John

Katz, Steve 1935-................. **CLC 47**
 See also CA 25-28R; CAAS 14; CANR 12;
 DLBY 83

Kauffman, Janet 1945-............ **CLC 42**
 See also CA 117; CANR 43; DLBY 86

Kaufman, Bob (Garnell)
 1925-1986 .... **CLC 49**
 See also BW; CA 41-44R; 118; CANR 22;
 DLB 16, 41

Kaufman, George S. 1889-1961..... **CLC 38**
 See also CA 108; 93-96; DLB 7

Kaufman, Sue .... **CLC 3, 8**
 See also Barondess, Sue K(aufman)

Kavafis, Konstantinos Petrou 1863-1933
 See Cavafy, C(onstantine) P(eter)
 See also CA 104

Kavan, Anna 1901-1968...... **CLC 5, 13, 82**
 See also CA 5-8R; CANR 6; MTCW

Kavanagh, Dan
 See Barnes, Julian

Kavanagh, Patrick (Joseph)
 1904-1967 .... **CLC 22**
 See also CA 123; 25-28R; DLB 15, 20;
 MTCW

Kawabata, Yasunari
 1899-1972 ....**CLC 2, 5, 9, 18**
 See also CA 93-96; 33-36R

Kaye, M(ary) M(argaret) 1909-..... **CLC 28**
 See also CA 89-92; CANR 24; MTCW;
 SATA 62

Kaye, Mollie
 See Kaye, M(ary) M(argaret)

Kaye-Smith, Sheila 1887-1956..... **TCLC 20**
 See also CA 118; DLB 36

Kaymor, Patrice Maguilene
 See Senghor, Leopold Sedar

Kazan, Elia 1909-........... **CLC 6, 16, 63**
 See also CA 21-24R; CANR 32

Kazantzakis, Nikos
 1883(?)-1957 .... **TCLC 2, 5, 33**
 See also CA 105; 132; MTCW

Kazin, Alfred 1915- .... **CLC 34, 38**
 See also CA 1-4R; CAAS 7; CANR 1;
 DLB 67

Keane, Mary Nesta (Skrine) 1904-
 See Keane, Molly
 See also CA 108; 114

Keane, Molly.................... **CLC 31**
 See also Keane, Mary Nesta (Skrine)

Keates, Jonathan 19(?)-........... **CLC 34**

Keaton, Buster 1895-1966 .... **CLC 20**

Keats, John
 1795-1821 ... **NCLC 8; DA; PC 1; WLC**
 See also CDBLB 1789-1832; DLB 96, 110

Keene, Donald 1922- .... **CLC 34**
 See also CA 1-4R; CANR 5

Keillor, Garrison .... **CLC 40**
 See also Keillor, Gary (Edward)
 See also AAYA 2; BEST 89:3; DLBY 87;
 SATA 58

Keillor, Gary (Edward) 1942-
 See Keillor, Garrison
 See also CA 111; 117; CANR 36; MTCW

Keith, Michael
 See Hubbard, L(afayette) Ron(ald)

Keller, Gottfried 1819-1890....... **NCLC 2**
 See also DLB 129

Kellerman, Jonathan 1949- .... **CLC 44**
 See also BEST 90:1; CA 106; CANR 29

Kelley, William Melvin 1937-...... **CLC 22**
 See also BW; CA 77-80; CANR 27; DLB 33

Kellogg, Marjorie 1922-........... **CLC 2**
 See also CA 81-84

Kellow, Kathleen
 See Hibbert, Eleanor Alice Burford

Kelly, M(ilton) T(erry) 1947-....... **CLC 55**
 See also CA 97-100; CANR 19, 43

Kelman, James 1946-............. **CLC 58**

Kemal, Yashar 1923- .... **CLC 14, 29**
 See also CA 89-92

Kemble, Fanny 1809-1893 .... **NCLC 18**
 See also DLB 32

Kemelman, Harry 1908-............ **CLC 2**
 See also AITN 1; CA 9-12R; CANR 6;
 DLB 28

Kempe, Margery 1373(?)-1440(?) ..... **LC 6**

Kempis, Thomas a 1380-1471 .... **LC 11**

Kendall, Henry 1839-1882....... **NCLC 12**

Keneally, Thomas (Michael)
 1935- ...... **CLC 5, 8, 10, 14, 19, 27, 43**
 See also CA 85-88; CANR 10; MTCW

Kennedy, Adrienne (Lita)
 1931- .... **CLC 66; BLC**
 See also BW; CA 103; CABS 3; CANR 26;
 DLB 38

Kennedy, John Pendleton
 1795-1870 .... **NCLC 2**
 See also DLB 3

Kennedy, Joseph Charles 1929-...... **CLC 8**
 See also Kennedy, X. J.
 See also CA 1-4R; CANR 4, 30, 40;
 SATA 14

Kennedy, William 1928-... **CLC 6, 28, 34, 53**
 See also AAYA 1; CA 85-88; CANR 14,
 31; DLBY 85; MTCW; SATA 57

Kennedy, X. J..................... **CLC 42**
 See also Kennedy, Joseph Charles
 See also CAAS 9; CLR 27; DLB 5

Kent, Kelvin
 See Kuttner, Henry

Kenton, Maxwell
 See Southern, Terry

Kenyon, Robert O.
See Kuttner, Henry

Kerouac, Jack ..... **CLC 1, 2, 3, 5, 14, 29, 61**
See also Kerouac, Jean-Louis Lebris de
See also CDALB 1941-1968; DLB 2, 16;
DLBD 3

Kerouac, Jean-Louis Lebris de 1922-1969
See Kerouac, Jack
See also AITN 1; CA 5-8R; 25-28R;
CANR 26; DA; MTCW; WLC

Kerr, Jean 1923- .... **CLC 22**
See also CA 5-8R; CANR 7

Kerr, M. E. .... **CLC 12, 35**
See also Meaker, Marijane (Agnes)
See also AAYA 2; CLR 29; SAAS 1

Kerr, Robert .... **CLC 55**

Kerrigan, (Thomas) Anthony
1918- .... **CLC 4, 6**
See also CA 49-52; CAAS 11; CANR 4

Kerry, Lois
See Duncan, Lois

Kesey, Ken (Elton)
1935- ...... **CLC 1, 3, 6, 11, 46, 64; DA;**
WLC
See also CA 1-4R; CANR 22, 38;
CDALB 1968-1988; DLB 2, 16; MTCW;
SATA 66

Kesselring, Joseph (Otto)
1902-1967 .... **CLC 45**

Kessler, Jascha (Frederick) 1929- .... **CLC 4**
See also CA 17-20R; CANR 8

Kettelkamp, Larry (Dale) 1933- .... **CLC 12**
See also CA 29-32R; CANR 16; SAAS 3;
SATA 2

Keyber, Conny
See Fielding, Henry

Keyes, Daniel 1927- .... **CLC 80; DA**
See also CA 17-20R; CANR 10, 26;
SATA 37

Khayyam, Omar
1048-1131 .... **CMLC 11; PC 8**

Kherdian, David 1931- .... **CLC 6, 9**
See also CA 21-24R; CAAS 2; CANR 39;
CLR 24; JRDA; MAICYA; SATA 16, 74

Khlebnikov, Velimir .... **TCLC 20**
See also Khlebnikov, Viktor Vladimirovich

Khlebnikov, Viktor Vladimirovich 1885-1922
See Khlebnikov, Velimir
See also CA 117

Khodasevich, Vladislav (Felitsianovich)
1886-1939 .... **TCLC 15**
See also CA 115

Kielland, Alexander Lange
1849-1906 .... **TCLC 5**
See also CA 104

Kiely, Benedict 1919- .... **CLC 23, 43**
See also CA 1-4R; CANR 2; DLB 15

Kienzle, William X(avier) 1928- .... **CLC 25**
See also CA 93-96; CAAS 1; CANR 9, 31;
MTCW

Kierkegaard, Soren 1813-1855 .... **NCLC 34**

Killens, John Oliver 1916-1987 ..... **CLC 10**
See also BW; CA 77-80; 123; CAAS 2;
CANR 26; DLB 33

Killigrew, Anne 1660-1685 .... **LC 4**
See also DLB 131

Kim
See Simenon, Georges (Jacques Christian)

Kincaid, Jamaica 1949- ... **CLC 43, 68; BLC**
See also BW; CA 125

King, Francis (Henry) 1923- ..... **CLC 8, 53**
See also CA 1-4R; CANR 1, 33; DLB 15;
MTCW

King, Stephen (Edwin)
1947- .... **CLC 12, 26, 37, 61**
See also AAYA 1; BEST 90:1; CA 61-64;
CANR 1, 30; DLBY 80; JRDA; MTCW;
SATA 9, 55

King, Steve
See King, Stephen (Edwin)

Kingman, Lee .... **CLC 17**
See also Natti, (Mary) Lee
See also SAAS 3; SATA 1, 67

Kingsley, Charles 1819-1875 ..... **NCLC 35**
See also DLB 21, 32; YABC 2

Kingsley, Sidney 1906- .... **CLC 44**
See also CA 85-88; DLB 7

Kingsolver, Barbara 1955- ...... **CLC 55, 81**
See also CA 129; 134

Kingston, Maxine (Ting Ting) Hong
1940- .... **CLC 12, 19, 58**
See also AAYA 8; CA 69-72; CANR 13,
38; DLBY 80; MTCW; SATA 53

Kinnell, Galway
1927- .... **CLC 1, 2, 3, 5, 13, 29**
See also CA 9-12R; CANR 10, 34; DLB 5;
DLBY 87; MTCW

Kinsella, Thomas 1928- .... **CLC 4, 19**
See also CA 17-20R; CANR 15; DLB 27;
MTCW

Kinsella, W(illiam) P(atrick)
1935- .... **CLC 27, 43**
See also AAYA 7; CA 97-100; CAAS 7;
CANR 21, 35; MTCW

Kipling, (Joseph) Rudyard
1865-1936 ...... **TCLC 8, 17; DA; PC 3;**
SSC 5; WLC
See also CA 105; 120; CANR 33;
CDBLB 1890-1914; DLB 19, 34;
MAICYA; MTCW; YABC 2

Kirkup, James 1918- .... **CLC 1**
See also CA 1-4R; CAAS 4; CANR 2;
DLB 27; SATA 12

Kirkwood, James 1930(?)-1989 ...... **CLC 9**
See also AITN 2; CA 1-4R; 128; CANR 6,
40

Kis, Danilo 1935-1989 .... **CLC 57**
See also CA 109; 118; 129; MTCW

Kivi, Aleksis 1834-1872 .... **NCLC 30**

Kizer, Carolyn (Ashley)
1925- .... **CLC 15, 39, 80**
See also CA 65-68; CAAS 5; CANR 24;
DLB 5

Klabund 1890-1928 .... **TCLC 44**
See also DLB 66

Klappert, Peter 1942- .... **CLC 57**
See also CA 33-36R; DLB 5

Klein, A(braham) M(oses)
1909-1972 .... **CLC 19**
See also CA 101; 37-40R; DLB 68

Klein, Norma 1938-1989 .... **CLC 30**
See also AAYA 2; CA 41-44R; 128;
CANR 15, 37; CLR 2, 19; JRDA;
MAICYA; SAAS 1; SATA 7, 57

Klein, T(heodore) E(ibon) D(onald)
1947- .... **CLC 34**
See also CA 119

Kleist, Heinrich von
1777-1811 .... **NCLC 2, 37**
See also DLB 90

Klima, Ivan 1931- .... **CLC 56**
See also CA 25-28R; CANR 17

Klimentov, Andrei Platonovich 1899-1951
See Platonov, Andrei
See also CA 108

Klinger, Friedrich Maximilian von
1752-1831 .... **NCLC 1**
See also DLB 94

Klopstock, Friedrich Gottlieb
1724-1803 .... **NCLC 11**
See also DLB 97

Knebel, Fletcher 1911-1993 .... **CLC 14**
See also AITN 1; CA 1-4R; 140; CAAS 3;
CANR 1, 36; SATA 36; SATA-Obit 75

Knickerbocker, Diedrich
See Irving, Washington

Knight, Etheridge
1931-1991 .... **CLC 40; BLC**
See also BW; CA 21-24R; 133; CANR 23;
DLB 41

Knight, Sarah Kemble 1666-1727 ..... **LC 7**
See also DLB 24

Knowles, John
1926- .... **CLC 1, 4, 10, 26; DA**
See also AAYA 10; CA 17-20R; CANR 40;
CDALB 1968-1988; DLB 6; MTCW;
SATA 8

Knox, Calvin M.
See Silverberg, Robert

Knye, Cassandra
See Disch, Thomas M(ichael)

Koch, C(hristopher) J(ohn) 1932- ... **CLC 42**
See also CA 127

Koch, Christopher
See Koch, C(hristopher) J(ohn)

Koch, Kenneth 1925- .... **CLC 5, 8, 44**
See also CA 1-4R; CANR 6, 36; DLB 5;
SATA 65

Kochanowski, Jan 1530-1584 .... **LC 10**

Kock, Charles Paul de
1794-1871 .... **NCLC 16**

Koda Shigeyuki 1867-1947
See Rohan, Koda
See also CA 121

Koestler, Arthur
1905-1983 .... **CLC 1, 3, 6, 8, 15, 33**
See also CA 1-4R; 109; CANR 1, 33;
CDBLB 1945-1960; DLBY 83; MTCW

Kogawa, Joy Nozomi 1935- .... **CLC 78**
See also CA 101; CANR 19

Kohout, Pavel 1928- .... **CLC 13**
See also CA 45-48; CANR 3

L'Amour, Louis (Dearborn)
1908-1988 . . . . **CLC 25, 55**
See also AITN 2; BEST 89:2; CA 1-4R;
125; CANR 3, 25, 40; DLBY 80; MTCW

Lampedusa, Giuseppe (Tomasi) di . . . **TCLC 13**
See also Tomasi di Lampedusa, Giuseppe

Lampman, Archibald 1861-1899 . . **NCLC 25**
See also DLB 92

Lancaster, Bruce 1896-1963. . . . . . . **CLC 36**
See also CA 9-10; CAP 1; SATA 9

Landau, Mark Alexandrovich
See Aldanov, Mark (Alexandrovich)

Landau-Aldanov, Mark Alexandrovich
See Aldanov, Mark (Alexandrovich)

Landis, John 1950- . . . . **CLC 26**
See also CA 112; 122

Landolfi, Tommaso 1908-1979. . . **CLC 11, 49**
See also CA 127; 117

Landon, Letitia Elizabeth
1802-1838 . . . . **NCLC 15**
See also DLB 96

Landor, Walter Savage
1775-1864 . . . . **NCLC 14**
See also DLB 93, 107

Landwirth, Heinz 1927-
See Lind, Jakov
See also CA 9-12R; CANR 7

Lane, Patrick 1939- . . . . **CLC 25**
See also CA 97-100; DLB 53

Lang, Andrew 1844-1912 . . . . **TCLC 16**
See also CA 114; 137; DLB 98; MAICYA;
SATA 16

Lang, Fritz 1890-1976 . . . . **CLC 20**
See also CA 77-80; 69-72; CANR 30

Lange, John
See Crichton, (John) Michael

Langer, Elinor 1939- . . . . **CLC 34**
See also CA 121

Langland, William
1330(?)-1400(?) . . . . **LC 19; DA**

Langstaff, Launcelot
See Irving, Washington

Lanier, Sidney 1842-1881 . . . . **NCLC 6**
See also DLB 64; MAICYA; SATA 18

Lanyer, Aemilia 1569-1645 . . . . **LC 10**

Lao Tzu . . . . **CMLC 7**

Lapine, James (Elliot) 1949- . . . . **CLC 39**
See also CA 123; 130

Larbaud, Valery (Nicolas)
1881-1957 . . . . **TCLC 9**
See also CA 106

Lardner, Ring
See Lardner, Ring(gold) W(ilmer)

Lardner, Ring W., Jr.
See Lardner, Ring(gold) W(ilmer)

Lardner, Ring(gold) W(ilmer)
1885-1933 . . . . **TCLC 2, 14**
See also CA 104; 131; CDALB 1917-1929;
DLB 11, 25, 86; MTCW

Laredo, Betty
See Codrescu, Andrei

Larkin, Maia
See Wojciechowska, Maia (Teresa)

Larkin, Philip (Arthur)
1922-1985 . . . . **CLC 3, 5, 8, 9, 13, 18, 33,
39, 64**
See also CA 5-8R; 117; CANR 24;
CDBLB 1960 to Present; DLB 27;
MTCW

Larra (y Sanchez de Castro), Mariano Jose de
1809-1837 . . . . **NCLC 17**

Larsen, Eric 1941- . . . . **CLC 55**
See also CA 132

Larsen, Nella 1891-1964 . . . . . **CLC 37; BLC**
See also BW; CA 125; DLB 51

Larson, Charles R(aymond) 1938-. . . **CLC 31**
See also CA 53-56; CANR 4

Latham, Jean Lee 1902-. . . . . **CLC 12**
See also AITN 1; CA 5-8R; CANR 7;
MAICYA; SATA 2, 68

Latham, Mavis
See Clark, Mavis Thorpe

Lathen, Emma . . . . **CLC 2**
See also Hennissart, Martha; Latsis, Mary
J(ane)

Lathrop, Francis
See Leiber, Fritz (Reuter, Jr.)

Latsis, Mary J(ane)
See Lathen, Emma
See also CA 85-88

Lattimore, Richmond (Alexander)
1906-1984 . . . . **CLC 3**
See also CA 1-4R; 112; CANR 1

Laughlin, James 1914-. . . . . **CLC 49**
See also CA 21-24R; CANR 9; DLB 48

Laurence, (Jean) Margaret (Wemyss)
1926-1987 . . **CLC 3, 6, 13, 50, 62; SSC 7**
See also CA 5-8R; 121; CANR 33; DLB 53;
MTCW; SATA 50

Laurent, Antoine 1952- . . . . **CLC 50**

Lauscher, Hermann
See Hesse, Hermann

Lautreamont, Comte de
1846-1870 . . . . **NCLC 12; SSC 14**

Laverty, Donald
See Blish, James (Benjamin)

Lavin, Mary 1912- . . . . . . **CLC 4, 18; SSC 4**
See also CA 9-12R; CANR 33; DLB 15;
MTCW

Lavond, Paul Dennis
See Kornbluth, C(yril) M.; Pohl, Frederik

Lawler, Raymond Evenor 1922- . . . . **CLC 58**
See also CA 103

Lawrence, D(avid) H(erbert Richards)
1885-1930 . . . . **TCLC 2, 9, 16, 33, 48;
DA; SSC 4; WLC**
See also CA 104; 121; CDBLB 1914-1945;
DLB 10, 19, 36, 98; MTCW

Lawrence, T(homas) E(dward)
1888-1935 . . . . **TCLC 18**
See also Dale, Colin
See also CA 115

Lawrence of Arabia
See Lawrence, T(homas) E(dward)

Lawson, Henry (Archibald Hertzberg)
1867-1922 . . . . **TCLC 27**
See also CA 120

Lawton, Dennis
See Faust, Frederick (Schiller)

Laxness, Halldor . . . . **CLC 25**
See also Gudjonsson, Halldor Kiljan

Layamon fl. c. 1200-. . . . . **CMLC 10**

Laye, Camara 1928-1980 . . . **CLC 4, 38; BLC**
See also BW; CA 85-88; 97-100; CANR 25;
MTCW

Layton, Irving (Peter) 1912- . . . . . **CLC 2, 15**
See also CA 1-4R; CANR 2, 33, 43;
DLB 88; MTCW

Lazarus, Emma 1849-1887. . . . . **NCLC 8**

Lazarus, Felix
See Cable, George Washington

Lazarus, Henry
See Slavitt, David R(ytman)

Lea, Joan
See Neufeld, John (Arthur)

Leacock, Stephen (Butler)
1869-1944 . . . . **TCLC 2**
See also CA 104; 141; DLB 92

Lear, Edward 1812-1888 . . . . **NCLC 3**
See also CLR 1; DLB 32; MAICYA;
SATA 18

Lear, Norman (Milton) 1922- . . . . . . **CLC 12**
See also CA 73-76

Leavis, F(rank) R(aymond)
1895-1978 . . . . **CLC 24**
See also CA 21-24R; 77-80; MTCW

Leavitt, David 1961-. . . . . **CLC 34**
See also CA 116; 122; DLB 130

Leblanc, Maurice (Marie Emile)
1864-1941 . . . . **TCLC 49**
See also CA 110

Lebowitz, Fran(ces Ann)
1951(?)- . . . . **CLC 11, 36**
See also CA 81-84; CANR 14; MTCW

le Carre, John . . . . **CLC 3, 5, 9, 15, 28**
See also Cornwell, David (John Moore)
See also BEST 89:4; CDBLB 1960 to
Present; DLB 87

Le Clezio, J(ean) M(arie) G(ustave)
1940- . . . . **CLC 31**
See also CA 116; 128; DLB 83

Leconte de Lisle, Charles-Marie-Rene
1818-1894 . . . . **NCLC 29**

Le Coq, Monsieur
See Simenon, Georges (Jacques Christian)

Leduc, Violette 1907-1972. . . . . **CLC 22**
See also CA 13-14; 33-36R; CAP 1

Ledwidge, Francis 1887(?)-1917 . . . **TCLC 23**
See also CA 123; DLB 20

Lee, Andrea 1953- . . . . **CLC 36; BLC**
See also BW; CA 125

Lee, Andrew
See Auchincloss, Louis (Stanton)

Lee, Don L. . . . . **CLC 2**
See also Madhubuti, Haki R.

Lee, George W(ashington)
1894-1976 . . . . **CLC 52; BLC**
See also BW; CA 125; DLB 51

Lee, (Nelle) Harper
1926- .... **CLC 12, 60; DA; WLC**
See also CA 13-16R; CDALB 1941-1968;
DLB 6; MTCW; SATA 11

Lee, Julian
See Latham, Jean Lee

Lee, Larry
See Lee, Lawrence

Lee, Lawrence 1941-1990......... **CLC 34**
See also CA 131; CANR 43

Lee, Manfred B(ennington)
1905-1971 .... **CLC 11**
See also Queen, Ellery
See also CA 1-4R; 29-32R; CANR 2

Lee, Stan 1922-................. **CLC 17**
See also AAYA 5; CA 108; 111

Lee, Tanith 1947-............... **CLC 46**
See also CA 37-40R; SATA 8

Lee, Vernon...................... **TCLC 5**
See also Paget, Violet
See also DLB 57

Lee, William
See Burroughs, William S(eward)

Lee, Willy
See Burroughs, William S(eward)

Lee-Hamilton, Eugene (Jacob)
1845-1907 .... **TCLC 22**
See also CA 117

Leet, Judith 1935- .... **CLC 11**

Le Fanu, Joseph Sheridan
1814-1873 .... **NCLC 9; SSC 14**
See also DLB 21, 70

Leffland, Ella 1931- .... **CLC 19**
See also CA 29-32R; CANR 35; DLBY 84;
SATA 65

Leger, Alexis
See Leger, (Marie-Rene Auguste) Alexis
Saint-Leger

Leger, (Marie-Rene Auguste) Alexis
Saint-Leger 1887-1975........ **CLC 11**
See also Perse, St.-John
See also CA 13-16R; 61-64; CANR 43;
MTCW

Leger, Saintleger
See Leger, (Marie-Rene Auguste) Alexis
Saint-Leger

Le Guin, Ursula K(roeber)
1929- .... **CLC 8, 13, 22, 45, 71; SSC 12**
See also AAYA 9; AITN 1; CA 21-24R;
CANR 9, 32; CDALB 1968-1988; CLR 3,
28; DLB 8, 52; JRDA; MAICYA;
MTCW; SATA 4, 52

Lehmann, Rosamond (Nina)
1901-1990 .... **CLC 5**
See also CA 77-80; 131; CANR 8; DLB 15

Leiber, Fritz (Reuter, Jr.)
1910-1992 .... **CLC 25**
See also CA 45-48; 139; CANR 2, 40;
DLB 8; MTCW; SATA 45;
SATA-Obit 73

Leimbach, Martha 1963-
See Leimbach, Marti
See also CA 130

Leimbach, Marti .... **CLC 65**
See also Leimbach, Martha

Leino, Eino .... **TCLC 24**
See also Loennbohm, Armas Eino Leopold

Leiris, Michel (Julien) 1901-1990... **CLC 61**
See also CA 119; 128; 132

Leithauser, Brad 1953-........... **CLC 27**
See also CA 107; CANR 27; DLB 120

Lelchuk, Alan 1938-............. **CLC 5**
See also CA 45-48; CANR 1

Lem, Stanislaw 1921-........ **CLC 8, 15, 40**
See also CA 105; CAAS 1; CANR 32;
MTCW

Lemann, Nancy 1956-............. **CLC 39**
See also CA 118; 136

Lemonnier, (Antoine Louis) Camille
1844-1913 .... **TCLC 22**
See also CA 121

Lenau, Nikolaus 1802-1850 ..... **NCLC 16**

L'Engle, Madeleine (Camp Franklin)
1918- .... **CLC 12**
See also AAYA 1; AITN 2; CA 1-4R;
CANR 3, 21, 39; CLR 1, 14; DLB 52;
JRDA; MAICYA; MTCW; SAAS 15;
SATA 1, 27, 75

Lengyel, Jozsef 1896-1975......... **CLC 7**
See also CA 85-88; 57-60

Lennon, John (Ono)
1940-1980 .... **CLC 12, 35**
See also CA 102

Lennox, Charlotte Ramsay
1729(?)-1804 .... **NCLC 23**
See also DLB 39

Lentricchia, Frank (Jr.) 1940-...... **CLC 34**
See also CA 25-28R; CANR 19

Lenz, Siegfried 1926-............ **CLC 27**
See also CA 89-92; DLB 75

Leonard, Elmore (John, Jr.)
1925- .... **CLC 28, 34, 71**
See also AITN 1; BEST 89:1, 90:4;
CA 81-84; CANR 12, 28; MTCW

Leonard, Hugh
See Byrne, John Keyes
See also DLB 13

Leopardi, (Conte) Giacomo (Talegardo
Francesco di Sales Save)
1798-1837 .... **NCLC 22**

Le Reveler
See Artaud, Antonin

Lerman, Eleanor 1952-............ **CLC 9**
See also CA 85-88

Lerman, Rhoda 1936-............ **CLC 56**
See also CA 49-52

Lermontov, Mikhail Yuryevich
1814-1841 .... **NCLC 5**

Leroux, Gaston 1868-1927....... **TCLC 25**
See also CA 108; 136; SATA 65

Lesage, Alain-Rene 1668-1747....... **LC 2**

Leskov, Nikolai (Semyonovich)
1831-1895 .... **NCLC 25**

Lessing, Doris (May)
1919- ..... **CLC 1, 2, 3, 6, 10, 15, 22, 40;**
DA; SSC 6
See also CA 9-12R; CAAS 14; CANR 33;
CDBLB 1960 to Present; DLB 15;
DLBY 85; MTCW

Lessing, Gotthold Ephraim
1729-1781 .... **LC 8**
See also DLB 97

Lester, Richard 1932-............ **CLC 20**

Lever, Charles (James)
1806-1872 .... **NCLC 23**
See also DLB 21

Leverson, Ada 1865(?)-1936(?) .... **TCLC 18**
See also Elaine
See also CA 117

Levertov, Denise
1923- ...... **CLC 1, 2, 3, 5, 8, 15, 28, 66**
See also CA 1-4R; CANR 3, 29; DLB 5;
MTCW

Levi, Jonathan.................... **CLC 76**

Levi, Peter (Chad Tigar) 1931-..... **CLC 41**
See also CA 5-8R; CANR 34; DLB 40

Levi, Primo
1919-1987 .... **CLC 37, 50; SSC 12**
See also CA 13-16R; 122; CANR 12, 33;
MTCW

Levin, Ira 1929- .... **CLC 3, 6**
See also CA 21-24R; CANR 17; MTCW;
SATA 66

Levin, Meyer 1905-1981 .... **CLC 7**
See also AITN 1; CA 9-12R; 104;
CANR 15; DLB 9, 28; DLBY 81;
SATA 21, 27

Levine, Norman 1924-............ **CLC 54**
See also CA 73-76; CANR 14; DLB 88

Levine, Philip 1928-... **CLC 2, 4, 5, 9, 14, 33**
See also CA 9-12R; CANR 9, 37; DLB 5

Levinson, Deirdre 1931-.......... **CLC 49**
See also CA 73-76

Levi-Strauss, Claude 1908-........ **CLC 38**
See also CA 1-4R; CANR 6, 32; MTCW

Levitin, Sonia (Wolff) 1934- .... **CLC 17**
See also CA 29-32R; CANR 14, 32; JRDA;
MAICYA; SAAS 2; SATA 4, 68

Levon, O. U.
See Kesey, Ken (Elton)

Lewes, George Henry
1817-1878 .... **NCLC 25**
See also DLB 55

Lewis, Alun 1915-1944............ **TCLC 3**
See also CA 104; DLB 20

Lewis, C. Day
See Day Lewis, C(ecil)

Lewis, C(live) S(taples)
1898-1963 ..... **CLC 1, 3, 6, 14, 27; DA;**
WLC
See also AAYA 3; CA 81-84; CANR 33;
CDBLB 1945-1960; CLR 3, 27; DLB 15,
100; JRDA; MAICYA; MTCW;
SATA 13

Lewis, Janet 1899-............... **CLC 41**
See also Winters, Janet Lewis
See also CA 9-12R; CANR 29; CAP 1;
DLBY 87

Lewis, Matthew Gregory
1775-1818 .... **NCLC 11**
See also DLB 39

Author Index

Lord Jeffrey
See Jeffrey, Francis

Lorenzo, Heberto Padilla
See Padilla (Lorenzo), Heberto

Loris
See Hofmannsthal, Hugo von

Loti, Pierre . . . . **TCLC 11**
See also Viaud, (Louis Marie) Julien
See also DLB 123

Louie, David Wong 1954- . . . . **CLC 70**
See also CA 139

Louis, Father M.
See Merton, Thomas

Lovecraft, H(oward) P(hillips)
1890-1937 . . . . **TCLC 4, 22; SSC 3**
See also CA 104; 133; MTCW

Lovelace, Earl 1935- . . . . **CLC 51**
See also CA 77-80; CANR 41; DLB 125;
MTCW

Lovelace, Richard 1618-1657 . . . . **LC 24**
See also DLB 131

Lowell, Amy 1874-1925 . . . . **TCLC 1, 8**
See also CA 104; DLB 54

Lowell, James Russell 1819-1891 . . **NCLC 2**
See also CDALB 1640-1865; DLB 1, 11, 64,
79

Lowell, Robert (Traill Spence, Jr.)
1917-1977 . . . **CLC 1, 2, 3, 4, 5, 8, 9, 11,
15, 37; DA; PC 3; WLC**
See also CA 9-12R; 73-76; CABS 2;
CANR 26; DLB 5; MTCW

Lowndes, Marie Adelaide (Belloc)
1868-1947 . . . . **TCLC 12**
See also CA 107; DLB 70

Lowry, (Clarence) Malcolm
1909-1957 . . . . **TCLC 6, 40**
See also CA 105; 131; CDBLB 1945-1960;
DLB 15; MTCW

Lowry, Mina Gertrude 1882-1966
See Loy, Mina
See also CA 113

Loxsmith, John
See Brunner, John (Kilian Houston)

Loy, Mina . . . . **CLC 28**
See also Lowry, Mina Gertrude
See also DLB 4, 54

Loyson-Bridet
See Schwob, (Mayer Andre) Marcel

Lucas, Craig 1951- . . . . **CLC 64**
See also CA 137

Lucas, George 1944- . . . . **CLC 16**
See also AAYA 1; CA 77-80; CANR 30;
SATA 56

Lucas, Hans
See Godard, Jean-Luc

Lucas, Victoria
See Plath, Sylvia

Ludlam, Charles 1943-1987 . . . . . **CLC 46, 50**
See also CA 85-88; 122

Ludlum, Robert 1927- . . . . **CLC 22, 43**
See also AAYA 10; BEST 89:1, 90:3;
CA 33-36R; CANR 25, 41; DLBY 82;
MTCW

Ludwig, Ken . . . . **CLC 60**

Ludwig, Otto 1813-1865 . . . . **NCLC 4**
See also DLB 129

Lugones, Leopoldo 1874-1938 . . . . . **TCLC 15**
See also CA 116; 131; HW

Lu Hsun 1881-1936 . . . . **TCLC 3**

Lukacs, George . . . . **CLC 24**
See also Lukacs, Gyorgy (Szegeny von)

Lukacs, Gyorgy (Szegeny von) 1885-1971
See Lukacs, George
See also CA 101; 29-32R

Luke, Peter (Ambrose Cyprian)
1919- . . . . **CLC 38**
See also CA 81-84; DLB 13

Lunar, Dennis
See Mungo, Raymond

Lurie, Alison 1926- . . . . **CLC 4, 5, 18, 39**
See also CA 1-4R; CANR 2, 17; DLB 2;
MTCW; SATA 46

Lustig, Arnost 1926- . . . . **CLC 56**
See also AAYA 3; CA 69-72; SATA 56

Luther, Martin 1483-1546 . . . . **LC 9**

Luzi, Mario 1914- . . . . **CLC 13**
See also CA 61-64; CANR 9; DLB 128

Lynch, B. Suarez
See Bioy Casares, Adolfo; Borges, Jorge
Luis

Lynch, David (K.) 1946- . . . . **CLC 66**
See also CA 124; 129

Lynch, James
See Andreyev, Leonid (Nikolaevich)

Lynch Davis, B.
See Bioy Casares, Adolfo; Borges, Jorge
Luis

Lyndsay, Sir David 1490-1555 . . . . . . **LC 20**

Lynn, Kenneth S(chuyler) 1923- . . . . **CLC 50**
See also CA 1-4R; CANR 3, 27

Lynx
See West, Rebecca

Lyons, Marcus
See Blish, James (Benjamin)

Lyre, Pinchbeck
See Sassoon, Siegfried (Lorraine)

Lytle, Andrew (Nelson) 1902- . . . . . . **CLC 22**
See also CA 9-12R; DLB 6

Lyttelton, George 1709-1773 . . . . **LC 10**

Maas, Peter 1929- . . . . **CLC 29**
See also CA 93-96

Macaulay, Rose 1881-1958 . . . . . **TCLC 7, 44**
See also CA 104; DLB 36

Macaulay, Thomas Babington
1800-1859 . . . . **NCLC 42**
See also CDBLB 1832-1890; DLB 32, 55

MacBeth, George (Mann)
1932-1992 . . . . **CLC 2, 5, 9**
See also CA 25-28R; 136; DLB 40; MTCW;
SATA 4; SATA-Obit 70

MacCaig, Norman (Alexander)
1910- . . . . **CLC 36**
See also CA 9-12R; CANR 3, 34; DLB 27

MacCarthy, (Sir Charles Otto) Desmond
1877-1952 . . . . **TCLC 36**

MacDiarmid, Hugh . . . . . **CLC 2, 4, 11, 19, 63**
See also Grieve, C(hristopher) M(urray)
See also CDBLB 1945-1960; DLB 20

MacDonald, Anson
See Heinlein, Robert A(nson)

Macdonald, Cynthia 1928- . . . . . . **CLC 13, 19**
See also CA 49-52; CANR 4; DLB 105

MacDonald, George 1824-1905 . . . . . **TCLC 9**
See also CA 106; 137; DLB 18; MAICYA;
SATA 33

Macdonald, John
See Millar, Kenneth

MacDonald, John D(ann)
1916-1986 . . . . **CLC 3, 27, 44**
See also CA 1-4R; 121; CANR 1, 19;
DLB 8; DLBY 86; MTCW

Macdonald, John Ross
See Millar, Kenneth

Macdonald, Ross . . . . . **CLC 1, 2, 3, 14, 34, 41**
See also Millar, Kenneth
See also DLBD 6

MacDougal, John
See Blish, James (Benjamin)

MacEwen, Gwendolyn (Margaret)
1941-1987 . . . . **CLC 13, 55**
See also CA 9-12R; 124; CANR 7, 22;
DLB 53; SATA 50, 55

Machado (y Ruiz), Antonio
1875-1939 . . . . **TCLC 3**
See also CA 104; DLB 108

Machado de Assis, Joaquim Maria
1839-1908 . . . . **TCLC 10; BLC**
See also CA 107

Machen, Arthur . . . . **TCLC 4**
See also Jones, Arthur Llewellyn
See also DLB 36

Machiavelli, Niccolo 1469-1527 . . **LC 8; DA**

MacInnes, Colin 1914-1976 . . . . . . **CLC 4, 23**
See also CA 69-72; 65-68; CANR 21;
DLB 14; MTCW

MacInnes, Helen (Clark)
1907-1985 . . . . **CLC 27, 39**
See also CA 1-4R; 117; CANR 1, 28;
DLB 87; MTCW; SATA 22, 44

Mackay, Mary 1855-1924
See Corelli, Marie
See also CA 118

Mackenzie, Compton (Edward Montague)
1883-1972 . . . . **CLC 18**
See also CA 21-22; 37-40R; CAP 2;
DLB 34, 100

Mackenzie, Henry 1745-1831 . . . . **NCLC 41**
See also DLB 39

Mackintosh, Elizabeth 1896(?)-1952
See Tey, Josephine
See also CA 110

MacLaren, James
See Grieve, C(hristopher) M(urray)

Mac Laverty, Bernard 1942- . . . . **CLC 31**
See also CA 116; 118; CANR 43

MacLean, Alistair (Stuart)
1922-1987 . . . . . **CLC 3, 13, 50, 63**
See also CA 57-60; 121; CANR 28; MTCW;
SATA 23, 50

Maclean, Norman (Fitzroy)
1902-1990 . . . . **CLC 78; SSC 13**
See also CA 102; 132

MacLeish, Archibald
1892-1982 . . . . **CLC 3, 8, 14, 68**
See also CA 9-12R; 106; CANR 33; DLB 4,
7, 45; DLBY 82; MTCW

MacLennan, (John) Hugh
1907-1990 . . . . **CLC 2, 14**
See also CA 5-8R; 142; CANR 33; DLB 68;
MTCW

MacLeod, Alistair 1936- . . . . **CLC 56**
See also CA 123; DLB 60

MacNeice, (Frederick) Louis
1907-1963 . . . . **CLC 1, 4, 10, 53**
See also CA 85-88; DLB 10, 20; MTCW

MacNeill, Dand
See Fraser, George MacDonald

Macpherson, (Jean) Jay 1931- . . . . . . **CLC 14**
See also CA 5-8R; DLB 53

MacShane, Frank 1927- . . . . **CLC 39**
See also CA 9-12R; CANR 3, 33; DLB 111

Macumber, Mari
See Sandoz, Mari(e Susette)

Madach, Imre 1823-1864 . . . . **NCLC 19**

Madden, (Jerry) David 1933- . . . . **CLC 5, 15**
See also CA 1-4R; CAAS 3; CANR 4;
DLB 6; MTCW

Maddern, Al(an)
See Ellison, Harlan

Madhubuti, Haki R.
1942- . . . . **CLC 6, 73; BLC; PC 5**
See also Lee, Don L.
See also BW; CA 73-76; CANR 24; DLB 5,
41; DLBD 8

Madow, Pauline (Reichberg) . . . . **CLC 1**
See also CA 9-12R

Maepenn, Hugh
See Kuttner, Henry

Maepenn, K. H.
See Kuttner, Henry

Maeterlinck, Maurice 1862-1949 . . . **TCLC 3**
See also CA 104; 136; SATA 66

Maginn, William 1794-1842 . . . . **NCLC 8**
See also DLB 110

Mahapatra, Jayanta 1928- . . . . **CLC 33**
See also CA 73-76; CAAS 9; CANR 15, 33

Mahfouz, Naguib (Abdel Aziz Al-Sabilgi)
1911(?)-
See Mahfuz, Najib
See also BEST 89:2; CA 128; MTCW

Mahfuz, Najib . . . . **CLC 52, 55**
See also Mahfouz, Naguib (Abdel Aziz
Al-Sabilgi)
See also DLBY 88

Mahon, Derek 1941- . . . . **CLC 27**
See also CA 113; 128; DLB 40

Mailer, Norman
1923- . . . . . . **CLC 1, 2, 3, 4, 5, 8, 11, 14,
28, 39, 74; DA**
See also AITN 2; CA 9-12R; CABS 1;
CANR 28; CDALB 1968-1988; DLB 2,
16, 28; DLBD 3; DLBY 80, 83; MTCW

Maillet, Antonine 1929- . . . . **CLC 54**
See also CA 115; 120; DLB 60

Mais, Roger 1905-1955 . . . . **TCLC 8**
See also BW; CA 105; 124; DLB 125;
MTCW

Maistre, Joseph de 1753-1821 . . . . **NCLC 37**

Maitland, Sara (Louise) 1950- . . . . . . **CLC 49**
See also CA 69-72; CANR 13

Major, Clarence
1936- . . . . **CLC 3, 19, 48; BLC**
See also BW; CA 21-24R; CAAS 6;
CANR 13, 25; DLB 33

Major, Kevin (Gerald) 1949- . . . . **CLC 26**
See also CA 97-100; CANR 21, 38;
CLR 11; DLB 60; JRDA; MAICYA;
SATA 32

Maki, James
See Ozu, Yasujiro

Malabaila, Damiano
See Levi, Primo

Malamud, Bernard
1914-1986 . . . . . . **CLC 1, 2, 3, 5, 8, 9, 11,
18, 27, 44, 78; DA; SSC 15; WLC**
See also CA 5-8R; 118; CABS 1; CANR 28;
CDALB 1941-1968; DLB 2, 28;
DLBY 80, 86; MTCW

Malaparte, Curzio 1898-1957 . . . . . **TCLC 52**

Malcolm, Dan
See Silverberg, Robert

Malcolm X . . . . **CLC 82; BLC**
See also Little, Malcolm

Malherbe, Francois de 1555-1628 . . . . . **LC 5**

Mallarme, Stephane
1842-1898 . . . . **NCLC 4, 41; PC 4**

Mallet-Joris, Francoise 1930- . . . . . . **CLC 11**
See also CA 65-68; CANR 17; DLB 83

Malley, Ern
See McAuley, James Phillip

Mallowan, Agatha Christie
See Christie, Agatha (Mary Clarissa)

Maloff, Saul 1922- . . . . **CLC 5**
See also CA 33-36R

Malone, Louis
See MacNeice, (Frederick) Louis

Malone, Michael (Christopher)
1942- . . . . **CLC 43**
See also CA 77-80; CANR 14, 32

Malory, (Sir) Thomas
1410(?)-1471(?) . . . . **LC 11; DA**
See also CDBLB Before 1660; SATA 33, 59

Malouf, (George Joseph) David
1934- . . . . **CLC 28**
See also CA 124

Malraux, (Georges-)Andre
1901-1976 . . . . . . **CLC 1, 4, 9, 13, 15, 57**
See also CA 21-22; 69-72; CANR 34;
CAP 2; DLB 72; MTCW

Malzberg, Barry N(athaniel) 1939- . . . **CLC 7**
See also CA 61-64; CAAS 4; CANR 16;
DLB 8

Mamet, David (Alan)
1947- . . . . **CLC 9, 15, 34, 46; DC 4**
See also AAYA 3; CA 81-84; CABS 3;
CANR 15, 41; DLB 7; MTCW

Mamoulian, Rouben (Zachary)
1897-1987 . . . . **CLC 16**
See also CA 25-28R; 124

Mandelstam, Osip (Emilievich)
1891(?)-1938(?) . . . . **TCLC 2, 6**
See also CA 104

Mander, (Mary) Jane 1877-1949 . . . **TCLC 31**

Mandiargues, Andre Pieyre de . . . . . . **CLC 41**
See also Pieyre de Mandiargues, Andre
See also DLB 83

Mandrake, Ethel Belle
See Thurman, Wallace (Henry)

Mangan, James Clarence
1803-1849 . . . . **NCLC 27**

Maniere, J.-E.
See Giraudoux, (Hippolyte) Jean

Manley, (Mary) Delariviere
1672(?)-1724 . . . . **LC 1**
See also DLB 39, 80

Mann, Abel
See Creasey, John

Mann, (Luiz) Heinrich 1871-1950 . . . **TCLC 9**
See also CA 106; DLB 66

Mann, (Paul) Thomas
1875-1955 . . . . **TCLC 2, 8, 14, 21, 35, 44;
DA; SSC 5; WLC**
See also CA 104; 128; DLB 66; MTCW

Manning, David
See Faust, Frederick (Schiller)

Manning, Frederic 1887(?)-1935 . . . **TCLC 25**
See also CA 124

Manning, Olivia 1915-1980 . . . . . . **CLC 5, 19**
See also CA 5-8R; 101; CANR 29; MTCW

Mano, D. Keith 1942- . . . . **CLC 2, 10**
See also CA 25-28R; CAAS 6; CANR 26;
DLB 6

Mansfield, Katherine
. . . . **TCLC 2, 8, 39; SSC 9; WLC**
See also Beauchamp, Kathleen Mansfield

Manso, Peter 1940- . . . . **CLC 39**
See also CA 29-32R

Mantecon, Juan Jimenez
See Jimenez (Mantecon), Juan Ramon

Manton, Peter
See Creasey, John

Man Without a Spleen, A
See Chekhov, Anton (Pavlovich)

Manzoni, Alessandro 1785-1873 . . **NCLC 29**

Mapu, Abraham (ben Jekutiel)
1808-1867 . . . . **NCLC 18**

Mara, Sally
See Queneau, Raymond

Marat, Jean Paul 1743-1793 . . . . **LC 10**

Marcel, Gabriel Honore
1889-1973 . . . . **CLC 15**
See also CA 102; 45-48; MTCW

Marchbanks, Samuel
See Davies, (William) Robertson

Marchi, Giacomo
See Bassani, Giorgio

Margulies, Donald . . . . **CLC 76**

Marie de France c. 12th cent. - . . . . **CMLC 8**

Marie de l'Incarnation 1599-1672 . . . . **LC 10**

Mariner, Scott
See Pohl, Frederik

Marinetti, Filippo Tommaso
1876-1944 .... **TCLC 10**
See also CA 107; DLB 114

Marivaux, Pierre Carlet de Chamblain de
1688-1763 .... **LC 4**

Markandaya, Kamala .... **CLC 8, 38**
See also Taylor, Kamala (Purnaiya)

Markfield, Wallace 1926-.......... **CLC 8**
See also CA 69-72; CAAS 3; DLB 2, 28

Markham, Edwin 1852-1940 ..... **TCLC 47**
See also DLB 54

Markham, Robert
See Amis, Kingsley (William)

Marks, J
See Highwater, Jamake (Mamake)

Marks-Highwater, J
See Highwater, Jamake (Mamake)

Markson, David M(errill) 1927-.... **CLC 67**
See also CA 49-52; CANR 1

Marley, Bob..................... **CLC 17**
See also Marley, Robert Nesta

Marley, Robert Nesta 1945-1981
See Marley, Bob
See also CA 107; 103

Marlowe, Christopher
1564-1593 ..... **LC 22; DA; DC 1; WLC**
See also CDBLB Before 1660; DLB 62

Marmontel, Jean-Francois
1723-1799 .... **LC 2**

Marquand, John P(hillips)
1893-1960 .... **CLC 2, 10**
See also CA 85-88; DLB 9, 102

Marquez, Gabriel (Jose) Garcia...... **CLC 68**
See also Garcia Marquez, Gabriel (Jose)

Marquis, Don(ald Robert Perry)
1878-1937 .... **TCLC 7**
See also CA 104; DLB 11, 25

Marric, J. J.
See Creasey, John

Marrow, Bernard
See Moore, Brian

Marryat, Frederick 1792-1848 .... **NCLC 3**
See also DLB 21

Marsden, James
See Creasey, John

Marsh, (Edith) Ngaio
1899-1982 .... **CLC 7, 53**
See also CA 9-12R; CANR 6; DLB 77;
MTCW

Marshall, Garry 1934-............ **CLC 17**
See also AAYA 3; CA 111; SATA 60

Marshall, Paule
1929- .... **CLC 27, 72; BLC; SSC 3**
See also BW; CA 77-80; CANR 25;
DLB 33; MTCW

Marsten, Richard
See Hunter, Evan

Martha, Henry
See Harris, Mark

Martin, Ken
See Hubbard, L(afayette) Ron(ald)

Martin, Richard
See Creasey, John

Martin, Steve 1945-.............. **CLC 30**
See also CA 97-100; CANR 30; MTCW

Martin, Violet Florence
1862-1915 .... **TCLC 51**

Martin, Webber
See Silverberg, Robert

Martindale, Patrick Victor
See White, Patrick (Victor Martindale)

Martin du Gard, Roger
1881-1958 .... **TCLC 24**
See also CA 118; DLB 65

Martineau, Harriet 1802-1876.... **NCLC 26**
See also DLB 21, 55; YABC 2

Martines, Julia
See O'Faolain, Julia

Martinez, Jacinto Benavente y
See Benavente (y Martinez), Jacinto

Martinez Ruiz, Jose 1873-1967
See Azorin; Ruiz, Jose Martinez
See also CA 93-96; HW

Martinez Sierra, Gregorio
1881-1947 .... **TCLC 6**
See also CA 115

Martinez Sierra, Maria (de la O'LeJarraga)
1874-1974 .... **TCLC 6**
See also CA 115

Martinsen, Martin
See Follett, Ken(neth Martin)

Martinson, Harry (Edmund)
1904-1978 .... **CLC 14**
See also CA 77-80; CANR 34

Marut, Ret
See Traven, B.

Marut, Robert
See Traven, B.

Marvell, Andrew
1621-1678 .... **LC 4; DA; WLC**
See also CDBLB 1660-1789; DLB 131

Marx, Karl (Heinrich)
1818-1883 .... **NCLC 17**
See also DLB 129

Masaoka Shiki................. **TCLC 18**
See also Masaoka Tsunenori

Masaoka Tsunenori 1867-1902
See Masaoka Shiki
See also CA 117

Masefield, John (Edward)
1878-1967 .... **CLC 11, 47**
See also CA 19-20; 25-28R; CANR 33;
CAP 2; CDBLB 1890-1914; DLB 10;
MTCW; SATA 19

Maso, Carole 19(?)-.............. **CLC 44**

Mason, Bobbie Ann
1940- .... **CLC 28, 43, 82; SSC 4**
See also AAYA 5; CA 53-56; CANR 11,
31; DLBY 87; MTCW

Mason, Ernst
See Pohl, Frederik

Mason, Lee W.
See Malzberg, Barry N(athaniel)

Mason, Nick 1945-.............. **CLC 35**
See also Pink Floyd

Mason, Tally
See Derleth, August (William)

Mass, William
See Gibson, William

Masters, Edgar Lee
1868-1950 ..... **TCLC 2, 25; DA; PC 1**
See also CA 104; 133; CDALB 1865-1917;
DLB 54; MTCW

Masters, Hilary 1928-............ **CLC 48**
See also CA 25-28R; CANR 13

Mastrosimone, William 19(?)-...... **CLC 36**

Mathe, Albert
See Camus, Albert

Matheson, Richard Burton 1926- ... **CLC 37**
See also CA 97-100; DLB 8, 44

Mathews, Harry 1930-.......... **CLC 6, 52**
See also CA 21-24R; CAAS 6; CANR 18,
40

Mathias, Roland (Glyn) 1915-...... **CLC 45**
See also CA 97-100; CANR 19, 41; DLB 27

Matsuo Basho 1644-1694........... **PC 3**

Mattheson, Rodney
See Creasey, John

Matthews, Greg 1949-............ **CLC 45**
See also CA 135

Matthews, William 1942-.......... **CLC 40**
See also CA 29-32R; CAAS 18; CANR 12;
DLB 5

Matthias, John (Edward) 1941-...... **CLC 9**
See also CA 33-36R

Matthiessen, Peter
1927- .... **CLC 5, 7, 11, 32, 64**
See also AAYA 6; BEST 90:4; CA 9-12R;
CANR 21; DLB 6; MTCW; SATA 27

Maturin, Charles Robert
1780(?)-1824 .... **NCLC 6**

Matute (Ausejo), Ana Maria
1925- .... **CLC 11**
See also CA 89-92; MTCW

Maugham, W. S.
See Maugham, W(illiam) Somerset

Maugham, W(illiam) Somerset
1874-1965 ...... **CLC 1, 11, 15, 67; DA;**
SSC 8; WLC
See also CA 5-8R; 25-28R; CANR 40;
CDBLB 1914-1945; DLB 10, 36, 77, 100;
MTCW; SATA 54

Maugham, William Somerset
See Maugham, W(illiam) Somerset

Maupassant, (Henri Rene Albert) Guy de
1850-1893 .... **NCLC 1, 42; DA; SSC 1;**
WLC
See also DLB 123

Maurhut, Richard
See Traven, B.

Mauriac, Claude 1914-............. **CLC 9**
See also CA 89-92; DLB 83

Mauriac, Francois (Charles)
1885-1970 .... **CLC 4, 9, 56**
See also CA 25-28; CAP 2; DLB 65;
MTCW

Mavor, Osborne Henry 1888-1951
See Bridie, James
See also CA 104

Maxwell, William (Keepers, Jr.)
1908- . . . . **CLC 19**
See also CA 93-96; DLBY 80

May, Elaine 1932- . . . . **CLC 16**
See also CA 124; 142; DLB 44

Mayakovski, Vladimir (Vladimirovich)
1893-1930 . . . . **TCLC 4, 18**
See also CA 104

Mayhew, Henry 1812-1887 . . . . . . **NCLC 31**
See also DLB 18, 55

Maynard, Joyce 1953- . . . . **CLC 23**
See also CA 111; 129

Mayne, William (James Carter)
1928- . . . . **CLC 12**
See also CA 9-12R; CANR 37; CLR 25;
JRDA; MAICYA; SAAS 11; SATA 6, 68

Mayo, Jim
See L'Amour, Louis (Dearborn)

Maysles, Albert 1926- . . . . **CLC 16**
See also CA 29-32R

Maysles, David 1932- . . . . **CLC 16**

Mazer, Norma Fox 1931- . . . . **CLC 26**
See also AAYA 5; CA 69-72; CANR 12,
32; CLR 23; JRDA; MAICYA; SAAS 1;
SATA 24, 67

Mazzini, Guiseppe 1805-1872 . . . . **NCLC 34**

McAuley, James Phillip
1917-1976 . . . . **CLC 45**
See also CA 97-100

McBain, Ed
See Hunter, Evan

McBrien, William Augustine
1930- . . . . **CLC 44**
See also CA 107

McCaffrey, Anne (Inez) 1926- . . . . . . **CLC 17**
See also AAYA 6; AITN 2; BEST 89:2;
CA 25-28R; CANR 15, 35; DLB 8;
JRDA; MAICYA; MTCW; SAAS 11;
SATA 8, 70

McCann, Arthur
See Campbell, John W(ood, Jr.)

McCann, Edson
See Pohl, Frederik

McCarthy, Charles, Jr. 1933-
See McCarthy, Cormac
See also CANR 42

McCarthy, Cormac . . . . **CLC 4, 57**
See also McCarthy, Charles, Jr.
See also DLB 6

McCarthy, Mary (Therese)
1912-1989 . . . **CLC 1, 3, 5, 14, 24, 39, 59**
See also CA 5-8R; 129; CANR 16; DLB 2;
DLBY 81; MTCW

McCartney, (James) Paul
1942- . . . . **CLC 12, 35**

McCauley, Stephen (D.) 1955- . . . . . **CLC 50**
See also CA 141

McClure, Michael (Thomas)
1932- . . . . **CLC 6, 10**
See also CA 21-24R; CANR 17; DLB 16

McCorkle, Jill (Collins) 1958- . . . . . **CLC 51**
See also CA 121; DLBY 87

McCourt, James 1941- . . . . **CLC 5**
See also CA 57-60

McCoy, Horace (Stanley)
1897-1955 . . . . **TCLC 28**
See also CA 108; DLB 9

McCrae, John 1872-1918 . . . . **TCLC 12**
See also CA 109; DLB 92

McCreigh, James
See Pohl, Frederik

McCullers, (Lula) Carson (Smith)
1917-1967 . . . . **CLC 1, 4, 10, 12, 48; DA;
SSC 9; WLC**
See also CA 5-8R; 25-28R; CABS 1, 3;
CANR 18; CDALB 1941-1968; DLB 2, 7;
MTCW; SATA 27

McCulloch, John Tyler
See Burroughs, Edgar Rice

McCullough, Colleen 1938(?)- . . . . . . **CLC 27**
See also CA 81-84; CANR 17; MTCW

McElroy, Joseph 1930- . . . . **CLC 5, 47**
See also CA 17-20R

McEwan, Ian (Russell) 1948- . . . **CLC 13, 66**
See also BEST 90:4; CA 61-64; CANR 14,
41; DLB 14; MTCW

McFadden, David 1940- . . . . **CLC 48**
See also CA 104; DLB 60

McFarland, Dennis 1950- . . . . **CLC 65**

McGahern, John 1934- . . . . **CLC 5, 9, 48**
See also CA 17-20R; CANR 29; DLB 14;
MTCW

McGinley, Patrick (Anthony)
1937- . . . . **CLC 41**
See also CA 120; 127

McGinley, Phyllis 1905-1978 . . . . . . **CLC 14**
See also CA 9-12R; 77-80; CANR 19;
DLB 11, 48; SATA 2, 24, 44

McGinniss, Joe 1942- . . . . **CLC 32**
See also AITN 2; BEST 89:2; CA 25-28R;
CANR 26

McGivern, Maureen Daly
See Daly, Maureen

McGrath, Patrick 1950- . . . . **CLC 55**
See also CA 136

McGrath, Thomas (Matthew)
1916-1990 . . . . **CLC 28, 59**
See also CA 9-12R; 132; CANR 6, 33;
MTCW; SATA 41; SATA-Obit 66

McGuane, Thomas (Francis III)
1939- . . . . **CLC 3, 7, 18, 45**
See also AITN 2; CA 49-52; CANR 5, 24;
DLB 2; DLBY 80; MTCW

McGuckian, Medbh 1950- . . . . **CLC 48**
See also CA 143; DLB 40

McHale, Tom 1942(?)-1982 . . . . **CLC 3, 5**
See also AITN 1; CA 77-80; 106

McIlvanney, William 1936- . . . . **CLC 42**
See also CA 25-28R; DLB 14

McIlwraith, Maureen Mollie Hunter
See Hunter, Mollie
See also SATA 2

McInerney, Jay 1955- . . . . **CLC 34**
See also CA 116; 123

McIntyre, Vonda N(eel) 1948- . . . . . **CLC 18**
See also CA 81-84; CANR 17, 34; MTCW

McKay, Claude . . . . . **TCLC 7, 41; BLC; PC 2**
See also McKay, Festus Claudius
See also DLB 4, 45, 51, 117

McKay, Festus Claudius 1889-1948
See McKay, Claude
See also BW; CA 104; 124; DA; MTCW;
WLC

McKuen, Rod 1933- . . . . **CLC 1, 3**
See also AITN 1; CA 41-44R; CANR 40

McLoughlin, R. B.
See Mencken, H(enry) L(ouis)

McLuhan, (Herbert) Marshall
1911-1980 . . . . **CLC 37**
See also CA 9-12R; 102; CANR 12, 34;
DLB 88; MTCW

McMillan, Terry (L.) 1951- . . . . . **CLC 50, 61**
See also CA 140

McMurtry, Larry (Jeff)
1936- . . . . **CLC 2, 3, 7, 11, 27, 44**
See also AITN 2; BEST 89:2; CA 5-8R;
CANR 19, 43; CDALB 1968-1988;
DLB 2; DLBY 80, 87; MTCW

McNally, T. M. 1961- . . . . **CLC 82**

McNally, Terrence 1939- . . . . . **CLC 4, 7, 41**
See also CA 45-48; CANR 2; DLB 7

McNamer, Deirdre 1950- . . . . **CLC 70**

McNeile, Herman Cyril 1888-1937
See Sapper
See also DLB 77

McPhee, John (Angus) 1931- . . . . . . **CLC 36**
See also BEST 90:1; CA 65-68; CANR 20;
MTCW

McPherson, James Alan
1943- . . . . **CLC 19, 77**
See also BW; CA 25-28R; CAAS 17;
CANR 24; DLB 38; MTCW

McPherson, William (Alexander)
1933- . . . . **CLC 34**
See also CA 69-72; CANR 28

McSweeney, Kerry . . . . **CLC 34**

Mead, Margaret 1901-1978 . . . . **CLC 37**
See also AITN 1; CA 1-4R; 81-84;
CANR 4; MTCW; SATA 20

Meaker, Marijane (Agnes) 1927-
See Kerr, M. E.
See also CA 107; CANR 37; JRDA;
MAICYA; MTCW; SATA 20, 61

Medoff, Mark (Howard) 1940- . . . **CLC 6, 23**
See also AITN 1; CA 53-56; CANR 5;
DLB 7

Meged, Aharon
See Megged, Aharon

Meged, Aron
See Megged, Aharon

Megged, Aharon 1920- . . . . **CLC 9**
See also CA 49-52; CAAS 13; CANR 1

Mehta, Ved (Parkash) 1934- . . . . **CLC 37**
See also CA 1-4R; CANR 2, 23; MTCW

Melanter
See Blackmore, R(ichard) D(oddridge)

Melikow, Loris
See Hofmannsthal, Hugo von

Melmoth, Sebastian
See Wilde, Oscar (Fingal O'Flahertie Wills)

Mitford, Nancy 1904-1973........ **CLC 44**
See also CA 9-12R

Miyamoto, Yuriko 1899-1951 ..... **TCLC 37**

Mo, Timothy (Peter) 1950(?)- ...... **CLC 46**
See also CA 117; MTCW

Modarressi, Taghi (M.) 1931- ...... **CLC 44**
See also CA 121; 134

Modiano, Patrick (Jean) 1945- ..... **CLC 18**
See also CA 85-88; CANR 17, 40; DLB 83

Moerck, Paal
See Roelvaag, O(le) E(dvart)

Mofolo, Thomas (Mokopu)
1875(?)-1948 .... **TCLC 22; BLC**
See also CA 121

Mohr, Nicholasa 1935- ...... **CLC 12; HLC**
See also AAYA 8; CA 49-52; CANR 1, 32;
CLR 22; HW; JRDA; SAAS 8; SATA 8

Mojtabai, A(nn) G(race)
1938- .... **CLC 5, 9, 15, 29**
See also CA 85-88

Moliere 1622-1673 .... **LC 10; DA; WLC**

Molin, Charles
See Mayne, William (James Carter)

Molnar, Ferenc 1878-1952....... **TCLC 20**
See also CA 109

Momaday, N(avarre) Scott
1934- .... **CLC 2, 19; DA**
See also CA 25-28R; CANR 14, 34;
MTCW; SATA 30, 48

Monette, Paul 1945- .... **CLC 82**
See also CA 139

Monroe, Harriet 1860-1936...... **TCLC 12**
See also CA 109; DLB 54, 91

Monroe, Lyle
See Heinlein, Robert A(nson)

Montagu, Elizabeth 1917- .... **NCLC 7**
See also CA 9-12R

Montagu, Mary (Pierrepont) Wortley
1689-1762 .... **LC 9**
See also DLB 95, 101

Montagu, W. H.
See Coleridge, Samuel Taylor

Montague, John (Patrick)
1929- .... **CLC 13, 46**
See also CA 9-12R; CANR 9; DLB 40;
MTCW

Montaigne, Michel (Eyquem) de
·1533-1592 .... **LC 8; DA; WLC**

Montale, Eugenio 1896-1981... **CLC 7, 9, 18**
See also CA 17-20R; 104; CANR 30;
DLB 114; MTCW

Montesquieu, Charles-Louis de Secondat
1689-1755 .... **LC 7**

Montgomery, (Robert) Bruce 1921-1978
See Crispin, Edmund
See also CA 104

Montgomery, L(ucy) M(aud)
1874-1942 .... **TCLC 51**
See also CA 108; 137; CLR 8; DLB 92;
JRDA; MAICYA; YABC 1

Montgomery, Marion H., Jr. 1925- .. **CLC 7**
See also AITN 1; CA 1-4R; CANR 3;
DLB 6

Montgomery, Max
See Davenport, Guy (Mattison, Jr.)

Montherlant, Henry (Milon) de
1896-1972 .... **CLC 8, 19**
See also CA 85-88; 37-40R; DLB 72;
MTCW

Monty Python .... **CLC 21**
See also Chapman, Graham; Cleese, John
(Marwood); Gilliam, Terry (Vance); Idle,
Eric; Jones, Terence Graham Parry; Palin,
Michael (Edward)
See also AAYA 7

Moodie, Susanna (Strickland)
1803-1885 .... **NCLC 14**
See also DLB 99

Mooney, Edward 1951- .... **CLC 25**
See also CA 130

Mooney, Ted
See Mooney, Edward

Moorcock, Michael (John)
1939- .... **CLC 5, 27, 58**
See also CA 45-48; CAAS 5; CANR 2, 17,
38; DLB 14; MTCW

Moore, Brian
1921- .... **CLC 1, 3, 5, 7, 8, 19, 32**
See also CA 1-4R; CANR 1, 25, 42; MTCW

Moore, Edward
See Muir, Edwin

Moore, George Augustus
1852-1933 .... **TCLC 7**
See also CA 104; DLB 10, 18, 57, 135

Moore, Lorrie .... **CLC 39, 45, 68**
See also Moore, Marie Lorena

Moore, Marianne (Craig)
1887-1972 .... **CLC 1, 2, 4, 8, 10, 13, 19,
47; DA; PC 4**
See also CA 1-4R; 33-36R; CANR 3;
CDALB 1929-1941; DLB 45; DLBD 7;
MTCW; SATA 20

Moore, Marie Lorena 1957-
See Moore, Lorrie
See also CA 116; CANR 39

Moore, Thomas 1779-1852....... **NCLC 6**
See also DLB 96

Morand, Paul 1888-1976......... **CLC 41**
See also CA 69-72; DLB 65

Morante, Elsa 1918-1985....... **CLC 8, 47**
See also CA 85-88; 117; CANR 35; MTCW

Moravia, Alberto...... CLC 2, 7, 11, 27, 46
See also Pincherle, Alberto

More, Hannah 1745-1833 .... **NCLC 27**
See also DLB 107, 109, 116

More, Henry 1614-1687............. **LC 9**
See also DLB 126

More, Sir Thomas 1478-1535 .... **LC 10**

Moreas, Jean.................... TCLC 18
See also Papadiamantopoulos, Johannes

Morgan, Berry 1919- .... **CLC 6**
See also CA 49-52; DLB 6

Morgan, Claire
See Highsmith, (Mary) Patricia

Morgan, Edwin (George) 1920- ..... **CLC 31**
See also CA 5-8R; CANR 3, 43; DLB 27

Morgan, (George) Frederick
1922- .... **CLC 23**
See also CA 17-20R; CANR 21

Morgan, Harriet
See Mencken, H(enry) L(ouis)

Morgan, Jane
See Cooper, James Fenimore

Morgan, Janet 1945- .... **CLC 39**
See also CA 65-68

Morgan, Lady 1776(?)-1859...... **NCLC 29**
See also DLB 116

Morgan, Robin 1941- .... **CLC 2**
See also CA 69-72; CANR 29; MTCW

Morgan, Scott
See Kuttner, Henry

Morgan, Seth 1949(?)-1990 .... **CLC 65**
See also CA 132

Morgenstern, Christian
1871-1914 .... **TCLC 8**
See also CA 105

Morgenstern, S.
See Goldman, William (W.)

Moricz, Zsigmond 1879-1942 ..... **TCLC 33**

Morike, Eduard (Friedrich)
1804-1875 .... **NCLC 10**
See also DLB 133

Mori Ogai .... TCLC 14
See also Mori Rintaro

Mori Rintaro 1862-1922
See Mori Ogai
See also CA 110

Moritz, Karl Philipp 1756-1793 ...... **LC 2**
See also DLB 94

Morland, Peter Henry
See Faust, Frederick (Schiller)

Morren, Theophil
See Hofmannsthal, Hugo von

Morris, Bill 1952-................ **CLC 76**

Morris, Julian
See West, Morris L(anglo)

Morris, Steveland Judkins 1950(?)-
See Wonder, Stevie
See also CA 111

Morris, William 1834-1896 .... **NCLC 4**
See also CDBLB 1832-1890; DLB 18, 35, 57

Morris, Wright 1910-... **CLC 1, 3, 7, 18, 37**
See also CA 9-12R; CANR 21; DLB 2;
DLBY 81; MTCW

Morrison, Chloe Anthony Wofford
See Morrison, Toni

Morrison, James Douglas 1943-1971
See Morrison, Jim
See also CA 73-76; CANR 40

Morrison, Jim .... CLC 17
See also Morrison, James Douglas

Morrison, Toni
1931- .. **CLC 4, 10, 22, 55, 81; BLC; DA**
See also AAYA 1; BW; CA 29-32R;
CANR 27, 42; CDALB 1968-1988;
DLB 6, 33; DLBY 81; MTCW; SATA 57

Morrison, Van 1945- .... **CLC 21**
See also CA 116

Nessi, Pio Baroja y
See Baroja (y Nessi), Pio

Nestroy, Johann 1801-1862 . . . . . . **NCLC 42**
See also DLB 133

Neufeld, John (Arthur) 1938- . . . . . . **CLC 17**
See also CA 25-28R; CANR 11, 37;
MAICYA; SAAS 3; SATA 6

Neville, Emily Cheney 1919- . . . . **CLC 12**
See also CA 5-8R; CANR 3, 37; JRDA;
MAICYA; SAAS 2; SATA 1

Newbound, Bernard Slade 1930-
See Slade, Bernard
See also CA 81-84

Newby, P(ercy) H(oward)
1918- . . . . **CLC 2, 13**
See also CA 5-8R; CANR 32; DLB 15;
MTCW

Newlove, Donald 1928- . . . . **CLC 6**
See also CA 29-32R; CANR 25

Newlove, John (Herbert) 1938- . . . . . **CLC 14**
See also CA 21-24R; CANR 9, 25

Newman, Charles 1938- . . . . **CLC 2, 8**
See also CA 21-24R

Newman, Edwin (Harold) 1919- . . . . **CLC 14**
See also AITN 1; CA 69-72; CANR 5

Newman, John Henry
1801-1890 . . . . **NCLC 38**
See also DLB 18, 32, 55

Newton, Suzanne 1936- . . . . **CLC 35**
See also CA 41-44R; CANR 14; JRDA;
SATA 5

Nexo, Martin Andersen
1869-1954 . . . . **TCLC 43**

Nezval, Vitezslav 1900-1958 . . . . . . **TCLC 44**
See also CA 123

Ng, Fae Myenne 1957(?)- . . . . **CLC 81**

Ngema, Mbongeni 1955- . . . . **CLC 57**
See also CA 143

Ngugi, James T(hiong'o) . . . . **CLC 3, 7, 13**
See also Ngugi wa Thiong'o

Ngugi wa Thiong'o 1938- . . . . . **CLC 36; BLC**
See also Ngugi, James T(hiong'o)
See also BW; CA 81-84; CANR 27;
DLB 125; MTCW

Nichol, B(arrie) P(hillip)
1944-1988 . . . . **CLC 18**
See also CA 53-56; DLB 53; SATA 66

Nichols, John (Treadwell) 1940- . . . . **CLC 38**
See also CA 9-12R; CAAS 2; CANR 6;
DLBY 82

Nichols, Leigh
See Koontz, Dean R(ay)

Nichols, Peter (Richard)
1927- . . . . **CLC 5, 36, 65**
See also CA 104; CANR 33; DLB 13;
MTCW

Nicolas, F. R. E.
See Freeling, Nicolas

Niedecker, Lorine 1903-1970 . . . . **CLC 10, 42**
See also CA 25-28; CAP 2; DLB 48

Nietzsche, Friedrich (Wilhelm)
1844-1900 . . . . **TCLC 10, 18**
See also CA 107; 121; DLB 129

Nievo, Ippolito 1831-1861 . . . . **NCLC 22**

Nightingale, Anne Redmon 1943-
See Redmon, Anne
See also CA 103

Nik.T.O.
See Annensky, Innokenty Fyodorovich

Nin, Anais
1903-1977 . . . . . . **CLC 1, 4, 8, 11, 14, 60;
SSC 10**
See also AITN 2; CA 13-16R; 69-72;
CANR 22; DLB 2, 4; MTCW

Nissenson, Hugh 1933- . . . . **CLC 4, 9**
See also CA 17-20R; CANR 27; DLB 28

Niven, Larry . . . . **CLC 8**
See also Niven, Laurence Van Cott
See also DLB 8

Niven, Laurence Van Cott 1938-
See Niven, Larry
See also CA 21-24R; CAAS 12; CANR 14;
MTCW

Nixon, Agnes Eckhardt 1927- . . . . . . **CLC 21**
See also CA 110

Nizan, Paul 1905-1940 . . . . **TCLC 40**
See also DLB 72

Nkosi, Lewis 1936- . . . . **CLC 45; BLC**
See also BW; CA 65-68; CANR 27

Nodier, (Jean) Charles (Emmanuel)
1780-1844 . . . . **NCLC 19**
See also DLB 119

Nolan, Christopher 1965- . . . . **CLC 58**
See also CA 111

Norden, Charles
See Durrell, Lawrence (George)

Nordhoff, Charles (Bernard)
1887-1947 . . . . **TCLC 23**
See also CA 108; DLB 9; SATA 23

Norfolk, Lawrence 1963- . . . . **CLC 76**

Norman, Marsha 1947- . . . . **CLC 28**
See also CA 105; CABS 3; CANR 41;
DLBY 84

Norris, Benjamin Franklin, Jr.
1870-1902 . . . . **TCLC 24**
See also Norris, Frank
See also CA 110

Norris, Frank
See Norris, Benjamin Franklin, Jr.
See also CDALB 1865-1917; DLB 12, 71

Norris, Leslie 1921- . . . . **CLC 14**
See also CA 11-12; CANR 14; CAP 1;
DLB 27

North, Andrew
See Norton, Andre

North, Anthony
See Koontz, Dean R(ay)

North, Captain George
See Stevenson, Robert Louis (Balfour)

North, Milou
See Erdrich, Louise

Northrup, B. A.
See Hubbard, L(afayette) Ron(ald)

North Staffs
See Hulme, T(homas) E(rnest)

Norton, Alice Mary
See Norton, Andre
See also MAICYA; SATA 1, 43

Norton, Andre 1912- . . . . **CLC 12**
See also Norton, Alice Mary
See also CA 1-4R; CANR 2, 31; DLB 8, 52;
JRDA; MTCW

Norway, Nevil Shute 1899-1960
See Shute, Nevil
See also CA 102; 93-96

Norwid, Cyprian Kamil
1821-1883 . . . . **NCLC 17**

Nosille, Nabrah
See Ellison, Harlan

Nossack, Hans Erich 1901-1978 . . . . . **CLC 6**
See also CA 93-96; 85-88; DLB 69

Nosu, Chuji
See Ozu, Yasujiro

Nova, Craig 1945- . . . . **CLC 7, 31**
See also CA 45-48; CANR 2

Novak, Joseph
See Kosinski, Jerzy (Nikodem)

Novalis 1772-1801 . . . . **NCLC 13**
See also DLB 90

Nowlan, Alden (Albert) 1933-1983 . . **CLC 15**
See also CA 9-12R; CANR 5; DLB 53

Noyes, Alfred 1880-1958 . . . . **TCLC 7**
See also CA 104; DLB 20

Nunn, Kem 19(?)- . . . . **CLC 34**

Nye, Robert 1939- . . . . **CLC 13, 42**
See also CA 33-36R; CANR 29; DLB 14;
MTCW; SATA 6

Nyro, Laura 1947- . . . . **CLC 17**

Oates, Joyce Carol
1938- . . . . . . **CLC 1, 2, 3, 6, 9, 11, 15, 19,
33, 52; DA; SSC 6; WLC**
See also AITN 1; BEST 89:2; CA 5-8R;
CANR 25; CDALB 1968-1988; DLB 2, 5,
130; DLBY 81; MTCW

O'Brien, E. G.
See Clarke, Arthur C(harles)

O'Brien, Edna
1936- . . . **CLC 3, 5, 8, 13, 36, 65; SSC 10**
See also CA 1-4R; CANR 6, 41;
CDBLB 1960 to Present; DLB 14;
MTCW

O'Brien, Fitz-James 1828-1862 . . . **NCLC 21**
See also DLB 74

O'Brien, Flann . . . . **CLC 1, 4, 5, 7, 10, 47**
See also O Nuallain, Brian

O'Brien, Richard 1942- . . . . **CLC 17**
See also CA 124

O'Brien, Tim 1946- . . . . **CLC 7, 19, 40**
See also CA 85-88; CANR 40; DLBD 9;
DLBY 80

Obstfelder, Sigbjoern 1866-1900 . . . **TCLC 23**
See also CA 123

O'Casey, Sean
1880-1964 . . . . **CLC 1, 5, 9, 11, 15**
See also CA 89-92; CDBLB 1914-1945;
DLB 10; MTCW

O'Cathasaigh, Sean
See O'Casey, Sean

Ochs, Phil 1940-1976 . . . . **CLC 17**
See also CA 65-68

O'Connor, Edwin (Greene)
1918-1968 . . . . **CLC 14**
See also CA 93-96; 25-28R

O'Connor, (Mary) Flannery
1925-1964 . . . . **CLC 1, 2, 3, 6, 10, 13, 15,**
21, 66; DA; SSC 1; WLC
See also AAYA 7; CA 1-4R; CANR 3, 41;
CDALB 1941-1968; DLB 2; DLBY 80;
MTCW

O'Connor, Frank . . . . **CLC 23; SSC 5**
See also O'Donovan, Michael John

O'Dell, Scott 1898-1989 . . . . **CLC 30**
See also AAYA 3; CA 61-64; 129;
CANR 12, 30; CLR 1, 16; DLB 52;
JRDA; MAICYA; SATA 12, 60

Odets, Clifford 1906-1963 . . . . **CLC 2, 28**
See also CA 85-88; DLB 7, 26; MTCW

O'Doherty, Brian 1934- . . . . **CLC 76**
See also CA 105

O'Donnell, K. M.
See Malzberg, Barry N(athaniel)

O'Donnell, Lawrence
See Kuttner, Henry

O'Donovan, Michael John
1903-1966 . . . . **CLC 14**
See also O'Connor, Frank
See also CA 93-96

Oe, Kenzaburo 1935- . . . . **CLC 10, 36**
See also CA 97-100; CANR 36; MTCW

O'Faolain, Julia 1932- . . . . **CLC 6, 19, 47**
See also CA 81-84; CAAS 2; CANR 12;
DLB 14; MTCW

O'Faolain, Sean
1900-1991 . . . . **CLC 1, 7, 14, 32, 70;**
SSC 13
See also CA 61-64; 134; CANR 12;
DLB 15; MTCW

O'Flaherty, Liam
1896-1984 . . . . **CLC 5, 34; SSC 6**
See also CA 101; 113; CANR 35; DLB 36;
DLBY 84; MTCW

Ogilvy, Gavin
See Barrie, J(ames) M(atthew)

O'Grady, Standish James
1846-1928 . . . . **TCLC 5**
See also CA 104

O'Grady, Timothy 1951- . . . . **CLC 59**
See also CA 138

O'Hara, Frank
1926-1966 . . . . **CLC 2, 5, 13, 78**
See also CA 9-12R; 25-28R; CANR 33;
DLB 5, 16; MTCW

O'Hara, John (Henry)
1905-1970 . . . . **CLC 1, 2, 3, 6, 11, 42;**
SSC 15
See also CA 5-8R; 25-28R; CANR 31;
CDALB 1929-1941; DLB 9, 86; DLBD 2;
MTCW

O Hehir, Diana 1922- . . . . **CLC 41**
See also CA 93-96

Okigbo, Christopher (Ifenayichukwu)
1932-1967 . . . . **CLC 25; BLC; PC 7**
See also BW; CA 77-80; DLB 125; MTCW

Olds, Sharon 1942- . . . . **CLC 32, 39**
See also CA 101; CANR 18, 41; DLB 120

Oldstyle, Jonathan
See Irving, Washington

Olesha, Yuri (Karlovich)
1899-1960 . . . . **CLC 8**
See also CA 85-88

Oliphant, Margaret (Oliphant Wilson)
1828-1897 . . . . **NCLC 11**
See also DLB 18

Oliver, Mary 1935- . . . . **CLC 19, 34**
See also CA 21-24R; CANR 9, 43; DLB 5

Olivier, Laurence (Kerr)
1907-1989 . . . . **CLC 20**
See also CA 111; 129

Olsen, Tillie
1913- . . . . **CLC 4, 13; DA; SSC 11**
See also CA 1-4R; CANR 1, 43; DLB 28;
DLBY 80; MTCW

Olson, Charles (John)
1910-1970 . . . . . **CLC 1, 2, 5, 6, 9, 11, 29**
See also CA 13-16; 25-28R; CABS 2;
CANR 35; CAP 1; DLB 5, 16; MTCW

Olson, Toby 1937- . . . . **CLC 28**
See also CA 65-68; CANR 9, 31

Olyesha, Yuri
See Olesha, Yuri (Karlovich)

Ondaatje, (Philip) Michael
1943- . . . . **CLC 14, 29, 51, 76**
See also CA 77-80; CANR 42; DLB 60

Oneal, Elizabeth 1934-
See Oneal, Zibby
See also CA 106; CANR 28; MAICYA;
SATA 30

Oneal, Zibby . . . . **CLC 30**
See also Oneal, Elizabeth
See also AAYA 5; CLR 13; JRDA

O'Neill, Eugene (Gladstone)
1888-1953 . . . . . . **TCLC 1, 6, 27, 49; DA;**
WLC
See also AITN 1; CA 110; 132;
CDALB 1929-1941; DLB 7; MTCW

Onetti, Juan Carlos 1909- . . . . **CLC 7, 10**
See also CA 85-88; CANR 32; DLB 113;
HW; MTCW

O Nuallain, Brian 1911-1966
See O'Brien, Flann
See also CA 21-22; 25-28R; CAP 2

Oppen, George 1908-1984 . . . . **CLC 7, 13, 34**
See also CA 13-16R; 113; CANR 8; DLB 5

Oppenheim, E(dward) Phillips
1866-1946 . . . . **TCLC 45**
See also CA 111; DLB 70

Orlovitz, Gil 1918-1973 . . . . **CLC 22**
See also CA 77-80; 45-48; DLB 2, 5

Orris
See Ingelow, Jean

Ortega y Gasset, Jose
1883-1955 . . . . **TCLC 9; HLC**
See also CA 106; 130; HW; MTCW

Ortiz, Simon J(oseph) 1941- . . . . **CLC 45**
See also CA 134; DLB 120

Orton, Joe . . . . **CLC 4, 13, 43; DC 3**
See also Orton, John Kingsley
See also CDBLB 1960 to Present; DLB 13

Orton, John Kingsley 1933-1967
See Orton, Joe
See also CA 85-88; CANR 35; MTCW

Orwell, George
. . . . **TCLC 2, 6, 15, 31, 51; WLC**
See also Blair, Eric (Arthur)
See also CDBLB 1945-1960; DLB 15, 98

Osborne, David
See Silverberg, Robert

Osborne, George
See Silverberg, Robert

Osborne, John (James)
1929- . . . . **CLC 1, 2, 5, 11, 45; DA; WLC**
See also CA 13-16R; CANR 21;
CDBLB 1945-1960; DLB 13; MTCW

Osborne, Lawrence 1958- . . . . **CLC 50**

Oshima, Nagisa 1932- . . . . **CLC 20**
See also CA 116; 121

Oskison, John M(ilton)
1874-1947 . . . . **TCLC 35**

Ossoli, Sarah Margaret (Fuller marchesa d')
1810-1850
See Fuller, Margaret
See also SATA 25

Ostrovsky, Alexander
1823-1886 . . . . **NCLC 30**

Otero, Blas de 1916-1979 . . . . **CLC 11**
See also CA 89-92; DLB 134

Otto, Whitney 1955- . . . . **CLC 70**
See also CA 140

Ouida . . . . **TCLC 43**
See also De La Ramee, (Marie) Louise
See also DLB 18

Ousmane, Sembene 1923- . . . . **CLC 66; BLC**
See also BW; CA 117; 125; MTCW

Ovid 43B.C.-18th cent. (?) . . . **CMLC 7; PC 2**

Owen, Hugh
See Faust, Frederick (Schiller)

Owen, Wilfred (Edward Salter)
1893-1918 . . . . . . **TCLC 5, 27; DA; WLC**
See also CA 104; 141; CDBLB 1914-1945;
DLB 20

Owens, Rochelle 1936- . . . . **CLC 8**
See also CA 17-20R; CAAS 2; CANR 39

Oz, Amos 1939- . . . **CLC 5, 8, 11, 27, 33, 54**
See also CA 53-56; CANR 27; MTCW

Ozick, Cynthia
1928- . . . . **CLC 3, 7, 28, 62; SSC 15**
See also BEST 90:1; CA 17-20R; CANR 23;
DLB 28; DLBY 82; MTCW

Ozu, Yasujiro 1903-1963 . . . . **CLC 16**
See also CA 112

Pacheco, C.
See Pessoa, Fernando (Antonio Nogueira)

Pa Chin
See Li Fei-kan

Pack, Robert 1929- . . . . **CLC 13**
See also CA 1-4R; CANR 3; DLB 5

Padgett, Lewis
See Kuttner, Henry

Padilla (Lorenzo), Heberto 1932- . . . **CLC 38**
See also AITN 1; CA 123; 131; HW

Page, Jimmy 1944- . . . . **CLC 12**

Page, Louise 1955-. . . . . CLC 40
See also CA 140

Page, P(atricia) K(athleen)
1916-. CLC 7, 18
See also CA 53-56; CANR 4, 22; DLB 68;
MTCW

Paget, Violet 1856-1935
See Lee, Vernon
See also CA 104

Paget-Lowe, Henry
See Lovecraft, H(oward) P(hillips)

Paglia, Camille (Anna) 1947-. . . . . . . CLC 68
See also CA 140

Paige, Richard
See Koontz, Dean R(ay)

Pakenham, Antonia
See Fraser, Antonia (Pakenham)

Palamas, Kostes 1859-1943 . . . . TCLC 5
See also CA 105

Palazzeschi, Aldo 1885-1974 . . . . CLC 11
See also CA 89-92; 53-56; DLB 114

Paley, Grace 1922-. . . . CLC 4, 6, 37; SSC 8
See also CA 25-28R; CANR 13; DLB 28;
MTCW

Palin, Michael (Edward) 1943-. . . . . CLC 21
See also Monty Python
See also CA 107; CANR 35; SATA 67

Palliser, Charles 1947-. . . . . CLC 65
See also CA 136

Palma, Ricardo 1833-1919. . . . . . . TCLC 29

Pancake, Breece Dexter 1952-1979
See Pancake, Breece D'J
See also CA 123; 109

Pancake, Breece D'J. . . . . CLC 29
See also Pancake, Breece Dexter
See also DLB 130

Panko, Rudy
See Gogol, Nikolai (Vasilyevich)

Papadiamantis, Alexandros
1851-1911 . . . . TCLC 29

Papadiamantopoulos, Johannes 1856-1910
See Moreas, Jean
See also CA 117

Papini, Giovanni 1881-1956. . . . . . . TCLC 22
See also CA 121

Paracelsus 1493-1541. . . . . LC 14

Parasol, Peter
See Stevens, Wallace

Parfenie, Maria
See Codrescu, Andrei

Parini, Jay (Lee) 1948- . . . . CLC 54
See also CA 97-100; CAAS 16; CANR 32

Park, Jordan
See Kornbluth, C(yril) M.; Pohl, Frederik

Parker, Bert
See Ellison, Harlan

Parker, Dorothy (Rothschild)
1893-1967 . . . . CLC 15, 68; SSC 2
See also CA 19-20; 25-28R; CAP 2;
DLB 11, 45, 86; MTCW

Parker, Robert B(rown) 1932-. . . . . . CLC 27
See also BEST 89:4; CA 49-52; CANR 1,
26; MTCW

Parkes, Lucas
See Harris, John (Wyndham Parkes Lucas)
Beynon

Parkin, Frank 1940-. . . . . CLC 43

Parkman, Francis, Jr.
1823-1893 . . . . NCLC 12
See also DLB 1, 30

Parks, Gordon (Alexander Buchanan)
1912-. . . . . CLC 1, 16; BLC
See also AITN 2; BW; CA 41-44R;
CANR 26; DLB 33; SATA 8

Parnell, Thomas 1679-1718. . . . . LC 3
See also DLB 94

Parra, Nicanor 1914-. . . . . CLC 2; HLC
See also CA 85-88; CANR 32; HW; MTCW

Parrish, Mary Frances
See Fisher, M(ary) F(rances) K(ennedy)

Parson
See Coleridge, Samuel Taylor

Parson Lot
See Kingsley, Charles

Partridge, Anthony
See Oppenheim, E(dward) Phillips

Pascoli, Giovanni 1855-1912 . . . . . . TCLC 45

Pasolini, Pier Paolo
1922-1975 . . . . CLC 20, 37
See also CA 93-96; 61-64; DLB 128;
MTCW

Pasquini
See Silone, Ignazio

Pastan, Linda (Olenik) 1932- . . . . . . CLC 27
See also CA 61-64; CANR 18, 40; DLB 5

Pasternak, Boris (Leonidovich)
1890-1960 . . . . . . CLC 7, 10, 18, 63; DA;
PC 6; WLC
See also CA 127; 116; MTCW

Patchen, Kenneth 1911-1972. . . CLC 1, 2, 18
See also CA 1-4R; 33-36R; CANR 3, 35;
DLB 16, 48; MTCW

Pater, Walter (Horatio)
1839-1894 . . . . NCLC 7
See also CDBLB 1832-1890; DLB 57

Paterson, A(ndrew) B(arton)
1864-1941 . . . . TCLC 32

Paterson, Katherine (Womeldorf)
1932-. . . . . CLC 12, 30
See also AAYA 1; CA 21-24R; CANR 28;
CLR 7; DLB 52; JRDA; MAICYA;
MTCW; SATA 13, 53

Patmore, Coventry Kersey Dighton
1823-1896 . . . . NCLC 9
See also DLB 35, 98

Paton, Alan (Stewart)
1903-1988 . . . . . . CLC 4, 10, 25, 55; DA;
WLC
See also CA 13-16; 125; CANR 22; CAP 1;
MTCW; SATA 11, 56

Paton Walsh, Gillian 1937-
See Walsh, Jill Paton
See also CANR 38; JRDA; MAICYA;
SAAS 3; SATA 4, 72

Paulding, James Kirke 1778-1860. . NCLC 2
See also DLB 3, 59, 74

Paulin, Thomas Neilson 1949-
See Paulin, Tom
See also CA 123; 128

Paulin, Tom. . . . . CLC 37
See also Paulin, Thomas Neilson
See also DLB 40

Paustovsky, Konstantin (Georgievich)
1892-1968 . . . . CLC 40
See also CA 93-96; 25-28R

Pavese, Cesare 1908-1950 . . . . TCLC 3
See also CA 104; DLB 128

Pavic, Milorad 1929-. . . . . CLC 60
See also CA 136

Payne, Alan
See Jakes, John (William)

Paz, Gil
See Lugones, Leopoldo

Paz, Octavio
1914-. . . . . . . CLC 3, 4, 6, 10, 19, 51, 65;
DA; HLC; PC 1; WLC
See also CA 73-76; CANR 32; DLBY 90;
HW; MTCW

Peacock, Molly 1947-. . . . . CLC 60
See also CA 103; DLB 120

Peacock, Thomas Love
1785-1866 . . . . NCLC 22
See also DLB 96, 116

Peake, Mervyn 1911-1968. . . . . . . CLC 7, 54
See also CA 5-8R; 25-28R; CANR 3;
DLB 15; MTCW; SATA 23

Pearce, Philippa . . . . CLC 21
See also Christie, (Ann) Philippa
See also CLR 9; MAICYA; SATA 1, 67

Pearl, Eric
See Elman, Richard

Pearson, T(homas) R(eid) 1956- . . . . CLC 39
See also CA 120; 130

Peck, Dale 1968(?)- . . . . CLC 81

Peck, John 1941-. . . . . CLC 3
See also CA 49-52; CANR 3

Peck, Richard (Wayne) 1934-. . . . . . CLC 21
See also AAYA 1; CA 85-88; CANR 19,
38; JRDA; MAICYA; SAAS 2; SATA 18,
55

Peck, Robert Newton 1928-. . . . CLC 17; DA
See also AAYA 3; CA 81-84; CANR 31;
JRDA; MAICYA; SAAS 1; SATA 21, 62

Peckinpah, (David) Sam(uel)
1925-1984 . . . . CLC 20
See also CA 109; 114

Pedersen, Knut 1859-1952
See Hamsun, Knut
See also CA 104; 119; MTCW

Peeslake, Gaffer
See Durrell, Lawrence (George)

Peguy, Charles Pierre
1873-1914 . . . . TCLC 10
See also CA 107

Pena, Ramon del Valle y
See Valle-Inclan, Ramon (Maria) del

Pendennis, Arthur Esquir
See Thackeray, William Makepeace

Penn, William 1644-1718. . . . . LC 25
See also DLB 24

Pepys, Samuel
1633-1703 . . . . **LC 11; DA; WLC**
See also CDBLB 1660-1789; DLB 101

Percy, Walker
1916-1990 . . . . **CLC 2, 3, 6, 8, 14, 18, 47,
65**
See also CA 1-4R; 131; CANR 1, 23;
DLB 2; DLBY 80, 90; MTCW

Perec, Georges 1936-1982 . . . . **CLC 56**
See also CA 141; DLB 83

Pereda (y Sanchez de Porrua), Jose Maria de
1833-1906 . . . . **TCLC 16**
See also CA 117

Pereda y Porrua, Jose Maria de
See Pereda (y Sanchez de Porrua), Jose
Maria de

Peregoy, George Weems
See Mencken, H(enry) L(ouis)

Perelman, S(idney) J(oseph)
1904-1979 . . . **CLC 3, 5, 9, 15, 23, 44, 49**
See also AITN 1, 2; CA 73-76; 89-92;
CANR 18; DLB 11, 44; MTCW

Peret, Benjamin 1899-1959 . . . . **TCLC 20**
See also CA 117

Peretz, Isaac Loeb 1851(?)-1915 . . . **TCLC 16**
See also CA 109

Peretz, Yitzkhok Leibush
See Peretz, Isaac Loeb

Perez Galdos, Benito 1843-1920 . . . **TCLC 27**
See also CA 125; HW

Perrault, Charles 1628-1703 . . . . **LC 2**
See also MAICYA; SATA 25

Perry, Brighton
See Sherwood, Robert E(mmet)

Perse, St.-John . . . . **CLC 4, 11, 46**
See also Leger, (Marie-Rene Auguste) Alexis
Saint-Leger

Peseenz, Tulio F.
See Lopez y Fuentes, Gregorio

Pesetsky, Bette 1932- . . . . **CLC 28**
See also CA 133; DLB 130

Peshkov, Alexei Maximovich 1868-1936
See Gorky, Maxim
See also CA 105; 141; DA

Pessoa, Fernando (Antonio Nogueira)
1888-1935 . . . . **TCLC 27; HLC**
See also CA 125

Peterkin, Julia Mood 1880-1961 . . . . **CLC 31**
See also CA 102; DLB 9

Peters, Joan K. 1945- . . . . **CLC 39**

Peters, Robert L(ouis) 1924- . . . . **CLC 7**
See also CA 13-16R; CAAS 8; DLB 105

Petofi, Sandor 1823-1849 . . . . **NCLC 21**

Petrakis, Harry Mark 1923- . . . . **CLC 3**
See also CA 9-12R; CANR 4, 30

Petrarch 1304-1374 . . . . **PC 8**

Petrov, Evgeny . . . . **TCLC 21**
See also Kataev, Evgeny Petrovich

Petry, Ann (Lane) 1908- . . . . . . **CLC 1, 7, 18**
See also BW; CA 5-8R; CAAS 6; CANR 4;
CLR 12; DLB 76; JRDA; MAICYA;
MTCW; SATA 5

Petursson, Halligrimur 1614-1674 . . . . **LC 8**

Philipson, Morris H. 1926- . . . . **CLC 53**
See also CA 1-4R; CANR 4

Phillips, David Graham
1867-1911 . . . . **TCLC 44**
See also CA 108; DLB 9, 12

Phillips, Jack
See Sandburg, Carl (August)

Phillips, Jayne Anne 1952- . . . . . **CLC 15, 33**
See also CA 101; CANR 24; DLBY 80;
MTCW

Phillips, Richard
See Dick, Philip K(indred)

Phillips, Robert (Schaeffer) 1938- . . . **CLC 28**
See also CA 17-20R; CAAS 13; CANR 8;
DLB 105

Phillips, Ward
See Lovecraft, H(oward) P(hillips)

Piccolo, Lucio 1901-1969 . . . . **CLC 13**
See also CA 97-100; DLB 114

Pickthall, Marjorie L(owry) C(hristie)
1883-1922 . . . . **TCLC 21**
See also CA 107; DLB 92

Pico della Mirandola, Giovanni
1463-1494 . . . . **LC 15**

Piercy, Marge
1936- . . . . **CLC 3, 6, 14, 18, 27, 62**
See also CA 21-24R; CAAS 1; CANR 13,
43; DLB 120; MTCW

Piers, Robert
See Anthony, Piers

Pieyre de Mandiargues, Andre 1909-1991
See Mandiargues, Andre Pieyre de
See also CA 103; 136; CANR 22

Pilnyak, Boris . . . . **TCLC 23**
See also Vogau, Boris Andreyevich

Pincherle, Alberto 1907-1990 . . . **CLC 11, 18**
See also Moravia, Alberto
See also CA 25-28R; 132; CANR 33;
MTCW

Pinckney, Darryl 1953- . . . . **CLC 76**
See also CA 143

Pindar 518B.C.-446B.C. . . . . **CMLC 12**

Pineda, Cecile 1942- . . . . **CLC 39**
See also CA 118

Pinero, Arthur Wing 1855-1934 . . . **TCLC 32**
See also CA 110; DLB 10

Pinero, Miguel (Antonio Gomez)
1946-1988 . . . . **CLC 4, 55**
See also CA 61-64; 125; CANR 29; HW

Pinget, Robert 1919- . . . . . . **CLC 7, 13, 37**
See also CA 85-88; DLB 83

Pink Floyd . . . . **CLC 35**
See also Barrett, (Roger) Syd; Gilmour,
David; Mason, Nick; Waters, Roger;
Wright, Rick

Pinkney, Edward 1802-1828 . . . . . **NCLC 31**

Pinkwater, Daniel Manus 1941- . . . . **CLC 35**
See also Pinkwater, Manus
See also AAYA 1; CA 29-32R; CANR 12,
38; CLR 4; JRDA; MAICYA; SAAS 3;
SATA 46

Pinkwater, Manus
See Pinkwater, Daniel Manus
See also SATA 8

Pinsky, Robert 1940- . . . . **CLC 9, 19, 38**
See also CA 29-32R; CAAS 4; DLBY 82

Pinta, Harold
See Pinter, Harold

Pinter, Harold
1930- . . . . . **CLC 1, 3, 6, 9, 11, 15, 27, 58,
73; DA; WLC**
See also CA 5-8R; CANR 33; CDBLB 1960
to Present; DLB 13; MTCW

Pirandello, Luigi
1867-1936 . . . . . . **TCLC 4, 29; DA; WLC**
See also CA 104

Pirsig, Robert M(aynard)
1928- . . . . **CLC 4, 6, 73**
See also CA 53-56; CANR 42; MTCW;
SATA 39

Pisarev, Dmitry Ivanovich
1840-1868 . . . . **NCLC 25**

Pix, Mary (Griffith) 1666-1709 . . . . . . **LC 8**
See also DLB 80

Pixerecourt, Guilbert de
1773-1844 . . . . **NCLC 39**

Plaidy, Jean
See Hibbert, Eleanor Alice Burford

Planche, James Robinson
1796-1880 . . . . **NCLC 42**

Plant, Robert 1948- . . . . **CLC 12**

Plante, David (Robert)
1940- . . . . **CLC 7, 23, 38**
See also CA 37-40R; CANR 12, 36;
DLBY 83; MTCW

Plath, Sylvia
1932-1963 . . . . . **CLC 1, 2, 3, 5, 9, 11, 14,
17, 50, 51, 62; DA; PC 1; WLC**
See also CA 19-20; CANR 34; CAP 2;
CDALB 1941-1968; DLB 5, 6; MTCW

Plato 428(?)B.C.-348(?)B.C. . . . . **CMLC 8; DA**

Platonov, Andrei . . . . **TCLC 14**
See also Klimentov, Andrei Platonovich

Platt, Kin 1911- . . . . **CLC 26**
See also CA 17-20R; CANR 11; JRDA;
SAAS 17; SATA 21

Plick et Plock
See Simenon, Georges (Jacques Christian)

Plimpton, George (Ames) 1927- . . . . . **CLC 36**
See also AITN 1; CA 21-24R; CANR 32;
MTCW; SATA 10

Plomer, William Charles Franklin
1903-1973 . . . . **CLC 4, 8**
See also CA 21-22; CANR 34; CAP 2;
DLB 20; MTCW; SATA 24

Plowman, Piers
See Kavanagh, Patrick (Joseph)

Plum, J.
See Wodehouse, P(elham) G(renville)

Plumly, Stanley (Ross) 1939- . . . . . . **CLC 33**
See also CA 108; 110; DLB 5

Plumpe, Friedrich Wilhelm
1888-1931 . . . . **TCLC 53**
See also CA 112

Poe, Edgar Allan
1809-1849 . . . . . **NCLC 1, 16; DA; PC 1;
SSC 1; WLC**
See also CDALB 1640-1865; DLB 3, 59, 73,
74; SATA 23

Poet of Titchfield Street, The
  See Pound, Ezra (Weston Loomis)

Pohl, Frederik 1919- .... **CLC 18**
  See also CA 61-64; CAAS 1; CANR 11, 37;
  DLB 8; MTCW; SATA 24

Poirier, Louis 1910-
  See Gracq, Julien
  See also CA 122; 126

Poitier, Sidney 1927-............. **CLC 26**
  See also BW; CA 117

Polanski, Roman 1933- .... **CLC 16**
  See also CA 77-80

Poliakoff, Stephen 1952- .... **CLC 38**
  See also CA 106; DLB 13

Police, The..................... **CLC 26**
  See also Copeland, Stewart (Armstrong);
  Summers, Andrew James; Sumner,
  Gordon Matthew

Pollitt, Katha 1949- .... **CLC 28**
  See also CA 120; 122; MTCW

Pollock, (Mary) Sharon 1936-...... **CLC 50**
  See also CA 141; DLB 60

Pomerance, Bernard 1940-........ **CLC 13**
  See also CA 101

Ponge, Francis (Jean Gaston Alfred)
  1899-1988 .... **CLC 6, 18**
  See also CA 85-88; 126; CANR 40

Pontoppidan, Henrik 1857-1943 ... **TCLC 29**

Poole, Josephine .... **CLC 17**
  See also Helyar, Jane Penelope Josephine
  See also SAAS 2; SATA 5

Popa, Vasko 1922-............... **CLC 19**
  See also CA 112

Pope, Alexander
  1688-1744 .... **LC 3; DA; WLC**
  See also CDBLB 1660-1789; DLB 95, 101

Porter, Connie (Rose) 1959(?)- ..... **CLC 70**
  See also CA 142

Porter, Gene(va Grace) Stratton
  1863(?)-1924 .... **TCLC 21**
  See also CA 112

Porter, Katherine Anne
  1890-1980 ...... **CLC 1, 3, 7, 10, 13, 15,**
              27; DA; SSC 4
  See also AITN 2; CA 1-4R; 101; CANR 1;
  DLB 4, 9, 102; DLBY 80; MTCW;
  SATA 23, 39

Porter, Peter (Neville Frederick)
  1929- .... **CLC 5, 13, 33**
  See also CA 85-88; DLB 40

Porter, William Sydney 1862-1910
  See Henry, O.
  See also CA 104; 131; CDALB 1865-1917;
  DA; DLB 12, 78, 79; MTCW; YABC 2

Portillo (y Pacheco), Jose Lopez
  See Lopez Portillo (y Pacheco), Jose

Post, Melville Davisson
  1869-1930 .... **TCLC 39**
  See also CA 110

Potok, Chaim 1929-....... **CLC 2, 7, 14, 26**
  See also AITN 1, 2; CA 17-20R; CANR 19,
  35; DLB 28; MTCW; SATA 33

Potter, Beatrice
  See Webb, (Martha) Beatrice (Potter)
  See also MAICYA

Potter, Dennis (Christopher George)
  1935- .... **CLC 58**
  See also CA 107; CANR 33; MTCW

Pound, Ezra (Weston Loomis)
  1885-1972 ...... **CLC 1, 2, 3, 4, 5, 7, 10,**
          13, 18, 34, 48, 50; DA; PC 4; WLC
  See also CA 5-8R; 37-40R; CANR 40;
  CDALB 1917-1929; DLB 4, 45, 63;
  MTCW

Povod, Reinaldo 1959-............ **CLC 44**
  See also CA 136

Powell, Anthony (Dymoke)
  1905- .... **CLC 1, 3, 7, 9, 10, 31**
  See also CA 1-4R; CANR 1, 32;
  CDBLB 1945-1960; DLB 15; MTCW

Powell, Dawn 1897-1965 .... **CLC 66**
  See also CA 5-8R

Powell, Padgett 1952-............ **CLC 34**
  See also CA 126

Powers, J(ames) F(arl)
  1917- .... **CLC 1, 4, 8, 57; SSC 4**
  See also CA 1-4R; CANR 2; DLB 130;
  MTCW

Powers, John J(ames) 1945-
  See Powers, John R.
  See also CA 69-72

Powers, John R. .... **CLC 66**
  See also Powers, John J(ames)

Pownall, David 1938-............. **CLC 10**
  See also CA 89-92; CAAS 18; DLB 14

Powys, John Cowper
  1872-1963 .... **CLC 7, 9, 15, 46**
  See also CA 85-88; DLB 15; MTCW

Powys, T(heodore) F(rancis)
  1875-1953 .... **TCLC 9**
  See also CA 106; DLB 36

Prager, Emily 1952-............. **CLC 56**

Pratt, E(dwin) J(ohn)
  1883(?)-1964 .... **CLC 19**
  See also CA 141; 93-96; DLB 92

Premchand.................... **TCLC 21**
  See also Srivastava, Dhanpat Rai

Preussler, Otfried 1923-........... **CLC 17**
  See also CA 77-80; SATA 24

Prevert, Jacques (Henri Marie)
  1900-1977 .... **CLC 15**
  See also CA 77-80; 69-72; CANR 29;
  MTCW; SATA 30

Prevost, Abbe (Antoine Francois)
  1697-1763 .... **LC 1**

Price, (Edward) Reynolds
  1933- .... **CLC 3, 6, 13, 43, 50, 63**
  See also CA 1-4R; CANR 1, 37; DLB 2

Price, Richard 1949- .... **CLC 6, 12**
  See also CA 49-52; CANR 3; DLBY 81

Prichard, Katharine Susannah
  1883-1969 .... **CLC 46**
  See also CA 11-12; CANR 33; CAP 1;
  MTCW; SATA 66

Priestley, J(ohn) B(oynton)
  1894-1984 ....**CLC 2, 5, 9, 34**
  See also CA 9-12R; 113; CANR 33;
  CDBLB 1914-1945; DLB 10, 34, 77, 100;
  DLBY 84; MTCW

Prince 1958(?)- .... **CLC 35**

Prince, F(rank) T(empleton) 1912- ... **CLC 22**
  See also CA 101; CANR 43; DLB 20

Prince Kropotkin
  See Kropotkin, Peter (Aleksieevich)

Prior, Matthew 1664-1721.......... **LC 4**
  See also DLB 95

Pritchard, William H(arrison)
  1932- .... **CLC 34**
  See also CA 65-68; CANR 23; DLB 111

Pritchett, V(ictor) S(awdon)
  1900- ..... **CLC 5, 13, 15, 41; SSC 14**
  See also CA 61-64; CANR 31; DLB 15;
  MTCW

Private 19022
  See Manning, Frederic

Probst, Mark 1925- .... **CLC 59**
  See also CA 130

Prokosch, Frederic 1908-1989.... **CLC 4, 48**
  See also CA 73-76; 128; DLB 48

Prophet, The
  See Dreiser, Theodore (Herman Albert)

Prose, Francine 1947-............. **CLC 45**
  See also CA 109; 112

Proudhon
  See Cunha, Euclides (Rodrigues Pimenta) da

Proulx, E. Annie 1935- .... **CLC 81**

Proust, (Valentin-Louis-George-Eugene-)
  Marcel
  1871-1922 ... **TCLC 7, 13, 33; DA; WLC**
  See also CA 104; 120; DLB 65; MTCW

Prowler, Harley
  See Masters, Edgar Lee

Prus, Boleslaw................... **TCLC 48**
  See also Glowacki, Aleksander

Pryor, Richard (Franklin Lenox Thomas)
  1940- .... **CLC 26**
  See also CA 122

Przybyszewski, Stanislaw
  1868-1927 .... **TCLC 36**
  See also DLB 66

Pteleon
  See Grieve, C(hristopher) M(urray)

Puckett, Lute
  See Masters, Edgar Lee

Puig, Manuel
  1932-1990 ... **CLC 3, 5, 10, 28, 65; HLC**
  See also CA 45-48; CANR 2, 32; DLB 113;
  HW; MTCW

Purdy, Al(fred Wellington)
  1918- ....**CLC 3, 6, 14, 50**
  See also CA 81-84; CAAS 17; CANR 42;
  DLB 88

Purdy, James (Amos)
  1923- .... **CLC 2, 4, 10, 28, 52**
  See also CA 33-36R; CAAS 1; CANR 19;
  DLB 2; MTCW

Pure, Simon
  See Swinnerton, Frank Arthur

Pushkin, Alexander (Sergeyevich)
  1799-1837 ...... **NCLC 3, 27; DA; WLC**
  See also SATA 61

P'u Sung-ling 1640-1715 .... **LC 3**

Putnam, Arthur Lee
  See Alger, Horatio, Jr.

Reid Banks, Lynne 1929-
See Banks, Lynne Reid
See also CA 1-4R; CANR 6, 22, 38;
CLR 24; JRDA; MAICYA; SATA 22, 75

Reilly, William K.
See Creasey, John

Reiner, Max
See Caldwell, (Janet Miriam) Taylor
(Holland)

Reis, Ricardo
See Pessoa, Fernando (Antonio Nogueira)

Remarque, Erich Maria
1898-1970 .... **CLC 21; DA**
See also CA 77-80; 29-32R; DLB 56;
MTCW

Remizov, A.
See Remizov, Aleksei (Mikhailovich)

Remizov, A. M.
See Remizov, Aleksei (Mikhailovich)

Remizov, Aleksei (Mikhailovich)
1877-1957 .... **TCLC 27**
See also CA 125; 133

Renan, Joseph Ernest
1823-1892 .... **NCLC 26**

Renard, Jules 1864-1910 .... **TCLC 17**
See also CA 117

Renault, Mary .... **CLC 3, 11, 17**
See also Challans, Mary
See also DLBY 83

Rendell, Ruth (Barbara) 1930- .. **CLC 28, 48**
See also Vine, Barbara
See also CA 109; CANR 32; DLB 87;
MTCW

Renoir, Jean 1894-1979 .... **CLC 20**
See also CA 129; 85-88

Resnais, Alain 1922-.............. **CLC 16**

Reverdy, Pierre 1889-1960 .... **CLC 53**
See also CA 97-100; 89-92

Rexroth, Kenneth
1905-1982 ...... **CLC 1, 2, 6, 11, 22, 49**
See also CA 5-8R; 107; CANR 14, 34;
CDALB 1941-1968; DLB 16, 48;
DLBY 82; MTCW

Reyes, Alfonso 1889-1959 .... **TCLC 33**
See also CA 131; HW

Reyes y Basoalto, Ricardo Eliecer Neftali
See Neruda, Pablo

Reymont, Wladyslaw (Stanislaw)
1868(?)-1925 .... **TCLC 5**
See also CA 104

Reynolds, Jonathan 1942-....... **CLC 6, 38**
See also CA 65-68; CANR 28

Reynolds, Joshua 1723-1792 .... **LC 15**
See also DLB 104

Reynolds, Michael Shane 1937- .... **CLC 44**
See also CA 65-68; CANR 9

Reznikoff, Charles 1894-1976 .... **CLC 9**
See also CA 33-36; 61-64; CAP 2; DLB 28,
45

Rezzori (d'Arezzo), Gregor von
1914- .... **CLC 25**
See also CA 122; 136

Rhine, Richard
See Silverstein, Alvin

Rhodes, Eugene Manlove
1869-1934 .... **TCLC 53**

R'hoone
See Balzac, Honore de

Rhys, Jean
1890(?)-1979 .... **CLC 2, 4, 6, 14, 19, 51**
See also CA 25-28R; 85-88; CANR 35;
CDBLB 1945-1960; DLB 36, 117; MTCW

Ribeiro, Darcy 1922- .... **CLC 34**
See also CA 33-36R

Ribeiro, Joao Ubaldo (Osorio Pimentel)
1941- .... **CLC 10, 67**
See also CA 81-84

Ribman, Ronald (Burt) 1932- .... **CLC 7**
See also CA 21-24R

Ricci, Nino 1959- .... **CLC 70**
See also CA 137

Rice, Anne 1941- .... **CLC 41**
See also AAYA 9; BEST 89:2; CA 65-68;
CANR 12, 36

Rice, Elmer (Leopold)
1892-1967 .... **CLC 7, 49**
See also CA 21-22; 25-28R; CAP 2; DLB 4,
7; MTCW

Rice, Tim 1944- .... **CLC 21**
See also CA 103

Rich, Adrienne (Cecile)
1929- .... **CLC 3, 6, 7, 11, 18, 36, 73, 76;
PC 5**
See also CA 9-12R; CANR 20; DLB 5, 67;
MTCW

Rich, Barbara
See Graves, Robert (von Ranke)

Rich, Robert
See Trumbo, Dalton

Richards, David Adams 1950-...... **CLC 59**
See also CA 93-96; DLB 53

Richards, I(vor) A(rmstrong)
1893-1979 .... **CLC 14, 24**
See also CA 41-44R; 89-92; CANR 34;
DLB 27

Richardson, Anne
See Roiphe, Anne Richardson

Richardson, Dorothy Miller
1873-1957 .... **TCLC 3**
See also CA 104; DLB 36

Richardson, Ethel Florence (Lindesay)
1870-1946
See Richardson, Henry Handel
See also CA 105

Richardson, Henry Handel .... **TCLC 4**
See also Richardson, Ethel Florence
(Lindesay)

Richardson, Samuel
1689-1761 .... **LC 1; DA; WLC**
See also CDBLB 1660-1789; DLB 39

Richler, Mordecai
1931- .... **CLC 3, 5, 9, 13, 18, 46, 70**
See also AITN 1; CA 65-68; CANR 31;
CLR 17; DLB 53; MAICYA; MTCW;
SATA 27, 44

Richter, Conrad (Michael)
1890-1968 .... **CLC 30**
See also CA 5-8R; 25-28R; CANR 23;
DLB 9; MTCW; SATA 3

Riddell, J. H. 1832-1906 .... **TCLC 40**

Riding, Laura................... **CLC 3, 7**
See also Jackson, Laura (Riding)

Riefenstahl, Berta Helene Amalia 1902-
See Riefenstahl, Leni
See also CA 108

Riefenstahl, Leni................. **CLC 16**
See also Riefenstahl, Berta Helene Amalia

Riffe, Ernest
See Bergman, (Ernst) Ingmar

Riley, James Whitcomb
1849-1916 .... **TCLC 51**
See also CA 118; 137; MAICYA; SATA 17

Riley, Tex
See Creasey, John

Rilke, Rainer Maria
1875-1926 .... **TCLC 1, 6, 19; PC 2**
See also CA 104; 132; DLB 81; MTCW

Rimbaud, (Jean Nicolas) Arthur
1854-1891 ..... **NCLC 4, 35; DA; PC 3;
WLC**

Rinehart, Mary Roberts
1876-1958 .... **TCLC 52**
See also CA 108

Ringmaster, The
See Mencken, H(enry) L(ouis)

Ringwood, Gwen(dolyn Margaret) Pharis
1910-1984 .... **CLC 48**
See also CA 112; DLB 88

Rio, Michel 19(?)-................ **CLC 43**

Ritsos, Giannes
See Ritsos, Yannis

Ritsos, Yannis 1909-1990..... **CLC 6, 13, 31**
See also CA 77-80; 133; CANR 39; MTCW

Ritter, Erika 1948(?)-............. **CLC 52**

Rivera, Jose Eustasio 1889-1928... **TCLC 35**
See also HW

Rivers, Conrad Kent 1933-1968...... **CLC 1**
See also BW; CA 85-88; DLB 41

Rivers, Elfrida
See Bradley, Marion Zimmer

Riverside, John
See Heinlein, Robert A(nson)

Rizal, Jose 1861-1896.......... **NCLC 27**

Roa Bastos, Augusto (Antonio)
1917- .... **CLC 45; HLC**
See also CA 131; DLB 113; HW

Robbe-Grillet, Alain
1922- ...... **CLC 1, 2, 4, 6, 8, 10, 14, 43**
See also CA 9-12R; CANR 33; DLB 83;
MTCW

Robbins, Harold 1916-............. **CLC 5**
See also CA 73-76; CANR 26; MTCW

Robbins, Thomas Eugene 1936-
See Robbins, Tom
See also CA 81-84; CANR 29; MTCW

Robbins, Tom................. **CLC 9, 32, 64**
See also Robbins, Thomas Eugene
See also BEST 90:3; DLBY 80

Robbins, Trina 1938- .... **CLC 21**
See also CA 128

Roberts, Charles G(eorge) D(ouglas)
1860-1943 . . . . TCLC 8
See also CA 105; CLR 33; DLB 92;
SATA 29

Roberts, Kate 1891-1985 . . . . CLC 15
See also CA 107; 116

Roberts, Keith (John Kingston)
1935- . . . . CLC 14
See also CA 25-28R

Roberts, Kenneth (Lewis)
1885-1957 . . . . TCLC 23
See also CA 109; DLB 9

Roberts, Michele (B.) 1949- . . . . CLC 48
See also CA 115

Robertson, Ellis
See Ellison, Harlan; Silverberg, Robert

Robertson, Thomas William
1829-1871 . . . . NCLC 35

Robinson, Edwin Arlington
1869-1935 . . . . TCLC 5; DA; PC 1
See also CA 104; 133; CDALB 1865-1917;
DLB 54; MTCW

Robinson, Henry Crabb
1775-1867 . . . . NCLC 15
See also DLB 107

Robinson, Jill 1936- . . . . CLC 10
See also CA 102

Robinson, Kim Stanley 1952- . . . . . . CLC 34
See also CA 126

Robinson, Lloyd
See Silverberg, Robert

Robinson, Marilynne 1944- . . . . CLC 25
See also CA 116

Robinson, Smokey . . . . CLC 21
See also Robinson, William, Jr.

Robinson, William, Jr. 1940-
See Robinson, Smokey
See also CA 116

Robison, Mary 1949- . . . . CLC 42
See also CA 113; 116; DLB 130

Rod, Edouard 1857-1910 . . . . TCLC 52

Roddenberry, Eugene Wesley 1921-1991
See Roddenberry, Gene
See also CA 110; 135; CANR 37; SATA 45

Roddenberry, Gene . . . . CLC 17
See also Roddenberry, Eugene Wesley
See also AAYA 5; SATA-Obit 69

Rodgers, Mary 1931- . . . . CLC 12
See also CA 49-52; CANR 8; CLR 20;
JRDA; MAICYA; SATA 8

Rodgers, W(illiam) R(obert)
1909-1969 . . . . CLC 7
See also CA 85-88; DLB 20

Rodman, Eric
See Silverberg, Robert

Rodman, Howard 1920(?)-1985 . . . . . CLC 65
See also CA 118

Rodman, Maia
See Wojciechowska, Maia (Teresa)

Rodriguez, Claudio 1934- . . . . CLC 10
See also DLB 134

Roelvaag, O(le) E(dvart)
1876-1931 . . . . TCLC 17
See also CA 117; DLB 9

Roethke, Theodore (Huebner)
1908-1963 . . . . . . CLC 1, 3, 8, 11, 19, 46
See also CA 81-84; CABS 2;
CDALB 1941-1968; DLB 5; MTCW

Rogers, Thomas Hunton 1927- . . . . . CLC 57
See also CA 89-92

Rogers, Will(iam Penn Adair)
1879-1935 . . . . TCLC 8
See also CA 105; DLB 11

Rogin, Gilbert 1929- . . . . CLC 18
See also CA 65-68; CANR 15

Rohan, Koda . . . . TCLC 22
See also Koda Shigeyuki

Rohmer, Eric . . . . CLC 16
See also Scherer, Jean-Marie Maurice

Rohmer, Sax . . . . TCLC 28
See also Ward, Arthur Henry Sarsfield
See also DLB 70

Roiphe, Anne Richardson 1935- . . . CLC 3, 9
See also CA 89-92; DLBY 80

Rojas, Fernando de 1465-1541 . . . . . LC 23

Rolfe, Frederick (William Serafino Austin
Lewis Mary) 1860-1913 . . . . . TCLC 12
See also CA 107; DLB 34

Rolland, Romain 1866-1944 . . . . . . TCLC 23
See also CA 118; DLB 65

Rolvaag, O(le) E(dvart)
See Roelvaag, O(le) E(dvart)

Romain Arnaud, Saint
See Aragon, Louis

Romains, Jules 1885-1972 . . . . CLC 7
See also CA 85-88; CANR 34; DLB 65;
MTCW

Romero, Jose Ruben 1890-1952 . . . TCLC 14
See also CA 114; 131; HW

Ronsard, Pierre de 1524-1585 . . . . LC 6

Rooke, Leon 1934- . . . . CLC 25, 34
See also CA 25-28R; CANR 23

Roper, William 1498-1578 . . . . LC 10

Roquelaure, A. N.
See Rice, Anne

Rosa, Joao Guimaraes 1908-1967 . . . CLC 23
See also CA 89-92; DLB 113

Rosen, Richard (Dean) 1949- . . . . . . CLC 39
See also CA 77-80

Rosenberg, Isaac 1890-1918 . . . . . . TCLC 12
See also CA 107; DLB 20

Rosenblatt, Joe . . . . CLC 15
See also Rosenblatt, Joseph

Rosenblatt, Joseph 1933-
See Rosenblatt, Joe
See also CA 89-92

Rosenfeld, Samuel 1896-1963
See Tzara, Tristan
See also CA 89-92

Rosenthal, M(acha) L(ouis) 1917- . . . CLC 28
See also CA 1-4R; CAAS 6; CANR 4;
DLB 5; SATA 59

Ross, Barnaby
See Dannay, Frederic

Ross, Bernard L.
See Follett, Ken(neth Martin)

Ross, J. H.
See Lawrence, T(homas) E(dward)

Ross, Martin
See Martin, Violet Florence
See also DLB 135

Ross, (James) Sinclair 1908- . . . . CLC 13
See also CA 73-76; DLB 88

Rossetti, Christina (Georgina)
1830-1894 . . . NCLC 2; DA; PC 7; WLC
See also DLB 35; MAICYA; SATA 20

Rossetti, Dante Gabriel
1828-1882 . . . . NCLC 4; DA; WLC
See also CDBLB 1832-1890; DLB 35

Rossner, Judith (Perelman)
1935- . . . . CLC 6, 9, 29
See also AITN 2; BEST 90:3; CA 17-20R;
CANR 18; DLB 6; MTCW

Rostand, Edmond (Eugene Alexis)
1868-1918 . . . . TCLC 6, 37; DA
See also CA 104; 126; MTCW

Roth, Henry 1906- . . . . CLC 2, 6, 11
See also CA 11-12; CANR 38; CAP 1;
DLB 28; MTCW

Roth, Joseph 1894-1939 . . . . TCLC 33
See also DLB 85

Roth, Philip (Milton)
1933- . . . . . . CLC 1, 2, 3, 4, 6, 9, 15, 22,
31, 47, 66; DA; WLC
See also BEST 90:3; CA 1-4R; CANR 1, 22,
36; CDALB 1968-1988; DLB 2, 28;
DLBY 82; MTCW

Rothenberg, Jerome 1931- . . . . CLC 6, 57
See also CA 45-48; CANR 1; DLB 5

Roumain, Jacques (Jean Baptiste)
1907-1944 . . . . TCLC 19; BLC
See also BW; CA 117; 125

Rourke, Constance (Mayfield)
1885-1941 . . . . TCLC 12
See also CA 107; YABC 1

Rousseau, Jean-Baptiste 1671-1741 . . . LC 9

Rousseau, Jean-Jacques
1712-1778 . . . . LC 14; DA; WLC

Roussel, Raymond 1877-1933 . . . . . TCLC 20
See also CA 117

Rovit, Earl (Herbert) 1927- . . . . CLC 7
See also CA 5-8R; CANR 12

Rowe, Nicholas 1674-1718 . . . . LC 8
See also DLB 84

Rowley, Ames Dorrance
See Lovecraft, H(oward) P(hillips)

Rowson, Susanna Haswell
1762(?)-1824 . . . . NCLC 5
See also DLB 37

Roy, Gabrielle 1909-1983 . . . . CLC 10, 14
See also CA 53-56; 110; CANR 5; DLB 68;
MTCW

Rozewicz, Tadeusz 1921- . . . . CLC 9, 23
See also CA 108; CANR 36; MTCW

Ruark, Gibbons 1941- . . . . CLC 3
See also CA 33-36R; CANR 14, 31;
DLB 120

Rubens, Bernice (Ruth) 1923- . . . CLC 19, 31
See also CA 25-28R; CANR 33; DLB 14;
MTCW

Rudkin, (James) David 1936- ...... **CLC 14**
See also CA 89-92; DLB 13

Rudnik, Raphael 1933- .... **CLC 7**
See also CA 29-32R

Ruffian, M.
See Hasek, Jaroslav (Matej Frantisek)

Ruiz, Jose Martinez .... **CLC 11**
See also Martinez Ruiz, Jose

Rukeyser, Muriel
1913-1980 .... **CLC 6, 10, 15, 27**
See also CA 5-8R; 93-96; CANR 26;
DLB 48; MTCW; SATA 22

Rule, Jane (Vance) 1931- .... **CLC 27**
See also CA 25-28R; CAAS 18; CANR 12;
DLB 60

Rulfo, Juan 1918-1986.... **CLC 8, 80; HLC**
See also CA 85-88; 118; CANR 26;
DLB 113; HW; MTCW

Runeberg, Johan 1804-1877...... **NCLC 41**

Runyon, (Alfred) Damon
1884(?)-1946 .... **TCLC 10**
See also CA 107; DLB 11, 86

Rush, Norman 1933- .... **CLC 44**
See also CA 121; 126

Rushdie, (Ahmed) Salman
1947- .... **CLC 23, 31, 55**
See also BEST 89:3; CA 108; 111;
CANR 33; MTCW

Rushforth, Peter (Scott) 1945- ..... **CLC 19**
See also CA 101

Ruskin, John 1819-1900......... **TCLC 20**
See also CA 114; 129; CDBLB 1832-1890;
DLB 55; SATA 24

Russ, Joanna 1937- .... **CLC 15**
See also CA 25-28R; CANR 11, 31; DLB 8;
MTCW

Russell, George William 1867-1935
See A. E.
See also CA 104; CDBLB 1890-1914

Russell, (Henry) Ken(neth Alfred)
1927- .... **CLC 16**
See also CA 105

Russell, Willy 1947- .... **CLC 60**

Rutherford, Mark .... **TCLC 25**
See also White, William Hale
See also DLB 18

Ruyslinck, Ward
See Belser, Reimond Karel Maria de

Ryan, Cornelius (John) 1920-1974 ... **CLC 7**
See also CA 69-72; 53-56; CANR 38

Ryan, Michael 1946- .... **CLC 65**
See also CA 49-52; DLBY 82

Rybakov, Anatoli (Naumovich)
1911- .... **CLC 23, 53**
See also CA 126; 135

Ryder, Jonathan
See Ludlum, Robert

Ryga, George 1932-1987 .... **CLC 14**
See also CA 101; 124; CANR 43; DLB 60

S. S.
See Sassoon, Siegfried (Lorraine)

Saba, Umberto 1883-1957 .... **TCLC 33**
See also DLB 114

Sabatini, Rafael 1875-1950 .... **TCLC 47**

Sabato, Ernesto (R.)
1911- .... **CLC 10, 23; HLC**
See also CA 97-100; CANR 32; HW;
MTCW

Sacastru, Martin
See Bioy Casares, Adolfo

Sacher-Masoch, Leopold von
1836(?)-1895 .... **NCLC 31**

Sachs, Marilyn (Stickle) 1927- ..... **CLC 35**
See also AAYA 2; CA 17-20R; CANR 13;
CLR 2; JRDA; MAICYA; SAAS 2;
SATA 3, 68

Sachs, Nelly 1891-1970 .... **CLC 14**
See also CA 17-18; 25-28R; CAP 2

Sackler, Howard (Oliver)
1929-1982 .... **CLC 14**
See also CA 61-64; 108; CANR 30; DLB 7

Sacks, Oliver (Wolf) 1933- .... **CLC 67**
See also CA 53-56; CANR 28; MTCW

Sade, Donatien Alphonse Francois Comte
1740-1814 .... **NCLC 3**

Sadoff, Ira 1945- .... **CLC 9**
See also CA 53-56; CANR 5, 21; DLB 120

Saetone
See Camus, Albert

Safire, William 1929- .... **CLC 10**
See also CA 17-20R; CANR 31

Sagan, Carl (Edward) 1934- .... **CLC 30**
See also AAYA 2; CA 25-28R; CANR 11,
36; MTCW; SATA 58

Sagan, Francoise .... **CLC 3, 6, 9, 17, 36**
See also Quoirez, Francoise
See also DLB 83

Sahgal, Nayantara (Pandit) 1927-... **CLC 41**
See also CA 9-12R; CANR 11

Saint, H(arry) F. 1941- .... **CLC 50**
See also CA 127

St. Aubin de Teran, Lisa 1953-
See Teran, Lisa St. Aubin de
See also CA 118; 126

Sainte-Beuve, Charles Augustin
1804-1869 .... **NCLC 5**

**Saint-Exupery, Antoine (Jean Baptiste Marie
Roger) de** 1900-1944 ... **TCLC 2; WLC**
See also CA 108; 132; CLR 10; DLB 72;
MAICYA; MTCW; SATA 20

St. John, David
See Hunt, E(verette) Howard, Jr.

Saint-John Perse
See Leger, (Marie-Rene Auguste) Alexis
Saint-Leger

Saintsbury, George (Edward Bateman)
1845-1933 .... **TCLC 31**
See also DLB 57

Sait Faik .... **TCLC 23**
See also Abasiyanik, Sait Faik

Saki .... **TCLC 3; SSC 12**
See also Munro, H(ector) H(ugh)

Salama, Hannu 1936- .... **CLC 18**

Salamanca, J(ack) R(ichard)
1922- .... **CLC 4, 15**
See also CA 25-28R

Sale, J. Kirkpatrick
See Sale, Kirkpatrick

Sale, Kirkpatrick 1937- .... **CLC 68**
See also CA 13-16R; CANR 10

Salinas (y Serrano), Pedro
1891(?)-1951 .... **TCLC 17**
See also CA 117; DLB 134

Salinger, J(erome) D(avid)
1919- ...... **CLC 1, 3, 8, 12, 55, 56; DA;
SSC 2; WLC**
See also AAYA 2; CA 5-8R; CANR 39;
CDALB 1941-1968; CLR 18; DLB 2, 102;
MAICYA; MTCW; SATA 67

Salisbury, John
See Caute, David

Salter, James 1925- .... **CLC 7, 52, 59**
See also CA 73-76; DLB 130

Saltus, Edgar (Everton)
1855-1921 .... **TCLC 8**
See also CA 105

Saltykov, Mikhail Evgrafovich
1826-1889 .... **NCLC 16**

Samarakis, Antonis 1919- .... **CLC 5**
See also CA 25-28R; CAAS 16; CANR 36

Sanchez, Florencio 1875-1910..... **TCLC 37**
See also HW

Sanchez, Luis Rafael 1936- .... **CLC 23**
See also CA 128; HW

Sanchez, Sonia 1934- .... **CLC 5; BLC**
See also BW; CA 33-36R; CANR 24;
CLR 18; DLB 41; DLBD 8; MAICYA;
MTCW; SATA 22

Sand, George
1804-1876 ...... **NCLC 2, 42; DA; WLC**
See also DLB 119

Sandburg, Carl (August)
1878-1967 .... **CLC 1, 4, 10, 15, 35; DA;
PC 2; WLC**
See also CA 5-8R; 25-28R; CANR 35;
CDALB 1865-1917; DLB 17, 54;
MAICYA; MTCW; SATA 8

Sandburg, Charles
See Sandburg, Carl (August)

Sandburg, Charles A.
See Sandburg, Carl (August)

Sanders, (James) Ed(ward) 1939- ... **CLC 53**
See also CA 13-16R; CANR 13; DLB 16

Sanders, Lawrence 1920- .... **CLC 41**
See also BEST 89:4; CA 81-84; CANR 33;
MTCW

Sanders, Noah
See Blount, Roy (Alton), Jr.

Sanders, Winston P.
See Anderson, Poul (William)

Sandoz, Mari(e Susette)
1896-1966 .... **CLC 28**
See also CA 1-4R; 25-28R; CANR 17;
DLB 9; MTCW; SATA 5

Saner, Reg(inald Anthony) 1931- .... **CLC 9**
See also CA 65-68

Sannazaro, Jacopo 1456(?)-1530...... **LC 8**

Sansom, William 1912-1976....... **CLC 2, 6**
See also CA 5-8R; 65-68; CANR 42;
MTCW

Santayana, George 1863-1952..... **TCLC 40**
See also CA 115; DLB 54, 71

Scrum, R.
See Crumb, R(obert)

Scudery, Madeleine de 1607-1701..... **LC 2**

Scum
See Crumb, R(obert)

Scumbag, Little Bobby
See Crumb, R(obert)

Seabrook, John
See Hubbard, L(afayette) Ron(ald)

Sealy, I. Allan 1951- .... **CLC 55**

Search, Alexander
See Pessoa, Fernando (Antonio Nogueira)

Sebastian, Lee
See Silverberg, Robert

Sebastian Owl
See Thompson, Hunter S(tockton)

Sebestyen, Ouida 1924- .... **CLC 30**
See also AAYA 8; CA 107; CANR 40;
CLR 17; JRDA; MAICYA; SAAS 10;
SATA 39

Secundus, H. Scriblerus
See Fielding, Henry

Sedges, John
See Buck, Pearl S(ydenstricker)

Sedgwick, Catharine Maria
1789-1867 .... **NCLC 19**
See also DLB 1, 74

Seelye, John 1931- .... **CLC 7**

Seferiades, Giorgos Stylianou 1900-1971
See Seferis, George
See also CA 5-8R; 33-36R; CANR 5, 36;
MTCW

Seferis, George .... **CLC 5, 11**
See also Seferiades, Giorgos Stylianou

Segal, Erich (Wolf) 1937- .... **CLC 3, 10**
See also BEST 89:1; CA 25-28R; CANR 20,
36; DLBY 86; MTCW

Seger, Bob 1945-................. **CLC 35**

Seghers, Anna .... **CLC 7**
See also Radvanyi, Netty
See also DLB 69

Seidel, Frederick (Lewis) 1936-..... **CLC 18**
See also CA 13-16R; CANR 8; DLBY 84

Seifert, Jaroslav 1901-1986..... **CLC 34, 44**
See also CA 127; MTCW

Sei Shonagon c. 966-1017(?) ...... **CMLC 6**

Selby, Hubert, Jr. 1928- ..... **CLC 1, 2, 4, 8**
See also CA 13-16R; CANR 33; DLB 2

Selzer, Richard 1928-............. **CLC 74**
See also CA 65-68; CANR 14

Sembene, Ousmane
See Ousmane, Sembene

Senancour, Etienne Pivert de
1770-1846 .... **NCLC 16**
See also DLB 119

Sender, Ramon (Jose)
1902-1982 .... **CLC 8; HLC**
See also CA 5-8R; 105; CANR 8; HW;
MTCW

Seneca, Lucius Annaeus
4B.C.-65.................... **CMLC 6**

Senghor, Leopold Sedar
1906- .... **CLC 54; BLC**
See also BW; CA 116; 125; MTCW

Serling, (Edward) Rod(man)
1924-1975 .... **CLC 30**
See also AITN 1; CA 65-68; 57-60; DLB 26

Serna, Ramon Gomez de la
See Gomez de la Serna, Ramon

Serpieres
See Guillevic, (Eugene)

Service, Robert
See Service, Robert W(illiam)
See also DLB 92

Service, Robert W(illiam)
1874(?)-1958 ...... **TCLC 15; DA; WLC**
See also Service, Robert
See also CA 115; 140; SATA 20

Seth, Vikram 1952-............... **CLC 43**
See also CA 121; 127; DLB 120

Seton, Cynthia Propper
1926-1982 .... **CLC 27**
See also CA 5-8R; 108; CANR 7

Seton, Ernest (Evan) Thompson
1860-1946 .... **TCLC 31**
See also CA 109; DLB 92; JRDA; SATA 18

Seton-Thompson, Ernest
See Seton, Ernest (Evan) Thompson

Settle, Mary Lee 1918- .... **CLC 19, 61**
See also CA 89-92; CAAS 1; DLB 6

Seuphor, Michel
See Arp, Jean

**Sevigne, Marie (de Rabutin-Chantal) Marquise
de** 1626-1696 .... **LC 11**

Sexton, Anne (Harvey)
1928-1974 .... **CLC 2, 4, 6, 8, 10, 15, 53;
DA; PC 2; WLC**
See also CA 1-4R; 53-56; CABS 2;
CANR 3, 36; CDALB 1941-1968; DLB 5;
MTCW; SATA 10

Shaara, Michael (Joseph Jr.)
1929-1988 .... **CLC 15**
See also AITN 1; CA 102; DLBY 83

Shackleton, C. C.
See Aldiss, Brian W(ilson)

Shacochis, Bob .... **CLC 39**
See also Shacochis, Robert G.

Shacochis, Robert G. 1951-
See Shacochis, Bob
See also CA 119; 124

Shaffer, Anthony (Joshua) 1926-.... **CLC 19**
See also CA 110; 116; DLB 13

Shaffer, Peter (Levin)
1926- .... **CLC 5, 14, 18, 37, 60**
See also CA 25-28R; CANR 25;
CDBLB 1960 to Present; DLB 13;
MTCW

Shakey, Bernard
See Young, Neil

Shalamov, Varlam (Tikhonovich)
1907(?)-1982 .... **CLC 18**
See also CA 129; 105

Shamlu, Ahmad 1925- .... **CLC 10**

Shammas, Anton 1951-............ **CLC 55**

Shange, Ntozake
1948- .... **CLC 8, 25, 38, 74; BLC; DC 3**
See also AAYA 9; BW; CA 85-88; CABS 3;
CANR 27; DLB 38; MTCW

Shanley, John Patrick 1950-....... **CLC 75**
See also CA 128; 133

Shapcott, Thomas William 1935- ... **CLC 38**
See also CA 69-72

Shapiro, Jane.................... **CLC 76**

Shapiro, Karl (Jay) 1913- ..**CLC 4, 8, 15, 53**
See also CA 1-4R; CAAS 6; CANR 1, 36;
DLB 48; MTCW

Sharp, William 1855-1905........ **TCLC 39**

Sharpe, Thomas Ridley 1928-
See Sharpe, Tom
See also CA 114; 122

Sharpe, Tom.................... **CLC 36**
See also Sharpe, Thomas Ridley
See also DLB 14

Shaw, Bernard.................... **TCLC 45**
See also Shaw, George Bernard

Shaw, G. Bernard
See Shaw, George Bernard

Shaw, George Bernard
1856-1950 .... **TCLC 3, 9, 21; DA; WLC**
See also Shaw, Bernard
See also CA 104; 128; CDBLB 1914-1945;
DLB 10, 57; MTCW

Shaw, Henry Wheeler
1818-1885 .... **NCLC 15**
See also DLB 11

Shaw, Irwin 1913-1984....... **CLC 7, 23, 34**
See also AITN 1; CA 13-16R; 112;
CANR 21; CDALB 1941-1968; DLB 6,
102; DLBY 84; MTCW

Shaw, Robert 1927-1978 .... **CLC 5**
See also AITN 1; CA 1-4R; 81-84;
CANR 4; DLB 13, 14

Shaw, T. E.
See Lawrence, T(homas) E(dward)

Shawn, Wallace 1943- .... **CLC 41**
See also CA 112

Sheed, Wilfrid (John Joseph)
1930- .... **CLC 2, 4, 10, 53**
See also CA 65-68; CANR 30; DLB 6;
MTCW

Sheldon, Alice Hastings Bradley
1915(?)-1987
See Tiptree, James, Jr.
See also CA 108; 122; CANR 34; MTCW

Sheldon, John
See Bloch, Robert (Albert)

Shelley, Mary Wollstonecraft (Godwin)
1797-1851 .... **NCLC 14; DA; WLC**
See also CDBLB 1789-1832; DLB 110, 116;
SATA 29

Shelley, Percy Bysshe
1792-1822 .... **NCLC 18; DA; WLC**
See also CDBLB 1789-1832; DLB 96, 110

Shepard, Jim 1956-............... **CLC 36**
See also CA 137

Shepard, Lucius 1947- .... **CLC 34**
See also CA 128; 141

Shepard, Sam
1943- . . . . **CLC 4, 6, 17, 34, 41, 44**
See also AAYA 1; CA 69-72; CABS 3;
CANR 22; DLB 7; MTCW

Shepherd, Michael
See Ludlum, Robert

Sherburne, Zoa (Morin) 1912- . . . . . . **CLC 30**
See also CA 1-4R; CANR 3, 37; MAICYA;
SATA 3

Sheridan, Frances 1724-1766 . . . . **LC 7**
See also DLB 39, 84

Sheridan, Richard Brinsley
1751-1816 . . . **NCLC 5; DA; DC 1; WLC**
See also CDBLB 1660-1789; DLB 89

Sherman, Jonathan Marc . . . . **CLC 55**

Sherman, Martin 1941(?)- . . . . **CLC 19**
See also CA 116; 123

Sherwin, Judith Johnson 1936- . . . **CLC 7, 15**
See also CA 25-28R; CANR 34

Sherwood, Frances 1940- . . . . **CLC 81**

Sherwood, Robert E(mmet)
1896-1955 . . . . **TCLC 3**
See also CA 104; DLB 7, 26

Shiel, M(atthew) P(hipps)
1865-1947 . . . . **TCLC 8**
See also CA 106

Shiga, Naoya 1883-1971 . . . . **CLC 33**
See also CA 101; 33-36R

Shimazaki Haruki 1872-1943
See Shimazaki Toson
See also CA 105; 134

Shimazaki Toson . . . . **TCLC 5**
See also Shimazaki Haruki

Sholokhov, Mikhail (Aleksandrovich)
1905-1984 . . . . **CLC 7, 15**
See also CA 101; 112; MTCW; SATA 36

Shone, Patric
See Hanley, James

Shreve, Susan Richards 1939- . . . . . . **CLC 23**
See also CA 49-52; CAAS 5; CANR 5, 38;
MAICYA; SATA 41, 46

Shue, Larry 1946-1985 . . . . **CLC 52**
See also CA 117

Shu-Jen, Chou 1881-1936
See Hsun, Lu
See also CA 104

Shulman, Alix Kates 1932- . . . . . . **CLC 2, 10**
See also CA 29-32R; CANR 43; SATA 7

Shuster, Joe 1914- . . . . **CLC 21**

Shute, Nevil . . . . **CLC 30**
See also Norway, Nevil Shute

Shuttle, Penelope (Diane) 1947- . . . . . **CLC 7**
See also CA 93-96; CANR 39; DLB 14, 40

Sidney, Mary 1561-1621 . . . . **LC 19**

Sidney, Sir Philip 1554-1586 . . . . **LC 19; DA**
See also CDBLB Before 1660

Siegel, Jerome 1914- . . . . **CLC 21**
See also CA 116

Siegel, Jerry
See Siegel, Jerome

Sienkiewicz, Henryk (Adam Alexander Pius)
1846-1916 . . . . **TCLC 3**
See also CA 104; 134

Sierra, Gregorio Martinez
See Martinez Sierra, Gregorio

Sierra, Maria (de la O'LeJarraga) Martinez
See Martinez Sierra, Maria (de la
O'LeJarraga)

Sigal, Clancy 1926- . . . . **CLC 7**
See also CA 1-4R

Sigourney, Lydia Howard (Huntley)
1791-1865 . . . . **NCLC 21**
See also DLB 1, 42, 73

Siguenza y Gongora, Carlos de
1645-1700 . . . . **LC 8**

Sigurjonsson, Johann 1880-1919 . . . **TCLC 27**

Sikelianos, Angelos 1884-1951 . . . . **TCLC 39**

Silkin, Jon 1930- . . . . **CLC 2, 6, 43**
See also CA 5-8R; CAAS 5; DLB 27

Silko, Leslie Marmon
1948- . . . . **CLC 23, 74; DA**
See also CA 115; 122

Sillanpaa, Frans Eemil 1888-1964 . . . **CLC 19**
See also CA 129; 93-96; MTCW

Sillitoe, Alan
1928- . . . . **CLC 1, 3, 6, 10, 19, 57**
See also AITN 1; CA 9-12R; CAAS 2;
CANR 8, 26; CDBLB 1960 to Present;
DLB 14; MTCW; SATA 61

Silone, Ignazio 1900-1978 . . . . **CLC 4**
See also CA 25-28; 81-84; CANR 34;
CAP 2; MTCW

Silver, Joan Micklin 1935- . . . . **CLC 20**
See also CA 114; 121

Silver, Nicholas
See Faust, Frederick (Schiller)

Silverberg, Robert 1935- . . . . **CLC 7**
See also CA 1-4R; CAAS 3; CANR 1, 20,
36; DLB 8; MAICYA; MTCW; SATA 13

Silverstein, Alvin 1933- . . . . **CLC 17**
See also CA 49-52; CANR 2; CLR 25;
JRDA; MAICYA; SATA 8, 69

Silverstein, Virginia B(arbara Opshelor)
1937- . . . . **CLC 17**
See also CA 49-52; CANR 2; CLR 25;
JRDA; MAICYA; SATA 8, 69

Sim, Georges
See Simenon, Georges (Jacques Christian)

Simak, Clifford D(onald)
1904-1988 . . . . **CLC 1, 55**
See also CA 1-4R; 125; CANR 1, 35;
DLB 8; MTCW; SATA 56

Simenon, Georges (Jacques Christian)
1903-1989 . . . . **CLC 1, 2, 3, 8, 18, 47**
See also CA 85-88; 129; CANR 35;
DLB 72; DLBY 89; MTCW

Simic, Charles 1938- . . . **CLC 6, 9, 22, 49, 68**
See also CA 29-32R; CAAS 4; CANR 12,
33; DLB 105

Simmons, Charles (Paul) 1924- . . . . . **CLC 57**
See also CA 89-92

Simmons, Dan 1948- . . . . **CLC 44**
See also CA 138

Simmons, James (Stewart Alexander)
1933- . . . . **CLC 43**
See also CA 105; DLB 40

Simms, William Gilmore
1806-1870 . . . . **NCLC 3**
See also DLB 3, 30, 59, 73

Simon, Carly 1945- . . . . **CLC 26**
See also CA 105

Simon, Claude 1913- . . . . . . **CLC 4, 9, 15, 39**
See also CA 89-92; CANR 33; DLB 83;
MTCW

Simon, (Marvin) Neil
1927- . . . . **CLC 6, 11, 31, 39, 70**
See also AITN 1; CA 21-24R; CANR 26;
DLB 7; MTCW

Simon, Paul 1942(?)- . . . . **CLC 17**
See also CA 116

Simonon, Paul 1956(?)- . . . . **CLC 30**
See also Clash, The

Simpson, Harriette
See Arnow, Harriette (Louisa) Simpson

Simpson, Louis (Aston Marantz)
1923- . . . . **CLC 4, 7, 9, 32**
See also CA 1-4R; CAAS 4; CANR 1;
DLB 5; MTCW

Simpson, Mona (Elizabeth) 1957- . . . **CLC 44**
See also CA 122; 135

Simpson, N(orman) F(rederick)
1919- . . . . **CLC 29**
See also CA 13-16R; DLB 13

Sinclair, Andrew (Annandale)
1935- . . . . **CLC 2, 14**
See also CA 9-12R; CAAS 5; CANR 14, 38;
DLB 14; MTCW

Sinclair, Emil
See Hesse, Hermann

Sinclair, Iain 1943- . . . . **CLC 76**
See also CA 132

Sinclair, Iain MacGregor
See Sinclair, Iain

Sinclair, Mary Amelia St. Clair 1865(?)-1946
See Sinclair, May
See also CA 104

Sinclair, May . . . . **TCLC 3, 11**
See also Sinclair, Mary Amelia St. Clair
See also DLB 36, 135

Sinclair, Upton (Beall)
1878-1968 . . . . . . **CLC 1, 11, 15, 63; DA;**
WLC
See also CA 5-8R; 25-28R; CANR 7;
CDALB 1929-1941; DLB 9; MTCW;
SATA 9

Singer, Isaac
See Singer, Isaac Bashevis

Singer, Isaac Bashevis
1904-1991 . . . . **CLC 1, 3, 6, 9, 11, 15, 23,**
38, 69; DA; SSC 3; WLC
See also AITN 1, 2; CA 1-4R; 134;
CANR 1, 39; CDALB 1941-1968; CLR 1;
DLB 6, 28, 52; DLBY 91; JRDA;
MAICYA; MTCW; SATA 3, 27;
SATA-Obit 68

Singer, Israel Joshua 1893-1944 . . . **TCLC 33**

Singh, Khushwant 1915- . . . . **CLC 11**
See also CA 9-12R; CAAS 9; CANR 6

Sinjohn, John
See Galsworthy, John

Sinyavsky, Andrei (Donatevich)
1925- . . . . CLC 8
See also CA 85-88

Sirin, V.
See Nabokov, Vladimir (Vladimirovich)

Sissman, L(ouis) E(dward)
1928-1976 . . . . CLC 9, 18
See also CA 21-24R; 65-68; CANR 13;
DLB 5

Sisson, C(harles) H(ubert)   1914- . . . . . CLC 8
See also CA 1-4R; CAAS 3; CANR 3;
DLB 27

Sitwell, Dame Edith
1887-1964 . . . . CLC 2, 9, 67; PC 3
See also CA 9-12R; CANR 35;
CDBLB 1945-1960; DLB 20; MTCW

Sjoewall, Maj   1935- . . . . CLC 7
See also CA 65-68

Sjowall, Maj
See Sjoewall, Maj

Skelton, Robin   1925- . . . . CLC 13
See also AITN 2; CA 5-8R; CAAS 5;
CANR 28; DLB 27, 53

Skolimowski, Jerzy   1938- . . . . CLC 20
See also CA 128

Skram, Amalie (Bertha)
1847-1905 . . . . TCLC 25

Skvorecky, Josef (Vaclav)
1924- . . . . CLC 15, 39, 69
See also CA 61-64; CAAS 1; CANR 10, 34;
MTCW

Slade, Bernard . . . . CLC 11, 46
See also Newbound, Bernard Slade
See also CAAS 9; DLB 53

Slaughter, Carolyn   1946- . . . . CLC 56
See also CA 85-88

Slaughter, Frank G(ill)   1908- . . . . . . CLC 29
See also AITN 2; CA 5-8R; CANR 5

Slavitt, David R(ytman)   1935- . . . . CLC 5, 14
See also CA 21-24R; CAAS 3; CANR 41;
DLB 5, 6

Slesinger, Tess   1905-1945 . . . . TCLC 10
See also CA 107; DLB 102

Slessor, Kenneth   1901-1971 . . . . CLC 14
See also CA 102; 89-92

Slowacki, Juliusz   1809-1849 . . . . . NCLC 15

Smart, Christopher   1722-1771 . . . . LC 3
See also DLB 109

Smart, Elizabeth   1913-1986 . . . . CLC 54
See also CA 81-84; 118; DLB 88

Smiley, Jane (Graves)   1949- . . . . CLC 53, 76
See also CA 104; CANR 30

Smith, A(rthur) J(ames) M(arshall)
1902-1980 . . . . CLC 15
See also CA 1-4R; 102; CANR 4; DLB 88

Smith, Betty (Wehner)   1896-1972 . . . CLC 19
See also CA 5-8R; 33-36R; DLBY 82;
SATA 6

Smith, Charlotte (Turner)
1749-1806 . . . . NCLC 23
See also DLB 39, 109

Smith, Clark Ashton   1893-1961 . . . . CLC 43
See also CA 143

Smith, Dave . . . . CLC 22, 42
See also Smith, David (Jeddie)
See also CAAS 7; DLB 5

Smith, David (Jeddie)   1942-
See Smith, Dave
See also CA 49-52; CANR 1

Smith, Florence Margaret
1902-1971 . . . . CLC 8
See also Smith, Stevie
See also CA 17-18; 29-32R; CANR 35;
CAP 2; MTCW

Smith, Iain Crichton   1928- . . . . CLC 64
See also CA 21-24R; DLB 40

Smith, John   1580(?)-1631 . . . . LC 9

Smith, Johnston
See Crane, Stephen (Townley)

Smith, Lee   1944- . . . . CLC 25, 73
See also CA 114; 119; DLBY 83

Smith, Martin
See Smith, Martin Cruz

Smith, Martin Cruz   1942- . . . . CLC 25
See also BEST 89:4; CA 85-88; CANR 6,
23, 43

Smith, Mary-Ann Tirone   1944- . . . . . CLC 39
See also CA 118; 136

Smith, Patti   1946- . . . . CLC 12
See also CA 93-96

Smith, Pauline (Urmson)
1882-1959 . . . . TCLC 25

Smith, Rosamond
See Oates, Joyce Carol

Smith, Sheila Kaye
See Kaye-Smith, Sheila

Smith, Stevie . . . . CLC 3, 8, 25, 44
See also Smith, Florence Margaret
See also DLB 20

Smith, Wilbur A(ddison)   1933- . . . . . CLC 33
See also CA 13-16R; CANR 7; MTCW

Smith, William Jay   1918- . . . . CLC 6
See also CA 5-8R; DLB 5; MAICYA;
SATA 2, 68

Smith, Woodrow Wilson
See Kuttner, Henry

Smolenskin, Peretz   1842-1885 . . . . NCLC 30

Smollett, Tobias (George)   1721-1771 . . LC 2
See also CDBLB 1660-1789; DLB 39, 104

Snodgrass, W(illiam) D(e Witt)
1926- . . . . CLC 2, 6, 10, 18, 68
See also CA 1-4R; CANR 6, 36; DLB 5;
MTCW

Snow, C(harles) P(ercy)
1905-1980 . . . . CLC 1, 4, 6, 9, 13, 19
See also CA 5-8R; 101; CANR 28;
CDBLB 1945-1960; DLB 15, 77; MTCW

Snow, Frances Compton
See Adams, Henry (Brooks)

Snyder, Gary (Sherman)
1930- . . . . CLC 1, 2, 5, 9, 32
See also CA 17-20R; CANR 30; DLB 5, 16

Snyder, Zilpha Keatley   1927- . . . . . . CLC 17
See also CA 9-12R; CANR 38; CLR 31;
JRDA; MAICYA; SAAS 2; SATA 1, 28,
75

Soares, Bernardo
See Pessoa, Fernando (Antonio Nogueira)

Sobh, A.
See Shamlu, Ahmad

Sobol, Joshua . . . . CLC 60

Soderberg, Hjalmar   1869-1941 . . . . TCLC 39

Sodergran, Edith (Irene)
See Soedergran, Edith (Irene)

Soedergran, Edith (Irene)
1892-1923 . . . . TCLC 31

Softly, Edgar
See Lovecraft, H(oward) P(hillips)

Softly, Edward
See Lovecraft, H(oward) P(hillips)

Sokolov, Raymond   1941- . . . . CLC 7
See also CA 85-88

Solo, Jay
See Ellison, Harlan

Sologub, Fyodor . . . . TCLC 9
See also Teternikov, Fyodor Kuzmich

Solomons, Ikey Esquir
See Thackeray, William Makepeace

Solomos, Dionysios   1798-1857 . . . NCLC 15

Solwoska, Mara
See French, Marilyn

Solzhenitsyn, Aleksandr I(sayevich)
1918- . . . . . . CLC 1, 2, 4, 7, 9, 10, 18, 26,
34, 78; DA; WLC
See also AITN 1; CA 69-72; CANR 40;
MTCW

Somers, Jane
See Lessing, Doris (May)

Somerville, Edith   1858-1949 . . . . . . TCLC 51
See also DLB 135

Somerville & Ross
See Martin, Violet Florence; Somerville,
Edith

Sommer, Scott   1951- . . . . CLC 25
See also CA 106

Sondheim, Stephen (Joshua)
1930- . . . . CLC 30, 39
See also CA 103

Sontag, Susan   1933- . . . CLC 1, 2, 10, 13, 31
See also CA 17-20R; CANR 25; DLB 2, 67;
MTCW

Sophocles
496(?)B.C.-406(?)B.C. . . . . CMLC 2; DA;
DC 1

Sorel, Julia
See Drexler, Rosalyn

Sorrentino, Gilbert
1929- . . . . CLC 3, 7, 14, 22, 40
See also CA 77-80; CANR 14, 33; DLB 5;
DLBY 80

Soto, Gary   1952- . . . . CLC 32, 80; HLC
See also AAYA 10; CA 119; 125; DLB 82;
HW; JRDA

Soupault, Philippe   1897-1990 . . . . . . CLC 68
See also CA 116; 131

Souster, (Holmes) Raymond
1921- . . . . CLC 5, 14
See also CA 13-16R; CAAS 14; CANR 13,
29; DLB 88; SATA 63

Southern, Terry 1926- . . . . **CLC 7**
See also CA 1-4R; CANR 1; DLB 2

Southey, Robert 1774-1843 . . . . **NCLC 8**
See also DLB 93, 107; SATA 54

Southworth, Emma Dorothy Eliza Nevitte
1819-1899 . . . . **NCLC 26**

Souza, Ernest
See Scott, Evelyn

Soyinka, Wole
1934- . . . . . . **CLC 3, 5, 14, 36, 44; BLC;
DA; DC 2; WLC**
See also BW; CA 13-16R; CANR 27, 39;
DLB 125; MTCW

Spackman, W(illiam) M(ode)
1905-1990 . . . . **CLC 46**
See also CA 81-84; 132

Spacks, Barry 1931- . . . . **CLC 14**
See also CA 29-32R; CANR 33; DLB 105

Spanidou, Irini 1946- . . . . **CLC 44**

Spark, Muriel (Sarah)
1918- . . . . **CLC 2, 3, 5, 8, 13, 18, 40;
SSC 10**
See also CA 5-8R; CANR 12, 36;
CDBLB 1945-1960; DLB 15; MTCW

Spaulding, Douglas
See Bradbury, Ray (Douglas)

Spaulding, Leonard
See Bradbury, Ray (Douglas)

Spence, J. A. D.
See Eliot, T(homas) S(tearns)

Spencer, Elizabeth 1921- . . . . **CLC 22**
See also CA 13-16R; CANR 32; DLB 6;
MTCW; SATA 14

Spencer, Leonard G.
See Silverberg, Robert

Spencer, Scott 1945- . . . . **CLC 30**
See also CA 113; DLBY 86

Spender, Stephen (Harold)
1909- . . . . **CLC 1, 2, 5, 10, 41**
See also CA 9-12R; CANR 31;
CDBLB 1945-1960; DLB 20; MTCW

Spengler, Oswald (Arnold Gottfried)
1880-1936 . . . . **TCLC 25**
See also CA 118

Spenser, Edmund
1552(?)-1599 . . . . **LC 5; DA; PC 8; WLC**
See also CDBLB Before 1660

Spicer, Jack 1925-1965 . . . . . . **CLC 8, 18, 72**
See also CA 85-88; DLB 5, 16

Spiegelman, Art 1948- . . . . **CLC 76**
See also AAYA 10; CA 125; CANR 41

Spielberg, Peter 1929- . . . . **CLC 6**
See also CA 5-8R; CANR 4; DLBY 81

Spielberg, Steven 1947- . . . . **CLC 20**
See also AAYA 8; CA 77-80; CANR 32;
SATA 32

Spillane, Frank Morrison 1918-
See Spillane, Mickey
See also CA 25-28R; CANR 28; MTCW;
SATA 66

Spillane, Mickey . . . . **CLC 3, 13**
See also Spillane, Frank Morrison

Spinoza, Benedictus de 1632-1677 . . . . **LC 9**

Spinrad, Norman (Richard) 1940- . . . **CLC 46**
See also CA 37-40R; CANR 20; DLB 8

Spitteler, Carl (Friedrich Georg)
1845-1924 . . . . **TCLC 12**
See also CA 109; DLB 129

Spivack, Kathleen (Romola Drucker)
1938- . . . . **CLC 6**
See also CA 49-52

Spoto, Donald 1941- . . . . **CLC 39**
See also CA 65-68; CANR 11

Springsteen, Bruce (F.) 1949- . . . . . . **CLC 17**
See also CA 111

Spurling, Hilary 1940- . . . . **CLC 34**
See also CA 104; CANR 25

Squires, (James) Radcliffe
1917-1993 . . . . **CLC 51**
See also CA 1-4R; 140; CANR 6, 21

Srivastava, Dhanpat Rai 1880(?)-1936
See Premchand
See also CA 118

Stacy, Donald
See Pohl, Frederik

Stael, Germaine de
See Stael-Holstein, Anne Louise Germaine
Necker Baronn
See also DLB 119

Stael-Holstein, Anne Louise Germaine Necker
Baronn 1766-1817 . . . . **NCLC 3**
See also Stael, Germaine de

Stafford, Jean 1915-1979 . . . **CLC 4, 7, 19, 68**
See also CA 1-4R; 85-88; CANR 3; DLB 2;
MTCW; SATA 22

Stafford, William (Edgar)
1914-1993 . . . . **CLC 4, 7, 29**
See also CA 5-8R; 142; CAAS 3; CANR 5,
22; DLB 5

Staines, Trevor
See Brunner, John (Kilian Houston)

Stairs, Gordon
See Austin, Mary (Hunter)

Stannard, Martin 1947- . . . . **CLC 44**
See also CA 142

Stanton, Maura 1946- . . . . **CLC 9**
See also CA 89-92; CANR 15; DLB 120

Stanton, Schuyler
See Baum, L(yman) Frank

Stapledon, (William) Olaf
1886-1950 . . . . **TCLC 22**
See also CA 111; DLB 15

Starbuck, George (Edwin) 1931- . . . . **CLC 53**
See also CA 21-24R; CANR 23

Stark, Richard
See Westlake, Donald E(dwin)

Staunton, Schuyler
See Baum, L(yman) Frank

Stead, Christina (Ellen)
1902-1983 . . . . **CLC 2, 5, 8, 32, 80**
See also CA 13-16R; 109; CANR 33, 40;
MTCW

Stead, William Thomas
1849-1912 . . . . **TCLC 48**

Steele, Richard 1672-1729 . . . . **LC 18**
See also CDBLB 1660-1789; DLB 84, 101

Steele, Timothy (Reid) 1948- . . . . **CLC 45**
See also CA 93-96; CANR 16; DLB 120

Steffens, (Joseph) Lincoln
1866-1936 . . . . **TCLC 20**
See also CA 117

Stegner, Wallace (Earle)
1909-1993 . . . . **CLC 9, 49, 81**
See also AITN 1; BEST 90:3; CA 1-4R;
141; CAAS 9; CANR 1, 21; DLB 9;
MTCW

Stein, Gertrude
1874-1946 . . . . . . **TCLC 1, 6, 28, 48; DA;
WLC**
See also CA 104; 132; CDALB 1917-1929;
DLB 4, 54, 86; MTCW

Steinbeck, John (Ernst)
1902-1968 . . . . . . **CLC 1, 5, 9, 13, 21, 34,
45, 75; DA; SSC 11; WLC**
See also CA 1-4R; 25-28R; CANR 1, 35;
CDALB 1929-1941; DLB 7, 9; DLBD 2;
MTCW; SATA 9

Steinem, Gloria 1934- . . . . **CLC 63**
See also CA 53-56; CANR 28; MTCW

Steiner, George 1929- . . . . **CLC 24**
See also CA 73-76; CANR 31; DLB 67;
MTCW; SATA 62

Steiner, K. Leslie
See Delany, Samuel R(ay, Jr.)

Steiner, Rudolf 1861-1925 . . . . **TCLC 13**
See also CA 107

Stendhal 1783-1842 . . . . **NCLC 23; DA; WLC**
See also DLB 119

Stephen, Leslie 1832-1904 . . . . **TCLC 23**
See also CA 123; DLB 57

Stephen, Sir Leslie
See Stephen, Leslie

Stephen, Virginia
See Woolf, (Adeline) Virginia

Stephens, James 1882(?)-1950 . . . . . . **TCLC 4**
See also CA 104; DLB 19

Stephens, Reed
See Donaldson, Stephen R.

Steptoe, Lydia
See Barnes, Djuna

Sterchi, Beat 1949- . . . . **CLC 65**

Sterling, Brett
See Bradbury, Ray (Douglas); Hamilton,
Edmond

Sterling, Bruce 1954- . . . . **CLC 72**
See also CA 119

Sterling, George 1869-1926 . . . . **TCLC 20**
See also CA 117; DLB 54

Stern, Gerald 1925- . . . . **CLC 40**
See also CA 81-84; CANR 28; DLB 105

Stern, Richard (Gustave) 1928- . . . **CLC 4, 39**
See also CA 1-4R; CANR 1, 25; DLBY 87

Sternberg, Josef von 1894-1969 . . . . . **CLC 20**
See also CA 81-84

Sterne, Laurence
1713-1768 . . . . **LC 2; DA; WLC**
See also CDBLB 1660-1789; DLB 39

Sternheim, (William Adolf) Carl
1878-1942 . . . . **TCLC 8**
See also CA 105; DLB 56, 118

Stevens, Mark 1951- .... **CLC 34**
See also CA 122

Stevens, Wallace
1879-1955 .... **TCLC 3, 12, 45; DA; PC 6; WLC**
See also CA 104; 124; CDALB 1929-1941; DLB 54; MTCW

Stevenson, Anne (Katharine)
1933- .... **CLC 7, 33**
See also CA 17-20R; CAAS 9; CANR 9, 33; DLB 40; MTCW

Stevenson, Robert Louis (Balfour)
1850-1894 .... **NCLC 5, 14; DA; SSC 11; WLC**
See also CDBLB 1890-1914; CLR 10, 11; DLB 18, 57; JRDA; MAICYA; YABC 2

Stewart, J(ohn) I(nnes) M(ackintosh)
1906- .... **CLC 7, 14, 32**
See also CA 85-88; CAAS 3; MTCW

Stewart, Mary (Florence Elinor)
1916- .... **CLC 7, 35**
See also CA 1-4R; CANR 1; SATA 12

Stewart, Mary Rainbow
See Stewart, Mary (Florence Elinor)

Stifter, Adalbert 1805-1868 ...... **NCLC 41**
See also DLB 133

Still, James 1906- .... **CLC 49**
See also CA 65-68; CAAS 17; CANR 10, 26; DLB 9; SATA 29

Sting
See Sumner, Gordon Matthew

Stirling, Arthur
See Sinclair, Upton (Beall)

Stitt, Milan 1941- .... **CLC 29**
See also CA 69-72

Stockton, Francis Richard 1834-1902
See Stockton, Frank R.
See also CA 108; 137; MAICYA; SATA 44

Stockton, Frank R. .... **TCLC 47**
See also Stockton, Francis Richard
See also DLB 42, 74; SATA 32

Stoddard, Charles
See Kuttner, Henry

Stoker, Abraham 1847-1912
See Stoker, Bram
See also CA 105; DA; SATA 29

Stoker, Bram .... **TCLC 8; WLC**
See also Stoker, Abraham
See also CDBLB 1890-1914; DLB 36, 70

Stolz, Mary (Slattery) 1920- .... **CLC 12**
See also AAYA 8; AITN 1; CA 5-8R; CANR 13, 41; JRDA; MAICYA; SAAS 3; SATA 10, 71

Stone, Irving 1903-1989 .... **CLC 7**
See also AITN 1; CA 1-4R; 129; CAAS 3; CANR 1, 23; MTCW; SATA 3; SATA-Obit 64

Stone, Oliver 1946- .... **CLC 73**
See also CA 110

Stone, Robert (Anthony)
1937- .... **CLC 5, 23, 42**
See also CA 85-88; CANR 23; MTCW

Stone, Zachary
See Follett, Ken(neth Martin)

Stoppard, Tom
1937- ...... **CLC 1, 3, 4, 5, 8, 15, 29, 34, 63; DA; WLC**
See also CA 81-84; CANR 39; CDBLB 1960 to Present; DLB 13; DLBY 85; MTCW

Storey, David (Malcolm)
1933- .... **CLC 2, 4, 5, 8**
See also CA 81-84; CANR 36; DLB 13, 14; MTCW

Storm, Hyemeyohsts 1935- .... **CLC 3**
See also CA 81-84

Storm, (Hans) Theodor (Woldsen)
1817-1888 .... **NCLC 1**

Storni, Alfonsina
1892-1938 .... **TCLC 5; HLC**
See also CA 104; 131; HW

Stout, Rex (Todhunter) 1886-1975 ... **CLC 3**
See also AITN 2; CA 61-64

Stow, (Julian) Randolph 1935- .. **CLC 23, 48**
See also CA 13-16R; CANR 33; MTCW

Stowe, Harriet (Elizabeth) Beecher
1811-1896 .... **NCLC 3; DA; WLC**
See also CDALB 1865-1917; DLB 1, 12, 42, 74; JRDA; MAICYA; YABC 1

Strachey, (Giles) Lytton
1880-1932 .... **TCLC 12**
See also CA 110; DLBD 10

Strand, Mark 1934- ...... **CLC 6, 18, 41, 71**
See also CA 21-24R; CANR 40; DLB 5; SATA 41

Straub, Peter (Francis) 1943- ...... **CLC 28**
See also BEST 89:1; CA 85-88; CANR 28; DLBY 84; MTCW

Strauss, Botho 1944- .... **CLC 22**
See also DLB 124

Streatfeild, (Mary) Noel
1895(?)-1986 .... **CLC 21**
See also CA 81-84; 120; CANR 31; CLR 17; MAICYA; SATA 20, 48

Stribling, T(homas) S(igismund)
1881-1965 .... **CLC 23**
See also CA 107; DLB 9

Strindberg, (Johan) August
1849-1912 ...... **TCLC 1, 8, 21, 47; DA; WLC**
See also CA 104; 135

Stringer, Arthur 1874-1950 ...... **TCLC 37**
See also DLB 92

Stringer, David
See Roberts, Keith (John Kingston)

Strugatskii, Arkadii (Natanovich)
1925-1991 .... **CLC 27**
See also CA 106; 135

Strugatskii, Boris (Natanovich)
1933- .... **CLC 27**
See also CA 106

Strummer, Joe 1953(?)- .... **CLC 30**
See also Clash, The

Stuart, Don A.
See Campbell, John W(ood, Jr.)

Stuart, Ian
See MacLean, Alistair (Stuart)

Stuart, Jesse (Hilton)
1906-1984 .... **CLC 1, 8, 11, 14, 34**
See also CA 5-8R; 112; CANR 31; DLB 9, 48, 102; DLBY 84; SATA 2, 36

Sturgeon, Theodore (Hamilton)
1918-1985 .... **CLC 22, 39**
See also Queen, Ellery
See also CA 81-84; 116; CANR 32; DLB 8; DLBY 85; MTCW

Sturges, Preston 1898-1959 .... **TCLC 48**
See also CA 114; DLB 26

Styron, William
1925- .... **CLC 1, 3, 5, 11, 15, 60**
See also BEST 90:4; CA 5-8R; CANR 6, 33; CDALB 1968-1988; DLB 2; DLBY 80; MTCW

Suarez Lynch, B.
See Bioy Casares, Adolfo; Borges, Jorge Luis

Suarez Lynch, B.
See Borges, Jorge Luis

Su Chien 1884-1918
See Su Man-shu
See also CA 123

Sudermann, Hermann 1857-1928 .. **TCLC 15**
See also CA 107; DLB 118

Sue, Eugene 1804-1857 .... **NCLC 1**
See also DLB 119

Sueskind, Patrick 1949- .... **CLC 44**

Sukenick, Ronald 1932- ..... **CLC 3, 4, 6, 48**
See also CA 25-28R; CAAS 8; CANR 32; DLBY 81

Suknaski, Andrew 1942- .... **CLC 19**
See also CA 101; DLB 53

Sullivan, Vernon
See Vian, Boris

Sully Prudhomme 1839-1907 ...... **TCLC 31**

Su Man-shu .... **TCLC 24**
See also Su Chien

Summerforest, Ivy B.
See Kirkup, James

Summers, Andrew James 1942- ..... **CLC 26**
See also Police, The

Summers, Andy
See Summers, Andrew James

Summers, Hollis (Spurgeon, Jr.)
1916- .... **CLC 10**
See also CA 5-8R; CANR 3; DLB 6

Summers, (Alphonsus Joseph-Mary Augustus)
Montague 1880-1948 .... **TCLC 16**
See also CA 118

Sumner, Gordon Matthew 1951- .... **CLC 26**
See also Police, The

Surtees, Robert Smith
1803-1864 .... **NCLC 14**
See also DLB 21

Susann, Jacqueline 1921-1974 .... **CLC 3**
See also AITN 1; CA 65-68; 53-56; MTCW

Suskind, Patrick
See Sueskind, Patrick

Sutcliff, Rosemary 1920-1992 ...... **CLC 26**
See also AAYA 10; CA 5-8R; 139; CANR 37; CLR 1; JRDA; MAICYA; SATA 6, 44; SATA-Obit 73

Thackeray, William Makepeace
    1811-1863 .... **NCLC 5, 14, 22, 43; DA;**
                                                WLC
    See also CDBLB 1832-1890; DLB 21, 55;
        SATA 23

Thakura, Ravindranatha
    See Tagore, Rabindranath

Tharoor, Shashi 1956- .... **CLC 70**
    See also CA 141

Thelwell, Michael Miles 1939- ..... **CLC 22**
    See also CA 101

Theobald, Lewis, Jr.
    See Lovecraft, H(oward) P(hillips)

Theodorescu, Ion N. 1880-1967
    See Arghezi, Tudor
    See also CA 116

Theriault, Yves 1915-1983 .... **CLC 79**
    See also CA 102; DLB 88

Theroux, Alexander (Louis)
    1939- .... **CLC 2, 25**
    See also CA 85-88; CANR 20

Theroux, Paul (Edward)
    1941- .... **CLC 5, 8, 11, 15, 28, 46**
    See also BEST 89:4; CA 33-36R; CANR 20;
        DLB 2; MTCW; SATA 44

Thesen, Sharon 1946- .... **CLC 56**

Thevenin, Denis
    See Duhamel, Georges

Thibault, Jacques Anatole Francois
    1844-1924
    See France, Anatole
    See also CA 106; 127; MTCW

Thiele, Colin (Milton) 1920- .... **CLC 17**
    See also CA 29-32R; CANR 12, 28;
        CLR 27; MAICYA; SAAS 2; SATA 14,
        72

Thomas, Audrey (Callahan)
    1935- .... **CLC 7, 13, 37**
    See also AITN 2; CA 21-24R; CANR 36;
        DLB 60; MTCW

Thomas, D(onald) M(ichael)
    1935- .... **CLC 13, 22, 31**
    See also CA 61-64; CAAS 11; CANR 17;
        CDBLB 1960 to Present; DLB 40;
        MTCW

Thomas, Dylan (Marlais)
    1914-1953 ... **TCLC 1, 8, 45; DA; PC 2;**
                                                SSC 3; WLC
    See also CA 104; 120; CDBLB 1945-1960;
        DLB 13, 20; MTCW; SATA 60

Thomas, (Philip) Edward
    1878-1917 .... **TCLC 10**
    See also CA 106; DLB 19

Thomas, Joyce Carol 1938- .... **CLC 35**
    See also BW; CA 113; 116; CLR 19;
        DLB 33; JRDA; MAICYA; MTCW;
        SAAS 7; SATA 40

Thomas, Lewis 1913-1993 .... **CLC 35**
    See also CA 85-88; 143; CANR 38; MTCW

Thomas, Paul
    See Mann, (Paul) Thomas

Thomas, Piri 1928- .... **CLC 17**
    See also CA 73-76; HW

Thomas, R(onald) S(tuart)
    1913- .... **CLC 6, 13, 48**
    See also CA 89-92; CAAS 4; CANR 30;
        CDBLB 1960 to Present; DLB 27;
        MTCW

Thomas, Ross (Elmore) 1926- ...... **CLC 39**
    See also CA 33-36R; CANR 22

Thompson, Francis Clegg
    See Mencken, H(enry) L(ouis)

Thompson, Francis Joseph
    1859-1907 .... **TCLC 4**
    See also CA 104; CDBLB 1890-1914;
        DLB 19

Thompson, Hunter S(tockton)
    1939- .... **CLC 9, 17, 40**
    See also BEST 89:1; CA 17-20R; CANR 23;
        MTCW

Thompson, James Myers
    See Thompson, Jim (Myers)

Thompson, Jim (Myers)
    1906-1977(?) .... **CLC 69**
    See also CA 140

Thompson, Judith .... **CLC 39**

Thomson, James 1700-1748 .... **LC 16**

Thomson, James 1834-1882 ...... **NCLC 18**

Thoreau, Henry David
    1817-1862 ...... **NCLC 7, 21; DA; WLC**
    See also CDALB 1640-1865; DLB 1

Thornton, Hall
    See Silverberg, Robert

Thurber, James (Grover)
    1894-1961 ... **CLC 5, 11, 25; DA; SSC 1**
    See also CA 73-76; CANR 17, 39;
        CDALB 1929-1941; DLB 4, 11, 22, 102;
        MAICYA; MTCW; SATA 13

Thurman, Wallace (Henry)
    1902-1934 .... **TCLC 6; BLC**
    See also BW; CA 104; 124; DLB 51

Ticheburn, Cheviot
    See Ainsworth, William Harrison

Tieck, (Johann) Ludwig
    1773-1853 .... **NCLC 5**
    See also DLB 90

Tiger, Derry
    See Ellison, Harlan

Tilghman, Christopher 1948(?)- ..... **CLC 65**

Tillinghast, Richard (Williford)
    1940- .... **CLC 29**
    See also CA 29-32R; CANR 26

Timrod, Henry 1828-1867 .... **NCLC 25**
    See also DLB 3

Tindall, Gillian 1938- .... **CLC 7**
    See also CA 21-24R; CANR 11

Tiptree, James, Jr. .... **CLC 48, 50**
    See also Sheldon, Alice Hastings Bradley
    See also DLB 8

Titmarsh, Michael Angelo
    See Thackeray, William Makepeace

Tocqueville, Alexis (Charles Henri Maurice
        Clerel Comte) 1805-1859 ..... **NCLC 7**

Tolkien, J(ohn) R(onald) R(euel)
    1892-1973 ...... **CLC 1, 2, 3, 8, 12, 38;**
                                                DA; WLC
    See also AAYA 10; AITN 1; CA 17-18;
        45-48; CANR 36; CAP 2;
        CDBLB 1914-1945; DLB 15; JRDA;
        MAICYA; MTCW; SATA 2, 24, 32

Toller, Ernst 1893-1939 .... **TCLC 10**
    See also CA 107; DLB 124

Tolson, M. B.
    See Tolson, Melvin B(eaunorus)

Tolson, Melvin B(eaunorus)
    1898(?)-1966 .... **CLC 36; BLC**
    See also BW; CA 124; 89-92; DLB 48, 76

Tolstoi, Aleksei Nikolaevich
    See Tolstoy, Alexey Nikolaevich

Tolstoy, Alexey Nikolaevich
    1882-1945 .... **TCLC 18**
    See also CA 107

Tolstoy, Count Leo
    See Tolstoy, Leo (Nikolaevich)

Tolstoy, Leo (Nikolaevich)
    1828-1910 ...... **TCLC 4, 11, 17, 28, 44;**
                                                DA; SSC 9; WLC
    See also CA 104; 123; SATA 26

Tomasi di Lampedusa, Giuseppe 1896-1957
    See Lampedusa, Giuseppe (Tomasi) di
    See also CA 111

Tomlin, Lily .... **CLC 17**
    See also Tomlin, Mary Jean

Tomlin, Mary Jean 1939(?)-
    See Tomlin, Lily
    See also CA 117

Tomlinson, (Alfred) Charles
    1927- .... **CLC 2, 4, 6, 13, 45**
    See also CA 5-8R; CANR 33; DLB 40

Tonson, Jacob
    See Bennett, (Enoch) Arnold

Toole, John Kennedy
    1937-1969 .... **CLC 19, 64**
    See also CA 104; DLBY 81

Toomer, Jean
    1894-1967 ...... **CLC 1, 4, 13, 22; BLC;**
                                                PC 7; SSC 1
    See also BW; CA 85-88;
        CDALB 1917-1929; DLB 45, 51; MTCW

Torley, Luke
    See Blish, James (Benjamin)

Tornimparte, Alessandra
    See Ginzburg, Natalia

Torre, Raoul della
    See Mencken, H(enry) L(ouis)

Torrey, E(dwin) Fuller 1937- .... **CLC 34**
    See also CA 119

Torsvan, Ben Traven
    See Traven, B.

Torsvan, Benno Traven
    See Traven, B.

Torsvan, Berick Traven
    See Traven, B.

Torsvan, Berwick Traven
    See Traven, B.

Torsvan, Bruno Traven
    See Traven, B.

Torsvan, Traven
See Traven, B.

Tournier, Michel (Edouard)
1924- . . . . **CLC 6, 23, 36**
See also CA 49-52; CANR 3, 36; DLB 83;
MTCW; SATA 23

Tournimparte, Alessandra
See Ginzburg, Natalia

Towers, Ivar
See Kornbluth, C(yril) M.

Townsend, Sue 1946- . . . . **CLC 61**
See also CA 119; 127; MTCW; SATA 48,
55

Townshend, Peter (Dennis Blandford)
1945- . . . . **CLC 17, 42**
See also CA 107

Tozzi, Federigo 1883-1920 . . . . **TCLC 31**

Traill, Catharine Parr
1802-1899 . . . . **NCLC 31**
See also DLB 99

Trakl, Georg 1887-1914 . . . . **TCLC 5**
See also CA 104

Transtroemer, Tomas (Goesta)
1931- . . . . **CLC 52, 65**
See also CA 117; 129; CAAS 17

Transtromer, Tomas Gosta
See Transtroemer, Tomas (Goesta)

Traven, B. (?)-1969 . . . . **CLC 8, 11**
See also CA 19-20; 25-28R; CAP 2; DLB 9,
56; MTCW

Treitel, Jonathan 1959- . . . . **CLC 70**

Tremain, Rose 1943- . . . . **CLC 42**
See also CA 97-100; DLB 14

Tremblay, Michel 1942- . . . . **CLC 29**
See also CA 116; 128; DLB 60; MTCW

Trevanian (a pseudonym) 1930(?)- . . . **CLC 29**
See also CA 108

Trevor, Glen
See Hilton, James

Trevor, William
1928- . . . . **CLC 7, 9, 14, 25, 71**
See also Cox, William Trevor
See also DLB 14

Trifonov, Yuri (Valentinovich)
1925-1981 . . . . **CLC 45**
See also CA 126; 103; MTCW

Trilling, Lionel 1905-1975 . . . . **CLC 9, 11, 24**
See also CA 9-12R; 61-64; CANR 10;
DLB 28, 63; MTCW

Trimball, W. H.
See Mencken, H(enry) L(ouis)

Tristan
See Gomez de la Serna, Ramon

Tristram
See Housman, A(lfred) E(dward)

Trogdon, William (Lewis) 1939-
See Heat-Moon, William Least
See also CA 115; 119

Trollope, Anthony
1815-1882 . . . . . . **NCLC 6, 33; DA; WLC**
See also CDBLB 1832-1890; DLB 21, 57;
SATA 22

Trollope, Frances 1779-1863 . . . . . **NCLC 30**
See also DLB 21

Trotsky, Leon 1879-1940 . . . . **TCLC 22**
See also CA 118

Trotter (Cockburn), Catharine
1679-1749 . . . . **LC 8**
See also DLB 84

Trout, Kilgore
See Farmer, Philip Jose

Trow, George W. S. 1943- . . . . **CLC 52**
See also CA 126

Troyat, Henri 1911- . . . . **CLC 23**
See also CA 45-48; CANR 2, 33; MTCW

Trudeau, G(arretson) B(eekman) 1948-
See Trudeau, Garry B.
See also CA 81-84; CANR 31; SATA 35

Trudeau, Garry B. . . . . **CLC 12**
See also Trudeau, G(arretson) B(eekman)
See also AAYA 10; AITN 2

Truffaut, Francois 1932-1984 . . . . . . **CLC 20**
See also CA 81-84; 113; CANR 34

Trumbo, Dalton 1905-1976 . . . . **CLC 19**
See also CA 21-24R; 69-72; CANR 10;
DLB 26

Trumbull, John 1750-1831 . . . . . . **NCLC 30**
See also DLB 31

Trundlett, Helen B.
See Eliot, T(homas) S(tearns)

Tryon, Thomas 1926-1991 . . . . **CLC 3, 11**
See also AITN 1; CA 29-32R; 135;
CANR 32; MTCW

Tryon, Tom
See Tryon, Thomas

Ts'ao Hsueh-ch'in 1715(?)-1763 . . . . . . **LC 1**

Tsushima, Shuji 1909-1948
See Dazai, Osamu
See also CA 107

Tsvetaeva (Efron), Marina (Ivanovna)
1892-1941 . . . . **TCLC 7, 35**
See also CA 104; 128; MTCW

Tuck, Lily 1938- . . . . **CLC 70**
See also CA 139

Tunis, John R(oberts) 1889-1975 . . . **CLC 12**
See also CA 61-64; DLB 22; JRDA;
MAICYA; SATA 30, 37

Tuohy, Frank . . . . **CLC 37**
See also Tuohy, John Francis
See also DLB 14

Tuohy, John Francis 1925-
See Tuohy, Frank
See also CA 5-8R; CANR 3

Turco, Lewis (Putnam) 1934- . . . **CLC 11, 63**
See also CA 13-16R; CANR 24; DLBY 84

Turgenev, Ivan
1818-1883 . . . . . . **NCLC 21; DA; SSC 7;
WLC**

Turner, Frederick 1943- . . . . **CLC 48**
See also CA 73-76; CAAS 10; CANR 12,
30; DLB 40

Tusan, Stan 1936- . . . . **CLC 22**
See also CA 105

Tutu, Desmond M(pilo)
1931- . . . . **CLC 80; BLC**
See also BW; CA 125

Tutuola, Amos 1920- . . . **CLC 5, 14, 29; BLC**
See also BW; CA 9-12R; CANR 27;
DLB 125; MTCW

Twain, Mark
. . . **TCLC 6, 12, 19, 36, 48; SSC 6; WLC**
See also Clemens, Samuel Langhorne
See also DLB 11, 12, 23, 64, 74

Tyler, Anne
1941- . . . . **CLC 7, 11, 18, 28, 44, 59**
See also BEST 89:1; CA 9-12R; CANR 11,
33; DLB 6; DLBY 82; MTCW; SATA 7

Tyler, Royall 1757-1826 . . . . **NCLC 3**
See also DLB 37

Tynan, Katharine 1861-1931 . . . . **TCLC 3**
See also CA 104

Tytell, John 1939- . . . . **CLC 50**
See also CA 29-32R

Tyutchev, Fyodor 1803-1873 . . . . . **NCLC 34**

Tzara, Tristan . . . . **CLC 47**
See also Rosenfeld, Samuel

Uhry, Alfred 1936- . . . . **CLC 55**
See also CA 127; 133

Ulf, Haerved
See Strindberg, (Johan) August

Ulf, Harved
See Strindberg, (Johan) August

Unamuno (y Jugo), Miguel de
1864-1936 . . . . **TCLC 2, 9; HLC; SSC 11**
See also CA 104; 131; DLB 108; HW;
MTCW

Undercliffe, Errol
See Campbell, (John) Ramsey

Underwood, Miles
See Glassco, John

Undset, Sigrid
1882-1949 . . . . **TCLC 3; DA; WLC**
See also CA 104; 129; MTCW

Ungaretti, Giuseppe
1888-1970 . . . . **CLC 7, 11, 15**
See also CA 19-20; 25-28R; CAP 2;
DLB 114

Unger, Douglas 1952- . . . . **CLC 34**
See also CA 130

Unsworth, Barry (Forster) 1930- . . . . **CLC 76**
See also CA 25-28R; CANR 30

Updike, John (Hoyer)
1932- . . . . . . **CLC 1, 2, 3, 5, 7, 9, 13, 15,
23, 34, 43, 70; DA; SSC 13; WLC**
See also CA 1-4R; CABS 1; CANR 4, 33;
CDALB 1968-1988; DLB 2, 5; DLBD 3;
DLBY 80, 82; MTCW

Upshaw, Margaret Mitchell
See Mitchell, Margaret (Munnerlyn)

Upton, Mark
See Sanders, Lawrence

Urdang, Constance (Henriette)
1922- . . . . **CLC 47**
See also CA 21-24R; CANR 9, 24

Uriel, Henry
See Faust, Frederick (Schiller)

Uris, Leon (Marcus) 1924- . . . . **CLC 7, 32**
See also AITN 1, 2; BEST 89:2; CA 1-4R;
CANR 1, 40; MTCW; SATA 49

Urmuz
See Codrescu, Andrei

Ustinov, Peter (Alexander) 1921- .... **CLC 1**
See also AITN 1; CA 13-16R; CANR 25;
DLB 13

V
See Chekhov, Anton (Pavlovich)

Vaculik, Ludvik 1926- .... **CLC 7**
See also CA 53-56

Valenzuela, Luisa 1938-... **CLC 31; SSC 14**
See also CA 101; CANR 32; DLB 113; HW

Valera y Alcala-Galiano, Juan
1824-1905 .... **TCLC 10**
See also CA 106

Valery, (Ambroise) Paul (Toussaint Jules)
1871-1945 .... **TCLC 4, 15**
See also CA 104; 122; MTCW

Valle-Inclan, Ramon (Maria) del
1866-1936 .... **TCLC 5; HLC**
See also CA 106; DLB 134

Vallejo, Antonio Buero
See Buero Vallejo, Antonio

Vallejo, Cesar (Abraham)
1892-1938 .... **TCLC 3; HLC**
See also CA 105; HW

Valle Y Pena, Ramon del
See Valle-Inclan, Ramon (Maria) del

Van Ash, Cay 1918- .... **CLC 34**

Vanbrugh, Sir John 1664-1726 ...... **LC 21**
See also DLB 80

Van Campen, Karl
See Campbell, John W(ood, Jr.)

Vance, Gerald
See Silverberg, Robert

Vance, Jack .... **CLC 35**
See also Vance, John Holbrook
See also DLB 8

Vance, John Holbrook 1916-
See Queen, Ellery; Vance, Jack
See also CA 29-32R; CANR 17; MTCW

Van Den Bogarde, Derek Jules Gaspard Ulric
Niven 1921-
See Bogarde, Dirk
See also CA 77-80

Vandenburgh, Jane .... **CLC 59**

Vanderhaeghe, Guy 1951- .... **CLC 41**
See also CA 113

van der Post, Laurens (Jan) 1906- ... **CLC 5**
See also CA 5-8R; CANR 35

van de Wetering, Janwillem 1931- .. **CLC 47**
See also CA 49-52; CANR 4

Van Dine, S. S. .... **TCLC 23**
See also Wright, Willard Huntington

Van Doren, Carl (Clinton)
1885-1950 .... **TCLC 18**
See also CA 111

Van Doren, Mark 1894-1972..... **CLC 6, 10**
See also CA 1-4R; 37-40R; CANR 3;
DLB 45; MTCW

Van Druten, John (William)
1901-1957 .... **TCLC 2**
See also CA 104; DLB 10

Van Duyn, Mona (Jane)
1921- .... **CLC 3, 7, 63**
See also CA 9-12R; CANR 7, 38; DLB 5

Van Dyne, Edith
See Baum, L(yman) Frank

van Itallie, Jean-Claude 1936- .... **CLC 3**
See also CA 45-48; CAAS 2; CANR 1;
DLB 7

van Ostaijen, Paul 1896-1928 ..... **TCLC 33**

Van Peebles, Melvin 1932- ...... **CLC 2, 20**
See also BW; CA 85-88; CANR 27

Vansittart, Peter 1920-.......... **CLC 42**
See also CA 1-4R; CANR 3

Van Vechten, Carl 1880-1964 ..... **CLC 33**
See also CA 89-92; DLB 4, 9, 51

Van Vogt, A(lfred) E(lton) 1912-.... **CLC 1**
See also CA 21-24R; CANR 28; DLB 8;
SATA 14

Varda, Agnes 1928- .... **CLC 16**
See also CA 116; 122

Vargas Llosa, (Jorge) Mario (Pedro)
1936- .... **CLC 3, 6, 9, 10, 15, 31, 42;**
DA; HLC
See also CA 73-76; CANR 18, 32, 42; HW;
MTCW

Vasiliu, Gheorghe 1881-1957
See Bacovia, George
See also CA 123

Vassa, Gustavus
See Equiano, Olaudah

Vassilikos, Vassilis 1933-......... **CLC 4, 8**
See also CA 81-84

Vaughn, Stephanie................ **CLC 62**

Vazov, Ivan (Minchov)
1850-1921 .... **TCLC 25**
See also CA 121

Veblen, Thorstein (Bunde)
1857-1929 .... **TCLC 31**
See also CA 115

Vega, Lope de 1562-1635........... **LC 23**

Venison, Alfred
See Pound, Ezra (Weston Loomis)

Verdi, Marie de
See Mencken, H(enry) L(ouis)

Verdu, Matilde
See Cela, Camilo Jose

Verga, Giovanni (Carmelo)
1840-1922 .... **TCLC 3**
See also CA 104; 123

Vergil 70B.C.-19B.C. .... **CMLC 9; DA**

Verhaeren, Emile (Adolphe Gustave)
1855-1916 .... **TCLC 12**
See also CA 109

Verlaine, Paul (Marie)
1844-1896 .... **NCLC 2; PC 2**

Verne, Jules (Gabriel)
1828-1905 .... **TCLC 6, 52**
See also CA 110; 131; DLB 123; JRDA;
MAICYA; SATA 21

Very, Jones 1813-1880........... **NCLC 9**
See also DLB 1

Vesaas, Tarjei 1897-1970......... **CLC 48**
See also CA 29-32R

Vialis, Gaston
See Simenon, Georges (Jacques Christian)

Vian, Boris 1920-1959 .... **TCLC 9**
See also CA 106; DLB 72

Viaud, (Louis Marie) Julien 1850-1923
See Loti, Pierre
See also CA 107

Vicar, Henry
See Felsen, Henry Gregor

Vicker, Angus
See Felsen, Henry Gregor

Vidal, Gore
1925- ..... **CLC 2, 4, 6, 8, 10, 22, 33, 72**
See also AITN 1; BEST 90:2; CA 5-8R;
CANR 13; DLB 6; MTCW

Viereck, Peter (Robert Edwin)
1916- .... **CLC 4**
See also CA 1-4R; CANR 1; DLB 5

Vigny, Alfred (Victor) de
1797-1863 .... **NCLC 7**
See also DLB 119

Vilakazi, Benedict Wallet
1906-1947 .... **TCLC 37**

Villiers de l'Isle Adam, Jean Marie Mathias
Philippe Auguste Comte
1838-1889 .... **NCLC 3; SSC 14**
See also DLB 123

Vincent, Gabrielle a pseudonym...... **CLC 13**
See also CA 126; CLR 13; MAICYA;
SATA 61

Vinci, Leonardo da 1452-1519....... **LC 12**

Vine, Barbara .... **CLC 50**
See also Rendell, Ruth (Barbara)
See also BEST 90:4

Vinge, Joan D(ennison) 1948-...... **CLC 30**
See also CA 93-96; SATA 36

Violis, G.
See Simenon, Georges (Jacques Christian)

Visconti, Luchino 1906-1976....... **CLC 16**
See also CA 81-84; 65-68; CANR 39

Vittorini, Elio 1908-1966...... **CLC 6, 9, 14**
See also CA 133; 25-28R

Vizinczey, Stephen 1933-.......... **CLC 40**
See also CA 128

Vliet, R(ussell) G(ordon)
1929-1984 .... **CLC 22**
See also CA 37-40R; 112; CANR 18

Vogau, Boris Andreyevich 1894-1937(?)
See Pilnyak, Boris
See also CA 123

Vogel, Paula A(nne) 1951-......... **CLC 76**
See also CA 108

Voight, Ellen Bryant 1943- .... **CLC 54**
See also CA 69-72; CANR 11, 29; DLB 120

Voigt, Cynthia 1942- .... **CLC 30**
See also AAYA 3; CA 106; CANR 18, 37,
40; CLR 13; JRDA; MAICYA;
SATA 33, 48

Voinovich, Vladimir (Nikolaevich)
1932- .... **CLC 10, 49**
See also CA 81-84; CAAS 12; CANR 33;
MTCW

Voltaire
1694-1778 ... **LC 14; DA; SSC 12; WLC**

Wasserstein, Wendy
1950- .... **CLC 32, 59; DC 4**
See also CA 121; 129; CABS 3

Waterhouse, Keith (Spencer)
1929- .... **CLC 47**
See also CA 5-8R; CANR 38; DLB 13, 15;
MTCW

Waters, Roger 1944- .... **CLC 35**
See also Pink Floyd

Watkins, Frances Ellen
See Harper, Frances Ellen Watkins

Watkins, Gerrold
See Malzberg, Barry N(athaniel)

Watkins, Paul 1964- .... **CLC 55**
See also CA 132

Watkins, Vernon Phillips
1906-1967 .... **CLC 43**
See also CA 9-10; 25-28R; CAP 1; DLB 20

Watson, Irving S.
See Mencken, H(enry) L(ouis)

Watson, John H.
See Farmer, Philip Jose

Watson, Richard F.
See Silverberg, Robert

Waugh, Auberon (Alexander) 1939- .. **CLC 7**
See also CA 45-48; CANR 6, 22; DLB 14

Waugh, Evelyn (Arthur St. John)
1903-1966 ...... **CLC 1, 3, 8, 13, 19, 27,
44; DA; WLC**
See also CA 85-88; 25-28R; CANR 22;
CDBLB 1914-1945; DLB 15; MTCW

Waugh, Harriet 1944- .... **CLC 6**
See also CA 85-88; CANR 22

Ways, C. R.
See Blount, Roy (Alton), Jr.

Waystaff, Simon
See Swift, Jonathan

Webb, (Martha) Beatrice (Potter)
1858-1943 .... **TCLC 22**
See also Potter, Beatrice
See also CA 117

Webb, Charles (Richard) 1939- ...... **CLC 7**
See also CA 25-28R

Webb, James H(enry), Jr. 1946- .... **CLC 22**
See also CA 81-84

Webb, Mary (Gladys Meredith)
1881-1927 .... **TCLC 24**
See also CA 123; DLB 34

Webb, Mrs. Sidney
See Webb, (Martha) Beatrice (Potter)

Webb, Phyllis 1927- .... **CLC 18**
See also CA 104; CANR 23; DLB 53

Webb, Sidney (James)
1859-1947 .... **TCLC 22**
See also CA 117

Webber, Andrew Lloyd............. **CLC 21
See also Lloyd Webber, Andrew

Weber, Lenora Mattingly
1895-1971 .... **CLC 12**
See also CA 19-20; 29-32R; CAP 1;
SATA 2, 26

Webster, John 1579(?)-1634(?) .... **DC 2**
See also CDBLB Before 1660; DA; DLB 58;
WLC

Webster, Noah 1758-1843 ...... **NCLC 30**

Wedekind, (Benjamin) Frank(lin)
1864-1918 .... **TCLC 7**
See also CA 104; DLB 118

Weidman, Jerome 1913-. .... **CLC 7**
See also AITN 2; CA 1-4R; CANR 1;
DLB 28

Weil, Simone (Adolphine)
1909-1943 .... **TCLC 23**
See also CA 117

Weinstein, Nathan
See West, Nathanael

Weinstein, Nathan von Wallenstein
See West, Nathanael

Weir, Peter (Lindsay) 1944- .... **CLC 20**
See also CA 113; 123

Weiss, Peter (Ulrich)
1916-1982 .... **CLC 3, 15, 51**
See also CA 45-48; 106; CANR 3; DLB 69,
124

Weiss, Theodore (Russell)
1916- .... **CLC 3, 8, 14**
See also CA 9-12R; CAAS 2; DLB 5

Welch, (Maurice) Denton
1915-1948 .... **TCLC 22**
See also CA 121

Welch, James 1940- .... **CLC 6, 14, 52**
See also CA 85-88; CANR 42

Weldon, Fay
1933(?)- .... **CLC 6, 9, 11, 19, 36, 59**
See also CA 21-24R; CANR 16;
CDBLB 1960 to Present; DLB 14;
MTCW

Wellek, Rene 1903- .... **CLC 28**
See also CA 5-8R; CAAS 7; CANR 8;
DLB 63

Weller, Michael 1942- .... **CLC 10, 53**
See also CA 85-88

Weller, Paul 1958- .... **CLC 26**

Wellershoff, Dieter 1925-......... **CLC 46**
See also CA 89-92; CANR 16, 37

Welles, (George) Orson
1915-1985 .... **CLC 20, 80**
See also CA 93-96; 117

Wellman, Mac 1945- .... **CLC 65**

Wellman, Manly Wade 1903-1986 .. **CLC 49**
See also CA 1-4R; 118; CANR 6, 16;
SATA 6, 47

Wells, Carolyn 1869(?)-1942 ...... **TCLC 35**
See also CA 113; DLB 11

Wells, H(erbert) G(eorge)
1866-1946 .... **TCLC 6, 12, 19; DA;
SSC 6; WLC**
See also CA 110; 121; CDBLB 1914-1945;
DLB 34, 70; MTCW; SATA 20

Wells, Rosemary 1943-. .... **CLC 12**
See also CA 85-88; CLR 16; MAICYA;
SAAS 1; SATA 18, 69

Welty, Eudora
1909- ...... **CLC 1, 2, 5, 14, 22, 33; DA;
SSC 1; WLC**
See also CA 9-12R; CABS 1; CANR 32;
CDALB 1941-1968; DLB 2, 102;
DLBY 87; MTCW

Wen I-to 1899-1946 .... **TCLC 28**

Wentworth, Robert
See Hamilton, Edmond

Werfel, Franz (V.) 1890-1945 ...... **TCLC 8**
See also CA 104; DLB 81, 124

Wergeland, Henrik Arnold
1808-1845 .... **NCLC 5**

Wersba, Barbara 1932-. .... **CLC 30**
See also AAYA 2; CA 29-32R; CANR 16,
38; CLR 3; DLB 52; JRDA; MAICYA;
SAAS 2; SATA 1, 58

Wertmueller, Lina 1928- .... **CLC 16**
See also CA 97-100; CANR 39

Wescott, Glenway 1901-1987....... **CLC 13**
See also CA 13-16R; 121; CANR 23;
DLB 4, 9, 102

Wesker, Arnold 1932- .... **CLC 3, 5, 42**
See also CA 1-4R; CAAS 7; CANR 1, 33;
CDBLB 1960 to Present; DLB 13;
MTCW

Wesley, Richard (Errol) 1945-....... **CLC 7**
See also BW; CA 57-60; CANR 27; DLB 38

Wessel, Johan Herman 1742-1785 .... **LC 7**

West, Anthony (Panther)
1914-1987 .... **CLC 50**
See also CA 45-48; 124; CANR 3, 19;
DLB 15

West, C. P.
See Wodehouse, P(elham) G(renville)

West, (Mary) Jessamyn
1902-1984 .... **CLC 7, 17**
See also CA 9-12R; 112; CANR 27; DLB 6;
DLBY 84; MTCW; SATA 37

West, Morris L(anglo) 1916-..... **CLC 6, 33**
See also CA 5-8R; CANR 24; MTCW

West, Nathanael
1903-1940 .... **TCLC 1, 14, 44**
See also CA 104; 125; CDALB 1929-1941;
DLB 4, 9, 28; MTCW

West, Owen
See Koontz, Dean R(ay)

West, Paul 1930- .... **CLC 7, 14**
See also CA 13-16R; CAAS 7; CANR 22;
DLB 14

West, Rebecca 1892-1983 .. **CLC 7, 9, 31, 50**
See also CA 5-8R; 109; CANR 19; DLB 36;
DLBY 83; MTCW

Westall, Robert (Atkinson)
1929-1993 .... **CLC 17**
See also CA 69-72; 141; CANR 18;
CLR 13; JRDA; MAICYA; SAAS 2;
SATA 23, 69; SATA-Obit 75

Westlake, Donald E(dwin)
1933- .... **CLC 7, 33**
See also CA 17-20R; CAAS 13; CANR 16

Westmacott, Mary
See Christie, Agatha (Mary Clarissa)

Weston, Allen
See Norton, Andre

Wetcheek, J. L.
See Feuchtwanger, Lion

Wetering, Janwillem van de
See van de Wetering, Janwillem

Wetherell, Elizabeth
See Warner, Susan (Bogert)

Whalen, Philip 1923- . . . . **CLC 6, 29**
See also CA 9-12R; CANR 5, 39; DLB 16

Wharton, Edith (Newbold Jones)
1862-1937 . . . . . . **TCLC 3, 9, 27, 53; DA;
SSC 6; WLC**
See also CA 104; 132; CDALB 1865-1917;
DLB 4, 9, 12, 78; MTCW

Wharton, James
See Mencken, H(enry) L(ouis)

Wharton, William (a pseudonym)
. . . . **CLC 18, 37**
See also CA 93-96; DLBY 80

Wheatley (Peters), Phillis
1754(?)-1784 . . . . **LC 3; BLC; DA; PC 3;
WLC**
See also CDALB 1640-1865; DLB 31, 50

Wheelock, John Hall 1886-1978 . . . . **CLC 14**
See also CA 13-16R; 77-80; CANR 14;
DLB 45

White, E(lwyn) B(rooks)
1899-1985 . . . . **CLC 10, 34, 39**
See also AITN 2; CA 13-16R; 116;
CANR 16, 37; CLR 1, 21; DLB 11, 22;
MAICYA; MTCW; SATA 2, 29, 44

White, Edmund (Valentine III)
1940- . . . . **CLC 27**
See also AAYA 7; CA 45-48; CANR 3, 19,
36; MTCW

White, Patrick (Victor Martindale)
1912-1990 . . **CLC 3, 4, 5, 7, 9, 18, 65, 69**
See also CA 81-84; 132; CANR 43; MTCW

White, Phyllis Dorothy James 1920-
See James, P. D.
See also CA 21-24R; CANR 17, 43; MTCW

White, T(erence) H(anbury)
1906-1964 . . . . **CLC 30**
See also CA 73-76; CANR 37; JRDA;
MAICYA; SATA 12

White, Terence de Vere 1912- . . . . . . **CLC 49**
See also CA 49-52; CANR 3

White, Walter F(rancis)
1893-1955 . . . . **TCLC 15**
See also White, Walter
See also CA 115; 124; DLB 51

White, William Hale 1831-1913
See Rutherford, Mark
See also CA 121

Whitehead, E(dward) A(nthony)
1933- . . . . **CLC 5**
See also CA 65-68

Whitemore, Hugh (John) 1936- . . . . . **CLC 37**
See also CA 132

Whitman, Sarah Helen (Power)
1803-1878 . . . . **NCLC 19**
See also DLB 1

Whitman, Walt(er)
1819-1892 . . . . . **NCLC 4, 31; DA; PC 3;
WLC**
See also CDALB 1640-1865; DLB 3, 64;
SATA 20

Whitney, Phyllis A(yame) 1903- . . . . **CLC 42**
See also AITN 2; BEST 90:3; CA 1-4R;
CANR 3, 25, 38; JRDA; MAICYA;
SATA 1, 30

Whittemore, (Edward) Reed (Jr.)
1919- . . . . **CLC 4**
See also CA 9-12R; CAAS 8; CANR 4;
DLB 5

Whittier, John Greenleaf
1807-1892 . . . . **NCLC 8**
See also CDALB 1640-1865; DLB 1

Whittlebot, Hernia
See Coward, Noel (Peirce)

Wicker, Thomas Grey 1926-
See Wicker, Tom
See also CA 65-68; CANR 21

Wicker, Tom . . . . **CLC 7**
See also Wicker, Thomas Grey

Wideman, John Edgar
1941- . . . . **CLC 5, 34, 36, 67; BLC**
See also BW; CA 85-88; CANR 14, 42;
DLB 33

Wiebe, Rudy (Henry) 1934- . . . **CLC 6, 11, 14**
See also CA 37-40R; CANR 42; DLB 60

Wieland, Christoph Martin
1733-1813 . . . . **NCLC 17**
See also DLB 97

Wieners, John 1934- . . . . **CLC 7**
See also CA 13-16R; DLB 16

Wiesel, Elie(zer)
1928- . . . . **CLC 3, 5, 11, 37; DA**
See also AAYA 7; AITN 1; CA 5-8R;
CAAS 4; CANR 8, 40; DLB 83;
DLBY 87; MTCW; SATA 56

Wiggins, Marianne 1947- . . . . **CLC 57**
See also BEST 89:3; CA 130

Wight, James Alfred 1916-
See Herriot, James
See also CA 77-80; SATA 44, 55

Wilbur, Richard (Purdy)
1921- . . . . **CLC 3, 6, 9, 14, 53; DA**
See also CA 1-4R; CABS 2; CANR 2, 29;
DLB 5; MTCW; SATA 9

Wild, Peter 1940- . . . . **CLC 14**
See also CA 37-40R; DLB 5

Wilde, Oscar (Fingal O'Flahertie Wills)
1854(?)-1900 . . . . **TCLC 1, 8, 23, 41; DA;
SSC 11; WLC**
See also CA 104; 119; CDBLB 1890-1914;
DLB 10, 19, 34, 57; SATA 24

Wilder, Billy . . . . **CLC 20**
See also Wilder, Samuel
See also DLB 26

Wilder, Samuel 1906-
See Wilder, Billy
See also CA 89-92

Wilder, Thornton (Niven)
1897-1975 . . . . . . **CLC 1, 5, 6, 10, 15, 35,
82; DA; DC 1; WLC**
See also AITN 2; CA 13-16R; 61-64;
CANR 40; DLB 4, 7, 9; MTCW

Wilding, Michael 1942- . . . . **CLC 73**
See also CA 104; CANR 24

Wiley, Richard 1944- . . . . **CLC 44**
See also CA 121; 129

Wilhelm, Kate . . . . **CLC 7**
See also Wilhelm, Katie Gertrude
See also CAAS 5; DLB 8

Wilhelm, Katie Gertrude 1928-
See Wilhelm, Kate
See also CA 37-40R; CANR 17, 36; MTCW

Wilkins, Mary
See Freeman, Mary Eleanor Wilkins

Willard, Nancy 1936- . . . . **CLC 7, 37**
See also CA 89-92; CANR 10, 39; CLR 5;
DLB 5, 52; MAICYA; MTCW;
SATA 30, 37, 71

Williams, C(harles) K(enneth)
1936- . . . . **CLC 33, 56**
See also CA 37-40R; DLB 5

Williams, Charles
See Collier, James L(incoln)

Williams, Charles (Walter Stansby)
1886-1945 . . . . **TCLC 1, 11**
See also CA 104; DLB 100

Williams, (George) Emlyn
1905-1987 . . . . **CLC 15**
See also CA 104; 123; CANR 36; DLB 10,
77; MTCW

Williams, Hugo 1942- . . . . **CLC 42**
See also CA 17-20R; DLB 40

Williams, J. Walker
See Wodehouse, P(elham) G(renville)

Williams, John A(lfred)
1925- . . . . **CLC 5, 13; BLC**
See also BW; CA 53-56; CAAS 3; CANR 6,
26; DLB 2, 33

Williams, Jonathan (Chamberlain)
1929- . . . . **CLC 13**
See also CA 9-12R; CAAS 12; CANR 8;
DLB 5

Williams, Joy 1944- . . . . **CLC 31**
See also CA 41-44R; CANR 22

Williams, Norman 1952- . . . . **CLC 39**
See also CA 118

Williams, Tennessee
1911-1983 . . . . . **CLC 1, 2, 5, 7, 8, 11, 15,
19, 30, 39, 45, 71; DA; DC 4; WLC**
See also AITN 1, 2; CA 5-8R; 108;
CABS 3; CANR 31; CDALB 1941-1968;
DLB 7; DLBD 4; DLBY 83; MTCW

Williams, Thomas (Alonzo)
1926-1990 . . . . **CLC 14**
See also CA 1-4R; 132; CANR 2

Williams, William C.
See Williams, William Carlos

Williams, William Carlos
1883-1963 . . . . **CLC 1, 2, 5, 9, 13, 22, 42,
67; DA; PC 7**
See also CA 89-92; CANR 34;
CDALB 1917-1929; DLB 4, 16, 54, 86;
MTCW

Williamson, David (Keith) 1942- . . . . **CLC 56**
See also CA 103; CANR 41

Williamson, Jack . . . . **CLC 29**
See also Williamson, John Stewart
See also CAAS 8; DLB 8

Williamson, John Stewart 1908-
See Williamson, Jack
See also CA 17-20R; CANR 23

Willie, Frederick
See Lovecraft, H(oward) P(hillips)

Willingham, Calder (Baynard, Jr.)
1922- . . . . CLC **5, 51**
See also CA 5-8R; CANR 3; DLB 2, 44;
MTCW

Willis, Charles
See Clarke, Arthur C(harles)

Willy
See Colette, (Sidonie-Gabrielle)

Willy, Colette
See Colette, (Sidonie-Gabrielle)

Wilson, A(ndrew) N(orman) 1950- . . CLC **33**
See also CA 112; 122; DLB 14

Wilson, Angus (Frank Johnstone)
1913-1991 . . . . CLC **2, 3, 5, 25, 34**
See also CA 5-8R; 134; CANR 21; DLB 15;
MTCW

Wilson, August
1945- . . CLC **39, 50, 63; BLC; DA; DC 2**
See also BW; CA 115; 122; CANR 42;
MTCW

Wilson, Brian 1942- . . . . CLC **12**

Wilson, Colin 1931- . . . . CLC **3, 14**
See also CA 1-4R; CAAS 5; CANR 1, 22,
33; DLB 14; MTCW

Wilson, Dirk
See Pohl, Frederik

Wilson, Edmund
1895-1972 . . . . CLC **1, 2, 3, 8, 24**
See also CA 1-4R; 37-40R; CANR 1;
DLB 63; MTCW

Wilson, Ethel Davis (Bryant)
1888(?)-1980 . . . . CLC **13**
See also CA 102; DLB 68; MTCW

Wilson, John 1785-1854 . . . . NCLC **5**

Wilson, John (Anthony) Burgess 1917-1993
See Burgess, Anthony
See also CA 1-4R; 143; CANR 2; MTCW

Wilson, Lanford 1937- . . . . CLC **7, 14, 36**
See also CA 17-20R; CABS 3; DLB 7

Wilson, Robert M. 1944- . . . . CLC **7, 9**
See also CA 49-52; CANR 2, 41; MTCW

Wilson, Robert McLiam 1964- . . . . . CLC **59**
See also CA 132

Wilson, Sloan 1920- . . . . CLC **32**
See also CA 1-4R; CANR 1

Wilson, Snoo 1948- . . . . CLC **33**
See also CA 69-72

Wilson, William S(mith) 1932- . . . . . CLC **49**
See also CA 81-84

Winchilsea, Anne (Kingsmill) Finch Counte
1661-1720 . . . . LC **3**

Windham, Basil
See Wodehouse, P(elham) G(renville)

Wingrove, David (John) 1954- . . . . . . CLC **68**
See also CA 133

Winters, Janet Lewis . . . . CLC **41**
See also Lewis, Janet
See also DLBY 87

Winters, (Arthur) Yvor
1900-1968 . . . . CLC **4, 8, 32**
See also CA 11-12; 25-28R; CAP 1;
DLB 48; MTCW

Winterson, Jeanette 1959- . . . . CLC **64**
See also CA 136

Wiseman, Frederick 1930- . . . . CLC **20**

Wister, Owen 1860-1938 . . . . TCLC **21**
See also CA 108; DLB 9, 78; SATA 62

Witkacy
See Witkiewicz, Stanislaw Ignacy

Witkiewicz, Stanislaw Ignacy
1885-1939 . . . . TCLC **8**
See also CA 105

Wittig, Monique 1935(?)- . . . . CLC **22**
See also CA 116; 135; DLB 83

Wittlin, Jozef 1896-1976 . . . . CLC **25**
See also CA 49-52; 65-68; CANR 3

Wodehouse, P(elham) G(renville)
1881-1975 . . . CLC **1, 2, 5, 10, 22; SSC 2**
See also AITN 2; CA 45-48; 57-60;
CANR 3, 33; CDBLB 1914-1945;
DLB 34; MTCW; SATA 22

Woiwode, L.
See Woiwode, Larry (Alfred)

Woiwode, Larry (Alfred) 1941- . . . CLC **6, 10**
See also CA 73-76; CANR 16; DLB 6

Wojciechowska, Maia (Teresa)
1927- . . . . CLC **26**
See also AAYA 8; CA 9-12R; CANR 4, 41;
CLR 1; JRDA; MAICYA; SAAS 1;
SATA 1, 28

Wolf, Christa 1929- . . . . CLC **14, 29, 58**
See also CA 85-88; DLB 75; MTCW

Wolfe, Gene (Rodman) 1931- . . . . . . CLC **25**
See also CA 57-60; CAAS 9; CANR 6, 32;
DLB 8

Wolfe, George C. 1954- . . . . CLC **49**

Wolfe, Thomas (Clayton)
1900-1938 . . . TCLC **4, 13, 29; DA; WLC**
See also CA 104; 132; CDALB 1929-1941;
DLB 9, 102; DLBD 2; DLBY 85; MTCW

Wolfe, Thomas Kennerly, Jr. 1931-
See Wolfe, Tom
See also CA 13-16R; CANR 9, 33; MTCW

Wolfe, Tom . . . . CLC **1, 2, 9, 15, 35, 51**
See also Wolfe, Thomas Kennerly, Jr.
See also AAYA 8; AITN 2; BEST 89:1

Wolff, Geoffrey (Ansell) 1937- . . . . . CLC **41**
See also CA 29-32R; CANR 29, 43

Wolff, Sonia
See Levitin, Sonia (Wolff)

Wolff, Tobias (Jonathan Ansell)
1945- . . . . CLC **39, 64**
See also BEST 90:2; CA 114; 117; DLB 130

Wolfram von Eschenbach
c. 1170-c. 1220 . . . . CMLC **5**

Wolitzer, Hilma 1930- . . . . CLC **17**
See also CA 65-68; CANR 18, 40; SATA 31

Wollstonecraft, Mary 1759-1797 . . . . . LC **5**
See also CDBLB 1789-1832; DLB 39, 104

Wonder, Stevie . . . . CLC **12**
See also Morris, Steveland Judkins

Wong, Jade Snow 1922- . . . . CLC **17**
See also CA 109

Woodcott, Keith
See Brunner, John (Kilian Houston)

Woodruff, Robert W.
See Mencken, H(enry) L(ouis)

Woolf, (Adeline) Virginia
1882-1941 . . . . . . TCLC **1, 5, 20, 43; DA;
SSC 7; WLC**
See also CA 104; 130; CDBLB 1914-1945;
DLB 36, 100; DLBD 10; MTCW

Woollcott, Alexander (Humphreys)
1887-1943 . . . . TCLC **5**
See also CA 105; DLB 29

Woolrich, Cornell 1903-1968 . . . . . . CLC **77**
See also Hopley-Woolrich, Cornell George

Wordsworth, Dorothy
1771-1855 . . . . NCLC **25**
See also DLB 107

Wordsworth, William
1770-1850 . . . . NCLC **12, 38; DA; PC 4;
WLC**
See also CDBLB 1789-1832; DLB 93, 107

Wouk, Herman 1915- . . . . CLC **1, 9, 38**
See also CA 5-8R; CANR 6, 33; DLBY 82;
MTCW

Wright, Charles (Penzel, Jr.)
1935- . . . . CLC **6, 13, 28**
See also CA 29-32R; CAAS 7; CANR 23,
36; DLBY 82; MTCW

Wright, Charles Stevenson
1932- . . . . CLC **49; BLC 3**
See also BW; CA 9-12R; CANR 26;
DLB 33

Wright, Jack R.
See Harris, Mark

Wright, James (Arlington)
1927-1980 . . . . CLC **3, 5, 10, 28**
See also AITN 2; CA 49-52; 97-100;
CANR 4, 34; DLB 5; MTCW

Wright, Judith (Arandell)
1915- . . . . CLC **11, 53**
See also CA 13-16R; CANR 31; MTCW;
SATA 14

Wright, L(aurali) R. 1939- . . . . CLC **44**
See also CA 138

Wright, Richard (Nathaniel)
1908-1960 . . . . CLC **1, 3, 4, 9, 14, 21, 48,
74; BLC; DA; SSC 2; WLC**
See also AAYA 5; BW; CA 108;
CDALB 1929-1941; DLB 76, 102;
DLBD 2; MTCW

Wright, Richard B(ruce) 1937- . . . . . . CLC **6**
See also CA 85-88; DLB 53

Wright, Rick 1945- . . . . CLC **35**
See also Pink Floyd

Wright, Rowland
See Wells, Carolyn

Wright, Stephen 1946- . . . . CLC **33**

Wright, Willard Huntington 1888-1939
See Van Dine, S. S.
See also CA 115

Wright, William 1930- . . . . CLC **44**
See also CA 53-56; CANR 7, 23

Wu Ch'eng-en 1500(?)-1582(?) . . . . LC **7**

Wu Ching-tzu 1701-1754 . . . . LC **2**

Wurlitzer, Rudolph 1938(?)- . . . CLC **2, 4, 15**
See also CA 85-88

Wycherley, William 1641-1715 . . . . LC **8, 21**
See also CDBLB 1660-1789; DLB 80

Wylie, Elinor (Morton Hoyt)
1885-1928 .... **TCLC 8**
See also CA 105; DLB 9, 45

Wylie, Philip (Gordon) 1902-1971... **CLC 43**
See also CA 21-22; 33-36R; CAP 2; DLB 9

Wyndham, John
See Harris, John (Wyndham Parkes Lucas)
Beynon

Wyss, Johann David Von
1743-1818 .... **NCLC 10**
See also JRDA; MAICYA; SATA 27, 29

Yakumo Koizumi
See Hearn, (Patricio) Lafcadio (Tessima
Carlos)

Yanez, Jose Donoso
See Donoso (Yanez), Jose

Yanovsky, Basile S.
See Yanovsky, V(assily) S(emenovich)

Yanovsky, V(assily) S(emenovich)
1906-1989 .... **CLC 2, 18**
See also CA 97-100; 129

Yates, Richard 1926-1992 ..... **CLC 7, 8, 23**
See also CA 5-8R; 139; CANR 10, 43;
DLB 2; DLBY 81, 92

Yeats, W. B.
See Yeats, William Butler

Yeats, William Butler
1865-1939 ..... **TCLC 1, 11, 18, 31; DA;**
WLC
See also CA 104; 127; CDBLB 1890-1914;
DLB 10, 19, 98; MTCW

Yehoshua, A(braham) B.
1936- .... **CLC 13, 31**
See also CA 33-36R; CANR 43

Yep, Laurence Michael 1948- ...... **CLC 35**
See also AAYA 5; CA 49-52; CANR 1;
CLR 3, 17; DLB 52; JRDA; MAICYA;
SATA 7, 69

Yerby, Frank G(arvin)
1916-1991 .... **CLC 1, 7, 22; BLC**
See also BW; CA 9-12R; 136; CANR 16;
DLB 76; MTCW

Yesenin, Sergei Alexandrovich
See Esenin, Sergei (Alexandrovich)

Yevtushenko, Yevgeny (Alexandrovich)
1933- .... **CLC 1, 3, 13, 26, 51**
See also CA 81-84; CANR 33; MTCW

Yezierska, Anzia 1885(?)-1970 ..... **CLC 46**
See also CA 126; 89-92; DLB 28; MTCW

Yglesias, Helen 1915- .... **CLC 7, 22**
See also CA 37-40R; CANR 15; MTCW

Yokomitsu Riichi 1898-1947 ..... **TCLC 47**

Yonge, Charlotte (Mary)
1823-1901 .... **TCLC 48**
See also CA 109; DLB 18; SATA 17

York, Jeremy
See Creasey, John

York, Simon
See Heinlein, Robert A(nson)

Yorke, Henry Vincent 1905-1974 ... **CLC 13**
See also Green, Henry
See also CA 85-88; 49-52

Young, Al(bert James)
1939- .... **CLC 19; BLC**
See also BW; CA 29-32R; CANR 26;
DLB 33

Young, Andrew (John) 1885-1971 .... **CLC 5**
See also CA 5-8R; CANR 7, 29

Young, Collier
See Bloch, Robert (Albert)

Young, Edward 1683-1765 .... **LC 3**
See also DLB 95

Young, Marguerite 1909- .... **CLC 82**
See also CA 13-16; CAP 1

Young, Neil 1945- .... **CLC 17**
See also CA 110

Yourcenar, Marguerite
1903-1987 .... **CLC 19, 38, 50**
See also CA 69-72; CANR 23; DLB 72;
DLBY 88; MTCW

Yurick, Sol 1925- .... **CLC 6**
See also CA 13-16R; CANR 25

Zabolotskii, Nikolai Alekseevich
1903-1958 .... **TCLC 52**
See also CA 116

Zamiatin, Yevgenii
See Zamyatin, Evgeny Ivanovich

Zamyatin, Evgeny Ivanovich
1884-1937 .... **TCLC 8, 37**
See also CA 105

Zangwill, Israel 1864-1926 .... **TCLC 16**
See also CA 109; DLB 10, 135

Zappa, Francis Vincent, Jr. 1940-1993
See Zappa, Frank
See also CA 108; 143

Zappa, Frank .... **CLC 17**
See also Zappa, Francis Vincent, Jr.

Zaturenska, Marya 1902-1982 .... **CLC 6, 11**
See also CA 13-16R; 105; CANR 22

Zelazny, Roger (Joseph) 1937- ..... **CLC 21**
See also AAYA 7; CA 21-24R; CANR 26;
DLB 8; MTCW; SATA 39, 57

Zhdanov, Andrei A(lexandrovich)
1896-1948 .... **TCLC 18**
See also CA 117

Zhukovsky, Vasily 1783-1852 .... **NCLC 35**

Ziegenhagen, Eric .... **CLC 55**

Zimmer, Jill Schary
See Robinson, Jill

Zimmerman, Robert
See Dylan, Bob

Zindel, Paul 1936- .... **CLC 6, 26; DA**
See also AAYA 2; CA 73-76; CANR 31;
CLR 3; DLB 7, 52; JRDA; MAICYA;
MTCW; SATA 16, 58

Zinov'Ev, A. A.
See Zinoviev, Alexander (Aleksandrovich)

Zinoviev, Alexander (Aleksandrovich)
1922- .... **CLC 19**
See also CA 116; 133; CAAS 10

Zoilus
See Lovecraft, H(oward) P(hillips)

Zola, Emile (Edouard Charles Antoine)
1840-1902 ...... **TCLC 1, 6, 21, 41; DA;**
WLC
See also CA 104; 138; DLB 123

Zoline, Pamela 1941- .... **CLC 62**

Zorrilla y Moral, Jose 1817-1893 .. **NCLC 6**

Zoshchenko, Mikhail (Mikhailovich)
1895-1958 .... **TCLC 15; SSC 15**
See also CA 115

Zuckmayer, Carl 1896-1977 .... **CLC 18**
See also CA 69-72; DLB 56, 124

Zuk, Georges
See Skelton, Robin

Zukofsky, Louis
1904-1978 .... **CLC 1, 2, 4, 7, 11, 18**
See also CA 9-12R; 77-80; CANR 39;
DLB 5; MTCW

Zweig, Paul 1935-1984 .... **CLC 34, 42**
See also CA 85-88; 113

Zweig, Stefan 1881-1942 .... **TCLC 17**
See also CA 112; DLB 81, 118

Literary Criticism Series
Cumulative Topic Index

This index lists all topic entries in the Gale Literary Criticism Series *Classical and Medieval Literature Criticism, Contemporary Literary Criticism, Literature Criticism from 1400 to 1800, Nineteenth-Century Literature Criticism,* and *Twentieth-Century Literary Criticism.*

NCLC Cumulative Nationality Index

Maturin, Charles Robert **6**
Moore, Thomas **6**
Morgan, Lady **29**
O'Brien, Fitz-James **21**
Sheridan, Richard Brinsley **5**

ITALIAN
Foscolo, Ugo **8**
Gozzi, Carlo **23**
Leopardi, Giacomo **22**
Manzoni, Alessandro **29**
Mazzini, Guiseppe **34**
Nievo, Ippolito **22**

LITHUANIAN
Mapu, Abraham **18**

MEXICAN
Lizardi, José Joaquin Fernández de **30**

NORWEGIAN
Collett, Camilla **22**
Wergeland, Henrik Arnold **5**

POLISH
Fredro, Aleksander **8**
Krasicki, Ignacy **8**
Krasiński, Zygmunt **4**
Mickiewicz, Adam **3**
Norwid, Cyprian Kamil **17**
Słowacki, Juliusz **15**

ROMANIAN
Eminescu, Mihail **33**

RUSSIAN
Aksakov, Sergei Timofeyvich **2**
Bakunin, Mikhail Alexandrovich **25**
Bashkirtseff, Marie **27**
Belinski, Vissarion Grigoryevich **5**
Chernyshevsky, Nikolay Gavrilovich **1**
Dobrolyubov, Nikolai Alexandrovich **5**
Dostoevsky, Fyodor **2, 7, 21, 33, 43**
Gogol, Nikolai **5, 15, 31**
Goncharov, Ivan Alexandrovich **1**
Herzen, Aleksandr Ivanovich **10**
Karamzin, Nikolai Mikhailovich **3**
Krylov, Ivan Andreevich **1**
Lermontov, Mikhail Yuryevich **5**
Leskov, Nikolai Semyonovich **25**
Nekrasov, Nikolai **11**
Ostrovsky, Alexander **30**
Pisarev, Dmitry Ivanovich **25**
Pushkin, Alexander **3, 27**
Saltykov, Mikhail Evgrafovich **16**
Smolenskin, Peretz **30**
Turgenev, Ivan **21, 37**
Tyutchev, Fyodor **34**
Zhukovsky, Vasily **35**

SCOTTISH
Baillie, Joanna **2**
Beattie, James **25**
Campbell, Thomas **19**
Ferrier, Susan **8**
Galt, John **1**
Hogg, James **4**
Jeffrey, Francis **33**
Lockhart, John Gibson **6**
Mackenzie, Henry **41**
Oliphant, Margaret **11**
Scott, Sir Walter **15**

Stevenson, Robert Louis **5, 14**
Thomson, James **18**
Wilson, John **5**

SPANISH
Alarcón, Pedro Antonio de **1**
Caballero, Fernán **10**
Castro, Rosalía de **3**
Espronceda, José de **39**
Larra, Mariano José de **17**
Tamayo y Baus, Manuel **1**
Zorrilla y Moral, José **6**

SWEDISH
Almqvist, Carl Jonas Love **42**
Bremer, Fredrika **11**
Tegnér, Esias **2**

SWISS
Amiel, Henri Frédéric **4**
Keller, Gottfried **2**
Wyss, Johann David **10**

Nationality Index

473

ISBN 0-8103-8477-9

90000

9 780810 384774

ISSN 0732-1864

R

Volume 78

Nineteenth-Century Literature Criticism

Excerpts from Criticism of the Works of Novelists, Poets, Playwrights, Short Story Writers, Philosophers, and Other Creative Writers Who Died between 1800 and 1899, from the First Published Critical Appraisals to Current Evaluations

Suzanne Dewsbury
Editor

GALE GROUP

Detroit
San Francisco
London
Boston
Woodbridge, CT

STAFF

Suzanne Dewsbury, *Editor*
Gianna Barberi, *Associate Editor*
Janet Witalec, *Managing Editor*

Maria L. Franklin, *Permissions Manager*
Kimberly F. Smilay, *Permissions Specialist*
Kelly A. Quin, *Permissions Associate*
Erin Bealmear, Sandra K. Gore, *Permissions Assistants*

Victoria B. Cariappa, *Research Manager*
Cheryl Warnock, *Research Specialist*
Corrine Boland, Tamara C. Nott, Tracie A. Richardson, *Research Associates*
Phyllis Blackman, Timothy Lehnerer, *Research Assistants*

Dorothy Maki, *Manufacturing Manager*
Cindy Range, *Buyer*

Gary Leach, *Graphic Artist*
Randy Bassett, *Image Database Supervisor*
Robert Duncan, Michael Logusz, *Imaging Specialists*
Pamela A. Reed, *Imaging Coordinator*

This book is printed on acid-free paper that meets the minimum requirements of American National Standard for Information Sciences—Permanence Paper for Printed Library Materials, ANSI Z39.48-1984.

Library of Congress Catalog Card Number 84-643008
ISBN 0-7876-1911-6
ISSN 0732-1864
Printed in the United States of America

10 9 8 7 6 5 4 3 2 1

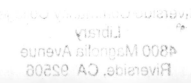

Contents

Preface vii

Acknowledgments xi

Preface

S ince its inception in 1981, *Nineteenth-Century Literature Criticism* has been a valuable resource for students and librarians seeking critical commentary on writers of this transitional period in world history. Designated an "Outstanding Reference Source" by the American Library Association with the publication of its first volume, *NCLC* has since been purchased by over 6,000 school, public, and university libraries. The series has covered more than 300 authors representing 29 nationalities and over 17,000 titles. No other reference source has surveyed the critical reaction to nineteenth-century authors and literature as thoroughly as *NCLC*.

Scope of the Series

NCLC is designed to introduce students and advanced readers to the authors of the nineteenth century, and to the most significant interpretations of these authors' works. The great poets, novelists, short story writers, playwrights, and philosophers of this period are frequently studied in high school and college literature courses. By organizing and reprinting commentary written on these authors, *NCLC* helps students develop valuable insight into literary history, promotes a better understanding of the texts, and sparks ideas for papers and assignments. Each entry in *NCLC* presents a comprehensive survey of an author's career or an individual work of literature and provides the user with a multiplicity of interpretations and assessments. Such variety allows students to pursue their own interests; furthermore, it fosters an awareness that literature is dynamic and responsive to many different opinions.

Every fourth volume of *NCLC* is devoted to literary topics that cannot be covered under the author approach used in the rest of the series. Such topics include literary movements, prominent themes in nineteenth-century literature, literary reaction to political and historical events, significant eras in literary history, prominent literary anniversaries, and the literatures of cultures that are often overlooked by English-speaking readers.

NCLC continues the survey of criticism of world literature begun by Gale's *Contemporary Literary Criticism (CLC)* and *Twentieth-Century Literary Criticism (TCLC),* both of which excerpt and reprint commentary on authors of the twentieth century. For additional information about *TCLC, CLC,* and Gale's other criticism series, users should consult the Guide to Gale Literary Criticism Series preceding the title page in this volume.

Coverage

Each volume of *NCLC* is carefully compiled to present:

- criticism of authors, or literary topics, representing a variety of genres and nationalities
- both major and lesser-known writers and literary works of the period
- 4-8 authors or 4-6 topics per volume
- individual entries that survey critical response to an author's work or a topic in literary history, including early criticism to reflect initial reactions, later criticism to represent any rise or decline in reputation, and current retrospective analyses.

Organization

An author entry consists of the following elements: author heading, biographical and critical introduction, list of principal works, excerpts of criticism (each preceded by a bibliographic citation and an annotation), and a bibliography of further reading.

- The **Author Heading** consists of the name under which the author most commonly wrote, followed by birth and death dates. If an author wrote consistently under a pseudonym, the pseudonym will be listed in the author heading and the real name given in parentheses on the first line of the biographical and critical introduction. Also located at the beginning of the introduction to the author entry are any name variations under which an author wrote, including transliterated forms for an author whose language uses a nonroman alphabet.

- The **Biographical and Critical Introduction** outlines the author's life and career, as well as the critical issues surrounding his or her work. References are provided to past volumes of *NCLC* in which further information about the author may be found.

- Most *NCLC* entries include a **Portrait** of the author. Many entries also contain reproductions of materials pertinent to an author's career, including manuscript pages, title pages, dust jackets, letters, and drawings, as well as photographs of important people, places, and events in an author's life.

- The list of **Principal Works** is chronological by date of first publication and identifies the genre of each work. In the case of foreign authors with both foreign-language publications and English translations, the English-language version is given in brackets. Unless otherwise indicated, dramas are dated by first performance, not first publication.

- **Criticism** in each author entry is arranged chronologically to provide a perspective on changes in critical evaluation over the years. All titles of works by the author featured in the entry are printed in boldface type to enable the user to easily locate discussion of particular works. Also for purposes of easier identification, the critic's name and the publication date of the essay are given at the beginning of each piece of criticism. Unsigned criticism is preceded by the title of the journal in which it appeared. Publication information (such as publisher names and book prices) and some parenthetical numerical references (such as page and line references to specific editions of works) have been deleted at the editors' discretion to provide smoother reading of the text. Footnotes that appear with previously published pieces of criticism are reprinted at the end of each essay or excerpt. In the case of excerpted criticism, only those footnotes that pertain to the excerpted text are included.

- A complete **Bibliographic Citation** provides original publication information for each piece of criticism.

- Critical excerpts are prefaced by **Annotations** providing the reader with a summary of the critical intent of the piece. Also included, when appropriate, is information about the critic's reputation, individual approach to literary criticism, and particular expertise in an author's works, as well as information about the relative importance of the critical excerpt. In some cases, the annotations cross-reference excerpts by critics who discuss each other's commentary.

- An annotated list of **Further Reading** appearing at the end of each entry suggests secondary sources on the author. In some cases it includes essays for which the editors could not obtain reprint rights.

Cumulative Indexes

- Each volume of *NCLC* contains a cumulative **Author Index** listing all authors who have appeared in Gale's Literary Criticism Series, along with cross-references to such biographical series as *Contemporary Authors* and *Dictionary of Literary Biography*. Useful for locating authors within the various series, this index is particularly valuable for those authors who are identified with a certain period but who, because of their death dates, are placed in another, or for those authors whose careers span two periods. For example, Fyodor Dostoevsky is found in *NCLC,* yet Leo Tolstoy, another major nineteenth-century Russian novelist, is found in *TCLC* because he died after 1899.

- Each *NCLC* volume includes a cumulative **Nationality Index** which lists all authors who have appeared in *NCLC*, arranged alphabetically under their respective nationalities.

- Each new volume in Gale's Literary Criticism Series includes a cumulative **Topic Index**, which lists all literary topics treated in *NCLC, TCLC, LC 1400-1800*, and the *CLC* Yearbook.

- Each new volume of *NCLC*, with the exception of the Topics volumes, contains a **Title Index** listing the titles of all literary works discussed in the volume. In response to numerous suggestions from librarians, Gale has also produced a **Special Paperbound Edition** of the *NCLC* title index. This annual cumulation lists all titles discussed in the series since its inception. Additional copies of the index are available on request. Librarians and patrons have welcomed this separate index: it saves shelf space, is easy to use, and is recyclable upon receipt of the following year's cumulation. Titles discussed in the Topics volume entries are not included in the *NCLC* cumulative index.

Citing *Nineteenth-Century Literature Criticism*

When writing papers, students who quote directly from any volume in Gale's Literary Criticism Series may use the following general forms to footnote reprinted criticism. The first example pertains to material drawn from periodicals, the second to material reprinted from books:

[1]Kim McQuaid, "William Apes, Pequot: An Indian Reformer in the Jackson Era," *The New England Quarterly*, 50 (December 1977), 605-25; excerpted and reprinted in *Nineteenth-Century Literature Criticism,* Vol. 73, ed. Janet Witalec (Farmington Hills, Mich.: The Gale Group, 1999), pp. 3-4.

[2]Richard Harter Fogle, *The Imagery of Keats and Shelley: A Comparative Study* (Archon Books, 1949); excerpted and reprinted in *Nineteenth-Century Literary Criticism,* Vol. 73, ed. Janet Witalec (Farmington Hills, Mich.: The Gale Group, 1999), pp. 157-69.

Suggestions Are Welcome

In response to suggestions, several features have been added to *NCLC* since the series began, including annotations to excerpted criticism, a cumulative index to authors in all Gale literary criticism series, entries devoted to criticism on a single work by a major author, more illustrations, and a title index listing all literary works discussed in the series.

Readers who wish to suggest authors, single works, or topics to appear in future volumes, or who have other suggestions, are cordially invited to write: The Editors, *Nineteenth-Century Literature Criticism,* The Gale Group, 27500 Drake Rd., Farmington Hills, MI 48331-3535; call toll-free at 1-800-347-GALE.

Acknowledgments

The editors wish to thank the copyright holders of the excerpted criticism included in this volume and the permissions managers of many book and magazine publishing companies for assisting us in securing reproduction rights. We are also grateful to the staffs of the Detroit Public Library, the Library of Congress, the University of Detroit Mercy Library, Wayne State University Purdy/Kresge Library Complex, and the University of Michigan Libraries for making their resources available to us. Following is a list of the copyright holders who have granted us permission to reproduce material in this volume of *NCLC*. Every effort has been made to trace copyright, but if omissions have been made, please let us know.

COPYRIGHTED MATERIAL IN *NCLC,* VOLUME 78, WERE REPRODUCED FROM THE FOLLOWING PERIODICALS:

African American Review, v. 16, Spring, 1993 for "Speaking the Body's Pain" by Cynthia J. Davis. Copyright © 1993 by the author. Reproduced by permission of the author.—*Callaloo*, v. 16, Spring, 1993. Copyright © 1993 by Charles H. Rowell. Reproduced by permission of The Johns Hopkins University Press.—*English Language Notes*, v. VII, March, 1970. © copyrighted 1970, Regents of the University of Colorado. Reproduced by permission.—*Faith and Philosophy*, v. 7, July, 1990. Reproduced by permission.—*Hispanofila*, September, 1984. Reproduced by permission.—*Indian Literature*, v. XI, 1968; v. XII, 1969. Both reproduced by permission.—*Kentucky Romance Quarterly*, v. 29, 1982. Copyright © 1982 Helen Dwight Reid Educational Foundation. Reproduced with permission of the Helen Dwight Reid Educational Foundation, published by Heldref Publications, 1319 18th Street, NW, Washington, DC 20036-1802.—*Kierkegaardiana*, v. 15, 1991 for "The Logic Soren Kierkegaard's Misogyny, 1854-1855" by Julia Watkin. Reproduced by permission of the publisher and the author.—*Legacy*, v. 13, 1996. Copyright 1996 by The Pennsylvania State University. Reproduced by permission.—*Modern Language Notes*, v. 112, December, 1997. Copyright © 1997 by The Johns Hopkins University Press. Reproduced by permission of The Johns Hopkins University Press.—*Mosaic*, v. 25, Spring, 1992. © Mosaic 1992. Acknowledgment of previous publication is herewith made.—*Nineteenth-Century Fiction*, v. 19, March, 1965. © 1965 by The Regents of the University of California. Reproduced by permission of the Regents.—*Papers on Language & Literature*, v. 24, Summer, 1988. Copyright © 1998 by The Board of Trustees, Southern Illinois University at Edwardsville. Reproduced by permission.—*Perspective*, v. II, February-March, 1969. Reproduced by permission.—*PMLA*, v. 109, May, 1994. Copyright © 1994 by the Modern Language Association of America. Reproduced by permission of the Modern Language Association of America.—*Studies in Short Fiction*, v. V, Summer, 1968; v. 22, Fall, 1985. Copyright 1968, 1985 by Newberry College. Both reproduced by permission.—*Symposium*, v. XXVI, Winter, 1972. Copyright © 1972 Helen Dwight Reid Educational Foundation. Reproduced with permission of the Helen Dwight Reid Educational Foundation, published by Heldref Publications, 1319 18th Street, NW, Washington, DC 20036-1802.—*Theory and History of Literature* - Kierkegaard: Construction of the Aesthetic, v. 61, University of Minnesota Press, 1989. © 1989 by the University of Minnesota. Reproduced by permission.—*Yale Journal of Criticism*, v. 5, 1992. © 1992. Reproduced by permission of The Johns Hopkins University Press.

Shelley. From *Rosalia de Castro and the Galician Revival*. Tamesis Books Limited, 1986. © Copyright by Tamesis Books Limited London, 1986. Reproduced by permission.—Sud, K.N. From *Eternal Flame: (Aspects of Ghalib's Life and Works)*. Sterling Publishers, 1969. © 1969 by K.N. Sud. Reproduced by permission.—Walsh, Sylvia I. From "On 'Feminine' and 'Masculine' Forms of Despair" in *International Kierkegaard Commentary: The Sickness unto Death*. Edited by Robert L. Perkins. Mercer University Press, 1987. © 1987 Mercer University Press, Macon, Georgia, 31207. All rights reserved. Reproduced by permission.—Westphal, Merold. From *Kierkegaard's Critique of Reason and Society*. Mercer University Press, 1987. © 1987 Mercer University Press, Macon, Georgia, 31207. All rights reserved. Reproduced by permission.—Wilcox, John C. From *Women Poets of Spain, 1860-1990: Toward a Gynocentric Vision*. University of Illinois Press, 1997. © 1997 by the Board of Trustees of the University of Illinois. Reproduced by permission of the publisher and the author.

PHOTOGRAPHS AND ILLUSTRATIONS APPEARING IN *NCLC*, VOLUME 78, WERE RECEIVED FROM THE FOLLOWING SOURCES:

de Castro, Rosalia, photograph. Ediciones Aguilar. Reproduced by permission.—A title page for "En Las Orillas Del Sar" by Rosalia De Castro, 1909 edition, photograph. The Department of Rare Books and Special Collections, The University of Michigan Library. Reproduced by permission.—Ghalib, drawing. Reproduced by permission.—Poe, Edgar Allan, photograph. AP/Wide World Photos. Reproduced by permission.